D0778893

A SECULAR AGE

A Secular Age

CHARLES TAYLOR

The Belknap Press of Harvard University Press

Cambridge, Massachusetts, and London, England · 2007

Design by Annamarie McMahon Why

Poems by Robinson Jeffers are quoted from *The Collected Poetry of Robinson Jeffers,* ed. Tim
Hunt (Stanford University Press, 2001). Copyright © 1927, 1955 by Robinson Jeffers; copyright Jeffers Literary Properties. All rights reserved. Used with the permission of Stanford
University Press. "Rock and Hawk," copyright 1934 and renewed 1962 by Donnan Jeffers
and Garth Jeffers, is quoted from *Selected Poetry of Robinson Jeffers* by Robinson Jeffers. Used
by permission of Random House, Inc.

Library of Congress Cataloging-in-Publication Data

Taylor, Charles, 1931–
A secular age / Charles Taylor.
    p. cm.
  Includes bibliographical references and index.
  ISBN-13: 978-0-674-02676-6 (alk. paper)
  ISBN-10: 0-674-02676-4 (alk. paper)
  1. Secularism.   2. Religion and culture.   I. Title.

  BL2747.8.T39 2007
  211'.6—dc22   2007008005

To my daughter Gretta

Contents

PART V   Conditions of Belief

Preface

This book emerges from my Gifford Lectures at Edinburgh in the spring of 1999, entitled "Living in a Secular Age?". It's been quite some time since then, and in fact the scope of the work has expanded. Basically, the lectures of 1999 covered Parts I–III of the present book, and Parts IV and V deal with matters I wanted to discuss then, but lacked the time and competence to treat properly. (I hope the passing years have helped in this regard.)

The book has grown since 1999, and also increased its scope. But the first process hasn't kept pace with the second: The larger scope would have demanded a much bigger book than I am now offering to the reader. I am telling a story, that of what we usually call "secularization" in the modern West. And in doing so, I am trying to clarify what this process, often invoked, but still not very clear, amounts to. To do this properly, I should have had to tell a denser and more continuous story, something I have neither the time nor the competence to do.

I ask the reader who picks up this book not to think of it as a continuous story-and-argument, but rather as a set of interlocking essays, which shed light on each other, and offer a context of relevance for each other. I hope the general thrust of my thesis will emerge from this sketchy treatment, and will suggest to others further ways of developing, applying, modifying, and transposing the argument.

I want to thank the Gifford Lectures Committee at Edinburgh for giving me the initial impetus to start on this project. I also owe a debt of gratitude to the Canada Council for an Isaac Killam Fellowship during 1996–1998, which allowed me to get started; and to the Social Science and Humanities Research Council of Canada for their Gold Medal Award of 2003. I benefited greatly from visits to the Institut für die Wissenschaften vom Menschen in Vienna in 2000 and 2001. The Wissenschaftskolleg zu Berlin gave me a fellowship in 2005–2006 that allowed me to complete the project in the best possible conditions, including discussions with José Casanova and Hans Joas, who have been working on parallel projects.

I must also express my gratitude to the members of the network around the Centre for Transcultural Studies. Some of the key concepts I use in this work have emerged during our exchanges.

In producing the book, I was greatly helped by Bryan Smyth, who made or discovered many of the translations as well as preparing the index. Unmarked translations are almost always by him, occasionally modified by myself.

A SECULAR AGE

Introduction

1

What does it mean to say that we live in a secular age? Almost everyone would agree that in some sense we do: I mean the "we" who live in the West, or perhaps Northwest, or otherwise put, the North Atlantic world—although secularity extends also partially, and in different ways, beyond this world. And the judgment of secularity seems hard to resist when we compare these societies with anything else in human history: that is, with almost all other contemporary societies (e.g., Islamic countries, India, Africa), on one hand; and with the rest of human history, Atlantic or otherwise, on the other.

But it's not so clear in what this secularity consists. There are two big candidates for its characterization—or perhaps, better, families of candidate. The first concentrates on the common institutions and practices—most obviously, but not only, the state. The difference would then consist in this, that whereas the political organization of all pre-modern societies was in some way connected to, based on, guaranteed by some faith in, or adherence to God, or some notion of ultimate reality, the modern Western state is free from this connection. Churches are now separate from political structures (with a couple of exceptions, in Britain and the Scandinavian countries, which are so low-key and undemanding as not really to constitute exceptions). Religion or its absence is largely a private matter. The political society is seen as that of believers (of all stripes) and non-believers alike.[1]

Put in another way, in our "secular" societies, you can engage fully in politics without ever encountering God, that is, coming to a point where the crucial importance of the God of Abraham for this whole enterprise is brought home forcefully and unmistakably. The few moments of vestigial ritual or prayer barely constitute such an encounter today, but this would have been inescapable in earlier centuries in Christendom.

This way of putting it allows us to see that more than the state is involved in this change. If we go back a few centuries in our civilization, we see that God was pres-

ent in the above sense in a whole host of social practices—not just the political—
and at all levels of society: for instance, when the functioning mode of local government was the parish, and the parish was still primarily a community of prayer; or
when guilds maintained a ritual life that was more than pro forma; or when the
only modes in which the society in all its components could display itself to itself
were religious feasts, like, for instance, the Corpus Christi procession. In those societies, you couldn't engage in any kind of public activity without "encountering
God" in the above sense. But the situation is totally different today.

And if you go back even farther in human history, you come to archaic societies
in which the whole set of distinctions we make between the religious, political, economic, social, etc., aspects of our society ceases to make sense. In these earlier societies, religion was "everywhere",[2] was interwoven with everything else, and in no
sense constituted a separate "sphere" of its own.

One understanding of secularity then is in terms of public spaces. These have
been allegedly emptied of God, or of any reference to ultimate reality. Or taken
from another side, as we function within various spheres of activity—economic, political, cultural, educational, professional, recreational—the norms and principles
we follow, the deliberations we engage in, generally don't refer us to God or to any
religious beliefs; the considerations we act on are internal to the "rationality" of each
sphere—maximum gain within the economy, the greatest benefit to the greatest
number in the political area, and so on. This is in striking contrast to earlier periods, when Christian faith laid down authoritative prescriptions, often through the
mouths of the clergy, which could not be easily ignored in any of these domains,
such as the ban on usury, or the obligation to enforce orthodoxy.[3]

But whether we see this in terms of prescriptions, or in terms of ritual or ceremonial presence, this emptying of religion from autonomous social spheres is, of
course, compatible with the vast majority of people still believing in God, and practising their religion vigorously. The case of Communist Poland springs to mind.
This is perhaps a bit of a red herring, because the public secularity was imposed
there by a dictatorial and unpopular régime. But the United States is rather striking
in this regard. One of the earliest societies to separate Church and State, it is also
the Western society with the highest statistics for religious belief and practice.

And yet this is the issue that people often want to get at when they speak of our
times as secular, and contrast them, nostalgically or with relief, with earlier ages of
faith or piety. In this second meaning, secularity consists in the falling off of religious belief and practice, in people turning away from God, and no longer going to
Church. In this sense, the countries of western Europe have mainly become secular—even those who retain the vestigial public reference to God in public space.

Now I believe that an examination of this age as secular is worth taking up in a third sense, closely related to the second, and not without connection to the first. This would focus on the conditions of belief. The shift to secularity in this sense consists, among other things, of a move from a society where belief in God is un-challenged and indeed, unproblematic, to one in which it is understood to be one option among others, and frequently not the easiest to embrace. In this meaning, as against sense 2, at least many milieux in the United States are secularized, and I would argue that the United States as a whole is. Clear contrast cases today would be the majority of Muslim societies, or the milieux in which the vast majority of Indians live. It wouldn't matter if one showed that the statistics for church/synagogue attendance in the U.S., or some regions of it, approached those for Friday mosque attendance in, say, Pakistan or Jordan (or this, plus daily prayer). That would be evidence towards classing these societies as the same in sense 2. Nevertheless, it seems to me evident that there are big differences between these societies in *what it is to believe,* stemming in part from the fact that belief is an option, and in some sense an embattled option in the Christian (or "post-Christian") society, and not (or not yet) in the Muslim ones.

So what I want to do is examine our society as secular in this third sense, which I could perhaps encapsulate in this way: the change I want to define and trace is one which takes us from a society in which it was virtually impossible not to believe in God, to one in which faith, even for the staunchest believer, is one human possibility among others. I may find it inconceivable that I would abandon my faith, but there are others, including possibly some very close to me, whose way of living I cannot in all honesty just dismiss as depraved, or blind, or unworthy, who have no faith (at least not in God, or the transcendent). Belief in God is no longer axiomatic. There are alternatives. And this will also likely mean that at least in certain milieux, it may be hard to sustain one's faith. There will be people who feel bound to give it up, even though they mourn its loss. This has been a recognizable experience in our societies, at least since the mid-nineteenth century. There will be many others to whom faith never even seems an eligible possibility. There are certainly millions today of whom this is true.

Secularity in this sense is a matter of the whole context of understanding in which our moral, spiritual or religious experience and search takes place. By 'context of understanding' here, I mean both matters that will probably have been explicitly formulated by almost everyone, such as the plurality of options, and some which form the implicit, largely unfocussed background of this experience and search, its "pre-ontology", to use a Heideggerian term.

An age or society would then be secular or not, in virtue of the conditions of experience of and search for the spiritual. Obviously, where it stood in this dimension would have a lot to do with how secular it was in the second sense, which turns on levels of belief and practice, but there is no simple correlation between the two, as the case of the U.S. shows. As for the first sense, which concerns public space, this may be uncorrelated with both the others (as might be argued for the case of India). But I will maintain that in fact, in the Western case, the shift to public secularity has been part of what helped to bring on a secular age in my third sense.

2

Articulating the conditions of experience turns out to be harder than one might think. This is partly because people tend to be focussed on belief itself. What people are usually interested in, what arouses a lot of the anguish and conflict, is the second issue: what do people believe and practice? How many believe in God? In which direction is the trend going? Concern for public secularity often relates to the issue of what people believe or practice, and of how they are treated in consequence: does our secularist régime marginalize believing Christians, as some claim in the U.S.A.? Or does it stigmatize hitherto unrecognized groups? African-Americans, Hispanics? or else gays and lesbians?

But in our societies, the big issue about religion is usually defined in terms of belief. First Christianity has always defined itself in relation to credal statements. And secularism in sense 2 has often been seen as the decline of Christian belief; and this decline as largely powered by the rise of other beliefs, in science, reason, or by the deliverances of particular sciences: for instance, evolutionary theory, or neuro-physiological explanations of mental functioning.

Part of my reason for wanting to shift the focus to the conditions of belief, experience and search is that I'm not satisfied with this explanation of secularism 2: science refutes and hence crowds out religious belief. I'm dissatisfied on two, related levels. First, I don't see the cogency of the supposed arguments from, say, the findings of Darwin to the alleged refutations of religion. And secondly, partly for this reason, I don't see this as an adequate explanation for why in fact people abandoned their faith, even when they themselves articulate what happened in such terms as "Darwin refuted the Bible", as allegedly said by a Harrow schoolboy in the 1890s.[4] Of course bad arguments can figure as crucial in perfectly good psychological or historical explanations. But bad arguments like this, which leave out so many viable possibilities between fundamentalism and atheism, cry out for some account why these other roads were not travelled. This deeper account, I think, is to be found at the level I'm trying to explore. I will return to this shortly.

In order to get a little bit clearer on this level, I want to talk about belief and unbelief, not as rival *theories*, that is, ways that people account for existence, or morality, whether by God or by something in nature, or whatever. Rather what I want to do is focus attention on the different kinds of lived experience involved in understanding your life in one way or the other, on what it's like to live as a believer or an unbeliever.

As a first rough indication of the direction I'm groping in, we could say that these are alternative ways of living our moral/spiritual life, in the broadest sense.

We all see our lives, and/or the space wherein we live our lives, as having a certain moral/spiritual shape. Somewhere, in some activity, or condition, lies a fullness, a richness; that is, in that place (activity or condition), life is fuller, richer, deeper, more worth while, more admirable, more what it should be. This is perhaps a place of power: we often experience this as deeply moving, as inspiring. Perhaps this sense of fullness is something we just catch glimpses of from afar off; we have the powerful intuition of what fullness would be, were we to be in that condition, e.g., of peace or wholeness; or able to act on that level, of integrity or generosity or abandonment or self-forgetfulness. But sometimes there will be moments of experienced fullness, of joy and fulfillment, where we feel ourselves there. Let one example, drawn from the autobiography of Bede Griffiths, stand for many:

One day during my last term at school I walked out alone in the evening and heard the birds singing in that full chorus of song, which can only be heard at that time of the year at dawn or at sunset. I remember now the shock of surprise with which the sound broke on my ears. It seemed to me that I had never heard the birds singing before and I wondered whether they sang like this all year round and I had never noticed it. As I walked I came upon some hawthorn trees in full bloom and again I thought that I had never seen such a sight or experienced such sweetness before. If I had been brought suddenly among the trees of the Garden of Paradise and heard a choir of angels singing I could not have been more surprised. I came then to where the sun was setting over the playing fields. A lark rose suddenly from the ground beside the tree where I was standing and poured out its song above my head, and then sank still singing to rest. Everything then grew still as the sunset faded and the veil of dusk began to cover the earth. I remember now the feeling of awe which came over me. I felt inclined to kneel on the ground, as though I had been standing in the presence of an angel; and I hardly dared to look on the face of the sky, because it seemed as though it was but a veil before the face of God.[5]

In this case, the sense of fullness came in an experience which unsettles and breaks through our ordinary sense of being in the world, with its familiar objects, activities and points of reference. These may be moments, as Peter Berger puts it, describing the work of Robert Musil, when "ordinary reality is 'abolished' and something terrifyingly *other* shines through", a state of consciousness which Musil describes as "der andere Zustand" (the other condition).[6]

But the identification of fullness may happen without a limit experience of this kind, whether uplifting or frightening. There may just be moments when the deep divisions, distractions, worries, sadnesses that seem to drag us down are somehow dissolved, or brought into alignment, so that we feel united, moving forward, suddenly capable and full of energy. Our highest aspirations and our life energies are somehow lined up, reinforcing each other, instead of producing psychic gridlock. This is the kind of experience which Schiller tried to understand with his notion of "play".[7]

These experiences, and others again which can't all be enumerated here, help us to situate a place of fullness,[8] to which we orient ourselves morally or spiritually. They can orient us because they offer some sense of what they are of: the presence of God, or the voice of nature, or the force which flows through everything, or the alignment in us of desire and the drive to form. But they are also often unsettling and enigmatic. Our sense of where they come from may also be unclear, confused, lacunary. We are deeply moved, but also puzzled and shaken. We struggle to articulate what we've been through. If we succeed in formulating it, however partially, we feel a release, as though the power of the experience was increased by having been focussed, articulated, and hence let fully be.

This can help define a direction to our lives. But the sense of orientation also has its negative slope; where we experience above all a distance, an absence, an exile, a seemingly irremediable incapacity ever to reach this place; an absence of power; a confusion, or worse, the condition often described in the tradition as melancholy, ennui (the "spleen" of Baudelaire). What is terrible in this latter condition is that we lose a sense of where the place of fullness is, even of what fullness could consist in; we feel we've forgotten what it would look like, or cannot believe in it any more. But the misery of absence, of loss, is still there, indeed, it is in some ways even more acute.[9]

There are other figures of exile, which we can see in the tradition, where what dominates is a sense of damnation, of deserved and decided exclusion forever from fullness; or images of captivity, within hideous forms which embody the very negation of fullness: the monstrous animal forms that we see in the paintings of Hieronymus Bosch, for instance.

Then thirdly, there is a kind of stabilized middle condition, to which we often aspire. This is one where we have found a way to escape the forms of negation, exile, emptiness, without having reached fullness. We come to terms with the middle position, often through some stable, even routine order in life, in which we are doing things which have some meaning for us; for instance, which contribute to our ordinary happiness, or which are fulfilling in various ways, or which contribute to what we conceive of as the good. Or often, in the best scenario, all three: for instance, we strive to live happily with spouse and children, while practising a vocation which we find fulfilling, and also which constitutes an obvious contribution to human welfare.

But it is essential to this middle condition, first that the routine, the order, the regular contact with meaning in our daily activities, somehow conjures, and keeps at bay the exile, or the ennui, or captivity in the monstrous; and second, that we have some sense of continuing contact with the place of fullness; and of slow movement towards it over the years. This place can't be renounced, or totally despaired of, without the equilibrium of the middle condition being undermined.[10]

Here's where it might appear that my description of this supposedly general structure of our moral/spiritual lives tilts towards the believer. It is clear that the last sentences of the previous paragraph fit rather well the state of mind of the believer in the middle condition. She goes on placing faith in a fuller condition, often described as salvation, and can't despair of it, and also would want to feel that she is at least open to progress towards it, if not already taking small steps thither.

But there are surely many unbelievers for whom this life in what I've described as the "middle condition" is all there is. This is the goal. Living this well and fully is what human life is about—for instance, the threefold scenario I described above. This is all that human life offers; but on this view this is a) no small thing, and b) to believe that there is something more, e.g., after death, or in some impossible condition of sanctity, is to run away from and undermine the search for this human excellence.

So describing fullness as another "place" from this middle condition may be misleading. And yet there is a structural analogy here. The unbeliever wants to be the kind of person for whom this life is fully satisfying, in which all of him can rejoice, in which his whole sense of fullness can find an adequate object. And he is not there yet. Either he's not really living the constitutive meanings in his life fully: he's not really happy in his marriage, or fulfilled in his job, or confident that this job really conduces to the benefit of humankind. Or else he is reasonably confident that he has the bases of all these, but contrary to his express view, cannot find the fullness of peace and a sense of satisfaction and completeness in this life. In other words, there is something he aspires to beyond where he's at. He perhaps hasn't yet fully conquered the nostalgia for something transcendent. In one way or another, he still has some way to go. And that's the point behind this image of place, even though this place isn't "other" in the obvious sense of involving quite different activities, or a condition beyond this life.

Now the point of describing these typical dimensions of human moral/spiritual

FULLNESS

belief vs. lived

life as identifications of fullness, modes of exile, and types of the middle condition, is to allow us to understand better belief and unbelief as lived conditions, not just as theories or sets of beliefs subscribed to.

Contrast bel/unbel. The big obvious contrast here is that for believers, the account of the place of fullness requires reference to God, that is, to something beyond human life and/or nature; where for unbelievers this is not the case; they rather will leave any account open, or understand fullness in terms of a potentiality of human beings understood naturalistically. But so far this description of the contrast seems to be still a belief description. What we need to do is to get a sense of the difference of lived experience.

Of course, this is incredibly various. But perhaps some recurring themes can be identified. For believers, often or typically, the sense is that fullness comes to them, that it is something they receive; moreover, receive in something like a personal relation, from another being capable of love and giving; approaching fullness involves among other things, practices of devotion and prayer (as well as charity, giving); and they are aware of being very far from the condition of full devotion and giving; they are aware of being self-enclosed, bound to lesser things and goals, not able to open themselves and receive/give as they would at the place of fullness. So there is the notion of receiving power or fullness in a relation; but the receiver isn't simply empowered in his/her present condition; he/she needs to be opened, transformed, brought out of self.

This is a very Christian formulation. In order to make the contrast with modern unbelief, perhaps it would be good to appose to it another formulation, more "Buddhist": here the personal relation might drop out as central. But the emphasis would be all the stronger on the direction of transcending the self, opening it out, receiving a power that goes beyond us.

KANT For modern unbelievers, the predicament is quite different. The power to reach fullness is within. There are different variations of this. One is that which centres on our nature as rational beings. The Kantian variant is the most upfront form of this. We have the power as rational agency to make the laws by which we live. This is something so greatly superior to the force of mere nature in us, in the form of desire, that when we contemplate it without distortion, we cannot but feel reverence (Achtung) for this power. The place of fullness is where we manage finally to give this power full reign, and so to live by it. We have a feeling of receptivity, when with our full sense of our own fragility and pathos as desiring beings, we look up to the power of law-giving with admiration and awe. But this doesn't in the end mean that there is any reception from outside; the power is within; and the more we realize this power, the more we become aware that it is within, that morality must be autonomous and not heteronomous.

(Later a Feuerbachian theory of alienation can be added to this: we project God because of our early sense of this awesome power which we mistakenly place outside us; we need to re-appropriate it for human beings. But Kant didn't take this step.)

Of course, there are also lots of more naturalistic variants of the power of reason, which depart from the dualistic, religious dimensions of Kant's thought, his belief in radical freedom of the moral agent, immortality, God—the three postulates of practical reason. There may be a more rigorous naturalism, which accords little room for manoeuvre for human reason, driven on one side by instinct, and on the other hemmed in by the exigencies of survival. There may be no explanation offered of why we have this power. It may consist largely in instrumental uses of reason, there again unlike Kant. But within this kind of naturalism, we often find an admiration for the power of cool, disengaged reason, capable of contemplating the world and human life without illusion, and of acting lucidly for the best in the interest of human flourishing. A certain awe still surrounds reason as a critical power, capable of liberating us from illusion and blind forces of instinct, as well as the phantasies bred of our fear and narrowness and pusillanimity. The nearest thing to fullness lies in this power of reason, and it is entirely ours, developed if it is through our own, often heroic action. (And here the giants of modern "scientific" reason are often named: Copernicus, Darwin, Freud.)

Indeed, this sense of ourselves as beings both frail and courageous, capable of facing a meaningless, hostile universe without faintness of heart, and of rising to the challenge of devising our own rules of life, can be an inspiring one, as we see in the writings of a Camus for instance.[11] Rising fully to this challenge, empowered by this sense of our own greatness in doing so, this condition we aspire to but only rarely, if ever, achieve, can function as its own place of fullness, in the sense of my discussion here.

Over against these modes of rejoicing in the self-sufficient power of reason, there are other modes of unbelief which, analogous to religious views, see us as needing to receive power from elsewhere than autonomous reason to achieve fullness. Reason by itself is narrow, blind to the demands of fullness, will run on perhaps to destruction, human and ecological, if it recognizes no limits; is perhaps actuated by a kind of pride, hubris. There are often echoes here of a religious critique of modern, disengaged, unbelieving reason. Except that the sources of power are not transcendent. They are to be found in Nature, or in our own inner depths, or in both. We can recognize here theories of immanence which emerge from the Romantic critique of disengaged reason, and most notably certain ecological ethics of our day, particularly deep ecology. Rational mind has to open itself to something deeper and fuller. This is something (at least partly) inner; our own deepest feelings or instincts. We have therefore to heal the division within us that disengaged reason has created, setting thinking in opposition to feeling or instinct or intuition.

So we have here views which, as just mentioned, have certain analogies to the religious reaction to the unbelieving Enlightenment, in that they stress reception over against self-sufficiency; but they are views which intend to remain immanent, and are often as hostile, if not more so, to religion than the disengaged ones.

There is a third category of outlook, which is hard to classify here, but which I hope to illuminate later in this discussion. These are views, like that of certain contemporary modes of post-modernism, which deny, attack or scoff at the claims of self-sufficient reason, but offer no outside source for the reception of power. They are as determined to undermine and deny Romantic notions of solace in feeling, or in recovered unity, as they are to attack the Enlightenment dream of pure thinking; and they seem often even more eager to underscore their atheist convictions. They want to make a point of stressing the irremediable nature of division, lack of centre, the perpetual absence of fullness; which is at best a necessary dream, something we may have to suppose to make minimum sense of our world, but which is always elsewhere, and which couldn't in principle ever be found.

This family of views seems to stand altogether outside the structures I'm talking about here. And yet I think one can show that in a number of ways it draws on them. In particular, it draws empowerment from the sense of our courage and greatness in being able to face the irremediable, and carry on nonetheless. I hope to come back to this later.

So we've made some progress in talking about belief and unbelief as ways of living or experiencing moral/spiritual life, in the three dimensions I talked about earlier. At least I drew some contrasts in the first dimension, the way of experiencing fullness; the source of the power which can bring us to this fullness; whether this is "within" or "without"; and in what sense. Corresponding differences follow about experiences of exile, and those of the middle condition.

More needs to be said about this distinction of within/without, but before elaborating further on this, there is another important facet of this experience of fullness as "placed" somewhere which we need to explore. We have gone beyond mere belief, and are closer to lived experience here, but there are still important differences in the way we live it which have to be brought out.

What does it mean to say that for me fullness comes from a power which is beyond me, that I have to receive it, etc.? Today, it is likely to mean something like this: the best sense I can make of my conflicting moral and spiritual experience is captured by a theological view of this kind. That is, in my own experience, in prayer, in moments of fullness, in experiences of exile overcome, in what I seem to observe around me in other people's lives—lives of exceptional spiritual fullness, or lives of maximum self-enclosedness, lives of demonic evil, etc.—this seems to be the picture which emerges. But I am never, or only rarely, really sure, free of all doubt, untroubled by some objection—by some experience which won't fit, some lives which exhibit fullness on another basis, some alternative mode of fullness which sometimes draws me, etc.

This is typical of the modern condition, and an analogous story could be told by many an unbeliever. We live in a condition where we cannot help but be aware that there are a number of different construals, views which intelligent, reasonably undeluded people, of good will, can and do disagree on. We cannot help looking over our shoulder from time to time, looking sideways, living our faith also in a condition of doubt and uncertainty.

It is this index of doubt, which induces people to speak of "theories" here. Because theories are often hypotheses, held in ultimate uncertainty, pending further evidence. I hope I have said something to show that we can't understand them as mere theories, that there is a way in which our whole experience is inflected if we live in one or another spirituality. But all the same we are aware today that one can live the spiritual life differently; that power, fullness, exile, etc., can take different shapes.

But there is clearly another way one can live these things, and many human beings did. This is a condition in which the immediate experience of power, a place of fullness, exile, is in terms which *we* would identify as one of the possible alternatives, but where for the people concerned no such distinction, between experience and its construal, arose. Let's recur to Hieronymus Bosch for instance. Those nightmare scenarios of possession, of evil spirits, of captivation in monstrous animal forms; we can imagine that these were not "theories" in any sense in the lived experience of many people in that age. They were objects of real fear, of such compelling fear, that it wasn't possible to entertain seriously the idea that they might be unreal. You or people you knew had experienced them. And perhaps no one in your milieu ever got around even to suggesting their unreality.

Analogously, the people of New Testament Palestine, when they saw someone possessed of an evil spirit, were too immediately at grips with the real suffering of this condition, in a neighbour, or a loved one, to be able to entertain the idea that this was an interesting explanation for a psychological condition, identifiable purely in intra-psychic terms, but that there were other, possibly more reliable aetiologies for this condition.

Or to take a contemporary example, from West Africa in this case, so it must have been for the Celestine, interviewed by Birgit Meyer,[12] who "walked home from Aventile with her mother, accompanied by a stranger dressed in a white northern gown." When asked afterwards, her mother denied having seen the man. He turned out to be the Akan spirit Sowlui, and Celestine was pressed into his service. In Celestine's world, perhaps the identification of the man with this spirit might be called a "belief", in that it came after the experience in an attempt to explain what it was all about. But the man accompanying her was just something that happened to her, a fact of her world.

So there is a condition of lived experience, where what we might call a construal of the moral/spiritual is lived not as such, but as immediate reality, like stones, rivers and mountains. And this plainly also goes for the positive side of things: e.g., people in earlier ages of our culture, for whom moving to fullness just meant getting closer to God. The alternatives they faced in life were: living a fuller devotion, or going on living for lesser goods, at a continuing distance from fullness; being "dévot" or "mondain", in the terms of seventeenth-century France; not taking off after a different construal of what fullness might mean.

Now part of what has happened in our civilization is that we have largely eroded these forms of immediate certainty. That is, it seems clear that they can never be as fully (to us) "naïve"[13] as they were at the time of Hieronymus Bosch. But we still have something analogous to that, though weaker. I'm talking about the way the moral/spiritual life tends to show up in certain milieux. That is, although everybody has now to be aware that there is more than one option, it may be that in our milieu one construal, believing or unbelieving, tends to show up as the overwhelmingly more plausible one. You know that there are other ones, and if you get interested, then drawn to another one, you can perhaps think/struggle your way through to it. You break with your believing community and become an atheist; or you go in the reverse direction. But one option is, as it were, the default option.

Now in this regard, there has been a titanic change in our western civilization. We have changed not just from a condition where most people lived "naïvely" in a construal (part Christian, part related to "spirits" of pagan origin) as simple reality, to one in which almost no one is capable of this, but all see their option as one among many. We all learn to navigate between two standpoints: an "engaged" one in which we live as best we can the reality our standpoint opens us to; and a "disengaged" one in which we are able to see ourselves as occupying one standpoint among a range of possible ones, with which we have in various ways to coexist.

But we have also changed from a condition in which belief was the default option, not just for the naïve but also for those who knew, considered, talked about atheism; to a condition in which for more and more people unbelieving construals seem at first blush the only plausible ones. They can only approach, without ever gaining the condition of "naïve" atheists, in the way that their ancestors were naïve, semi-pagan believers; but this seems to them the overwhelmingly plausible construal, and it is difficult to understand people adopting another. So much so that they easily reach for rather gross error theories to explain religious belief: people are afraid of uncertainty, the unknown; they're weak in the head, crippled by guilt, etc.

This is not to say that everyone is in this condition. Our modern civilization is made up of a host of societies, sub-societies and milieux, all rather different from each other. But the presumption of unbelief has become dominant in more and more of these milieux; and has achieved hegemony in certain crucial ones, in the academic and intellectual life, for instance; whence it can more easily extend itself to others.

In order to place the discussion between belief and unbelief in our day and age, we have to put it in the context of this lived experience, and the construals that shape this experience. And this means not only seeing this as more than a matter of different "theories" to explain the same experiences. It also means understanding the differential position of different construals; how they can be lived "naïvely" or "reflectively"; how one or another can become the default option for many people or milieux.

To put the point in different terms, belief in God isn't quite the same thing in 1500 and 2000. I am not referring to the fact that even orthodox Christianity has undergone important changes (e.g., the "decline of Hell", new understandings of the atonement). Even in regard to identical credal propositions, there is an important difference. This emerges as soon as we take account of the fact that all beliefs are held within a context or framework of the taken-for-granted, which usually remains tacit, and may even be as yet unacknowledged by the agent, because never formulated. This is what philosophers, influenced by Wittgenstein, Heidegger or Polanyi, have called the "background".[14] As Wittgenstein points out,[15] my research into rock formations takes as granted that the world didn't start five minutes ago, complete with all the fossils and striations, but it would never occur to me to formulate and acknowledge this, until some crazed philosophers, obsessively riding their epistemological hobby-horses, put the proposition to me.

But now perhaps I have caught the bug, and I can no longer be naïvely into my research, but now take account of what I have been leaning on, perhaps entertain the possibility that it might be wrong. This breach of naïveté is often the path to fuller understanding (even if not in this case). You might be just operating in a framework in which all moves would be in one of the cardinal directions or up or down; but in order to function in a space ship, even to conceive one, you have to see how relative and constrained this framework is.

The difference I've been talking about above is one of the whole background framework in which one believes or refuses to believe in God. The frameworks of yesterday and today are related as "naïve" and "reflective", because the latter has opened a question which had been foreclosed in the former by the unacknowledged shape of the background.

The shift in background, or better the disruption of the earlier background, comes best to light when we focus on certain distinctions we make today; for instance, that between the immanent and the transcendent, the natural and the supernatural. Everyone understands these, both those who affirm and those who deny the second term of each pair. This hiving off of an independent, free-standing level, that of "nature", which may or may not be in interaction with something further or beyond, is a crucial bit of modern theorizing, which in turn corresponds to a constitutive dimension of modern experience, as I hope to show in greater detail below.

It is this shift in background, in the whole context in which we experience and search for fullness, that I am calling the coming of a secular age, in my third sense. How did we move from a condition where, in Christendom, people lived naïvely within a theistic construal, to one in which we all shunt between two stances, in which everyone's construal shows up as such; and in which moreover, unbelief has become for many the major default option? This is the transformation that I want to describe, and perhaps also (very partially) explain in the following chapters.

This will not be easy to do, but only by identifying the change as one of lived experience, can we even begin to put the right questions properly, and avoid the naïvetés on all sides: either that unbelief is just the falling away of any sense of fullness, or the betrayal of it (what theists sometimes are tempted to think of atheists); or that belief is just a set of theories attempting to make sense of experiences which we all have, and whose real nature can be understood purely immanently (what atheists are sometimes tempted to think about theists).

In fact, we have to understand the differences between these options not just in terms of creeds, but also in terms of differences of experience and sensibility. And on this latter level, we have to take account of two important differences: first, there is the massive change in the whole background of belief or unbelief, that is, the passing of the earlier "naïve" framework, and the rise of our "reflective" one. And secondly, we have to be aware of how believers and unbelievers can experience their world very differently. The sense that fullness is to be found in something beyond us can break in on us as a fact of experience, as in the case of Bede Griffiths quoted above, or in the moment of conversion that Claudel lived in Notre Dame at Vespers. This experience may then be articulated, rationalized; it may generate particular beliefs. This process may take time, and the beliefs in question may change over the years, even though the experience remains in memory as a paradigm moment. This is what happened to Bede, who came to a fully theistic reading of that crucial moment only some years later; and a similar "lag" can be seen in the case of Claudel.[16] The condition of secularity 3 has thus to be described in terms of the possibility or impossibility of certain kinds of experience in our age.

3

I have been struggling above with the term "secular", or "secularity". It seems obvious before you start thinking about it, but as soon as you do, all sorts of problems arise. I tried to conjure some of these by distinguishing three senses in which I will use the term. This by no means gets rid of all problems, but it may be enough to allow for some progress in my enquiry.

But all three modes of secularity make reference to "religion": as that which is retreating in public space (1), or as a type of belief and practice which is or is not in regression (2), and as a certain kind of belief or commitment whose conditions in this age are being examined (3). But what is "religion"? This famously defies definition, largely because the phenomena we are tempted to call religious are so tremendously varied in human life. When we try to think what there is in common between the lives of archaic societies where "religion is everywhere", and the clearly demarcated set of beliefs, practices and institutions which exist under this title in our society, we are facing a hard, perhaps insuperable task.

But if we are prudent (or perhaps cowardly), and reflect that we are trying to understand a set of forms and changes which have arisen in one particular civilization, that of the modern West—or in an earlier incarnation, Latin Christendom—we see to our relief that we don't need to forge a definition which covers everything "religious" in all human societies in all ages. The change which mattered to people in our (North Atlantic, or "Western") civilization, and still matters today, concerning the status of religion in the three dimensions of secularity I identified, is the one I have already started to explore in one of its central facets: we have moved from a world in which the place of fullness was understood as unproblematically outside of or "beyond" human life, to a conflicted age in which this construal is challenged by others which place it (in a wide range of different ways) "within" human life. This is what a lot of the important fights have been about more recently (as against an earlier time when people fought to the death over different readings of the Christian construal).

In other words, a reading of "religion" in terms of the distinction transcendent/ immanent is going to serve our purposes here. This is the beauty of the prudent (or cowardly) move I'm proposing here. It is far from being the case that religion in general can be defined in terms of this distinction. One could even argue that marking our particular hard-and-fast distinction here is something which we (Westerners, Latin Christians) alone have done, be it to our intellectual glory or stultification (some of each, I will argue later). You couldn't foist this on Plato, for instance, not because you can't distinguish the Ideas from the things in the flux which "copy" them, but precisely because these changing realities can only be understood through the Ideas. The great invention of the West was that of an immanent order in Nature, whose working could be systematically understood and explained on its own terms, leaving open the question whether this whole order had a deeper significance, and whether, if it did, we should infer a transcendent Creator beyond it. This notion of the "immanent" involved denying—or at least isolating and problematizing—any form of interpenetration between the things of Nature, on one hand, and "the supernatural" on the other, be this understood in terms of the one transcendent God, or of Gods or spirits, or magic forces, or whatever.[17]

So defining religion in terms of the distinction immanent/transcendent is a move tailor-made for our culture. This may be seen as parochial, incestuous, navel-gazing, but I would argue that this is a wise move, since we are trying to understand changes in a culture for which this distinction has become foundational.

So instead of asking whether the source of fullness is seen/lived as within or without, as we did in the above discussion, we could ask whether people recognize something beyond or transcendent to their lives. This is the way the matter is usually put, and I want to adopt it in what follows. I will offer a somewhat fuller account of what I mean by this distinction several chapters down the road, when we come to examine modern theories of secularization. I fully recognize that a word like "transcendent" is very slippery—partly because, as I hinted just now, these distinctions have been constructed or redefined in the very process of modernity and secularization. But I believe that in all its vagueness, it can serve in our context.

But precisely for the reasons that I explored above, I want to supplement the usual account of "religion" in terms of belief in the transcendent, with one more focussed on the sense we have of our practical context. Here is one way of making sense of this.

Every person, and every society, lives with or by some conception(s) of what human flourishing is: what constitutes a fulfilled life? what makes life really worth living? What would we most admire people for? We can't help asking these and related questions in our lives. And our struggles to answer them define the view or views that we try to live by, or between which we haver. At another level, these views are codified, sometimes in philosophical theories, sometimes in moral codes, sometimes in religious practices and devotion. These and the various ill-formulated practices which people around us engage in constitute the resources that our society offers each one of us as we try to lead our lives.

Another way of getting at something like the issue raised above in terms of within/without is to ask: does the highest, the best life involve our seeking, or acknowledging, or serving a good which is beyond, in the sense of independent of human flourishing? In which case, the highest, most real, authentic or adequate human flourishing could include our aiming (also) in our range of final goals at something other than human flourishing. I say "final goals", because even the most self-suffing humanism has to be concerned with the condition of some non-human things instrumentally, e.g., the condition of the natural environment. The issue is whether they matter also finally.

It's clear that in the Judaeo-Christian religious tradition the answer to this question is affirmative. Loving, worshipping God is the ultimate end. Of course, in this tradition God is seen as willing human flourishing, but devotion to God is not seen as contingent on this. The injunction "Thy will be done" isn't equivalent to "Let humans flourish", even though we know that God wills human flourishing.

This is a very familiar case for us. But there are other ways in which we can be taken beyond ordinary human flourishing. Buddhism is an example. In one way, we could construe the message of the Buddha as telling us how to achieve true happiness, that is, how to avoid suffering, and attain bliss.[18] But it is clear that the understanding of the conditions of bliss is so "revisionist" that it amounts to a departure from what we normally understand as human flourishing. The departure here can be put in terms of a radical change of identity. Normal understandings of flourishing assume a continuing self, its beneficiary, or in the case of its failure the sufferer. The Buddhist doctrine of anatta aims to bring us beyond this illusion. The way to Nirvana involves renouncing, or at least going beyond, all forms of recognizable human flourishing.

In both Buddhism and Christianity, there is something similar in spite of the great difference in doctrine. This is that the believer or devout person is called on to make a profound inner break with the goals of flourishing in their own case; they are called on, that is, to detach themselves from their own flourishing, to the point of the extinction of self in one case, or to that of renunciation of human fulfillment to serve God in the other. The respective patterns are clearly visible in the exemplary figures. The Buddha achieves Enlightenment; Christ consents to a degrading death to follow his father's will.

But can't we just follow the hint above, and reconstrue "true" flourishing as involving renunciation, as Stoicism seems to do, for example? This won't work for Christianity, and I suspect also not for Buddhism. In the Christian case, the very point of renunciation requires that the ordinary flourishing forgone be confirmed as valid. Unless living the full span were a good, Christ's giving of himself to death couldn't have the meaning it does. In this it is utterly different from Socrates' death, which the latter portrays as leaving this condition for a better one. Here we see the unbridgeable gulf between Christianity and Greek philosophy. God wills ordinary human flourishing, and a great part of what is reported in the Gospels consists in Christ making this possible for the people whose afflictions he heals. The call to renounce doesn't negate the value of flourishing; it is rather a call to centre everything on God, even if it be at the cost of forgoing this unsubstitutable good; and the fruit of this forgoing is that it become on one level the source of flourishing to others, and on another level, a collaboration with the restoration of a fuller flourishing by God. It is a mode of healing wounds and "repairing the world" (I am here borrowing the Hebrew phrase *tikkun olam*).

This means that flourishing and renunciation cannot simply be collapsed into each other to make a single goal, by as it were, pitching the renounced goods overboard as unnecessary ballast on the journey of life, in the manner of Stoicism. There remains a fundamental tension in Christianity. Flourishing is good, nevertheless seeking it is not our ultimate goal. But even where we renounce it, we re-affirm it, because we follow God's will in being a channel for it to others, and ultimately to all.

Can a similar, paradoxical relation be seen in Buddhism? I'm not sure, but Buddhism also has this notion that the renouncer is a source of compassion for those who suffer. There is an analogy between karuna and agape. And over the centuries in Buddhist civilization there developed, parallel with Christendom, a distinction of vocation between radical renouncers, and those who go on living within the forms of life aiming at ordinary flourishing, while trying to accumulate "merit" for a future life. (Of course, this distinction was radically "deconstructed" in the Protestant Reformation, with what fateful results for our story here we are all in some way aware, even though the task of tracing its connections to modern secularism is still very far from completed.)

Now the point of bringing out this distinction between human flourishing and goals which go beyond it is this. I would like to claim that the coming of modern secularity in my sense has been coterminous with the rise of a society in which for the first time in history a purely self-sufficient humanism came to be a widely available option. I mean by this a humanism accepting no final goals beyond human flourishing, nor any allegiance to anything else beyond this flourishing. Of no previous society was this true.

Although this humanism arose out of a religious tradition in which flourishing and the transcendent goal were distinguished and paradoxically related (and this was of some importance for our story), this doesn't mean that all previous societies projected a duality in this domain, as I have argued for Buddhism and Christianity. There were also outlooks, like Taoism seems to be, where flourishing was conceived in a unitary way, including reverence for the higher. But in these cases, this reverence, although essential for flourishing, couldn't be undertaken in a purely instrumental spirit. That is, it couldn't be *reverence* if it were so understood.

In other words, the general understanding of the human predicament before modernity placed us in an order where we were not at the top. Higher beings, like Gods or spirits, or a higher kind of being, like the Ideas or the cosmopolis of Gods and humans, demanded and deserved our worship, reverence, devotion or love. In some cases, this reverence or devotion was itself seen as integral to human flourishing; it was a proper part of the human good. Taoism is an example, as are such ancient philosophies as Platonism and Stoicism. In other cases, the devotion was called for even though it be at our expense, or conduce to our good only through winning the favour of a God. But even here the reverence called for was real. These beings commanded our awe. There was no question of treating them as we treat the forces of nature we harness for energy.

In this kind of case, we might speak of a humanism, but not of a self-sufficing or exclusive humanism, which is the contrast case which is at the heart of modern secularity.

This thesis, placing exclusive humanism only within modernity, may seem too bald and exceptionless to be true. And indeed, there are exceptions. By my account, ancient Epicureanism was a self-sufficing humanism. It admitted Gods, but denied them relevance to human life. My plea here is that one swallow doesn't make a summer. I'm talking about an age when self-sufficing humanism becomes a widely available option, which it never was in the ancient world, where only a small minority of the élite which was itself a minority espoused it.

I also don't want to claim that modern secularity is somehow coterminous with exclusive humanism. For one thing, the way I'm defining it, secularity is a condition in which our experience of and search for fullness occurs; and this is something we all share, believers and unbelievers alike. But also, it is not my intention to claim that exclusive humanisms offer the only alternatives to religion. Our age has seen a strong set of currents which one might call non-religious anti-humanisms, which fly under various names today, like "deconstruction" and "post-structuralism", and which find their roots in immensely influential writings of the nineteenth century, especially those of Nietzsche. At the same time, there are attempts to reconstruct a non-exclusive humanism on a non-religious basis, which one sees in various forms of deep ecology.

My claim will rather be something of this nature: secularity 3 came to be along with the possibility of exclusive humanism, which thus for the first time widened the range of possible options, ending the era of "naïve" religious faith. Exclusive humanism in a sense crept up on us through an intermediate form, Providential Deism; and both the Deism and the humanism were made possible by earlier developments within orthodox Christianity. Once this humanism is on the scene, the new plural, non-naïve predicament allows for multiplying the options beyond the original gamut. But the crucial transforming move in the process is the coming of exclusive humanism.

From this point of view, one could offer this one-line description of the difference between earlier times and the secular age: a secular age is one in which the eclipse of all goals beyond human flourishing becomes conceivable; or better, it falls within the range of an imaginable life for masses of people. This is the crucial link between secularity and a self-sufficing humanism.[19]

So "religion" for our purposes can be defined in terms of "transcendence", but this latter term has to be understood in more than one dimension. Whether one believes in some agency or power transcending the immanent order is indeed, a crucial feature of "religion", as this has figured in secularization theories. It is our relation to a transcendent God which has been displaced at the centre of social life (secularity 1); it is faith in this God whose decline is tracked in these theories (secularity 2). But in order to understand better the phenomena we want to explain, we should see religion's relation to a "beyond" in three dimensions. And the crucial one, that which makes its impact on our lives understandable, is the one I have just been exploring: the sense that there is some good higher than, beyond human flourishing. In the Christian case, we could think of this as agape, the love which God has for us, and which we can partake of through his power. In other words, a possibility of transformation is offered, which takes us beyond merely human perfection. But of course, this notion of a higher good as attainable by us could only make sense in the context of belief in a higher power, the transcendent God of faith which appears in most definitions of religion. But then thirdly, the Christian story of our potential transformation by agape requires that we see our life as going beyond the bounds of its "natural" scope between birth and death; our lives extend beyond "this life".

For purposes of understanding the struggle, rivalry, or debate between religion and unbelief in our culture, we have to understand religion as combining these three dimensions of transcendence. This is not because there are not other possibilities which are being explored in our society, options somewhere between this triple transcendence perspective, and the total denial of religion. On the contrary, these options abound. It is rather because, in a way I shall explain many chapters down the road, the multi-cornered debate is shaped by the two extremes, transcendent religion, on one hand, and its frontal denial, on the other. It is perfectly legitimate to think that this is a misfortune about modern culture; but I would like to argue that it is a fact.

4

So secularity 3, which is my interest here, as against 1 (secularized public spaces), and 2 (the decline of belief and practice), consists of new conditions of belief; it consists in a new shape to the experience which prompts to and is defined by belief; in a new context in which all search and questioning about the moral and spiritual must proceed.

The main feature of this new context is that it puts an end to the naïve acknowl-edgment of the transcendent, or of goals or claims which go beyond human flour-ishing. But this is quite unlike religious turnovers in the past, where one naïve hori-zon ends up replacing another, or the two fuse syncretistically—as with, say, the conversion of Asia Minor from Christianity to Islam in the wake of the Turkish conquest. Naïveté is now unavailable to anyone, believer or unbeliever alike.

This is the global context in a society which contains different milieux, within each of which the default option may be different from others, although the dwell-ers within each are very aware of the options favoured by the others, and cannot just dismiss them as inexplicable exotic error.

The crucial change which brought us into this new condition was the coming of exclusive humanism as a widely available option. How did all this happen? Or oth-erwise put, what exactly is it which has happened, such that the conditions of belief are altered in the way I've been describing? These are not easy questions to answer.

That is, I think they aren't easy. But for many people in our day, the answer seems, at least in its general lines, fairly obvious. Modernity brings about secularity, in all its three forms. This causal connection is ineluctable, and mainline seculariza-tion theory is concerned to explain why it had to be. Modern civilization cannot but bring about a "death of God".

I find this theory very unconvincing, but in order to show why, I have to launch myself into my own story, which I shall be telling in the following chapters. At a later phase I shall return to the issue of what a convincing theory of secularization might look like.

But first, a word about the debate I shall be developing. In fact, two words. First, I shall be concerned, as I said above, with the West, or the North Atlantic world; or in other terms, I shall be dealing with the civilization whose principal roots lie in what used to be called "Latin Christendom". Of course, secularization and secularity are phenomena which exist today well beyond the boundaries of this world. It should be possible some day to undertake a study of the whole phe-nomenon on a global scale. But I don't think one can start there. This is be-cause secularity, like other features of "modernity"—political structures, democratic forms, uses of media, to cite a few other examples—in fact find rather different ex-pression, and develop under the pressure of different demands and aspirations in different civilizations. We are more and more living in a world of "multiple mod-ernities".[20] These crucial changes need to be studied in their different civilizational sites before we rush to global generalization. Already my canvas is on the verge of being too broad; there are many regional and national paths to secularity within the North Atlantic world, and I haven't been able to do justice to all of them. But I hope some light can be cast on general features of the process nonetheless.[21] In following this path, I am repeating what I attempted in *Sources of the Self*,[22] which also took up a set of issues of universal human concern, but dealt with them within a regional compass.

Secondly, in the following chapters, I will be making a continuing polemic against what I call "subtraction stories". Concisely put, I mean by this stories of modernity in general, and secularity in particular, which explain them by human beings having lost, or sloughed off, or liberated themselves from certain earlier, confining horizons, or illusions, or limitations of knowledge. What emerges from this process—modernity or secularity—is to be understood in terms of underlying features of human nature which were there all along, but had been impeded by what is now set aside. Against this kind of story, I will steadily be arguing that Western modernity, including its secularity, is the fruit of new inventions, newly constructed self-understandings and related practices, and can't be explained in terms of perennial features of human life.

I hope that the detailed discussion which follows will make clearer what is involved in this issue, and I shall also return to it more systematically towards the end, in Chapter 15.

PART I

The Work of Reform

1   The Bulwarks of Belief

1

One way to put the question that I want to answer here is this: why was it virtually impossible not to believe in God in, say, 1500 in our Western society, while in 2000 many of us find this not only easy, but even inescapable?

Part of the answer, no doubt, is that in those days everyone believed, and so the alternatives seemed outlandish. But this just pushes the question further back. We need to understand how things changed. How did the alternatives become thinkable?

One important part of the picture is that so many features of their world told in favour of belief, made the presence of God seemingly undeniable. I will mention three, which will play a part in the story I want to tell.

(1) The natural world they lived in, which had its place in the cosmos they imagined, testified to divine purpose and action; and not just in the obvious way which we can still understand and (at least many of us) appreciate today, that its order and design bespeaks creation; but also because the great events in this natural order, storms, droughts, floods, plagues, as well as years of exceptional fertility and flourishing, were seen as acts of God, as the now dead metaphor of our legal language still bears witness.

(2) God was also implicated in the very existence of society (but not described as such—this is a modern term—rather as polis, kingdom, church, or whatever). A kingdom could only be conceived as grounded in something higher than mere human action in secular time. And beyond that, the life of the various associations which made up society, parishes, boroughs, guilds, and so on, were interwoven with ritual and worship, as I mentioned in the previous chapter. One could not but encounter God everywhere.

(3) People lived in an "enchanted" world. This is perhaps not the best expression; it seems to evoke light and fairies. But I am invoking here its negation, Weber's expression "disenchantment" as a description of our modern condition. This term has

achieved such wide currency in our discussion of these matters, that I'm going to use its antonym to describe a crucial feature of the pre-modern condition. The enchanted world in this sense is the world of spirits, demons, and moral forces which our ancestors lived in.

People who live in this kind of world don't necessarily believe in God, certainly not in the God of Abraham, as the existence of countless "pagan" societies shows. But in the outlook of European peasants in 1500, beyond all the inevitable ambivalences, the Christian God was the ultimate guarantee that good would triumph or at least hold the plentiful forces of darkness at bay.

Atheism comes close to being inconceivable in a world with these three features. It just seems so obvious that God is there, acting in the cosmos, founding and sustaining societies, acting as a bulwark against evil. So part of the answer to my opening question, what happened between 1500 and 2000? is that these three features have vanished.

But that can't be the whole story, as I argued in the previous chapter. The rise of modernity isn't just a story of loss, of subtraction. The key difference we're looking at between our two marker dates is a shift in the understanding of what I called "fullness", between a condition in which our highest spiritual and moral aspirations point us inescapably to God, one might say, make no sense without God, to one in which they can be related to a host of different sources, and frequently are referred to sources which deny God. Now the disappearance of these three modes of God's felt presence in our world, while it certainly facilitates this change, couldn't by itself bring it about. Because we can certainly go on experiencing fullness as a gift from God, even in a disenchanted world, a secular society, and a post-cosmic universe. In order to be able not to, we needed an alternative.

And so the story I have to tell will relate not only how God's presence receded in these three dimensions; it also has to explain how something other than God could become the necessary objective pole of moral or spiritual aspiration, of "fullness". In a sense, the big question of what happened is, how did alternatives to the God-reference of fullness arise? What I'll be concerned with is the Entstehungsgeschichte of exclusive humanism.

A common "subtraction" story attributes everything to disenchantment. First, science gave us "naturalistic" explanation of the world. And then people began to look for alternatives to God. But things didn't work that way. The new mechanistic science of the seventeenth century wasn't seen as necessarily threatening to God. It was to the enchanted universe and magic. It also began to pose a problem for particular providences. But there were important Christian motives for going the route of disenchantment. Darwin was not even on the horizon in the eighteenth century.

Then, of course, society comes to be seen in secular terms. People make revolutions. In certain cases, this involved rebelling against churches. But it could be in the name of other church structures, as in the 1640s, and with a strong sense of Providence guiding us.

A fuller subtraction story holds that not just disenchantment, but the fading of God's presence in all three domains made us look afresh at the alternative possible reference-points for fullness. As though these were already there, just waiting to be invited in.

My point is that, in an important sense, they weren't yet there. True, there were various doctrines, which some people had imagined, even which orthodox writers had inveighed against; in some cases, which ancient authors had spelled out. But these weren't yet really available alternatives. I mean alternative construals of fullness which could really make sense to people, outside of a few very original spirits.

Negatively, it was very hard to see how an exclusive humanism could fill this role, as long as people had an enchanted view of the universe; that is, saw us human beings as in a field of spirits, some of whom were malign. In this respect, of course, science in helping to disenchant the universe, contributed to opening the way for exclusive humanism. A crucial condition for this was a new sense of the self and its place in the cosmos: not open and porous and vulnerable to a world of spirits and powers, but what I want to call "buffered". But it took more than disenchantment to produce the buffered self; it was also necessary to have confidence in our own powers of moral ordering.

But surely, the resources for that were available, in the non-theistic ethics of the pagan ancient world? Only very partially, I believe. First, some of those views also placed us in a larger spiritual or cosmic order. Platonism, Stoicism, for instance. True, they had no necessary truck with magic and wood spirits, but they resisted disenchantment and the mechanistic universe in their own ways. They were not really exclusive humanisms in my sense. I would argue this even for Aristotle, because of the important role for contemplation of a larger order as something divine in us.

Where an exclusive humanism was undoubtedly available was in Epicureanism. And it is no surprise that Lucretius was one of the inspirations for explorations in the direction of naturalism, e.g., with Hume. But Epicureanism just as it was couldn't really do the trick. It could teach us to achieve ataraxia by overcoming our illusions about the Gods. But this wasn't what was needed for a humanism which could flourish in the modern context. For this was becoming one in which the power to create moral order in one's life had a rather different shape. It had to include the active capacity to shape and fashion our world, natural and social; and it had to be actuated by some drive to human beneficence. To put this second requirement in a way which refers back to the religious tradition, modern humanism, in addition to being activist and interventionist, had to produce some substitute for agape.

All this means that an acceptable form of exclusive humanism had to be imagined. And this couldn't be done overnight. Nor could it arise in one leap, but it came to be in a series of phases, emerging out of earlier Christian forms. This is the story I'm going to try to tell.

As of the late nineteenth century, indeed, we have fully-formed alternatives which are there before us. And people can be influenced towards one or the other, partly in terms of their views of science—even though, as I shall argue, here too, a crucial role is still played by their moral ontologies. But today, for instance, when a naturalistic materialism is not only on offer, but presents itself as the only view compatible with the most prestigious institution of the modern world, viz., science; it is quite conceivable that one's doubts about one's own faith, about one's ability to be transformed, or one's sense of how one's own faith is indeed, childish and inadequate, could mesh with this powerful ideology, and send one off along the path of unbelief, even though with regret and nostalgia. But it is wildly anachronistic to project this very familiar scenario of Victorian times, or today, onto earlier centuries, when the rival outlooks between which we hesitate today were still being forged.

2

My opening question stated a contrast, between the conditions of belief in 1500 and 2000. And then I talked about the story I want to tell to clarify this contrast. But why tell a story? Why not just extract the analytic contrast, state what things were like then, and how they are now, and let the linking narrative go? Who needs all this detail, this history? Haven't I already made a satisfactory start on such an analytic contrast in identifying the three ways of God's presence then which have faded by now?

Now in a way, the ultimate goal is to arrive at such a contrast, or at least to get into focus our situation in 2000 by means of such a comparative description. But I don't think it can properly be done if one tries to elide the history. I hope the reasons for this will become clearer and more convincing as I proceed. But just to give the general shape of them here: it is a crucial fact of our present spiritual predicament that it is historical; that is, our understanding of ourselves and where we stand is partly defined by our sense of having come to where we are, of having overcome a previous condition. Thus we are widely aware of living in a "disenchanted" universe; and our use of this word bespeaks our sense that it was once enchanted. More, we are not only aware that it used to be so, but also that it was a struggle and an achievement to get to where we are; and that in some respects this achievement is fragile. We know this because each one of us as we grew up has had to take on the disciplines of disenchantment, and we regularly reproach each other for our failings in this regard, and accuse each other of "magical" thinking, of indulging in "myth", of giving way to "fantasy"; we say that X isn't living in our century, that Y has a "mediaeval" mind, while Z, whom we admire, is way ahead of her time.

In other words, our sense of where we are is crucially defined in part by a story of how we got there. In that sense, there is an inescapable (though often negative) God-reference in the very nature of our secular age. And just because we describe where we are in relating the journey, we can misdescribe it grievously by misidentifying the itinerary. This is what the "subtraction" accounts of modernity have in fact done. To get straight where we are, we have to go back and tell the story properly.

Our past is sedimented in our present, and we are doomed to misidentify ourselves, as long as we can't do justice to where we come from. This is why the narrative is not an optional extra, why I believe that I have to tell a story here.

That enlarges the task, potentially without limit. The story of what happened in the secularization of Western Christendom is so broad, and so multi-faceted, that one could write several books this length and still not do justice to it. This is the more so, in that my chosen area, Latin Christendom, is not homogeneous. As we will see below, there is more than one path here, and different nations and regions have trodden their own way at different speeds and times. I can only give the barest bones of the story, and touch on some of the major transitions. My hope is that a general picture of the dynamic involved will emerge from this skeleton account. But some such diachronic account is indispensable.

3

Telling the story can't be elided; but it isn't sufficient of itself. In fact, the whole discussion has to tack back and forth between the analytical and the historical. And at this point I want to start by laying out some broad features of the contrast between then and now, which will be filled in and enriched by the story. They fall in the range of the three big negative changes I alluded to above, but I'll be proceeding from last to first, and in fact I want to mention five changes.

The first is disenchantment, the undoing of obstacle 3 above to unbelief (I). Then entering the terrain of obstacle 2 (II), I want also to look at the way in which earlier society held certain profound tensions in equilibrium (III). This in turn was linked to a common understanding of time, which has since been done away with (IV). And lastly, I want to deal with the erosion of obstacle 1, in the way in which the old idea of cosmos has been replaced by the modern neutral universe (V).

I. Let me start with the enchanted world, the world of spirits, demons, moral forces which our predecessors acknowledged. The process of disenchantment is the disappearance of this world, and the substitution of what we live today: a world in which the only locus of thoughts, feelings, spiritual élan is what we call minds; the only minds in the cosmos are those of humans (grosso modo, with apologies to possible Martians or extra-terrestrials); and minds are bounded, so that these thoughts, feelings, etc., are situated "within" them.

This space within is constituted by the possibility of introspective self-awareness. This doesn't mean that everything within is capable of being brought to this awareness. The possibility remains that some things "in the mind" are so deep, and perhaps hidden (repressed), that we can never bring them to consciousness. But these belong to this inner space, because they lie beyond and help shape the things we can grasp introspectively; as the things just beyond the horizon we see have their place in the world of the visible, even though we may never be able to go there to witness them. The "inward" in this sense is constituted by what I have called "radical reflexivity".[1]

What I am trying to describe here is not a theory. Rather my target is our contemporary lived understanding; that is, the way we naïvely take things to be. We might say: the construal we just live in, without ever being aware of it as a construal, or—for most of us—without ever even formulating it. This means that I am not taking on board the various philosophical theories which have been offered to explain and articulate the "mind" and its relation to the "body". I am not attributing to our lived understanding some kind of Cartesian dualism, or its monist materialist rivals, identity theory, or whatever; or even a more sophisticated and adequate theory of embodied agency. I am trying to capture the level of understanding prior to philosophical puzzlement. And while this modern understanding of the mind certainly opens itself to Cartesian type theories in a way that the earlier "enchanted" understanding does not, it isn't itself such a theory. Put another way, the modern idea of mind makes something like the "mind-body problem" conceivable, indeed, in a way inescapable, where on the earlier understanding it didn't really make sense. But by itself it doesn't offer an answer to that problem.

I am interested in the naïve understanding, because my claim will be that a fundamental shift has occurred in naïve understanding in the move to disenchantment. This is unlike what I said above on the issue of the existence of God and other spiritual creatures. There we have moved from a naïve acceptance of their reality, to a sense that either to affirm or deny them is to enter a disputed terrain; there are no more naïve theists, just as there are no naïve atheists. But underlying this change is the one I am now talking about in our sense of our world, from one in which these spirits were just unproblematically there, impinging on us, to one in which they are no longer so, and indeed, in which many of the ways they were there have become inconceivable. Their not so impinging is what we experience naïvely.

Of course, this doesn't mean that we experience them naïvely as being non-existent. The scope of the negative operator is broad here. We do not (no longer) experience their existence; it is not true that we experience their non-existence. Analogously, on the naïve level, I have no experience of the molecular constitution of things. But that is no bar to my believing what I am taught in physics class. Only these beliefs have a certain specific locus in my picture of the world; I know that they are available to me only through a complex theoretical activity of search, which has been carried through by others. Similarly here, the existence of God or other spirits is not negated by the modern world-understanding; but this understanding situates belief in a realm where it is open to doubt, argument, mediating explanations, and the like.

This shift in naïve understanding is therefore very important for my purpose here. Getting a clearer view of it will be to have a better grasp on the change in the conditions of belief. We get to the heart of secularity in my third sense.

I started off explicating this understanding with the notion of mind. Thoughts, etc., occur in minds; minds are (grosso modo) only human; and they are bounded: they are inward spaces.

Let's start from the first principle. What am I gesturing at with the expression "thoughts, etc."? I mean, of course, the perceptions we have, as well as the beliefs or propositions which we hold or entertain about the world and ourselves. But I also mean our responses, the significance, importance, meaning, we find in things. I want to use for these the generic term 'meaning', even though there is in principle a danger of confusion with linguistic meaning. Here I'm using it in the sense in which we talk about "the meaning of life", or of a relationship as having great "meaning" for us.

Now the crucial difference between the mind-centred view and the enchanted world emerges when we look at meanings in this sense. On the former view meanings are "in the mind", in the sense that things only have the meaning they do in that they awaken a certain response in us, and this has to do with our nature as creatures who are thus capable of such responses, which means creatures with feelings, with desires, aversions, i.e., beings endowed with minds, in the broadest sense.

I must stress again that this is a way of understanding things which is prior to explication in different philosophical theories, materialist, idealist, monist, dualist. We can take a strict materialist view, and hold that our responses are to be explained by the functions things have for us as organisms, and further by the kinds of neurophysiological responses which their perception triggers off. We are still explaining the meanings of things by our responses, and these responses are "within" us, in the sense that they depend on the way we have been "programmed" or "wired up" inside.

The materialist fantasy, that we could for all we know be brains in a vat, being manipulated by some mad scientist, depends for its sense on this view that the material sufficient condition for thoughts of all kinds is within the cranium. Hence convincing thoughts about a non-existent world could be produced by generating the right brain states. The inside/outside geography, and the boundary dividing them, which is crucial to the mind-outlook is reproduced in this materialist explication of it.

But in the enchanted world, meanings are not in the mind in this sense, certainly not in the human mind. If we look at the lives of ordinary people—and even to a large degree of élites—500 years ago, we can see in a myriad ways how this was so. First, they lived in a world of spirits, both good and bad. The bad ones include Satan, of course, but beside him, the world was full of a host of demons, threatening from all sides: demons and spirits of the forest, and wilderness, but also those which can threaten us in our everyday lives.

Spirit agents were also numerous on the good side. Not just God, but also his saints, to whom one prayed, and whose shrines one visited in certain cases, in hopes of a cure, or in thanks for a cure already prayed for and granted, or for rescue from extreme danger, e.g., at sea.

These extra-human agencies are perhaps not so strange to us. They violate the second point of the modern outlook I mentioned above, viz., that (as we ordinarily tend to believe) the only minds in the cosmos are humans; but they nevertheless seem to offer a picture of minds, somewhat like ours, in which meanings, in the form of benevolent or malevolent intent can reside.

But seeing things this way understates the strangeness of the enchanted world. Thus precisely in this cult of the saints, we can see how the forces here were not all agents, subjectivities, who could decide to confer a favour. But power also resided in things.[2] For the curative action of saints was often linked to centres where their relics resided; either some piece of their body (supposedly), or some object which had been connected with them in life, like (in the case of Christ), pieces of the true cross, or the sweat-cloth which Saint Veronica had used to wipe his face, and which was on display on certain occasions in Rome. And we can add to this other objects which had been endowed with sacramental power, like the Host, or candles which had been blessed at Candlemas, and the like. These objects were loci of spiritual power; which is why they had to be treated with care, and if abused could wreak terrible damage.

In fact, in the enchanted world, the line between personal agency and impersonal force was not at all clearly drawn. We see this again in the case of relics. The cures effected by them, or the curse laid on people who stole them or otherwise mishandled them, were seen both as emanating from them, as loci of power, and also as coming from the good will, or anger, of the saint they belonged to. Indeed, we can say that in this world, there is a whole gamut of forces, ranging from (to take the evil side for a moment) super-agents like Satan himself, forever plotting to encompass our damnation, down to minor demons, like spirits of the wood, which are almost indistinguishable from the loci they inhabit, and ending in magic potions which bring sickness or death. This illustrates a point which I want to bring out here, and to which I will recur shortly, that the enchanted world, in contrast to our universe of buffered selves and "minds", shows a perplexing absence of certain boundaries which seem to us essential.

So in the pre-modern world, meanings are not only in minds, but can reside in things, or in various kinds of extra-human but intra-cosmic subjects. We can bring out the contrast with today in two dimensions, by looking at two kinds of powers that these things/subjects possess.

The first is the power to impose a certain meaning on us. Now in a sense, something like this happens today all the time, in the sense that certain responses are involuntarily triggered in us by what happens in our world. Misfortunes befall us, and we are sad; great events befall and we rejoice. But the way in which things with power affected us in the enchanted world has no analogies in our understanding today.

For us, things in the world, those which are neither human beings, nor expressions of human beings, are "outside" of mind. They may in their own way impinge on mind—really, in two possible ways:

(1) We may observe these things, and therefore change our view of the world, or be stirred up in ways that we otherwise wouldn't be. (2) Since we are ourselves as bodies continuous with these external things, and in constant exchange with them, and since our mental condition is responsive causally to our bodily condition in a host of ways (something we are aware of without espousing any particular theory of what exactly causes what), our strength, moods, motivations, etc. can be affected, and are continually being affected, by what happens outside.

But in all these cases, that these responses arise in us, that things take on these meanings, is a function of how we as minds, or organisms secreting minds, operate. By contrast, in the enchanted world, the meaning is already there in the object/agent, it is there quite independently of us; it would be there even if we didn't exist. And this means that the object/agent can communicate this meaning to us, impose it on us, in a third way, by bringing us as it were into its field of force. It can in this way even impose quite alien meanings on us, ones that we would not normally have, given our nature; as well as, in positive cases, strengthening our endogenous good responses.

In other words, the world doesn't just affect us by presenting us with certain states of affairs, which we react to from out of our own nature, or by bringing about some chemical-organic condition in us, which in virtue of the way we operate produces, say, euphoria or depression. In all these cases, the meaning as it were only comes into existence as the world impinges on the mind/organism. It is in this sense endogenous. But in the enchanted world, the meaning exists already outside of us, prior to contact; it can take us over, we can fall into its field of force. It comes on us from the outside.

In a way, this sounds weird. But in another way, there is an analogy which is quite understandable to us today, and which helps. We just have to think what happens between humans. Say I am in a terrible mood. I walk around the house full of anger and despair. You started off the morning full of optimism and energy; but you gradually feel yourself drained, drawn down into my pit of despair. (Or maybe it works happily, and you draw me up.) The mood which falls on you is, in a sense, exogenous.

But of course, you have it in your repertory to be in a black mood. I'm just responsible for bringing it on today, not for your being susceptible to it as such. However, we also see cases of more fundamental exogenous change. Perhaps I have learned from you a certain kind of open, giving love, which I was quite incapable of before, whose existence I even wanted to deny; it wasn't on my map of possibilities. Or more fundamentally again, we both have come to a love, one essentially involving sharing, communication, which neither one of us could have had unilaterally. For each of us this is in a sense the gift of the other. Rather than existing within each of us, we might want to say that it happens in the interspace between us.

But this is not the enchanted world, of course; because we are remaining within the human realm, human agents, human potentialities. It only can look like the enchanted world, if we understand disenchantment through the prism of an atomistic view of the human subject: thoughts only exist within individual minds. This is, alas, all too common. There is something in the move to the mind-centred view which has given us a fatal susceptibility to atomistic theories. Philosophy keeps having to climb out of them. But once again, I'm trying to deal with a whole framework of understanding, abstracting from the philosophical theories which articulate it.

These common human happenings don't give us the enchanted world, but they offer an analogy which helps us to understand it. The pre-modern understanding allows this inter-human power of inducing meanings in each other (exogenously, relative to the individual) to roam beyond the human sphere, or at least something analogous to this power.

So we can explicate the idea that meaning is in things partly in terms of this power of exogenously inducing or imposing meaning. But in the enchanted world, the meaning in things also includes another power. These "charged" objects can affect not only us but other things in the world. They can effect cures, save ships from wreck, end hail and lightning, and so on. They have what we usually call "magic" powers. Blessed objects, e.g., relics of saints, the Host, candles, are full of God-power, and can do some of the good things which God's power does, like heal diseases, and fight off disasters. Sources of evil power correspondingly wreak malevolent ends, make us sick, weaken our cattle, blight our crops, and the like.

Once again, to point up the contrast with our world, we can say that in the enchanted world, charged things have a causal power which matches their incorporated meaning. The High Renaissance theory of the correspondences, which while more an élite than a popular belief, partakes of the same enchanted logic, is full of such causal links mediated by meaning. Why does mercury cure venereal disease? Because this is contracted in the market, and Hermes is the God of markets (Hacking). This way of thinking is totally different from our post-Galilean, mind-centred disenchantment. If thoughts and meanings are only in minds, then there can be no "charged" objects, and the causal relations between things cannot be in any way dependent on their meanings, which must be projected on them from our minds. In other words, the physical world, outside the mind, must proceed by causal laws which in no way turn on the moral meanings things have for us.

Thus in the enchanted world, charged things can impose meanings, and bring about physical outcomes proportionate to their meanings. Let me call these two respectively influence and causal power.

I want now to try to bring out how in this world, certain boundaries which are both familiar and crucial to us seem to fade. I have already spoken about the line between subjects and things among these charged beings. But more centrally, the clear boundary between mind and world which we mark was much hazier in this earlier understanding.

This follows from the fact of influence. Once meanings are not exclusively in the mind, once we can fall under the spell, enter the zone of power of exogenous meaning, then we think of this meaning as including us, or perhaps penetrating us. We are in as it were a kind of space defined by this influence. The meaning can no longer be placed simply within; but nor can it be located exclusively without. Rather it is in a kind of interspace which straddles what for us is a clear boundary. Or the boundary is, in an image I want to use here, porous.[3]

This porousness is most clearly in evidence in the fear of possession. Demons can take us over. And indeed, five centuries ago, many of the more spectacular manifestations of mental illness, what we would class as psychotic behaviour, were laid at the door of possession, as in the New Testament times. One "cure" on offer for this condition was to beat the patient; the idea being that by making this site acutely uncomfortable for the demon, one would induce him to leave.

But the fuzziness is even greater than that. Even the line between ordinary cases of influence and full possession was not totally sharp. There is a gamut of cases. People spoke of possession when our higher faculties and powers seemed totally eclipsed; for instance, when people fell into delirium. But in a sense, any evil influence involves some eclipse of the highest capacities in us. Only in the case of good influence, for instance, when we are filled with grace, do we become one with the agent/force through what is best and highest in us. Demons may possess us, but God or the Holy Spirit enter us, or quicken us from within.

Whether for good or evil, influence does away with sharp boundaries. Say someone falls in love. And this has an impact, good or ill, on his life. An "internal" event, we think, albeit susceptible to pressures from outside in the two ways I mentioned above, and although it certainly has effects.

But now let's say that we see this whole side of life as under the aegis of a goddess, Aphrodite. That means that its going well is its being smiled on by Aphrodite. This means not only that she is keeping the external dangers at bay; like a human patron, she is in this aspect causally responsible for the conditions being propitious. It also means that the blooming of the right internal motivation is a gift from her. In other words, my being in the highest motivational condition is not just a fact about my inner realm of desires; it is my being the recipient of the gift of the goddess. The highest condition can't just be placed unambiguously within; it is placed in that interspace, where the gift is received.

Now imagine that this is not a theory, but how we sense things to be; and thus how we seem to experience them. Then the inside is no longer just inside; it is also outside. That is, emotions which are in the very depths of human life exist in a space which takes us beyond ourselves, which is porous to some outside power, a person-like power.

Let's turn to the opposite pole: evil spirits, those which tend to do us harm. Here too, there is a dimension in which we can make this familiar: there are beings who will us evil, and can bring about conditions in which evil befalls. It sounds just like a human enemy, only this one has a repertory of evil tricks which go way beyond the human. This would be symmetrical to the external protection of Aphrodite.

But once again, the evil spirit has more than just weird and impressive external powers. The malevolence is more invasive than this. It can sap our very will to resist, our will to survive. It can penetrate us as living, willing beings, with our own purposes and intent. We can't restrict its action to the "external" realm.

As a mode of experience, rather than as theory, this can be captured by saying that we feel ourselves vulnerable or "healable" (this is meant to be the favourable antonym to "vulnerable") to benevolence or malevolence which is more than human, which resides in the cosmos or even beyond it. This sense of vulnerability is one of the principal features which have gone with disenchantment. Any particular attribution of danger, e.g., to a witch, fits in that world into a generalized sense of vulnerability which this attribution specifies. This is what makes it credible. The enchanted world provides a framework in which these attributions make sense and can be fully believable. They are analogous in this way to an attribution of hostile intent to an armed person in one of those zones of urban lawlessness which exist in our world.

Along with vulnerability to malevolence goes the need to propitiate, action to buy or win the friendship, or at least de-activate the enmity of these forces. And connected to this are notions of what it is normal to do to propitiate, hence notions of ought, debt; hence notions of guilt and punishment; which thus play a large part in this world.

Of course, talk of gods and spirits can be grasped on the analogy of human amity/enmity. But this doesn't capture the whole of the pre-modern world view, as I pointed out above. This opens us to a universe which is much more alien than this. Cosmic forces which breach the boundary and can act within are not only personalized creatures like us. There is a whole gamut of them, which progressively depart from the personal, until we need a quite different model; that of cosmic realities which nevertheless incorporate certain meanings; and hence can affect us, make us live these meanings in certain circumstances.

Now all this has very important consequences for the whole way we live our experience. I'd like to try to spell out this crucial difference a bit more fully.

Let us take a well-known example of influence inhering in an inanimate substance; again like the correspondences above, this is drawn from élite theory rather than popular belief; but the principle is the same. Consider melancholy: black bile is not the cause of melancholy, it embodies it, it *is* melancholy. The emotional life is porous here again; it doesn't simply exist in an inner, mental space. Our vulnerability to the evil, the inwardly destructive, extends to more than just spirits which are malevolent. It goes beyond them to things which have no wills, but are nevertheless redolent with the evil meanings.

See the contrast. A modern is feeling depressed, melancholy. He is told: it's just your body chemistry, you're hungry, or there is a hormone malfunction, or whatever. Straightaway, he feels relieved. He can take a distance from this feeling, which is ipso facto declared not justified. Things don't really have this meaning; it just feels this way, which is the result of a causal action utterly unrelated to the meanings of things. This step of disengagement depends on our modern mind/body distinction, and the relegation of the physical to being "just" a contingent cause of the psychic.

But a pre-modern may not be helped by learning that his mood comes from black bile. Because this doesn't permit a distancing. Black bile *is* melancholy. Now he just knows that he's in the grips of the real thing.

Here is the contrast between the modern, bounded self—I want to say "buffered"

BLACK BILE

BUFFERED MODERN

self—and the "porous" self of the earlier enchanted world. What difference does this make?

A very different existential condition. The last example about melancholy and its causes illustrates this well. For the modern, buffered self, the possibility exists of taking a distance from, disengaging from everything outside the mind. My ultimate purposes are those which arise within me, the crucial meanings of things are those defined in my responses to them. These purposes and meanings may be vulnerable to manipulation in the two ways described above; but this can in principle be met with a counter-manipulation: I avoid distressing or tempting experiences, I don't shoot up the wrong substances, etc.

This is not to say that the buffered understanding necessitates your taking this stance. It is just that it allows it as a possibility, whereas the porous one does not. By definition for the porous self, the source of its most powerful and important emotions are outside the "mind"; or better put, the very notion that there is a clear boundary, allowing us to define an inner base area, grounded in which we can disengage from the rest, has no sense.

As a bounded self I can see the boundary as a buffer, such that the things beyond don't need to "get to me", to use the contemporary expression. That's the sense to my use of the term "buffered" here. This self can see itself as invulnerable, as master of the meanings of things for it.

These two descriptions get at, respectively, the two important facets of this contrast. First, the porous self is vulnerable, to spirits, demons, cosmic forces. And along with this go certain fears which can grip it in certain circumstances. The buffered self has been taken out of the world of this kind of fear. For instance, the kind of thing vividly portrayed in some of the paintings of Bosch.

True, something analogous can take its place. These images can also be seen as coded manifestations of inner depths, repressed thoughts and feelings. But the point is that in this quite transformed understanding of self and world, we define these as inner, and naturally, we deal with them very differently. And indeed, an important part of the treatment is designed to make disengagement possible.

Perhaps the clearest sign of the transformation in our world is that today many people look back to the world of the porous self with nostalgia. As though the creation of a thick emotional boundary between us and the cosmos were now lived as a loss. The aim is to try to recover some measure of this lost feeling. So people go to movies about the uncanny in order to experience a frisson. Our peasant ancestors would have thought us insane. You can't get a frisson from what is really in fact terrifying you.

The second facet is that the buffered self can form the ambition of disengaging from whatever is beyond the boundary, and of giving its own autonomous order to its life. The absence of fear can be not just enjoyed, but seen as an opportunity for self-control or self-direction.

And so the boundary between agents and forces is fuzzy in the enchanted world; and the boundary between mind and world is porous, as we see in the way that charged objects can influence us. I have just been speaking about the moral influence of substances, like black bile. But a similar point can be made about the relation to spirits. The porousness of the boundary emerges here in the various kinds of "possession", all the way from a full taking over of the person, as with a medium, to various kinds of domination by, or partial fusion with, a spirit or God.[4] Here again, the boundary between self and other is fuzzy, porous. And this has to be seen as a fact of *experience,* not a matter of "theory", or "belief".

Yet another clear boundary of today, that between the laws of physical science and the meanings things have for us, is also not respected. Charged objects have causal power in virtue of their intrinsic meanings. Indeed, the absence of boundary can be put in a more thoroughgoing way; for even the distinction that I as a typical modern have been using as an expository device, that between the two powers of charged objects, influence and causal power; even this falls afoul of the enchanted world. Not that the distinction could not be made in that world for it was, as we shall see; but that it didn't necessarily correspond to two types of event which were really, as against analytically, distinct. That is, the same force that healed you could also make you a better, or more holy person; and that in one act, so to speak. For the two disabilities were often seen as not really distinct.[5] This shows that in, for instance, the healing at and by shrines, relics, sacred objects, etc., we are dealing with something different from modern medicine, even where the analogy seems closest. The way people carried away from Canterbury phials of water supposedly mixed with the blood of the martyr Thomas à Becket, and then drank the water to effect a cure of something, may seem at first sight rather similar to finding a rare medicine at a special pharmacy today. But the modern boundary wasn't there, whereby the remedy is meant to be for the body, not the mind, or if the mind, only because this is affected by changes in the organism in the canonical way described above. This comes out in the way in which illness and sin were often seen as inextricably related. We are ill, because we are sapped inwardly by our sinful condition. In cases like this, we might say that sin was playing the role which we would attribute today to a failure of the immune system.[6] It was commonly believed that certain conditions would clear up after absolution. The close link between sin and illness also explains the decisions of the Lateran and other councils warning against recourse to ordinary medicine in place of spiritual remedies, and forbidding altogether the frequenting of infidel doctors (e.g., Jews).

Of course, in practice, lots of people treated the remedies as though they would work of themselves, regardless of the spiritual condition of the recipient. Just this was the cause of repeated complaints by clergy and educated observers. But this was not because they had the attitude of modern buffered selves to prescription medicine from the drug store. Rather it was that they hoped that the spiritual and physical change would come together, from drinking the water, or putting their hand in the reliquary, without needing serious spiritual input on their part. In a very similar way, many people ignored the condition of indulgences, that one should be shriven before engaging in the pilgrimage or other indulgence-earning act; they treated it as sufficient of itself to bring them God's forgiveness. This was the scandal which Luther protested against; and he was far from being the first to do so.

But just as there were people then who in their crass use of sacred objects or acts seemed to approach the modern instrumentalization of healing substances; so there are remains today of the stance which links illness to sin. Think of the reaction of some people to the AIDS epidemic; or the way people with cancer are often told that they are stricken because of their bad life style (Susan Sontag protested against this). Some of the old attitudes are not beyond recovery, in a sense. It is just that in espousing them seriously one goes against the grain of the modern identity in a fundamental way. One adopts beliefs which most people will castigate as weird.

In the enchanted world of 500 years ago, a clear line between the physical and the moral wasn't drawn. But this is just another facet of the basic fact that the boundary around the mind was constitutionally porous. Things and agencies which are clearly extra-human could alter or shape our spiritual and emotional condition, and not just our physical state (and hence mediately our spiritual or emotional condition), but both together in one act. These agencies didn't simply operate from outside the "mind", they helped to constitute us emotionally and spiritually.

This is not the only way in which we draw this physical/moral boundary today that wasn't recognized then. Connected to our firm placing of the non-human world outside the mind, is our perception of it as the domain of exceptionless natural law. The modern post-Newtonian outlook reigns supreme here. Now even if we are theoretically committed to treat the human world in the same "scientific" way, we don't manage ever in practice to frame our interaction with others in this mould. In fact, we live the domain of human action as one in which a big difference can be made by an exceptional effort of will, or charismatic appeal, or superlative judgment irreducible to rules or formulae. And so we often see outcomes as arising from exceptionally effective (or ineffective) action, without being able to state them all as instances of a single set of laws.

But it was in exactly this way that our ancestors saw the significant natural events of their world: the cures or their failure, the bumper harvest or famine, plagues or storms, rescue at sea or foundering. These were not instances of exceptionless laws, but actions; sometimes of evil agents, sometimes of saints, and sometimes of God. The term "act of God" had its real meaning then.

This persisted right up to the Renaissance. Bouwsma points out that Calvin sees storms and floods as special Providences, literally acts of God, responding to ours.[7] The exceptionless order was still a thing of the future. It is a facet of the disenchanted world.

How does all this then relate to the conditions of belief? This relation can be stated in two ways, corresponding to the two facets of the contrast buffered/porous above.

First, disbelief is hard in the enchanted world. This is not so much because spirits are part of the undeniable furniture of things and God is a spirit, ergo undeniable. Much more important, God figures in this world as the dominant spirit, and moreover, as the only thing that guarantees that in this awe-inspiring and frightening field of forces, good will triumph. Of course, just this will mean that our relations with, feelings about God will probably be tinged with ambiguity, as they always are. But it will also mean that the prospect of rejecting God does not involve retiring to the safe redoubt of the buffered self, but rather chancing ourselves in the field of forces without him. Practically our only recourse can be to seek another protector; and in this case the most likely candidate is his arch-enemy, Satan. Although it's hard to tell through all the trumped up accusations, possibly a small number of brave souls really took an option something like this in the Middle Ages, but it's obviously not one which is likely to attract masses of people.

In general, going against God is not an option in the enchanted world. That is one way the change to the buffered self has impinged. It removes a tremendous obstacle to unbelief. But as I argued above, this was not enough. There has still to be a positive option of exclusive humanism on offer. And here the significance of the change is evident. It opened the way to the kind of disengagement from cosmos and God which made exclusive humanism a possibility.

A possibility, but still not a reality. In order to see how it became that, we have to follow a bit more closely the actual progress of disenchantment. How it actually worked out has marked, in many ways, the actual condition of modern Western secularity, and the terms in which the struggles of belief and unbelief now occur.

4

H. I have been speaking of the modern self as "buffered", and the earlier mode of existence as that of a "porous self". But the use of the substantive here may mislead. Someone can live the modern sense of self as buffered, while being very conscious of himself as an individual. Indeed, this understanding lends itself to individuality, even atomism; sometimes we may wonder if it can be made hospitable to a sense of community. The buffered self is essentially the self which is aware of the possibility of disengagement. And disengagement is frequently carried out in relation to one's whole surroundings, natural and social.

But living in the enchanted, porous world of our ancestors was inherently living socially. It was not just that the spiritual forces which impinged on me often emanated from people around me; e.g., the spell cast by my enemy, or the protection afforded by a candle which has been blessed in the parish church. Much more fundamental, these forces often impinged on us as a society, and were defended against by us as a society.

To take the latter first: much of the "good magic" was that of the church. This is intrinsic to the sense that God is the ultimate guarantee that good will triumph. So we ring the church bells when lightning threatens. Or more fundamentally, the whole community turns out in procession to "beat the bounds" of the parish on rogation days. Carrying the host and whatever relics we possess, we march around the boundaries, in this way warding off evil spirits for another season. In one such rite in England, the Gospels were read "in the wide field among the corn and grass, that by virtue of the operation of God's word, the power of the wicked spirits, which keep in the air and infect the same . . . may be laid down . . . to the intent the corn may remain unharmed, and not infected . . . but serve us for our use and bodily sustenance."[8] Our defense here is collective, deploying a power that we can only draw on as a community, on one level, that of the parish, but more broadly that of the Church in its full extent.

So we're all in this together. This has two consequences. First, it puts a tremendous premium on holding to the consensus. Turning "heretic" and rejecting this power, or condemning the practice as idolatrous, is not just a personal matter. Villagers who hold out, or even denounce the common rites, put the efficacy of these rites in danger, and hence pose a menace to everyone.

This is something we constantly tend to forget when we look back condescendingly on the intolerance of earlier ages. As long as the common weal was bound up in collective rites, devotions, allegiances, it couldn't be seen just as an individual's own business that he break ranks, even less that he blaspheme or try to desecrate the rite. There was an immense common motivation to bring him back into line.

In these earlier days, societies, and not just parishes but whole kingdoms, were seen as standing together towards God, responsible for the "orthodoxy" (right praise) of their members. The deviancy of some would call down punishment on all. At a certain point, God even owes it to himself, as it were, to his honour, we might say, to strike. This is how it seemed to Luther, for instance.[9] Even as late and (in some ways, anyway) enlightened a figure as Jean Bodin, at the end of the sixteenth century, in his writings on the necessary repression of witches, says that we must "venger à toute rigueur afin de faire cesser l'ire de Dieu"[10] (exact rigorous vengeance in order to stay the anger of God).

The idea died hard that a society containing heretics, even unbelievers, must fall into disorder. It even hangs on in a semi-rationalized form into the Age of Enlightenment, in the view, for instance, that oaths of allegiance would have to be null and void for atheists, who by definition fear no retribution in the after-life. Locke thought so, and even Voltaire came close to it.

This means that there was great pressure towards orthodoxy. This was one consequence. But the other was perhaps more important for our purposes here, tracing the way in which God was, as it were, an object of "naïve" experience for people of that day. This brings us into what we identified as dimension (2) above. When such crucial social action involves deploying together this kind of "magic" or spiritual power, then society itself is seen, is experienced as a locus of this power. How can you be fully "into" a collective rite like beating the bounds, and yet skeptical of the power of God and the Sacrament? It would be like fixing the socket today while doubting the existence of electricity. God's power was there for you in the microfunctioning of your society.

This example relates to the level of the parish. But the point is just as true of the higher levels of society, e.g., the universal church, or the kingdom. This latter, like the former, but in its own way, can only exist thanks to sacred power, the "divinity which doth hedge a king", his anointment, certain thaumaturgical powers thought to inhere in the king, etc.

The social bond at all these levels was intertwined in the sacred, and indeed, it was unimaginable otherwise. How could a society not so sustained exist in the enchanted world? If not rooted in the sacred of God, it would have to be grounded in the counter-sacred of the Evil one.

And so society, this utterly solid and indispensable reality, argues for God. Not only does it follow: I have moral and spiritual aspirations, therefore God is; but also: we are linked in society, therefore God is. It is this facet, God's existential-foundational role in society, which perhaps best explains how difficult it was to get our minds around the possibility that a society might exist which was not grounded in common religious beliefs.[11]

III. Now there is another feature, or set of features, which is crucial to this world of our ancestors, and which has also been done away with. The story of the undoing of this feature is central to the transformation. This is a feature which mediaeval Christendom had in common with many (perhaps most) civilizations dominated by a "higher" religion.

We could call this feature an equilibrium in tension between two kinds of goals. On one hand, the Christian faith pointed towards a self-transcendence, a turning of life towards something beyond ordinary human flourishing, as we discussed in an earlier section. On the other, the institutions and practices of mediaeval society, as with all human societies, were at least partly attuned to foster at least some human flourishing. This sets up a tension, between the demands of the total transformation which the faith calls to, and the requirements of ordinary ongoing human life.

The tension emerges in various ways. One of the most common and best known centres around the celibate vocations which became important first in the eastern Church in the very first centuries. The understanding behind these first waves of hermitic and monastic lives was that celibacy enabled a total turning of the heart to God. Procreation is our answer to the Fall, and the death which it introduces into the world. By procreating, we go on perpetuating the species in fallen time. But through celibacy, we can attempt to leap out of fallen time, and return to God's eternity.[12]

The tension would be overcome in a church which enjoined celibacy on everyone, as the Shakers did in our time. Or else, it could be overcome in the way the Reformers would eventually do, by rejecting celibate vocations altogether. Only in this later case, the strain between the demands of perfection and those of everyday life breaks out in other forms.

But the mainline Catholic and Orthodox churches combined both celibate and married modes of life. Moreover, with time, the distinction begins to grow into a complementarity. So that in the Latin Church a (in theory) celibate clergy prays and fulfills priestly and pastoral functions for a married laity, which in turn supports the clergy. On a broader scale, monks pray for all, mendicant orders preach; others provide alms, hospitals, etc. Over time, the tension is overlaid with an equilibrium, based on a complementarity of functions.

Naturally, this doesn't do away with continuing sources of tension. For one thing, there is a continuing lack of fit between the dominant, accepted notions of flourishing and the demands of the gospel. The honour ethic, the demands of pride and station, are built in to the model of flourishing of at least the upper castes. And the warrior life, the central vocation of the lay nobility, has its demands as well, which are very hard to square with the gospel, in spite of attempted syntheses, as in the ideal of the monk-crusader.

Added to this source of contention, and compounding it, are issues about the role and place of the sacraments and "sacramentals". These are meant to serve the salvation of the faithful. But they also are the very heart of the "white magic" by which ordinary human flourishing is defended against threats, and enhanced. So the blessed sacrament will be part of the procession around the boundaries of the parish. And "sacramentals", like blessed candles, will be used to conjure evil spells, and ward off sickness.

Now in principle, this continues the Gospels, where Jesus' power heals sickness and restores people to flourishing life. But where do these uses of sacred power cross a line where their purpose in the order of salvation is lost sight of, or even profaned in the name of flourishing? What if the sacrament is carried home, and applied as powerful substance to some end? What if sacred power is captured as a love charm?[13]

Erasmus was repelled by the sheerly *interested* nature of much popular piety, as he saw it.

> There are those who worship certain heavenly powers with special rites. One salutes Christopher daily, though only when he sees his image, because he has persuaded himself that on such days he will be insured against an evil death. Another worships St Roch—but why? Because he thinks to drive away the plague. Another mumbles prayers to Barbara or George, lest they fall into the hands of an enemy. This man vows to Apollonia to fast in order to escape toothache; that one gazes on the image of St Job to get rid of the itch. Some give part of their profits to the poor in order to keep their business from mishap; some light candles to Jerome to restore a business already bad.

All this for Erasmus was on a par with idolatry.[14]

Now without overlooking these points of tension, we can read mediaeval Catholicism in one way as incorporating a kind of equilibrium based on hierarchical complementarity. This was certainly recognized as an organizing principle for the society as a whole. For instance, the famous formula: the clergy pray for all, the lords defend all, the peasants labour for all, encapsulates the idea that society is organized in complementary functions, which nevertheless are of unequal dignity. Similarly, the celibate vocations can be seen as higher, and undeniably the sacerdotal ones were so seen; but this doesn't prevent them balancing the other, lower modes of life in a functional whole.

What this means is that there is in principle a place for something less than the highest vocation and aspirations. The tension resolves into an equilibrium. We'll see in a minute that this was not the whole truth of the late Middle Ages, but it was part of it.

Another way in which this feature of equilibrium in tension emerges in this society became evident in Carnival and similar festivities, such as the feasts of misrule, or boy bishops, and the like. These were periods in which the ordinary order of things

Festival

was inverted, or "the world was turned upside down". For a while, there was a ludic interval, in which people played out a condition of reversal of the usual order. Boys wore the mitre, or fools were made kings for a day; what was ordinarily revered was mocked, people permitted themselves various forms of licence, not just sexually but also in close-to-violent acts, and the like.

These festivals are fascinating, because their human meaning was at once very powerfully felt in them—people threw themselves into these feasts with gusto—and yet also enigmatic.[15] The enigma is particularly strong for us moderns, in that the festivals were not putting forward an alternative to the established order, in anything like the sense we understand in modern politics, that is, presenting an antithetical order of things which might replace the prevailing dispensation. The mockery was enframed by a understanding that betters, superiors, virtue, ecclesial charisma, etc. ought to rule; the humour was in that sense not ultimately serious.[16]

Natalie Davis had argued for an origin of these feasts of the urban setting in the villages, where there was recognized licence for the class of young unmarried males to indulge in mockery and mayhem, like the charivari. But as she points out, this mockery was exercised very much in support of the ruling moral values.[17]

And yet, for all this acceptance of order, plainly something else showed through the display and the laughter, some deeply felt longings, at variance with this order. What was going on? I don't know, but some interesting and suggestive ideas have been put forward which are worth noting.

Even at the time, the explanation was offered that people needed this as a safety valve. The weight of virtue and good order was so heavy, and so much steam built up under this suppression of instinct, that there had to be periodic blow-outs if the whole system were not to fly apart. Of course, they didn't think in terms of steam at the time, but a French cleric expressed the point clearly in the technology of the day.

> We do these things in jest and not in earnest, as the ancient custom is, so that once a year the foolishness innate in us can come out and evaporate. Don't wine skins and barrels burst open very often if the air-hole is not opened from time to time? We too are old barrels . . .[18]

Also at the time, and more since, people have related these festivals to the Roman Saturnalia. There seems no good ground to trace a real historical connection, but the supposition that something similar is resurfacing here is perfectly acceptable in principle. The thinking behind this parallel draws on theories about the Saturnalia, and other similar festivals (e.g., in ancient Mesopotamia, and also the Aztec renewals of the world). The intuition supposedly underlying these is that order binds a primitive chaos, which is both its enemy but also the source of all energy, including that of order. The binding has to capture that energy, and in the supreme moments of founding it does this. But the years of routine crush this force and drain it; so that order itself can only survive through periodic renewal, in which the forces of chaos are first unleashed anew, and then brought into a new founding of order. As though the effort to maintain order against chaos could not but in the end weaken, tire, unless this order were replunged into the primal energies of chaos to emerge with renewed strength. Or something like this; it's hard to get it entirely clear.

Then, of course, there is Bakhtin, who brings out the utopian strain in laughter. Laughter as the solvent of all boundaries; the body which connects us to everyone and everything; these are celebrated in Carnival. A kind of carnal Parousia is adumbrated.[19]

Victor Turner proposes another theory. The order we are mocking is important but not ultimate; what is ultimate is the community it serves; and this community is fundamentally egalitarian; it includes everyone. Yet we cannot do away with the order. So we periodically renew it, rededicate it, return it to its original meaning, by suspending it in the name of the community, which is fundamentally, ultimately of equals, and which underlies it.[20]

I've laid all these out, because whatever the merits of each one, they point up an important feature of the world in which these festivals occurred. It incorporates some sense of the complementarity, the mutual necessity of opposites, that is, of states which are antithetical, can't be lived at the same time. Of course, we all live this at some level: we work for x hours, relax for y hours, sleep for z hours. But what is unsettling to the modern mind is that the complementarity behind carnival exists on the moral or spiritual level. We're not just dealing with a de facto incompatibility, like that of sleeping and watching television at the same time. We're dealing with things which are enjoined and those condemned, with the licit and illicit, order and chaos. All the above accounts have this in common, that they postulate a world, and underlying this perhaps a cosmos, in which order needs chaos, in which we have to give place to contradictory principles.

Victor Turner's discussion of this is especially interesting, because he tries to put this phenomenon of Carnival in a wider perspective. It is one manifestation of a relationship which turns up in a tremendous range of pre-modern societies in all parts of the world. In its general form, the relationship could be put in this way: all structure needs anti-structure. By 'structure', Turner means, borrowing a phrase from Merton, "the patterned arrangements of role-sets, status-sets and status-sequences' *consciously* recognized and regularly operative in a given society."[21] We could perhaps rephrase this, and speak of the code of behaviour of a society, in which are defined the different roles and statuses, and their rights, duties, powers, vulnerabilities.

Turner's point is that in many societies where this code is taken perfectly seriously, and enforced, even harshly most of the time, there are nevertheless moments or situations in which it is suspended, neutralized, or even transgressed. Plainly Carnival and Feasts of Misrule constituted such moments in mediaeval Europe. But these "rituals of reversal" are in fact very widespread. For instance, in the enthroning ritual of the king in various African societies, the candidate must pass through an ordeal, in which he is reviled, hectored, and even kicked and shoved by his subjects to be.[22]

This kind of reversal has analogies to another kind of relation in which people who according to the dominant jural-political code are weak or of low status can exercise another kind of power in a complementary domain. Turner cites a number of African societies formed by militarily dominant invaders who have conquered the indigenous people. "The invaders control high political office, such as the kingship, provincial governorships, and headmanships. On the other hand, the indigenous people, through their leaders, frequently are held to have a mystical power over the fertility of the earth and of all on it. These autochthonous people have religious power, the 'power of the weak' as against the jural-political power of the strong, and represent the undivided land itself against the political system with its internal segmentation and hierarchies of authority."[23]

This situation has analogies in turn to all those societies in which various classes of powerless and low-status people can exercise a certain authority in their sphere, as is sometimes the case for women, for instance; or in which the weak, the indigent, the outsider is surrounded with a certain charisma, like holy madmen, or indeed, the poor in mediaeval society—whose altered fate in early modern society I will discuss below.

Turner further extends the range of analogies to include societies with "rites of passage" of the kind studied by Arnold van Gennep.[24] The point of contact here is that these rituals by which people move from one status to the next—say, circumcision rites for young men, who thereby become adults—involve the neophytes stepping out of their earlier role and entering a kind of limbo, in which they are stripped of all the marks of status. Their earlier identity is in a sense obliterated, and they pass a period on the "threshold", undergoing trials and ordeals, before they step into the new identity. The threshold image is van Gennep's, who coined the term "liminality" for this condition. Turner sees liminality as a kind of "anti-structure", because it's a condition in which the markers of the ordinary code, with its rights, duties and status criteria, have been temporarily wiped away.

What all these situations have in common is that there is a play of structure and anti-structure, code and anti-code; this either takes the form of the code's being momentarily suspended or transgressed; or else, as with the relation between conquerors and autochthonous above, the code itself allows for a counter-principle to the dominant source of power; it opens space for a complementary "power of the weak". It's as though there were a felt need to complement the structure of power with its opposite. Otherwise . . . what?

The basic intuitions here are hard to define. I mentioned some possibilities above in connection with Carnival. One is certainly the idea that the pressure of the code needs to be relaxed from time to time; we need to let off steam. But then the further idea often seems to be there, that the code relentlessly applied would drain us of all energy; that the code needs to recapture some of the untamed force of the contrary principle. Commenting a paper by Evans-Pritchard on rituals which prescribe obscenity, Turner says:

> The raw energies released in overt symbolisms of sexuality and hostility between the sexes are channelled toward master symbols representative of structural order, and values and virtues on which that order depends. Every opposition is overcome or transcended in a recovered unity, a unity that, moreover, is reinforced by the very potencies which endanger it. One aspect of the ritual is shown by these rites to be a means of putting at the service of the social order the very forces of disorder that inhere in man's mammalian constitution.[25]

These explanations still sound rather "functionalist"; the aim of the exercise seems still to be the preservation of the society. But Turner puts them in the context of the pull of "communitas", which takes us beyond this level of explanation. The sense of "communitas" is the intuition we all share that, beyond the way we relate to each other through our diversified coded roles, we also are a community of many-sided human beings, fundamentally equal, who are associated together. It is this underlying community which breaks out in moments of reversal or transgression, and which gives legitimacy to the power of the weak.

Now this account also has its "functionalist" face. When we curse and swear at the king-elect, we remind him and us that the ruler's rights and prerogatives have a further purpose which is the weal of the whole. But in Turner's view, the draw to communitas can go way beyond the boundaries of our society. It can be activated by the sense that we are all human beings, equals, that we belong together. The pull to anti-structure can come from beyond the society, and even from beyond humanity. From this point of view, it would be legitimate to see the first tension I mentioned above, that between ordinary flourishing and the higher, renunciative vocations, as another example of structure versus anti-structure. The structures of power, property, warrior dominance, are challenged by a life which claims to be higher, and yet which couldn't simply replace the established order. They are forced into co-existence, and hence some kind of complementarity.

This enables us to see that the play of structure and anti-structure can take place on more than one level, because it is this whole complementarity of state and church together which plays the structural pole to the anti-structure of carnival.

So the pull of communitas is potentially multi-valenced. It can not only bring to the fore our community, but that of humankind. And in breaking us out of coded roles, it also does a number of other things besides releasing fellowship. It also sets free our spontaneity and creativity. It allows free reign to the imagination.

Seen in this perspective, the power of anti-structure comes also from the sense that all codes limit us, shut us out from something important, prevent us from seeing and feeling things of great moment. We remember that in some of the rites of passage, the elders take advantage of this liminal condition to instruct the youth in the deepest lore of the society; as if these things can't be learned except by those who have become receptive through stepping out of their normal coded roles. We recognize here the principle behind the "retreat", both religious and secular.

The general phenomenon here is thus a sense of the necessity of anti-structure. All codes need to be countervailed, sometimes even swamped in their negation, on pain of rigidity, enervation, the atrophy of social cohesion, blindness, perhaps ultimately self-destruction. Both the tension between temporal and spiritual, and the existence of carnival and other rites of reversal, show that this sense used to be very alive in Latin Christendom. What has happened to it today?

Well, as the reference above to retreats shows, it is not wholly gone. We have a sense of it in our daily lives. We still feel the need to "get away from it all", to cut out and "recharge our batteries", away, on holiday, outside our usual roles. There are certainly carnival-type moments: public holidays, football matches—here, like their predecessors, hovering on the brink, sometimes over the brink of violence. Communitas breaks out in moments of exceptional danger or bereavement, as with the crowds mourning Princess Di.

What is different is that this need for anti-structure is no longer recognized at the level of the whole society, and in relation to its official, political-jural structure. One might ask: how could it be? In all the cases mentioned above, the need for anti-structure was understood in terms of a spiritual context: the human code exists within a larger spiritual cosmos, and its opening to anti-structure is what is required to keep the society in true with the cosmos, or to draw on its forces. Seen from this point of view, the eclipse of this felt need is a simple corollary of the secularization of public space (sense 1 of the first chapter above).

I draw attention to it here, because I think that it played a very important role in the rise of secularity 1. That is, it was the eclipse of this sense of necessary complementarity, of the need for anti-structure, which preceded and helped to bring about the secularization of public space. The idea that a code need leave no space for the principle that contradicts it, that there need be no limit to its enforcement, which is the spirit of totalitarianism, is not just one of the consequences of the eclipse of anti-structure in modernity. That is certainly true. But it is also the case that the temptation to put into effect a code which brooks no limit came first. Yielding to this temptation is what helped bring modern secularity, in all its senses, into being.

That belongs to the story I want to tell shortly. For the moment I want just to complete the contrast I was making between then and now.

Certainly one consequence of the eclipse of anti-structure was this propensity to believe that the perfect code wouldn't need to be limited, that one could and should enforce it without restriction. This has been one of the driving ideas behind the various totalitarian movements and régimes of our time. Society had to be totally made over, and none of the traditional restraints on action should be allowed to hamper this enterprise. In a less dramatic way, it encourages the tunnel vision with which the various "speech codes" of political correctness are applied on certain campuses, and lends the positive ring to such slogans as "zero tolerance".

The epoch of the French Revolution is perhaps the moment in which at one and the same moment anti-structure goes into eclipse, and the project of applying a code without moral boundaries is seriously contemplated. This emerges most clearly in the attempts of the various revolutionary governments to design festivals which would express and entrench the new society. In these attempts, they drew heavily on earlier feasts, for instance, on Carnival, on pilgrimages (the model for the Fête de la Fédération), and the processions of Corpus Christi (la Fête Dieu). But the nature of the enterprise was in a certain sense reversed.

That is because the dimension of anti-structure was totally missing. The aim of the exercise was not to open a hiatus in the now reigning code, but to give expression to its spirit, and inspire identification with it. The anti-structural elements of Carnival were sometimes borrowed, as in the dechristianization of Year II, but this destructive mockery was directed against the old religion and the ancien régime in general. It aimed to complete the destruction of the reigning code's enemies, not to suspend the code itself.[26]

As befits celebrations of the official reality these feasts were generally well ordered; they were meant to celebrate the social bond itself, or else "nature"; and they were rigorously egalitarian and reciprocal. They tried to meet the Rousseauian requirement that the distinction between spectators and actors be abolished. As a report on one of these feasts had it: "La fête de la liberté du 15 mai fut du moins nationale, en ce que le peuple y était tout à la fois acteur et spectateur." (The Festival of Liberty on May 15 was at least national, in that in it the people were at once both actors and spectators.)[27] They were determinedly anthropocentric. "La seule vraie religion est celle qui annoblit l'homme, en lui donnant une idée sublime de la dignité de son être et des belles destinées auxquelles il est appelé par l'ordinateur humain." (The only true religion is that which ennobles man by giving him a sublime idea of the dignity of his being and of the great destinies to which he is called by the designer of the human condition.)[28]

No wonder that they were deathly dull, and disappeared, along with the new calendar designed to contain them, with the fall of the régime which sponsored them. They are harbingers of similar attempts at self-celebration by this century's communist régimes, which have met a similar fate. And they tell us something about what happens to traditional anti-structures in our age, as we can see with the use made of aspects of Carnival in the dechristianization of 1793. They can offer guidelines for Utopia, or for a new and totally harmonious régime. I will return to this below.

But erecting a structure without moral boundaries is a temptation of an age which has forgotten anti-structure; it is not a fatality. It can be avoided, and generally has been. A principle of opposition can be built into our reigning political code, as with the division of powers; and this has generally been done in the name of a principle of limitation, the negative freedom of the subject. Of course, an attempt may still be made on the intellectual plane to show how these free, self-limiting régimes flow from a single principle, as we see, for instance, with the contemporary "liberalism" of Rawls and Dworkin. This shows how deeply modernity has invested in the myth of the single, omnicompetent code.[29] But there are theorists, such as Benjamin Constant, Alexis de Tocqueville, and in our century, Isaiah Berlin, who have recognized that we have to give our allegiance to more than one principle, and that those we essentially hold to are frequently in conflict.

Where in theory and in practice, liberal régimes of this pluralist kind have been developed, the consequences of the eclipse of anti-structure have been much mitigated. We might even say that anti-structure has been given a new kind of place in these societies, in the private domain. The public/private distinction, and the wide area of negative freedom, is the equivalent zone in these societies to the festivals of reversal in their predecessors. It is here, on our own, among friends and family, or in voluntary associations, that we can "drop out", throw off our coded roles, think and feel with our whole being, and find various intense forms of community. Without this zone, life in modern society would be unliveable.

This unofficial zone has developed its own public spheres, in which the imagination is nourished, and ideas and images circulate: the spheres of art, music, literature, thought, religious life, without which our personal dropping out would be radically impoverished. This modern space for anti-structure opens up unprecedented possibilities for untrammeled creation, and at the same time hitherto unexperienced dangers of isolation and loss of meaning. Both of these come from the fact that this space is "private", its public spheres sustained by purely voluntary participation.[30]

The modern predicament is in this way structurally different from anything which went before. And this means that one part of the traditional play of structure and anti-structure is no longer available to us. In rituals of reversal, or in the rites of obscenity in African societies I alluded to earlier, we have not only the airing of opposed principles, which are allowed to emerge and engage in mock battle. The aim is frequently also to bring them to some kind of synergy; to make the structure less self-enclosed, and at the same time to allow it to draw on the energy of anti-structure in order to renew itself.

This is something which seems beyond our capacity in the modern age. Or at least not by means of ritual. Sometimes the antagonistic forces in a society are brought together to recognize their commonalty by some common threat, or in moments of common grief. But that is a rather different thing. The fact that external danger is what so often is needed to unite us explains to some degree the continuing force of nationalism in our time.

So one of the places that anti-structure has migrated is into the private domain, and the public spheres sustained out of this. But that is not all. The call of anti-structure is still strong in our highly interdependent, technological, super-bureaucratized world. In some ways, more powerful than ever. A stream of protests, against central control, regimentation, the tyranny of instrumental reason, the forces of conformity, the rape of nature, the euthanasia of the imagination, have accompanied the development of this society over the last two centuries. They came to one climax recently, in the sixties and seventies, and we can be sure this is not their last. At that time, many aspects of Carnival were revisited and re-edited. Think of May '68 in Paris, with its denunciation of structure (le cloisonnement), and the energy of communitas that it thought it was releasing. The "Soixante-huitards" wanted precisely to eschew the anti-structure of private space; they wanted to make it central to public space, indeed, to abolish the distinction between the two.

But this too, is importantly different from the place of anti-structure earlier. Here the negation of the code is being drawn on as a source for utopias, and new projects, which are meant to replace the existing society, as I mentioned above. Carnival and Revolution can never coincide, no matter how close playful revolutionaries try to bring them. The aim of revolution is to replace the present order. It mines previous anti-structures to design a new code of freedom, community, radical fraternity. It is the birthplace of a new and perfect code, one that will need no moral boundaries, that will brook no anti-structure. It is the anti-structure to end all anti-structure. The dream if carried through (which fortunately it wasn't in '68) turns into a nightmare.

At this point, we become aware of a wisdom in the earlier play of code and negation that we are in danger of losing sight of. All structures need to be limited, if not suspended. Yet we can't do without structure altogether. We need to tack back and forth between codes and their limitation, seeking the better society, without ever falling into the illusion that we might leap out of this tension of opposites into pure anti-structure, which could reign alone, a purified non-code, forever.[31]

But it is extraordinary how often this dream has been generated afresh in our age, even by otherwise hard-headed people, like the inventors of "scientific socialism", dreaming of a "withering away of the state". This is because the pains of structure, its rigidities, injustices, insensitivity to human aspiration and suffering, having lost their earlier social outlet, drive us back to this dream. We have probably not seen the last of it.

5

IV. It is obvious that time in this world of reversal and anti-structure can't be the "homogeneous, empty time" which Benjamin makes central to modernity.[32] The time of carnival, for instance, is kairotic; that is, the time line encounters kairotic knots, moments whose nature and placing calls for reversal, followed by others demanding rededication, and others still which approach Parousia: Shrove Tuesday, Lent, Easter.

Now there are kairotic knots in the stories we tell about ourselves in our time. Revolutions themselves are understood by their heirs and supporters as such kairotic moments. And nationalist historiography is full of such moments. But what has changed is that around which these moments gather. In the pre-modern era, the organizing field for ordinary time came from what I want to call higher times.

The most obvious term to introduce here would be 'eternity'. And that isn't wrong, because it is the philosophically and theologically consecrated term for higher time. But I need the more general term, because (a) there was more than one kind of eternity, and (b) these didn't exhaust the higher times.

What did higher times do? One might say, they gathered, assembled, reordered, punctuated profane, ordinary time. Let me grasp a nettle and call this latter 'secular time'. There is a risk here, because I'm already using the word 'secular' (and in three senses, already!) for features of our age. If I feel impelled to introduce it in a fourth sense, it's because this is the original one, that from which my three meanings of chapter one are derived.

'Secular', as we all know, comes from 'saeculum', a century or age. When it begins to be used as one term in an opposition, like secular/regular clergy; or being in the saeculum, as against in religion (that is, some monastic order), the original meaning is being drawn on in a very specific way. People who are in the saeculum, are embedded in ordinary time, they are living the life of ordinary time; as against those who have turned away from this in order to live closer to eternity. The word is thus used for ordinary as against higher time. A parallel distinction is temporal/spiritual. One is concerned with things in ordinary time, the other with the affairs of eternity.

So it is hard to sideline the term when discussing pre-modern time-consciousness. Best to have things straight out, and use it.

"Secular" time is what to us is ordinary time, indeed, to *us* it's just time, period. One thing happens after another, and when something is past, it's past. Time placings are consistently transitive. If A is before B and B before C, then A is before C. The same goes if we quantify these relations: if A is long before B, and B long before C, then A is very long before C.

Now higher times gather and re-order secular time. They introduce "warps" and seeming inconsistencies in profane time-ordering. Events which were far apart in profane time could nevertheless be closely linked. Benedict Anderson in a penetrating discussion of the some of the same issues I am trying to describe here,[33] quotes Auerbach on the relation prefiguring-fulfilling in which events of the old Testament were held to stand to those in the New, for instance the sacrifice of Isaac and the Crucifixion of Christ. These two events were linked through their immediate contiguous places in the divine plan. They are drawn close to identity in eternity, even though they are centuries (that is, "aeons" or "saecula") apart. In God's time there is a sort of simultaneity of sacrifice and Crucifixion.

Similarly, Good Friday 1998 is closer in a way to the original day of the Crucifixion than mid-summer's day 1997. Once events are situated in relation to more than one kind of time, the issue of time-placing becomes quite transformed.

Why are higher times higher? The answer is easy for the eternity which Europe inherits from Plato and Greek philosophy. The really real, full being is outside of time, unchanging. Time is a moving image of eternity. It is imperfect, or tends to imperfection.

For Aristotle, this is very true of the sub-lunar. Nothing here can be counted on to be quite totally conformed to its nature. But there were some processes which reflected eternity without flaw: for instance, the stars in their circular courses, without beginning nor end.

The general tendency of this thought was to go for a sempiternal universe, that is, one which underwent change, but in which there was neither beginning nor end. True eternity was beyond this; it was fixed and unvarying.

This was the realm of Ideas. Below these lay their embodiments in the world, which begin to exhibit imperfections. These become really serious in ordinary, sub-lunar time, where everything deviates to a certain degree from its Form.

Thus what happens in time is less real than the timeless. A limit is set to this devi-ancy because the course of time is held in place by higher movements which are closer to eternity (like the rotation of the stars). On some versions, it is also held in place by circular "great years", huge cycles of time after which everything returns to its original state. This was a common idea borrowed from mythology. Thus for the Stoics, after each such cycle everything returns to its original undifferentiated state in a great conflagration.

Without fully abandoning this idea of eternity, Christianity developed a some-what different one. The Bible sees the universe as made by God. It also tells a story of God's dealings with humans. This divine-human history is incompatible with the idea that there are ever-repeating cycles. It also means that what happens in time matters. God enters into drama in time. The Incarnation, the Crucifixion hap-pened in time, and so what occurs here can no longer be seen as less than fully real.

Out of this emerges another idea of eternity. As long as it is conceived after the fashion of Plato, and after him Plotinus, our way to God lies in our rising out of time. And also God, as impassible, beyond time, can't really be a player in history. The Christian conception has to be different from this. It evolves slowly, but its best known formulation in Latin Christendom comes from Augustine. With him eter-nity is reconceived as gathered time.

Unlike his Greek sources, who looked at objective time, the time of processes and movement, Augustine in his famous discussion in *Confessions* XI examines lived time. His instant is not the "nun" of Aristotle, which is a limit, like a point, an extensionless boundary of time periods. Rather it is the gathering together of past into present to project a future. The past, which "objectively" exists no more, is here in my present; it shapes this moment in which I turn to a future, which "objec-tively" is not yet, but which is here qua project.[34] In a sense, Augustine may be thought to have foreshadowed the three ekstaseis of Heidegger.[35]

This creates a kind of simultaneity between the components of an action; my ac-tion knits together my situation as it emerges from my past with the future I project as a response to it. They make sense of each other. They cannot be dissociated, and in this way there is a certain minimum consistency in the now of action, a minimal thickness, below which time cannot be further dissected without disaggregating the coherence of action. This is the kind of coherence we find in a melody or a poem, favourite examples of Augustine.[36] There is a kind of simultaneity of the first note with the last, because all have to sound in the presence of the others in order for the melody to be heard. In this micro-environment, time is crucial because it gives us the order of notes which is constitutive of the melody. But it is not here playing the

role of time the destroyer, which has carried my youth off to an inaccessible distance, and closed the door on bygone ages.

There is thus a kind of extended simultaneity of the moment of action or enjoyment, which we see also, for instance, in a conversation which really engages us. Your question, my reply, your rejoinder occur in this sense together, even though like the melody, their ordering in time is of the essence.

Now Augustine holds that God can and does make all time such an instant of action. So all times are present to him, and he holds them in his extended simultaneity. His now contains all time. It is a "nunc stans".

So rising to eternity is rising to participate in God's instant. Augustine sees ordinary time as dispersal, distensio, losing the unity, being cut off from our past and out of touch with our future. We get lost in our little parcel of time. But we have an irrepressible craving for eternity, and so we strive to go beyond this. Unfortunately, this all too often takes the form of our trying to invest our little parcel with eternal significance, and therefore divinising things, and therefore falling deeper into sin.[37]

The Middle Ages had therefore two models of eternity: what we might call Plato eternity, that of perfect immobility, impassivity, which we aspire to by rising out of time; and God's eternity, which doesn't abolish time, but gathers it into an instant. This we can only have access to by participating in God's life.

To this we have to add a third kind of higher time, which we can call, following Eliade, a "time of origins".[38] Unlike the two eternities, this was not developed by philosophers and theologians, but belongs to the folk tradition of peoples, and indeed, not only in Europe, but almost everywhere.

The idea is of a Great Time, an "illud tempus", when the order of things was established, whether that of the creation of the present world, or the founding of our people with its Law. The agents in this time were on a larger scale than people today, perhaps gods, but at least heroes. In terms of secular time, this origin is in a remote past, it is "time out of mind". But it is not simply in the past, because it is also something that we can re-approach, can get closer to again. This may be by ritual only, but this ritual may also have an effect of renewing and rededicating, hence coming closer to the origin. The Great Time is thus behind us, but it is also in a sense above us. It is what happened at the beginning, but it is also the great Exemplar, which we can be closer to or farther away from as we move through history.

Now some aspects of each of these three kinds of higher time helped form the time-consciousness of our mediaeval predecessors. In each case, as well as the "horizontal" dimension of merely secular time, there is a "vertical" dimension, which can allow for the "warps" and foreshortening of time which I mentioned above. The flow of secular time occurs in a multiplex vertical context, so that everything relates to more than one kind of time.

Thus a late mediaeval kingdom, in which the king has two "bodies", has to be conceived as existing also in Plato eternity. The body which can never die is not subject to time and change. At the same time, many of these kingdoms saw their Law as laid down since time out of mind, a notion which comes from the framework of a Time of Origins. While also, as part of Christendom, they were related through the Church to God's eternity.

Meanwhile the Church, in its liturgical year, remembers and re-enacts what happened in illo tempore when Christ was on earth. Which is why this year's Good Friday can be closer to the Crucifixion than last year's mid-summer day. And the Crucifixion itself, since Christ's action/passion here participates in God's eternity, is closer to all times than they in secular terms are to each other.

Put in other terms, on this view tracts of secular time were not homogeneous, mutually interchangeable. They were coloured by their placing in relation to higher times. I am evoking the contrast case here, Benjamin's "homogeneous, empty time", as the mark of modern consciousness. On this view, time like space has become a container, indifferent to what fills it.

I'm not sure that this take on our contemporary outlook is quite right as it stands. It's true that the shift from ancient and mediaeval "place" to modern "space" involved a dissociation of segments of space from what happens to be filling them. While a "place" is identified by what's there, Newtonian space and time were mere containers, within which objects could be moved around (and even non-objects, i.e., vacua, could fit there). But many contemporary understandings of time take it as indissociable from cosmic processes, like entropy.

However, this identification of time in cosmic terms makes it an indifferent container of the human and historical events which our species lives out on this planet. In that sense, cosmic time is (for us) homogeneous and empty.

But that is far from being true of the earlier, complex time-consciousness. If a tract of time is identified not just by its placing in secular time order, but also by its proximity to higher times, then what happens within it is no longer indifferent to its placing. A time which has fallen away from the eternal paradigms of order will exhibit more disorder. A time-place which is closer to God's eternity will be more gathered. At the pilgrimage centre on the saint's feast day, it is the time itself which is hallowed.[39] When Hamlet says that "the times are out of joint", we could take this remark literally, and not just as a metonym for "the condition of Danish society which happens to be filling this time-slice is lamentable". "Out of joint" means that things don't fit together in the proper fashion, as they do in times which are closer to the ordering paradigms of eternity. Just as we should take Marcellus' earlier remark literally, that ghosts and goblins don't dare walk the earth on Christmas Eve, "so hallow'd and so gracious is the time".[40]

Now homogeneity and emptiness don't tell the full story of modern time-consciousness. I want to argue later that we have forms of narrativity, gathered around notions of potential and maturation, which make different time-placings significant in a sense. But certainly, in relation to the earlier complex consciousness of higher times, our outlook enshrines homogeneity and indifference to content. We now find it very hard even to understand what Hamlet may have been getting at.

That is because, unlike our ancestors, we tend to see our lives exclusively within the horizontal flow of secular time. I don't mean, once again, that people don't believe in, say, God's eternity. Many do. But the imbrication of secular in higher times is no longer for many people today a matter of common, "naïve" experience, something not yet a candidate for belief or disbelief because it is just obviously there; as it was for pilgrims at Compostela or Canterbury in the fourteenth century. (And as it may be today for many at Częstachowa and Guadalupe; our secular age has geographical and social as well as temporal boundaries.)

This is another of the great shifts, along with disenchantment, and the eclipse of anti-structure, which have helped to set the conditions for modern secular society. Obviously modern natural science has had something to do with the change. Seventeenth-century mechanistic science offered a completely different notion of the stable reality behind change. This was no longer eternity; the stable is not something beyond time, nor is it gathered time, but just the law of changes in time. This is like ancient objective time, except now there is no deviancy. The sub-lunar obeys these laws exactly, just as the stars do. The eternity of mathematics is not beyond change, but constantly rules change. It is equidistant from all times. It is not in this sense a "higher" time.

But important as science is to our present outlook, we mustn't exaggerate its causal role here, and make it the main motor of the transformation. Our encasing in secular time is also something we have brought about in the way we live and order our lives. It has been brought about by the same social and ideological changes which have wrought disenchantment. In particular, the disciplines of our modern civilized order have led us to measure and organize time as never before in human history. Time has become a precious resource, not to be "wasted". The result has been the creation of a tight, ordered time environment. This has enveloped us, until it comes to seem like nature. We have constructed an environment in which we live a uniform, univocal secular time, which we try to measure and control in order to get things done. This "time frame" deserves, perhaps more than any other facet of modernity, Weber's famous description of a "stahlhartes Gehäuse" (iron cage).[41] It occludes all higher times, makes them even hard to conceive. This will be part of my story below.

V. Interwoven with this change in time-consciousness is a transformation in our understanding of the universe in which we live. We might say that we moved from living in a cosmos to being included in a universe.

I use 'cosmos' for our forebears' idea of the totality of existence because it contains the sense of ordered whole. It is not that our universe isn't in its own way ordered, but in the cosmos the order of things was a humanly meaningful one. That is, the principle of order in the cosmos was closely related to, often identical with that which gave shape to our lives.

Thus Aristotle's cosmos has at its apex and centre God, whose ceaseless and unvarying action exemplifies something close to Plato's eternity. But this action, a kind of thinking, is also at the centre of our lives. Theoretical thought is in us that which is "most divine".[42] And for Plato, and this whole mode of thought in general, the cosmos exhibits the order which we should exemplify in our own lives, both individually and as societies.

It belongs to this understanding of order that the cosmos was limited and bounded. At least it did for the Greeks, for whom order and limit were inextricably linked; and our civilization was in this sense heir to the Greeks.

This kind of cosmos is a hierarchy; it has higher and lower levels of being. And it reaches its apex in eternity; it is indeed, held together by what exists on the level of eternity, the Ideas, or God, or both together—Ideas as the thoughts of the creator.

Partly as a result of the scientific revolution, the cosmos idea faded, and we find ourselves in a universe. This has its own kind of order, that exhibited in exceptionless natural laws. But it is no longer a hierarchy of being, and it doesn't obviously point to eternity as the locus of its principle of cohesion. The universe flows on in secular time. Above all, its principles of order are not related to human meaning, at any rate not immediately or evidently.

Biblical religion, in entering the Graeco-Roman, later Arab, worlds, develops within the cosmos idea. So we come to see ourselves as situated in a defined history, which unfolds within a bounded setting. So the whole sweep of cosmic-divine history can be rendered in the stained glass of a large cathedral. But the universe approaches the limitless, or at any rate its limits are not easily encompassable in time or space. Our planet, our solar system is set in a galaxy, which is one of an as yet uncounted number of galaxies. Our origins go back into the mists of evolutionary time, so that we become unclear as to what could count as the beginning of our human story, many of the features of which are irretrievably lost.

Many of the spectacular battles between belief and unbelief in the last two centuries have turned on the challenge to Biblical religion from the universe idea. But in spite of the headline-grabbing nature of these fights, I doubt whether the relevance of the universe conception for unbelief lies here. The battles only arose because and where Biblical religion was held prisoner to the cosmos idea. Placing the creation of the world on a certain day in 4004 B.C. is a prime example of this kind of thinking, paradoxically using the modes of exact calculation developed in modernity to entrench oneself in the cosmos bastion. As is the refusal of the very idea of an evolution of species (as against the more implausible aspects of neo-Darwinianism).

There is no bar as such to rethinking Biblical religion within the universe. And some earlier thinkers—Origen, Nicholas of Cusa—already had done something of this kind. Not to speak of Pascal, whose invocation of the eternal silence of infinite spaces places him firmly beyond the range of the cosmos and the music of its spheres.

The real relevance of the universe understanding is more subtle and indirect. It lies in the way it has altered the terms of the debate, and reshaped the possibilities both of belief and unbelief, opened up new loci of mystery, as well as offering new ways of denying transcendence. We will see specifically later on how the universe, seen as a great clockwork-like order, whose parts are made to mesh perfectly, can be the basis for a certain kind of doctrine of Providence.

But the new understanding of our spatio-temporal setting worked alongside the other changes I have been describing here to generate this new context. Let me move on to the story of how this arose.

6

I have been drawing a portrait of the world we have lost, one in which spiritual forces impinged on porous agents, in which the social was grounded in the sacred and secular time in higher times, a society moreover in which the play of structure and anti-structure was held in equilibrium; and this human drama unfolded within a cosmos. All this has been dismantled and replaced by something quite different in the transformation we often roughly call disenchantment.

How did this arise? There were many causes. People cite: Renaissance humanism, the scientific revolution, the rise of the "police state", the Reformation. All of these are right. But to understand them all, we have to appreciate the importance of a movement which gathers steam in the late mediaeval period, and which aimed to remake European society to meet the demands of the Gospel, and later of "civilization". It would perhaps not be wrong to apply the overworked word 'revolutionary' here, because this drive to Reform was the matrix out of which the modern European idea of Revolution emerges. To misuse the rhetoric of Saddam Hussein, we can say that it was "the mother of Revolutions".

What I'm calling "Reform" here expressed a profound dissatisfaction with the hierarchical equilibrium between lay life and the renunciative vocations. In one way, this was quite understandable. This equilibrium involved accepting that masses of people were not going to live up to the demands of perfection. They were being "carried", in a sense, by the perfect. And there is something in this which runs against the very spirit of Christian faith.

But this doesn't explain the unease, the growing demand to close the gap. All civilizations which have been organized around a "higher" religion have shown a great spread between the dedicated and the less committed, between highly demanding forms of devotion and more perfunctory practice, between paths of renunciation and those in which religious ritual served more the needs of prosperity and flourishing. To borrow a term from the jargon of European integration, these religious civilizations operated "at several speeds".

As we saw above these differences of "speed" can end up being ambiguously accepted, even given some recognition in theories of complementarity between the laity and the clergy, or other religious "virtuosi", like monks or hermits or wandering saints. People see the relationship in terms of a kind of exchange. For instance, in many Buddhist societies, the laity feed the monks, and thereby gain merit against better future rebirths.

The Latin Christendom which emerged from the "Dark Ages" was of this type. But in this it was not alone. Many "speeds" were also very much in evidence in the Eastern Churches; not to speak of the other major civilizations. What seems peculiar to Latin Christendom is rather the deep and growing dissatisfaction with it. Although the aim at first was not to abolish the difference altogether, serious attempts were made to narrow the gap between the fastest and the slowest. The dissatisfaction grew, and manifested itself in different movements, some among élites, and some among the people—at both levels therefore.

The boundary between élite and people was not neat, of course. In a sense, the clergy belonged to the élite, but there were very ill-schooled parish clergy at the base, who thought and acted more like their parishioners than like their bishops or educated confrères in universities or mendicant orders. At the same time, there was a growing educated laity; not only, perhaps not especially, the gentry, but the new "middle class", rising through commerce, or the practice of the law, or administration in state and church, and through the spread of grammar schools.

What I'm calling "Reform", with a capital 'R', is to be distinguished from attempts by more dedicated people to spread their forms of practice and devotion, by preaching, encouragement, example. These reform movements (with a small 'r') may even be organized or sponsored by the official hierarchy, without this amounting to "Reform". Proselytizing and renewal movements have cropped up periodically in all the higher civilizations. What distinguishes them from Reform is that they do not try to delegitimate less dedicated forms, but only to convert more people from these to the higher "speeds".

Now there was also lots of reform in late mediaeval Europe. Think only of the preaching of the mendicant friars. But what is peculiar to Latin Christendom is a growing concern with Reform, a drive to make over the whole society to higher standards. I don't pretend to have the explanation of this "rage for order", but it seems to me to be a fact about the late-mediaeval and early modern period, and moreover one which has carried over into the modern period in the partly secularized ideal of "civilization". I want to argue that this "rage" has been crucial to the destruction of the old enchanted cosmos, and to the creation of a viable alternative in exclusive humanism.

What were the differences in religious life which constituted the spread? They are not easy to pin down exactly. But one important divergence lay on one hand between a faith in which the doctrinal element was more developed, and in which devotional life took to some degree the form of inner prayer, and later even meditative practices; contrasted on the other to a faith where the belief content was very rudimentary, and devotional practice was largely a matter of what one did. As Pierre Chaunu puts it, the people had "une religion du faire, non du savoir".[43]

The actions were extremely various. They included things like fasting, and also abstaining from work, at the appropriate times, related to Sundays and feast-days, as well as seasons like Lent and Advent. They included attendance at Mass on Sunday, Penance and Communion at least once a year at Easter time. These were prescribed actions. But there was as well a rich gamut of devotional acts which people threw themselves into; liturgical acts, like "creeping to the Cross" on Good Friday, blessing candles on Candlemas, taking part in Corpus Christi parades; and then there was the whole host of devotions to saints, cults of relics, prayers to the Virgin, in which we shade off into an area which was more and more a field of controversy.

Now in a sense, this two-tiered religion, that is, dual system of religious practice, hierarchically arranged, had made much sense in the Dark Ages. Take the newly converted Germanic tribes of the eighth century, for instance; they were often brought into the Church through some decision of their leaders. To the extent that they were willing converts, they were deeply impressed by the miracle-making power (as they saw it) of the missionaries; just like the Anglo-Saxon converts of the seventh century, won over in large part by the alleged miracle-working powers of Christian saints;[44] as well as the rustici which St. Martin of Tours wanted to Christianize in fourth-century Gaul. All these must have seen the new religion in terms of those categories of sacred power that they were already familiar with; a superior version, perhaps, but one in the same register. It is obvious that the meaning of the new rites for them would be different from the correct, canonical meaning held by the clerical missionaries.[45]

To the extent that this difference of wave-length remains in place throughout the

Middle Ages, as it seems to have done for certain, sometimes sizeable, marginal populations;[46] and zones of recent conversion (Scandinavia, the Baltic lands); the two-tiered system was stable; indeed, irreplaceable.

But in fact, the gap becomes steadily smaller, and that in a number of ways.

First, the years after 1000 see the steady growth of a widely popular, specifically Christocentric spirituality, focussed on the suffering humanity of Jesus; which we can see in religious art (the growing importance and centrality of depictions of the Crucifixion); in practices of identification with his suffering (the stigmata of St. Francis, and on a quite different level, movements of Flagellants); in the growing focus of piety on Christ, or Christ and his mother, or the Holy Family, in relation to other saints, as the Middle Ages come to a close.[47] Even in the league of miracle-working relics and objects, there is a shift in these centuries towards those connected to Christ and Mary: the pieces of the Holy Rood, Christ's blood (Hailes), Mary's milk, the Five Wounds.[48]

As Eamon Duffy puts it, "Lay people wanted to cultivate that intense relationship of affectionate, penitential intimacy with Christ and his Mother which was the devotional lingua franca of the late Middle Ages".[49] The focus of devotion was more and more on the Passion; the death of Christ who as a loving brother pays the debt owed by humanity. Implicit in this is a move from a triumphal theology of the crucifixion towards a theology of suffering. The prayer "adoro te in cruce ascendentem" is altered so that the last word reads "pendentem". We can see why images of the Five Wounds took on such power. They provided the banner under which the Pilgrimage of Grace marched.[50]

The practices still may have been different from those of certain élites—e.g., the devotion to relics at shrines, which alienated humanists like Erasmus and Colet[51]—but there was not much left of paganism in the religion of the central areas of Latin Christendom at the end of the Middle Ages, in spite of what these disapproving humanists and reformers were wont to say.[52]

But even this difference in practice becomes problematic in the centuries before the climacteric of the early 1500s. It is attacked, as I indicated above, from both directions. There were movements from below, which I want to come to; but there seems also to have been a concerted effort, on the part of the hierarchical-clerical church, (as they saw it) to raise standards. One might say, an effort to align the masses on the religion of the élites. For instance, the Lateran Council of 1215 laid down the requirement of auricular confession for all the laity, at least once a year. Along with this went efforts to train priests, and the making of manuals, so that the clergy could better form the conscience of the faithful.

Then the action of mendicant preachers, which had more than one kind of impact on the hierarchical church, not all by any means stabilizing. But one effect was certainly to open up new and very effective channels of communication with the base, through the preaching of itinerant friars, often better educated than the parish clergy (and often in a condition of rivalry with these poor secular priests). Through them the message of the new, more exigent practice was very effectively spread throughout the length and breadth of Latin Christendom. If we see this attempt by an élite to make over the base as a kind of distant preparation for a world in which something like the Bolshevik party can emerge, then we can see the friars as a form of late-mediaeval agit-prop. (There are of course many intermediate stages, including later orders, like the Jesuits, then the Jacobins, etc.) The friars actually changed the consciousness of many people. They were a crucial part of the metamorphosis which culminates in the dual Reformation.

One of the most striking changes, for which the mendicant preaching was at partly responsible, concerns the attitude to death. As Ariès and others have noted,[53] the late Middle Ages sees what seems to us today a growing concern, even fear of death. The message of the endless preaching and writing on the theme of memento mori, of the iconography of the dance of death, of the endless repetition of the *Dict des trois morts et des trois vifs*,[54] was the vanity of life, prosperity, pleasure, the "good things", in face of approaching death. What's the good? it will all disappear; it will turn into its opposite. The beautiful flesh of that desirable woman or man, will turn into its opposite, putrefying flesh. Indeed, it is in a sense already that, beneath the surface appearance.

La beauté du corps est toute entière dans la peau. En effet, si les hommes, doués, comme les lynx de Béotie, d'intérieure pénétration visuelle, voyaient ce qui est sous la peau, la vue seule des femmes leur serait nauséabonde: cette grâce féminine n'est que saburre, sang, humeur, fiel. Considérez ce qui se cache dans les narines, dans la gorge, dans le ventre: saletés partout. . . . Et nous qui répugnons à toucher, même du bout du doigt, de la vomissure et du fumier, comment pouvons-nous désirer serrer dans nos bras le sac d'excréments lui-même?[55]

(The beauty of the body is found entirely in the skin. If people could see what is underneath the skin, as it is said in Boethia that the lynx can do, they would find the sight of women sickening. Her charm consists of slime and blood, of wetness and gall. Consider what lies hidden in the nostrils, in the throat, and in the belly: nothing but filth. . . . And if we cannot bring ourselves to touch vomit and feces, not even with our fingertips, how can we bring ourselves to embrace the dirt bag itself?)[56]

But the point is not just, of course, that these pleasures of the flesh pass, are barely real, it is that in turning to them we are neglecting what is really important, the issue that we face beyond our death, the judgment of God on our whole life. What emerges in this century as a mass phenomenon is a kind of stance towards death which has been repeatedly evoked among a certain spiritual élite since the first centuries. If St. Jerome is often depicted with a skull, it is because he was thought to be meditating on death; and why? precisely to turn away from the things that don't matter to the issue that does; which question requires an answer whereby we die to the world and live for God.

So in a sense, this late-mediaeval spirituality of death meant an important step towards overcoming the multi-speed system. Whether we think of it as coming as a result of efforts of the hierarchy and clergy (which it probably did in part), or as arising from a deeper spontaneous movement among the faithful (which it clearly also was in great part), it brought both levels of the church together on something like the same wave-length on an important issue.

I say "something like", because still there were important differences. Or perhaps better, the élites themselves evolved, and new differences emerged; the most important of which exploded eventually in 1517, with cataclysmic consequences for Latin Christendom.

But before exploring this, I want to look closer at the new stance towards death. It represents both a Christianization, and an individuation.

First, the Christianization is evident. In the pagan religious outlooks, from which the people of Latin Christendom had been converted, death was in a sense a further stage in the career of existence; generally a reduced stage, as famously with the early Greek notion of Hades. This loss complicates our relation to our dead, because we can easily imagine that they resent leaving the land of the living, that they envy us our continuing good fortune, that they can be tempted to return to haunt us. A goodly part of our funeral rites are propitiatory, or otherwise designed to nudge our forebears on, so that they remain securely within the next phase. So our relationship with them is complex: we need their good-will, but we don't want them too close. We are ambivalent.

In this dispensation, although we may fear the dead, we have no great reason to fear death. We don't welcome it, but it is part of the natural order of things, an appointed stage.

Now the Christian outlook introduces something quite different, something incommensurable. Although Christian faith has incorporated and at times elaborated different conceptions of the natural order of things, it focusses on another dimension, the eschatological. We are called to live a quite transformed life, one in which death has been overcome. This transformation involves our living for something beyond the human flourishing, as defined by the natural order, whatever it be.

This idea of a beyond of human flourishing, which I argued above is crucial to Christianity, is also found in a number of other "higher" religions—very obviously, for instance, in Buddhism—and is one of the reasons why they have often been considered "higher". The relation between this call to live beyond, on one hand, and the eschatological transformation, on the other, is complicated and enveloped in controversy throughout the Christian centuries. According to a recurring sense among the faithful, even if not in line with orthodox theology, we earn or fail to earn entry into the ultimate transformation through our adequate or inadequate response to the call. Theologians point out that this simple picture leaves out the action of God in making us capable of responding to the call, but this generally just displaces the definition of the test which we can fail, and passage of which is necessary for entry into the Kingdom.

In terms of a central image of Christian history, a judgment intervenes before our full entry into the Kingdom. In some way or other, our life will be weighed, and can be found wanting. Now there *is* a reason to fear death; death as the end of life, therefore as the completion, as it were, of the dossier with which we will affront judgment.

So the anxious turning towards death and judgment represents a Christianization of people's way of living mortality. Not that a lot of the old ways didn't continue. People were still afraid of ghosts, of their unwillingness to accept their death, and their frightening desire to remain with us.[57] Montaigne talked of a familiarity and acceptance of death among the common people of his own day, something he wanted to imitate.[58] Many people still lived death not as something frightening, or which called life into question, but as part of the round of life. We live, and then die. Moreover, the dead were still in many ways part of the society of the living. They were buried in a common plot, often in the centre of the village. In some places, the dead were thought to return to us on certain festivals; there were reports of dances in cemeteries. The presence of the dead was both a little frightening and comforting, as they were when alive too.[59]

But nevertheless, the new outlook steadily makes progress. And with it, a certain individuation. Was this essentially linked? In a sense, yes. The whole dimension of response to the call, judgment, transformation is one which appeals to individual responsibility. I mentioned above how this new concern for death takes up the basic forms of the minority spirituality of monks and ascetics of earlier ages.

But the dislocation of the older, communal approach to death went farther and affected the received version of Christian belief as well. The notion of a common judgment, englobing everyone, at the end of time was a central part of Christian belief from the earliest ages. In the later Middle Ages, the church begins to give currency to the idea that each individual will face as well his/her own judgment, immediately on their death. This in a sense dramatized and made more urgent the whole issue of my "dossier" at the moment of my demise. Previously, the belief in a Last Judgment could be added on, as it were, to older, pre-Christian ideas of death as part of the round of life. The ultimate transformation was put off into a deeper distance, where the issue of its articulation onto our present experience of death can be left vague. The new belief in immediate individual judgment brought it up close, sometimes terrifyingly so. As Delumeau puts it: "mépris du monde, dramatisation de la mort et insistance sur le salut personnel ont émergé ensemble"[60] (contempt for the world, dramatisation of death, and the insistence on personal salvation, emerged together).

Here's where the whole issue of understanding why this change took place shows its complexity. There is no single answer. There is no doubt that it was in part induced by clerical élites, as part of the whole effort of Latin Christendom towards raising the level of religious devotion and practice of the whole society. The start of the movement can be identified at various moments, but one good beginning point could be 1215, the Lateran Council which decides to make auricular confession universal. In any case, there was something like an "internal crusade" from the thirteenth century on, mainly carried by the preaching of the mendicant orders. A crusade against real heresies, in the case of the Dominicans in Albigensian country; but also a standing campaign towards repentance, towards facing the facts of death and judgment, and acting accordingly. Perhaps the teaching on individual judgment could be seen as part of the armory of this crusade.

But on the other side, we could argue that it wasn't just eschatology which fostered individuation, but just as much the reverse. The breaking up of certain traditional cadres of life: peasants who left the village to live in towns, new socially mobile groups who staffed the institutions of commerce, or the law, or administration; condottieri who lived by arms and their wits, new self-made rulers in Renaissance Italy; that all these and others were no longer so deeply embedded in the communal forms of life within which the dead were still treated as part of an ongoing community in the old way.

These were people who could be tempted to think of themselves as working out an individual destiny, aiming at riches, or power, or glory. But exactly these people were the prime targets for the preaching of memento mori, of the vanity of all earthly success, of the inevitable putrefaction of all life and beauty. This inescapable reversal is all the more dramatic in the life of one who follows a personal destiny to the heights. Which is why it is a favourite subject of preaching; and why some of the great wanted to make a public display of their having taken this point: a great bishop will have represented on his tombstone himself not only in his regalia, but also as a corpse being eaten by worms (Wells Cathedral).

Whatever the motor, the new spirituality had an individuating side. This was perhaps also reflected in an increasing emphasis on sexual purity, which begins to gain on sins of anger, violence, the dislocation of fraternal bonds.[61] Bossy speaks of an early emphasis on sins of aversion, sins against charity and solidarity, which gradually makes place for an increasing concern with sins of concupiscence, sins against chastity, seen as pollution, and as a negation of personal holiness.[62] Bossy also notes a shift in the main thrust of penances, from those which involve making up, restituting damage, as their end, to those which involve metanoia and reform.[63]

But at the same time, by a turn which we see repeatedly in our history, a new individuality brought with it a new kind of social bonding. Around the very individuating concern for death and judgment arose the new solidarity of intercession. The living can pray for and otherwise bring relief to the souls of the dead. The terrifying individual destiny can be met by mutual help.

This is part of what is involved in the tremendous growth of Purgatory as a focal point of spiritual concern and action. There had been earlier, since the first centuries, some notion that all of those who avoid damnation are not yet ready for Heaven, some vague conception of purifying fire. But it is only in mediaeval Latin Christendom that this develops not only into a full-fledged doctrine, but into a new temporality. Between our temporal existence here, and the eternity of God which is contemporaneous to all times, a new domain of quasi-time is inserted, in which souls exist between the immediate judgment after death and the Last Judgment. It is a place of purification, necessary for all but the saints on one hand (who don't need it), and the damned on the other (who don't deserve it); in short for just about everybody's dead relations and friends.

The prayer of the living can affect the suffering of those in Purgatory; as can the intercession of saints, and the Virgin Mary. Out of this, a whole theory develops about the treasury of merits of the saints, and the possibility of redistributing this to the benefit of sinners. This underpinned the institution of indulgences, which in the end came to be calculated in the coin of this quasi-time: such and such an act earned one year and forty days' remission for your mother in Purgatory.[64]

That this got out of hand, went beyond the bounds of any sane theology or Christian practice, and in the end set fire to the whole structure of the mediaeval church, is well-known. The image we have in the light of the ultimate revolt is of a rich, powerful, and greedy hierarchy, battening on the ignorance and fears of the laity to drain vast sums of money towards the purposes of Rome, principally maintaining and expanding the Papal state and building magnificent Renaissance churches.

There is much truth in this view, but it masks a movement in the other direction. How much was the hierarchy responding to, in a sense following a popular piety which demanded a means of acting in solidarity in face of death? Chaunu and Duffy both point out how important the associations were which arose or partly structured themselves around this goal. The guilds, confréries,[65] and even the life of the parish itself, e.g., in the reading of the bede-roll.[66] Purgatory became the focal point for a very large part of Christian practice in the late mediaeval church. It channeled an immense charge of anxiety, towards intercessory prayers and acts, towards charitable donations to the poor,[67] or to chantries, which would pray for the soul of the departed.

To the point where the big question of the early sixteenth century is, what happened to this immense energy, this charge of anxiety and hope, when the Reformers tried to abolish the whole system, root and branch? Did people react with a visceral refusal of this destructive act? Or did they follow the reformers in channelling that energy into a new direction, a new register? This was undoubtedly crucial for the fate of the Reformation in many places.

But in any case, this new spirituality of death and judgment, which ought in a sense to have brought élite and mass closer together, to a more Christian focus on death, and which was vigorously preached with this end in view; all this had the opposite effect: it opened a widening breach between certain élites and the mass of the faithful, which was in the end the casus belli which broke the church apart. Why was this?

Because along with the new devotion to the crucified Christ, along with the new concern with death, there were also other movements which were widening the gap between certain élite minorities and the practice of the great majority of the people.

First there were a number of attempts, emanating from different sources, to develop a more intense, inward, devotional life. The tradition of German mystics, beginning with Meister Eckhart, is perhaps the best known in this field, but it was far from alone. More widespread and influential, in the fourteenth century, was the devotio moderna of the Brethren of the Common Life, whose most famous figure was Thomas à Kempis, the author of *The Imitation of Christ*. This devotion put more emphasis on private prayer, on introspection; even encouraging the keeping of a journal.

But there were a great number of initiatives in this direction which had no connection to these or any other movements, arising among the minor clergy, but also among the growing number of more educated and reflective laity. People were seeking a more personal religious life, wanted a new kind of prayer, wanted to read and meditate the Bible themselves.

Here was a new élite, not necessarily coterminous with the hierarchical and clerical Church leadership. Indeed, this often looked with suspicion on these new forms of inwardness. Some of Eckhart's writings were condemned. Some of the movements of prayer, like the Béguines, fell afoul of the Church and were declared deviant. This suspicion of inwardness continued till very late in the Catholic Church. Ignatius and Teresa were harassed at various times by the Spanish Inquisition, which had marked an earlier wave of inward piety, that of the so-called "Alumbrados" as heretical, and was on the watch for any recrudescence of it in its true paranoid style. Things got somewhat better after the Council of Trent, but even then the fear of new forms of inwardness didn't cease.

But while potentially falling afoul of the hierarchy, this kind of spirituality could also detach itself from the base. It was developing on a different line than mainstream popular piety, which was so much a practice of doing, rather than one of reflection and silent prayer. The doing included public prayer, the saying of Paters and Aves, as well as the liturgical prayer of the Church, not to speak of individualizable actions like fasting, going on pilgrimage, etc. But it was a mode of piety which was acted out.

Now turning inward didn't necessarily mean abandoning these active forms of devotion, much less turning against them. But some of the adepts of a more inward devotion felt an aversion to these forms, saw them as mindless diversion from real piety. This was a common reaction among Christian humanists. Erasmus is a good example. They fell into the negative judgment that élites all too easily make on popular piety, seeing it from the outside, and missing all too often the spirit which animated it. In this way, a new gap began to open between educated minorities and mass practice.

But this practice could not only be attacked as external diversion. There was also a growing unease about it, which went right to the heart of its embedding in the enchanted world. In this world, as we saw, in which charged objects have influence and causal power, "holy" objects, emanating from God and his saints, are our bulwark against malificent beings and things charged with their malevolent power. And so relics of saints have this power of "good magic"; as have candles blessed on Candlemas; crosses made during the reading of the Passion narrative on Palm Sunday; holy water, pieces of bread blessed at Mass (not the Host);[68] written prayers used as amulets; "agnus dei"; church bells whose ringing can drive away thunder;[69] and above all, of course, the Sacrament of the altar itself.

Now this became deeply disturbing to growing minorities of people, who were not necessarily drawn from social élites. And this on a variety of grounds, more or less radical. Even on the most uncritical assumptions, there were bound to be problems with certain popular practices. Causal power exercised in a good cause, like healing, was perfectly all right; even more so when it was inseparable from positive influence, as when the healing was effected partly by undergoing confession and absolution. But there always were dubious uses of causal power, like employing the Host as a love charm; and frankly evil ones, like having a Mass for the dead said for a living person, in order to hasten his demise. And then there were uses of sacred power in league with the forces of darkness, of which the Black Mass is the most famous. So even before more fundamental doubts arose about the uses of sacramental power, the church always had to police the boundary here between the licit and the illicit.

More radically, there was unease at the use of causal powers, even for unexceptionable ends. We saw this above with Erasmus. As long as the sacrament is used for purposes of good influence, to bring us more into the ambit of grace, that is acceptable. But the focus on a scatter of worldly ends, even though good in themselves, diverts us from true piety. Praying to saints should have as goal purely our own spiritual betterment. "The true way to worship saints is to imitate their virtues, and they care more for this than for a hundred candles . . . You venerate the bones of Paul laid away in a shrine, but not the mind of Paul, enshrined in his writings".[70] The crucial point here is, not so much the practice, but the end we have in view. But of course, to follow through on this, a great many practices will straight away fall by the wayside. If the aim is to become more inwardly like Paul, you are less likely to see touching a relic as the appropriate action. This is not because on the long-existing pious understanding, the relic did nothing to make you spiritually better, but because it belonged in a world where this boundary between spiritual and material benefit, which Erasmus is so eager to police, went usually unremarked.

Most radically of all, a deep theological objection arose to the "white magic" of the church, whatever its purpose. Treating anything as a charged object, even the sacrament, and even if its purpose is to make me more holy, and not to protect against disease or crop failure, is in principle wrong. God's power can't be contained like this, controlled as it were, through its confinement in things, and thus "aimed" by us in one direction or another.

This rejection of the church's good magic arises early on. It recurs in almost all the heresies of the Middle Ages, even quite far back, as with the Waldensians. It is prominent among the Lollards, and the more radical Hussites; and then it takes over the Reformation churches. And because it concerns not just outlying abuses, but the heart of the system itself, a central issue is always made of the Eucharist. Wycliffe rejects the power of the priest to consecrate the elements ex opere operato, that is, in virtue of the power of the rite, regardless of the spiritual condition of the officiant. The fundamental idea is the one I've just mentioned, concerning the power of God. God could be understood to respond to the prayers of a holy person, but the notion that any old priest, however debauched, can control God's movements was utterly unacceptable. But then the same goes a fortiori for the manipulation of any charged objects, or for prayer to the Virgin or saints. God is free of his actions. This belongs to his sovereignty.

(We can see a certain affinity between this spiritual sense and Scotist-Occamite theology, which also stressed the unfettered sovereign power of God. That this was more than just an affinity can be seen in the way Luther drew on this stream of thought.)

There was something more here than humanist fastidiousness at the clutter of popular practices, although the two streams could merge, and did at the Reformation. But this rejection of church magic also appears at the popular level, as I indicated. The Lollards were often quite simple people; and the radical Taborites drew in the lowest orders of society. What drove these movements?

Among many, I want to single out two factors, which are in a sense facets of each other. One is social, the other is what I will call a reversal of the field of fear.

First, the social dimension. Church magic was an illegitimate claim to control the power of God. Who made this claim? The hierarchical church. One vector of the revolt was directed at the claimants, who were often personally far from holy, wielding great power over ordinary people's lives, and abusing this power. The magic was discredited by the magician.

But it wasn't so easy to revolt, and to reject magic in the enchanted world. This was a world full of dark magic, which only white magic could keep at bay. Moreover, even good magic was charged with a power which could also be dangerous. Chaunu writes convincingly of the popular attitude to the Eucharist. It was exalted so high as a concentration of God's power, and ordinary people's sense of their own unworthiness, constantly renewed by preaching, put them so low, that they feared to take communion. They were forced to once a year by the rules of the Church, but this minimum in fact remained a maximum for most people. We have to bear in mind that charged objects, however good their magic, can be dangerous if taken from the wrong side—in that sense very much like electric wires in our own world. To take communion unworthily was seen as highly perilous, and the church's preaching reinforced this.

But that the sacrament remains an object of power can be seen by the growth of another practice, that of adoring the Blessed Sacrament as it is exposed to view. This became more and more widespread in the late Middle Ages; as did the Corpus Christi processions. It's as though its power could be allowed to work at this safe distance, but for them taking communion was too close.[71]

Revolting against all this meant facing a barrier of fear. But one of the potentialities of Christian faith was a reversal of the field of fear. The power of God will be victorious over all evil magic. So much is common to all variants of the faith. But this victory can be understood as that of white magic over dark magic. Or it can be understood as that of God's naked power over all magic. To draw on this power, you have to leap out of the field of magic altogether, and throw yourself on the power of God alone.

This "disenchanting" move is implicit in the tradition of Judaism, and later Christianity. Fundamental to both is a break with a world in which what they judge to be bad magic, the worship of pagan Gods and forces, is rampant. But this breach can take one of two forms; in a sense, it hovers between them. We can see this when Elijah humbles the prophets of Baal on Mount Carmel. In challenging them to see which God will bring down fire on the offerings, and showing that they can't deliver, while he can, he is in a sense deploying a victorious counter-magic to theirs. But the point of the story, which Elijah drives home, is that their magic is empty; it is utterly ineffective; their Gods have no power.

God's power conquers the pagan enchanted world. And this can proceed either through a good, God-willed enchantment; or else by annihilating all enchantment, and in the end emptying the world of it. But to flip from one of these tracks to another requires a reversal of the field of fear. Beforehand, what you fear most is this magic power; the bad kind, of course, that of demons, but you also have a healthy fear of the good kind, and keep a safe distance from it. The flip comes when you take all that fear and transpose it into a fear of God, sole rightful object of fear, confident that it can arm you against all magic.

In a sense, you might say that fear drives out fear. But this is not quite right. It's not like when my fear of making a fool of myself in our conversation is driven out by the fear of a fatal accident, as we find ourselves drawn into a multi-car crash on the autoroute. Because the fear of God is something higher, something which exalts us, where the fear of magic seems to lower us. So what is needed is a kind of reversed field, where precisely what you most feared before is that the facing of which, we should say: the facing down of which, now fills you with courage and energy. This reversed field draws on the power of God in a new register.

(This energy released by facing the fear and reversing it is what must have powered some of the acts of bravado by which heretics flouted the sacred, such as profaning the sacrament, or the Lollard who burnt the statue of Ste. Catherine to fry his supper, and joked that she was undergoing a second martyrdom.)[72]

In these early heresies, the fear of magic and the fear of hierarchical power are reversed together. This is what powers the most radical challenge to mass piety in the Middle Ages. It gravitates towards a quite different form of liturgy and church life, in which the sacraments tend to become purely symbolic, authority slides away from a hierarchy, and is placed back in Scripture, and the visible church is more sharply distinguished from the true community of the saved.

In a sense, the stage seems set for the Reformation; and these early movements have been thought of as Proto-Reformations (Hudson's book about Lollardry is entitled *The Premature Reformation*). But there was one big element missing; and that was the doctrine of salvation by faith. It fits well with the denial of church magic, and the recurrence to pure Biblical authority, but it doesn't absolutely have to be linked with them. One can even imagine another chain of events, in which at least some important elements of the Reformation didn't have to be driven out of the Catholic Church, and to a denial of the sacraments (which Luther for his part never agreed to) and of the value of tradition (which Luther was not as such against). But it would have required a rather different Rome, less absorbed with its power trip than it has tended to be these last centuries.

But the important point is that in propounding salvation by faith, Luther was touching on *the* nevralgic issue of his day, the central concern and fear, which dominated so much lay piety, and drove the whole indulgences racket, the issue of judgment, damnation, salvation. In raising his standard on this issue, Luther was on to something which could move masses of people, unlike the humanist critique of mass piety, or the rejection of the sacred.

And in taking it up, Luther operated another reversal of the field of fear, analogous to that involved in denying church magic. The sale of indulgences was driven by a fear of punishment. But Luther's message was that we are all sinners, and deserve punishment. Salvation involves facing and accepting this fully. Only in facing our full sinfulness, can we throw ourselves on the mercy of God, by which alone we are justified. "Who fears Hell runs towards it".[73] We have to face down our fears, and this transmutes them into confidence in the saving power of God.

There is perhaps an irony here. A great deal of Catholic preaching on sin and repentance was based on the principle that the ordinary person was so insensitive that they had to be terrified into responding. They had to be woken with strong effects.[74] Preachers tried to culpabilize their audiences to the extreme. Even venial sins were talked up as something terrible, because after all, they also involve offense to God.[75] But just this cranking up of fear may have helped to prepare people to respond to Luther's reversal of the field.

The irony is perhaps compounded when we see how some Protestant preaching repeats the same pattern. You're supposed to be confident in your salvation, but not flatly complacent.[76] But because many ministers saw their flocks as leaning towards the second danger, they too cranked up the terrifying visions of damnation.[77] Did this prepare the desertion of a goodly part of their flock to humanism? I believe this to have been so; but we'll return to this later.

7

So there were strong urges for religious renewal, on at least the three axes I have been describing: the turn to a more inward and intense personal devotion, a greater uneasiness at "sacramentals" and church-controlled magic, and then latterly the new inspiring idea of salvation by faith, which erupted into a world riven with anxiety about judgment and a sense of unworthiness.

These aspirations inspired various reforms; people made over their lives, formed associations like the Brethren of the Common Life, developed new practices of prayer and contemplation. Why didn't they stay on this level? Why did they have to spill over into Reform, that is, the attempt to make over the whole Church, and to outlaw and abolish the lower "speeds"? Small-r reformers, like Erasmus, would have been happy with the less radical solution. What frightened him was precisely the "rage for order", the need Reformers felt to smash the old dispensation, even literally in the form of iconoclasm.

> The mass has been abolished, but what more holy has been put in its place? . . . I have never entered your churches, but now and then I have seen the hearers of your sermons come out like men possessed, with anger and rage on their faces . . . They came out like warriors, animated by the oration of the general to some mighty attack. When did your sermons ever produce penitence and remorse? Are they not more concerned with suppression of the clergy and the sacerdotal life? Do they not make more for sedition than for piety? Are not riots common among this evangelical people? Do they not for small causes betake themselves to force?[78]

One issue which was hard to settle by reform was that of the sacred in the church. In the term 'sacred', I'm pointing to the belief that God's power is somehow concentrated in certain people, times, places or actions. Divine power is in these, in a way it is not in other people, times, etc., which are "profane". The sacred played a central role in the practices of the mediaeval church. Churches were holy places, made more so by the presence of relics; feasts were holy times, and the sacraments of the church were holy actions, which supposed a clergy with special powers. So the uneasiness over sacramentals and relics was not easy to contain, especially if it went so far as to deny the sacred in the sacrament of the altar itself. A peaceful, "comprehending" solution to these issues was conceivable, but it would have taken a much more open and comprehending Catholic Church, which was not so concerned to ferret out difference and root out heresy; a Church in which the representative figure would have been Erasmus, instead of John Eck.

But this was not all. It would also have taken a Protestant side who did not respond to the practices of the sacred as an abomination, as idolatry in the sight of God. Lutherans and moderate Catholics could have agreed on this whole range of issues, even the Eucharist, and various formulae were even worked out. But the temptation to see the other on both sides in the perspective of irreconcilable difference—as rejecting the sacrament utterly, or else falling into papist idolatry—was too strong.

This is where one can ask whether the triumph of the hard line wasn't already programmed, as it were, in the very climate of Reform in which both sides bathed at the end of the Middle Ages. If the point was to make the Church over to uniformly higher standards, so that the spread between higher and lower would be less, it would not be auspicious to start with allowing an even greater diversity of practices. And, indeed, it is clear that the Reformation was driven by the spirit of Reform in an even more uncompromising mode. One of its principal talking points from the very beginning was the refusal to accept special vocations and counsels of perfection. There were not to be any more ordinary Christians and super-Christians. The renunciative vocations were abolished. All Christians alike were to be totally dedicated.

Seen in this light, the Reformation is the ultimate fruit of the Reform spirit, producing for the first time a true uniformity of believers, a levelling up which left no further room for different speeds. If salvation by faith had been the issue of ultimate importance, co-existence might have been conceivable. But where the driving force was Reform, the split in Christendom was inevitable. It was Reform, further inflamed by a hatred of idolatry, which animated the grim-faced worshippers Erasmus saw emerging from the Church in Basel.

The Reformation as Reform is central to the story I want to tell—that of the abolition of the enchanted cosmos, and the eventual creation of a humanist alternative to faith. The first consequence seems evident enough; the Reformation is known as an engine of disenchantment. The second is less obvious, and more indirect. It passes through the attempts to re-order whole societies which emerge in the radical, Calvinist wing of Protestantism. I will take these each in turn.

First, disenchantment. We can see the immense energy behind the denial of the sacred, if we look at Calvin. He was an inspired religious visionary. Like many great reformers, including, for instance, St. Francis, his vision proposes a radical simplification, in which the essentials of the faith stand out from behind the clutter of secondary concerns. These reformers all see the reigning equilibrium as a bad compromise, at least for them. Their vision has three facets: (1) they see more acutely what transformation we're called to; (2) they see more acutely our imperfections; (3) they see clearer the greatness of God. These belong together; (1) and (2) are just facets of the same insight, as Calvin himself says.[79]

It is this sense of the essentials which permits the radical simplification; it shows the irrelevance of much religious practice, even if it's not counter-purpose (Erasmus).

The Reformers come after many attempts to mobilize everyone to higher transformation. They have a history behind them of late-mediaeval Reform. These earlier attempts had bogged down; first in compromise; then they themselves developed mechanical, routinized sides—e.g., confession, distinguishing kinds of sin, etc. These are perhaps inseparable from any régime designed to produce transformation. But Calvin wanted to make a radical break.

Calvin's radical simplification could perhaps be put this way: We are depraved; and thus in the work of our salvation God does everything. Man "cannot, without sacrilege, claim for himself even a crumb of righteousness, for just so much is plucked and taken away from the glory of God's righteousness."[80]

God's honour and glory is paramount.[81] But the honour of God is attacked by the sin of Adam.[82] God owes it to his justice, and his glory to reject such creatures. But he is merciful. He gets satisfaction he must have for our sin through Christ; he works off the required punishment on him, and this allows us to be imputed just.

I want to digress a moment to note here the fateful fact that Calvin, like the other Reformers, casts his doctrine of our incapacity and God's remedy for it in the juridical-penal framework that he takes over from Augustine and later Anselm. There is one enigma which Christians (and perhaps realists of any persuasion) have to recognize, and that is the puzzle of evil; why, in spite of knowing that we are born for the highest, we sometimes not only inexplicably choose against it, but even feel that we cannot do otherwise. The symmetrical mystery (now for Christians alone) is that God can act to overcome this incapacity—the doctrine of grace.

Anselm expressed this double mystery in terms of crime and punishment. The incapacity is explained as our just desert for our original falling away (which founding act remains shrouded in mystery, of course). Being inveterate sinners, we now deserve damnation. Not only is our punishment now permissible, but some has to be exacted as reparation for our fault, according to the juridical logic of this conception. God is nevertheless merciful, wants to save some of us. But in order to do this he has to have the reparation paid by his son, and then count it as satisfaction for our sins, in an act of gratuitous mercy.

Needless to say, this wasn't the only way that the double mystery could be articulated. Eastern fathers, like Gregory of Nyssa, put things differently. But Augustine and Anselm shaped the theology of Latin Christendom in this regard, and the Reformation, far from correcting this imbalance, aggravated it. The sense that this language, above all others, has got a lock on the mysteries, is an invitation to drive its logic through to the most counter-intuitive, not to say horrifying conclusions, like the doctrine of the damnation of the majority of humans, or double predestination. The confidence—not to say arrogance—with which these conclusions were drawn anticipates and offers a model for the later humanist hostility to mystery.[83]

I mention this here because the hegemony of this juridical-penal model plays an important role in the later rise of unbelief, both in repelling people from the faith, and in modifying it in the direction of Deism.

But to return to the drive to disenchantment, this incapacity, countered by God's mercy, was received as good news. For provided we see how hopeless our case is, how we can't give satisfaction ourselves, by works, how the Law must condemn us, the news that we are saved by Christ takes us out of despair. Or if we are still struggling, it takes us out of anxiety. Of course, the question is always put, how we know we are saved if so few are? The answer is that having faith, responding to the call, is itself a sign that we are among the lucky ones. Then we should be confident, because otherwise we are failing in faith.

This now changes the centre of gravity of the religious life. The power of God doesn't operate through various "sacramentals", or locations of sacred power which we can draw on. These are seen to be something which we can control, and hence blasphemous. In one way, we can say that the sacred/profane distinction breaks down, insofar as it can be placed in person, time, space, gesture. This means that the sacred is suddenly broadened: for the saved, God is sanctifying us everywhere, hence also in ordinary life, our work, in marriage, and so on.

But in another way, the channels are radically narrowed, because this sanctification depends entirely now on our inner transformation, our throwing ourselves on God's mercy in faith. Otherwise nothing works, and we create no valid order.

This doesn't mean that everything happens in our heads. That is a later aberration, a total subjectivization of religion. Calvin stresses that God really acts, he communicates grace and sanctification to us. We are fed by God through Christ; and in a sense by his body and blood, because it is his bodily existence which gave satisfaction, culminating in the shedding of his blood. So the Eucharist is the sign of something real, something which has exactly that form, our being fed by God. But what he can't admit is that God could have released something of his saving efficacy out there into the world, at the mercy of human action, because that is the cost of really sanctifying creatures like us which are bodily, social, historical. The whole efficacy of the sacrament is contingent on the connection between God and my faith, a speech act made and uptaken. And we have to see and accept the full meaning for uptake to happen. "Les Sacremens n'ont d'autre office que la parolle de Dieu".[84]

So we disenchant the world; we reject the sacramentals; all the elements of "magic" in the old religion. They are not only useless, but blasphemous, because they are arrogating power to us, and hence "plucking" it away "from the glory of God's righteousness". This also means that intercession by saints is of no effect. In face of the world of spirits and powers, this gives us great freedom. Christian liberty for Calvin consists in this: that one see salvation in faith; that one serve God with one's whole heart; and that one no longer be scrupled by indifferent things.[85] We can cast aside all the myriad rituals and acts of propitiation of the old religion. Serving God now in our ordinary life, guided by the spirit, we can re-order things freely. We don't need to be too impressed by custom; this can lead us terribly astray.[86]

The energy of disenchantment is double. First negative, we must reject everything which smacks of idolatry. We combat the enchanted world, without quarter. At first, this fight is not carried on because enchantment is totally untrue, but rather because it is necessarily ungodly. If we are not allowed to look for help to the sacred, to a "white" magic of the church, then all magic must be black. All spirits now are ranged under the devil, the one great enemy. Even supposedly good magic must really be serving him.[87]

So in the short run this could lead to an intensification of certain of the old beliefs, particularly in witches, who were now redefined in a much more sinister role as helpmeets of the devil. Salem becomes possible. But in the longer run, this attack could not but undermine the whole outlook within which these persecutions made sense.

The more so, in that the second energy was positive. We feel a new freedom in a world shorn of the sacred, and the limits it set for us, to re-order things as seems best. We take the crucial stance, for faith and glory of God. Acting out of this, we order things for the best. We are not deterred by the older tabus, or supposedly sacred orderings. So we can rationalise the world, expel the mystery from it (because it is all now concentrated in the will of God). A great energy is released to re-order affairs in secular time.

This brings us to the second great consequence of this turn, its long-term contribution to the rise of humanism. This came about precisely through the drive to re-order society, not only in its church structure, but in its secular life as well. What drives this activism, which we see in certain Calvinist societies, Geneva, New England, Puritan-governed England of the mid-sixteenth century? It continues the Reform traditions of the late Middle Ages, but on a much more ambitious level.

We can understand this drive to re-order if we see it against the background of the tensions inherent in Christian faith, and the forms they took in this period.

One perennial tension we have already visited. It is the one which is resolved, or at least relaxed, by formulae of hierarchical complementarity between vocations at different "speeds". We could describe it as lying between the demand to love God, which means to follow him even to the cross, to be ready to renounce everything, on one hand; and the demand to affirm ordinary human life and flourishing, on the other. The two come together in that the path of giving to God often takes the form of feeding, healing, clothing; fending off suffering and death, and thus making human flourishing possible. This is clear in the life of Christ.

The tension arises when it comes to determining what is the Christian life for those who are engaged in full human flourishing, through work, family, civic life, friends, building for society and the future, and so on. The holy renouncer puts the two together in that his/her renunciation can directly serve works of mercy, healing. But how about the person engaged in ordinary life, married, with children, living from the land or from a trade?

An answer can be given valid in theory for everyone: Go beyond the kind of affirmation of the good of life which the ordinary homme moyen sensuel makes, which is very much focussed on my own good, my own life, and might even be willing to sacrifice endless others to this; and connect to the affirmation of God, his agape, which loves all mankind, and is ready to give without stint, to let go of what I hold in order to be part of the movement of love.

But for the ordinary householder this answer seems to require something paradoxical: living in all the practices and institutions of flourishing, but at the same time not fully in them. Being in them but not of them; being in them, but yet at a distance, ready to lose them. Augustine put it: use the things of this world, but don't enjoy them; uti, not frui. Or do it all for the glory of God, in the Loyola-Calvin formulation.

The big problem is working out what this means. Any attempt to tie it down faces two opposite dangers. One is to set the element of renunciation so high as to make the life of flourishing a travesty of itself. In particular, think of the teaching to the laity in the Middle Ages about married sexuality. It totally excluded any sexual joy. The other is, to set a bare minimum. Think of the minimum necessary for salvation: keeping certain important commandments. But then we know even these will often be broken; so in the end the minimum demands simply that you repent in time.

The end result here is that an inherent danger built into this tension itself now befalls us. We clearly set the renunciative vocations above the ordinary lay ones. There are first- and second-class Christians; the second being in a sense carried by the first. We fall back into hierarchical complementarity.

Whereas the crucial truth that we wanted to hold on to was the complementarity of all lives and vocations, where we all serve under God, and can't put some above others.

So there seems to be a dilemma here, between demanding too much renunciation from the ordinary person, on one hand, and relaxing these demands, but at the cost of a multi-speed system, on the other.

Radical Protestantism utterly rejects the multi-speed system, and in the name of this abolishes the supposedly higher, renunciative vocations; but also builds renunciation into ordinary life. It avoids the second horn, but comes close to the first danger above: loading ordinary flourishing with a burden of renunciation it cannot carry. It in fact fills out the picture of what the properly sanctified life would be with a severe set of moral demands. This seems to be unavoidable in the logic of rejecting complementarity, because if we really must hold that all vocations are equally demanding, and don't want this to be a levelling down, then all must be at the most exigent pitch.

Images of order and disorder were important here. The justified, sanctified person eschewed disordered conduct, put his/her life in order, made an end of drunkenness, fornication, unbridled speech, immoderate laughter, fights, violence, etc.[88]

Moreover, Calvinists shared with many people of the day, particularly élites, a strong sense of the scandal of social disorder, that the general behaviour was sinful in the above ways, and that society as a whole was given over to disorder, vice, injustice, blasphemy, etc. It was an important goal to remedy this, on the social and not only the personal level.

Here is where it becomes significant[89] that Protestantism is in the line of continuity with mediaeval reform, attempting to raise general standards, not satisfied with a world in which only a few integrally fulfill the gospel, but trying to make certain pious practices absolutely general.

But in view of the importance now given to social order, the generalization of moral demands involved not only placing high moral demands on one's own life, but also putting order into society. This was not seen as involving a watering down of the standards of personal morality, but as completing them. Calvin held that we have to control the vices of the whole society, lest the vicious infect the others. We are all responsible for each other, and for society as a whole.[90]

And indeed, getting the degree of order which Calvinist societies often aimed at—e.g., Geneva, New England—was quite exceptional in history, and was unprecedented. It involved a leap higher than what had gone before, and was understood as such.

But, of course, the idea was not that human beings could do this on their own. Only the power of God could make this possible. We had to recognize our own helplessness, and turn to God in faith, in order to achieve this. This is what made the whole enterprise utterly different from a new and more highly moralized view about human flourishing. Only those who were turned quite beyond human flourishing, to God, building this order for the glory of God and not for human convenience, could pull it off.

The inner motive was key here. But this meant that for actually living this out, a third level of order had to be added to the other two: a disciplined personal life, and a well-ordered society. It was also necessary that one's inner stance to all this be correct. One had to avoid building this on a sense of one's own unaided powers; that would be blind, presumptuous, ungodly. But at the same time, one had to avoid the sense that one was indeed, powerless, because in the irrevocable grip of sin. The sanctified necessarily had a sense that they were saved by God, empowered by God to build the godly order.

Puritan spiritual life moved between a Scylla and a Charybdis. On one hand, one had to have confidence in one's salvation. Too much anxious doubt amounted to a turning away of God's gift, and could even be a sign that one was not saved after all. But at the same time, an utterly unruffled confidence showed that you were altogether forgetting the theological stakes involved, forgetting that one was a sinner who richly deserved eternal damnation, and was only saved from this by God's gratuitous grace; that one was in fact hanging over a cliff, and was only held back by God's outstretched hand.

Puritan preaching went back and forth in recognition of these two dangers. On one hand, people were shown how deeply they had offended God, and how powerless they were to amend themselves; on the other, they were assured that God had rescued them from damnation. But again, lest they take all this for granted, they must be reminded how helpless, etc. they were.[91]

Since it was a general belief of Protestants that one of the usual signs of salvation was a certain confidence in God's saving action, there was understandably much soul-searching to see what one's inner dispositions were. But the line between searching to see whether one has certain inner feelings and reactions, and trying to bring them on, is very hard to draw, particularly when so much rides on the answer. And this is all the more so, when one is also being exhorted to feel these things.

Consequently, a third level of order-building arises in Protestant (and also some Catholic) spirituality: building the right inner attitude. Being able to avoid despair, or paralyzing melancholy, on one side, and a facile, unthinking confidence on the other.

Now I think one can see how all this disciplined order-building prepared a great reversal. On one hand, we have people who develop the disciplines of character, so that they can put some (for the time) impressive degree of moral order in their conduct. On the other, some of these people in association find ways to impose an unprecedented degree of order on society, or at least come to believe that they can do so, given the right conditions.

Now both their action in expelling the sacred from worship and social life, and the instrumental stance they take to things and to society in the course of building their order, tends to drive out the enchantment from the world. This becomes progressively voided of its spirits and meaningful forces, and more and more the disenchanted world we are familiar with. In consequence the understanding of the subject as porous fades more and more away.

However, the immediate effect is not to put the place of God in any doubt. God is no longer needed as the guarantee that good will triumph in a world of multiple spirits and forces. But in the first instance, this multiplicity is denied in favour of a single rival source, the devil. All magic becomes black, and the workings of the devil. In face of universally deserved damnation, the power of God is all the more dramatically necessary that evil not triumph. The sense of God is all the more acute.

But the reversal is prepared in the fact that as an order is built in conduct, and at least seen as within our power to encompass in society, and more crucially, as people learn the secret of a kind of motivational equilibrium whereby they can keep themselves on the track to both of these external orders, the possibility is opened to slide de facto, without even feeling it, into the Scylla mentioned above, that is, into a confidence that we have these things under control, we can pull it off.

Of course, we go on holding to the express belief that only God's power makes this possible; but in fact the confidence has grown that we, people like us, successful, well-behaved people, in our well-ordered society/stratum, are beneficiaries of God's grace—as against those depraved, disordered classes, marginal groups, Papists, or whatever. It is hard to dent this confidence as long as we can keep the triple-level order in being. As a *general* proposition, of course, it remains true that the majority of humankind is destined for damnation, and that the minority of the saved are very lucky; but in practice, we are confident that we belong in this minority; and that the universe is unfolding as it should. The declarations that we are helpless sinners become more and more pro forma.

I have described a change as it might happen among the less reflective and devout members of the community. But the sense of greater control also effected the more reflective and devout. Thus Arminianism arises after a time in all Calvinist societies, provoking as it does revivals of predestinarian orthodoxy, but then returning in force again. This development was inevitable, in view of the very success of Calvinism in changing people's lives.

We can see how from this confidence in our capacity to achieve the three-fold order, a move to an exclusive humanism could be made. What is required is that the reference to God be lopped off, at two points.

First the goal of order is redefined as a matter purely of human flourishing. We no longer see the pursuit of it as a way of following God, let alone glorifying him. And secondly, the power to pursue it is no longer something that we receive from God, but is a purely human capacity.

But as a consequence of this double movement towards immanence, a new conception of human flourishing is born, which is in some ways without precedent. The new understanding is frequently expressed in terms of "nature", following the philosophical tradition which comes down to us from the ancients.

8

But I am running ahead of my story. Before we can see how the Reformation played a role in the disenchantment of the world, and the creation of an exclusive humanism, we should get a sense of the whole period which enframes it, before and after, the period from, say (all dates are arbitrary here), 1450–1650. Three centuries of Reform, we might say, including the various phases of what we call THE Reformation, and also the counter-Reformation. But it also includes the drives beforehand, in the late Middle Ages, to reform lay piety, and bring it up to a "higher" standard. There is a continuity here. The Reformation, in closing the gap (at least in theory) between élite and ordinary, clerical and lay piety, was continuing an enterprise which had been launched in different form before.

Now in this period, three kinds of change are happening together, mixed into each other, and hampering or furthering each other. So mixed that they can often only be analytically separated. There are, first, autonomous changes in popular piety, which may be encouraged from on high, but are not mainly powered from above, like the devotion to the crucified Christ, and the practices of solidarity before death and Purgatory. There are, second, the rise and development of new élites, with a different outlook, or different social base, as with the educated laity who more and more mark the religious picture of Latin Christendom through this period.

And then there is, third, the deliberate attempts by élites, whether old or new, to make over the whole society, to change the lives of the mass of people, and make then conform better to certain models which carried strong conviction among these élites. This we see from the very beginning of the period, even before the period as I have drawn it, in the series of measures undertaken by the mediaeval church to raise the standards of religious practice and piety. This is a very important fact I mentioned above, without being able to explain it; the "rage for order" of Latin Christendom, whereby the dissatisfaction grew with the hierarchical equilibrium between religious leaders and people, hierarchy and laity, which has been the rule rather than the exception among civilizations dominated by "higher" religions.[92]

This was far from being simply a passing phase, for attempts of this kind are repeatedly made. First, they go on being made by this same élite, the hierarchy of the Catholic church, through the Council of Trent, and into the various ramifications of the counter-Reformation church. The standards of clerical education are constantly raised, as are the standards of lay practice.

But secondly, analogous attempts are made by other élites, in some cases but not always in rivalry with the hierarchy. The rivalry is clear in the case of those who reorganized societies under the aegis of the Reformation: the church and state leaders of Lutheran lands, the Christian humanists who opted for the Reform, and helped to create the synthesis of the Reformed Churches, in first place, of course, Jean Cal-vin; their spiritual affines who re-organized the English church after the Henrician break with Rome. Again and again, semi-refractory masses were forced to shape up to a new régime, sometimes rudely, sometimes by gentle persuasion, while the rise of new élites often facilitated the process.

But thirdly, we see another series of attempts to remake society carried out by sec-ular authorities, in the name of good social order; in which there is always a reli-gious component, but which is never exclusively defined in religious terms. The sit-uation of the poor and of mendicants undergoes a re-evaluation. They begin to lose their evangelical aura, are less seen as occasions of charity, and more as social prob-lems which need to be dealt with. They are dealt with by being organized, taken in hand, disciplined, sometimes semi-incarcerated.[93]

This is only one facet of the new "police state", which undertakes to organize the lives of its citizens in rational ways; ensure that they are properly educated, that they belong to churches, that they lead sober and productive economic lives. It is also an organization which effectively combats various social disasters, as plague is con-trolled by more rigorous quarantine.

Here there is not necessarily rivalry. These secular authorities worked closely in co-operation with some church or other. Charles Borromeo, the great counter-Ref-ormation bishop of Milan, both carried out a reform of many church practices in keeping with more advanced models: condemning carnivals, and other vestiges of paganism, which mix sacred and profane, trying to exclude animals from churches, end dancing in cemeteries, ban charivaris, etc.; in short, establish a more ordered and less "enchanted" version of Christian practice; and he also encouraged munici-pal measures to organize and discipline the poor and vagabonds.

There are certain common features running through all these attempts at reform and organization: (1) they are activist; they seek effective measures to re-order soci-ety; they are highly interventionist; (2) they are uniformizing: they aim to apply a single model or schema to everything and everybody; they attempt to eliminate anomalies, exceptions, marginal populations, and all kinds of non-conformists; (3) they are homogenizing; although they still operate in societies based on differences of rank, their general tendency is to reduce differences, to educate the masses, and to make them conform more and more to the standards governing their betters. This is very clear in the church reformations; but it also is true of the attempts to or-der people's lives by the "police states"; (4) they are "rationalizing" in Weber's dou-ble sense: that is, they not only involve an increased use of instrumental reason, in the very process of activist reform, as well as in designing some of the ends of reform (e.g., in the economic sphere); but they also try to order society by a coherent set of rules (Weber's second dimension of rationality, *Wertrationalität*).

This, plus the inherent drive of the religious reformations, made them work towards the disenchantment of the world, and the abolition of society based on hierarchical equilibrium, whether that of élite and mass, or that we find reflected in the
Carnival, and the "world turned upside down". Indeed, the hostility to Carnival
and such-like remains of popular culture is one of the evident points in common
between religious and secular re-orderings. In the perspective of élites of the sixteenth and seventeenth centuries, the world upside down of Carnival was neither a
subject of amusement, nor a salutary correction for élite pride, nor an "air-hole"
(safety valve), nor a recognition of the depth and many-sidedness of human life. It
was simply an image of, and an invitation to sin. Starting with Brant's *Ship of Fools*,
a stream of writing, painting (Bosch, Breughel), illustrations begin to moralize this
theme of reversal. It is in the end no laughing matter. Indeed, the world upside
down is the one we daily live in, in which sin has upset all order. A humourless determination to castigate sin and disorder takes over, a denial of ambiguity and complexity in an unmixed condemnation, which reflects the attempts by controlling
élites to abolish carnivalesque and ludic practices, on the grounds that they sew disorder, mix pagan and Christian elements, and are a breeding ground of vice. (We
are witnessing the birth of what will become in our day p.c.) Delumeau relates this
to a parallel shift in attitude to madness;[94] where previously this could be seen as the
site of vision, even holiness, it now comes more and more to be judged unambiguously as the fruit of sin.

Which brings me to a very important feature of this whole period. It is marked at
the beginning by a growing split between élite and popular culture. Peter Burke has
traced the major lineaments of this. Of course, there are dangers in distinguishing
élite and popular culture. From way back, there have been elements of culture confined to an élite, such as theology, scholastic philosophy, humanist letters; but in the
Middle Ages, one could perhaps argue that the symmetrical condition didn't really
hold. That is, there wasn't a popular culture from which the élites were excluded.
Popular modes of piety, for instance, were shared in by gentry and clergy; everyone
participated in Carnival.

But from the late Renaissance, we find a growing split. We might say a kind of secession of the élites from popular culture; be it the devotion to images in the religious sphere, or Carnival and popular amusements. This secession marks the development of élite ideals of life which are seen as incompatible with much of popular
culture, ideals of piety in the religious sphere, and of "civility" in the secular domain. This secession doesn't remain at that stage, but is the basis for the attempt to
remake society, the active re-ordering of mass life, which has had such fateful consequences.

This is the context in which we have to see the transformation which does away with the enchanted world, and brings on stage the first viable forms of exclusive humanism. This latter is marked by the process which brings it about, by its activism, uniformization, homogenization, rationalization, and of course by its hostility to enchantment and equilibrium.

Ideally, we should be able to follow the whole process of re-ordering in its different facets, the two reformations and the "police state". But before doing this, we have to describe some of the background to the lay attempts at Reform. We need to factor in some of the modern history of the philosophical concepts of nature which underlay these efforts. We need to look at some of the late mediaeval and early modern developments of humanism; because these also contributed heavily to the attempt at a disciplined re-ordering of life and society. I want to turn now to take up this thread.

9

But first, one more general remark about this whole period. It is, as Delumeau argues, an age of anxiety.[95] An age of great fears. Fear of magic, of outsiders, of disorders, and of course of sin, death, and judgment. This is particularly marked after the great disasters of the fourteenth century; famines, wars, and above all the Black Death. It is sometimes just explained by these disasters.

But it seems plausible that the fear was multiplied by the transitions this society was going through. Not only the slow disenchantment, but also the destabilization involved in the continuing attempts to re-order it, abolishing the familiar, and starting something new.

The first effect of disenchantment was not to do away with demons, let us remember. Since in the radical form, it eschewed all church magic, it branded all magic as black. Everything of this sort now belonged to the devil, and all sorcerers, cunning women, healers, etc., were now in danger of being branded as confederates of the devil.

In a sense, the demons get concentrated, even as the positive energy of God is concentrating out of its dispersal in charged objects and church magic. There is one enemy, THE devil, Satan.

This change also raises anxiety. There is greater fear of the devil, fear for our salvation. The emphasis on struggle increases.

So it is perhaps not surprising that this age is one intensified persecutions, some of which seem close to mad to us. There is perhaps a phenomenon here, which we could call social panic. The so-called "Grande Peur" of Revolutionary France in 1789 is perhaps an example. Just because we fight evil forces through social order, or see this as our protection against these, there can be a certain kind of tremendous fear when what we identify as crucial to this social order is being undermined. I mean what is crucial to achieve whatever protection we need. We can argue that this kind of fear survives into the secular age. A modern society can be deeply shaken when it learns that some of its young people have taken up terrorism, just because this undercuts the very bulwark of what they understand as order, which is the security of the person. Or think of the over-reaction in the McCarthy era to the idea that some hitherto trusted milieux harboured Communists.

It is perhaps for analogous reasons to these that the late Middle Ages and early modern period sees an intensification of the persecution of marginals, including those which had been allowed to exist peaceably before. The hunt for witches steadily escalated. Heretics were more vigorously hunted down. Fear of vagabonds increased (but here there was objective change also). The hypothesis is that there was more free-floating anxiety, really about one's own salvation; and so more likelihood that people would react violently to pollution threats to what they dimly saw as bulwarks in the social sacred against whatever menaces arose.

I will return to this issue towards the end of the book.

2 The Rise of the Disciplinary Society

1

Part of our story seems to lie in the increasing interest in nature, as it were, for its own sake, not simply as a manifestation of God; an interest which can be seen in science (e.g., the recovery of Aristotle in the thirteenth/fourteenth centuries); in art (e.g., the new "realism" of Giotto, who seems to have put the people around him, closely observed, into his painting); in ethics (the recovery of ancient ethics of "nature", Aristotle, the Stoics). This process starts far back, and goes through several stages. It is one crucial facet of the "Twelfth Century Renaissance". But then another kind of interest in nature is evident among the nominalists of the fifteenth century; another again among Renaissance humanists; something further is evident in the great revolution in scientific outlook, the Galilean-Newtonian turn of the seventeenth century; and there is more to come.

Now the relationship of this to modern secularism can seem obvious. As I put it above, following a very common way of telling the story, people begin to be interested in nature, in the life around them, "for their own sakes", and not just in reference to God. Where before they had one goal in portraying or thinking about nature or human life, now they have two. They have taken the first step on a journey which leads to us. It suffices that they take more and more interest in nature-for-its-own-sake, and gradually this will grow, while the reference to the divine atrophies. Until finally, they are modern exclusive humanists, or at least secularists. Of course, this story is underlain by the sense that this terminus is the obviously correct one; that being interested in nature without external reference, or with reference only to us humans, is the only sensible stance. And this cannot but dawn, slowly, and against resistance, and with some steps forward, and some back, but overall, over time, it must prevail.

This straight path account is another "subtraction" story, of the kind I discussed above (Introduction, last page). We just need to slough off the reference to God, and an interest in nature for its own sake—or in the light of our interests—emerges as the "natural" stance.

This seems to me to be wrong. The real story is much more interesting. The first thing which is clearly wrong with it, is that it contrasts interest in nature-for-itself with reference to God; whereas in fact these two went together. Take the new Aristotelian-Christian synthesis which takes its most influential form in Thomas. This brought about what one could call an autonomization of nature. The things around us have their own natures, the forms which they strive to embody, and hence their own kind of perfection. They are also called to exhibit another kind of perfection in the dimension of grace, but this doesn't cancel or set aside their inherent, natural perfection. Gratia non tollit naturam, sed perficit.

But to contemplate things in the perfection of their natures, although it brackets the work of grace, doesn't turn us away from God. Nature offers another way of encountering God, because it is his creation. Its order bespeaks his goodness. That is why Aquinas says: "Detrahere ergo perfectioni creaturarum est detrahere perfectioni divinae virtutis"[1] (Consequently to detract from the creature's perfection is to detract from the perfection of the divine power).[2]

Of course, everyone knows that this is the doctrine. The difference between the straight path view and myself here lies in the issue, how seriously to take this as an account of the motivation of the change. One can hold that the natural pull of the only sensible view was beginning to make itself felt. Autonomization of nature was the first timid step towards the negation of all super-nature. Of course, people at the time wouldn't have put it in these terms; they had to have some acceptable reason relating to God. But what was really pulling them was a growing interest in nature-for-itself.

This is what I want to contest. But to clear the road to the issue here, we have to deal with an obvious feature of the situation then and now, which can confuse us. Even in an "age of faith", not everyone is equally devout. Indeed, we may even wonder whether the proportion of people who are deeply into whatever spirituality(ies) are accessible in any given epoch is not fairly constant. Belief is not the issue. Presumably the person who used the Host as a love-charm had a pretty high view of the power of consecration. But the level of devotion, or the "reference to God" wasn't very conspicuous.

Similarly, views of the autonomy of nature could have a whole gamut of meanings. Contemplating it or learning about it could be part of a variety of projects, all the way from glorifying God, to finding the most effective way of doing things, passing through ethical reflection and aesthetic appreciation. We can't speak of a single goal here.

The interesting question is, what goal(s) was (were) hegemonic; what explains the original shift to autonomy, among those who made it? what explains its continuing impact? what meanings are defined as the proper or highest ones? Of course, here too, there is no more reason to look for one unique cause than there is anywhere else; but my claim would be that the meanings involving reference to God played a very important role.

Clearly this is so among the clerical scholar-intellectuals who articulated this shift, from Aquinas on down. What the straight path view can't really take account of is the way in which the autonomization of nature makes possible its own kind of devotion. This can indeed, come into conflict with other kinds of devotion, and that is why the change can (and did) evoke resistance, why it can be *castigated* as impious, which it most certainly was not.

We can try to get a sense of these different ways of devotion. One focusses on things as the loci of the great acts, the marvels that God has wrought. This is largely Biblically-nourished, but also feeds on miracles and marvels which have occurred since Biblical times. To think of bread is to relate it to the manna which fell in the desert, the Passover rites of the Jews, the last supper, the celestial banquet.[3] The focus on its role in these gesta Dei leaves no place for a consideration of its nature, in the sense of a stable way of being which governs it in abstraction from these acts. This was a spirituality widely followed by the scholar-monks of the high Middle Ages, focussed as they were on the Scriptures, and on an allegorization of the events they read about there.

But what goes missing here is a sense of the universe as an ordered whole, the cosmos, or universitas mundi, as it came to be called. We might say that one way focusses on God's speech acts, the other on the marvellous systematic language which makes these acts possible. Carrying this image forward, we can say that for those on the first path, the second seems to downplay God's power and his marvels; to confine him too much, as though he couldn't neologize; while for those on the second path, the first seems blind to one of God's greatest marvels, the creation of the ordered whole.[4] This emerges in Honorius of Autun's use of the image of the world as an immense cithar.

> Summus namque opifex universitatem quasi magnam citharam condidit, in qua veluti chordas ad multiplices sonos reddendos posuit.[5]
>
> (The supreme artisan made the universe like a great cithar upon which he placed as it were strings to yield a variety of sounds.)[6]

It goes without saying that for those in the second way, the autonomy of nature didn't in any sense involve a denial of the symbolic or allegorical meanings of things. Only these meanings were now to be understood against the background of the harmonious order. The speech acts drew on the syntax and vocabulary of an ordered language. That things have a stable nature doesn't prevent them from still being signs pointing us to God. In the words of Hugues of St. Victor, "Universus mundus iste sensibilis quasi quidam liber est scriptus digito Dei . . ."[7] (The entire sense-perceptible world is like a sort of book written by the finger of God.)[8]

So the autonomy of nature had genuine and powerful spiritual sources. But so did the new "realism" in painting and sculpture. This too is often portrayed as an add-on. That the portrayal of the Virgin and Child shows real observation of contemporary models, that there is variety and individual portraiture in religious painting, that what is represented is no longer just some universal, normative feature of the person or being concerned, as in the awesome Christ Pantocrator on the cupola of Byzantine churches, but the traits of live individuals begin to appear; all this is frequently taken as the emergence of an extra-religious motive, alongside the religious purpose.[9]

But here again the contrast seems mistaken. Apart from the impact on visual art of the sense of nature as an ordered whole, we can see other spiritual reasons in the twelfth and thirteenth centuries for this change.

Where monastic spirituality of the high Middle Ages tended to focus on the cloister as the site of a life which approached closest to the vita apostolica,[10] led by minorities away from the world, we see movements of lay people in the late twelfth century crying out for a new mode of apostolic existence within the world, and indeed for the world. That is, the new life would involve going out and preaching to the world; it would be apostolic in a sense which the word has (partly as a result of these movements) acquired (or re-acquired). Some of these movements ended up turning heretical, like that led by Peter Waldo; others revolutionized the life of the Church, notably the new orders founded by Francis and Dominic.[11]

This new turn can probably be connected to the spiritual development I talked about above, whereby a devotion grows during these centuries to the human Christ, the suffering Christ, where before it had been the Christ of Judgment (reflected for instance in the Pantocrator) which predominated in Latin Christendom. St. Francis reflects this too, for instance in the stigmata which he bore. The stress on the human suffering Christ obviously fits with the aspiration to bring Christ to the suffering humans of our time. They are two facets of the same leading idea, that Christ is our brother, our neighbour, is among us.

And that is what this new spiritual direction was about. It is one of the main themes of Christianity, as faith in the Incarnation, which keeps recurring in form after form in Christian history: the aspiration to bring Christ to the people, among the people, who have been left out or kept at a distance in the previous spiritual dispensation, especially to the poor. These new movements aim to shift the centre of gravity of the "apostolic life" out of the monastery and among the laity, particularly in those new milieux of the towns, with their merchants, artisans, and also their destitute. Both Waldo and Francis were children of artisans.

So it is not altogether surprising that this attempt to bring Christ to the world, the lay world, the previously unhallowed world, should inspire a new focus on this world. On one side, this involved a new vision of nature, as we see in the rich Franciscan spirituality of the life of God in the animate and inanimate things which surround us; on another it brought ordinary people into focus.

And we might add, ordinary people in their individuality. Because another important facet of Franciscan spirituality was its intense focus on the person of Jesus Christ. This devotion, as Louis Dupré argues, ends up opening "a new perspective on the unique particularity of the person." On the intellectual level, this takes time to work its way out, in the writings of the great Franciscan thinkers, Bonaventure, Duns Scotus, Occam, but it ends up giving a new status to the particular, as something more than a mere instantiation of the universal. Perfect knowledge will mean now grasping the "individual form", the haecceitas, in Scotus' language.[12]

Though it couldn't be clear at the time, we with hindsight can recognize this as a major turning point in the history of Western civilization, an important step towards that primacy of the individual which defines our culture. But of course, it could only have this significance because it was more than a mere intellectual shift, reflected in the invention of new unpronounceable scholastic terms. It was primarily a revolution in devotion, in the focus of prayer and love: the paradigm human individual, the God-Man, in relation to whom alone the humanity of all the others can be truly known, begins to emerge more into the light.

And so it seems to be no coincidence that one of the first reflections of this focus in painting should have been Giotto's murals in the church at Assisi. This interest in the variety and detailed features of real contemporary people did not arise alongside and extrinsic to the religious point of the painting; it was intrinsic to the new spiritual stance to the world.

I have been identifying two spiritual motives for the renewed interest in nature as autonomous: devotion to God as the creator of an ordered cosmos, whose parts themselves exhibited standing marvels of micro-order (this applies, of course, especially to human beings, but not only to them); and a new evangelical turning to the world, to bring Christ among the people. It is clear that these can fit well together; the evangelical turn to a society or milieu previously inadequately touched by the Gospel, of itself invites us to see how God is already present in the lives of our addressees, so as the better to address them. The best practice of missionaries after the Reformation will constantly keep account of this, trying to adapt the Gospel to the culture and traditions of the people it is being preached to. One might make this general point, that the preaching of the Gospel, if it is to be other than an expression of the felt superiority of the preacher, demands this close and respectful attention to the life of the addressees as it is prior to the grace which the Gospel will bring. Once again, it ought to come as no surprise that some of the great formulations of the new understanding of nature as autonomous come from members of an order whose official name is the Ordo Predicatorum.

The coming of this new double orientation obviously had a lot to do with the sociological evolution of these centuries, particularly the development of new urban milieux relatively free from the feudal structures of society, with new sites for self-government, of town, guild, confrérie, and with a new sense of lateral connections extending beyond the locality. And indeed, the new orders, being precisely made up of itinerant preachers, do a great deal to extend this sense of broader connectedness throughout the countryside. They become the conduits which disseminate both ideas and images, and a sense of links which bind to others similarly situated elsewhere. The travelling friars were in a sense media of communication, through which a more vivid social imaginary of linkage could grow among ordinary people, until the invention of printing intensified the process many fold in a quantum leap.[13]

But to understand the social basis is not to take away from the prominence of the religious motives which were at work here. The new interest in nature was not a step outside of a religious outlook, even partially; it was a mutation within this outlook. The straight path account of modern secularity can't be sustained. Instead, what I'm offering here is a zig-zag account, one full of unintended consequences. That the autonomy of nature eventually (after a number of further transpositions, of which more anon) came to serve as grist to the mill of exclusive humanism is clearly true. That establishing it was already a step in that direction is profoundly false. This move had a quite different meaning at the time, and in other circumstances might never have come to have the meaning that it bears for unbelievers today.

Another way of coming at the point that I'm trying to make here would be to say that an interest in nature for itself, either in scientific study, or aesthetic portrayal, or ethical reflection, isn't always the same kind of thing. It can be something very different, depending on the background understanding within which the things of nature show up for us. There is a Heideggerian resonance to that last phrase, which is intended. Heidegger has raised this issue of the "meaning of being", the usually unspoken, background understanding of what entities are, which can change from epoch to epoch.

For the period we have been looking at, it went without saying that the things of nature were created beings, showing in some way the fact that they issued from the hand of God. As Heidegger often says, in the Middle Ages entities were understood under the master description of "ens creatum". He seems to have had mainly the scholastic period in mind, on which he did his first work. But in fact, as we have seen, there was more than one framework understanding which met this master description. The focus on things as the loci of God's marvellous acts also took them as creatures, but it was very different from the view which brought out their inclusion in an ordered cosmos.

Now it is important for our story that the framework descriptions evolved further, and in a number of ways. I have already mentioned the impact on visual art of the new turning to the world. But the connected view of nature as regular order, as a coherent cosmos, seems also to have been at work over time. An art which remains within the understanding of things as loci of transcendent power need not concern itself with their relative placing in some coherent order. It doesn't matter that heads aren't what we would see as proportional to bodies, or figures to background. But with the painting of the fifteenth century, with the achievement of perspective, we get objects which are clearly ranged in a single coherent space.[14] This new way of imitating nature clearly springs from a quite different framework understanding of what it is to be a thing, of what is important in thinghood.

The coherence of space has to mean the coherence of time too. Earlier, as we have discussed elsewhere, time was understood as complex. As well as secular time, the time of ordinary "temporal" existence, in which things happen one after another in an even rhythm, there were higher times, modes of eternity. There was what I have called Platonic eternity, the ever unchanging realm of essences, of which the ever-flowing ectypes were pale images. There was the eternity of God, where he stands contemporary with the whole flow of history, the time of nunc stans. And there was also the time of origins, a higher time of original founding events, which we can periodically re-approach at certain high moments.

As this last phrase suggests, the understanding of time saw these higher modes as woven into secular time, interfering with the simple coherent order of secular time-place. Two events very far apart in secular time might nevertheless be close because one of them approaches the time of origins. This Easter Vigil, for instance, brings us back into the vicinity of the original Easter, closer than last year's summer day—although that was closer in terms of secular time alone. The original Passover in Egypt, and the last supper, are brought into close proximity by typology, although they are aeons apart in secular time. And so on.

But the non-homogeneity of time entails a non-homogeneity of space. Certain sacred places—a church, a shrine, a site of pilgrimage—are closer to higher time than everyday places. Really to capture this complexity, or rather to capture the hierarchy here, one has to disrupt space, or else make no attempt to render it coherently. This latter is the option enshrined in the iconic tradition, which strongly influences pre-Renaissance church painting.

But the former option comes to the fore after the coherence is established in painting, and we can see it in some of the painting of the Catholic baroque age. For instance Tintoretto's Resurrection in the Scuola di San Rocco. The figure of Christ emerging from the tomb is in a zone of sharp discontinuity from the rest of the picture where the guards are. This is a good example of how the same profound religious meaning can re-emerge in a quite different form after the autonomy of nature has been established.

There is another series of shifts which cumulatively take the master description of the world as ens creatum in a radically different direction, and one crucial to our story. This begins with the nominalist revolution against the reigning, Thomistic idea of the autonomy of nature. Again, the basic motive is theological. The Aristotelian notion of nature seems to define for each thing its natural perfection, its proper good. This would be independent of God's will, except that he it is who has created the thing thus. But once created, it would appear that God cannot further redefine what the good is for the thing. One might be tempted to say that God as the supremely good being, who always necessarily wills the good, is constrained to will G for object O, where G is the natural good of O.

Of course, the crucial O here is the human being, and it thus appears that once having created humans, God cannot but will what their nature defines as their good. But this seemed to some thinkers an unacceptable attempt to limit God's sovereignty. God must always remain free to determine what is good. The good is whatever God wills; not God must will whatever is (determined by nature as) good. This was the most powerful motive to reject the "realism" of essences for Occam and his followers.

Here another supremely important aspect of this whole dimension of human thinking comes to the fore. The framework, the meaning of being, is relative not just to a vision of the world, but also to an understanding of the stance of the agent in the world. Realism about essences bespeaks the predicament of an agent who sees rightful action as following patterns (essences) which must first be descried in things. As against this, in nominalism, the super-agent who is God relates to things as freely to be disposed of according to his autonomous purposes.

But if this is right, then we, the dependent, created agents, have also to relate to these things not in terms of the normative patterns they reveal, but in terms of the autonomous super-purposes of our creator. The purposes things serve are extrinsic to them. The stance is fundamentally one of instrumental reason.

Now this, of course, is at first in the service of God's purposes; but the shift will not be long in coming to a new understanding of being, according to which, all intrinsic purpose having been expelled, final causation drops out, and efficient causation alone remains. There comes about what has been called "the mechanization of the world picture". And this in turn opens the way for a view of science in which a good test of the truth of a hypothesis is what it enables you to effect. This is the Baconian view.

A radical shift has taken place. We are still in the domain of the ens creatum. The world is God's creature. Moreover, it is an ordered whole. But now the order is no longer normative, in the sense that the world exhibits the (more or less imperfect) instantiations of a system of normative patterns, on which we should model ourselves. Rather the world is a vast field of mutually affecting parts. This has been designed to work in certain ways, that is, to produce certain results.

The purposes are extrinsic, in the sense that we can't understand things in terms of supposedly normative patterns at work in them. But we can grasp the purposes if we can discern what ends a mechanism of this kind is well designed to serve. There is no normative pattern, but things do work smoothly when set to produce certain results.

These are the results which God has established. This we can know either from scripture; or from examining what he has made. It is up to us to strive to encompass these purposes.

Living a godly life in this world is something very different from living in the ordered Aristotelian Cosmos of Aquinas, or the hierarchy of Pseudo-Dionysios. It is no longer a matter of admiring a normative order, in which God has revealed himself through signs and symbols. We rather have to inhabit it as agents of instrumental reason, working the system effectively in order to bring about God's purposes; because it is through these purposes, and not through signs, that God reveals himself in his world. These are not just two different stances, but two incompatible ones. We have to abandon the attempt to read the cosmos as the locus of signs, reject this as illusion, in order to adopt the instrumental stance effectively. Not just on a level of popular belief, as a world of spirits, do we have to disenchant the universe; we have also to bring about the analogous shift on the high cultural level of science, and trade in a universe of ordered signs, in which everything has a meaning, for a silent but beneficent machine.

We can see how this turn runs well together with the drive to disenchantment implicit in Reformation theology. It is not an accident that this kind of science flourished in England and Holland. The same crucial features recur here as in the story of the ultimate effects of the Reformation: disenchantment, the active instrumental stance towards the world, and the following of God's purposes, which means beneficence. And these are the key features of the new emergent exclusive humanism.

But this section of our story is still incomplete. As it stands, it sounds as though the shift from symbol to mechanism was mainly powered by a theological demand. A view of what alone is compatible with God's sovereignty ends up making a new human stance to the world normative. Now certainly there is something to this story; and its close affinity to the Reformation insistence on the sovereign power of God is unmistakable. But nevertheless, there were other forces pushing towards this redefinition of human agency in instrumental terms; this rewriting of humanism in terms of ordering action. This new humanism has deep roots in the Renaissance era, which dovetail with but are partly independent of religious belief.

First, we see a new idea emerging of what we are doing when we do science. Coming to understand requires that we construct an order in thought. Nicholas of Cusa in the fifteenth century developed an account of this kind. This constructivism hadn't yet challenged the view of the cosmos as meaningful order. Ficino, who articulated a very influential version of Platonism first for his circle in Florence, and then well beyond, adopted it.

Since man has observed the order of the heavens, when they move, whither they proceed and with what measures, and what they produce, who could deny that man possesses as it were almost the same genius as the Author of the heavens? And who could deny that man could somehow also make the heavens, could he only obtain the instruments and the heavenly material, since even now he makes them, though of a different material, but with a very similar order.[15]

Leonardo later develops a similar thought. We have to find the "ragioni" in things. But this involves a second creation; in fact two kinds of creation; one in reason, which is science, and the second in imagination, which is art.

But the vision of human agency as active, constructive, shaping, isn't confined to the activities which subserve a contemplative grasp of the world, viz., science and art; it also begins to take a greater place in ethics, in the form of a new understanding of ethical improvement, of how to reach the good life. This is what I would now like to examine.

2

A crucial strand in this story starts from the Renaissance notion of civility. Renaissance 'civility' is the ancestor of our 'civilization', and has much the same force. It is what we have, and those others don't, who lack the excellences, the refinements, the important achievements which we value in our way of life. The others were the "savages". As we can see from the terms, the underlying epitomizing contrast is between life in the forest and life in the city.

The city, following the ancients, is seen as the site of human life at its best and highest. Aristotle had made clear that humans reach the fullness of their nature only in the polis. 'Civility' connects to the Latin word which translates 'polis' (civitas); and in fact derivations of the Greek word were also used with closely related sense: in the seventeenth century, the French spoke of an "état policé" as something they had and the "sauvages" didn't.

So part of what this term designated was the mode of government. One must be governed in orderly fashion, under a code of law, according to which rulers and "magistrates" exercised their functions. Because of the projection onto them of the image of "natural man", savages were held to lack these things. But what they really did lack in most cases, were the makings of what we think of as a modern state, a continuing instrument of government in whose hands was concentrated a great deal of power over the society, so that it was capable of remoulding this society in important ways.[16] As this state developed, so it came to be seen as a defining feature of an "état policé".

Thirdly, the mode of government required by civility assured some degree of domestic peace. It didn't consort with rowdiness, random and unauthorized violence, or public brawls, either in young aristocratic bloods, or among the people. Of course, in early modern times, there was lots of all this. And this alerts us to an important difference between the place 'civility' had in Renaissance discourse, and that which 'civilization' holds in ours. As we read in our morning papers about the massacres in Bosnia or Rwanda, or the breakdown of government in Liberia, we tend to feel ourselves in tranquil possession of what we call "civilization", even though we may feel a little embarrassed to say so out loud. A race riot at home may disturb our equanimity, but we rapidly revert.

In Renaissance times, the élites among which this ideal circulated were all too aware that it was not only absent abroad, but all too imperfectly realized at home. The common people, while not on the level of savages in America, and even being far above the European savage peoples of the margins (e.g., the Irish, the Russians),[17] still had a long way to go. And even the members of ruling élites needed to be subjected to firm discipline in each new generation, as a Venetian law of public education in 1551 proposed.[18] Civility was not something you attained at a certain stage in history, and then relaxed into, which is the way we tend to think about civilization.

This reflected the transition that European societies were going through from about 1400. The new (or newly recovered) ideal reflected a new way of life. If we compare the life of, say, the English nobility and gentry before the Wars of the Roses with the way they lived under the Tudors, the difference is striking. Fighting is no longer part of the normal way of life of this class, unless it be for wars in the service of the Crown. Something like this process continues over four centuries, until by 1800, a normal "civilized" country is one which can ensure continuing domestic peace, and in which commerce has largely replaced war as the paramount activity with which political society concerns itself; or at least shares the pre-eminence with war.

But this change didn't come about without resistance. Young nobles were capable of outbursts of mayhem, carnivals teetered on the thin line between mock and real violence, brigands were rife, vagabonds could be dangerous, city riots and peasant uprisings, provoked by unbearable conditions of life, were recurrent. Civility had to be to some degree a fighting creed.

Ordered government was one facet of civility. But there were others. They included a certain development of the arts and sciences, what we would call today, technology (here again, like our 'civilization'). It included the development of rational moral self-control; and also, crucially, taste, manners, refinement; in short, sound education and polite manners.[19]

But these, no less than ordered government and domestic peace, were seen as the fruits of discipline, training. A fundamental image was of civility as the result of nurture, or taming, of an originally wild, raw nature.[20] This is what underlies the to us striking ethnocentricity of our ancestors. They didn't see their difference from, say, Amerindians as that between two "cultures", as we would say today; but rather as that between culture and nature. We are trained, disciplined, formed, and they are not. The raw meet the cooked.

It is important not to forget that there was an ambivalence in this contrast. Many were tempted to hold that civility enervates us, renders us effete. Perhaps the height of virtue is to be found precisely in unspoiled nature.[21] And of course, there were honourable exceptions to this whole ethnocentric take, such as Montaigne.[22] But the general understanding of those who did think within the contrast wild/tamed, whatever side they came down on, cast the process which brought us from one to the other as one involving severe discipline. Lipsius defined it as "the rod of Circe which tameth both man and beast that are touched therewith, whereby each one is brought in awe and due obedience where before they were all fierce and unruly."[23] The "rod of Circe" is a great literary image, and makes it sound easy, but the latter part of the phrase indicates that this transformation is a hard slog. Civility requires working on yourself, not just leaving things as they are, but making them over. It involves a struggle to reshape ourselves.

Now I suggested above that this emphasis on struggle in part reflected the perception of civility as an embattled ideal; to some extent among the élite, but unquestionably among the people. But then we can ask the question, why involve the people? Lots of élites in history have had a sense of the superiority of their way of life, and have been content to build it on the control and/or exploitation of lower orders whom they never dream of seeing as potential participants in this way of life. All slave societies have been like this; but so have a great many others. The early Islamic empire is a good example; the Arab rulers didn't feel called upon to proselytize among their Christian subjects. They were content to live the new revelation themselves. Mass conversions came later, and on the initiative of the subject populations.

Of course, at the beginning, members of élite groups tended to take the same attitude towards civility. But what is remarkable is how, gathering pace in the sixteenth century in the wake of the Reforms, and then continuing at higher intensities, attempts are undertaken to make over the lower orders. They are precisely not left as they are, but badgered, bullied, pushed, preached at, drilled and organized to abandon their lax and disordered folkways and conform to one or another feature of civil behaviour. At the beginning, of course, there is no thought of making them over utterly to meet the full ideal; but nor did it seem acceptable just to leave them as they were. And by the end of this process, we enter a world, ours, where everyone among us is supposed to be "civilized".

Why this pro-active stance? The motivation seems complex. One strand is readily understandable on the part of any élite anywhere: the people had to be disciplined because their disorder threatened the élite. This seems particularly evident in the brace of reforms of what were called in England the "poor laws", whereby the conditions of relief for the indigent were strictly defined, begging forbidden or severely restricted, vagabondage outlawed, etc. It would appear that a rise in population, coupled with more difficult economic conditions in the sixteenth century, meant that the number of indigent increased; and their mobility did as well, as they gravitated to larger cities in search of the aid and sustenance they could no longer find at home. This larger, destitute and mobile population brought about conditions which were threatening to public order, facilitating crime and the spread of disease. The attempts to control relief, stop free-lance begging, prevent people from moving, can perhaps be understood as a response to these threats.

Later on, however, the motivation shifts from this negative concern to a positive one. The reform of society comes to be seen as an essential part of statecraft, as crucial to the maintenance and increase of state power. This comes with the dawning realization, first, that governmental action can help to improve economic performance, and second, that this performance was the essential precondition of military power. This latter was still the decisive domain for state policy, as rulers sought to resist the encroachments of others, or expand their own power. But the sinews of war were tax revenues; and tax revenues couldn't be increased in anything but the short run unless production grew, or greater trade surpluses were won. Previously, rulers had been concerned with what we might call questions of distribution: shortages of grain in the capital could send the price soaring, with potentially grave consequences to public order; a shortage of workers could send the price of labour to heights that gentry and town employers found impossible; a mass of paupers could converge on the towns requiring relief, as I have just described; all these could call for measures of control of prices, or of the sale of goods.

But with the seventeenth century, as military technology advances, and as some states began obviously to win great advantage from their higher production (e.g., Holland, England), the pressure was on to intervene on the supply side. Governments became concerned with productivity; and in fact with a whole host of measures to do with the size, health, prosperity, and even mores of populations, all of which had a powerful, direct or indirect effect on military might.

One needed a healthy, numerous, and disciplined population from which to draw good fighting men; one needed a numerous and productive people to get the revenues needed to arm and sustain these men; one needed a sober, ordered and industrious population to keep production high. Governments were more and more concerned to make over their subjects in a more thoroughgoing way, not just to maintain order, and prevent riots, but to participate in the ever-higher stakes of the balance of military power in Europe.

So intervention was driven by fear, and ambition; to head off disorder, and to increase power; a negative and a positive motive. But it seems to me that this can't be the whole story. There was also another fear, and another positive goal.

First, there was another kind of fear operative among élites. This is the kind we feel when, struggling with a difficult discipline ourselves, we see others flaunting their untamed conduct; the kind of disturbance that overt sexual licence arouses among those who are striving to control desire in their own lives. If the straight fear of crime, disease and disorder can account for the poor laws, what explains the attempts to suppress elements of popular culture, like Carnival, feasts of "misrule", various kinds of dancing, and the like?

Of course, here we come to a place where the objective is no longer simply civility. This kind of change was often driven by the demands of religious reforms. But this brings us to one of the main points I want to make. Although the goals of civility and religious reform (whether Protestant or Catholic) can be clearly distinguished in definition, they were frequently seamlessly combined in practice. Attempts to discipline a population, and reduce it to order, almost always had a religious component, requiring people to hear sermons, or learn catechism, for example; and how could it be otherwise in a civilization where good conduct was inseparable from religion? At the same time, religious reforms had a public order component; and this seemed inescapable, since the fruits of religious conversion were supposed to include an ordered life, and this involved conforming to a certain social order as well. Some of the most celebrated attempts to reform people in the sixteenth century, Calvin's Geneva on the Protestant side, and Charles Borromeo's Milan on the Catholic side, were all-in efforts, in which issues of religion, morality and good public order were lumped together; and many of their measures were over-determined; one can't neatly distinguish issues of religion from those of good civic order. St. Charles attacked Carnival and dancing, and he also tried to organize and discipline the poor. All this was part of a single programme of reform.

But it is not just that the two notionally distinct programmes of reform tended to merge in certain contexts. I believe also that the two ideals influenced and inflected each other. Religious Reform, as I argued above, was inhabited by a demand, felt with increasing power during the late Middle Ages and the early modern period, that not just an élite, but as far as possible all the faithful live up to the demands of the Gospel. The demand had been there before; something like it underlay the mediaeval attempts to remake the practice and devotion of the laity. But it took a quantum leap with the reformations of the sixteenth century; to the point where, on the Protestant side, there was an in principle denial of any hierarchy of vocations. Everyone was called on to live their faith to the full. And this meant that the lives and practices of ordinary people couldn't just be left as they were. They had to be exhorted, commanded, and sometimes forced and bullied into giving up, e.g., the veneration of saints, the adoration of the Sacrament, dancing around the maypole, and so on. There was a drive here to make certain norms universal, conceived in part as a demand of charity towards fellow human beings, but given an edge or urgency by the thought that God will punish our community for the blasphemy of its wayward members.

My claim is that some of this did and had to rub off on the lay goal of imposing some of the demands of civility on the general population. The two goals were not generally seen as in conflict (outside of some special contexts, which I shall mention), which is what you might expect today of a "secular" and "religious" objective. They were generally lived as compatible, and parts of a coherent normative outlook. It should not be surprising if some sense of an obligation to universalize, which surrounded the religious reform, should rub off onto secular reform. So that, alongside the two kinds of fear above, the agenda of civility was also imposed partly in the name of the supposed good of the people themselves; and not just as a hypocritical rationalization (although there was always lots of this), but as a felt duty.

But the inflection goes in the other direction as well. I said above that, of course, religious conversion was thought to produce an ordered life. Or to put the same point negatively, the inevitable fruit of sin is disorder, conflict. For Calvin, fallen man constantly tries to dominate others. "I say that the nature of man is such that every man would be lord and master over his neighbours and no man by his good will would be a subject."[24] But social order doesn't have to be a prominent part of what we expect from personal sanctity, not, in any case, in this fallen world.

Thus if our model of the apostolic life is monks living in a monastery off in the wilderness, we wouldn't think that even the highest degree of sanctity would necessarily put an end to violence and disorder in the world. The situation is, of course, very different if we think of the Christian life not in terms of minority communities, but as embracing everyone. But even this doesn't mean that social order must accrue to sanctity; we have to remember that all parties during the Reformation, but especially the Protestants, held to a hyper-Augustinian position, according to which only a small minority were saved. The way in which Christian living could bring about order in society was thus not, in all consistency, that every member was a saint. That was the path of the separatist sects, firmly refused by both Luther and Calvin. Rather it would have to be that the Godly minority control things and keep them on the right track.

Now we can see some of the rationale for this in the belief I mentioned above, that God will punish us collectively for the faults of our wayward compatriots. But in spite of this, it is hard to argue that it follows inescapably from Christian faith that the Godly have a duty to take over and bring things into line. Minority for minority, mediaeval monks took a somewhat different position.[25]

That, therefore, at least some branches of the Protestant family (in particular, Calvinists) took responsibility in this way for the world needs explaining. And it is likely that part of the explanation here is the same as accounts for the political élites of the day imposing their agenda of social and economic reform.

In other words, the good order of civility, and the good order of piety, didn't remain in separate uncommunicating compartments. They to some extent merged, and inflected each other. The drive to piety, to bring all real Christians (which were, of course, a minority, the saved, and didn't include the foreknown to damnation, even if they were nominally members of the Church) up to the fully Godly life, inflects the agenda of social reform, and gives it a universalist-philanthropic thrust. And the demands of civility, which entailed some reordering of society, in turn give a new social dimension to the pious, ordered life.

This seamless connection of piety and social order finds expression in a book by one of the itinerant apostles of Reform in the mid-sixteenth century, the Polish divine Jan Łąski. In a properly reformed society, he argued,

Princes and magistrates would be more peaceful; wars would cease among the nobility; the ambition of prelates would be punished; and all would do their duty in their calling. Children would be instructed from a young age in holy discipline; doctrine would be purely preached; the sacraments properly administered; the populace held in check; virtue would be prized; vices corrected; true penance restored and excommunication pronounced on the obstinate and rebellious; God's honour would be advanced together with the proper invocation of his holy name; the most honourable estate of marriage would be restored to its original form; brothels would be abolished; the poor would be cared for and all begging eliminated; the sick would be visited and consoled; and the dead honoured with an honest burial devoid of superstition.[26]

This global agenda was perhaps more in evidence in Calvinist societies, and was at its most marked among the Puritans of late-sixteenth and seventeenth-century England and America. The same disorder, violence, vagabonds, "masterless men" that frightened almost everyone at some time or other, frightened Puritans. They saw it naturally in the prism of sin; nothing different could be expected from fallen men. But they also saw the reform of life following conversion as the remedy for this disorder. And this view of the consequences of sanctity, as we have seen, doesn't necessarily follow from their view about the consequences of sin. Others have held that the believing Christian ought to opt out, or live on alms, or adopt a quietist stance, or espouse anarchism. It is not only Machiavelli who has thought that believing Christians make bad citizens.

The Puritan notion of the good life, by contrast, saw the "saint" as a pillar of a new social order. As against the indolence and disorder of monks, beggars, vagabonds and idle gentlemen, he "betakes himself to some honest and seemly trade, and [does] not suffer his senses to be mortified with idleness."[27] This means not just any activity, but one to which he has given himself as a lifetime's vocation. "He that hath no honest business about which ordinarily to be employed, no settled course to which he may betake himself, cannot please God." So the Puritan preacher, Samuel Hieron.[28]

These men are industrious, disciplined, do useful work, and above all can be relied upon. They have "settled courses", and are thus mutually predictable. You can build a solid, dependable social order on the covenants they make with each other. They are not tempted to mischief, because it is idleness which is the principal breeding ground of all sorts of evils. "An idle man's brain becometh quickly the shop of the devil . . . Whereof rise mutinies and mutterings in cities against magistrates? You can give no greater cause thereof, than idleness."[29]

With such men, a safe, well-ordered society can be built. But, of course, everyone will not be like them. However, the Puritan project can cope with this difficulty: the godly were to rule; the unregenerate were to be kept in check. The magistrate, as Baxter thought, must force all men "to learn the word of God and to walk orderly and quietly . . . till they are brought to a voluntary, personal profession of Christianity."[30] This was, of course, basically the same as the order Calvin erected in Geneva.

Thus while the Calvinist Reformation was defining the path to true Christian obedience, it also seemed to be offering the solution to the grave, even frightening social crises of the age. A very human social anxiety could enter, along with the hunger for salvation and the fear of damnation, into the reasons for espousing a faith, which would both regenerate the believer, and perhaps also put bounds to a threatening condition of disorder. Spiritual recovery and the rescue of civil order go together.

To put this another way, we can say that while late mediaeval élites, clerical of course, but with a growing lay component, were developing ideals of more intense devotion, and were coming to demand church reform, members of the same élites—sometimes others, sometimes the same people—were developing/recovering the ideal of civility, with its demands for a more ordered, less violent social existence. There was some tension between the two, but also symbiosis, and they came to inflect each other; and indeed, came to have an overlapping agenda.

Thus, in this context, there is a complex causal story behind the fact that the ideal of civility develops an active, transformatory agenda. As time goes on, it is undoubtedly powered by the escalating demand for military, and hence fiscal power, and hence economic performance by industrious, educated, disciplined populations. But it is also partly the result of the symbiosis and mutual inflection with the agenda of religious reform, whereby "improvement" came to be seen as a duty for itself—as shall see with the ethic of neo-Stoicism.

Negatively, it is partly an attempt to fend off real dangers to social order; and partly a reaction to practices, like carnival, feasts of misrule, etc., which had been accepted in the past, but had become profoundly disturbing to those striving for the new ideals. Here's where the symbiosis with religious reform plays an obvious role again, because this kind of susceptibility to be upset by the display of vice has been very much a feature of the stringent religious conscience.

We see clear examples from the field of sexual morality. The Middle Ages in many parts of Europe tolerated prostitution, which seemed a sensible prophylactic against adultery and rape, with all their disruptive consequences.[31] Even the Council of Konstanz organized temporary brothels for the large number of participants which flooded into the town. But the new trends in devotion tended to emphasize sexual purity, and to turn the main focus away from sins of violence and social division; and so the attitude to prostitution changes. It becomes inconceivable to countenance it, but it is also deeply disturbing. A sort of fascination-repulsion arises which expresses itself in widespread and continued efforts to redeem fallen women. One cannot just let this go on; one has to act.

The upshot is that in the early modern period, élites, under the combined force of these two ideals, turn more and more against popular practices along a wide range. Their tolerance for what they see as disorder, rowdiness, uncontrolled violence diminishes. What previously was accepted as normal is now seen as unacceptable, even scandalous. Already during the sixteenth century, and sometimes continuing afterwards, the complex motives I have been describing lead to the launching of five types of programmes.

1. The first are the new kinds of poor laws, mentioned above. These involve an important shift, even reversal, from what went before. For the Middle Ages, there was an aura of sanctity around poverty. It was not that this extremely rank-conscious society did not have a healthy contempt for the destitute and powerless, at the absolute bottom of the social ladder. But precisely because of this, the poor person offered an occasion of sanctification. Following the discourse of Matthew 25, to help a person in need was to help Christ. One of the things which the powerful of that world did to offset their pride and their trespasses was to offer distributions to the poor. Kings did this, as did monasteries, and later also rich bourgeois. Well-off people left a provision in their wills that alms should be given to a certain number of paupers at their funeral, and these should in turn pray for their soul. Contrary to the Gospel story, the prayer of Lazarus, heard in heaven, might hasten Dives to Abraham's bosom.[32]

But in the fifteenth century, partly as a result of a rise in population, and crop failures, and a consequent flow of the destitute towards the towns, there is a radical change in attitude. A new series of poor laws is adopted, whose principle is sharply to distinguish those who are capable of work from those who genuinely have no recourse but charity. The former are expelled or put to work, for very low pay, and often in stringent conditions. The incapable poor are to be given relief, but again in highly controlled conditions, which often ended up involving confinement in institutions which in some ways resembled prisons. Efforts were also made to rehabilitate the children of beggars, to teach them a trade, to make them useful and industrious members of society.[33]

All these operations: providing work, giving relief, training and rehabilitation, could entail confinement, both as a measure of economy, and as a measure of control. This begins the period of what has been called, following Michel Foucault, "le grand renfermement", which came to involve other classes of helpless people, most famously the insane.[34]

Now whatever the motives, it is clear that there is a profound shift in attitude; one might say, in the whole register in which poverty is understood. In the Middle Ages, as Geremek points out,[35] it was voluntary poverty which was the path to holiness. The involuntary poor were not seen in general as saints. Instead of bearing their lot with patience as they ought, they could feel envy, or turn to crime. But

nevertheless, the poor person was an occasion of sanctification. In g
you give to Christ. The new stance set that aside and looked at the pau   ....ui-
cally different register, which was double: on the one hand he was tested for desert;
did he merit, warrant aid, or should he be working for himself? And secondly, the
dealings with him were assessed instrumental-rationally. Great attention was paid to
getting the most bang for their buck (or florin or ducat or livre tournois). In seventeenth-century English work-houses, people are put to work producing what the
economy needs. They thread wool, which was the bottleneck in the industry at the
time. In this way, they pay for their keep, and they help society. Rehabilitation is
pursued with the same instrumental rigour. In the Amsterdam Rasphuis, the habitually idle are put in cells where the water slowly rises as long as they are inactive.
Their breaks can't be too long, or else . . .[36]

The extreme Puritan view was even harsher than this. The judgment rendered on
the beggar was stonily adverse. Beggars, for Perkins, "are as rotten legs and arms,
that drop from the body."[37] There was no place for them in a well-ordered commonwealth.

It was this radical shift in orientation which gave rise to resistances. In Catholic
countries, there was opposition from some of the clergy, on doctrinal grounds, particularly the mendicant orders. And in Spain, a more "backward" country in terms
of economic development, the reforms were stopped altogether.[38] The break with
the whole Mediaeval theology of poverty was too great. But in most of Catholic Europe, this wasn't enough to stop the advance of the new approach. It was practised
in Paris, and figured in Charles Borromeo's programme for Milan.

The second source of opposition was even less capable of stopping the change. It
came from the people themselves, who would sometimes demonstrate when a pau-
per was dragged off, or even protect or hide him.

2. National government, city governments, church authorities, or some combination of them, often came down hard on certain elements of popular culture:
charivaris, carnival, feasts of "misrule", dancing in church. Here also we see a reversal. What had previously been seen as normal, which everybody had been prepared
to participate in, now seems utterly condemnable, and also, in one sense, profoundly disturbing.

Erasmus condemned the Carnival he saw in Siena in 1509 as "unchristian", and
that on two grounds: first, it contains "traces of ancient paganism"; and secondly,
"the people over-indulge in licence".[39] The Elizabethan Puritan, Philip Stubbes, attacked "the horrible vice of pestiferous dancing", which led to "filthy groping and
unclean handling" and so became "an introduction to whoredom, a preparative
to wantonnesse, a provocative of uncleanness, and an introit to all kinds of lewd-
ness."[40]

Now as Burke points out, churchmen had been criticizing these aspects of popular culture for centuries.[41] What is new is (a) that the religious attack is intensified, because of the new worries about the place of the sacred; and (b) that the ideal of civility, and its norms of orderliness, polish, refinement, have alienated the leading classes from these practices.

Civility by itself would have led to what Burke calls the "withdrawal of the upper classes" from popular culture.

> In 1500 . . . popular culture was everyone's culture; a second culture for the educated, and the only culture for everyone else. By 1800, however, in most parts of Europe, the clergy, the nobility, the merchants, the professional men—and their wives—had abandoned popular culture to the lower classes, from whom they were now separated, as never before, by profound differences in world view.[42]

Civility meant that, in the sixteenth century,

> The nobles were adopting more "polished" manners, a new and more self-conscious style of behaviour, modelled on the courtesy-book, of which the most famous was Castiglione's *Courtier*. Noblemen were learning to exercise self-control, to behave with a studied nonchalance, to cultivate a sense of style, and to move in a dignified manner as if engaging in a formal dance. Treatises on dancing also multiplied and court dancing diverged from country dancing. Noblemen stopped eating in great dining halls with their retainers and withdrew into separate dining rooms (not to mention "drawing rooms", that is "withdrawing rooms"). They stopped wrestling with their peasants, as they used to do in Lombardy, and they stopped killing bulls in public, as they used to do in Spain. The nobleman learned to speak and write "correctly", according to formal rules, and to avoid technical terms and dialect words used by craftsmen and peasants.[43]

By itself, the ideal of civility would have been sufficient to bring about this withdrawal, which actually came in the eighteenth century to distance itself as well from elements of traditional piety, as too "enthusiastic". But interwoven with religious reform it went beyond withdrawal into attempts to suppress and remake the culture of the people; attempts like that of Maximilian of Bavaria, whose programme of reform in the early seventeenth century forbade, inter alia: magic, masquerades, short dresses, mixed bathing, fortune-telling, excessive eating and drinking, and "shameful" language at weddings.[44]

3. During the seventeenth century, these first two kinds of action become sub-

sumed under a third: the attempts by the developing state structures of absolutist or dirigiste bent, in France and Central Europe, to shape through ordinances
the economic, educational, spiritual and material well-being of their subjects, in
the interests of power, but also of improvement. The ideal of the well-ordered
"Polizeistaat"[45] was uppermost in Germany from the fifteenth to the eighteenth
century. The impetus to this dirigiste activity was given by the situation in the wake
of the Reformation, in which the ruler of each territory had to see to the re-organization of the Church (in Protestant territories), and enforce conformity (in all territories). But the attempts at control are extended in the next century, and encompass
economic, social, educational and moral goals. These covered some of the same territory we have already explored under (1) and (2), the regulation of relief, and the
suppression of some traditional festivals and practices.[46] But in the sixteenth century, they branch out, try to establish schooling, to increase productivity, and to inculcate a more rational, hard-working, industrious and production-oriented outlook in their subjects. Society was to be disciplined, but with the aim of inducing
self-discipline.[47]

In short, this meant imposing some features of the ideal of civility on wider and
wider strata of the population. Undoubtedly an important motive here was to create a population from which obedient and effective soldiers could be drawn, and
the resources to pay them and arm them. But many of these ordinances posit improvement (as they see it) as an end in itself. As we move into the eighteenth century, the ends of legislation come more and more to incorporate the ideas of the Enlightenment, putting increasing emphasis on the productive, material aspects of
human activity, in the name of the benefits which would accrue to individuals and
to society as a whole.[48]

4. What made these social reforms possible was the development of effective governing structures imbued with the right spirit and discipline. These might be local
and more voluntary, as in the Low Countries, or they might consist in central state
bureaucracies of a more and more rationalized kind. Perhaps the most spectacular
creation of the latter kind was in Prussia, which managed from the late seventeenth
century to win a place among the major powers in Europe on a base of population
and riches that was much less than all other states in that league.

What made these structures possible in turn was a mix of discipline and dedication, which allowed Prussia, for instance, to raise more money, and train more soldiers, in relation to population and wealth than any of its rivals. Philip Gorski has
argued convincingly that the sources of this extraordinary performance were to be
found in part in the neo-Stoic philosophy that was very widespread among élites,
but even more so in the Calvinist or Pietist faith of the dynasty and leading political
figures. The drive for Reform was thus a key factor in this extraordinary story.[49]

5. We see this whole development from another angle, if we look at the prolifera-

tion of modes of discipline, of "methods", of procedures. Some of these arise in the individual sphere, as methods of self-control, of intellectual or spiritual development; some of these are taken on collectively, as with the political élites in Holland and Prussia; others again are inculcated and imposed in a context of hierarchical control. Foucault notes how programmes of training based on the close analysis of physical movement, breaking it down into parts and then drilling people in a standardized form of it, multiply in the sixteenth century. Their primary locus is, of course, armies, which inaugurate new modes of military training, but then some of the principles come to be applied to schools, and hospitals, and later factories.[50]

Among methodical programmes aimed at the transformation of the self, one of the best known was the spiritual exercises of Loyola, meditation directed to spiritual change. But these two key ideas, meditation directed by method, also crop up a century later in the programme proposed by Descartes (who was, after all, educated by the Jesuits at Laflèche).

3

The ideal of civility, with its core image of taming raw nature, already involves what we might call a stance of reconstruction towards ourselves. It takes form in programmes and methods of "self-fashioning",[51] as we see especially in group 5 just described. We treat our own baser nature as raw matter to be controlled, reshaped, and in certain cases eliminated, in order to impose a higher form on our lives. Of course, there are affinities to traditional ethical outlooks, Christian and ancient. All these involve in some way controlling or eliminating the base in the name of the higher. But what is special about this new outlook is the emphasis on will, and on the imposition of form on an inert or refractory matter.

The great ancient ethics, those of Plato, Aristotle, the Stoics, called for the subordination, or even, in the case of the Stoics, the elimination of baser desires (in the Stoic case, passion, as a kind of false opinion, disappears altogether from the soul of the wise). But the dominant image of virtue was that of a soul in harmony. The master idea was of a form which was already at work in human nature, which the virtuous person has to help emerge, rather than of a pattern imposed ab extra. Images of reshaping matter, of imposing form, which were the key terms in which they understand human productive activity, didn't have a place in ethics. Praxis and poiesis were clearly distinguished; and as has been repeatedly noted, these ethics didn't have a place for what we designate by the modern term will.

This operates for us in two dimensions: we sometimes distinguish good from bad will; and sometimes strong from weak will. The first contrast undoubtedly comes to us from Christianity; and in the West, its most famous formulation was that of Augustine's two loves, charity and concupiscence. But the main axis of this new modern climate of thought is the other contrast. Virtue requires a strong will, one which can impose the good against powerful resistance. There is thus not just a move away from the ancients, in making thus central a concept of will, but a shift of axis within this concept from the main line of Christian thought.

This crucial role of the will is not always explicitly made in the formulations of this modern outlook, and nor are ancient notions of harmony entirely absent, as we will see in a minute in the case of neo-Stoicism, but in one form or other the shift is evident.

My claim is that this introduction of a stance of poiesis into the domain of praxis is in a relation of mutual facilitation with the changes I mentioned in the previous section; with the view of Cusanus, Ficino, Leonardo, that science is made possible by our own constructive activity, and with the shift in natural science to what Scheler called a "Leistungswissen", a science in which truth is confirmed by instrumental efficacy. There were, of course, also the theological reasons I described above for this last change. And retrospectively, there was the very success of the new science itself (not immediately, to be sure, in terms of instrumental efficacy). Now we can see that a constellation of key concepts about the good life must also have played a part. Two modes of poiesis, the reconstructive stance in ethics, and an instrumental rather than a contemplative understanding of science, lent each other mutual support.

This epochal change in our understanding of and stance towards nature, within us and without, is the overdetermined result of a number of independent changes, and cannot be laid at the door of one crucial factor. Obviously, the sense of the unlimited sovereignty of God was instrumental in destroying the older view of the cosmos as the realization of Form. We see this with the nominalist writers, and later with many of the seventeenth century champions of the new science, e.g., Descartes and Mersenne. If God has a potentia absoluta over Creation, and this mean that he cannot be seen as bound by the inherent bent, even of things he has created in the first place, then reality must be seen as infinitely manipulable by him, and this requirement can best be met by a view of nature as mechanism, from which all hint of intrinsic teleology has been expelled.

But if this is the nature of things, then this has consequences for our stance towards the world as well. Not only must we alter our model of science—no longer the search for Aristotelian or Platonic form, it must search for relations of efficient causality; but the manipulable universe invites us to develop a Leistungswissen, or a science of control. It suggests the goal of becoming "maîtres et possesseurs de la nature", in Descartes' famous phrase.[52] More, it can invite us to imitate God, in obedience to him, in using things to the effects that he intended for us.

It might be tempting to find here the key to the epochal shift from finding our place in the cosmos to constructing an order within the universe; either as a new way of following God, or in a kind of reaction against the all-invasive power of God, which seems to leave us no place, and which has indeed destroyed the former sense of our having our rightful place within the ordered cosmos. Something like this latter, "reactive" account in terms of human "self-assertion" seems to be espoused by Blumenberg.[53]

And yet it seems plain that the drive to reconstruction also had other sources, and sprang also from less reactive motives. It didn't wait for the destruction of the old cosmos. There developed, even within a Platonic idea of the world as shaped by Form, the idea that human beings have to co-operate with this shaping, are called upon to complete it. The Renaissance gave an important role in this respect to the artist. Marsilio Ficino expressed this idea: "the human person imitates all the works of divine nature; those of inferior nature he brings to perfection, corrects, and improves" (Homo omnia divinae naturae opera imitatur et naturae inferioris opera perficit, corrigit et emendat). Michelangelo saw himself as working in this way. Leonardo sees that the artist must submit to the "ragioni" that we find in nature, but our task must be to bring these out fully through our own rational and constructive activity. Experience needs reason, "maestra e tutatrice della natura". So the human artist himself in his own way "creates". They are not just servile imitators of nature, but its competitors, as Pico put it: "non servi naturae, sed aemuli".[54]

In a similar way, on the threshold of the revolution of modern science, we find the Renaissance "magi", people like Dee, Bruno, Fludd, and assorted alchemists, who combine a strong belief in the primacy of Form, or even soul, in nature, with an agenda of transformation and amelioration. The discovery of the philosopher's stone will allow us to make gold, and also to bring human life to perfection.[55]

It is important, of course, that these modes of non-mechanistic poiesis were not to be the wave of the future, that they were soon superseded by the Galilean-Baconian stance, to be retrieved later, in a quite different form, by the Romantic generation. But they, along with many other phenomena, are enough to show that the drive to reconstruction was not inseparable from the move to mechanism, nor tied necessarily to a revolt against God's absolute power.

Now if this multi-stranded poiesis is central to civility as an ideal, how much more prominent must the reconstructive stance become when the practice of self-refashioning is applied to society as a whole, when the nascent state becomes more and more an engineer of morals and social practice.

In order to illustrate the shift I've been talking about, I'd like to look at the views of the most influential neo-Stoic writer of the sixteenth century, Justus Lipsius. He is a key figure in my story, not only because he articulates an ethical theory of this new, reconstructive range, but also because he led the way in showing how to apply this view in the political-military realm.

Lipsius invents a (sort of) Christianized Stoicism. It leans to the Stoic side. There are two striking differences between Christianity and Stoicism in the ethical realm: a) Christianity sees us as in need of God's grace, as needing God's help to liberate the good will which is potentially ours; where Stoicism appeals purely to our powers of reason and self-control; b) Christianity sees the fullest realization of the good will in us in agape, our love for our neighbour. Stoicism sees the wise person as having attained apatheia, a condition beyond passion. Now these two are not necessarily incompatible; agape could be conceived as a kind of passionless condition of strenuous benevolence. But Christian theology has steered away from this Stoicised reading, and with good Biblical reason. Christ in the Gospels is portrayed as being moved "in the bowels" by compassion *(splangnizesthai);* and his cries on the cross were hardly manifestations of apatheia. This has given the greatest difficulty to Christian theology in the early centuries, precisely because of the force of the Greek-derived idea that God is apathes; Jesus' obvious failure to meet this standard even became an argument for Arianism. But in the end orthodoxy refused the Stoicised solution.

But this is just what Lipsius espouses. He rejects miseratio, or misericordia, the compassion of feeling, in favour of the compassion of active intervention, but on the basis of a full inner detachment. The nuance was not lost on theologians of his day, and the sentences criticizing miseratio were deleted in the Spanish translation of *De Constantia.*[56]

As for the other issue, neo-Stoicism is silent on the need for grace. We are still not dealing, however, with an exclusive humanism. As with the classical model, God plays a central role; he is the source of the ratio on which we base our lives. "Reason comes from heaven, from God himself—Seneca extolled it as a part of the divine spirit implanted in man". For "Deus ipse per hanc sui imaginem ad nos venit, imo quod proprius est, in nos"[57] (God himself approaches us by this his image; or rather, he comes into us).

Here the Stoic idea is put in the Biblical term of the image of God. Lipsius also puts a great deal of emphasis on another doctrine common to Stoicism and Christianity, God's Providence. Everything that happens comes about through the Providence of God. God has his own purposes in putting us through the trials we suffer. It is vain and foolish to resist. Rather we should obey, like soldiers in camp or field. Quoting Seneca: "We are born into a kingdom; to obey God is to be free."[58]

And what is it to obey God or reason? The answer is in its essence Stoic: opinion, which comes from the earth and the body, misleads us; external calamities, loss of fortune, health, even life, only affect changeable things, which have of necessity to pass anyway. Reason tells us to hang on to what is unchanging. To quote Lipsius' predecessor and compatriot, who was one of the foundational influences of six-teenth-century humanism, "Transfer your love to something permanent, some-thing celestial, something incorruptible, and you will love more coolly this transi-tory and fleeting form of the body".[59] By cleaving to what is permanent, we will attain constancy, the central virtue of Lipsius' vision. "Constantiam hic appello rec-tum at immotum robur animi, non elati externis aut fortuitis non depressi. Robur dixi et intelligo firmitudinem insitam animo, non ab Opinione, sed a judicio et recta Ratione."[60] (Constancy denotes the proper and immovable strength of the mind that is neither elated nor downcast by outward or fortuitous circumstances. Strength is a firmness implanted in the mind, not by opinion, but by judgment and right reason.)

Constancy offers us a criterion of the right path. But on this path, we shall also encounter harmony. And if we choose to make our basic principle following God, we will be on the same road; as also if we take nature, or reason, as our guides. All these criteria line up.

The good man shows constantia, patientia, firmitas. He is not moved by the chaos, disorder, violence, suffering. But that means that he is not upset, disturbed. It doesn't mean that he doesn't react. On the contrary, Lipsius, in a way which is typical of this whole modern epoch, departs from Stoicism in his activism. We might say that he is closer to the Roman, or Senecan, version than to that of Epictetus, although he cites both these authors as his inspiration. But in fact he goes beyond even the Romans. It is not a matter just of doing one's duty in the world, but of waging active struggle for the good. Lipsius' work is full of military meta-phors, and some of his earliest enthusiastic readers were concerned with military af-fairs, as we shall see.

There is even here an important doctrinal departure from the Stoa. Lipsius firmly believes in our free will. We are responsible for our world. Reason should galvanize will, and will impose discipline, which will arm us for the struggle with evil and dis-order. The firmness or perseverance doesn't just denote the strength passively to bear suffering; but it means the power to engage unrelentingly in the good fight.

Why did this (semi)-Christianized Stoicism have such an impact in its time? And on both sides of the confessional barrier; in Lipsius' native Netherlands, in Ger-many, in France? Calvinists, Lutherans, Catholics praised it. And indeed, Lipsius managed to teach at Universities of all three faiths: Louvain, Jena, Leiden—a very rare feat at the time.

There were two obvious reasons: First, if many members of the élite, under the impress of the ideal of civility, were less tolerant of violence and disorder than their forebears, then they were doubly appalled to see that the cause of Reform, instead of bringing greater peace and order, had been in many cases, the occasion of greater strife and conflict, and often of a particularly vicious kind. These people were looking for a version of their faith which would be less obsessed with confessional orthodoxy, and more concerned with the essentials that all churches shared. In a sense, these were people who shared some of the spirit of Erasmus, but in the circumstances, they had frequently become what in France were known as "les politiques". They were concerned above all with peace and accommodation, and they strongly opposed the sectarian fanatics of the Ligue. Two of Lipsius' most prominent French followers were Catholics of this stamp, Charron and du Vair, one a priest and the other a bishop.

Secondly, like the politiques, Lipsius' readers wanted to do more than bemoan the vicious conflict; they wanted to put an end to it, and build a new political order. These were often people with military and governmental responsibility; rulers, generals, and civil servants. They were engaged or about to engage in programmes of the five kinds I outlined above. They were looking for a philosophy to guide them in this enterprise, and many of them found it in Justus Lipsius' work.

I want to try to examine in a minute why this modernized Stoicism provided the basis for this kind of state activism. But first I want to register the shift that has taken place, one which in fact moves in the direction of the later Deism, and eventually exclusive humanism.

Once again, we have to avoid the anachronism of seeing this as a step along a straight path. Lipsius' view was at its core theistic; and his God was not presiding over the benign, harmonious universe of eighteenth-century Deism. But the eclipse of certain crucial Christian elements, those of grace and of agape, already changed quite decisively the centre of gravity of this outlook. Moreover, there didn't seem to be an essential place for the worship of God, other than through the cultivation of reason and constancy; that was in a sense, the strength of this philosophy, because the worship of God was exactly what all the fighting was supposed to be about in the sixteenth century. This silence could be seen as an invitation to belong to "the church of your choice", to use a somewhat anachronistic expression (more aptly, the church of your ruler's choice). But it could also be seen as a relegation of worship as ultimately unnecessary and irrelevant.

God is still very crucial, because he is the source of reason, and in following it we are following his image in us. But it appears that what we have to do to do his will is to become an excellent human being, and nothing further. This prepares the ground for the anthropocentrism of later Deism, after this has made a further shift towards disconnecting our reasoning powers from the work of God in us. An important turning has been made. Neo-Stoicism is the zig to which Deism will be the zag.

Lipsius' work was important for the programmes of military and social reconstruction which were launched towards the end of the century, because his ethical view called for active intervention in public life, and because he provided the key notion of discipline.

Lipsius' political doctrine in his *Politicorum sive civilis doctrinae, libri sex* of 1589 takes the stance that I've been calling "politique", that is, he is concerned to recover order and stability out of the reigning condition of confessional civil war in much of Europe. He favours a monarchical form of government, and gives little attention to the claims of the estates. But his prince is to be guided by strict moral principles, and is to dedicate his efforts to the public weal.

This work, however, goes beyond giving general advice, and contains detailed prescriptions for army reform. These stress the importance of drill and order in forming an effective armed force. But his conception of discipline goes beyond this; he wants to inculcate moral change. His idea is to create a professional army, where the old values of personal honour and plunder would be sidelined, and the soldiers would be actuated by the Stoic principles of continentia, modestia, abstinentia— self-control, moderation, and abstinence.[61]

In other words, the aim of training is not only to produce the discipline of co-ordinated movement and obedience to command, but also to make the soldier over morally, and inculcate a professional ethic of service and self-control. The irresponsible mercenary armies, which were often as much a danger to the subjects of their employer as to his enemies, are to be replaced by disciplined troops, who will make it a point of honour to refrain from rapine and plunder.

Now the importance of this was twofold, on a particular, and on a more general level. The particular result was that Lipsius' advice was taken by the initiators of the military reforms in the Netherlands in the 1590s, which included some of his ex-pupils (especially Maurice of Orange). These by introducing strict training created an effective military force which was then widely imitated in Europe—in the Swedish army of Gustavus Adolphus, and in Cromwell's New Model Army, for example.

On a more general level, Lipsius set the tone for serious reformers of high moral purpose in the next century, be they (as they sometimes were) rulers, or more often high civil servants, administrators, generals, who initiated reforms aiming to reconstruct various dimensions of society. He proposed, first, a lofty moral goal of service to the general weal, to be grounded in a personal ethic of austerity and self-discipline; this was to be the basis of a far-reaching remaking of institutional and social life, through the discipline and training of the subordinate population; and it was to result in the internalization of the values of self-control and industriousness among these subjects.

In short, something like what has been called the "protestant work ethic", in an atmosphere comparable to the "inner-worldly asceticism" (innerweltliche Askese) of which Max Weber talked,[62] was to be created, but very much through the active, re-constructive efforts of political authority. It may indeed, be argued that this ethic of active state intervention, in the period of absolute governments, did as much to in-troduce a rationalized, disciplined, and professionalized mode of life as the Calvinist ethic of the calling. Neo-Stoicism very much strengthened by Calvinism, worked in some places from above by means of state bureaucracies, to bring about the changes that Calvinism and Pietism wrought in other places from below, through dedicated, self-denying entrepreneurs and voluntary associations.[63]

In their activism, and their dedicated asceticism, neo-Stoicism and Calvinism were very similar. And indeed, Calvin too started his life by publishing a study of Seneca. In spite of the differences of doctrine, it was easy for people in Calvinist so-cieties without a strong sense of theological orthodoxy to hold them together. (And indeed, it was not too difficult for many Catholics and Lutherans to do the same.) The ordering impulses were very similar: create a stable order in society by training people into "settled courses", through dedication to some profession, whose goals were defined in terms of service to our fellow human beings: in the private sector, through productive labour; and in the public sector through government dedicated to the subjects' good. In the political sphere, indeed, Calvinism produced some rather different forms, some deeply antithetical to absolute rule. But the pictures of social order, of the kind of activism required to produce it, and of the necessity to this end of the domination of the godly/virtuous, ran closely parallel.

And what also ran parallel, and which perhaps doesn't astonish us enough, was the belief that all this could be accomplished. How was it, that in the face of so much violence and disorder, both in history and the present, in the face of such ob-viously refractory human material, that people could entertain serious hopes of making a decisive, even irreversible change for the better?

Plainly there has been a major change in outlook. The Middle Ages seems steeped in the view, which has probably been the way most people in most ages have seen this question, that there are severe limits to the degree in which sin and disor-der can be done away with in this world. Of course, many, perhaps most epochs posit a golden age somewhere in the past; and sometimes this as seen as some-thing which can, in favourable circumstances, be recovered. This what Renaissance humanists thought in relation to the apogee of classical culture. But it was also the spirit in which the Carolingian restoration of the "Roman Empire" was car-ried through. Successive Byzantine Emperors dreamed of re-enacting the reign of Justinian.

But this high point had rarely been defined so ambitiously as the Calvinist or neo-Stoic programmes of the seventeenth century. This was so in two respects: first, in that the aim was to do away with violence and social disorder altogether, leaving only individual crime at one end of the spectrum, and the legitimate violence of the state in war and the repression of crime on the other; secondly, in that the goal was to inculcate at least some of the norms of civility and a properly ordered life in *everyone*. These goals were, of course, linked, in that it is only through attaining something like the second that one could hope to realize the first.

An ambition of this kind is unprecedented in European history, although there seem to have been comparable attempts in China at different moments. And, in fact, its protagonists were aware of innovating. That is, while they did take inspiration from various "golden ages" in the past, they were conscious that they were proposing to surpass them in important respects, and not just to recreate them.

Thus Calvinists looked back to the days of the early church. Now although they may have felt inferior to the Christians of this age in holiness, they knew that the establishment of a whole Christian society had been impossible in those earlier days. That is why we find that they frequently found models in Old Testament Israel, which at least offered the image of a godly society, embattled on all sides by enemies. But the respect in which they were meant to surpass Israel was defined in the central tenets of Christian theology.

Similarly, Lipsius and his neo-Stoic successors looked back to the Roman Empire, and its great legal, military and political achievements. There is in a sense a shift here in humanist interest, from Latin and Greek literature to the historians of Rome, including the Greek Polybius, and concentrating on Tacitus. In rhetoric, Tacitus too comes to be preferred to the more effusive style of Cicero. And the Stoicism they drew on was that of Seneca. People have even spoken of the seventeenth century as a "Roman century".[64] But for all their admiration for Roman statecraft, military discipline, and Stoic philosophy, they were increasingly aware that the programmes which were intended to reform the mores and change the outlook of the whole population were entering new territory.

There was another model of (in one sense) an entire society of high, austere morals, and that was provided by early Republican Rome, or (more rarely) of the Greek poleis at their height. This played a big role at other moments in modern European history: among the civic humanists of Italian cities in the Renaissance, and of course, in the great American and French Revolutions of the eighteenth century. But here again, at least in the later period, the consciousness was acute that one couldn't just go back to these small, face-to-face societies of direct self-rule;[65] and moreover, that one of the reasons why this was impossible, beyond the larger size of modern states, lay just in the fact that the ancient republics had *not* incorporated all their population, that a substantial part of their workers, the slave population, had been left out.[66]

So where did they get the confidence to enter this uncharted terrain? This question may sound strange to us, because we live very much in the age they have created. We in the North Atlantic world take for granted that "normally" violence and disorder should be effectively eliminated, pushed to the two limits of individual crime and state-conducted war. We are not only shocked and traumatized by riots in South L.A., or the suburbs of Paris, but consider it to be a sign of grievous malfunction in our society. We look with horror at some of the successor states of the ex-Soviet Union, and see there something more closely resembling our pre-modern past. And we have in a sense achieved the goal of inculcating "civility" in everyone, with the vast majority of the population literate, having many years of schooling, sharing certain norms of disciplined work and ordered peaceful life. So much so that we are shocked and horrified at signs that some youth are regressing to violence and a way of life which utterly abandons family life and the work ethic. Our unreflecting norm is even beyond the point that the reforms of Calvinist divines and neo-Stoic ministeriales aimed at starting four centuries ago.

And yet we have to conquer anachronism, and realize how important, and even astonishing the change was here. The question returns again: how did they come to believe that they could do it?

Because what all these programmes betoken, and what underlies this drive to make over, is an extraordinary confidence in the capacity to remodel human beings. We cannot but be struck by the sheer ambition of some Puritan projects to control sinful nature by force of law. William Stoughton declared in a 1604 treatise: "There is no crime respecting any commandment contained with either of the two tables of the holy law of God but . . . that hath been evermore and is now punishable by the king's regal and temporal jurisdiction." So the whole Decalogue is already to be criminalized. Stoughton goes on to discuss heresy and absence from church; while other Puritans of the day proposed laws forbidding bear-baiting, dancing, swearing, Sunday sports, church-ales, and so on.[67]

But in another way, a comparably great ambition is evident in the ordinances of the Polizeistaat. The drive to remould subjects through the fine regulation of details of their lives bespeaks an almost unbounded confidence in the power to shape people to a new mould. As Raeff puts it, "implicit though almost never stated in so many words was . . . the assumption of human nature's malleability." The claim was "that human nature was essentially malleable, that it could be fashioned by will and external circumstances".[68]

Of course, by some this remodelling was just seen as a possibility in principle, without much hope that one really could get all that far with the masses; but nevertheless, the belief was that nothing in principle stood in the way of this social engineering.

What could stand in the way? Well, first of all, there was the traditional understanding of things, which set limits to the possibilities of total reform. In the case of the European Middle Ages, this was articulated in the formulations of Augustine. Two societies, the city of god and the earthly city lived side by side, intermingled. The earthly city was the site of sin. It had an inherent tendency to violence and strife. Government itself could be conceived as an agent of violence on a grander scale. But it was nevertheless indispensable. Only such a powerful agent could keep in awe all the lesser ones, who otherwise would reduce social life to an unliveable chaos.

On this rather low view of the state, its role was to keep some kind of order within a fallen world, but actually imparting virtue to the citizens was beyond its powers, and hence its brief.

Of course, the city of God was also among us in Christian lands. Perhaps a Christian state could do better? This Augustine, who lived under the Christian Empire, did not believe. A Christian state could help the church, repress heretics and false cults, but it couldn't improve its citizens; only the city of God, represented by the Church, could aspire to that.

Moreover, the relation of numbers told heavily against the city of God. For Augustine, and he was followed in this by late mediaeval Catholicism, and even more by Calvinism, the number of the saved was very small. They were a small élite among the mass of the damned.

Since Augustine was the maître à penser of the Reformers, how did they imagine that they could step beyond the limits that he so persuasively defined? The answer is not that they believed the elect were more numerous, but rather, as we saw above, that they saw a dispensation in which the elect would rule, and discipline the whole society.

Later, of course, they slid into seeing things in a rather different way. The line between the few saved and the many damned, instead of running within each society more or less equally, ended up running between godly societies, which were implicitly taken as containing mostly elect, and those dominated by Rome and its imitators, or the darkness of paganism. There a few brave souls might struggle against persecution, but most were clearly heading for perdition. This slide was inevitable. It is extremely difficult to preach to an audience without taking at least as one's working hypothesis that everyone has at least a chance to be among the elect. Moreover, the small and embattled position of many Calvinist communities contributed to this "us versus them" view, which also favoured the analogy with ancient Israel.

Thus were the Augustinian limits by-passed among Calvinists. In the less orthodox climate of neo-Stoicism, they seem rather to have faded from view.

But there was more than a change in beliefs about the potential for change. It took the fading of an entire inarticulate understanding of the structure of society and its relation to evil for the new confidence to arise.

I have already mentioned some profound shifts in the way of looking at certain facets of society. For instance, the changed register in which poverty was now placed, and the alienation from and rejection of old social rituals as mere vice and disorder. What underlay the earlier stance in each case was something more than a doctrine; it was rather a whole framework of understanding.

Perhaps we could formulate this by saying that it tended to see society as articulated into orders, hierarchically ranked, and at the same time complementary in their functioning. We are familiar with examples of explicitly held doctrine which reflect this framework; for instance, the society of the three orders, those who pray (monks and ecclesiastics), those who fight (nobility), and those who work (peasants); or the various analogies between the kingdom and the human body, each estate being aligned to its own part of the body (the king to the head, the nobility to the arms, etc.).

The point about these articulations is that, while there are clearly differences of worth between different strata—we're dealing with a hierarchical order, after all—there cannot be any question of improving things by eliminating the lower strata, or making everybody over as monks or knights, for example. Every stratum is needed for the whole.

Now my suggestion is that something of this understanding applied in the general consciousness also to other differentiations, even where there may not have been an explicit doctrine to this effect. Thus the stance to the poor had the sense it did partly because it was taken for granted that "the poor ye have always with you". More, this made sense, because the poor, while being succoured by the fortunate, were also an occasion of the salvation of these latter. There was a complementarity here, alongside a difference in worth. (Although the difference could tell in both directions: the lord or burgess who gave was certainly higher in worldly rank to the beggar; but this latter might be on a higher religious plane.) Within this way of understanding, it was unthinkable that one try actually to abolish poverty.

Something similar applies, I believe, to the relation between austere sanctity and the unbuttoned release of boisterous spirits, or even the sensuous enjoyment of the things of the flesh. This is a harder case to make, of course, because there are no explicit doctrines to point to, as with the case of the poor. But something like this seems implicit in the ritual of Carnival, or the various feasts of "misrule", all those rituals in which the "world was turned upside down", after which the order of things was restored. Or at least, so I was arguing in the previous segment.

Of course, one explanation for all this is the "air-hole" (safety valve) theory: society needed this temporary licence to let off steam, built up through the repression of ordinary life, in order to return refreshed to the standard disciplines. But perhaps this ritual can be given another reading. The Carnival play with eating, sex and (mostly mock) violence was a recognition that these cravings of the flesh, while obviously lower than the asceticism of Lent, could not be totally done away with, that they have also to be given their due. Of course, the "air-hole" explanation is saying this in one form. But I mean they have to be let out, not just because the barrel will burst otherwise, but because they are part of the unalterable equilibrium of things, at least until the Parousia. They are what make our world go around. And so we celebrate their place at these ritually appointed times, knowing full well that as lower, they must cede their place to the higher, when the world is turned back aright.

Or perhaps the equilibrium reflects something deeper still, some Turnerian idea that society has two registers; it is order and it is communitas; it is structure, but this must find periodically its roots in anti-structure. This latter can't be totally lost from view. We have to give it outlet.

In either case, Carnival supposes, as I argued above (Chapter 1), an understanding of time as kairotic and many-levelled.

This understanding would be in many ways pre-Christian, and in origin extra-Christian; but not necessarily anti-Christian. There also is Gospel warrant for the idea that evil is so bound up with good that it can't just be eliminated, until we reach the end of things, in evangelical terms, that the wheat and the tares are together till the harvest.

Plainly in the modern period élites totally lose touch with this understanding. Gradually a new conception of the world and time begins to gain ground, according to which the complementarity of order and chaos is no longer necessary. Conceding a place to this chaos is no longer an inescapable alternation, going with the kairotic shape of time, but a gratuitous concession to that which we are trying to extirpate, a compromise with evil. And so the voices critical of these elements of popular culture become more and more frequent, and reach a deafening chorus among élites in the sixteenth-seventeenth centuries.

There's a long story here; but very shortly put, we can see that this new understanding of world and time, originally arising within a Christian outlook, is taken over by secular variants; we might better say, gradually slips over more and more in a secular direction, starting perhaps with the neo-Stoicism of Justus Lipsius. Indeed, we might say that it helps to constitute the modern secular outlook, of which "homogeneous, empty time" is a crucial constituent. And along with this come new uncompromising conceptions of order: order in our lives; and social order.

Among other things, modern versions of this latter are much less tolerant of violence and social disorder than earlier variants. The sixteenth century sees the taming of the unruly military aristocracy, and its domestication in court service, court attendance, or estate management. The eighteenth century begins to see the taming of the general population. Riots, peasant rebellions, social disorders begin to become rarer in Northwest Europe. Until we reach the rather high standards of non-violence which most Atlantic societies expect in their domestic life. (In this, as in other respects, the U.S. is a curious throw-back to an earlier epoch.)

And growing through all this development, partly driving it, partly strengthened by it, is a growing sense of our *ability* to put this kind of order in our lives. This confidence is at the heart of the various programmes of discipline, both individual and social; religious, economic and political, which begin to make us over from the sixteenth-seventeenth centuries. This confidence is consubstantial with the belief that we don't have to compromise, that we don't need complementarity, that the erecting of order doesn't need to acknowledge limits in any opposing principle of chaos. And because of this, this drive to order is both offended and rendered insecure by the traditional festivals of reversal. It cannot stomach the "world turned upside down".

Thus it becomes easier to lose the sense that there is a limit in principle to the malleability of people, to the advance of the higher over the lower. Raw savage nature may resist civility, but there is no such thing as irreparable loss, as a fatal disequilibrium, as the destruction of something essential to the whole. You go as far as you can. This applies to Jesuit Utopias in Paraguay, just as much to Polizeistaate in Central Europe.

Later on, psychological theories will arise which consecrate this view. The human being is a bundle of habits, stamped in to a tabula rasa; there is no limit to reform. But the imprudent ignoring of limits doesn't originate in these. It comes rather with a new understanding of order, one which gave an essential place to the willed constructive effort in the remaking of human life.

We can best give an account of this, if we ask the question: what gave these élites the positive hope that they could really transform society? In the case of Calvinists, there was the belief the God's providence would give them rulership, at least in the societies which had been elected as God's chosen. But in the climate of thought which was influenced by neo-Stoicism, a new idea developed, a conception of natural order, which seemed to offer a basis for hope in a reformed world.

A natural order, this seems a traditional idea. What after all did Plato teach, or Aristotle, as well as all their followers in the Middle Ages and after? But this was an order of a quite different kind. It was normative, but in a very different way.

The older conception of order, derived ultimately from Plato, whether in the Aristotelian renewal of Thomas, or in the world of Pseudo-Dionysios, was one of forms which were seen as already at work in reality. The visible world we see around us expresses or manifests these forms, whether this is understood as the result of some emanation, or in a more orthodox way, in terms of creation on the basis of ideas in the mind of God.

The notion that the forms are at work, this was essential to the ancient ethical tradition, with which I was contrasting above a modern reconstructivist view, which sees a form imposed ab extra on nature by human will. Now the new notion of nature remains within this reconstructivist perspective. The order is not itself at work, striving for realization. Rather, it is a way in which things have been designed by God to fit together, so that when they follow this plan, they are plainly serving as they were meant to. But this plan is not itself in operation in nature, pushing towards its own realization. It rather corresponds, in certain departments, simply to the way things de facto work; while in other areas, it can only be brought about if it is seen and acted upon by rational beings endowed with will.

The principal area of the latter sort is human society; here the plan is a norm proposed to reason, and not one which is already at work in being. Or again, the only way it can be operative in being is via its being taken up and willed by rational beings. It is not only compatible with, but requires a stance of reconstruction towards the world and society.[69]

One very influential conceptual form in which this idea was put forward in the seventeenth century was that of Natural Law. This had played an important role in Thomist thought; and was still doing so among the great Spanish thinkers, like Suarez, and their following. But the thinkers we now deem foundational for modern natural law theory, Grotius, Pufendorf and Locke, for instance, gave it a new twist.

Grotius' derivation of Natural Law doesn't follow the path of an Aristotelian-Thomist definition of the ends of human nature. It proceeds almost more geometrico. In the first pages of *De jure belli ac pacis,* Grotius derives natural law as what "suits" (convenit)[70] a being who is both rational and sociable. The derivation is extremely terse, but unpacked a little it would seem to go like this: a rational being means one who proceeds by rules, laws, principles; a rational being who is also sociable would have to have laws which made living together possible. Most of the standard prohibitions and injunctions of traditional natural law can be derived on this basis. No form is proposed as already at work here, but there is a way that things (in this case, humans) fit together "rationally", which is proposed as a binding norm.

Grotius, who was a follower of Lipsius, thinks that this law is binding in reason alone (hence his famous assertion, that the Law would hold, "etsi Deus non daretur" [even if God did not exist]);[71] while Pufendorf and later Locke see it as binding qua command of God. But the basic argument is the same. God made man rational, and he made him sociable, and with an instinct to his own conservation. It is plain from this what norms he held binding on his creatures. Plainly they must respect each other's life, liberty and estate.

These laws are binding on us, because the maker can set the rules for his products. But we didn't need revelation to tell us what the rules are. They are plain given the nature of these products.

This conception of a natural law, or a natural order, grows along with the programmes of reconstruction which are reshaping European societies. Locke brings the stance of reconstruction to a new pitch, with his psychology of the human mind as a tabula rasa, waiting to have its habits imprinted on it. He took a vivid interest in the remaking of his society, putting forward his views on education, for instance. It is no accident that he is one of the major defining figures in the modern natural law tradition.

Why did these two go together? Why did the reconstructors need something like natural law? Why didn't they just develop a theory of human nature as malleable (as Locke most strikingly did), and leave it at that?

Because they needed a firm underpinning for an agreed public order. Neo-Stoicism was born in the midst of bitter and violent inter-confessional strife. One of the most important things it was meant to offer was a basis for rational agreement on the foundations of political life, beyond and in spite of confessional differences. Grotius followed Lipsius, developing a full theory not only of obedience to the state, but of international law, which was meant to be valid across the confessional divide. The aim of Natural Law theory was to provide a rational terrain d'entente, replacing not only the ex parte theories of extremist religious partisans, but later on, in its Lockean variant, also setting aside other, dangerously flawed reactions to the religious strife, such as theories of sovereignty unbound by any law.

I mention these, because we have to bear in mind that order drawn from natural law had rivals, which were also designed to meet the critical conditions of religious strife, and give a basis to the state's reconstructive activity. We have forgotten, because the losers tend to slip out of sight in history, but the most prominent answer in seventeenth-century Europe to the disorder of religious war was the absolute state. And this tended to be grounded on its own conception of order. This has also tended to slip out of our sight, because it was less radically different from the pre-modern ideas. It was, for one thing, still hierarchical: it saw society as made up of tiered ranks or orders, largely derived from the earlier mediaeval dispensation. And it was content to sustain the earlier organic understanding of society as hierarchical complementarity among the common people. But it was in other ways very modern in the élite formulations of what it was all about, the kind of thing one sees, for instance, in the writings of Bossuet.

These formulations start from the modern notion of agency as constructing orders, rather than conforming to those already in "nature". Like the natural law view, it sees the political order as an answer to a problem: how to maintain peace and civility among diverse and potentially rival agents. Absolute rule and a fixed social hierarchy are the answers to this problem, rather than being given in the nature of the cosmos. The first answers to the purpose by submitting everyone to one single, unchallengeable will, providing a locus of "sovereignty", without which on this modern will-centred view, society cannot subsist at all. The hierarchy serves the end of order by allocating to everyone their proper situation and role, and by putting in place a chain of command through which the impulses from the top can be carried down through the whole society.

For many people in the seventeenth century, this answer to the threat of disorder seemed both more intellectually cogent and more politically effective than those grounded on theories of Natural Rights. And indeed, the earlier, pre-Lockean versions of Natural Law theory compromised with this ideal of clear, undivided sovereignty: the purpose of the social contract for Grotius and Pufendorf was precisely to establish a sovereign rule of this kind.

Moreover, this hierarchical, command conception of order also drew on a doctrine of Providence. In obeying this kind of sovereign one was following God's will, most clearly in the variant of this notion which still is notorious today, the theory of the Divine Right of Kings.

From our standpoint today, this command conception seems like a kind of halfway house between the mediaeval dispensation and a modernity dominated by Natural Law. This is an anachronistic judgment in a way, since this view dominated its age, and didn't seem at all at the time like a transitional form. But the truth in this judgment is that the command notion did keep certain facets of the earlier dispensation, and saw itself as in continuity with earlier royal régimes.

As a command structure in supposed continuity with an earlier one based more on complementarity, the absolute state showed a certain analogy to the post-Tridentine Catholic church. And while this parallel could spell rivalry, it also could generate an affinity between the Church and the monarchies which espoused this outlook. The fatal enmeshing of the Church in the ancien régime becomes denser with this affinity. In the light of this, it may not perhaps be too far-fetched to give this command-hierarchical conception of order the name 'baroque', even though the art and architecture which flourished under this name didn't dominate all the societies which adopted this political-theoretical formula. (Louis XIV's France saw itself rather as "classical".) But the art forms undoubtedly reflect this mixture of hierarchy and of an impulse from on high which defines the formula.

As it developed from its Lockean version, the Natural Law theory took a very different direction. This theory, of course, had, and needed, a voluntarist side stressing the power of reconstruction; but it also needed a notion of normative order to set the rules and the goals for this reconstruction. The crucial concepts defining this are not hierarchy and command. The starting point is rather a race of equal individuals designed to enter with each other into a society of mutual benefit.

Gradually this normative order turns into a blueprint for the kind of society the reconstruction aims at. These rational, sociable beings, meant to live together in respect for each other's life and liberty, are also meant to preserve themselves by industrious exploitation of their natural surroundings.[72] Properly carried out, this exploitation leads to economic growth. The right to property both follows immediately from this exploitation of nature, and also makes possible improvement and hence economic growth.

And so what emerges out of this reflection on Natural Law is the norm of a stable order of industrious men in the settled courses of their callings, dedicating themselves to growth and prosperity, rather than war and plunder, and accepting a morality of mutual respect and an ethic of self-improvement. This order seemed to be more than just a good idea; it was the rational, and God-given, way of living. To aim for this is not to follow a whim, or a particular preference; it is to head to where things were destined to go, a terminus ad quem in which everything is in its proper place.

This is the natural order of things, not in the sense that it is at work in history—that idea will come when Hegel re-integrates Aristotelian teleology into this constructivist outlook—but rather in that it is the reasonable, even providential goal of our efforts.

These efforts can now be conceived as taking place over a long time horizon. We are at the birth of the concept which now goes under the name "development". It has become difficult for us to conceive human society and history without this concept. It almost seems that we wouldn't know what to do, or how to define the social good, without it.

Our time understanding has evidently radically altered. The framework understanding of hierarchical equilibrium went with a time understanding in which cycles played an important part, and in which tracts of time were qualitatively distinct: now is the time for Carnival or "misrule"; and then there is the time for the re-enactment of order. The long time horizon of modern reconstruction is linear, and it is made up of "homogeneous, empty time".[73]

In the eighteenth century, this notion of natural order will develop further, and complete the transformation of the old conception of the Great Chain of Being, from the hierarchical order, whose forms are at work in reality, to the universe of natures, created so that in the operation of meeting their needs, their activities mesh. In their perpetual change, they support and help each other.

Rather significantly, the balance in the original seventeenth-century idea will have been lost. There the sense of hard struggle with a refractory nature was balanced by the harmony of our ultimate destination. But in the eighteenth century, the harmony is more and more seen as one which is already there. The harmony of interests is written into human nature from the start. Sympathy, and a community of interests, should have been enough to establish a non-conflictual order of things. The search is on for the sinister agencies which made things go wrong: kings, priests, enclosers of land?

One mustn't exaggerate. The shift was far from total. But the hard slog was frequently lost from view. And this reflected a new situation, in which for many among the expanding European élites, "civilization" had arrived; the fully reformed society was close to hand, rather than a distant prospect; requiring only one more package of reforms: political (e.g., representative government), economic (e.g., laissez-faire), social (e.g., an end to castes and privileges). Indeed, some of these final programmes were even defined as against "civilization" as this had been understood. (Many of the writings of Jean-Jacques Rousseau have this thrust).

This was the predicament, marked by a sense of order achieved, a feeling that the powers of reconstruction had been successfully exercised, in which anthropocentrism could flourish, and the conditions were created at last in which a live option of exclusive humanism could emerge from the womb of history.

4

But before turning to this, I want to double back and examine how some of the bases for this humanism emerged out of the neo-Stoic tradition.

I noted above how neo-Stoicism gives an important place to a stance of reconstruction. The emphasis shifts from the notion of a form which tends to realize itself, but requires our collaboration, to that of a form imposed ab extra on our life by the power of will. In the seventeenth century, this move towards an ethic of poiesis is consummated in a new coherent theory of disengaged agency, and a new understanding of virtue as dominance of the will over passion. One of the most influential formulations of this is provided by Descartes.

Descartes clearly stands in the neo-Stoic stream of thought. He was influenced by Lipsius' French disciples, du Vair and Charron; and there is no doubt that he would have been exposed to Lipsius' thought at Laflèche at the hands of his Jesuit teachers. Neo-Stoicism in Lipsius' formulation had already departed from the original model, as we saw: in its emphasis on the will, and in its mind/body dualism. Descartes pushes further along these lines of departure, and develops a quite different view.

The transition can be conceived as one which takes us from an ethic grounded on an order which is at work in reality, to an ethic which sees order as imposed by will. Descartes utterly ruins any conceivable basis for the first, by adopting a consistently mechanistic view of the material universe. It no longer makes sense to speak of the things of nature as expressing or realizing a form. No causal explanation of them in these terms can be made intelligible any more. Forms and their expression belong exclusively in the domain of minds. Matter is to be explained as mechanism.

Moreover, getting this distinction clear is essential for ethics. Because virtue consists in mind, in the form of will, exercising sovereign control over the body, and the domain of things which arise from the union of soul and body, in particular the passions. To remain confused about the distinctions here is not to see clearly what should control what.

Both science and virtue require that we disenchant the world, that we make the rigorous distinction between mind and body, and relegate all thought and meaning to the realm of the intra-mental. We have to set up a firm boundary, the one, as we have seen, which defines the buffered self. For Descartes, seeing reality as pure mechanism is the way of establishing that boundary, it is indispensable to it.

In the ethical dimension, where we are dealing with praxis, the requirement is that we be able to *treat* the extra-mental as mechanism, and that means taking an instrumental stance, or a stance of reconstruction towards it. But this stance must englobe not only the bodily, but also whatever is not pure mind; that is, it must include the things which arise in the mind only because of the union of soul and body, and that means especially, the passions.

Descartes thus develops a quite different theory of the passions from the Stoics. For the latter, the passions were false opinions. When we achieve wisdom, we free ourselves altogether from them. They disappear, like the illusions they are. Descartes understands the passions in a quite different register; not in terms of what they say, but in terms of their function. They are responses we are endowed with by the Creator to help us respond with appropriate vigour in certain, appropriate circumstances. The goal is not to do away with them, but to bring them under the instrumental control of reason.

Passions not only are not meant to disappear, but in the best people they are even more powerful than in most. The crucial point is, however, that they are controlled by the will. Descartes admires "les plus grandes âmes", who "ont des raisonnements si forts & si puissans que, bien qu'elles ayent aussi des passions, & mesme souvent de plus violentes que celles du commun, leur raison demeure neantmoins tousiours la maistresse"[74] (the greatest souls . . . whose reasoning powers are so strong and powerful, that although they also have passions, and often even more violent than is common, nonetheless their reason remains sovereign). So that far from having to get rid of passions, "il suffit qu'on les rende suiettes a la raison, & lorsqu'on les a ainsy apprivoisées, elles sont quelquefois d'autant plus utiles qu'elles penchent vers l'exces"[75] (it is enough to subject one's passions to reason; and once they are thus tamed they are sometimes useful precisely to the degree that they tend to excess).

What Descartes does very much retain of Stoic and neo-Stoic thought is the norm of detachment. Reason tells us what is for the best, and we act to bring it about. But all the while, we are fully detached from the outcome. Thus the passage I quoted above about "les plus grandes âmes" continues:

> Elles font bien tout ce qui est en leur pouvoir pour se rendre la Fortune favorable en cette vie, mais neantmoins elles l'estiment si peu, au regard de l'Éternité, qu'elles n'en considerent quasi les evenemens que comme nous faisons ceux des Comedies.

> (They do everything in their power to make fortune favour them in this life, but nevertheless they think so little of it, in relation to eternity, that they view the events of the world as we do those of a play.)

What emerges here is a kind of Stoicism. The central ideas of detachment, of constancy, of steadfastness, and control by reason have remained. But the underlying anthropology has been crucially transformed.

The difference can be seen clearest when we ask what is good about the good life; or from a slightly different angle, what is the nature of the joy or satisfaction which draws us to it.

For the ancient ethics of forms-at-work, this can be found at two levels. First, since we are instantiations of the form of a human being, leading the good life brings us into true with the bent of our natures; and so we escape division, inner tumult, and enjoy harmony; we are no longer riven by opposing forces, and so we are capable of constancy. We are no longer pining after what doesn't suit us, and so have realized self-sufficiency.

At a second level, forms are also at work in the whole cosmos around us, and in some ethical theories this plays a role. For instance, with Plato, reason in us just is the power to see the order in the cosmos and to love it. Our love of it makes us want to imitate it, and therefore live ordered lives ourselves.[76] The motive force for goodness comes not only from the form we instantiate, but also from the whole ensemble, ordered by the Form of the Good. In other words, the joy or satisfaction comes not only from our following our own nature, but from our being in line also with the whole.

Not all ancient ethics had recourse to this detour through the whole. Perhaps Aristotle did not, for instance. But the Stoics had their own variant of it. The wise person is happy, because following her nature; but she is also rejoicing at everything which befalls, because this is part of the unfolding of God's providence.

Now for Descartes, much of this either falls away, or is given a quite different basis. Steadfastness, indeed, remains; as does a notion of Providence. But the universe can no longer offer a picture of an order at work in things. All we can glean from it is insight into how things were meant to function, and that is then something which we have to put into effect, as we see with the paradigm case of the passions.

What is crucial now are the joys within. But these are no longer really those of harmony, or absence of strife. Because the good person is precisely embattled. She is called upon to exercise all her strength. In a field of passion, more violent than the ordinary person's, her "raison demeure neantmoins tousiours la maistresse". She is not going with the bent of nature, but imposing through struggle an order, which is indeed the one designed for, but which can only be achieved through this triumph of the will.[77]

Not conflict-free harmony, but struggled-for domination is now the acme of virtue, and the joy which flows from this is the satisfaction at the victory of reason. Because what I am most fundamentally is rational will.

Outre que le libre arbitre est de soy la chose la plus noble qui puisse estre en nous, d'autant qu'il nous rend en quelque façon pareils à Dieu & semble nous exempter de luy estre sujets, & que, par consequent, son bon usage est le plus grand de tous nos biens, il est aussi celuy qui est le plus nostre & qui nous importe le plus, d'où il suit que ce n'est que de luy que nos plus grands contentemens peuvent proceder.[78]

(Now freewill is in itself the noblest thing we can have because it makes us in a certain manner equal to God and exempts us from being his subjects; and so its rightful use is the greatest of all the goods we possess, and further there is nothing that is more our own or that matters more to us. From all this it follows that nothing but freewill can produce our greatest contentments.)

The "contentment" here is the sense of having lived up to my dignity as a rational being, which demands that I be ruled by reason.

In what might seem like a surprising turn, Descartes at this point introduces a key term of the honour ethic, "generosity". This word meant something different in the seventeenth century. It designates the lively sense one has of one's rank, and of the honour which attaches to it, which motivates one to live up to the demands of one's station. Corneille's heroes are always declaring their "générosité" as the reason for the striking, courageous and often gruesome acts they are about to commit.

But Descartes takes the notion out of public space, and the field of socially defined ranks, into the internal realm of self-knowledge. True generosity

> qui fait qu'un homme s'estime au plus haut point qu'il se peut legitimement estimer, consiste seulement, partie en ce qu'il connoist qu'il n'y a rien que veritablement luy appartiene que cette libre disposition de ses volontez, ny pourquoi il doive estre loüé ou blasmé sinon pour ce qu'il en use bien ou mal; & partie en ce qu'il sent en soy mesme une ferme & constante resolution d'en bien user, c'est à dire de manquer jamais de volonté, pour entreprendre & exe-cuter toutes les choses qu'il jugera estre les meilleurs.[79]

> (True generosity, which causes a man to esteem himself as highly as he legiti-mately can, consists alone partly in the fact that he knows that there is nothing that truly pertains to him but this free disposition of the will, and that there is no reason why he should be praised or blamed unless it is because he uses it well or ill; and partly in the fact that he is sensible in himself of a firm and con-stant resolution to use it well, that is to say, never to fail of his own will to un-dertake and execute all the things which he judges to be the best.)

The rank I must live up to is the non-socially-defined one of rational agent. It is this sense of my own dignity which Descartes says is "comme la clef de toutes les autres vertus, & un remede general contre tous les dereglements des Passions"[80] (the key of all other virtues, and a general remedy for all the disorders of the passions). In other words, the central place, the virtue which can uphold and sustain the others, which Socrates gave to wisdom, for instance, and others have given to temperance, for Descartes falls to generosity. The key motivation here is the demands laid on me by my own status as rational being, and the satisfaction is that of having lived up to the dignity of this station.

What moves us now is no longer a sense of being in tune with nature, our own and/or that in the cosmos. It is something more like the sense of our own intrinsic worth; something clearly self-referential. The Kantian notion of "Würde" is not far off. A crucial element of the coming exclusive humanism is in place.[81]

This new ethic of rational control supposes disenchantment, as we saw above. Indeed, it is one of the forces bringing it about, operating in this respect alongside the Reformation rejection of the old sacred. It contributes thus to the creation of the new identity which I have called the buffered self. But it also intensifies it.

The buffered self is the agent who no longer fears demons, spirits, magic forces. More radically, these no longer impinge; they don't exist for him; whatever threat or other meaning they proffer doesn't "get to" him. Now the disengaged rational agent carries out an analogous operation on desire.

Of course, our desires still impinge, as de facto inclinations. But they are deprived of any higher meaning or aura. They are just de facto solicitations. We ought to be able to stand back from all of them, and determine rationally how we should best dispose them.

Le vraye usage de nostre raison pour la conduite de la vie ne consiste qu'a examiner & considerer sans passions les valeurs de toutes les perfections, tant du corps que de l'esprit . . . afin qu'estant ordinairement obligez de nous priver de quelques unes, pour avoir les autres, nous choisissions tousiours les meilleures.[82]

(The true function of reason, then, in the conduct of life is to examine and consider without passion the value of all perfections of body and soul that can be acquired by our conduct, so that since we are commonly obliged to deprive ourselves of some goods in order to acquire others, we shall always choose the better.)

Now it is true that any higher morality, which proposes to control passions, will have to bring about a debunking operation of this kind. Because in fact our "lower" passions are often surrounded with a very powerful aura. The impulse to violence, for instance, is frequently invested by a sense of great moment. I have been insulted, my honour is at stake; or this act that I am about to strike is for a noble cause. And on top of all that, violence can be exciting, can seem to lift us out of the banality of everyday existence, onto a higher, more exalted plane. And here's where violence comes close to the domain of sexual desire, so that the two are often interwoven. Separately, or interwoven, they can give us a sense of release from the everyday, from the monotony of the ordinary world. That's why they can appear, separately or together, in rituals—such for instance as Carnival.

An important theme which runs through all the traditional ethical views is the debunking of the false prestige of these desires, the dissipation of their aura. In this regard, the ethic of rational control is not different. Plato and the Stoics also laboured to show that what seems to shine in these dark realms is only illusion, that in the cold light of day, the aura utterly disappears. And this debunking is even more in evidence in the long attack against the honour ethic, from Plato, through the Stoics, through Augustine, and to the modern day. I mean the ethic in its original form, which makes public recognition, glory, a worthy end; I am not talking about its sublimated, internalized form, as with Descartes, which is meant to replace the original, public one. Glory is castigated as mere appearance (Plato), as an end posited by pride, the source of evil (Augustine), as "vain-glory" (Hobbes).

But this debunking can still leave desire with some aura in the older theories. For Plato, my sexual desire for a beautiful person is a dim, distorted recognition of the idea of beauty, which my soul longs for. In its present form, this desire has to be shown up as incapable of realizing its promise, but the promise was not totally wrong. For the ethic of rational control, nothing like this remains. There is just a field of de facto solicitations, which no more than the external, mechanized world can be considered a locus of higher meanings, even confused and distorted ones. This field is utterly stripped of any such meaning. It is not that the false prestige of desire distorts the real ground for the aura. The aura is total illusion.

It follows that it needs no special insight to see through this prestige. One just has to take once for all the right stance, that of instrumental, rational control, and this world of feeling goes expressively dead; which is just to say that it shows up in its true, disenchanted nature.

This agent is in a sense super-buffered. He is not only not "got at" by demons and spirits; he is also utterly unmoved by the aura of desire. In a mechanistic universe, and in a field of functionally understood passions, there is no more ontological room for such an aura. There is nothing it could correspond to. It is just a disturbing, supercharged feeling, which somehow grips us until we can come to our senses, and take on our full, buffered identity.

Needless to remind ourselves, modernity didn't stop at the ethic of rational control. This is just one of the burning points of dissatisfaction with this reading of the modern identity, which was taken up in that broad stream of thought and sensibility sometimes called "Romanticism". The very idea that feeling could be stripped of all aura came to seem not only erroneous, but terribly impoverishing, a denial of our humanity.

But within this identity of disengaged reason, disenchantment and instrumental control go closely together. And it was this which helped prepare the ground for the new option of exclusive humanism.

5

This disengaged, disciplined stance to self and society has become part of the essential defining repertory of the modern identity. It is also a central feature of secularity 3. The disciplined stance helps to build a second facet of what I've been calling the buffered self. I discussed above how disenchantment involves a drawing of boundaries, an end to porousness in relation to the world of spirits.

Now the disengaged stance also leads to the drawing of boundaries, and a withdrawal from certain modes of intimacy, as well as taking a distance from certain bodily functions. This has been admirably explored by Norbert Elias in his masterful book.[83]

We stand in a relation of intimacy with someone when there is a flow of feeling between us, when our barriers are down, and we can sense each other's emotions. It's the relation we usually stand in with family and close friends.

Ontogenetically, these relations are crucial, since in our infancy and childhood, the recognition we need to flourish and become human passes through intimate relations. If sufficiently deprived of them we cannot come to know who we are; or else our world goes dead.

Now our identity, our sense of what is really important, may go on being crucially linked to certain relations: we only really have a grasp on who we are, and what is crucial within this relation; it can be a love relation, or one to a hero, saint, guru, role model. So this identity can be threatened when something happens to the relation. When they die, it can be hard, but we often rise to this, and go on living in relation to them. The worst is when it goes sour, they repudiate us, or we change our view of them. These are defining relations.

All this is, of course, overwhelmingly true when we are small. But later, certain people are trained into an identity which is detached from these early close, intimate relations. For instance, young boys in warrior societies are detached from women at a certain age. You still need recognition, but now from others, warrior leaders, and your relations with them abstract from certain dimensions of intimacy, as also do relations with peers. There is gruff joking, horseplay, boasting, but not tender openness, vulnerability, as earlier with the womenfolk. Those earlier relations are no longer admitted as defining.

Now disengagement takes us a step further in this direction. It has indeed, a certain affinity with the warrior ethic (as we can see in Descartes' invocation of "générosité").[84] Except that now all discipline is around an impersonal principle. Carried to the limit, the injunction would now be: as much as possible, be self-reliant; relate to God or the principle alone. You are allowed tenderness, but not in a defining relation. Indeed, in the limit all defining relations are meant to be "sublated" (aufgehoben) in God/principle.

Of course, it is very hard to get to that final point; and it only can be a final point of aspiration, not a beginning. We all need recognition to hold our identity at the beginning, and most never can do without it. Their identity can flourish only in their relations to leaders, or colleagues. But these still defining relations are stiff, gruff, restrained, unintimate. And what is being aimed at is already reflected in the character of these relations; it is a kind of self-reliance, self-sufficiency, autarky, autonomy. We need recognition to get there, but we try to transcend this, to throw away the ladder.

So disengaged discipline frames a new experience of the self as having a telos of autarky. Freud's sense of the proud loneliness of the ego is an example of this. The interspaces between human beings are no longer important. Our great emotions are inner.

Later, in the reaction against this kind of discipline, we rediscover our deep emotions, our intimacy, as a kind of lost continent. We experience all this in a new way, see it in a new light. Think of the triumphant rediscovery of emotional depth in D. H. Lawrence. (There is perhaps a disturbing parallel to our being excited by ghost stories, after we can no longer really believe in ghosts.)

Elias has noted and recorded the tremendous shift in manners which accompanies the developing ideal of civility, and later civilization. This starts off among élites, of course, but then spreads during the nineteenth century virtually to the whole society. The shift involves a steady raising of the threshold of embarrassment, one might even say, disgust, which is quite remarkable. It is with surprise, and not a little shock, that we discover how things were back in 1500.

Early books of etiquette admonish people not to blow their nose on the table-cloth (143–144). A book of 1558 tells us that it is not a "very fine habit", when one comes across excrement in the street to point it out to another, and hold it up for him to smell (177). People are told not to defecate in public places (177). Clearly we are in an age whose standards in this regard are far removed from our own.

Elias traces, not an abrupt change, but a gradual raising of the thresholds. Where earlier the standard books advise against blowing your nose in the table-cloth, later ones demand the use of handkerchiefs, tell you not to blow at table, etc. Where at one point you are asked not to defecate in the hallways, by the end of the process, it would be an indelicacy even to mention such a thing in a book of etiquette. There falls a "Bann des Schweigens". People shouldn't even mention such bodily functions (183–184).

Elias attributes this whole movement to two main factors. First, the demands of living together in large numbers in courts forced the imposition of stricter rules; and this movement carries on as people come more and more to live in denser, more interactive societies. This necessary disciplining of behaviour is the "civilizing process" (E332).

But alongside this, Elias sees another dynamic at work, that of the class or status differentiation. The demands of refinement serve to distinguish upper strata from their inferiors; and these become the more necessary as nobles are being forced into a courtly, urban way of life where their resources and the powers at their disposal no longer clearly mark them off from bourgeois. This sets in chain, of course, a desire to imitate the higher strata on the part of "bourgeois gentilshommes" and others; which requires a further step in the chain of refinement to keep the distance intact (136–139, E83–85). Elias gives what seems a good example of this in the courtly modelling of the French language, and the subsequent total hegemony of this dialect over the language we now all have come to speak (145–152).

Now I think there is truth in both these accounts. But I think the developments he describes can also be understood in two other, related contexts. I want to see them as reflecting the way in which the disengaged, disciplined stance first restricts intimacy, and then makes us take a distance from our powerful emotions and our bodily functions.

If we look at how these changes strike us, what leaps to the fore is the rise in the threshold of fastidiousness; something we feel particularly when we read of the more disgusting practices, like those I have just mentioned. But in fact, in some earlier books of manners, the advice to avoid these practices not only seems to assume that the average addressee was not put off by them, but doesn't even seem to be advising against them because they are revolting. Something else is at stake, which has to do with permitted relations of intimacy.

In fact, many of the issues which are raised in these books have an obvious relation to intimacy, such as being naked in the presence of others, allowing them to see one doing one's bodily functions, eating out of the same dish. It is obvious that the objection to all these falls away with people we're on intimate terms with. The objection to "mixing fluids" with a stranger, by sharing, say, the same spoon, disappears altogether between lovers. Love-making itself is a mixing of fluids with abandon.

The first admonitions against this kind of thing, from the advice books of the late Middle Ages and the early modern period, often seem to be concerned with unjustified presumptions of intimacy. They are not symmetrical, but warn inferiors against presuming on close relations with their superiors.

Thus, *Galateo,* an advice book from the sixteenth century: "Nor do I believe that it is fitting to serve from the common dish intended for all the guests, unless the server is of higher rank so that the other, who is served, is thereby especially honoured. For when this is done among equals, it appears as if the server is partly placing himself above the others" (E114). Here clearly the prohibition surrounds presuming intimacy. If someone superior to you offers this kind of closeness, far from being repelled, you are honoured. But just for that reason, it is utterly inadmissible to initiate this yourself. *Galateo* also advises against showing one's intimate parts to thers, but then continues: "for this and similar things are not done, except among people before whom one is not ashamed. It is true that a great lord might do so before one of his servants or in the presence of a friend of lower rank; for in this he would not show him arrogance but rather a particular affection and friendship" (E113).

Earlier manners offer all sorts of examples of asymmetrical restrictions on intimacy, which today have become thoroughly bilateral. Kings would dress in the company of their courtiers; they would even sit on the "chaise-percée" in company. The same kind of hierarchical asymmetry is operative when the Marquise de Châtelet, Voltaire's mistress, shows herself naked to her servant while bathing, throwing him into confusion, only to scold him because he is not pouring the hot water properly (E113).

With the progress of equal relations these prohibitions are not relaxed, but on the contrary, are generalized between people of equal rank, and finally become universal. The restrictions on bodily intimacy, which start as measures of respect for superiors, become internalized as tabus in relation to everyone. Now we have learned to feel embarrassment at the exposure, or even disgust at the contact (when, say, using someone else's spoon). We read of the eighteenth-century self-exposure of the great with surprise, astonished that *they* didn't feel embarrassed, vulnerable. We think of this self-exposure as something that those with arbitrary power might cruelly impose on their underlings, in order to humiliate them, or that jailers do to their prisoners; the idea that the most powerful might do it themselves seems bizarre.

This reversal of the meaning of exposure into a generalized tabu reflects on one level, I believe, the withdrawal from promiscuous intimacy which is part of the modern disciplined stance. Henceforth, this kind of closeness is reserved for a small circle of people, generally the immediate family; and even there the tabus are partly effective. You keep the multifarious functions of your body, its fluids and secretions, very much to yourself, you keep a respectful distance, and you relate to others through voice and visage, via sight and sound, reserving touch for intimates, or for certain ritually permitted moments, like shaking hands.

This development had its flip side, which was the greater intensity of intimate relations which can grow within the family or between lovers, walled off from the outside world by the new spaces and conventions of privacy. Indeed, we can say that what we can mean by intimacy changes profoundly at this time. Whereas the previous relations of promiscuous contact, say, between masters and servants reflected perhaps a certain closeness, anyway a lack of guardedness; in the new, narrower circle of more intense relations, intimacy takes on the sense that it has with us, implying the openness and sharing of our deepest and strongest, most "private" feelings. The dimension of shared feeling, which is part of our modern concept, arises, of course, in an age where the having of certain profound and intense feelings comes to be seen as a central human fulfillment. The new companionate marriage and the family it creates requires a privacy which earlier ages didn't seek, just because it is the locus of shared sentiment, which is now understood to be an important human good, indeed, for many, an essential part of a full human life. We are on the road to our contemporary age, where creating a harmonious household, having children, carrying on the line, no longer define the point of marriage, but this finds its main goal in an emotional fulfillment which is identified as one of the central human goods.[85]

But in general, we relate to the world as more disembodied beings than our ancestors; that is, the centre of gravity of the person each one of us is, as we interact with others, has moved out of the body. It stands outside, in the agent of disengaged discipline, capable of dispassionate control. This is the persona we project towards others, and they towards us, and in this mutual projection we help each other to see ourselves as having attained this rational distance, and hence help each other to live up to this exalted ideal.

That is why the person who breaks the tabus is so disturbing. He not only makes a fool of himself, but also subverts the commonly-maintained discipline. Because this is not easy. Elias shows that the "civilizing process" involved our taking this distance from a whole range of powerful emotions: rage and the fascination with violence, sexual desire, and our fascination with bodily processes and excretions, which is in some way related to sexual feeling. Our ancestors permitted themselves accesses of rage, they more frankly gloried in violence, they flocked to scenes of cruel punishment, inflicted on humans and animals; all things that tend to horrify us today. These things too, as well as bodily intimacy, have been strongly suppressed. It is not just that we tend to control our anger better, or at least to demand this of each other; we also learn to damp our feelings of rage and resentment. We allow ourselves to enjoy violence only when it is derealized, in fiction, or television presentations which have the same feel as fiction (280).

But the only way to maintain this control is to awaken the disgust or the fastidious distaste of our disciplined or refined self at the feelings which are complicit with this bodily, sexual or violent abandon. "Civilization" in this sense has gone beyond the mere interdict of actions, which of themselves arouse no aversion, in order to show proper respect for others. The march of disengaged discipline demands that we keep our distance from this abandon, and this requires that we call on the sense of being besmirched or lowered which attaches to abandon when it is framed in the perspective of the dignity of rational control.

In this sense, the two feelings go together, sides of the same coin: on one side, the exalted sense of dispassionate impartiality; on the other, the sense of rage and sexual esire as a kind of imprisonment, dragging us down, away from the heights where we can survey everything. In the last century, attempts have been made (and not least, by Bertrand Russell himself) to lift the tabu on raw sexual desire, to see only rage and violence as the besmirchers of dispassionate reason, while cleaving to an ethic of disinterested benevolence. This may be possible, although there are obvious dangers of cooling out and objectifying sexual desire in the process. If it were, it would be another innovation of modernity. But in fact, the civilizing process we have been through in the last centuries took its distance from sex and violence alike.

So this civilization advances by raising the threshold of fastidiousness or disgust before bodily intimacy, raw sexual desire, and violence. "Delicacy", "Feingefühl", become the virtues of polite society. Clean your spoon before reaching again for the common dish, says Courtin in 1672, "y ayant des gens si délicats qu'ils ne voudraient pas manger du potage où vous l'auriez mise, après l'avoir portée à la bouche" (154). It is no longer a question of not presuming on your superiors, but of behaviour which awakens disgust.

And since, as I said above, civilization is a game we play together, relating to each other through our disengaged persona, and thus maintaining the standards; when we violate one of these tabus, we not only arouse disgust, but we feel terrible shame. Civilization is in a sense a matter of feeling shame in the appropriate places.

In this way, the disciplined, disengaged agent completes another facet of what I've been calling the buffered self. Not only is there a firm inner/outer boundary in a world which has been disenchanted, but further barriers are raised against strong physical desires and the fascination with the body. The barriers are raised by and in the name of the central identity as agent of disengaged discipline, keeping its distance from this zone of abandon. But since this is also a zone in which feelings flow between people, and a kind of intimacy of mutual arousal can easily arise, this distance also drastically narrows the range of permitted intimacy. Outside the narrow circles of intimacy which remain, we are trained to relate to each other as dignified subjects of rational control, whose defining relations are no longer intimate ones, and indeed, which prepare each other eventually to transcend defining relations altogether.

The buffering here is not only against a zone of bodily life, but also to some degree against the other. It is not surprising that the agent trained in this discipline falls easily prey to ideologies of atomism, in which men might as well have "grown like mushrooms out of the earth".

6

We are now ready to go on with the story, and see what made possible the shift to an exclusive humanism. But before proceeding, I want to pause and put the whole

imanent vs transcender
NATURE   Supl

sweep of things in another framework, which sheds important light on it. Our question is how we moved from a condition in 1500 in which it was hard not to believe in God, to our present situation just after 2000, where this has become quite easy for many. A way of putting our present condition is to say that many people are happy living for goals which are purely immanent; they live in a way that takes no account of the transcendent.

What I'm proposing here is a two-stage account. In the first stage, we developed an outlook and mode of life (mainly at first confined to élites), which clearly distinguished immanent from transcendent; or to speak the intellectual dialect of Western Christendom, natural from supernatural. I don't only mean that this distinction was drawn in (theological) theory, although it is also significant that Latin Christians did mark the boundary (quite early on, in fact, during the high Middle Ages). This is itself is worthy of note; it singles out this civilization among others, and was a harbinger of things to come.

But what is important for us is not the theoretical distinction, but a sorting out in experience, by which it became possible to relate to certain realities as purely "natural", and disintricate them from the transcendent; whereby it eventually became possible to see the immediate surroundings of our lives as existing on this "natural" plane, however much we might believe that they indicated something beyond.

It is clear that one cannot experience one's surroundings this way in an enchanted world, full of spirits and forces, nor in a world shaped by the Ideas and the Correspondences, nor in one in which one could encounter the sacred. So first, these worlds had to be destroyed or undermined, rendered experience-far; the levels, immanent and transcendent, had to be sorted out.

This sorting out was the first stage. But this was at first compatible with a continuing belief in God. Indeed, it was accompanied by a more conscious and zealous dedication to God. It was this dedication which largely fuelled the processes of disenchantment, by which the sorting out was effected.

It has often been noted how secularization went along with an intensification of religious faith. The "message and driving force behind Reformation and Counter-Reformation" was that "religion was on its way to becoming a matter of intense personal decision." In the seventeenth and eighteenth centuries, there was a "new Christianity of personal commitment which was evolving in an increasingly secularized society".[86] One clear reason for this connection between disenchantment and personal faith is that in the beginning the latter drove the former through its "rage for order". Later on, the causal arrow will also move in the other direction: Christians in a world which less and less reflects God are thrown back on their own resources.

But the Christian drive to sort things out came not only from the rage for order.

This new, more personal, more intense Christian faith, was also moving in another vector. Since the High Middle Ages, there have been repeated attempts in Western Christendom to integrate faith more fully in ordinary life. This often went along with the goal of reducing the distance between different "speeds" in the Church, but it isn't really the same thing. I mean rather attempts to bring a more intense devotional life into niches of personal and social existence where they had hitherto been absent.

One fruit of this is the founding of new orders, who took on some of the disciplines of monasticism, including poverty and celibacy, but took them out of cloister into the world, like the mendicant friars of the thirteenth century, and later on the Jesuits. This is a movement which continues in the Catholic Church to this day, for instance, in orders like that founded by Mother Teresa.

On another level, we have the late mediaeval movements like the Brethren of the Common Life, which aim precisely to integrate the life of prayer more closely into everyday life. The Reformation itself is strongly marked by this goal, which emerges in what I have called the affirmation of ordinary life. A Christian worships God in his everyday existence, in work and family life. None of this is to be considered profane.

Now I believe there is a connection between this aspiration, and some of the profound shifts in representation, which one can see in Western painting in these centuries. I followed Louis Dupré above in positing a connection between the Franciscan movement, and the new "realism", the new interest in portraying the particular people around one in religious painting, which we see beginning with Giotto. In the centuries which follow, Renaissance Italian and later Netherlands painting moves out of the orbit of the icon, which tends to portray Christ, Mary, and the Saints as almost archetypical figures, lodged in higher time, and paint them as human beings very much present in our time, as people whom we might meet in our own world.

This is often presented by critics as itself a kind of secularization, a shift of interest towards the things of this world for their own sake. There must have been some of this, if we think for instance of the portraiture of powerful princes. But it is a mistake, I believe, to see much of the religious painting in this light. On the contrary, it should rather be seen as part of the attempt to bring faith closer to everyday life. It bespeaks rather a strong Incarnational spirituality, an attempt to see/imagine Jesus and Mary as having really been among us, hallowing the ordinary contexts of life, in which we also live.

So the realism, tenderness, physicality, particularity of much of this painting (see the "Northern Renaissance" expo), instead of being read as a turning away from transcendence, should be grasped in a devotional context, as a powerful affirmation of the Incarnation, an attempt to live it more fully by bringing it completely into our world.

In this painting, transcendence and immanence are together. But it is in the nature of things that as the interest in immanence grows, frequently for its own sake, a tension should arise. The connection is in danger of being broken. There comes a felt need to portray the higher reality breaking through, as in Mannerism, and much Baroque painting. The figures strain beyond our condition, or some break in the painting allows us to see the irruption of higher time, as in the Tintoretto depiction of the Resurrection I mentioned above. Or the connection may be maintained through allegory.

How does this fit into our story? I think this focus on the here and now eventually contributed to the sorting out. I mentioned above how the discovery of perspective, and the interest in spatial relations, contributes to a sense of the coherence of space. The properly ordered scene, as witnessed from a certain spot, as though one were looking at it through a window, "una finestra aperta", made of "vetro tralucente", in Alberti's famous phrase,[87] presents a solid world, no longer broken through by figures who dwell in a higher time, which can't be related coherently to ours. The world as so represented comes more and more to be the world as lived, in which spirits, forces and higher times are less and less directly encountered. They become relatively experience-far objects of belief.

And so more than one vector in Western Christendom contributed to the cut between immanence and transcendence; not just the rage for order which was implicit in much of the more intense piety, and whose drive to disenchantment is clear; but also the need to make God more fully present in everyday life and all its contexts, which led people to invest these contexts with a new significance and solidity.

The irony is that just this, so much the fruit of devotion and faith, prepares the ground for an escape from faith, into a purely immanent world. Just how this happened is the subject of the following chapters.

3 The Great Disembedding

We have seen the development among important élites in Latin Christendom of a buffered identity, impervious to the enchanted cosmos. This both animated and was rendered firmer by disciplines of thought and conduct. These disciplines in turn aimed not only at the reform of personal conduct, but at reforming and remaking societies so as to render them more peaceful, more ordered, more industrious.

The newly remade society was to embody unequivocally the demands of the gospel in a stable and, as it was increasingly understood, a rational order. This had no place for the ambivalent complementarities of the older enchanted world: between worldly life and monastic renunciation, between proper order and its periodic suspension in carnival, between the acknowledged power of spirits and forces and their relegation by divine power. The new order was coherent, uncompromising, all of a piece. Disenchantment brought a new uniformity of purpose and principle.

The progressive imposition of this order meant the end of the unstable post-Axial equilibrium. The compromise between the individuated religion of devotion or obedience or rationally understood virtue, on one hand, and the collective often cosmos-related rituals of whole societies, on the other, was broken, and in favour of the former. Disenchantment, Reform, and personal religion went together. Just as the church was at its most perfect when each of its members adhered to it on their own individual responsibility—and in certain places, like Congregational Connecticut, this became an explicit requirement of membership—so society itself comes to be reconceived as made up of individuals. The Great Disembedding, as I propose to call it, implicit in the Axial revolution, reaches its logical conclusion.

This involved the growth and entrenchment of a new self-understanding of our social existence, one which gave an unprecedented primacy to the individual. This is the story whose broad lines I want to sketch here.

In talking of our self-understanding, I am particularly concerned with what I will call our "social imaginary", that is, the way that we collectively imagine, even pretheoretically, our social life in the contemporary Western world. I will expand on this notion later, and the roles it plays in our lives.

But first, I want to place the revolution in our imaginary of the last few centuries in the broader sweep of cultural-religious development, as this has generally come to be understood. The full scale of this millennial change comes clearer if we focus first on some features of the religious life of earlier, smaller-scale societies, in so far as we can trace this. There must have been a phase in which all humans lived in such small-scale societies, even though much of the life of this epoch can only be guessed at.

But if we focus on what I will call "early religion" (which covers partly what Robert Bellah, for instance, calls "archaic religion"),[1] we note how profoundly these forms of life "embed" the agent. And that in three crucial ways.

First, socially: in paleolithic, and even certain neolithic, tribal societies, religious life is inseparably linked with social life. Of course, there is a sense in which this is true which is not particular to early religion. This consists in the obvious fact that the very basic language, categories of the sacred, the forms of religious experience, modes of ritual action, etc. available to agents in these societies, is found in their socially established religious life. It is as though each such small-scale society has shaped, articulated, some common human capacity in its own original fashion. There have been diffusions and borrowings, but the differences of vocabulary, and the gamut of possibilities, remain extraordinarily various.

What this common human religious capacity is; whether ontically it is to be placed exhaustively within the psyches of human beings, or whether they must be seen as responding differently to some human-transcending spiritual reality, we can leave unresolved. Whether something like this is an inescapable dimension of human life, or whether humans can eventually quite put it behind them, we can also leave open (although obviously the present writer has strong hunches on both these issues). What stands out however, is first, the ubiquity of something like a relation to spirits, or forces, or powers, which are recognized as being in some sense higher, not the ordinary forces and animals of everyday; and second, how differently these forces and powers are conceived and related to. This is more than just a difference of "theory", or "belief"; it is reflected in a striking difference of capacities and experience; in the repertory of ways of living religion.

Thus among some peoples, agents fall into trance-like conditions which are understood as possession; among others (sometimes the same ones), powerful portentous dreams occur to certain people, among others, shamans feel themselves to have been transported to a higher world, with others again, surprising cures are effected in certain conditions; and so on. All of these are beyond the range of most people in our modern civilization, as each of them is beyond the range of other earlier peoples in whose life this capacity doesn't figure. Thus for some people, portentous dreams may be possible, but not possession; for others possession, but not certain kinds of cure, and so on.

Now this fact, that the religious language, capacities, modes of experience that are available to each of us come from the society in which we are born, remains true in a sense of all human beings. Even great innovative religious founders have to draw on a pre-existing vocabulary available in their society. This in the end shades into the obvious point about human language in general, that we all acquire it from the language-groups we grow up in, and can only transcend what we are given by leaning on it. But it is clear that we have moved into a world where spiritual vocabularies have more and more travelled, in which more than one is available to each person, where each vocabulary has already been influenced by many others; where, in short, the rather abrupt differences between the religious lives of people living far from each other are being eroded.

But what is crucially relevant to the Great Disembedding is a second way in which early religion was social, that the primary agency of important religious action: invoking, praying to, sacrificing to, or propitiating Gods or spirits; coming close to these powers, getting healing, protection from them, divining under their guidance, etc.—this primary agency was the social group as a whole, or some more specialized agency recognized as acting for the group. In early religion, we primarily relate to God as a society.

We see both aspects of this in, for example, ritual sacrifices among the Dinka, as they were described a half century ago by Godfrey Lienhardt. On one hand, the major agents of the sacrifice, the "masters of the fishing spear", are in a sense "functionaries", acting for the whole society; while on the other, the whole community becomes involved, repeating the invocations of the masters, until everyone's attention is focussed and concentrated on the single ritual action. It is at the climax "that those attending the ceremony are most palpably members of a single undifferentiated body". This participation often takes the form of possession by the Divinity being invoked.[2]

Nor is this just the way things happen to be in a certain community. This collective action is essential for the efficacy of the ritual. You can't mount a powerful invocation of the Divinities like this on your own in the Dinka world. This "importance of corporate action by a community of which the individual is really and traditionally a member is the reason for the fear which individual Dinka feel when they suffer misfortune away from home and kin."[3]

This kind of collective ritual action, where the principal agents are acting on behalf of a community, which also in its own way becomes involved in the action, seems to figure virtually everywhere in early religion, and continues in some ways up till our day. Certainly it goes on occupying an important place as long as people live in an enchanted world, as I remarked earlier in the discussion of disenchantment. The ceremony of "beating the bounds" of the agricultural village, for instance, involved the whole parish, and could only be effective as a collective act of this whole.[4]

This embedding in social ritual usually carries with it another feature. Just because the most important religious action was that of the collective, and because it often required that certain functionaries—priests, shamans, medicine men, diviners, chiefs, etc.—fill crucial roles in the action, the social order in which these roles were defined tended to be sacrosanct. This is, of course, the aspect of religious life which was most centrally identified and pilloried by the radical Enlightenment. The crime laid bare here was the entrenchment of forms of inequality, domination and exploitation through their identification with the untouchable, sacred structure of things. Hence the longing to see the day "when the last king had been strangled in the entrails of the last priest". But this identification is in fact very old, and goes back to a time when many of the later, more egregious and vicious forms of inequality had not yet been developed, before there were kings and hierarchies of priests.

Behind the issue of inequality and justice lies something deeper, which touches what we would call today the "identity" of the human beings in those earlier societies. Just because their most important actions were the doings of whole groups (tribe, clan, sub-tribe, lineage), articulated in a certain way (the actions were led by chiefs, shamans, masters of the fishing-spear), they couldn't conceive themselves as potentially disconnected from this social matrix. It would probably never even occur to them to try.

To get a sense of what this means, we can think of contexts that even for us can't easily be thought away. What would I be like if I had been born to different parents? As an abstract exercise, this question can be addressed (answer: like the people who were in fact born to those other parents). But if I try to get a grip on this, probing my own sense of identity, on the analogy with: what would I be like if I hadn't taken that job? married that woman? and the like, then my head begins to swim. I am getting too deep into the very formative horizon of my identity to be able to make sense of the question. For most people, something like this is also true of their gender.

The point I am trying to make here is that in earlier societies this inability to imagine the self outside of a particular context extended to membership of our society in its essential order. That this is no longer so with us, that many of these "what would it be like if I were . . .?" questions are not only conceivable but arise as burning practical issues (should I emigrate? should I convert to another religion/no religion?), is the measure of our disembedding. And another fruit of this is our ability to entertain the abstract question, even where we cannot make it imaginatively real.

What I'm calling social embeddedness is thus partly an identity thing. From the standpoint of the individual's sense of self, it means the inability to imagine oneself outside a certain matrix. But it also can be understood as a social reality; and here it refers to the way we together imagine our social existence, for instance, that our most important actions are those of the whole society, which must be structured in a certain way to carry them out. And we can see that it is growing up in a world where this kind of social imaginary reigns which sets the limits to our sense of self.

Embedding thus in society. But this also brings with it an embedding in the cosmos. For in early religion, the spirits and forces with whom we are dealing are in numerous ways intricated in the world. We saw some of these in the discussion earlier of the enchanted world of our medieval ancestors: for all that the God they worshipped transcended the world, they nevertheless also had to do with intra-cosmic spirits, and they dealt with causal powers which were embedded in things: relics, sacred places, and the like. In early religion, even the high gods are often identified with certain features of the world; and where the phenomenon which has come to be called "totemism" exists, we can even say that some feature of the world, an animal or plant species, for instance, is central to the identity of a group.[5] It may even be that a particular geographical terrain is essential to our religious life. Certain places are sacred. Or the layout of the land speaks to us of the original disposition of things in sacred time. We relate to the ancestors and to this higher time through this landscape.[6]

Besides this relation to society and the cosmos, there is a third form of embedding in existing reality which we can see in early religion. This is what makes the most striking contrast with what we tend to think of as the "higher" religions. What the people ask for when they invoke or placate divinities and powers is prosperity, health, long life, fertility; what they ask to be preserved from is disease, dearth, sterility, premature death. There is a certain understanding of human flourishing here which we can immediately understand, and which, however much we might want to add to it, seems to us quite "natural". What there isn't, and what seems central to the later "higher" religions, as I mentioned in Chapter 1, is the idea that we have to question radically this ordinary understanding, that we are called in some way to go beyond it.

This is not to say that human flourishing is the end sought by all things. The Divine may also have other purposes, some of which impact harmfully on us. There is a sense in which, for early religions, the Divine is always more than just well-disposed towards us; it may also be in some ways indifferent; or there may also be hostility, or jealousy, or anger, which we have to deflect. Although benevolence, in principle, may have the upper hand, this process may have to be helped along, by propitiation, or even by the action of "trickster" figures. But through all this, what remains true is that Divinity's benign purposes are defined in terms of ordinary human flourishing. Again, there may be capacities which some people can attain, which go way beyond the ordinary human ones, which say, prophets or shamans have. But these in the end subserve well-being as ordinarily understood.

By contrast, with Christianity or Buddhism, for instance, as we saw in the first chapter, there is a notion of our good which goes beyond human flourishing, which we may gain even while failing utterly on the scales of human flourishing, even *through* such a failing (like dying young on a cross); or which involves leaving the field of flourishing altogether (ending the cycle of rebirth). The paradox of Christianity, in relation to early religion, is that on one hand, it seems to assert the unconditional benevolence of God towards humans; there is none of the ambivalence of early Divinity in this respect; and yet it redefines our ends so as to take us beyond flourishing.

In this respect, early religion has something in common with modern exclusive humanism; and this has been felt, and expressed in the sympathy of many modern post-Enlightenment people for "paganism"; "pagan self-assertion", thought John Stuart Mill, was much superior to "Christian self-denial".[7] (This is related to, but not quite the same as the sympathy felt for "polytheism", which I want to discuss later.) What makes modern humanism unprecedented, of course, is the idea that this flourishing involves no relation to anything higher.

Now, as earlier mentions suggest, I have been speaking of "early religion" to contrast with what many people have called "post-Axial" religions.[8] The reference is to what Karl Jaspers called the "Axial Age",[9] the extraordinary period in the last millennium B.C.E., when various "higher" forms of religion appeared seemingly independently in different civilizations, marked by such founding figures as Confucius, Gautama, Socrates, the Hebrew prophets.

The surprising feature of the Axial religions, compared with what went before, what would in other words have made them hard to predict beforehand, is that they initiate a break in all three dimensions of embeddedness: social order, cosmos, human good. Not in all cases and all at once: perhaps in some ways Buddhism is the most far-reaching, because it radically undercuts the second dimension: the order of the world itself is called into question, because the wheel of rebirth means suffering. In Christianity, there is something analogous: our world is disordered and must be made anew. But some post-Axial outlooks keep the sense of relation to an ordered cosmos, as we see in very different ways with Confucius and Plato; however, they mark a distinction between this and the actual, highly imperfect social order, so that the close link to the cosmos through collective religious life is made problematic.

The portrait of the early triple embeddedness is well drawn by Francis Oakley, in his discussion of the history of monarchy:

> Kingship . . . emerged from an "archaic" mentality that appears to have been thoroughly monistic, to have perceived no impermeable barrier between the

human and divine, to have intuited the divine as immanent in the cyclic rhythms of the natural world and civil society as somehow enmeshed in these natural processes, and to have viewed its primary function, therefore, as a fundamentally religious one, involving the preservation of the cosmic order and the "harmonious integration" of human beings with the natural world.[10]

Human agents are embedded in society, society in the cosmos, and the cosmos incorporates the divine. What I've been describing as the Axial transformations breaks this chain at least at one point, if not more. Oakley argues that the break point which was particularly fateful for our development in the West was the rupture, as it were, at the top, the Jewish idea of (what we now call) creation ex nihilo, which took God quite out of the cosmos, and placed him above it. This meant that potentially God can become the source of demands that we break with "the way of the world"; that what Brague refers to as "the wisdom of the world" no longer constrains us.[11]

But perhaps the most fundamental novelty of all is the revisionary stance towards the human good in Axial religions. More or less radically, they all call into question the received, seemingly unquestionable understandings of human flourishing, and hence inevitably also the structures of society and the features of the cosmos through which this flourishing was supposedly achieved. The change was double, as I mentioned above. On one hand, the "transcendent" realm, the world of God, or gods, of spirits, or Heaven, however defined, which previously contained elements which were both favourable and unfavourable to the human good, becomes unambiguously affirmative of this good. But on the other hand, both the crucial terms here, both the transcendent and the human good are reconceived in the process.

We have already noted the changes in the first term. The transcendent may now be quite beyond or outside of the cosmos, as with the Creator God of Genesis, or the Nirvana of Buddhism. Or if it remains cosmic, it loses its original ambivalent character, and exhibits an order of unalloyed goodness, as with the "Heaven", guarantor of just rule in Chinese thought,[12] or the order of Ideas of Plato, whose key is the Good.

But the second term must perforce also change. The highest human goal can no longer just be to flourish, as it was before. Either a new goal is posited, of a salvation which takes us beyond what we usually understand as human flourishing. Or else Heaven, or the Good, lays the demand on us to imitate or embody its unambiguous goodness, and hence to alter the mundane order of things down here. This may, indeed usually does involve flourishing on a wider scale, but our own flourishing (as individual, family, clan or tribe) can no longer be our highest goal. And of course, this may be expressed by a redefinition of what "flourishing" consists in.

Seen from another angle, this means a change in our attitude to evil, as the destructive, harm-inflicting side of things. This is no longer just part of the order of things, to be accepted as such. Something has to be done about it. This may be conceived as an escape through self-transformation, or it may be seen as a struggle to contain or eliminate the bad, but in either case evil is not something just to be lived with as part of the inevitable balance of things. Of course, the very sense of the term "evil" also changes here, once it is no longer just the negative side of the cosmos, and comes to be branded as an imperfection.[13]

We might try to put the contrast in this way: unlike post-Axial religion, early religion involved an acceptance of the order of things, in the three dimensions I have been discussing. In a remarkable series of articles on Australian aboriginal religion, W. E. H. Stanner speaks of "the mood of assent" which is central to this spirituality. Aboriginals had not set up the "kind of quarrel with life" which springs from the various post-Axial religious initiatives.[14] The contrast is in some ways easy to miss, because aboriginal mythology, in relating the way in which the order of things came to be in the Dream Time—the original time out of time, which is also "everywhen"—contains a number of stories of catastrophe, brought on by trickery, deceit and violence, from which human life recouped and re-emerged, but in an impaired and divided fashion, so that there remains the intrinsic connection between life and suffering, and unity is inseparable from division. Now this may seem reminiscent of other stories of a Fall, including that related in Genesis I. But in contrast with what Christianity has made of this last, for the Aboriginals the imperative to "follow up" the Dreaming, to recover through ritual and insight their contact with the order of the original time, relates to this riven and impaired dispensation, in which good and evil are interwoven. There is no question of reparation of the original rift, or of a compensation, or making good of the original loss. More, ritual and the wisdom that goes with it can even bring them to accept the inexorable, and "celebrate joyously what could not be changed".[15] The original Catastrophe doesn't separate or alienate us from the sacred or Higher, as in the Genesis story; it rather contributes to shaping the sacred order we are trying to "follow up".

Now Axial religion didn't do away with early religious life. In many ways, features of this continued in modified form to define majority religious life for centuries. Modifications arose, of course, not just from the Axial formulations, but also from the growth of large-scale, more differentiated, often urban-centred societies, with more hierarchical organization and embryonic state structures. Indeed, it has been argued that these too, played a part in the process of disembedding, because the very existence of state power entails some attempt to control and shape religious life and the social structures it requires, and hence undercuts the sense of intangibility surrounding this life and these structures.[16] I think there is a lot to this thesis, and indeed, I invoke something like it later on, but for the moment I want to focus on the significance of the Axial changes.

These don't at once totally change the religious life of whole societies. But they do open new possibilities of disembedded religion: seeking a relation to the Divine or the Higher, which severely revises the going notions of flourishing, or even goes beyond them, and can be carried through by individuals on their own, and/or in new kinds of sociality, unlinked to the established sacred order. So monks, bhikhus, sanyassi, devotees of some avatar or God, strike out on their own; and from this springs unprecedented modes of sociality: initiation groups, sects of devotees, the sangha, monastic orders, and so on.

In all these cases, there is some kind of hiatus, difference, or even break in relation to the religious life of the whole larger society. This may itself be to some extent differentiated, with different strata or castes or classes, and a new religious outlook may lodge in one of them. But very often a new devotion may cut across all of these, particularly where there is a break in the third dimension, with a "higher" idea of the human good.

There is inevitably a tension here, but there often is also an attempt to secure the unity of the whole, to recover some sense of complementarity between the different religious forms. So that those who are fully dedicated to the "higher" forms, while on one hand they can be seen as a standing reproach to those who remain in the earlier forms, supplicating the Powers for human flourishing, nevertheless can also be seen as in a relationship of mutual help with them. The laity feed the monks, and by this they earn "merit", which can be understood as taking them a little farther along the "higher" road, but also serves to protect them against the dangers of life, and increases their health, prosperity, fertility.

So strong is the pull towards complementarity that even in those cases where a "higher" religion took over the whole society, as we see with Buddhism, Christianity, and Islam, and there is nothing supposedly left to contrast with, the difference between dedicated minorities of religious "virtuosi" (to use Max Weber's term), and the mass religion of the social sacred, still largely oriented to flourishing, survived or reconstituted itself, with the same combination of strain on one hand, and hierarchical complementarity on the other.

From our modern perspective, with 20/20 hindsight, it appears as though the Axial spiritualities were prevented from producing their full disembedding effect because they were so to speak hemmed in by the force of the majority religious life which remained firmly in the old mould. They did bring about a certain form of religious individualism, but this was what Louis Dumont called the charter for "l'individu hors du monde",[17] that is, it was the way of life of élite minorities, and it was in some ways marginal to, or in some tension with the "world", where this means not just the cosmos which is ordered in relation to the Higher or the Sacred, but also the society which is ordered in relation to both cosmos and sacred. This "world" was still a matrix of embeddedness, and it still provided the inescapable framework for social life, including that of the individuals who tried to turn their backs on it, insofar as they remained in some sense within its reach.[18]

What had yet to happen was for this matrix to be itself transformed, to be made over according to some of the principles of Axial spirituality, so that the "world" itself would come to be seen as constituted by individuals. This would be the charter for "l'individu dans le monde" in Dumont's terms, the agent who in his ordinary "worldly" life sees himself as primordially an individual, that is, the human agent of modernity.

But this project of transformation is the one I have been describing in the previous chapters, the attempt to make over society in a thoroughgoing way according to the demands of a Christian order, while purging it of its connection to an enchanted cosmos, and removing all vestiges of the old complementarities, between spiritual and temporal, between life devoted to God and life in the "world", between order and the chaos on which it draws.

This project was thoroughly disembedding just by virtue of its form or mode of operation: the disciplined remaking of behaviour and social forms through objectification and an instrumental stance. But its ends were also intrinsically concerned to disembed. This is clear with the drive to disenchantment, which destroys the second dimension of embeddedness; but we can also see it in the Christian context. In one way, Christianity here operates like any Axial spirituality; indeed, it operates in conjunction with another such, namely Stoicism. But there also were specifically Christian modes. The New Testament is full of calls to leave or relativize solidarities of family, clan, society, and be part of the Kingdom. We see this seriously reflected in the way of operating of certain Protestant churches, where one was not simply a member in virtue of birth, but where one had to join by answering a personal call. This in turn helped to give force to a conception of society as founded on covenant, and hence as ultimately constituted by the decision of free individuals.

This is a relatively obvious filiation. But my thesis is that the effect of the Christian, or Christian-Stoic, attempt to remake society in bringing about the modern "individual in the world" was much more pervasive, and multitracked. It helped to nudge first the moral, then the social imaginary in the direction of modern individualism. This becomes evident in the new conception of moral order which we see emerging in modern Natural Law theory, and which I mentioned in the previous chapter.[19] This was heavily indebted to Stoicism, and its originators were arguably the Netherlands neo-Stoics, Justus Lipsius and Hugo Grotius. But this was a Christianized Stoicism, and a modern one, in the sense that it gave a crucial place to a willed remaking of human society.

We could say that both the buffered identity and the project of Reform contributed to the disembedding. Embeddedness, as I said above, is both a matter of identity—the contextual limits to the imagination of the self—and of the social imaginary: the ways we are able to think or imagine the whole of society. But the new buffered identity, with its insistence on personal devotion and discipline, increased the distance, the disidentification, even the hostility to the older forms of collective ritual and belonging; while the drive to Reform came to envisage their abolition. Both in their sense of self, and in their project for society, the disciplined élites moved towards a conception of the social world as constituted by individuals.

There is a problem with this kind of broad gauge historical interpretation, which has already been recognized in the discussion of Weber's thesis about the development of the Protestant ethic and its relation to capitalism. This indeed, is close to what I am saying here; it is a kind of specification of the broader connection I am asserting here. Weber is obviously one of my sources.

Now people often object to Weber's thesis that they can't verify it in terms of clearly traceable correlations, say, between confessional allegiances and capitalist development. But it is in the nature of this kind of relation between spiritual outlook and economic and political performance that the influence may also be much more diffuse and indirect. If we really believed, following the most vulgar forms of Marxism, that all change can be explained by non-spiritual factors, say in terms of economic motives, so that spiritual changes were always dependent variables, this wouldn't matter. But in fact, the relationship is much more intimate and reciprocal. Certain moral self-understandings are embedded in certain practices, which can mean both that they are promoted by the spread of these practices, and that they shape the practices and help them get established. It is equally absurd to believe that the practices always come first, or to adopt the opposite views that "ideas" somehow drive history.

But this doesn't stop us over the long run from making sensible judgments about the relation of certain social forms and certain spiritual traditions. If Anglo-Saxon forms of capitalist entrepreneurship are much less connected to family relations than, say, Chinese forms, which seems undeniable,[20] has this really nothing to do with the difference between the Protestant conceptions of individual church membership versus the Confucian centrality of the family? This seems hard to credit, even if the micro-links can't all be traced.

Similarly, my thesis here tries to link the undoubted primacy of the individual in modern Western culture, which we shall shortly explore in the form of the modern conception of moral order, to the earlier radical attempts to transform society along the principles of Axial spirituality, tracing in other words, how our present self-understandings grew.

It might easily seem that we don't need to trace this kind of genealogy, because of the hold of subtraction stories. And these are strong, because individualism has come to seem to us just common sense. The mistake of moderns is to take this understanding of the individual so much for granted, that it is taken to be our first-off self-understanding "naturally". Just as, in modern epistemological thinking, a neutral description of things is thought to impinge first on us, and then "values" are "added"; so here, we seize ourselves first as individuals, then become aware of others, and of forms of sociality. This makes it easy to understand the emergence of modern individualism by a kind of subtraction story: the old horizons were eroded, burned away, and what emerges is the underlying sense of ourselves as individuals.

On the contrary, what we propose here is the idea that our first self-understanding was deeply embedded in society. Our essential identity was as father, son, etc., and member of this tribe. Only later did we come to conceive ourselves as free individuals first. This was not just a revolution in our neutral view of ourselves, but involved a profound change in our moral world, as is always the case with identity shifts.

This means that we have here too to distinguish between a formal and material mode of social embedding, corresponding to the first two facets I described above. On the first level, we are always socially embedded; we learn our identities in dialogue, by being inducted into a certain language. But on the level of content, what we may learn is to be an individual, to have our own opinions, to attain to our own relation to God, our own conversion experience.

So the great disembedding occurs as a revolution in our understanding of moral order. And it goes on being accompanied by ideas of moral order. To be an individual is not to be a Robinson Crusoe, but to be placed in a certain way among other humans. This is the reflection of the transcendental necessity of holism just mentioned.

This revolution disembeds us from the cosmic sacred; altogether, and not just partially and for certain people as in earlier post-Axial moves. It disembeds us from the social sacred; and posits a new relation to God, as designer. This new relation will in fact turn out to be dispensable, because the Design underlying the moral order can be seen as directed to ordinary human flourishing. This, the transcendent, aspect of the Axial revolution is partly rolled back, or can be, given a neat separation of this-worldly from other-worldly good. But only partly, because notions of flourishing remain under surveillance in our modern moral view: they have to fit with the demands of the moral order itself, of justice, equality, non-domination, if they are to escape condemnation. Our notions of flourishing can thus always be revised. This belongs to our post-Axial condition.

This final phase of the Great Disembedding was largely powered by Christianity. But it was also in a sense a "corruption" of it, in Ivan Illich's memorable phrase.[21] Powered by it, because the gospel also is a disembedding. I mentioned above the calls to break away from the established solidarities. But this demand is there even more strongly in a parable like the story of the Good Samaritan, as Illich explains. It is not said, but inescapably implied. If the Samaritan had followed the demands of sacred social boundaries, he would never have stopped to help the wounded Jew. It is plain that the Kingdom involves another kind of solidarity altogether, one which would bring us into a network of agape.

Here's where the corruption comes in: what we got was not a network of agape, but rather a disciplined society in which categorial relations have primacy, and therefore norms. But it nevertheless all started by the laudable attempt to fight back the demands of the "world", and then make it over. 'World' (cosmos) in the New Testament has on one hand a positive meaning, as in, e.g., "God so loved the world" (John 3.16), and on the other a negative one: judge not as the world judges, etc. This latter sense of 'world' can be understood as the present sacralized order of things, and its embedding in the cosmos.[22] In this sense, the church is rightly at odds with the world. It was this which Hildebrand clearly saw when he fought to keep episcopal appointments out of the invasive power field of dynastic drive and ambition in the Investiture Controversy.

It might have seemed obvious that one should build on this defensive victory with an attempt to change and purify the power field of the "world", make it more and more consonant with the demands of Christian spirituality. But this naturally didn't happen all at once. The changes were incremental, but the project was somehow continually re-ignited in more radical form, through the various Reformations, and down to the present age. The irony is that it somehow turned into something quite different; in another, rather different sense, the "world" won after all. Perhaps the contradiction lay in the very idea of a disciplined imposition of the Kingdom of God. The temptation of power was after all, too strong, as Dostoyevsky saw in the Legend of the Grand Inquisitor. Here lay the corruption.

Let us turn now to follow the way that the Great Disembedding came about in our modern social imaginary.

4 Modern Social Imaginaries

1. The Modern Moral Order[1]

I will start with the new vision of moral order, which I claim played a central role in the development of modern Western society. This was most clearly stated in the new theories of Natural Law which emerged in the seventeenth century, largely as a response to the domestic and international disorder wrought by the wars of religion. Grotius and Locke are the most important theorists of reference for our purposes here.

Grotius derives the normative order underlying political society from the nature of its constitutive members. Human beings are rational, sociable agents who are meant to collaborate in peace to their mutual benefit.

Starting from the seventeenth century, this idea has come more and more to dominate our political thinking, and the way we imagine our society. It starts off in Grotius' version as a theory of what political society is, that is, what it is in aid of, and how it comes to be. But any theory of this kind also offers inescapably an idea of moral order. It tells us something about how we ought to live together in society.

The picture of society is that of individuals who come together to form a political entity, against a certain pre-existing moral background, and with certain ends in view. The moral background is one of natural rights; these people already have certain moral obligations towards each other. The ends sought are certain common benefits, of which security is the most important.

The underlying idea of moral order stresses the rights and obligations which we have as individuals in regard to each other, even prior to or outside of the political bond. Political obligations are seen as an extension or application of these more fundamental moral ties. Political authority itself is legitimate only because it was consented to by individuals (the original contract), and this contract creates binding obligations in virtue of the pre-existing principle that promises ought to be kept.

In the light of what has later been made of this Contract theory, even later in the same century by Locke, it is astonishing to us how tame the moral-political conclusions are which Grotius draws from it. The grounding of political legitimacy in consent is not put forward in order to question the credentials of existing govern-ments. The aim of the exercise is rather to undercut the reasons for rebellion being all too irresponsibly urged by confessional zealots; the assumption being that exist-ing legitimate régimes were ultimately founded on some consent of this kind. Grotius also seeks to give a firm foundation, beyond confessional cavil, to the basic rules of war and peace. In the context of the early seventeenth century, with its con-tinuing bitterly fought wars of religion, this emphasis was entirely understandable.

It is Locke who first uses this theory as a justification of "revolution", and as a ground for limited government. Rights can now be seriously pleaded against power. Consent is not just an original agreement to set up government, but a continuing right to agree to taxation.

In the next three centuries, from Locke to our day, although the contract lan-guage may fall away, and be used only by a minority of theorists, the underlying idea of society as existing for the (mutual) benefit of individuals, and the defense of their rights, takes on more and more importance. That is, it both comes to be the dominant view, pushing older theories of society, or newer rivals, to the margins of political life and discourse; and it also generates more and more far-reaching claims on political life. The requirement of original consent, via the halfway house of Locke's consent to taxation, becomes the full-fledged doctrine of popular sover-eignty under which we now live. The theory of natural rights ends up spawning a dense web of limits to legislative and executive action, via the entrenched charters which have become an important feature of contemporary government. The pre-sumption of equality, implicit in the starting point of the State of Nature, where people stand outside of all relations of superiority and inferiority,[2] has been applied in more and more contexts, ending with the multiple equal treatment or non-dis-crimination provisions, which are an integral part of most entrenched charters.

In other words, during these last four centuries, the idea of moral order implicit in this view of society has undergone a double expansion: in extension, on one hand (more people live by it, it has become dominant), and in intensity, on the other (the demands it makes are heavier and more ramified). The idea has gone, as it were, through a series of "redactions", each richer and more demanding than the previous one, up to the present day.

This double expansion can be traced in a number of ways. The modern discourse of natural law started off in a rather specialized niche. It provided philosophers and legal theorists a language in which to talk about the legitimacy of governments, and the rules of war and peace, the nascent doctrines of modern international law. But then it begins to infiltrate and transform the discourse in other niches. One such case, which plays a crucial role in the story I'm telling, is the way that the new idea of moral order begins to inflect and reformulate the descriptions of God's providence, and the order he has established between humans and in the cosmos. I'll return to this below.

Even more important to our lives today is the manner in which this idea of order has become more and more central to our notions of society and polity, remaking them in the process. And in the course of this expansion, it has moved from being a theory, animating the discourse of a few experts, and become integral to our social imaginary, that is, the way in which our contemporaries imagine the societies they inhabit and sustain. I want to describe this process in more detail later.

Migrating from one niche to many, and from theory to social imaginary, the expansion is also visible along a third axis, as defined by the kind of demands this moral order makes on us.

Sometimes a conception of moral order may not carry with it a real expectation of its integral fulfillment. This does not mean no expectation at all, for otherwise it wouldn't be an idea of moral order, in the sense I'm using the term here. It will be seen as something to strive for, and it will be realized by some, but the general sense may be that only a minority will really succeed in following it, at least under present conditions.

Thus the Gospel generates the idea of a community of saints, inspired by love for God, for each other, and for humankind, whose members were devoid of rivalry, mutual resentment, love of gain, ambition to rule, and the like. The general expectation in the Middle Ages was that only a minority of saints really aspired to this, and that they had to live in a world which heavily deviated from this ideal. But in the fullness of time, this would be the order of those gathered around God in the final dispensation. We can speak of a moral order here, and not just a gratuitous ideal, because it is thought to be in the process of full realization, but the time for this is not yet.

A distant analogy in another context would be some modern definitions of Utopia, which refer us to a way of things which may be realized in some eventually possible conditions; but which meanwhile serves as a standard to steer by.

Rather different from this are the orders which demand a more or less full realization here and now. But this can be understood in two rather different ways. In one, the order is held to be realized; it underlies the normal way of things. Mediaeval conceptions of political order were often of this kind. In the understanding of the "King's Two Bodies", his individual biological existence realizes and instantiates an undying royal "body". In the absence of highly exceptional and scandalously disordered circumstances, on the occasion of some terrible usurpation, for instance, the order is fully realized. It offers us not so much a prescription, as a key to understanding reality, rather as the Chain of Being does in relation to the cosmos which surrounds us. It provides us the hermeneutic clue to understanding the real.

But a moral order can stand in another relation to reality, as one not yet realized, but demanding to be integrally carried out. It provides an imperative prescription.

Summing up these distinctions, we can say that an idea of moral or political order can either be ultimate, like the community of saints, or for the here-and-now; and if the latter, it can either be hermeneutic or prescriptive.

Now the modern idea of order, in contradistinction to the mediaeval Christian ideal, was seen from the beginning as for the here-and-now. But it definitely migrates along a path, running from the more hermeneutic to the more prescriptive. As used in its original niche by thinkers like Grotius and Pufendorf, it offered an interpretation of what must underlie established governments; grounded on a supposed founding contract, these enjoyed unquestioned legitimacy. Natural Law theory at its origin was a hermeneutic of legitimation.

But already with Locke, the political theory can justify revolution, indeed, make this morally imperative in certain circumstances; while at the same time, other general features of the human moral predicament provide a hermeneutic of legitimacy in relation to, for instance, property. Later on down the line, this notion of order will be woven into "redactions" demanding even more "revolutionary" changes, including in relations of property, as reflected in influential theories, such as those of Rousseau and Marx, for instance.

Thus while moving from one niche to many, and migrating from theory into social imaginary, the modern idea of order also travels on a third axis, and the discourses it generates are strung out along the path from the hermeneutic to the prescriptive. In the process it comes to be intricated with a wide range of ethical concepts, but the resulting amalgams have in common that they make essential use of this understanding of political and moral order which descends from modern Natural Law theory.

This three-axis expansion is certainly remarkable. It cries out for explanation. It is unfortunately not part of my rather narrowly focussed intentions to offer a causal explanation of the rise of the modern social imaginary. I will be happy if I can clarify somewhat the forms it has taken. But this will by its very nature help to focus more sharply the issues of causal explanation, on which I will offer some random thoughts somewhat later. For the moment, however, I want to explore further the peculiar features of this modern order.

A crucial point which ought to be evident from the foregoing is that the notion of moral order I am using here goes beyond some proposed schedule of norms which ought to govern our mutual relations and/or political life. What an understanding of moral order adds to an awareness and acceptance of norms is an identification of features of the world, or divine action, or human life which make certain norms both right and (up to the point indicated) realizable. In other words the image of order not only carries a definition of what is right, but of the context in which it makes sense to strive for, and hope to realize the right (at least partially).

Now it is clear that the images of moral order which descend through a series of transformations from that inscribed in the Natural Law theories of Grotius and Locke are rather different from those embedded in the social imaginary of the premodern age.

Two important types of pre-modern moral order are worth singling out here, because we can see them being gradually taken over, displaced or marginalized by the Grotian-Lockean strand during the transition to political modernity. One is based on the idea of the Law of a people, which has governed this people since time out of mind, and which in a sense defines it as a people. This idea seems to have been widespread among the Indo-European tribes who at various stages erupted into Europe. It was very powerful in seventeenth-century England, under the guise of the Ancient Constitution, and became one of the key justifying ideas of the rebellion against the King.[3]

This case should be enough to show that these notions are not always conservative in import; but we should also include in this category the sense of normative order which seems to have been carried on through generations in peasant communities, and out of which they developed a picture of the "moral economy", from which they could criticize the burdens laid on them by landlords, or the exactions levied on them by state and church.[4] Here again, the recurring idea seems to have been that an original acceptable distribution of burdens had been displaced by usurpation, and ought to be rolled back.

The other type is organized around a notion of a hierarchy in society which expresses and corresponds to a hierarchy in the cosmos. These were often theorized in language drawn from the Platonic-Aristotelian concept of Form, but the underlying notion also emerges strongly in theories of correspondence: e.g., the king is in his kingdom, as the lion among animals, the eagle among birds, etc. It is out of this outlook that the idea emerges that disorders in the human realm will resonate in nature, because the very order of things is threatened. The night on which Duncan was murdered was disturbed by "lamenting heard i' the air; strange screams of death", and it remained dark even though day should have started. On the previous Tuesday a falcon had been killed by a mousing owl; and Duncan's horses turned wild in the night, "Contending 'gainst obedience, as they would / Make war with mankind".[5]

In both these cases, and particularly in the second, we have an order which tends to impose itself by the course of things; violations are met with backlash which transcends the merely human realm. This seems to be a very common feature in pre-modern ideas of moral order. Anaximander likens any deviation from the course of nature to injustice, and says that things which resist it must eventually "pay penalty and retribution to each other for their injustice according to the assessment of time."[6] Heraclitus speaks of the order of things in similar terms, when he says that if ever the sun should deviate from its appointed course, the Furies would seize it and drag it back.[7] And of course, the Platonic forms are active in shaping the things and events in the world of change.

In these cases, it is very clear that a moral order is more than just a set of norms; that it also contains what we might call an "ontic" component, identifying features of the world which make the norms realizable. Now, as I argued above in Chapter 2, the modern order which descends from Grotius and Locke is not self-realizing in the sense invoked by Hesiod or Plato, or the cosmic reactions to Duncan's murder. It is therefore tempting to think that our modern notions of moral order lack altogether an ontic component. But this would be a mistake, as I hope to show later. There is an important difference, but it lies in the fact that this component is now a feature about us humans, rather than one touching God or the cosmos, and not in the supposed absence altogether of an ontic dimension.

Now what is peculiar to our modern understanding of order stands out most clearly if we focus on how the idealizations of Natural Law theory differ from those which were dominant before. Pre-modern social imaginaries, especially those of the second type mentioned above, were structured by various modes of hierarchical complementarity. Society was seen as made up of different orders. These needed and complemented each other. But this didn't mean that their relations were truly mutual, because they didn't exist on the same level. They formed rather a hierarchy in which some had greater dignity and value than the others. An example is the often repeated mediaeval idealization of the society of three orders, oratores, bellatores, laboratores: those who pray, those who fight, and those who work. It was clear that each needed the others, but there was no doubt that we have here a descending scale of dignity; some functions were in their essence higher than others.

Now it is crucial to this kind of ideal that the distribution of functions is itself a key part of the normative order. It is not just that each order ought to perform its characteristic function for the others, granted they have entered these relations of exchange, while we keep the possibility open that things might be arranged rather differently, e.g., in a world where everyone does some praying, some fighting and some working. No, the hierarchical differentiation itself is seen as the proper order of things. It was part of the nature, or form of society. In the Platonic and neo-Platonic traditions, as I have just mentioned, this form was already at work in the world, and any attempt to deviate from it turned reality against itself. Society would be denatured in the attempt. Hence the tremendous power of the organic metaphor in these earlier theories. The organism seems the paradigm locus of forms at work, striving to heal its wounds and cure its maladies. And at the same time, the arrangement of functions which it exhibits is not simply contingent; it is "normal" and right. That the feet are below the head is how it should be.

The modern idealization of order departs radically from this. It is not just that there is no place for a Platonic-type form at work; but connected to this, whatever distribution of functions a society might develop is deemed contingent; it will be justified or not instrumentally; it cannot itself define the good. The basic normative principle is, indeed, that the members of society serve each other's needs, help each other, in short, behave like the rational and sociable creatures that they are. In this way, they complement each other. But the particular functional differentiation which they need to take on to do this most effectively is endowed with no essential worth. It is adventitious, and potentially changeable. In some cases, it may be merely temporary, as with the principle of the ancient polis, that we may be rulers and ruled in turn. In other cases, it requires lifetime specialization, but there is no inherent value in this, and all callings are equal in the sight of God. In one way or the other, the modern order gives no ontological status to hierarchy, or any particular structure of differentiation.

In other words, the basic point of the new normative order was the mutual respect and mutual service of the individuals who make up society. The actual structures were meant to serve these ends, and were judged instrumentally in this light. The difference might be obscured by the fact that the older orders also ensured a kind of mutual service; the clergy prays for the laity, and the laity defend/work for the clergy. But the crucial point is just this division into types in their hierarchical ordering; whereas on the new understanding we start with individuals and their debt of mutual service, and the divisions fall out as they can most effectively discharge this debt.

Thus Plato, in Book II of the *Republic,* starts out by reasoning from the non-self-sufficiency of the individual to the need for an order of mutual service. But quite rapidly it becomes clear that it is the structure of this order which is the basic point. And the last doubt is removed when we see that this order is meant to stand in analogy and interaction with the normative order in the soul. By contrast, in the modern ideal, the whole point is the mutual respect and service, however achieved.

I have mentioned two differences which distinguish this ideal from the earlier, Platonic-modelled orders of hierarchical complementarity: the Form is no longer at work in reality, and the distribution of functions is not itself normative. A third difference goes along with this. For the Platonic-derived theories, the mutual service which the classes render to each other when they stand in the right relation includes bringing them to the condition of their highest virtue; indeed, this is the service which the whole order, as it were, renders to all its members. But in the modern ideal, the mutual respect and service is directed towards serving our ordinary goals, life, liberty, sustenance of self and family. The organization of society, I said above, is judged not on its inherent form, but instrumentally. But now we can add that what this organization is instrumental to concerns the very basic conditions of existence as free agents, rather than the excellence of virtue—although we may judge that we need a high degree of virtue to play our proper part in this.

Our primary service to each other was thus (to use the language of a later age) the provision of collective security, to render our lives and property safe under law. But we also serve each other in practising economic exchange. These two main ends, security and prosperity, are now the principal goals of organized society, which itself can come to be seen as something in the nature of a profitable exchange between its constituent members. The ideal social order is one in which our purposes mesh, and each in furthering himself helps the others.

This ideal order was not thought to be a mere human invention. Rather it was designed by God, an order in which everything coheres according to God's purposes. Later in the eighteenth century, the same model is projected on the cosmos, in a vision of the universe as a set of perfectly interlocking parts, in which the purposes of each kind of creature mesh with those of all the others.

This order sets the goal for our constructive activity, insofar as it lies within our power to upset it, or realize it. Of course, when we look at the whole, we see how much the order is already realized; but when we cast our eye on human affairs, we see how much we have deviated from it and upset it; it becomes the norm to which we should strive to return.

This order was thought to be evident in the nature of things. Of course, if we consult revelation, we will also find the demand formulated there that we abide by it. But reason alone can tell us God's purposes. Living things, including ourselves, strive to preserve themselves. This is God's doing.

> God having made Man, and planted in him, as in all other Animals, a strong desire of Self-preservation, and furnished the World with things fit for Food and Rayment and other Necessaries of Life, Subservient to his design, that Man should live and abide for some time upon the Face of the Earth, and not that so curious and wonderful a piece of Workmanship by its own Negligence, or want of Necessities, should perish again . . .: God . . . spoke to him, (that is) directed him by his Senses and Reason, . . . to the use of those things which were serviceable for his Subsistence, and given him as the means of his Preservation. . . . For the desire, strong desire of Preserving his Life and Being having been planted in him, as a Principle of Action by God himself, Reason, which

was the voice of God in him, could not but teach him and assure him, that pursuing that natural Inclination he had to preserve his Being, he followed the Will of his Maker.[8]

Being endowed with reason, we see that not only our lives but that of all humans are to be preserved. And in addition, God made us sociable beings. So that "every one as he is bound to preserve himself, and not quit his Station wilfully; so by the like reason when his Preservation comes not in competition, ought he, as much as he can, to preserve the rest of Mankind."[9]

Similarly Locke reasons that God gave us our powers of reason and discipline so that we could most effectively go about the business of preserving ourselves. It follows that we ought to be "Industrious and Rational".[10] The ethic of discipline and improvement is itself a requirement of the natural order that God had designed. The imposition of order by human will is itself called for by his scheme.

We can see in Locke's formulation how much he sees mutual service in terms of profitable exchange. "Economic" (that is, ordered, peaceful, productive) activity has become the model for human behaviour, and the key for harmonious co-existence. In contrast to the theories of hierarchical complementarity, we meet in a zone of concord and mutual service, not to the extent that we transcend our ordinary goals and purposes, but on the contrary, in the process of carrying them out according to God's design.

Now this idealization was at the outset profoundly out of synch with the way things in fact ran, thus with the effective social imaginary on just about every level of society. Hierarchical complementarity was the principle on which people's lives effectively operated, all the way from the kingdom, to the city, to the diocese, to the parish, to the clan and the family. We still have some lively sense of this disparity in the case of the family, because it is really only in our time that the older images of hierarchical complementarity between men and women are being comprehensively challenged. But this is a late stage on a "long march", a process in which the modern idealization, advancing along the three axes I mentioned above, has connected up with and transformed our social imaginary on virtually every level, with revolutionary consequences.

The very revolutionary nature of the consequences ensured that those who first took up this theory would fail to see its application in a host of areas which seem obvious to us today. The powerful hold of hierarchically complementary forms of life, in the family, between master and servant in the household, between lord and peasant on the domain, between educated élite and the masses, made it seem "evident" that the new principle of order ought to be applied within certain bounds.

This was often not even perceived as a restriction. What seems to us flagrant inconsistency, when eighteenth-century Whigs defended their oligarchic power in the name of the "people", for instance, was for the Whig leaders themselves just common sense.

In fact, they were drawing on an older understanding of "people", one stemming from a pre-modern notion of order, of the first type I mentioned above, where a people is constituted as such by a Law which always already exists, "since time out of mind". This law can confer leadership on some elements, who thus quite naturally speak for the "people". Even revolutions (or what we consider such) in early modern Europe were carried out under this understanding—as for instance, the monarchomachs in the French Wars of Religion, who accorded the right to rebel not to the unorganized masses, but to the "subordinate magistrates". This was also the basis of Parliament's rebellion against Charles I.

And this long march is perhaps only ending today. Or perhaps we too are victims of a mental restriction, for which our posterity will accuse us of inconsistency or hypocrisy. In any case, some very important tracts of this journey happened very recently. I have mentioned contemporary gender relations in this regard. But we should also remember that it wasn't very long ago when whole segments of our supposedly modern society remained outside of this modern social imaginary. Eugen Weber has shown[11] how many communities of French peasants were transformed only late in the last century, and inducted into France as a nation of 40 million individual citizens. He makes plain how much their previous mode of life depended on complementary modes of action which were far from equal; especially, but not only between the sexes: there was also the fate of younger siblings, who renounced their share of the inheritance, in order to keep the family property together and viable. In a world of indigence and insecurity, of perpetually threatening dearth, the rules of family and community seemed the only guarantee of survival. Modern modes of individualism seemed a luxury, a dangerous indulgence.

This is easy to forget, because once we are well installed in the modern social imaginary, it seems the only possible one, the only one which makes sense. After all, are we not all individuals? Do we not associate in society for our mutual benefit? How else to measure social life?

This makes it very easy for us to entertain a quite distorted view of the process; and this in two respects. First, we tend to read the march of this new principle of order, and its displacing of traditional modes of complementarity, as the rise of "individualism" at the expense of "community". Whereas the new understanding of the individual has as its inevitable flip side a new understanding of sociality, the society of mutual benefit, whose functional differentiations are ultimately contingent, and whose members are fundamentally equal. This is what I have been insisting on in these pages, just because it generally gets lost from view. The individual seems primary, because we read the displacement of older forms of complementarity as the erosion of community as such. We seem to be left with a standing problem of how to induce or force the individual into some kind of social order, make him conform and obey the rules.

This recurrent experience of breakdown is real enough. But it shouldn't mask from us the fact that modernity is also the rise of new principles of sociality. Breakdown occurs, as we can see with the case of the French Revolution, because people are often expelled from their old forms, through war, revolution, or rapid economic change, before they can find their feet in the new structures, that is, connect some transformed practices to the new principles to form a viable social imaginary. But this doesn't show that modern individualism is by its very essence a solvent of community. Nor that the modern political predicament is that defined by Hobbes: how do we rescue atomic individuals from the prisoners' dilemma? The real, recurring problem has been better defined by Tocqueville, or in our day François Furet.

The second distortion is the familiar one. The modern principle seems to us so self-evident: are we not by nature and essence individuals? that we are tempted by a "subtraction" account of the rise of modernity. We just needed to liberate ourselves from the old horizons, and then the mutual service conception of order was the obvious alternative left. It needed no inventive insight, or constructive effort. Individualism and mutual benefit are the evident residual ideas which remain after you have sloughed off the older religions and metaphysics.

But the reverse is the case. Humans have lived for most of their history in modes of complementarity, mixed with a greater or lesser degree of hierarchy. There have been islands of equality, like that of the citizens of the polis, but they are set in a sea of hierarchy, once you replace them in the bigger picture. Not to speak of how alien these societies were to modern individualism. What is rather surprising is that it was possible to win through to modern individualism; not just on the level of theory, but also transforming and penetrating the social imaginary. Now that this imaginary has become linked with societies of unprecedented power in human history, it seems impossible and mad to try to resist. But we mustn't fall into the anachronism of thinking that this was always the case.

The best antidote to this error is to bring to mind again some of the phases of the long, and often conflictual, march by which this theory has ended up achieving such a hold on our imagination.

I will be doing some of this as my argument proceeds. But at this stage, I want to pull together the preceding discussion and outline the main features of this modern understanding of moral order.

This can be sketched in three points, to which I will then add a fourth:

(1) The original idealization of this order of mutual benefit comes in a theory of rights and of legitimate rule. It starts with individuals, and conceives society as established for their sake. Political society is seen as an instrument for something pre-political.

This individualism signifies a rejection of the previously dominant notion of hierarchy, according to which a human being can only be a proper moral agent embedded in a larger social whole, whose very nature is to exhibit a hierarchical complementarity. In its original form, the Grotian-Lockean theory stands against all those views, of which Aristotle's is the most prominent, which deny that one can be a fully competent human subject outside of society.

As this idea of order advances, and generates new "redactions", it becomes connected again with a philosophical anthropology which once again defines humans as social beings, incapable of functioning morally on their own. Rousseau, Hegel, Marx provide earlier examples, and they are followed by a host of thinkers in our day. But I see these still as redactions of the modern idea, because what they posit as a well-ordered society incorporates relations of mutual service between equal individuals as a crucial element. This is the goal, even for those who think that the "bourgeois individual" is a fiction, and that the goal can only be achieved in a communist society. Even connected to ethical concepts antithetical to those of the Natural Law theorists, and indeed, closer to the Aristotle they rejected, the kernel of the modern idea remains an idée-force in our world.

(2) As an instrument, political society enables these individuals to serve each other for mutual benefit; both in providing security, and in fostering exchange and prosperity. Any differentiations within it are to be justified by this telos; no hierarchical or other form is intrinsically good.

The significance of this, as we saw above, is that the mutual service centres on the needs of ordinary life, rather than aiming to secure for them the highest virtue. It aims to secure their conditions of existence as free agents. Now here, too, later redactions involve a revision. With Rousseau, for instance, freedom itself becomes the basis for a new definition of virtue, and an order of true mutual benefit becomes inseparable from one which secures the virtue of self-dependence. But Rousseau and those who followed him still put the central emphasis on securing freedom, equality and the needs of ordinary life.

(3) The theory starts with individuals, which political society must serve. More important, this service is defined in terms of the defense of individuals' rights. And freedom is central to these rights. The importance of freedom is attested in the requirement that political society be founded on the consent of those bound by it.

If we reflect on the context in which this theory was operative, we can see that the crucial emphasis on freedom was overdetermined. The order of mutual benefit is an ideal to be constructed. It serves as a guide for those who want to establish a stable peace, and then remake society to bring it closer to its norms. The proponents of the theory already see themselves as agents who through disengaged, disciplined action can reform their own lives, as well as the larger social order. They are buffered, disciplined selves. Free agency is central to their self-understanding. The emphasis on rights, and the primacy of freedom among them, doesn't just stem from the principle that society should exist for the sake of its members; it also reflects the holders' sense of their own agency, and of the situation which that agency normatively demands in the world, viz., freedom.

Thus the ethic at work here should be defined just as much in terms of this condition of agency, as in terms of the demands of the ideal order. We should best think of it as an ethic of freedom and mutual benefit. Both terms in this expression are essential. And that is why consent plays such an important role in the political theories which derive from this ethic.

Summing up, we can say that the order of mutual benefit holds (1) between individuals (or at least moral agents who are independent of larger hierarchical orders); the benefits (2) crucially include life and the means to life, however securing these relates to the practice of virtue; it is meant (3) to secure freedom, and easily finds expression in terms of rights. To these we can add a fourth point: (4) these rights, this freedom, this mutual benefit is to be secured to all participants equally. Exactly what is meant by equality will vary, but that it must be affirmed in some form follows from the rejection of hierarchical order. These are the crucial features, the constants that recur in the modern idea of moral order, through its varying "redactions".

2. What Is a "Social Imaginary"?

I have several times used the term 'social imaginary' in the preceding pages. Perhaps the time has come to make a little clearer what is involved.

What I'm trying to get at with this term is something much broader and deeper than the intellectual schemes people may entertain when they think about social reality in a disengaged mode. I am thinking rather of the ways in which they imagine their social existence, how they fit together with others, how things go on between them and their fellows, the expectations which are normally met, and the deeper normative notions and images which underlie these expectations.

I want to speak of "social imaginary" here, rather than social theory, because there are important differences between the two. There are, in fact, several differences. I speak of "imaginary" (i) because I'm talking about the way ordinary people "imagine" their social surroundings, and this is often not expressed in theoretical terms, it is carried in images, stories, legends, etc. But it is also the case that (ii) theory is often the possession of a small minority, whereas what is interesting in the social imaginary is that it is shared by large groups of people, if not the whole society. Which leads to a third difference: (iii) the social imaginary is that common understanding which makes possible common practices, and a widely shared sense of legitimacy.

Now it very often happens that what start off as theories held by a few people may come to infiltrate the social imaginary, first of élites perhaps, and then of the whole society. This is what has happened, grosso modo, to the theories of Grotius and Locke, although the transformations have been many along the way, and the ultimate forms are rather varied.

Our social imaginary at any given time is complex. It incorporates a sense of the normal expectations that we have of each other; the kind of common understanding which enables us to carry out the collective practices which make up our social life. This incorporates some sense of how we all fit together in carrying out the common practice. This understanding is both factual and "normative"; that is, we have a sense of how things usually go, but this is interwoven with an idea of how they ought to go, of what mis-steps would invalidate the practice. Take our practice of choosing governments through general elections. Part of the background understanding which makes sense of our act of voting for each one of us is our awareness of the whole action, involving all citizens, choosing each individually, but from among the same alternatives, and the compounding of these micro-choices into one binding, collective decision. Essential to our understanding what is involved in this kind of macro-decision is our ability to identify what would constitute a foul: certain kinds of influence, buying votes, threats, and the like. This kind of macro-decision has, in other words, to meet certain norms, if it is to be what it is meant to be. If a minority could force all others to conform to their orders, it would cease to be a democratic decision, for instance.

Now implicit in this understanding of the norms is the ability to recognize ideal cases, e.g., an election in which each citizen exercised to the maximum his/her judgment autonomously, in which everyone was heard, etc. And beyond the ideal stands some notion of a moral or metaphysical order, in the context of which the norms and ideals make sense.

What I'm calling the social imaginary extends beyond the immediate background understanding which makes sense of our particular practices. This is not an arbitrary extension of the concept, because just as the practice without the understanding wouldn't make sense for us, and thus wouldn't be possible, so this understanding supposes, if it is to make sense, a wider grasp of our whole predicament, how we stand to each other, how we got to where we are, how we relate to other groups, etc.

This wider grasp has no clear limits. That's the very nature of what contemporary philosophers have described as the "background".[12] It is in fact that largely unstructured and inarticulate understanding of our whole situation, within which particular features of our world show up for us in the sense they have. It can never be adequately expressed in the form of explicit doctrines, because of its very unlimited and indefinite nature. That is another reason for speaking here of an "imaginary", and not a theory.

The relation between practices and the background understanding behind them is therefore not one-sided. If the understanding makes the practice possible, it is also true that it is the practice which largely carries the understanding. At any given time, we can speak of the "repertory" of collective actions at the disposal of a given group of society. These are the common actions which they know how to undertake, all the way from the general election, involving the whole society, to knowing how to strike up a polite but uninvolved conversation with a casual group in the reception hall. The discriminations we have to make to carry these off, knowing whom to speak to and when and how, carry an implicit "map" of social space, of what kinds of people we can associate with in what ways in what circumstances. Perhaps I don't initiate the conversation at all, if the group are all socially superior to me, or outrank me in the bureaucracy, or consist entirely of women.

This implicit grasp of social space is unlike a theoretical description of this space, distinguishing different kinds of people, and the norms connected to them. The understanding implicit in practice stands to social theory the way that my ability to get around a familiar environment stands to a (literal) map of this area. I am very well able to orient myself without ever having adopted the standpoint of overview which the map offers me. And similarly, for most of human history, and for most of social life, we function through the grasp we have on the common repertory, without benefit of theoretical overview. Humans operated with a social imaginary, well before they ever got into the business of theorizing about themselves.[13]

Another example might help to make more palpable the width and depth of this implicit understanding. Let's say we organize a demonstration. This means that this act is already in our repertory. We know how to assemble, pick up banners, and march. We know that this is meant to remain within certain bounds, both spatially (don't invade certain spaces), and in the way it impinges on others (this side of a threshold of aggressivity—no violence). We understand the ritual.

The background understanding which makes this act possible for us is complex, but part of what makes sense of it is some picture of ourselves as speaking to others, to which we are related in a certain way—say, compatriots, or the human race.

There is a speech act here, addresser and addressees, and some understanding of how they can stand in this relation to each other. There are public spaces; we are already in some kind of conversation with each other. Like all speech acts, it is addressed to a previously spoken word, in the prospect of a to-be-spoken word.[14]

The mode of address says something about the footing we stand on with our addressees. The action is forceful; it is meant to impress, perhaps even to threaten certain consequences if our message is not heard. But it is also meant to persuade; it remains this side of violence. It figures the addressee as one who can be, must be reasoned with.

The immediate sense of what we're doing, getting the message to the government and our fellow citizens that the cuts must stop, say, makes sense in a wider context, in which we see ourselves as standing in a continuing relation with others, in which it is appropriate to address them in this manner, and not say, by humble supplication, or by threats of armed insurrection. We can gesture quickly at all this by saying that this kind of demonstration has its normal place in a stable, ordered, democratic society.

This does not mean that there are not cases where we might do this—Manila 1986, TienAnMen 1989—where armed insurrection would be perfectly justified. But precisely, the point of this act in those circumstances is to invite tyranny to open up to a democratic transition.

We can see here how the understanding of what we're doing right now (without which we couldn't be doing *this* action) makes the sense it does, because of our grasp on the wider predicament: how we continuingly stand, or have stood to others and to power. This in turn opens out wider perspectives on where we stand in space and time: our relation to other nations and peoples, e.g., to external models of democratic life we are trying to imitate, or of tyranny we are trying to distance ourselves from; and also of where we stand in our history, in the narrative of our becoming, whereby we recognize this capacity to demonstrate peacefully as an achievement of democracy, hard-won by our ancestors, or something we aspire to become capable of through this common action.

This sense of standing internationally and in history can be invoked in the iconography of the demonstration itself, as in TienAnMen 1989, with its references to the French Revolution, and its "citation" of the American case through the Statue of Liberty.

The background which makes sense of any given act is thus wide and deep. It doesn't include everything in our world, but the relevant sense-giving features can't be circumscribed; and because of this we can say that sense-giving draws on our whole world, that is, our sense of our whole predicament in time and space, among others and in history.

Now an important part of this wider background is what I called above a sense of moral order. I mean by this more than just a grasp on the norms underlying our social practice, which are part of the immediate understanding which makes this practice possible. There also must be a sense, as I stated above, of what makes these norms realizable. This too, is an essential part of the context of action. People don't demonstrate for the impossible, for the utopic[15]—or if they do, then this becomes ipso facto a rather different action. Part of what we're saying as we march on TienAnMen is that a (somewhat more) democratic society is possible for us, that we could bring it off, in spite of the skepticism of our gerontocratic rulers.

Just what this confidence is based on, for instance, that we as other human beings can sustain a democratic order together, that this is within our human possibilities, this will include the images of moral order through which we understand human life and history. It ought to be clear from the above that our images of moral order, although they make sense of some of our actions, are by no means necessarily tilted towards the status quo. They may also underlie revolutionary practice, as at Manila and Beijing, just as they may underwrite the established order.

Now what I want to do, in the following pages, is sketch the change-over, the process in which the modern theory of moral order gradually infiltrates and transforms our social imaginary. In this process, what is originally just an idealization grows into a complex imaginary through being taken up and associated with social practices, in part traditional ones, but often transformed by the contact. This is crucial to what I called above the extension of the understanding of moral order. It couldn't have become the dominant view in our culture without this penetration/transformation of our imaginary.

We see transitions of this kind happening, for instance, in the great founding revolutions of our contemporary world, the American and the French. The transition was much smoother and less catastrophic in one case, because the idealization of popular sovereignty connected up relatively unproblematically with an existing practice of popular election of assemblies; whereas in the other case, the inability to "translate" the same principle into a stable and agreed set of practices was an immense source of conflict and uncertainty for more than a century. But in both these great events, there was some awareness of the historical primacy of theory, which is central to the modern idea of a "revolution", whereby we set out to remake our political life according to agreed principles. This "constructivism" has become a central feature of modern political culture.

What exactly is involved, when a theory penetrates and transforms the social imaginary? Well for the most part, people take up, improvise, or are inducted into new practices. These are made sense of by the new outlook, the one first articulated in the theory; this outlook is the context that gives sense to the practices. And hence the new understanding comes to be accessible to the participants in a way it wasn't before. It begins to define the contours of their world, and can eventually come to count as the taken-for-granted shape of things, too obvious to mention.

But this process isn't just one-sided; a theory making over a social imaginary. The theory in coming to make sense of the action is "glossed", as it were, given a particular shape as the context of these practices. Rather like Kant's notion of an abstract category becoming "schematized" when it is applied to reality in space and time,[16] the theory is schematized in the dense sphere of common practice.

Nor need the process end here. The new practice, with the implicit understanding it generates, can be the basis for modifications of theory, which in turn can inflect practice, and so on.

What I'm calling the "long march" is a process whereby new practices, or modifications of old ones, either developed through improvisation among certain groups and strata of the population (e.g., the public sphere among educated élites in the eighteenth century, trade unions among workers in the nineteenth); or else were launched by élites in such a way as to recruit a larger and larger base (e.g., the Jacobin organization of the "sections" in Paris). Or alternatively, a set of practices in the course of their slow development and ramification gradually changed their meaning for people, and hence helped to constitute a new social imaginary (the "economy"). The result in all these cases was a profound transformation of the social imaginary in Western societies, and thus of the world in which we live.

3. The Economy as Objectified Reality

There are in fact three important forms of social self-understanding which I want to deal with in this essay. They are crucial to modernity, and each of them represents a penetration or transformation of the social imaginary by the Grotian-Lockean theory of moral order. They are respectively (1) the "economy", (2) the public sphere, and (3) the practices and outlooks of democratic self-rule.

I start with (1). This was obviously linked with the self-understanding of "polite" civilization as grounded in a commercial society. But we can find the roots of this understanding further back, in the Grotian-Lockean idea of order itself.

I mentioned above that this new notion of order brought about a change in the understanding of the cosmos as the work of God's Providence. We have here in fact one of the earliest examples of the new model of order moving beyond its original niche and reshaping the image of God's providential rule.

The notion that God governs the world according to a benign plan was ancient, even pre-Christian, with roots in Judaism, as well as Stoicism. What is new is the way of conceiving his benevolent scheme. We can see this in the arguments from the design of the world to the existence of a good Creator God. These too were very old. But formerly, they insisted on the magnificent design of the whole framework in which our world was set, the stars, the planets, etc.; and then on the admirable micro-design of creatures, including ourselves, with our organs fitted for their functions, as well as on the general way in which life was sustained by the processes of nature.

These certainly continue, but what is added in the eighteenth century is an appreciation of the way in which human life is designed so as to produce mutual benefit. Emphasis is sometimes laid on mutual benevolence. But very often the happy design is identified in the existence of what one might call "invisible hand" factors. I mean by this actions and attitudes which we are "programmed" for, which have systematically beneficent results for the general happiness, even though these are not part of what is intended in the action or affirmed in the attitude. Adam Smith in his *Wealth of Nations* has provided us with the most famous of these mechanisms, whereby our search for our own individual prosperity redounds to the general welfare. But there are other examples; for instance, one drawn from his *Theory of Moral Sentiments,* where Smith argues that Nature has made us admire greatly rank and fortune, because social order is much more secure if it rests on the respect for visible distinctions, rather than on the less striking qualities of virtue and wisdom.[17]

The order here is that of a good engineering design, in which efficient causation plays the crucial role. In this it differs from earlier notions of order, where the harmony comes from the consonance between the Ideas or Forms manifested in the different levels of being or ranks in society. The crucial thing in the new conception is that our purposes mesh, however divergent they may be in the conscious awareness of each of us. They involve us in an exchange of advantages. We admire and support the rich and well-born, and in return we enjoy the kind of stable order without which prosperity would be impossible. God's design is one of interlocking causes, not of harmonized meanings.

Otherwise put, humans are engaged in an exchange of services. The fundamental model seems to be what we have come to call an economy.

This new understanding of Providence is already evident in Locke's formulation of Natural Law theory in the *Second Treatise.* We can already see here how much importance the economic dimension is taking on in the new notion of order. There are two facets to this. The two main goals of organized society were security and economic prosperity. But because the whole theory emphasized a kind of profitable exchange, one could begin to see political society itself through a quasi-economic metaphor.

Thus no less a personage than Louis XIV, in the advice he offers to his dauphin, subscribes to something like an exchange view: "All these different conditions that compose the world are united to each other only by an exchange of reciprocal obligations. The deference and respect that we receive from our subjects are not a free gift from them but payment for the justice and protection they expect to receive from us".[18]

This, incidentally, offers some insight into (what turned out to be) an important transition stage on the "long march" of the order of mutual benefit into our social imaginary. This was a rival model of order based on command and hierarchy. What Louis and others of his time were offering could be seen as a kind of compromise between the new and the old. The basic justifying reasoning of the different functions, here ruler and subject, is new, viz., the necessary and fruitful exchange of services. But what is justified is still a hierarchical society, and above all, the most radical hierarchical relation, that of absolute monarch to subject. The justification is more and more in terms of functional necessity, but the master images still reflect something of inherent superiority, an ontological hierarchy. The king, by being above everyone else, can hold society together, and sustain everything. He is like the Sun, to use Louis' favourite image.[19]

We might call this the "baroque"[20] solution, except that its most spectacular example, at Versailles, saw itself in "classical" terms. It is this compromise which reigns for a while over most of Europe, sustaining régimes with much of the pomp, ritual and imagery of hierarchical complementarity, but on the basis of a justification drawn more and more from the modern order. Bossuet's defense of Louis' absolute rule falls in the same register.

But secondly, the economy could become more than a metaphor. It came to be seen more and more as the dominant end of society. Contemporary with Louis' memoir of advice, Montchrétien offers a theory of the state which sees it primarily as the orchestrating power which can make an economy flourish. (It is he, incidentally, who seems to have coined the term 'political economy'.) Merchants act for love of gain, but good policy by the ruler (here a very visible hand) can draw this towards the common good.[21]

This second shift reflects feature (2) of the modern order in my sketch above: the mutual benefit we are meant to confer on each other gives a crucial place to the securing of life and the means to life. This is not an isolated change within theories of Providence; it goes along with a major trend of the age.

This trend is often understood in terms of the standard "materialist" explanations, which I evoked in my discussion in Chapter 3; for instance, the old Marxist account that business classes, merchants, later manufacturers, were becoming more numerous, and gaining greater power. Even on its own level, this account needs to be supplemented with a reference to the changing demands of state power. It more and more dawned on governing élites that increased production, and favourable exchange, was a key condition of political and military power. The experience of Holland and England demonstrated that. And, of course, once some nations began to "develop" economically, their rivals were forced to follow suit, or to be relegated to dependent status. This, as much if not more than growing numbers and wealth, was responsible for the enhanced position of commercial classes.

These factors were important, but they cannot provide the whole explanation of the change for reasons which I intimated earlier. What started us on this path were changes on several levels, not only economic, but political and spiritual. In this I think Weber is right, even if not all the detail of his theory can be salvaged.

The original importance of people working steadily in a profession came from the fact that they thereby placed themselves in "settled courses", to use the Puritan expression mentioned above. If ordered life became a demand, not just for a military or spiritual/intellectual élite, but for the mass of ordinary people, then they had to become ordered and serious about what they were doing, and of necessity had to be doing, in life, viz., working in some productive occupation. A really ordered society requires that one take these economic occupations seriously, and prescribe a discipline for them. This was the "political" ground.

But in Reformed Christianity, and to a growing extent among Catholics as well, there was a pressing spiritual reason to make this demand, which was the one Weber picked up on. To put it in the Reformed variant, if we are going to reject the Catholic idea that there are some higher vocations, to the celibate or monastic life, following "counsels of perfection", if one claims that all Christians must be 100 percent Christian, that one can be so in any vocation, then one must claim that ordinary life, the life that the vast majority cannot help leading, the life of production and the family, work and sex, is as hallowed as any other. Indeed, more so than monastic celibacy, because this is based on the vain and prideful claim to have found a higher way.

This is the basis for that sanctification of ordinary life, which I want to claim has had a tremendous formative effect on our civilization, spilling beyond the original religious variant into a myriad secular forms. It has two facets: it promotes ordinary life, as a site for the highest forms of Christian life; and it also has an anti-élitist thrust: it takes down those allegedly higher modes of existence, whether in the Church (monastic vocations), or in the world (ancient-derived ethics which place contemplation higher than productive existence). The mighty are cast down from their seats, and the humble and meek are exalted.

Both these facets have been formative of modern civilization. The first is part of the background to the central place given to the economic in our lives, as also for the tremendous importance we put on family life, or "relationships". The second underlies the fundamental importance of equality in our social and political lives.[22]

All these factors, material and spiritual, help explain the gradual promotion of the economic to its central place, a promotion already clearly visible in the eighteenth century. And at that time, another factor enters; or perhaps it is simply an extension of the "political" one above. The notion becomes more and more accredited that commerce and economic activity is the path to peace and orderly existence. "Le doux commerce" is contrasted to the wild destructiveness of the aristocratic search for military glory. The more a society turns to commerce, the more "polished" and civilized it becomes, the more it excels in the arts of peace. The impetus to money-making is seen as a "calm passion". When it takes hold in a society, it can help to control and inhibit the violent passions. Or put in other language, money-making serves our "interest", and interest can check and control passion.[23] Kant even believed that as nations become republics, and hence more under the control of their ordinary tax-payers, actuated by economic interests, recourse to war will become rarer and rarer.

The new economically-centred notion of natural order underlies the doctrines of harmony of interest. It even came to be projected onto the universe, for it is this which is reflected in the eighteenth-century vision of cosmic order, not as a hierarchy of forms-at-work, but as a chain of beings whose purposes mesh with each other. Things cohere, because they serve each other in their survival and flourishing. They form an ideal economy.

> See dying vegetables life sustain,
> See life dissolving vegetate again:
> All forms that perish other forms supply,
> (By turns we catch the vital breath, and die)
> Like bubbles on the sea of Matter born,
> They rise, they break, and to that sea return.
> Nothing is foreign: Parts relate to whole;
> One all-extending, all preserving Soul
>
> Connects each being, greatest with the least;
> Made Beast in aid of Man, and Man of Beast;
> All served, all serving: nothing stands alone;
> The chain holds on, and where it ends, unknown.
> . . . . .
> God in nature of each being founds
> Its proper bliss, and sets its proper bounds;
> But as he framed a Whole, the Whole to bless,

> On mutual Wants built mutual Happiness:
> So from the first, eternal ORDER ran,
> And creature linked to creature, man to man.

From all this, Pope triumphantly concludes "that true SELF-LOVE and SOCIAL are the same."[24]

And so perhaps the first big shift wrought by this new idea of order, both in theory and in social imaginary, consists in our coming to see our society as an "economy", an interlocking set of activities of production, exchange and consumption, which form a system with its own laws and its own dynamic. Instead of being merely the management, by those in authority, of the resources we collectively need, in household or state, the "economic" now defines a way in which we are linked together, a sphere of coexistence which could in principle suffice to itself, if only disorder and conflict didn't threaten. Conceiving of the economy as a system is an achievement of eighteenth-century theory, with the Physiocrats and Adam Smith; but coming to see the most important purpose and agenda of society as economic collaboration and exchange is a drift in our social imaginary which begins in that period and continues to this day. From that point on, organized society is no longer equivalent to the polity; other dimensions of social existence are seen as having their own forms and integrity. The very shift in this period of the meaning of the term 'civil society' reflects this.

This is the first of the three forms of social imaginary I want to discuss. But before passing to the second, I want to bring out a general feature of our modern self-understanding which comes to light when we contrast the economy with the other two forms. Both of these—the public sphere and the self-ruling "people"—imagine us as collective agencies. And it is these new modes of collective agency which are among the most striking feature of Western modernity and beyond; we understand ourselves after all to be living in a democratic age.

But the account of economic life in terms of an invisible hand is quite different. There is no collective agent here, indeed, the account amounts to a denial of such. There are agents, individuals acting on their own behalf, but the global upshot happens behind their backs. It has a certain predictable form, because there are certain laws governing the way in which their myriad individual actions concatenate.

This is an objectifying account, one which treats social events like other processes in nature, following laws of a similar sort. But this objectifying take on social life is just as much part of the modern understanding, derived from the modern moral order, as the new modes of imagining social agency. The two belong together as part of the same package. Once one is dealing with an idea of social order no longer as Forms-at-work in reality, of the kind invoked by Plato, but as forms imposed on inert reality by human agency, we need pictures of the lay-out of this inert reality, and the causal connections which structure it, just as much as we need models of our collective action on it. The engineer needs to know the laws of the domain he is going to work on, just as much as he needs a plan of what he is trying to achieve; indeed, the second can't be drawn up unless the first is known.

And so this age also sees the beginnings of a new kind of objectifying social science, starting from William Petty's Survey in Ireland in the mid-seventeenth century, the collection of facts and statistics about wealth, production and demography, as the basis for policy. Objectifying pictures of social reality are just as prominent a feature of western modernity as the constitution of large-scale collective agencies.[25] The modern grasp of society is ineradicably bi-focal.

To understand better this change in the nature of science, we should see it from the other side of the divide. As long as society was understood in terms of something resembling a Platonic- or Aristotelian-type teleology, this kind of bi-focal take was not possible. In speaking of teleology, I don't want to invoke any heavy metaphysical doctrines, I am talking of a widespread understanding of society as having a "normal" order, which tended to maintain itself over time, but which could be threatened by certain developments, which taken beyond a certain point could precipitate a slide towards destruction, civil strife, or the utter loss of the proper form. We can see this as an understanding of society very analogous to our understanding ourselves as organisms, in terms of the key concepts of health and sickness.

Even Machiavelli still has an understanding of this kind when it comes to Republican forms. There is a certain equilibrium-in-tension which needs to be maintained between the "grandi" and the people, if these forms are to survive. In healthy polities, this equilibrium is maintained by the play or rivalry and mutual surveillance between the orders. But there are certain developments which threaten this, such as an excessive interest on the part of citizens in their private wealth and property. This constitutes "corruzione", and unless dealt with in time, and severely, will bring about the end of republican liberty. There is a causal attribution here: wealth undermines liberty; but the term used, with its strong normative resonances, shows that the understanding of society is being organized around a concept of normal form.

As long as social thought is organized in this way, the bi-focal take can't get a hold. Reality is not understood as inert, but as shaped by a normal form, which maintains itself within certain limits of distance from its proper shape, and beyond them spirals off to destruction, just as the healthy human body does. Successful collective action is seen as taking place within a field shaped by this form; indeed, this form is its condition; once we lose it, collective action disintegrates into the corrupt strivings of self-regarding individuals. There is neither inert reality, nor action ab extra imposing some shape on this reality.

One might think that the Smithian notion of an invisible hand defines a new "normal" order, one of mutual enrichment; and in some ways it can be treated as such, and is so invoked by various neo-liberal boosters of "the market" in our day. But it is not an order of collective action; for the "market" is the negation of collective action. It requires, to operate properly, a certain pattern of interventions (keeping order, enforcing contracts, setting weights and measures, etc.), and (tirelessly stressed) non-interventions (get the government off our backs). What is striking about the Smithian invisible hand, from the standpoint of the old science, is that it is a spontaneous order arising among *corrupt,* that is, purely self-regarding actors. It is not a finding which, like Machiavelli's link between wealth and corruption, pertains to the normative conditions of proper collective action.

In a science concerned with these, there is place neither for action unenframed by a normatively constituted reality, nor for a study of a normatively neutral, inert social field. Neither component of the modern bi-focal take can find a niche.

This shift in the nature of "science" is also connected to the change I noted a few paragraphs back. For moderns, organized society is no longer equivalent to the polity. Once we turn to discover the impersonal processes happening behind the backs of agents, there may well be other aspects of society which show some law-like systematicity. The invisible-hand-guided "economy" is one such aspect; but other facets of social life, or culture, or demography will later be singled out for scientific treatment. There will be more than one way in which the same body of systematically interacting human beings can be considered as forming an entity, a "society". We can speak of them as an "economy", or a "state", or a "civil society" (now identified in its non-political aspects), or just as a "society", or a "culture", and so on. 'Society' has been unhooked from 'polity', and now floats free, through a number of different applications.

A lot in this scientific revolution turns on the rejection of a mode of normative thinking in terms of *tele.* Now this rejection was also a central part of much of the moral thinking which emerges from the modern idea of order. This found expression in the anti-Aristotelian animus of Locke and those he influenced. Of course, the rejection of teleology was famously motivated by a stance supporting the new, mechanistic science. But it was also animated by the emerging moral theory. What distinguished the new, atomist, Natural Law theory from its predecessor as formulated by Aquinas, for instance, was its thoroughgoing detachment from the Aristotelian matrix which had been central for Thomas. The correct political forms were not deducible from a telos at work in human society. What justified the law was either its being commanded by God (Locke), or its making logical sense, given the rational and social nature of humans (Grotius), or (later) its providing a way of securing the harmony of interests.[26]

We have to note that the modern bi-focal take is not without its tensions. I mentioned earlier that freedom as a central good is over-determined in the modern moral order: it is both one of the central properties of the humans who consent to and thus constitute society; and it is inscribed in their condition as the artificers who build their own social world, as against being born into one which already has its own "normal" form. Indeed, one of the reasons for the vigorous rejection of Aristotelian teleology was that it was seen, then as now, as potentially circumscribing our freedom to determine our own lives and build our own societies.

But just for this reason, a battle could break out between the two takes. What for one school falls into the domain of an objective take on unavoidable reality, may seem to another to be a surrender of the human capacity to design our world before a false "positivity". The very importance given to freedom is bound to give rise to this kind of challenge. This sort of critique has been central to the work of Rousseau, and beyond him to Fichte, Hegel, Marx. We don't need to underline the importance that they have had in our civilization. The ambition to transform what is lived just "an sich" into something assumed "für sich", to use the Hegel-Marx terminology, is an ever-recurring one. We see this in the constant attempts to transform what are at first merely objective sociological categories, e.g., "handicapped" or "welfare recipients", into collective agencies through mobilizing movements.

But before these philosophers wrote, and influencing their work, was the civic humanist tradition, the ethic of republican self-rule. Here we come to a tension which has been inseparable from the modern moral order itself. Even while it has advanced and colonized our modern social imaginaries, it has awakened unease and suspicion. We saw above that its entrenchment was connected to the self-understanding of modern society as commercial; and that the transition to the commercial stage was understood as having effected the great internal pacification of modern states. This society dethroned war as the highest human activity, and put in its place production. It was hostile to the older codes of warrior honour, and it tended towards a certain levelling.

But all this could not but provoke resistance. This came not just from the orders which had a stake in the old way of things, the noblesse de l'épée; many people from all stations were ambivalent about it. With the coming of a commercial society, it seemed that greatness, heroism, full-hearted dedication to a non-utilitarian cause, were in danger of atrophy, even of disappearing from the world.

One form which this worry took was the concern about men, following the ethos of polite society, becoming "effeminate", losing their manly virtues, which was an important recurring theme in the eighteenth century. At the most primitive level, this could emerge in a rebellion of upper-class rowdies against the polite conventions of the age; at a slightly higher level perhaps, in the return of duelling in eighteenth-century England.[27] But at the highest level, it promoted the ethic of civic humanism as a rival to the ethos of commercial society; or perhaps as a compensation for the dangers, of enervation, corruption, loss of liberty, which this modern form brought with it. This was not a marginal concern; it occupied some of the most influential thinkers of the age, such as Adam Smith.[28]

These worries and tensions have remained a central part of modern culture. In one form, they could lead to a transformed "redaction" of the modern idea of order, in order to save civic virtue, or freedom, or non-alienated self-rule, as we find in the philosophies of Rousseau or Marx. Or else, they were indeed, seen as a potential threat of degeneracy inherent in the order, but by people who in no way wanted to reject this order, merely to find some prophylactic for its dangerous potentialities. Smith, and later Tocqueville, belong to this category.

But the concern about levelling, the end of heroism, of greatness, has also been turned into a fierce denunciation of the modern moral order, and everything it stands for, as we see with Nietzsche. Attempts to build a polity around a rival notion of order in the very heart of modern civilization, most notably the various forms of fascism and related authoritarianism, have failed. But the continued popularity of Nietzsche shows that his devastating critique still speaks to many people today. The modern order, though entrenched—perhaps even because entrenched—still awakens much resistance.

4. The Public Sphere

(2) The economic was perhaps the first dimension of "civil society" to achieve an identity independent from the polity. But it was followed shortly afterwards by the public sphere.

I want to describe the public sphere as a common space in which the members of society are deemed to meet through a variety of media: print, electronic, and also face-to-face encounters; to discuss matters of common interest; and thus to be able to form a common mind about these. I say "*a* common space", because although the media are multiple, as well as the exchanges which take place in them, these are deemed to be in principle intercommunicating. The discussion we're having on television now takes account of what was said in the newspaper this morning, which in turn reports on the radio debate yesterday, and so on. That's why we usually speak of the public sphere, in the singular.

The public sphere is a central feature of modern society. So much so, that even where it is in fact suppressed or manipulated it has to be faked. Modern despotic so-

cieties have generally felt compelled to go through the motions. Editorials appear in
the party newspapers, purporting to express the opinions of the writers, offered for
the consideration of their fellow citizens; mass demonstrations are organized, purporting to give vent to the felt indignation of large numbers of people. All this takes
place as though a genuine process were in train of forming a common mind
through exchange, even though the result is carefully controlled from the beginning.

In this discussion, I want to draw in particular on two very interesting books, one
published almost thirty years ago but recently translated into English, Jürgen
Habermas' *The Structural Transformation of the Public Sphere*,[29] which deals with the
development of public opinion in eighteenth-century Western Europe; the other a
very recent publication by Michael Warner, *The Letters of the Republic*,[30] which describes the analogous phenomenon in the British-American colonies.

A central theme of Habermas' book is the emergence in Western Europe in the
eighteenth century of a new concept of public opinion. Dispersed publications and
small group or local exchanges come to be construed as one big debate, from which
the "public opinion" of a whole society emerges. In other words, it is understood
that widely separated people sharing the same view have been linked in a kind of
space of discussion, wherein they have been able to exchange ideas together with
others and reach this common end-point.

What is this common space? It's a rather strange thing, when one comes to think
of it. The people involved here have by hypothesis never met. But they are seen as
linked in a common space of discussion through media—in the eighteenth century,
print media. Books, pamphlets, newspapers circulated among the educated public,
vehiculing theses, analyses, arguments, counter-arguments, referring to and refuting
each other. These were widely read, and often discussed in face-to-face gatherings,
in drawing rooms, coffee houses, salons, and/or in more (authoritatively) "public"
places, like Parliament. The sensed general view which resulted from all this, if any,
counted as "public opinion" in this new sense.

This space is a "public sphere", in the sense I'm using it here. Now in the previous
paragraph, I talked of a conclusion "counting as" public opinion. This reflects the
fact that a public sphere can only exist if it is imagined as such. Unless all the dispersed discussions are seen by their participants as linked in one great exchange,
there can be no sense of their upshot as "public opinion". This doesn't mean that
imagination is all-powerful here. There are objective conditions; internal: for instance, that the fragmentary local discussions inter-refer; external: there had to be
printed materials, circulating from a plurality of independent sources, for there to
be the bases of what could be seen as a common discussion. As is often said, the
modern public sphere relied on "print capitalism" to get going. But as Warner

shows, printing itself, and even print capitalism, didn't provide a sufficient condition. They had to be taken up in the right cultural context, where the essential common understandings could arise.[31] The public sphere was a mutation of the social imaginary, one crucial to the development of modern society. It was an important step on the long march.

We are now in a slightly better position to understand what kind of thing a public sphere is, and why it was new in the eighteenth century. It's a kind of common space, I have been saying, in which people who never meet understand themselves to be engaged in discussion, and capable of reaching a common mind. Let me introduce some new terminology. We can speak of "common space" when people come together in a common act of focus for whatever purpose, be it ritual, the enjoyment of a play, conversation, the celebration of a major event, or whatever. Their focus is common, as against merely convergent, because it is part of what is commonly understood that they are attending to the common object, or purpose, together, as against each person just happening, on his or her own, to be concerned with the same thing. In this sense, the "opinion of mankind" offers a merely convergent unity, while public opinion is supposedly generated out of a series of common actions.

Now an intuitively understandable kind of common space is set up when people are assembled for some purpose, be it on an intimate level for conversation, or on a larger, more "public" scale for a deliberative assembly, or a ritual, or a celebration, or the enjoyment of a football match or an opera, and the like. Common space arising from assembly in some locale, I want to call "topical common space".

But the public sphere, as we have been defining it, is something different. It transcends such topical spaces. We might say that it knits together a plurality of such spaces into one larger space of non-assembly. The same public discussion is deemed to pass through our debate today, and someone else's earnest conversation tomorrow, and the newspaper interview Thursday, and so on. I want to call this larger kind of non-local common space "meta-topical". The public sphere which emerges in the eighteenth century is a meta-topical common space.

What we have been discovering about such spaces is that they are partly constituted by common understandings; that is, they are not reducible to, but cannot exist without such understandings. New, unprecedented kinds of spaces require new and unprecedented understandings. Such is the case for the public sphere.

What is new is not meta-topicality. The Church, the state were already existing meta-topical spaces. But getting clear about the novelty brings us to the essential features of the public sphere as a step in the long march.

I see it as a step in this march, because this mutation in the social imaginary was inspired by the modern idea of order. Two features of it stand out in this regard.

One has just been implied: its independent identity from the political. The other is its force as a benchmark of legitimacy. Why these are important will be clear if we recur to the original idealization, say, with Grotius or Locke.

First, as I made clear in the pencil sketch above (point 1), in the Grotius-Locke idealization, political society is seen as an instrument for something pre-political; there is a place to stand, mentally, outside of the polity, as it were, from which to judge its performance. This is what is reflected in the new ways of imagining social life independent of the political, viz., the economy and the public sphere.

Secondly, freedom is central to the rights society exists to defend (point 3). Responding both to this, and to the underlying notion of agency, the theory puts great importance on the requirement that political society be founded on the consent of those bound by it.

Now contract theories of legitimate government had existed before. But what was new with the theories of this century is that they put the requirement of consent at a more fundamental level. It was not just that a people, conceived already as existing, had to give consent to those who would claim to rule it. Now the original contract brings us out of the state of nature, and founds even the existence of a collectivity which has some claim on its member individuals.

This original demand for once-for-all historical consent, as a condition of legitimacy, can easily develop into a requirement of current consent. Government must win the consent of the governed; not just originally, but as an ongoing condition of legitimacy. This is what begins to surface in the legitimation function of public opinion.

I will bring out these features of the public sphere, in reverse order. This can perhaps best be done by articulating what is new about it on two levels: what the public sphere *does;* and what it *is.*

First, what it does; or rather, what is done in it. The public sphere is the locus of a discussion potentially engaging everyone (although in the eighteenth century the claim was only to involve the educated or "enlightened" minority) in which the society can come to a common mind about important matters. This common mind is a reflective view, emerging from critical debate, and not just a summation of whatever views happen to be held in the population.[32] As a consequence it has a normative status: government ought to listen to it. There were two reasons for this, of which one tended to gain ground and ultimately swallow up the other. The first is, that this opinion is likely to be enlightened, and hence government would be well-advised to follow it. This statement by Louis Sébastien Mercier, quoted by Habermas,[33] give clear expression to this idea:

Les bons livres dépendent des lumières dans toutes les classes du peuple; ils ornent la vérité. Ce sont eux qui déjà gouvernent l'Europe; ils éclairent le gouvernement sur ses devoirs, sur sa faute, sur son véritable intérêt, sur l'opinion publique qu'il doit écouter et suivre: ces bons livres sont des maîtres patients qui attendent le réveil des administrateurs des États et le calme de leurs passions.

(Good books depend on enlightenment in all classes of the people; they adorn the truth. It is they who already govern Europe; they enlighten the government about its duties, its shortcomings, its true interest, and the public opinion to which it must listen and conform: these good books are patient masters that wait for the state administrators to awaken and for their passions to subside.)

Kant famously had a similar view.

The second reason emerges with the view that the people is sovereign. Government is then not only wise to follow opinion; it is morally bound to do so. Governments ought to legislate and rule in the midst of a reasoning public. Parliament, or the court, in taking its decisions ought to be concentrating together and enacting what has already been emerging out of enlightened debate among the people. From this arises what Warner, following Habermas, calls the "principle of supervision", which insists that the proceedings of governing bodies be public, open to the scrutiny of discerning citizens.[34] By going public, legislative deliberation informs public opinion and allows it to be maximally rational, while at the same time exposing itself to its pressure, and thus acknowledging that legislation should ultimately bow to the clear mandates of this opinion.[35]

The public sphere is, then, a locus in which rational views are elaborated which should guide government. This comes to be seen as an essential feature of a free society. As Burke put it, "in a free country, every man thinks he has a concern in all public matters".[36] There is, of course, something very new about this in the eighteenth century, compared to the immediate past of Europe. But one might ask, is this new in history? Isn't this a feature of all free societies?

No; there is a subtle but important difference. Let's compare the modern society with a public sphere with an ancient republic or polis. In this latter, we can imagine that debate on public affairs may be carried on in a host of settings: among friends at a symposium, between those who meet in the agora, and then of course in the ekklesia where the thing is finally decided. The debate swirls around and ultimately reaches its conclusion in the competent decision-making body. Now the difference is that the discussions outside this body prepare for the action ultimately taken by the same people within it. The "unofficial" discussions are not separated off, given a status of their own, and seen to constitute a kind of meta-topical space.

But that is what happens with the modern public sphere. It is a space of discussion which is self-consciously seen as being outside power. It is supposed to be listened to by power, but it is not itself an exercise of power. Its in this sense extra-political status is crucial. As we shall see below, it links the public sphere with other facets of modern society which also are seen as essentially extra-political. The extra-political status is not just defined negatively, as a lack of power. It is also seen positively: just because public opinion is not an exercise of power, it can be ideally disengaged from both partisan spirit and rational.

In other words, with the modern public sphere comes the idea that political power must be supervised and checked by something outside. What was new, of course, was not that there was an outside check, but rather the nature of this instance. It is not defined as the will of God, or the Law of Nature (although it could be thought to articulate these), but as a kind of discourse, emanating from reason and not from power or traditional authority. As Habermas puts it, power was to be tamed by reason. The notion was that "veritas non auctoritas facit legem".[37]

In this way, the public sphere was different from everything preceding it. An "unofficial" discussion, which nevertheless can come to a verdict of great importance, it is defined outside the sphere of power. It borrows some of the images from ancient assemblies—this was especially prominent in the American case—to project the whole public as one space of discussion. But as Warner shows, it innovates in relation to this model. Those who intervene are, as it were, like speakers before an assembly. But unlike their models in real ancient assemblies, they strive for a certain impersonality, a certain impartiality, an eschewing of party spirit. They strive to negate their own particularity, and thus to rise above "any private or partial view". This is what Warner calls "the principle of negativity". And we can see it not only as suiting with the print, as against spoken, medium, but also as giving expression to this crucial feature of the new public sphere as extra-political, as a discourse of reason *on* and *to* power, rather than *by* power.[38]

As Warner points out, the rise of the public sphere involves a breach in the old ideal of a social order undivided by conflict and difference. On the contrary, it means that debate breaks out, and continues, involving in principle everybody, and this is perfectly legitimate. The old unity will be gone forever. But a new unity is to be substituted. For the ever-continuing controversy is not meant to be an exercise in power, a quasi-civil war carried on by dialectical means. Its potentially divisive and destructive consequences are offset by the fact that it is a debate outside of power, a rational debate, striving without parti pris to define the common good. "The language of resistance to controversy articulates a norm for controversy. It silently transforms the ideal of a social order free from conflictual debate into an ideal of debate free from social conflict."[39]

So what the public sphere does, is enable the society to come to a common mind, without the mediation of the political sphere, in a discourse of reason outside power, which nevertheless is normative for power. Now let's try to see what, in order to do this, it has to *be*.

We can perhaps best do this by trying to define what is new and unprecedented in it. And I want to get to this in two steps, as it were. First, there is the aspect of its novelty which has already been touched on. When we compare the public sphere with one of the important sources of its constitutive images, viz., the ancient republic, what springs to our notice is its extra-political locus. The "Republic of Letters" was a common term which the members of the international society of savants in interchange gave themselves towards the end of the seventeenth century. This was a precursor phenomenon to the public sphere; indeed, it contributed to shaping it. Here was a "republic" constituted outside of the political.

Both the analogy and the difference gave its force and point to this image: it was a republic as a unified association, grouping all enlightened participants, across political boundaries; but it was also a republic in being free from subjection; its "citizens" owed no allegiance but to it, as long as they went about the business of Letters.

Something of this is inherited by the eighteenth-century public sphere. Within it, the members of society come together and pursue a common end; they form and understand themselves to form an association, which is nevertheless not constituted by its political structure. This was not true of the ancient polis or republic. Athens was a society, a koinonia, only as constituted politically. And the same was true of Rome. The ancient society was given its identity by its laws. On the banners of the legions, "SPQR" stood for "Senatus populusque romanus", but the "populus" here was the ensemble of Roman citizens, that is, those defined as such by the laws. The people didn't have an identity, didn't constitute a unity prior to and outside of these laws. This reflected, as we saw above, a common pre-modern understanding of the moral/metaphysical order underlying social practice.

By contrast, in projecting a public sphere, our eighteenth-century forebears were placing themselves in an association, this common space of discussion, which owed nothing to political structures, but was seen as existing independently of them.

This extra-political status is one aspect of the newness: that all the members of a political society (or at least, all the competent and "enlightened" members) should be seen as also forming a society outside the state. Indeed, this society was wider than any one state; it extended for some purposes to all of civilized Europe. This is an extremely important aspect, and corresponds to a crucial feature of our contemporary civilization, which emerges at this time, and which is visible in more than the public sphere. I want to take this up in a minute, but first we have to take the second step.

For it is obvious that an extra-political, international society is by itself not new.

It is preceded by the Stoic cosmopolis, and more immediately, by the Christian Church. Europeans were used to living in a dual society, one organized by two mutually irreducible principles. So the second facet of the newness of the public sphere has to be defined as its radical secularity.

Here I am recurring to a very particular use of this term, in which it stands close to its original meaning as an expression for a certain kind of time. It is obviously intimately related to the one common meaning of 'secularity', which focusses on the removal of God, or religion or the spiritual, from public space. What I am talking about here is not exactly that, but something which has contributed to it; viz., a shift in our understanding of what society is grounded on. In spite of all the risks of confusion, there is a reason to use the term 'secular' here because it marks in its very etymology what is at stake in this context, which has something to do with the way human society inhabits time. But this way of describing the difference can only be brought in later, after some preliminary exploration.

The notion of secularity I'm using here is radical, because it stands not only in contrast with a divine foundation for society, but with any idea of society as constituted in something which transcends contemporary common action. If we recur to the pre-modern ideas of order which were described in chapter 1, we find, for instance, hierarchical societies which conceive themselves as bodying forth some part of the Chain of Being. Behind the empirical fillers of the slots of kingship, aristocracy, and so on, lie the Ideas, or the persisting metaphysical Realities that these people are momentarily embodying. The King has two bodies, only one being the particular, perishable one, which is now being fed and clothed, and will later be buried.[40] Within this outlook, what constitutes a society as such is the metaphysical order it embodies.[41] People act within a framework which is there prior to and independent of their action.

But secularity contrasts not only with divinely-established churches, or Great Chains. It is also different from an understanding of our society as constituted by a law which has been ours since time out of mind. Because this too, places our action within a framework, one which binds us together and makes us a society, and which transcends our common action.

In contradistinction to all this, the public sphere is an association which is constituted by nothing outside of the common action we carry out in it: coming to a common mind, where possible, through the exchange of ideas. Its existence as an association is just our acting together in this way. This common action is not made possible by a framework which needs to be established in some action-transcendent dimension: either by an act of God, or in a Great Chain, or by a law which comes down to us since time out of mind. This is what makes it radically secular. And this, I want to claim, gets us to the heart of what is new and unprecedented in it.

This is baldly stated. Obviously, this notion of secularity still needs to be made clearer. Perhaps the contrast is obvious enough with Mystical Bodies and Great Chains. But I am claiming a difference from traditional tribal society as well, the kind of thing the German peoples had who founded our modern North Atlantic polities, or in another form what constituted the ancient republics and poleis. And this might be challenged.

These societies were defined by a law. But is that all that different from the public sphere? After all, whenever we want to act in this sphere, we meet a number of structures already in place: there are certain newspapers, television networks, publishing houses, and the rest. We act within the channels that these provide. Is this not rather analogous to any member of a tribe, who also has to act within established structures, of chieftainships, councils, annual meetings, and the rest? Of course, the institutions of the public sphere change; newspapers go broke, television networks merge, and the like. But no tribe remains absolutely fixed in its forms; these too evolve over time. If one wanted to claim that this pre-existing structure is valid for ongoing action, but not for the founding acts which set up the public sphere, the answer might be that these are impossible to identify in the stream of time, any more than they are for the tribe. And if we want to insist that there must be such a moment, then we should remark that many tribes as well hand down legends of a founding act, when a Lycurgus, for instance, laid down their laws. Surely he acted outside of existing structures.

Talking of actions within structures brings out the similarities. But there is an important difference which resides in the respective common understandings. It is true that in a functioning public sphere, action at any time is carried out within structures laid down earlier. There is a de facto arrangement of things. But this arrangement doesn't enjoy any privilege over the action carried out within it. The structures were set up during previous acts of communication in common space, on all fours with those we are carrying out now. Our present action may modify these structures, and that is perfectly legitimate, because these are seen as nothing more than precipitates and facilitators of such communicative action.

But the traditional law of a tribe usually enjoys a different status. We may, of course, alter it over time, following the prescription it itself provides. But it is not seen just as a precipitate and facilitator of action. The abolition of the law would mean the abolition of the subject of common action, because the law defines the tribe as an entity. Whereas a public sphere could start up again, even where all media had been abolished, simply by founding new ones, a tribe can only resume its life on the understanding that the law, although perhaps interrupted in its efficacy by foreign conquest, is still in force.

That's what I mean when I say that what constitutes the society, what makes the common agency possible, transcends the common actions carried out within it. It is not just that the structures we need for today's common action arose as a consequence of yesterday's, which however was no different in nature from today's. Rather the traditional law is a precondition of any common action, at whatever time, because this common agency couldn't exist without it. It is in this sense transcendent. By contrast, in a purely secular association (in my sense), common agency arises simply in and as a precipitate of common action.

The crucial distinction underlying the concept of secularity I'm trying to define here can thus be related to this issue: what constitutes the association? or otherwise put, what makes this group of people as they continue over time a common agent? Where this is something which transcends the realm of those common actions this agency engages in, the association is non-secular. Where the constituting factor is nothing other than such common action—whether the founding acts have already occurred in the past, or are now coming about is immaterial—we have secularity.

Now the claim I want to make is that this kind of secularity is modern; that it comes about very recently in the history of mankind. Of course, there have been all sorts of momentary and topical common agents which have arisen just from common action. A crowd gathers, people shout protests, and then the governor's house is stoned, or the chateau is burned down. But prior to the modern day, enduring, metatopical common agency was inconceivable on a purely secular basis. People could only see themselves as constituted into such by something action-transcendent, be it a foundation by God, or a Chain of Being which society bodied forth, or some traditional law which defined our people. The eighteenth century public sphere thus represents an instance of a new kind: a metatopical common space and common agency without an action-transcendent constitution, an agency grounded purely in its own common actions.

But how about the founding moments which traditional societies often "remembered"? What about Lycurgus' action in giving Sparta its laws? Surely these show us examples of the constituting factor (here law) issuing from common action: Lycurgus proposes, the Spartans accept. But it is in the nature of such founding moments that they are not put on the same plane as contemporary common action. The foundation acts are displaced onto a higher plane, into a heroic time, an illud tempus which is not seen as qualitatively on a level with what we do today. The founding action is not just like our action, not just an earlier similar act whose precipitate structures ours. It is not just earlier, but in another kind of time, an exemplary time.[42]

And this is why I am tempted to use the term 'secular', in spite of all the misunderstandings which may arise. Because it's clear that I don't only mean: 'not tied to religion'.[43] The exclusion is much broader. For the original sense of 'secular' was 'of the age', that is, pertaining to profane time. It was close to the sense of 'temporal' in the opposition temporal/spiritual, as we saw earlier.

Now in earlier ages, the understanding was that this profane time existed in relation to (surrounded by, penetrated by: it is hard to find the right words here) higher times. Pre-modern understandings of time seem to have been always multi-dimensional. Time was transcended and held in place by eternity; whether that of Greek philosophy, or that of the Biblical God. In either case, eternity was not just endless profane time, but an ascent into the unchanging, or a kind of gathering of time into a unity; hence the expression "hoi aiones ton aionon", or "saecula saeculorum".

The Platonic or Christian relating of time and eternity were not the only games in town, even in Christendom. There was also the much more widespread sense of a foundation time, a "time of origins" as Eliade used to call it,[44] which was complexly related to the present moment in ordinary time, in that it frequently could be ritually approached and its force partly re-appropriated at certain privileged moments. That's why it could not simply be unambiguously placed in the past (in ordinary time). The Christian liturgical year draws on this kind of time-consciousness, widely shared by other religious outlooks, in re-enacting the "founding" events of Christ's life.

Now it seems to have been the universal norm to see the important meta-topical spaces and agencies as constituted in some mode of higher time. States, churches, were seen to exist almost necessarily in more than one time-dimension, as though it were inconceivable that they have their being purely in the profane or ordinary time. A state which bodied forth the Great Chain was connected to the eternal realm of the Ideas; a people defined by its law communicated with the founding time where this was laid down; and so on.

Modern "secularization" can be seen from one angle as the rejection of higher times, and the positing of time as purely profane. Events now exist only in this one dimension, in which they stand at greater and lesser temporal distance, and in relations of causality with other events of the same kind. The modern notion of simultaneity comes to be, in which events utterly unrelated in cause or meaning are held together simply by their co-occurrence at the same point in this single profane time-line. Modern literature, as well as news media, seconded by social science, has accustomed us to think of society in terms of vertical time-slices, holding together myriad happenings, related and unrelated. I think Anderson is right that this is a typically modern mode of social imagination, which our mediaeval forebears would have found difficult to understand, for where events in profane time are very differently related to higher time, it seems unnatural just to group them side by side in the modern relation of simultaneity. This carries a presumption of homogeneity which was essentially negated by the dominant time-consciousness.[45] I will recur to this below.

Now the move to what I am calling "secularity" is obviously related to this radically purged time-consciousness. It comes when associations are placed firmly and wholly in homogeneous, profane time, whether or not the higher time is negated altogether, or other associations are still admitted to exist in it. Such I want to argue is the case with the public sphere, and therein lies its new and (close to) unprecedented nature.

I can now perhaps draw this discussion together, and try to state what the public sphere *was*. It was a new meta-topical space, in which members of society could exchange ideas and come to a common mind. As such it constituted a meta-topical agency, but one which was understood to exist independent of the political constitution of society and completely in profane time.

An extra-political, secular, meta-topical space, this is what the public sphere was and is. And the importance of understanding this lies partly in the fact that it was not the only such, that it was part of a development which transformed our whole understanding of time and society, so that we have trouble even recalling what it was like before.

5. The Sovereign People

(3) This latter is the third in the great connected chain of mutations in the social imaginary which have helped constitute modern society. This too starts off as a theory, and then gradually infiltrates and transmutes social imaginaries. But how does this come about? We can in fact distinguish two rather different paths. I will define them here as ideal types, recognizing that in real historical developments they are often combined and sometimes difficult to disentangle.

On one hand, a theory may inspire a new kind of activity with new practices, and in this way form the imaginary of whatever groups adopt these practices. The first puritan churches formed around the idea of a "Covenant" provide examples of this. A new ecclesial structure flowed from a theological innovation; and this becomes part of the story of political change, because the civil structures themselves were influenced in certain American colonies by the ways churches were governed, as with Connecticut Congregationalism, where only the "converted" enjoyed full citizenship.

Or else the change in the social imaginary comes with a re-interpretation of a practice which already existed in the old dispensation. Older forms of legitimacy are colonized, as it were, with the new understandings of order, and then transformed; in certain cases, without a clear break.

The United States is a case in point. The reigning notions of legitimacy in Britain and America, the ones which fired the English Civil War, for instance, as well as the beginnings of the Colonies' rebellion, were basically backward-looking. They turned around the idea of an "ancient constitution", an order based on law holding "since time out of mind", in which Parliament had its rightful place beside the King. This was typical of one of the most widespread pre-modern understandings of order, which referred back to a "time of origins" (Eliade's phrase), which was not in ordinary time.

This older idea emerges from the American Revolution transformed into a full-fledged foundation in popular sovereignty, whereby the U.S. constitution is put in the mouth of "We, the people". This was preceded by an appeal to the idealized order of Natural Law, in the invocation of "truths held self-evident" in the Declaration of Independence.[46] The transition was the easier, because what was understood as the traditional law gave an important place to elected assemblies and their consent to taxation. All that was needed was to shift the balance in these so as to make elections the only source of legitimate power.

But what has to take place for this change to come off is a transformed social imaginary, in which the idea of foundation is taken out of the mythical early time, and seen as something that people can do today. In other words, it becomes something that can be brought about by collective action in contemporary, purely secular time. This happened sometime in the eighteenth century, but really more towards its end than its beginning. Élites propounded *theories* of founding action beforehand, but these hadn't adequately sunk into the general social imaginary for them to be acted on. So that 1688, radical departure as it may seem to us in retrospect, was presented as an act of continuity, of return to a pre-existent legality. (We are fooled by a change in semantics. The "Glorious Revolution" had the original sense of a return to the original position; not the modern sense of a innovative turn-over. Of course, it helped by its Wirkungsgeschichte to alter the sense.)

This fit between new theory and traditional practices was crucial to the outcome. Popular Sovereignty could be invoked in the American case, because it could find a generally agreed institutional meaning. All colonists agreed that the way to found a new constitution was through some kind of assembly, perhaps slightly larger than the normal one, such as in Massachusetts in 1779. The force of the old representative institutions helped to "interpret" in practical terms the new concept.

We can say that the American Revolution started on the basis of one legitimacy idea, and finished by engendering another very different one; while somehow avoiding a radical break. The colonists started by asserting the traditional "rights of Englishmen" against an arrogant and insensitive imperial government. Once the break with King in Parliament consummated, and the governors no longer to be

obeyed, the leadership of the resistance passed naturally to the existing elected legislatures, associated in a Continental Congress. The analogy with the Civil War of the
1640s was evident.

But war has always been a source of radicalization. The breach itself was made
through a Declaration which affirmed universal human rights, no longer simply
those of Englishmen. Certain states adopted new constitutions based on the popular will. And ultimately the whole movement culminates in a Constitution which
places the new Republic squarely within the modern moral order, as the will of a
people which had no need of some pre-existing law to act as a people, but could see
itself as the source of law.

The new social imaginary comes essentially through a retrospective re-interpretation. The revolutionary forces were mobilized largely on the basis of the old, backward-looking legitimacy idea. This will later be seen as the exercise of a power inherent in a sovereign people. The proof of its existence and legitimacy lies in the
new polity it has erected. But popular sovereignty would have been incapable of doing this job, if it had entered the scene too soon. The predecessor idea, invoking the
traditional rights of a people defined by its ancient constitution, had to do the original heavy lifting, mobilizing the colonists for the struggle, before being relegated to
oblivion, with the pitiless ingratitude towards the past which defines modern revolutions.

This of course didn't mean that nothing changed in the practices, only the legitimating discourse. On the contrary, certain important new steps were taken, which
only the new discourse could justify. I've already mentioned the new state constitutions, such as that of Massachusetts in 1779. But the federal Constitution itself is
the most striking example. In the Federalist view, it was imperative to create a new
central power which wasn't simply a creature of the states; this had been the principal fault of the Confederal régime they were trying to replace. There had to be
something more than the "peoples" of the different states, creating a common instrument. The new union government had to have its own base of legitimacy in a
"people of the United States". This was integral to the whole Federalist project.

But at the same time, this projection backwards of the action of a sovereign people wouldn't have been possible without the continuity in institutions and practices
which allowed for the reinterpretation of past actions as the fruit of the new principles. The essence of this continuity resided in the virtually universal acceptance
among the colonists of elected assemblies as legitimate forms of power. This was the
more heartfelt, in that their elected legislatures had long been the main bulwark of
their local liberties, against the encroachments of an executive under royal, or imperial control. At most, come a crucial turning point like the adoption of a new state

constitution, they had recourse to special enlarged assemblies. Popular sovereignty could be embraced because it had a clear and uncontested institutional meaning. This was the basis of the new order.[47]

Quite different was the case in the French Revolution, with fateful effects. The impossibility remarked by all historians of "bringing the Revolution to an end"[48] came partly from this, that any particular expression of popular sovereignty could be challenged by some other, with substantial support. Part of the terrifying instability of the first years of the Revolution stemmed from this negative fact, that the shift from the legitimacy of dynastic rule to that of the nation had no agreed meaning in a broadly based social imaginary.

This is not to be understood as the global "explanation" of this instability, but as telling us something about the way in which the different factors we cite to explain it worked together to produce the result we know. Of course, the fact that substantial parts of the King's entourage, the army and the nobility did not accept the new principles created a tremendous obstacle to stabilization. And even those who were for the new legitimacy were divided among themselves. But what made these latter divisions so deadly was the absence of any agreed understanding on the institutional meaning of the sovereignty of the nation.

Burke's advice to the revolutionaries was to stick to their traditional constitution, and amend it piecemeal. But this was already beyond their powers. It was not just that the representative institutions of this constitution, the Estates General, had been in abeyance for 175 years. They were also profoundly out of synch with the aspiration to equal citizenship which had developed among the educated classes, the bourgeoisie and a good part of the aristocracy, which found expression in a number of ways; negatively through the attack on aristocratic privilege, and positively in the enthusiasm for Republican Rome and its ideals.[49] That is why virtually the first demand of the Third Estate in 1789 was to abolish the separate chambers, and bring all the delegates together in a single National Assembly.

Even more gravely, outside of these educated élites, there was very little sense of what a representative constitution might mean. True, masses of people responded to the calling of the Estates General, with their cahiers de doléance, but this whole procedure supposed the continuance of royal sovereignty; it wasn't at all suited to serve as a channel for the popular will.

What the moderates hoped for was something along the lines of Burke's prescription: an evolution of the traditional constitution to fashion the kind of representative institutions which would precisely be understood by all as the expression of the nation's will, through the votes of the citizens. This is what the House of Commons had become in the eighteenth century, even though the "people" here was a small élite, deemed to speak for the whole through various modes of virtual representation.

The evolution which had brought this about in Britain had created a sense of the forms of self-rule which was part of the social imaginary of the broader society. That's why the demands for broader popular participation took the form in England of proposals to extend the franchise. The people wanted in to the established representative structure, as most notably in the Chartist agitation of the 1830s and 1840s. The American case discussed above was a stage ahead on this same evolution; their representative assemblies were generally elected on the basis of manhood suffrage.

These forms of self-rule through elected assembly were part of the generally available repertory in the Anglo-Saxon societies. Not only were they absent in that of the popular classes in France, but these had developed their own forms of popular protest which were structured by a quite different logic. But before turning to examine these, there is a general point to be made about modern revolutionary transitions, carried out on the basis of novel theories.

The transition can only come off, in anything like the desired sense, if the "people", or at least important minorities of activists, understand and internalize the theory. But for political actors understanding a theory is being able to put it into practice in their world. They understand it through the practices which put it into effect. These practices have to make sense to them, the kind of sense which the theory prescribes. But what makes sense of our practices is our social imaginary. And so what is crucial to this kind of transition is that the people (or its active segments) share a social imaginary which can fill this requirement, that is, which includes ways of realizing the new theory.

So we can think of the social imaginary of a people at a given time as a kind of repertory, as I suggested in Chapter 2, including the ensemble of practices which they can make sense of. To transform society according to a new principle of legitimacy, we have to have a repertory which includes ways of meeting this principle. This requirement can be broken down into two facets: (1) the actors have to know what to do, have to have practices in their repertory which put the new order into effect; and (2) the ensemble of actors have to agree on what these practices are.

To evoke an analogy, drawn from Kantian philosophy: theories are like abstract categories; they need to be "schematized", to receive some concrete interpretation in the domain of practice, if they are to be operative in history.

There have been certain modern revolutionary situations where (1) has been virtually completely missing. Take the Russian case, for instance: the collapse of Tsarist rule in 1917 was supposed to open the way to a new republican legitimacy, which the Provisional Government supposed would be defined in the Constituent Assembly they called for the following year. But if we follow the analysis of Orlando Figes,[50] the mass of the peasant population couldn't conceive of the Russian people as a whole as a sovereign agent. What they did perfectly well understand, and what they sought, was the freedom for the *mir* to act on its own, to divide the land which the nobles (in their view) had usurped, and no longer to suffer repression at the hands of the central government. Their social imaginary included a *local* collective agency, the people of the village or *mir*. They knew that this agency had to deal with a national government which could do them a lot of harm, and even occasionally some good. But they had no conception of a national *people* which could take over sovereign power from the despotic government. Their repertory didn't include collective actions of this type at this national level; what they could understand was large-scale insurrections, like the Pugachovschina, whose goal was not to take over and replace central power, but to force it to be less malignant and invasive.

By contrast, what was missing in the period of the French Revolution was (2). More than one formula was on offer to realize popular sovereignty. On one side, the traditional institutions of the Estates General were unsuited for this purpose; the (common) people only elected one chamber out of three; and the whole system was meant to represent subjects making supplication to a sovereign monarch.

But on the other, the gamut of theories on offer was much wider than in the American case. This was partly due to the fact that in the Anglo-Saxon world, the powerful hold of representative institutions on the imaginary inhibited the theoretical imagination; but it also arises out of the peculiar trajectories of French culture and thought.

Of particular importance in the French case was a range of theories influenced by Rousseau. These had two features which were fateful for the course of the Revolution. The first was what underlay Rousseau's conception of la volonté générale. This reflected Rousseau's new and more radical "redaction" of the modern idea of order.

The principle of this idea of order, as we have seen, is that we are each meant to pursue freely the means to life, but in such a way that each in seeking his own aids, or at least refrains from hindering, the parallel search of others. In other words, our pursuit of our life plans must harmonize. But this harmony was variously conceived. It can come about through invisible hand processes, as with the celebrated theory of Adam Smith.[51] But since this was never thought to suffice, harmonization was also to be brought about consciously, through our following natural law. Locke saw this as given by God, and the motivation for obeying it was whatever makes us obey God: a sense of obligation to our Creator, and the fear of eternal punishment.

Later, the fear of God is replaced by the idea of impersonal benevolence, or else by a notion of natural sympathy. But what all these earlier conceptions have in common is that they suppose a duality of motivations in us. We can be tempted to serve our interest at the expense of others; and then we can also be moved—through fear of God, impersonal benevolence, or whatever—to act for the general good. It is this dualism which Rousseau wanted to set aside. True harmony can only come when we can overcome this duality, when my love of myself coincides with my desire to fulfill the legitimate goals of my co-agents (those participating with me in this harmonization). In Rousseau's language, the primitive instincts of self-love (amour de soi) and sympathy (pitié) fuse together in the rational and virtuous human being into a love of the common good, which in the political context is known as the "general will".

In other words, in the perfectly virtuous man, self-love is no longer distinct from love of others. But the overcoming of this distinction brings with it a new dualism which arises at another point. If self-love is also love of humanity, how to explain the egoistic tendencies which fight in us against virtue? These must come from another motive which Rousseau calls "pride" (amour propre). So my concern for myself can take two different forms, which are opposed to each other, as good is to evil.

This distinction is new in the context of the Enlightenment. But in another sense it involves a return to a way of thinking deeply anchored in tradition. We distinguish two qualities in the will. We're back in the moral world of Augustine: humans are capable of two loves, one good, the other evil. But it's a revised Augustine, a Pelagian Augustine, if the paradox is not too shocking, because the good will is now innate, natural, entirely anthropocentric, as Monseigneur de Beaumont saw very clearly.

And the theory itself is very modern, placed within the modern moral order. The goal is to harmonize individual wills, even if this can't be done without creating a new identity, a "moi commun" ("common self").[52] What has to be rescued is liberty, the individual liberty of each and every one. Freedom is the supreme good, to the point where Rousseau reinterprets the opposition of virtue and vice to align it with that of liberty and slavery. "Car l'impulsion de l'appétit est esclavage, et l'obéissance à une loi qu'on s'est préscrite est liberté" ("for impulsion by appetite alone is slavery, and obedience to self-imposed law is freedom").[53] The law we love, because it aims at the good of all, is not a brake on freedom. On the contrary, it comes from what is most authentic in us, from a self-love which is enlarged and transposed into the higher register of morality. It's the fruit of the passage from solitude to society, which is also that from the animal condition to that of humanity.

> Ce passage de l'état de nature à l'état civil produit dans l'homme un changement très remarquable, en substituant dans sa conduite la justice à l'instinct, et donnant à ses actions la moralité qui leur manquait auparavant.
> . . . Quoiqu'il se prive dans cet état de plusieurs avantages qu'il tient de la na-

ture, il en regagne de si grands, ses facultés s'exercent et se développent, ses idées s'étendent, ses sentiments s'ennoblissent, son âme toute entière s'élève à tel point que si les abus de cette nouvelle condition ne le dégradait souvent au-dessous de celle dont il est sorti, il devrait bénir sans cesse l'instant heureux qui l'en arracha pour jamais, et qui, d'un animal stupide et borné en fit un être in-telligent et un homme.

(The passage from the state of nature to the civil state produces a remarkable change in man by substituting justice for instinct in his conduct and giving his acts the morality they previously lacked. . . . In this state he is deprived of some advantages given to him by nature, but he gains others so great—his fac-ulties are exercised and developed, his ideas are broadened, his feelings are en-nobled, his whole soul is uplifted—that if the abuses of this new state did not often degrade him below his previous level, he would constantly have reason to bless the happy moment when he was drawn out of the state of nature for-ever and changed from a stupid, short-sighted animal into an intelligent being and a man.)[54]

What opposes this law, on the other hand, is not the authentic self, but a will which has been corrupted and turned from its proper course through other-dependence.

The Rousseau "redaction" gives us a moral psychology very different from the standard conception of the Enlightenment period, which came down to them from Locke. It not only returns to a will with potentially two qualities, good and evil. It also presents the relation between reason and the good will in a quite different way. Where the mainstream version sees disengaged reason, which lifts us to a universal standpoint, and makes us impartial spectators, as liberating a general benevolence in us, or at least teaches us to recognize our enlightened self-interest, for Rousseau this objectifying reason is the servant of strategic thinking, and only serves to em-broil us more fully in the power calculations which, by trying to control others, in fact make us more and more dependent on them.

This strategic self, which is at one and the same time isolated and eager for oth-ers' approval, represses ever further the true self. The struggle for virtue is that at-tempt to recover a voice which has been buried and almost silenced deep within us. What we need is the exact opposite of disengagement; we need rather a re-engagement with what is most intimate and essential in ourselves, rendered inaudi-ble by the clamour of the world, for which Rousseau uses the traditional term "con-science".

Conscience! Conscience! instinct divin, immortelle et céleste voix; guide assuré d'un être ignorant et borné, mais intelligent et libre; juge infaillible du bien et du mal, qui rends l'homme semblable à Dieu, c'est toi qui fais l'excellence de sa nature et la moralité de ses actions; sans toi je ne sens rien en moi qui m'élève au-dessus des bêtes, que le triste privilège de m'égarer d'erreurs en erreurs à l'aide d'un entendement sans règle et d'une raison sans principe.

(Conscience! Conscience! Divine instinct, immortal voice from heaven; sure guide for a creature ignorant and finite indeed, yet intelligent and free; infallible judge of good and evil, making man like to God! In thee consists the excellence of man's nature and the morality of his actions; apart from thee, I find nothing in myself to raise me above the beasts—nothing but the sad privilege of wandering from one error to another, by the help of an unbridled understanding and a reason which knows no principle.)[55]

This theory suggested a new kind of politics, which we in fact see enacted in the climactic period of the Revolution, 1792–94. It is a politics which (a) makes virtue a central concept, a virtue which consists in the fusion of self-love and love of country. As Robespierre put in 1792: "L'âme de la République, c'est la vertu, c'est l'amour de la patrie, le dévouement magnanime qui confond tous les intérêts dans l'intérêt général" ("The soul of the Republic is virtue, it's the love of the fatherland, the magnanimous devotion which subsumes all particular interests in the general one").[56] In one sense, this was a return to an ancient notion of virtue, which Montesquieu had identified as the "mainspring" of Republics, "une préférence continuelle de l'intérêt public au sien propre" ("A continuing preference of the public interest over one's own").[57] But it has been re-edited in the new Rousseauian terms of fusion ("qui confond tous les intérêts dans l'intérêt général").

(b) It tends to manicheism. The gray areas between virtue and vice tend to disappear. There is no legitimate place for private interest alongside, even if subordinate to, the love of the general good. Self-interest is a sign of corruption, thus of vice, and at the limit can become inseparable from opposition. The egoist becomes identified as traitor.

(c) The discourse of this politics has a quasi-religious tenor. This has often been remarked.[58] The "sacred" is often evoked (l'union sacrée, the "sacrilegious hand" which killed Marat, etc.)

(d) But one of the most fateful features of this politics is its complex notion of representation. For Rousseau, of course—and this is the second important feature of his theory—political representation in its normal sense through elected assemblies was anathema. This is connected with his insistence on transparency.[59] The general will is the site of maximum transparency, in this sense, that we are maximally present and open to each other when our wills fuse into one. Opacity is inherent to particular wills, which we often try to realize by indirect strategies, using manipulation and false appearances (which touches on another form of "representation", of a quasi-theatrical type, which is also bad and harmful). That is why this political outlook so easily assimilates disaffection with hidden and non-avowable action, even with plots, hence at the limit with treason. The general will, on the other hand, is created openly, in the sight of everyone. Which is why in this type of politics, the general will always has to be defined, declared, one might even say produced before the people, in another kind of theatre which Rousseau had clearly described. This is not one where actors present themselves before spectators, but rather one modelled on the public festival, where everyone is both performer and spectator. This is what distinguishes the true republican festival from the modern degraded forms of theatre. In the former, one may well ask:

> Mais quels seront enfin les objets de ces spectacles? Rien, si l'on veut. Avec la liberté, partout où règne l'affluence, le bien-être y règne aussi. Plantez au milieu d'une place publique un piquet couronné de fleurs, rassemblez-y le peuple, et vous aurez une fête. Faites mieux encore: donnez les spectateurs en spectacle; rendez-les acteurs eux-mêmes; faites que chacun se voie et s'aime dans les autres, afin que tous en soient mieux unis.

> (But what will be the objects of these entertainments? What will be shown in them? Nothing, if you please. With liberty, wherever abundance reigns, well-being also reigns. Plant a stake crowned with flowers in the middle of a square; gather the people together there, and you will have a festival. Do better yet; let the spectators become an entertainment to themselves; make them actors themselves; do it so that each sees and loves himself in the others so that all will be better united.)[60]

Transparency, that is non-representation, requires a certain form of discourse, where the common will is defined publicly; and even forms of liturgy where it is made manifest for and by the people, and that not once and for all but repeatedly, one might even think obsessively. This makes sense of a crucial dimension of revolutionary discourse in these fateful years in Paris, where legitimacy was meant to be won through a (finally right) formulation of that general will which is already, ex ante, that of the healthy and virtuous Republic. This goes some way to explain the striking verboseness of the struggle between the factions in 1792–94. But it also shows the importance given to revolutionary festivals, which Mona Ozouf has studied.[61] These were attempts to make the Republic manifest to the people, or the people manifest to itself, following Rousseau; these festivals often borrowed their forms from earlier religious ceremonies, such as Corpus Christi processions.

I say that the Rousseauian notion of representation was complex, because it involved more than the negative point, the interdict on representative assemblies. We can see in the revolutionary discourse itself, and in the festivals, another kind of "representation", discursive or quasi-theatrical. Fair enough, one might say; this doesn't infringe the Rousseauian interdict; the festivals even follow his plan. But there was already something less avowable and more potentially dangerous here. Insofar as the general will only exists where there is real virtue, that is, the real fusion of individual and common wills, what can we say of a situation in which many, perhaps even most people are still "corrupt", that is, have not yet achieved this fusion? Its only locus now will be the minority of virtuous. They will be the vehicles of the genuine common will, which is objectively that of everyone, that is, the common goals which everyone would subscribe to if virtuous.

What is this minority supposed to do with this insight into its own correctness? Just let a corrupt majority "will of all" take its course through the working of certain formally agreed procedures of voting? What would be the value of this, for there can as yet by hypothesis be no true Republic where the will of all coincides with the general will? Surely the minority is called on to act so as to bring about the true Republic, which means to combat corruption and establish virtue.

We can see here the temptation to vanguard politics which has been such a fateful part of our world. This kind of politics involves a claim to "representation" of a new kind. It's not the old pre-modern kind, where in virtue of the structure of things the kind "represents" his kingdom, the bishop his church, the duke his rear-vassals, and so on, because in occupying their place they constitute their subordinates as representable collectivities. It is very different from this, but like these older forms, Revolutionary power will use quasi-theatrical forms of self-presentation to make the representative function manifest.

Nor is it representation in the modern sense, which Rousseau condemned, where deputies are chosen by constituents to make decisions binding on all. We might say that this novel, not fully avowed, form is rather a kind of representation by "incarnation". The minority embodies the general will, and is the only place where this is embodied. But this makes the claim hard to formulate. Not only because the minority want to distinguish themselves from the "formal" model of elected representatives, but also because there is something inherently provisional about this claim to speak for the whole. By hypothesis, it could have no place in a functioning Republic. It can only play a role in the revolutionary transition. It is part of the theory of Revolution; it has no place in the theory of government.[62] This is the root of that incoherence which we always see in the politics of the vanguard, right up to the major twentieth century example of Bolshevism.

In any case, this only semi-avowed theory of representation by incarnation engendered new political forms. It is what lay behind the new kind of active vanguard "clubs", of which the Jacobins are the most celebrated example. Furet, following Augustin Cochin, has shown how important were the "sociétés de pensée" in the run-up to the calling of the Estates-General.[63]

We can see here the theoretical basis for a kind of politics which the heady climax of 1792–94 has made familiar to us, and which created a modern tradition which we see continued for instance in Leninist Communism. It is a politics of virtue, as the fusion of individual and general will, and it is Manichean, highly "ideological", even quasi-religious in tone. It seeks transparency, and hence fears its polar opposite, hidden agendas and plots. And it practices two forms of "representation": first in both discursive and quasi-theatrical forms, it makes manifest the general will; and secondly, even if only implicitly, it lays claim to a kind of representation by incarnation.

Obviously, the birth of this style of politics out of theory, along with the absence of an existing repertory of representative government, cannot suffice to explain the terrible events of 1792–94. We also have to take account of other existing repertories of common action, in particular the forms of popular revolt which were familiar in France. These heavily influenced what we call the Terror, which was in a sense a joint creation of the new ideology and these powerfully entrenched folk-ways.[64]

But we can see the contrast between the two rather different paths by which theories expressive of the modern moral order came to inform the social imaginaries, and hence the repertory of practices, at first of élites, and then of whole societies. We can also see how the paths affected the outcomes. For the forms which "took" in France turned out to be interestingly different from the Anglo-American mode. Pierre Rosanvallon has traced the peculiar path by which universal suffrage was achieved in France, and he brings to light the different shape of the social imaginary in this republican tradition.[65]

6. The Direct-Access Society

I have been describing our modern social imaginary in terms of the underlying idea of moral order, one which has captured in our characteristic social practices and forms the salient features of seventeenth-century Natural Law theory, while transforming this in the process. But it is clear that the change in the underlying notion of order has brought a number of other changes with it.

I have already mentioned the absence of an action-transcendent grounding, the fact that modern social forms exist exclusively in secular time. The modern social imaginary no longer sees the greater trans-local entities as grounded in something other, something higher, than common action in secular time. This was not true of the pre-modern state, as I argued above. The hierarchical order of the kingdom was seen as based in the Great Chain of Being. The tribal unit was seen as constituted as such by its law, which went back "since time out of mind", or perhaps to some founding moment which had the status of a "time of origins" in Eliade's sense. The importance in pre-modern revolutions, up to and including the English civil war, of the backward look, of establishing an original law, comes from this sense that the political entity is in this sense action-transcendent. It cannot simply create itself by its own action. On the contrary, it can act as an entity because it is already constituted as such; and that is why such legitimacy attaches to returning to the original constitution.

Seventeenth-century social contact theory, which sees a people as coming together out of a state of nature, obviously belongs to another order of thought. But, if my argument above is right, it wasn't until the late eighteenth century that this new way of conceiving things entered the social imaginary. The American Revolution is in a sense the watershed. It was undertaken in a backward-looking spirit, in the sense that the colonists were fighting for their established rights as Englishmen. Moreover they were fighting under their established colonial legislatures, associated in a Congress. But out of the whole process emerges the crucial fiction of "we, the people", into whose mouth the declaration of the new constitution is placed.

Here the idea is invoked that a people, or as it was also called at the time, a "nation", can exist prior to and independently of its political constitution. So that this people can give itself its own constitution by its own free action in secular time. Of course the epoch-making action comes rapidly to be invested with images drawn from older notions of higher time. The "Novus Ordo seclorum", just like the new French revolutionary calendar, draws heavily on Judaeo-Christian apocalyptic. The constitution-founding comes to be invested with something of the force of a "time of origins", a higher time, filled with agents of a superior kind, which we should ceaselessly try to re-approach. But nevertheless, a new way of conceiving things is abroad. Nations, people, can have a personality, can act together outside of any prior political ordering. One of the key premises of modern nationalism is in place, because without this the demand for self-determination of nations would make no sense. This just is the right for peoples to make their own constitution, unfettered by their historical political organization.

In order to see how this new idea of collective agency, the "nation" or "people", articulates into a new understanding of time, I want to recur to Benedict Anderson's very insightful discussion.[66] Anderson stresses how the new sense of belonging to a nation was prepared by a new way of grasping society under the category of simultaneity:[67] society as the whole consisting of the simultaneous happening of all the myriad events which mark the lives of its members at that moment. These events are the fillers of this segment of a kind of homogeneous time. This very clear, unambiguous concept of simultaneity belongs to an understanding of time as exclusively secular. As long as secular time is interwoven with various kinds of higher time, there is no guarantee that all events can be placed in unambiguous relations of simultaneity and succession. The high feast is in one way contemporaneous with my life and that of my fellow pilgrims, but in another way it is close to eternity, or the time of origins, or the events it prefigures.

A purely secular time-understanding allows us to imagine society "horizontally", unrelated to any "high points", where the ordinary sequence of events touches higher time, and therefore without recognizing any privileged persons or agencies—such as kings or priests—who stand and mediate at such alleged points. This radical horizontality is precisely what is implied in the direct access society, where each member is "immediate to the whole". Anderson is undoubtedly right to argue that this new understanding couldn't have arisen without social developments, like that of print capitalism, but he doesn't want to imply by this that the transformations of the social imaginary are sufficiently explained by these developments. Modern society required also transformations in the way we figure ourselves as societies. Crucial among these has been this ability to grasp society from a decentred view which is no one's. That is, the search for a truer and more authoritative perspective than my own doesn't lead me to centre society on a king or sacred assembly, or whatever, but allows for this lateral, horizontal view, which an unsituated observer might have—society as it might be laid out in a tableau without privileged nodal points. There is a close inner link between modern societies, their self-understandings, and modern synoptic modes of representation in "the Age of the World Picture":[68] society as simultaneous happenings, social interchange as impersonal "system", the social terrain as what is mapped, historical culture as what shows up in museums, etc.

There was thus a certain "verticality" of society, which depended on a grounding in higher time, and which has disappeared in modern society. But this was also, seen from another angle, a society of mediated access. In an ancien régime kingdom, like France, the subjects are only held together within an order which coheres through its apex, in the person of the King, through whom this order connects to higher time and the order of things. We are members of this order through our relation to the king. As we saw in the previous chapter, earlier hierarchical societies tended to personalize relations of power and subordination.

The principle of a modern horizontal society is radically different. Each of us is equidistant from the centre, we are immediate to the whole. This describes what we could call a "direct-access" society. We have moved from a hierarchical order of personalized links to an impersonal egalitarian one; from a vertical world of mediated-access to horizontal, direct-access societies.

In the earlier form, hierarchy and what I am calling mediacy of access went together. A society of ranks—"society of orders", to use Tocqueville's phrase—like seventeenth-century France, for instance, was hierarchical in an obvious sense. But this
also meant that one belonged to this society via belonging to some component of it.
As a peasant one was linked to a lord who in turn held from the king. One was a
member of a municipal corporation which had a standing in the kingdom, or exercised some function in a Parliament with its recognized status, and so on. By contrast, the modern notion of citizenship is direct. In whatever many ways I am related to the rest of society through intermediary organizations, I think of my
citizenship as separate from all these. My fundamental way of belonging to the state
is not dependent on, or mediated by any of these other belongings. I stand, alongside all my fellow citizens, in direct relationship to the state which is the object of
our common allegiance.

Of course, this doesn't necessarily change the way things get done. I know someone whose brother-in-law is a judge, or an MP, and so I phone her up when I'm in a
jam. We might say that what has changed is the normative picture. But underlying
this, without which the new norm couldn't exist for us, is a change in the way people imagine belonging. There were certainly people in seventeenth-century France,
and before, for whom the very idea of direct access would have been foreign, impossible to clearly grasp. The educated had the model of the ancient republic. But for
many others, the only way they could understand belonging to a larger whole, like a
kingdom, or a universal church, was through the imbrication of more immediate,
understandable units of belonging—parish, lord—into the greater entity. Modernity has involved, among other things, a revolution in our social imaginary, the relegation of these forms of mediacy to the margins, and the diffusion of images of direct access.

This has come through the rise of the social forms which I have been describing: the public sphere, in which people conceive themselves as participating directly
in a nation-wide (sometimes even international) discussion; market economies, in
which all economic agents are seen as entering into contractual relations with others
on an equal footing; and, of course, the modern citizenship state. But we can think
of other ways as well in which immediacy of access takes hold of our imaginations.
We see ourselves as in spaces of fashion, for instance, taking up and handing on
styles. We see ourselves as part of the world-wide audience of media stars. And
while these spaces are in their own sense hierarchical—they centre on quasi-legend-
ary figures—they offer all participants an access unmediated by any of their other
allegiances or belongings. Something of the same kind, along with a more substantial mode of participation, is available in the various movements, social, political,

religious, which are a crucial feature of modern life, and which link people translocally and internationally into a single collective agency.

These modes of imagined direct access are linked to, indeed are just different facets of, modern equality and individualism. Directness of access abolishes the heterogeneity of hierarchical belonging. It makes us uniform, and that is one way of becoming equal. (Whether it is the only way is the fateful issue at stake in much of today's struggles over multi-culturalism.) At the same time, the relegation of various mediations reduces their importance in our lives; the individual stands more and more free of them, and hence has a growing self-consciousness as an individual. Modern individualism, as a moral idea, doesn't mean ceasing to belong at all—that's the individualism of anomie and break-down—but imagining oneself as belonging to ever wider and more impersonal entities: the state, the movement, the community of humankind. This is the change that has been described from another angle as the shift from "network" or "relational" identities to "categorical" ones.[69]

We can see right away that in an important sense, modern direct-access societies are more homogeneous than pre-modern ones. But this doesn't mean that there tends to be less de facto differentiation in culture and life style between different strata than there was a few centuries ago, although this is undoubtedly true. It is also the case that the social imaginaries of different classes have come much closer together. It was a feature of hierarchical, mediated societies, that the people in a local community, a village or parish, for instance, might have only the most hazy idea of the rest of their society. They would have some image of central authority, some mixture of good king and evil ministers, but very little notion of how to fill in the rest of the picture. In particular, their sense was rather vague of what other people and regions made up the kingdom. There was in fact a wide gap between the theory and social imaginary of political élites, and that of the less educated classes, or those in rural areas. This state of affairs lasted until comparatively recently in many countries. It has been well documented for France during most of the nineteenth century, in spite of the confident remarks of Republican leaders about the nation "one and indivisible".[70] This split consciousness is quite incompatible with the existence of a direct-access society. The necessary transformation was ultimately wrought by the Third Republic, and the modern France theorized by the Revolution became real and all-embracing for the first time. This (in more than one sense) revolutionary change in the social imaginary is what Weber captures in his title: *Peasants into Frenchmen*.[71]

5 The Spectre of Idealism

The fact that I have started this discussion of Western modernity with an underlying idea of order, which first was a theory, and later helped shaped social imaginaries, may smack to some readers of "idealism", the attributing to "ideas" of an independent force in history. But surely, one might argue, the causal arrow runs in the reverse direction. For instance, the importance I mentioned above of the "economic" model in the modern understanding of order, surely this must reflect what was happening on the ground, for instance the rise of merchants, of capitalist forms of agriculture, the extension of markets. This gives the correct, "materialist" explanation.

Now I think this kind of objection is based on a false dichotomy, that between "ideas" and "material factors" as rival causal agencies. But in fact, what we see in human history is ranges of human practices which are both at once, that is, "material" practices carried out by human beings in space and time, and very often coercively maintained, and at the same time, self-conceptions, modes of understanding. These are often quite inseparable, in the way described in the previous chapter's discussion of social imaginaries, just because the self-understandings are the essential condition of the practice making the sense that it does to the participants. Just because human practices are the kind of thing which make sense, certain "ideas" are internal to them; one cannot distinguish the two in order to ask the question, which causes which.

"Materialism", if it is to make any sense, has to be formulated differently, somewhat in the way G. A. Cohen does in his masterful account of historical materialism.[1] It would be a thesis to the effect that certain motivations are dominant in history, those for "material" things, say, economic ones, for the means to life, or perhaps power. This might explain a progressive transformation of the modes of production, towards "higher" forms. Now in any given case, a certain mode would require certain "ideas", legal forms, generally accepted norms, and the rest. Thus, it is recognized in Marxist theory that fully developed capitalism is incompatible with feudal conditions of labour; it requires formally (legally) free labourers, who can move and sell their labour as they see fit.

The "materialist" thesis here says that in any such "package" of mode of production and legal forms and ideas, it is the former which is the crucial explanatory factor. The underlying motivation pushing agents to adopt the new mode also led them to adopt the new legal forms, because these were essential to that mode. The form of the explanation here is teleological, not a matter of efficient causation. An efficient causal relation is supposed, and incorporated in the historical account: because the legal forms facilitate the capitalist mode (efficient causation), therefore agents whose fundamental draw was to this mode were induced to favour the new legal forms (even if at first unconscious of what they were doing). This is an in-order-to explanation, or in other words, a teleological account.

It must be said that materialism, as so formulated, becomes coherent, but at the cost of being implausible as a universal principle. There are lots of contexts in which we can discern that the economic motive is primary, and explains the adoption of certain moral ideas; as when advertisers in the 1960s adopt the new language of expressive individualism, and become eventually inducted into the new ideals. But an account of the spread of the Reformation doctrine of salvation by faith in economic terms is not very plausible. The only general rule in history is that there is no general rule identifying one order of motivation as always the driving force. "Ideas" always come in history wrapped up in certain practices, even if these are only discursive practices. But the motivations which drive towards the adoption and spread of these packages may be very varied; and indeed, it is not even clear that we have a typology of such motivations ("economic" v. "political", v. "ideal", etc.) which is valid throughout human history.

The same point could be made in a different fashion. Any new practice or institution has obviously "material" conditions. Modern capitalism could not have arisen without a thriving set of commercial practices—trade, money, banks, bookkeeping methods, and so on. But these from another point of view pose conditions in the realm of "ideas". People have to share certain understandings of how they can function with others, and what the norms are, if they are to engage in these practices. We fail to notice this, because we take it for granted. Or we assume, like Adam Smith, that people always had a propensity to "truck and barter",[2] and just may have lacked some skills, or detailed knowledge of certain procedures, to engage in these activities.

But if we were thrown back into gift-exchange societies, of the kind that Marcel Mauss writes about,[3] we would see that we had the greatest difficulty in explaining our "trade", which might even appear something monstrous and insulting to them—for instance, if we immediately returned a money equivalent of their gift; or worse, handed it back, and asked for something more.

When it comes to inaugurating a new political practice, like democratic self-rule, we see many contexts where what is missing is not certain "material" conditions, like mutual proximity of the population concerned, or good communications, and what might be thought of as "material" motivations, like anger at royal oppression, or exploitation by aristocrats, but rather the issue is a lack of a commonly understood repertory of self-rule, as in the cases discussed in the previous chapter.

In general, a new practice will have both "material" and "ideal" conditions; which we try to explain may depend on which is problematic. Why did a democratic revolution occur just then, and not before? The answer may be: because the people hadn't suffered from monarchical rule as much as they came to on the eve of the turn-over; or it may be: because they began to see from some striking examples that democracy brings prosperity (the draw of Europe?). But it might also be: because at that moment they had developed the repertory which allowed for a self-sustaining democracy, as against just a revolt which changed one mode of despotism for another. And it may also be: because democratic forms of rule came to seem right, and in keeping with their dignity, around that time. There is no good empirically-based reason to think that the second kind of explanation must always give way to the first. The weighting between the two can't be determined a priori, but will be different from case to case.

But just because of this interweaving of the two levels, it might be helpful here, and also dissipate any unease over "idealism", without offering anything like a causal explanation of the changes I have been describing, to say a little bit about how the new idea of moral order came to acquire the strength which eventually allows it to shape the social imaginaries of modernity.

I have already mentioned one context, in a sense the original home of this modern idea of order, in the discursive practices of theorists reacting to the destruction wrought by the Wars of Religion. Their aim was to find a stable basis of legitimacy beyond confessional differences. But this whole attempt needs to be placed in a broader context still: what one might call the taming or domestication of the feudal nobility, which went on from the end of the fourteenth and into the sixteenth century. I mean the transformation of the noble class from semi-independent warrior chieftains, often with extensive followings, who in theory owed allegiance to the King, but in practice were quite capable of using their coercive power for all sorts of ends unsanctioned by royal power, to a nobility of servants of the Crown/nation, who might often serve in a military capacity, but were no longer capable of acting independently in this capacity.

In England, the change came about essentially under the Tudors, who raised a new service nobility over the remnants of the old warrior caste which had laid waste the Kingdom in the Wars of the Roses. In France, the process was longer and more conflictual, involving the creation of a new noblesse de robe alongside the older noblesse d'épée.

This altered the self-understanding of noble and gentry élites, their social imaginary not of the whole society, but of themselves as a class or order within it. It brought with it new models of sociability, new ideals, and new notions of the training required to fulfill their role. The ideal was no longer that of the semi-independent warrior, the "preux chevalier", with the associated honour code, but rather that of the courtier, acting alongside others in advising/serving royal power. The new gentleman required not principally a training in arms, but a humanistic education which would enable him to become a "civil" governor. The function was now advising, persuading, first colleagues, and ultimately ruling power. It was necessary to cultivate the capacities of self-presentation, rhetoric, persuasion, winning friendships, looking formidable, accommodating, pleasing. Where the old nobles lived on their estates, surrounded by retainers, who were their subordinates, the new top people had to operate in courts or cities, where the hierarchical relations were more complex, frequently ambiguous, sometimes as yet indeterminate, because adept manoeuvring could bring you to the top in a trice (and mistakes could precipitate an abrupt fall).[4]

Hence the new importance of humanist training for élites. Instead of teaching your boy to joust, get him reading Erasmus, or Castiglione, so that he knows how to speak properly, make a good impression, converse persuasively with others in a wide variety of situations. This training made sense in the new kind of social space, the new modes of sociability, in which noble or gentry children would have to make their way. The paradigm defining the new sociability is not ritualized combat, but rather conversation, talking, pleasing, being persuasive, in a context of quasi-equality. I mean by this latter term not an absence of hierarchy, because court society was full of this, but rather a context in which hierarchy has to be partly bracketed, because of the complexity, ambiguity, and indeterminacy noted above. So that one learns to talk to people at a great range of levels within certain common constraints of politeness, because this is what being pleasing and persuasive require. You can't get anywhere either if you're always pulling rank and ignoring those beneath you, or so tongue-tied you can't talk to those above.

These qualities were often packed into the term 'courtesy', whose etymology points to the space where they had to be displayed. The term was an old one, going back to the time of the troubadours, and passing through the flourishing Burgundian court of the fifteenth century. But its meaning changed. The older courts were places where semi-independent warriors congregated from time to time for jousts and hierarchical displays around the royal household. But when Castiglione writes his bestselling *Courtier,* the context is the city-court of the Duchess of Urbino, where the courtier has his permanent abode, and where his occupation is advising his ruler. Life is a continuous conversation.

In its later meaning, 'courtesy' comes to be associated with another term, 'civility'. This too invokes a dense background, which I tried to describe in Chapter 2, section 2. It was, indeed, also concerned, as we saw, with ordered government, and the repression of excessive violence.

So the high Renaissance understanding of "courtesy" brings it close to the same age's understanding of "civility".[5] This convergence reflects the taming of the aristocracy, and the great internal pacification of society under the nascent modern state (external war was a different matter). Both virtues designate the qualities one needs to bring about cohesion in the new élite social space. "By courtesie and humanitie, all societies among men are maintained and preserved"; and "the chiefe signs of civilitie [are] quietness, concord, agreiment, fellowship and friendship". The virtues promoting social harmony and over-all peace include, as well as civility, "Courtesie, Gentlenesse, Affabilitie, Clemencie, Humanitie".[6]

The discussion above of civility points us to a third facet of the transition to a pacified élite. Civility was not a natural condition of human beings. Nor was it easily attained. It required great efforts of discipline, the taming of raw nature. The child embodies the "natural" condition of lawlessness, and has to be made over.[7]

So we need to understand the notion of civility not just in the context of the taming of the nobility, but in relation to the much more widespread and ambitious attempt to make over all classes of society through new forms of discipline, economic, military, religious, moral, which are a striking feature of European society from at least the seventeenth century. This was powered both by the aspiration to a more complete religious reform, both Protestant and Catholic; and by the ambitions of states to achieve more military power, and hence as a necessary condition, a more productive economy. Indeed, these two programmes were often interwoven; reforming governments saw religion as a very good source of discipline, and churches as handy instruments. And many religious reformers, in turn, saw ordered social life as the essential expression of conversion.

So we see the interwoven operation of the ideals of courtesy, civility and (religious) Reform, and we see the vectors of change in European society with which they are connected: ordered government, reduction of violence, disciplines of self-control, and economic reform, new institutions/practices based on such disciplines, like changed modes of economic entrepreneurship, new forms of "confinement"—hospitals, schools, workhouses—new modes of military organization, and the like.

Is this idealism? I suppose it would be, if anyone were foolish enough to see these ideals as impinging from nowhere on European society, and driving these changes forward. But in fact, nothing like this is really conceivable. At every stage we have an inextricable interweaving of plural motivations: royal governments striving to keep order, these same governments struggling to find the sinews of war, and realizing more and more that they needed economic improvement to get them; new non-noble strata which could rise by serving these royal governments, or by trade; and then of course, there is the powerful impulse given by the drive to Reform itself, which engaged a great many people and frequently commanded changes which were difficult to resist. All these helped advance the changes which gave expression to the ideals.

All this helped create a new mental world, one in which the modern ideal of order was at home. The connections and affinities are not hard to trace. We see on one hand, the development of a new model of élite sociability, connected to the notion of civility, in which the paradigm is conversation under conditions of quasi-equality; on the other hand, we see the project of extending this civility beyond the ruling strata to much broader sections of the society. There are affinities here with the modern notion of moral order. Sociability as conversation could suggest a model of society as mutual exchange rather than hierarchical order; while the project of transforming non-élites through discipline can mean that the features of civility will not remain forever the property of a single class, but are meant to be spread wider. At the same time, the very goal of making people over suggests a break with the older notions of order, in the semi-Platonic mode of an ideal Form underlying the real, and working for its own realization—or at least against whatever infringes it, as the elements expressed their horror at Macbeth's crime. It fits rather with the notion of order as a formula to be realized in constructive artifice, which is just what the modern order offers; societies emerge from human agency, through contract; but God has given us the model we should follow.

These are possible affinities; but at the same time, there are others. For instance, society as conversation can give a new relevance to the ideal of republican self-rule, as it did in Renaissance Italy, and then later in northern Europe, particularly in England during and after the Civil War.[8] Or else it can remain captured within that other agent of social transformation, the "absolute" monarchical state.

What seems to have pushed the élite social consciousness we have been describing decisively into the ambit of the modern social imaginary were the developments of the new sociability which occurred in the eighteenth century, particularly in England where they start a little earlier. This period saw a broadening of the élite social stratum, those involved in ruling or administering the society, to include those occupied essentially with "economic" functions, either because members of the already dominant class turned themselves towards these functions, became improving landlords, for instance; or through opening a place for merchants, bankers and the propertied generally.

Now the conditions which I called above quasi-equality have to bridge a wider gap. Without engendering the full-scale contemporary notion of equality, the understanding of membership in "society" was broadened, and detached from specific gentry or noble features, even while keeping the language of "gentility". The extended understanding of civility, now called frequently "politeness", remained directed to the goal of producing harmony and easing social relations, but it had now to hold together people from different classes, and operate in a number of new venues, including coffee houses, theatres, gardens.⁹ As in the earlier idea of civility, too, entering polite society involved broadening one's perspective, and entering into a higher mode of being than the merely private; but the emphasis now is on the virtue of benevolence, and a mode of life less overtly competitive than those fostered by earlier warrior or courtier codes. Eighteenth century polite society even gave rise to an ethic of "sensibility".

This relative distancing from hierarchy, and the new centrality of benevolence, brought the age closer to the modern model of order described above. At the same time, the inclusion of economic functions in "society" intensified the affinity between civility and this notion of order.

This eighteenth century transition is in a sense a crucial one in the development of Western modernity. "Polite" society had a new kind of self-consciousness, which one could call "historical" in a new sense. It was not only unprecedentedly aware of the importance of its economic underpinnings; it also had a new understanding of its place in history, as a way of life which belonged to "commercial" society, a stage of history recently arrived at. The eighteenth century generated new, stadial theories of history, which saw human society developing through a series of stages, defined by the form of their economy: e.g., hunter-gatherer, agricultural, etc., culminating in the contemporary commercial society.¹⁰ This made people see the whole transition I have called the taming of the nobility, as well as the internal pacification of modern societies, in a new light. Commerce, "le doux commerce," was endowed with this power to relegate martial values and the military way of life to a subordinate role, ending their age-old dominance of human culture.¹¹ Political societies could no longer be understood simply in perennial terms; one had to take account of the epoch in which things happened. Modernity was an epoch without precedent.¹²

PART II

The Turning Point

6 Providential Deism

Let us return now to the main line of our story: how did an exclusive humanism become a live option for large numbers of people, first among élites, and then more generally?[1]

The genesis comes about through an intermediate stage, which is often referred to as "Deism". There are many facets of this, and I want to single out three in the chapters of this part. The first turns around the notion of the world as designed by God. This understanding, which of course is perfectly orthodox as a general notion, goes through an anthropocentric shift in the late seventeenth and eighteenth century. I will call the upshot of this shift "Providential Deism". The second facet of Deism is the shift towards the primacy of impersonal order. God relates to us primarily by establishing a certain order of things, whose moral shape we can easily grasp, if we are not misled by false and superstitious notions. We obey God in following the demands of this order. We see a third facet of Deism in the idea of a true, original natural religion, which has been obscured by accretions and corruptions, and which must now be laid clear again.

1

We saw above how the discourse of the modern moral order reshaped the understanding of Providence. It led in a sense to an "economistic" view of it. But the change which is fateful for the story I'm following here is the narrowing of the purposes of Divine Providence. God's goals for us shrink to the single end of our encompassing this order of mutual benefit he has designed for us.

Of course, a crucial feature of God's order, deriving from the very way in which we discover and define it, is that it is directed to the good of the creatures which make it up, and especially ourselves. This is not new in the Judaeo-Christian tradition. But it had always been thought that God had further purposes as well in his creation; that these were largely inscrutable, but that they included our love and worship of him. So that a recognition of God and our dependence on him places immediately on us a demand which goes beyond human flourishing.

But now a striking anthropocentric shift occurs, around the turn of the seventeenth/eighteenth centuries, give or take a couple of decades. We can in fact get a fuller view of this shift, if we discern four directions of change in it, each one reducing the role and place of the transcendent.

Now the first anthropocentric shift comes with the eclipse of this sense of further purpose; and hence of the idea that we owe God anything further than the realization of his plan. Which means fundamentally that we owe him essentially the achievement of our own good. This was formulated by Tindal in his *Christianity as Old as the Creation*, a title which itself reflects the third facet of Deism, the appeal to an original natural religion. For Tindal, God's purposes for us are confined to the encompassing of "the common Interest, and mutual Happiness of his rational Creatures."[2]

Now Tindal was an extreme case, and not many agreed with his book when it came out in the early eighteenth century. Tindal went all the way, while I am talking about a trend here. But Tindal was far from alone in giving voice to this trend. There were the Huguenot exiles in Holland, Jean Leclerc and Jacques Bernard; somewhat later in France, the Abbé de Saint-Pierre adopted the position that the practice of virtue was the only form of cult worthy of God. The goals of religion and politics are the same, "l'observation de la justice et la pratique de la bienfaisance." The Abbé, whose outlook was immensely influential, coined this term "bienfaisance", which became a key notion of the Enlightenment. His favourite appellations for God were indeed "l'Être souverainement bienfaisant" and "l'Être infiniment bienfaisant".[3]

But beyond those who subscribed to these unambiguous formulations, even people who held to orthodox beliefs were influenced by this humanizing trend; frequently the transcendent dimension of their faith became less central.

The second anthropocentric shift was the eclipse of grace. The order God designed was there for reason to see. By reason and discipline, humans could rise to the challenge and realize it. Now even those orthodox thinkers in the past who might have agreed with such a high view of the power of reason would have wanted to add at this point that the full measure of good will required for carrying out the programme of rational discipline, given our fallen condition, required God's grace. Without this always being denied, it fades in the spiritual climate I'm calling "Deist".

God still has a role, of course; indeed, he often is given two. First he made us, and endowed us with reason, and in some cases also, with benevolence, and it is these faculties which enable us to get things together, and carry out his plan. And secondly, in case this didn't suffice, he stands at the end of time as judge, promising to distribute rewards of unimaginable joy, and punishments of unspeakable agony; and these will concentrate our minds on the task at hand.

Authors differed on whether they relied more on inherent benevolence, or on the rewards and punishments. Locke stands at one extreme. He sees us as being so susceptible to being driven from the path of right reason by sloth, covetousness, passion, ambition, superstition, and bad education and customs, that God has acted providentially in establishing and publishing (through revelation) such rewards and pains, without which we wouldn't be able to muster the motivation to comply.

> The Philosophers, indeed, showed the beauty of virtue: they set her off and drew men's eyes and approbation to her; but leaving her unendowed, very few were willing to espouse her . . . But now there being put into the scales, on her side, "an exceeding and immortal weight of glory", interest is come about to her; and virtue now is visibly the most enriching purchase, and by much the best bargain . . . It has another relish and efficacy to persuade men, that if they live well here, they shall be happy hereafter. Open their eyes to the endless unspeakable joys of another life; and their hearts will find something solid to move them . . . Upon this foundation, and upon this only, morality stands firm, and may defy all competition.[4]

This position repelled others, for instance, Shaftesbury, and after him Hutcheson, and they insisted rather on the force of the motives of love, benevolence and solidarity within us. This second variant gains ground throughout the century, in keeping with "the decline of Hell", the greater and greater reluctance to accept traditional beliefs about an implacable punishing God. But in neither one form or the other, is there a role for grace.

The third shift follows from the first two. The sense of mystery fades. Here again, there is an extreme statement at the turn of the century, Toland's *Christianity not mysterious;* a book which was much excoriated, and even burned by the public hangman in Ireland. But it too captured and pushed to its full conclusion, a broader trend, which others were reluctant to articulate.

This in a way follows from the other two changes, and the general way in which natural order is understood. If God's purposes for us encompass only our own good, and this can be read from the design of our nature, then no further mystery can hide here. If we set aside one of the central mysteries of traditional Christian faith, that of evil, of our estrangement from God, and inability to return to him unaided, but we see all the motivation we need already there, either in our self-interest well understood, or in our feelings of benevolence, then there is no further mystery in the human heart.

That other great niche of mystery, God's Providence, has also been emptied. His Providence consists simply in his plan for us, which we understand. "Particular providences", unforeseeable interventions in specific cases, have no more place in the scheme; no more than miracles. Indeed, if God is relying on our reason to grasp the laws of his universe, and hence carry out his plan, it would be irresponsible of him and defeat his purpose to be intervening miraculously. If God were to adjust laws to particular cases, then this "would immediately supersede all contrivance and forethought of men, and all prudent action", as Hutcheson argues.[5]

The fourth shift came with the eclipse of the idea that God was planning a transformation of human beings, which would take them beyond the limitations which inhere in their present condition. In the Christian tradition, this has usually been expressed in terms of humans becoming partakers in the life of God. The Greek fathers, followed by the Cambridge Platonists, spoke of "theiosis", a "becoming divine", which was part of human destiny. This prospect is, in a sense, a counterpart to the demand to go beyond merely human flourishing. The call to love God, and love Creatures in the fulsome way that God does, is matched by the promise of a change which will make these heights attainable for us.

This prospect survives longest as an account of the after-life. The transformation, which will take us beyond our limitations in this life, will be realized in another life after death. Figures like Butler and Kant, for instance, hang on to this vestige of the traditional Christian doctrine, even when they have given ground on some of the other shifts. In this form, of course, the doctrine of transformation is safely insulated from Christian life in this world, being quite relegated to the next.

What underlay these shifts? There were many factors at the time which undoubtedly help to explain it (always remembering that the explanations offered here will be of the partial and fragmentary type I mentioned above).

Chaunu has talked about the "high tides" of religious fervour and controversy, which after a century and a half of intense flow, begin to ebb. We are familiar with this kind of fatigue reaction from powerful ideological mobilization in our own century; something of the kind seems to have been taking place in the latter part of the seventeenth century, in both England and France. The leading classes of both countries began to have less and less sympathy for aggressive religious partisanship. Tolerance was more and more an accepted norm. The general European reaction to Louis' Revocation of the Edict of Nantes in 1685 showed it to be quite out of tune with powerful currents of European élite opinion.[6]

More particularly, the English had cause to reflect on the costs of intense partisanship after their Civil War. The Restoration sees a reaction against fanaticism and "enthusiasm". At the same time, partly for this reason, and partly perhaps because of the success of the new science, there was an insistence on a simpler, doctrinally less elaborated religion, and one more accessible to reason.

All these factors played a role; but I do not think that they can fully illuminate the fourfold anthropocentric shift I've been describing. It is certain that religious fervour fell off among the leading strata of many European countries. A certain skepticism, even a scoffing attitude could be discerned in many a coffee-house conversation or salon. It was this general climate, rather than widespread unambiguously espoused unbelief, which explains the sense we frequently meet among concerned clergy and other serious believers that they had an important apologetic task on their hands. Major figures, like Boyle and Clarke, were concerned to produce solid proofs of the existence and goodness of God. Butler's writings were largely apologetic in intent.

Indeed, Butler, in his charge to his diocesan clergy in 1751 speaks of "the general decay of religion in this nation, which is now observed by every one and has been for some time the complaint of all serious persons." The number of those who think seriously about these issues, Butler declared, "and who profess themselves unbelievers, increases, and with their numbers, their zeal."[7]

Real unbelievers, such as the world knows in profusion today, that is, people who clearly in their own mind reject a belief in God, were not all that numerous in 1751, though the few who fit the description were highly placed. Butler was reacting to a decline in zeal, even a disaffection with religion. But this has existed in many epochs in history, without bringing about an actual rise in a rival belief system.

More significant, as Michael Buckley points out in his penetrating book, is the fact that the great apologetic effort called forth by this disaffection itself narrowed its focus so drastically. It barely invoked the saving action of Christ, nor did it dwell on the life of devotion and prayer, although the seventeenth century was rich in this. The arguments turned exclusively on demonstrating God as Creator, and showing his Providence.[8]

Whence this narrowing? I believe it reflects in part the hold of the new idea of moral order. It was perhaps more than understandable that, after the terrible struggles around deep theological issues to do with grace, free will, and predestination, many people should hunger for a less theologically elaborate faith which would guide them towards holy living. The Cambridge Platonists made this kind of plea. But so also did such figures as Jeremy Taylor, Tillotson, and Locke. What is significant is that the plea for a holy life came to be reductively seen as a call to centre on morality, and morality in turn as a matter of conduct.

As we move from the Cambridge Platonists through Tillotson to Locke and the eighteenth century, apologetics, and indeed, much preaching, is less and less concerned with sin as a condition we need to be rescued from through some transformation of our being, and more and more with sin as wrong behaviour which we can be persuaded, trained or disciplined to turn our backs on. This concern with a morality of correct conduct has been observed by many historians of the period. Religion is narrowed to moralism.[9]

This morality in turn was cast in terms of the modern notion of order, one in which our purposes mesh to our mutual benefit. Self-love and social were ultimately at one. That this harmony had been wrought by God in his providence was a key part of apologetics. As Tillotson put it: "And nothing is more likely to prevail with wise and considerate men to become religious, than to be thoroughly convinced, that religion and happiness, our duty and our interest, are but one and the same thing considered under different notions."[10]

An observer today looks with stupefaction on this pre-shrunk religion,[11] anticipating the root and branch rejection from both sides, by Wesley from one direction, and later secular humanists from the other. How could it be conceived thus narrowly?

A common explanation often given here is the demands of reason. It is certainly true that Restoration clerics appealed frequently to reason. It was a way of returning to a simpler, less theologically elaborate religion, which would give less purchase to divisive disputes. Through reason one could hope to define a compact core of unquestionable belief. For the Anglican Establishment, it might appear that reason would undercut their enemies on both sides, both Papist and Puritan, by refuting "superstition", and showing the groundlessness of "fanaticism". Thomas Sprat, a strong clerical supporter of the Royal Society, argued that those who put their trust in "implicit faith and enthusiasm" might fear the advance of science, but "our church . . . can never be prejudiced in the light of reason, not by the improvements of knowledge, nor by the advancement of the works of men's hands, . . . From whence may be concluded that we cannot make war against reason, without undermining our own strength."[12]

With benefit of hindsight, we know how this kind of reasoning would be later turned against Sprat's Church; but unless we accept a simple secularization thesis, that religion must retreat before reason, it is hard to see this as a cogent explanation for the narrowing of much official religion in his time. For one thing, 'reason' does not have a single, unambiguous meaning. It was appealed to by the Cambridge Platonists, also in an attempt to define a simpler, purer religion which would nourish holy living. But their account of reason had a place for an intuition of the divine. Of course, this Cartesian-Platonic understanding was undermined by the success of the new natural science. But even if we accept the new account of knowledge, empirical and focussed on the evidence of the senses, we still can't find sufficient ground for the exclusion of Christology, devotion and religious experience from apologetics and much preaching.

The new natural science did indeed, threaten some of the outlying forms which had become intricated with religion, e.g., the Ptolemaic system, and the scholastic method; it did, of course, hasten the disenchantment of the world, helping to split spirit from matter; more seriously, its conception of exceptionless natural law would later raise questions about the possibility of miracles. But this by itself can't explain the turning from devotion and religious experience to an external moralism.

True, the receding of Chaunu's "high tides" meant that there was a falling off in devotion. But this still doesn't explain why what there was so often took this moralistic form, why a figure for instance, like William Law, whose devotional life was so reminiscent of the theocentrism of the seventeenth century, was such a marginal figure in the first half of the eighteenth, until the preaching of Wesley, who admired him, brought something of this life of prayer back to the forefront.

The early modern period was rich in the development of devotional practices. It was a continuation of this greater flowering of inward religion which marks the end of the Middle Ages. Discipline, method, the new sense of human agency was turned to account by Ignatius Loyola in the form of spiritual exercises which were intended to open us to God. The "devout humanism" of early seventeenth century France, which has been so well described by Henri Bremond,[13] explored the ways of achieving a "theocentrism" of one's life. It supposes, and at the same time intensifies, a high degree of reflectiveness about one's own orientation, a consciousness of the distraction and self-absorption that currently dominates, and proposes ways to nourish a dedication to and love of God which will take us beyond these. In these practices of prayer and devotion, and in the reflections, say, of St. François de Sales, in his *Traité de l'Amour de Dieu,* God's presence in the world, however narrowed in the theories of theologians, is still very much felt.[14]

But devout humanism supposes that we can find within us that élan towards God on which we can build, the seed which we can nourish. Now this falls afoul of the strand of hyper-Augustinian spirituality which was so powerful in that age. If our nature is really quite depraved, then the hope of finding this élan within us can be a snare and a delusion, a figment of our own pride. Recognizing our distance from God, we can only throw ourselves on his mercy, hoping that he will heal our ruined nature. We must obey his commandments from a distance in fear, rather than presume to approach him in love.

This, of course, was the standpoint generally adopted by the stream of spirituality that we call Jansenist. St. Cyran, Arnauld, Nicole, and others were highly suspicious of devout humanism, and very critical of it.[15] But the outlook was much wider than the sect. We see this affirmation of a religion of fear in Bossuet, in his struggle with that late defender of devout humanism, Fénelon, over the issue of "amour pur".

This was a spirituality which put the emphasis on external conduct, both moral and ritual. So that the Jansenists laid great emphasis on the prayer of the church, and introduced a number of liturgical reforms; they demanded the most excruciatingly high standards of ethical conduct. They undoubtedly contributed to the great achievements of the age in organization and self-discipline. But they probably also contributed to the atrophy of the inner devotional life based on a sense of our inner link with God. And in this way, they may have accredited, when the high tides of devotion subsided, an understanding of religion so one-sidedly in terms of a morality of correct conduct.

There is a paradox here, because in the Jansenist view, it is precisely the confidence of devout humanism which ends up fostering the later exclusive variety, indeed is already a step on the road towards it. And we can certainly argue that the later sense of the goodness of nature, both within and without, probably drew on the heritage of humanist devotion. There seems on the surface much more continuity between the two humanisms than between the religious consciousness of depravity and fear and the sunny affirmation of nature's innocence. But one can nonetheless claim that this latter paradoxical pairing shows up some of the dynamic of the connection. It may help reveal: how it came about that a religion of external conduct comes to be so important in the eighteenth century; how the conduct it prescribed was already so entrenched by discipline in many strata of the population. And it certainly helps explain how the new affirmation of human innocence arose as a reaction to this sense of depravity and fear, once the inner devotion it animated was no longer widely and deeply felt.

Whatever the truth of these speculations, it is clear that the narrower religion and apologetics of the early eighteenth century fits well within a conception of the buffered self and an understanding of providence shaped by the modern moral order. And so perhaps the question we ought to ask is: Why after all did this order so strongly mark the hermeneutic of legitimacy of this age?

To find the answer, we have to look at another facet of the experience of the time. I refer to the experience on the part of élites of success in imposing the order they sought on themselves and on society. First, the training in a disciplined, sober, industrious life came to be widespread enough that for lots of people this became a second nature, from which individuals would deviate, but which was not under perpetual threat of being cast off and abandoned. The situation among the dominant classes in, say, eighteenth century England, was in this respect very different from that of the raw knights, prone to violence and disorder, of early Tudor times, from which some of them were descended. At the same time, some headway was being made in educating other classes, and instilling some facets of this ordered existence in them. There still was a long way to go, in the eyes of the dominant classes, as witness the draconian laws to protect property; but there was some sense that a "civilizing process" had been begun, that could continue further.

Hence the tone, very much present in early neo-Stoicism, of the intense struggle that the disciplined life requires, both within the agent and in relation to society, fades in the eighteenth century. Locke still has a lively sense of what a hard slog it was, but a half century later lots of influential writers offer a very much more eirenic picture. Order is now seen more often as in the cards, either because self-interest is thought to conduce to public good of its own bent; or because the standard human motivation is seen as being much more benign and benevolent.

The first of these grounds, what Halévy called "the harmony of interests", took a more and more prominent place in the thinking of the age. We find it with Nicole in the seventeenth century, in the notion that society can be so organized that even our lower motives can conduce to order. The idea was made notorious in Mandeville's *The Fable of the Bees,* in the shocking thought that private vices conduce to public benefit. It was finally given canonical form in the invisible hand doctrine of Adam Smith, and was henceforth almost universally admitted.

That this shift reflects an experience of the successful inculcation of a disciplined, industrious and productive form of life seems evident. Although these truths were often presented as timeless, in fact they assumed that self-interest would find its normal expression in productive work and fair exchange, rather than in military exploits and pillage. They assumed a population already imbued with a "bourgeois" ethic of disciplined production, rather than an ethic of military adventure. The very fact that the first of these came to be seen as "natural" says volumes for the confidence that West European élites were beginning to have in the orders that they had been building. They felt secure enough in them to begin to see them as first, rather than second nature.

Or, on another widespread view, these orders were seen as secure once humans had emerged out of savagery and had tasted the benefits of civilization. This sense of the importance of peaceful industry and exchange was part of what it meant to live in a "polite" age, along with a free sociability of intellectual discussion and a more refined sensibility.

This elision is still an illusion that we, their descendants, are vulnerable to. We still can experience surprise when the "privatization", recommended by the best Harvard economists to some republic of the former Soviet Union, ends up putting criminal syndicates in charge of most enterprises, or simply installs a kleptocracy of the previous ruling clique.

The spreading doctrines of the harmony of interests reflect the shift in the idea of natural order which we described in the previous part, in which the economic dimension takes on greater and greater importance, and "economic" (that is, ordered, peaceful, productive) activity is more and more the model for human behaviour.

We can perhaps see how this economic-centred idea of harmony could contribute to the fourfold anthropocentric shift I described above. The confidence in our own order-creating powers which the belief in harmony betokens made the help of grace seem less necessary. The very scrutability of the whole system left little place for mystery. And the very idea that peace and order depend not on some high heroic aspiration, but on the lowly, interest-driven self-love in us, seems to render otiose any attempt to transcend ourselves, to aim beyond ordinary human flourishing.

In fact, this is not only unnecessary, but even potentially dangerous. Heroics are more at home in the aristocratic-warrior honour ethic. They threaten to disrupt the orderly exchange of services actuated by mutual interest. If God's purpose for us really is simply that we flourish, and we flourish by judicious use of industry and instrumental reason, then what possible use could he have for a Saint Francis, who in a great élan of love calls on his followers to dedicate themselves to a life of poverty? At best, this must lower GNP, by withdrawing these mendicants from the workforce; but worse, it can lower the morale of the productive.[16] Better to accept the limitations of our nature as self-loving creatures, and make the best of it.

This seems to be Tindal's view. He holds that God is capable of disinterested love, in a way that we are not. We can only love God, because he's good to us. God's greatness exists precisely in his not needing us, but being disposed nevertheless to think exclusively of our good. Tindal doesn't see that we are called on in any way to participate in this self-giving love.[17]

But at this point, something else becomes evident. The shift to Deism was also justified by arguments which are central to the Christian tradition, often those which had been used by the Reformers. Take this matter of abjuring false heroics for our ordinary, self-loving nature. This parallels closely the Reformers' defense of ordinary life, and the vocations of work and family, against the supposedly exceptional vocations of celibacy. These high-flyers were seen as being filled with prideful illusion, as though they could do without what ordinary human beings need as God made them. They scorn God's gifts, for "God hath given us Temporals to enjoy . . . We should therefore suck the sweet of them, and so slack our thirst with them, as not to be Insatiably craving after more."[18] Tindal carries this argument farther; one might think that he carries it beyond the bounds of recognizable Christian faith, but he appeals to a Christian reaction—against presumptuous claims to unfounded purity made by an élite.[19]

Even the more radical idea, espoused later by exclusive humanism, the rehabilitation of ordinary, even sensuous, desire as good, against the "calumnies" of orthodox religion; even this, although directed against mainline Protestants as much as Catholics, took up and transposed one of the main themes of the Reformation. This claimed to liberate the Christian from the weight of a gratuitous, and presumptuous, asceticism. The liberty of the Christian, says Calvin, means not being scrupled by indifferent things.[20] Now this same sense of liberation is mobilized around the innocence of desire. We release this part of us which lay, as it were, under an ancient curse. We might almost say that humanism redeems it from bondage, in hallowing it as good. And with desire, we redeem the humble, the ordinary in human life, the hitherto despised sensuous and material.

Similarly, the rejection of mystery carried further a line of criticism levied by the Reformers against the Catholic Church. The attacks on the Church's sacred, and in particular on the Mass, made light of the claim that there was a mystery here. How could a piece of bread be the body of Christ? These mysteries were branded as an excuse for what we would call today mystification, with the aim of holding Christians in thrall to a usurped power. The ordinary Christian could read the Scripture and grasp its plain sense. He had no need of this authority. What Calvin did to the mysteries of the Catholic Church, Toland did to mystery as such.[21]

Tindal also uses an argument which had been levied against the extreme Augustinianism of the Reformers, but by other Christians, whose orthodoxy was undiminished. Whichcote and others had argued that it was demeaning to God to suppose that he was concerned in relation to us with anything but our good; that, for instance, he might need our service, and might be angry if we didn't satisfy the demands of his honour. Tindal takes up this point in his book: we shouldn't think of God as injured by human wrongdoing. It is wrong and demeaning to God to think that he punishes us to restore his own honour. He does it purely for our sake.[22]

Here we see another facet of the debate. Tindal is using an argument drawn from a counter-current to the dominating Augustinianism of both major segments of Christendom in the early modern period. He is part, in a sense, of a strong *reaction* against mainstream Christianity. We'll have to take account of that too, when we come to describe the rise of exclusive humanism. But although a minority view at the time, this stance of Whichcote's remains very much within the broader tradition. For him, the good of ours which God pursues includes "deification", the raising of human nature to participate in the divine.[23] For Tindal, on the other hand, he purposes nothing beyond ordinary human flourishing.

For many people, then as now, the view articulated by Tindal has seemed to be a gratuitous reduction of human scope. There is a long train of thinkers, from the Romantic period on, who have reacted against this excision of the heroic dimension from human life, including Tocqueville and Nietzsche. The reduction may even seem humanly incomprehensible. But we have to remember that it entailed a kind of self-transcendence in another direction. The rational agent, who is capable of seeing that self-love and social are the same, and designing a social order on this basis, has already stepped way beyond the narrow point of view of the single being that he/she is. As an agent of instrumental reason, he/she stands at the point of view of the whole, and is moved by the greatness and design of this whole. Theorists sometimes commit a kind of pragmatic contradiction in not taking account, in their theory of the human agent, of the motives which actuate them as theorists and overall planners. But this mode of transcendence is still there, and one of the motive forces behind their position.

This may put us on the track of another reason for this surprising narrowing of the religious outlook, this time focussing on the buffered self, and in particular, on its disengaged reason. The apologetics of this period focusses on the universe as an order of mutual benefit. Much like the new natural science, and partly inspired by it, it presents the universe as a system before our gaze, whereby we can grasp the whole in a kind of tableau. Indeed, according to the dominant moral theory developed in this period, the truly moral agent should be able to abstract from his own situation, and adopt the standpoint of the "impartial spectator" that Hutcheson introduced into the debate, followed later by Smith, and then by the Utilitarians.

This is, of course, the classic stand of disengagement, laying out the universe as a tableau, from which the thinker is disintricated; even though he may also recognize that he figures as a small component within it, this is not the vantage from which he is now contemplating the whole. We are in what Heidegger has called "the Age of the World-picture".[24]

Something rather different happens within an understanding of the cosmos as a hierarchy of forms. There it is obvious that the human observer is on a certain level, and while he is aware that there are levels which are higher, and has some idea of their nature, it is also accepted that his grasp of them will be imperfect. In this sense, seeing the whole in a tableau, in which all parts and levels are equally intelligible, because identically placed in relation to the thinker, is obviously impossible. The view of the whole is from a certain position within it, and it essentially reflects that placing.

How does this affect the religion and apologetics of this time? Well, perhaps the confident way in which God's purposes are being read off the Universe, and his good intentions demonstrated, reflects precisely this stance of the World-picture, the disengaged grasp of the whole, which has put behind it the sense that the higher levels may not be fully scrutable.

More, perhaps the very emphasis on theodicy, on proving the goodness and justice of God from the universe, which dominates the apologetics of this age, reflects this disengaged stance. One can always be induced to question God's rightness. After all, Abraham and Moses started way back arguing with God about his intentions. But the certainty that we have all the elements we need to carry out a trial of God (and triumphantly acquit him by our apologetic) can only come in the Age of the World-picture. Indeed, an increased preoccupation with theodicy seems to be a feature of this age. Earlier, in dire straits in the world he made, we can more easily be inclined to appeal to him as helper and saviour, while accepting that we can't understand how his creation got into this fix, and whose fault it is (presumably ours). Now that we think we see how it all works, the argument gets displaced. People in coffee-houses and salons begin to express their disaffection in reflections on divine justice, and the theologians begin to feel that this is the challenge they must meet to fight back the coming wave of unbelief. The burning concern with theodicy is enframed by the new imagined epistemic predicament.

So we can get a sense of the complex forces which brought about the fourfold eclipse I'm capturing in my ideal type of "Providential Deism". Partly the social experience of successful imposition of order and discipline, on self and on society; partly the carrying forward of reflections which were already very much part of anyway, Reformed Christianity, and pushing them on to a more radical stage; partly a reaction against the juridical-penal framework which Mediaeval and Reformed Christianity had made into an exclusive horizon. This reaction had its profound Christian sources, in the Greek Fathers, for instance; but it served as well to bolster Deism; as it would serve soon to power exclusive humanism.

What remained for God after the "Deist" fourfold eclipse? Still something significant. God remains the Creator, and hence our benefactor, to whom we owe gratitude beyond all measure. We are grateful for his Providence, which has designed our good; but this Providence remains exclusively general: particular providences, and miracles, are out. They would, indeed, defeat the kind of good which God has planned for us. And he has prepared for us an afterlife, with rewards and punishments. This, too, is for our good, because it is what motivates us to fulfill his beneficent plan.

But not enough to block exclusive humanism. We can run through the reasoning again. Once disenchantment has befallen the world, the sense that God is an indispensable source for our spiritual and moral life migrates. From being the guarantor that good will triumph, or at least hold its own, in a world of spirits and meaningful forces, he becomes (1) the essential energizer of that ordering power through which we disenchant the world, and turn it to our purposes. As the very origin of our being, spiritual and material, he (2) commands our allegiance and worship, a worship which is now purer through being disintricated from the enchanted world.

But with the fourfold eclipse, the very notion that God has purposes for us beyond fulfilling his plan in the world, equated with our good, begins to fade. Worship shrinks to carrying out God's goals (= our goals) in the world. So element (2) becomes weaker and weaker.

As to element (1), this was expressed principally in terms of a doctrine of grace. This was seconded in lay ethics, like neo-Stoicism, by a sense that the power to impose order on self and world is God's power in us, which we have to recognize and nurture. With growing confidence, reflected in the new harmonious, economic-centred order, neither grace nor the nurture of God's power in us seem all that indispensable. Space has been created for a shift, in which the power to order will be seen as purely intra-human.

It is true that on the Deist view, God can also help us in another way. The very contemplation of his goodness in his works inspires us, and energizes us to do his will.

> Thus as the calm and most extensive determination of the soul towards the universal happiness can have no other centre of rest and joy than the original independent omnipotent Goodness; so without the knowledge of it, and the most ardent love and resignation to it, the soul cannot attain to its most stable and highest perfection and excellence.[25]

The strength that this can impart to us is not negligible, and perhaps most people will recognize the need for some source like this. But having got this far, it is not clear why something of the same inspiring power cannot come from the contemplation of the order of nature itself, without reference to a Creator. And this idea has recurred in exclusive humanisms.

And so exclusive humanism could take hold, as more than a theory held by a tiny minority, but as a more and more viable spiritual outlook. There needed two conditions for its appearance: the negative one, that the enchanted world fade; and also the positive one, that a viable conception of our highest spiritual and moral aspirations arise such that we could conceive of doing without God in acknowledging and pursuing them. This came about in the ethic of imposed order (which also played an essential role in disenchantment), and in an experience with this ethic which made it seem possible to rely exclusively on intra-human powers to carry it through. The points at which God had seemed an indispensable source for this ordering power were the ones which began to fade and become invisible. The hitherto unthought became thinkable.

2

Thinkable perhaps, but not yet thought. I want to look more closely at the transition from the first to the second. It occurs within the culture which developed among the élites of the advanced societies of Western Europe in the eighteenth century, the culture of "polite" society.

What was this idea of polite society? It was part of the self-understanding of their own world among Western (and principally English-French-Scottish) élite strata. It was a self-understanding cast in historical form, of a kind which has become all-pervasive in modern society. Polite society had emerged recently out of an earlier form, and was defined by the contrast.

Mediaeval society had been violent, full of the disordered clashes of an armed aristocracy, whose members defined themselves as warriors; the ancient poleis and republics had also been led by a warrior class, and had been in their own way dedicated to war. The members of a "polite" society were dedicated primarily to the arts of peace.

First, this society was a productive one, which gave an important place to the useful arts, and to their steady improvement. In modern terms, the economic dimension of society, and economic progress in particular, was highly valued. It was a general belief that an important cause of the transition to polite society had been the development of commerce.

But this society also defined itself by its devotion to the finer arts, to what we now sometimes call "fine art", to literature, to conversation, to philosophy. Polite society was civilized, and this meant that it had reached a higher level of refinement than its immediate predecessor (whether or not it had surpassed the heights of classical civilization was a matter of dispute).

But this meant that it defined itself not only by its crucial goals (peace rather than fighting, self-improvement in the arts rather than in warrior skills), but also that it prided itself on its characteristic styles of action. Refined or polite "manners" were the key, and indeed, the term 'polite' has survived in our language in this context, even while it has disappeared in the manifold other uses of the eighteenth century. "Manners" defined a certain kind of sociability, a way we relate to each other, approach each other, converse with each other.

The polite style or manner was to approach the other as an independent agent, with his (and now also her) own legitimate views and interests, and enter into courteous exchange for mutual benefit; be it on one level economic exchange for mutual enrichment; or conversational exchange for mutual enlightenment or amusement. Thus a paradigm locus for this kind of sociability, apart from the market, was the salon or coffeehouse, in which enlightened conversation took place, extended through the growing range of publications which were meant to aliment these exchanges. Polite society showed itself above all in the refinement of this kind of meeting and exchange, in which of course a new kind of disrespect and agonism could emerge, but one situated within the forms and goals of polite repartee. Your deliciously ironic remark cuts me down to size and ensures that the Countess will focus on you for the rest of the soirée, but this remark was designed to amuse, and perhaps even instruct, and in this is light-years away from the rapier thrust I am dreaming of giving you, if I can induce you to meet me at dawn in an earlier form of agonic encounter.

Similarly, mutual respect for each other as equals had strict limits. It did not include the mass of peasants or artisans, but it did rather remarkably manage to gather together, without excessive distance of rank, nobles and well-placed commoners.

Beneath manners, although the line between the two is hard to draw, was what was called by French writers 'les moeurs', the complex of largely unarticulated values and norms which guided the members of polite society in their mutual dealings. It was a matter of moeurs what was required and what permitted, what was beneath one's dignity or demanded by it, what was shameful or honourable, unconscionable or laudatory. Polite culture was very conscious of moeurs, because they were rightly aware that what had changed in the immediately preceding centuries was very often not so much the laws of their country, and not the established religious forms, and often not the basis of authority and sovereignty. Voltaire praised the age of Louis XIV as the time when polite society becomes established in France, its premier seat in Europe (as all Frenchmen, and even many Britons, saw it).[26] But what changed in that time was not so much the explicitly valid rules of society, but the spirit, the unofficial and largely implicit norms of élite exchange. Nothing legally prevented Louis from revoking the Edict of Nantes and persecuting his Protestant subjects, but such a flagrant disrespect for free opinion was seen as unconscionable within the prism of politeness.[27]

Thus the transition which brought about this new culture was seen partly in economic and political terms: the extension of commerce, wider travel and "discoveries"; the rise of stronger states which could force the warring nobles to disband their irregular forces and keep the peace; but was also seen as a change in outlook: a widening of the mind, refinement of sensibility, greater interest in the sciences and philosophy. As Hume put it in his *History of Great Britain,*

> About this period [after about 1500], the minds of men, throughout Europe, especially in England, seem to have undergone a general, but insensible revolution. Though letters had been revived in the preceding age, they were chiefly cultivated by sedentary professions; nor had they, till now, begun to spread themselves, in any degree, among men of the world. Arts, both mechanical and liberal, were every day receiving great improvements. Navigation had extended itself over the whole globe. Travelling was become more secure and agreeable. And the general system of politics, in Europe, was become more enlarged and comprehensive. In consequence of this universal fermentation, the ideas of men enlarged themselves on all sides.[28]

We can see, in this self-understanding as polite society, the central role played by what I called above the modern moral order, which is refracted in this civilizational ideal. The importance accorded to liberty, to a mode of sociability which respects the independent interest and opinion of the other; the understanding that social intercourse is designed for mutual benefit; the high place given to commerce and productive activities, all these reflect features of the modern order.

But what is even more significant is that there is here an ideal of sociability, derived from this order, which has been erected into an independent criterion for social relations. "Independent" here means first of all from the political structure. This is not at first a revolutionary threat, of course. Indeed, in this first self-understanding of polite society, through a view about its own genesis, the rise of strong, even "absolute" states was considered a crucial cause of the pacification of society which made this new higher phase possible. It was natural that Voltaire should write in praise of Louis XIV as the main agent of this change. But even those writing in the British context, with a strong sense of their "liberties", also had a lively sense of the need for authority. Certainly Hume had, although we must bear in mind that he was more skeptical of the Whig line than most authors in this field.

But through this understanding of politeness, the modern moral order becomes for Enlightened opinion a criterion of good government which well-advised rulers, even "despots" ought to hearken to. This was how Voltaire saw it, and even some "despots"—Frederick, Joseph, Catherine—began partly to respond. We are already on the slope which will make "public opinion" the arbiter of the King's action in the dying years of the ancien régime.

The link established here between the modern moral order and "civilization" also illustrates one of the principal theses I am defending in this work, the close connection between the ideal of order and the disciplines and modes of organization by which society was to be "civilized". It was, in fact, the felt success of these forms of self-refashioning which underwrote the confidence in this sociability as an independent criterion. In terms of our discussion above, we might say that the culture of politeness was the first stage in the passage of the modern moral order from a mere theory to a form of social imaginary, here underpinning the practices of an educated and "polished" élite.

But "independent" also meant something more. It meant independent from ecclesiastical or particular-doctrinal authority. This didn't have to mean, of course, independence from religion; because one could easily conceive of the modern moral order in a providentialist framework, as God's design for humans, as I have described it above. But this just strengthens the point: to see the order as God's design gives it an authority which cannot be overturned by the deliverances of any magisterium, nor set aside in the name of any doctrine particular to one or other denomination. We can recall here that the modern moral order, in its earliest formulations, with Grotius, for instance, was meant to give political authority a place to stand, independent of confessional strife.

To follow through on the logic of this position is to come to hold that the normative force of this sociability cannot be over-ruled by the deliverances of any church, which is why the reaction of polite society to an act like the Revocation of the Edict of Nantes was negative, and becomes overwhelmingly so as we enter the eighteenth century. Such brutal enforcement of a difference in doctrine, irrelevant to the general truths about God as the designer of the moral order, is itself a breach of the order—unless, of course, it was necessary to assure public tranquillity and obedience, which was manifestly not so in this case. Enlightened Europe could have understood the—even bloody—suppression of a sect whose doctrine justified subversion of established authority or property, but not the gratuitous coercion of law-abiding subjects with a slightly deviant theology.

So within the framework of polite society, there come to be a set of normative limits on the action and intervention of churches, and the playing out of religious differences: largely overlapping with those with which we have become familiar in contemporary society. State power should operate independent of ecclesiastical control, and public order should be maintained without disturbance by ecclesiastical-doctrinal strife, whether this originates from below, among sects, or from above by gratuitous state coercion or persecution.[29]

This means that there is a strong potential conflict between this ideal of sociality and the kind of sacral authority claimed by, e.g., the magisterium of the Catholic Church, or the "High" interpretations of authority in the Church of England. The actual coming-to-be of a range of non-Christian and anti-Christian positions, ranging from various forms of Deism and Unitarianism to exclusive humanism, can best be understood within this field of potential and frequently actualized conflict.

Polite sociability puts a strain on allegiance to strong forms of sacral authority, claiming a right to intervene in society and politics in ways which go beyond, or even cut across the order. By the same token it puts a strain on the various beliefs and practices which could be the basis of such strong sacral authority. These include a strong notion of the sacred, as defined in our earlier chapter, as situated in some people, places, times, or acts, as against others defined as "profane". Hence the polite outlook is more hospitable to what I have called disenchantment, and this new culture is a continuation of the process of sidelining the sacred.

Further, insofar as the figure of Christ, as divine, stands behind claims to sacral authority, while the issue whether Jesus was God or simply a great prophet or teacher is not relevant to the question whether God is the Designer of the order of mutual benefit, there is a temptation to abandon either the question or the doctrine of Christ's divinity, to slide towards Socianism, or Deism; or else to adopt a skeptical stance towards such questions.

Polite civilization, and the moral order it entrenches, can easily become lived as a self-sufficient framework within which to find the standards of our social, moral and political life; the only transcendent references admitted being those which underpin the order and do not justify infringing it. On the social and civilizational level, it fits perfectly with, indeed expresses, what I called above the "buffered identity", the self-understanding which arises out of disenchantment. Otherwise put, it is a social and civilizational framework which inhibits or blocks out certain of the ways in which transcendence has historically impinged on humans, and been present in their lives. It tends to complete and entrench on a civilizational level the anthropocentric shift I described in the previous section. It builds for the buffered identity a buffered world.

We can see the outlook emerging from this logic in some of the key terms used by writers of the eighteenth century to describe the history and present state of polite civilization. Three kinds of dangerous religion were categorized as "superstition", "fanaticism", and "enthusiasm". The first designated the enchanted dimension of religion, the rites and cults and practices which partook of magic in their understanding. In this, they were continuing and extending an existing Protestant vocabulary of condemnation of Catholicism.

'Fanaticism' designated the kind of religious certainty that seemed to the agent concerned to licence going well beyond, and even committing gross violations against the order of mutual benefit. While 'enthusiasm' meant the certainty that one heard the voice of God, and could act on it, without having to rely on external authority, ecclesiastical or civil. Enthusiasm could lead to fanaticism, but it could also turn people away from it, as with certain pacifist sects like the Quakers; while fanaticism could also be generated, of course, out of religions with strong authority structures, like the Catholic Church, that had no truck with enthusiasm.

The Abbé Raynal, in a very influential work, makes it clear that conformity to this modern idea of order, which he calls "l'intérêt général", is the supreme principle of civil society. "L'intérêt général est la règle de tout ce qui doit subsister dans l'État" (the general interest is the rule of everything which should subsist in the State). From which it follows that "le peuple ou l'autorité souveraine, dépositaire de la sienne, a seule le droit de juger de la conformité de quelque institution que ce soit avec l'intérêt général" (the people, or the sovereign power in which its authority is invested, alone has the right to judge of any institution whatever whether it conforms to the general interest). In the ensuing discussion, he makes clear what kinds of dangers he fears that religion might pose to this order:

C'est à cette autorité, et à cette autorité seule qu'il appartient d'examiner les dogmes et les disciplines d'une religion; les dogmes, pour s'assurer si, contraires su sens commun, ils n'exposeraient point la tranquillité à des troubles d'autant plus dangereux que les idées d'un bonheur à venir s'y compliqueront avec le zèle pour la gloire de Dieu et la soumission à des vérités qu'on regardera comme révélées; la discipline, pour voir si elle ne choque pas les mœurs régnantes, n'éteint pas l'esprit patriotique, n'affaiblit pas le courage, ne dégoûte point de l'industrie, du mariage et des affaires publiques, ne nuit pas à la population et à la sociabilité, n'inspire pas le fanatisme et l'intolérance, ne sème point la division entre les proches de la même famille, entre les familles d'une même cité, entre les cités d'un même royaume, entre les royaumes de la terre, ne diminue point le respect dû au souverain et aux magistrats, et ne prêche ni des maximes d'une austérité qui attriste, ni des conseils qui amènent à la folie.[30]

(It pertains to this authority, and to this authority alone, to examine the dogmas and the disciplines of a religion: dogmas, to make sure that, contrary to common sense, they would not expose peaceful order to disturbances made all the more dangerous by the fact that dogmatic ideas of a happiness to come are combined with the zeal for God's glory and the submission to truths that are regarded as revelation; and discipline, to ascertain that it does not offend prevailing mores, dampen patriotic spirit, enfeeble courage, nor turn people away from industry, marriage, and public affairs; that it harm neither the population nor sociability, that it not inspire fanaticism and intolerance, sow division between family members, between families in the same city, between cities within a kingdom, between kingdoms on Earth; that it does not diminish the respect due to the sovereign and to the magistrates, and that it advocates neither maxims of a demoralizing austerity, nor counsel that leads to madness.)

The less radical wing of the Enlightenment could be much softer on superstition than on the other two deviations, because writers like Hume or Gibbon seemed to take for granted that Enlightenment and politeness would remain élite possessions, and the problem remained of how to keep order among the masses. For these, a little superstition could be a good thing, satisfying their religious impulses without inculcating rebellion. This supposed that the religion would be primarily defined by cult, and not by doctrines, which could be the source of disputation with believers of other creeds.

The anti-model here was Catholic Christianity, whose superstition was indeed, linked with a militant doctrine. But the model for Gibbon was the ancient world, whose unbelieving élites, in his view, were sophisticated enough to conform outwardly to the national cults, and leave the people undisturbed in their sacred practices. "The various modes of worship, which prevailed in the Roman world, were all considered by the people, as equally true; by the philosophers, as equally false; and by the magistrates, as equally useful."[31] Gibbon can't help showing his sympathy with these ancient magistrates, confronted with the fanatical refusal of Christians to pay their dues by a similar outward conformity to essential public rites. He portrays them as reluctant persecutors, contrasting them favourably with such modern enforcers of orthodoxy as Louis XIV. They were more puzzled than scandalized; they really had trouble understanding these sectaries. He concludes that they were also much less severe than their modern counterparts in Christendom. "As they were actuated, not by the furious zeal of bigots, but by the temperate policy of legislators, contempt must often have relaxed, and humanity must frequently have suspended the execution of those laws, which they enacted against the humble and obscure followers of Christ."[32] These Roman magistrates get a high rating on the polite ethic, because their motivation was purely public order, in no way mixed with doctrinal zeal; they pass where Louis ignominiously flunks.

The version of polite culture embodied by Gibbon and Hume is not only averse to "enthusiasm" in the sense the term had, but also to what the term means today. Politeness and refinement entailed also a stance of cool and ironic distance from the heated, ugly, and frequently cruel and destructive actions of those in the grips of religious fervour. Though plainly their condemnation of these acts was strong, these writers expressed the superiority of their civilized stance by maintaining a cool distance from their object, laced periodically with ironic wit. This unflappable stance was itself to them one emblem of Enlightened politeness, and it is integral to the power and influence of Gibbon's striking style.

In another passage in which he compares ancient pagan thinkers to Christian sectaries, he describes the pain of the former at the suppression of pagan religion under the Christian emperors.

> The ruins of the Pagan religion is described by the sophists, as a dreadful and amazing prodigy, which covered the earth with darkness, and restored the ancient dominion of chaos and of night. They relate, in solemn and pathetic strains, that the temples were converted into sepulchres, and that the holy places, which had been adorned by the statues of the gods, were basely polluted by the relics of Christian martyrs.

It is typical of Gibbon, and of his ironic self-positioning, that the last part of this quote, and particularly the strong term "polluted", can be easily read as a bit of early *style indirect libre:* the word is being put in the mouths of the sophists. But later on, Gibbon seems to enter his own comment with the dry remark: "Without approving the malice, it is natural enough to share the surprise, of the Sophist, the spectator of a revolution, which raised these obscure victims of the laws of Rome, to the rank of celestial and invisible protectors of the Roman empire."[33] From a lofty height above these calamitous events, we the enlightened readers are being invited to savour the absurdity of it all, sine ira ac studio.

Polite civilization provides the stage, a site of potential grave conflict with Christianity, in which different reactions were possible. Some strove to accommodate the two; some felt the clash, and became critics of "politeness"; some felt it and were propelled into various modes of rejection of Christian orthodoxy. But politeness by itself doesn't provide the background to understand the more far-reaching rejections. It can help us understand élite skeptics like Gibbon and Hume, but not those whose reactions were more radical. I mean this is a double sense, that these positions were sometimes more radical politically, that they were less accommodating of established orders than the Enlightenment of Voltaire and Gibbon; but I also mean that they frequently went farther into the fashioning of a militant exclusive humanism, which sometimes could extend even to materialism. More needs to be said of how exclusive humanism could come onto the scene as a real alternative, and for masses of people.

3

I have been trying to show, in the preceding pages, how exclusive humanism could arise. But this isn't yet an account of its actual arising, what it meant for it to come on the scene as a real alternative.

Let me try to bring out the main lines of my account again, in order to delineate better what remains to be said. I have been speaking of a fourfold anthropocentric shift in the eighteenth century, which I'm associating with my construct "Providential Deism". In a sense, the first two can be seen as crucial, carrying the others with them.

The first was that the plan of God for human beings was reduced to their coming to realize the order in their lives which he had planned for their happiness and well-being. Essentially, the carrying out of the order of mutual benefit was what God created us for. The sense that there is a further vocation for human being, beyond human flourishing, atrophies in the climate of "Deism".

This shift in turn is set in a very long-lasting bent in European culture towards Reform, in the widest sense. I mean by this, the attempt by élites to make over society, and the life and practices of non-élites, so as to conform to what the élites identify as higher standards. This is a remarkable fact. I don't pretend to have an explanation for it, but I offer it as a fact, that ever since the great Hildebrandine Reform of the eleventh century, there were recurrent attempts to raise the standards of mass practice. At first, these were religious reforms; they attempted to raise the whole body of the clergy, and later even the mass of the laity, to the higher standard of devotion and pious life which was largely defined by the best of monastic and clerical practice. The goal set by the Fourth Lateran Council in 1215, to impose a régime of once-yearly confession, absolution and communion on all lay people was an instance of this raising of the standards universally demanded.

The idea behind the Hildebrandine reform has been called by Arquillière "political Augustinianism". This is slightly unfair to Augustine, as Arquillière admits.[34] Augustine had a much stronger sense of the gap between the city of God and the earthly city, so that the attempt by the magisterium, seconded by state power, to bring society more into line with the heavenly city would have certainly appeared extremely hazardous to him, at the least.[35] Of course, reforming Popes accepted that the fullness of justice, which for Augustine must include giving to God his due, cannot be expected in this world. Sinners will abound until the end. But a régime can be envisaged in which people are subordinated to rule which models itself on full justice. If kingly power really follows the injunctions of those speaking with the authority of God's will (the hierarchy of the Church), then an order can be established in which those truly good will rule, and the bad will be forced to conform.[36]

The idea begins slowly to arise, developing through stages over several centuries, of a world here and now in which no compromises need to be made with any alternative principle. The promise of the Parousia, that God will be all in all, can be realized here, albeit in the reduced form which requires constraint. The drive of Christian reform from this point onward tends to take this direction: the mass of the faithful must be made over to come as close as possible to the minority of dedicated Christians. Foucault was right, that the decision of the Fourth Lateran Council in 1215, prescribing one-on-one confession for the entire laity, was part of this project of making over.

The reforms, of course, never work as planned. But what is striking is the degree to which church élites recurrently return to the attempt, after periods of laxity and corruption. Hildebrand himself followed such a lax period, and reacts to it. And so did successive waves of reformers, operating both on the level of the rules imposed on clergy and laity, and also through movements of preachers, calling on people to convert, and face the dread responsibilities of personal judgment.

In a sense, what we think of as THE Reformation has to be seen in this context. True, it reacts to another period of shocking laxity and corruption in high ecclesiastical places, but the Catholic Church it rejected had itself been the locus of reform efforts for several centuries, and under the impact of heresy and schism, then underwent another gigantic reform. Probably no other branch of Christendom went through such repeated, far-reaching and global attempts of reform as Latin

Christendom has done in this second millennium of our era, and continues to do today. In a sense, one might argue that reform, re-awakening, re-organization, re-newed dedication and discipline has become part of the standing culture of all the Churches which have issued out of Western Christendom. Again, I don't pretend to understand why; but it seems to me that this is a fact, and a rather significant one.[37]

Around 1500, this drive begins to take a slightly different direction. It begins to take up a more ambitious goal, to change the habits and life-practices, not only religious but civil, of whole populations; to instil orderly, sober, disciplined, productive ways of living in everyone. This is the point where the religious drive to reform begins to become interwoven into the attempts to introduce civility, thus to "civilize", as the key term came to be. This was not a simple take-over, a deviation imposed on the drive to religious reform; because religious reformers themselves concurred that the undeniable fruit of Godliness would be ordered, disciplined lives. They also sought to civilize, for good theological reasons.[38]

And yet, over the longue durée, there was arguably a deviation here. At least a terrible irony. Because what was seen as an unfailing mark of Godliness, and thus very much worth pursuing, somehow comes to infiltrate the very essence of Godliness, becomes gradually indistinguishable from it. The tremendous investment in reform, and hence discipline, which inspires such a sense of their spiritual superiority in the breasts of Latin, and ex-Latin Christians, when they contemplate those of other faiths, or even other Christian churches, this immense effort seems itself to have obscured the essentials of the faith, and to have led to a substitution of something secondary for the primary goal of centring everything on God. This was the first anthropocentric shift.

The second one complements this. Once the goal is shrunk, it can begin to seem that we can encompass it with our unaided forces. Grace seems less essential. We can see where exclusive humanism can arise. The stage is set, as it were, for its entrance. But in order for it effectively to come on stage, we need more than just the negative fact that grace doesn't seem such a dire necessity; that it cease to be what it must have been for Calvin and his colleagues in the sixteenth century, as they contemplated the disorder, violence, vice, debauchery and danger endemic in their society, and knew that only strong spiritual medicine could bring order. (And, indeed, we might add, as a Brasilian worker knows today, when he breaks a crippling drinking habit in joining a Pentecostal church; as an African-American adolescent in a ghetto knows as he escapes the drug culture by joining the Nation of Islam.)

Beyond this negative change, we also need the positive move that moral/spiritual resources can be experienced as purely immanent. This is also a crucial part of our story. What does this entail? To formulate it in the way I put the question in the introduction: we need to see how it became possible to experience moral fullness, to identify the locus of our highest moral capacity and inspiration, without reference to God, but within the range of purely intra-human powers.

However, in the context we are describing, not just any such experience could do the trick. Since that time, we have seen many formulations of fullness with an exclusively human reference; for instance, Nietzsche writing about the eternal return in the last entry in *The Will to Power;* where we sense that what is being captured here is a heightened moment of inspiration, but in which the understanding which underpins it is rigorously atheist.[39] But this couldn't have been the first mode of exclusive humanism. That's because the context in which this arose was defined by a sense of the over-riding moral importance of the order of mutual benefit, the sense that this order had to be realized as far as possible, and that it was within our power to do so. The identification of moral fullness, of the highest moral sources, had to be adequate to this task. It had to be something which could energize us to act for its realization, a functional replacement either for Christian agape, or the disinterested benevolence of the neo-Stoics.

This means that it had not only to incorporate the confidence that we can actually re-order and reshape our lives, but also the motivation to carry this out for the benefit of all. The locus of the highest moral capacity had to be a source of benevolence, and of the aspiration to universal justice. Now benevolence and universal concern are precisely the hallmarks of eighteenth century exclusive humanism, or perhaps we might say, of the humanism which turned exclusive; of utilitarianism, or the theory of Kant; or the Enlightenment proponents of the rights of man, and of a new dispensation based on general human happiness and welfare. As Bentham famously put it: "Is there one of these my pages in which the love of humankind has for a moment been forgotten? Show it me, and this hand shall be the first to tear it out."[40]

These moral sources had to be created/discovered. A standard subtractionist story would convince us that once the old religious and metaphysical beliefs withered away, room was finally made for the existing, purely human moral motivation. But this was not the case. It may seem to be, because the locus now of the highest moral capacities was identified as in "human nature". And that links up with centuries of non-exclusive humanism, and in particular with the moral theories that came down to us from the ancients. And these were certainly already available.

But it is already evident that, in one sense, this modern humanism is different from most ancient ethics of human nature, in that it is exclusive, that is, its notion of human flourishing makes no reference to something higher which humans should reverence or love or acknowledge. And this clearly distinguishes it from, say, Plato, or the Stoics. On the other hand, there is the case of the Epicurean-Lucretian philosophy, which does seem genuinely exclusive in my sense (and which just for this reason was the reference point of a number of modern thinkers, e.g., Hume). Now if we take this as our comparison, two differences stand out sharply.

First, the modern image of human flourishing incorporates an activist, interventionist stance, both towards nature and to human society. Both are to be re-ordered, in the light of instrumental reason, to suit human purposes. The theories developed about human society approach it instrumentally; e.g., it exists to protect life and property. It is understood functionally. Activist re-ordering and instrumental reason are key categories.

Secondly, the new humanism has taken over universalism from its Christian roots; or else moves to retrieve it from Stoic sources, as with an influential modern school of thought in the sixteenth and seventeenth centuries (often called "neo-Stoicism"). By this, I mean that it accepts in principle that the good of everyone must be served in the re-ordering of things. Of course, this "in principle" is in fact breached in numerous ways, corresponding to the cultural restrictions of the time, be they of class, birth, gender, confession. But the principle nevertheless mattered, because these breaches and exclusions came in time under pressure, had to be justified, and failed to sustain themselves.

But more, the new humanism supposes that we are motivated to act for the good of our fellow human beings. We are endowed with a specific bent in this direction. In this way the moral psychology of modern humanism is strikingly different from the ancients. For the latter, we are bound to (some) others in ties of friendship or common citizenship, because we can only pursue our good in common. The desire to act beneficently arises out of the recognition of these common goals. For Aristotle, even distributive justice only makes sense within the framework of the common project of the polis. Only Stoicism offers an exception to this narrow focus of beneficence among the ancients. But even here, the Stoics, who really did conceive of solidarity as species-wide, in a sense held to the same framework: they simply extended it, seeing us as part of the great cosmopolis of all Gods and humans.

On the contrary, what has always been stressed in Christian agape is the way in which it can take us beyond the bounds of any already existing solidarity. The Good Samaritan was in no way bound to the man he helped. That was, indeed, part of the point of the story. Of course, this active charity, stepping beyond the bounds of community can be placed in the context of a super-community of all the children of God, thus replicating something close to the Stoic cosmopolis. But this is seen more as something to be built, an eschatological concept. And the paradigmatic stepping beyond of agape, the incarnation and submission to death of Christ, is not motivated by a pre-existing community or solidarity. It is free gift of God.

This active, community-transcendent beneficence is reflected in the moral psychologies of modern exclusive humanism, in the frequently recurring idea that human beings are endowed with a capacity of benevolence, or altruism, which will emerge if it is not stifled by unfavourable conditions. Even where an attempt is made to give a naturalistic explanation to this, for instance, in a theory of sympathy, the idea is there that human motivation includes a bent to act for the good of others, just in virtue of their being fellow humans, independently of any perception of common interest or purpose.

In other words, there is a specific drive to beneficence in modern humanist moral psychology, independent of pre-existing ties. Its scope is in principle universal. This is the historical trace, as it were, of agape. Or otherwise put, this is the upshot of the second immanentizing move I mentioned above, which no longer seeks the power to build the order in our individual and collective lives in God and grace. But we can't just describe this move negatively. It not only shuts out God, it attributes this great power of benevolence or altruism to humans. It would be one thing to reject Christianity in the name of a real return to a pre-modern exclusive humanism, like that of Lucretius. Some were tempted by this, and moved in this direction, e.g., Hume. But the main thrust of modern exclusive humanism has tried rather to immanentize this capacity of beneficence, and this is very far from being a return to ancient wisdom. Nietzsche tirelessly made this point. And even Hume incorporates into his theory a very modern notion of sympathy.

I have been stressing the way in which modern humanisms innovated in relation to the ancients, drawing on the forms of Christian faith they emerged from: active re-ordering; instrumental rationality; universalism; benevolence. But of course, their aim was also to reject the Christian aspiration to transcend flourishing. Hence only the self-giving which conduced to general flourishing as now defined was allowed as rational and natural, and even that within reasonable bounds. The rest was condemned as extravagance, or "enthusiasm". Think of the contempt of a Hume or a Gibbon for the Christian ascetic traditions, for monasticism, for missionaries, for prophesying, for the emotional preaching of the Wesleyans. The successor to agape was to be held strictly within the bounds of measure, instrumental reason, and perhaps also good taste.

Nevertheless, there is something remarkable in this retention of an agape-analogue. And I think it tells us two important things about this transition, and hence about ourselves.

The first is that it would probably not have been possible to make the transition to an exclusive humanism on any other basis. My supposition here is that the transition built on the confidence acquired in effecting orders in life and society, which at least began to approximate closer the ideal model of mutual benefit. But agape or beneficence was built into this ideal model at three levels. Charity was part of the ideal of personal conduct; good social order must involve taking care of all members of society; and the proper inward dispositions of a decent man included charitable ones. The basic move in the transition was the recognition that the power to create this order resides in all of us; and since the order is constituted in part by agape or benevolence, then this power must reside in us.

The move to a straight Lucretian outlook would have involved a much bigger break with the whole thrust of society and morality, a break for which none of the groundwork had been laid. Later on, of course, when unbelief had acquired its place within our culture, this and other possibilities began to open up.

The second point takes up this issue from another angle. I have just argued that only this transition was then possible—I mean as more than a marginal, exceptional phenomenon—and not a supposed shift to pure Lucretianism. But it is significant that it *was* possible. Some of the background which had to be prepared was negative. I've mentioned the disenchantment of the world which this ordering helped to bring about. Plainly, in the world of spirits and forces, it was hard to envisage a universe without God. But the short-term effects of disenchantment, and the consequent high demands on our powers to transform ourselves and society, seemed to make God's active grace even more necessary. It was with a certain success and routinization of this ordering process that space was opened for a world without God.

But even taking this into account, the transition didn't have to happen. It also required something positive, viz., that in what turned out to be a gamut of different ways people actually could acquire the conviction that these powers resided in them. They could find within their own human resources the motivation to universal beneficence and justice.

Now one obvious place they might find these resources was in pride. Not the negatively judged pride of Christian preaching, but the positive force which was central to the warrior-aristocratic ethic, whereby one is moved by the sense of one's own dignity to live up to the demands of one's estate. This motive in seventeenth-century French was called "générosité". Corneille's characters incessantly evoked it. Here is Cleopatra's speech from *Pompée:*

> Les Princes ont cela de leur haute naissance
> Leur âme dans leur sang prend des impressions
> Qui dessous leur vertu rangent les passions.
> Leur générosité soumet tout à leur gloire.[41]

> (This to their high extraction Princes owe,
> That by the assistance of their royal blood
> Their passions are more easily subdued.
> Their magnanimity subjects all to their glory.)[42]

The motivation here to control the baser passions is precisely the sense of what they owe to their high birth, the glory which alone suits their station.

Now as we saw with Descartes above, it was possible to take over a transformed version of this ethic. Descartes, as I noted (Chapter 2, section 4), makes generosity "comme la clef de toutes les autres vertus, & le remede general contre tous les dereglemens des Passions" (the key of all the other virtues, and a general remedy for all disorders of the passions). But now the high station whose demands we must live up to is not a social rank. It is the estate of the human being as such, as an agent of rational control. And what it commands is to obey the demands of rational disengagement.

Now the affinities between the honour ethic and the ideal of disengaged self-discipline that emerges from neo-Stoicism were obvious enough. Descartes was not the only person to make the link. There is a parallel I noted above between the demands of discipline and those of warrior training, in the distance they demand from certain intimate relations.

Montesquieu notes that "une noble fierté qui vient de cette satisfaction intérieure que laisse la vertu" is a sentiment which "sied aux grands". "Une grande âme ne saurait s'empêcher de se montrer tout entière: elle sent la dignité de son être."[43] (A noble pride that stems from this internal satisfaction that virtue brings is a sentiment that befits great men. A great soul cannot help showing itself completely; it feels the dignity of its being.) Later this sense of internal satisfaction is recruited for a hedonist philosophy; it is considered one of the greatest pleasures. "Oui! voluptés, c'est le nom que je donne aux témoignages flatteurs qu'on se rend à soi-même, après une action vertueuse", affirms Marivaux (Yes! sensual pleasure, that is what I call the flattering testimony one gives of oneself after a virtuous action). And Diderot concurs, holding that "la félicité que procure la vertu est durable, et que ces plaisirs si purs qui en dérivent sont les délices du sentiment"[44] (the bliss brought by virtue is enduring, and the pleasures so pure which derive from it are the delights of feeling).

This motivation certainly meets the requirement of being a purely intra-human moral source. No one can doubt that, if the older warrior ethics had stood alone, had not been part of an outlook which also recognized a God or gods, they would have been exclusive humanisms; as indeed, the later attempt by Nietzsche at a transposed aristocratic ethic undoubtedly was exclusive. But the problem was that the new ethic of universal benevolence needed something more and other than a motive which was in its essence self-regarding.

Montesquieu himself puts the point pithily. In the school of honour,

les vertus qu'on nous y montre sont toujours moins ce que l'on doit aux autres, que ce que l'on se doit à soi-même: elles ne sont pas tant ce qui nous appelle vers nos concitoyens, que ce qui nous en distingue. On n'y juge pas les actions des hommes comme bonnes, mais comme belles; comme justes, mais comme grandes; comme raisonnables, mais comme extraordinaires.[45]

(The virtues we are shown here are always less what one owes others than what one owes oneself; they are not so much what calls us to our fellow citizens as what distinguishes us from them. Here men's actions are judged not as good but as fine, not as just but as great; not as reasonable but as extraordinary.)[46]

Of course, Montesquieu was speaking of the original ethic of the "honnête homme", not of the transposed variant which Descartes and he took up, and which was supposed to animate the agent of disciplined rational benevolence. But it is clear that the point must partly carry over.

If living up to my dignity as a rational being involves acting for universal beneficence and justice, then a bent to these must be part of what rationality requires, part of what a rational agent finds in herself as a defining feature. There is no way around it. A sense of pride cannot fully replace universal benevolence. It can only second it, give me a reason for living up to it even when it flags; but it cannot operate in the total absence of this benevolence. Or at least, it would then be a quite different ethic, one in which beneficence no longer figured among the things my dignity calls me to; as with Nietzsche's Übermensch, for instance.

Once again, Montesquieu says it best:

Rien n'est plus près de la Providence divine que cette bienveillance générale et cette grande capacité d'aimer qui embrasse tous les hommes, et rien n'approche plus de l'instinct des bêtes que ces bornes que le coeur se donne lorsqu'il n'est touché que de son intérêt propre, ou de ce qui est autour de lui.[47]

(Nothing is closer to divine Providence than this general benevolence and this great capacity to love that encompasses all men; and nothing comes nearer to animal instinct than these limits that the heart gives itself when it is affected only by its own interest or by that which is around it.)

And so the new humanism needed, and found, inner sources of benevolence. And this in more than one way.

One was through a strong sense of the powers of disengaged instrumental reason, whose dispassionate impersonality was taken as sufficient for universal beneficence. This is where modern humanism shows its roots in neo-Stoicism; except, of course, that what has been lost is the idea of a providential course of things, designed by a beneficent God, which the wise person must learn to accept and endorse. Now the idea is advanced that disengaged reason itself, by freeing us from enmiring in our own narrow perspective, and allowing us a view of the whole, must kindle the desire to serve that whole. The impartial spectator will be by this very fact benevolent; seeing what the greatest happiness would amount to, he wants to encompass it.

There are perhaps dangerous illusions attaching to this outlook. But it undoubtedly corresponds to a powerful moral experience in the modern world. Disengagement itself, by freeing us from the confused, perturbed mass of personal desires, cravings, envy, liberates a universal benevolence in us. Bertrand Russell has given expression to this in our century. In "The Essence of Religion", he distinguishes two natures in human beings, one "particular, finite, self-centred; the other universal, infinite, impartial". The infinite part "shines impartially";

> Distant ages and remote regions of space are as real to it as what is present and near. In thought, it rises above the life of the senses, seeking always what is general and open to all men. In desire and will, it aims simply at the good, without regarding the good as mine or yours. In feeling, it gives love to all, not only to those who further the purposes of the self. Unlike the finite self, it is impartial; its impartiality leads to truth in thought, justice in action, and universal love in feeling.[48]

Another way of immanentizing moral power was through a sense of a pure, universal will, an inner power before which we stand in awe, as with Kant. This is a close relation to the disengaged reason I have just described, except that the source of benevolence is not the width of things surveyed. It is rather that the very power to act by universal law is an object of wonder and infinite respect. Kant invokes in the same breath "the starry skies above, and the moral law within".[49] It is this which lifts and inspires us to rise to the full demands of justice and benevolence.

A third way was through a sense of universal sympathy, which only needed the right conditions to flourish into virtue. The source of the love is no longer seen here as residing in dispassionate reason, or in our own awesome capacity to act on universal principles. It lies deep in our emotional make-up; but it has been suppressed, distorted, covered over by the false and denaturing conditions which have developed in history. Our task is to find the conditions which can liberate it. Rousseau, in particular with his notion of pitié, is one of the inspirational writers in this vein.[50]

Another view which arises a little later is the Feuerbachian vision that the powers we have attributed to God are really human potentialities. This rich treasure of moral inspiration can be rediscovered within us.

What was new here was not only the theoretical account of the sources of morality. These are new modes of moral experience. We may be led to think that the feeling, the sense of moral strength, is the same before and after; it is just explained differently, in one case as agape, in the other, say, as the "moral law within". After all, some of the earlier views also placed these sources in a sense within us; the neo-Stoic idea, for instance, that reason was a spark of God within us. Doesn't a Kantian sense the same spark, and just give a different explanation for it?

Now there is undoubtedly something to this idea. There are, for instance, clearly continuities between Kantian moral experience and that of the Stoics and neo-Stoics, on whom Kant drew heavily. But it is quite wrong to think that the difference is *just* a matter of background explanations; that there is something like a raw feel which Lipsius and Kant share, only differing in their attributions of underlying causal mechanisms; as two people might have the same sore throat while proposing different aetiologies of their malady.

When we hear Bertrand Russell articulating his sense of moral inspiration in the quote above, he is not just offering an underlying explanation, he is giving expression to the experience of being lifted to a higher, more universal moral plane. Its being understood in this way is integral to the experience. That is why, for all the analogies, it has to be different from the experience of a Kantian contemplating the moral law within, or of a believer listening to a Bach cantata. In each case the inspiration comes with and from the particular understanding of our human predicament. That is why it can be intensified when we bring this predicament into clearer focus, or when a particularly striking sense of its reality overwhelms us.

This is not to say that this is simply a brute fact of experience, which offers no purchase for criticism, as when I offer the autobiographical detail that such-and-such an idea excites me, I know not why. Because there also is an explanation offered here, and it can turn out wrong. I am after all claiming to identify what is *moving* here; and this claim can fail in a number of ways. The inspiration may fail as we understand things better; what it inspired us to may no longer seem as worthy as we formerly thought; or the claims about reality (e.g., the existence of God) may no longer seem founded. In all these cases, the experience goes dead.

Or else, without repudiating the original experience we may come to reinterpret it. This is what happened with Bede Griffiths, whose description of a marking moment of fullness I quoted in the first chapter. At first what this persuaded him to was a kind of "worship of nature", given shape by his reading of the Romantic poets, Wordsworth, Shelley, and Keats. Later on, he became a Catholic monk, and saw this as a moment in which he was turned to the search of God. But the reinterpretation doesn't align the original experience with the sore throat, of which we now have an alternative explanation. Because the meaning is integral to, it is constituent of the experience. It is not only that reinterpreting it one becomes incapable of living it again in quite the same way; it is also that the change may consist in our seeing in it now a deeper, richer meaning than we were able to take in then. This is how the mature Bede saw the moment the schoolboy had lived decades ago.

What we have here in this discovery of new moral motivations is a composite, experience and reality claim together, amounting to new modes of moral life, which in placing the moral sources within us constitute forms of exclusive humanism. This is what the subtraction story has difficulty accounting for.

I tried to show above that the new modes of moral life innovated in relation to the traditional humanist ethics, drawn from the ancient world. But the most common subtraction story doesn't give much importance to these. The idea is that once religious and metaphysical beliefs fall away, we are left with ordinary human desires, and these are the basis of our modern humanism. This is the residuum, once the false mythologies are subtracted. In the most radical version of the story, ordinary desire undergoes a reversal in value. Formerly it was comprehensively condemned in the name of an other-worldly salvation. Now it is affirmed. Sexual fulfillment, instead of being condemned as a path to perdition, is now seen as one of our greatest joys. Ordinary self-love is no longer sin, but the very basis of healthy human life. The core of the subtraction story consists in this, that we only needed to get these perverse and illusory condemnations off our back, and the value of ordinary human desire shines out, in its true nature, as it has always been.

Now the rehabilitation of human nature was certainly an important strand of the Enlightenment; and it is clear that this reversal, get-off-our-backs story was how many of its protagonists saw, and see themselves. But it is also obvious that this story leaves out something crucial.

There are two ways in which the reversal was conceived in the Enlightenment. I'm really invoking two ideal types here, because most thinkers took some from each. These offer each their own way of casting the motivation to justice/benevolence as immanent, while they also bring about a revolution in relation to the earlier Christian and Stoic understandings of this motivation; the revolution consists in a rehabilitation of ordinary, untransformed human desire and self-love, previously seen as an obstacle to universal justice/benevolence, which now is cast either as innocent, or as a positive force for good.

1. The "innocentizing" strategy paints human motivation as neutral; always a mode of self-love, it can either be well or badly, irrationally or rationally directed. Guided by reason it leads to justice and mutual aid. The extreme case, where this ideal type is virtually unalloyed is, for example, Helvétius: "La douleur et le plaisir physique est le principe ignoré de toutes les actions des hommes"[51] (physical pain and pleasure, this is the as yet unrecognized principle of all human action). Here the issue of the nature of our motivation disappears altogether. Everything depends on what guides it.

There is something here, analogous to the rise out of base, sensual self-absorption into a broader, higher, purer perspective, which figured in the traditional, non-exclusive humanisms derived from the ancients; this is the move from narrow, irrational, brutish, unenlightened ways of seeing the world to enlightenment and science. Science by its very nature involves our taking an objective, and in this sense universal perspective on things. To see human life in the view from nowhere, or to use a term of the epoch, from the standpoint of the "impartial spectator", is to think in universal, and no longer parochial terms. But this rise is now coded as exclusively in the register of the understanding; the will remains constant.

Within this framework, it is clear why the quality of the will is irrelevant to ethics. What is needed to work out what we ought to do is purely disengaged reason.

2. The "positive" strategy is to paint original, unspoiled human motivation as including a bent to solidarity with all others. The notion of sympathy was frequently invoked in this context in the eighteenth century. The extreme case of this ideal type can be seen in certain forms of primitivism: the noble savage has been corrupted, the original straight and healthy reactions have been overlaid. Rousseau in his primitivist moments reflects this (see the description of the unreflecting reactions of pitié in the original state of nature, in the second *Discourse*),[52] although his full theory is much more complicated.

Now what is clear is that we don't have here a simple affirmation of ordinary human desire, as it has always been understood and lived. In each case, a special context has been built within which it can show up as innocent or good. The first shows desire to be innocent, because it can be guided into the channels of beneficent order by disengaged reason. If it weren't docile in this way, it would obviously be terribly bad in the eyes of anyone committed to this order, as all proponents of the Enlightenment were. In the context of this universal, dispassionate, impartial will to good, which supposedly arises out of disengaged reason, nature does indeed, seem to recover its innocence. But it is a little too quick to say that this is a simple discovery of what was always there. That is how things appear within the Helvétian picture. But our experience of lust, greed, anger and the rest of the Seven Deadly Sins, was very different before we adopted this picture, and remains different for those who find the picture implausible. What we have is a view which can arise within our first (Bertrand Russell) mode of moral life referred to above, and which—and here is the important fact—can in fact empower some people to beneficent action. And this was a new development of this period.

The case is even clearer with the second strategy. This involves a quite novel insight into an alleged potentiality of ordinary desire, its ability to align itself spontaneously with a kind of agape (pitié, sympathy). This ability is of its essence, but has been lost or overlaid, and needs to be retrieved. Here again was no simple affirmation of ordinary desire as it always had been lived, rescuing it from the calumnies of religion. This "agapized" desire belongs to a new mode of moral life, the third referred to above (Rousseau).

So exclusive humanism wasn't just something we fell into, once the old myths dissolved, or the "infamous" ancien régime church was crushed. It opened up new human potentialities, viz., to live in these modes of moral life in which the sources are radically immanentized. The subtraction story doesn't allow us to be as surprised as we ought to be at this achievement—or as admiring of it; because it is after all one of the great realizations in the history of human development, whatever our ultimate views about its scope or limitations.

It is an achievement, because getting to the point where we can be inspired and empowered to beneficence by an impartial view of things, or a sense of buried sympathy within, requires training, or inculcated insight, and frequently much work on ourselves. It is in this respect like being moved by other great moral sources in our tradition, be they the Idea of the Good, or God's agape, or the Tao, or humanheartedness. These things are not just given to us by birth, as is our fear of the dark, or of falling, or our response to a parent's smile. Making the new sources available was thus a step in an unprecedented direction, something not to be dismissed lightly.

We might look at Russell's idea of universal benevolence through disengagement in the light of other similar transformations in the history of human spirituality. There are other shifts of this kind, where we suddenly feel the call to go beyond our narrower circles of solidarity, to embrace a wider range of people, even all of humanity, in the scope of our beneficent action. Examples are, for instance, the New Testament, the call by Mohammad to go beyond tribe or nation in founding the new Umma, Stoicism, the Buddha's stepping beyond caste and other ritual distinctions. These moves always arouse both opposition, resistance, from some people, but open up new vistas, a higher plane of spiritual aspiration for others. This is something that, in various forms, human beings are capable of responding to. The newness of the modern form which Russell articulates is this: that for the first time, we have such an opening to the universal which is not based in some way on a connection to the transcendent. Even if we think that this appeal is insufficient, because it leaves something important out, we have to recognize that the development of this purely immanent sense of universal solidarity is an important achievement, a milestone in human history.[53]

At this point I can recur to a matter I left insufficiently explored above. What is the "ontic component" in the modern understanding of moral order? I argued earlier that our notions of moral order contain more than just a definition of norms or ideals; they also offer us a picture of what it is in God's will, or the universe, or ourselves, which makes these norms appropriate and possible of realization. This seems clear enough for the earlier, pre-modern ideas. An order anchored in the cosmos, which tends to realize itself, and reacts to any breach as the animal kingdom did to Duncan's murder, this clearly has a very real "ontic component". But we are tempted to believe that the move to human-centred definitions, particularly those which see the order not as self-realizing but as to be constructed, leaves this component quite aside; it offers nothing but a set of norms.

We can now see what is wrong with this view. The modern understanding of the order of mutual benefit central to the exclusive humanisms which arise out of the Enlightenment has indeed, such a component. The difference is that it is now intra-human. This order is appropriate and realizable by us, precisely because we are, under certain circumstances, capable of universal benevolence and justice. On the more radically materialist variants, this order may find no more succour in nature, now "red in tooth and claw". We may see the human family surrounded by an indifferent, even hostile universe. We may even come to see what terrible, destructive desires human beings are capable of. But through all this, the idea can remain that certain conditions of training, discipline, "civilization", or affirming, non-punitive upbringing will release the motivations of detached benevolence, or awe for the moral law, or universal sympathy, on which this order can be built.

Put in other terms, the confidence can remain that this order speaks to something profound in us, so that building towards it is not like constructing sand-castles. On the contrary, it can be self-stabilizing, its realization making us see how much we cherish it. The conditions of a stable, even if only partial realization of this order are therefore those in which that in us which it speaks to can be released, developed, matured. But what gives the echo in us to the order is these motivations of benevolence. These are thus the ontic component which remains in the modern, unbelieving understandings of order.[54]

This explains why they are not easy to repudiate. Nietzsche indeed did, as did Fascism after him. But you have to go very far along this track to follow them. You have to repudiate also all the norms and ideals of universality. You can't keep the standards of this order while jettisoning all ontic component. This might seem to be the case with certain contemporaries who invoke the name of Nietzsche, and which are sometimes called "post-modernists". But the demands that they make, e.g., for a universal recognition of "differences", show that they are constructing their own variant of the modern understanding of moral order. Why denounce people for failing in this recognition, if it is not possible? And what makes it possible? To what in us does it speak?

The two strategies I noted above which show benevolence to be an inner capacity correspond to the two major views about its ontic placement in our nature. The first of these sees benevolence as a fruit of our escaping our narrow particular standpoint. We rise to it through enlightenment and discipline. The second sees the root of it in our deep nature, in an original propensity to sympathy, which may then get lost and covered over. These yield rather different ways of understanding the historical and personal narratives of our rising to virtue, or falling into vice. Thus discipline and rational self-control plays an entirely positive role in the first account; but it is often seen as what leads us away from our original, spontaneous good nature on the second, as we see for example with Rousseau. On the other side, the very idea of a deep inborn nature is often anathema to the ethics of rational discipline which descend from Locke and Helvétius.

There are two types of story here, but this doesn't mean that a synthesis cannot be attempted. Indeed, some of the most powerful and arresting modern theories are attempts to combine them. Kant is a good example: our noumenal nature is indeed, something innate to us; but it takes a long discipline of reason to emerge. All of German Idealism embroiders and develops Kant's insight here; and Marx, too, draws on this tradition. In a rather different way, John Stuart Mill tries to combine the two traditions.

But however it is conceived, the discovery/definition of these intra-human sources of benevolence is one of the great achievements of our civilization, and the charter of modern unbelief. What has made this great shift possible? This is the question which I've been struggling with through the preceding pages. Clearly, the context for the leap into exclusive humanism was set by the "Deism" which I described earlier: the focus more and more on the order of mutual benefit, or even on "civilization", as the agenda of humanity; and then the very relative, but nevertheless unprecedented, progress in realizing this order; the confidence this generated in human powers, and in the tractability of the universe to human ends. "Deism" provides the framework, but this progress supplied the "material conditions" for the leap.

But there were obviously other conditions: for instance, disengagement, and the secularization of public space. To these, however, we have to add something further, which has to do with the self-understanding of agency. It is clear that this immanentization of moral sources was prepared by the inward turn in modern culture. I have dealt with this extensively elsewhere;[55] I just want to mention a few salient points here.

Clearly the inward turn in the form of disengaged reason directly prepared some of these new modes of moral life—at least the first (B. Russell). The disengaged, disciplined agent, capable of remaking the self, who has discovered and thus released in himself the awesome power of control, is obviously one of the crucial supports of modern exclusive humanism.

Disengagement also contributes in another way. The crucial démarche, as we see it in Descartes, is to isolate the agent from its field, to zero in on it, and to bring out what it has in itself, in abstraction from the surroundings. This is central to Descartes' strategy in the *cogito:* see first the ideas which are "in" us, then raise the issue whether they correspond to what is "out" there.

In a parallel fashion, we can trace the developing notion that the nature of things is "within" them, in an exclusive way quite at variance with the theories of traditional philosophy.[56] This, interwoven with the reaction against disengagement, brings about a new focus on our sentiments as inner. So that we can have an influential ethical theory in the eighteenth century centring on "moral sentiments", and later our moral salvation can be seen in the voice of nature within.[57]

All this created the cultural resources for the immanentization of moral sources. Here is perhaps the locus of another irony. Because this inward turn is also evident in religious life; indeed, the whole turn was largely driven by religious motives.

Mediaeval popular religion was, as we saw above, mainly a devotion of deeds; one fasted, took part in collective rituals and prayers, attended Mass, etc. But in the later Middle Ages, there was a strong move towards more inner devotion, that is, where the focus was self-consciously on God and his goodness. Later Erasmian piety stressed that what matters is the spirit, the intention, not the external practice. Then the Reformation trumpets salvation by faith, and the issue of the quality of my faith becomes central to the lives of countless believers.

In the seventeenth century, the question of "theocentrism" is posed in France by Bérulle and others; the focus is now even more acutely on my inner dispositions: is the centre of my existence myself, or am I centring on God? From this point there are movements which parallel those we see in humanist culture. Corresponding to the stress on moral sentiments, there develop devotions of sentiment: Pietism, Methodism, and on the Catholic side that to the Sacred Heart.

The story of a rejection of the old, unchanging religion, which uncovers and releases the perennial human, is wrong on both counts. Re-invention, innovation exist on both sides, and continuing mutual influence links them.

We can set the stage as well as we can; we can never fully explain the rise of exclusive humanism; certainly not, if explanation means: showing its inevitability, given certain conditions. Like all striking human achievements, there is something in it which resists reduction to these enabling conditions.

That this achievement was possible is an important fact about human beings, albeit it is open to different interpretations. We can hold that, of *course,* we could find our moral sources within, since our conception of these powers was only ever an alienated consciousness of our own human potential, à la Feuerbach. We can hold on the other extreme that this supposed perception is a delusion, a shadow cast by human pride and presumption. Or we can argue, as I would, that neither of these readings is really convincing. The Feuerbachian view can't account for all the malaise that we have experienced around purely immanent humanism. If it really were the triumphantly achieved truth, dispelling error, it should be more self-stabilizing, more all-convincing. The pure delusion view on its side cannot account for the way that people have been strengthened to do good by various versions of this humanism.

But whatever the ultimate verdict, this shift to exclusive humanism is one of the facts of the case, one of the things we have to make sense of in orienting ourselves in and about our modern secular age. How does it help us to understand our present predicament?

4

But does it help us to understand the present age? We might protest that that was then and now is now. There is at present a whole gamut of unbelieving positions, including many which seem to owe little to the Enlightenment humanism, among them those which are frankly hostile to the Enlightenment, and some which present themselves as anti-humanist. What to make of the whole range of views inspired by Nietzsche, who denounced the modern order of mutual benefit root and branch?

The claim I'm making here can be broken down into three sub-parts. First, I've been saying that what I'm calling exclusive humanism arose in connection with, indeed, as an alternative set of moral sources for, the ethic of freedom and mutual benefit. Second, I want to say that it couldn't have arisen any other way at the time. But third, I want to make the further claim that this origin still counts today; that the much wider range of unbelieving positions available today is still somehow marked by this origin point in the ethic of beneficent order.

The first claim will probably be generally accepted. The transition I'm talking about begins in the latter part of the seventeenth century and continues in the eighteenth. One of the first clear signs that something had changed was the reaction to Louis XIV's Revocation of the Edict of Nantes. There was an outcry in educated Europe. This violence done to the free conscience of so many ordered and loyal French subjects seemed gratuitous and savage. Bayle in particular gave expression to the indignation which many felt.

In the early part of the century, a reaction like this wouldn't have been possible. True, many were even then in favour of tolerance. If Richelieu had revoked the Edict at the time of the troubles at La Rochelle, the act would have been regretted by many, widely criticized, it would have stirred up the confessional indignation among Protestants at Catholic oppression. But what would have been missing was the sense that freedom of conscience was a value that should be espoused, independent of confessional adherence, that there was something retrograde in its violation, something uncivilized. This new sense continued to gain strength throughout the next century, culminating in the famous campaigns of Voltaire, particularly in the Calas case.

When we look at this event in the long sweep of changing mentalities in which it figures, and which it helped to further, we can see a decisive shift in the centre of gravity of élite moral sensibility in Western Europe. Freedom, in particular freedom of belief, is beginning to become a value in itself, a crucial feature of any acceptable political order.

We are talking about a quasi-geological movement in the outlook of a whole society, which is very difficult to explain, may not be evident if we focus just on short spans of time, but which seems quite undeniable if we take say, the century which follows 1685—or perhaps, better, the century and a half after 1650.

Alongside or following this growing emphasis on freedom, comes a greater concern with what we might call welfare, with economic prosperity and growth—as the possibilities of this latter come to be more and more understood. This was, of course, partly motivated by the need of governments to create the fiscal and economic sinews of war, but educated Europe begins to be pre-occupied with it for its own sake. Above all, a sense of the new possibilities here begins to spread throughout the eighteenth century.

The emphases on freedom and welfare take a more radical turn in the later eighteenth century. I mean that proposals are put forward and canvassed which involve some quite radical departures from existing practice. We see this, for instance, with laissez-faire economics, coming from Physiocrats, and Adam Smith—admittedly a more far-reaching proposal in the French than in the British context. But the new radicality extends to law reform (Bentham, Beccaria), and eventually to politics as we enter the last quarter of the century, and the great epoch of Revolutions. The modern idea of moral order shifts in this century from a mainly hermeneutic to a more and more prescriptive role.

It is these connected shifts in élite public opinion—and along with this, of course, the emergence of the recognized phenomenon of public opinion, endowed with legitimating force—which I have been interpreting in the light of the ethic of freedom and beneficent order. It seems to me that we can understand this whole movement as a continued working out of the demands of this ethic, together with an ever more insistent demand that it be put into practice.

Now it is within this movement that first, Providential "Deism", and then the early influential formulations of exclusive humanism arise. The coincidence in time seems undeniable, but I am pleading for a closer connection. What is it?

It is, to recap what I argued above, that exclusive humanism begins to look plausible because of the anthropocentric shifts which I described there. These involved, first, that the central moral concern becomes the imposition of a disciplined order on personal and social life, ensuring high standards of self-control and good behaviour in the individual, and peace, order and prosperity in society. Even many of the devout came to place great importance on this ordering project. The highest goals of human beings seem, even in the sphere of religion, to aim at purely human goods. When, on top of this, there begins to be serious progress towards these goals, the idea can gain currency that these ends are within the scope of unaided human powers.

But if God's help in the form of miraculous or providential interventions seem less and less necessary and important, it was still a central tenet of the religious tradition that humans cannot muster the will to act for these ends without God's help, in the form of grace. Here is where a second shift opens a field of purely intra-human moral sources. At this point, the need for God's aid in order to achieve the highest moral/spiritual goals ceases to be something obvious, undeniable, a matter of felt experience for most. People can come to sense themselves as actuated by purely human motives, like a sense of impartial benevolence, or purely human sympathy, in their action to further the ordering project; while at the same time they feel that there is nothing higher or more important than this project.

It is clear that it took both shifts to bring this about. The highest goals had to be brought down into the human realm, as it were, ends beyond human flourishing had to fade from view, even in the outlook of many of the devout, in order that the enhanced human moral powers could meet them half-way, and establish a kind of equilibrium between our goals and our moral abilities. The third anthropocentric shift I described above, the dispelling of mystery, shows the same double movement in a connected domain. On one hand, what is to be understood is now defined in relation to purely human goals: we have to see how human life can be organized so as to bring about fulfillment and happiness. At the same time, we seem to have come into greatly increased cognitive powers, thanks to the methods of the new sciences. Between these two movements, the realm of mystery shrinks, even approaches zero.

It then only requires the prospect of the after-life to fade, in the climate created by the first two changes, and the fourth shift will be completed. Already in this period there is a tendency to conceive of life after death in terms of peace, repose, the reunion with loved ones. The horizon of transformation, in particular in relation to our life here, recedes.

The double movement begins to make exclusive humanism a conceivable option. This suggests a positive motive for embracing this new humanism. It was accompanied by an increased sense of human power, that of the disengaged, impartial ordering agent, or of the self-giver of law, or of an agent who could tap immense inner resources of benevolence and sympathy, empowering him/her to act for universal human good on an unprecedented scale. Put another way, this self-sufficient agent could face down and set aside age-old human fears, of malevolent spirits, of not being chosen by God, of the blind, overwhelming forces of nature.

In short, the buffered identity, capable of disciplined control and benevolence, generated its own sense of dignity and power, its own inner satisfactions, and these could tilt in favour of exclusive humanism.

But there was also a negative motive. We can notice, running through much of the Enlightenment a motif of anger at, even hatred of orthodox Christianity. This was more powerful in some places than others; more so, for instance, in Catholic countries, or in general where the influence of "Deism" wasn't strong enough to soften the opposition between anthropocentrism and Christian faith. When the proponents of Enlightenment were angry and hostile to religion, they attacked it for its obscurantism and irrationality, but this in turn was condemned in large part because it served to justify oppression and the imposition of suffering. The proposing of goals beyond human flourishing were seen as denials of the right to happiness.

What made Christianity particularly repulsive to the Enlightenment mind was the whole juridical-penal way in which the doctrine of original sin and the atonement were cast during the high middle ages and the Reformation. Our distance from perfection was glossed as just punishment for earlier sin; and our salvation through Christ as his offering satisfaction for this fault, paying the fine, as it were.[58]

There were some repugnant aspects of this just in itself. But it became connected to two doctrines which were potentially deeply offensive. The first was the belief that only a few are saved. The second was the doctrine of predestination, which seemed to be generated inevitably from a belief in divine omnipotence in the context of the juridical-penal model.[59]

Now in fact, opinion begins to move against these doctrines in the seventeenth and eighteenth centuries. On the one hand, there is the "decline of hell", and the rise of universalism; on the other, there is growing revulsion at predestined damnation, even within Calvinist societies. Of course, these developments were surely not independent of the one I was tracing above, viz., the growth of confidence in the human power to do good. But they add an extra level of motivation, a revulsion at the orthodox formulations, which must either lead to a revised faith, or in certain cases, to a sharp break with it.

Again, as confidence in human powers grows, and in particular, in the powers of reason, the claims of Churches to authority on behalf of a faith which partly consists of mysteries, becomes harder and harder to accept. This is another way in which a modern rationalism based on science can argue that the rise of science refutes religion.

But this still doesn't capture fully the negative movement, the hostility to Christianity which spread among élites at this time. It wasn't just the particular doctrines of the juridical-penal model, nor the rationalist rejection of mystery.

We saw that much of the historical practice of Christianity ran afoul of the new ethic of purely immanent human good: all striving for something beyond this, be it monasticism, or the life of contemplation, be it Franciscan spirituality or Wesleyan dedication, everything which took us out of the path of ordinary human enjoyments and productive activity, seemed a threat to the good life, and was condemned under the names of "fanaticism" or "enthusiasm". Hume distinguishes the genuine virtues (which are qualities useful to others and to oneself) from the "monkish virtues" ("celibacy, fasting, penance, mortification, self-denial, humility, silence, solitude"), which contribute nothing to, even detract from human welfare. These are rejected by "men of sense", because they serve no manner of purpose; neither advance one's fortune, nor render one more valuable to society, neither entertain others nor bring self-enjoyment. "The gloomy, hare-brained enthusiast, after his death, may have a place in a calendar; but will scarcely ever be admitted, when alive, into intimacy and society, except by those who are as delirious and dismal as himself".[60]

This rejection of much historical practice was implicit in the adoption and radicalization by Providential Deism of the standard Protestant critique of Catholicism. It just took an identification of Christianity itself with these "enthusiastic" practices, in fact its identification with some or other aspiration beyond human flourishing as defined in the modern moral order, for this modern humanism to define itself as anti-Christian, whether it remained in some weak sense "Deist" or flipped over into outright atheism.

For those of us today, for whom it seems evident that Christianity must be identified with such further aspiration, this flip-over appears inevitable. But it was possible at the time to tread a path which identified Christian faith with this stripped-down variant, from Tindal through to Paley. Among those élites who had taken on the new buffered identity of discipline and benevolence, it was a nice hermeneutical issue whether this should strengthen or weaken one's adherence to the ancestral faith.

We see three positions being taken. (1) Some aligned the "true", reformed faith with civilization and "politeness"; others (2) reacted against this alignment, and insisted that faith must carry one beyond this beautifully self-controlled and self-sufficient mode of life, that it requires some giving of self, some surrender of autonomy. We see this in the Evangelical reaction at the end of the century, and even before in Wesleyanism. (3) There is the response of those who agreed in this more demanding definition of the faith, but just for that reason rejected it as the enemy of politeness, even as ultimately a force for barbarism; people like Edward Gibbon, for example.

Those in the first category had no difficulty combining their adherence to faith and civilization. But nor did many in the second category, whose sense of a vocation beyond didn't involve rejecting (what they saw as true) civilization. We can think of many Evangelicals here, who worked to radicalize the going definitions of reform and benevolence, for instance, in the campaigns to abolish slavery.

On the other side, Christians with a strong sense of mystery, or those tempted by Catholic sacramentalism, or those of a Pietist or Methodist persuasion frequently were at one with unbelievers in sensing the incompatibility of their faith with the dominant ethic.

So it could depend very much on personal experience, temperament, and the affinities one felt, how one came down on this issue. Someone deeply into the buffered identity could feel quite secure in his Christian allegiance, say as an Anglican. But someone who ended up identifying just as strongly with this identity, but who had felt at some point in his life the pull of a more demanding faith, could quite easily feel that Christianity was the enemy. In this regard, it might not be irrelevant that Gibbon, who did so much to articulate and define eighteenth-century anti-Christianity, had been tempted into a teenage conversion to Catholicism.

Thus, by a variety of routes, one could end up rejecting Christianity, because in calling for something more than human flourishing, it was the implacable enemy of the human good; and at the same time a denial of the dignity of the self-sufficient buffered identity.

What emerges clearly from this, however, is that, in both its positive and its negative motives, the rise of exclusive humanism was closely tied to the ethic of freedom and beneficent order. It was the centrality of this ethic, and the relative success in carrying it out, which fostered the anthropocentric turn. And it was the strong moral satisfactions of this successful ordering which positively motivated the embracing of the new humanism; while it was the failings of religion in relation to this ethic which often negatively motivated the move.

This account I am offering runs athwart the widespread subtraction story which sees the development of unbelief as coming simply from the progress of science and rational inquiry. This raises a crucial issue, which I want to return to shortly.

There is another way of putting my point about the relation between Reform and what we today call "secularization", starting from this last term itself. Its root is in 'saeculum', the Latin word for a big tract of time, an age. The Greek term it often translates is 'aion' (English 'aeon'). More recently, the term in modern languages (*siècle, siglo*) comes to a fixed quantity, of 100 years, what in English we call a century.

Now 'saeculum', and the adjective 'secular', come to be used in Latin Christendom as one term in a contrast; in fact, several related contrasts. As a description of time, it comes to mean ordinary time, the time which is measured in ages, over against higher time, God's time, or eternity. And so it can also mean the condition of living in this ordinary time, which in some respects differs radically from those in eternity, the conditions we will be in when we are fully gathered in God's time. Two obvious features of our condition here, which are not part of God's ultimate plan for us, are that we live in states, that is, under political power; and that we live under régimes of property; and there are many others.

In this sense the saeculum is resistant to the form of life which will prevail in the fullness of our restored condition, and which is at work even now. This higher form is what Augustine spoke of as the "City of God". It lives in some tension with the saeculum, just because the two conditions of life are very different, a tension which can flare into opposition when humans cling to their "secular" condition as ultimate.

Or, by an easy extension, "secular" can refer to the affairs of this world, "temporal" affairs, and it contrasts with the affairs of the City of God, which are "spiritual". And from there it extends to the occupations and people belonging to these different spheres. And so the House of Lords was made up of "the Lords spiritual and temporal" (Bishops and lay lords). Heretics were "handed over to the secular arm" to be punished. In general, clergy and monks belong to the "spiritual" side, but there also is a distinction between "secular" and "regular" clergy. The latter are monks, living separately from the "world", under monastic rules; the former are parish clergy, ministering to their flocks, and so "in the world".

In the original mediaeval form, we have two spheres of life, with their proper activities and offices, corresponding to two "cities" which coexist in history, the City of God, and the earthly city. They have their special rules and norms. For instance, the "spiritual" powers are not supposed to shed blood, and that is why heretics have to be turned over to the "secular arm".

The process I have been calling Reform alters the terms of this coexistence; in the end it comes close to wiping out the duality altogether. This happens along three vectors which are closely related to each other, and which I have been describing in the above pages.

1. The first starts not long after the Hildebrandine reforms of the eleventh century; it is an attempt to make the mass of the laity, living in the saeculum, shape up more fully as Christians. The norms defining this fuller life resemble in some respects those which have already developed among the "spiritual" vocations; in particular, they stress more and more personal devotion and ascetic discipline. A crucial phase is marked by the rule of the Fourth Lateran Council of 1215 that all the faithful should confess and take communion once a year

2. The second comes with the Protestant Reformation, and is a frontal attack on the dualism itself. It not only rejects the notion that the "spiritual" vocations of monks are higher than the lay ones. It rejects these as utterly invalid. You cannot be a proper Christian by stepping out of the saeculum. This ascetic withdrawal reflects only spiritual pride, and the false belief that you can win salvation by your own efforts. All valid Christian vocations are those of ordinary life, or production and reproduction in the world. The crucial issue is how you live these vocations. The two spheres are collapsed into each other. Monastic rules disappear, but ordinary lay life is now under more stringent demands. Some of the ascetic norms of monastic life are now transferred to the secular. Weber spoke in this connection of an "innerworldly asceticism".[61] This obviously continues, and even ratchets up trend 1.

3. Third, all branches of Reform push towards disenchantment, Protestants in a more radical fashion. This enormously facilitates the collapse of the two spheres into each other, because a great deal of what marked off the "spiritual" sphere was that its members dealt with the sacred, present in concentrated form in certain times, places, persons and actions, in feasts and churches, clergy and sacraments. To the extent that the sacred/profane description fades from our lives, it comes to seem all the more obvious that the Christian life can only consist in a certain manner of living in the "world".

Now one could go this far, and still not have the turn-over I have been describing here, in which the secular world declares, as it were, its independence from "spiritual" demands. It could be that this ideal of living non-sacramentally as a Christian in the world remain largely a matter of deep inspiration, without being reduced to a code, or organization, or detailed discipline. One strand coming from the Reformation stressed the important of Inner Light; and something like this inspired the original Quakers.

But to the extent that churches, and later states with churches, set themselves the goal of mobilizing and organizing and actively bringing about these higher levels of conformity to (what was seen as) the Christian life, this latter comes to be codified, laid out in a set of norms. Reform comes to be seen as a serious business, brooking no alternatives. There is no more separate sphere of the "spiritual" where one may go to pursue a life of prayer outside the saeculum; and nor is there the other alternation, between order and anti-order, which Carnival represented. There is just this one relentless order of right thought and action, which must occupy all social and personal space.

How then does the break-out occur? Because the very attempt to express what the Christian life means in terms of a code of action in the saeculum opens the possibility of devising a code whose main aim is to encompass the basic goods of life in the saeculum: life, prosperity, peace, mutual benefit. In other words, it makes possible what I called the anthropocentric shift. Once this happens then the break-out is ready to occur. It just needs the step to holding that these "secular" goods are the point of the whole code. Pushed by annoyance and resentment at the ascetic demands of ultra-conformity, many will be willing to take this step.

When we do, the dualistic world of mediaeval Christianity, already compressed into a spiritual-secular whole, at least in Protestant countries, comes close to being unitary. It can't fully do so, because the sense of the spiritual is still alive in our society, at least as a source of division. And beyond that, there are modes of anti-religion which try to recapture something of a higher purpose for secular life in purely immanent terms, for instance, in Communism or Fascism.

So much for my first thesis. But how about the second claim, that it could not have been otherwise; that an unbelieving ethos couldn't have arisen in any other form? In the very nature of things, this kind of claim is very hard to demonstrate. But it nevertheless seems to me overwhelmingly plausible. How could the immense force of religion in human life in that age be countered, except by using a modality of the most powerful ethical ideas, which this religion itself had helped to entrench? I mean as a widespread phenomenon. Plainly, virtually any shift in view is possible for exceptional individuals. Some of these seem to have been able to stand aside both from Christian faith, and from the modern commitment to beneficent order; and adopt a kind of discrete, quietistic Epicureanism; St. Evremond, for instance, or Fontenelle. This was an obvious intellectual alternative to Christianity, something which didn't require to be invented from scratch; the model is already there in the ancient world. But it was inconceivable that this could have been a mass movement, even among the educated, in a society where Christianity, sometimes mixed with neo-Stoicism, had up till recently defined the parameters of spiritual life, and was still clearly dominant.

There is a subtraction story, which I referred to above, which explains the shift primarily in cognitive terms. The claims of Christianity came to be less credible in an age where science was advancing. And so people were left with purely human values. I have already said why I think this is woefully inadequate. But we can understand why people in the grips of this story today should retrospectively give a greater importance to the Lucretian dissidents of the time than they deserve. Because these "libertins" were primarily free-thinkers; they were not primarily concerned with the beneficent order. But just for this reason, they were not the movers and shakers of the time. Fontenelle even proposes a strategy of retreat as a route to happiness. Take up as little place as possible in the world. Most of what we do to change reality increases our "volume" in the world, as it were.

Mais ce volume donne plus de prise aux coups de la Fortune. Un soldat qui va à la tranchée voudrait-il devenir un géant pour attraper les coups de mousquet? Celui qui veut être heureux se réduit et se resserre autant qu'il est possible. Il a ces deux caractères, il change peu de place, et en tient peu.[62]

(But this volume increases exposure to the blows of Fortune. Would a soldier fighting in the trenches want to become a giant in order to catch the musket shots? He who wants to be happy reduces and restricts himself as much as possible. He has these two characteristics, he moves around little, and takes up little space.)

This is hardly a philosophy for reconstructing the world.

To shift to a slightly later date, in the light of the dominant subtraction story, Hume's *Dialogues Concerning Natural Religion,* with its arguments against miracles, may seem to us today a crucial blow in the battle for unbelief. But my hypothesis is, that without the new moral understandings I have been describing, it would have had little impact. Bishops could have slept peacefully in their beds, if they had only had to face Lucretian-inspired skeptics. Other modes of unbelief could arise later; but they needed the humanism of beneficent order to blaze the trail.

To approach this point from a slightly different direction, there was indeed a pattern of minority élite unbelief in this age, which saw in the ancients an inspiring model antithetical to Christianity. They include those just mentioned, and others, like Shaftesbury and Gibbon. But their outlook was often shaped by the modern, and Christian-derived, value of benevolence; Shaftesbury is a good example of this. Where this modern element burned weakly, the influence was small. It wasn't the Gibbons who would set the world alight, but the Voltaires. For with all their similarity, the latter has a passionate commitment to the ethic of freedom and mutual benefit, where for the former, the best periods of history were those which lived under the "deathlike trance of enlightened despotism", in Leslie Stephen's phrase.[63]

This brings me to my third claim, that all contemporary unbelief is still marked by that origin. What I'm offering here is another thesis about the historicity of our contemporary options, about the sedimentation of the past in the present. I touched on this briefly at the beginning of Part I, where I argued that our understanding of ourselves as secular is defined by the (often terribly vague) historical sense that we have come to be that way through overcoming and rising out of earlier modes of belief. That is why God is still a reference point for even the most untroubled unbelievers, because he helps define the temptation you have to overcome and set aside to rise to the heights of rationality on which they dwell. That is why 'disenchantment' is still a description of our age which everyone understands, centuries after the practitioners of magic have ceased to be indispensable figures in our social life.

Perhaps one might imagine a society in which people would live without any reference to God, without any awareness of this negative fact; as for instance, we live in societies which are not led by a strategos, or a High Priest, without awareness of this (except for students of ancient history). Perhaps an atheist might look forward to this utterly Godless society. Whether it ever could exist or not, it plainly is very different from our present society.

But there are serious reasons to doubt whether it could exist. Of course, there could be a society without any sense that they do not believe in the God of Abraham. There are many such today. But the interesting issue is whether there could be unbelief without any sense of some religious view which is being negated. A condition of absence of religion which would no longer deserve the name unbelief. If so, it would be different from our present world in one crucial respect. Unbelief for great numbers of contemporary unbelievers, is understood as an achievement of rationality. It cannot have this without a continuing historical awareness. It is a condition which can't only be described in the present tense, but which also needs the perfect tense: a condition of "having overcome" the irrationality of belief. It is this perfect-tensed consciousness which underlies unbelievers' use of 'disenchantment' today. It is difficult to imagine a world in which this consciousness might have disappeared.

Now in a similar way, the founding importance of the exclusive humanism of freedom, discipline, and beneficent order remains ineradicable in our present world. Other modes of unbelief—as well as many forms of belief—understand themselves as having overcome or refuted it. The whole Nietzschean stream is a case in point, depending as it does on seeing the filiation between Christian belief and beneficent order, and then defining itself against both.

In fact the project of freedom and beneficent order is so central to our civilization, that all possible positions define themselves in relation to it; either as modes of affirming while interpreting it, like Marxism and other offshoots of the Enlightenment; or as critiques of it which want to open space for something else, as with the multiform progeny of the Romantic rebellion.

This is why the narrative history of the rise of unbelief does not merely relate an irrelevant past, an optional extra for history buffs. Rather, all present issues around secularism and belief are affected by a double historicity, a two-tiered perfect-tensedness. On one hand, unbelief and exclusive humanism defined itself in relation to earlier modes of belief, both orthodox theism and enchanted understandings of the world; and this definition remains inseparable from unbelief today. On the other hand, later-arising forms of unbelief, as well as all attempts to redefine and recover belief, define themselves in relation to this first path-breaking humanism of freedom, discipline, and order.

7 The Impersonal Order

I have been dealing with the first facet of my construct of "Deism", the anthropocentric shift in the ends of human life. Let me turn to the second facet, which is in a central feature of Deism, as this term is usually defined.

The crucial feature here is a change in the understanding of God, and his relation to the world. That is, there is a drift away from orthodox Christian conceptions of God as an agent interacting with humans and intervening in human history; and towards God as architect of a universe operating by unchanging laws, which humans have to conform to or suffer the consequences. In a wider perspective, this can be seen as a move along a continuum from a view of the supreme being with powers analogous to what we know as agency and personality, and exercising them continually in relation to us, to a view of this being as related to us only through the law-governed structure he has created, and ending with a view of our condition as at grips with an indifferent universe, with God either indifferent or non-existent. From this perspective, Deism can be seen as a half-way house on the road to contemporary atheism.

According to a conception widely canvassed in the Enlightenment and since, what powers the movement along this continuum, either to its half-way mark or all the way, is reason itself. We discover that certain of the features of the original view are untenable, and we end up adopting what remains after the unacceptable elements have been peeled off, be this some kind of Deism, or world-soul, or cosmic force, or blank atheism. Each variant has its designated end-point; that of Voltaire is not that of today's scientific materialists. But whatever end-point a variant enshrines is seen as the truth, the residual kernel of fact underlying the husk of invention or superstition which used to surround it. We're dealing with the classic subtraction story.

I want to contest this. Not that it doesn't contain important elements of truth; but rather because it is too crude and global, and runs together a number of factors which we need to separate. Let's try to separate some of the strands.

One is inseparable from disenchantment. To the extent that a view of the cosmos as the locus of spirits and meaningful causal powers declines, this opens space for, and is indeed partly caused by the growth of a picture of the universe as governed by universal causal laws. And the post-Galilean conception of these laws, which had no place for purpose, utterly excludes the kind of causal powers supposedly embodied in, say, relics or sacred spaces. Scientific reason was at once an engine and beneficiary of disenchantment, and its progress led people to brand all sorts of traditional beliefs and practices as superstition.

Another strand was the new stance towards history. Bernard Williams has spoken of the difference in ancient historiography between Herodotus and Thucydides as the step whereby people began to demand an account of remote, "legendary" events of the same kind as one would offer of what happened around here yesterday.[1] I could gloss this by saying that this demand amounted to a refusal to consider certain "legendary" events as taking place in some higher time, or on some unspecified higher plane of being, that of, say, Gods or heroes. Time is homogenized.

Something similar comes about in the eighteenth century. One place one can see this is the various attempts to give an account of the origins of human culture, or of human language.[2] Instead of the static theories of language of the previous century, such as those by Hobbes and Locke, which give an account of language in terms of its functions (ordering of our thoughts, communication), and just take for granted that it arose at some time in order to fulfill these, there is a felt need to give a psycho- and sociologically realistic picture of how this genesis could have taken place, and to fill in some of the stages of language and culture between the supposed origin point and the present. Crude and a priori as these accounts appear to us today, they were placing themselves in this new framework, and thus inviting the criticism which later thinkers made of them.

But another place in which this new historical sense arises is in Biblical criticism, with beginnings even in the seventeenth century. Biblical accounts begin to be weighed in terms of what was considered plausible; allowances begin to be made for the limitations of agents' understanding in the ages that they were drafted; and the like. One of the first (and most scandalous) forays of this kind was made by Spinoza in his *Tractatus Theologico-politicus*.[3]

This strand and the previous natural-science-driven one could combine in calling in doubt certain miraculous happenings in the Biblical story. Hume famously does this when he asks whether we really find it more reasonable to accept that this exceptional event took place, than we do to challenge the veracity or accuracy of the witnesses who have relayed it to us. He is clearly taking (what we might call) the Williams principle of the homogeneity of time as the unspoken background of his argument (as he must do to counter the defense that there was an "Age of Miracles" which is now past).

On some accounts these two strands, the operation, one might say, of "science", natural and historical, are sufficient to explain the slide to Deism; and granted other premises about science and materialism, even the slide to contemporary atheism. But (leaving aside this latter claim for the moment) this seems to me clearly inadequate. The relegation of "superstition" and the challenging of the Biblical account don't bar the door to all conceptions of God as an interlocutor to humans and intervening in history. People could and did go on sensing that they were in dialogue with God, and/or called by God, and/or comforted or strengthened by God, either as individuals, or in groups. Giving an account of things compatible with natural science and the best historiography can only rule out the Biblical stories of Abraham's or Moses' calling on a very narrow and reductive reading of what these sciences require; and a similar point can be made of events like God giving the victory to Israel over its enemies. To explain Deism in these terms is to fall into an implicit petitio principii.

In his Introduction to the work of Gibbon, Trevor-Roper speaks of the philosophical historians which influenced him in terms of the kind of homogeneity I have been invoking above—not that simply of time, but one grouping all institutions, secular and sacred under the same explanatory principles. In Trevor-Roper's words, Gibbon in projecting his "philosophical history", followed his predecessors, in venturing to "handle Church history in a secular spirit, to see the Church not as a repository of truth (or error), but as a human society subject to the same social laws as other societies".[4]

What the claim means here that Trevor-Roper makes on behalf of Gibbon depends on the force given to the expression "same social laws". Gibbon tends to account for the actions of ecclesiastics, when he doesn't invoke fanaticism and superstition, in terms of motives of power, prestige, rivalry. One might even claim that he violates Trevor-Roper's homogeneity principle, in that he sometimes gives to the actions of secular rulers and agents a more charitable explanation. But we drive closer to the main point I want to make here if we question Gibbon's exclusion from his account of human actions—and passions—motivated by an agent's relation to God: be this inspiration, strength, reactions of anger and spite, or whatever. No one who believes that these can figure in human action wants to reserve their action to ecclesiastics or "religious" leaders; the issue is whether we give them any status in our "social laws" in general (the scare quotes indicate that I don't want to concede the nomothetic bias encoded in Trevor-Roper's expression).

Of course, Trevor-Roper is right in this sense, that Gibbon treats ecclesiastical history as though we could disregard altogether whether the religious doctrines in contest are true or false. He declares none of them false, but he writes as though any truth they might contain can be disregarded for the purposes of explaining what happened. But this is not just the termination of an (unjustified) exceptional status, which brings all institutions under what are identified as "the same social laws". No one writes history like that, i.e., in a way which factors out the truth of any and all beliefs that people have about their condition. Everyone writes history within some understanding of the human condition, in which the agents are struggling with their fate, either advancing, or retarding or moving forward and back, but in virtue of our understanding of their condition, not all movements are seen as explanatorily on the same footing.

If we write like Gibbon out of the "Enlightened narrative" of the rise of polite society,[5] we cannot consider moments of rising to and those of sliding back from this height on the same footing. I don't mean just normatively—that is obviously so—but also explanatorily. Typically we shall understand the moments of rise as our responding in part to perceived reality. These moments are often explained in part in terms of "enlargement of the mind", or the "development of philosophy" in Enlightenment historiography.[6] And Gibbon himself seems to believe that some human advances are hardy enough to provide a ratchet effect and prevent backsliding. Even when there is a decline of civilization, the most useful and necessary arts survive. "Private genius and public industry may be extirpated; but these hardy plants survive the tempest, and strike everlasting root in unfavourable soil. . . . We may therefore acquiesce in the pleasing conclusion, that every age of the world has increased, and still increases, the real wealth, the happiness, the knowledge, and perhaps the virtue of the human race." And a little earlier: "We cannot determine to what height the human species may aspire in their advances towards perfection, but it may safely be presumed, that no people, unless the face of nature is changed, will relapse into their original barbarism."[7]

No meaningful narrative can treat all the beliefs of the agents described as equally explanatorily irrelevant. Gibbon's move was to write as though he were indeed, bracketing questions of the truth or falsehood of religious beliefs for explanatory purposes; but this couldn't be described as treating the institutions carrying those beliefs on the same footing as others, e.g., the institutions and practices of polite civilization, whose rise is partly explained by their validity. In fact, religious beliefs themselves are not really bracketed in this account; the understanding in many cases is that they are false, once the heavy irony is peeled off.

The Trevor-Roper interpretation is part of the modern subtraction story of the Enlightenment, that people started using Reason and Science, instead of Religion and Superstition, and that the conclusions they then came to simply reflect this salutary shift in method. Once you let the facts speak, Gibbonian conclusions ineluctably emerge. This is, of course, not a neutral and uncontestable fact, but part of the self-image of Enlightened unbelief. And before this, it was one of the self-images generated in polite civilization itself, which saw philosophical method, à la Descartes, or better Locke, as the royal road to knowledge. Gibbon seems himself to have attributed his shuffling off his early adherence to Rome to the effect that the "universal instrument" (Lockean epistemology) exercised "on my catholic opinions".[8]

So something else is operating in the making of eighteenth-century Deists like (we presume) Gibbon than simply the demands of (natural and human) science. They have a deep distaste for action (putatively) inspired by God; indeed, they have a (derogatory) word for it, "enthusiasm". On the surface it seems obvious why. The people they pick out as "enthusiasts" are often those who make clamorous and self-assured claims to divine inspiration, and on the strength of this frequently engage in aggressive behaviour or in other ways threaten the established order. In other words, they are people who put in danger the order of mutual benefit. These people were a menace, and to be opposed or contained, wherever quietism didn't render them harmless. But to explain Gibbon's exclusion of God (as against fanatical or enthusiastic beliefs about God) as a factor in human history in terms of his distaste for these subversive elements is once more to beg the question. If one accepts that God can work in human history in other, less noisy and obvious (and also more inspiring) ways, then one's reactions to "enthusiasts" will no longer determine how one reads ecclesiastical history in general. We have a phenomenon analogous to that in our day, whereby "secular" Americans judge the influence of religion on the basis of their (justifiably) negative views of Jerry Falwell and Pat Robertson. That their paradigm of "religion" is a negative one is not the result of empirical discovery, but of their pre-existing framework.

I could generalize this point. The slide to Deism was not just the result of "reason" and "science", but reflected a deep-seated moral distaste for the old religion that sees God as an agent in history. This is easy to lose sight of, because many of the examples of God's activity that were propounded by the orthodox could be made to look (or indeed, were) tawdry or morally offensive. The prevailing doctrines of majority damnation and divine grace were calculated to make God look an arbitrary tyrant, playing favourites in a capricious manner, and more concerned with arcane points of honour than with the good of his creatures. Many of the stories in the Old Testament portrayed God as egging the people of Israel on to terrible deeds, not excluding genocide. Where the stories of God's intervention didn't pose ethical problems, they often seem to be tainted with the particular and not very enlightened wishes of their supposed beneficiaries. People pray for and believe they receive things that are not really to their good, let alone good from a more general viewpoint. From a philosophical perspective, such as that of Spinoza, historical religion could be written off as a pandering to popular fears and illusions, offering an utterly unworthy picture of God.[9]

But of course, what doesn't figure in this kind of indictment is the (alleged) interventions spoken of in the autobiography of Santa Teresa, or the writings of John Wesley, nor a fortiori the myriad of unknown, less awe-inspiring acts and experiences of ordinary people which they have understood as related to God. Presumably the people who nod in agreement with Spinoza's analysis either don't believe these accounts, or reinterpret them in a derogatory light. But that's just the point: their stance is not forced on them by the "facts", but flows from a certain interpretive grid.

The interesting question is: what generates and motivates this grid? But before trying to describe this, it might help to get a deeper historical perspective on the issues involved here. What Deism in its various forms wanted to reject was seeing God as an agent intervening in history. He could be agent qua original Architect of the universe, but not as the author of myriad particular interventions, "miraculous" or not, which were the stuff of popular piety and orthodox religion (even though these two didn't agree on the details).

The issue here was in some ways a replay of the one the early church wrestled with in the Patristic period, defining a Christian outlook using the terminology of Greek philosophy, but attempting all the while to demarcate Christian doctrine from the dominant outlook which this terminology had hitherto been used to formulate. The philosophy which at first seemed to recommend itself as the most apt to express the Christian kerygma was (in a loose sense) Platonism. This had already been used by Philo to reformulate Judaism in Greek terms. In the third century, it was made use of by Clement and Origen to work out some of the basic doctrines of Christianity. Later on, a derived doctrine—which we call "neo-Platonism", but which was thought of at the time simply as "Platonism"—was a principal source of inspiration for Augustine.

All of the thinkers in this early period were aware that there were crucial features of Christian doctrine which were in danger of distortion in this language as they found it in the schools. Their effort was to struggle against the medium, as it were, to give it a new shape, in order to be able to say what they saw as the truth of Christian faith. And of course, they argued among themselves as to who had managed to do this. Some writers, notably Origen, were accused by later thinkers of having conceded too much.

I want to look here at some of the principal points of tension, which defined the crucial axes of change.

First, (1) the body: for the Platonist, we reach our highest state in a condition beyond the body; being incarnate is a hindrance. The body needs to be controlled by discipline in this life, but the contact through intelligence with the highest is at its most complete beyond this life. This stress on disembodiment is, of course, an extreme position in the ancient world. Other philosophies didn't follow Plato here (and there are certain interpretations of Plato which don't see him as this extreme). But the pagan culture of the ancient world nevertheless subscribed to a view of the body as subordinate. "In the pagan notion of the person, the soul had been thought of as ruling the body with the same alert, if occasionally tolerant, authority as the well-born male ruled those inferior and alien to himself—his wife, his slaves, and the populace of his city."[10]

As Peter Brown points out, in the Palestine of Jesus' time, this kind of dualism was, if present at all, secondary to another one, which turned on the "heart". The heart in this sense is seen as the site of our most profound and basic orientation, of our love and concern. The dualism was not between the "heart" and something else, but rather between different kinds or direction of heart. To use a Biblical image, the human heart could turn to stone, unmoved by the call of God or the needs of neighbour, "clenched in a state of mute rebellion to God's will". Against this, we have God's eschatological promise, as expressed by Ezekiel: "A new heart will I give you, and a new spirit will I put within you; and I will take out of your flesh the heart of stone."[11]

The direction of the heart is that of the whole person, body and soul. As Brown shows, this is the basis of a completely different form of bodily and sexual asceticism that we find among the Essenes, and of another kind again among Christians. Sexual abstinence, for instance, was not just a way of getting troublesome desires out of the way, which were impeding the soul's ascent. The new ascetic way of being was itself part of the new orientation to God, a way of belonging to the Kingdom.[12] Of course, the old dualism died hard; throughout the ages, it has constantly infiltrated Christian thought and practice. But a fundamental paradigm shift had taken place. The crucial issue henceforth is that of the nature of the heart (flesh or stone), or the direction of its concern (Augustine's "two loves"), or whether it is divided or single.

(2) The re-entry of the body also brought with it a new significance of history. Here too, we have a Jewish understanding seeking a Greek expression. The relation of the human heart to God was a story of falling away and returning. This was inseparable from human history; it was the central narrative of this history. Where at its most extreme—in Plotinus for instance—the Platonist ascent ends in a timeless condition beyond history, the Jewish story has an ending, which in some variants is within history. And where, as in Christianity, the eschaton is beyond history, the understanding of eternity is very different from the Platonic. As I described it earlier, the site of God, the nunc stans, is a point of gathering of all time; rather than an ever-unchanging point outside of time.

The idea here is that the whole story belongs to the end, and not just the last state it arrives at. Hence the importance of the lives of the saints. This is not just meant as a set of examples offering models and encouragement to the faithful. These are the paths to God of different people, and it is the paths which are being gathered, not just their upshots. The stories are also stories of sin, but the sin is also the occasion of mercy, of turning, and as such can be taken up. The final meaning of any incident is given in the whole, the "judgment" on it is made in the light of the whole. The Gospel records Peter's thrice-repeated denial of Christ, but also that the incident ends with his bitter weeping.

(3) The significance of history, which enters eternity as gathered story, entails the significance of the individuals whose identities are worked out in these stories. Here again, the contrast with Plotinus is striking: to accede to the eternal is to lose individuation. Even in Aristotle, individuation is seen as secured by the matter, the embodiment of a form. On the level of the Forms, there are no individuals, only a single archetype. For Aristotle, immortality could only be that of our active intellect, but this would be indistinguishable from any other person's intellect.

(4) This means as well a new significance for contingency. The accidents arising from the condition of matter, and the flow of events, can indeed, affect how Forms are embodied, for good or ill, but the Forms themselves remain quite unaffected. This is true for Aristotle as well as for Plato. Nor does contingency affect our existence in the highest state, where this is seen as beyond time, as with Plotinus. But the Christian eschaton is made up of paths, of stories. And these are shaped by contingencies. That the stories end well is sometimes seen as their having been rigorously scripted from the beginning. This is often what people call Providence, following the Stoics. God plans sins, so that he can script in some mercy.

But a rather different model is suggested by the Bible. God's Providence is his ability to respond to whatever the universe and human agency throw up. God is like a skilled tennis player, who can always return the serve.[13] We can see this model, for instance, in the famous phrase of the Preface of Easter Vigil: "O felix culpa" (happy fault), applied to Adam's sin; happy because it brought such a response from God to redeem it. This also seems the obvious reading of the parable of the Good Samaritan. The question it is supposed to answer is: who is my neighbour? The answer surprises, in part because it takes us out of the skein of social relations in which we're embedded, and we're told of a Samaritan who rescues a Jew. But it also takes us beyond any established relation into the domain of accident or contingency: my neighbour is someone I come across, bleeding in the road. It was sheer accident that I came along at just that time; but this accident can be the occasion for rebuilding a skein of human relations animated by agape. The Samaritan's action is part of God's response to the skewed serve the robbers have lobbed into history.

Of course, in order to take up this understanding, one has to abandon the notion that somewhere, there is a Total Plan; and of course, a fortiori, that we can figure it out. But this has been a tremendous temptation, particularly in Latin Christendom, and particularly in modern times. This was the stock in trade of certain theologians, e.g., Calvin, Janssen, who produced such repulsive results, that the main claimants to the Total Picture are now atheists, wielding theodicy like a club.[14]

The body, the heart, the individual; when these become central, so also do (5) the emotions. And here is another difference from classical thought. For Plotinus, and in another way for the Stoics, our highest condition is one which is purged of emotion. And even for Aristotle, who defended a place for emotion in the good life, they are clearly out of place in that activity where we come closest to the divine, contemplation. But here they are part of our relation to the highest being. I quote from Martha Nussbaum's extremely interesting discussion of Augustine:

> We hear sighs of longing and groans of profound desolation. We hear love songs composed in anguish, as the singer's heart strains upward in desire. We hear of a hunger than cannot be satisfied, of a thirst that torments, of the taste of a lover's body that kindles inexpressible longing. We hear of an opening that longs for penetration, of a burning fire that ignites the body and the heart. All of these are images of a profound erotic passion. And all of these are images of Christian love.[15]

This was one of the points of tension with Greek thought where the struggle was the most intense. Because it was essential to the educated, philosophical concept of God that he be beyond emotion, that he be apathes. The tremendous difficulty was to connect the Jesus on the cross, crying out in pain, with a God, one of whose defining characteristics was apatheia. This was one of the motives for the Aryan refusal of identification of Christ and God. The ensuing struggles over the Trinity and Christology were attempts to resolve this tension.

Body, heart, emotion, history; all these make sense only in the context of (6) the belief that the highest being is a personal being, not just in the sense of possessing agency, but also in that of being capable of communion. Indeed, the definitions of the Trinity in Athanasius and the Cappadocian Fathers made central use of this notion (Koinonia). The new sense of "hypostasis" which was developed by the Cappadocians, which we translate no longer as "substance", but as "person", was part of this new theology. The notion of person was correlative to that of communion; the person is the kind of being which can partake in communion.

God's intervention in history, and in particular the Incarnation, was intended to transform us, through making us partakers of the communion which God already is and lives. It was meant to effect our "deification" (theiosis).[16] In this crucial sense, salvation is thwarted to the extent that we treat God as an impersonal being, or as merely the creator of an impersonal order to which we have to adjust. Salvation is only effected by, one might say is, our being in communion with God through the community of humans in communion, viz., the church.

This is the central idea which makes sense of all the other modifications of pagan thought which I have just been describing. This is clear for the last one mentioned: emotions have their proper place in the love of God, where love describes the nature of the communion. But it also underlies all the other changes: communion has to integrate persons in their true identities, as bodily beings who establish their identities in their histories, in which contingency has a place. In this way, the central concept which makes sense of the whole is communion, or love, defining both the nature of God, and our relation to him.

The whole package, 1–6, arose out of a struggle, that of Patristic theology, with earlier ideals of impersonal order, be it that which identified the highest with an Idea (the Idea of the Good), or with Plotinus' One, or with a God, but one whose defining characteristic was apatheia. Now in the modern period, we see this package challenged by new understandings of order, running at one end of the spectrum from Deism, to modern atheist materialism, on the other.

But these understandings integrate the greater part of 1–5. They offer a picture of human order, either as normative, or as the end-point of historical development, or both, which sees us as historical agents, bodies in a material world, which move towards modes of common life in which our individuality is respected (at first as free rights-bearers, then later there are versions which want to make place for individual, original identities). The emotions are held under a rather tight rein in the earlier variants (neo-Stoicism, Locke), but then can take on a greater and greater role in the post-Rousseauian, post-Romantic era.

Of course, they often integrate a Providence-surrogate, in the form of a theory of progress, or picture of the "laws of history", and this can give rather little place to contingency. Accidental events can derail the process (colliding with a meteor, for instance), but the ultimate shape of civilization is often conceived in rather tightly-defined terms. There is little room for the idea, central to Christianity, that the path we take can help shape the goal. There is naturally, a more robust idea of contingency among those who react against the modern idea of order, for instance, in our day, certain "post-modernists", but this is because they want to reject the notion of a potential highest condition altogether, not because they have place for contingency within it.

But unlike the Christian package, the elements 1–5 which are taken up are utterly removed from their context in communion. There is, of course, an agape-surrogate, benevolence; but communion itself has little or no place in the picture: little enough even on the human level—the hegemony of atomist pictures of agency in modern culture militates against this; and no place at all for communion with God as a transforming relation.

Indeed, this last is so far off the map that it is rarely mentioned, even to be argued against. The main attack against orthodoxy concerns the agency of God, as wielder of extra-systemic causal power, bringing about miracles, special providences, acts of favour and punishment, and the like. Hence as we saw above, the "refutation" of orthodox religion barely notices the Loyolas, Ste. Teresas, or St. François de Sales; or when it does, can only see them as "enthusiastic" claimants to special revelations or divine commands. The grid that Deism, and its successors, operate with blanks out communion almost totally.

So we return to the question above: what made this grid so powerful? No one can claim to have the ultimate answer, but we can identify certain features of the situation in the eighteenth century, at least among élites (many of which continue today for a much broader segment of the population), which made the idea of God as a personal agent unattractive or threatening, and pushed people along the continuum in the direction of Deism, or even farther. Put positively, we could say that more attractive than the orthodox view was the idea of God as relating to us through an impersonal order, or perhaps even God as nothing but the indwelling spirit of an impersonal order (one of the ways in which Spinoza was taken, and of particular importance in late eighteenth century Germany); or perhaps even further an impersonal order without God.

The pull towards the "impersonal" pole of this continuum becomes more understandable when one takes account of the way in which the human condition was more and more understood in terms of impersonal orders; and this process was grasped in a historical consciousness which saw the impersonal as superseding earlier, more personal forms.

This was first of all evident in the natural-cosmic order in the way I described above. Disenchantment dissolved the cosmos, whose levels reflected higher and lower kinds of being, distinctions which had undeniable meaning and relevance for human beings, and which moreover contained spirits and meaningful causal forces, which made things respond to us in their human meanings (relics which could cure, for instance). In its stead was a universe ruled by causal laws, utterly unresponsive to human meanings, even if one believed that the whole was designed in the general case and the long run for our good. The universe itself was unresponsive, or indifferent, like a machine, even if we held that it was designed as a machine for our benefit.

We are not yet at the point where this universe begins to be seen as not just indifferent, but in a sense malign and cruel, "nature red in tooth and claw". That comes in the nineteenth century, and severely challenges the belief of providential Deism in benign design. This poses another set of issues to Christian faith, which belong to what we think of as the Age of Darwin, but in the eighteenth century we are not yet there.

I am not reverting to the idea that I rejected above, that the prevalence of impersonal law in nature refutes the orthodox idea of God as person and agent. My point is the logically weaker but hermeneutically understandable one that the predominance of impersonal, unrespondent order in the universe, which was known to follow an age in which people had believed in a meaningful cosmos, can be felt to accredit the idea that we have entered a new age in which the older religion is no more at home.

This reading would be strengthened by the nature of modern social imaginaries, which present society in its dominant, enframing structure, not as a network of personal relations of lordship, fealty, and tenure, but rather as a categorical, egalitarian order, in which we are all related in the same direct-access way to the society, which itself must be understood also objectively, as well as being the product of our coming together. Modern society is a united we/they of similar units, equal citizens; something utterly different from a tissue of feudal relations.[17] The transition from one to the other was going on in the eighteenth century, and was taking place slowly in the (sometimes accelerated) social imaginary of élites. Once more, we see not only a congruence of orthodox religion with monarchy, something the partisans of monarchy did not fail to trade on, but also a consciousness of change in which the rising force can seem more congruent with a religion of impersonal order.

Again, there are no tight relations of entailment here; and even the hermeneutical connection can easily be blocked by other roles which religion could play. Modern society, for instance, as in the American case, could be seen as following a design of God, so that God's presence was there in our institutions, which followed his prescription. This also, in a way, relates us to God via an impersonal order, the institutions of our society, but we can still conceive of the God with whom we are thus related in orthodox terms. Interestingly, in the American case, though many of the major figures of the founding generation tended to Deism (Washington, Jefferson), the first decades of the new Republic saw a second Great Awakening which cemented the link for many between orthodox religion and American freedom.

There is thus no iron link, but there is also here a possible affinity, which in the absence of other factors can lead people into the sense that a more impersonal reading of Christianity, or Deism, or even something further removed from orthodoxy, is more suitable to their age. This link is invoked in another form by David Martin when he remarks about the eighteenth-century British scene "that latitudinarian clergy deployed a public version of Isaac Newton to promote a separation of creation from its Creator in order the better to ensure that rationality ruled both the natural *and* the social universes".[18]

This affinity becomes stronger when one thinks of the ethical consequences of the two kinds of belief. At the heart of orthodox Christianity, seen in terms of communion, is the coming of God through Christ into a personal relation with disciples, and beyond them others, eventually ramifying through the church to humanity as a whole. God establishes the new relationship with us by loving us, in a way we cannot unaided love each other. (John 15: God loved us first.) The lifeblood of this new relation is agape, which can't ever be understood simply in terms of a set of rules, but rather as the extension of a certain kind of relation, spreading outward in a network. The church is in this sense a quintessentially network society, even though of an utterly unparalleled kind, in that the relations are not mediated by any of the historical forms of relatedness: kinship, fealty to a chief, or whatever. It transcends all these, but not into a categorical society based on similarity of members, like citizenship; but rather into a network of ever different relations of agape.[19]

Of course, the church lamentably and spectacularly fails to live up to this model; but this is the kind of society that it is meant to be.

By contrast, categorical societies are bound together by codes; law codes in the first instance. But to the extent that an ethic springs up which is congruent with, inspired by or modeled on categorical society, it will similarly be one of rules, of do's and don'ts, as we can see in the history of modern ethics which has developed in the wake of the Grotian understanding of the human predicament.[20] The dominant philosophical ethics today, divided into the two major branches of Utilitarianism and post-Kantianism, both conceive of morality as determining through some criterion what an agent ought to do. They are rather hostile to an ethics of virtue or the good, such as that of Aristotle. And a Christian conception, where the highest way of life can't be explained in terms of rules, but rather is rooted in a certain relation to God, is entirely off the screen.

Now one of the attractive features in modernity for an ethic of the code, or law, what one ought to do, is that it can offer a view of the agent as entirely free, unconstrained by authority. This notion of an ethic of freedom was implicit in the Grotian enterprise almost from the beginning. For Locke the law constrains, but it is itself the deliverance of reason. For Utilitarians, it is based on what human beings in fact want, and not on demands imposed from without. For Rousseau and Kant, the very nature of law is to be self-imposed. By contrast, orthodox Christianity sees our highest mode of being (and also our freedom, but this is in virtue of a rather different conception) as arising in a relation, moreover one which is not equal, but on which we draw to know and be ourselves.

Thus here, too, modernity, as the era of freedom, can be seen to be congruent with our relating ourselves to an impersonal law, not to the goals which arise out of a personal relation. All these forms of impersonal order: the natural, the political and the ethical can be made to speak together against orthodox Christianity, and its understanding of God as personal agent. There is a certain idea of human dignity, indeed, the one propounded by, among others, Kant, which seems incombinable with Christian faith.

Orthodox Christianity sees us as needing rescue. In this it can seem to treat us as children. Mercy, as a personal connection conflicts with the supremacy of a high code. Christianity seems not compatible with human dignity.

This (as I think) misprision has been a powerful force working in modern Christendom. The notion of dignity as agency involved here was for a long time identified as primarily male. The male role as self-given lawmaker was in many parts of Christendom difficult to combine with Christian faith. Christianity in modern times has often become feminized; with women practising more than men, and with many forms of piety appealing more to women (such as devotion to the Sacred Heart). This wasn't so in pre-modern Christendom, where there was an important role for the Christian warrior (perhaps too important a role, but this is not the place for theological judgments); even as there is much less feminization, where this role remains important—as in much contemporary Islam, and in the bellicose, hegemony-loving parts of U.S. society which President Bush speaks to. The feminization of western Christianity until recently, when many women began to aspire after (what had previously been seen as) "male" modes of being, has been an important sign of this deep tension between the modern sense of impersonal order and Christian faith.[21]

The natural, social, ethical orders all tend to further this slide towards the impersonal. But we can see this slide from another angle as well, as driven by our self-understanding as disengaged, rational agents. Disengagement is correlative to what I have called "objectification".[22] To objectify a given domain is to deprive it of normative force for us, or at least to bracket the meanings it has for us in our lives. If we take a domain of being in which hitherto the way things are has defined meanings or set standards for us, and we now take a new stance towards it as neutral, without meaning or normative force, we can speak of objectifying it.

The great mechanization of the scientific world picture in the seventeenth century was an objectification in this sense. Formerly, the cosmic order was seen as the embodiment of the Ideas. There is a double teleology here. First, the things that surround us take the form they do in order to exemplify ideas or archetypes; this is what underlies the Renaissance doctrine of the "correspondences", whereby, e.g., the king in the realm corresponds to the lion among animals, the eagle among birds, the dolphin among fishes, and so on. Each is a manifestation of the same Idea in its respective domain.

But on a second level, the whole order itself is as it is because it exhibits certain perfections; everything is ordered under the Idea of the Good, in Plato's variant. And it is meant to exhibit Reason as well. The Platonic Idea is a self-manifesting reality. Things are as they are in order to conform to a pattern of rational self-manifestation, in which the One turns into the Many, in which all possible niches are occupied (Lovejoy's "principle of plenitude"), and the like. This order *defines* excellence on several levels. First, the Idea of each kind of thing exhibits the good of that thing (and that, of course, includes humans); second, the whole cosmos exhibits a hierarchy of beings, from the lowest to the highest, and hence defines the rank of different things; and thirdly, the whole exhibits its own kind of goodness: plenitude, reason, or the benevolence of the Creator (in the Christian version).

An order conceived in this way can be called a "meaningful" order; one involving an "ontic logos". It sets the paradigm purposes for the beings within it. As humans we are to conform to our Idea, and this in turn must play its part in the whole, which among other things involves our being "rational", i.e., capable of seeing the self-manifesting order. No one can understand this order while being indifferent to it or failing to recognize its normative force. Indifference is a sign that one has not understood, that one is in error, as Epicureans and other atomists were widely condemned as being by the pre-modern mainstream.

The move to mechanism neutralizes this whole domain. It no longer sets norms for us, or defines crucial life meanings. The moral consequences were, of course, part of the story of the mechanization of the world picture. The nominalist revolt against Aristotelian realism, by figures like William of Occam, was motivated by the sense that propounding an ethic founded on the supposed bent of nature was attempting to set limits to the sovereignty of God. The further developments of this Occamist line of thought played an important role in the scientific revolution.[23] This is the move I'm calling 'objectification'. But I want also to speak of it as 'disengagement', because it involves a withdrawal of a certain sort. I said above that in the framework of the ontic logos, you couldn't understand reality without seeing its meaning or normative force. Crucial to a correct grasp is that we perceive things through their meanings. Objectification brackets these meanings, and sets them aside. They no longer animate our enquiry. We as agents-living-meaning withdraw, as it were, from this enquiry. We place ourselves outside a certain space of meanings while examining the things of this domain. This withdrawal I want to speak of as "disengagement".

The mechanization of the world picture involved one such withdrawal. But Descartes takes us farther than this. He calls on us also to withdraw from the meanings correlative with our existence as embodied agents. The normal, unreflecting person thinks of colour as in the dress, or sweetness as in the candy; she locates the pain in the tooth, or the tingling in the foot. But this is to see them obscurely and confusedly. The real ontological locus of all these experiences is in the mind, although they are caused by features of the object or organ concerned. And the correct understanding of what is happening when we have these experiences is the one available from a third person perspective, where we note the causal relations here.

Descartes' objectification involves withdrawal not just from the field of cosmic meanings, but also from the body. And further, in taking a firm stand in favour of a monological, self-responsible construction of certain knowledge for myself, he calls on us to withdraw from tradition and social authority, and the whole domain of what is experienced in common. We can't take the truths we have learned on trust, we have to generate them, each for ourselves, in a process of certain reasoning from clear and distinct ideas.

This powerful model of all-around disengagement gets handed down in the tradition of modernity; not indeed, without contestation, but with a tremendous power attaching to it. This stems partly from the crucial role of disengaged thinking in the most prestigious and impressive epistemic activity of modern civilization, viz., natural science. But partly also, as I have argued, in the close fit of disengagement and the buffered self, and the attached sense of freedom, control, invulnerability, and hence dignity. It was easy to take the prestige of the disengaged stance, based on the successes of natural science, and the sense of moral superiority attaching to it, and leap (often implicitly and semi-consciously) to the conclusion that it is the correct stance for all modes of enquiry. This (I think) illegitimate extension is one of the strong trends in our culture, from the seventeenth century up to the present, as the continuing battle in the humanities and human sciences attests. The argument has to be made again and again, that "experience-far" methods based on the natural sciences risk distorting and missing the point when applied to the phenomena of psychology, politics, language, historical interpretation, and so on.

Not that it isn't evident in ordinary life that disengagement may be quite the wrong way to go about increasing understanding. When we want to understand what someone is trying to tell us in a conversation; or to grasp what motivates some person or group, how they see the world, and what kinds of things are important to them, disengagement will almost certainly be a self-stultifying strategy. We have to be open to the person or event, allowing our responses to meaning full reign, which generally means our feelings, which reflect these responses. Of course, our feelings, or understanding of human meanings, may also be what is blocking us in these cases. We fail to grasp how different they are from us. But as Gadamer has shown so well, the remedy for this is not to jump out of the range of human meanings altogether, and try to take things in through a bleached, neutralized language of "social science". That just bolts the door against new insight. It is by allowing ourselves to be challenged by the ways they fail to fit into our recognized range of meanings, that we can begin to discern how this range has to be broken open and transformed if we are to understand them.[24]

But as clear as it might be in ordinary situations, the prestige of the disengaged model can easily override this everyday experience. Reality is summoned, as it were, to conform to what this stance can pick up. A powerful homogenizing a priori is at work here (perhaps a little too reminiscent of Kant), perverse in its effect. I say 'perverse', because we ought to hold that method and stance be adapted to the nature of the reality concerned, whereas here, albeit unwittingly, reality is being arraigned before the bar of Method; what doesn't shape up is condemned to a shadow-zone of the unreal.

We can call this perverse movement the spill-over effect of disengagement. Whereas the withdrawal from cosmic meanings is a move which is properly motivated by the nature of the reality which natural science studies, the spill-over occurs where the prestige of the stance begins to dictate what we can take in as reality. We can note too that the "sciences" structured by the spill-over are understood by their practitioners to be motivated by fully epistemic considerations, whereas in fact (if I am right) a big part of the motivation resides in the prestige and admiration surrounding the stance itself, with the sense of freedom, power, control, invulnerability, dignity, which it radiates. In other words, what operate here are *ethical* considerations (those to do with the ends of life, or what is a higher form of life). This is masked by a certain ideological consciousness.

To return to our main subject, think of Gibbon. Think of the force of his style, which broadcasts an irenic distance, what will later be called "unflappability". It is so judiciously disengaged, only allowing the meanings which structure the narrative to emerge in understated, straight-faced irony. Part of the power of this style for those whom it grips comes from the stance itself, which can seem (if you're at all inclined this way) so superior to the hot, hyper-engaged "fanaticism" of so many of the people described. How can you not admire this? How can you not feel that this is a superior epistemic stance?

We can see how this stance of general disengagement was in great tension with orthodox Christianity with its sense of God as personal agency, in relation to us. This sense gives rise to the notion that the grasp of things which arises from our engagement in relation with God, our communion with Him, and others under Him, will be different and superior to what we can grasp outside of, or withdrawn from this relation. If the spill-over effect from disengaged science goes far enough, it threatens this crucial feature of the understanding of faith.

Seen from within general disengagement, the case seems clear enough. The ensemble of supposed actions of God are dubious, if not incredible. The key case is miracles. See how Hume argues, entirely on a disengaged plane. The question is, which sort of hypothesis is more open to question: that some natural law suffered an exception, or that some human beings in the chain of transmission were less than fully accurate, either through confusion, credulity, or pious fraud? If we look at the human story in a disengaged manner, the question answers itself.

But let's look at the same issue from another perspective, say the miracles of healing in the Gospel story. Look at these through the eyes of a St. François de Sales. From this point of view, the notion that a closer relation to God can transform us is more than credible; it seems undeniable. That means transform us spiritually, one might say. Yes, but how clear is the boundary in this domain between the "spiritual" or "psychological", on one hand, and the "physical" on the other? Quite unbelieving doctors acknowledge that a strong will to live, or a condition of inner peace, can affect the course of a disease, even perhaps effect a regression or cure. Where exactly can the line be drawn here?

The point here is just to suggest that the Humean argument, which seems so certain and undeniable on its own terms, begins to shake on its foundations within the other perspective. For one thing, it is not so obvious what is "natural law" here, and what is breach thereof. And of course, it also matters where you stand in the chain of transmission, how trustworthy you judge the particular links in this chain to be. Both sides of the Humean argument cease to play the fixed and persuasive role assigned to them, once you desert the disengaged stance.

Another powerful factor was going for the disengaged stance in that epoch. What weighed with Hume and Gibbon was not so much St. François de Sales, but their perception of "superstition" in general. In other words, their sense of what it was to believe in God's intervention was shaped by popular and mass beliefs about miracle cures, and other stories of divine or saintly intervention, as relayed by the credulous. Even if we try to allow for the blindness to the phenomena of popular religion which was inseparable from their sense of intellectual/human superiority, tinged with fear, many of these stories and legends are not very convincing. It helped their case, if they could assimilate all the piety connected to a personal God to one or other of their negative categories: "superstition", "fanaticism", "enthusiasm", and just range the St. François figures under these, or forget about them altogether.

In the then condition of Europe, with a mass religion which even many of the clergy judged superstitious, with churches often carrying out acts of persecution against heretics and unbelievers, this assimilation was not hard to make, if one was oneself untouched by personal piety (or reacted against a youth where one was so touched—perhaps Gibbon?).

I said above that the modern slide to Deism, and later atheism, integrated a great deal of the original package of changes effected by the Fathers in the philosophy they inherited. Modern Deism integrated the first five in my list: the body, history, the place of individuals, contingency, and the emotions. That is, it integrated these as essential dimensions of our understanding of human life, but it excluded them altogether from our relation to God. But of course, these two levels can't be neatly separated. The stance of disengagement tends to pry us out of some of these when it comes to accounting for what is highest in our lives. This, with the eclipse of God, turns out to be morality, the law which binds us. This will often be seen as revealed to us by Reason, following a study of reality, or else of the very structure of Reason itself. But to the extent that disengagement is seen as essential to Reason, then the body tends to fall away. So we gravitate towards two possible positions; one tells us that we have to factor out our embodied feeling, our "gut reactions" in determining what is right, even set aside our desires and emotions. This move finds a paradigm statement in the work of Kant. Or else, we turn against the excessive claims of reason, and base morality on emotions, as we find with Hume. But just for that reason we undercut the aura of the higher that usually surrounds these feelings, giving them a purely naturalistic explanation. Embodied feeling is no longer a medium in which we relate to what we recognize as rightly bearing an aura of the higher; either we do recognize something like this, and we see reason as our unique access to it; or we tend to reject this kind of higher altogether, reducing it through naturalistic explanation.

This is the move which I want to call "excarnation", and which I will discuss later in the last part. It is, of course, vigorously combated in modern culture. One of the most important sites of resistance to it is aesthetic experience, where embodied feeling can still be allowed to open us to something higher.

So putting this all together, we can see how a certain kind of framework understanding came to be constituted: fed by the powerful presence of impersonal orders, cosmic, social, and moral; drawn by the power of the disengaged stance, and its ethical prestige, and ratified by a sense of what the alternative was, based on an élite's derogatory and somewhat fearful portrait of popular religion, an unshakeable sense could arise of our inhabiting an immanent, impersonal order, which screened out, for those who inhabited it, all phenomena which failed to fit this framework.

We just need to add one thing, which puts the lock on the door, as it were. Once one has adopted this take, one can be firmly entrenched in it by the enframing historical consciousness which was developed in polite, commercial society. Expressed in terms of theory, it emerges in the "stadial" accounts that we see in the Scottish Enlightenment, with for instance Smith and Ferguson,[25] which I invoked in an earlier section. Human society passes through certain stages, e.g., hunter-gatherer, agricultural, commercial. These stages, usually defined ultimately in economic terms, describe an advance. Higher ones represent a development, a gain, from which it would be quite irrational to try to retreat once they have come about (although there is room for some ambivalence, and regret at what is lost; this, as we shall see, is deeply rooted in modern culture). All this clearly applies to the current stage, just recently acceded to: commercial society.

I have described this in terms of certain important theories, but there was a more widespread outlook or temper, which understood recent history as gain or progress, based on some big structural changes: e.g., displacement of a feudal, warrior aristocracy, with a commercial, production-oriented élite, consequent pacification, economic prosperity, softening of manners, "politeness", and so on. It was easy to take on board the idea that along with different cultural features and practices which belonged to different eras—groups of feudal retainers versus joint stock companies, training in warfare versus training in the arts of administration or commerce, exaggerated insistence on honour, as against a more egalitarian sense of dignity—modes of religion too must change. From here it would be easy to take the step that orthodox, communion-defined Christianity really belongs to an earlier age; that it makes little sense, and is hard to sustain today.

This conclusion out of "stadial" consciousness wasn't drawn immediately, but it clearly was a possibility, and it in fact becomes a factor of greater and greater importance through the nineteenth century up to our day. If the anthropocentric take involves, as I claim, that one ignore a great many religious phenomena and possibilities, then some background understanding which tells you that indeed, you ought to ignore them, that you have no reason to take account of them, because they're "outdated" and impossible today, can play a crucial role in stabilizing the take, and arming it against all potential eruptions from outside. The sense is, that the superiority of our present outlook over other earlier forms of understanding is part of what defines the advance of the present stage over all earlier ones. That it seems right to us is not just a fact about us, but reflects the progress we have made. Intellectual regression would be unthinkable; it would involve pretending that we could go back.

This stadial consciousness is, so to speak, the ratchet at the end of the anthropocentric shift, which makes it (near) impossible to go back on it.

This powerful understanding of an inescapable impersonal order, uniting social imaginary, epistemic ethic, and historical consciousness, becomes one of the (in a sense unrecognized) *idées forces* of the modern age. Up till our time.

We can thus discern, across a number of different confessions, but stronger (or at least less vigorously contested) among Protestant English-speaking, and to a lesser extent German-speaking societies than elsewhere, the growth of a certain temper among élites. This was far from being the unanimous view, even among élites, and in terms of the whole societies in which it existed, it was very far from their religious centres of gravity, and often had to hide its more radical facets. But because it was well entrenched among élites, it played an important role.

I began by describing one facet of this temper: the "anthropocentric shift". This is first of all, a revision downward of God's purposes for us, inscribing these within an immanent order which allows for a certain kind of human flourishing, consonant with the order of mutual benefit. Alongside this, I spoke of the lesser importance of grace in this scheme, the eclipse of mystery, and the foreshortening of earlier views of eventual human transformation at the hands of God, evoked by the patristic notion of "theiosis". From another side, we can describe this new temper in the terms of the preceding paragraphs. God's relation with us comes to be seen as mediated by an impersonal, immanent order. As an immanent order, it is self-contained; that is, apart from the issue of how it arose, its workings can be understood in its own terms. On one level, we have the natural order, the universe, purged of enchantment, and freed from miraculous interventions and special providences from God, operating by universal, unrespondent causal laws. On another level, we have a social order, designed for us, which we have to come to discern by reason, and establish by constructive activity and discipline. Finally the Law which defines this order, whether as political/constitutional law, or ethical norms, can be expressed in rational codes, which can be grasped quite independent of any special relationship we might establish with God, and by extension with each other. The human relationships which matter are those prescribed in the codes (e.g., Natural Law, the Utilitarian principle, the Categorical Imperative).

These codes, of course, centre on the purely human flourishing which I invoked earlier in talking of the anthropocentric shift. We might just as well talk of a drift towards impersonal, immanent order. These are facets of the same movement. The shift or drift, I am suggesting, arises out of the larger development of earlier modernity, the growth of new modes of social organization and discipline, designed to be productive, instrumentally effective, fostering peace and economic development, and submitted to codes of conduct, political and ethical, aimed at mutual benefit. This comprises a large part of what we usually call "modernity". My thesis here is that, although reformed Christianity (and not only its Protestant variants) was a large part of the motor behind this development, its successful advance creates a predicament—where we in fact *do* live in an immanent order, of law, ethics, and a universe governed by natural law—which can be read in terms of the anthropocentric shift. Indeed, in the absence of some strong sense of what is being excluded, it even could be said to invite this reading.

The shift (or drift) can be seen as a reading, a take, on modernity; not the only possible one, as is supposed in some master narratives of secularization, and their subtraction stories, because it involves occluding, or belittling, whole dimensions of possible religious life and experience; but one which can look plausible, once you make these occlusions; and can even be highly understandable wherever the occlusions seem normal or forced on one by circumstances (if one is witnessing the execution of Calas, for instance, or learning of the Revocation of the Edict of Nantes, or engaged in a struggle against clerical reaction, and so on). Which way people go is never entirely explicable, but can be more or less understandable in defined circumstances.

The slide towards the impersonal can be seen in another development of the eighteenth century, continuing into the nineteenth. Parallel to and overlapping with Deism was a drift towards Unitarianism. The temper I am talking about, and even a lot of the theological beliefs, were found in other churches as well, but the defining theological beliefs of Unitarianism reflect the shift clearly.

Seen in this light, Unitarianism, like the Arianism which inspired it, can be seen as an attempt to hold on to the central figure of Jesus, while cutting loose from the main soteriological doctrines of historical Christianity. What is important about Jesus is not that he inaugurates a new relation with and among us, restoring or transforming our relation to God. That is not what salvation can mean. What it properly amounts to is our acceding to rational principles of conduct in law and ethics, and our becoming able to act on these. Jesus' role in this is that of a teacher, by precept and example. His importance is as an inspiring trailblazer of what we will later call Enlightenment. For this he doesn't need to be divine; indeed, he had better not be, if we want to maintain the notion of a self-contained impersonal order which God in his wisdom has set up, both in nature and for human society. Incarnation would blur the edges of this.

In this sense, Unitarianism wasn't confined to Unitarians. But it is not surprising to see that the members of this confession were among the social élites of Dissent, both in England and America; and also that they contained a disproportionate number of the élite figures involved in reform of various kinds in nineteenth-century Britain (closely followed by the Quakers). Martin quotes the claim that "relative to their size, which was never very great, Unitarians have acquired more entries in the *Dictionary of National Biography* than any other body."[26]

It may also be significant for the thesis I am defending here, that the switch to professed Unitarianism often took place among Presbyterians, or other Calvinists, whose official doctrines, with their stress on the Atonement, were at the antipodes to this new view.[27] This polar shift, however, seems to occur mainly among élites, those who have most successfully adopted and interiorized the new, disciplined, rational, code-defined ethos.

Whether through Unitarianism, or some other route, the primacy given to impersonal order ended up producing in the nineteenth century a tamed version of Christianity, tailored to suit its demands. The result was pithily described by George Tyrrell, a Catholic priest and scholar who, ironically, was silenced as a "modernist" under the hermetically self-enclosed Papacy of Pius X. This view contrived to find

> a moralist in a visionary; a professor in a prophet; the nineteenth century in the first; the natural in the supernatural. Christ was the ideal man; the Kingdom of Heaven, the ideal humanity. As the rationalistic presupposition had strained out, as spurious, the miraculous elements in the Gospel, so the moralistic presupposition strained out everything but modern morality. That alone was the substance, the essence of Christianity.[28]

2

The anthropocentric shift, and the slide to impersonal order; we can see how the movement with these two facets would also show us a third. Such a purified religion, where God reveals himself through His Creation, making demands on us which this Creation itself reveals to our rational scrutiny, and also making otiose all the forms of personal relation between Creator and creatures: personal fidelity, petitionary prayer, attempts to placate or implicate God in our fate, and the like; this is a religion founded on reality. It is based on Nature, or on Reason alone.

This religion doesn't need revelation; and it is scarcely conceivable that the Author of such an order would stoop to such a personalized communication as a short cut, if virtuous reason alone can suffice to tell us all we need to know.

On an optimistic view of humans' original capacities, this must have been the first religion of humankind. If we see it everywhere covered with distorting accretions, this must be because of some degeneration in virtue or enlightenment, perhaps aided by sinister forces which profited from darkness and ignorance (often castigated as "priestcraft"). The differences between religions, which consist in varied such accretions, are all false. We must return to the simple underlying common truth.

This truth is available to calm, dispassionate reason. So the royal road to true religion is right belief. We cannot access it by some relation of devotion which can supposedly yield more intimate insights into the will of God. That is the path of "mysticism", which has no legitimacy on this view. Theology is correct description, and loses any dimension of allocution, as it still had for Anselm.[29]

Again, on optimistic assumptions about humanity, the main cause of our so lamentably falling short of God's law is the operation of false religions, which not only lead us into quite irrelevant actions, like cult and sacrifice, but also put us against each other, introducing strife where there should be concord. Rid the world of these superstitions, and humans will find peace, concord, and mutual help.

This very "excarnate" religious life only needs one more transposition, into a register of total unbelief, and we can get the kind of thesis put forward by La Mettrie in *L'Homme Machine:*

> If atheism were generally accepted, every form of religion would be destroyed, and cut off at its roots. There would be no more theological wars, no more soldiers of religion—such terrible soldiers! Nature, having been infected with sacred poison, would regain its rights and purity. Deaf to all other voices, tranquil mortals would follow only the spontaneous dictates of their own being, the only commands . . . which can lead us to happiness.[30]

Here we can see the shift from belief to atheism, via the intermediary stage of what I've been calling "Providential Deism". It is through this intermediary that a place was opened for unbelief in our civilization.

The move to Deism involves more than just a change of belief; more even than a shift in what was taken to be rational argument (the kind of thing we see in Hume's discrediting of miracles). It really reflects a major shift in our background understanding of the human epistemic predicament. I have already described one facet of this above in my discussion of objectification and disengagement. But from another point of view it can be seen as a change in horizon which profoundly alters what it means to reason about God, or "religion".

The background assumption of the Deist standpoint involves disintricating the issue of religious truth from participation in a certain community practice of religious life, into which facets of prayer, faith, hope are woven. As we saw Buckley argue in the previous chapter, previous theology, including attempts to "prove" the existence of God, has to be understood as deployed within the horizon of such a common life, in this case, Christian. The same point is made by Stanley Hauerwas in his recent Gifford Lectures.[31]

In the new dispensation, the issues of God's existence, our relation to him, what we owe him, and the like, are put by Deism quite outside this horizon. We imagine that we have to start elsewhere, first showing that God exists, then that he is benevolent, then the nature of his commandments, and that they are to be obeyed. This was the new understanding which we saw in the new apologetics which Buckley described, an apologetics that with hindsight seems to be opening the door to atheism at the very moment when it thinks most effectively to have barred it. The barring is meant to come through strenuous argument, but the opening comes from the shift in standpoint. Both the proposers of these arguments from benevolent design of the universe, and their addressees, are presumed to stand outside of the previous Christian horizon of practice, prayer and hope, at least for the sake of argument. God is not essential to the very framework of their lives, but an entity (albeit an important one) which we have to *reason towards* out of this framework.

What is the new framework? It is the one I have been striving to define here. Human beings, forming societies under the normative provisions of the Modern Moral Order, and fulfilling their purposes by using what Nature provides, through the aid of accurate knowledge of this Nature, and the contrivances which we will later call Technology. Moreover, these agents acquire knowledge by exploring impersonal orders with the aid of disengaged reason. This now defines the human epistemic predicament.

This is the massive shift in horizon, which has been identified as the rise of modernity. It has been differently understood. By secular humanists, it is often framed by what I call a "subtraction" story: the religio-metaphysical illusions fall away, and human beings discover that they just *are* humans united in societies which can have no other normative principles but those of the MMO, and so on for the other features of the newly defined predicament. Or else, in a Blumenbergian twist, this is what they reveal themselves to be once they take a stance of self-assertion *(Selbstbehauptung)*. As should be clear from the above argument, I cannot accept this kind of account because it utterly passes over the ways in which this new self-understanding has been constructed in our history.

From the opposed perspective, we can trace the way in which the theological understanding of an Aquinas was lost, and arguments for the existence of God came to take on the quite different meaning in the new horizon. Since radically new constructions tend to seem "natural" after the fact, and thus to misunderstand how radical and innovative they are, many of the major thinkers of this new mode of argument, and also we their successors, often fail to see how much they have "changed the subject". We tend to think, for instance, that moderns differ from Aquinas on the validity of the proofs for God's existence (that is, we see how he was wrong in thinking them convincing), but cannot grasp that these arguments were doing something rather different in the earlier horizon.

Hence the importance of studies which show how the subject was changed through a series of steps involving late Scholasticism, Duns Scotus, nominalism, "possibilism", Occam, Cajetan and Suarez, Descartes, where each stage appeared to be addressing the same issues as the predecessors it criticized, while in fact the whole framework slid away and came to be replaced by another. Buckley has contributed to this critique of this unconscious distortion of the mediaeval sources, as have Hauerwas, MacIntyre, Milbank, Pickstock, Kerr, Burrell.[32] I haven't been able to do justice to this work here, but the story I have been telling is in a sense complementary to theirs. I have been trying to understand some of the changes in social practice and hence also social imaginary that helped bring about the shift of horizon. (I will say a few words about this at the end, in the epilogue, "The Many Stories".)

Meanwhile, glancing forward, we can see how this new framework, granted the important place it gave to the natural universe, seen as basically benign and ordered, was bound to be profoundly disturbed by the developments of the succeeding centuries, most dramatically epitomized by the findings of Darwin, and the picture of a Nature "red in tooth and claw". The updated form of the classical early-modern horizon of metaphysical argument still contains human beings uniting in societies under (contemporary understandings of) the MMO, but these are now set in an indifferent, even hostile universe. Now any metaphysical view (other, of course, than that of the instrumentally rational subject in the modern order, which is embedded in the framework) has to be established starting from the considerations which lie to hand within this horizon. We will see what this means for metaphysical and religious thinking below.

The development of the disciplined, instrumentally rational order of mutual benefit has been the matrix within which the shift could take place. This shift is the heartland and origin of modern "secularization", in the third sense in which I have been using this term: that is, of the new conditions in which belief and unbelief uneasily coexist, and often struggle with each other in contemporary society. But this matrix does more than illuminate the shift; it can also help account for some of the struggle. In its light, we can understand some of the reactions against "modernity", and the impact they have had on modern belief, both for and against. To a consideration of this, I now turn.

PART III

The Nova Effect

8   The Malaises of Modernity

We will get a sense of this as we follow, at least in summary over-view, the currents and cross-currents in the polemics around belief and unbelief in the last two centuries. This will be part of the story I now want to tell. I am trying to give an account of the development of contemporary secularity 3, which can be presented in three stages.

The first I have just completed: an explanation of how there came to be an exclusive humanist alternative to Christian faith. The second phase sees a further diversification. The multiple critiques levelled at orthodox religion, Deism, and the new humanism, and their cross-polemics, end up generating a number of new positions, including modes of unbelief which have broken out of the humanism of freedom and mutual benefit (e.g., Nietzsche and his followers)—and lots else besides. So that our present predicament offers a gamut of possible positions which extend way beyond the options available in the late eighteenth century. It's as though the original duality, the positing of a viable humanist alternative, set in train a dynamic, something like a nova effect, spawning an ever-widening variety of moral/spiritual options, across the span of the thinkable and perhaps even beyond. This phase extends up to the present.

The third, overlapping with the second, is relatively recent. The fractured culture of the nova, which was originally that of élites only, becomes generalized to whole societies. This reaches its culmination in the latter half of the twentieth century. And along with this, and integral to it, there arises in Western societies a generalized culture of "authenticity", or expressive individualism, in which people are encouraged to find their own way, discover their own fulfillment, "do their own thing". The ethic of authenticity originates in the Romantic period, but it has utterly penetrated popular culture only in recent decades, in the time since the Second World War, if not even closer to the present.

This turn has plainly altered the shape of secularity 3, mainly by shifting the place of the spiritual in human life, at least as lived by many. The connection between pursuing a moral or spiritual path and belonging to larger ensembles—state, church, even denomination—has been further loosened; and as a result the nova effect has been intensified. We are now living in a spiritual super-nova, a kind of galloping pluralism on the spiritual plane.

1

I start with the nova effect. Can we describe the predicament created by the move to Deism and then to exclusive humanism? I mean the predicament as experienced, primarily by members of the élite, who were alone concerned by these changes in the eighteenth century?

The ethic of freedom and order has arisen in a culture which puts at its centre a buffered self. This term, as I've been using it, has in fact a complex meaning. The phenomenon has, as it were, objective and subjective sides. To be a buffered subject, to have closed the porous boundary between inside (thought) and outside (nature, the physical) is partly a matter of living in a disenchanted world. It comes about through a number of the changes described above: the replacement of a cosmos of spirits and forces by a mechanistic universe, the fading of higher times, the recession of a sense of complementarities, which found expression, for instance, in Carnival.

But these changes were furthered, and in turn intensified by subjective changes, shifts in identity, like the rise of disengaged reason, and the transformations wrought by disciplined self-remaking, including the narrowing and intensifying of intimacy, and Elias' "civilizing process".

For élites, these two facets generally went together, but more popular strata could suffer the first without being inducted into the second. That is, their world could be disenchanted by Reform from on top, banning and disrupting the customs and rituals which carried their sense of the sacred, higher time, complementarity. I will return to this common predicament of ordinary people later. For the moment, I want to describe the culture or conditions of belief among those strata which carried the Deist-humanist shifts.

What did (does) this buffered, anthropocentric identity have going for it? Its attractions are fairly obvious, at least to us. A sense of power, of capacity, in being able to order our world and ourselves. To the extent that this power was connected with reason and science, a sense of having made great gains in knowledge and understanding.

But beyond power and reason, there is something else very strong going for this anthropocentrism: a sense of invulnerability. Living in a disenchanted world, the buffered self is no longer open, vulnerable to a world of spirits and forces which cross the boundary of the mind, indeed, negate the very idea of there being a secure boundary. The fears, anxieties, even terrors that belong to the porous self are behind it. This sense of self-possession, of a secure inner mental realm, is all the stronger, if in addition to disenchanting the world, we have also taken the anthropocentric turn, and no longer even draw on the power of God.

Power, reason, invulnerability, a decisive distancing from age-old fears, of which we all still have some sense, not only from history, and not only from the as yet unenlightened masses, but also because they resonated somehow in our own childhood; all this belongs to the sense of self of those who have made the anthropocentric turn. And there are strong satisfactions which attend this.

Above all, there is a certain pride, and sense of one's own worth; which is the stronger, the more acutely one is aware of what an achievement this is, of the unreasoning fears from which one has freed oneself. Part of the self-consciousness of modern anthropocentrism is this sense of achievement, of having won through to this invulnerability out of an earlier state of captivity in an enchanted world. In this sense, modern self-consciousness has a historical dimension, even for those—who are, alas, many today—who know next to nothing about history. They know that certain things are "modern", that other practices are "backward", that this idea is positively "mediaeval", and that other one is "progressive". The sense of historical placement can accommodate itself to a bare skeletal minimum of fact.

The stance which this consciousness takes towards the past is that "enormous condescension of posterity" of which Edward Thompson spoke.[1] We can see classic expression of this in the great era in which this anthropocentric consciousness comes into its own, the eighteenth-century Enlightenment. Gibbon is an excellent example. The sense of invulnerability and distance from the unreason of the past finds expression in the cool self-possession, the "unflappable" tone in which the wild and disturbing antics of monks and bishops in Byzantium are recounted. Invulnerability is enacted in the style, in which the violent, extreme, God-haunted acts of our forebears are held at a fastidious distance through the unperturbable voice of a dry, ironic wit. This tone tells us: We no longer belong to this world; we have transcended it.

This buffered distance becomes part of the complex modern-European concept of "civilization", developing since the Renaissance notion of "civility", and becoming a crucial part of our own historicized self-awareness, whereby we place ourselves to our own "barbarian" past, and to other, less fortunate peoples. Woven into the other elements—literacy and education, personal self-discipline, development of the productive arts, a sense of decorum, government and the respect of law—which make up this developing ideal of civility[2] (or what it is to live in an "état policé"), this new kind of invulnerability and distance takes its place, inflecting the ideals of discipline, education, decorum, and good political order.[3]

So much for the positive side. But there is also a negative side. The buffered identity is deeply anchored in our social order, our embedding in secular time, the disengaged disciplines we have taken on. This anchoring ensures our invulnerability. But it can also be lived as a limit, even a prison, making us blind or insensitive to whatever lies beyond this ordered human world and its instrumental-rational projects. The sense can easily arise that we are missing something, cut off from something, that we are living behind a screen.

I am not just referring to the way many people reacted against Deism, and even more against humanism, out of a strong sense of God, or the transcendent; the kind of reaction we see among Wesleyans, Pietists, later among Evangelicals. I am thinking much more of a wide sense of malaise at the disenchanted world, a sense of it as flat, empty, a multiform search for something within, or beyond it, which could compensate for the meaning lost with transcendence; and this not only as a feature of that time, but as one which continues into ours.

My point is not that everybody feels this, but rather, first, that many people do, and far beyond the ranks of card-carrying theists. Indeed, what is noticeable from the very beginning is the constitution of a growing category of people who while unable to accept orthodox Christianity are seeking some alternative spiritual sources. Shaftesbury was an early, one might say proto-member of this class, which includes many of the great Romantic writers. (The relation of some of these to orthodoxy was complex, since there were those who evolved towards it—Wordsworth, Friedrich Schlegel—and those who evolved out of it—Lamartine, Victor Hugo.) And then there was the milieu of Mme de Staël in the Restoration, Carlyle, Arnold, and so on.

What this reflects is that in face of the opposition between orthodoxy and unbelief, many, and among them the best and most sensitive minds, were cross-pressured, looking for a third way. This cross-pressure is, of course, part of the dynamic which generates the nova effect, as more and more third ways are created.

I think that this says something about the predicament itself of being a buffered self, within the ethic of freedom and mutual benefit, with all the reasons which this supplied to resent the unacceptable faces of orthodoxy: the authoritarianism, the placing conformity before well-being, the sense of human guilt and evil, damnation, and so on. It tells us that this predicament was spiritually unstable, offering on one side motives not to go back to the earlier established faiths, and on the other (among other things), a sense of malaise, emptiness, a need for meaning.

Again, this doesn't mean that everyone will go on being pulled both ways. Many, perhaps most, will end up opting for some solution, including the extreme ones of authoritarian orthodoxy and materialist atheism. But the situation as a whole remains unstable, in the sense that there is no long term movement towards a resolution of whatever kind. Successive generations keep re-opening the issues in new ways; children desert the solutions of their parents: one generation reacts to the Gibbonian high culture of the eighteenth century by turning evangelical; not very long after their descendants have become unbelievers, and so on. Both those who hope that unbelief will encounter its own limitations and aridity, and will peter out in a general return to orthodoxy; and those who think that all this represents an historic march towards reason and science, seem doomed to disappointment. Over time, there seems no stable resolution.

Secondly, we can read the cross-pressure within the buffered identity, if we stand back from the see-sawing battle, and look at certain features of the culture as a whole. Although we respond to it very differently, everyone understands the complaint that our disenchanted world lacks meaning, that in this world, particularly youth suffer from a lack of strong purposes in their lives, and so on. This is, after all a remarkable fact. You couldn't even have explained this problem to people in Luther's age. What worried them was, if anything, an excess of "meaning", the sense of one over-bearing issue—am I saved or damned?—which wouldn't leave them alone. One can hear all sorts of complaints about "the present age" throughout history: that it is fickle, full of vice and disorder, lacking in greatness or high deeds, full of blasphemy and viciousness. But what you won't hear at other times and places is one of the commonplaces of our day (right or wrong, that is beside my point), that our age suffers from a threatened loss of meaning. This malaise is specific to a buffered identity, whose very invulnerability opens it to the danger that not just evil spirits, cosmic forces or gods won't "get to" it, but that nothing significant will stand out for it.

There was indeed, a predecessor condition with some analogies to this one, and that was "melancholy" or "acedia". But this was, of course, enframed very differently. It was a specific condition, one might say, a spiritual pathology of the agent himself; it said nothing at all about the nature of things. It cast no doubt on the ontic grounding of meaning. But this ontic doubt about meaning itself is integral to the modern malaise. We can understand, however, why melancholy (or "ennui" or "spleen") can take an important place in the art which has formed the consciousness of our age, as with Baudelaire. I will return to this question of the place of art below.

Meanwhile, this malaise, and other similar ones, speak to the condition of the buffered identity. This condition is defined by a kind of cross-pressure: a deep embedding in this identity, and its relative invulnerability to anything beyond the human world, while at the same time a sense that something may be occluded in the very closure which guarantees this safety. This is one source, as I mentioned above, of the nova effect; it pushes us to explore and try out new solutions, new formulae.

But it also helps explain the fragility of any particular formula or solution, whether believing or unbelieving. This mutual fragilization of all the different views in presence, the undermining sense that others think differently, is certainly one of the main features of the world of 2000, in contrast to that of 1500.

Pluralism is certainly an important part of the answer, how things are different today. When everybody believes, questions don't as easily arise. But we have to say that pluralism in the sense meant here doesn't just mean the co-existence of many faiths in the same society, or the same city. Because we have often seen this in pre-modern contexts, or in other parts of the world, with relatively little fragilizing effects.

The fact is that this kind of multiplicity of faiths has little effect as long as it is neutralized by the sense that being like them is not really an option for me. As long as the alternative is strange and other, perhaps despised, but perhaps just too different, too weird, too incomprehensible, so that becoming *that* isn't really conceivable for me, so long will their difference not undermine my embedding in my own faith.

This changes when through increased contact, interchange, even perhaps inter-marriage, the other becomes more and more like me, in everything else but faith: same activities, professions, opinions, tastes, etc. Then the issue posed by difference becomes more insistent: why my way, and not hers? There is no other difference left to make the shift preposterous or unimaginable.

Now the condition of modern society, within the modern idea of moral order, and the democratic, direct-access society which has entrenched this, is one of maximum homogeneity. We are more and more like each other. The distances which keep the issue between us at bay get closer and closer. Mutual fragilization is at its maximum.[4]

But this effect is now further intensified by what I have been calling the instability in the buffered identity. Cross-pressured, we are prone to change, and even multiple changes over generations. This means that the other path I confront may be that of my brother, my father, my cousin, my aunt. The distances have vanished. If there were at least greater stability across generations, and little inter-marriage, at least the Xs and the Ys would grow different, would add more and more distances to the original divergence in faith. But this is impossible in modern society. Homogeneity and instability work together to bring the fragilizing effect of pluralism to a maximum.

2

I have been exploring how the nova effect arises out of the cross-pressures in the buffered identity. But it is also generated in a whole host of other ways, which emerge when we look at the dynamic of this instability in somewhat finer detail. The whole package: buffered identity, with its disengaged subjectivity, and its supporting disciplines, all sustaining an order of freedom and mutual benefit, has given rise to a gamut of negative reactions, sometimes levelled at the package itself, sometimes against one or other part of it, sometimes against particular solutions which arise from it. I want to look at least at some of these, and follow out a little the path of the polemics.

This will allow us to get some idea of the breadth of the nova effect, since within the ambivalence of the buffered identity a given reaction or objection can often give rise to more than one response. What may seem to call for a return to belief may give rise also to new forms of unbelief, and vice versa.

Because we have to bear in mind that it is not only the modern buffered identity which is triggering negative reactions. There is also at work in the culture since the eighteenth century strong objections against Christianity. Before we enumerate the axes of attack against the whole modern package, let's set out once more the indictments against orthodox religion.

Tersely put, the main points of accusation are:

1. It offends against reason (harbouring a role for mystery, proposing paradoxical notions, such as the God-man).
2. It is authoritarian (that is, it offends both freedom *and* reason).
3. It poses impossible problems of theodicy. Or it tries to avoid them; being often pusillanimous in proposing to compensate for the most terrible events in history in a future life; or else bowdlerizing in covering up how terrible these events are.
4. It threatens the order of mutual benefit:
   (i)   in mortifying the self: it inveighs against the body, sensual satisfaction, etc.,
   (ii) in mortifying others: in the ordinary case, as well, by its condemnation of the body and sensual satisfaction; but rising to an extreme in actual persecution (Calas case);
   (iii) in threatening legitimate authority in societies dedicated to furthering the order of mutual benefit.

We can see the connection of all of these with the understanding of the immanent, impersonal, rationally understandable order we live in which is meant to secure our freedom and relations of mutual benefit. The connections of (1), (2), and (4) are evident. But perhaps a word can be said about theodicy.

This in a sense seems to raise a separate set of arguments quite independent from notions of immanent order. But in fact, the problems of theodicy become at once more salient, and harder to answer, in the context of Deism and the new understanding of the human epistemic predicament.

It is obvious that theodicy, while it is always a possibility within theistic modes of belief, can be less acute if we see ourselves as in an inscrutable world, at threat, but having God as our helper. Once we claim to understand the universe, and how it works; once we even try to explain how it works by invoking its being created for our benefit, then this explanation is open to clear challenge: we know how things go, and we know why they were set up, and we can judge whether the first meets the purpose defined in the second. In Lisbon 1755, it seems clearly not to have. So the immanent order ups the ante.

But there is another connection. The failure of theodicy can now more readily lead to rebellion, because of our heightened sense of ourselves as free agents. The connection here is not one of logical argument so much as of existential attitude. Let us try to follow this:

Someone close to you dies. You may want to hang on to the love of God, to the faith that they and you are still with God, that love will conquer death, even though you don't understand how. What do you say to the challenge of theodicy? One answer could be: that in a sense, God is powerless; that is, he cannot just undo this process without abolishing our condition, and hence our coming to him from out, or through of this bodily condition—although occasionally this spark of our coming to him lights up, and there can be surprising cures.

Or on the other hand, it can be too painful, maddening, full of self-torture to feel that God could have helped but didn't; or that God somehow couldn't help, but is supposed to be all-loving father. There is a fight to go on remaining in the love of God. It's a relief to flip over and to give vent to anger. You can say, I don't want to pardon God; but in another way, you can say: I see it all as blind nature, and I can let myself go to hate this, or consider it my enemy; I no longer have the burden of having to see it as benign. I can just let fly, take it as my implacable adversary; and there is relief in this.

There is a kind of peace in being on my/our (human) own, in solidarity against the blind universe which wrought this horror. We fall back into this. This possibility has been opened by the modern sense of immanent order.

As this last point suggests, which way one goes may have a lot to do with preexisting solidarity groups. If one is in a profoundly believing/practising way of life, then this hanging in to trust in God may seem the obvious way, and is made easier by the fact that everyone is with you in this; and the same goes for the rebellion against God.

But an important point is that, once again as with "scientific" proofs of atheism, it is not the cast-iron intellectual reasoning which convinces, but the relief of revolt.

Whether one wants to take refuge in this will depend, first, on how much one has already felt the inner point of our being nevertheless in the love of God, that God suffered with us. It is easier if one hasn't, and even easier if one's sense of the love of God was of a protecting father who could easily prevent this (a sense strengthened by the anthropocentric shift). Then the painful paradox is at its worst, and it can become unbearable to go on holding on to this, and one flips over. Which means that, parallel to the case of becoming atheist through "science", the more childish one's faith, the easier the flip-over.

Which is not to say that death isn't a terrible trial for anyone.

Keeping this set of indictments in mind, let us turn to see those directed against the buffered identity within the immanent, impersonal order. They lie along several axes.

There is one central axis with which we are all familiar. There is a generalized sense in our culture that with the eclipse of the transcendent, something may have been lost. I put it in the optative mood, because people react very differently to this; some endorse this idea of loss, and seek to define what it is. Others want to downplay it, and paint it as an optional reaction, something we are in for only as long as we allow ourselves to wallow in nostalgia. Still others again, while standing as firmly on the side of disenchantment as the critics of nostalgia, nevertheless accept that this sense of loss is inevitable; it is the price we pay for modernity and rationality, but we must courageously accept this bargain, and lucidly opt for what we have inevitably become. One of the most influential proponents of this latter position was Max Weber.[5] But wherever people stand on this issue, everyone understands, or feels they understand what is being talked about here. This is a sense which, at least in its optative form, seems available to everyone, whatever interpretation they end up putting on it.

To get farther with this, and bring out more what it involves, we have to venture on some phenomenology, and this is always hazardous. How to describe this sense? Perhaps in terms like these: our actions, goals, achievements, and the like, have a lack of weight, gravity, thickness, substance. There is a deeper resonance which they lack, which we feel should be there.

This is the kind of lack which can show up with adolescence, and be the origin of an identity crisis. But it can also show up later, as the basis of a "mid-life crisis", where what previously satisfied us, gave us a sense of solidity, seems not really to match up, not to deserve what we put into it. The things which mattered up to now fail.

This is just an attempt to give some shape to a general malaise, and I recognize how questionable it is, and how many other descriptions could have been offered here. But the malaise also takes a number of more definite forms, in terms of defined issues, or felt lacks.

One way of framing this issue is in terms of "the meaning of life", Luc Ferry's "le sens du sens", the basic point which gives real significance to our lives.[6] Almost every action of ours has a point; we're trying to get to work, or to find a place to buy a bottle of milk after hours. But we can stop and ask why we're doing these things, and that points us beyond to the significance of these significances. The issue may arise for us in a crisis, where we feel that what has been orienting our life up to now lacks real value, weight. So a successful doctor may desert a highly paid and technically demanding position, and go off with Médecins Sans Frontières to Africa, with a sense that *this* is really significant. A crucial feature of the malaise of immanence is the sense that all these answers are fragile, or uncertain; that a moment may come, where we no longer feel that our chosen path is compelling, or cannot justify it to ourselves or others. There is a fragility of meaning, analogous to the existential fragility we always live with: that suddenly an accident, earthquake, flood, a fatal disease, some terrible betrayal, may jolt us off our path of life, definitively and without return. Only the fragility that I am talking about concerns the significance of it all; the path is still open, possible, supported by circumstances, the doubt concerns its worth.

Once again the stances we take to this can vary enormously. Some people are unruffled, even as others are by the existential dangers. They see the possibility as "only theoretical". But everyone understands this kind of issue, as they do people raising questions about "the meaning of life". This was not true in earlier epochs. True there was the danger of "acedia", the inexplicable loss of all motivation, or joy in one's activity. But this is a quite different experience, because it doesn't involve doubt and questioning about the value of the activity in question. For a monk to suffer from acedia in his vocation was a sin; it was not a form of questioning of God.

This way of framing the issue partakes of the post-Axial outlook, which opened up the idea that there is "one thing needful", some higher goal which transcends, or gives sense to all the lower ones. But the sense of emptiness, or non-resonance, may arise in a quite different way. It can come in the feeling that the quotidian is emptied of deeper resonance, is dry, flat; the things which surround us are dead, ugly, empty; and the way we organize them, shape them, arrange them, in order to live has no meaning, beauty, depth, sense. There can be a kind of "nausée" before this meaningless world.[7]

Some people indeed, want to reject the first way of framing the issue, the "one thing needful" way, the way of post-Axial culture. We shouldn't try to force life into a single over-riding purpose; we should be suspicious of questions about *the* meaning of life. These people want to take up an anti-Axial position, they want to rehabilitate "paganism", or "polytheism". But whatever one's stand on this polemic, the malaise is felt on both these levels, and we all can recognize what is going on when it is.

We can feel this emptiness in the everyday, but also it comes out with particular force in what should be the crucial moments of life: birth, marriage, death. These are the important turning points of our lives, and we want to mark them as such; we want to feel that they are of particular moment, something solemn. So we talk of "solemnizing" a marriage. The way we have always done this is by linking these moments up with the transcendent, the highest, the holy, the sacred. Pre-Axial religions did this. But the enclosure in the immanent leaves a hole here. Many people, who have no other connection or felt affinity with religion, go on using the ritual of the church for these rites de passage.

But we can also just feel the lack in the everyday. This can be where it most hurts. This seems to be felt particularly by people of some leisure and culture. For instance, some people sense a terrible flatness in the everyday, and this experience has been identified particularly with commercial, industrial, or consumer society. They feel emptiness of the repeated, accelerating cycle of desire and fulfillment in consumer culture; the cardboard quality of bright supermarkets, or neat row housing in a clean suburb; the ugliness of slag heaps, or an aging industrial townscape. We may respond negatively to the outsider's élite stance, the judging of ordinary people's lives without real knowledge, that these feelings seem to reflect. But however mixed with unacceptable social distance and superiority, these feelings are easy to understand and hard to shake off. And if we think of the immense popularity in our civilization of the flight away from certain townscapes, to the country, the suburb, even to wilderness, we have to admit the virtual universality of some reactions of this range. The irony of the suburb, or garden city, is that it provokes in more fortunate others some of the same feelings, viz., of the emptiness and flatness of an urban environment, which were responsible for its existence in the first place.[8]

I have distinguished three forms which the malaise of immanence may take: (1) the sense of the fragility of meaning, the search for an over-arching significance; (2) the felt flatness of our attempts to solemnize the crucial moments of passage in our lives; and (3) the utter flatness, emptiness of the ordinary.

Now I have been calling these "malaises of immanence", because everyone recognizes that they come onto our horizon, or onto our agenda, with the eclipse of transcendence. But it doesn't follow that the only cure for them is a return to transcendence. The dissatisfaction they give rise to can send people back to seek some relation to the transcendent, but it is also felt by those who for one reason or another cannot countenance such a return, or only in forms which are very far from traditional established religion. They too seek solutions, or ways of filling the lack, but within immanence; and thus the gamut of new positions multiplies. There is not only the traditional faith, and the modern anthropocentric shift to an immanent order; the felt dissatisfaction at this immanent order motivates not only new forms of religion, but also different readings of immanence. This expanding gamut is what I am trying to gesture at with the term "nova".

So the need for meaning can be met by a recovery of transcendence, but we can also try to define the "one thing needful" in purely immanent terms, say, in the project of creating a new world of justice and prosperity. And similarly, without appeal to religion, we can seek to give resonance to the everyday, to nature and the things around us, by calling on our own depth sense. In one such attempt, which has had a great impact on our history, "Nature" becomes not just the ensemble of natural reality, but a deep source in us. Corresponding to the depth of instinct in us and other animals, corresponding to the anchoring of certain patterns in animate nature in general, should be a sense of their deep significance in us; so the striving to feed our families, to love and have children, to listen to the wisdom of the old, to protect the young, etc., should, must have a deeper resonance in us. If we fail to sense this, it is because we are cut off, divided from ourselves; we have to be brought back to the "natural". One of the pioneers of this notion of disalienation as a recovery of contact with our own deeper purposes was Jean-Jacques Rousseau. And this notion of the joys and deep resonance of our natural form of life, returning to which out of the alienated forms of aristocratic society is the source of virtue, was one of the key themes of the French Revolution. One can see it in the rituals and festivals through which they tried to give substance and force to their new institutions. The names of the months reflected the natural round of the year; the festivals grouped people into the natural categories of their normal life, age, type of work, sex, and so on.[9]

My aim here will not so much be to canvass some of the different solutions offered, many of which are familiar enough, but rather to articulate further the dissatisfactions and felt lacks to which they respond. In this way, we will better be able to appreciate the dynamic which is driving the nova. This will involve stating in more detail what some people found objectionable or lacking in the buffered, disengaged, disciplined identity sustaining the modern moral order (hereafter referred to just as the "buffered identity"), or in one or another of its more powerful, widely diffused forms.

I have already started on this above, in breaking down the general malaise of immanence in three general areas, by defining different issues or sensed lacks. But we can take this farther, and define the different axes of criticism or objection. Disintricating these axes may sometimes be difficult. In the actual struggles, there has often been more than one issue at stake. I am going to have to make a number of analytic distinctions, which are bound to seem rather artificial when we look at any particular thinker or movement. But this move is justified, because the strands, while always connected, combine in a number of different ways.

The axes naturally group themselves, by the affinities of the different issues raised.

I. The principal group, which I have been discussing above, we could think of as axes of resonance, to give them a handy title. (In a sense, though, we could sum up the malaise of immanence in the words of a famous song by Peggy Lee: "Is that all there is?" Perhaps we should even speak of a "Peggy Lee" axis in honour of the singer. But this may not sound serious enough.)

The concern, whether we have identified a satisfactory purpose to our lives, can also arise in more specialized form, challenging specific aspects of the buffered, etc. identity. Thus, (1) starting in the late eighteenth century, we frequently encounter the sense that the understanding of benevolence, of charity, is too pale and tame in mainstream Deism/humanism. We saw that the movement to Deism involved some exclusion of practices which were previously seen as central to the love of/devotion to God, and their condemnation as excessive, extravagant, harmful, or "enthusiastic". A more demanding piety rebels at these restrictions. And so Evangelicals felt called upon to throw themselves into causes which most mainstream churchmen were willing to leave alone, most notably the abolition of slavery. To the less stringent, more Establishment-friendly mainstream notion of order, it seemed excessive to upset production and property rights, and long-settled ways, to such an extent, for such a reason.

But the call of a more demanding form of justice/benevolence also gave rise to new and more radical modes of humanism. As I remarked above, Rousseau is a hinge figure in this. He spoke up, very eloquently and persuasively, for a more demanding standard of justice and benevolence; and he was the inspiration of a whole tradition of radical humanist views, starting with those of the French Revolutionaries who swore by him.

(2) And the succession from Rousseau also has to include Kant. Here again, someone on the verge of Deism, in a sense; but one who very sharply defined the inner source of the moral law, and made morality identical to autonomy. Here we see a slightly different tilt to this axis: the indictment is not that the notion of benevolence is too tame; there is rather a revulsion against the flattening of human motivation which is inseparable from the utilitarian philosophy. Many felt a profound malaise at the idea that the sources of benevolence should be just enlightened self-interest, or simply feelings of sympathy. This seemed to neglect altogether the human power of self-transcendence, the capacity to go beyond self-related desire al-

together and follow a higher aspiration. This sense that the modern notion of order involves an eclipse of the human potential for moral ascent, either in theory or in the practice of commercial society, has been an important driving force in modern culture, as we shall see below.

It could and did generate believing forms of reaction, where the ascent which is being occluded here is identified as that to agape. But it also took humanist forms, and generated as well a host of intermediate variants, on the borderline of religion, as it were. Kant is an important resource for a whole gamut of these. In spite of the continuing place of God and immortality in his scheme, he is a crucial figure also in the development of exclusive humanism, just because he articulates so strongly the power of inner sources of morality.

And yet, we cannot be surprised when we learn that Kant came from a Pietist background. His philosophy goes on breathing this sense of the stringent demands of God and the good, even while he puts his Pietistic faith through an anthropocentric turn. We have a moving field of forces here, in which more than one constellation is possible, and more, in which the constellations frequently mutate.

(3) Another closely related line of attack against the buffered identity and its model of order charged them with moralism. In a sense, this too goes quite far back. I already mentioned how the "reasonable" religion which emerges out of the Civil War and its aftermath in England tended towards moralism. Our duty to God consisted in establishing and conforming to the moral order he had designed for us. The proofs of his existence and goodness pointed to his design of a world in which this order was appropriate, and his endorsing of it through the rewards and punishments he offers us. And I showed how the impersonal immanent order tended to focus its ethos in a code. What had got lost was the sense that devotion to God, for its own sake, was the centre of the religious life.

We can see how this objection runs parallel to the previous one; they both challenge the view that what is offered as our highest goal can really hold this place. The protest here is against a life totally absorbed in conforming to certain rules. The sense is that something central is missing, some great purpose, some élan, some fulfillment, without which life has lost its point.

Seen in a Christian perspective, this missing centrepiece is the love of God, and this could give us an alternative way of describing Wesley's rebellion against the established piety of his day. But the same charge can be taken up in a different perspective, in the name of an integral, fulfilled human nature, for instance, as we see it with Schiller. Simply imposing moral rules gives us a kind of unfreedom, a realm of necessity. If we impose them on ourselves, this means that we have created a kind of "master within".[10] True freedom requires that we go beyond morality to the harmonious realization of our whole nature, which we achieve in "play".

This appeal against the moral to a genuine self-realization can then be played out in a host of forms, both spiritual and naturalistic, as we see with Nietzsche, among others—and, of course, with Lawrence. Indeed, since moralism is one of the recurring forms generated out of the modern order of freedom and benefit, including its contemporary unbelieving Utilitarian and post-Kantian modes, this response is still being generated, and in a host of different directions. The nova effect goes on.

II. The reference to Schiller brings us to another constellation of axes, which I will call "Romantic", although given the role of Schiller and also Goethe in defining these, this might seem an inappropriate name. But the constellation arises in the Romantic period, and defines central concerns of the members of this, admittedly loose, group of writers and thinkers.

I mentioned above the attempt to find a weighty enough meaning to life in humanist terms, within the agent, and within nature. (1) One form in which this came to be defined, again following Rousseau, was through an ideal of harmonious unity. This would be both like and unlike Plato's: the crucial difference is that it would not involve rising beyond or sublimating ordinary natural desires. But operating fully in their ordinary forms, as sexual love, or enjoyment of beautiful surroundings, they would be transfigured by the sense of their higher significance. The ideal is thus of a fusion of ordinary desire and the sense of a higher goal, rather than an opposition in which harmony is achieved by the relegation or subordination of desire.

In the Romantic period, this ideal comes to be identified with beauty. Schiller takes on board the notion he finds in Shaftesbury and Kant, that our response to beauty is distinct from desire; it is, to use the common term of the time, "disinterested"; just as it is also distinct, as Kant said as well, from the moral imperative in us. But then Schiller argues that the highest mode of being comes where the moral and the appetitive are perfectly aligned in us, where our action for the good is overdetermined; and the response which expresses this alignment is just the proper response to beauty, what Schiller calls "play" (Spiel). We might even say that it is beauty which aligns us.[11]

This doctrine had a tremendous impact on the thinkers of the time; on Goethe (who was in a sense, one of its co-producers, in intensive exchange with Schiller), and on those we consider "Romantics" in the generally accepted sense. Beauty as the fullest form of unity, which was also the highest form of being, offers the definition of the true end of life; it is this which calls us to go beyond moralism, on one side, or a mere pursuit of enlightened interest, on the other. The Plato of the *Symposium* returns, but without the dualism and the sublimation. Hölderlin will call his ideal female companion, at first in theory, and then in the reality of Suzette

Gontard, "Diotima". But this name returns not as that of an older, wiser teacher, but in the form of a (hoped for) mate. (Of course, it ended tragically, but that's because reality cannot live up to such an ideal.)

From the standpoint of this anthropology of fusion and beauty, we can understand one of the central criticisms that the Romantic age levelled at the disengaged, disciplined, buffered self, and the world it had built. Beauty required the harmonious fusion of moral aspiration and desire, hence of reason and appetite. The accusation against the dominant conceptions of disciplined self and rational order was that they had divided these, that they had demanded that reason repress, deny feeling; or alternatively, that they had divided us, confined us in a desiccating reason which had alienated us from our deeper emotions.

Now this critique in fact went back some considerable way. Shaftesbury had reacted to the calculating hedonism of Locke, and rehabilitated the "generous affection" of which the soul is capable.[12] His was part of the inspiration behind the moral sense school. Later Rousseau in his own eloquent way protested against the narrow reasons of self-interest, which divide us from each other and stifle the reasons of the heart. The great importance laid on deep feeling as a facet of human excellence, on sentiment, on sensibility, reflected in part a reaction to the excessive demands of ordering reason. All this forms the background to the classical statements of the Romantic period, including the formulations of Schiller in his *Aesthetic Education,* which we have just adumbrated.

Now in one form this protest against division could be part of a way back out of rationalist Deism into orthodox belief. This is what it was for the Pietist movement. True religion couldn't consist in this intellectual fascination with doctrine; it had to engage the whole heart, or it was nothing. Count Zinzendorf pronounced a terse and final judgment on the apologetic obsessions of establishment theologians: "Whoso wishes to grasp God with his intellect becomes an atheist."[13] This religion of the heart was passed on to Wesley and Methodism, where it took ecstatic, often spectacular forms, deeply disturbing to those who feared above all "enthusiasm".

But the same reaction could lead in a quite different direction. The tyranny of reason over feeling in the context of much traditional morality involved a condemnation of base desire. The rehabilitation of ordinary feeling could therefore take the form of a rejection of this moral tradition, and also of the Christianity which seemed to underlie it, with its picture of human nature as damaged and depraved. So Rousseau's Deism sloughed off the doctrine of Original Sin. And others would follow this lead down the path to a humanism in which natural, spontaneous desire was the source of healing.

The same response could lead in two diametrically opposed directions—could bring us John Wesley (and today's Pentecostal movements), and D. H. Lawrence (and various twentieth-century cults of liberated sexuality). Not to speak of all the mediating links between these two Englishmen living a century and a half apart.

As for the writers of the Romantic period, they ended up going some in one direction, some eventually in the other. This is perhaps not hard to understand. Even though there was plainly a powerful immanent-humanist appeal to the original ideal of beauty, it also incorporated a very exalted conception of the highest in us, which was supposed to fuse with desire. This was often articulated in Platonic (Shelley) or Christian (Novalis) terms, or in both together (Hölderlin).

(2) But the Romantic protest was not only against the division within us. This could be seen as dividing us as moral reasoning agents from our own nature, nature within; but this was also frequently seen as a division from the great unity of nature outside us. And in another sense, the same emphasis on calculating reason cut us off from sympathetic union with others. What the modern forms of reason and disciplined order had put asunder could thus be seen as threefold: the reasoning mind was divided from his own desiring nature, from the community, which thus threatened to disintegrate, and from the great current of life in nature.

Schiller in the Sixth Letter of his work on *Aesthetic Education* offers a brilliant and immensely influential account of how the divisions in the individual interact with and strengthen those in the community, and how similarly, the healing of each can further that of the other.[14] This account continues to resonate in modern culture, as one could see as recently as the student protests of May 1968 in Paris.

But this sense of loss does not only power a humanist programme of recovery, in for example a future socialist society; it has also fuelled a backward-looking belief that the paradigm lies behind us, sometimes in an ideal Greek polis, sometimes in what was seen as a truly integrated mediaeval society; as with Novalis in his *Christenheit, oder Europa;* or even, in another form, Carlyle in *Past and Present.* Moreover, to complicate things, both forward and backward looking models could be combined, as again in the Romantic period, some hoped to recover the beautiful unity of the Greeks, which the progress of Christian society had disrupted, but which could be regained as part of a higher synthesis (Hölderlin, the young Hegel).

In fact, these master narratives of a spiral form were very widespread in this period.[15] They saw an original unity, followed by a division which sets its two terms in opposition: reason versus feeling, humans versus nature, etc. This in turn allowed for a recovered, more complex and richer unity, which resolved the opposition while preserving the terms. Through Hegel, this narrative form was passed on to Marx, and has exerted an immense force in modern history.

(3) If we focus on one facet of this triple division, we can discern a protest against the buffered self as such. The sense is here that in closing ourselves to the enchanted world, we have been cut off from a great source of life and meaning, which is there

for us in nature. Not that this was necessarily seen as an invitation to return to the past. On the contrary, the Romantics rather explored new ways to recover the link with nature, mediated by our expressive powers.

Once again the model for unity with nature in the Romantic period was frequently the Greeks. This is well articulated in a very influential poem of Schiller, *The Gods of Greece*. In ancient times, the unity with self and communion with nature in feeling was a given of life:

> Da der Dichtung zauberische Hülle
> Sich noch lieblich um die Wahrheit wand,
> Durch die Schöpfung floss da Lebensfülle,
> Und was nie empfinden wird, empfand.
> An der Liebe Busen sie zu drücken,
> Gab man höhern Adel der Natur,
> Alles wies den eingeweihten Blicken,
> Alles eines Gottes Spur.

> (When poetry's magic cloak
> Still with delight enfolded truth
> Life's fulness flowed through creation
> And there felt what never more will feel.
> Man acknowledged a higher nobility in Nature
> To press her to love's breast;
> Everything to the initiate's eye
> Showed the trace of a God.)

But this communion has now been destroyed; we face a "God-shorn nature":

> Unbewusst der Freuden die sie schenket,
> Nie entzückt von ihrer Herrlichkeit,
> Nie gewahr des Geistes, der sie lenket,
> Sel'ger nie durch meine Seligkeit,
> Fühllos selbst für ihres Künstlers Ehre,
> Gleich dem toten Schlag der Pendeluhr,
> Dient sie knechtisch dem Gesetzt der Schwere,
> Die entgötterte Natur.

> (Unconscious of the joys she dispenses
> Never enraptured by her own magnificence
> Never aware of the spirit which guides her

Never more blessed through my blessedness
Insensible of her maker's glory
Like the dead stroke of the pendulum
She slavishly obeys the law of gravity,
A Nature shorn of the divine.)

Notwithstanding the pessimism of these stanzas, this division too could form part of a spiral narrative of recovered unity.

(4) Now there is a particular way of framing this issue of division from nature which is especially worth mention. It is the malaise at the adoption of a purely instrumental, "rational" stance towards the world or human life. The close link to (3) comes in the fact that it is usually this stance which is indicted as what has in fact closed us off from nature and the current of life within us and without. But still, the attack on the instrumental stance takes up another side of this self-closure which has had its own devastating consequences. In the effort to control our lives, or control nature, we have destroyed much that is deep and valuable in them. We have been blinded to the importance of equilibria which can be upset, but can't be created by instrumental rationality. The most important of these in the contemporary debates is obviously the one touching the ecological balance of our entire biosphere. The line of protest which I am invoking here has been absolutely crucial to the ecological movements of our time. Some of these are grounded, of course, on instrumental rational considerations; but an important part of the whole ecological movement draws on the sense that there is something fundamentally wrong, blind, hubristic, even impious in taking this stance to the world, in which the environment is seen exclusively in terms of the human purposes to which it can be put.

Needless to say, this reaction too can take unbelieving as well as Christian forms.

III. Over against this "Romantic" group of axes, there is another which opposes it on many scores. Where the Romantic critique of division seems to suggest a healing remedy, the critiques I want to describe now tend to see this modern outlook as too facile and optimistic. They frequently point to irremediable division, and can introduce a note of tragedy.

(1) Something which may also go with a strong piety, but may not, is the rejection of the Deistic notion of Providence as just too absurdly, self-indulgently optimistic. Everything fits together for the good. It is all too pat, and seems to deny the tragedy, the pain, the unresolved suffering which we all know is there. The most famous occasion for this objection was the Lisbon earthquake of 1755. And the most famous articulation of it is probably Voltaire's in *Candide*, which shows right off how this response doesn't have to feed a sense of piety. On the contrary, it can be

used to put the whole notion of Providence on trial, and beyond it, belief in God as such. This has perhaps been its most important effect in the last two centuries. A very common objection of unbelief to Christianity has been that it offers a childishly benign view of human life, where everything will come right in the end, something which the really mature person cannot believe, and is willing to do without, having the courage to face reality as it is. This was in fact one of the main motors impelling those who moved from Deism to exclusive humanism in the eighteenth century.

In part, this bespeaks a one-sided definition of Christianity in terms of Providential Deism, particularly in the context of apologetic, as Buckley has shown.[16] It shows the importance of the order of historical events, and the key role played by Deism in the development of the modern debate. But it also is somewhat justified by the continuing place of a liberal, sanitized Christianity, which doesn't quite know what to do with suffering.

There is something deep in this objection. Deism or Christianity is taxed with unrealism; but there is also a moral objection here. Unrealism doesn't always have to be a moral fault. Some may even admire Christians or anarchists for their utopian hopes, and their willingness to fight for things which others recognize as impossible of attainment. But in the case of Panglossian optimism, the unrealism is held to betoken an immaturity, a lack of courage, and inability to face things.

Moreover, it is held in some way to cheapen life, to render it shallow. Recognizing the tragedy in life is not just having the nerve to face it; it is also acknowledging some of its depth and grandeur. There is depth, because suffering can make plain to us some of the meaning of life which we couldn't appreciate before, when it all seemed swimmingly benign; this is after all what tragedy as an art form explores. There is grandeur because of the way suffering is sometimes borne, or fought against. So in a curious way, a picture of life as potentially frictionless bliss robs us of something.

This is undoubtedly what Nietzsche was getting at in *The Genealogy of Morals*, where he says that what humans can't stand is not suffering, but meaningless suffering. They need to give a meaning to it. And he mentions specifically what I'm calling the judicial-penal model, the idea that we suffer because we have sinned, as an example of a belief which comes to be accredited partly because it makes sense of what is otherwise unbearable.[17]

Nietzsche is on to something here, although I have reservations about the idea that there is a demand for meaning as such, as it were, any meaning, as against something more specific. This, as we have seen and will see again, is rather endemic to our modern humanist consciousness of religion, and gives a particular (and I think dubious) twist to the hunger for religion in human beings. Nietzsche is followed in this, among others, by Weber, and also Gauchet.[18]

But nevertheless there is something important here. A too benign picture of the human condition leaves something crucial out, something that matters to us. There is a dark side to creation, to use this (Barthian) expression; along with joy, there is massive innocent suffering; and then on top of this, the suffering is denied, the story of the victims is distorted, eventually forgotten, never rectified or compensated. Along with communion, there is division, alienation, spite, mutual forgetfulness, never reconciled and brought together again.

Even where a voice of faith wants to deny that this is the last word, as with Christianity, we cannot set aside the fact that this is what we live, that we regularly experience this as ultimate. All great religions recognize this, and place their hopes in a beyond which doesn't simply deny this, which takes its reality seriously.

An image like the dance of Shiva, which brings destruction as well as creation in its wake, or a goddess like Kali, are a reflection of this. And so, for all its faults, was the juridical-penal model. It offered an articulation of the dark side of creation. Simply negating it, as many of us modern Christians are tempted to do, leaves a vacuum. Or it leaves rather an unbelievably benign picture, which cannot but provoke people either to unbelief, or to a return to this hyper-Augustinian mode of faith, unless it leads to a recovery of the mystery of the Crucifixion, of world-healing through the suffering of the God-man. Certainly this central mystery of Christian faith becomes invisible, if one tries to paint the dark out of Creation.

(2) There is another reaction which has arisen against precisely the models of benevolence and universalism in Deism and humanism. This is an attack that sees them as levelling down. Everybody is to be equal, and the old virtues of aristocracy are no longer valued: the virtues of heroism, for instance, the warrior virtues.

In this objection, the tilt in modern humanism and "civilization" towards equality is taken together with the valuing of peace over war, with the affirmation of the "bourgeois" virtues of production, and the relief of suffering; this is put in the context of the rejection of "extravagance" and "excess"; and the whole is condemned for levelling, for pusillanimity, for a negation of any high, demanding ideal, for the negation of all heroism.

We can see this in reactionary thinkers, like de Maistre, but also in Tocqueville; in Baudelaire, but also in Nietzsche; in Maurras, and also in Sorel. It can not only place itself on Left and Right (although perhaps it has been more evident in the twentieth century on the Right); but it also can take pious forms (where are the great vocations of asceticism and self-giving?), as well as fiercely anti-Christian forms (Nietzsche, who sees all this modern liberal egalitarianism as Christianity continued by other means).

It goes without saying that (2) easily combines with (1), but the objection lies on a different axis, and therefore I distinguish them.

(3) Closely related to both of these is a critique of the understanding of happiness

implicit in modern ideas of order. This, especially in its most simplistic, down-to-earth, or sensuous forms, as with certain kinds of utilitarianism, is often attacked as too flat, shallow, even demeaning. Moreover, it is held not just to reflect an intellectual error, an erroneous theory of happiness; it can also be the charter of a debased practice which threatens to spread in the modern world and to degrade human life. Humans so reduced will end up finding the point of their existence in "les petits et vulgaires plaisirs" which Tocqueville saw as the only remaining concern of the subjects of soft despotism;[19] or in the even more horrifying vision of Nietzsche, these reduced beings would end up as "last men".[20]

In the curved space of modern controversy, this axis clearly interweaves with the previous two. In one way, it clearly lies close to (2), in that this idea of happiness is being judged as base, unworthy of humanity; in another way, it can connect to (1), and be denounced as profoundly illusory, unrealistic. Human beings, however much they try, cannot really be happy this way. Their attempt to be so will be frustrated, either by the natural, unavoidable occurrence of suffering and death, or by the stifled sense within them that they were born for something higher. This latter criticism has been frequently levelled by Christian writers; but it can also be seen as implicit in Nietzsche's scornful picture of the last man.

These last three axes define types of controversy, rather than identifying fixed positions. That is, a given critical position may itself be attacked from a more exigent standpoint as being open to the same criticism. Thus, taking (3) as our example, the lowest-level hedonistic definition of a Helvétius, can be spurned as debased by a Rousseau, who will introduce a range of higher sentiments as well as an intrinsic love of virtue into his picture of human happiness. But from a more tragic standpoint, this harmonious fulfillment in a virtuous republic may seem quite utopian, and in the light of a more stringent demand for self-overcoming, it may seem too indulgent, insufficiently heroic, all-too-human.

These potential shifts in a more or less radical direction crop up in most of the axes I am identifying here. The Utilitarian Enlightenment was insufficiently spiritual for Mme de Staël and Benjamin Constant, but they in turn appeared too crassly humanist to a Chateaubriand. And so on.

(4) Another related line of attack concerns death. Modern humanism tends to develop a notion of human flourishing which has no place for death. Death is simply the negation, the ultimate negation, of flourishing; it must be combated, and held off till the very last moment. Against this, there have developed a whole range of views in the post-Enlightenment world, which while remaining atheist, or at least ambivalent and unclear about transcendence, have seen in death, at least the moment of death, or the standpoint of death, a privileged position, one at which the meaning, the point of life comes clear, or can be more closely attained than in the fullness of life.

Mallarmé, Heidegger, Camus, Celan, Beckett: the important thing is that these have not been marginal, forgotten figures, but their work has seized the imagination of their age. We don't fully understand this, but we have to take it into account in any attempt to understand the face-off between humanism and faith. Strangely, many things reminiscent of the religious tradition emerge in these and other writers, while it is also in some cases clear that they mean to reject religion, at least as it has been understood.

9 The Dark Abyss of Time

These axes of contention that I have sketched in the last chapter define a good part of the debate today in which belief and unbelief are implicated. But, as I have argued, it is not simply a debate between belief and unbelief, faith in God versus exclusive humanism. Currents swirl in different directions.

Thus the nineteenth century saw a great rise in unbelief. I mean by this not only that many people lost their faith, and abandoned churches or synagogues, but also that new positions were devised, new niches or spaces for unbelief. If the crucial story of the rise of secularity 3 over the centuries is the creation of an exclusive humanist alternative to faith, then this is a period in which the gamut of alternatives of this range becomes richer and wider.

In one way, we could see this period as a kind of reprise of the eighteenth-century slide to anthropocentrism, rather than simply as a continuation of it. That is because in between the two lies a strong surge of piety. This begins in England about the time of the French Revolutionary Wars (and partly in reaction to that display of militant unbelief), and strongly marks British society up to the last decades of Victoria's reign. First Evangelicalism, then later also High Church piety in the Established Church run alongside a surge of membership among dissident Churches. In France, it begins, of course, with the Restoration. The Church tries to regain the lost terrain, and to increase the level of practice; and they manage steadily to extend this, up till the third quarter of the century. In the U.S.A., the country from about 1800 is in the grips of the "Second Awakening" and the forming of an evangelical consensus, which somewhat marginalizes the Deistic outlook of so many of the founding Fathers of the Republic. Church membership begins its steady rise, which continues into the twentieth century.

So the turn to unbelief in the middle or later nineteenth century is in a way something new. It's not just that the movement is wider than its eighteenth-century predecessor; still within the élite of these advanced societies, but nevertheless more widespread. It's also that the turn is qualitatively different. It is in a sense deeper. I don't just mean that the intellectual formulations of a Comte or a Mill, or a Renan or Feuerbach were more profound than those of Bentham, Helvétius or Holbach, though I also think that this is so. But this depth is a reflection of something else, viz., that the unbelieving outlooks were more deeply anchored in the lifeworld and background sense of reality of nineteenth-century people than the analogous views of their eighteenth-century predecessors.

This is so in a number of ways, but I want to single out two here. The first consists in the fact that the shift from cosmos to universe, that I invoked above, had progressed farther.

Cosmos to universe: the way the world is imagined changed. By 'imagined' here, I mean two things, one of which is a specification of the other.

The first is analogous to what was described above as the "social imaginary". Indeed, it might be seen as a specification of this. The social imaginary consists of the generally shared background understandings of society, which make it possible for it to function as it does. It is "social" in two ways: in that it is generally shared, and in that it is about society. But there are also generally shared understandings about other things as well, and these are 'social' only in the first way. Among these is the ensemble of ways we imagine the world we live in.

And just as the social imaginary consists of the understandings which make sense of our social practices, so the "cosmic imaginary" makes sense of the ways in which the surrounding world figures in our lives: the ways, for instance, that it figures in our religious images and practices, including explicit cosmological doctrines; in the stories we tell about other lands and other ages; in our ways of marking the seasons and the passage of time; in the place of "nature" in our moral and/or aesthetic sensibility; and in our attempts to develop a "scientific" cosmology, if any.

The second and more specific sense in which our way of imagining the world has changed concerns the second-to-last item in this list, the way in which nature figures in our moral and aesthetic imagination. This is just one of the many ways in which our sense of the world comes to be formed, but it has been especially important in the change which I'm trying to delineate here, and I want to single it out for special attention.

Now this change, which has taken place over the last half millennium in our civilization, has been immense. We move from an enchanted world, inhabited by spirits and forces, to a disenchanted one; but perhaps more important, we have moved from a world which is encompassed within certain bounds and static to one which is vast, feels infinite, and is in the midst of an evolution spread over aeons.

The earlier world was limited and encompassed by certain notions of cosmos, world orders which imposed a boundary by attributing a shape to things. The Platonic-derived notion of the cosmos as a chain of being is one such: the cosmos in virtue of what Lovejoy called the "principle of plenitude" exhibits all the possible forms of being; it is as rich as it can be. But the number of these forms is finite, and they can be generated from a single basic set of principles. However vast and varied the world may appear to the untrained eye, we know that it is contained within the plan these principles define for us. No matter how deep and unfathomable it may appear, we know that we hit bottom, that we touch the outer edge, in this rational order.

Here I am talking about a kind of theory. But on the level of what I'm calling the imaginary, these theories draw on a general kind of understanding, one which can see the sensual, material world as contained in this way by the Ideas, because the things which surround us are understood as embodiments or expressions of these Ideas, or as signs of a higher reality which cannot be directly seen. In an enchanted universe, this kind of understanding is unproblematic. Things can show up as the loci of spirits or forces, and they do so unreflectingly, as a matter of immediate "experience", because they are generally understood to do so. A powerful relic, from which I hope for the cure of a debilitating illness, doesn't appear to me as just another bone, about which one might emit the hypothesis that touching it may have curative power. It is phenomenally filled with this power.[1]

Now what has happened is that for many, even most people in our civilization, that whole way of understanding things has fallen away. The world for them shows up as disenchanted. It's not just that the cosmos theories are no longer believed; they are even no longer fully intelligible. Seeing physical realities as embodiments or expressions doesn't fully make sense.

The cosmic imaginary of our ancestors was also shaped by another kind of idea, the Judaeo-Christian picture of the world as created by God, and as the locus of the story linking God and humans in the Fall and Redemption. This too, imposed a shape on things which sets an outer limit to any sense of unfathomable, bewildering depths in physical reality.

The limits were set in time. Even before the modern scientific spirit led theologians to calculate exactly when the Creation occurred (at 6 P.M. on October 22, 4004 B.C., according to Archbishop James Ussher), the depths of the past were already given shape by the divine-human drama played out in it. But this meant also that the limits were set in variety: the world we see is the one God created, with the same species of animals, birds and fishes. The world has always been inhabited by these animate creatures, even as it has always been the home of humans.

This Scripture-framework came to be interwoven with the cosmos one. There were tensions, of course: Aristotle had held that the world was eternal, and this was hard to square with creation ex nihilo. But Aristotle had also turned his back on evolution, and plumped for a fixed hierarchy of species.

At the same time, the understanding of things as signs or expressions of a higher reality could easily be taken over into a vision of the world as created. What God created had also a meaning, even as the words do which we produce. A vision of the world, drawing on neo-Platonism, and given early paradigm expression in the work of "Dionysius the Areopagite", becomes one of the leading ideas of mediaeval theology.

Now this Scripture-derived framework also sustained a certain kind of understanding of the world, interwoven with those underlying the cosmos ideas. The understanding of things as signs, and as signs addressed to us by God, entrenches the fixity of the cosmos in its short time scale. The world around us is God's speech act, and in the context of the Bible story this seemed to leave no room for any other story but the standard one, that the world as we see it issued in the beginning from the hand of God. Beyond the indices of change, of bewildering difference, must lie the limits laid down in the original creation.

But this whole understanding, defined by this sense of limits, has been swept away. Our sense of the universe now is precisely defined by the vast and the unfathomable: vastness in space, and above all in time; unfathomability in the long chain of changes out of which present forms evolve. But what is unprecedented in human history, there is no longer a clear and obvious sense that this vastness is shaped and limited by an antecedent plan. Earlier images of the universe as running through immense aeons—e.g., in Stoic or Hindu thought—were nevertheless limited by a notion of recurring cycles—like the Great Years of the Stoics. Our present sense of things fails to touch bottom anywhere.

I want to emphasize that I am talking about our *sense* of things. I'm not talking about what people believe. Many still hold that the universe is created by God, that in some sense it is governed by his Providence. What I am talking about is the way the universe is spontaneously imagined, and therefore experienced. It is no longer usual to sense the universe immediately and unproblematically as purposefully ordered, although reflection, meditation, spiritual development may lead one to see it this way.

Now the story of this change is the often told one—at least a part of it—of how the Biblical cosmology was replaced by the march of science, in the form of evolutionary theory. This is an important component; scientific discovery did indeed play a salient, even decisive, role in the change-over. My problem with this story is that it tells how one *theory* displaced another; whereas what I'm interested in is how our sense of things, our cosmic imaginary, in other words, our whole background understanding and feel of the world has been transformed.

These are not at all the same thing. Some theoretical change may leave our imaginary unaffected; this is true of much of the more refined and esoteric developments in contemporary science. Sometimes scientific change may help to undermine or destroy an earlier imaginary; and this is certainly true of the cosmological and bio-logical discoveries that led up to Darwin. But even in these cases, the science doesn't simply determine what imaginary develops in the place of the earlier one. For this we need to follow the fuller and richer story, englobing the transformations of both science and imaginary.

For our purposes here, we have to take up the richer account. Only if we accept the simplest "secularization" story, that "science" by itself determines modern unbe-lief, can we even imagine that we can neglect the fuller story. But I hope it will be evident in what follows how far this would be from a satisfactory account.

Even the actual course of the scientific story is hard to understand if we neglect the broader context.

The change-over on the level of theory is easy enough to trace. It can be set out in two categories. First, the immense increase in the dimensions of the old cosmos, centring on the Earth, which was orbited by the planets and the fixed stars. Vast as this was to earlier imaginations, it reached its limit in the outer spheres, and the Biblical story set its earlier limit in time. But now the idea grows that our solar sys-tem is just the immediate surrounding of one star in a galaxy; and then later that this galaxy is also one among countless others. Already in the late sixteenth century, Giordano Bruno postulated this infinite universe of uncountable worlds.

But the extension in space not only flees outward into the immense, it also opens an inner frontier of the microscopic. The things we are aware of in our everyday life not only are affected and determined by an immense surrounding universe, but also the nature of each one is shaped by a micro-constitution whose detailed make-up lies in the unexplored terrain of the infinitesimal. Reality in all directions plunges its roots into the unknown and as yet unmappable. It is this sense which defines the grasp of the world as 'universe' and not 'cosmos'; and this is what I mean when I say that the universe outlook was "deep" in a way the cosmos picture was not.

But much as we are overwhelmed by this opening onto unencompassable space, the extension in time has perhaps had an even deeper impact. From a contained cosmos of a mere 5,000–6,000 years, we come to see ourselves as issuing from what Buffon called "le sombre abîme du temps".[2] This arresting image derives its force from the fact that the vast expanse of time which lies behind us, unlike the tracts of space which lie around us, hides the process of our genesis, of our coming to be. The immense universe of galaxies can indeed, be thought of as dark, insofar as most of it is empty; but it can also be thought of as lit up by the countless stars. The countless aeons of time which lie behind us are dark in another sense; in attempting to explore them we meet the twilight of our own dawn, and then beyond that the night from which we conscious—light-bearing—animals emerged.

The continuous Biblical narrative was like a shaft of light right to the bottom of a (in retrospect rather shallow-seeming) well. Once this is abandoned, or no longer taken as straight chronicle, the remote past becomes dark. It is dark because unfathomable—this is undoubtedly part of Buffon's meaning. But it is also dark because it precedes the emergence of the light we know: conscious awareness of things. And this emergence itself is "dark", in the sense of hard to understand, or even imagine.

Humans are no longer charter members of the cosmos, but occupy merely a narrow band of recent time. As Diderot put it:

> Qu'est-ce que notre durée en comparaison de l'éternité des temps? . . . Suite indéfinie d'animalcules dans l'atome qui fermente, même suite indéfinie dans l'autre atome qu'on appelle la Terre. Qui sait les races d'animaux qui nous ont précédés? qui sait les races d'animaux qui succéderont aux nôtres?[3]

> (What is our human lifetime in comparison with the eternity of time? . . . There is an infinite series of tiny animals inside the fermenting atom, and the same infinite series inside that other atom called Earth. Who knows what races of animals preceded us? Who knows what races of animals will follow those that now exist?)[4]

This passage, written the better part of a century before Darwin, brings us to our second category of change. The earlier cosmos ideas saw the world as fixed, unvarying. But our consciousness of the universe is dominated by the sense that things evolve. The evolutionary process is as vast and hard to fathom as the abyss of time in which it unfolded. We can divide this category into two sub-categories: coming to see the world in which we live as having developed from an earlier state; and coming to see the life forms on it as evolving, changing, and in particular human life.

The transformation in outlook from a limited, fixed cosmos to a vast, evolving universe starts in the early seventeenth century, and is essentially completed in the early nineteenth century, though the final terminus might be fixed with the publication of Darwin's *Origin of Species* in 1859.

We can look at this as the classic success story, in which the responsible attempt to account for the facts wins out in the end over traditional, authoritative belief. There is some truth in this, in that certain discoveries were difficult to assimilate into the traditional story. Fossils in rocks were one case in point. But also the time-perspective of other peoples, of the Egyptians, Chaldeans, Chinese, referred to a much greater stretch of past time than the 5,000–6,000 which the Mosaic story was thought to record. And then the discovery of the New World, of new peoples, and as yet unknown species of animals, was hard to combine with the story of the

Flood. If all humans and animals today descend from those who survived in the ark, how did they get to America? Perhaps the humans sailed there, but the moose?

But the philosophy of science of recent decades has taught us that without an adequate alternative framework of explanation, the most refractory facts will not budge us from our established beliefs, that they can indeed, often be recuperated by these old beliefs.

Thus fossils were thought to be geological formations arising in the rocks themselves. The accounts of the Chaldeans could be rejected as so much vain and idle speculation by peoples who had lost contact with the true religion, and were trying to boost their own importance by giving themselves an ancient pedigree.[5]

What was needed before these "facts" could bear scientific fruit were two things, the availability of alternative frameworks, and the waning of the hold of the older cosmos ideas on the imagination.

Now the first were in a sense already there. Lucretius in the ancient world offered an "evolutionary" picture, of animals and humans arising by spontaneous generation out of the soil. And the beginnings of modern mechanistic physics, which was in a sense a return of certain Epicurean-Lucretian ideas, opened the way for a theory of physical change. Descartes presented an account by which one could understand how the present world order would come about, regardless of the original distribution of matter, following the operation of constant physical laws.

As to the second, we can easily understand how the hold of the earlier cosmos ideas was weakened—at least among the educated élites who proposed and debated these scientific theories. These cosmos ideas were closely connected to two features: a perception of the world as enchanted, of things as the expression-embodiment of spirits and forces, as I explained above; and a complex understanding of time, in which the secular chain of events was interwoven with higher times, be it Platonic eternity or God's eternity. The disenchantment of the world, the relegation of higher times, couldn't but weaken the traditional outlook.

A short 6,000-year span, set in the matrix of God's eternity, from which it emerges as a purposeful creation, this was a belief which it was hard to demur from as long as that eternity was a felt presence, whose concentrated power could be felt in certain places, times and actions. But once people come to live more and more in purely secular time, when God's eternity and the attendant span of creation becomes merely a *belief*, however well backed up with reasons, the imagination can easily be nudged towards other ways of accounting for the awkward facts.

This was the background to the striking fact pointed out by Michael Buckley,[6] and which I discussed earlier, the seemingly disproportionate concentration of Christian apologetics in these centuries on the proofs of God and God's benevolence through the design of the universe. To a modern believer, who will probably have been much more brought to the faith through reflections on the meaning of life and a sense of the love of God, this focus on the externals of cosmic design seems bizarre to say the least; most likely it will be seen as dry and irrelevant.

And yet we see Robert Boyle leaving a bequest with an annual income of £50, for a "learned theologian" to give "eight sermons a year proving the *Christian Religion* against Infidels, viz., Atheists, Theists [i.e., Deists], Pagans, Jews and Mohametans".[7] Some of the great thinkers of the day were Boyle lecturers, and they overwhelmingly concentrated on the attempt to prove God, his goodness, and the Biblical story through the design of things.

Does it mean that these people were without depths of religious feeling? Not at all. It was hardly an accident that this fund was set up by Boyle, the great theorist of atomist mechanism, the "corpuscularian philosophy". This move to a disenchanted universe in purely secular time couldn't but fragilize a belief which had been closely linked with an experience-near sense of the cosmos.

Mechanistic theory in fact refuted one facet of the earlier cosmos idea, that which drew on the Platonic view that things were ordered by the Ideas. But it could perfectly well accommodate the other facet, viz., that this world was created by a benevolent God, in part to succour his human creatures. This assertion of purpose could now be recaptured in a mechanist mode, through the idea that things are designed to produce beneficent results for us. This is one of the ideas underlying the modern moral order, which I described earlier.

But mechanistic theory fragilized faith not principally by refuting Plato and Aristotle. It was really because mechanism undermines enchantment, the expression-embodiment of higher reality in the things which surround us, and thus made the presence of God in the cosmos something which was no longer experience-near, or at least not at all in the same way. God's power was no longer something you could feel or see in the old way; it now had to be discerned in the design of things, the way we see the purposes of the maker or user in some artificial contrivance, a machine—an image which recurs again and again in the discourse of the time, particularly in the simile likening the universe to a clock.

What made for the intense concentration on design in Christian apologetics was not just that there is an intellectual problem here: one can doubt, and need to be shown that the design is purposeful and benevolent. What makes for the heat at this nevralgic point is that there is a strong sense of deficit in a world where people used to feel a presence here, and were accustomed to this support; often couldn't help feeling the lack of this support as undermining their whole faith; and very much needed to be reassured that it oughtn't to.

And of course, I'm not just talking about a need among the auditors of the Boyle Lectures, but quite possibly among the lecturers and with Boyle himself. It takes a later age, in which everyone has become accustomed to an disenchanted universe, and believers now have a mind set that puts a greater emphasis on other ways of sensing the presence of God, for this obsession with design to seem as strange as it does to us.

These unsettling effects of the sudden withdrawal of age-old supports have been repeated in a host of contexts during the last centuries, in e.g., Reforms from above, where the public authorities suddenly cease to sustain sacred space (the English Reformation, the French Revolution, etc.), or in the decay of rural parish society, as we shall see later on in discussing our century. It is this context of felt need, rather than the sempiternal issue between Belief and Unbelief, which determines how people respond. Seventeenth-century apologetics are no exception to this rule.

Having dropped the Platonic facet of the cosmos idea, many believers felt that they had to hold on all the more rigidly to the Biblical facet, in all its details. But this rigidity also springs from the scientific context itself. The older cosmos idea made heavy use of signs, and correspondences. The new science wanted to sweep this away as so many Idols, in Baconian terms, and propound a literal account of physical reality, seen as a domain of asemeiotic things. This, along with the Protestant emphasis on the Bible as the ultimate authority, led to a suppression of the older many-levelled Biblical commentary, with its analogies, correspondences and relations of typicality. Hence the idea of fastening on the Bible primarily as a chronicle of events, and trying to extract the maximum of exactitude from the accounts one finds there: a project typical of the post-Galilean age, and which ends up in the ludicrous precision of Archbishop Ussher's calculations.

Seen within this framework, the whole of Christian faith stands or falls with the exact historicity of the detailed accounts of the Book of Genesis. There has, e.g., to be a universal flood 1,656 years after Creation, or close thereabouts; or else the Bible is "refuted".

What is remarkable about this outlook, in relation to what preceded it, is the elimination of mystery. More exactly, mystery is tolerated in the designs of God; we cannot hope to understand them; but it is banished from His creation. In this way, the new outlook works analogously to, and goes farther than, the Protestant Reformation, which tended to expel the sacred from created things, on the grounds that placing it there is a form of idolatry.

On this view, the actual events themselves that make up our history are perfectly comprehensible. Where we will fail to understand is where God intervenes, and even this will be partly understood insofar as God reveals his purposes. Newton distinguishes between explaining the ordinary course of things, which can be done according to the natural laws we can discover, and trying to explain the origin of this world, which comes about through an act of creation which is beyond our understanding. The mystery, that things were made to cohere the way they do, is firmly placed in the intentions of God, and indeed, partly grasped insofar as his purposes have been revealed. Understanding how things run is within our powers, and no mystery need remain; understanding their origin is quite beyond our unaided powers, and we shouldn't attempt it; the answer lies beyond the world. There is no intra-cosmic mystery.[8]

This hostility to mystery on the part of the defenders of religion is rather strange, and it has very paradoxical consequences, which we shall explore more fully in a minute. But one immediate such consequence is that these defenders of the faith share a temper with its most implacable enemies. The existence of such defenders has been a constant of the modern debate, through all its transformations, right down to the present day.

The battle between ideological Darwinians and certain Biblical fundamentalists on the U.S. scene is a case in point. By ideological Darwinians, I mean those who not only accept the well-established facts of evolution, i.e., the descent of species including the human from one another, but make the dogmatic negative claim that the ultimate account of how evolution works, if we ever attain it, will make no reference to design in any shape or form. Design must purely figure among the explananda, never among the explanantia, of evolutionary theory. They face off against "creationists", who wish to deny altogether the descent of species, at least as far as humans are concerned. The locus of intra-cosmic mystery here, which most people feel who aren't in the grip of either ideology, viz., how it is that somehow design emerges in a universe of contingency, is rigorously banned by both sides. Creationists follow Newton here: the mystery is located totally in the Divine will, which erupts fully formed into history in the form of a special creation. The post-Galilean hostility to mystery couldn't find more forceful expression. The same thing can be said for the apocalyptic predictions of certain Protestant sects, which are science-fiction-like in combining realistic detail with the surprising improbability of the over-all dénouement.[9]

So then as now, in post-Galilean Europe and post–Scopes trial America, a fragilization of faith partly due to disenchantment, combined with an internalization of this disenchantment, produces a face-off between "religion" and "science" of a strangely intra-mural quality. This is the face-off which figures so prominently in the ex parte "death of God" story so popular among unbelievers. One party, moved purely by the interests of "science", that is, finding an adequate explanation for the undeniable facts, squares off against another, mainly actuated by an extra-scientific agenda, that of maintaining cherished beliefs and/or traditional authority.

But the actual history doesn't fit this dramatic picture. If we look at the period we're examining, we see that the mantle of sober scientists was often seized by the defenders of orthodoxy. The Newtonian distinction between explaining the origin of the world and its continuing function was meant to underline the impossibility of the first operation. This was directed against the Epicurean model, lately revived by Descartes, which would explain the present state of things as evolved from an earlier condition. The orthodox feared this as a regression to an Epicurean recourse to chance and necessity, which would negate design, or even as a step towards rehabilitating the Aristotelian idea of an eternal universe. The cause of design seemed better served by a picture of the universe which exhibits this design from the beginning.

But so, many claimed, was the cause of science. Newton's laws of mechanics could be clearly established, whereas any account of origins seemed condemned to be wildly speculative. Whoever engaged in this was trying to "deduce the world", to "construct hypotheses", to build systems, all things that sober scientists in the spirit of Newton eschewed. Turgot asks Buffon why he wants even to try to explain the origin of the solar system. Why "do you wish to deprive Newtonian science of that simplicity and wise restraint which characterize it? By plunging us back into the obscurity of hypotheses, do you want to give justification to the Cartesians, with their three elements and their formation of the world?" As Condillac put the case:

> If a philosopher, deep within his study, should try to move matter, he can do with it what he wishes: nothing resists him. This is because the imagination sees whatever it wishes to, and sees nothing more. But such arbitrary hypotheses throw light on no verity; on the contrary, they retard the progress of science and become most dangerous through the errors they lead us to adopt.[10]

These attempts were condemned as "romances", the very opposite of responsible science. But does this mean that Newton, Turgot, Condillac et al. were the ones purely actuated by the interests of science, while their opponents had a further agenda? Surely not. It rather means that everyone's motives were mixed; or better, that the pure love of truth, uncoloured by any passionately held beliefs, is a reality of some other universe, not ours.

The pure face-off between "religion" and "science" is a chimaera, or rather, an ideological construct. In reality, there is a struggle between thinkers with complex, many-levelled agendas, which is why the real story seems so confused and untidy in the light of the ideal confrontation, as Rossi so well shows.

Take Thomas Burnet, the late seventeenth century author of *The Sacred Theory of the Earth*. He was in many ways a Deist, willing to amend the Biblical account. But he did believe he could recapture the main lines of this story, the Creation, the Flood and the coming Apocalypse, in a scientific account. But this meant that he presented our existing world not as what issued from the hand of God at Creation, but rather as a ruined version of the original, devastated by the Flood. In other words, in the course of establishing the main lines of Judaeo-Christian history, Burnet broke with the picture of a fixed, unchanging world, and took a big step in the direction of an evolutionary history, from which our present world must have emerged.[11] He doesn't stand simply on one or other side of the face-off.

In another way, this is also true of Vico. He was actuated i.a. by the orthodox concern to discredit the chronologies of the Chinese, Chaldeans, etc., which cast doubt on the shorter Biblical story. But his solution was to hold that only the Hebrews, that is, the descendants of Shem, had held on to the original chronology. The other children of Noah had suffered a catastrophic regression, back to a bestial stage, from which they rebuilt civilization, but inevitably with a large reliance on myth, including their fantastic chronologies.

Again Vico can't be classed on either side. His intentions are orthodox, but he is one of the pioneers in developing a theory of the origins of human culture from a virtually pre-human, bestial stage. This means he helped to bury the picture of humanity as fixed from the beginning. He is an important originating figure in our modern sense of our history, whose roots are plunged in darkness.[12]

So what is going on with Burnet and Vico? We could understand them as just cross-pressured. They really want to defend (some part of) the orthodox view, but they have to face some stubborn facts, so they make adjustments, and this is what makes both of them originating figures in what we think of as the "scientific" outlook which won out over "religion". But this doesn't remotely capture the views of either of them. Burnet didn't need the world-as-ruin hypothesis to demonstrate the Flood, nor Vico the hypothesis of a feral period to discredit the old chronologies.

In fact, we can't understand what's going on until we enlarge our range of considerations. Neither "science", as the desire to give a credible account of the undeniable facts, nor "religion", as the attempt to hold on at all costs to received orthodoxy, come close to making sense of these two thinkers. We have to take account of how the universe and history figured in their moral and aesthetic imaginations. Certainly they had a belief in (some part of) orthodoxy. But their religious beliefs were not something separate from their moral imagination, rather their very idea of orthodoxy was inflected by this imagination.

If we understand them on this level, we can see them as key figures in the transformation of the cosmic imaginary. We can see in other words how what we now see as a modern cosmic imaginary is beginning to shape their religious outlook and sensibility.

The mountains of the earth are for Burnet "the ruins of a broken world". They show "a certain magnificence in Nature, as from old Temples and broken Amphitheatres of the *Romans* we collect the greatness of that people." Ruins are one of our routes of access to deep time; they connect us to an unrecoverable past, a partly lost world, existing in a kind of penumbra. To be moved by ruins is to feel the sense of loss, to savour what was great, but also its transiency. It is to be plunged into time with an acute sense of our incompleteness within it. These are the emotions which the Renaissance began to feel precisely around the "Temples and Amphitheatres of the Romans". That this sense can now be aroused by the natural world is a sign that a new sense of deep time is at work; that there is a profound and moving truth in the construal of the world not as fixed but as evolving. In Burnet's work this truth is articulated as a kind of Fall, a catastrophic reduction of our world as a punishment for our failings. A new cosmic imaginary is in the making, even if this articulation will undergo far-reaching change.

But this ruin strikes us in another way as well. We are over-awed by its greatness. In its mountains, deserts, oceans, we sense a vastness which is alien and strange, which dwarfs us, passes our understanding, and seems to take no heed of us. Now the arguments from design of contemporary apologetics concentrated on the way in which our world was made to suit us. They tended to portray nature as orderly, comprehensible and human-friendly, as garden rather than wilderness.

Burnet's picture of the world runs against this human-centred way of discovering God's presence in nature. But it discloses Him in another way:

> The greatest objects of Nature are, methinks, the most pleasing to behold; and next to the great Concave of the Heavens, and those boundless Regions where the Stars inhabit, there is nothing that I look upon with more pleasure than the wide Sea and the Mountains of the Earth. There is something august and stately in the Air of these things, that inspires the mind with great thoughts and passions; We do naturally, upon such occasions, think of God and his greatness; and whatsoever hath but a shadow and appearance of INFINITE, as all things have that are too big for our comprehension, they fill and overbear the mind with their Excess, and cast it into a pleasing kind of stupor and admiration.[13]

Burnet is turning to what in the eighteenth century will be called the "sublime".

Vico as we saw opens the space for an account of the rise of human beings from the bestial to the human. But this is not a concession he is forced to make to save the truth of the Biblical picture. It is rather the field for a new understanding of Providence, capable of guiding these blind creatures through their own limited passions back towards humanity and civilization. The world of gentile nations recov-

THE DARK ABYSS OF TIME

ered its order because "some bestial men were brought together by a certain human sense or instinct."[14]

Vico is trying to trace the genesis of humanity out of lower nature, something which can perhaps never be fully understood, and certainly cannot be grasped if we insist on a rationalist account of human action. This is mainly how Vico is known today, as one of the leaders of the reaction against a shallowly rationalist explanation of human action. At the centre of his theory is a kind of intra-cosmic mystery, how reason, consciousness, civilized order come to be out of their absence. He introduces another kind of deep time than that which ruins open us onto, a time that leads back into darkness, the "sombre abîme" prior to light.

We have found in these two authors three themes: that of ruins and deep time, that of the "sublime", and that of the dark genesis of humanity—as against the shaft of light to the very bottom of the well that Genesis 1 seemed to offer. These have become part of our cosmic imaginary today. Each conflicts with a major feature of the previous imaginary. And yet we can't think of them as coming about simply as by-products of scientific discovery.

For one thing, if we think of how the scientific progress came about, it is just as if not more true that a shift in our imaginary enabled us to come up with the scientific theories which we now accept. The shift in imagination is one of the prime movers here. But perhaps more important, we can't just see these new forms of moral imagination as a simple consequence of scientific change. It is true that the new scientific theories upset the older moral imagination which centred around the cosmos ideas and the Bible-derived chronology. But this fact by itself doesn't dictate the new responses to vastness and deep time. The old meanings may be destroyed, but this of itself doesn't create the new ones. We still have to understand what these are, and why they came to be.

Let's try to explore this in connection with the rise of the "sublime". The experience of what Burnet called "Excess" was aroused by the boundlessness of the heavens, or by high mountains, vast oceans, trackless deserts. In terrestrial terms, it attaches to wilderness.

Now the cosmos idea derived from the ancients best fitted cultivated land. This fully met the norms of order which are built etymologically into the very term. Wilderness and desert places could be seen as in a sense unfinished, that is, not yet fully brought into conformity with the shaping Ideas. In ancient Babylon, "wild, uncultivated regions and the like are assimilated to chaos; they still participate in the undifferentiated, formless modality of pre-Creation. This is why, when possession is taken of a territory—that is, when its exploitation begins—rites are performed that symbolically repeat the act of Creation: the uncultivated zone is first 'cosmicized', then inhabited." Hence "Settlement in a new, unknown, uncultivated country is equivalent to an act of Creation."[15]

We find something of this idea recurring in the European Middle Ages, when religious orders moved into forests or wastes and turned them into cultivated land. It was claimed on behalf of these monasteries in Carolingian times that they brought it about that "Horridae quondam solitudines ferarum nunc amoenissima diversiora hominum". And this work was sometimes represented as like creation, a human participation in God's work.[16]

This idea that humans were God's co-workers in ordering the world was understandably also strong in the Renaissance. Sir Matthew Hale speaks of Man as "the Vice-Roy of the great God of Heaven and Earth in this inferior World; his Steward, villicus, Bayliff and Farmer of this goodly Farm of the lower World", whose task is to cultivate it, and prevent it from reverting to wilderness. John Ray too sees man as being there to ensure that things don't revert to "a barbarous and inhospitable *Scythia,* without Houses, without Plantations, without Corn-fields or Vineyards . . . , or a rude and unpolished *America* peopled with slothful and naked *Indians.*"[17]

The reference earlier to "sometime horrible deserts of wild beasts" shows another aspect of wilderness in the older outlook. It was not just unfinished; it was also the abode of dangerous forces; of beasts, of course, but also of the bestiality that they incarnate; hence the place of devils and malign spirits. Wilderness reflected not just incompleteness, but the Fall, not just a further agenda in God's plan, but an opposition to it. In this perspective the power of the sainted monk in the wilderness is shown not in his transforming it but in his taming the wild beasts. The lives of the saints are full of such stories of anchorites befriending otherwise dangerous animals, including St. Anthony and St. Jerome, and of course, St. Francis.[18]

But the idea of deserts as the abode of demons is not simply a Christian one. The ancients placed Pan, satyrs and centaurs in wild places. The folklore of many peoples sees them inhabited by evil spirits, trolls, and the like.[19] But for Christians, there is a double meaning: the desert, that is, at a distance from cultivated soil and the society that reigns there, is the place where one can find God. The people of Israel were called out of Egypt, so that could worship God in the desert. Christ after his baptism spent 40 days in the desert.

This latter event shows the double significance, because Christ was tempted by the devil on his retreat. Breaking out of the confines of the all-too-human order can be a condition of finding God; but the very same act exposes one to all the destructive forces which that order binds. The struggle with demons in lonely places is repeated again and again in the lives of the saints.

Unformed and demonic, these are the meanings of wilderness within the frame of the cosmos ideas of Christendom. So it is not surprising that the first reactions to the breaking open of the cosmos into an infinite universe included horror and fear. Kepler expressed his "secret and hidden horror" at Bruno's infinite space, where "we feel ourselves lost". Pascal's cri de coeur: "le silence éternel des espaces infinis m'effraye" is well known.[20]

How did things change? How did the "sublime" become one of the central categories of aesthetics in the eighteenth century?

The shift didn't come about directly. At first, the horror was neutralized, by the disenchantment of the world and the development of a buffered self. The agent of disengaged reason was no longer "got to" by the eternal silences of alien vastness. Wild places were exorcized, the scary legends connected to them were debunked by humanist thinkers. Mountains and plains were harmonized, brought together in the single ordered space of maps, and scientific theory.[21]

But the horror returns, albeit in a different register. Schama shows how in the later seventeenth century, styles of painting return in which the alien and threatening vastness of mountains is again thrust upon us. "The sixteenth-century humanist vision, from the heights, of an intelligible, harmonized universe has been superseded, yet again, by the more histrionic view up from the dale where expendable man is trapped between the horrid crag and the rock of faith."[22]

But the horror is now pleasing in a certain way. Schama quotes an English traveller in the Alps in the late seventeenth century: he thought he had "walkd upon the very brink in a literal sense, of Destruction. . . . The sense of all this produced in me . . . a delightful Horrour, a terrible Joy and at the same time that I was infinitely pleased, I trembled." Joseph Addison later comments that the "Alps are broken into so many steps and precipices that they fill the mind with an agreeable kind of horror and form one of the most irregular and mis-shapen scenes in the world."[23]

How to understand this? Partly from the very success of the buffered identity. The vogue of such films as *Titanic* shows the pleasure we can take in contemplating terrible dangers, as long as we ourselves are in security. In relation to the horrors of craggy mountain fastnesses, the distance won by disengagement performs the same office as being safely in a warm cinema does for those enjoying the spectacle of the Titanic dragging hundreds of people to their watery grave.

This is certainly part of the story. Both Burke and Kant, in their writings on the sublime, see this element of personal safety as a necessary condition of being moved by it.[24] But it is far from being the whole story. The sublime can give us an agreeable frisson; and it is a feature of the buffered identity that we often experience such a frisson where our ancestors were genuinely terrified, as in horror movies about witches and possession. But this can't adequately explain the place of wilderness in our moral imagination. How to understand this?

I think that this too can be understood as a response of the modern buffered identity. In the previous chapter, I mentioned the reactions which arose against this identity and the anthropocentric understanding of order in Providential Deism and exclusive humanism. To many this seemed to draw the compass of human life too narrowly. Pursuing the goods of life and prosperity, while eschewing "enthusiasm", in a world designed especially to favour these ends, seemed to make life shallow, devoid of deep resonance and meaning; it seemed to exclude transports of devotion, of self-giving, to deny a heroic dimension to our existence; it reduces us by enclosing us in a too-rosy picture of the human condition, shorn of tragedy, irreparable loss, meaningless suffering, cruelty and horror.

These are several of the "axes" on which people were induced to attack the dominant view of human agency and order, the order on which, in a sense, modern European economic and political civilization was being largely built. Not all critics attacked on all axes, of course; but what they had in common was the sense that the danger which awaits us in our culture takes a certain form. We are tempted to draw the limits of our life too narrowly, to be concerned exclusively with a narrow range of internally-generated goals. In doing this we are closing ourselves to other, greater goals. These might be seen as originating outside of us, from God, or from the whole of nature, or from humanity; or they might be seen as goals which arise indeed within, but which push us to greatness, heroism, dedication, devotion to our fellow human beings, and which are now being suppressed and denied.[25]

As a consequence, a commonly-understood image of a remedy to this ill was the breaking in on this narrow self-absorption of some such larger purpose. We need to have our petty circle of life broken open. The membrane of self-absorption has to be broken from the outside, even if what it liberates is internal to our more authentic selves.

The moral meaning of the sublime is to be found here. Particularly for those attacking on the axes which exalted heroism, and shied away from a bowdlerized view of life which hid from sight the dark side of creation, the very terror of wilderness, or vast unmeasurable distances and powers, awakens us from petty self-concern, and sets to work our aspirations to what is higher. For Burke, terror and pain (provided they are below the necessary threshold) produce delight, because they provide the exercise necessary for our finer organs. Kant, who builds on Burke, while escaping the somewhat reductive-physiological bent of the Irishman's theory, claims that the sight of an overwhelming power in Nature, which we could never resist, like volcanoes or waterfalls, awakens an awareness of ourselves as noumenal beings, who stand as high above all this merely sensible reality, as within the sensible realm the threatening phenomenon stands above our puny phenomenal selves.[26]

The moral meaning of the sublime can vary with the different views about what is our higher purpose, but in its general form it fits into the self-perception of buffered selves engaged with merely human goods that they stand in danger of narrow self-absorption. The sight of "Excess", vast, strange, unencompassable, provoking fear, even horror, breaks through this self-absorption and awakens our sense of what is really important, whether this be the infinity of God, as with Burnet, our supersensible moral vocation, as with Kant; or, as with later thinkers, our capacity for heroic affirmation of meaning in the face of a world without telos—the truth of eternal recurrence.

We can see this if we look at another development which reflects the new place of wilderness. Schama has some interesting pages[27] on the evolution of the idea of arcadia, which has always been on the limit of the wild and the cultivated, moving back and forth between wilderness and garden. It perhaps begins on the wilderness side with Pan and Silenus, where the wildness includes bestial desire, as well as untamed nature. But there is also a tamer version of the pre-agricultural world, in which the earth produces fruit and grain in abundance, without human labour, and wild beasts do not threaten, a sort of idyllic Age of Saturn, such as Virgil paints in his *Eclogues*. By the time of the Renaissance, Arcadia has grown even closer to the garden. But in the eighteenth century, the reaction sets in, and "rudeness" and "confusion" become terms of appreciation for gardens. "Neatness and Elegancy" become less appreciated than a "mixture of garden and forest".

What is relevant for our argument here is not just the renewed value of wildness, which one could have predicted in the age of the sublime. But seeing this interest in the Arcadian tradition shows up an important difference. The interest in Arcadia in the late ancient world is part of the longing to return to nature which begins to crop up in the Hellenic world, presumably because at that stage city/political life becomes complex, all-consuming and intrigue-ridden enough to make people dream of an escape. But this escape, as we see it, for instance, in Virgil, both in the *Georgics* and the *Eclogues*, stresses the escape from the city's vices, and the return to a simpler, more wholesome way of life.

But the importance of wilderness in the period after 1700 is not that it offers us an alternative way of life. It has perhaps come to do so for a relatively small fringe of protesters at the evils of civilization in recent times, but the overwhelming thrust of the concern for wilderness is elsewhere. The idea is that being in touch with, being open to it awakens or strengthens something in us which enables us to live proper lives, which perforce will be led almost entirely in "civilization". Wilderness is not the locus of an alternative life to the "city", although Virgil-like we often still believe that the (cultivated) country can provide this. Rather it communicates or imparts something to us which awakens a power in us of living better where we are.

Thus the new feeling for nature moves beyond the well-ordered garden, which had always been understood as a kind of microcosm, beyond even the English garden, beyond even the valleys of Switzerland where the wilderness touches human habitation and which Rousseau made famous, and comes finally to the inhospitable heights, where it meets in awe an immensity which seems utterly indifferent to human life. Ramond journeyed into these regions, and his books gave expression to this exaltation before the vastness of the untamed heights. They place us before the unchartable immensity of time.

> Tout concourt à rendre les méditations plus profondes, à leur donner cette teinte sombre, ce caractère sublime qu'elles acquièrent, quand l'âme, prenant cet essor qui la rend contemporaine de tous les siècles, et coexistante avec tous les êtres, plane sur l'abîme des temps.[28]

> (Everything conspires to make our meditation deeper, to give it the somber hue, the sublime character it takes on, when the soul, taking a leap which makes it contemporary with all centuries and coexistent with all being, soars over the abyss of time.)

And from the nineteenth century on, Europeans were deeply struck by the wilderness of America. Chateaubriand, reporting on his travels in northern New York, says: "in vain does the imagination try to roam at large midst [Europe's] cultivated plains . . . but in this deserted region the soul delights to bury and lose itself amidst boundless forests . . . to mix and confound . . . with the wild sublimities of Nature." Speaking of his tour in 1803 in the upper Ohio Valley, the American Thaddeus Mason Harris declares: "there is something which impresses the mind with awe in the shade and silence of these vast forests. In the deep solitude, alone with nature, we converse with GOD." "[T]he majestic features of the uncultivated wilderness" produced "an expansion of fancy and an elevation of thought more dignified and noble". "THE SUBLIME IN NATURE captivates while it awes, and charms while it elevates and expands the soul." As another American put it: "How great are the advantages of solitude!—How sublime is the silence of nature's ever-active energies! There is something in the very name of wilderness, which charms the ear, and soothes the spirit of man. There is religion in it."[29]

Nash notes what he calls the "ambivalence" of many of these lovers of the wild. Thus the Reverend Harris, who felt he conversed with God on the Upper Ohio, also found the "lonesome woods" at times depressing and forbidding. "There is something very animating to the feelings, when a traveller, after traversing a region without culture, emerges from the depths of solitude, and comes upon an open, pleasant, cultivated country." Harris was cheered by the sight of settlement rising in the "desolate wilds"; "when we behold competence and plenty springing from the bosom of dreary forests—what a lesson is afforded of the benevolent intentions of Providence!"

But this ambivalence shouldn't be seen as a contradiction. It may be so noticed among us today, when the expansion of human cultivation threatens the very existence of wilderness areas. But in Harris' context there was no conflict. The praise of wilderness didn't imply that it offered an alternative site for a better life. Its importance was that it put us in touch with something greater, which we could easily lose sight of. The wilds being "desolate" and "lonesome", fearful and forbidding, was essential to their having this effect. As another American put it, the wild Adirondacks manifested "vagueness, terror, sublimity, strength and beauty", and this is why they could speak to us of God, as "a symbol of His omnipotence."[30]

Part of the sublimity of wilderness consisted in its otherness, its inhospitality to humans; in the fact that you couldn't really live there. But opening to it makes it possible for you to live properly outside of it.

This is the meaning of Thoreau's dictum: "In Wildness is the Preservation of the World". Oelschlaeger recounts Thoreau's encounter with Mount Ktaadn in Maine. A rather shaking experience for Thoreau, who hadn't perhaps anticipated the raw danger of it.

> Perhaps I most fully realized that this was primeval, untamed nature, . . . while coming down. . . . And yet we have not seen pure Nature, unless we have seen her thus vast and drear and inhuman. . . . Nature was here something savage and awful, though beautiful. . . . Here was no man's garden, but the unhandseled globe. . . . Man was not to be associated with it. It was Matter, vast, terrific,—not his Mother Earth that we have heard of, not for him to tread on or be buried in,—no, it were being too familiar even to let his bones lie there,—the home, this, of Necessity and Fate. It was a place for heathenism and superstitious rites,—to be inhabited by men nearer of kin to the rocks and wild animals than we.[31]

The point of Thoreau's famous dictum is that, in spite of its hostility to man, or just because of this, we have to live in contact with this inhuman force, if we want to live well, "to live deep and suck all the marrow out of life", as against "the mass of men [who] lead lives of quiet desperation". Nature is the perennial source of our life, which we cannot turn our backs on. "Shall I not have intelligence with the earth? Am I not partly leaves and vegetable mould myself?"[32]

I have been placing sublimity, and the moral meaning of wilderness, within the context of the felt inadequacies of modern anthropocentrism, and the need to recover contact with a greater force. In the context of the above discussion of wilderness as inhuman, we can see the sublime in a narrower focus: very often it is opposed to a sense of life which is too shallow and human-centred—shallow because human-centred.

Anthropocentrism was the creation of what I called above "Providential Deism" (one crucial facet of what is usually known as Deism). One of the loci where this position was worked out was precisely the apologetics I discussed above which concentrated on arguments from design.

Now these have existed since before Christianity. Plato inaugurated this form of argument to counter those who think that the world comes from "chance and necessity" *(Laws)*. And they have virtually never argued that the end of the design was purely the good of human beings. Augustine says, for instance: "Therefore, it is not with respect to our convenience or discomfort, but with respect to their own nature, that the creatures are glorifying to their Artificer."[33]

Now modern apologists also made the same protestation. But as a matter of fact, they concentrate very heavily on the advantages to human beings of the universe. And in a sense, this was inevitable. Once the cosmos ceases to be lived and experienced as the locus of spiritual forces, once you have to prove that it is God-given by its design, then the detail of the argument is inevitably going to focus on the implications for human beings. Burnet breaks out of the mould by presenting the mountains as ruins of the original earth. They show up not as helps, but as inhospitable, menaces to human life. To answer him, we need arguments showing why God had to make mountains. These can be devised. The whole hydrological cycle requires high and low ground, otherwise how could water flow through rivers and irrigate the earth? But how about the inclination of the earth? A good story can be told for this too. And how about insects, spiders, etc.?

The story runs on, accumulating more and more detail, and gradually gets ridiculous. God appears as a fussy parent, anxiously moulding every detail of creation to our well-being and comfort. The rebellion cannot but come, but it often is made by people who still believe in design in general, like Voltaire, but cannot stomach the ludicrous detail, and above all, the absence of any place in the story for the tragedies that life itself produces, like the famous earthquake at Lisbon.[34]

Now the earlier understanding of the world as God-produced cosmos wasn't open to these attacks. This earlier view wove the history of world events in secular time into the framework of higher times. The things and happenings of our world had a depth in God's eternity which they lost when the sense of this faded. At the same time, it was understood that God had other purposes than our well-being; and indeed, some of his purposes for us included chastisement, both as retribution and as training. What was abundantly clear was that we couldn't hope to reason all this out on our own. Much of the modern design-argument would have been unthinkable earlier. It arose in the context of a post-Galilean or -Newtonian science, which hoped to fathom God's providence in its own terms.

The moral meaning of the sublime, and much of the post-eighteenth century cosmic imaginary, can be seen as a reaction to this shallowness and anthropocentrism. But it can't just react by moving backward. The sense of depth cannot be found in an eternity which is no longer a felt reality. It is now found in the vastness of space and the abyss of time. It is no longer unproblematic to find the more-than-human in God, but it shows up in the frightening otherness of huge mountains and raging torrents. These latter in turn may be understood in terms of God and creation, but the experience can also be led in other directions.

My thread in the above discussion has been the sublime. But we can see how the Viconian dark genesis of humanity opens an analogous kind of depth, and a relation to the non-human reality out of which we emerge. And in fact the eighteenth century follows Vico, though not necessarily under his influence, in probing the mysteries of human evolution. Thus while seventeenth century theories of language—Locke and Hobbes, for instance—try to get clear on what language does, what role it plays in human life, the eighteenth century tries to carry these insights into an account of how humans actually came to be language beings, and what stages they went through in the process. We see this with Condillac, Warburton, Herder, Rousseau, Hamann, and others. And as Paolo Rossi points out, we can't understand these genesis stories as narrowly linguistic; they are always part of an overall theory of our becoming fully human.[35]

We can see how this development too could be told in a story of scientific advance, powered by the confrontation with new anthropological facts in the newly discovered continents. But it should be evident that here, too, the scientific story was interwoven with a transformation in the moral imaginary.

Thus the anthropological battles between, say, Condillac on one side, and Herder and Rousseau on the other, about the origins of language, were plainly related to different moral understandings of the human condition. In Condillac, human genesis is aided by the Lockean disciplines of reason. We advance as we adopt and put into effect a Lockean rational control of the signs we use. The dark genesis is left behind.

For both Herder and Rousseau, on the other hand, something is there at the beginning, an expressive-communicative power, which can be lost, or weakened, or covered over by the subsequent development of civilization. The genesis is not left behind, but rather progressively darkened, by rationalist "progress". Here the theory of genesis is inseparably also a theory of human depths, which are moreover threatened with a denial or forgetfulness, which the right genetic account can help us combat. Imagining ourselves in deep time is imagining us with deep natures, and hence helping to rescue these natures.

We can see how theories of this kind can open other axes of attack against the self-absorption of a too narrow anthropocentrism. The greater concerns which are being denied in this narrow focus are those of our deeper natures. These are what have to break through. The voice of nature is being stifled in us. This is one of the standard themes in those streams of Romanticism which were influenced by Rousseau.

These two kinds of theory, represented here respectively by Condillac and Herder/Rousseau, are clearly aligned with the two major accounts I described earlier of our moral sources as inner: in one of which benevolence comes from the disciplining of disengaged reason, which detaches us from particularity, while for the other, the well-springs of sympathy need to be recovered from deep within us.

In the sublime, something greater breaks through our self-absorption in a too narrow mode of gratification. It comes as it were from the outside. In the recovery of our inner depths, the breakthrough comes from within. But it is plain that these are not simply alternatives. For many in the Romantic period and after, the movement is in both directions at once. The rediscovery of what I really am within is made possible by the resonance I feel with the great current of nature outside of me.

And this idea of resonance is also given its sense by the dark genesis. As creatures who come to be who we are out of animal nature, which in turn arises from the non-animate, we cannot but feel a kinship with all living things, and beyond them with the whole of nature. Herder depicts nature as a great current of sympathy, running through all things. "Siehe die ganze Natur, betrachte die grosse Analogie der Schöpfung. Alles fühlt sich und seines Gleichen, Leben wallet zu Leben."[36] ("See the whole of nature, behold the great analogy of creation. Everything feels itself and its like, life reverberates to life.") Coleridge, who was very influenced by German thought, expressed a similar idea: "Everything has a life of its own . . . and we are all *One Life*."[37] Wordsworth speaks of "A motion and a spirit, that impels / All thinking things, all objects of all thought, / And rolls through all things."[38] Hölderlin speaks of a longing "Eines zu sein mit Allem, was lebt, in seiner Selbstvergessenheit wiederzukehren ins All der Natur"[39] ("to be at one with everything which lives, to return in self-forgetfulness to the All of Nature").

Now this sense of our connection with the universal current of life certainly has its roots in some of the older cosmos ideas. We can think for instance of the neo-Platonic notion that all reality emanates from the One. But the sense of kinship was greatly strengthened by what I've been calling our dark genesis, the idea that our humanity emerged out of an animal life which we share with other living things, and this is given even greater resonance if we see ourselves as evolving out of these other life-forms. That is why this sensibility of kinship has grown if anything even more powerful in our time, even while some of the ideas of design and Providence which Herder, for instance, still drew on have receded. It has become one of the crucial underpinnings of much contemporary ecological consciousness and concern.[40]

Thus Thoreau, who was an originator and still is a paradigm protagonist of this consciousness, saw himself as standing in Walden Pond close "to the perennial source of our life". "I was so distinctly made aware of the presence of something kindred to me, even in scenes which we are accustomed to call wild and dreary, and also that the nearest of blood to me and the humanest was not a person or a villager, that I thought no place could ever be strange to me again." That is why Thoreau asks, in the line I cited above: "Shall I not have intelligence with the earth? Am I not partly leaves and vegetable mould myself?"[41]

We can see a complexity, a tension, almost at times a contradiction in the moral imagination of nature I've been describing. We have a kinship with this nature; it is the source of our life, hence "near of blood", nearer we sometimes think than the "persons or villagers" we may live among. But at the same time, this Nature can be "vast and drear and inhuman", other, hostile, indifferent.

The conflict seems to emerge here out of our kinship to a nature which is also in other ways alien to us. But it can also surface in another form in Thoreau's writing. Here we are kin to all of nature, even the wild alien part. In his description of the inhuman on Mount Ktaadn, Thoreau says that "it was a place for heathenism and superstitious rites,—to be inhabited by men nearer of kin to the rocks and wild animals than we". Here the wildness is portrayed as something which could be, indeed in earlier "heathen" times was part of us. And at other places, Thoreau seems to be saying that this possibility does not only lie in our past. In *Walden* he reports the "wildness" in himself, and speaks about the "animal in us, which awakens in proportion as our higher nature slumbers. It is reptile and sensual, and perhaps cannot be wholly expelled; like the worms which, even in life and health, occupy our bodies".[42]

This is a worrying fact for Thoreau, but one that we cannot entirely turn our backs on. Indeed, the attempt to deny "wildness" both without and within is what is degrading our lives. It can only lead to stagnation.

My spirits infallibly rise in proportion to outward dreariness. Give me the ocean, the desert, or the wilderness! . . . When I would recreate myself, I seek the darkest wood, the thickest and most interminable and, to the citizen, most dismal swamp. I enter a swamp as a sacred place, a sanctum sanctorum. There is the strength, the marrow, of Nature. The wildwood covers the virgin mould,

and the same soil is good for men and for trees. . . . The civilized nations—
Greece, Rome, England—have been sustained by the primitive forests which
anciently rotted where they stand. They survive as long as the soil is not exhausted. Alas for human culture! little is to be expected of a nation, where the
vegetable mould is exhausted, and it is compelled to make manure of the
bones of its fathers.[43]

The idea here is that our existence, or vitality, or creativity depends, not just on
the inhuman outside of us—for instance, on the overwhelming power of raw nature
which awakens heroism in us—but on the wild and pre-human in us which resonates to that alien external power. We have gone beyond Kant, where the sublime
awakens our suprasensible moral agency, and where the "starry skies above" can be
linked together with "the moral law within", as two realities which fill us alike with
"wonder and respect".[44] We are now rather in the domain of Schopenhauer, where
our vital energy comes from a Will which is wild, unprincipled, amoral. This belief
in our reliance on the forces of irrationality, darkness, aggression, sacrifice has become widespread in our culture; partly in the wake of Schopenhauer—say, with
Nietzsche, Thomas Mann—but also beyond, with Conrad, D. H. Lawrence, Robinson Jeffers—the writers and contexts in which this sensibility surfaces are too numerous to count. Whole epochs seem saturated with it, like Europe in the aftermath of the First World War; and it is still powerful today.

Now this range of ideas and the modes of sensibility it inspires can be understood
partly in terms of the rebellion against modern anthropocentrism, particularly on
the "tragic" axes which react to the bowdlerized pictures of life, in which evil, suffering and violence have been painted out. But they have also to be related to the modern cosmic imaginary. In the context of the old cosmos ideas, the remedy to a
flattened, Panglossian perspective would have been to turn us again to the depths of
eternity and the anger of God. Renewed variants of this remedy are not inaccessible
today, but the fact that the (let us call it) post-Schopenhauerian one is also available,
is in fact a major source of rival recourses to the traditional believing ones; the fact
that we can conceive of giving this kind of moral meaning to the wilderness within
us—this is only comprehensible within the world animated by the modern cosmic
imaginary. This is one which relates to a universe which is not necessarily structured
and limited by a rational, benign plan, one where we cannot touch bottom, but
which is nevertheless the locus of our dark genesis.

I have been arguing here that to understand the transformation in our outlook
from cosmos to universe, we cannot just limit ourselves to the changes in our theoretical beliefs. These have taken us from pictures of a limited, ordered and static
cosmos to a universe which is immeasurably vast, and in constant evolution. It is

not just that our theories have changed, but the spontaneous, unreflecting understanding which provides the context for these beliefs has also altered. Where our ancestors used to see their world as the locus of spirits and forces, and understood it as a fixed, ordered cosmos, independently of whether they grasped and accepted any particular picture of this cosmos, we experience the universe as limitless, that is, unencompassable in imagination, but only at best in highly abstract theory, which is beyond most of us; and we feel it to be changing, evolving. Where our ancestors were able to ignore without difficulty the signs which point us to these two features—vastness and evolution—they stand out for us. This is not just a matter of regnant *theories* affirming these features—although that is obviously part of the reason for the change. It is also a matter of the way we see and experience things. Glaciers now speak to us of aeons and slow, "glacial" movement. We find this new sensibility arising already in the late eighteenth century, for instance in Ramond's descriptions of the Alps and Pyrenees, which I quoted above. These brought to immediate visibility, as it were, in the accounts of different layers of rock and ice, the widely separated ages of their genesis.

But what is also important is the way that our natural world figures in our moral imagination, and it is the change in this which I have mainly been trying to describe in the preceding pages. We live in a nature of deep time and unfathomable spaces, from which we emerged. It is a universe which is in many ways strange and alien, and certainly unfathomable. This nourishes on one hand a sense of kinship and filiation. We belong to the earth; it is our home. This sensibility is a powerful source of ecological consciousness. It also means that we are led to think of ourselves as having a deep nature, which we need to retrieve, or perhaps overcome, something which we can find out how to do by examining our dark genesis.

On the other hand, the unfathomable and the alien facets of this universe bring us up against the gigantic, the immeasurable, the inhuman, and this moves us in different ways. As the sublime it may fill us with awe, and while reminding us how little we are, paradoxically make us aware of our greatness. The paradigm expression of this double consciousness is Pascal's image of the reed: the human being in the universe has all the fragility of a mere reed, but its greatness lies in the fact that it is a thinking reed. But at the same time, we can sense a kinship also with the inhuman, violent, disordered in the universe; and this can trouble us, and/or utterly transform our understanding of our deep nature, discrediting the benign images of the Rousseauian tradition, and relating us to the wild, amoral, violent forces projected by post-Schopenhauerian visions.

This complex of theories, unreflective understanding and moral imagination is the dominant one in Western Civilization in our time. It saturates our world. We can see it everywhere. It is evident, for instance, in post-Freudian psychology. Many people may reject Freud's theories, but the surrounding context of understanding which makes sense of these theories is very deeply entrenched. The idea of a deep nature, which we have lost sight of, and may find it difficult to recover, the idea that this has to be recovered, understood, mainly through retelling our story, the idea that this deep nature may be in part wild and amoral, all these are obvious frameworks for self-understanding, intuitively understandable to almost everyone, whatever one thinks of particular theories—or even if one wants to combat the whole framework on philosophical grounds.

Marcel Gauchet has shown, in a very suggestive work,[45] how this key idea of the unconscious had multiple sources. It draws not only on the well-documented Romantic origins: the sense that there are as yet unsaid depths in us, as well as the strong idea of the continuity of all living forms. It also builds on the idea of a "cerebral unconscious". This grows in the nineteenth century with the understanding that our highest functions, thinking, willing, are in some sense the product of neuro-physiological functions in us.

The development of this idea shows in one compass the combined effect of a number of the changes which I have been trying to delineate here. First, it builds on a profound shift in the way of locating the nature of things. Under the old cosmos notions, particularly the "Platonic" cosmos defined by Ideas, the nature of thing was in a sense not within it, but belonged to the structure of the cosmos. Thus a Form, even for Aristotle, wasn't ontically totally dependent on the particulars it informed. Even though it couldn't exist outside of such instantiations, it had its own integrity independent of them; it was the Form which imparted their common shape to all these particular realizations of it. In the disenchanted universe, on the other hand, "nature", as the ensemble of causal powers producing the characteristic behaviour of this or that kind of thing, cannot be separated from the things in question. It no longer has an ontic niche outside of them.[46]

This, of course, was the same change which expelled the spirits and meaningful causal influences and forces out of the world. It sharply divided mind from non-mental reality. This division was the basis of a conception of thought and will as something self-contained, in principle quite clear and present to themselves, and capable of establishing their independence from the world of matter; the understanding which we identify with Descartes.

Now the shift in cosmic imaginary deeply undermined this view. The Cartesian subject had lost the kind of depth which belonged to a "nature" which was part of a cosmic order, where the discovery of what I really am requires that I come to grasp this nature by studying the orders of human social life and the cosmos. I can now supposedly make this discovery by purely immanent self-clarity, clear and distinct self-consciousness.

But within the context of a dark genesis, the subject acquires a new kind of depth, in evolutionary time, in personal time, and in her relation to her material embodiment. The Cartesian picture of total self-possession was only perhaps possible in the transition between the two great cosmic outlooks, that structured by the order of ideas, and the vast universe of abysses which we inhabit. Or otherwise put, it belonged to the relatively shallow cosmos idea which dominated the period between these two: a mechanistic universe, providentially ordered for the sake of souls whose destiny was elsewhere.

Gauchet shows how in the nineteenth century, one facet of this new depth develops, namely the sense that our thinking and willing emerges out of cerebral/nervous function, through the concepts of the reflex arc and sensori-motor scheme. The second half of the century comes to be dominated by a psycho-physiological outlook, which tries to place consciousness, thinking and will within its bodily realization.

But as Gauchet points out, this is more than just a change of theory. It is a shift in the whole framework in which theories are propounded, frameworks which define what is thinkable, and what questions have to be asked.[47] The relation of thought to its material substrate, from being an issue of external relations for Descartes, has now become the key question about its very nature. On the new understanding, conscious willing grows out of the reflex arc, and is of the same nature as it.[48] More than a theory, this outlook defines a set of difficult and conflicted problems, with which we are still at grips today. Scientific discovery and profound cultural change interacted and inflected each other to produce this new understanding of the cerebral unconscious.

This, along with the idea derived from evolution that ontogenesis recapitulates phylogenesis, married to the power of the Romantic legacy, has helped to produce our sense of the deep subject, opaque to herself, the locus of unconscious and partly impersonal processes, who must try to find herself in the unmeasurable time of a dark genesis out of the pre-human, without and within.

At the same time, the moral significance of nature that I have been describing is clearly also widely felt: the awe at wilderness; the sense of kinship and ecological concern with nature; the desire to renew oneself by leaving the city and visiting wilderness, or living in the country; all these are features of our world. We still have the longing for the bucolic which Virgil celebrated, but we have added the awe at the wilds.

The fact is that this sensibility, which used to be that of a minority in the eighteenth century, has become generalized. Not everyone shares it, of course; there are always opponents, as there were among eighteenth-century élites. But everyone understands it. An amusing story from Tocqueville's relation of his visit to America in 1831 says it all. A young Frenchman of the Romantic era, who had read

Chateaubriand, out in the Michigan territory, he obviously wanted to see the wilderness. But when he tried to explain his project to the local frontiersmen to enlist their help, he met a wall of incomprehension. Somebody wanting to enter the primeval forest just *to behold it;* this made no sense. He must have had some undeclared agenda, like lumbering or land speculation.[49] An analogous gap in sensibility exists in our day between, say, loggers in British Columbia, and ecology-concerned "tree huggers". But loggers today are all-too-familiar with ecological militants, and no longer need to have explained to them that such people exist.

One could go on. Travel, both to beautiful countryside, or beaches, or wilderness areas, has become just about universal in our culture. There are no classes or groups where lots of people don't either go, or want to go. Millions in North America have second residences in the country. And most telling of all, the need to escape the crowded city and get back in contact with nature has brought about the creation of the suburb, the flight to which has become a mass movement. Randy Connolly has shown how the suburb idea comes in the U.S. from the attempt to have it both ways, to unite the advantages of both city and country.[50]

Now we can see how the modern cosmic imaginary can foster the spread of materialism. Indeed, materialists often have trouble imagining how it can fail to do this. This limit on the materialist imagination is something I want to explain in what follows. But provisionally here I will say that it ought to be obvious from the above how this imaginary also can push in the other direction.

The link with materialism is clear enough. This imaginary has rendered close to incomprehensible the old cosmos ideas. It certainly has discredited the limited-scale Biblical cosmos idea. A vast and unfathomable universe, from which we have made a dark genesis, is obviously compatible with materialism. Indeed, the development of this imaginary owes something to ancient Epicurean ideas which were proto-materialist.

What tells the other way are precisely the moral meanings of the universe: the sense of our deep nature, of a current running through all things, which also resonates in us; the experience of being opened up to something deeper and fuller by the contact with Nature; the sense of intra-cosmic mystery, which was quite missing from Providential Deism, and from the apologetics of the age of Newton and the Boyle lecturers, even as it is today from the scientistic outlook and that of much Christian fundamentalism. But all these can be worked out in a number of different ways.

Some people may even want to claim that we cannot make sense of them within a totally materialist outlook; and some materialists agree, arguing that this is so much the worse for these moral meanings. But some people do try to give sense to them within this framework, and provisionally let us note this fact. However, it is also clear that many try to work things out in other ways. Some will understand our experience of these meanings in a theistic, even orthodox Christian frame, as Bede Griffiths came to understand his epiphanic experience that I cited in the Introduction.

But the striking fact about the modern cosmic imaginary is that it is uncapturable by any one range of views. It has moved people in a whole range of directions, from (almost) the hardest materialism through to Christian orthodoxy; passing by a whole range of intermediate positions. Some of these, like that of Goethe for instance, or in another way, Emerson, are in some clear sense spiritual, without being Christian or even theistic. But other ways of relating to a deep nature, or a current running through nature, have been really unclassifiable. We will see in a minute how the development of modern poetics, and in general the languages of art, has enabled people to explore these meanings with their ontological commitments as it were in suspense.

Thus the salient feature of the modern cosmic imaginary is not that it has fostered materialism, or enabled people to recover a spiritual outlook beyond materialism, to return as it were to religion, though it has done both these things. But the most important fact about it which is relevant to our enquiry here is that it has opened a space in which people can wander between and around all these options without having to land clearly and definitively in any one. In the wars between belief and unbelief, this can be seen as a kind of no-man's-land; except that it has got wide enough to take on the character rather of a neutral zone, where one can escape the war altogether. Indeed, this is part of the reason why the war is constantly running out of steam in modern civilization, in spite of the efforts of zealous minorities.

I will try to explain some of this more fully.

10 The Expanding Universe of Unbelief

1

The creation of this free space has been made possible in large part by the shift in the place and understanding of art that came in the Romantic period. This is related to the shift from an understanding of art as mimesis to one that stresses creation. It concerns what one could call the languages of art, that is, the publicly available reference points that, say, poets and painters draw on. As Shakespeare could draw on the correspondences to make us feel the full horror of the act of regicide, to recur to the case I cited above. He has a servant report the "unnatural" events that have been evoked in sympathy with this terrible deed: the night in which Duncan is murdered is an unruly one, with "lamentings heard i' the air; strange screams of death", and it remains dark even though the day should have started. On the previous Tuesday a falcon had been killed by a mousing owl, and Duncan's horses turned wild in the night, "Contending 'gainst obedience, as they would / Make war with mankind." In a similar way, painting could draw on the publicly understood objects of divine and secular history, events and personages which had heightened meaning, as it were, built into them, like the Madonna and Child or the oath of the Horatii.

But for a couple of centuries now we have been living in a world in which these points of reference no longer hold for us. Few now believe the doctrine of the correspondences, as this was accepted in the Renaissance, and neither divine or secular history has a generally accepted significance. It is not that one cannot write a poem about the correspondences. Precisely, Baudelaire did.[1] It is rather that this can't draw on the simple acceptance of the formerly public doctrines. The poet himself didn't subscribe to them in their canonical form. He is getting at something different, some personal vision he is trying to triangulate to through this historical reference, the "forest of symbols" that he sees in the world around him. But to grasp this forest, we need to understand not so much the erstwhile public doctrine (about which no one remembers any details anyway) but, as we might put it, the way it resonates in the poet's sensibility.

To take another example, Rilke speaks of angels. But his angels are not to be understood by their place in the traditionally defined order. Rather, we have to triangulate to the meaning of the term through the whole range of images with which Rilke articulates his sense of things. "Wer, wenn Ich schrie, hörte mich, aus der Engel Ordnungen?", begin the *Duino Elegies.* Their being beyond these cries partly defines these angels. We cannot get at them through a mediaeval treatise on the ranks of cherubim and seraphim, but we have to pass through this articulation of Rilke's sensibility.

We could describe the change in this way: where formerly poetic language could rely on certain publicly available orders of meaning, it now has to consist in a language of articulated sensibility. Earl Wasserman has shown how the decline of the old order with its established background of meanings made necessary the development of new poetic languages in the Romantic period. Pope, for instance, in his *Windsor Forest,* could draw on age-old views of the order of nature as a commonly available source of poetic images. For Shelley, this resource is no longer available; the poet must articulate his own world of references, and make them believable. As Wasserman explains it, "Until the end of the eighteenth century there was sufficient intellectual homogeneity for men to share certain assumptions . . . In varying degrees, . . . men accepted . . . the Christian interpretation of history, the sacramentalism of nature, the Great Chain of Being, the analogy of the various planes of creation, the conception of man as microcosm. . . . These were cosmic syntaxes in the public domain; and the poet could afford to think of his art as imitative of 'nature' since these patterns were what he meant by 'nature'.

"By the nineteenth century these world-pictures had passed from consciousness. The change from a mimetic to a creative conception of poetry is not merely a critical philosophical phenomenon . . . Now . . . an additional formulative act was required of the poet. . . . Within itself the modern poem must both formulate its cosmic syntax and shape the autonomous poetic reality that the cosmic syntax permits; 'nature', which was once prior to the poem and available for imitation, now shares with the poem a common origin in the poet's creativity."[2]

The Romantic poets and their successors have to articulate an original vision of the cosmos. When Wordsworth and Hölderlin describe the natural world around us, in *The Prelude, The Rhine,* or *Homecoming,* they no longer play on an established gamut of references, as Pope could still do in *Windsor Forest.* They make us aware of something in nature for which there are as yet no established words.[3] The poems are finding words for us. In this "subtler language"—the term is borrowed from Shelley—something is defined and created as well as manifested. A watershed has been passed in the history of literature.

Something similar happens in painting in the early nineteenth century. Caspar David Friedrich, for instance, distances himself from the traditional iconography.

He is searching for a symbolism in nature that is not based on the accepted conventions. The ambition is to let "the forms of nature speak directly, their power released by the ordering within the work of art".[4] Friedrich too is seeking a subtler language; he is trying to say something for which no adequate terms exist and whose meaning has to be sought in his works rather than in a pre-existing lexicon of references.[5] He builds on the late eighteenth-century sense of the affinity between our feelings and natural scenes, but in an attempt to articulate more than a subjective reaction. "Feeling can never be contrary to nature, is always consistent with nature."[6]

And of course, music too. But here we can see another facet of the development of subtler languages. This comes partly, as we saw, from the fading of metaphysical beliefs, about the Great Chain of Being, the order of things, and the like; partly from the end of consensus on metaphysics and religion. But first in the realm of music, and then also later elsewhere, we can see a move towards more "absolute" forms. These arise in a kind of further development out of the process by which poetry and music becomes "art" in the first place.

When we think of chanted prayer in a liturgical setting, or bardic recitation praising heroes at a banquet, we think of poetry and music as in the category "art". But as is well known, in the original societies, there may have been no such category, or if so, these activities may not have belonged to it. We think of them as "art", not only because of their resemblance (and sometimes ancestral relation) to our poetry and music, but also because we think of art as surrounded by an aura, and these too had their aura.

But this is not to say that we could explain their aura in the terms that we do that of our art, that is, in what we have come to call "aesthetic" categories. The liturgy is indeed, something special; it is singing in a special register. But this is because it is a privileged way of speaking to God, or being in communion with him. The bardic song is a uniquely solemn way of remembering and honouring our heroes.

In other words, what is special here is not to be understood aesthetically, in terms of the way in which the listener is (or ought to be) moved, but ontically: a specially important kind of action is being carried out (worshipping God, praising heroes).

In the original context, even telling a story within certain canonical forms, singing a love song, can be understood in this earlier "ontic" way. It lifts the events to a higher plane; there is now something archetypical, something close to the universal human grain, in this love, or this story. It places them in a higher register.

Then with song and story, we sooner or later come to a shift. In chant and bardic recitation, we have well understood social action. We don't yet have "art" in the modern sense, as a separate activity from religion, praising heroes, etc. The separate activity arises when we come to value creations because they allow us to contemplate, that is, to hold before ourselves so that we can appreciate whatever it is (greatness of God, or of the sense of the divine; greatness of heroes, or their admiration; the archetypes of love and suffering, etc.), without participating in the actions they were originally embedded in, e.g., praying or publicly praising our heroes at the feast.

So a first disembedding takes place. This is theorized, for instance, in Aristotle's *Poetics.* Art, as allowing this kind of contemplation, holding things up before us, can be described as mimetic. This is how Aristotle is understanding tragedy, rather than as a species of liturgy, as it was earlier. We are now entering the domain of (what will later be classified as) "art", as with, in more recent centuries, opera, the practice of playing Masses in concerts; nineteenth-century musical performances; and the like.

But there is a second disembedding, which arises with the subtler languages. We see this clearest in the case of music. Music develops over the history of its use in heightened action, and later in mimesis—love song, prayer, opera, etc.—a kind of "semanticisation". This is partly motivated; clearly the tones chosen for the love song and the chant felt right. But they weren't the only possibilities, and there is a great deal of historic association and accretion here.

The first, contemplative disembedding left the music with a clear context of human action: prayer, love declarations, dance, the plot of the opera, etc. These actions were not being done, but contemplated, but still they formed the context. The second disembedding is the step to "absolute" music. This creeps up in the instrumental music of the baroque and classical ages, before being theorized in the Romantic period.

There is a kind of desemanticisation and resemanticisation. The Mozart G Minor Quintet gives us a powerful sense of being moved by something profound and archetypical, not trivial and passing, which is both immensely sad, but also beautiful, moving, and arresting. We could imagine being moved in some analogous kind of way by some beautiful story of star-crossed love, of loss or parting. But the story isn't there. We have something like the essence of the response, without the story.

To put it another way: A love song evokes our being moved profoundly by some love story which seems to express a human archetype: Romeo and Juliet, say. The love song, play, opera gives us both the response expressed, and the intentional object of this response. Now with the new absolute music, we have the response in some way captured, made real, there unfolding before us; but the object isn't there. The music moves us very strongly, because it is moved, as it were; it captures, expresses, incarnates being profoundly moved. (Think of Beethoven quartets.) But what at? What is the object? Is there an object?

Or to come at this resemanticisation from another direction, we might think of the attempts to describe the opening bars of Beethoven's Fifth Symphony as the call of fate. Here the music is not capturing our being moved, but rather the meaning of intentional object itself. What people are saying is that this is the kind of music you might want to write for an opera for the moment in which fate calls. Only this is "absolute", not "programme" music; unlike in the opera, the object is left unportrayed.

Nevertheless we feel that there must be an object, an adequate object; or else this would be deception, play-acting. But we don't necessarily have any (other) language for it. Certainly not an assertoric language. This opens the way for Schopenhauer's theory of music. And then the practice of Wagner, which brings "absolute" music back into the story context of opera, but now enriched.

Semanticisation works thus at least in part, by capturing modes of being moved. But also perhaps by trying to express what is chthonic, cosmic. Here it trades on resonances of the cosmic in us.

This is a new kind of semantic freedom of exploration. Other arts imitate this. Mallarmé is a paradigm example in poetry. Then non-representational painting moves into a new space.

Subtler languages which have taken this "absolute" turn, unhooked themselves from intentional objects (music), or the assertoric (poetry), or the object represented (painting), are moving in a new field. The ontic commitments are very unclear. This means that such art can serve to disclose very deep truths which in the nature of things can never be obvious, nor available to everyone, regardless of spiritual condition. Thus Beethoven; and certainly Hopkins. But it can also combine with a denial of deep ontic realities out there. There is only le Néant. This leaves a residual mystery: why are we so moved? But this mystery is now replaced within us. It is the mystery of anthropological depth. This is what we have with Mallarmé. But the explorations here can then be re-used by those who see a reality outside, like Eliot; and those who want to point to one: Celan?

We can thus see how subtler languages operating in the "absolute" mode can offer a place to go for modern unbelief. In particular, for those who are moved by critiques on the "Romantic" axes: the modern identity and outlook flattens the world, leaves no place for the spiritual, the higher, for mystery. This doesn't need to send us back to religious belief. There is another direction.

The idea is: the mystery, the depth, the profoundly moving, can be, for all we know, entirely anthropological. Atheists, humanists cling on to this, as they go to concerts, operas, read great literature. So one can complement an ethic and a scientific anthropology which remain very reductive and flat.

All this shows how the new recourse to "subtler languages" reflects the predicament of the buffered identity. First, in an obvious negative way: the increasing unavailability of the earlier languages of objective reference, connected to sacred history, the correspondences, the Great Chain, is the ineluctable consequence of disenchantment, the recession of the cosmos before a universe to be understood in mechanistic terms. But the aspiration to create new languages shows the unwillingness to leave matters there. It reflects the force, in part, of the new cosmic imaginary, the struggle to articulate the new moral meanings in nature. This is plain in the work of Friedrich just mentioned, as well as in the poems of Wordsworth and Hölderlin, and in a host of other places. In more general terms, the struggle is to recover a kind of vision of something deeper, fuller, in the recognition that this cannot be easy, that it requires insight and creative power.

The enframing understanding is that our epistemic predicament is different. Where before the languages of theology and metaphysics confidently mapped out the domain of the deeper, the "invisible", now the thought is that these domains can only be made indirectly accessible through a language of "symbols". This polysemic word took on a special sense for the generation of German Romantics of the 1790s, which was later reflected in Goethe's writings. The "symbol" in this sense reveals something which can't be made accessible in any other way; unlike the "allegory", whose images refer us to a domain which we could also describe directly, in literal language.

The symbol is in fact constitutive of what Wasserman calls a "subtler language". It first and only gives access to what it refers to. It cannot simply rely on established languages. And that is why making/finding a symbol is so difficult; why it needs creative power, even genius. But this also means that what has been revealed is also partly concealed; it cannot be simply detached from the symbol, and be open to scrutiny as the ordinary referents are in our everyday world.

Now there is a close connection between the modern cosmic imaginary and the subtler languages of the last two centuries, particularly the poetry. The earlier imaginary was articulated and given shape by the cosmos ideas which animated it. There is nothing analogous for the new imaginary, save science; and important as this is, it cannot suffice to articulate the moral meanings of things. At the moment when the hermeneutic of nature as the embodiment of the forms and the Great Chain begins to falter, probing its half-hidden meanings becomes one of the major themes of subtler languages, as in this passage from *Tintern Abbey*, where Wordsworth speaks of

> A presence that disturbs me with the joy
> Of elevated thoughts; a sense sublime
> Of something far more deeply interfused,
> Whose dwelling is the light of setting suns,
> And the round ocean and the living air,

And the blue sky, and the mind of man;
A motion and a spirit, that impels
All thinking things, all objects of all thought,
And rolls through all things. (ll. 94–102)

The idea that nature has something to say to us hovers there in our culture, too far out for the buffered identity to be uncomfortable with it, but powerful enough to be evoked in a number of indirect ways—in art, in our feelings of renewal as we enter countryside or forest, in some of our responses of alarm at its destruction.

As I argued above, this sense of the need to open to nature is a counterpart to the feeling that there is something inadequate in our way of life, that we live by an order which represses what is really important. One of the paradigm places in which this sense of inadequacy was articulated was in Schiller's *Letters on the Aesthetic Education of Man.*[7] This was a critique of the dominant form of Enlightenment anthropocentrism, mainly on the second axis discussed in Chapter 8, section 2. It was a critique of this outlook as a moralism. The imposition of morality by the will on our refractory desires (Schiller plainly has Kant in mind here) divides reason and sensibility, and in effect enslaves one side of our nature to the other. But the simple affirmation of desire against morality divides us no less, and simply reverses the relation of master and slave. What we need to seek is a spontaneous unity, a harmony of all our faculties, and this we find in beauty. In beauty, form and content, will and desire, come of themselves together, indeed they merge inseparably.

At first, it seems that Schiller is talking about beauty as an aid to being moral; it enables one more effectively to live up to the moral law, because one goes along willingly, so to speak. But as the work proceeds, it more and more appears that Schiller sees the stage of aesthetic unity as a higher stage, beyond moralism. It is an integral fulfillment, in which all sides of our nature come together harmoniously, in which we achieve full freedom, since one side of us is no longer forced to submit to the demands of the other, and in which we experience the fullness of joy. This is the fulfillment, going beyond morality, which is really the point of our existence.

This is what Schiller seems to be saying. He introduces his new term 'play', which was to be taken up by so many writers after him in the last two centuries. It designates the activities by which we create and respond to beauty, and it is chosen to carry the sense of gratuitous, spontaneous freedom which is lacking in the imposition of law by the will. Schiller asserts that human beings "are only human insofar as they play".[8] This is the apex of human self-realization.

Schiller thus gave a wonderfully clear, convincing and influential formulation to a central idea of the Romantic period, that the answer to the felt inadequacy of moralism, the important defining goal or fulfillment which it leaves out and represses, was to be found in the aesthetic realm. This went beyond the moral, but in Schiller's case wasn't seen as contradicting it. Rather it complements morality in completing human fulfillment. Later, a doctrine which derives a great deal from Schiller's theory, one which also makes crucial use of the notion of 'play', will set the aesthetic against the moral. It finds its most important spokesman in Nietzsche.

So the aesthetic was established as an ethical category, as a source of answers to the question, how should we live? what is our greatest goal or fulfillment? This gives a crucial place to art. Beauty is what will save us, complete us. This can be found outside us, in nature, or in the grandeur of the cosmos (especially if we also incorporate the sublime in this regenerating power). But in order to open ourselves fully to this, we need to be fully aware of it, and for this we need to articulate it in the languages of art. So created beauty, works of art, are not only important loci of that beauty which can transform us, they are also essential ways of acceding to the beauty which we don't create. In the Romantic period, artistic creation comes to be the highest domain of human activity.

If we reach our highest goal through art and the aesthetic, then this goal, it would appear, must be immanent. It would represent an alternative to the love of God as a way of transcending moralism. But things are not so simple. God is not excluded. Nothing has ruled out an understanding of beauty as reflecting God's work in creating and redeeming the world. A theological aesthetic in von Balthasar's terms[9] is still an open possibility after Schiller.

The important change is rather that this issue now must remain open. This is what marks us off from earlier times. In pre-modern times, the beauty of art was understood in terms of mimesis: the imitation of reality which was set in an ordered cosmos, with its levels of being, which was further understood as God's creation; or the imitation of a divine history, in portrayals, say, of Mary and her Son, or of the Crucifixion. It went without saying that great art refers us to the correspondences, to the order of being, to sacred history. With the fading of these backgrounds, with the coming of a buffered self, for whom this larger spiritual environment was no longer a matter of untheorized experience, though it might still be an object of reasoned belief, we have the growth of what I have been calling, following Wasserman, "subtler languages". This was the second important creation of the Romantic period, complementing the identification of beauty as the key to restoring our lost unity.

Now as I argued above, these languages function, have power, move us, but without having to identify their ontic commitments. "Absolute" music expresses being moved by what is powerful and deep, but does not need to identify where this is to be found, whether in heaven, or on earth, or in the depths of our own being—or even whether these alternatives are exclusive. The consummation of subtler languages is when, in Pater's words, all arts strive to approach the condition of music. Now to enter in this medium does not mean to deny God. On the contrary, many great modern artists—Eliot, Messiaen—have tried to make their medium a locus of epiphany. This is perfectly possible. But it is not necessary. The ontic commitments can be other, or they can remain largely unidentified.

And this is what offers a place to go for modern unbelief. As a response to the inadequacies of moralism, the missing goal can be identified with the experience of beauty, in the realm of the aesthetic. But this is now unhooked from the ordered cosmos and/or the divine. It can be grounded anew in some purely immanent outlook, such as that offered by Freud, for instance. But it can also be left unspecified, and that is in fact the option most frequently taken.

It is largely thanks to the languages of art that our relation to nature can so often remain in this middle realm, this free and neutral space, between religious commitment and materialism. Something similar can perhaps be said of our relation to music. I am thinking of the way in which publicly performed music, in concert hall and opera house, becomes an especially important and serious activity in nineteenth century bourgeois Europe and America. People begin to listen to concerts with an almost religious intensity. The analogy is not out of place. The performance has taken on something of a rite, and has kept it to this day. There is a sense that something great is being said in this music. This too has helped create a kind of middle space, neither explicitly believing, but not atheistic either, a kind of undefined spirituality.[10]

Other features of our world seem to exist in the same ambiguous space. For instance, tourism, an activity involving masses of people in the late twentieth century; people travel for all sorts of reasons, but one is to see the important "sights" of our and other civilizations. Now these are overwhelmingly churches, temples, sites in which the strong transcendent meanings of the past are embedded. Perhaps one might reply that this proves nothing, except that the civilizations of the past invested heavily in the transcendent; those who want to see the monuments of the past, admire its art, etc., don't have the choice; they have to find these in cathedrals, mosques, temples. But I don't believe that this is all there is to it, but that there is also a certain admiration, wonder, mixed with some nostalgia, at these sites where the contact with the transcendent was/is so much firmer, surer.

The existence of this middle space is a reflection of what I called above, in Chapter 8, section 1, the cross-pressure felt by the modern buffered identity, on the one hand drawn towards unbelief, while on the other, feeling the solicitations of the spiritual—be they in nature, in art, in some contact with religious faith, or in a sense of God which may break through the membrane.

The continued search for what can be revealed by "symbols" (however this notion is phrased) in the art of the last two centuries, the very prominence of this understanding of art, even as something to rebel against, through a denial of "meaning", says something about our predicament. The loss of pre-modern languages shows how embedded we are in the buffered identity, but the continued attempt to devise subtler languages shows how difficult it is just to leave things there, not to try to compensate for, to replace those earlier vehicles of now problematic insight. This is another cultural fact about modernity, which testifies in the same sense as the concern for lost meaning. It bespeaks the malaise, the uncertainties, which inhabit the buffered identity.

The shift from cosmos to universe did two important things. It allowed for the development of deeper and more solid forms of materialism and unbelief, and it also gave a new shape to the cross-pressure felt by the buffered identity between belief and unbelief. Along with the development of post-Romantic art, it helps to create a neutral space between these.

2

I have been discussing this second development in the last pages. I now want to connect up to the beginning of this section by examining the maturing of unbelief in this period.

Of course, if we're looking for the reasons which made people renounce their religious belief in the nineteenth century, the gamut is very wide. Some of them are similar to these we have already rehearsed in the discussion of the rise of an option of unbelief in the eighteenth century. It is clear, for instance, that people who felt strongly the satisfactions of the buffered identity—power, invulnerability—and were not very sensitive to its narrowing effect, tended to opt more easily for the materialist side. Then there are all the reasons which made people reject Christianity: its counter-Enlightenment doctrines of human evil, and of divine punishment; the Church's practices of exclusion, its siding with obscurantism.

To take up this point from the other side, it could easily appear that the values of the modern moral order could only be carried out fully and radically by the step into unbelief. In the nineteenth century, one of the key values was understood to be altruism. And in this regard exclusive humanism could claim to be superior to Christianity. First, Christianity offers extrinsic rewards for altruism in the hereafter, where humanism makes benevolence its own reward; and secondly it sometimes can be tempted to exclude heretics and unbelievers from its purview whereas humanism can be truly universal. Mill, for instance, put forward these arguments.[11]

In other ways too, materialism seemed to complete a movement implicit in the modern order. The rehabilitation of ordinary, sensuous nature against the calumnies laid on it by those outlooks which aspire to some "higher" or "spiritual" level of existence, seems to take its most radical, thoroughgoing form in a doctrine which denies flatly all such higher levels. The defense of ordinary human desire against the demands of the supposedly superior renunciative vocations, which was undertaken by the Reformers, seems to reach its final end and logical conclusion in materialism. It is a declaration of the innocence of sensuous nature, of solidarity with it against the tortured demands of an illusory inhuman perfection.

All these factors had already been operative in the eighteenth century, although perhaps not focussed in quite the same way in the case of altruism. But now there entered two new factors, which both shifted the argument somewhat, and also contributed to the new depth and solidity of materialist positions. They are obviously linked. I am thinking of the impact of science and scholarship, on one hand, and the new cosmic imaginary, on the other.

Both science and scholarship had considerably developed. The latter was principally relevant in the form of Biblical criticism, which called into question the sources of the Bible. But far more important was the support which science was purported to offer to a materialist view of the universe, principally in connection with Darwin's work on evolution.

I don't mean by this that the "scientific" argument from evolutionary theory to atheism is convincing, or even that just as a scientific argument it convinced. My view, as I shall argue below (Chapter 15), is that the shift in world views turned rather on ethical considerations. I don't just mean ethical considerations extraneous to the "scientific" argument, such as those concerning altruism just mentioned. I mean that what began to look more plausible was the whole stance underlying the epistemology of materialism, over against that underlying the epistemology of Christian faith.

It is not hard to see why this was (and still is) so. Even where the conclusions of science seem to be doing the work of conversion, it is very often not the detailed findings so much as the form. Modern science offers us a view of the universe framed in general laws. The ultimate is an impersonal order of regularities in which all particular things exist, over-arching all space and time. This seems in conflict with Christian faith, which relates us to a personal Creator-God, and which explains our predicament in terms of a developing exchange of divine action and human reaction to his interventions in history, culminating in the Incarnation and Atonement.

Now there is a deep conflict in Western intellectual sensibility, going way back, between those who respond to this personal-historical faith, and those whose sense of what is plausible leads them to seek as ultimate framework an impersonal order. Many "philosophical" minds, even in the great religions which descend from Abraham, have been drawn in this direction. The attraction in the Middle Ages of the Aristotelian idea of an eternal universe, even though (seemingly) incombinable with the belief in the creation, on thinkers like Maimonides and Ibn Rushd, is a case in point.

The draw to the impersonal framework also helped to promote Deism and eventually unbelief, as I described in Chapter 7. We saw how for Providential Deism the principal claim to God's benevolence is precisely the nature of his unchanging order in creation. Lessing speaks of the "broad ditch" that separates the general truths of morality and religion from any particular facts of history.[12]

For those who take this view, the noblest, highest truths *must* have this general form. Personal interventions, even those of a God, would introduce something arbitrary, some element of subjective desire, into the picture, and the highest truths about reality must be beyond this element. From this standpoint, a faith in a personal God belongs to a less mature standpoint, where one still needs the sense of a personal relation to things; one is not yet ready to face the ultimate truth. A line of thinking of this nature, steadily gathering strength, runs through modern thought and culture, from Spinoza, through Goethe, to our present time.

Now I think that an important part of the force which drove many people to see science and religion as incompatible, and to opt for the former, comes from this crucial difference in form. In other words, the success of science built on and helped to entrench in them the sense that the Christian religion they were familiar with belonged to an earlier, more primitive or less mature form of understanding.

Now this bent to impersonality was greatly reinforced by the new cosmic imaginary. The vast universe, in which one could easily feel no sense of a personal God or a benign purpose, seemed to be impersonal in the most forbidding sense, blind and indifferent to our fate. An account in terms of impersonal causal law seemed called for by the new depth sense of reality in the universe.

This inference was all the stronger in that the stance of disengaged reason, construing the world as it does as devoid of human meaning, fits better with the impersonal picture. But this stance is part of the modern identity of the buffered self, which thus finds a natural affinity for the impersonal order.

But the affinity was not just epistemic. In a sense the moral outlook of modernity—the modern social imaginary with its stranger sociability, the great centrality of the moral code which articulates the modern moral order—calls on us to rise to a universal standpoint. The new morality comes to be identified with the standpoint of the "impartial spectator", as Hutcheson phrased it. We have to rise above and beyond our particular, narrow, biased view on things, to a view from everywhere, or for everyman, the analogue of the "view from nowhere" which natural science strives to occupy.

Seen from this perspective, the real telos implicit in the earlier forward steps of humanity—the Axial period, the end of paganism and polytheism, the Reformation—was the bringing of disenchantment, the end of a cosmos of spirits respondent to humans, and the coming of the impersonal order defined by the moral code. Straight line orthodox monotheism was not yet at the goal of this development. It turned the many gods into one, but is still seen as posing the moral issue too much in terms of the favour or disfavour of a capricious tyrant. We are now beyond this.

We shall see later that one of the crucial issues today is precisely whether this relegation of the personal relation in favour of the supremacy of an unchallengeable moral code is really as unproblematic as so many moderns, utilitarians and neo-Kantians, but not only they, seem to think.

In any case, this general parti pris for the impersonal may then spill over onto materialism, as the outlook which "science" has developed. But it is interesting that this is not always so. Some people who opted for science over religion were later influenced by the sense of spiritual flatness which I mentioned above. They felt both sides of the cross-pressure. Indeed, this malaise seems to grow among educated élites in the late nineteenth century. They turned to various forms of spiritualism, para-scientific researches, para-psychology and the like. In one case, that of Frederick Myers, the two moves were successive; first a loss of Christian faith owing to Darwinism, then a return to the spiritual, but within the bounds of an impersonal framework. He spoke of himself as "re-entering through the scullery the heavenly mansion out of which I had been kicked through the front door."[13] A spiritual-but-not-Christian (or Jewish or Muslim) position, adopted on something like these grounds, has remained a very widespread option in our culture.

But other things too, tend to make us align materialism with adulthood. A religious outlook may easily be painted as one which offers greater comfort, which shields us from the truth of an indifferent universe, which is now felt as a strong possibility within the modern cosmic imaginary. Religion is afraid to face the fact that we are alone in the universe, and without cosmic support. As children, we do indeed, find this hard to face, but growing up is becoming ready to look reality in the face.

Of course, this story will probably make little sense to someone who is deeply engaged in a life of prayer or meditation, or other serious spiritual discipline, because this involves in its own way growing beyond and letting go of more childish images of God. But if our faith has remained at the stage of the immature images, then the story that materialism equals maturity can seem plausible. And if in addition, one has been convinced that manliness is the key virtue, then the appeal to go over can appear irresistible. The appeal of science for Mill was precisely that of "good downright hard logic, with a minimum of sentimentalism"; it enables you to "look facts in the face".[14]

We can see from all this how much the appeal of scientific materialism is not so much the cogency of its detailed findings as that of the underlying epistemological stance, and that for ethical reasons. It is seen as the stance of maturity, of courage, of manliness, over against childish fears and sentimentality.

We can say in general terms that, where there was a conversion from faith to "science" which was undertaken reluctantly, and with a sense of loss, the kind of faith involved played an important role. On one hand, there were those who were very deeply wedded to certain particular beliefs, and couldn't conceive their faith without them. Thus, to the extent to which Christian faith was totally identified with certain dogmas or cosmic theories—e.g., the literal belief that Creation occurred in 4004 B.C., or the neat intermeshing of Deist Providential order—the new depth reality could appear as a decisive refutation. Or to the extent that the drama of Fall, Incarnation, Redemption was understood as incompatible with the slow evolution of human culture, refutation threatened.

And then there were those who felt the accusations of childishness levelled against faith as hitting a target in their own religious life. The presumption of immaturity deeply shook them because of this inner insecurity, and they ended up resolving the tension by abandoning their religion, even if with sadness and a sense of irreparable loss.

In the first case, we can really speak of a conversion brought about by certain scientific conclusions. But then the question must remain: why did they need to identify their faith with these particular doctrines? Why were they so deaf to the moral meanings of the new cosmic imaginary which might have led them back to God?

This fits, of course, with my general position here, that conversions from religion under the influence of "science" turn not on the alleged scientific proofs of materialism or the impossibility of God (which turn out on examination not to go through anyway), but rather on other factors which in this case consist in attachment to inessential doctrines which can be refuted.

In the second case, what happens is that people are convinced that there is something more mature, more courageous, readier to face unvarnished reality in the scientific stance. The superiority is an ethical one, and of course, is heavily influenced by the person's own sense of his/her own childhood faith, which may well have remained a childish one.

However, we can easily understand that, having gone though this conversion, the way it will appear to the convert will fit the standard story which makes scientific truth the decisive agency. If I become convinced that the ancient faith reflects a more immature outlook on things, in comparison to modern science, then I will indeed see myself as abandoning the first to cleave to the second. The fact that I have not made the move following some rigorously demonstrated scientific conclusion will escape me, either because, having already taken my side, I am easily convinced by its "arguments", or because, also owing to this parti pris, I am ready to have faith in science's ability to come up one day with the conclusive proofs of God's inexistence.

To put the point in another way, the story that a convert to unbelief may tell, about being convinced to abandon religion by science, is in a sense really true. This person does see himself as abandoning one world view ("religion") because another incompatible one ("science") seemed more believable. But what made it in fact more believable was not "scientific" proofs; it is rather that one whole package: science, plus a picture of our epistemic-moral predicament in which science represents a mature facing of hard reality, beats out another package: religion, plus a rival picture of our epistemic-moral predicament in which religion, say, represents true humility, and many of the claims of science unwarranted arrogance. But the decisive consideration here was the reading of the moral predicament proposed by "science", which struck home as true to the convert's experience (of a faith which was still childish—and whose faith is not, to one or another degree?), rather than the actual findings of science. This is the sense in which what I've been calling moral considerations played a crucial role; not that the convert necessarily found the morality of "science" of itself more attractive—one can assume that in a sense the opposite was the case, where he bemoaned loss of faith—but that it offered a more convincing story about his moral/spiritual life.

As I stated above, in commenting on the long evolution of the universe idea out of the cosmos, there are no important scientific moves which are not also motivated by a strongly held vision, which in turn has spiritual implications. When "science" beats out "religion", it is one such vision which expels another, and in this victory the moral/spiritual implications are probably playing a role. But once this happens, then the very ethic of "science" requires that the move be justified retrospectively in terms of "proofs". The official story takes over.

This whole way of seeing things, which comes about through the joint effect of science and the new cosmic imaginary, helped along by a notion of maturity which they generate along with the buffered identity, has brought about modes of unbelief which are much more solid. They are more firmly anchored, both in our sense of our world, and in the scientific and technological practices by which we know it and deal with it. This is why for whole milieux today materialism has become the obvious, the default position. It is no longer a wild, far-out theory, but creeps close to what is seen as common sense.

But materialism has not only solidified, it has also deepened. As we saw in the above discussion, the new cosmic imaginary carried further what the mechanistic view of the universe had already started. This world-picture had dissipated totally the earlier view of a meaning in things captured in the Platonic-Aristotelian idea that the world around us was the realization of Forms, the theory of ontic logos. But there was still room for other kinds of meaning: for instance, the purposes which God furthers in creating the mechanistic universe, or those which we have in virtue of having souls. Thoroughgoing materialism wipes these away as well.

Now an utter absence of purpose can be experienced as a terrible loss, as the most dire threat levelled at us by the disenchanted world. But it can also be seen in the other positive perspective, that of invulnerability. In such a universe, nothing is demanded of us; we have no destiny which we are called on to achieve, on pain of damnation, or divine retribution, or some terminal discord with ourselves. Already the Epicureans had made this point in one form. To know that all comes from atoms and their swervings, that the Gods are utterly unconcerned with us, is to liberate us from fear of the beyond, and thus allow us to achieve ataraxia. Modern materialism takes up this legacy, but gives it the characteristically modern activist twist: in this purposeless universe, we decide what goals to pursue. Or else we find them in the depths, our depths, that is, something we can recognize as coming from deep within us. In either case, it is we who determine the order of human things—and who can thus discover in ourselves the motivation, and the capacity, to build the order of freedom and mutual benefit, in the teeth of an indifferent and even hostile universe.

We are alone in the universe, and this is frightening; but it can also be exhilarating. There is a certain joy in solitude, particularly for the buffered identity. The thrill at being alone is part sense of freedom, part the intense poignancy of this fragile moment, the "dies" (day) that you must "carpere" (seize). All meaning is here, in this small speck. Pascal got at some of this with his image of the human being as a thinking reed.

The new cosmic imaginary adds a further dimension to this. Having come to sense how vast the universe is in time and space, how deep its micro-constitution goes into the infinitesimal, and feeling thus both our insignificance and fragility, we also see what a remarkable thing it is that out of this immense, purposeless machine, life, and then feeling, imagination and thought emerge.

Here is where a religious person will easily confess a sense of mystery. Materialists usually want to repudiate this; science in its progress recognizes no mysteries, only temporary puzzles. But nevertheless, the sense that our thinking, feeling life plunges its roots into a system of such unimaginable depths, that consciousness can emerge out of this, fills them too with awe.

Our wonder at our dark genesis, and the conflict we can feel around it, is well captured by a writer of our day. Douglas Hofstadter recognizes that certain people have an instinctive horror of any "explaining away" of the soul. I don't know why some people have this horror while others, like me, find in reductionism the ultimate religion. Perhaps my lifelong training in physics and science in general has given me a deep awe at seeing how the most substantial and familiar of objects or experiences fades away, as one approaches the infinitesimal scale, into an eerily insubstantial ether, a myriad of ephemeral swirling vortices of nearly incomprehensible mathematical activity. This in me evokes a cosmic awe. To me, reductionism doesn't "explain away"; rather, it adds mystery.[15]

But this awe is modulated, and intensified, by a sense of kinship, of belonging integrally to these depths. And this allows us to recapture the sense of connection and solidarity with all existence which arose in the eighteenth century out of our sense of dark genesis, but now with an incomparably greater sense of the width and profundity of its reach.[16]

And so materialism has become deeper, richer, but also more varied in its forms, as protagonists take different stands to the complex facets I have just been trying to lay out. The reasons to opt for unbelief go beyond our judgments about religion, and the supposed deliverances of "science". They include also the moral meanings which we now find in the universe and our genesis out of it. Materialism is now nourished by certain ways of living in, and further developing, our cosmic imaginary; certain ways of inflecting our sense of the purposelessness of this vast universe, our awe at, and sense of kinship with it.

This was one way, through science and the cosmic imaginary, in which unbelief deepened and solidified in the nineteenth century. Another, which I will just mention here, is that the forms of social imaginary built around simultaneity and action in purely secular time—the market economy, the public sphere, the polity of popular sovereignty—were becoming more and more dominant. Once again, we have a sense of social reality, parallel to the cosmic imaginary's sense of natural reality, which by no means must command an unbelieving outlook; but it certainly can consort with one, and on certain readings of the issue can be made to seem alone compatible with such an outlook. Certainly Pius IX thought so.

But whatever we think of nineteenth-century Papal politics (and they certainly don't convince anyone today), there is a deeper point here, which is analogous to our discussion of the cosmic imaginary. Modern societies are impersonal in an important sense; that is, they are based on stranger sociability, and involve the creation of collective agency among equals; they privilege categorical identities, in which people are linked through shared properties (being Americans, Frenchmen, Muslims, Catholics), rather than through a network of personal relations, as in kinship, or the relations of fealty central to pre-modern European societies ("feudal", as they were called.) People whose religious life was bound up with the forms of life of a network society—for instance peasants living in the hierarchical world of a country parish—once transferred to an industrializing city in the nineteenth century, would be profoundly disoriented, and unable to live their traditional religion. They may easily fall away from churches altogether, or else invent quite new forms of religious life. I shall explore this in a later chapter.

3

The deeper, more anchored forms of unbelief arising in the nineteenth century are basically the same as those which are held today. We can see the Victorians as our contemporaries in a way which we cannot easily extend to the men of the Enlightenment. Foucault and others have noticed the watershed that the Romantic age made in European thought, accrediting a sense of reality as deep, systematic, as finding its mainsprings well below an immediately available surface, whether it be in the economic theories of a Marx, the "depth psychology" of a Freud, or the genealogies of a Nietzsche.[17] We are still living in the aftermath of this shift to depth, even though we may contest these particular theories. In this respect, we might be tempted to say that modern unbelief starts then, and not really in the Age of the Enlightenment. The nineteenth century would be the moment when "the Modern Schism" occurred.[18]

The mention of Nietzsche in the preceding paragraph brings us to an extremely important turn in the moral imagination of unbelief in the nineteenth century. I talked of the "post-Schopenhauerian" visions earlier, which give a positive significance to the irrational, amoral, even violent forces within us. The idea is, in various forms, that these cannot simply be condemned and uprooted, because our existence, and/or vitality, creativity, strength, ability to create beauty depend on them. This turn finds a new moral meaning in our dark genesis out of the wild and prehuman. It comes of a rebellion against the standard form of modern anthropocentrism, along the "tragic" axis, rejecting the too-harmonized picture of life, in which suffering, evil and violence have been painted out.

This is a turn against the values of the Enlightenment. But unlike what we usually call the counter-Enlightenment—thinkers like Bonald and de Maistre—it is not in any sense a return to religion or the transcendent. It remains resolutely naturalist. That's why I will refer to it as the "immanent counter-Enlightenment".

What it is rebelling against is a crucial strand of modern exclusive humanism, which in turn draws on the religious tradition which preceded it. This is, in fact, a powerful constitutive strand of modern western spirituality as a whole: an affirmation of the value of life, of succouring life and sustaining it, healing and feeding. This was intensified by the anthropocentric turn, where the purposes of God were narrowed to this one goal of sustaining human life. The continuing power of this idea is perhaps evident in the contemporary concern to preserve life, to bring prosperity, to reduce suffering, world-wide, which is I believe without precedent in history.

This concern reflects, on one hand, the modern idea of moral order; while on the other, it arises historically out of what I have called elsewhere "the affirmation of ordinary life".[19] What I was trying to gesture at with this term is the cultural revolution of the early modern period, which dethroned the supposedly higher activities of contemplation and the citizen life, and put the centre of gravity of goodness in ordinary living, production and the family. It belongs to this spiritual outlook that our first concern ought to be to increase life, relieve suffering, foster prosperity. Concern above all for the "good life" smacked of pride, of self-absorption. And beyond that, it was inherently inegalitarian, since the alleged "higher" activities could only be carried out by an élite minority, whereas leading rightly one's ordinary life was open to everyone. This is a moral temper to which it seems obvious that our major concern must be our dealings with others, in justice and benevolence; and these dealings must be on a level of equality.

This affirmation, which constitutes a major component of our modern ethical outlook, was originally inspired by a mode of Christian piety. It exalted practical agape, and was polemically directed against the pride, élitism, one might say, self-absorption of those who believed in "higher" activities or spiritualities.

Consider the Reformers' attack on the supposedly "higher" vocations of the monastic life. These were meant to mark out élite paths of superior dedication, but were in fact deviations into pride and self-delusion. The really holy life for the Christian was within ordinary life itself, living in work and household in a Christian and worshipful manner.

There was an earthly, one might say, earthy critique of the allegedly "higher" here which was then transposed, and used as a secular critique of Christianity, and indeed, religion in general. Something of the same rhetorical stance adopted by Reformers against monks and nuns is taken up by secularists and unbelievers against Christian faith itself. This allegedly scorns the real, sensual, earthly human good for some purely imaginary higher end, the pursuit of which can only lead to the frustration of the real, earthly good, to suffering, mortification, repression, etc. The motivations of those who espouse this "higher" path are thus, indeed, suspect. Pride, élitism, the desire to dominate play a part in this story too, along with fear and timidity (also present in the earlier Reformers' story, but less prominent).

Exclusive humanism has inherited both the allegiance to the moral order, and the affirmation of ordinary life. And this has provoked, as it were, a revolt from within.

The revolt has been against what one could call a secular religion of life, which is one of the most striking features of the modern world.

We live in an extraordinary moral culture, measured against the norm of human history, in which suffering and death, through famine, flood, earthquake, pestilence or war, can awaken world-wide movements of sympathy and practical solidarity. Granted, of course, that this is made possible by modern media and modes of transportation, not to speak of surpluses. These shouldn't blind us to the importance of the cultural-moral change. The same media and means of transport don't awaken the same response everywhere; it is disproportionately strong in ex-Latin Christendom.

Let us grant also the distortions produced by media hype and the media-gazer's short attention span, the way dramatic pictures produce the strongest response, often relegating even more needy cases to a zone of neglect from which only the cameras of CNN can rescue them. Nevertheless, the phenomenon is remarkable. The age of Hiroshima and Auschwitz has also produced Amnesty International and Médecins Sans Frontières.

Of course, the Christian roots of all this run deep. First, there is the extraordinary missionary effort of the Counter-Reformation Church, taken up later by the Protestant denominations. Then there were the mass-mobilization campaigns of the early nineteenth century—the anti-slavery movement in England, largely inspired and led by Evangelicals; the parallel abolitionist movement in the United States, also largely Christian-inspired. Then this habit of mobilizing for the redress of injustice and the relief of suffering world-wide becomes part of our political culture. Somewhere along the road, this culture ceases to be simply Christian-inspired—although people of deep Christian faith continue to be important in today's movements. Moreover, it probably needed this breach with the culture of Christendom for the impulse of solidarity to transcend the frontier of Christendom itself.

This is the complex legacy of the Enlightenment which I am trying to describe here. It incorporates a powerful humanism, affirming the importance of preserving and enhancing life, of avoiding death and suffering, an eclipse/denial of transcendence which tends to make this humanism an exclusive one, and a dim historical sense that the first of these came about through and depends on the second.

From its beginnings two and a half centuries ago, this developing ethos encountered resistance. In its very influential Utilitarian variant, it was seen as a kind of flattening of human life, rendering it "one-dimensional", to use an expression which gained wide currency later. Life in the "Crystal Palace", to quote Dostoyevsky's protagonist in *Notes from Underground*, was felt as stifling, as diminishing, as deadening, or as levelling. There were clearly at least two important sources of this reaction, though they could sometimes be (uneasily) combined.

One was the continuing spiritual concern with the transcendent, which could never accept that flourishing human life was all there is, and bridled at the reduction. The other sprang from the older aristocratic ethos, and protested against the levelling effects of the culture of equality and benevolence. It apprehended a loss of the heroic dimension of human life, and a consequent levelling down of human beings to the bourgeois, utilitarian mean. That this concern went well beyond reactionary circles, we can see from the case of Tocqueville, who was very worried by this kind of reduction of humanity which threatens us in a democratic age. He feared a world in which people would end up being occupied exclusively with their "petits et vulgaires plaisirs", and would lose the love of freedom.[20]

Now these resistances were nourished by long-standing traditions, those of the transcendent on one hand, and certain long-existing standards of honour and excellence on the other. What I am calling the immanent revolt is a resistance against the primacy of life, but which has abandoned these traditional sources. It is neither grounded in transcendence, nor based on the historically received understandings of social hierarchy—though it may be inspired by earlier versions of the warrior ethic, as we see with Nietzsche.

It is the revolt from within unbelief, as it were, against the primacy of life. Not now in the name of something beyond, but really more just from a sense of being confined, diminished by the acknowledgment of this primacy.

So as well as an external counter-Enlightenment, nourished by the traditions that the Enlightenment relegated to the zone of illusion, there has grown an immanent counter-Enlightenment, which shares in, even sometimes intensifies this rejection of the past. But just as the secular Enlightenment humanism grew out of the earlier Christian, agape-inspired affirmation of ordinary life, so the immanent counter-Enlightenment grew out of its transcendent-inspired predecessor.

Where this primarily happened was in the literary and artistic domains that grew out of Romanticism and its successors. The Romantic movement was one of the important loci of the Counter-Enlightenment, even if it was also always much more than this. Protest against a flattened world, one which had been denuded of meaning, was a recurring theme of Romantic writers and artists, and this could go together with counter-Enlightenment commitments, although it didn't have to. At least it made it impossible to align oneself with the crasser variants of Enlightenment secularism, such as Utilitarianism.

The immanent counter-Enlightenment comes to existence within this domain of Western culture. From the beginning, it has been linked with a primacy of the aesthetic. Even where it rejects the category, and speaks of an "aesthetic illusion" (as with Paul de Man), it remains centrally concerned with art, and especially modern, post-Romantic art. Its big battalions within the modern academy are found in literature departments.

One of its major themes is a new understanding of the centrality of death, a kind of answer to the inability of mainstream exclusive humanism to cope with mortality. This finds some of its sources in the religious tradition. I will discuss this in Chapter 19.

Alongside that, and interwoven with it, is another kind of revolt against the primacy of life, inspired mainly by the other source of resistance in the external counter-Enlightenment, the resistance against levelling, in the name of the great, the exceptional, the heroic.

The most influential proponent of this kind of view has undoubtedly been Nietzsche. And it is significant that the most important anti-humanist thinkers of our time: e.g., Foucault, Derrida, behind them, Bataille, all draw heavily on Nietzsche.

Nietzsche, of course, rebelled against the idea that our highest goal is to preserve and increase life, to prevent suffering. He rejects this both metaphysically and practically. He rejects the egalitarianism underlying this whole affirmation of ordinary life. But his rebellion is in a sense also internal. Life itself can push to cruelty, to domination, to exclusion, and indeed does so in its moments of most exuberant affirmation.

So this move remains within the modern affirmation of life in a sense. There is nothing higher than the movement of life itself (the Will to Power). But it chafes at the benevolence, the universalism, the harmony, the order. It wants to rehabilitate destruction and chaos, the infliction of suffering and exploitation, as part of the life to be affirmed. Life properly understood also affirms death and destruction. To pretend otherwise is to try to restrict it, tame it, hem it in, deprive it of its highest manifestations, what makes it something you can say "yes" to.

A religion of life which would proscribe death-dealing, and the infliction of suffering, is confining and demeaning. Nietzsche thinks of himself as having taken up some of the legacy of pre-Platonic and pre-Christian warrior ethics, their exaltation of courage, greatness, élite excellence. And central to that has always been a paradigm place for death. The willingness to face death, the ability to set life lower than honour and reputation, has always been the mark of the warrior, his claim to superiority.[21] Modern life-affirming humanism breeds pusillanimity. This accusation frequently recurs in the culture of counter-Enlightenment.

Of course, one of the fruits of this counter-culture was Fascism—to which Nietzsche's influence was not entirely foreign, however true and valid is Walter Kaufman's refutation of the simple myth of Nietzsche as a proto-Nazi. But in spite of this, the fascination with death and violence recurs, e.g., in the interest in Bataille, shared by Derrida and Foucault. James Miller's book on Foucault shows the depths of this rebellion against "humanism", as a stifling, confining space one has to break out of.[22]

My point here is not to score off neo-Nietzscheanism, as some kind of antechamber to Fascism. As though any of the main spiritual tendencies of our civilization was totally free of responsibility for Fascism. The point is to allow us to recognize that there is an anti-humanism which rebels precisely against the unrelenting concern with life, the proscription of violence, the imposition of equality.

The Nietzschean understanding of enhanced life, which can fully affirm itself, also in a sense takes us beyond life; and in this it is analogous with other, religious notions of enhanced life (like the New Testament's "eternal life"). But it takes us beyond by incorporating a fascination with the negation of life, with death and suffering. It doesn't acknowledge some supreme good beyond life, and in that sense sees itself rightly as utterly antithetical to religion. The "transcendence" is, once again in an important sense and paradoxically, immanent.

What I have been calling the immanent counter-Enlightenment thus involves a new valorization of, even fascination with death and sometimes violence. It rebels against the exclusive humanism that dominates modern culture. But it also rejects all previous, ontically-grounded understandings of transcendence. If we took account of this, we might perhaps change our picture of modern culture. Instead of seeing it as the scene of a two-sided battle, between "tradition", especially religious tradition, and secular humanism, we might rather see it as a kind of free-for-all, the scene of a three-cornered—perhaps ultimately, a four-cornered—battle.

This would allow us to see how greatly what I've called the nova has expanded; positions have multiplied. Their affinities and oppositions become ever more complex. We have just seen this with materialism and unbelief. But a similar multiplication is taking place in other basic positions, and so the debate swirls on among a wider and wider range of participants, between whom a multiplicity of lateral, cross-cutting affinities arises—such as we sensed above between Pascal (of all people) and one strand of modern materialism, as the nova expands.

4

In the nineteenth century, one might say, unbelief comes of age. It develops a solidity, and a depth, but also and perhaps above all, a variety, a complex of internal differences. So that for many people in many milieux in our day, it can become a world unto itself. That is, for them it circumscribes the horizon of the potentially believable. There are exclusive humanists who are unsure of their position; but the direction from which they feel vulnerable is neo-Nietzschean anti-humanism. Or these "post-modernists" themselves have occasional pangs of doubt when they read John Stuart Mill or Karl Marx. The transcendent is off their map.

This is perhaps a moment, then, to recur to my original question: what has changed between 1500, when unbelief was virtually impossible, and (just about)

2000, when there are not only lots of happy atheists, but in certain milieux faith is bucking a powerful current?

Our discussion of the modern cosmic imaginary has helped us to understand this further. At our starting point in 1500, the enchanted world, in which nature and social life were interwoven with higher times, left little room for unbelief. Theologians distinguished between the natural and the supernatural level, but it was not possible to live experientially with one's awareness confined to the first. Spirits, forces, powers, higher times were always obtruding.

With the disenchantment of the world, and the marginalization of higher times, this kind of extrusion of the higher became in principle possible. But it was held off by the sense that the inspiration, strength and discipline we needed to re-order this world as disenchanted and moral came to us from God. It came as grace in individual lives, and it came as divinely ordained disciplines and structures in public life. And central to both individual morality and public order was a sense of a cosmic disposition of things which was providentially established by God for our good.

God was in our conscience, in our social order, in our cosmos; not in the obtrusive fashion of the immediate experience of certain things, places and times, as in the enchanted world; but rather as the ordering power which made sense of the shape of things in morality, society and world.

So the immediate encounter with spirits and forces gives way, but this opens space for that much more powerful a sense of God's ordering will. And indeed, it is partly our sense of this ordering will which has driven enchantment to the margins.

With the anthropocentric turn, this sense of God's ordering presence begins to fade. The sense begins to arise that we can sustain the order on our own. For some, God retreats to a distance, in the beginning or the end (Deists); for others, he fades altogether. Others again aggressively deny him.

The shift in cosmic imaginaries intensifies and completes this undermining of our sense of ordering presence. It is not just that this presence was over-heavily identified with the early modern apologetics of design. It is also that the vast, unfathomable universe in its dark abyss of time makes it all too possible to lose sight of this ordering presence altogether. Indeed, it can make it hard to hang on to this idea.

Our sense of the universe is not unequivocal, as I tried to explain earlier. It can occlude all sense of order and meaning, but it also can be the locus of powerful spiritual meanings. When these are denied, the result is often a narrow and philistine scientism. But if we are open to them, the outcomes can be very varied: read one way, in an Epicurean-naturalist direction, they lead us towards a deep and rich materialism; taken another way, they can open us to a range of spirituality, and for some people, to God.

But if one goes one of the first two ways—either refusing the meanings, or taking them in the Epicurean-naturalist sense—then one can indeed live in a world which seems to proclaim everywhere the absence of God. It is a universe whose outer limits touch nothing but absolute darkness; a universe with its corresponding human world in which we can really experience Godlessness.

This is not the way in which our forebears in 1500 could experience spirits and powers, in an encounter with particular things and places. It is more like the way our (élite) forebears in 1700 experienced God's ordering presence, that is, as a diffuse, structuring principle, rather than an object which can be foregrounded.

But it is different from this again, because it is the sense of an absence; it is the sense that all order, all meaning comes from us. We encounter no echo outside. In the world read this way, as so many of our contemporaries live it, the natural/supernatural distinction is no mere intellectual abstraction. A race of humans has arisen which has managed to experience its world entirely as immanent. In some respects, we may judge this achievement as a victory for darkness, but it is a remarkable achievement nonetheless.

11 Nineteenth-Century Trajectories

It would be ideal if we could follow the development of the nova in the late nineteenth and early twentieth centuries, because it is then that the alternatives open to unbelief are multiplied and enriched, prior to their diffusion to society as a whole in the process I'm calling "super-nova", which mainly takes place after the Second World War.

Here the trajectories differ significantly between national cultures. A really satisfactory account would have to follow all of these. But alas, I lack the space and the competence, and probably the reader lacks the patience, to accomplish this. And so I want to concentrate on a couple of interesting, illustrative cases. I will look first at England (sometimes also Britain, but mainly England) from roughly 1840 to 1940. And then I will take a brief look at France around the turn of the twentieth century. After which I will turn in the next part to try to draw some general conclusions about the coming of the "secular age" in the West.

1

The early nineteenth century saw a resurgence in belief and practice associated with the Evangelicals, and partly driven by the shock of the Revolutionary and Napoleonic Wars. But in the 1830s, orthodox belief among intellectual and social élites comes once again under pressure. Some of the same philosophical considerations were at work as earlier. Philosophical Radicalism, with its Utilitarian principles, was very much an intellectual product of the eighteenth century. But as I mentioned earlier (Chapter 10, section 2), we should perhaps see the new regression of Christian faith rather as a reprise than as a simple continuation of the developments of the previous century. That's because the line of attack was in some ways new. The old arguments continued, but they were supplemented by a new approach.

An important retreat occurred; so that by mid-century John Stuart Mill (true, not quite a neutral observer) could say that "the old opinions in religion, morals and politics, are so much discredited in the more intellectual minds as to have lost the greater part of their efficacy for good."[1] But one of the most important vectors by which this roll back occurred was new to the age. We can perhaps best understand it as the resolution of a cross-pressure which many people felt at the time. It is the one I described in the previous section between the seemingly inescapable idea of an impersonal order, on one hand, and the need above all to avoid the flatness, the emptiness, the fragmentation, which only too obviously seemed to accompany the social and cultural order which was emerging around them, on the other. The pull to impersonality dictated or reflected a rejection of orthodox Christianity; but in face of what seemed like the loss of so many crucial goods, it seemed imperative to save certain values of historical Christianity.

Thus for many whatever in the traditional faith went beyond or contradicted the notion of impersonal order was no longer believable; but at the same time, their sense of the weaknesses, ugliness, or evils of their age forbade them to accept the more reductive, scientist or Utilitarian modes of order.

A good reason for looking at the advance of unbelief in these terms is the influence and impact of Carlyle. This is hard to understand today, not just because of Carlyle's over-the-top polemical style (that might of itself keep us interested), but largely because at the end of his career he attacked some of the most basic values of modern liberalism, and this makes him hard to forgive. Indeed, one can argue that his eclipse occurred very shortly after his death.[2] But in the 1830s and 40s, he was immensely popular. When I speak here of a vector of the advance of unbelief, I mean that Carlyle's solution to the cross-pressures which he was responding to provided the bridge by which many members of the élite public could distance themselves from their ancestral faith. In this, he was followed by Arnold, who in a certain sense extended the bridge, or rebuilt it in a rather different, in the end more palatable way. (Another bridge of this kind was offered by George Eliot, again following in the wake of Carlyle.)

In giving Carlyle such a central role, I am deviating from what is often seen as the standard story of the Victorians' loss of faith. Somewhat oversimplifying, this is thought to have been caused by the impact of Darwinian evolution, which is held so directly to have refuted the Bible. This created an agonizing conflict for many people of devout upbringing, which was in the end resolved by many, often with a poignant sense of loss, by the abandonment of their faith. There is some truth in this story, especially about the agonizing, and sense of loss (which seems to have been felt by Darwin himself). But it leaves out something crucial: that evolutionary theory didn't emerge in a world where almost everyone still took the Bible story simply and literally; that among other things, this world was already strongly marked by the ideas of impersonal order, not to speak of the dark abyss of time; and that an influential formulation had already been given to the displacement of Christianity by a cosmic vision of impersonal order, that of Carlyle.

This doesn't mean that Darwin was without impact. His theory gave an important push towards a materialist, reductive view of the cosmos, from which all teleology was purged (because explained away on a deeper level). But it enters a field in which many people had already felt the pull of the primacy of impersonal order; it did not initiate this pull on its own.

Carlyle, formed in large part by Goethe, and partly through him by Schiller and the German Romantics,[3] reacted against all those features of Christianity uncombinable with impersonal order: the crucial importance of a personal relation to God, particular providences, Divine judgment as a personal decision of God, and above all, miracles (those "old Hebrew clothes").[4] Moreover, he didn't understand this as his own personal reaction. He shared the view which I described in an earlier chapter, based on a stadial conception of history, that the pieces he rejected were basically unacceptable to the mind of his age, however much some people, in their failure to understand their times, hung on to them. Whatever could be saved in Christianity couldn't be preserved in that form. "The Mythus of the Christian Religion looks not in the eighteenth Century as it did in the eighth"; who will help us "to embody the divine Spirit of that Religion in a new Mythus, in a new vehicle and vesture, that our Souls, otherwise too like perishing, may live?"[5] As we can already guess from the invocation of the term 'myth', the doctrines of this new form were not very definite, but they seemed to involve the existence of some not purely human spiritual force, which could help humanity to move forward to higher forms of life. They involved some form of Providence, History, Moral Absolutes, as Wilson puts it.[6] These higher forms would allow us really to affirm the goodness and rightness of all being, in what Carlyle called "the everlasting Yea".

This faith was of the greatest importance to Carlyle, because otherwise the trends of the time pointed towards a degradation of human life: the ugliness and egoism of commercial-industrial society, the atomism and lack of common concern that this society bred, held together only by the "cash nexus", the absence of any larger, more heroic perspective on life, beyond a myopic hedonism, which it tends to inculcate in us. (Carlyle, prefiguring Nietzsche, sarcastically defines organized philanthropy as "the Universal Abolition of Pain Association".) In this age, the universe and society appear as merely mechanical, devoid of meaning. "To me the Universe was all void of Life, of Purpose, of Volition, even of Hostility; it was one huge, dead, immeasurable Steam-engine, rolling on, in its dead indifference, to grind me limb from limb. O the vast, Gloomy, solitary Golgotha, and Mill of Death."[7] Everything, even the sublimest issues, are being reduced to calculation: "Benthamee Utility, virtue by profit and Loss; reducing this God's-World to a dead brute Steam-engine, the infinite celestial Soul of Man to a kind of Hay-balance for weighing hay and thistles on, pleasures and pains on."[8]

All this would be unbearable, if there weren't some assurance that we could move to a higher stage. We can see here reflected a broad brace of those dissatisfactions with the buffered identity and modern order that I distinguished in the different "axes" of an earlier chapter. But in particular, we see reflected in the last quote axis I.2 in my scheme, the need to rescue some sense of the human potential for spiritual/moral ascent, in face of the degrading theory and practice of utilitarian-commercial-industrial society.

One had thus to be both against Christianity and for it. Carlyle's (not very definite) doctrine was a resolution of this cross-pressure. And the tension was reflected in his own life, in his inability to tell his devout mother straight out that he had abandoned his faith. The formulation he offered, that he had not abandoned, but redefined it, gave some colour to the attempted deception (but not much).

Arnold follows after, in his own way, and responds to the same pulls. The old faith is unbelievable, but much of what it offered is essential. An atomized commercial society is threatened with "anarchy", and only the diffusion of high culture can combat this. The inculcation of this culture by a clerisy is very much like the maintenance of certain forms of worship by a national church. The two enterprises can be seen as overlapping, and in this way Arnold too could tell his mother that he was carrying on the work of his Broad Church father.

Arnold lost the faith he was brought up in during his early 20s, and that for the reasons which we have already seen in Carlyle. But this was not an easy step for him, for reasons analogous to Carlyle's. On the personal level, he was distancing himself from his father, who was a strongly committed Broad Church Anglican. But more, he felt that the decline of that faith he could no longer accept had brought terrible consequences in its wake.

Arnold felt acutely a sense that the modern world lacked depth, and the modern self, wholeness. We tend to live on the surface, and are therefore cut off from the greater currents of meaning which could transform our lives: "you must plunge yourself down to the depths of the sea of intuition; all other men are trying as far as in them lies to keep you at the barren surface."[9]

This sense of being cut off from some great source can also be felt as a division from self: "The misery of the present age is not in the intensity of men's suffering—but in their incapacity to suffer, enjoy, feel at all, wholly and profoundly . . . in their having one moment the commencement of a feeling, at the next moment the commencement of an imagination, & the eternal tumult of the world mingling, breaking in upon, hurrying away all. . . . The disease of the world is divorce from oneself".[10]

As Honan puts it, Arnold concluded that "man lacks a deep identity; he suffers from disorientation and ennui, shifting and unsatisfying feelings, shallowness of being, dissatisfaction with his own endeavours . . . debilities caused by the lack of any compelling authority for the spiritual life".[11]

Arnold felt to the full what I called in Chapter 8, section 2, the absence of resonance in the modern world, and he felt it particularly through the axes of the "Romantic" dimension; a sense of ourselves as divided, cut off from a great stream of life without. Like Carlyle, an important source for him was Goethe and the thinkers of the Romantic period. And like them as well, he saw a healing power in beauty; in practice in literature, and what he came to define as "culture".

This was not just the tragedy of the lone thinker, or person of exceptional awareness and feeling. The emptiness was reflected in the age. We live in a civilization that values the mechanical and material, that encourages narrow specialization for advantage, and encourages individual action without a sense of the whole. In England, this latter fault was at its most serious: "we are in danger of drifting towards anarchy. We have not the notion, so familiar on the Continent and to antiquity, of the *State*—the nation in its collective and corporate character, entrusted with stringent powers for the general advantage, and controlling individual wills in the name of an interest wider than individuals."[12]

This civilization was both philistine and atomistic. A fragmented society was the counterpart to a fragmented self. Arnold takes up the basic idea of Schiller in his *Aesthetic Education*.

This fragmentation and loss of depth is part of the price we pay for the ending of the Christian era. Arnold is as clear and sure as Carlyle that this is not a personal option of his, but reflects a change in epoch, which no one can in the end gainsay. His later poem, "Obermann once More",[13] lays out a kind of capsule sketch of our spiritual history. After the flowering of the pagan period, with its great achievements and beauty, a sense of "secret loathing fell / Deep weariness and sated lust / Made human life a hell" (ll. 94–96). But Christianity came, and conferred a great boon on the world. The Obermann figure cries:

'Oh, had I lived in that great day,
How had its glory new
Filled earth and heaven, and caught away
My ravished spirit too!

'No thoughts that to the world belong
Had stood against the wave
Of love which set so deep and strong
From Christ's then open grave.' (ll. 141–148)

. . . . .

'While we believed, on earth he went,
And open stood his grave,
Men called from chamber, church, and tent;
And Christ was by to save.

'Now he is dead! Far hence he lies
In the lorn Syrian town;
And on his grave, with shining eyes,
The Syrian stars look down.

'In vain men still, with hoping new,
Regard his death-place dumb,
And say the stone is not yet to,
And wait for words to come.' (ll. 169–180)

. . . . .

'Its frame yet stood without a breach
When blood and warmth were fled;
And still it spake its wonted speech—
But every word was dead.' (ll. 193–196)

Arnold's profound ambivalence, his sense of the impossibility of faith, whose departure has nonetheless left a great void, comes out most forcefully in the "Stanzas from the Grande Chartreuse".[14] The speaker feels, for all his powerful sense of sympathy, that he cannot return to the world in which the monastery's life of prayer played such an important part.

For rigorous teachers seized my youth,
And purged my faith, and trimmed its fire,
Showed me the high, white star of Truth,
There bade me gaze, and there aspire.
Even now their whispers pierce my gloom:
What dost thou in this living tomb?

Forgive me, masters of the mind!
At whose behest I long ago
So much unlearnt, so much resigned—
I come not here to be your foe!
I seek these anchorites, not in ruth,
To curse and to deny your truth;

Not as their friend, or child, I speak!
But as, on some far northern strand,

Thinking of his own Gods, a Greek
In pity and mournful awe might stand
Before some fallen Runic stone—
For both were faiths, and both are gone.

Wandering between two worlds, one dead,
The other powerless to be born,
With nowhere yet to rest my head,
Like these, on earth I wait forlorn.
Their faith, my tears, the world deride—
I come to shed them at their side. (ll. 67–90)

Arnold gives expression here to a very widely felt sentiment, certainly in the Europe of the early nineteenth century, but in some ways also today. As Lionel Trilling points out,[15] there were various ways of responding to this sense of, as it were, self-legislated, yet nevertheless irrevocable abandonment. One way is to explore this condition of despair, almost to wallow in it, as in their different ways do Goethe's Werther, Chateaubriand's René, and Senancour's Obermann. Modern melancholy seeks in these works for its definition; and the plangent picture at least provides this. Another response is titanic action, defiant, possibly even destructive and immoral; the kind of self-affirmation we see in Byron. This in a certain way answers the concerns of what I called above the "tragic" axis.

Arnold recognizes both these roads, and they are mentioned in this poem. One of them, the first, had a strong attraction for him, and he dwelt lovingly on it. But both are rejected here; the second a little dismissively: "What helps it now, that Byron bore, / . . . The pageant of his bleeding heart?" (ll. 133, 136); while the first is parted from with regret:

Or are we easier, to have read,
O Obermann, the sad stern page,
Which tells us how thou hidd'st thy head
From the fierce tempest of thine age
In the lone brakes of Fontainebleau,
Or chalets near the Alpine snow? (ll. 145–150)

But there is also a third path: the search for a new age of faith, a new positive form of religion. Here is where Carlyle, Arnold, Emerson situate themselves.

I can't go into great detail here, but Arnold's hope was that the new age, at present "powerless to be born", could be brought nearer by literature and education. "Culture" is what Arnold came to count on to wreak this change. This means Culture defined as "a pursuit of our total perfection by means of getting to know, on all matters which most concern us, the best which has been thought and said in the world; and through this knowledge, turning a stream of fresh and free thought upon our stock notions and habits, which we now follow staunchly and mechanically."[16] Our perfection means the growth of our humanity, as against our animality. It consists in "the ever-increasing efficacy and in the general harmonious expansion of those gifts of thought and feeling, which make the particular dignity, wealth and happiness of human nature."[17] This perfection is to be realized not just in the isolated individual; rather the goal is to bring about "a *harmonious* perfection, developing all sides of our humanity", which would also be "a *general* perfection, developing all parts of our society."[18] Culture in this sense was close to religion, but could not be subordinated to it. "Culture, disinterestedly seeking in its aim at perfection to see things as they really are, shows us how worthy and divine a thing is the religious side in man, though it is not the whole of man."[19]

But the two are brought closer together when, late in life, Arnold defines religion as "morality touched with emotion"; and describes God as "the enduring power, not ourselves, which makes for righteousness".[20] The consubstantiality of this religion with the code which springs from an impersonal order is evident, as is the attempt to retain some vestige of transcendence (through the expression "not ourselves").

But this attempted resolution of the dilemma was a hope, which didn't attenuate the powerful sense of division and loss, which resonates throughout the poetry, and must have been felt by the man.

It is worth looking at one more document here, a novel which had an immense success both in Britain and America at the end of the nineteenth and beginning of the twentieth century. The novel is *Robert Elsmere,* and the author is Mrs. Humphry Ward, a niece of Matthew Arnold.[21] The protagonist, Elsmere, is an Anglican clergyman who loses his faith in orthodox Christianity. But instead of falling into indifference, or even becoming an open enemy of Christianity (or even worse, cynically carrying on a comfortable career as a clergyman, hiding his true beliefs), he struggles to an Arnoldian position. He wants to redefine the faith, free of its—now indefensible—supernatural myths, and make it once more the vehicle by which humans can accede to a higher moral life.

In a moment of great inner turmoil and suffering at the loss of his early faith, Robert sees the new vision, of a "purely human Christ—a purely human, explicable, yet always wonderful Christianity" (321). He finds that he believes in Christ "in the teacher, the martyr, the symbol to us Westerns of all things heavenly and abiding, the image and pledge of the invisible life of the spirit—with all my soul and mind!" But he cannot accept "the Man-God, the Word from Eternity—. . . a wonder-working Christ, in a risen and ascended Jesus, in the living Intercessor and Mediator for the lives of his doomed brethren" (342).

He believes in God, but this God is something like an impersonal force. He is "an Eternal Goodness—and an Eternal Mind—of which Nature and Man are the continuous and only revelation" (494). Here the author seems to have borrowed less from her uncle, and more from the philosopher T. H. Green. Green appears in the story, under the (rather transparent) name "Grey", a fellow of Robert's college in Oxford, who befriends him and acts as his mentor at crucial moments. Green's philosophy emerged as well out of the same cross-pressures that I have been describing. On the one hand, a strong reaction against Hume and Utilitarianism, as theories which deny the human potentiality for moral ascent; on the other hand, an inability to accept God as a supernatural agent, intervening in human history. Green found in the work of Kant and Hegel a way of articulating his position. God was in a sense the lodestone which draws us higher, and also the ontic guarantee that this ascent will be possible. But the ascent is towards an impersonal moral order, prefigured in Hegel's notion of Geist, rather than in the God of Abraham, Isaac and Jacob.

As Robert puts it from his deathbed: "*personality,* or *intelligence,* or what not! What meaning can they have as applied to *God?*" (603).

But we need God: "Love and revere *something* we must, if we are to be men and not beasts" (498–499). And this God is not only indispensable for personal moral ascent. We also need him if we are to find a way of binding together our society. Here he takes up a crucial theme for Arnold. We need a new religion, because we need "a new social bond". We need it, for "that diminution of the self in man which is to enable the individual to see the *world's* ends clearly, and to care not only for his but for his neighbour's interest, which is to make the rich devote themselves to the poor, and the poor bear with the rich. . . . It is man's will which is eternally defective, eternally inadequate. Well, the great religions of the world are the stimulants by which the power at the root of things has worked upon this sluggish instrument of human destiny. Without religion you cannot make the will equal to its tasks. Our present religion fails us; we must, we will have another!" (572).

In Arnoldian terms, religion is portrayed here as the essential bulwark of Culture against Anarchy.

The novel, as we can see, contains lots of intellectual exchanges on a very high level. How did it nevertheless manage to be a runaway best-seller? Because it portrays so vividly the inner conflict, the intense suffering, which accompanied this de-conversion and reconstruction. It is not only that Robert is dismayed himself by the need to abandon his early faith. His marriage to Catherine is almost destroyed by it. Catherine is herself deeply anchored in an orthodox Evangelical position. For her there is nothing between cleaving to this faith on one hand, and open, scoffing disbelief on the other. She can't see the point of Robert's reconstructed religion of a purely human Jesus. "How can that help them? . . . Your historical Christ, Robert, will never win souls. If he was God, every word you speak will insult him. If he was man, he was not a good man!" (480).

The novel is set in the mid-1880s, and reflects the times. Thus Robert's early faith follows a contemporary trend, the reaction against the "overdriven rationalism" of Mill and Spencer among many young people of the time (62–63). And again, it is clear that the crucial issues that his de-conversion turns on are not those of natural science and evolution, but those raised by Biblical scholarship. It is these that are pressed on him by Roger Wendover, the squire-scholar who is the major agent of the change.[22] The crucial question might be said to be that of miracles, but in a broad sense; that is, not just the miracles performed by the Christ of the Gospels, but all the Christological doctrines which affirm divine intervention in history: the Incarnation, the Resurrection and Ascension, atonement and intercession, etc. And the squire in his arguments is firmly in the space in which Trevor-Roper placed Gibbon; "My object has been to help in making it discreditable . . . to refuse to read . . . Christian documents in the light of trained scientific criticism" (318). In other words, the "same social laws" are to be applied to all historical events, including those foundational to Christianity. The assumption is that we, in our rational age of impersonal orders, know perfectly well what these laws are, and have nothing to learn from first-century Palestinian fishermen. The squire is writing a "History of Testimony", which has a clear master narrative, in which science emerges out of earlier ignorance and irrationality (317–318).

The novel illustrates the force of this historicized framework, in which history is read as an ascent to a consciousness of impersonal orders, on which there is no turning back. Or rather, that is my reading; it would seem that Mrs. Ward accepts this framework as an unquestioned background of her own thinking. The novel, read in the way I am suggesting, can help us break free from that. But it also helps us break free of an equal and opposite simplification, and this is one which Mrs. Ward plainly wanted to challenge.

Where the Wendovers think their judgments are unproblematically scientific and rational, many of the orthodox of the day saw this kind of apostasy in equally stark terms as the simple fruit of pride. It is related that Mrs. Ward attended the first set of Bampton Lectures in 1881, at which the speaker, himself a nephew of Wordsworth, explained the abandonment of orthodox Christianity by a number of intellectual faults, including indolence, coldness, recklessness, pride, and avarice. It was this attack which spurred Mrs. Ward to write her novel, which would show that this was a caricature.[23] And indeed, what emerges from the novel is that good faith and honesty can be found on all sides of this controversy, even though the story awards the ultimate palm for courage and integrity to Robert.

This is a place where I might clarify further my own understanding of these conversions and deconversions. I cannot accept the Whiggish master narrative that they are determined by clear reason. They look rational within a certain framework, indeed, but this framework attracts us for a host of reasons, including ethical ones. Among the ethical attractions is certainly that of the free, invulnerable, disengaged agent. Being one of these is something in which moderns take a certain pride. But to leap from this to saying, simply, that the move from orthodoxy is actuated by pride is quite invalid. In some cases, undoubtedly. But what we're dealing with in talking of these frameworks is complex environing backgrounds of our thought and action, which impinge on our lives in a host of ways. In one respect, yes, this modern sense of impersonal orders can give us a sense of our dignity as free agents. But it also offers us powerful ideals, of honesty and integrity, as well as of benevolence and solidarity, just to name some of the most prominent. In the whole aetiological story of how these frameworks arose, pride has its place. But in individual cases, the stories can be as many and as different as there are people who inhabit them. In some cases, for a variety of reasons, the sense of an alternative was so far off the screen, that the principal response was determined by the ideals: say, honesty, integrity, and a sense of the human potential for moral ascent. This is what one sees with T. H. Green; and this is what Mrs. Ward shows us in her protagonist.

We are in fact all acting, thinking, and feeling out of backgrounds and frameworks which we do not fully understand. To ascribe total personal responsibility to us for these is to want to leap out of the human condition. At the same time, no background leaves us utterly without room for movement and change. The realities of human life are messier than is dreamed of either by dogmatic rationalists, or in the manichean rigidities of embattled orthodoxy.

But what Mrs. Ward shows best of all is the intense anguish of the cross-pressures here. As with Carlyle and Arnold, so with Robert Elsmere: the agony cannot just be explained by the rational considerations that were in play: the impersonal order pushes to deny Christianity, the need for some purpose or direction in history calls for it. There also were deep personal emotions involved, as we see in Carlyle's exchange with his mother. The pain was often great of deserting a childhood faith. As Wilson says in describing this retreat of belief, "this is a story of bereavement as much as of adventure".[24]

These reflections of Carlyle and Arnold were the bridges which people started to cross out of Christianity to some religion of impersonal order, before their structure was shaken by the controversy over evolution, which threatened one side of the synthesis—the saving of (impersonalized) Christianity as a bulwark against materialism and reductivism. This crisis eventually pointed the way to other compromises, which promised to save the (moral and cultural) furniture from the burning (theological) house.

But in the short run, it upped the ante. I have described the controversy between science and faith in Victorian times in the previous chapter, and what I think were the decisive considerations which settled it, one way or another. Briefly, my point is that it was not so much the science which decided things, as it was a battle between two understandings of our epistemological predicament, tinged with moral import, and related to images of adulthood and childishness. But the issue of theodicy also played a role. It already had in the earlier, pre-Darwin phase: the more austere faith of Carlyle in something like a direction of history could accommodate without difficulty Lisbon earthquakes, and this was seen as part of its superiority to Christianity.

But the Darwinian picture tended to shatter even those theories of general design which concentrated on the benevolent over-all drift of things. We have not just nature "red in tooth and claw", but a system which operates through extinctions, through the winnowing of the unfit. This could be very shaking to Christian faith, but it also undermined the more impersonal conception of Providence, as a cosmically-anchored vector in history towards higher modes of being. In the end, it is this kind of view, involving a world-soul or cosmic force, which seems to have suffered, more than orthodox Christianity. Not that there are not many people today who believe in a God conceived as an impersonal force; contemporary surveys show this (as we will see in the next chapter); and popular movies invoke it ("The Force be with you"). But as an explicitly espoused, intellectually defended view, it has greatly receded, where atheist materialism and orthodox Christianity still polemic against each other.

This may have partly to do with the theodicy issue. As I argued earlier (Chapter 7), while the issue of theodicy may always be raised in a theistic context, there are certain conditions for its being felt as a real problem, which have not always been met. Pressed by a sense of menace, both natural (famine, disease) and spiritual (devils, goblins, wood spirits, etc.), the pre-modern in an enchanted world could be more concerned with appealing to God as helper, or saviour, while acknowledging that it was quite beyond her to explain how things had come to this pass. The idea of blaming God gets a clearer sense and becomes much more salient in the modern era where people begin to think they know just what God was purposing in creating the world, and can check the results against the intention. The issue as posed in an atheist context inherits this clarity; only now it is we who are setting the standards, while assuming that what we know and can discern about human fate is all there is to know—in particular that there is nothing after or beyond our traceable life-path here, or that if there were, it would have to be of such and such a nature. God is set up to flunk the atheist exam, as surely as He was set up to pass that of Providential Deism with flying colours.

The atheist and the Deist are arguing within similar frameworks: we know the standards, and we know what happens to people. And they can thus score points against each other. And when we look at the most horrifying sides of nature and history, it is the atheist who tends to score. For the Christian, these arguments to a negative theodicy, a condemnation of any God who might claim to exist, are deeply disturbing, as is indeed, any tragic event seen up close: the death of a loved one, for example. But they realize that they are helpless to argue against these accusations. To do so, one would have to know, that means be able to exhibit or demonstrate, things we will never know. The case for the defense depends on there being more to human fate than we can exhibit as undeniable in history: that these people died in the earthquake, and those in gas chambers, and no-one came to rescue them. Christians can only reply to the accusations with hope.

In a sense, the only possible stance for a Christian is to recover something like the pre-modern one I described above, to see God as helper, and not cruel puppet-master. Only where earlier this was often adopted naïvely, that is, without the sense that there was an alternative, it now has to be recovered in full awareness. This is perhaps what Dostoyevsky was telling us in *The Brothers Karamazov*, in the dialogue between Ivan and Alyosha which culminates in the "Legend of the Grand Inquisitor". Ivan has all the arguments; Alyosha's only response is to be profoundly perturbed: "Blasphemy", he says; or pitiful attempts to deflect the force of the arguments. But the ultimate issue is, which stance can begin to transform the savage and cruel plight which Ivan so tellingly describes? The rest of the novel is meant to offer an answer to this question.

Theodicy thus may have played some role in the recession of these theories of cosmic force. But this cannot be the whole story. Perhaps the crucial point was this: as attempts to hold on to some of the force of Christian piety, while dropping the Christian God of personal agency, these middle positions didn't have the staying power. In the end they could win minds but not hearts.

This judgment gets some support, if we look beyond Britain for a moment to France. The "Religion of Humanity", if we take this in a broad sense, including Saint-Simon and the various offshoots of his movement, as well as Comte and his positivism, could be seen as another such attempt to retain some of the force of Christian piety while denying the dogmatic basis for it. Like Carlyle and Arnold, too, they found some of the sources of their new religion in German thought of the Romantic period. Only here the compromise didn't lie on the ontological plane, as it were, scaling God down to some cosmic force, rather the attempt was to keep the institutions, practices and attitudes of piety, without any of the dogma at all. Comte proposed to institute a hierarchy and sacraments, to offer a series of rituals for the crucial transition moments in life. He was ready in a sense to match Catholicism point for point. But the doctrinal core centred on Humanity, and its Progress through science.

Positivism did take off as a movement and quasi-religion, and even played an important role in Mexico (Porfirio Diaz was a positivist), and Brazil. But in the longer run, it withered away. The ritual couldn't sustain itself on such a weak basis, any more than that of the French Revolutionaries, complete with festivals and calendar, had been able to.

Perhaps we might think of Carlyle and Comte in another European context, that of the powerful personalities of the Romantic era which had such an impact on the thought, life and art of the nineteenth century and beyond; people like Wagner, Bakunin, Marx, Berlioz, Hugo.[25] Each was responding to some part of that range of dissatisfactions of the age, articulated in the "axes" of Chapter 8, in lines of attack which differed but over-lapped, and which included the emptiness, lack of beauty, division from self and nature, atomism, and injustice of the contemporary world, and this is what gave them their impact on this world. Only Comte, Marx and Bakunin started movements, and only Marx's had staying power, although Wagner and Hugo remain important figures in our canon to this day. But the point of the comparison is that the only cases in which their outlook could be seen as continuing today (perhaps only Marx is in this category) lie at the materialist end of the spectrum. As has often been pointed out, militant Marxism has very often taken on some of the trappings of a religion, but it has done so while vigorously denying that this is what it is about. And as we enter the twenty-first century, the staying power even of this quasi-religion seems in sharp decline.

Of course, at the turn of the twentieth century, we see Hardy recurring to a Prime Force underlying the universe. But this is already in a different moral space than Carlyle and Arnold. The Prime Will can be seen as blind and cruel. And although Hardy late in life puts forward the notion that it may grow and improve along with the humans whose lives it has so roughly handled, we have moved into the company of Schopenhauer (who influenced Hardy), rather than of the Goethe-plus-Transcendental-Idealism which inspired Carlyle. And even then, this meta-physical-cosmological dimension of Hardy's thought has been largely forgotten in the reception of his novels and poetry.

So dogmatic-metaphysical compromises between Christianity and materialism, based on the modern sense of an impersonal immanent order, don't seem to have a very long shelf life. Or do appearances deceive? If, as I want to argue, these compromises arise from a deep cross-pressure, between the unacceptability of Christianity for those who have deeply internalized the immanent order (or come to see themselves totally within it), on one hand, and a strong dissatisfaction with the flatness, emptiness of the world, and/or the inner division, atomism, ugliness or self-enclosed nature of human life in modernity, on the other; then we might ask, where has the second set of considerations gone in an age where materialism is incomparably stronger than in the nineteenth century, and seemingly without major rivals outside of orthodox religion? Does this mean that the second set of considerations no longer weigh with many people? That, unlike these great nineteenth-century prophets, we have adjusted to the purely immanent world?

Certainly some people have, or at least understand themselves to have so adjusted. One master narrative of "secularization" would hold that there is a trend here, and that more and more people will just turn away altogether from the issues to which Goethe, Carlyle, Hardy, etc., in one way, and orthodox Christianity, in another, offer answers.[26] Certainly more people would declare themselves in this category than in the nineteenth century. But the evidence of a continuing trend here doesn't seem strong. The sense of emptiness, flatness, the dissatisfactions raised in the whole group of resonance axes, seem still with us. Rebellions occur among the younger generation, of which the most spectacular in recent times was that of the 1960s. Surveys tell us that lots of people still situate themselves in this metaphysical middle ground, where they accept some impersonal force at work in the universe and/or their lives. The short shelf life of these compromise metaphysics is a phenomenon of the intellectual-academic world, on one hand, and that of religious-ideological institutions on the other. There is an important disconnect between these on one side, and the spiritual life of people in general on the other. This will be explored (even if not satisfactorily explained) in the next chapter.

But still we might ask the question again: where has the set of dissatisfactions of the Romantic age gone among contemporary materialists? Are they all unproblematically adjusted? And the answer here too, seems to be negative. The need to articulate a sense of something fuller, deeper, often drawing on the same Romantic sources, continues, as we see with Hardy, and those who continue to draw on him today. Only it has to be reinterpreted, so as to disconnect it from any extra-human source. I will return to this below.

2

At the same time as these conceptions of impersonal order on the cosmic level, variants of the modern order of mutual benefit, as well as the reactions against it, have played an important role in the development of what I'm calling the nova, the multiplication of new options around the polemic between belief and unbelief in the last two centuries. Thus the picture of order invoked in the American Declaration of Independence, which foregrounds the notion of inalienable rights, was originally placed within a version of what I called "Providential Deism". Human beings were "endowed by their Creator" with these rights. The order was providential, designed by God. This would eventually feed a social imaginary in which the sovereign nation was "one people under God": although divided by denominations, its unity was grounded in belief in this benign Creator who designed human beings for this free way of life.

This theistic underpinning has since fragmented. For a lot of Americans, the reference to God is irrelevant, even threatening. But the original social imaginary continues among important segments of the population.

One could argue that there was a somewhat analogous social imaginary in British society, in which its law and free institutions were identified with Protestant Christianity, itself tightly identified with an ethic of "decency". This too has now fragmented, but has by no means entirely disappeared.

In these "Anglo-Saxon" societies, and in other similar ones, the modern idea of an order of equal-rights-bearing individuals, related so as to further mutual benefit, has gradually colonized the social imaginary. It takes over and gives a new meaning to traditional features of the polity, like representative institutions and the primacy of law. In so doing, it replaces earlier visions of order, which are hierarchical and holist, rather than individualist and egalitarian.

The modern idea of order animates a social imaginary which presents society as a "horizontal" reality, to which each has direct access, created and sustained by common action in secular time, as we see in forms like the public sphere, the market economy, the sovereign people. By contrast, the earlier "vertical" vision presents society as articulated into hierarchically-ordered parts, which determine the identity of those who make them up, so that they relate to the whole only mediatedly, through the part. They belong to the kingdom as lord or peasant, clergy or layperson, member of an order or corporation. This complex unity is not created by the secular action of its members, but precedes them. It is grounded in the order of things itself (like the kingdom with the "Two Bodies"), or else is there since time out of mind. The polity requires the hierarchy, and particularly its apex, in order to be. Without the King, there is no France; the kingdom only holds together as an entity under its monarch.

The story of the last three centuries has been the sometimes gradual, sometimes rapid replacement of the vertical model with the horizontal one. This can be gradual, and can even pass in some respects unnoticed, because the lived social imaginary of peoples or groups is a complex thing, and can combine what may ultimately seem incompatible elements, sometimes sliding from one to another without much fuss, almost it seems without explicit awareness, as we see with the American recontextualizing of their representative institutions after the War of Independence in the framework of the new notion of popular sovereignty.

And for similar reasons, the two models can co-exist, as they clearly do in British history. Here we can't say that the difference is unnoticed, because there is an ideological struggle in the eighteenth century, between Tories and Whigs, about how to interpret the body of law and constitutional practice which they for the most part agree on. "Whigs" tend to want to cast the justification for their mixed constitution in terms of a doctrine of contract; they are reaching for the modern model. "Tories" want to stick with some kind of earlier "vertical" model, even sometimes toying with more recent, radicalized versions of this, like the Divine Right of Kings. Their actual political differences are supposedly justified by these different theories, but they also offer different ways of understanding the whole constitution and legal system.

If we move out of the pure sky of theory, it is probable that at the level of social imaginary, many Britons lived in these last centuries in a hybrid world. Social forms, like the public sphere, the market economy, which made sense only on the horizontal model, occupied a growing place in their world. Their political institutions, with successive widenings of the franchise, progressively came to meet the demands of popular sovereignty. And yet the polity itself remained a monarchy, with hierarchical elements, and with much ceremonial invocation of vertical modes of grounding, a church-blessed monarchy rooted in a time out of mind. All this can be held together by a (in its very nature modern) national consciousness, which I described above, in which this constitutional monarchy, the rights and freedoms it enshrines, the Protestant religion, and a certain ethic of "decency" are all seen as inextricably intertwined elements of British identity. In this and similar cases, the erosion of this identity can have important (negative) consequences for belief, as we shall see in the next part.

But within this hybrid, the balance between the elements can slowly and imperceptibly shift. There is, indeed, bound to be a slide, as the forms which embody a modern, horizontal imaginary take up more and more space. At first, the vertical model was the enframing one; England (Britain) was of its essence a monarchy; the horizontal elements fit within this without challenging its fundamental status. Even the challenge to monarchy in the Civil War didn't put this in question; on the contrary, the negative experience of the Commonwealth seems to have strengthened it.

But over time, the balance shifts. In the mid-Victorian period, Republicanism began to be an option for Britons. And although this was beaten back at the time, it has once more become one today. The British social imaginary has become predominantly horizontal. The enframing understanding is of a people (or more than one, if we think in terms of devolution), which has given itself a monarchical constitution, and which could in the future change this. It is this slow slide which is not necessarily noticeable as it happens, but whose direction appears with hindsight as inevitable, granted the spread of modern forms.

In Britain as a whole, the resurgence of belief and practice associated with the Evangelicals in the early part of the nineteenth century helped consolidate the synthesis I mentioned above, between British (or English) identity and a certain kind of piety. This synthesis englobed a certain version of the modern order of freedom and mutual benefit, that variant which was thought to be incorporated in British law and British ways—a certain individualism, conception of rights, parliamentary government, the rule of law—and which contrasted so favourably with the arbitrary and tyrannical forms of government that Continental powers were prone to, particularly the Papist ones. A certain law, a certain morality of "decency" were thought to be quintessentially British, and they were also seen as inextricably linked to the kind of freedom-valuing, Protestant Christianity which had grown up in the larger Island (in Ireland, alas, it had failed to take root).

The synthesis thus incorporated three facets: British, Protestant, decent. But it also connected to a fourth. The ideal of civilization which Britons accepted was heavily coloured by it. The notion of "civilization" which develops in modern Europe has a number of facets, as we discussed earlier (Chapter 2). It incorporated on one side economic and technical development: arts, crafts, industry, technology, science; on another sensibility: art, beauty, refinement of feeling and expression, wider consciousness. But then it also had a political dimension: "civilized" societies, as the very word implies, were governed in an orderly way; they had a state, law and order, internal peace, unlike "savage" tribes. Closely connected to this was a fourth, disciplinary dimension: to be civilized means to have internalized a demanding discipline, self-control, high standards of behaviour governed by ethics, manners, and other necessary conventions.

These four facets were thought to be linked, hence the unitary concept. How can you have scientific or economic progress without peace and law? How develop refinement without these? But the third and fourth were thought to be particularly closely linked. Civilized government and the rule of law were the external expressions of a certain mode of self-discipline.

But just because the British saw themselves as having a different kind of government and law than most of their Continental neighbours, they also gave a particular inflection to their notion of civilization. Whereas Europe as a whole was "civilized" in comparison to Asia, let alone Africa, the British variant was itself superior. This national inflection, within a general European sense of superiority, helps explain the unedifying spectacle during the First World War of countries on each side claiming to fight for "civilization", the British against the "Huns", and the Germans against the semi-Asiatic Tsarist hordes.

This close connection between law and discipline reflects the continuing sense that this civilization had been built by deliberate efforts of Reform, that people had been made over in recent history to meet the high demands of "civilized", decent or "Christian" life. That one had reached this level was an unprecedented, still (in global terms) rare, and recent achievement, the fruits in part of intellectual progress, but in even greater measure of organized self-discipline and social transformation. As Macaulay once said, "No ordinary misfortune, no ordinary misgovernment will do so much to make a nation wretched, as the constant progress of physical knowledge and the constant effort of every man to better himself will do to make a nation prosperous."[27] This was part of the background understanding of the European, and more particularly British idea/ideal of civilization.

Now in its original, high-Victorian form, for most people, this was inextricably Christian civilization. Its ethic of discipline and decency, freedom and benevolence was powered for many by an Evangelical Christianity. For Evangelicals, following God meant disciplining the self, creating by constant effort and exercise a character which would suppress the lower drives and strive to benefit mankind. Macaulay's mother enjoined him to strengthen the powers of his mind by exercise so that "in future you will better be able to glorify God with all your powers and talents", and then be received into the "everlasting habitations".[28] The glorifying God with one's talents was to be done mainly through beneficent action. The seriousness of this Evangelical dedication to universal benevolence can be seen in their political achievements, which included successful anti-slavery campaigns on both sides of the Atlantic, as well as—less fortunately—in service in the Empire, devoted to "improvements".[29]

But just as the earlier form of piety I've called "Providential Deism" prepared the ground for an exclusive humanism, so this strenuous Evangelicalism opened the road to an unbelieving philosophy of self-control. The very success in self-remaking encouraged, as the creation of a disciplined, buffered agent invited a reinterpretation in purely human terms.

This was the rewriting of the ethic of self-control which occurs in the high Victorian period through such major figures as Leslie Stephen and John Stuart Mill. This was an ethic of duty and altruism. It had a sense of the polar opposition between the obligation of benevolence, on one hand, and selfish desire on the other, which had affinities to Kant's philosophy.

This is what made this turn to immanence a reprise rather than a straight continuation of the eighteenth-century slide to anthropocentrism. Earlier, it had been all too easy to believe that "self-love and social" were "the same", that human egoism was either neutral, or even predisposed through sympathy to benevolence. But in the nineteenth-century turn, it was recognized that the climb to the new and more stringent ideal of altruism was a hard slog. This is not to say that Evangelicals reverted to the sixteenth-century view that in their society civility had to be inculcated by harsh discipline, against the grain of nature. On the contrary, they tended to assume like their contemporaries that certain basic standards were already met there. It is just that with altruism, the ante was upped. Like others in their day, they understood their predicament historically; that was the framework in which they understood the pre-eminence of British civilization.

But as a general proposition, they believed that character had to be formed by building good habits. This took time, both for the individual to reach the going standard, and for the standard to evolve historically.[30] It required a great effort to build a strong will, and continuing exercise of this to keep selfishness at bay. Egoism was ever a slough into which one could find oneself falling.

This moral psychology of will and struggle reflects the Evangelical outlook out of which the new humanism emerged, of which it was in a sense a transposition into an immanent key. The ever vigilant fight against temptation and weakness, which originally made sense in the Evangelical outlook of spiritual struggle, carried over into the new humanism as the continual need to form and steel the will, to fight off baser desire in the name of duty. That's why "manliness" was such an important quality—or rather, bundle of virtues—in the eyes of Leslie Stephen. One should be courageous, independent in spirit, frank, upright, in contrast to the childlike, effeminate, sentimental. It is not surprising that Stephen, before he lost his faith, was an associate of Kingsley, who propounded a "muscular Christianity". For Stephen, this quality was the key to all the virtues; it took the place that Socrates/Plato ascribed to wisdom: "One virtue lies at the base of all the others: call it force, energy, vitality, or manliness, or whatever you please."[31]

We can see how the Victorian Christianity of self-discipline created a space for the move to a humanism of duty, will and altruism. They had a lot in common, particularly the opposition between egoism and benevolence, but the ontic basis for the move from the first to the second was quite different. For Christian faith, benevolence was possible first, because of the pristine human nature which God created before the Fall. But then since this had been perverted by that Fall, it also required grace to restore it.

For humanism, altruism was possible, because once humans rise to it, they see it to be a higher, more evolved way of being. Stephen thought that as we become stronger and more vital, altruism will come to appeal more to us. A higher self, which can think in terms of universal good, arises out of the process of enlightenment and character formation. This is a recognizable form of the eighteenth century idea that disengaged reason will free us from the particular, and make us want to live up to the demands of a more universal good, or act on impersonal principles. Kant is one source here.

But there also was an important borrowing from Romantic sources. George Eliot, for instance, was inspired by Feuerbach, and believed that we have the power within us to sustain an all-encompassing love. At a certain stage of development, we can bring this power to fruition, and thus come to recognize that what we have previously attributed to the divine is really a human capacity.

Both Mill and Stephen in different ways drew on the English Romantics. There are emotional resources deep within us which can be released by contact with unspoiled nature, and these can be articulated and thus strengthened by a poetry which celebrates them, and our relation with nature. Wordsworth was obviously an important influence here. So for Mill, sublime natural beauty can raise us above the petty objects which usually occupy us. And for Stephen, great literature (he specifically mentions Wordsworth) can help to keep us in touch with our vital feelings.[32]

But in appealing to inner sources, these writers introduced a certain tension in their position. The search for the release of spontaneous feeling can easily come in conflict with the demand for discipline. If our salvation lies in tapping these inner resources, then the attempt at all costs to make the will dominant over desire may end up stifling the saving impulses. Both Mill and Matthew Arnold felt the tension. Mill speaks of the danger of a "pinched and hidebound type of human character". Rigidity could destroy creativity and inhibit a wider sympathy.

So both feel the need to supplement the formation of good habits with something else; and here they draw on the thinkers of the Romantic age in Germany. Arnold looks for a Goethian serenity, a rounded harmony, as against just seeking "self-conquest". Mill, for his part, drew on Wilhelm von Humboldt's expressivist ideal of "human development in its richest diversity". And this could easily be seen as thwarting the demands of character. Humboldtian Bildung suggests openness to experience, the cultivation of a subjective response, the elevation of the aesthetic, the exploration of my own potential. All these can undermine the single-minded pursuit of the primacy of the will over desire, especially when this is defined in terms of a "manliness" which is opposed to the effeminate and sentimental.[33] I want to return to this tension below, when we look at some of the reactions against this ethic of duty and the will.

Victorian Christianity created the space for humanism, but this by itself doesn't explain what motivated the shift. In the nature of things, this kind of move is impossible to explain exhaustively, and the reasons vary tremendously from one individual to the other. But it is clear that the entire range of motivations which I reviewed in the previous chapter came into play here: the reactions against Christianity, the impact of science, particularly Darwinian evolutionism, and the development of the modern cosmic imaginary.

And we have just seen how the major figures of Victorian unbelief, feeling the cross-pressures attendant on the anthropocentric turn, had recourse to some of the moral meanings of this imaginary, for instance in a Wordsworthian sense of nature.

But one motivation which was particularly strong in the British cultural context was an argument based on the primacy of altruism. Christianity could be thought inferior to humanism on this register for two reasons. First, Christianity offers extrinsic rewards for altruism in the hereafter, where humanism makes benevolence its own reward; and secondly it sometimes can be tempted to exclude heretics and unbelievers from its purview whereas humanism can be truly universal. Mill, for instance, put forward these arguments.[34]

And so a new space for unbelief emerges, a humanism of altruism and duty, often rooted in an enriched materialism. This leaves much of the reigning synthesis intact, which linked Britishness, law, decency, civilization and religion. It lops off the last element, but insists just as much on discipline, will, character-formation, and the long but successful historical struggle to realize the synthesis in this happy Isle. A quite new set of spaces open up, however, when this synthesis is challenged.

There are a number of obvious reasons why it was bound to be. I have already mentioned the tension in J. S. Mill's position between character-formation and human development. Others were concerned that the stress on discipline would inhibit the growth of imagination and intelligence; or that it would crush spontaneity and emotional development. The stress on manliness simply intensified this danger, since it frowned on sentiment, self-exploration, an exploration of the aesthetic for its own sake, and a host of other such directions of growth.

Indeed, the rebellion against this manly discipline can be better understood if we consider one of its most important institutional settings, the public school. These schools were reformed in the mid-nineteenth century, most notably by Arnold of Rugby, and they became training grounds of character in the Victorian sense. As Annan puts it, they principally inculcated two ideals: manliness and loyalty. They had replaced Athens with Sparta as the ideal ancient city.[35] The stress on team sports was a crucial part of this training.

This education was very successful, in the sense that the élite male youth who attended these schools carried these ideals with them into their later lives, in regiments, board rooms, and politics, as well in public service at home and in the Empire. Its success is perhaps best attested by the importance that the game-playing image took on in English élite imagination. The idea that battles could be won "on the playing fields of Eton", that "playing the game" was the ultimate social virtue, always astonished foreigners, but it expressed a powerful ethos for Englishmen.

But one can see right away how this kind of training was in danger of producing ultra-loyal hearties, with underdeveloped intelligence and imagination—not to speak of the "underdeveloped hearts" of which Forster complained. It could easily generate philistinism, a contempt for or disinterest in outsiders, a calm assumption of English superiority allied with blank ignorance of other societies.

All this provoked a lot of reactions, along all the possible axes implied in the pencil sketch I've offered here. But perhaps the most important for our purposes was the protest against a narrowing of the ends of life to a code of conduct: This ethic of discipline, in both believing and unbelieving variants, was a moralism. It put discipline, self-control, the achieving of a high moral standard as the supreme goal. This tended to be true even of the Evangelical modes, which had after all started in the previous century as a reaction against narrow moralism, for instance in the emotionally liberating preaching of Wesley. Like all moralisms, it could come to seem too thin, too dry, concerned so exclusively with behaviour, discipline, control, that it left no space for some great élan or purpose which would transform our lives and take us out of the narrow focus on control. The obsession with getting myself to act right seems to leave no place for some overwhelmingly important goal or fulfillment, which is the one which gives point to my existence.

This complaint, sometimes interwoven with the "Romantic" one, that modern moral, disciplined life represses feeling, recurs again and again in the last two centuries. It is one of the defining concerns of the modern world. It is related to that other great defining concern, the worry about meaning, that is, about the possible meaninglessness of life. Indeed, these two are closely linked; they come at the same issue from different directions. The attack on our form of life as having left no place for what is the essential purpose of life, can from another angle be taken up as the anguished question whether there is still such an essential purpose, or whether they have not rather been all equally rendered nugatory by our way of life. It is just that, while the reproach against dry-as-dust moralism has analogies in earlier centuries, the anguish about meaning is quintessentially modern.

Now the protest against moralism is not only a recurring concern of our culture, but it comes particularly strongly to the fore in this period, the late nineteenth century. It forms part of the "fin-de-siècle" mood where such exists, and this on a European scale. Society was attacked by the young in France, Germany, England, and other countries as being too "materialist" in both senses: proffering a too reductive account of human life, and being too concerned with material acquisition, getting and spending. It was also attacked for stifling and denying heroism, dedication, commitment, sacrifice. It was this which created the mood in which the First World War was welcomed by many élite youths as the long-awaited opportunity for great deeds in a great cause.

Of course, within a widespread agreement that something was missing, there was no consensus on what it was. Some turned again to religion, but in forms generally different from those established in society; some turned to the new philosophies of self-affirmation which descended largely from Nietzsche; others found an outlet in politics, generally at the extremes, right or left. But there was one line of exploration which was especially important in English culture at this time, and this involved seeking the essential but marginalized fulfillment in art and the aesthetic.

The new spaces in this direction had been opened up by the writers of the Romantic generation—even though not all of them wanted to identify with this label. An important step had been taken by Schiller in his *Aesthetic Education,* which, as I indicated above, was a direct response to the inadequacies of moralism. The force to which we have to open ourselves to break out of the narrow focus of anthropocentrism can itself be identified with beauty, as in Schiller's treatise, or else we can see the languages of art as our privileged channel to it, whatever it be—nature, the Will, or God.

Now, as I argued above, these languages function, have power, move us, but without our having to identify their ontic commitments. And this is what offers a place to go for modern unbelief. As a response to the inadequacies of moralism, the missing goal can be identified with the experience of beauty, in the realm of the aesthetic. But this is now unhooked from the ordered cosmos and/or the divine. It can be grounded anew in some purely immanent outlook, such as that offered by Freud, for instance. But it can also be left unspecified, and that is in fact the option most frequently taken.

We connect up here with what I said above about the richer forms of materialism, with their sense if not of mystery (this word touches too many hot buttons among unbelievers), then of awe at the emergence of human consciousness and sensibility out of the depths of the material universe. The human depths are there, and they connect somehow to stars, molecules, and cells, even though we cannot fully see how. This connection, and the wider kinship it reflects, moves us, even though we cannot understand it. These human depths, or our strange capacity to be surprised and overwhelmed by beauty, can be articulated and celebrated in languages which are not undermined or weakened by the uncertainty of our ontic commitments, if we are this kind of materialist—or even if we are not certain whether we subscribe to materialism at all.

In fact, this opening to the aesthetic founded a broad church, as it were, in modern culture, in England and elsewhere. Some within it were drawn to Catholicism,

of both the Anglo- and the Roman variety. Some espoused a less defined spiritualism, or even a manner of materialism. And even more disconcertingly, some seemed
not to feel excessive strain in moving between these utterly opposed commitments.
Oscar Wilde was interested for a while in Catholicism, Hopkins was a student of
Pater's, and so on.

Besides this establishing of the aesthetic as an ethical category, and the subtler
languages, there is another legacy of the Romantic period to the English culture
of this generation. I have already mentioned it above. It is the sense that there is
a power in unspoiled nature which speaks to something deep in us. This was
paradigmatically articulated by Wordsworth, as for instance, in the passage from
"Tintern Abbey" I quoted in the previous chapter. In a sense, this also reflects in its
way the two other legacies. It is an example of the power of beauty to restore us and
make us whole; while at the same time, the ontic commitments of the poetry are
minimal and supremely hard to specify. It is "A presence that disturbs me with the
joy / Of elevated thoughts", which dwells in nature "and the mind of man", "A motion and a spirit".

This sense of nature, and the anguish at its potential loss through industrialization and economic development, is a continuing theme, which awakens a deep response in the English of the last two centuries, across wide differences of belief and
unbelief. It is a recurring focus of poetry, either directly, or in the shattering invocation of its absence. It has helped to shape the culture.

3

With this as background, I want now to look at how the reaction against moralism
found new spaces for unbelief in the later nineteenth and earlier twentieth centuries
in England. This reaction was not just against the ethic of duty and altruism, and its
institutional manifestations in public school, regiment, government, and so on. We
saw earlier that the widespread protest among European youth at that time was
against the society also in its heavy focus on production, material wealth-getting,
and its foregrounding of economic priorities. Or otherwise put, the rejection was
not only of the ethic of self-control in its altruistic, public-spirited facet, but also
against its individualistic, self-improving, "self-help" aspect; targeting Samuel
Smiles as much if not more than, say, Leslie Stephen.

I want to mention a number of responses, starting with the less radical. But first
a word about their relation to each other. They all grew out of a wider climate of
dissatisfaction with the reigning moralism/materialism, as I have just mentioned.
This produced two in a sense opposite effects. On one hand, there is frequently
an affinity between different responses, even though the answers they give differ

widely; so much so at times that people can hover on the boundary between two (to us clearly) incompatible positions, or move through one to the other. This is particularly striking when one of the positions involves belief and the other espouses unbelief. But on the other hand, just because these responses are rival answers to the same question, they can be bitterly opposed. Indeed, one can denounce another as being part of the (commonly identified) problem, rather than a solution to it. So D. H. Lawrence fulminates against Bloomsbury, as being unfeeling, dissociated from their own deeper emotions, just as though they were integrally part of the uptight, disciplined culture that they thought they were breaking away from.

On the less radical end, we have people that are very conscious of the inadequacies of moralism and the focus on production and acquisition, but don't want to reject the morality or the production, but rather to supplement it with a higher, cultural dimension. Matthew Arnold and arguably J. S. Mill belong here. I have already mentioned them, and the tensions that this double allegiance creates in their positions. Arnold hoped to supply the missing dimension in the life of discipline and production through a kind of Bildung, which was explicitly seen as filling the slot that religion could no longer occupy. This culture would offer a higher goal to our lives, as religion did in earlier times. He was one of the first to create, using the materials bequeathed from the Romantic period, a space for unbelief to go in its reaction against the inadequacies or moralism.

Another much younger figure who had a similarly complex position is George Macaulay Trevelyan. Trevelyan was another of those, like Stephen, who issuing from a strong Evangelical family, abandoned his faith. And yet he maintained the synthesis: Britishness, Protestantism, law, freedom, decency, civilization constructed over centuries on the favoured Isle, almost intact. Indeed, he became as a historian a great articulator and celebrator of this synthesis, only amended to make Protestantism the penultimate stage before a liberal, disciplined unbelief. As regards the Christian religion, "the only thing I can believe in for certain—the progress of the human race. What people usually call religion, the immortality of the soul and so on, I am in absolute darkness about these things. But in Democracy I have got hold of something definite."[36]

Christianity had nobly organized Europe "politically and socially in the dark ages . . . yet failed in what it chiefly pretended to do, to make men love one another. . . . Philanthropy" has been furthered in the modern world not so much by churchmen as by the great agnostics, like Voltaire.[37]

But at the same time, Trevelyan saw like Wordsworth something sublime in nature:

> In Northumberland alone both heaven and earth are seen; we walk all day along ridges, high enough to give far views of moor and valley, and the sense of

solitude above the world below . . . It is the land of far horizons, where the piled and drifted shapes of gathered vapour are for ever moving along the far-thest ridge of hills, like the procession of long primaeval ages that is written in the tribal mounds and Roman camps and Border towers on the breast of Northumberland.[38]

He tells his brother Charles, in a period of deep trouble, to

lean on the hills and the lakes and the stars as symbolic of all that is noble . . . Wordsworth leant on them fifty years. I believe he really leant comparatively little on God. He could not realize God in the abstract. He had to see him in the Hills.[39]

As the reference to Wordsworth implies, the recourse to nature went along with recourse to the literature which opens us to nature; not only the earlier writer, but for Macaulay particularly Meredith. The modern passion for untamed nature, for mountains, rocks and moors, as articulated in literature is "one of the sacraments prepared for man or discovered by man".[40]

But this relation to nature remains within a zone where its ontic commitments are uncertain and undefined. In a sermon he preached as Master of Trinity in 1945, Trevelyan stated that there is in the spiritual and imaginative power of man some-thing which "forbids him to take a purely material view of the world, and gives him glimpses of something divine, either external to, or immanent in, nature and hu-mankind."[41] And in describing his passion for history, he confessed a sense of mystery:

The dead were and are not. Their place knows them no more and it is ours to-day. Yet they were once as real as we and we shall tomorrow be shadows like them. In men's first astonishment over that unchanging mystery lie the origins of poetry, philosophy and religion.[42]

Somewhat more radical were the aestheticisms of Pater and later Wilde. True, they were quietistic; they didn't launch a challenge to the existing ethic in the sense of proposing to overturn it. But they intended to opt out in the name of a rival comprehensive view, which was in a sense even more subversive. The aesthetic was now really placed outside of and above the moral.

But this was an aesthetic which was in a sense close to the religious. It made use of religious forms and symbols, and drew inspiration from earlier ages of faith and metaphysical belief. People who were drawn to it often hovered on the brink of reli-gious commitment, to non-established forms, principally High Church or Catholic. So, as I mentioned above, Hopkins was a student of Pater, and Wilde ended by converting to Catholicism. (There are parallels to contemporary France, with a figure like Huysmans who was both aesthete and Catholic combined.)

And yet thanks to the suspension of ontic commitment in modern languages of art, it could open a space outside both morality and religion, using the second to lever free of the tyranny of the first, but then swinging free of faith in turn to make the aesthetic realm ultimate and self-sufficient.

One might say that the ontological indeterminacy of the "subtler languages" of post-Romantic literature allowed for three kinds of position. One could remain with the indeterminacy, as much of Wordsworth's poetry seems to do and as well as the quotes I have just given from Trevelyan; one leaves the issue undecided, to what extent one is invoking an extra-human spiritual reality, or rather pointing to something wholly within experience. But one can also firmly disambiguate one's position: on one hand, in favour of the first position, as did those who opted for Catholicism, for instance; and of course, Wordsworth himself in his later life as an orthodox Anglican. Or else, one can opt for the second. Pater's aestheticism seems to have been of this latter kind (with perhaps some second thoughts towards the end of his life). The stated ideal: "to burn always with this hard gem-like flame, to maintain this ecstasy, is success in life", is fulfilled at the level of experience; no claim is made about our relation to a transcendent object.

> High passions give one this quickened sense of life, ecstasy, the sorrow of love, political or religious enthusiasm, or "the enthusiasm of humanity". Only, be sure it is passion, that it does yield you this fruit of a quickened, multiplied consciousness. Of this wisdom, the poetic passion, the desire of beauty, the love of art for art's sake, has most; for art comes to us professing frankly to give nothing but the highest quality to your moments as they pass, and simply for those moments' sake.[43]

Hopkins, as we will see below (Chapter 20) ends up taking explicitly the other option, and this is clearly reflected in his work. But he goes on drawing on the stock of post-Romantic images and understanding of language, as well as on the aversion to the modes of disciplined, instrumental moralism which he shares with Pater, Ruskin, and many others.

Bloomsbury was in a way less and in a way more radical than this. More so in that it really offered what amounted to a serious amendment of the reigning ethic, which emerged most clearly in the opposition of many of its members to participation in the War.

The alternative ethic was the one articulated by Moore, which identified the only intrinsically good things as personal relations and beautiful states of mind. Or as Forster put it, "Personal relations are the most important thing for ever and ever, and not this outer life of telegrams and anger".[44] We could perhaps better sum it up by saying that friendship and honest, strong feelings were major goods; Noel Annan describes Virginia Woolf's conviction that integrity demanded that "you should detect exactly what you felt and should then, having realized what sort of a person you were, live up to it."[45] But aesthetic experience was also crucial, since it was one of the most important sources of strong feeling. Each of these could intensify the others: friendship was intensified by shared experience, and the experiences were rendered all the deeper by being shared.

These were the ultimate goods. All others were to be judged, Moore argued, consequentially by how much they promoted or obstructed these intrinsic goods. And this is where the less radical side of Bloomsbury emerged. For most of the ethic of decency, the structures of law and freedom, many of the disciplines, and much of the institutional framework around this, were recaptured as valuable in this instrumental way. Keynes is here the paradigm figure. He fully subscribed to the Bloomsbury ethic, but he was happy to operate within the government as civil servant and adviser for many years—all except for the latter part of the First World War, and the Peace Conference, whose results he famously denounced in an influential book. The point was to impart a different spirit to all this, to move it towards different ultimate goals.

But by not being radical, Bloomsbury was in a sense all the more subversive; since the spirit which they advocated was poles apart from the ethic of discipline and manliness, which were very much taken as goods in themselves. Discipline yes, but only where it conduces to friendship and beautiful states of mind. In this way, they dismantled, by downgrading and rendering conditional, great parts of the reigning synthesis: its religion was utterly sidelined, its sexual ethic was declared bankrupt, its patriotism was severely chastened, most of its conventions were mocked.

Apart from the repression of feeling and free self-expression, Bloomsbury's principal targets were the philistinism that reigned in so much of English life, and the chauvinism that made people incapable of appreciating the artistic and cultural achievements of other countries. Virginia Woolf's famous reminiscence: "On or about December 1910 human nature changed" was an indirect reference to an exhibition of post-Impressionist painting which was showing in London at that time, and which helped to break somewhat the barrier both against new experimental art, and against foreign painting.

So one thing this response conserved intact, indeed intensified, was the link between the ethic of decency and the modern moral order of mutual benefit. In fact, it helped to alter our understanding of this order by moving it farther along two of the vectors of change I identified above. First, it advanced on the vector of authenticity, prizing the individual self-expression of each person in their difference from others, the "integrity" invoked by Noel Annan above to describe Virginia Woolf's position. And second, they radicalized the claims of ordinary human sensual desire against the supposedly "higher" demands of discipline or abstinence. For instance, Blooms-bury homosexuals threw off the restrictions of their society. They all "came out", not, indeed, before the general public—homosexual relations were still a criminal offence in those days—but in the society they frequented. They helped to set the climate of the latter half of the century, in England and elsewhere.

I have been describing some ways in which the reaction against moralism helped to open new spaces for unbelief, all in different ways drawing on the post-Romantic understanding of the aesthetic as an ethical category. That this reaction went so much to unbelief is partly due to the fact that the reigning synthesis supposedly in-corporated Christian faith. But this was not a fatality; it could and sometimes did inspire people to explore forms of faith other than those of the established synthesis. More important was the affinity between many responses and the earlier mid-Vic-torian turn to exclusive humanism.

Bloomsbury especially reflects this. It is tempting, particularly if we focus on the Stephen family, to see it as a third-generation phenomenon. A revolt within a revolt, which kept much of the first phase intact. The father rebels against Victorian faith, largely because it seems so much less humane than humanism, but keeps the ethic and discipline. The daughters then rebel against this, but don't revise the original judgment of religion. On the contrary, they go farther and define humaneness in terms, e.g., of sexual freedom, which carry them even farther from the established religion.

Indeed, they even carry immanence a step farther; not only do they adopt an ethic purely in terms of human good; but this good is itself immanentized in an-other sense. The intrinsically valuable is identified with the inner, the mental, with experience and sensibility. They very much subjectivized ethics, not in the sense that external action was unimportant, but that it was all instrumentalized to goods which were experiential. In this way, too, they anticipate an important shift in the later twentieth century.

It was this immanentization which many people reacted to when they accused Bloomsbury of trivializing the human condition, of immuring themselves against deep and powerful forces, and reducing the issues of human life to what can be encompassed by individual feeling. Whether one is coming from a religious perspective, or from an atheist invocation of a life force, like D. H. Lawrence, or the Will to Power, or the forces of history, one finds something irritatingly precious and reductive in Bloomsbury. Lytton Strachey's take-down of his "eminent Victorians", all of whom saw themselves as at grips with such larger realities, strikes one not so much as witty and perceptive, but as obtusely reductive and trivializing.

Here is the source of a continuing twentieth-century quarrel. On behalf of Bloomsbury, one can point to the great crimes which have been committed in the name of such larger realities, not only of God, but of History and the Race, and how the ethic of decency has led people to stand against these. This point is certainly well-taken. In fact, perhaps both points are; which leaves us in a dilemma, which I want to return to later.

In the meantime, I want just to appreciate the importance of these new spaces for unbelief, whereby the reaction even against "materialism" (in the sense of the focus on purely material well-being) isn't driven to religious forms, but can find atheist expression. In terms of my original question, how things differ now in regard to belief/unbelief from what they were like 500 years ago, we can see how the map of experience has changed. I cited Bede Griffiths' great experience as a school-boy, which he later saw as the beginning of his faith. In the light of these new spaces, we can see how an analogous experience, of a sense of something incomparably higher, which quite breaks with the ordinary sense of things we are brought up with, can now occur within an unbelieving perspective. And indeed, Bede's experience is a good example, because he originally saw in it that perspective of post-Wordsworthian Romanticism which played such an important part in the development of English sensibility in the last two centuries.

4

We have followed two important shifts: the turn to exclusive humanism within the reigning synthesis; the reaction against the moralism and restrictions of that synthesis, whose most important strand was Bloomsbury. But then came the trauma of the First World War. This damaged the credibility of the synthesis as nothing earlier could have done. The synthesis incorporated "civilization", one of whose key components was to protect life from violence through order and law. The war was supposedly fought for "civilization", at least in its British variant. And yet the massive slaughter turned out to be a greater negation of civilized life than any foe threatened. The attempt to salvage a justification by promising a quantum leap in peace and welfare and social justice in the aftermath just made things worse when none of these promises could be made good on.

There is some evidence that the majority of Britons went on believing in the synthesis, but for an influential minority of the young, who had served in the trenches, or who came along after, it shattered their faith in the whole complex. In particular, British patriotism was badly shaken. The ethic of manliness and loyalty, taught in the public school and carried into the regiment, seemed utterly discredited. The Big Words that encased it and gave it meaning—Honour, Sacrifice, for God King and Country, for Loved Ones Home and Empire (to quote from the inscription on the monument to the Unknown Warrior)[46]—rang hollow.

If one was shaken in this way, there were various directions one could go. One was to try to reconstruct the synthesis, keeping decency and law, but shedding the jingoist patriotism and mindless commitment to struggle. One could turn to an internationalist liberalism, the kind that sustained the League of Nations and the various attempts at disarmament. Or else one could go more radically Left or Right, reject the synthesis for either Communism or Fascism. In the Thirties, when these two seemed to be lined up against each other in a struggle for world power, many young people did pick one of the sides, overwhelmingly the Left in fact.

But instead of this, or perhaps even alongside it, the trauma could create a sense of uncertainty, of disbelief and even cynicism. The idea could be accredited that there is no morally credible publicly established order, the diametrical opposite of the previously established synthesis. Part of what Hynes calls the "Myth of the War" is this sense that it created a radical discontinuity in history, that we are cut off from the order enjoyed by our predecessors by an impassable gulf.[47]

Pound summed up this mood of despair, loss, and cynicism in a stanza of his "Hugh Selwyn Mauberly":

> There died a myriad,
> And the best, among them,
> For an old bitch gone in the teeth,
> For a botched civilization.[48]

How to respond to *this* sense, the idea that we are living after the demise of a viable order? We might surmise that this was particularly hard to accept in an English context, just because people had lived with such confidence for so long within the synthesis. Contrast this with the French case, where for a century there had been a struggle between rival conceptions of order, and where the idea of combatting "le désordre établi" was already quite familiar.

One reaction in the English case, which wouldn't have made the same sense in France, was to see the moral order as totally disintegrated, fallen into a "heap of broken fragments". This, whatever the intentions of its author, was the sense given to Eliot's "Waste Land" when it was published in 1922; it was seen as an attempt to articulate our shattered condition, after the historical break.[49] And from here, one could go in different directions. One was to see the only hope for integration in personal experience. Poetry can bring us closer to this by articulating the fragmentation, building it into its very form, as Eliot seemed to have done. "These fragments have I shored against my ruin." The answer was in inner, individual experience, in personalized meaning, which might then inspire others and give them the means to do the same; but a renewed public order was abandoned as a possibility.

The other was to go for a radical re-ordering, to leap into one of the extreme solutions of Left or Right. This is where more and more of the young élite were drawn in the 1930s, as I said above. And in spite of the fact that some of the most famous poets writing in English tended to the Right—Yeats, Pound, Eliot—the great majority went Left.

In a sense, the terrible trauma of the First World War was paradoxically resolved at least in part by the Second. This is because it really was a war to defend civilization. Hitler brought reality down to match and surpass the war propaganda of the previous conflict. This, plus the moral discrediting of Communism, emptied the ranks of extreme Left and Right, and the War itself restored some sense to British patriotism, and recovered the link with the past.

But the synthesis could never recover its unshakeable force that it had prior to 1914. Any sense that one was living in continuity with that order had to include the understanding that one was also evolving out of it, moving in a more liberal, internationalist direction, for a long time also, until the Thatcher revolution, in a more social-democratic direction, sliding further along the vectors of authenticity and the defense of ordinary, sensual desire, allowing individuals more space to lead their lives as they want, in a more permissive climate. In spite of the glories of the Second War, the generals of the First retain their unenviable (if perhaps not fully deserved) reputation for mindless, insensitive sacrifice of lives to outmoded strategy. *That* kind of patriotism cannot be rehabilitated.

What then was the legacy of the inter-war years? A further retreat from belief because of the implication of Christian faith in the discredited synthesis; a relative decline of insularity, and a greater cultural integration of England into Europe, which has been proceeding apace ever since that time. The subtler languages of Continental Modernism, e.g., Proust; even the views of Continental theorists, e.g., Weber, Freud, are more and more part of the conversation. But also the sense of living in a shattered order has remained at some level as a truth of experience. Even with a reconstituted confidence in some kind of modified synthesis, the sense remains that in some register the sense of disintegration also has validity. It is difficult for intellectuals and artists to inhabit a public order in the old Victorian-Edwardian way any more.

It still astonishes us when we catch a glimpse of the mental world of those who went to war in 1914, through the sonnets of Rupert Brooke, or in a host of contemporary comments and letters. It's not just the heightened language in which they talked of war: honour, valour, sacrifice, staunch and gallant. It was also the way they saw the conflict through images of a glorious national history, preserved in the greatest literature (e.g., Shakespeare's *Henry V*), or in the writings of the Classical authors they were steeped in at school ("dulce et decorum est / pro patria mori"). We realize with a shock that they were totally, unselfconsciously *into* this imagery. "The British intercourse with literature . . . was instinctive and unapologetic—indeed, shameless."[50]

Of course, this doesn't disappear at once; for the majority these images and their resonance remain authoritative through the inter-War commemorations. And after 1945, Laurence Olivier can produce an immense successful film version of *Henry V*. But among educated and sophisticated people, it has become impossible to use this language and deploy these images without some distancing—through irony, unease, semi-parody, citation, Bakhtinian "voicing".

And yet some attachment remains. Contemporaries are ambivalent about this earlier age, or at least their reactions are complex. We feel wider, less naïve, and somewhat patronizing towards our patriotic forebears, but also somewhat envious of their certainties, and perhaps even in some way dependent on them for an anchoring point, since some of their reference points: dedication, sacrifice to protect others, cannot just be sloughed off, however awkward we feel pronouncing the words.

I said above that unease was felt among élites; it wasn't necessarily where the mass of people were in the '20s and '30s; even less so in 1945. But the line between élite and mass has been steadily eroding in the twentieth century; formerly minority reactions are spreading. And so something of the same complex relations of the past now reappear in popular culture. Take the various nostalgia trips which occur from time to time: a vogue for First World War reminiscences or memories, or for military uniforms of earlier days. Here there is often an element of irony, even camp, but also nostalgia for a lost age of certainty; and alongside all this even a sort of comfort in rootedness in this lost past. This ambivalence about the former synthesis now seems to have penetrated the whole culture.

All this has tended on balance to widen the spaces of unbelief. And it appears obvious that England in the post-war period has had an élite, academic-artistic culture which is predominantly and increasingly unbelieving. Noel Annan's interesting and insightful book, *Our Age,* gives a insider's portrait of the generations which led England in the thirty years after the War.[51]

One thing that strikes the reader is the continuity with the objectives of Bloomsbury. There is the same aspiration to "transform philistine Britain into a country in which the arts were enjoyed and artists respected as in other European countries". There was the aspiration to give "the greatest possible freedom to people in their private lives, and in the way they expressed that life through the arts". "The will was suspect"; imposing a form by sheer will power seemed a formula for destruction rather than virtue; and the gentlemanly ideal and its public school manifestation comes in for searching criticism.[52]

What is quite outside the Bloomsbury purview, and which is the legacy of the Second World War, is what Annan calls "collectivism", the belief "that the state should intervene to promote greater social justice", and the egalitarianism: "we wanted all classes in society to enjoy what had formerly been the privileges of the rich".[53] Stemming from the inter-war years is the recognition of the reality of alienation in our societies.[54]

The spaces for unbelief are more varied and complex, and there is more acceptance of the irrational and negative elements they involve. But fundamentally, the buffered identity is inhabited with the same unruffled confidence. Early on, Annan quotes Forster: "Lord I disbelieve, help thou mine unbelief". He adds, "Our Age were often sceptics, but self-confident sceptics".[55] The implication here is that there is some global option possible to "believe", which is here being wisely and bravely refused, presumably involving unnecessary, gratuitous, unfounded beliefs, about things that the buffered identity happily considers as external and ignorable. Whether this really makes sense of the human condition is not so obvious.

Towards the end, Annan takes up an attack by Roger Scruton on the consensus of the Age, in which he accuses the liberal mind-set of lacking "experience of the sacred and the erotic, of mourning and holy dread". He sees this as an imputation of shallowness and triviality, in a sense a reprise of the Lawrentian attack against Bloomsbury. His reply is that "they read poetry for consolation and to stir their sense of wonder . . . They grew up when Hardy and Housman were still living or only recently dead; when Yeats was reminding them of the mysteries of life, when Eliot's exquisite ear kept his revolution in prosody within the poetic tradition."[56] The dimension of profundity is entered through art, whose subtler language can open us to mystery, but with its ontic commitments suspended and undefined. The post-Romantic space that the nineteenth century carved out is still being occupied. And it is good that it should be; many of us need it to live. But Scruton is surely right that there cannot be "holy dread", where ontic commitments are suspended, and the buffered self lives secure.

But this is just the beginning of the argument. Whether and in what way this is a loss still has to be established. And there is in fact a lot to be said on both sides.

What is clear, however, is the present condition of belief and unbelief can't be described purely in terms of élite culture. One of the important events of the twenti-eth century is that the nova has come to involve whole societies. It has become the "super-nova". This is what I will examine in Part IV.

5

Now this shift I mentioned at the beginning of section 2, between earlier vertical notions of order, and the modern horizontal ones, was occurring also, at least for significant periods, in a number of European societies. Indeed, if one takes the long view, say a school textbook in the twenty-second century, this will probably be the dominant phenomenon. But these shifts have not always been silent, and difficult to notice, as in the U.K. There have been struggles around ideas of order in Euro-pean, particularly Latin cultures, and these have been directly relevant to the bal-ance between belief and unbelief.

A certain variant of the modern order of mutual benefit, heavily influenced by Rousseau, becomes the basis for a Republican tradition in France, and then else-where, which is explicitly anti-Christian, if not always clearly atheist. Democracy and human rights are conceived as inseparable from a view of humans as innocent or fundamentally good by nature. The proper political order can only thrive if it ac-knowledges and celebrates this nature, and the virtues which belong to it. Religion, particularly the Christian doctrine of original sin, cannot but undermine it, sap its foundations. The free society must inculcate a philosophy, and build a social imagi-nary, which is grounded in exclusive humanism.

So the original Revolutionaries, in their radical period, attacked the Church, tried to bring about a "dechristianization", under Robespierre's rule tried even to substitute a new religion of the "Supreme Being". And even after Thermidor, the at-tempt goes on, through the new calendar, through state-organized festivals, to in-culcate a new outlook in the place of the traditional Christian one.

This Republican hostility to religion was later radicalized, both socially and metaphysically, in Marxist socialism, which was explicitly committed to an atheist outlook. Many socialist régimes and revolutionary movements have attacked the Church even more vigorously than the Jacobins, both within the Communist world, as well as beyond, in places like Mexico and Spain.

This line-up between moral order, human rights and democracy, and atheism, helped to provoke the counter-line-up, that of "Reaction". The Catholic ancien régime was already heavily committed to an alternative notion of order, which I called above, rather loosely "baroque". This was vertical, in that it stressed the im-portance of hierarchy; order as such, that is, the fending off of chaos, could only subsist where differences of rank were respected, where each person had a place to which he belonged, and where the whole was held in place by over-arching monarchical power. Bossuet had been a major spokesman of this outlook.

What was "modern" about this idea was that the actual hierarchy was less and less justified by some metaphysical notion of the ontic logos, some doctrine of the levels of being as reflected in the orders of society, and more and more explained and defended in terms of its beneficial consequences, mainly stable order itself. Seen from today's perspective, it appears a kind of hybrid: on one hand, the actual differences were surrounded by an aura of higher meaning, a sense of originating in a distant time of origins; they were celebrated with an impressive ceremonial, and monarchy atop hierarchy could be claimed to reflect God's relation to his creation. On the other hand, since the main justification was consequentialist, the possibility was implicitly opened that other forms might be justified, if they turned out to work better.

The Restoration tried to restore this outlook integrally, but this proved impossible. Too much of the older order had been swept away. It was no longer what had been there since time out of mind; the ceremonial just couldn't have the same meaning, as Charles X discovered when he tried to re-enact the full ancient coronation rite in Rheims in 1825. The justification for hierarchy under monarchy now has to rely much more clearly and frankly on the claim that it and it alone works to produce order. This is what emerges in the major articulation of the Restoration outlook in de Maistre. The eulogy of the hangman is meant to drive home the point that without this kind of threat hanging over them, men would be ungovernable. And of course, after the chaos of the French Revolution, many, particularly among the aristocratic class, found this a very plausible view.

The justification then came more and more to centre on order, and a respect for rightful authority. But this latter was also seen to include religious, ecclesial authority. Democracy, the handing over of the right to judge to just anyone and everyone, seemed naturally allied with free thought and heresy. If the truth were not to be lost in an unending proliferation of unfounded opinion, there must be a single authority which can enforce its rulings. This had been the essence of Bossuet's argument against the Protestants: once you break with Rome, it's continuous, unending fission.

So Pius VI in 1791, commenting the National Assembly's declaration of rights, condemned "cette licence de penser, de dire, d'écrire et même de faire imprimer impunément, en matière de religion, tout ce que peut suggérer l'imagination la plus déréglée, . . . cette liberté de penser et d'agir que l'Assemblée nationale accorde à l'homme en société comme un droit imprescriptible de la nature." And his successor Pius IX in 1864 condemned in his *Syllabus* among other outrageous propositions that "Le Pontife Romain peut et doit se réconcilier et transiger avec le progrès, le libéralisme et la civilisation moderne."[57]

So an ideal order in its different variants, starting from the individual, and stressing rights, liberties and democracy, squares off against a counter-ideal which stresses obedience, hierarchy, belonging to, even sacrifice for a larger whole. For the proponents of the counter-ideal, this seemed to be the obvious way to avoid chaos, both politically and religiously. But more than this, the stress on obedience and on sacrifice gave it an obvious congruence in their minds with religion as they understood it, that is, not the anthropocentric faith of Providential Deism, but the Augustinian understanding of sin and the need for submission to God.

Of course, we with hindsight can confidently predict that the ideal would win out over the counter-ideal, for the reasons rehearsed above. And this is what has in fact happened. But the path to this end was much more bumpy and circuitous than one would assume from today's perspective. And that is because it didn't remain a simple matter of atheist republicans or socialists against clerical hierarchs. The picture was already more complicated than that, in that there were already variants of the order of mutual benefit which were related to a Christian outlook, as in the U.S.A.; and there came to be more in Catholic Europe, from Lammenais to Péguy, and then up to the triumph of Christian democracy in the middle of this century. This of course, merely hastened the victory of the modern moral order.

What delayed it, on the other hand, were the cross-overs in the other direction: that is, the development of variants of the counter-ideal which were to a greater or lesser degree delinked from Catholicism or Christianity. Already an intellectual cross-over position is staked out in mid-century by Auguste Comte, who looks to an authoritative religion to provide social cohesion, but devises one from science to replace Christianity.

More seriously, towards the end of the century movements arise which are based on some variant of the counter-ideal, but which break progressively loose from their Christian moorings. The attraction of these comes only partly from the consequentialist justification that hierarchy assures order. Much more important is an intrinsic admiration for the way of life which centres on hierarchy, obedience, sacrifice. I mentioned in the last segment the axes of criticism of modern humanism which come at it from the "tragic" direction, which attack it as levelling, destroying heroism, greatness, the exceptional; or which see it as bowdlerizing life, trying to write out the ineradicable suffering, tragedy, conflict.

Now one can make this critique from a Christian perspective, where the heroes are saints, and the essential suffering is that of the Cross. But a crucial aspect of what I'm calling the nova is that they come to be mounted also from an unbelieving direction, where the heroes are closer to the warriors of old, and the suffering is an ineradicable dimension of the human condition which these heroes learn to face and surmount. From this point of view, Christianity, with its stress on peace and humility, and its hope of ultimate union with God, can easily be seen as the enemy, the original source of this enervating modern humanism. Nietzsche was the most prominent spokesman of this kind of view, and remains in many ways the most influential.

This is what I called in the previous chapter the "immanent counter-Enlightenment"; 'immanent', because it makes no reference to transcendent reality. This century has been wracked by struggles between the two ideals of order, where what I am calling the counter-ideal was not always or even mainly supported by a Christian outlook, but more and more drew on non-Christian, even atheist sources.

We have, in fact, the whole gamut, from one extreme to the other. Take a figure like Charles Maurras. He animates a movement which mainly appeals to Catholics. But he himself is not a believer, and his reasons for wanting to return France to the Monarchy are not simply to restore order and the faith. Indeed, the restoration of faith is itself instrumental to something else. Maurras' belief is that France can only be great again under the monarchy. The order this régime will bring will conduce to this. But that is not all; it is its ethos of discipline, obedience, dedication, which will form and give an outlet to a higher type of human being. The ultimate goal is human greatness.

How was it possible for Maurras to remain the mentor of a movement so overwhelmingly made up of Catholics, some of whom didn't desert him even when he was condemned by the Pope in 1926? Well, partly because the Church did have an important place in his plans, even though he had an ulterior motive; partly because there was an important overlap between Christians and non-Christians in their valuation of discipline, sacrifice, dedication to a larger community. But it was also undoubtedly because many of his Catholic followers were themselves attracted by the ethic of heroism. It was, after all, the ethos of their caste if they were nobles. It was certainly what they aspired to if they were bourgeois who were repelled by (what they saw as) the morally flabby, egoistic, utilitarian outlook of their society.

We can see this if we look at a book, *Les Jeunes Gens d'aujourd'hui*, published in 1912, which was one of the expressions of the protest against spiritual flatness at the turn of the century, which I mentioned above. Its authors, Henri Massis and Alfred de Tarde, claim to be speaking for a generation of youth among whom they carried out a survey. Of course, the scientific credentials of the survey are very much in doubt. But what is interesting from our point of view is the rhetoric and the aspirations. They contrast themselves with the "generation of 1885", which seem to them to be "overly intellectual and introspective, relativistic, incapable of energetic action, lacking faith, obsessed with decadence". They are ultimately "dilettantes". What was needed was a new discipline, which would "create order and hierarchy", and would lead to a life of commitment.[58] Faith against skepticism and science, dedication to the nation against individualism, commitment and discipline against individual choice, hierarchy against equality, these were the lines of attraction for young people of this tendency.

Some of them, like Massis, ended up converting to Catholicism, but it's clear that there was a rival moral aspiration here, a yearning for some major cause to give meaning to life, for an object of dedication and sacrifice, for action and life as against simple reflection, for great-hearted action. One sees these among the youth of other European societies in this same period, for instance in the Jugendbewegung in Germany, with its cult of nature, of the community, of Lebensphilosophie. So much so, that many élite members of this generation will see in the war itself the outlet for community, sacrifice, great deeds which they were waiting for. "Now God be thanked Who has matched us with His hour", writes Rupert Brooke, and the same exultation can be heard from many young Frenchmen and Germans.[59] Hans Castorp runs to the battlefield, singing the *Ode to Joy*.

Now the War was a shattering experience, as I mentioned above. It was one of the great traumas of modern history. Just because it was entered into by so many young men, from all belligerent countries, with the sense that at last they had found an outlet for the heroism and dedication they had been yearning for, the actual fighting on the Western Front, years of monotony and boredom in appalling conditions, punctuated by orgies of indiscriminate, mechanized slaughter, came as a terrible awakening.

At a deeper level, the War was a crisis of civilization, that is, it called into question the basic assumption that the belligerent states were truly civilized, or else more deeply, the very idea of civilization itself. With hindsight, it seems extraordinary to us now that so many Edwardians could have assumed that a war between the major powers could somehow fit into a civilized world, that it wasn't bound to shake the very framework of this world.

There were two sides to this illusion, a military expectation, and its moral meaning. The military error was to see the 1870 Franco-Prussian conflict, rather than the Boer War or the U.S. Civil War, as the precedents. Both sides imagined a lightning campaign, full of cavalry charges and heroic action, after which there would be a clear winner. It would all be over before Christmas. The moral meaning was that there would be an outlet for the hunger for heroism; some young men would lay down their lives, but it would be done in a worthy setting: they would throw themselves deliberately into danger for the sake of the cause, and would die in an act of individual self-dedication, cut down by the bullet or blade they had consciously risked. They would deserve and achieve the status of glorious dead, as understood in the archetypes of military valour which went back to the ancients. Dulce et decorum est pro patria mori.

Behind this, there was often the further moral reflection, that without periodic opportunities of this kind for heroism and dedication, civilization itself would stagnate, go flabby and decadent. Indeed, this was what many feared was already happening in the long peace at the end of the nineteenth century. Of course, there were weighty philosophical arguments for this thesis of the necessity of war, most notably from Hegel. But we are horrified to read today how many respectable thinkers on both sides espoused this view in August 1914. For instance, Edmund Gosse, a prominent critic of the Edwardian era, wrote that autumn:

> War is a great scavenger of thought. It is the sovereign disinfectant, and its red stream of blood is the Condy's Fluid that cleans out the stagnant pools and clotted channels of the intellect. . . . We have awakened from an opium-dream of comfort, of ease, or that miserable poltroonery of "the sheltered life". Our wish for indulgence of every sort, our laxity of manners, our wretched sensitiveness to personal inconvenience, these are suddenly lifted before us in their true guise as the spectres of national decay; and we have risen from the lethargy of our dilettantism to lay them, before it is too late, by the flashing of the unsheathed sword.[60]

But the reality of the long, mass mechanized slaughter, where men were sent wholesale to anonymous deaths in seas of mud, utterly belied these moral meanings. Moreover, one the constituent meanings of 'civilization', as this concept had developed in modern Europe, was that it was meant to protect life from violence through order and law. The concept was after all, partly shaped by the modern moral order. This could find a place for some young men laying down their lives heroically, in order to ensure the safety of others. And indeed, the belligerent powers made implausibly horrifying claims about the danger their enemies represented to precisely this feature of civilized life. The Germans in English war propaganda rapidly became the "Huns". But the actual slaughter made a mockery of this goal. To justify grinding a generation to powder in a virtually stationary battle zone over four years you would have to be fighting at least against real Huns, if not something considerably worse. The reality made the stated reasons look farcical.

One way to cope with this, was to up the ante; to promise an ever higher civilization after the war: more democratic, more egalitarian, more caring for its less affluent citizens, and definitively peaceful. The war became that to end all wars; the state would build homes fit for heroes. Instinctively governments knew that the purposes of the conflict had to be jacked up to match the suffering. The war radicalized politics. But of course, the upshot of all this was even more crushing disappointment, as the promised changes failed to materialize.

Now the crisis of civilization played out in various ways: in cynicism and despair for some, in radical redefinitions of the goals of society on both Left and Right, as I mentioned above, in internal emigration, in counter-cultural forms of art. I want to mention two kinds of reaction which are relevant to the spreading nova of belief and unbelief.

The first is that the crisis of civilization was also a crisis of a certain kind of Christian culture. To the extent that Christian faith has become married to modern civilization—and it was, of course, this marriage which had opened the way for the anthropomorphic turn—it too was shaken. Britain was a case in point, as I argued in the previous section, where for many the national identity so tightly associated British political order, decency and a certain Protestant Christianity, all of which were felt to be the established values. For those within this identity, that's what the war was being fought for. If all this made the civilization look dubious, where did it leave the faith? This was a danger to which various oppositional forms of Christianity, as in suppressed nations like Poland and Ireland, or among anti-Republican French Catholics who inveighed against "le désordre établi", were less vulnerable. Elsewhere, the civilizational crisis of the First World War was a body blow to established faiths, from which they have never recovered.

The second reaction I want to mention takes us back to the cross-over I was talking about earlier: the development of new, unbelieving variants of the vertical ideal of order.

The war was for most a terrible experience, but for some, like Ernst Jünger, it did offer a field for daring deeds and self-sacrifice, and for even more, it offered an experience of companionship, which they hadn't had and couldn't recreate in civilian life. The aftermath was a terrible disappointment, in view of the promises made for renewal. And so the spiritual hunger with which many entered the war remained unsatisfied. Various extremist movements built themselves on this continuing aspiration, both communist and fascist. Hitler and Mussolini spoke directly to the experience of the former front-line fighter, who felt disoriented back in civilian life, unappreciated, and had a lingering sense of having been betrayed by the people behind the lines.

Fascism gives us the paradigm of a counter-ideal of the modern order, one which extolled command, leadership, dedication, obedience, over individualism, rights and democracy, but which did so out of a cult for greatness, will, action, life. There was no place left for the morality of Christianity, and certainly not of liberalism; the ultimate goal was to make something great out of one's life. Greatness was measured partly in the impact of power, through domination, conquest; partly in the pitch of dedication, and here the giving and risking of death was the measure; and partly in aesthetic categories.

As Eksteins points out, the propaganda of fascist and Nazi régimes was not simply a means. This celebration of power, of the triumph of the will, was partly that in aid of which the whole operation was undertaken. This is what Benjamin had pointed to in talking of "the aestheticization of politics". And the celebrations turned to a surprising degree on death. "The grandest of Nazi ceremonies seemed to focus on the laying of wreaths, on the celebration of heroes or martyrs, whether they were Frederick the Great, the fallen of the war, the party dead of the 1923 Munich Putsch, or Horst Wessel. 'Propaganda of the corpse' was how Harry Kessler described this aspect of Nazism."[61]

By the 1930s, even Catholic societies where the counter-ideal is powerful, like Spain, Portugal, later Vichy France, not to speak of Italy, see a strong influence and role of this new kind of worship of power in the face of death.

We see from these short reflections that an important facet of the struggle between belief and unbelief, as well as the development of new forms of both, has been connected with ideals and counter-ideals of the moral order of society. It is necessary to say this today, because we seem in the West largely to have left the age behind in which this was true—although a glance at Islamic societies shows that this is far from universal. But in the West, some kind of uncoupling has taken place, which would have been inconceivable for many of our forebears—Catholics of Action Française for instance, for whom "le Catholicisme intégral" was inseparable from a change of régime, Communists whose whole faith in man demanded the Revolution. We mustn't exaggerate. Even back in the France of the early twentieth century, there were Catholics for whom the faith was delinked from the Right: Péguy, Claudel, later Bernanos and Maritain. But it appears that in the last half-century, we have entered a new world, in which the old links have virtually disappeared.

How did the delinking of the polemic from these ideals occur? It is not that modern forms of humanism or faith are unconnected to ideals of order. On the contrary. But they are now connected to the same one. The modern ideal has triumphed. We are all partisans of human rights.

This is part of the explanation. But there has also been a delinking of religion from society, or rather a transfer of spirituality to a new kind of niche in society. This is the transition that I will try to describe below, in the next part.

PART IV

Narratives of Secularization

12 The Age of Mobilization

1

Let's try to see where we have got to in this story of the rise of modern secularity in the West. The end of the eighteenth century saw the emergence of a viable alternative to Christianity in exclusive humanism; it also saw a number of reactions against this, and the understanding of human life which produced it. This was the beginning of what I'm calling the nova effect, the steadily widening gamut of new positions—some believing, some unbelieving, some hard to classify—which have become available options for us. But all this is happening among social élites, sometimes—when it comes to the development of new forms of unbelief—only among the intelligentsia. And this process of élite pluralization continues throughout the nineteenth century, at different paces, and with differently spaced interruptions in different societies. It is this process that I have been following, at least in some of its aspects, in the preceding chapters.

But somehow, in the intervening two centuries, the predicament of the then upper strata has become that of whole societies. Not only has the palette of options (religious and areligious) widened, but the very locus of the religious, or the spiritual, in social life has shifted. How did this come about?

Here we enter onto the terrain of "secularization theory". This has been mainly concerned with explaining various facets of secularity 1 (the retreat of religion in public life) and 2 (the decline in belief and practice), but obviously, there is going to be a lot of overlap between these and secularity 3 (the change in the conditions of belief). In particular, the relation of this latter with secularity 2 is bound to be close. This is not because the two changes are identical, or even bound to go together. But the change I am interested in here, (3), involves among other things the arising of a humanist alternative. This is a precondition for (2) the rise of actual unbelief, which in turn often contributes to (2) the decline of practice. Nothing makes these consequences ineluctable, but they cannot happen at all unless the original pluralization of alternatives occurs.

So in order to understand how what were alternatives for the few became so for the many, it will be helpful to lean on what is known about the decline or lack of decline of belief. The story here is incredibly complicated, with wide variations between different countries, regions, classes, milieux, etc. And as in the preceding chapters, my discussion here will mainly focus on some phases of the process, in some societies (mainly Britain, France and sometimes the U.S.A., with occasional side glances elsewhere). So needless to say, my remarks here will be very provisional. But I venture to hope that they can nevertheless be helpful, that some general lines of change can be made visible, at least in the countries mainly discussed, and that in this way they may make a small contribution to the general story of secularization in the West.

Now we might be tempted to think that the spiritual condition of the élite became that of the masses largely through diffusion. This was aided by the expansion of standard education, the spread of literacy, and then of higher levels of schooling, and more recently through the great growth in university training. The élite condition often became generalized too, by the fact that modern society inducts everyone into the same mode of life, tends to wipe out the distinction between town and country, and inculcates in everyone the same social imaginary, relating to the society as a whole, particularly with the penetration everywhere of electronic media.

Now all these have played an important role, particularly recently. But the actual road from there to here has been much more bumpy and indirect than a simple diffusion story can capture. To begin with, in a number of countries, religious practice rose in the nineteenth and sometimes also the twentieth century. Some people calculate that the apogee of Catholic practice in France comes around 1870, after the crisis of the Revolution with its "dechristianization" campaigns, constitutional church, and other such traumas.[1]

Thereafter there is decline, which becomes steep in the 1960s. Figures for adherence to churches rise in England during the nineteenth century, reaching a peak round the beginning of the twentieth century, before a slow decline sets in, which becomes faster after the Second World War, and quite precipitate after the 1960s.[2] As for the U.S.A., some calculate a steady rise in religious adherence from the Revolution right through to the 1960s, with only a relatively small decline since.[3]

This, of course, shouldn't surprise us. We should put it in the context of the drive to Reform, which arguably underlies the whole movement of which "secularization" is an offshoot. All earlier efforts at remaking the church aimed at increasing levels of orthodox practice. The last great drive of French Catholicism, previous to the nineteenth-century effort, was the Counter-Reformation of the seventeenth century, which succeeded in reaching people who had previously been marginal practitioners, and integrating them. It carried out wide ranging internal missions. And something analogous takes place in the more Protestant cultures of Britain and America, with missions and revival movements moving out to church the unchurched.

In the British and French cases, one clear aim of those who sponsored these missions in, roughly, the nineteenth century was to prevent the diffusion of the fractured metaphysical-religious culture of the upper crust and intelligentsia, for whom unbelief was a real option. No one can doubt that this was a primary objective of Restoration French Catholicism, but it also figured in the Evangelical movement of late-eighteenth century England, in Chalmers' efforts in Scotland in the early nineteenth century, and elsewhere. Why were these movements successful, where they were successful? And why did it all collapse in recent decades? We can see from the above figures that the 1960s or thereabouts is a watershed moment in all three countries, and in fact in many others in the western world; what happened? And, of course, the great enigma of secularization theory remains the United States. Why does this society so flagrantly stand out from other Atlantic countries?

I would be crazy even to pretend for a minute that I could answer these questions. They are perhaps even unanswerable in the terms in which they are often put by sociologists, who are induced by their discipline to seek explanations by general factors. But these regularly turn out to have less than meets the eye.

Thus one of the factors often referred to in secularization theory is "differentiation", the process by which functions which are originally carried out together crystallize out and fall into separate spheres, with their own norms, rules, and institutions.[4] For instance, the household was once both a site for living and a site for production. But this latter function has since moved out of it, and the enterprises where it now takes place form the sphere we think of as "the economy", with its own intrinsic rationality. In a similar way, the church used to provide education and "health care", and these now take place in specialized institutions which are often state-financed and -run.

Now these developments are certainly relevant to our whole subject. If nothing else, some of them could perhaps be taken as a description of secularity 1, relegating God and religion to the margins of various public spheres. But even this equation raises problems, and when one tries to use differentiation to explain secularity 2, objections must arise. The difficulty with the equation of differentiation and secularity 1 is this: the fact that activity in a given sphere follows its own inherent rationality and doesn't permit of the older kind of faith-based norming doesn't mean that it cannot still be very much shaped by faith. Thus an entrepreneur in a modern economy couldn't accommodate the mediaeval Church interdict on usury, but that wouldn't prevent a devout Calvinist from carrying on his business to the glory of God, giving much of the proceeds to charity, etc. Similarly, a modern doctor will not usually send her patient to touch a relic, but her vocation to medicine may be deeply grounded in her faith. Obvious problems relating differentiation to secularity 2 follow.[5]

The mistake in this latter case, involving the doctor, is to identify secularization with disenchantment. But if secularization (in our civilization) is supposed to include some kind of decline or recession of Christian (and/or Jewish) faith, this identification cannot stand. As Weber, Gauchet, Berger, and many others have repeatedly stated,[6] both Judaism and Christianity have themselves at different times fostered various kinds of disenchantment.

José Casanova has persuasively argued against the identification of differentiation and privatization. A separation out and emancipation of secular spheres, like the state, the economy, and science, has undoubtedly occurred. But it doesn't follow at all "that the process of secularization would bring in its wake the privatization and, some added, the marginalization of religion in the modern world". On the contrary, claims Casanova, today "we are witnessing the 'deprivatization' of religion. . . . Religious traditions throughout the world are refusing to accept the marginal and privatized role which theories of modernity as well as theories of secularization had reserved for them."[7]

Difficulties of another kind arise with generalizations which look plausible in a number of salient cases, but turn out not to hold more widely, such as that linking urbanization and secularity 2. Some have argued that the reverse seems to be true for the U.S.A.[8] And the generalization may not have held of the U.K. during the nineteenth century.[9]

Here we get to a key point with this kind of historical thinking. Situations are so various and sui generis, and recognizably repeatable factors may be understood and lived so differently in these situations, that in the end we can be surer of certain particular causal attributions than we ever can of what appear to be the generalizations based on them. Weber was aware of this predicament, and Bruce brings it forcefully to bear in criticizing some of his critics.[10]

So what does all this mean for the idea of "secularization"? It is a commonplace that something that deserves this title has taken place in our civilization; although sometimes this will be contested by scholars.[11] But the problem is defining exactly what it is that has happened. Indeed, even the demurrals about whether "secularization" has occurred turn on these issues of interpretation.

Everyone can see that there have been declines in practice and declared belief in many countries, particularly in recent decades; that God is not present in public space as in past centuries, and so on for a host of other changes. But how to understand and interpret these changes may not be evident.

There are in fact two big grounds for demurral. 'Secularization' is generally thought of as the name for some kind of decline in religion. So you can question whether religion has really receded in our era as much as appears; or while accepting that it doesn't occupy all that much space, you can wonder whether it ever did. You can question, in other words, our images of a past golden age of religion, an "age of faith"; perhaps things are after all not that different, beneath a changed exterior.

Both these claims turn on questions of interpretation. What is religion? If one identifies this with the great historic faiths, or even with explicit belief in supernatural beings, then it seems to have declined. But if you include a wide range of spiritual and semi-spiritual beliefs; or if you cast your net even wider and think of someone's religion as the shape of their ultimate concern, then indeed, one can make a case that religion is as present as ever.

On the second score, what is the past we are comparing ourselves with? Even in ages of faith, everybody wasn't really devout. What about the reluctant parishioners who rarely attended? Are they really so different from people who declare themselves non-religious today?

I believe myself that the secularization thesis can resist most of these challenges. But this is not to say that something important is not gained by going through them. It allows us to refine our account of exactly what has happened. There is after all, more than one change which has gone on; what do we want to include under the title "secularization"? Does the fact that clergy can no longer haul people before church courts for not paying their tithes mean that we are less religious? Not certainly by itself. There are very devout societies today where this doesn't happen and can't happen. And of course, no Pope or bishop could bring a ruler to beg penance on his knees, as happened to Henry II of England and Henry IV of the Empire. But this had already become impossible by the time that Henry VIII of England rammed through his supremacy act, or the troops of the Emperor Charles V sacked Rome. Does this mean that "secularization" had essentially happened by the early sixteenth century? We can't just identify "religion" and twelfth-century Catholicism, and then count every move away from this as decline, as David Martin has persuasively argued.[12]

Part of the intellectual problem here, and certainly much of the reason for the emotional reaction, is that there is also an important "unthought" (if I can use this Foucauldian term) which underpins much secularization theory. Opponents of the theory speak of an "ideology" of secularization, one that judges religion false and therefore inexorably in decline. The various "death of God" scenarios I mentioned earlier could be seen as variants of this. But the term "ideology" is misplaced here. It implies that partisanship has overwhelmed scholarship, that bad faith reigns. Bruce is quite right to rebut this suggestion.[13]

But this doesn't dispose of the suggestion that much of the sociology/history of secularization has been affected/shaped by an "unthought", which is related in a more complex way to the outlook of the author in question, that is, not simply as a polemical extension of one's views, but in the more subtle way that one's own framework beliefs and values can constrict one's theoretical imagination.

This, rather than flaming, polemical partisanship is the real stumbling block of neutral social science. One can read in the Preface to a contemporary work: "Which, if any, of the religions treated here is 'true' is no business of the social scientist, who should always aspire to value neutrality, even if that state is difficult to attain."[14] The emphasis should be on this last clause. Determining just what has happened depends on a host of interpretive judgments, on issues such as the exact nature of religion, or the content of Christian faith, and these will be deeply coloured by our substantive beliefs. Thus the author of the above quote goes on in his book to give some of the reasons for the decline in religion. He mentions the development of science and technology. This is not because he holds the standard "death of God" theory that science disproved religion, which thus disappears. On the contrary, he explicitly rejects this. People are too good at insulating their "beliefs from apparently contradictory evidence". But he does think that the availability of technical solutions to life problems tends to turn us away from religion. "There is no need for religious rites or spells to protect cattle against ringworm when you can buy a drench which has proven over and over to be an excellent cure for the condition."[15]

But this seems to me to confound disenchantment with the decline of religion, and thus to fudge again the complex, sometimes contradictory relation between the religions dominant in our civilization, Judaism and Christianity, and the enchanted world which I referred to above. Our disagreement here turns on our respective understandings of religion, which cannot but be initially very much shaped by our substantive beliefs.

I am not arguing some "post-modern" thesis that we are each imprisoned in our own outlook, and can do nothing to rationally convince each other. On the contrary, I think we can marshal arguments to induce others to modify their judgments and (what is closely connected) to widen their sympathies. But this task is very difficult, and what is more important, it is never complete. We don't just decide once and for all when we enter sociology class to leave our "values" at the door. They don't just enter as conscious premises which we can discount. They continue to shape our thought at a much deeper level, and it is only a continuing open exchange with those of different standpoints which will help us to correct some of the distortions they engender.[16]

For this reason we have to be aware of the ways in which an "unthought" of secularization, as well as various modes of religious belief, can bedevil the debate. There is, indeed, a powerful such unthought operative: an outlook which holds that religion must decline either (a) because it is false, and science shows this to be so; or (b) because it is increasingly irrelevant now that we can cure ringworm by drenches; or (c) because religion is based on authority, and modern societies give an increasingly important place to individual autonomy; or some combination of the above. This is strong not so much because it is widely supported in the population at large—how widely seems to vary from society to society—but because it is very strong among intellectuals and academics, even in countries like the U.S.A. where general religious practice is very high. Indeed, the exclusion/irrelevance of religion is often part of the unnoticed background of social science, history, philosophy, psychology. In fact, even unbelieving sociologists of religion often remark how their colleagues in other parts of the discipline express surprise at the attention devoted to such a marginal phenomenon.[17] In this kind of climate, distortive judgments unconsciously engendered out of this outlook can often thrive unchallenged. This was the well-taken point of David Martin's cri de coeur about "eliminating secularization".[18]

Now of course, my writing is also shaped by a different "unthought", and I want to try to articulate some of that here, because I think that this is the way to advance the debate. But I can best do this by contrasting it with that implicit in much mainstream secularization theory.

The basic insight underlying the "orthodox" modes of theory in this domain[19] is that "modernity" (in some sense) tends to repress or reduce "religion" (in some sense). I have no quarrel with this; there is a sense in which I concur. It is one of the main aims of this book to define this sense more exactly. Nor do I quarrel with the definition of religion which many orthodox theorists offer. Thus Bruce offers the following defining description: "Religion for us consists of actions, beliefs and institutions predicated upon the assumption of the existence of either supernatural entities with powers of agency, or impersonal powers or processes possessed of moral purpose, which have the capacity to set the conditions of, or to intervene in, human affairs."[20]

Of course, there is a lot one could cavil at in detail. One of the big problems with this definition is drawing the line: there are various forms of "spiritual" outlook today which don't seem to invoke the "supernatural", but it is often hard to say. But this kind of problem will affect any definition. More troubling, 'supernatural' is a term which has developed in Christian civilization; the sharp line between the "natural" and what is beyond is not marked elsewhere. That would be an objection if this definition were meant to serve a sociology/history of the world; but in fact, we are really looking at the history of the West, of the former Latin Christendom, and within this domain, 'supernatural' offers a good first approximation.

Moreover, I agree with Bruce's intent here, which is to prevent such a broad and inclusive definition of 'religion' that we end up arguing that nothing has changed. Plainly something important has happened; there has been a decline in something very significant, which most people recognize under the term 'religion'. We don't have to follow the masses in our use of this term, but we need *some* word if we are to try to understand the significance of this decline, and 'religion' is certainly the handiest one.[21]

Another thing that I like about Bruce's definition is that it includes the "impersonal powers", and thus recognizes the important place of what I called in Chapter 2 "moral forces" in our "enchanted" religious past.

With this definition in mind, I can agree with Bruce on the crucial phenomenon:

> Although it is possible to conceptualize it in other ways, secularization primarily refers to the beliefs of people. The core of what we mean when we talk of this society being more "secular" than that is that the lives of fewer people in the former than in the latter are influenced by religious beliefs.[22]

Having abandoned the attempt to define religion in a way which would be universally applicable, I would like to particularize even more what has come under pressure through modernity. Drawing on the discussion in the first chapter, I want to come at the phenomenon from two directions at once. I want to focus not only on beliefs and actions "predicated on the existence of supernatural entities" (a.k.a. "God"), but also on the perspective of a transformation of human beings which takes them beyond or outside of whatever is normally understood as human flourishing, even in a context of reasonable mutuality (that is, where we work for each other's flourishing). In the Christian case, this means our participating in the love (agape) of God for human beings, which is by definition a love which goes way beyond any possible mutuality, a self-giving not bounded by some measure of fairness. We grasp the specificity of this belief only by taking it from two sides, as it were, in terms of what it supposes as a supra-human power (God), and in terms of what this power calls us to, the perspective of transformation it opens.[23]

I descend to this level of specificity because I believe that the main struggle, both between and within groups and individuals, has been shaped by a polarization between this kind of transformation perspective, and a view which emerges in the eighteenth century in the context of the Modern Moral Order and commercial society, and which I described in Chapter 4. This is a view which sees our highest goal in terms of a certain kind of human flourishing, in a context of mutuality, pursuing each his/her own happiness on the basis of assured life and liberty, in a society of mutual benefit. Although this was first of all a providentialist view, with a place for some kind of God, variants arose which set their face against any illusions of higher transformation, which they saw as a danger to the order of mutuality, in short as "fanaticism" or "enthusiasm". There very soon developed atheist or agnostic forms.

There seem to be two very different stances in our civilization, which one can describe both as tempers and as outlooks. What does one think of Francis of Assisi, with his renunciation of his potential life as a merchant, his austerities, his stigmata? One can be deeply moved by this call to go beyond flourishing, and then one is tempted by the transformation perspective; or one can see him as a paradigm exemplar of what Hume calls "the monkish virtues", a practitioner of senseless self-denial and a threat to civil mutuality.

Of course, there are lots of people who want to situate themselves between what we might call the transformation and the immanence perspectives. This is particularly so in our age when the latter perspective tends to be supported by a materialist outlook. Many have taken a position between the two extremes, shying away from materialism, or from a narrow view of the morality of mutual benefit, and yet not wanting to return to the strong claims of the transformation view, with its far-reaching beliefs about the power of God in our lives. In the nineteenth century, Victor Hugo comes to mind; or Unitarians and ex-Unitarians like Emerson, or Matthew Arnold. The list could go on indefinitely. This kind of position is not insignificant; indeed, in some contemporary societies, in one or other variant, it may be a majority (but when you take account of people's ambivalences, counting is far from easy in this area). But people take up a stance of this kind in a field which is polarized by the two extreme perspectives; they define themselves in relation to the polar opposites, whereas the people in polar opposition don't return the favour, but usually define themselves in relation to each other, ignoring the middle (or abusively assimilating it to the other side). It is in this sense that the two extreme perspectives define the field.

So we could zero in on the following proposition as the heart of "secularization": modernity has led to a decline in the transformation perspective. So far orthodox secularization theorists would agree with me, even if they might have no interest in singling out transformation as a central issue. So what beef do I have with (orthodox) secularization theory?

A difficulty in this whole discussion is that there is some unclarity as to what exactly the "secularization" thesis amounts to. There are in fact, thinner and wider versions. What I'm calling the mainstream secularization thesis might be likened to a three-storey dwelling. The ground floor represents the factual claim that religious belief and practice have declined, and that "the scope and influence of religious institutions" is now less than in the past.[24] The basement contains some claims about how to explain these changes. In Bruce's case, the account is in terms of social fragmentation (including what is often called "differentiation"), the disappearance of community (and the growth of bureaucracy), and increasing rationalization.[25]

But this doesn't exhaust the richest versions. These add a storey above the ground floor, about the place of religion today. Where has the whole movement left us? What is the predicament, what are the vulnerabilities and strengths of religion and unbelief today? Here we are in the domain that I have designated secularity 3, and of course, it is the answers in this domain, the upper storey, that interest most people, non-scholars, but not only them.

Now much of the confusion about whether or not one agrees with "secularization" comes from the imprecision about how much of the building we're concerned with. If it's just the ground floor we're talking about, then there is wide agreement on the general drift, even though there be some cavilling at the details. Bruce often ropes in a broad church of scholars who allegedly agree on secularization, including, for instance, Martin and Berger. If this claim holds, it only extends to the ground floor. Once we get to the basement and the upper storey, divergences are evident.

Let's see what the "revisionists" reproach mainline theorists for. As we saw above, a big objection is that they take some feature of modernization, like urbanization, or industrialization, or the development of class society, or the rise of science/technology, and see them as working steadily to undermine and sideline religious faith; whereas, argue the revisionists, the actual movement is not at all linear in many cases. Sometimes, as in Britain, urbanization and industrialization led to the development of new forms which actually grew during the nineteenth century. A similar case might be made for Belgium, and for some parts of France. Then there are specific ethnic groups, like the Irish working class, the Welsh, and so on.

The accusation thrown at orthodox theorists is that they must somehow believe that these modern developments of themselves undermine belief, or make it harder; rather than seeing that the new structures indeed, undermine old forms, but leave open the possibility of new forms which can flourish. The attribution seems justified, because otherwise they wouldn't have so easily overlooked this contrary evidence. In other words, the revisionists are laying the mistake at the door of the "unthought" of mainline theorists.

This may be thought unfair, particularly to sociologists, whose field is not the nineteenth century, and who often feel that they don't have to concern themselves with history. But nevertheless, there does seem something to it. The impression is strengthened when one looks at the answer that Wallis and Bruce offer to the exceptions. They agree that churches can find a role which slows down or inhibits secularization, as the Irish and Polish cases show, but then they conclude

> These specific historical and cultural patterns suggest a simple heuristic principle, namely that social differentiation, societalization and rationalization generate secularization except where religion finds and retains work to do other than relating individuals to the supernatural.[26]

The last clause has to be read in the light of the definition of religion earlier, in terms of "supernatural entities". To say that religion finds other things to do than relating us to these, is to say that religious bodies find other functions or tasks, by definition, non-religious ones. Here religion is not functioning on its own, but as a support to something else. It has a "function" in another domain, here "cultural defense".

What this seems to imply is that "religion" is no longer an independent motivating force in conditions of modernity. Translated into the terms of my polarity above, the transformation perspective, it is assumed, has lost most of its power to draw people in modernity; so that something like the same actions and institutions which it used to sustain can only remain if they are powered by some other motive.

But with this kind of claim, we are already in the upper storey. It turns out that basement and higher floor are intimately linked; that is, that the explanation one gives for the declines registered by "secularization" relate closely to one's picture of the place of religion today. This is hardly surprising; any explanation in history takes as its background a certain view of the gamut of human motivations, in whose context the particular explanatory theses make sense. For instance, various "materialist" accounts, for whom religion is always "superstructure", its forms always to be explained by, say, economic structures and processes, are in effect denying any independent efficacy to religious aspirations. They are asserting for all time what I have just claimed mainline secularization seems to be saying about the modern age.[27]

Thus one very important focus of disagreement, even among those who are together on the ground floor, arises from their respective pictures of the upper storey, which must also set them at odds in the historically explanatory basement. This to a large extent underlies the historical disputes I alluded to above.

If we take this seeming denial of independent motivating force to religion, and put it together with the elision I referred to above, which took the thesis that modern technology makes it difficult to believe in magic and the enchanted world, and make this a thesis about religion in general ("There is no need for religious rites or spells to protect cattle against ringworm . . ."), we seem to be dealing with powerful enframing assumptions. We could perhaps articulate them in two (connected) propositions: (1) the disappearance thesis, (2) the epiphenomenal thesis.

The first says that the independent motivation to religious belief and action (if, indeed, it hasn't always been epiphenomenal) tends to disappear in conditions of modernity. The second says that in conditions of modernity (if not always), religious belief and action can only be epiphenomenal, that is, functional to some distinct goals or purposes. The second thesis seems implicit in the "heuristic principle" cited above; and the first seems implied by Bruce's rejection of a view he attributes to "the critics of the secularization approach", that there is "an enduring latent demand for religion".[28]

But I am also attributing these theses to Bruce and Wallis and Bruce not because they have (fully and clearly) stated them, but on the (admittedly indirect) grounds that if they held the negation of these propositions they would not argue the way they do; or at least would feel that some of their statements need more defense. But of course, lots of people do hold something like these two propositions. And we can understand why they might appear plausible to people firmly occupying the immanent perspective. It can appear plausible, either (a) because it seems to people in this standpoint that science has already refuted religion, and/or (b) because the religious motive was only ever tied to the misery, suffering, and despair of the human condition ("heart of a heartless world"—Marx; despair—E. P. Thompson); when humans come to control their world and society, the religious impulse must atrophy.[29]

What then does Bruce seem to be suggesting about the place of religion today? The quote about ringworm in cattle does seem to align him with a modified version of (a). The position sounds like a chastened, late-twentieth-century cousin to Renan's robust prediction: "il viendra un jour où l'humanité ne croira plus, mais où elle saura; un jour où elle saura le monde métaphysique et moral, comme elle sait déjà le monde physique";[30] as it were, what Renan might have said if he had appreciated how good people actually are at insulating their "beliefs from apparently contradicting evidence". But Bruce vigorously wants to separate himself from the old materialist-rationalist position, the Comtean idea that science will eventually do away with religion.[31]

Rather he seems to see a different end point to the whole development; not universal materialism, but widespread indifference.

> The fragmentation of the religious culture was, in time, to see the widespread, taken-for-granted and unexamined Christianity of the pre-Reformation period replaced by an equally widespread, taken-for-granted, and unexamined indifference to religion.[32]

Principled atheism and agnosticism will probably not become the default positions, for they "are features of religious cultures and were at their height in the Victorian era".[33] Rather, the suggestion seems to be, the whole issue will fade. It will be with religion as such, rather as it has been with certain political issues surrounding religion, like the fierce battle in France between monarchist Catholics and anti-clerical Republicans. Committed partisans on both sides dwindle, and eventually (we hope) later generations will wonder what the fuss was all about.

Or, as Bruce puts it in a later book:

> In so far as I can imagine an endpoint, it would not be self-conscious irreligion; you have to care too much about religion to be irreligious. It would be widespread indifference (what Weber called being religiously unmusical); no socially significant shared religion; and religious ideas being no more common than would be the case if all minds were wiped blank and people began from scratch to think about the world and their place in it.[34]

This, of course, might be right, but it seems to me deeply implausible. But this is because I cannot see the "demand for religion" just disappearing like that. It seems to me that our situation (the perennial human situation?) is to be open to two solicitations. One (in our civilization, anyway) is the draw to a transformation perspective. The other comes from a congeries of resistances to this kind of solicitation. These arise partly from the abuses and distortions which affect the going versions of the transformation perspective in our culture; and partly from the fact that following this perspective risks pulling us away from the modes of human flourishing which have developed in our culture, and to which we are deeply committed.

In our society (the West, I mean), the first draw is to some form of Christian faith, or in our increasingly plural world, a Jewish, or Muslim, or Buddhist commitment. The second response has taken form in the "laïque" or "secular" critique/rejection of religion, as a danger, even enemy to human flourishing. The second response entrenches one in a certain definition of this flourishing, which is made the absolute standard of good and bad, right and wrong. Each of these positions is inherently fragile, more particularly, open to destabilization by the other. The second can be upset by the draw to a transformation perspective, or something which claims the far-reaching, absolute nature of this perspective. The first is vulnerable to all the doubts and second thoughts arising from strong images of flourishing in our culture.

This doesn't mean that everybody is troubled. People often manage for big parts of their lives anyway, to be calm and well-entrenched in one or other of these positions, or in the various compromise postures I mentioned earlier. There are untroubled exclusive humanists; and also unruffled believers, who are even very satisfied with their own performance. These latter may have adopted a transformation perspective without fully measuring what it means. (In fact, this applies in some degree to virtually all believers). But they all remain vulnerable, in the sense that circumstances may arise in which they feel the force of the opposite solicitation. And if they don't, often their children will. This seems to me to be one of the lessons of the

1960s, where the thirst for the absolute was very evident, even though it often didn't take a "religious" form.

Now I am not claiming for myself in all this a position of objectivity, free from any "unthought". On the contrary, I stand in the other perspective; I am moved by the life of Francis of Assisi, for instance; and that has something to do with why this picture of the disappearance of independent religious aspiration seems to me so implausible.[35] But that doesn't mean that we have simply a stand-off here, where we make declarations to each other from out of our respective ultimate premises. Presumably, one or other view about religious aspiration can allow us to make better sense of what has actually happened. Being in one or other perspective makes it easier for some or other insights to come to you; but there is still the question of how these insights pan out in the actual account of history.

So let me try to set out an alternative take on the last centuries, which offers a different picture of secularization. Briefly, the mainline thesis is right to this extent, that most of the changes they identify (e.g., urbanization, industrialization, migration, the fracturing of earlier communities) had a negative effect on the previously existing religious forms. They often made some of the earlier practices impossible, while others lost their meaning or their force. This did sometimes lead whole groups to adopt some quite other outlook, antithetical to Christianity, or indeed, to any religion: such as Jacobinism, Marxism or anarchism (as in Spain); but it also happened that people responded to the breakdown by developing new religious forms. This happened partly through the founding of new denominations, such as Methodism and its off-shoots. But it also could happen through new modes of organization and new spiritual directions in older established churches, the Catholic Church for instance.

Our contemporary situation results from a further development, which can be dated to the period after the Second World War, more precisely, the 1960s and their aftermath. In this the nineteenth and early-twentieth century constructions, which responded to the earlier breakdown, were themselves undermined, in what can only be described as a cultural revolution of some magnitude. As we analyse and discuss this, new forms again are evolving.

This reading allows us to see certain things which the mainline reading occludes. First, it doesn't see the decline as linear, that is, the decline of one unchanging thing, over centuries, under the steady operation of a single set of causes. The continuity consists in the fact that earlier forms were undermined both in (roughly) the earlier nineteenth and the late twentieth century. But the discontinuity resides in the fact that the forms concerned, and the forces undermining them, were different.[36] Second, it allows us to appreciate that and how the forms of religion actually changed, and are changing again today.

In brief, I come closest to agreement with the mainline thesis on the ground floor; as to the basement, there is some convergence: factors like urbanization, migration, etc. did count. But the way they counted was not by bringing about an atrophy of independent religious motivation. On the contrary, this was and is evident in the creation of new forms, replacing those disrupted or rendered unviable by these "secularizing" agents. The vector of this whole development does not point towards a kind of heat death of faith.

It should thus be clear that this is not an attempt to show that religion remains constant, that, suitably defined, its continuance refutes secularization (the ground floor). On the contrary, the present scene, shorn of the earlier forms, is different and unrecognizable to any earlier epoch. It is marked by an unheard of pluralism of outlooks, religious and non- and anti-religious, in which the number of possible positions seems to be increasing without end. It is marked in consequence by a great deal of mutual fragilization, and hence movement between different outlooks. It naturally depends on one's milieu, but it is harder and harder to find a niche where either belief or unbelief go without saying. And as a consequence, the proportion of belief is smaller and that of unbelief is larger than ever before; and this is even more clearly the case, if you define religion in terms of the transformation perspective.

Thus my own view of "secularization", which I freely confess has been shaped by my own perspective as a believer (but that I would nevertheless hope to be able to defend with arguments), is that there has certainly been a "decline" of religion. Religious belief now exists in a field of choices which include various forms of demurral and rejection; Christian faith exists in a field where there is also a wide range of other spiritual options. But the interesting story is not simply one of decline, but also of a new placement of the sacred or spiritual in relation to individual and social life. This new placement is now the occasion for recompositions of spiritual life in new forms, and for new ways of existing both in and out of relation to God.

2

Perhaps I can give a better idea of what this reading involves by offering an outrageously simplified potted history of the last two-and-some centuries, the move from an age of some élite unbelief (the eighteenth century) to that of mass secularization (the twenty-first). I want to introduce some Weber-style ideal types in order to mark the distinction between the different stages.[37] I talked earlier of religious forms which were undermined by later developments. These can perhaps best be defined in terms of two aspects: the social matrix within which religious life was carried on, and the forms of spirituality which this life consisted in.

The first ideal type is the "ancien régime" matrix. Here, invoking my discussion above about the development of modern social imaginaries, we can say that the understanding of order widespread among the people (as against the Enlightenment conceptions circulating among élites) is of a pre-modern kind, an order of hierarchical complementarity, which is grounded in the Divine Will, or the Law which holds since time out of mind, or the nature of things. This notion of order holds both for the larger society: we are subordinated to King, Lord, Bishops, nobility, each in their rank; and also for the microcosm of the village or the parish, where priest and noble (or in England, squire and parson) hold sway, and each person has their place. Indeed, we only belong to the larger society through our membership in this local microcosm.

In this parish world, collective ritual still has a large place, even in societies which have undergone Reform. This is partly to do with what rituals have been handed down, and here there is a gamut, where the list will obviously differ from Catholic to Protestant societies. But in spite of all attempts in the latter (and even in some Catholic areas, e.g., those dominated by Jansenists) to expunge "magical" and "pagan" elements,[38] there were substantial elements of "folk religion" in England, for instance. This might consist not so much in forbidden rituals (though those existed, in the consulting of "cunning women" for instance), as in an unorthodox meaning given to church feasts. Thus in some parts of England, Good Friday was important, not only for the theologically orthodox reason, but because the power it carried made it a good day for planting crops, and enabled hot cross buns to save houses from fire. Similar unofficial meanings inhered in New Year's Eve, St. Mark's Eve (April 24), Hallowe'en, and St. John's Eve (June 23). These rituals often had their origin in earlier pagan customs (for instance, Hallowe'en drew partly on the Celtic festival of Samhain) and they were concerned "to ward off evil, bring good luck and cement the solidarity of the community".[39] Unless they were persecuted and harried by the authorities, most parishioners felt no opposition between their more orthodox liturgical life and these unofficial beliefs and rituals. It was part of the sanctity of a particular time, like Good Friday, that it could have these other beneficent effects. Pre- and post-Axial religious elements co-existed without unease.

It is worth making this point, because successive reforming élites, clerical and lay, have tended to dismiss much folk religion as "pagan" and "superstitious"; and in this they have been followed by later "Enlightenment" critics of religion; as though the popular understanding of Good Friday were limited to its crop-enhancing power. There is a temptation in a modern "disenchanted" framework to follow the most severe reforming clerics of earlier times, and consider folk religion as utterly distinct from Christian faith; our peasant ancestors would be engaged on this view in a kind of happy syncretism, but the elements combined would be quite distinct, and animated by different principles: Christianity is about devotion, the love of God, folk ritual is about control, manipulation. Among the authors I am drawing on here, Obelkevich sometimes seems to come close to this perspective.[40]

But this is to misunderstand the nature of the pre-Axial stratum of popular Christianity. As we saw above, the rituals of pre-Axial religion were concerned with securing human flourishing, and protecting against the threats of disease, famine, flood, etc. These survive in what I called in Chapter 2 the post-Axial compromise, in which they are combined with a religious form which includes an aspiration to some higher good than flourishing, salvation, or eternal life, or Nirvana. This latter is usually sought more single-mindedly by élites, what Weber called religious "virtuosi": monks, sanyassi, Bhikhus. But the combination is not just a juxtaposition of alien elements. There is generally a real symbiosis.

Even in the pre-Axial period, ritual was not simply an attempt at manipulation of higher powers, as we would understand this today, because it was accompanied by a sense of awe at these higher powers, and often a sense of wrongness in going against them, captured by a term like 'hubris' for instance, as well as feelings of devotion and gratitude for favours conferred.[41] A fortiori, within the framework of post-Axial religions, these modes of awe and devotion were made over. Take a case like the crop-enhancing power of sowing on Good Friday. What the manipulative interpretation neglects is that the popular understanding of what conferred power on that day was basically the orthodox one: that this is the day on which Christ died for us. We see this again and again in Christian history, in the cult of relics for instance. We can think of a modern instance, related by Philippe Boutry in his book on the Ain department in the nineteenth century. Even in his lifetime, parishioners began to collect "relics" of the curé d'Ars. But that was because he became for them the paradigm of a "saint curé"; and the criteria for sanctity here were very much those of the universal church: charity, prayer, abnegation, etc. Williams makes a similar point in stressing the importance of the "good vicar", and the value of a blessing from him. But the criteria of goodness were profoundly Christian: kindness, openness, concern for his flock, self-sacrificial giving.[42]

In a similar way, the rites of passage had additional meanings: baptism marked entry into the community, Confirmation was a symbolic rite of entry into adulthood. Sarah Williams has shown how important the ceremony of "churching" was for non-élite Anglicans right up to the twentieth century. You weren't supposed to go out again after childbirth, before you brought the child to church. Breaches would often be sanctioned by the neighbours. But the "protective" force of these rituals didn't stand apart from, but rather built on their "Christian" meaning, e.g., giving thanks to God for the birth of a child.[43]

We can't neatly separate the Christian from the "pagan" in this religious form; but nevertheless, there was an important gap in this "ancien régime" mode of religious life. The same rituals were lived and understood rather differently by élites, clerical and/or other, on one hand, and by the popular majority on the other. The élites as we saw were made uneasy by many of the popular rituals and practices, and were often tempted to remake or even abolish them. From the popular side, we have in the nature of things less evidence of how they understood their religious life. But it seems clear from the examples we have cited, and others, that they valued and responded to the marks of personal sanctity in their priests; that for them these marks had more to do with charity, devotion to their flock, an openness to everyone (as against a too close relation to the squire or notable), and were less concerned with heroic forms of self-abnegation, sexual or otherwise (except insofar as abnegation directly served charity). For the rest, popular religion had a very important festive dimension: saints' days, pilgrimages to shrines, celebrations, in which religious ceremonies and more earthy festivities: banquets, dancing, were combined—too promiscuously combined, in the eyes of many clerics. Here was another source of friction with clergy, and a target for the latter's Reforming zeal.[44]

In this "ancien régime" form, we have a close connection between church membership and being part of a national, but particularly a local community; this connection was cemented in part by the coexistence of official orthodox ritual and prayer, on one hand, with, on the other, ritual forms concerned with defense, luck, warding off evil. These latter were designed to protect individuals, but also the community. At this deep, pre-Axial level, we are all in it together, when it comes to certain practices. The abstainer lets down the whole body. This synthesis of the pre- and post-Axial long continues even in societies which had passed through a process of Reform, whose goal was to raise personal commitment over (much) community ritual; and to purge the magical and pagan elements of the latter.

But these local community forms are disrupted. In a sense, the disruption starts with the Reformation itself, but the force of popular religion allows them to be reconstituted, often on an altered basis. It is a feature of the whole modern period, as we saw above (Chapter 2), that social élites become detached from, even hostile to much of popular culture, and attempt to make it over. One of the things they have frequently imposed is disenchantment, the suppression of "magic" and unofficial religion. And this by itself is disruptive of what we have called "ancien régime" forms.

Élites can often have tremendous power to impose these changes; their very secession from the popular forms can destabilize them. It is in the very nature of religion in an enchanted world, as I have just mentioned, that it defines the practice not simply or even primarily of individuals, but of whole societies.

A religion of this kind is uniquely vulnerable to the defection of élites, since they are often in a position severely to restrict, if not to put an end altogether to the central collective rituals. If the king himself will no longer play his role, what can one do? Or if the relics and statues of saints are burned, how go on drawing on their power?

Reform from on top can thus put a brutal end to a great deal of popular religion, without necessarily putting anything in its place for many of the people concerned. And this was not only an end de facto, it could also be seen as a kind of refutation. For those who believed in the influences and forces residing in certain places and things, the very fact that they could be destroyed without terrible retribution seemed to indicate that their power had fled. In this way, the reformers carried on a practice which had already been used time and again to spread the faith. When St. Boniface felled the sacred oak groves of the pagan Germans, just this demonstration effect was what was intended. And the missionaries who followed the Conquistadores in Mexico hastened to destroy the temples and cults of the natives, with the same intention, and similar results.[45]

We, alas, don't have a great deal of insight into the process from that point, because the reflections and deliberations of non-élites are almost by definition not lavishly recorded. But it would appear likely, both a priori and in terms of what we know, that they begin to fill the vacuum by weaving together a new outlook and a set of practices, drawn partly from the old, and partly from what has been offered in the way of new faith or faiths.

The English Reformation provides an early example of this for which we have some sense of its different phases. At first imposed by élites, it suppressed by force the main practices of a Catholicism which was the living faith of the majority.[46] There was a minority of non-élites who went along out of conviction; indeed, in the form of Lollardry, some among the people had anticipated Cromwell and Cranmer by almost two centuries. But for most people, a void was opened, a sense of loss which created the conditions for a restoration of the old faith, only slightly altered, under Mary. But later in the century, we find that the majority have come to find themselves at home within the Church of England, on the basis of a compromise between old practices and the new liturgy, which itself becomes and remains the target of critical, mainly Puritan minorities.

Now this process of élite-engendered destruction and popular recreation happened again and again in the centuries which follow. To mention only the history of France, the seventeenth century Counter-Reformation, particularly under Jansenist clergy, often involved the forbidding or abolition of popular practices; then the

Revolution and the dechristianization of the Jacobin period, not to speak of the imprisoning and exile of priests and bishops, brought about a severe disruption of religious practice.

With this last event, we obviously come to a new era. For the first time, the destroyers offer a new anti-Christian ideology to fill the gap. They were in the short term remarkably unsuccessful: the Republic and its new calendar didn't take hold. But a long-term battle is joined, between Catholic and "Republican" élites to make over France in their image.

It starts with the fall of Napoleon. The Restoration Catholic Church tries to win back the lost terrain, and it is supported by many leading groups, out of piety and/ or concern for social order.

But by and large the efforts of the Restoration Church remained within what I called above the "baroque" social imaginary. Indeed, the ultramontane church which emerges from the Revolution gives a new form to this imaginary; the flow of command is downward, from God through the hierarchy, and the aim is the reconstitution of a total Christian society, seen as one of hierarchical complementarity, in which each order plays its part for the good of the whole. At first the alliance of throne and altar is re-affirmed, but the goal of preserving the crucial place of the Church obviously permits of a more "democratic" variant, in which the other hierarchies are abandoned, and the Church alone retains the role of guide in a society otherwise based on complementary equality—the formula of early twentieth century "Christian Democracy".

Now like other "baroque" imaginaries, in spite of the damage caused by the Revolution, this one at first still embeds a lot of the older hierarchical understandings based on the Forms, and at the popular level, much of the enchanted world, albeit policed for orthodoxy. Society is still seen as organic, and one's place in this organic whole is the essential definer of obligation and duty. The Church is that of the whole society, to which everyone must belong; and moreover, the force which inheres in social obligations comes from the sacred of which the Church is guardian and articulator. Societies organized by such a church are in this (loose) meaning "Durkheimian", in the sense that church and social sacred are one—although the relation of primary and secondary focus is reversed, since for Durkheim the social is the principal focus, reflected in the divine, while the opposite is true for ultramontane Catholicism.

This kind of attempt to re-establish Christendom everywhere generated counter-efforts, which took the form of secularist liberal or radical movements, and often found their inspiration in the French Revolution. The result was a deep rift, and important levels of dissidence in the middle classes. Moreover, this dissidence often spread downward to lower or working classes, particularly to the latter. One reason for this was fairly evident, that the ultramontane church generally stood with the monarchical-hierarchical status quo, and thus drove those who suffered from this to oppose it.[47]

But there was probably something deeper at work here, which comes clearer to light when the Church switched to the "Christian Democratic" philosophy. The cultural gap between élite and mass, which is characteristic of the modern age, makes it difficult to sustain a church which is really for everyone in society. That is, the devotional lives of different milieux are likely to diverge more than they did in the Middle Ages, where most of the élites still participated in the pilgrimage-going, relic-visiting religious culture of ordinary people. Moreover, whatever differences there may have been in that age, they were over-arched by the sense of common plight which is inescapable from religion in an enchanted world. When we have to "beat the bounds" of the parish to protect our crops, or ring the carillon de tonnerre to ward off hail, then we are all in this together, squire as well as cottager.

But of course, cultural-devotional estrangement was further exacerbated by class conflict. Once the sense arises that we are not part of an organic community, but suffer from exploitation—and we can see that this sense was never very far from the surface even at the height of the ancien régime—then the issue arises of whose side the established church is on. For the most part, the answer was clear in much of Europe: the hierarchy came down on the side of the established order, or landlords and employers. There were just enough counter cases to show that the resulting alienation of non-élites from the church didn't have to happen.

This is where the processes of urbanization and industrialization enter our explanatory picture. They further the process of disintegration of the ancien régime forms, partly just through dislocation and great transfers to areas where there were few churches, but more profoundly by taking masses of people out of the parish context in which these forms had made sense. Much of the folk religion was tied to the agricultural context, or related to the customs of a particular community, and can't be recovered in the new context (though much also survived). Shifting forward to the time of the Third Republic, we can see that the opening up of the countryside, the drift to the cities, the impact of new national institutions, like the Army, all have an effect of disrupting the old ways. In spite of the efforts of Jansenists and Jacobins, many of the forms of mediaeval Catholicism remain alive in mid-nineteenth-century rural France.[48] People would still ring the carillon de tonnerre when hail threatened, for instance. But this entire range of practices was not only linked to a collectivity, as we have seen is typical for "enchanted" religion; it was linked to the specific type of community which was the parish. The erosion and breaking open of this community, the displacement of its members into cities, undermined and sidelined its practices as effectively as élite-imposed Reform, and sometimes even more so.

Then add to this that the relation with the élites that now have to be dealt with:

urban employers and magistrates, soon slides towards class war. Once the enchanted world fades, or we relate to it quite differently, as with urban workers, and once élite culture has gone its own way, and this way has come to dominate the official church, and once class conflict arises with employers, then inevitably a sense of religious alienation will rise among the people. And they can then be recruited to some opposing view, which in these ultramontane societies was generally a secular humanist one.

This brace of causes converges on the main effect. That is, the new city-dweller, no longer relating back to a living community, as some of the earlier temporary migrants had,[49] would find himself with a void in his spiritual life, and have to find a way of weaving new forms and community allegiances in the new situation. The "dechristianization" of the urban working classes in the later nineteenth century had often more to do with this than with an actual conversion to the new lay ideologies. Something similar might perhaps be said about the decline in practice among working class urban English people in the same period.

However, the void demands to be filled; and the new lay ideologies are possible, sometimes strong candidates; particularly where the leaders and organizers of the new working class and socialist movements were inspired by them. In late-sixteenth century England, there were still only forms of Christianity which could be drawn on to fill the gap. In late-nineteenth-century Europe, the gamut of choices had been crucially widened. Modalities of exclusive humanism were now options. And the often reactionary stance of the Church could only help to make them more plausible.

This kind of development occurred in France, and in Spain; and something similar even took place in certain Protestant societies, like Prussia-Germany, where the working class turned to a Social Democratic movement, philosophically committed to materialism.[50]

The remarkable fact was that this was not the whole story. The ultramontane church of the nineteenth century was also remarkably successful with masses of people, rural certainly, but also urban, including workers. It did so, because in spite of its claims to be the unchanging church, facing an apostate world, it adapted in certain crucial ways. It abandoned the kind of rigorism, the harsh stance towards sinners, of which Jansenism had been a leading form, and took on the more compassionate stance that Alfonso de Liguori had already advocated in the eighteenth century. It was more tolerant and open to popular modes of piety, including alleged miracle sites, like (most famously) Lourdes. And it proposed a warmer, more emotional piety, of which the devotion to the Sacred Heart was a prime example. Some of this change might have been tactical, but much must be put to the account of post-Romantic currents which were already strong in Europe as a whole, and which were inevitably present in the Church as well. Whatever the reasons, it turned its back on some of the more condemnatory and contemptuous stances of earlier Reforming élites for the masses.

But it also adapted in another crucial way. I said above that the imaginary which it officially adopted was an "ancien régime" one, based on hierarchy, an organic society in which each found his/her place, and in which obedience was owed to the hierarchy. But in fact, it began in practice to subvert this stance, because so much of what it wanted to do required not the re-enactment of existing orders in age-old hierarchies, but the organization of laypeople in new bodies, be it for fund-raising (as with the gigantic campaign to build Sacré Coeur de Montmartre), pilgrimages, and various forms of lay apostolates, some of which later came to be called collectively "Catholic Action". The Catholic church was unavoidably in the business of mobilizing, by which I mean organizing and recruiting people into membership organizations with some definite purpose. But this means new forms of collective action, created by the participants themselves; and this has no proper place in the ancien régime model. Gradually content began to break through form. In order to see better what this involved, let me now introduce a second ideal type.

3

This type essentially belongs to what we can call the Age of Mobilization.

What do I mean by 'mobilization' here? One obvious facet of its meaning is that it designates a process whereby people are persuaded, pushed, dragooned, or bullied into new forms of society, church, association. This generally means that they are induced through the actions of governments, church hierarchies, and/or other élites, not only to adopt new structures, but also to some extent to alter their social imaginaries, and sense of legitimacy, as well as their sense of what is crucially important in their lives or society. Described in this way, mobilization was already taking place during the English Reformation, or the French Counter-Reformation of the seventeenth century—indeed, the Crusades might be seen as an even earlier example. But these changes were taking place within a wider social context, that of Kingdom and Church, which were not themselves seen as the products of mobilization, but on the contrary as already there, the unchanging and unchangeable backdrop of all legitimacy.

But in an "age of mobilization", this backdrop is no longer there. It becomes clearer and clearer that whatever political, social, ecclesial structures we aspire to have to be mobilized into existence. This becomes evident eventually even to "reactionaries", whose paradigms are found in the ancien régime. They are often forced to act on this understanding before they can bring themselves to recognize it. But sooner or later, their discourse changes, and the features they want to reinstate of the old order become forms to be established, eternally valid perhaps, because willed by God, or in conformity with Nature, but still an ideal yet to be realized, and not already there. As this understanding dawns across the political/ecclesial spectrum, we enter the Age of Mobilization.

The ancien régime model interwove church and state, presented us as living in a hierarchical order, which had divine endorsement. In societies on this model, the presence of God was unavoidable; authority itself was bound up with the divine, and various invocations of God were inseparable from public life. But there was more than one form of this in our past. Between the sixteenth and the nineteenth centuries, we moved from an original model, which was alive in the Middle Ages, and in a number of non-Western cultures, to another very different one. It is this second one which defines what I want to call the Mobilization type.

The earlier, "ancien régime" form was connected to what one might call an "enchanted world". This is obviously borrowing from Max Weber, and introducing the antonym to his term "disenchanted". In an enchanted world there is a strong contrast between sacred and profane. By the sacred, I mean certain places: like churches, certain agents: priests, certain times: high feasts, certain actions: saying the Mass, in which the divine or the holy is present. As against these, other places, persons, times, actions count as profane.

In an enchanted world, there is an obvious way in which God can be present in society; in the loci of the sacred. And the political society can be closely connected to these, and can itself be thought to exist on a higher plane. Ernst Kantorowicz tells us that one of the first uses of the term 'mystical body' in European history referred to the French kingdom.[51] The king himself could be one of the links between the planes, represented respectively by the king's mortal and undying bodies.

Or to talk a slightly different language, in these earlier societies, the kingdom existed not only in ordinary, secular time, in which a strong transitivity rule held, but also existed in higher times. There are, of course, different kinds of higher times— Platonic eternity, where there is a level in which we are beyond the flux altogether; God's eternity as understood in the Christian tradition, a kind of gathering of time together; and various times of origins, in Mircea Eliade's sense.[52]

Now with advancing disenchantment, especially in Protestant societies, another model took shape, with relation both to the cosmos and the polity. In this the notion of Design was crucial. To take the cosmos, there was a shift from the enchanted world to a cosmos conceived in conformity with post-Newtonian science, in which there is absolutely no question of higher meanings being *expressed* in the universe around us. But there is still, with someone like Newton himself, for instance, a strong sense that the universe declares the glory of God. This is evident in its Design, its beauty, its regularity, but also in its having evidently been shaped to conduce to the welfare of His creatures, particularly of ourselves, the superior creatures who cap it all off. Now the presence of God no longer lies in the sacred, because this category fades in a disenchanted world. But He can be thought to be no less powerfully present through His Design.

This presence of God in the cosmos is matched by another idea: His presence in the polity. Here an analogous change takes place. The divine isn't there in a King who straddles the planes. But it can be present to the extent that we build a society which plainly follows God's design. This can be filled in with an idea of moral order which is seen as established by God, in the way invoked, for instance, in the American Declaration of Independence: Men have been created equal, and have been endowed by their creator with certain inalienable rights.

The idea of moral order which is expressed in this Declaration, and which has since become dominant in our world, is what I have been calling the Modern Moral Order. It is quite different from the orders which preceded it, because it starts from individuals, and doesn't see these as set a priori within a hierarchical order, outside of which they wouldn't be fully human agents. Its members are not agents who are essentially embedded in a society which in turn reflects and connects with the cosmos, but rather disembedded individuals who come to associate together. The design underlying the association is that each, in pursuing his or her own purposes in life, act to benefit others mutually. It calls for a society structured for mutual benefit, in which each respects the rights of others, and offers them mutual help of certain kinds. The most influential early articulator of this formula is John Locke, but the basic conception of such an order of mutual service has come down to us through a series of variants, including more radical ones, such as those presented by Rousseau and Marx.

But in the earlier days, when the plan was understood as Providential, and the order seen as Natural Law, which is the same as the law of God, building a society which fulfills these requirements was seen as fulfilling the design of God. To live in such a society was to live in one where God was present, not at all in the way that belonged to the enchanted world, through the sacred, but because we were following His design. God is present as the designer of the way we live. We see ourselves, to quote a famous phrase, as "one people under God".

In thus taking the United States as a paradigm case of this new idea of order, I am following Robert Bellah's tremendously fertile idea of an American "civil religion". Of course, the concept is understandably and rightly contested today, because some of the conditions of this religion are now being challenged, but there is no doubt that Bellah has captured something essential about American society, both at its inception, and for about two centuries thereafter.

The fundamental idea, that America had a vocation to carry out God's purposes, which alone makes sense of the passages Bellah quotes, for instance, from Kennedy's Inaugural Address, and even more from Lincoln's second Inaugural, and which can seem strange and threatening to many unbelievers in America today, has to be understood in relation to this conception of an order of free, rights-bearing individuals. This was what was invoked in the Declaration of Independence, which appealed to "the Laws of Nature and of Nature's God". The rightness of these laws, for both Deists and Theists, was grounded in their being part of the Providential Design. What the activism of the American Revolutionaries added to this was a view of history as the theatre in which this Design was to be progressively realized, and of their own society as the place where this realization was to be consummated—what Lincoln will later refer to as "the last best hope on earth". It was this notion of themselves as fulfilling Divine purposes which, along with the Biblical culture of Protestant America, facilitated the analogy with ancient Israel that often recurs in American official rhetoric of the early days.[53]

The confusion today arises from the fact that there is both continuity and discontinuity. What continues is the importance of some form of the modern idea of moral order. It is this which gives the sense that Americans are still operating on the same principles as the Founders. The rift comes from the fact that what makes this order the right one is, for many though not by any means for all, no longer God's Providence; the order is grounded in nature alone, or in some concept of civilization, or even in supposedly unchallengeable a priori principles, often inspired by Kant. So that some Americans want to rescue the Constitution from God, whereas others, with deeper historical roots, see this as doing violence to it. Hence the contemporary American Kulturkampf.

But the United States' path to modernity, although considered paradigmatic by many Americans, is in fact rather exceptional. All Western societies have trodden the path out of the ancien régime form into the Age of Mobilization, and beyond to our present predicament, which I will describe below. But the ride was much bumpier and more conflictual in old Europe. This was particularly the case in Catholic societies, as I indicated above, where the old model of presence lasted much longer. True, it was affected by disenchantment, and became more and more a compromise, in which the hierarchical order was in some sense treated as untouchable and the King as sacred, but in which also elements of functional justification began to creep in, where monarchical rule was argued to be indispensable for order, for example. We can think of this as the "baroque" compromise.

The path to what we are now living today passes out of both of these forms of divine presence in society into something different, which I want to define below. The path out of the Catholic "baroque" went through a catastrophic revolutionary overturn. But the "Protestant" one was smoother, and therefore harder in some ways to trace.

David Martin, in a number of insightful works,[54] has developed an interesting account of the "Protestant", more particularly "Anglophone" path. This comes about in societies in which the reigning forms of social imaginary centre more and more on the order of mutual benefit, and the "baroque" order is seen as distant and somewhat abhorrent, in short "Papist".

In keeping with this outlook, it seems more and more evident in these cultures that valid religious adherence can only be voluntary. Forcing it has less and less legitimacy. And so popular alienation from élite-dominated religion can take the form of new voluntary associations, rather different from the earlier churches. The prototype of these is the Wesleyan Methodists, but the real explosion in such free churches occurs in the United States at the end of the eighteenth century, and this transforms the face of American religion.

With the Methodists, we have something new, neither a church nor a sect, but a proto-form of what we now call a "denomination". A "church" in this Troeltschian sense claims to gather within it all members of society; as with the Catholic church, it sees its vocation as being the church for everyone. Some of the main Reformation churches had the same aspiration, and often managed to take with them into dissidence whole societies, for instance, in Germany, Scandinavia, and initially England as well.

But even what we call "sects" after Troeltsch, which concentrated on the "saved", those who really deserved to be members, were in a sense frustrated churches. That is, either like Presbyterians in England, they aspired to take over the one national church; or like some Anabaptists, they despaired of the larger society, but just for that reason tried to reduce their contacts with it to a minimum. They still tried to circumscribe a zone in which they defined religious life.

At its beginning, the Methodist movement didn't aspire to churchhood, just to being a current within the national Church of England. They would practise their own kind of spirituality, but within a broader body which included others. Their desired status was analogous in some ways to that of religious orders in the Catholic Church. Something of this sense of legitimate difference carries over when they are forced out, and becomes the standard outlook which distinguishes the denomination, dominant on the U.S. scene.

Denominations are like affinity groups. They don't see their differences from (at least some) others as make-or-break, salvation-or-damnation issues. Their way is better for them, may even be seen as better tout court, but doesn't cut them off from other recognized denominations. They thus exist in a space of other "churches", such that in another, more general sense, the whole group of these make up "the church". The injunction to worship in the church of your choice is an injunction to belong to the "church" in this broader sense, the limits of permitted choice defining its boundaries.

The denomination clearly belongs to the Age of Mobilization. It is not a divinely established body (though in another sense, the broader "church" may be seen as such), but something that we have to create—not just at our whim, but to fulfill the plan of God. In this, it resembles the new Republic as Providentially conceived in its civil religion. There is an affinity between the two, and each strengthened the other. That is, the voluntaristic dimension of the Great Awakening in the mid-eighteenth century obviously prepared the way for the revolutionary break of 1776; and in turn, the ethos of self-governing "independence" in the new Republic meant that the second Awakening in the early nineteenth century involved an even greater profusion of denominational initiatives than before.[55]

Now it is clear that this kind of spontaneously created affinity group offered unique advantages when migration, social change or class conflict rendered older, more inclusive churches in one way or another alien and forbidding for non-élites. Methodism was certainly not devised in order to accommodate class division; Wesley himself clove to the most unshakeable Tory convictions about social order, and even condemned the American Revolution in which so many of his transatlantic followers enthusiastically participated. And later, the main Methodist connections in England tried to damp down worker militancy against employers (although they were ready to mobilize both sides of industry against Tory landowners).

But nevertheless, whatever the original idea of the founders, the form was there ready to give shape and expression to the religious aspirations and insights of some group, whether defined by class, or by locality (such as mining villages in Northern England), or of region (like Wales), or region plus ideological affinity (e.g., the splits between Northern and Southern Methodists and Baptists in the U.S.A.), or even race (again the U.S. case). Whereas in societies where the model of one big, society-wide Church, in continuity with the original divine foundation, dominated the imagination (i.e., Catholic societies, but also some Lutheran ones, and even to a lesser degree some Calvinist ones [Scotland]) finding a creative solution to non-élite alienation within the compass of Christian faith was extremely difficult (but not impossible, as we shall see from certain examples below), where the voluntarist culture of mobilization was already part of religious self-understanding, new faith initiatives could more easily arise. The denominational imaginary made possible a flexibility unknown in most Continental societies.[56]

A number of different initiatives in fact took place, but the most impressive class was made up of what are loosely called "evangelical" modes of revival, which were widespread in Britain and America from the end of the eighteenth century.[57] At their most intense, these centred on certain central doctrines of the Reformation: our sinful condition, and the need for conversion, for a turning to God in faith, which would open us to His grace. The stress was often on this conversion as a personal act, undertaken for oneself, rather than as a disposition inhering in the group; and it was often taken, dramatically, under the press of powerful emotions, and in public.

Here was a powerful transformation perspective, in the terms of my earlier discussion, defined on one side by a deep, potentially overpowering sense of sin and imperfection, and on the other by an overwhelming feeling of the love of God and its power to heal; in a word, of "amazing grace". As in the earlier Reformation, this new empowerment was meant to yield fruit in an ordered life. And order and disorder were conceived in terms which were very understandable in the existing predicament of the popular strata of the time, often struggling to find their feet in a more and more market-driven economy, where survival often depended on adaptation to new conditions, migration, adopting new work disciplines, outside of traditional social forms. The danger was of sinking into forms of behaviour that were idle, irresponsible, undisciplined and wasteful. And behind these lay the lure of traditional modes of recreation and conviviality which could immure you in these dysfunctional forms—in the first place, drink and the tavern. That is why temperance was one of the central goals of evangelical cultures, in a way that sounds totally excessive to many contemporary ears. We are perhaps sobered (if that's the word), however, when we learn how much of a curse drink could be; for instance, that in the U.S.A. in the 1820s, the liquor consumption per capita was four times what it is today.[58]

And along with drink, aiding and abetting it, were other favoured activities: cruel sports, gambling, sexual promiscuity. This understanding of disorder targeted certain long-standing male forms of conviviality outside the family. The new understanding of order was family-centred, and often involved identifying the male as the source of potential disruption, and the female as victim and guardian of this ordered domestic space. Callum Brown even speaks here of a "demonization" of male qualities, and a "feminization of piety".[59] Order required the male to be a family man and a good provider; and this required that he become educated, disciplined, and a hard worker. Sobriety, industry, discipline were the principal virtues. Education and self-help were highly valued qualities. By attaining these, the man acquired a certain dignity, that of a free, self-governing agent. The goal could be captured in two terms: on the one hand, the "respectability" which went with an ordered life has been much stressed; but along with this, we should place free agency, the dignity of the citizen. Evangelicalism was basically an anti-hierarchical force, part of the drive for democracy.

This connection of salvation and sanctity with a certain moral order in our lives reminds us of the first Reformation, of which evangelicalism is in a sense a reprise, in different circumstances and with an even more central emphasis on personal commitment. And we can also look in the other direction and note how this movement carries on in our day, not so much in its home terrain of Britain and the U.S.A. (though it is still very strong in the latter), but nowadays in Latin America, Africa, Asia.[60] And we can note the same connection between accepting salvation and putting a certain kind of order in one's life. So that men in Latin America become more family centred, deserting certain kinds of male conviviality which stress machismo, becoming sober and good providers. Indeed, we might even extend the comparison to include non-Christian movements like the Nation of Islam in the U.S.A.[61]

We can see that these movements have a powerful effect in "secular" history, that of enabling certain populations to become capable of functioning as productive, ordered agents in a new non-traditional environment, be it nineteenth-century Manchester, or twentieth-century São Paulo, or twenty-first-century Lagos. And this gives rise to two reflections. First, will this tight identification of faith and a certain morality or order end up undercutting faith, as I have already argued it did among élites in the seventeenth and eighteenth century, and as it seems to have done, anyway in Britain, in the twentieth? It does indeed, seem that a faith which was originally connected with a sense of one's own powerlessness unaided to bring order to one's life, contrasted with the efficacy of grace to do this, will lose some of its relevance and convincing power if/when the required disciplines become second nature, and instead of feeling powerless, one feels in control of one's life. But however this may seem borne out by the long-term fate of earlier waves, we would be very foolish to predict what will happen to current waves of Pentecostalism in the Third World, not only because they have features of their own, unmatched by their predecessors, but because they are happening in a quite different social context, and our past experience concerns only the West.

The second reflection brings us back to the discussion in the first section about the power of an independent religious motivation. The history I have just been resuming might be summed up in social science language by saying that the (latent) function of the faith in these cases has been the inculcation of a productive, adaptive character structure. This might explain why faith declines once the function has been fulfilled. And all this might be grist to an epiphenomenalist mill, and entrench the two theses I mentioned above, in short the view that religion has no more independent force in modernity.

But looking at this case of evangelicalism-pentecostalism shows how misguided this would be. If "latent function" means de facto, not necessarily intended result, then the above claim is right. But if we are looking at the force of different motivations, in order to assess the independent power of religion in modernity, evangelicalism is far from an example of religion riding on the back of some other goal or purpose. Let us take a clear case of the latter in order to show the contrast. Some of the haute bourgeoisie in France, who were Voltairean in the late eighteenth century, became supporters of the Church after the Restoration, and even more after 1848. It was said of many of them that they were mainly influenced by the reflection that the Church was a good guarantor of order. I'm not hazarding a guess about how much genuine piety and how much social interest underlay this turn. Undoubtedly there was some of the latter, and let that serve as our contrast case.

The claim would be in this French case that genuine piety would not have to be strong, might indeed be close to absent altogether; fear of disorder would bring the bourgeois back to the pews, might even inculcate a sense of the rightness of this move. The evangelical case shows precisely the opposite. We can suppose that with part of himself, a pre-conversion worker as he tarried in the pub, drinking away his pay, wished that he could become a good provider (the analogue to the Paris bourgeois' desire for a docile working class). But this desire was not effective in producing the change. What turned out to be was the religious conversion, which shows itself to be an incomparably more powerful motive force in his life. Any theory which subordinates this to an ulterior motive has a heavy burden of proof. Of course, theories of a depth psychological nature might do the trick, and some have been thought of; but theories which invoke the latent social function cannot wash in this case.

We have been describing two ways in which religious faith might re-establish itself within the Mobilization model, after the break with the ancien régime. The first involved a presence of God at the level of the whole society, as the author of a Design which this society is undertaking to carry out. The Design of God, as it were, defines the political identity of this society. The second consists in "free" churches, set up as instruments of mutual help whereby individuals are brought in contact with the Word of God and mutually strengthen each other in ordering their lives along Godly lines. They consist very well together. Not only are they both organized on similar principles: mobilizing to carry out the will of God; but they can also be seen as mutually strengthening. This was the case in the early U.S.A. The Republic secures the freedom of the churches; and the churches sustain the Godly ethos which the Republic requires.

Here is the sense behind the injunction quoted above to worship in the church of your choice. This supposes that each church doesn't just operate for its own ends, in competition, even hostility to others. There will inevitably be lots of that. But the idea is that there will also be a convergence, a synergy in their ethical effect. So that together, they constitute a wider body, a "church"—or at least those of them do which fit within certain tolerable limits.

In earlier days on the American scene, Catholics were outside these limits, as they are still for many today. But for others, the limits have widened to include Jews as part of a common adhesion to Judaeo-Christian theism. (And more recently, they have widened again, to include Muslims and others, particularly after September 11, 2001.)

So it is a feature of denominationalism that, just because one's own church does not include all the faithful, there is a sense of belonging to a wider, less structured whole which does. And this can find at least partial expression in the state. That is, the members of mutually recognizing denominations can form a people "under God", with the sense of acting according to the demands of God in forming and maintaining their state, as in the case of the American "civil religion" alluded to above. Indeed, insofar as the divine Design includes freedom, this can be interpreted as calling for an openness to a plurality of denominations.

This sense of a providential political mission has been very strong among American Protestants, and remains alive till this day. But something analogous also developed in Britain. Linda Colley has claimed that a kind of British nationalism developed in the eighteenth century, part of which formed around the sense of a shared Protestantism, which over-arched differences in actual confession.[62] This built on a previous self-identification of Englishmen with the Protestant cause, in a world where the major threats to national security came from large "Papist" powers.

So in one way, a denominational identity tends to separate religion from the state. A denomination cannot be a national church, and its members can't accept and join whatever claims to be the national church. Denominationalism implies that churches are all equally options, and thrives best in a régime of separation of church and state, de facto if not de jure. But on another level, the political entity can be identified with the broader, over-arching "church", and this can be a crucial element in its patriotism.

This of course gives us a situation very different from the "Durkheimian" one prevailing in some Catholic countries, where the social sacred is defined and served by the Church. For one thing, in this disenchanted Protestant setting, there is no more sacred in the earlier sense, in which certain places, times, people, acts are distinguished as such from the profane. For another, no one church can uniquely define and celebrate the link of the political society and divine providence.

Of course, I am speaking here of an ideal type; one which in this regard is fully realized in the United States. The British situation is muddied by the continued existence of national churches, which in one case (the Anglican Church) goes on assuming a ceremonial role, which in type and even in many of its ritual details is a legacy of its Catholic, mediaeval past. But mass enjoyment of this ceremonial has long been unhooked from identification with this Church.

I will call this kind of link between religion and the state "neo-Durkheimian", contrasting on the one hand to the "paleo-Durkheimian" mode of "baroque" Catholic societies, and on the other to more recent forms in which the spiritual dimension of existence is quite unhooked from the political. The "paleo" phase corresponds to a situation in which a sense of the ontic dependence of the state on God and higher times is still alive, even though it may be weakened by disenchantment and an instrumental spirit; whereas in "neo" societies, God is present because it is his Design around which society is organized. It is this which we concur on as the identifying common description of our society, what we could call its "political identity."

Now if we look at this "Anglophone" trajectory, we can see that, unlike the "baroque" one, where the Church almost inevitably generated counter-forces, it can sustain a high level of religious belief and practice. Resentment at the power of élites, and estrangement from their spiritual style, can find expression in another mode of Christian life and worship. Popular groups can find and live by their own spiritual style, as the "enthusiastic" Methodists did in eighteenth-century England, and the Baptists did in the rural U.S., and Evangelicals and Pentecostals are doing today in Latin America, Africa, and Asia. Alienation from a Northeast dominated by genteel Episcopalians and Presbyterians can take the form of passionate born-again Evangelicalism in the South and West.

At the same time, belief is sustained by the "neo-Durkheimian" identification with the state. Over a long period, for many of the English, Christianity of a certain Protestant variety was identified with certain moral standards, often summed in the word "decency",[63] and England was thought to be the pre-eminent carrier of this variety on the world scene. This was what we could call the "established synthesis". English patriotism was built for many around this complex of beliefs and norms. Many Protestant Americans, and latterly some Catholic ones, have thought that the U.S.A. has a providential mission to spread liberal democracy among the rest of humankind.

In this neo-Durkheimian form, religious belonging is central to political identity. But the religious dimension also figures in what we might call the "civilizational" identity, the sense people have of the basic order by which they live, even imperfectly, as good, and (usually) as superior to the ways of life of outsiders, be they "barbarians", or "savages", or (in the more polite contemporary language) "less developed" peoples.

In fact, most of the time, we relate to the order established in our "civilization" the way people have always related to their most fundamental sense of order; we have both a sense of security in believing that it is really in effect in our world; and also a sense of our own superiority and goodness deriving from the confidence that we participate in it and uphold it. Which means that we can react with great insecurity when we see that it can be breached from outside, as at the World Trade Centre; but also that we are even more shaken when we feel that it might be undermined from within, or that we might be betraying it. There it is not only our security which is threatened; it is also our sense of our own integrity and goodness. To see this questioned is profoundly unsettling, threatening ultimately our ability to act.

Which is why in earlier times, we see people lashing out at such moments of threat, in scapegoating violence against "the enemy within", meeting the threat to our security by finessing that to our integrity, deflecting it onto the scapegoats. In earlier periods of Latin Christendom, Jews and witches were cast in this unenviable role. The evidence that we are still tempted to have recourse to similar mechanisms in our "enlightened" age is unsettling. But it would not be the first such paradox in history, if a doctrine of peaceful universalism were invoked to mobilize scapegoating violence.[64]

The point I want to make about British and later American patriotism, based as it was at first on the sense of fulfilling God's design, is that national identity was based on a self-ascribed pre-eminence in realizing a certain civilizational superiority. The superiority may have ultimately been understood as that of "Christendom" over infidel religions, but within Christendom, Britain/America stood at the cutting edge.

This sense of superiority, originally religious in essence, can and does undergo a "secularization", as the sense of civilizational superiority becomes detached from Providence, and attributed to race, or Enlightenment, or even some combination of the two. But the point of identifying here this sense of order is that it provides another niche, as it were, in which God can be present in our lives, or in our social imaginary; not just as the author of the Design which defines our political identity, but also of the Design which defines civilizational order.

But why distinguish them when they so obviously go together in the paradigm case of the U.S.A.? Because they don't always fit together in this way, but can operate separately. It is absolutely crucial to much Christian apologetics from the French Revolution onwards, that the Christian faith is essential to the maintenance of civilizational order, whether this is defined in terms of the Modern Moral Order, or in terms of their earlier hierarchical complementarity. This is the very staple of counter-Revolutionary thought, as it flows from the pen, for instance, of Joseph de Maistre. But one can hear something similar today, in a quite neo-Durkheimian context, from some parts of the religious Right in the U.S.A. The doctrine is, that our order is not stable unless based on an explicit recognition that we are following God's plan. So much for the belief involved.

But this can issue in a social imaginary, that our order is now stable, because we are following God's plan; or alternatively, that our order is threatened, because we are deviating from the plan. This sense of the presence, or the threatened absence, of God in our world, as the designer/guarantor of the civilizational order can be very present, even where it is not linked with a sense that our nation singles itself out by its pre-eminence in realizing His order. It may be relatively unhooked from our political identity. This view may reflect my own national identity, but it seems to me that the self-arrogation of such vanguard station is more likely (at least over the long run) among hegemonic powers. It's more difficult to think that you are at the cutting edge of human history, if you come from Norway, or Belgium (or Canada). But people in these smaller nations can still have a sense of God as the basis of their civilizational order.

But also, it may work the other way around; God may be central to our political identity, without this being linked to any pre-eminence in the broader order. Thus, in the course of modern history, confessional allegiances have come to be woven into the sense of identity of certain ethnic, national, class or regional groups.

We can discern here one application of a pattern which is central to what we might call the Age of Mobilization. The modern citizen social imaginary contrasts with various pre-modern forms in that these reflect an "embedded" understanding of human life. In relation to an ancien régime kingdom, we are seen as already, since time out of mind, defined as subjects of the King, and indeed, even placed more exactly, as serfs of this Lord, who holds from a Duke, who holds from the King; or as bourgeois of this city, who holds from, etc.; or members of this Cathedral chapter, which is under this Bishop, who relates to both Pope and King; and so on. Our relation to the whole is mediated. The modern citizen imaginary, on the other hand, sees us all as coming together to form this political entity, to which we all relate in the same way, as equal members. This entity has to be (or had to be, if it's already up and running) constructed. However much various modern ideologies, like nationalism, may convince us that we were always, since time out of mind, members of the X people (even though our ancestors didn't fully realize it, and even were forced/induced to speak the Y's language), and however much this gives us the vocation to construct our own state, X-land, nevertheless this state has (had) to be constructed. People need(ed) to be convinced that they were really Xes, and not Ys (Ukrainians and not Poles).

Two related features are crucial to this self-understanding. The first is that realizing who we really are (Xes) requires (required) mobilization. We had to be brought to act together to erect our state: rebel against the Ys, or appeal to the League of Nations, or whatever. And the second is that this mobilization is inseparable from a (re)definition of identity: we have to define ourselves, saliently, even sometimes primarily, as Xes, and not as a host of other things which we also are or could be (Poles, or Catholic-Uniates, or just members of this village, or just peasants, etc.).

These new entities—citizen states or other products of mobilization—are ordered around certain common poles of identity, let's call them "political identities". This doesn't have to be a linguistically-defined nation of course (though it often has been in the West). It can be a religious confession; it can be certain principles of government (Revolutionary France and U.S.A.); it can be historical links; and so on. This allows us to see the U.S. case as one example of a widespread feature of the modern world, in the Age of Mobilization. Political identities can also be woven around religious or confessional definitions, even where the reference to divine Design, as we see it in the U.S. case, is absent or secondary. Again, Britain and the U.S.A. are powerful, independent nations. But the confessional kind of identification often happens with marginal or oppressed populations. The Polish and Irish Catholic identities are well-known cases in point. The erstwhile French-Canadian one is another.

The link here between group and confession is not of the "ancien régime" type that we saw in counter-Revolutionary France, even though it is the same Catholic Church which is involved. Throne and altar can't be allied, because the throne is alien, not just when it is Lutheran, Anglican, or Orthodox, but even where it is Catholic (Vienna). Resentment at élites becomes marginal to the extent that these élites lose power and privilege. But the sense of national domination and oppression, the sense of virtue in suffering and struggle is deeply interwoven with the religious belief and allegiance—even to the point of such rhetorical excesses as the depiction of Poland as "Christ crucified among the nations". The result is what I'm calling a "neo-Durkheimian" effect, where the senses of belonging to group and confession are fused, and the moral issues of the group's history tend to be coded in religious categories. (The rival language for oppressed people was always that of the French Revolution. This had its moments in each of the subaltern nations mentioned here: the United Irish, Papineau's rebellion in 1837, Dąbrowski's legion; but in each case, the Catholic coding later took the upper hand.)

My "neo-Durkheimian" category can even be expanded to include a founding of political identity on an anti-religious philosophical stance, such as we saw with the long-standing "republican" French identity. The long-standing "guerre franco-française" was in this sense fought between two neo-Durkheimian identities. These then contrast with other kinds of political identities, those founded on a supposed linguistic-historical nation, for instance, or on a certain constitutional order.

This last, French, case shows that neo-Durkheimian identity mobilization extends well beyond established nations, or even wannabe nations, like Poland or Ireland. There are also cases of confessional mobilization which aims at political impact, even where this is purely defensive, and can't hope to issue in independent nationhood, as with Catholics in Germany during the Kulturkampf, and Dutch pillarization.

Now this phenomenon, religiously-defined political identity-mobilization, obviously has a tremendous present and (I fear) future in our world. I want to return to this in a later section. But for the moment, I want to point out that, where this effect takes hold, a potential decline in belief and practice is retarded or fails to occur. This easily gives rise to a misunderstanding in the climate of contemporary sociology with its rather "secular" mind-set. Once again, as with Evangelicalism above, we may be tempted to say of these situations, as well as the Anglophone nations above, that religion is performing an "integrating function", or in Bruce's language, that of "cultural defense". The slide is easy to the thesis that religious belief is the dependent variable here, its integrative function being the explanatory factor.

But I think it would be less distortive to say that the religious language is the one in which people find it meaningful to code their strong moral and political experience, either of oppression or of successful state building, around certain moral principles. The point of citing the different predicaments of Polish or Irish peasants or workers, on one hand, and their Spanish or French counterparts on the other, is that the first offered inducements and little resistance to coding in a Catholic language, whereas life in a "baroque" régime generates experiences which are strong deterrents to doing so.

Invoking Ireland and Poland brings us back to the attempts of the Catholic Church to recover the ground lost in the Revolutionary period and its aftermath. We could say of these that they were a triumph of mobilization, in a sense malgré elle.

4

But before I expand on this point, it might be useful to bring together the different facets of my distinction between "ancien régime" forms and "paleo-Durkheimian" polities on one hand, and the era of Mobilization with its "neo-Durkheimian" forms, on the other. These, I repeat, are ideal types; perhaps never completely instantiated—although the pre-Revolutionary French monarchy and the early nineteenth century American Republic can be taken as paradigms of each type.

The differences between the first (AR) and the second (M) can be laid out in the following list of contrasts:

(i) AR forms are based on a pre-modern idea of order, grounded in the cosmos and/or in higher time; whereas M is related to the modern Moral idea of order, as a way of coexistence among equals, based on principles of mutual benefit.

(ii) AR forms pre-exist the actual human beings which belong to them, and define their status and role; they are already there "since time out of mind"; whereas M offers a model which we are called upon to realize; human agency puts this design into effect in secular time. This is the intrinsic connection between M and what I have been calling "mobilization"; instead of being enjoined to remain in (or, after an unfortunate revolutionary hiatus) to return to their pre-existing places, people have to be induced, or forced, or organized to take their parts in the new structure; they have to be recruited into the creation of new structures.

(iii) AR forms are "organic", in the sense that society is articulated into constituent "orders" (nobility, clergy, bourgeoisie, peasants), and institutions (Assembly of clergy, Parliaments, estates), and smaller societies (parishes, communes, provinces), such that one only belongs to the whole through belonging to one of these constituent parts; whereas M societies are "direct-access"; the individual is a citizen "immediately", without reference to these different groupings, which can be made and unmade at will.

(iv) The world of AR forms is generally an enchanted world; whereas the move towards M involves a greater and greater disenchantment.

These ideal types of AR and "Mobilization" have helped to clarify the transitions I have been describing. In the way I have been using them here, they apply most centrally to the paths taken towards modernity and secularity in France and the Anglo-Saxon countries. More narrowly, my focus has been on certain key stages in the history of those societies, when the dissatisfaction with national, long-established churches made inevitable the development of new forms.

These stories I have been telling clearly have limitations, as does the particular ideal type "neo-Durkheimian", which I have made lavish use of in telling them. They cannot suffice to understand all the different national itineraries, nor all the stages within these. There are, for instance, a brace of Lutheran societies, in Germany and Scandinavia, which retained national, established churches, unaffected by large-scale dissidence, in some cases up to the present day. There are the other Latin societies, Italy, Spain, where developments bore some analogy to the French case, but are far from identical with it.

One can say that the AR ideal type had application everywhere in Europe, if we go back far enough. It is for cultural reasons quite understandable that the English and French monarchies had similar notions of the sacrality of kingship, of the King's Two Bodies, even of the power to cure the "King's evil" by touch. And both these societies understand themselves today thoroughly in terms of the Age of Mobilization. But their paths from the mediaeval starting point to the present were very different. Certainly, in the English case, the "ancien régime" monarchy of the eighteenth century had lost many of the sacralizing features of its mediaeval original. A really thorough study of all the diverse paths, across all of Latin Christendom would require an immense enlargement of our theoretical apparatus.[65]

This is unfortunately beyond my scope here (and certainly beyond my powers, at least for the moment). But the transitions I have been describing suffice for my limited purposes here. These are, negatively, to cast down on the formerly dominant, unilinear secularization theory, which sees the retreat of faith as a steady function of certain modernizing trends, such as the class differentiation of society, or the movement out of the countryside into the cities. The contrast between the French and the Anglo-American cases should be enough to challenge this view, since similar developments led in one case to a break-away from Christianity, and in another to the development of vigorous new forms of piety and church life. Indeed, it is clear that mobility itself doesn't tell in one direction or the other. As the French sociologist of religion Gabriel le Bras put it, when the French peasant in the late nineteenth century arrived at the Gare de Montparnasse, he was already lost to the church. But the migration of similar peasants to North America often brought about a new and more vigorous form of practice.

Positively, my aim is to suggest, in place of the supposed uniform and unilinear effect of modernity on religious belief and practice, another model, in which these changes do, indeed, frequently destabilize older forms, but where what follows depends heavily on what alternatives are available or can be invented out of the repertory of the populations concerned. In some cases, this turns out to be new religious forms. The pattern of modern religious life under "secularization" is one of destabilization and recomposition, a process which can be repeated many times.

A fully convincing proof of this would require the fuller study which I have admitted is beyond me here. But I think the results of the narrower comparisons I have made are quite convincing, and the addition of further varied itineraries could only add confirmation to my basic thesis.

Let me make one more caveat. Since I am dealing with ideal types, it will obviously be the case, even where they best apply, that plenty of the forms we can observe during the last three centuries lie in some ways athwart these distinctions. The point of the distinction is first, to identify the long term movement, "la tendance lourde", which is taking us from AR to M, but secondly, to be able to discriminate the different kinds of social matrix within which a common sense of belonging to the Christian church was maintained, and to see the rather different kind of belonging which was sustained in each.

But clearly there is something over-simple in speaking of pre-twentieth-century Britain as "neo-Durkheimian" sans phrase, when there were obviously important strands of deference, and hierarchy, and a reverence for the ancient constitution up to very recently (even now perhaps?); where there were still parishes of the Church of England, where community impregnated with folk religion was alive until quite recently. In a symmetrical way, it is too simple to speak of nineteenth-century France as continuing AR forms, when this was only partly true, and a new urban culture was arising and new institutions developing which belonged to the Age of Mobilization.

The point of the distinction is not to put whole societies and/or whole time-slices into one or another slot, but to show how the weighting of AR and M forms in each gave a different shape and curvature to a movement which at a very general level was common to all: the evacuation of AR forms in favour of M ones, followed by the undermining even of these latter in the second half of the twentieth century.

And here I come to my point about the Catholic reaction of the nineteenth century being a triumph of mobilization in spite of itself. To take the French case first, the original attempt was certainly to reconstitute a church around the defense of hierarchy, not just clerical but also lay. The trauma of the Revolutionary period drove the Church back to the alliance of throne and altar, in spite of the more insightful proposals of people like Ozanam and Lammenais. But first, the rebuilding eventually came to require far-reaching organization, involving lay men and women, as well as regulars and nuns. And second, the features of the nineteenth-century Church which fitted best with the goal of Restoration were vulnerable to the developments of modernity in that century: towns, industry, communications, mobility. Then third, the very attempt to defend these features involved organization, recruiting, in brief mobilization, which itself undermined these forms.

Taking the second and third points together, the features which I am speaking about here were most in evidence in the rural parishes of nineteenth-century France. At the antipodes from the mode of belonging to a Methodist church in America, for instance, which was compatible with almost infinite mobility, the primary locus of Catholic life for rural folk was the parish (line (iii) of the contrast above). The religious life of this parish brought together Catholic liturgy and practice with folk religion, as I described above, the latter operating very much in an enchanted world (line (iv) above). Moreover, each parish had its own mix of these two elements: for instance its own special saints, pilgrimages, cults of saints as healers and protectors, and the like (line (iii) again).

As Boutry puts it,

Il convient de marquer combien "naturellement" cette "religion populaire" s'insère, s'intègre, dans la vie religieuse paroissiale, requiert même avec insistance l'office et les bénédictions des prêtres. La pregnance du surnaturel, l'union intime d'un culte, d'une date, d'un terroir, tels sont les traits communs à cet ensemble complexe de pratiques cultuelles, qui ne sont pas à ce titre si éloignées de la pratique paroissiale des sacrements. De cet ensemble de rites se dégage l'image d'une *religion du terroir*, fondement des mentalités religieuse de la chrétienneté rurale tout au long du siècle.[66]

(It should be noted how "naturally" this "popular religion" fits and integrates itself into the religious life of the parish, and even insistently calls upon the prayers and blessings of the priests. The saturation with the supernatural, the intimate union of a cult with a date and a locality, these are the common features of this complex set of ritual practices, which as such are not so far removed from the official parish practice of the sacrament. From this set of rites emerges the image of a *religion of the soil*, which is the foundation of the religious mentalities of rural Christianity throughout the century.)

This religion "of the soil" *(du terroir)* was lived in each village as a collective norm. It didn't simply reflect the upshot of the different individual forms and levels of devotion of the inhabitants. On the contrary, collective rituals were important to everybody, because on them depended the general welfare, success of crops, health of animals, protection against cholera (line (i) of the contrasts). And indeed, this range of practices was thought to hold "depuis des temps immémoriaux" (since time immemorial).[67]

But beyond this, even the level and type of liturgical devotion was prescribed for everyone. Priests who wanted to raise this level came up against a normative barrier, what was called by their parishioners "le respect humain". Our neo-Kantian ears quite mislead us as to the meaning of this expression. It doesn't designate what each of us is in conscience bound to do in order to respect our fellows. Rather it defines what each must do to gain and keep the respect of his co-parishioners. At the antipodes to Kant, it is a law of conformity, not autonomy. In many parishes, for instance, the norm was understood to be taking communion once a year, usually at Easter time. This was the essential, what we would call today, "paying your dues"; but going beyond this was frowned upon. When the movement developed in mid-century in the Church at large in favour of frequent communion, priests who tried to inculcate this ran up against the norms of "respect humain". Parishioners frequently couldn't be budged; they couldn't see this as a matter for individual decision, and felt quite unjustified in breaking with the usual practice. The only way an important change could be brought about, as it sometimes was by a charismatic curé (such as the curé d'Ars), was through a change in the collective mind. As an observer said about Ars, "Le respect humain était renversé. On avait honte de ne pas faire le bien et de ne pas pratiquer sa religion."[68] (The pressure to conformity began to operate in the reverse direction. One felt ashamed of not doing good and not practising one's religion.)

Here was a very important social matrix, of a fundamentally AR type, which held people together in their belonging to the Catholic church.[69] But various developments of the century were threatening to undermine it; the religious and political life of urban and élite France ran on quite different principles. People were divided, had divergent opinions, formed parties, fought each other. The two types of milieux couldn't be kept in isolation. Urban élites settled, or rural notables changed their views; some towns developed industries; people travelled. In the end the countryside was opened up not only by the railway, but by the anti-clerical governments of the Third Republic, which conscripted the young men into the Army, and sent teachers into the villages to wean people away from the Church.

In the end, the Republicans were successful. They divided these rural communities, and came out with a majority in the crucial elections of 1877. But the point made by Boutry, following Agulhon, is that this doesn't mean simply a regression of the same form of religion which has existed before 1860. Rather it means a shift from the strong community form, which Boutry and Agulhon call a "mentalité", to a new understanding of religion as something on which we all have to have an "opinion". "La paroisse [éclatée] n'est plus que le cadre collectif de dévotions individuelles" (the [fragmented] parish is nothing more than the collective framework of individual devotions). An ancien régime form has been replaced by one which belongs to the Age of Mobilization.[70]

With hindsight, we can see that this was going to happen anyway. But the pathos of this passage is that the clergy themselves contributed to it. They did this partly through their attempts to change and reform the elements of popular religion they didn't approve of. Of course, in this they were just following the centuries-old practice of Reform. Their seventeenth-century forebears had done the same thing, especially if they were Jansenists. If anything, the nineteenth-century clergy were much more cautious. They saw how excess of reforming zeal could alienate whole populations from Catholicism, and they had felt on their own backs what this could mean in the Revolutionary period. They were much more tolerant of folk religion than their predecessors; but nevertheless, they couldn't resist interfering.[71]

And one of their most important targets was the "christianisme festif" of their flock. It wasn't just that many of the festivals were around some dubious focus, for instance, a pilgrimage to a site of healing, where the rite seemed to have little to do with orthodox Christianity. It wasn't only that the State, using the powers of the Napoleonic Concordat, wanted to cut down on the number of feast days, in the name of greater productivity (and in this following a path already trodden by Protestant countries centuries earlier). What often troubled the clergy was the culture of the feast itself, which mixed some sacred ritual with a lot of very earthy eating, drinking, and dancing, with often unmentionable consequences for the sexual morality of young and old alike. They wanted to clean the feasts up, disengage their properly religious significance from the rather riotous community celebrations, and tone these down as much as possible. We connect up here with a long-standing vector of the centuries-long process of Reform; visible, for instance, on both the Catholic and Protestant side in the suppression of the "excesses" of Carnival, of which I spoke in Chapter 3; visible also in the attempts to suppress rowdiness and drinking at the statute fairs and village feasts which Obelkevich describes in nineteenth-century Lincolnshire.[72]

Secondly, the very attempt of the clergy to make their people over, and raise their level of practice and morality, meant that they were constantly pushing, reprimanding, demanding that some cabaret or dance hall be closed, that money be spent on a new church. Conflicts inevitably arose between priests and communities. At first these revolts were quite independent of any philosophical foundation. But through them, a new outlook, denouncing clerical power, and exalting the moral independence of the laity could enter. As Maurice Agulhon put it,

> Pour que l'influence de la libre pensée puisse jouer à plein, il fallait que celle de l'Église fût préalablement ébranlée par des raisons internes. . . . au premier rang de ces conditions, la naissance de conflits entre peuple et clergé.[73]

> (The influence of free-thinking could not have taken full effect had not the Church's influence already been undermined for internal reasons. . . . One of the most important of these conditions was the rise of conflicts between the people and the clergy.)[74]

And of course, once the division had set in, the Church could only defend itself by mobilizing its own partisans. So its response to the crisis itself augmented the break, and helped to push along the dissolution of the earlier parish consensus. Religion is now not a community mentalité, but a partisan stance.[75]

The pathos of this self-defeating action shows with hindsight that the Catholic Church was engaged in a mission impossible. But this is of wider significance than just the contradictions of Pius IX and the ultramontane Church in the nineteenth century. In a way it shows up the tensions in the whole project of Reform. The strength of the rural parish was its collective ritual and its strong consensual notion of "respect humain". But the whole drive of the Reform movement, from the high Middle Ages, right through Reformation and counter-Reformation, right up through evangelical renewal and the post-Restoration Church, was to make Christians with a strong personal and devotional commitment to God and the faith. But strong personal faith and all-powerful community consensus can't ultimately consist together. If the aim is to encourage Christians in their strong devotional lives to come to frequent communion, then this must in the end mean that they break out of the restraining force of "respect humain". In theory any one of these conflicts on the ground could be resolved by a reversal of the local consensus; but in the long run it is impossible that it should always be this way: there can't be a Jean Vianney in every parish (and even he took decades to turn the village of Ars around).

Unless, that is, one wants to erect a totalitarian system; at which point one has fundamentally changed the nature of the enterprise. The ultramontane church has not always seen the strength of this last point, and has betimes felt the totalitarian temptation; but it has also been the victim of this temptation as felt by others, and it has been cured of its illusions on this score. It has had trouble however, seeing how contradictory the goal ultimately is, of a Church tightly held together by a strong hierarchical authority, which will nevertheless be filled with practitioners of heartfelt devotion. There are, of course, people whose devotional life is enhanced by the sense that they live under this kind of authority, but for the masses who do not respond this way the choices are either to knuckle under, or leave, or live a semi-clandestine life. The irreversible aspect of Vatican II is that it brought this contradiction to the surface.

But to return to France in the nineteenth century, we should recognize that the reconstitution of the parish and its religion du terroir after the Revolution is in a way a remarkable fact. It shows how deeply this mode of community life was anchored in the mores of the people that it could come together again after the hiatus of the 1790s. It is all the more remarkable in that the Ain Department studied by Boutry was strongly for the Emperor, and rather refractory at the beginning of the Restoration. The victory of Republicans in the 1870s might be seen as the return to an original stance. But it is clear that something more important and irreversible happened the second time: the undermining of AR forms and the move into an Age of Mobilization.

This is not to say that all such cohesive parishes were broken open at that time. There were the regions, in the West for instance, where the Republican offensive was resisted. Later on, we will look at a Breton parish, Limerzel, where this undermining or dissolution of parish life only happened in the cultural revolution following the Second World War.

However, to the extent that the AR forms were undermined, and that Republicans themselves mobilized, the Catholic Church in France had no choice. Boutry is perhaps right; the crucial turning may be 1848, where universal male suffrage was introduced, never to be rescinded (and for a long time, not augmented either; women didn't get the vote till 1945—and the Republic-Church quarrel was part of the cause of this delay). Catholics couldn't stand aside from political mobilization.[76]

Already, the organizational needs were wide-ranging: raising money, founding and running schools, hospitals, universities; setting up organs of lay apostolate to give the Church a presence where it might otherwise have been absent—among students, professionals, workers; these latter organs also served another purpose, which was to insulate the faithful as much as possible from outside influences (perceived to be) of a hostile nature: liberalism, socialism, Protestantism. This latter goal also required a whole range of organizations, like Catholic sports clubs and other recreational groups. Lastly, and far from least, Catholic political parties were founded.

Of course, the Catholic Church has always had lay organizations: sodalities, guilds, etc. But what was peculiar to the situation in the nineteenth and twentieth centuries was that they were operating in societies with a more and more modern social imaginary, in which independent voluntary associations and political parties played a bigger and bigger role. It proved impossible not to accommodate to this context.

This eventually led to contextually-determined abandonments of the alliance with thrones—especially where these left no choice by attacking the Church themselves, as in Germany under Bismarck; and also later to hesitant and localized abandonment of the alignment with employers, which opened the road for the beginnings of Christian Democracy, most notably in Belgium. These showed that the alienation of the working class was far from an ineluctable consequence of industrialization.[77]

But the exigencies of operating in the Age of Mobilization meant inevitably the loosening of clerical control as well. Trade Unions and political parties had to be cut some slack if they were to be effective. The irony is reflected in an incident during the Kulturkampf, Bismarck's attack on the German Catholic Church. This sparked a strong sense of union and solidarity among German Catholics, in a sense doing the work of the church for her. As the Archbishop of Köln was being dragged off to imprisonment, masses of faithful turned out and lined the streets, kneeling as he passed. This strong political demonstration of loyalty to established church authority had, however, necessarily another side. The continued political resistance could only be carried out by a political party, and in the long run this gave greater and greater importance to its lay leadership.

There were, in the end, strong analogies between evangelicalism and reconstituted post-Revolutionary Catholicism, for all the differences. We should mention, first of all, new or renewed forms of spirituality, with a strong emotional appeal:

conversion to a loving God on one side, and devotions such as the Sacred Heart, and that mobilized around the life and example of Thérèse de Lisieux, on the other; it would be a mistake to focus, as perhaps our sociological sensibility invites us to do, simply on the "functional" features of these faith forms, their providing people with the skills and disciplines they needed to operate in their changed circumstances. All may share a certain liturgy and ethos. But various people will feel the need for some special, stronger, more focussed, concentrated and/or disciplined form of devotion/prayer/meditation/dedication. It may be that they affront a crisis or a tough period in their lives, and they need to concentrate their spiritual resources to meet it. It may be that they feel their lives are too shallow or unfocussed, or all over the place; they need a stronger centre, a point of concentration. It may be just that they feel the need to give some expression, some vent to powerful feelings of gratitude, to acknowledge and rejoice in the gifts of God.

These forms of spirituality were on both the Protestant and the Catholic side combined with attempts to inculcate the new ethos and disciplines necessary to function in the changed economy and society. The battle against drunkenness was also waged by priests in Irish parishes, at the same time as Nonconformity was campaigning for Temperance.[78] On both sides, the attempts to set up the necessary organs of economic survival, such as friendly societies, credit unions, were often linked with churches.

The various successful forms of faith in the age of mobilization combine these two strands; not only ethical/disciplinary, in which all (or most) partake, but also a series of special devotions, services, modes of prayer, etc., for those who from time to time feel the need for some special form of dedication. These arise from individual choices, though they often are carried out in groups, and they can be indefinitely varied, and allow of new forms being created. A principal site of these on the Protestant side is, of course, the revival. On the Catholic side, we have novenas, retreats, special devotions, as to the Sacred Heart, pilgrimages, the steps of the Oratoire St.-Joseph; forms of service, to priests, parish, and the like. Ste. Thérèse de Lisieux was an important trail-blazer in this last kind of devotion.

These special forms were often gendered: Sacred Heart for the women, whereas the men would either opt out altogether from this dimension, or else do something "active", like running Catholic Trade Unions.

One thing stands out on the Catholic side, which at first blush doesn't seem to have an analogue in Protestant countries. The new building of a mass movement around ultramontane Catholicism didn't just repress or sideline the old festive Christianity which had been so important in the "religions du terroir" of the parish community. It recreated its own versions. Already on the parish level, priests tried not so much to suppress popular feasts and pilgrimages as to gain control of them, redirect them, clean them up, as I described above. One common attempt was to shift the focus from local traditional sites to important regional centres of pilgrimage. As Ralph Gibson puts it, "the clergy tried to redirect the characteristic localism of popular religion in a more universalist direction".[79] In the course of the nineteenth century, there developed in France important national sites, tied to recent apparitions of the Virgin, at for instance, La Salette, Lourdes, and Paray le Monial. By the end of the century, people were going to Lourdes every year in hundreds of thousands, travelling in organized groups, mostly by train.

This was on one level a triumph of mobilization. It appears as the ultimate success of the clergy's attempt to supplant local cults, jealously controlled by the parish community, with trans-local ones, blessed by the hierarchy. But like all the other forms of Catholic mobilization, this one too was ambiguous. In fact, the apparitions of the Virgin start locally; she appears to peasants, shepherds. The hierarchy are at first wary; and anyway, they have to put these new claims to the test. The great trans-local sites of Marian pilgrimage of the last two centuries, from Guadalupe to Medjugorje, all start as new departures in popular religion, and they take off because they speak to masses of ordinary believers. The clergy can sometimes kill these movements, but they don't create them.[80]

The notion of the "festive" I'm invoking here has to be understood in a broad sense. It includes feasts and pilgrimages. It involves, first, large numbers of people coming together outside of quotidian routine, whether the "outside" is geographic, as in the case of pilgrimage, or resides in the ritual of the feast which breaks with the everyday order of things. We can recognize as another species of this genus the Carnivals of yore, which still survive in some form in Brazil, for instance. But secondly, this assembly is felt to put them in touch with the sacred, or at least, some greater power. This may manifest itself in the form of healing, as at Lourdes. But even where it does not, the sense of tapping into something deeper or higher is present. That's why it is not stretching things to include Carnival in this category. If we follow Turner's account that I outlined in Chapter 3, this world "turned upside down" connects us again to the "communitas" dimension of our society, where beyond the hierarchical divisions of the established order, we are together as equal human beings.

I raise this, because I believe that the festive, in this sense, is an important continuing form of religious and quasi-religious life in our own day. It has to be part of any description of the place of the spiritual in our society. I said at the outset of this discussion of the festive that these nineteenth century Catholic forms didn't seem to have any analogue on the Protestant side. But on a second look, this can be challenged. The revival meeting presents obvious analogues. And when we think of the explosion of Pentecostalism during the last century, now spreading to many parts of the world, we have all the more reason to see the festive as a crucial dimension of contemporary religious life.

I will return to this in the next chapter. But continuing our discussion of the analogies between Catholic and Protestant mobilizations, we can see that on both sides spirituality and modes of self-discipline were often in turn connected, although in very different ways, to political identities. In the U.K. and the U.S., this relationship was seen as positive, and as linked firmly to the sense of civilizational order. Evangelicals felt that they were fostering the ethos that their society needed to live up to its highest vocation and ideals. That's what gave them the confidence and sense of mission to demand that the whole society live up to certain of their standards, e.g., Temperance, and observance of the Sabbath. While there was lots of opposition to these goals, and a sense that Puritans were ramming unacceptable restrictions down everyone's throats, there was enough congruence between Nonconformity and the political identities of both Britain and America, defined as they originally were over against Catholicism and authoritarianism, for Evangelicals to have a sense that these were nations basically aligned on their fundamental values.[81]

Another quite different kind of relation, this time negative, is evident among minorities like the Poles and the Irish above. Faith connects to a political identity here too, but one in opposition to the established authorities, and more and more dreaming of an independent state. A third kind of relation is evident among Catholic minorities, or at least beleaguered churches (such as France) on the Continent; resistance is organized, either in the hopes of defining the nation's political identity against a rival (France), or of assuring an acceptable status for the minority, as in Germany. Another variant of this can be found in the Low Countries, both Belgium and the Netherlands, where "pillarization" ("verzuiling", the Dutch term) takes place. All spiritual families, in a sense, behave like minorities, demanding their recognized place. The consequence of many of the Continental arrangements was often political parties defined by spiritual option: Catholic, sometimes Protestant, or Liberal (i.e., anti-confessional) parties.

And in all these beleaguered and embattled Catholic churches, the sense was strong that they offered the only possible bulwark of civilizational order. The claim was frequently made by the Church in France, and accepted by many in the possessing classes, that Catholicism was the only defense against the destructive disorders of Revolution, whose return was a constant menace. But the idea was not just that only the Church could persuade people to obey due authority; it was also that the very basis of morality, social and family life, would crumble away without the constant and patient work of dedicated clergy. As the curé d'Ars himself once put it: "Laissez une paroisse vingt ans sans prêtre, on y adorera des bêtes".[82]

Here was a strongly clericalist form of the doctrine; but without this nuance, there were analogies to views held across the Channel by Evangelicals, and indeed many others, to the effect that basic morality could not long survive the demise of religion. A common view among churchgoers was, as Jeffrey Cox put it, that "Society would fall apart without morality, morality was impossible without religion, and religion would disappear without the churches." To quote from the Duke of Devonshire in a speech to supporters of the South London Church Fund,

> Can you imagine for one moment what England would have been like today without those churches and all that those churches mean? . . . Certainly it would not have been safe to walk the streets. All respect, decency, all those things which tend to make modern civilization what it is would not have been in existence. You can imagine what we should have had to pay for our police, for lunatic asylums, for criminal asylums . . . The charges would have been increased hundredfold if it had not been for the work the church has done and is doing today.[83]

The Duke was perhaps mainly referring to the churches' philanthropic work in this speech, but this was plainly part of a more fundamental point about the moral bases of civilizational order.

For the majority Christian sentiment of this age, the issue was not the one I posed above about religion: whether one should restrict one's goals to a purely human fulfillment, or open a transcendent perspective to something more than this. For the dominant outlook then, this first option didn't exist. Unless one reached out to something beyond, to God and salvation through Jesus Christ, the conditions of even the most basic human fulfillment would crumble in immorality and disorder. This view is still defended in some circles today, but a century ago it was standard and hegemonic among Christian believers.

If we take my ideal type of Mobilization, and try to determine the period when it was more and more dominant, we can fix the limits of the Age of Mobilization from roughly 1800 to 1950 (perhaps more exactly 1960). If we survey this period, we can see religious forms everywhere suffering decay and loss, those of the ancien régime type; and almost everywhere too, new forms being developed which can fit the age. Some of these recruited and mobilized people on an impressive scale, surpassing their ancien régime counterparts (e.g., the Irish Church, which went through a reform process after the Famine).

Indeed, some scholars speak of a "Second Confessional Age" (the first one being the sixteenth century, of course),[84] because churches managed to organize so much of their members' lives, and hence became the focus of often intense loyalty, a sentiment akin to nationalism.[85] Indeed, outside the Anglo-Saxon world, this organization often took the form of a ghetto, which was meant to ensure that people would be schooled, play football, take their recreation, etc., exclusively among co-religionists. The Catholic Church was the major architect of such ghettos, building them even in the Anglo-Saxon world; but in the Netherlands, for instance, Protestants did likewise. As a matter of fact, one might even claim that the "Confessional Age" extends beyond the boundaries of Christian Churches. One can see certain analogies with Social Democratic and later Communist parties, with their women and youth groups, sports clubs, cultural organizations, and the like. The aims here were not dissimilar to those underlying Catholic "ghettos": to penetrate more deeply the lives of the followers, to bond them more closely together, and to minimize contact with outsiders.[86]

Thus the powerful forms of faith wove four strands together in this age: spirituality, discipline, political identity, and an image of civilizational order. These four strands had been present in élite religion in the two preceding centuries, but now this had become a mass phenomenon. They strengthened each other, made a whole.

But these tightly organized churches, often suspicious of outsiders, with their strongly puritanical codes, their inherent links, of whatever sort, to political identities, and their claims to ground civilizational order, were perfectly set up for a precipitate fall in the next age which was beginning to dawn at mid-century. To this I now turn.

13 The Age of Authenticity

5

Let's call this the Age of Authenticity. It appears that something has happened in the last half-century, perhaps even less, which has profoundly altered the conditions of belief in our societies.

I believe, along with many others, that our North Atlantic civilization has been undergoing a cultural revolution in recent decades. The 60s provide perhaps the hinge moment, at least symbolically. It is on one hand an individuating revolution, which may sound strange, because our modern age was already based on a certain individualism. But this has shifted on to a new axis, without deserting the others. As well as moral/spiritual and instrumental individualisms, we now have a widespread "expressive" individualism. This is, of course, not totally new. Expressivism was the invention of the Romantic period in the late eighteenth century. Intellectual and artistic élites have been searching for the authentic way of living or expressing themselves throughout the nineteenth century. What is new is that this kind of self-orientation seems to have become a mass phenomenon.

Everyone senses that something has changed. Often this is experienced as loss, break-up. A majority of Americans believe that communities are eroding, families, neighbourhoods, even the polity; they sense that people are less willing to participate, to do their bit; and they are less trusting of others.[1] Scholars don't necessarily agree with this assessment,[2] but the perception itself is an important fact about today's society. No doubt there are analogous perceptions widespread in other Western societies.

The causes cited for these changes are many: affluence and the continued extension of consumer life styles; social and geographic mobility; outsourcing and downsizing by corporations; new family patterns, particularly the growth of the two-income household, with the resulting overwork and burnout; suburban spread, whereby people often live, work, and shop in three separate areas; the rise of television, and others.[3] But whatever the correct list of such precipitating factors, what interests me here is the understandings of human life, agency, and the good which both encourage this new (at least seeming) individuation, and also make us morally uneasy about it.

The shift is often understood, particularly by those most disturbed by it, as an outbreak of mere egoism, or a turn to hedonism. In other words, two things which were identified clearly as vices in a traditional ethic of community service and self-discipline are targeted as the motors of change. But I think this misses an important point. Egoism and the mere search for pleasure (whatever exactly these amount to) may play a larger or smaller role in the motivation of different individuals, but a large-scale shift in general understandings of the good requires some new under-standing of the good. Whether in a given individual case this functions more as ra-tionalization or as animating ideal is neither here nor there; the ideal itself becomes a crucial facilitating factor.

Thus one of the most obvious manifestations of the individuation in question here has been the consumer revolution. With post-war affluence, and the diffusion of what many had considered luxuries before, came a new concentration on private space, and the means to fill it, which began distending the relations of previously close-knit working-class[4] or peasant communities,[5] even of extended families. Older modes of mutual help dropped off, perhaps partly because of the receding of dire necessity. People concentrated more on their own lives, and that of their nuclear families. They moved to new towns or suburbs, lived more on their own, tried to make a life out of the ever-growing gamut of new goods and services on offer, from washing-machines to packaged holidays, and the freer individual life-styles they fa-cilitated. The "pursuit of happiness" took on new, more immediate meaning, with a growing range of easily available means. And in this newly individuated space, the customer was encouraged more and more to express her taste, furnishing her space according to her own needs and affinities, as only the rich had been able to do in previous eras.

One important facet of this new consumer culture was the creation of a special youth market, with a flood of new goods, from clothes to records, aimed at an age bracket which ranged over adolescents and young adults. The advertising deployed to sell these goods in symbiosis with the youth culture which develops helped create a new kind of consciousness of youth as a stage in life, between childhood and an adulthood tied down by responsibility. This was not, of course, without precedent. Many earlier societies had marked out such a stage in the life cycle, with its own special groupings and rituals; and upper-class youth had enjoyed their student days and (sometimes) fraternities. Indeed, with the expansion of urban life and the con-solidation of national cultures, upper- and middle-class youth began to become conscious of itself as a social reality towards the end of the nineteenth century.

Youth even becomes a political reference point, or a basis of mobilization, as one sees with the German Jugendbewegung, and later with Fascist invocation of "Giovinezza" in their famous marching song. But this self-demarcation of youth was a break with the working class culture of the nineteenth and early twentieth century, where the necessities of life seemed to exclude such a time out after childhood and before the serious business of earning began.

The present youth culture is defined, both by the way advertising is pitched at it, and to a great degree autonomously, as expressivist. The styles of dress adopted, the kinds of music listened to, give expression to the personality, to the affinities of the chooser, within a wide space of fashion in which one's choice could align one with thousands, even millions of others.

I want to talk about this space of fashion in a minute, but if we move from these external facts about post-war consumerism to the self-understandings that went along with them, we see a steady spread of what I have called the culture of "authenticity".[6] I mean the understanding of life which emerges with the Romantic expressivism of the late-eighteenth century, that each one of us has his/her own way of realizing our humanity, and that it is important to find and live out one's own, as against surrendering to conformity with a model imposed on us from outside, by society, or the previous generation, or religious or political authority.

This had been the standpoint of many intellectuals and artists during the nineteenth and early twentieth centuries. One can trace the strengthening, even radicalization of this ethos among some cultural élites throughout this period, a growing sense of the right, even duty, to resist "bourgeois" or established codes and standards, to declare openly for the art and the mode of life that they felt inspired to create and live. The defining of its own ethos by the Bloomsbury milieu was an important stage on this road in early twentieth century England, and the sense of the epochal change is reflected in the famous phrase of Virginia Woolf: "On or about December 1910, human nature changed".[7] A somewhat parallel moment comes with André Gide's "coming out" as a homosexual in the 1920s, a move in which desire, morality, and a sense of integrity came together. It is not just that Gide no longer feels the need to maintain a false front; it is that after a long struggle he sees this front as a wrong that he is inflicting on himself, and on others who labour under similar disguises.[8]

But it is only in the era after the Second World War, that this ethic of authenticity begins to shape the outlook of society in general. Expressions like "do your own thing" become current; a beer commercial of the early 70s enjoined us to "be yourselves in the world of today". A simplified expressivism infiltrates everywhere. Therapies multiply which promise to help you find yourself, realize yourself, release your true self, and so on.

The contemporary ethic of authenticity thus has a long pre-history; and if we look at this, we can see that it is set in a wider critique of the buffered, disciplined self, concerned above all with instrumental rational control. If we think of the 60s as our hinge moment, we note a widespread critique of our society in the period immediately preceding it among leading intellectuals. The society of the 1950s was castigated as conformist, crushing individuality and creativity, as too concerned with production and concrete results, as repressing feeling and spontaneity, as exalting the mechanical over the organic. Writers like Theodor Roszak and Herbert Marcuse turned out to be prophets of the coming revolution. As Paul Tillich said to a graduating class in 1957: "We hope for more non-conformists among you, for your sake, for the sake of the nation, and for the sake of humanity." In one sense (perhaps not the one he intended), his wish was granted in profusion in the following decade.[9]

The revolts of young people in the "60s" (which really extended into the 70s, but I am using what has become the standard term) were indeed, directed against a "system" which smothered creativity, individuality and imagination. They rebelled against a "mechanical" system in the name of more "organic" ties; against the instrumental, and for lives devoted to things of intrinsic value; against privilege, and for equality; and against the repression of the body by reason, and for the fullness of sensuality. But these were not seen just as a list of separate goals or demands. Following axes of criticism already laid down in the Romantic period, their understanding was that inner divisions, like reason as against feeling, and social divisions, like between students and workers, as well as divisions between spheres of life, like work/play, were both intrinsically linked with each other, and inseparable from modes of domination and oppression (reason over feeling, those who think dominating those who work with their hands, the work of "serious" work marginalizing play). An integral revolution will undo all these divisions/oppressions at once. This clearly was the outlook which came to expression in the May 1968 student movement in Paris. An equal society was meant to emerge from a simultaneous breaking down of the three barriers just mentioned (le "décloisonnement"). And although the theory didn't come to exactly this articulation everywhere, it is clear that the May event had an immense resonance throughout the world; and that in turn it reflected some of the themes of the earlier movement in the U.S. which started at Berkeley in 1964.

This outlook goes back to the Romantic period; it is articulated among other places in Schiller's *Letters on the Aesthetic Education of Man.*[10] It is carried down into the 1960s in part through the continuing chain of related counter-cultures, and in part expressly through the influence of writers like Marcuse. Like the ethic of authenticity which is embedded in it, it moves in this period out of élite milieux to become a much more widely available option, a stance and sensibility recognizable to the society as a whole (however much disliked and maligned).

But of course, we can't read the culture of the succeeding decades simply through the aspirations of the 60s. We have to factor in, not only the reactions of those who opposed, and still oppose, this whole outlook, but also the contradictions and dilemmas that these aspirations themselves generate. Perhaps everyone would now recognize the Utopian nature of the ideals of May 1968.[11] In a sense, this was even so at the time; the "soixante-huitards" lacked completely the steely political determination of Lenin and the Bolsheviks; indeed, the movement emerged partly in criticism of the French Communist Party. In this sense, their hands were clean. But Utopianism has its costs. To the extent that the goals of integral self-expression, sensual release, equal relations, and social bonding cannot be easily realized together—and it seems that they can only be united with difficulty, and for a time, in small communities at best—the attempt to realize them will involve sacrificing some elements of the package for others.

And this, of course, is what we see happening in the aftermath. David Brooks sets out the synthesis between "bourgeois" and "bohemian" which he sees in the contemporary U.S. upper class. These "BoBos", as he calls them, have made their peace with capitalism and productivity, but they retain their over-riding sense of the importance of personal development and self-expression. They retain the whole-hearted embrace of sex and sensuality as a good in itself, but they pursue it with the kind of earnest concern for self-improvement which is light-years away from the Dionysian spontaneity of the 60s. They have developed what he calls the "higher selfishness": "Self-cultivation is the imperative. . . . So this isn't a crass and vulgar selfishness, about narrow self-interest or mindless accumulation. This is a higher selfishness. It's about making sure you get the most out of yourself, which means putting yourself in a job which is spiritually fulfilling, socially constructive, experientially diverse, emotionally enriching, self-esteem boosting, perpetually challenging, and eternally edifying."

Among the things that get lost in the original package are, on one hand, social equality; BoBos have made their peace with the Reagan-Thatcher revolution, the slimming down of the welfare state, and increasing income inequality, where they sit at the upper end. And on the other hand, their highly mobile life-style has helped to erode community. But there is more than a residual unease about this among many of these high-flyers. They want to believe that they are contributing to the welfare of everyone; and they yearn for more meaningful community relations.[12]

In fact, this kind of capitalist sub-culture, which one found mainly in the IT world, is not unanimously accepted among the rich and powerful. There still exists a culture of the big vertical corporations; and there is a tension between the two.

What this shows, however, is that fragments of the ideal, selectively acted on, remain powerful; and even the abandoned segments may still tug at our conscience. The ideal, however distorted, is still powerful enough in a society like the U.S. to awaken strong resistance in certain quarters, and to be the object of what have been called "culture wars". This latter term may be in some sense an exaggeration, because there is some evidence that the number of full-scale, utterly down-the-line warriors on each side may be relatively small; in fact, the great majority of Americans are caught in the middle. But the dynamic of the system, the interaction between single-issue organizations, the media, and the American party system, and perhaps the American obsession with "rights", keeps the polarization at fever heat, and prevents saner and lower-key treatment of the issues.[13]

The fact that the ideal can only be selectively fulfilled also changes the significance of those parts we do act on. Self-expression has a weight and significance when we see it as not just compatible with, but even as the road towards a true community of equals. It has to lose much of this when it turns out to concern only ourselves. Hence the invitation to irony which, for instance, David Brooks responds to in the quote above about the "higher selfishness" (and indeed, throughout his book). Selectivity not only takes a toll in the loss of the abandoned bits, but also in the potential trivialization or banalization of what remains. It also carries the danger that in holding on to our now reduced goals, we will hide from ourselves the dilemmas involved here: that we are willy-nilly impeding other valid aims, and reducing the ones we espouse and proclaim. The reduced and simplified fragment becomes the limit of our moral world, the basis of an all-encompassing slogan.

A good example of this is "choice", that is bare choice as a prime value, irrespective of what it is a choice between, or in what domain. Yet we have to admit that this is regularly invoked in our society as an all-trumping argument in weighty contexts. I can think of a number of reasons against the idea of forbidding by law at least, say, first-trimester abortions; including the fact that in our present society the burden of bearing the child falls almost totally on the pregnant woman; or the high likelihood that the law would be widely evaded, and the operations carried out in much more perilous conditions. But being in favour of choice as such has nothing to do with it—unless one would like equally to legitimate the choice of prospective parents to selectively abort female fetuses to reduce their eventual dowry costs. This kind of appeal trivializes the issue. It trades on the favourable resonances of a word which is also invoked in other contexts: for instance, in advertising where it serves to invoke the sense that there are no barriers to my desires, the child-in-the-candy-store feeling of hovering alongside a limitless field of pleasurable options. It is a word which occludes almost everything important: the sacrificed alternatives in a dilemmatic situation, and the real moral weight of the situation.

And yet we find these words surfacing again and again, slogan terms like "freedom", "rights", "respect", "non-discrimination", and so on. Of course, none of these is empty in the way "choice" is; but they too are often deployed as argument-stopping universals, without any consideration of the where and how of their application to the case at hand. This has something to do with the dynamic of our political process in many Western democracies (I'm not taking a stand one way or another on whether it's better elsewhere); the way in which advocacy groups, media, political parties both generate and feed off a dumbed down political culture. Hunter relates the poignant fact that studies showed the "pro-life" side of the abortion debate that the best way they could make their case was in terms of "rights" and "choice".[14] These favoured terms acquire a Procrustean force. Shallowness and dominance are two sides of the same coin.

But for that very reason, one can wonder how much they reflect real-life deliberation of the human beings in the society. Hunter reveals how complex and nuanced is the thinking of people who can be lined up on one side of the other by some simplifying question, like "are you pro-life or pro-choice?"[15]

We find another interesting reflection of this in Alan Ehrenhalt's fascinating study of 1950s Chicago, and of what became of the life in America since.[16] The book starts:

> Most of us in America believe a few simple propositions that seem so clear and self-evident they scarcely need to be said. Choice is a good thing in life, and the more of it we have, the happier we are. Authority is inherently suspect; nobody should have the right to tell others what to think or how to behave. Sin isn't personal, it's social; individual human beings are creatures of the society they live in.[17]

Anyone can recognize here widespread ideas that are often used as trumps in arguments, or enframing assumptions, even though they are often contested. Ehrenhalt's main point is very convincing here. It is absurd to adopt any of these three propositions as universal truths. It is clear that to have any kind of liveable society some choices have to be restricted, some authorities have to be respected, and some individual responsibility has to be assumed. The issue should always be which choices, authorities and responsibilities, and at what cost. In other words, falling back on slogans like these hides from us the dilemmas we have to navigate between in our choices. Properly understood, what happened in the last half of the twentieth century in America was that some choices were freed, and some authorities over-thrown, with some resultant gains, and at the cost of some losses. And most of the people who help these slogans to circulate are at some level aware of this, because they may also in another context bemoan the loss of stable, reliable and safe communities. We saw above how the majority of Americans believe that community has been undermined and that people are less trustworthy today.

In a way, the costs may be hidden by the fact that we are especially indignant, even today, about some of the restrictions and oppressions of the 50s: women confined to the home, children being forced into moulds in school. We feel these things should never occur again. Whereas the costs, like the unravelling of social connections in the ghetto, or the way so many of us "channel surf" through life, come across either as bearable, or perhaps as simply "systemic", and thus to be borne regardless.

But what emerges through all the muddle and evasion is that there has been a real value shift here. We see this in the fact that things which were borne for centuries are now declared unbearable, for instance, the restrictions on women's options in life. And so there are two points to be made about our situation. One is to pick up on the flattening and trivialization of many of the key terms of public discourse; another is to see that our actual deliberations, while distorted and partly captive of such illusions, nevertheless are always richer and deeper than these allow.

I make this point because I think we need to allow a similar double assessment of a turn like that which inaugurates the Age of Authenticity. It is tempting for those out of sympathy with this turn to see it simply in the light of its illusions; to see authenticity, or the affirmation of sensuality, as simply egoism and the pursuit of pleasure, for example; or to see the aspiration to self-expression exclusively in the light of consumer choice. It is tempting on the other side for proponents of the turn to affirm the values of the new ideal as though they were unproblematic, cost-free and could never be trivialized. Both see the turn as a move within a stable, perennial game. For the critics, it involves the embracing of vices which were and are the main threats to virtue; for the boosters, we have reversed age-old forms which were and are modes of oppression.

I want to view the turn differently. When we undergo some such transformation, the moral stakes change. I don't mean that we cannot make a reasoned over-all judgment about the gains and losses in the transition. (I believe that this one has been on balance positive, while involving palpable costs.) But I do mean that the available options have changed. This means, first, that some options available in earlier days are not possible today, like a general return to the ideal of clear and fixed gender roles in the family. And secondly, it means that there are options today, within the new context, and that some of them are better than others. This is something which the constant harping on the most degraded forms by critics tends to occlude. These critics become unwitting allies of the trivialized forms, because they attack the new context as a whole as though it were defined by these. That one side in the abortion debate calls itself "pro-choice" has something to do with the dynamic of its battle with its polar opposite. Root and branch attacks on authenticity help to make our lives worse, while being powerless to put the clock back to an earlier time.

What are the consequences of the turn for our social imaginary? One important facet of these harks back to our discussion above about youth culture. It also constitutes an important locus of possible trivialization.

I have spoken elsewhere[18] about the typically modern, "horizontal" forms of social imaginary, in which people grasp themselves and great numbers of others as existing and acting simultaneously. The three widely-recognized such forms are: the economy, the public sphere, and the sovereign people. But the space of fashion alluded to above is an example of a fourth structure of simultaneity. It is unlike the public sphere and the sovereign people, because these are sites of common action. In this respect, it is like the economy, where a host of individual actions concatenate. But it is different from this as well, because our actions relate in the space of fashion in a particular way. I wear my own kind of hat, but in doing so I am displaying my style to all of you, and in this, I am responding to your self-display, even as you will respond to mine. The space of fashion is one in which we sustain a language together of signs and meanings, which is constantly changing, but which at any moment is the background needed to give our gestures the sense they have. If my hat can express my particular kind of cocky, yet understated self-display, then this is because of how the common language of style has evolved between us up to this point. My gesture can change it, and then your responding stylistic move will take its meaning from the new contour the language takes on.

The general structure I want to draw from this example of the space of fashion is that of a horizontal, simultaneous mutual presence, which is not that of a common action, but rather of mutual display. It matters to each one of us as we act that the others are there, as witness of what we are doing, and thus as co-determiners of the meaning of our action.

Spaces of this kind become more and more important in modern urban society, where large numbers of people rub shoulders, unknown to each other, without dealings with each other, and yet affecting each other, forming the inescapable context of each other's lives. As against the everyday rush to work in the Metro, where the others can sink to the status of obstacles in my way, city life has developed other ways of being-with, for instance, as we each take our Sunday walk in the park; or as we mingle at the summer street-festival, or in the stadium before the play-off game.

Here each individual or small group acts on their own, but aware that their display says something to the others, will be responded to by them, will help build a common mood or tone which will colour everyone's actions.

Here a host of urban monads hover on the boundary between solipsism and communication. My loud remarks and gestures are overtly addressed only to my immediate companions, my family group is sedately walking, engaged in our own Sunday outing, but all the time we are aware of this common space that we are building, in which the messages that cross take their meaning. This strange zone between loneliness and communication strongly impressed many of the early observers of this phenomenon as it arose in the nineteenth century. We can think of some of the paintings of Manet, or of Baudelaire's fascination with the urban scene, in the roles of flâneur and dandy, uniting observation and display.

Of course, these nineteenth-century urban spaces were topical, that is, all the participants were in the same place, in sight of each other. But twentieth-century communications has produced meta-topical variants, when for instance, we watch the Olympics or Princess Di's funeral on television, aware that millions of others are with us in this. The meaning of our participation in the event is shaped by the whole vast dispersed audience we share it with.

Just because these spaces hover between solitude and togetherness, they may sometimes flip over into common action; and indeed, the moment when they do so may be hard to pin-point. As we rise as one to cheer the crucial third-period goal, we have undoubtedly become a common agent; and we may try to prolong this when we leave the stadium by marching and chanting, or even wreaking various forms of mayhem together. The cheering crowd at a rock festival is similarly fused. There is a heightened excitement at these moments of fusion, reminiscent of Carnival, or of some of the great collective rituals of earlier days. Durkheim gave an important place to these times of collective effervescence as founding moments of society and the sacred.[19] In any case, these moments seem to respond to some important felt need of today's "lonely crowd".

I have just spoken here of "common action", but this is not always the right category. It is the right word, perhaps, when the mob smashes the police cars, or throws stones at the soldiers. But at the rock concert, at the Princess' funeral, what is shared is something else. Not so much an action, as an emotion, a powerful common feeling. What is happening is that we are all being touched together, moved as one, sensing ourselves as fused in our contact with something greater, deeply moving, or admirable; whose power to move us has been immensely magnified by the fusion.

This brings us back into the category of the "festive", which I invoked above: moments of fusion in a common action/feeling, which both wrench us out of the everyday, and seem to put us in touch with something exceptional, beyond ourselves. Which is why some have seen these moments as among the new forms of religion in our world.[20] I think there is something to this idea, and I'd like to examine it later on.

Now consumer culture, expressivism and spaces of mutual display connect in our world to produce their own kind of synergy. Commodities become vehicles of individual expression, even the self-definition of identity. But however this may be ideologically presented, this doesn't amount to some declaration of real individual autonomy. The language of self-definition is defined in the spaces of mutual display, which have now gone meta-topical; they relate us to prestigious centres of style-creation, usually in rich and powerful nations and milieux. And this language is the object of constant attempted manipulation by large corporations.

My buying Nike running shoes may say something about how I want to be/appear, the kind of empowered agent who can take "just do it!" as my motto. And in doing this, I identify myself with those heroes of sport and the great leagues they play in. In so doing, I join millions of others in expressing my "individuality". Moreover, I express it by linking myself to some higher world, the locus of stars and heroes, which is largely a construct of fantasy.

Modern consumer society is inseparable from the construction of spaces of display: topical spaces, palaces of consumption, like the arcades of nineteenth-century Paris thematized by Walter Benjamin, and the giant malls of today; and also meta-topical spaces which link us through commodities to an imagined higher existence elsewhere.

But all this conformity and alienation may nevertheless feel like choice and self-determination; not only because consumer spaces with their multiplying options celebrate choice, but also because in embracing some style within them, I may feel myself to be breaking out of some more confining space of family or tradition.[21]

Of course, it goes without saying that a more genuine search for authenticity begins only where one can break out of the Logo-centric[22] language generated by trans-national corporations. This language occupies a large place in meta-topical spaces of display, but it is not the whole story. Admired stars, heroes, political slogans and modes of demonstration also circulate. These can suffer their own distortions (think of Che Guevara T-shirts), but they can also connect us to trans-national movements around genuine issues.

How else is the advance of expressive individualism altering our social imaginary? Here I can once again only sketch an ideal type, because we're dealing with a gradual process, in which the new co-exists with the old.

Our self-understandings as sovereign peoples haven't been displaced by this new individualism. But perhaps there has been a shift of emphasis. A human identity is a complex thing, made up of many reference points. It still seems important for many of us that we are Canadians, Americans, Britons or French. Just watch us when the Olympics are on. But the weighting, the importance of this in our over-all sense of identity can shift.

One could argue that for many young people today, certain styles, which they enjoy and display in their more immediate circle, but which are defined through the media, in relation to admired stars—or even products—occupy a bigger place in their sense of self, and that this has tended to displace in importance the sense of belonging to large scale collective agencies, like nations, not to speak of churches, political parties, agencies of advocacy, and the like.

As for the modern moral order of mutual benefit, this has been if anything strengthened. Or perhaps, better put, it has taken on a somewhat different form. Certainly it is clear that the ideals of fairness, of the mutual respect of each other's freedom, are as strong among young people today as they ever were. Indeed, precisely the soft relativism that seems to accompany the ethic of authenticity: let each person do their own thing, and we shouldn't criticise each other's "values"; this is predicated on a firm ethical base, indeed, demanded by it. One shouldn't criticise the others' values, because they have a right to live their own life as you do. The sin which is not tolerated is intolerance. This injunction emerges clearly from the ethic of freedom and mutual benefit, although one might easily cavil at this application of it.[23]

Where the new twist comes in, evident in the "relativism", is that this injunction stands alone where it used to be surrounded and contained by others. For Locke, the Law of Nature needed to be inculcated in people by strong discipline; so although the goal was individual freedom, there was no felt incompatibility between this and the need for strong, commonly enforced virtues of character. On the contrary, it seemed evident that without these, the régime of mutual respect couldn't survive. It took a long time before John Stuart Mill could enunciate what has come to be called the "harm principle", that no one has a right to interfere with me for my own good, but only to prevent harm to others. In his day, this was far from generally accepted; it seemed the path to libertinism.

But today, the harm principle is widely endorsed, and seems the formula demanded by the dominant expressive individualism. (It is perhaps not an accident that Mill's arguments also drew on expressivist sources, in the person of Humboldt.)

Indeed, the "pursuit of (individual) happiness" takes on a new meaning in the after-war period. Of course, it is integral to Liberalism since the American Revolution, which enshrined it as one of a trinity of basic rights. But in the first century of the American Republic, it was inscribed within certain taken-for-granted boundaries. First there was the citizen ethic, centred on the good of self-rule, which Americans were meant to live up to. But beyond this, there were certain basic demands of sexual morality, of what later would be called "family values", as well as the values of hard work and productivity, which gave a framework to the pursuit of individual good. To move outside of these was not so much to seek one's happiness, as to head towards perdition. There seemed therefore nothing contrary to the three basic rights enshrined by the Declaration of Independence in society's striving to inculcate, even in certain cases (e.g., sexual morality) to enforce these norms. European societies were perhaps less keen than the Americans to enforce various modes of social conformity, but their code was if anything even more restrictive.

The erosion of these limits on individual fulfillment has been in some cases gradual, with oscillations forward and backward, but with an unmistakable general tendency over the long run. Michael Sandel has noted how the concern for the citizen ethic was much more prominent in the first century of American history. Brandeis could argue the anti-trust case at the beginning of the twentieth century partly on the ground that large combines "erod[e] the moral and civic capacities that equip workers to think like citizens".[24] But as the twentieth century advances, such considerations take more and more a back seat. Courts become more concerned to defend the "privacy" of the individual.

But it is really in the period after the Second World War that the limits on the pursuit of individual happiness have been most clearly set aside, particularly in sexual matters, but also in other domains as well. The U.S. Supreme Court decisions invoking privacy, and thereby restricting the range of the criminal law, provide a clear example. Something similar happens with the revisions of the Canadian Criminal Code under Trudeau, which expressed his principle that "the State has no business in the bedrooms of the nation." Michel Winock notes the change in "mentalités" in France during the 70s: "La levée des censures, la 'libéralisation des moeurs', . . . entra dans la loi", with the legalization of abortion, divorce reform, authorization of pornographic films, and so on.[25] This evolution takes place in virtually all Atlantic societies.

The heart of this revolution lies in sexual mores. This was a long time a-building, as the previous paragraph indicates, but the development took place earlier among cultural élites. In the 1960s, it was generalized to all classes. This is obviously a profound shift. The relativization of chastity and monogamy, the affirmation of homosexuality as a legitimate option, all these have a tremendous impact on churches whose stance in recent centuries has laid so much stress on these issues, and where piety has often been identified with a very stringent sexual code. I shall return to this shortly.

In fact, the need to train character has receded even farther into the background, as though the morality of mutual respect were embedded in the ideal of authentic self-fulfillment itself; which is how undoubtedly many young people experience it today, oblivious of how the terrible twentieth-century aberrations of Fascism and extreme nationalism have also drunk at the expressivist source.

All this perhaps reflects the degree to which these principles of mutual respect for rights have become embedded in our cultures in the Atlantic world, forming the background against which many of our political and legal procedures of rights-retrieval and non-discrimination seem totally legitimate, even though we vigorously dispute their detailed application. But it also reflects the way in which rights-consciousness has become more loosely linked to the sense of belonging to a particular political community, which has both positive and negative sides.[26]

I leave aside the pros and cons here to concentrate on what is relevant to our purposes, which we could describe as the imagined place of the sacred, in the widest sense. Drawing an ideal type of this new social imaginary of expressive individualism, we could say that it was quite non-Durkheimian.

Under the paleo-Durkheimian dispensation, my connection to the sacred entailed my belonging to a church, in principle co-extensive with society, although in fact there were perhaps tolerated outsiders, and as yet undisciplined heretics. The neo-Durkheimian dispensation saw me enter the denomination of my choice, but that in turn connected me to a broader, more elusive "church", and more importantly, to a political entity with a providential role to play. In both these cases, there was a link between adhering to God and belonging to the state—hence my epithet "Durkheimian".

The neo-Durkheimian mode involves an important step towards the individual and the right of choice. One joins a denomination because it seems right to one. And indeed, it now comes to seem that there is no way of being in the "church" except through such a choice. Where under paleo-Durkheimian rules one can—and did—demand that people be forcibly integrated, be rightly connected with God against their will, this now makes no sense. Coercion comes to seem not only wrong, but absurd and thus obscene. We saw an important watershed in the development of this consciousness in the reaction of educated Europe to the Revocation of the Edict of Nantes. Even the Pope thought it was a mistake.

But the expressivist outlook takes this a stage farther. The religious life or practice that I become part of must not only be my choice, but it must speak to me, it must make sense in terms of my spiritual development as I understand this. This takes us farther. The choice of denomination was understood to take place within a fixed cadre, say that of the apostles' creed, the faith of the broader "church". Within this framework of belief, I choose the church in which I feel most comfortable. But if the focus is going now to be on my spiritual path, thus on what insights come to me in the subtler languages that I find meaningful, then maintaining this or any other framework becomes increasingly difficult.

But this means that my placing in the broader "church" may not be that relevant for me, and along with this, my placing in the "nation under God", or other such political agency with a providential role. In the new expressivist dispensation, there is no necessary embedding of our link to the sacred in any particular broader framework, whether "church" or state.

This is why the developments of recent decades in France have been so destabilizing for both sides of the old "guerre franco-française". Not only did the church see a sharp drop in adherence, but young people began to drop out of the rival Jacobin and/or communist world-views as well. In keeping with the dynamic of baroque, paleo-Durkheimian clericalism, the struggle threw up a kind of humanism which aspired in its own way to be a kind of national "church", that of the Republic and its principles, the framework within which people would hold their different metaphysical and (if they insisted) religious views. The Republic played a kind of neo-Durkheimian dispensation against the paleo-Durkheimianism of the clerical monarchists. This tradition even took over the term 'sacred' for itself. (Think of "l'union sacrée", of "la main sacrilège" which killed Marat, etc. This usage obviously facilitated Durkheim's theoretical use of the term to over-arch both ancien régime and republic.) It is not surprising that both Catholicism and this brand of republicanism undergo defections in the new post-Durkheimian dispensation of expressive individualism.[27]

This changes utterly the ways in which ideals of order used to be interwoven with the polemic between belief and unbelief. What has changed to make this much less the case is not only that we have achieved a broad consensus on our ideal of moral order. It is also that in our post-Durkheimian dispensation, the "sacred", either religious or "laïque", has become uncoupled from our political allegiance. It was the rivalry between two such kinds of global allegiance that animated the "guerre franco-française". It was also this older dispensation which could send masses of men into the trenches to fight for their country in 1914, and keep them there, with few desertions and rare instances of mutiny for over four years.[28]

I speak of this in the past tense, because in many of these same countries which were the prime belligerents in this war the new dispensation has probably made this kind of thing impossible. But it is also clear that the geographic area for which this holds true is limited. Down in the Balkans, not that much has changed since the wars which broke out in 1911. And we should not be too sanguine in believing that the change is irreversible even in the core North Atlantic societies.

Paleo-, neo-, post-Durkheimian describe ideal types. My claim is not that any of these provides the total description, but that our history has moved through these dispensations, and that the latter has come to colour more and more our age.

That the new dispensation doesn't provide the whole story is readily evident from the struggles in contemporary society. In a sense, part of what drove the Moral Majority and motivates the Christian Right in the U.S.A. is an aspiration to re-estab-lish something of the fractured neo-Durkheimian understanding that used to define the nation, where being American would once more have a connection with theism, with being "one nation under God", or at least with the ethic which was interwoven with this. Similarly, much of the leadership of the Catholic Church, led by the Vati-can, is trying to resist the challenge to monolithic authority which is implicit in the new expressivist understanding of spirituality. And the Catholic Church in the U.S. frequently lines up with the Christian Right in attempts to re-establish earlier ver-sions of the moral consensus which enjoyed in their day neo-Durkheimian religious grounding.[29] For all these groups, the idea remains strong that there is a link be-tween Christian faith and civilizational order.

But the very embattled nature of these attempts shows how we have slid out of the old dispensation. This shift goes a long way to explain the conditions of belief in our day. But it also underlines a point I made earlier. My terms "neo-Durkheimian" and "post-Durkheimian" designate ideal types. My claim is not that our present day is unambiguously post-Durkheimian, as say, mediaeval France was unquestionably paleo-Durkheimian, and say, the nineteenth-century U.S.A. was neo-Durkheimian. Rather there is a struggle going on between these two dispensations. But it is just this, the availability of a post-Durkheimian dispensation, which destabilizes us and provokes the conflict.

Before examining the embattled link between faith and civilizational order, how-ever, I want to bring out how much the shift I have been talking about consorts with the logic of modern subjectification, and with what we might call the "buf-fered self". We already saw in the eighteenth century, at one of the important "branching points" mentioned in the preceding Part, that one reaction to the cool, measured religion of the buffered identity was to stress feeling, emotion, a living faith which moves us. This was the case, for instance, with Pietism and Methodism, for whom a powerful emotional response to God's saving action was more impor-tant than theological correctness.

Of course, these movements wished to remain within orthodoxy, but it wouldn't be long before the emphasis will shift more and more towards the strength and the genuineness of the feelings, rather than the nature of their object. Later in the cen-tury, the readers of *Émile* will admire above all the deep authentic sentiments of the characters.

There is a certain logic in this. Where before there was lots of passionate belief, and the life and death issues were doctrinal; now there comes to be a widespread feeling that the very point of religion is being lost in the cool distance of even im-peccable intellectual orthodoxy. One can only connect with God through passion. For those who feel this, the intensity of the passion becomes a major virtue, well worth some lack of accuracy in theological formulation. In an age dominated by disengaged reason, this virtue comes to seem more and more crucial.

By the time of the Romantic period, the same issue has been somewhat transposed. Now it appears to many that desiccated reason cannot reach the ultimate truths in any form. What is needed is a subtler language which can make manifest the higher or the divine. But this language requires for its force that it resonate with the writer or reader. Getting assent to some external formula is not the main thing, but being able to generate the moving insight into higher reality is what is important. Deeply felt personal insight now becomes our most precious spiritual resource. For Schleiermacher, the crucial thing to explore is the powerful feeling of dependence on something greater. To give this reign and voice in oneself is more crucial than getting the right formula.

I believe that the present expressive outlook comes from that shift having penetrated in some general form deep into our culture. In an age which seems dominated by the "learned despisers of religion", in Schleiermacher's phrase, what is really valuable is spiritual insight/feeling. This will inevitably draw on a language which resonates very much with the person who possesses it. Thus the injunction would seem to be: let everyone follow his/her own path of spiritual inspiration. Don't be led off yours by the allegation that it doesn't fit with some orthodoxy.

Hence while in the original paleo-Durkheimian dispensation, people could easily feel that they had to obey the command to abandon their own religious instincts, because these being at variance with orthodoxy must be heretical or at least inferior; and while those inhabiting a neo-Durkheimian world felt that their choice had to conform to the over-all framework of the "church" or favoured nation, so that even Unitarians and ethical societies presented themselves as denominations with services and sermons on Sunday; in the post-Durkheimian age many people are uncomprehending in face of the demand to conform. Just as in the neo-Durkheimian world, joining a church you don't believe in seems not just wrong, but absurd, contradictory, so in the post-Durkheimian age seems the idea of adhering to a spirituality which doesn't present itself as your path, the one which moves and inspires you. For many people today, to set aside their own path in order to conform to some external authority just doesn't seem comprehensible as a form of spiritual life.[30] The injunction is, in the words of a speaker at a New Age festival: "Only accept what rings true to your own inner Self."[31]

Of course, this understanding of the place and nature of spirituality has pluralism built into it, not just pluralism within a certain doctrinal framework, but unlimited. Or rather, the limits are of another order, they are in a sense political, and flow from the moral order of freedom and mutual benefit. My spiritual path has to respect those of others; it must abide by the harm principle. With this restriction, one's path can range through those which require some community to live out, even national communities or would-be state churches, but it can also range beyond to those which require only the loosest of affinity groups, or just some servicing agency, like a source of advice and literature.

The a priori principle, that a valid answer to the religious quest must meet either the paleo- or neo-Durkheimian conditions (a church, or a "church" and/or society) has been abandoned in the new dispensation. The spiritual as such is no longer intrinsically related to society.

So much for the logic of the expressivist response to the buffered identity. But of course, this didn't have to work itself out as it has done. In certain societies at least, the principal catalyst for its having done so in recent decades seems to have been the new individual consumer culture released by post-war affluence. This seems to have had a tremendous appeal for populations which had been living since time out of mind under the grip of what appeared unchanging necessity, where the most optimistic horizon was maintaining a level of modest sufficiency and avoiding disaster. Yves Lambert has shown how this new culture at once loosened the tight community life of a Breton parish, and turned people from their dense communal-ritual life to the vigorous pursuit of personal prosperity. As one of his informants put it, "On n'a plus le temps de se soucier de ça [la religion], il y a trop de travail. Il faut de l'argent, du confort, tout ça, tout le monde est lancé là-dedans, et le reste, pffft!"[32] (We no longer have time to care about that [religion]. One seeks money, comfort, and all that; everyone is now into that, and the rest, bah!)

These are connected movements. The new prosperity came along with better communications, and this opened horizons; but then the new pursuit of happiness drew people so strongly that they began to desert the older ritual life which was built around the community and its common efforts to survive in the physical and spiritual world. This ritual life then itself begins to shrink, in part disappear, and there is less and less to hold those who might want to stay within it.[33]

It is almost as though the "conversion" was a response to a stronger form of magic, as earlier conversions had been. It is not that the religion of the villagers in Limerzel was exclusively concerned with economic survival and the defense against disaster, but their faith had so woven together the concern for salvation with that for well-being, that the prospect of a new individual road to prosperity, proven and impressive, dislocated their whole previous outlook. Said another informant: "Pourquoi j'irais à la messe, qu'ils se disent, le voisin qui est à côté de moi, il réussit aussi bien que moi, peut-être même mieux, et il n'y va pas."[34] (Why would I go to mass, they say to themselves, when my next-door neighbour is doing as well as me, perhaps even better, and he doesn't go.)

In other words, in the late-surviving AR form of this Breton parish, the old outlook bound together a composite of concerns, worldly and other-worldly, which now fell apart quite decisively. It couldn't be reconstituted, and the faith has only survived among those who hold to it by evolving, as Lambert describes.[35] Something analogous happened in Québec, though this was a much more urbanized society, in the 1960s. Here the effect was delayed by the neo-Durkheimian link between national identity and Catholicism, but when this knot was untied, the falling off happened with a bewildering rapidity. The development has perhaps some affinities with what is taking place in contemporary Ireland, or what is beginning to emerge in Poland.

The corresponding slide in other, Protestant, especially Anglophone, societies has been more gradual and less dramatic, perhaps because the new consumer culture developed more slowly and over a longer period of time. But in both Britain and America, the expressivist revolution of the 60s seems to have accelerated things.

How to understand the impact of this whole shift on the place of religion in public space? It can perhaps be envisaged in this way. The invention of exclusive humanism in the eighteenth century created a new situation of pluralism, a culture fractured between religion and areligion (phase 1). The reactions not only to this humanism, but to the matrix (buffered identity, moral order) out of which it grew, multiplied the options in all directions (phase 2). But this pluralism operated and generated its new options for a long time largely within certain élite groups, intellectuals and artists.

Early on, especially in Catholic countries, there arose political movements of militant humanism which tried to carry unbelief to the masses, with rather modest success; and religious alienation also detached some strata of the common people from the church without necessarily offering them an alternative. On the other side, large numbers of people were either held outside this pluralist, fractured culture; or if on the fringes of it, were held strongly within the believing option, by different modes of Durkheimian dispensation, whereby a given religious option was closely linked to their insertion in their society. This could be of the paleo type, which although it began to decay rapidly on the level of the whole society could still be very operative in rural areas at the level of the local community, as in Lambert's Limerzel. Or it can be of the neo type, as in the triumphant sense of national providence, or among oppressed groups, defending a threatened identity against power of another religious stripe (including atheism in the case of recent Poland), or among immigrant groups. Or the sense of necessary insertion in the faith community could be underpinned by the unchallenged belief that Christianity, in whatever locally dominant form, was the indispensable matrix of civilizational order.

My hypothesis is that the post-war slide in our social imaginary more and more into a post-Durkheimian age has destabilized and undermined the various

Durkheimian dispensations. This has had the effect of either gradually releasing people to be recruited into the fractured culture, or in the case where the new consumer culture has quite dislocated the earlier outlook, of explosively expelling people into this fractured world. For, while remaining aware of the attractions of the new culture, we must never underestimate the ways in which one can also be forced into it: the village community disintegrates, the local factory closes, jobs disappear in "downsizing", the immense weight of social approval and opprobrium begins to tell on the side of the new individualism.

So the expressivist revolution has undermined some of the large-scale religious forms of the Age of Mobilization: churches whose claim on our allegiance comes partly through their connection to a political identity. Even where this identity remains strong, the connection to the spiritual has been broken for those in the new post-Durkheimian dispensation.

But there is more than this. The expressive revolution has also undermined the link between Christian faith and civilizational order. A leading feature of many of the religious forms of the Age of Mobilization described above was their strong sense of an ordered life, and their attempts to aid/persuade/pressure their members into realizing this. As I indicated above, it was perhaps inevitable, as the new disciplines became internalized, that this disciplining function would be less valued, that some of the rigid measures earlier seen as essential, such as absolute temperance, or total Sabbath observance, would appear irksome to the descendants of those who had put them in place. There was always a certain resistance to evangelicals, on the alleged grounds that they were puritans, spoil sports, sowers of division. Fictional portrayals like Dickens' Melchisedech Howler and Jabez Fireworks, as well as George Eliot's Bulstrode, express some of this hostility, and there were sometimes criticisms of Methodists, with their insistence on temperance and banning village sports, as disrupting convivial community culture, and setting people against each other.[36] A more general reaction set in towards the end of the nineteenth century against evangelical morality as desiccating, repressing freedom and self-development, uniformizing us, denying beauty, and the like. Writers like Shaw, Ibsen, and Nietzsche articulated this very powerfully; and something of this is expressed in J. S. Mill's famous "pagan self-assertion is better than Christian self-denial".[37] For his part, Arnold bemoaned the lack of cultivation of the Nonconformist Middle Class. And the culture of Bloomsbury can be seen as formed partly in reaction to this whole religious climate.

But all this was intensified by the cultural revolution of the 1960s, not only in that more people were swept into a stance in opposition to much of the religious ethic, but also in that the new sexual mores were even more strongly at odds with it.

There was a tripartite connection which seemed to many absolutely unquestionable in the past: between Christian faith and an ethic of discipline and self-control, even of abnegation, on one hand; and between this ethic and civilizational order on the other. But as I described above, this second link has come to seem less and less credible to more and more people. The pursuit of happiness has come to seem not only not to need a restrictive sexual ethic and the disciplines of deferred gratification, but actually to demand their transgression in the name of self-fulfillment. The people who feel this most strongly are, of course, precisely those for whom many of these disciplines have become second nature, not needing a strong ethical/spiritual backing to maintain themselves. To the surprise of many Weberian sociologists of my generation, the children of the 1960s and 70s managed to relax many of the traditional disciplines in their lives, while keeping them in their work life. This is not necessarily easy to manage; some people can't make it. There are moreover whole milieux, where the disciplines are still too new and distant from their way of life, for this kind of picking and choosing to be possible. As David Martin puts it, in describing the advance of Pentecostalism in the global South,

> In the developed world the permissions and releases can be pursued by quite large numbers of people while ignoring the economic disciplines, at least for a quite extended period of licence, but in the developing world the economic disciplines cannot be evaded. Though in the developed world you can accept the disciplines in your working life and ignore them elsewhere, in the developing world your disciplines must govern your whole life, or you fall by the wayside—or fall into crime.[38]

This feat of selective assumption of disciplines, which supposes a long, often multi-generational interiorization, is a crucial facilitating condition of the new stance; even though the expressive revolution provided the reason to transgress the old boundaries. At other times and places, such principled transgression seems insane, almost suicidal.

Now where the link between disciplines and civilizational order is broken, but that between Christian faith and the disciplines remains unchallenged, expressivism and the conjoined sexual revolution has alienated many people from the churches. And this on two scores. First, those who have gone along with the current changes find themselves profoundly at odds with the sexual ethic which churches have been propounding. But second, their sense of following their own path is offended by what they experience as the "authoritarian" approach of churches, laying down the law, and not waiting for a reply.

Churches find it hard to talk to people in this mindset. Talking to them is not a matter of simply agreeing with what they say. There has been too much hype, uto-pian illusion, and reacting to old tabus in the sexual revolution for this to make sense. And indeed, 40 years on this is more and more evident to lots of young people. (Which is not to say that churches don't also have something to learn from this whole transition.)[39]

But just as in face of any responsible agent, those who claim to possess some wis-dom have an obligation to explain it persuasively, starting from where their interloc-utor is, so here. The attachment to a rigid code, as well as the sense of being an em-battled band of the faithful, developed through the defensive postures of the last two centuries, makes it almost impossible to find the language.

The break has been very profound. As Callum Brown has shown for the evangeli-cal case, the ethical stance was predicated on an idea of women as wanting a stable family life, which was constantly endangered by male temptation, to drink, gam-bling, infidelity. And we see similar ideas propounded on the Catholic side. This way of defining the issues was not without basis in the past; where women feared the consequences for themselves and their children of male irresponsibility, and even violence. And it is not without basis in many milieux in the present, especially in the global South, as David Martin has pointed out.[40]

We connect up here with a profound development, evident across the con-fessional divide over the last two or three centuries, which has been called the "feminization" of Christianity, about which Callum Brown speaks in his interesting recent book.[41] It obviously has something to do with the close symbiosis established between Christian faith and the ethic of "family values" and disciplined work, which has downgraded if not been directed against military and combative modes of life, as well as forms of male sociability: drinking, gambling, sport, which took them outside the arenas of both work and home. This has not just been an issue for churches; we can see the conflict—and the ambivalence—reflected in the whole society, with the development of the ideal of "polite" society, based on commerce in the eighteenth century. Even some of the intellectual figures who defined and welcomed this new development, like Adam Smith or Adam Ferguson, expressed their misgivings about it. It might lead to an atrophy of the martial virtues neces-sary to the self-governing citizen. Others feared an "effeminization" of the male.[42] Feminization of the culture went parallel to feminization of the faith.

In the Christian context, this was reflected, as well as further entrenched, by a rel-ative drop in male practice as against female. "Les hommes s'en vont" is the unani-mous lament of priests in the Ain Department in the nineteenth century, particu-larly in the latter half.[43] This absence reflects often a sense of male pride and dignity, which is seen as incompatible with a too unbridled devotion; there is something "womanly" about this kind of dedication. This sense was connected to, fed and was fed by a certain mistrust of clerical power: the priest (whose habit resembled that of a woman) had perhaps too much power over wives and daughters; but on the other hand, that was no bad thing, because he taught them chastity and fidelity, and offered security to the male head of household. But at the same time, however good for women, this kind of acceptance of clerical leadership was incompatible with the independence which was a crucial part of male dignity. Obviously, this attitude could give a point of purchase to the philosophical anti-clericalism of the Republican.[44]

But the present sexual revolution in the West has challenged the whole picture of male and female on which this understanding of civilizational order reposed. It has brought with it a gamut of feminist positions, and for some of these, women should demand for themselves the same right to sexual exploration and unfettered fulfillment which were previously thought central to male desire. This totally undercuts the conceptual base of the hitherto dominant ethic. In a line from a 1970 Church of Scotland report on the issue: "It is the promiscuous girl who is the real problem here."[45]

Of course, not everybody agrees with this account of female desire. But it shows a new uncertainty about the forms of women's identity—matched by corresponding uncertainty among men. It is not possible to address the question of sexual ethics without engaging with these issues.

6

Thus the generations which have been formed in the cultural revolution of the 1960s are in some respects deeply alienated from a strong traditional model of Christian faith in the West. We have already seen how they are refractory to the sexual disciplines which were part of the good Christian life as understood, for instance, in the nineteenth century Evangelical revivals in English-speaking countries. Indeed, the contemporary swing goes beyond just repudiating these very high standards. Even the limitations which were accepted generally among traditional peasant communities, which clerical minorities thought were terribly lax, and which they were always trying to get to shape up; even these have been set aside by large numbers of people in our society today. For instance, the clergy used to frown on pre-marital sex, and were concerned when couples came to be married already expecting a child. But these same peasant communities, although they thought it quite normal to try things out beforehand, particularly to be sure that they could have children, accepted that it was mandatory to confirm their union by a ceremony. Those who try to step outside these limits were brought back into line by strong social pressure, charivaris, or "rough music".[46]

But we have clearly stepped way beyond these limits today. Not only do people experiment widely before settling down in a stable couple, but they also form couples without ever marrying; in addition, they form, then break, then reform these relationships. Now our peasant ancestors also engaged in a kind of "serial monogamy", but in their cases the earlier unions were always broken by death, while in ours it is divorce (or in the case of unmarried partners just moving out) which ends them.[47]

There is something here deeply at odds with all forms of sexual ethic—be it folk tradition or Christian doctrine—which saw the stability of marriage as essential to social order. But there is more than this. Christians did see their faith as essential to civilizational order, but this was not the only source of the sexual ethic which has dominated modern Western Christianity. There were also strong images of spirituality which enshrined particular images of sexual purity. We can see these developing in the early modern period. John Bossy has argued that in the mediaeval understanding of the seven deadly sins, the sins of the spirit (pride, envy, anger) were seen as more grievous than those of the flesh (gluttony, lechery, sloth: avarice could be put in either column). But during the Catholic Reformation, emphasis came to be more and more on concupiscence as the crucial obstacle to sanctity.[48]

What was perhaps ancient was seeing sexual ethics through a prism of pollution and purity. "Hence the ban on marriage during Lent and at other seasons, the doctrine that sexual acts between the married were always venially sinful, the purification of women after childbirth, the peculiar preoccupation with sexuality among priests."[49] The modern age seems to have spiritualized the underlying notion of purity, and made it the principal gateway (or its opposite the principal obstacle) to our approach to God.

We can think of the Catholic Reformation, and in particular in France, in the terms I have been using in this study, as an attempt to inculcate a deep, personal, devotion to God (through Christ, or Mary) in (potentially) everyone; an attempt, moreover, which was to be carried out mainly through the agency of the clergy, who would preach, persuade, cajole, push their charges towards this new, higher orientation, and away from the traditional, community, pre-Axial forms of the sacred. If we posit this as the goal, we can think of various ways in which one might try to encompass it. A heavy emphasis might be put on certain examples of sanctity, in the hope of awakening a desire to follow them. Or else, the major thrust might be to bring people by fear to shape up at least minimally. Of course, both of these paths were tried, but the overwhelming weight fell on the negative one. This was, indeed, part of the whole process of Reform from the High Middle Ages. Jean Delumeau has spoken of "la pastorale de la peur" (a pastoral policy of fear).[50]

Perhaps we might just take this as a given, particularly as the tradition goes so far back before the modern period. But we can perhaps also see it as inseparable from the Reforming enterprise itself. If the aim is not just to make certain forms of spirituality shine forth, and draw as many people as possible to them; if the goal is really to make everybody over (or everybody who is not heading for damnation), then perhaps the only way you can ever hope to produce this kind of mass movement is by leaning heavily on threat and fear. This is certainly the pattern set up very early on in the process of Reform, in the preaching mission of wandering friars from the thirteenth century.

The irony is that where clerical leadership really managed to transform a community, it was through the personal holiness of the incumbent, and not through his parading the horrors of Hell. I mentioned in the previous section the case of the curé d'Ars. But, as I said then, you can't expect a Jean Vianney in every parish. If the goal is to move everyone, even through spiritually unimpressive agents, then fear is your best bet.

To quote a mission preacher at the time of the Restoration in France:

Soon the hour of your death will sound; continue the web of your disorders; sink yourselves deeper in the mire of your shameful passions; insult by the impiety of your heart Him who judges even the just. Soon you will fall under the pitiless blows of death, and the measure of your iniquities will be that of the fearful torments which will then be inflicted upon you.[51]

Once one goes this route, something else follows. The threat has to attach to very clearly defined failures. Do this, or else (damnation will follow). The "this" has to be clearly definable. Of course, there were periods, particularly in the Calvinist theological context, in which it has to remain ultimately uncertain whether anyone had really been chosen by God. But as Weber pointed out, this is an unlivable predicament, and very soon certain signs of election crystallize out, whatever the lack of theological warrant. In the context of the Catholic Reformation, the relevant standards are not signs of election, but minimal conformity to the demands of God: the avoidance of mortal sin, or at least doing whatever is necessary to have these sins remitted.

What emerges from all this is what we might call "moralism", that is, the crucial importance given to a certain code in our spiritual lives. We should all come closer to God; but a crucial stage on this road has to be the minimal conformity to the code. Without this, you aren't even at the starting line, as it were, of this crucial journey. You are not in the game at all. This is perhaps not an outlook which it is easy to square with a reading of the New Testament, but it nevertheless achieved a kind of hegemony across broad reaches of the Christian church in the modern era.

This outlook ends up putting all the emphasis on what we should do, and/ or what we should believe, to the detriment of spiritual growth. Sister Elisabeth Germain, analyzing a representative catechism in wide use in the nineteenth century, concludes that

> morality takes precedence over everything, and religion becomes its servant. Faith and the sacraments are no longer understood as the basis of the moral life, but as duties to be carried out, as truths that we must believe, and as means to help us fulfill these moral obligations.[52]

Now one can have clerically-driven Reform, powered by fear of damnation, and hence moralism, and the code around which this crystallizes can nevertheless take different forms. The central issues could be questions of charity versus aggression, anger, vengeance; or a central vector can be this issue of sexual purity. Again, both are present, but with a surprisingly strong emphasis on the sexual. We saw above that in a sense, the emphasis shifted in this direction with the Catholic Reformation. It is not that sins of aggression, violence, injustice were neglected. On the contrary. It is just that the code, the definition of what it is to get to the starting line, was extremely rigid on sexual matters. There were mortal sins in the other dimensions as well, for instance, murder, and there were many in the domain of church rules (skipping Mass, for instance); but you could go quite far in being unjust and hard-hearted in your dealings with subordinates and others, without incurring the automatic exclusion you incur by sexual license. Sexual deviation, and not listening to the church, seemed to be the major domains where automatic excluders lurked. Sexual purity, along with obedience, were therefore given extraordinary salience.

Hence the tremendous (as it seems to us) disproportionate fuss which clergy made in nineteenth-century France about banning dancing, cleaning up folk festivals, and the like. (There are analogues, of course, among Evangelicals in Protestant countries.) Young people were refused communion, or absolution, unless they gave it up altogether. The concern with this issue appears at certain moments obsessive.

I can't pretend to be able to explain this; but perhaps a couple of considerations can put it in context. The first is the pacification of modern society that I discussed in previous chapters; the fact that the level of everyday domestic violence, caused by brigands, feuds, rebellions, clan rivalries, and the like, declined between the fifteenth and the nineteenth centuries. As violence and anger became less overwhelming realities of life, the attention could shift towards purity. The second is the obvious remark that sexual abstinence was a central fact of life for a celibate clergy. It is perhaps not surprising that they made a lot of it.

In any case, it was clearly fated that this combination of clerical Reform from the top, moralism, and repression of sexual life, would come into conflict with the developing modernity that I have been describing in these pages. The emphasis on individual responsibility and freedom will eventually run athwart the claims of clerical control. And the post-Romantic reactions against the disciplines of modernity, the attempts to rehabilitate the body and the life of feeling, will eventually fuel a reaction against sexual repression.

These tensions were already evident before the mid-twentieth century. I mentioned above the decline in male practice, in relation to females, from the late eighteenth century on. One common explanation I mentioned there invoked images of male pride and dignity. But we might also come at the same phenomenon from another direction, stressing that this more rigid sexual code frontally attacked certain male practices, particularly the rowdy life-style of young men. And perhaps more profoundly, it seems that the combination of sexual repression and clerical control, as it was felt in the practice of confession, drove men away. Clerical control went against their sense of independence, but this became doubly intolerable when the control took the form of opening up the most reserved and intimate facet of their lives. Hence the immense resistance to confession, at just about any period, and the attempt to confess, if one had to, not to one's own curé, but to a visiting priest on mission to whom one was unknown. As Delumeau put it, "la raison principale des silences volontaires au confessional fut la honte d'avouer des péchés d'ordre sexuel". Eventually, this tension drove men out of the confessional; as Gibson describes the sequel in the nineteenth century, "unable to take communion, and angry at the prying of the clergy, they increasingly abandoned the Church".[53]

In order better to understand the gap in outlook here, it might be useful to review some of the features of the sexual revolution, which up to now I have just been invoking globally. It too has a pre-history, some of which I have invoked. We might even stretch this history out over centuries, and take as our starting point certain mediaeval Catholic teachings which looked askance at sexual pleasure, even among married couples in the process of procreation. Over against this, Reform thinkers rehabilitated married love as a good of its own. The "mutual comfort" that marriage gave included sexual intercourse, which was given a positive evaluation by this phrase. But sex still had its primary goal in procreation. "Unnatural" acts were those which broke with any procreative purpose. For these reasons, and because they could lead us away from a centring of our lives on God, the sensual or erotic side of love was considered dangerous and questionable.[54]

An analogous view was very strong in the Victorian era, in both England and America. Sex was meant to bond the couple. Sex is healthy, and hence pleasure is attached to it, but pleasure shouldn't be its main object.[55] However, the framework in which this understanding stood was very different. It was, of course, still considered a Christian doctrine. But it was also, and mainly, justified in terms of science. Medical experts, and their ideas of health, were as important if not more so than divines with their notions about God's will.

We can see here a further development of the crucial turn in the seventeenth and eighteenth centuries which I described above: the equation of God's will for us with the reigning conception of human flourishing, in that case defined by the Modern Moral Order. God designs Nature, and he does so with our good in mind. His will can therefore be read off this design. We put ourselves in tune with its benign functioning, and we are following His will. Locke argues this way in his *Treatises of Civil Government*. With the advance of science, this opens the way for a naturalization, a medicalization of sexual ethics, without any sense that this is somehow displacing faith.

But the background assumptions are very different. For the Puritan, the right ordering of our sexual lives can only come with grace and sanctification. It's not something available to the ordinary, non-deviant or non-depraved person. (In a parallel way, one might say, ancient ethics based on Nature were thought to propound a perfection which the vast majority of ordinary human beings couldn't attain to; that's why whole classes of people: non-Hellenes, slaves, workmen, women, weren't really candidates for virtue.) By contrast, the medicalized view offers us a picture of health, which ought to be attainable by the average person, bar some terrible defect in nature, or depraved training. The point where, as it were, the demands of the good and our sexual lives meet should be right here in everyday life, and not at the end of a transformation which takes us beyond ordinary flourishing.

Thus the medicalizing nineteenth century needed an explanation why normal sexual fulfillment was not very widespread, although this need could be hidden by a lot of the reticence and cover-up which surrounded the lives of the respectable. But when the issue was faced, a lot of weight was put on depraved training (evident in immigrants, natives of colonies, the working classes, etc.); and also as the century goes on, more ominously, on supposed differences of race. There were certain "degenerate types" and certain inferior races.

We are still living with the consequences of this elision of virtue, health, and even sanctity, opposing together vice, sickness and sin. For one, it can generate the negative moral aura which surrounds sickness, the notion that those who suffer from cancer are somehow themselves to blame, which Susan Sontag has so vigorously protested against.[56] The healthy feel a morally-tinged goodness, and the sick a vice-tainted badness. We are very far from the older Christian perception of the ill as a locus of suffering which brings Christ close to them, and hence also the rest of us.

Moreover, there is a crucial difference between health as conceived by modern medicine and the older (and I think deeper) notions of virtue. In the case of health, what is required for the fullness of excellence is split in two. There is a knowledge component and a practice component. But these may reside in quite different people. The expert may be leading the most "unhealthy" life, without ceasing to be an expert; whereas the dutiful patient, who (we hope) is brimming with health, understands very little why his régime is a good one. We are in a different universe from that of, say, Aristotelian ethics, where a concept like 'phronesis' doesn't allow us to separate a knowledge component from the practice of virtue.[57] This becomes possible with modern science, construed as knowledge of an objectified domain, as with our contemporary Western medicine. Even more striking, this recourse to objectified knowledge begins in modern culture to take over ethics. On the utilitarian viewpoint, for example, the knowledge/expertise necessary to make the calculus which will reveal the right action is quite unconnected from one's own motivation in relation to the good. It is the kind of knowledge which can permit the bad person to do harm, just as much as the well-disposed agent to do good. This is precisely the kind of knowledge which Aristotle *contrasted* to practical wisdom (phronesis). Analogously, for many contemporary neo-Kantians, it might seem that what you need is the sharpness to follow the logic of an argument, another capacity which seems detachable from moral insight.

It goes without saying that this emphasis on objectified expertise over moral insight is the charter for new and more powerful forms of paternalism in our world. Who dares argue with "science", whether delivered by doctors, psychiatrists, or visiting economists from the IMF telling you to slash health care in order to achieve fiscal "balance"?

But then, to return to our story, in the hands of certain writers at the turn of the century, "science" itself began to break the alliance with religion. For thinkers like Freud, Havelock Ellis, Edward Carpenter, sexual gratification was either itself good, or at least seen as a virtually unstoppable force. This fed into a counter-culture, some strands of which saw sexuality as a form of Dionysian release from discipline and repression. Around the beginning of the twentieth century, all this came together with new social conditions, mainly in cities, where young people could pair off without supervision. The 1920s was aware of a new kind of freedom which young people, particularly women, were enjoying, which took the form of a sensuality unconnected to marriage or procreation.

All this involved: (a) a hesitant lifting of the age-old denigration of sensuality (at least in white, middle-class circles), and (b) a hesitant affirmation of women's desire (often denied in the high Victorian period), and of their right to seek pleasure as well. This was, of course, still fraught with danger, because women still had to bear the brunt of any negative consequences of pregnancy.

If we fast-forward to the 1960s, we have, of course, to take account of new social factors: women in the work-force, the contraceptive revolution, and others. But just as above, my interest here is to articulate the ethical changes of this time, rather than enumerating the facilitating causes. What were the main strands of this revolution?

There was indeed, one which was characterized by a supposedly worldly-wise hedonism, the one associated with *Playboy.* But the main ones associated with the movements of students and young people were fourfold: (1) a continuation and radicalization of (a) above, the rehabilitation of sensuality as a good in itself; (2) the radicalization of (b): affirming the equality of the sexes, and in particular articulating a new ideal in which men and women come together as partners, freed of their gender roles;[58] (3) a widespread sense of Dionysian, even "transgressive" sex as liberating; and (4) a new conception of one's sexuality as an essential part of one's identity, which not only gave an additional meaning to sexual liberation, but also became the basis for gay liberation, and the emancipation of a whole host of previously condemned forms of sexual life.[59]

All this shows that the sexual revolution was an integral part of the 60s, as I defined them above; that is, that it was moved by the same complex of moral ideas, in which discovering one's authentic identity and demanding that it be recognized (strand 4) was connected to the goals of equality (strand 2), and of the rehabilitation of the body and sensuality, the overcoming of the divisions between mind and body, reason and feeling (strands 1 and 3). We cannot simply treat it as an outbreak of hedonism, as though its total definition could fit into the discourse of Hefner and *Playboy.*

But just as above, the fact that there was one interconnected ideal here did nothing to guarantee its realization. The hard discontinuities and dilemmas which beset human sexual life, and which most ethics tend to ignore or downplay, had to assert themselves: the impossibility of integrating the Dionysian into a continuing way of life, the difficulty of containing the sensual within a continuing really intimate relation, the impossibility of escaping gender roles altogether, and the great obstacles to redefining them, at least in the short run. Not to mention that the celebration of sexual release could generate new ways in which men could objectify and exploit women.[60] A lot of people discovered the hard way that there were dangers as well as liberation in throwing over the codes of their parents.

However, once again as in the earlier discussion, we have to recognize that the moral landscape has changed. People who have been through the upheaval have to find forms which can allow for long-term loving relations between equal partners, who will in many cases also want to become parents, and bring up their children in love and security. But these can't be simply identical to the codes of the past; insofar as these were connected with, e.g., the denigration of sexuality, horror at the Dionysian, fixed gender roles, or a refusal to discuss identity issues. It is a tragedy that the codes which churches want to urge on people still (at least seem to) suffer from one or more, even sometimes all, of these defects.

The inability is made the more irremediable by the unfortunate fusion of Christian sexual ethics with certain models of the "natural", even in the medical sense. This not only makes them hard to redefine; it also hides from view how contingent and questionable this elision is, how little it can be justified as intrinsically and essentially Christian. Once again, the eighteenth century identification of God's will with certain supposed human goods is operating as a great engine of secularization (engendering secularity 2).

The repellent effect of this fused vision is clearly at its maximum in the Age of Authenticity, with a widespread popular culture in which individual self-realization and sexual fulfillment are interwoven. The irony is that this alienation takes place just when so many of the features of the Reform-clerical complex were called into question at Vatican II. Unquestionably, clericalism, moralism, and the primacy of fear were largely repudiated. Other elements of the complex were less clearly addressed. It's not clear that the full negative consequences of the drive to Reform itself, with its constant attempt to purge popular religion of its "unchristian" elements, were properly understood. Certain attempts at Reform in Latin America, post-Vatican II and in its spirit, like those around "liberation theology" seem to have repeated the old pattern of "clerical dechristianization", depreciating and banning popular cults, and alienating many of the faithful, some of whom—ironically—have turned to Protestant churches in the region, who have a greater place for the miraculous and the festive than the progressive "liberators" had.[61] A strange turn of events, which would surprise Calvin, were he to return! As to the issue of sexual morality, attempts to review this, in the question of birth control, were abandoned in a fit of clerical nerves about the "authority" of the Church.

In fact, the present position of the Vatican seems to want to retain the most rigid moralism in the sexual field, relaxing nothing of the rules, with the result that people with "irregular" sexual lives are (supposed to be) automatically denied the sacraments, while as-yet-unconvicted mafiosi, not to speak of unrepentant latifundistas in the Third World, and Roman aristocrats with enough clout to wangle an "annulment", find no bar.

But however incomplete and hesitantly followed the turnings taken at Vatican II, it has clearly relativized the old Reform-clerical complex. It has opened a field in which you don't have to be deeply read in the history of the Church to see that the dominant spiritual fashion of recent centuries is not normative. Which is not to say that this whole spirituality, aspiring to a full devotion to God, and fuelled by abnegation and a strong image of sexual purity, is to be in turn condemned. This would be a clerical-Reform way of dealing with the Reform-clerical complex! It is clear that there have been and are today celibate vocations which are extremely spiritually fertile, and many of these turn centrally on aspirations to sexual abstinence and purity. It would just repeat the mistake of the Protestant Reformers to turn around and depreciate these. The fateful feature of Reform-clericalism, which erects such a barrier between the Church and contemporary society, is not its animating spirituality; our world is if anything drowned in exalted images of sexual fulfillment, and needs to hear about paths of renunciation. The deviation was to make this take on sexuality mandatory for everyone, through a moralistic code which made a certain kind of purity a base condition for relating to God through the sacraments. What Vatican rule-makers and secularist ideologies unite in not being able to see, is that there are more ways of being a Catholic Christian than either have yet imagined. And yet this shouldn't be so hard to grasp. Even during those centuries when the Reform-clerical outlook has dominated pastoral policy, there were always other paths present, represented sometimes by the most prominent figures, including (to remain with the French Catholic Reformation) St. François de Sales and Fénelon, not to speak of Pascal, who though he gave comfort to the fear-mongers, offered an incomparably deeper vision.

But as long as this monolithic image dominates the scene, the Christian message as vehicled by the Catholic Church will not be easy to hear in wide zones of the Age of Authenticity. But then these are not very hospitable to a narrow secularism either.

14 Religion Today

7

So the dominant religious forms of the Mobilization Age have been destabilized by the current cultural revolution, even as those of the ancien régime were by the onset of the Age of Mobilization. The forms of the last two centuries have taken a double whammy: on one side, an undermining of churches connected to strong national or minority identities, on the other, an estrangement from much of the ethic and style of authority of these same churches.

We might even speak of a triple whammy, if we think of the way in which the neo-Durkheimian embedding of religion in a state, and its role as the mainstay of a civilization morality, especially its sexual ethic, intersect in the family.

The best-known case of this double embedding is perhaps the U.S.A., particularly in the immediate post-war era; for this was a time in which American patriotism, religion, and sense of family values seemed to be in perfect lock step. On the one hand, the new opportunities for a large segment of the population to live to the full the life of the nuclear family in the growing suburbs was seen as a realization of the American dream. What America was about was the opening of this kind of opportunity, in which eventually all could prosper. That life in a suburb should have seemed to so many people as the acme of prosperity makes sense if one asks where they were coming from. Some had a past, especially recent immigrants, of dense insertion in extended families and kin networks, in relation to which this new life seemed a liberation, which also brought their lives into line with a hallowed model in established American society. For others, this life had been impeded by poverty and the dangers that beset poverty: unemployment, lack of discipline, drink. At last they had acceded to respectability. Moreover, these people were emerging from a catastrophic depression and a world war, and it seemed that at last green fields were opening before them.

If this kind of prosperity was central to the American way of life, so was religion. For it could be seen as following God's design, and America as a nation was especially founded to realize this design. The three sides of this triangle mutually supported each other: the family was the matrix in which the young were brought up to be good citizens and believing worshippers; religion was the source of the values that animated both family and society; and the state was the realization and bulwark of the values central to both family and churches. And this was all the more starkly underlined by the fact that American freedom needed to defend itself against "Godless Communism". It was no wonder that the residents of the new Chicago suburb, Elmhurst, crowned their community-building achievements in the erection of a new church, Elmhurst Presbyterian. This was seen as a central part of what was involved in building their new life.

Of course, this close interweaving of religion, life-style and patriotism was frowned on by many observers. Will Herberg, in his *Protestant, Catholic, and Jew,* saw these new churches as more about social identity than about God. And in founding a new Presbyterian church, the new residents were taking their distance from the existing church of that denomination in the area, one which was much more fire-and-brimstone in its tone. In fact, the Presbyterian identity was not chosen for its theology, but because it was right in the middle of the social spectrum of denominations; not as stuffy as the Episcopalians, not as undignified and popular as the Baptists.[1]

This tight interweaving of family, religion, and state is the more remarkable in that, unknown to anyone at the time, it was about to suffer simultaneous blows to each of its constituent parts. Indeed, it has been referred to by unsympathetic historians as "the last-gasp orgy of modern nuclear family domesticity".[2] The unsullied goodness of the American Way of Life was called into question in the struggle against Jim Crow, and in the agony about the Vietnam War; the positive image of the nuclear family was questioned by feminism, and the new expressive culture and sexual revolution of the 1960s; and the bland religion of American conformity was roundly repudiated in that turbulent decade.

Now in these last chapters, I have been describing this crucial transition as a breakout, or break-down of previous religious forms, those of the Age of Mobilization. This gives us the negative side, what our present situation is not. But we should also fill out more of a positive characterization. What is the spiritual life like which emerges from the expressive revolution, with its altered sexual ethic?

Many young people are following their own spiritual instincts, as it were, but what are they looking for? Many are "looking for a more direct experience of the sacred, for greater immediacy, spontaneity, and spiritual depth", in the words of an astute observer of the American scene.[3] This often springs from a profound dissatisfaction with a life encased entirely in the immanent order. The sense is that this life is empty, flat, devoid of higher purpose.

This, of course, has been a widespread response to the world created by Western modernity over at least the last two centuries. We might borrow as its slogan the title of a song by the American singer Peggy Lee, "Is that all there is?" There has to be more to life than our current definitions of social and individual success define for us. This was always a factor in previous returns to religion, like the conversions to Catholicism in nineteenth and early twentieth century France I mentioned above. But it was interwoven there with a neo-Durkheimian identity, and even more a project for restoring civilizational order. When these fall away, this search occurs for its own sake. It is a personal search, and can easily be coded in the language of authenticity: I am trying to find my path, or find myself.

Moreover the seekers in this case are the heirs of the expressive revolution, with its roots in the reactions of the Romantic period against the disciplined, instrumental self connected to the modern moral order. This means not only that they resonate with the "Peggy Lee" response, but also that they are seeking a kind of unity and wholeness of the self, a reclaiming of the place of feeling, against the one-sided pre-eminence of reason, and a reclaiming of the body and its pleasures from the inferior and often guilt-ridden place it has been allowed in the disciplined, instrumental identity.[4] The stress is on unity, integrity, holism, individuality; their language often invokes "harmony, balance, flow, integrations, being at one, centred".[5]

Because of this, the search for spiritual wholeness is often closely related to the search for health. We seem to have something akin to the medicalization of sin and vice in the nineteenth century that I described in a previous chapter. A link is created here between spiritual and physical health, but its basis is entirely different. Mainstream medicine objectifies the body and its processes, and what I called medicalization extends this objectification to vice. But contemporary links between health and spirituality usually take off from alternative kinds of medicine. Far from seeing the body just as an object of natural science, they see it as the site of spiritual currents and flows. Recovering health requires that one put oneself right with these, and this can only be done by opening oneself to them, the very opposite stance from objectification.

Roof points to new approaches to dieting, and the control of obesity, in contemporary spiritual culture. On the older "deadly sin" understanding, obesity comes from gluttony, a temptation which must be rigorously controlled. Medicalization resituated this temptation as a kind of abnormality, the kind of thing which arises with deviant kinds of development. The contemporary understanding will often look beyond the craving to the deeper unmet spiritual needs that trigger anxious eating.[6]

And, crucially, this is a culture informed by an ethic of authenticity. I have to discover my route to wholeness and spiritual depth. The focus is on the individual, and on his/her experience. Spirituality must speak to this experience. The basic mode of spiritual life is thus the quest, as Roof argues.[7] It is a quest which can't start with a priori exclusions or inescapable starting points, which could pre-empt this experience.

This kind of search is often called by its practitioners "spirituality", and is opposed to "religion". This contrast reflects the rejection of "institutional religion", that is, the authority claims made by churches which see it as their mandate to pre-empt the search, or to maintain it within certain definite limits, and above all to dictate a certain code of behaviour. Roof quotes one of the people he interviewed:

> Well, religion, I feel, is doctrine and tradition, genuflecting, and you have to do things this way. Spirituality is an inner feeling, an allowance of however you perceive it in your world, in your mind, and however it feels is okay. . . . There's not these parameters on it. That you have to believe in this way and only in this way. Spirituality, I think, is what enters you and lifts you up and moves you to be a better person, a more open person. I don't think religion does that. Religion tells you what to do and when to do it, when to kneel, when to stand up, all of that stuff. Lots of rules.[8]

These features of "spirituality", its subjectivism, its focus on the self and its wholeness, its emphasis on feeling, has led many to see the new forms of spiritual quest which arise on our society as intrinsically trivial or privatised. I believe that this is part and parcel of the common error which I criticized in the previous chapter: the widespread propensity to identify the main phenomena of the Age of Authenticity with their most simple and flattened forms. This flattening effect arises out of the polemic which opposes critics of authenticity on one hand, and the boosters of these trivialized forms on the other—like the purveyors of the discourse of "choice" in the earlier discussion. These unwittingly conspire to offer a simplified and distorted view of what is happening in our civilization.

In particular, in this case, the new kinds of spiritual quest, which include without being limited to those often lumped together under the term "New Age", are often taxed with being mere extensions of the human potential movement, hence totally focussed on the immanent, and/or being a variety of invitations to self-absorption, without any concern for anything beyond the agent, whether the surrounding society, or the transcendent. And, of course, lots of phenomena in this general range do meet these specifications. But the idea that all of them do, that this kind of question by its very nature must gravitate towards immanent self-concern, is an illusion which arises from the often raucous debate between those whose sense of religious authority is offended by this kind of quest, on one hand, and the proponents of the most self- and immanent-centred forms, on the other, each of which likes to target the other as their main rival. "Look what happens when you abandon proper authority" (i.e., the Bible, or the Pope, or the tradition, according to the point of view), say the first; "don't you see that we alone offer an alternative to mindless authoritarianism", say the second. Each is comforted in their position by the thought that the only alternative is so utterly repulsive.

But this misses a good part of the spiritual reality of our age. Picturing this contemporary form of spiritual quest as a move towards immanence confuses it with a tendency which has been around for a lot longer, throughout most of the modern age. A figure like Norman Vincent Peale in the post-war period, with his "power of positive thinking", represents this kind of move; religious language and images are used in a project which promises fuller human flourishing. We can think of his offering as a part of the "human potential movement" avant la lettre. But lots of seekers today are looking for something more than that, as Roof among others persuasively argues. Very often after confining themselves to self-development, they sense the inadequacy of this; this itself awakens the "Peggy Lee" response, and they want to move on.[9]

Again, even as acute an observer as Paul Heelas, in a very interesting recent book,[10] seems to me to foreshorten a little the reality he is studying. The kind of quest which I am invoking here, and which is central to what the authors call "spirituality", which they oppose to "religion", is indeed defined by a kind of autonomous exploration, which is opposed to a simple surrender to authority; and people who engage in this kind of spiritual path are indeed, put off by the moralism and code-fetishism which they find in the churches. But these ways of putting the crucial issue do not necessarily run parallel to others which the authors also offer as more or less equivalent: for instance, that between "heeding and conforming to a source of significance which ultimately transcends the life of this world", as against . . . "seeking out, experiencing and expressing a source of significance which lies within the process of life itself."[11] Many of the young visitors to Taizé will end up opting for the first alternative here, as must many of the Buddhists who figured in the authors' surveys, but they remain as allergic to moralism and a pre-emption of their quest by authority as all other such seekers.

Again, "finding out about oneself, expressing oneself, discovering one's own way of becoming all that one can . . . be" is opposed to "denying or sacrificing oneself for the sake of a super-self order of things, or even . . . living by reference to such an order".[12] But this contrast can't be considered exhaustive. The first term could be seen as a definition of the contemporary ethic of authenticity; the second invokes one view of what is supremely important in life. The question set in the first can initiate a quest, and this *can* end in the second as an answer. Nothing guarantees this, but nothing ensures its opposite either.

Indeed, the authors correctly see that much of the spirituality we call "New Age" is informed by a humanism which is inspired by the Romantic critique of the modern disciplined, instrumental agent, which was central as we saw above to the 60s; the stress is on unity, integrity, holism, individuality.[13] But they also point out that the spirituality they study differentiates itself from the "general subjective wellbeing culture" by the generalized desire to go beyond this. It involves "deepening the quest".[14] For some people, this will go no farther than some immanently-conceived life force, but it doesn't need to stop there. Some people want, of course, to declare a fundamental opposition between this search for integrity and the transcendent: the authors quote a minister who told his congregation that "wholeness" should matter to them less than "holiness",[15] but that is what one might expect from a hostile observer for whom religious authority renders this kind of quest useless and dangerous. There is no reason to buy into this kind of myopia.

I insist on this point because in a way this whole book is an attempt to study the fate in the modern West of religious faith in a strong sense. This strong sense I define, to repeat, by a double criterion: the belief in transcendent reality, on one hand, and the connected aspiration to a transformation which goes beyond ordinary human flourishing on the other. One would be seriously mistaken about the fate of religion so defined if one accepts the flattened view that I have been combating here.

There is unquestionably a tension in our time, which is the site of a battle between neo- and post-Durkheimian construals of our condition, between different forms of religion or spirituality, those which place authority first, and hence are suspicious and hostile of contemporary modes of quest; and those which are embarked on these, and may or may not in the course of searching come to recognize one or another form of authority. Now this opposition has some affinities with a division which goes back 500 years in our civilization, to about the time of the Reformation.

The spiritual ancestors of our seekers belonged to the stream for which Abbé Henri Bremond found the name "humanisme dévot" in his massive work on the French seventeenth century.[16] Their opponents in that country and century were the Jansenists. The battles which come immediately to mind are those between Jesuits and Jansenists, and we usually define these in terms of the doctrines, political positions and strategic stances and alliances that each side adopted. But I am thinking of something more basic: a difference in profound attitude in one's spiritual life. For the devout humanists, the principal goal was to cultivate in oneself the love of God, to use the crucial term of one of their founding figures in this century, St. François de Sales. This meant that they were ready to trust the first promptings of this love in themselves; they set out to cultivate a germ which could already be identified.[17]

We can get a good example of what this involved if we look a century earlier, to one of their sources, which we find in a story about the conversion of Ignatius Loyola, founder of the Jesuits. While recovering from the wound sustained in battle, he was desperately bored, and wanted something to read. Specifically, he wanted some of the novels of chivalry which were the staple of knights and ladies of his days, and which would later be lampooned by Cervantes. But there weren't any in the castle where he was staying, and all he could put his hands on were lives of the saints. After a while, he began to notice something: whereas reading the novels was gripping and exciting, afterwards it left you feeling arid and unsatisfied; when he read the stories of saints, he was greatly uplifted, but here there was no let-down afterwards; he remained with a sense of satisfaction, even joy. This became the basis for a crucial form of discernment in his later *Spiritual Exercises*. There was an intimation here of which path to follow. This inner sense of joy he called "consolation", and its opposite "desolation". The first was produced in relation to his reading by "las hazañas de Dios"; the second often arose after stories of "las hazañas humanas". This was the reflection which started him on the path for which we now know him in history.[18]

The opponents of this devout humanism strongly objected to the kind of trust which it seemed willing to repose in one's own intimations. How could fallen men ever presume this? They were potentially sources of endless self-deceit. What was required was something external to latch on to, some authority beyond one's own sense of the direction in which God was to be found. This might be the Bible, or the authority of the Church, but the crucial thing was that it was not based on one's own intimations.

The same issue arose in a famous dispute in the late seventeenth century between two French Bishops, Bossuet and Fénelon, over whether one should aspire to a truly pure love of God, one which could hold even if it should appear to one that one was damned. A crucial moment in the life of St. François de Sales, after a long period when he felt that he might be damned, came when he sensed that even this would not stop him from loving God. Fénelon embraced this ideal, and Bossuet held that it implied a presumption that we could rise above our sinful condition.

Now these disputes were fought out in terms of doctrines in the seventeenth century, in particular, hyper-Augustinian doctrines of human depravity, and the inability to escape it without efficacious grace. But I'm talking about the underlying attitudes. Once one frames these as doctrines, one betrays them, loses the nuances that they incorporated. Of course, no one ever thought that one's own intimations were sufficient as indicators, that they were valid against the whole weight of Christian doctrine; and those on the other side were capable of recognizing and drawing strength from moments of spiritual uplift. One might even argue that the valid position was to recognize a complementarity here, and to combine some features of each: within a basic stance of self-trust, to be aware of the multiple possibilities of complacency and self-deception, as indeed, people like Loyola and St. François were. This is the position that Wuthnow takes up between the two spiritual stances which he calls "dwelling" and "seeking".[19] But there still remain two directions in which one can lean.

My contention is that these remain till this day the basis of two kinds of religious sensibility, those which underlie respectively the new kinds of spiritual quest, on one side, and the prior option for an authority which forecloses them on the other. And we can make some very partial and hesitant attempts to understand why this might be so. Take for example the kind of conversion in which people are rescued from a deep disorder in their lives, the kind which often accompanied revivals in the U.S.A. in the last two centuries, or the kind which one sees in Evangelical and Pentecostal churches in today's Brazil or West Africa. It is surely very understandable that these should often be felt as a surrender to an external authority which overcomes the self-destructive drives in oneself. This should neither invalidate, nor be invalidated by another kind of itinerary, in which a seeker might come to the same Christian faith after following earlier intimations which seemed not to lead there: the kind of life history of Bede Griffiths, for instance, from whose autobiography I quoted in the first chapter.

Once again, these alternatives are hardened by various doctrines which make them polar opposites, and have the obfuscatory effect of forcing people to the extremes, to peremptory authority on one side, and self-sufficiency on the other; either utter self-suspicion or total self-trust. This is, of course, in keeping with the long-standing obsession in Latin Christendom to nail down with ultimate, unattainable and finally self-destructive precision the bases of final, unchallengeable, inerrant authority, be it in a certain form of Papal decision, or a literal reading of the Bible.

But if one can escape from this dialectic which propels people to these extremes, it should be clear that there are other alternatives, and that much of today's spiritual/religious life is to be found in this middle ground.

This is not to say that there is no connection between a post-Durkheimian dispensation, on one hand, and the tendency to an individualized experience of the spiritual which often slides towards the feel-good and the superficial. For clearly, this kind of undemanding spirituality is what a lot of people will understand as following their own way. But this is far from being the whole story. It is indeed true that, if one could in some way leap back to some earlier century, the number of self-indulgent seekers would radically decline. But this in no way justifies our identifying the injunction to follow one's own spiritual path with the more flaccid and superficial options visible today.

Some conservative souls feel that it is sufficient to condemn this age to note that it has led great numbers into modes of free floating not very exigent spirituality. But they should ask themselves two questions: First, is it conceivable that one could return to a paleo- or even neo-Durkheimian dispensation? And secondly, and more profoundly, doesn't every dispensation have its own favoured forms of deviation? If ours tends to multiply somewhat shallow and undemanding spiritual options, we shouldn't forget the spiritual costs of various kinds of forced conformity: hypocrisy, spiritual stultification, inner revolt against the Gospel, the confusion of faith and power, and even worse. Even if we had a choice, I'm not sure we wouldn't be wiser to stick with the present dispensation.

8

What are the features of this new spiritual landscape? First, one that everybody will welcome, a breaking down of barriers between different religious groups, a deconstruction of ghetto walls where such existed, as Michael Hornsby-Smith reports for the English Catholic Church after Vatican II.[20] And, of course, the effects of this are even more palpable in what were previously denominationally partitioned societies, like Holland.

But the flip side of this is a decline. The measurable, external results are as we might expect: first, a rise in the number of those who state themselves to be atheists, agnostics, or to have no religion, in many countries, including Britain, France, the U.S., and Australia.[21] But beyond this, the gamut of intermediate positions greatly widens: many people drop out of active practice while still declaring themselves as belonging to some confession, or believing in God. On another dimension, the gamut of beliefs in something beyond widens, fewer declaring belief in a personal God, while more hold to something like an impersonal force;[22] in other words a wider range of people express religious beliefs which move outside Christian orthodoxy. Following in this line is the growth of non-Christian religions, particularly those originating in the Orient, and the proliferation of New Age modes of practice, of views which bridge the humanist/spiritual boundary, of practices which link spirituality and therapy. On top of this more and more people adopt what would earlier have been seen as untenable positions, e.g., they consider themselves Catholic while not accepting many crucial dogmas, or they combine Christianity with Buddhism, or they pray while not being certain they believe. This is not to say that people didn't occupy positions like this in the past. Just that now it seems to be easier to be upfront about it. In reaction to all this, Christian faith is in the process of redefining and recomposing itself in various ways, from Vatican II to the charismatic movements. All this represents the consequence of expressivist culture as it impacts on our world. It has created a quite new predicament.[23]

Danièle Hervieu-Léger speaks of a "découplage de la croyance et de la pratique", of a "désemboîtement de la croyance, de l'appartenance et de la référence iden-titaire". Grace Davie speaks of "believing without belonging". The tight normative link between a certain religious identity, the belief in certain theological proposi-tions, and a standard practice, no longer holds for great numbers of people. Many of these are engaged in assembling their own personal outlook, through a kind of "bricolage"; but there also some widespread patterns which run athwart the tradi-tional constellations. Not only declaring some faith in God, and identifying with a church, without actually attending its services ("believing without belonging"), but also a Scandinavian pattern of identifying with the national church, which one only attends for the crucial rites of passage, while professing widespread skepticism about the theology. The tight connection between national identity, a certain ecclesial tra-dition, strong common beliefs, and sense of civilizational order, which was standard for the Age of Mobilization, has given way, weakening crucially the hold of the the-ology. But whereas in other countries this has also meant a decline in identification with the church, this latter connection seems strong in Scandinavian countries, but deprived of its original theological connotations. The churches are seen, one might say, as a crucial element in the historical-cultural identity. This pattern can also be found in other European countries, but in the Nordic nations seems dominant.[24]

What lies behind these figures and trends? We cannot understand our present sit-uation by a single ideal type, but if we understand ourselves to be moving away from an Age of Mobilization and more into an Age of Authenticity, then we can see this whole move as in a sense a retreat of Christendom. I mean by Christendom a civilization where society and culture are profoundly informed by Christian faith. This retreat is a shattering development, if we think of the way until quite recently, that Christian churches conceived their task. If we just take the Catholic Church (and there were analogues with the inter-denominational "church" in pluralist Prot-estant societies), the goal was to provide a common religious home for the whole so-ciety. We can think in the French case of the seventeenth century Catholic Refor-mation, trying to win back ground lost to the Reformed Church, as well as to penetrate segments of rural society which had never been properly Christianized; then in the nineteenth century, the Church tried again, to make up the ravages of the Revolution; the goal of Action Catholique in the early twentieth century was to missionize the milieux which had slipped away. But it is clear today that this ambi-tion is unrealizable.

Now our societies in the West will forever remain historically informed by Chris-tianity. I will return below to some of the significance of this. But what I mean by the retreat of Christendom is that it will be less and less common for people to be drawn into or kept within a faith by some strong political or group identity, or by the sense that they are sustaining a socially essential ethic. There will obviously still be lots of both of these things: at the very least, group identity may be important for immigrants, particularly of recent provenance—and even more among non-Christians, say, Muslims or Hindus, who feel their difference from the established majority religion. And there will certainly remain a core of people both members and regular attenders of churches, larger or smaller from country to country (vast in the U.S.A., minuscule in Sweden).

And there is another reason which assures the continuing importance of the neo-Durkheimian identities. In some societies these are in a quasi-agonistic relation to the post-Durkheimian climate. Think for instance of the United States, and certain demands of the Christian Right, for, e.g., school prayer. But these identities are perhaps even more in evidence among groups which feel suppressed or threatened (perhaps also the case of the Christian Right?), and often people of a certain ethnic or historical identity will look to some religious marker to gather around. I mentioned, e.g., the Poles and Irish above. These were peoples cast into the modern political form because they were mobilized to attain their independence or establish their integrity, in the context of being ruled from outside and sometimes being very heavily oppressed. They therefore took on the modern language and the modern conceptions of a political entity; they became in a modern sense peoples. And modern peoples, that is collectivities that strive to be agents in history, need some understanding of what they're about, what I'm calling political identity. In the two cases mentioned, being Catholic was an important part of that identity.

This phenomenon remains important in the modern world, although from a faith perspective one might be ambivalent about it. Because there are a gamut of cases, from a deeply felt religious allegiance, all the way to situations in which the religious marker is cynically manipulated in order to mobilize people. Think of Milošević, and the BJP. But whatever one's ethical judgments, this is a powerful reality in today's world, and one that is not about to disappear.

But in general, we can say that in twenty-first-century North Atlantic societies not riven by ethnic-confessional differences (e.g., we're NOT talking about Northern Ireland), the recently dominant forms of the Age of Mobilization will have difficulty holding their members, whether to a greater (Europe) or lesser (U.S.A.) degree.

Now if we don't accept the view that the human aspiration to religion will flag, and I do not, then where will the access lie to practice of and deeper engagement with religion? The answer is the various forms of spiritual practice to which each is drawn in his/her own spiritual life. These may involve meditation, or some charitable work, or a study group, or a pilgrimage, or some special form of prayer, or a host of such things.

A range of such forms has always existed, of course, as optional extras as it were, for those who are already and primarily embedded in ordinary church practice. But now it is frequently the reverse. First people are drawn to a pilgrimage, or a World Youth Day, or a meditation group, or a prayer circle; and then later, if they move along in the appropriate direction, they will find themselves embedded in ordinary practice.

And there will be much movement between such forms of practice, and between the associated faiths.

This shows once more the error of confusing the post-Durkheimian dispensation with a trivialized and utterly privatized spirituality. Of course, there will exist lots of both. These are the dangers which attend our present predicament. A post-Durkheimian world means, as I said above, that our relation to the spiritual is being more and more unhooked from our relation to our political societies. But that by itself doesn't say anything about whether or how our relation to the sacred will be mediated by collective connections. A thoroughly post-Durkheimian society would be one in which our religious belonging would be unconnected to our national identity. It will almost certainly be one in which the gamut of such religious allegiances will be wide and varied. It will also almost certainly have lots of people who are following a religious life centred on personal experience in the sense that William James made famous.[25] But it doesn't follow that everyone, or even that most people, will be doing this. Many people will find their spiritual home in churches, for instance, including the Catholic Church. In a post-Durkheimian world, this allegiance will be unhooked from that to a sacralized society (paleo-style), or some national identity (neo-style); or from the (now arrogant-sounding) claim to provide the indispensable matrix for the common civilizational order; and if I am right above, the mode of access will be different; but it will still be a collective connection.

These connections, sacramental or through a common practice, are obviously still powerful in the modern world. We have to avoid an easy error here; that of confusing the new place of religion in our personal and social lives, the framework understanding that we should be following our own spiritual sense, from the issue of what paths we will follow. The new framework has a strongly individualist component, but this will not necessarily mean that the content will be individuating. Many people will find themselves joining extremely powerful religious communities. Because that's where many people's sense of the spiritual will lead them.

Of course, they won't necessarily sit easily in these communities as their forebears did. And in particular, a post-Durkheimian age may mean a much lower rate of inter-generational continuity of religious allegiance. But the strongly collective options will not lose adherents. Perhaps even the contrary trend might declare itself.

One reason to take this latter idea seriously is the continuing importance of the festive. People still seek those moments of fusion, which wrench us out of the everyday, and put us in contact with something beyond ourselves. We see this in pilgrimages, mass assemblies like World Youth Days, in one-off gatherings of people moved by some highly resonating event, like the funeral of Princess Diana, as well as in rock concerts, raves, and the like. What has all this got to do with religion? The relationship is complex. On one hand, some of these events are unquestionably "religious", in the sense I adopted at the beginning of this discussion, that is oriented to something putatively transcendent (a pilgrimage to Medjugorje, or a World Youth Day). And what has perhaps not sufficiently been remarked is the way in which this dimension of religion, which goes back to its earliest forms, well before the Axial age, is still alive and well today, in spite of all attempts by Reforming élites over many centuries to render our religious and/or moral lives more personal and inward, to disenchant the universe and downplay the collective.

In some respects, these forms are well adapted to the contemporary predicament. Hervieu-Léger points out how the traditional figure of the pilgrim can be given a new sense today, as young people travel in search of faith or meaning in their lives. The pilgrimage is also a quest. The example of Taizé is striking in this regard. An interconfessional Christian centre in Burgundy, with at its core a community of monks, gathered around the late Roger Schütz, it draws thousands of young people from a great range of countries in the summer months, and tens of thousands to its international gatherings. The drawing power lies partly in the fact that they are received as searchers, that they can express themselves, without being "confrontés à un dispositif normatif du croire, ni même à un discours du sens préconstitué". And yet at the same time, the centre is clearly rooted in Christianity, and in values of international understanding and reconciliation, whose religious roots are explored through Bible study and liturgy. This whole combination is what attracts young people, who want to meet their counterparts from other lands, and explore Christian faith without any preconditions as to the outcome. As one visitor put it, "A Taizé, on ne vous donne pas la réponse avant que vous ayez posé la question, et surtout, c'est à chacun de chercher sa réponse."

Of course, the Taizé experience is not simply and totally in the category of the festive. There certainly is the departure from the everyday, and the contact with something greater, a sense of universal brotherhood, even if not always its source in the fatherhood of God; but the sense of fusion is not always prominent. It is not, however, totally absent; a central part of the Taizé experience is singing together, chants especially designed by the community, each in his/her own language, a model and foretaste of the reconciliation sought between peoples and cultures. It is not surprising that Taizé should provide the template from which World Youth Days were developed; a form of Christian pilgrimage/assembly for the Age of Authenticity.[26]

But how about rock concerts and raves? In terms of our criterion, they are plainly "non-religious"; and yet they also sit uneasily in the secular, disenchanted world. Fusions in common action/feeling, which take us out of the everyday, they often generate the powerful phenomenological sense that we are in contact with something greater, however we ultimately want to explain or understand this. A disenchanted view of the world needs a theory to explain the continuing power of this kind of experience. Now of course, such theories can be devised; some already have been: e.g., Durkheim, Freud, Bataille. But it remains true that the state of mind of the participant is far removed from the disengaged, objectifying stance, from which the alleged truth of the immanent, naturalistic world-view is supposed to be convincingly evident. It is not obvious a priori that the sense of something beyond, inherent in these fusions, can be ultimately explained (away) in naturalistic categories. The festive remains a niche in our world, where the (putatively) transcendent can erupt into our lives, however well we have organized them around immanent understandings of order.

The other thing that it is easy to under-rate, if one confuses framework with content, is the way in which our response to our original spiritual intuitions may continue into formal spiritual practices. Our path may start in a moment of inspiration, a strong feeling of spiritual affinity or moment of blinding insight, but it may then continue through some, perhaps very demanding spiritual discipline. It can be in meditation; it can be prayer. One develops a religious life. Arguably this kind of path is becoming more and more prominent and widespread in our (largely) post-Durkheimian age. Many people are not satisfied with a momentary sense of wow! They want to take it further, and they're looking for ways of doing so.[27] That is what leads them into the practices which are their main access to traditional forms of faith.[28]

If this retreat from Christendom offers one key to our situation, if the connections between faith and national/group political identities and ways of life steadily weaken, if as part consequence, we now are witnessing a polarity between spiritualities of quest and of peremptory authority; this still leaves much which is enigmatic and difficult to understand. Many people have taken a distance from their ancestral churches without altogether breaking off. They retain some of the beliefs of Christianity, for instance, and/or they retain some nominal tie with the church, still identify in some way with it: they will reply, say, to a poll by saying that they are Anglican, or Catholic. Sociologists are forced to invent new terms, such as "believing without belonging", or "diffusive Christianity", to come to grips with this.[29] This phenomenon is particularly in evidence in Western Europe.

Now something like this has always existed. That is, churches have always had a penumbra around the core of orthodox, fully practising believers, whose beliefs shade off into heterodoxy, and/or whose practice was partial or fragmentary. We saw examples of this above in the "folk religion" of populations still living partly or largely within "ancien régime" forms. Now in fact, the term "diffusive Christianity" was coined for the unofficial popular religion of a more modern, but still not contemporary period, the late nineteenth and early twentieth centuries in the U.K. John Wolffe, following Cox, tries to give a sense of one version of this outlook. It was

> a vague non-doctrinal kind of belief: God exists; Christ was a good man and an example to be followed; people should lead decent lives on charitable terms with their neighbours, and those who do so will go to Heaven when they die. Those who suffer in this world will receive compensation in the next. The churches were regarded with apathy rather than hostility: their social activities made some contribution to the community. Sunday School was felt to provide a necessary part of the upbringing of children, and the rites of passage required formal religious sanction. Association was maintained by attendance at certain annual and seasonal festivals, but weekly participation in worship was felt to be unnecessary and excessive. Women and children were more likely than men to be regularly involved, but this did not imply that adult males were hostile; merely—it can be surmised—that they tended to see themselves as the main breadwinners, and felt that women should therefore represent the family's interests in the religious arena. The emphasis was on the practical and the communal rather than on the theological and the individual.[30]

Perhaps this kind of penumbra was bigger in 1900, and the core it surrounded somewhat smaller than at the high tide of the evangelical wave, around 1850. But there has always been such a hinterland, surrounding the central zones of belief and practice in any large membership church. Only small committed minorities, battling with their surroundings, have been able to maintain 100 percent commitment by 100 percent of members. In earlier times, the hinterland of lesser orthodoxy lay more in the dimension of folk religion, semi-magical beliefs and practices surrounding the liturgy and festivals of the church. And even some of this survived into the early twentieth century, as the work of Sarah Williams attests, though the "diffusive Christianity" of 1900 was in its essentials different from the religious penumbra of earlier times. But penumbra it was nonetheless. When one compares these different stages of British Christianity, there is "some foundation for the judgment", Wolffe opines, "that around 1900 the British people were, albeit in a diffuse and passive sense, closer to Christian orthodoxy than they had ever been in their history."[31]

What then has happened since 1960? Well, clearly some of the penumbra has been lost; people now stand clearly outside Christian belief, no longer identifying with any church, that were in the hinterland before (or their parents were). Some of these people have consciously adopted some quite different outlook, materialist for instance, or have adopted a non-Christian religion. Some of this shift is reflected in the rise in numbers of those who declare themselves to have no religion. But that still doesn't account for the substantial number of those who declare themselves still to believe in God, and/or to identify with some church, even though they stand at a much greater distance from it than the "diffused" Christians of a century ago. For instance, their views are more heterodox (God is often conceived more like a life force), and they no longer participate in many of the rites of passage, e.g., baptism and marriage. (In Britain, unlike in Germany, religious funerals hold up better than the other rites.)

In other words, the falling off, or alienation, from the Church and from some aspects of orthodox Christianity has taken more the form of what Grace Davie calls "Christian nominalism". Committed secularism "remains the creed of a relatively small minority. . . . In terms of belief, nominalism rather than secularism is the residual category".[32]

How to understand this is yet unclear. A great deal of ambivalence, of different kinds, inhabits this distancing stance, which Davie calls "believing without belonging". Is it a mere transitional phenomenon, as secularists hold? For some people, undoubtedly. But for all?

In some ways, this phenomenon can perhaps best be described in terms of past forms of Christian collective life. It stands at a distance from "diffusive Christianity", which itself stood at a certain distance from the models of totally committed practice. It is orbiting farther out from a star which is still a key reference point. In this way, the forms of the Age of Mobilization remain still alive at the margins of contemporary life. This becomes evident at certain moments, for instance when people feel a desire to be connected to their past; to take the British case, at moments of royal ceremonial, such as the Jubilee and the funeral of the Queen Mum. Here it is as though the full force of the old neo-Durkheimian identity, linking Britishness to a certain form of Protestant Christianity, where oddly, the Anglican Church is allowed to perform ceremonies for everyone (even Catholics!), relives for a day. Our eccentric orbit, which normally carries us far into outer space, passes close to the original sun on those occasions. This is part of the significance, which I mentioned earlier, of the fact that our past is irrevocably within Christendom. A similar moment occurred in France recently, in the celebrations of the 1500th anniversary of the baptism of Clovis. Various "laïque" figures grumbled, but the ceremonies went on regardless. History is hard to deny.

The other kind of occasion arises when disaster strikes, such as September 11, 2001, in the U.S.A.; or the Hillsborough football tragedy in England in April 1989, where 94 people died, mostly Liverpool supporters. Grace Davie describes the ceremonies which followed in Liverpool.[33] Again, a recent German case is the school massacre which occurred at Erfurt in April 2002. Here in former East Germany, where the level of practice has fallen lower than anywhere else in the world, there was a rush to churches which are normally deserted. Something similar happened when the ferry *Estonia* sank in the Baltic with many Swedes on board; the churches were packed for memorial services in Sweden.[34]

And of course, there are events which combine both of the above, such as the mourning and funeral for Princess Di in 1997.

So it appears that the religious or spiritual identity of masses of people still remains defined by religious forms from which they normally keep themselves at a good distance. We still need some attempt to articulate this stance, to describe it from the inside, as it were, as Wolffe attempted in the passage quoted above about diffusive Christianity. There is perhaps also one other clue we can use here. It is after all a quite well known stance to be holding oneself at some distance from a spiritual demand which one nevertheless acknowledges. The famous Augustinian: "Lord, make me chaste, but not yet" encapsulates some of this. But it is normally less dramatic; we all have important things to get on with in our lives, and we feel we can't give our full attention and effort to spiritual or moral demands that we hold in some sense valid, that we may admire others for giving themselves to more fully.

Our attachment to these comes in our not wanting to lose sight of these, our resistance to denying them or seeing them denigrated by others. This may be part of what lies behind someone answering a survey by saying that they believe in God (or angels, or an afterlife), even though they don't, say, baptize their children or marry in Church, or perhaps do anything else which clearly reflects this belief. It would also explain why the same people may be very moved by the actions of others which do manifest their relation to that spiritual source. In the language of my earlier discussion, people may retain an attachment to a perspective of transformation which they are not presently acting on; they may even find themselves losing sight of it from time to time. The reception, as it were, fades in and out, like a city FM station in the countryside. When they see or hear of people's lives which seem really to have been touched by these sources of transformation, they can be strongly moved. The broadcast is now loud and clear. They are moved, and curiously grateful. I remember the response to the life, and particularly the death, of Pope John XXIII. And something similar has happened with some of the actions of John Paul II. These reactions often went well beyond the borders of the Catholic Church. We are dealing with a phenomenon which is not confined to religion. A figure like Nelson Mandela has awakened the same kind of response of confirmation and gratitude.

Perhaps what we need here is a new concept, which can capture the inner dynamic underlying this phenomenon. Grace Davie and Danièle Hervieu-Léger seem to have been working towards this in their writings. We might borrow from Davie the term "vicarious religion".[35] What she is trying to capture here is the relationship of people to a church, from which they stand at a certain distance, but which they nevertheless in some sense cherish; which they want to be there, partly as a holder of ancestral memory, partly as a resource against some future need (e.g., their need for a rite of passage, especially a funeral); or as a source of comfort and orientation in the face of some collective disaster.

In this case, we shouldn't perhaps speak simply of the loss of a neo-Durkheimian identity, or connection to religion through our allegiance to civilizational order, but rather of a kind of mutation. The religious reference in our national identity (and/ or sense of civilizational order) doesn't so much disappear, as change, retreat to a certain distance. It remains powerful in memory; but also as a kind of reserve fund of spiritual force or consolation. It mutates from a "hot" to a "cold" form (with apologies to Marshall McLuhan). The hot form demands a strong, participating identity, and/or an acute sense of Christianity as the bulwark of moral order. The colder form allows a certain ambivalence about the historical identity, as well as a certain degree of dissidence from the Church's official morality (which these days will be strongest in the domain of sexual ethics).

To take Britain as an example, the original hot form of the synthesis between being British, decent and Christian was damaged in a number of ways in the twentieth century, perhaps most of all by the experience of the First World War. And on the European scene in general, hot, militant nationalism has suffered a great loss of credit through both World Wars. But these identities, both national and civilizational, have not just vanished. And the new, fledgling European identity, where it exists, unites these two dimensions; Europe is a supra-national community, which is to be defined by certain "values". But the older identities take a new form, involving distance, passivity, and above all a certain queasiness in face of assertions of their erstwhile "hot" variants.

And indeed, educated, cultivated Europeans are extremely uncomfortable with any overt manifestations of either strong nationalism or religious sentiment. The contrast to the U.S. in this regard has often been remarked. And it might help to take up here one of the most debated issues in the field of secularization theory, that of the "American exception"—or, if one likes, seen from a broader perspective, the "European exception". Put either way, we are faced with a strong even if not uniform pattern of decline in European societies, and virtually nothing of the sort in the U.S.A. How can this difference be explained?

9

Various attempts have been made. (1) For instance, Bruce attributes the strength of religion in America partly to the immigrant context. Immigrants needed to group together with those of similar origins in order to ease their transition into American society. The rallying point was often a shared religion, and the main agency a church.[36]

But this explanation stops too short. Why should emigration consolidate church membership and attendance? The idea must be that churches can be handy support groups. But the evidence shows that they are not always seen that way. Indeed, emigration can produce the opposite effect, as very often happens when peasants move from country to city. This phenomenon has been so widespread that certain variants of secularization theory have taken it as a basic rule that mobility is one of those things, like education and industrial development, which tend to "secularize" a population.

But the truth is, there is no general rule here. The same population source, like Southern Italy, can send people to different destinations, e.g., Northern Italy, Argentina, and the United States, with differing results.

> Rural Italian immigrants from the south at the turn of the twentieth century . . . tended to adopt anti-clerical socialist and anarchist identities when they migrated to urban industrial centres in Northern Italy or in Catholic Argentina, while they tended to become "better" practising Catholics when they migrated to urban industrial centres in the United States. One could make similar comparisons in the present between Hindu immigrants in London and New York, or between francophone West African Muslims in Paris and New York.[37]

What makes the difference? We are thrown back onto our original question. There is some difference in the "social imaginary" of the two kinds of destination societies. I mean in particular their understanding of the place of religion in society. We seem back at square one; but perhaps we can get a little farther if we probe this difference more.

American society from the very beginning has seen itself as integrating different elements. "E pluribus Unum" is the motto. Of course, at first these elements were states. But then very soon one of the models of integration was of "denominations". As the old established churches were sidelined, and the population broke up into a host of churches, unity was nevertheless recovered by seeing all of these as part of a broader "church", which related people together in a consensual "civil religion", as I described above. At first this only included Protestant Christians, and there was widespread feeling among these that new arrivals, particularly Catholics, were only dubiously "American". But somehow the Republic managed to expand its base, and in the course of the twentieth century, Catholics and Jews came to be seen as included.

This means that a way that Americans can understand their fitting together in society although of different faiths, is through these faiths themselves being seen as in this consensual relation to the common civil religion. Go to the church of your choice, but go. Later this expands to include synagogues. When imams also begin to appear at prayer breakfasts, along with priests, pastors, and rabbis, the signal is that Islam is being invited into the consensus.

That means that one can be integrated as an American *through* one's faith or religious identity. This contrasts with the Jacobin-republican formula of "laïcité", where the integration takes place by ignoring, sidelining or privatising the religious identity, if any.

The fact that a very large consensus in the U.S. accepts this old formula of integration, suitably expanded, makes it advantageous for immigrant minorities to further their own entry into U.S. society through a foregrounding of their religious identities. And this becomes true in spades for some minorities, where the alternative is to be perceived in terms of race, that other major dimension of U.S. diversity, where the relationships tend to be fraught and conflictual.

One crucial feature of U.S. society, which may help to explain the American (or European) exception, is that it has a long and positive experience of integration through religious identities, whereas in Europe these have been factors of division: either between dissenters and the national church, or between the church and lay forces. And this relatively positive experience sits alongside that other dimension of diversity, race, which has continued to be deeply problematical. Indeed, the notion of "whiteness" has evolved in American history. Some previously excluded groups, like swarthy South European Catholics, eventually enter the category precisely because their faith becomes included in the consensual civil religion.[38]

So it is not only, or even mainly, the plight of the immigrant as such (e.g., the necessity of networking, and the like) which is operative here; rather the crucial factor is a structural feature of the host society, the way it integrates through religious identity. But this historical experience itself begins to explain the difference with Europe.

(2) Another important differentiating factor may have been the hierarchical nature of European societies. British élites, for instance, and particularly the intelligentsia have been living a fractured culture since the eighteenth century; the saliency of unbelief may have been lower in certain periods of strong piety, but it was always there. Now something similar may also have been true of the American intelligentsia, but the position this occupied in its own society was very different. In deferential British society, the pattern of élite life has a prestige which it largely lacks in the U.S.A. This means that élite unbelief can both more effectively resist conforming, and can also more readily provide models for people at other levels. Again there

are parallels with other European societies, which all in this respect contrast with the U.S.A.[39]

The capacity of élites to set the tone of a whole society, to define its "religious imaginary", may turn out to be a very important factor. The American academic world is probably as deeply invested in unbelief as its European counterpart. Certainly, the basic assumptions in, say, social science and history, seem to be equally secularist. But in the American case, this seems without effect on large segments of the greater society, whereas in European countries, the élite outlook seems to have defined the generally accepted picture of the place of religion. European publics seem to have interiorised the mainline secularization story of steady decline, which I have been arguing against here, in a way that Americans have not.

The strength of these different stories on each side of the Atlantic seems to emerge in a peculiar feature of polling data. It has been noticed that in surveys to ascertain the level of religious involvement—say, how often one goes to church—Americans tend to exaggerate the frequency of their attendance, while Europeans tend to understate it. On this level, some sense of what should "normally" be happening is intervening to affect the data. But perhaps it goes farther than this. Perhaps the sense that religion is declining, and that this is a sign of "modernity", not only makes people downplay their religious beliefs and involvements, but acts as a damper on these as well. A belief in secularization theory would be acting here in part as a "self-fulfilling prophecy".[40]

(3) But perhaps the heart of the American exception is that this society is the only one that from the beginning (if we leave aside the countries of the "old" British Commonwealth) was entirely within the neo-Durkheimian mould. All European societies had some element of the "ancien régime" or the paleo-Durkheimian, perhaps more vestigial than real, like the ritual surrounding even constitutional monarchies; but often important enough—such as the presence of (at least would be) state churches, or of rural communities with their "religion du terroir". The proportions of paleo and neo were very different as we move from Spain to Britain or Sweden, but all European states alike contain some mix of the two, whereas American religious life was entirely in the Age of Mobilization.

This means that in varying degrees some of the dynamic arising from ancien régime (AR) structures will take place in all the Old World societies. One of these is the reaction against a state church in the context of an inegalitarian society, where the temptation to align established religion with power and privilege is almost irresistible. This cannot fail to produce anti-clerical reactions, which can easily turn, given the availability of exclusive humanist options since the eighteenth century, into militant unbelief; which is then available to canalize the full force of popular discontent with established clergy. We see this dynamic played out in France and

Spain, even to some extent in Prussia. In Britain, on the other hand, we saw that much popular anti-clericalism found expression in Nonconformity. But even here an alternative stream was there from the beginning, in figures like Tom Paine and Godwin; whereas ideas of this sort didn't have the same impact in the early history of the United States. The imprint of an impressive array of Deists among the founders, most notably Jefferson, seems to have been largely effaced by the second Great Awakening.

The other dynamic which is important in these cases, is that the perturbing effect on religious belief of a shake-out which is affecting both AR forms and Mobilization forms at one and the same time is obviously greater than a challenge addressed to neo-Durkheimian structures alone. If peasants being turned into Frenchmen can only be rescued from unbelief by modes of neo-Durkheimian mobilization, then the undermining of these latter has a much more profoundly destabilizing effect on belief, or at least practice. In a society, on the other hand, where the move to the Age of Mobilization has been completed without any significant fall-off in belief, the effect of undermining the previously dominant modes of this mobilization will obviously be much less.

(4) We can perhaps sharpen our question of the difference between America and Europe if we put it in the following way. My main line of argument has been here that the cultural revolution of the 60s destabilized earlier forms of religion, and therefore was followed by the development of new forms. The newly powerful ethic of authenticity, accompanied by a sexual revolution, worked in two ways to upset powerful religious forms of the nineteenth and early twentieth centuries. First, it undermined the neo-Durkheimian alignments of faith with political identity; and second, it undercut the close connection of religious faith and a certain sexual morality, one of the important fusions of religion with supposedly civilization-bearing morality.

So our question can be put this way: why did this destabilization give rise to a decline of religious allegiance and practice, even to some extent in religious belief, in Europe and not in the U.S.A.?

As far as the U.S.A. is concerned, at least one facet of the answer leaps out. In that country, there was a strong reaction of resistance against loosening the ties of religion, political identity and civilizational morality. Indeed, the mode of American patriotism which sees the country as essentially a nation under God, and certain "family values" as essential to its greatness, remains very strong. It is ready to fight back at what it sees as a denaturing of America. This is one mode of religion which remains powerful in the United States.

By contrast, the constitutional-moral patriotism, what I called above the reigning synthesis between nation, morality and religion, which earlier was very similar in

Britain and the United States, was nevertheless much less strong in Britain, indeed, it was much more strongly contested. This was particularly so in the aftermath of the First World War, which was much more traumatic for British than American society. The challenge to civilization in Britain that this cataclysm represented was certainly lived by many as a challenge to their faith, as I argued above. The strong sense generated by a neo-Durkheimian effect, that everyone shares a certain moral or spiritual coding, that this is how you understand our strong collective moral experience, thus faded more rapidly in Britain, and weakened the code; whereas in the American case, many people felt and have gone on feeling that you can show your Americanness by joining a church, partly for reasons I have just outlined above. In this respect, following the above argument, other European societies are similar to Britain, have gone through the same historical experiences, with similar results.[41]

Against this argument has to be set the triple attack which the family-religion-patriotism complex of the 1950s suffered in the era of civil rights, Vietnam and the expressive revolution. Was this not the analogue in the American case to the First World War for the British? Perhaps, but plainly not everyone sees it this way. Indeed, the different reactions to this era seem to underlie the "culture wars" of contemporary U.S. politics. It seems that that fusion of faith, family values and patriotism is still extremely important to one half of American society, that they are dismayed to see it challenged, both in its central values (e.g., the fight over abortion or gay marriage), and in the link between their faith and the polity (fights over school prayer, the phrase "under God", and the like).

In addition, lots of Americans, even those who are not on the Right, still feel quite at home with the idea of the U.S. as "one nation under God". Those whom this identity makes uncomfortable are vocal and dominant in universities and (some) media, but are not all that numerous. This is the more so, in that the groups of non-Christian and non-Jewish immigrants, who might be thought natural allies of those who want to resist a Biblical coding of the American identity, are themselves anxious to be co-opted into a suitably widened variation of it. Imams are now alongside priests and rabbis at public prayers, and this pan-religious unity surfaces especially at moments of crisis or disaster, as after 9/11.

In other words, the continuing importance of religious identity in national integration keeps a majority of Americans happy in "one nation under God", even while they are disputing bitterly with others about the supposed entailments of this, in areas like abortion or gay marriage. Lots of voters in "blue" states, who abominate the zealots of the Religious Right, are in their majority members of mainline churches, who will still happily sign on to the hallowed formulae of harmoniously co-existing denominations.

Now this is partly the result of the sheer difference in numbers of people who adhere to some religion in the U.S., as against Europe. But it has also to do with the respective attitudes towards national identity. Europe in the second half of the twentieth century has been full of reticence about its erstwhile senses of nationhood; and the events of the first half of this century explain why. The European Union is built on the attempt to go beyond the earlier forms, in the full consciousness of how destructive they have been. The full-throated assertion of the older self-exalting nationalisms are now reserved for the radical Right, which is felt by everyone else to represent a pestilence, a possibly deadly disease, and which in turn is anti-European. War, even "righteous" war, as an expression of the superiority of the national project, makes most Europeans profoundly uneasy.

Quite different is the attitude of the United States. This may be partly because they have fewer skeletons in the family closet to confront than their European cousins. But I think the answer is simpler. It is easier to be unreservedly confident in your own rightness when you are the hegemonic power. The skeletons are there, but they can be resolutely ignored, in spite of the efforts of a gallant band of scholars, who are engaged in the "history wars". Most Germans have to cringe when they are reminded of the First World War slogan "Gott mit uns" (about the Second World War, the less said the better).[42] But most Americans have few doubts about whose side God is on. In this context, the traditional neo-Durkheimian definition is far easier to live with.[43]

So in terms of my discussion a few paragraphs back, the traditional American synthesis of "civil religion", a strong neo-Durkheimian identity, originally around a non-denominational Christianity, with a strong connection to civilizational order, is still in a "hot" phase, unlike its British counterpart. The original civil religion gradually moved wider than its Protestant base, but it has now come to a stage where, while the link to civilizational order remains strong, the connection to religion is now challenged by a broad range of secularists and Liberal believers. Issues like the banning of school prayer, abortion, and more recently, homosexual marriage become highly charged. I spoke above of a "culture war", but another analogy might be "la guerre franco-française", two strong opposed ideological codings of the same nation's identity, in a context where nationalism (not to say great power chauvinism) remains powerful. This is the recipe for bitter struggles.[44]

(5) That provides one half of the answer. The other half is that, for those who are willing to move to a post-Durkheimian stance, and are critical of traditional sexual morality, the history of American religious pluralism affords them the model of numerous options of more personalized and experimental religious forms. William James' celebrated, century-old book already provided us with many examples of this well before the twentieth-century cultural revolution.[45] In other words, models of religious life which had broken out of the neo-Durkheimian and moralistic modes

were already common and familiar on the U.S. scene. People who now wanted to explore in these directions had examples to follow.

The U.S. since the early nineteenth century has been a home of religious freedom, expressed in a very American way: that is, it has been a country of religious choice. People move, form new denominations, join ones that they weren't brought up in, break away from existing ones, and so on. Their whole religious culture was in some way prepared for the Age of Authenticity, even before this became a facet of mass culture in the latter part of the twentieth century. It is true that the ethic of authenticity was before the 1960s present among cultured élites on both sides of the Atlantic, but the educated were a much larger proportion of U.S. population even before the post-war expansion of universities.

This whole shift was therefore much less destabilizing in America. By contrast, in Europe precedents for the more novel post-Durkheimian forms were thin or nonexistent. We have just to think of, for instance, Germany and France, where new "cults" deeply disturb people. Even French atheists are a trifle horrified when religion doesn't take the standard Catholic form that they love to hate.

So much for the answer to this question which emerges from my argument above. I confess that I am only half-satisfied with this answer; perhaps three-quarters satisfied, to be more exact. I think the reasoning about the U.S.A. is right; and the lack of a neo-Durkheimian reaction in Europe seems to me correct and understandable. But one might still ask: why were Europeans not more inventive in creating new forms? Why did they not even copy American models, which are after all not unknown in this age of rapid communication and international travel?

Perhaps the answer can only be sought in long-term factors. One of these might be the continuing historical shadow of the ancien régime in Europe which I invoked above. The hegemony of national (or nationally-established trans-national) churches still shapes people's outlook even centuries after they have ceased to play any controlling role; and perhaps even in places like Britain where the hegemony was very mitigated by religious pluralism. Whereas not even a vestige of this existed in the U.S.A. This might have been determining for the impact of an ethic of authenticity on the two continents. Whereas this new value could easily be associated with religious modes of expression in America, in Europe it was easier to link religion with authority, with conformity to society-wide standards, not to speak of hostile divisions between people, and even violence. Churches and religion still carried this baggage of submission and conformity for many people, including the young, that it had long lost for many Americans. In this situation, the invitation to find one's own way was bound to lead a larger number of people to seek extra-religious forms of meaning in Europe than in the U.S.A.

Moreover this identification of religion as the enemy of authenticity helped to accredit the secularization story, that a growth of autonomy and freely-sought identities was bound to lead to a decline in religion. And the general acceptance of this story contributed in its turn to a decline in belief and practice as a self-fulfilling prophesy.

Here I confess that I am making stabs in the dark. A fully satisfactory account of this difference, which is in a sense the crucial question facing secularization theory, escapes me.[46]

10

Perhaps I can try to gather together some of the threads of this discussion. I have been trying to describe how we got from the (partial) élite unbelief of the eighteenth century to the (wider but still partial) unbelief, but also disaffection and distance from religion, in the twenty-first century. This brought me into the area of secularization theory; and here I declared my disagreement with the "orthodox" version, and my concurrence with the criticisms of "revisionist" historians and sociologists. We are not dealing with a linear regression (I'm not talking statistics here!) in belief/practice, caused by the incompatibility between some features of "modernity" and religious belief. I don't accept what often seems to be an unspoken premise about human motivation which underlies this master narrative of secularization. In particular, I hold that religious longing, the longing for and response to a more-than-immanent transformation perspective, what Chantal Milon-Delsol calls a "désir d'éternité",[47] remains a strong independent source of motivation in modernity.[48]

Nevertheless, it is obvious that a decline in belief and practice has occurred, and beyond this, that the unchallengeable status that belief enjoyed in earlier centuries has been lost. This is the major phenomenon of "secularization". It remains to understand just what it consists in. One way my thesis could be constructed, for simplicity's sake, would be as another "subtraction story". This would involve ignoring for the moment the way in which each stage of this process has involved new constructions of identity, social imaginary, institutions and practices. But it will bring out clearer the contrast with mainline theory if I focus on the negative side.

Put this way, and very schematically, we can ask: what stopped people (that is, almost everybody) from being able to adopt stances of unbelief in 1500? One answer is: the enchanted world; in a cosmos of spirits and forces, some of them evil and destructive, one had to hold on to whatever was conceived to be the mainstay of good power, our bulwark against evil. Another answer was: that belief was so interwoven with social life that one was hardly conceivable without the other. And these two answers were originally connected: some of the interweaving involved collective uses of good, Godly power against the dangers of the spirit world; ceremonies like "beating the bounds" of the parish illustrate this.

Negatively, and leaving aside all the construction that went into this, the intervening centuries have seen the dissipation of the enchanted cosmos (some elements of belief in enchantment remain, but they don't form a system, and are held by individuals here and there, rather than being socially shared). Then there came the introduction, within the context of the modern moral order, of a viable alternative to belief, of forms of exclusive humanism, in turn followed by a multiplication of both believing and unbelieving positions, which I have called the "nova". This all generated the challenge, undermining, and dissolution of the early social forms which embedded God's presence in social space: the paleo-Durkheimian, and more generally "ancien régime" forms. At first, the major beneficiaries of this decline were the neo-Durkheimian and other forms of the Age of Mobilization which were constructed on the ruins of the ancien régime structures and communities. But then subsequent developments undermined these as well, including the claim that civilization had to be Christian to be ordered. We no longer live in societies in which the widespread sense can be maintained that faith in God is central to the ordered life we (partially) enjoy.[49]

It is a pluralist world, in which many forms of belief and unbelief jostle, and hence fragilize each other. It is a world in which belief has lost many of the social matrices which made it seem "obvious" and unchallengeable. Not all, of course; there are still milieux in which it is the "default" solution: unless you have powerful intuitions to the contrary, it will seem to you that you ought to go along. But then we also have milieux in which unbelief is close to being the default solution (including important parts of the academy). So over-all fragilization has increased.

If we want to carry this account on as a "subtraction story", we might say that secularization, defined as the loss of social matrices of belief, hence decline and fragilization, has at last brought about a "level playing field", because these matrices previously conferred a preferential advantage on belief. But this very idea is absurd, since what we really have is not a playing field at all, but a very accidented terrain; there are lots of tilts, but they don't all slide in the same direction. The tilt of the Bible Belt is not that of the urban university.

We could say that this is a world in which the fate of belief depends much more than before on powerful intuitions of individuals, radiating out to others. And these intuitions will be far from self-evident to others again. To some, including many believers, this epochal development will seem like a regression of Christianity. To others, the retreat of Christendom involves both loss and gain. Some great realizations of collective life are lost, but other facets of our predicament in relation to God come to the fore; for instance what Isaiah meant when he talked of a "hidden God". In the seventeenth century, you had to be a Pascal to appreciate that. Now we live it daily.

The outcome of this pluralism and mutual fragilization will often be a retreat of religion from the public square. In one way this is inevitable and in the circumstances good. Justice requires that a modern democracy keep an equal distance from different faith positions. The language of some public bodies, for instance courts, has to be free from premises drawn from one or other position. Our cohesion depends on a political ethic, democracy and human rights, basically drawn from the Modern Moral Order, to which different faith and non-faith communities subscribe, each for their own divergent reason. We live in a world of what John Rawls has described as "overlapping consensus".[50]

But in another way, as José Casanova has argued,[51] religious discourse will be very much in the public square. Democracy requires that each citizen or group of citizens speak the language in public debate that is most meaningful to them. Prudence may urge us to put things in terms which others relate to, but to require this would be an intolerable imposition on citizen speech. As the sense of living in Christendom fades, and we recognize that no spiritual family is in charge, or speaks for the whole, there will be a greater sense of freedom to speak our own minds, and in some cases these will inescapably be formulated in religious discourse.

This development lies behind, I believe, a seeming paradox which Grace Davie notes; that it was precisely after the great decline post-1960 that certain Anglican Bishops began to intervene strongly in public criticism of the Thatcher government.[52] Perhaps we can say that it was only after the sharp decline that Anglican leaders were unshackled from the mental weight of being an established church, and could feel free to speak their minds.

So much for the negative story as master narrative. But we could also add a complementary narrative which emphasizes the positive features of the present spirituality of search. By "positive", I don't mean features that we necessarily want to endorse; just that we focus not on what our Age has displaced, but on what characterizes it. Here what springs out is the long-term vector in Latin Christendom, moving steadily over a half millennium towards more personal, committed forms of religious devotion and practice. The spirituality of quest that we see today could be understood as the form that this movement takes in an Age of Authenticity. The same long-term trend which produced the disciplined, conscious, committed individual believer, Calvinist, Jansenist, devout humanist, Methodist; which later gives us the "born-again" Christian, now has brought forth today's pilgrim seeker, attempting to discern and follow his/her own path. The future of North Atlantic religion depends for one part on the concatenated outcomes of a whole host of such quests; and for another, on the relations, hostile, indifferent, or (hopefully) symbiotic, which will develop between modes of quest and centres of traditional religious authority, between what Wuthnow calls dwellers and seekers.

For some, this will not be an encouraging thought. Whatever the level of religious belief and practice, on an uneven but many-sloped playing field, the debate between different forms of belief and unbelief goes on. In this debate, modes of belief are disadvantaged by the memory of their previously dominant forms, which in many ways run athwart the ethos of the times, and which many people are still reacting against. They are even more severely disadvantaged by an unintended by-product of the climate of fragmented search: the fact that the falling off of practice has meant that rising generations have often lost touch with traditional religious languages.[53] As Paul Valadier put it, "c'est en bien des cas l'ouverture même au sens religieux, la compréhension minimale de ce qu'il en est d'un acte de foi, l'expérience toute simple du sacré, ou de Dieu . . . , l'apperception que la foi n'est pas pure absurdité mais démarche sensée et exaltante qui font défaut, . . . le geste même par lequel quelque chose se laisse pressentir de l'univers religieux."[54]

On the other side, what tells against forms of unbelief is the series of nagging dissatisfactions with the modern moral order, and its attendant disciplines, the rapid wearing out of its Utopian versions, the continuing sense that there is something more. These can send people off in many directions, including those of the immanent counter-Enlightenment, but they also can open avenues to faith. Here is where one of the disadvantages of belief above has a flip side which is positive. The very fact that its forms are not absolutely in true with much of the spirit of the age; a spirit in which people can be imprisoned, and feel the need to break out; the fact that faith connects us to so many spiritual avenues across different ages; this can over time draw people towards it. La lotta continua.

So far as the heartland of Latin Christendom is concerned, that is, Western Europe, as against its outlying areas in the Americas, North and South, the future is very unclear. The fading contact of many with the traditional languages of faith seems to presage a declining future. But the very intensity of the search for adequate forms of spiritual life that this loss occasions may be full of promise. Perhaps the "cool" phase of European religious identities can be interpreted in terms somewhat like those proposed by Mikhaïl Epstein to describe the situation in post-Soviet Russia.

In a pair of interesting papers,[55] Epstein introduces the concept of "minimal religion". He also speaks of an overlapping category, the people who declare themselves "just Christians" in surveys of religious allegiance, as against those who adhere to one or other Christian confession, like Orthodox, or Catholic. This kind of religious position Epstein sees as "post-atheist"; and this in two senses. The people concerned were brought up under a militantly atheist régime, which denied and repressed all religious forms, so that they are equidistant from, and equally ignorant of, all the confessional options. But the position is also post-atheist in the stronger sense that those concerned have reacted against their training; they have acquired in some fashion a sense of God, which however ill-defined places them outside the space of their upbringing.

"Minimal religion" is a spirituality lived in one's immediate circle, with family and friends, rather than in churches, one especially aware of the particular, both in individual human beings, and in the places and things which surround us. In response to the universalist concern for the "distant one" stressed in Marxist communism, it seeks to honour the "image and likeness of God" in the particular people who share our lives.[56]

But because this religion was born outside of any confessional structures, it has its own kind of universalism, a sort of spontaneous and unreflective ecumenicism, in which the coexistence of plural forms of spirituality and worship is taken for granted. Even when people who start with this kind of spirituality end up joining a church, as many of them do, they retain something of their original outlook.

> Sooner or later, a minimal believer usually joins a specific religious tradition, becoming an Orthodox Christian, a Baptist, or a Jew. But after having experienced this resonant space of the void, of the wilderness, . . . s/he preserves the new feeling of openness forever. It is there, in a wasteland of spirit, without any preparations, baptisms, catechisms, that God suddenly grabs hold of him.
>
> One might speculate that this thrust toward religious reformation will dominate the spirit of twenty-first century Russia. The restoration of pre-atheist traditions is the focus of the current [1995] religious revival, but the atheistic past, the experience of the wilderness, cannot pass without a trace, and this trace of "the void" will manifest itself in a striving for fullness of spirit, transcending the boundaries of historical denominations. These people who have found God in the wilderness feel that the walls of the existing temples are too narrow for them and should be expanded.[57]

Perhaps something analogous can be said about the situation in "post-secular" Europe. I use this term not as designating an age in which the declines in belief and practice of the last century would have been reversed, because this doesn't seem likely, at least for the moment; I rather mean a time in which the hegemony of the mainstream master narrative of secularization will be more and more challenged.

This I think is now happening. But because, as I believe, this hegemony has helped to effect the decline, its overcoming would open new possibilities.

Being "spiritual but not religious" is one of the western phenomena which has some affinity with Epstein's "minimal religion" in Russia; it usually designates a spiritual life which retains some distance from the disciplines and authority of religious confessions. Of course, the distance here reflects a reaction to religious authority claims, and a wariness of confessional leadership; whereas the reaction in Russia is against the "wasteland" left by militant atheism, and the distance from confessions is at first a matter of ignorance and unfamiliarity. But in both cases, a certain diffuse ecumenical sense is widespread, and even those who subsequently take on some confessional life, and thus become "religious", retain something of this original freedom from sectarianism. What also remains important, in both East and West, is some continuing sense of the importance of following one's own spiritual itinerary, and the sense that, in a saying of Berdyaev which Epstein reproduces: "Knowledge, morality, art, government and the economy should become religious, but freely and from inside, not by compulsion from outside."[58]

In any case, we are just at the beginning of a new age of religious searching, whose outcome no one can foresee.

PART V

Conditions of Belief

15 The Immanent Frame

1

So we can return to our original question about secularity 3, the conditions of belief which obtain in the modern West. Put simply, the original question was: why is it so hard to believe in God in (many milieux of) the modern West, while in 1500 it was virtually impossible not to?

In the previous chapters, I have been trying to give an answer in terms of the story of how we got to where we are. But "secularization" stories also involve some picture of where this is, of the spiritual shape of the present age (the third story of such theories, as I described this in Chapter 12). That is what I would like to address in this chapter.

We can assemble the pieces of an answer, if we pick up some of the themes that have been discussed in earlier chapters, and lay out the interlocking and mutually reinforcing changes described there.

We spoke about disenchantment. This has many facets. Here I want to mention first its "inner" side, the replacement of the porous self by the buffered self, for whom it comes to seem axiomatic that all thought, feeling and purpose, all the features we normally can ascribe to agents, must be in minds, which are distinct from the "outer" world. The buffered self begins to find the idea of spirits, moral forces, causal powers with a purposive bent, close to incomprehensible.

The rise of the buffered identity has been accompanied by an interiorization; that is, not only the Inner/Outer distinction, that between Mind and World as separate loci, which is central to the buffer itself; and not only the development of this Inner/Outer distinction in a whole range of epistemological theories of a mediational type from Descartes to Rorty;[1] but also the growth of a rich vocabulary of interiority, an inner realm of thought and feeling to be explored. This frontier of self-exploration has grown, through various spiritual disciplines of self-examination, through Montaigne, the development of the modern novel, the rise of Romanticism, the ethic of authenticity, to the point where we now conceive of ourselves as having inner depths. We might even say that the depths which were previously located in the cosmos, the enchanted world, are now more readily placed within. Where earlier people spoke of possession by evil spirits, we think of mental illness. Or again, the rich symbolism of the enchanted world is located by Freud in the depths of the psyche; and we all find this move very natural and convincing, whatever we might think of his detailed theories.[2]

The buffered identity with its internal spaces has gone along with the changes which have been most suggestively described by Norbert Elias.[3] These involved the development of discipline, of self-control, particularly in the areas of sex and anger. There is an overlap here in the changes described by Elias with those which have been examined by Michel Foucault.[4] But Elias also points to the striking development of a sense of fastidiousness, which involved a withdrawal from earlier forms of promiscuous contact with others, in which people carried out bodily functions before others which are now strictly tabued. People of breeding and education come to insist on privacy, which begins to transform living arrangements in the seventeenth and eighteenth centuries. Privacy allows intimacy, but this is now no longer indiscriminate, but reserved for "intimates". We might say that the earlier field of more promiscuous contact, in which nobles mingled at table and elsewhere with a host of retainers, is now split by a new distinction intimacy/distance.

Intimate space is, of course, social space, in that it is shared with (a few, privileged) others. But there is a close connection between inner space and zones of intimacy. It is in these latter that we share something of the depths of feeling, affinity, susceptibility, that we discover within ourselves. Indeed, without this sharing, be it in prayer, conversation, letters, without the sympathetic reception by close interlocutors, much of our inner exploration couldn't take place. The habits of inwardness are learned partly in intimate exchange, and the modes of exchange themselves become common property through the circulation of new texts, like novels (of which an early form consisted largely or entirely in epistolary exchange).

The buffered, disciplined self, seeking intimacy (although discipline and intimacy can be in tension), also sees him/herself more and more as an individual. We saw this clearly reflected in the understanding of society implicit in what we called the Modern Moral Order. The social orders we live in are not grounded cosmically, prior to us, there as it were, waiting for us to take up our allotted place; rather society is made by individuals, or at least for individuals, and their place in it should reflect the reasons why they joined in the first place, or why God appointed this form of common existence for them. These reasons in the end come down to the good of human beings, not qua fillers of this or that role, but just simpliciter, a human good which is that of all of them equally, even if they don't achieve it in equal measure. (And of course, modern social theory will be split on the issue whether they can achieve this good as individuals [e.g., Locke, Bentham], or whether they have rather to realize it as some shared, common good [e.g., Rousseau, Hegel, Marx, Humboldt]; but in either case we're talking about a good which pertains to human beings as such.)

Buffer, discipline, and individuality not only interlock and mutually reinforce, but their coming can be seen as largely driven by the process of Reform, as I have been describing it here. The drive to a new form of religious life, more personal, committed, devoted; more christocentric; one which will largely replace the older forms which centred on collective ritual; the drive moreover, to wreak this change for everyone, not just certain religious élites; all this not only powers disenchantment (hence the buffer), and new disciplines of self-control, but also ends up making older holistic understandings of society less and less believable, even in the end nigh incomprehensible.

Individualism, as it emerges from the process of Reform, is first of all that of responsibility. I have to adhere, in a personal commitment, to God, to Christ, to the Church. This can go so far as to put in question the practice of infant baptism, or to make of a personal conversion the condition for Church membership (as in colonial Connecticut). But even where it isn't pushed this far, it plays a crucial role. Each Catholic must confess and be absolved so as to fulfill his Easter duties; one can no longer just go along with the group. But this first individualism develops through that of self-examination, and then self-development, ultimately to that of authenticity. And along the way, it naturally spawns an instrumental individualism, which is implicit in the idea that society is there for the good of individuals.

The obverse of this view of society as made of individuals is the atrophy of earlier ideas of cosmic order, such as those which underlay traditional monarchies. This, in a sense, was another facet of disenchantment, since these notions of cosmic order invoked a teleology in nature, and purposive forces underlying social reality. They form, in a sense, the higher, élite and intellectualized range of the enchanted world, which the peasants lived in the mode of relics and wood sprites.

Cosmic orders were inseparable from earlier understandings of higher time. The modern idea of order thus places us deeply and comprehensively in secular time. But as we saw above, while cosmic orders are thought to maintain themselves, the new Providential social order is meant to be established by human action. It offers a blueprint for constructive action, rather than a matrix of purposive forces already in nature. The new context puts a premium on constructive action, on an instrumental stance towards the world, which the new disciplines have already inculcated.

Now the instrumental stance, and the thoroughgoing secularization of time, go together. Our sense of being comprehensively in secular time is very much reinforced by the very thick environment of measured time which we have woven around ourselves in our civilization. Our lives are measured and shaped by accurate clock-readings, without which we couldn't function as we do. This thick environment is both the condition and the consequence of our far-reaching attempt to make the best of time, to use it well, not to waste it. It is the condition and consequence of time becoming for us a resource, which we have to make use of wisely and to advantage. And we remember that this too was one of the modes of discipline inculcated by the Puritan Reformers.[5] The dominance of instrumental rationality in our world, and the pervasiveness of secular time go together.

So the buffered identity of the disciplined individual moves in a constructed social space, where instrumental rationality is a key value, and time is pervasively secular. All of this makes up what I want to call "the immanent frame". There remains to add just one background idea: that this frame constitutes a "natural" order, to be contrasted to a "supernatural" one, an "immanent" world, over against a possible "transcendent" one.

Now the irony is, that this clear distinction of natural from supernatural, which was an achievement of Latin Christendom in the late Middle Ages and early modern period, was originally made in order to mark clearly the autonomy of the supernatural. The rebellion of the "nominalists" against Aquinas' "realism" was meant to establish the sovereign power of God, whose judgments made right and wrong, and could not be chained by the bent of "nature". Likewise the Reformers did everything they could to disentangle the order of grace from that of nature.

But this idea, which runs so much against the understandings of an enchanted world, and of cosmic orders, which have been dominant in all previous civilizations, only becomes deeply established in our understanding of our world through the set of connected changes I have just been describing. These represent profound changes in our practical self-understanding, how we fit into our world (as buffered, disciplined, instrumental agents) and into society (as responsible individuals, constituting societies designed for mutual benefit). But they are all the more firmly entrenched in that they dovetail perfectly with the major theoretical transformation of Western modernity, viz., the rise of post-Galilean natural science. This finally yielded our familiar picture of the natural, "physical" universe as governed by exceptionless laws, which may reflect the wisdom and benevolence of the creator, but don't require in order to be understood—or (at least on a first level) explained—any reference to a good aimed at, whether in the form of a Platonic Idea, or of Ideas in the mind of God.

This move was, of course, connected to some of those resumed above. In particular, there was a close connection between modern post-Baconian science and the instrumental stance: Bacon insists that the goal of science is not to discover a noble over-all pattern in things (as he somewhat tendentiously describes the sciences of

Aristotle), which we can take pride in making evident, but the making of experiments which permit us to "improve the condition of mankind". That is why Scheler describes the new sciences as modes of "Leistungswissen".[6]

Now while the new science gave a clear theoretical form to the idea of an immanent order which could be understood on its own, without reference to interventions from outside (even if we might reason from it to a Creator, and even a benevolent Creator), the life of the buffered individual, instrumentally effective in secular time, created the practical context within which the self-sufficiency of this immanent realm could become a matter of experience. And as I indicated above, the new understanding of society allowed space not just for new collective agents (we who come together to found a state, create a movement, set up a church), but also for an objectification of social reality as governed by its own laws (as exceptionless and clear, we hope, as Newton's); and indeed, this objective understanding is essential for the efficacy of our collective action.

And so we come to understand our lives as taking place within a self-sufficient immanent order;[7] or better, a constellation of orders, cosmic, social and moral. As I described them in Chapter 7, these orders are understood as impersonal. This understanding of our predicament has as background a sense of our history: we have advanced to this grasp of our predicament through earlier more primitive stages of society and self-understanding. In this process, we have come of age.

At first, the social order is seen as offering us a blueprint for how things, in the human realm, can hang together to our mutual benefit, and this is identified with the plan of Providence, what God asks us to realize. But it is in the nature of a self-sufficient immanent order that it can be envisaged without reference to God; and very soon the proper blueprint is attributed to Nature. This change can, of course, involve nothing of importance, if we go on seeing God as the Author of Nature, just a notational variant on the first view. But following a path opened by Spinoza, we can also see Nature as identical with God, and then as independent from God. The Plan is without a planner. A further step can then be taken, where we see the Plan as what we come to share and adhere to in the process of civilization and Enlightenment; either because we are capable of rising to a universal view, to the outlook, for instance, of the "impartial spectator"; or because our innate sympathy extends to all human beings; or because our attachment to rational freedom in the end shows us how we ought to behave. These are the most common paths whereby the notion of a normative arrangement of things among humans can be entirely immanentized, no longer to "nature" in general, but to developing human motivation.

The immanent order can thus slough off the transcendent. But it doesn't necessarily do so. What I have been describing as the immanent frame is common to all of us in the modern West, or at least that is what I am trying to portray. Some of us want to live it as open to something beyond; some live it as closed. It is something which permits closure, without demanding it. Let me try to explore this further.

2

First of all, let me explore the main motivations that people feel on one side or the other. Let's start by asking: how does the immanent frame remain open?

We've already seen various elements of the answer to this in the preceding pages. A good example was the paradigm of what I called in the previous chapter the "neo-Durkheimian" understanding, the "civil religion" of the U.S.A. at its foundation. Here we have the Providentialist reading of the plan that we should follow. God (or Deistically, the Architect of the Universe) is whom we are following in erecting our social order. The general feature that I want to extract from this example is that for many Americans then (and for lots still now) their very sense that there was something higher to aim at, some better and more moral way of life, was indissolubly connected to God.

We might put it this way. It is in the nature of what I have called "strong evaluation", whereby we distinguish good and evil, noble and base, virtuous and vicious, and the like, that it distinguish between terms, one (or some) of which are in some way incommensurably higher than the other(s). That is, the lower are not just quantitatively inferior; there is no way of compensating for the lack of the higher through any accumulation of the lower. On the contrary.

Now wherever the sense of the higher which constitutes such distinctions is somehow ineradicably linked to God, or something ontically higher (transcendent), belief in this higher seems obviously right, founded, even undeniable. For many, their highest sense of the good has been developed in a profoundly religious context: it has been formed, for instance, around images of sainthood; or their strongest sense of it comes in moment of prayer, or liturgy, or perhaps religious music; or their role models were people of strong religious faith. Their sense of the highest good, formed before any defined theological "ideas", is of something consubstantial with God; by that I mean that this good is inconceivable without God, or some relation to the higher. Of course, 'inconceivable' doesn't mean here what it usually means in philosophical discourse, where we are talking about conceptual incoherence, as when someone speaks of "round squares", or "married bachelors". It rather means that they cannot make sense of the good as they experience it without reference to the transcendent in some form.

This connection may be broken by further experience. We may change our view of the highest good; or come to see it as possible in an immanent context. Or we may come to see from our relations to others how experience might be construed differently, even though we go on feeling that the reference to God makes the best sense of it. Morality without God may be no longer inconceivable, even though still not fully credible for us.

But further experience may also entrench it. And there are cases where it greatly strengthens it, even converts us from an initial stance of immanence. A good example, discussed in the previous chapter, were the conversion experiences of the Great Awakening and its successors, whereby people felt empowered by God or Christ to live up to the demands of discipline and effort that their life laid on them, becoming sober, productive providers, for instance. This kind of experience continues today, as we saw in the spreading wave of Pentecostalism, as well as in extra-Christian forms, as with Black Muslims in the U.S.A. But this is only one among many forms of conversion narrative in modern times.

The neo-Durkheimian case mentioned above provides a further entrenchment. It is not just a matter of my own experience of the good, but something which is woven into a cherished and crucial collective identity, whether it be that of a nation, or an ethnic group, or religious movement. Here is a crucial collective good which seems "consubstantial" with God, or in some essential relation to transcendence.

This kind of consubstantiality is one, positive set of ways in which the immanent frame may be lived as inherently open to transcendence. But it may also be present for us negatively, as something whose lack we feel. I discussed earlier the multiple reactions against what people feel are the reductive forms of the modern moral order and its attendant disciplines and instrumentalities. Certain modes, like utilitarianism, have attracted this kind of hostile reaction, and offer an easy illustration, even though not the only one. We can have a sense of stifling in an order thus reductively conceived: is that all there is? There seems to be no room for generous action, heroism, the warrior virtues, a higher sensibility; or else for a real dedication to humanity, a more demanding ethic of sacrifice; or a sense of a greater whole, a relation to the universe; and the like.

This range of reactions, for instance to utilitarianism, may take us in a number of directions. Some remain within the immanent order, find a more radical and far-reaching understanding of the good, as we have for instance with Rousseau and Marx. But they want to respect the limits set by natural science and law-like social sciences modeled on it; as well as those of the buffered identity. Others remain within immanence, but at the cost of rejecting the moral order of equality and universal welfare, and exalt higher forms of life available only to the minority; here we have forms of the immanent counter-Enlightenment. But some also press towards some recognition of transcendence, or remain in the uncertain border zone opened by Romantic forms of art.

As for the positive forms in which transcendence impinges, we see that they are connected to what we see as the highest good; they figure in the ethical or spiritual dimensions. This is something which applies to our age, to life in the immanent frame, but not at all times and all places. Think of the story told of Boniface among the pagan Germans. He had their sacred oak groves felled—and nothing happened. This was taken as a sign of great power, and led to many conversions, or so we are told. Pre-Axial understandings of power were at work there, a situation so removed from our own as to be difficult to imagine.

But this is not to say that we are utterly confined to factors that fit within the immanent frame, like moral goodness. Sometimes suppressed elements which were prominent in the past and have been sidelined by modern Reform seem to break through again. New centres of pilgrimage arise, out of apparitions of the Virgin: Lourdes, Fatima, Medjugorje, in continuity with much older sites, like Częstachowa and Guadalupe. These pilgrimages themselves are sites of power for those who participate in them. These phenomena have to be put into the context of what Yves-Marie Hilaire calls the "festive",[8] which can also be observed in certain moments of mass celebration which seem to take us out of the everyday. We are not necessarily as "modern" as we think we are.

3

And what pushes to closure, when we go in that direction? Well clearly, corresponding to goods which are consubstantial with the transcendent, stand notions of the good which are intrinsically seen as immanent. From the eighteenth century, from the time of Gibbon, Voltaire, and Hume, we see the reaction which identifies in a strongly transcendent version of Christianity a danger for the goods of the modern moral order. Strong Christianity will demand allegiance to certain theological beliefs or ecclesiastical structures, and this will split a society which should be intent simply on securing mutual benefit. Or else, the demand that we reach for some higher good, beyond human flourishing, at best will distract us, at worst will become the basis for demands which will again endanger the well-oiled order of mutual benefit. Religion in all these menacing forms is what the men of the Enlightenment called "fanaticism".

The sense of being menaced by fanaticism is one great source of the closure of immanence. In many cases we have an initial movement of anti-clericalism, which ends up turning into a rejection of Christianity, or later into atheism. We can trace this, for instance, in the story of anti-clericalism in nineteenth-century France.[9]

But this movement can go farther. It is not just that the good is allegedly threatened by the supposedly better, higher. It may also come to be identified with the rejection of the higher. There is a discourse of Protestantism, in rejection of Catholic asceticism, which chides monks with refusing the gifts of God in the name of a bogus higher vocation. This is continued in the last two centuries by a discourse, now of anti-Christianity, because of its supposed rejection, or relegation, of the sensual. The human good is in its very essence sensual, earthly; whoever identifies a transcendent goal departs from it, betrays it.

We touch here on one of the deep sources of the moral attraction of immanence, even materialism; something we can already feel with Lucretius. There is a strong attraction to the idea that we are in an order of "nature", in which we are part of this greater whole, arise from it, and don't escape or transcend it, even though we rise above everything else in it. One side of this attraction is the sense of belonging, being part of our native land; we are one with this nature. We feel this most palpably on summer days, as we sit in a garden, hearing the birds singing and the bees humming. We belong to the earth. Camus evokes this sense most powerfully in his *Noces*.[10] This feeling can only be further strengthened when we reflect how believing we are above this has often pushed us to inhumanity.

Another facet of this same belonging is our sense of wonder that something like ourselves arose out of lower nature. There is a mysterious process here; something deep to understand. We are very drawn to this; we want to explore it. The mechanical outlook which splits nature from supernature voids all this mystery. This split generates the modern concept of the "miracle"; a kind of punctual hole blown in the regular order of things from outside, that is, from the transcendent. Whatever is higher must thus come about through the holes pierced in the regular, natural order, within whose normal operation there is no mystery. This is curiously enough, a view of things shared between materialists and Christian Fundamentalists. Only for these, it provides proof of "miracles", because certain things are unexplained by the normal course of natural causation. For the materialist, it is a proof that anything transcendent is excluded by "science".

This often brings a tension into materialist discourse, because on one hand they want to stress that in scientifically understood nature, there are no "mysteries". But on the other hand, many feel a strong sense of mystery before the genesis of mind and purpose out of inanimate nature. They are deeply drawn to this dark genesis, and want to try to go further into it, understand it more fully. What is clear is that you altogether void the question with the standard modern notion of "miracle", as punctual intervention interrupting a regular order.

This rejection of "miracle" was a great passion of Ernest Renan, as we can see from his life's work tracing the origin of religions. He couldn't but see the faith as denying the very basic premises of this search, viz., that there is something deep to understand here, which we can only grasp by digging into nature and history. So he was pulled out of faith, and into his own version of "science".[11]

Of course, these latter considerations: belonging to the earth, the sense of our dark genesis, can also be part of Christian faith, but only when it has broken with certain features of the immanent frame, especially the distinction nature/supernature. It is perhaps precisely the ordinary operation of things which constitutes the "miracle".

But leaving this aside for the moment, we can see in the naturalistic rejection of the transcendent that I have been describing the ethical outlook which pushes to closure. Now while many have felt a sense of unease within the modern order with its disciplines and instrumental reason, and have been driven towards an opening to the transcendent, there is also a set of ways in which we can feel comfortable and empowered within this order. I have enumerated them frequently above. The buffered self feels invulnerable before the world of spirits and magic forces, which still can haunt us in our dreams, particularly those of childhood. Objectification of the world gives a sense of power, and control, which is intensified by every victory of instrumental reason.

And then the colossal success of modern natural science and the associated technology can lead us to feel that it unlocks all mysteries, that it will ultimately explain everything, that human science must be developed on the same basic plan, or even ultimately reduced to physics, or at least organic chemistry.

And so we can come to see the growth of civilization, or modernity, as synonymous with the laying out of a closed immanent frame; within this civilized values develop, and a single-minded focus on the human good, aided by the fuller and fuller use of scientific reason, permits the greatest flourishing possible of human beings. Religion not only menaces these goals with its fanaticism, but it also undercuts reason, which comes to be seen as rigorously requiring scientific materialism.

I have been describing here the basic motivations of the two great polar positions. But we must also remember that there always have been a great many people who have been cross-pressured between the two basic orientations; who want to respect as much as they can the "scientific" shape of the immanent order, as they have been led to see it; or who fear the effect of religious "fanaticism"; but who still cannot help believing that there is something more than the merely immanent. The kind of "spiritualist" position that we see with Victor Hugo, for instance, or alternatively with Jean Jaurès, are striking examples.

What emerges from all this is that we can either see the transcendent as a threat, a dangerous temptation, a distraction, or an obstacle to our greatest good. Or we can read it as answering to our deepest craving, need, fulfillment of the good. Or else, since religion has very often been the first: think of the long line that runs from Aztec sacrifice, through Torquemada, to Bin Laden; the question really is whether it is only threat, or doesn't also offer a promise. (And we might add the question whether *only* religion poses this kind of threat; the twentieth century, through the figures of Stalin, Hitler, and Pol Pot, seems to indicate the contrary.)

I think that which way we go ultimately comes down to our answer to this question. But this doesn't mean that everyone who goes one way or the other, even everyone who makes some kind of crucial turning in life in one direction or the other, has faced this issue in its clearest and starkest way. They have not necessarily stood in that open space where you can feel the winds pulling you, now to belief, now to unbelief, which I described in my lectures on William James as the site he has so masterfully explored.[12]

We don't stand there, because not only is the immanent frame itself not usually, or even mainly a set of *beliefs* which we entertain about our predicament, however it may have started out; rather it is the sensed context in which we develop our beliefs; but in the same way, one or other of these takes on the immanent frame, as open or closed, has usually sunk to the level of such an unchallenged framework, something we have trouble often thinking ourselves outside of, even as an imaginative exercise.

I have already described on the believing side people for whom the good is consubstantial to God, for whom another construal makes no sense. And there are corresponding positions on the side of closure, which I will explore in a minute. In general, we have here what Wittgenstein calls a "picture", a background to our thinking, within whose terms it is carried on, but which is often largely unformulated, and to which we can frequently, just for this reason, imagine no alternative. As he once famously put it, "a picture held us captive".[13] We can sometimes be completely captured by the picture, not even able to imagine what an alternative would look like; or we can be in somewhat better shape: capable of seeing that there is another way of construing things, but still having great difficulty making sense of it—in a sense, the standard predicament in ethnology.

Standing in the Jamesian open space requires that you have gone farther than this second state, and can actually feel some of the force of each opposing position. But so far apart are belief and unbelief, openness and closure here, that this feat is relatively rare. Most of us are at level one or two, either unable to see how the other view makes sense at all, or else struggling to make sense of it.

Our predicament in the modern West is, therefore, not only characterized by what I have called the immanent frame, which we all more or less share—although some features of this need to be challenged or re-interpreted, as we shall see below. It also consists of more specific pictures, the immanent frame as "spun" in ways of openness and closure, which are often dominant in certain milieux. This local dominance obviously strengthens their hold as pictures. The spin of closure which is hegemonic in the Academy is a case in point.

4

But my whole reading here will be challenged. I have distinguished the immanent frame, on one hand, and two equally possible "spins", open and closed, on the other. Some people will undoubtedly feel that the immanent frame calls out for one reading. True, we can adopt the other view by dint of determined (and not quite intellectually honest) "spinning", but one reading is the obvious, the "natural" one. In the nature of things, that claim is made today most often by protagonists of the "closed" reading, those who see immanence as admitting of no beyond. This is an effect of the hegemony of this reading, especially in intellectual and academic milieux. The sense that this reading is natural, logically unavoidable, underpins the power of the mainstream secularization theory, the view that modernity must bring secularity in its train, that I have been arguing against here. This understanding goes back at least to Weber, who speaks sneeringly of those who would go on believing in face of "disenchantment" as having to make an "Opfer des Intellekts" (a sacrifice of the intellect). "To the person who cannot bear the fate of the times like a man, one must say: may he rather return silently, . . . The arms of the Churches are open widely and compassionately for him".[14]

By contrast, my understanding of the immanent frame is that, properly understood, it allows of both readings, without compelling us to either. If you grasp our predicament without ideological distortion, and without blinders, then you see that going one way or another requires what is often called a "leap of faith". But it's worth examining a bit more closely what I mean by that here.

What pushes us one way or the other is what we might describe as our over-all take on human life, and its cosmic and (if any) spiritual surroundings. People's stance on the issue of belief in God, or of an open versus closed understanding of the immanent frame, usually emerge out of this general sense of things.

This take can hardly be simply arbitrary. If pressed, one can often articulate a whole host of considerations which motivate this stance, such as our sense of what is really important in human life, or the ways we think that human life can be transformed, or the constants, if any, of human history, and so on.

But the take goes beyond these particulate insights. Moreover, these themselves can be changed through further events and experience. In this way, our over-all sense of things anticipates or leaps ahead of the reasons we can muster for it. It is something in the nature of a hunch; perhaps we might better speak here of "anticipatory confidence". This is what it means to talk of a "leap of faith" here.

But of course, the term "faith" has a different meaning when we speak of theistic religion. Here it refers to a crucial feature of our over-all sense of things, namely the personal relation of trust and confidence in God, rather than to our motives for taking this stance. It describes the *content* of our position, not the *reasons* for it.

Of course, experience can bring an increase in our confidence in our stance. But we never move to a point beyond all anticipation, beyond all hunches, to the kind of certainty that we can enjoy in certain narrower questions, say, in natural science or ordinary life.

Thus although faith in our second, theistic sense, is peculiar to a certain kind of stance of openness in the immanent frame, both open and closed stances involve a step beyond available reasons into the realm of anticipatory confidence.

And so full lucidity would involve recognizing that one's confidence is at least partly anticipatory, and hence being aware of the Jamesian open space. What I am calling "spin" is a way of avoiding entering this space, a way of convincing oneself that one's reading is obvious, compelling, allowing of no cavil or demurral. I invoked in the previous paragraph the accusation of intellectual dishonesty often hurled at believers from Weber on down to today. My concept of spin here involves something of this kind, but much less dramatic and insulting; it implies that one's thinking is clouded or cramped by a powerful picture which prevents one seeing important aspects of reality. I want to argue that those who think the closed reading of immanence is "natural" and obvious are suffering from this kind of disability.

Of course, so are those who think that the open reading is obvious and inescapable, because, for instance, the existence of God can be "proven". But such people are perhaps less numerous today than their secularist opposite numbers, and certainly cannot approach the intellectual hegemony their opponents enjoy, and so my arguments here will mainly address these latter.

The force of secularist spin can be understood in terms of what I will call "closed world structures" (CWSs), that is, ways of restricting our grasp of things which are not recognized as such. I want in the course of the following pages to examine three broad categories of these, which go a long way to explaining the unjustified force of the mainstream account of secularization, as well as the disinterest in and contempt for religion which frequently accompanies it. Of course, nothing that I will say in the course of this analysis, and hence also exposé of these structures, impugns in any way the conclusions which they support. All CWSs may be illegitimate, and yet there may be nothing beyond the immanent frame. I will not be arguing either for or against an open or closed reading, just trying to dissipate the false aura of the obvious that surrounds one of these.

But before entering on this analysis, another possible misunderstanding must be laid to rest. Surely, our modern man-made world declares the absence of God in something like the same sense that the Heavens for the psalmist declared his glory. As A. N. Wilson put it,

> The nineteenth century had created a climate for itself—philosophical, politico-sociological, literary, artistic, personal—in which God had become

unknowable, His voice inaudible against the din of machines and the atonal banshee of the emerging egomania called The Modern. The cohesive social force which religion had once provided was broken up. The nature of society itself, urban, industrialized, materialistic, was the background for the godlessness which philosophy and science did not so much discover as ratify.[15]

Wilson's portrait of "godlessness" has many facets. On one level, there is the change in urban environment: contrast a mediaeval city crowded around its Gothic cathedral with a modern metropolis. It's not just that skyscrapers now dwarf the cathedral, if one remains. This might be seen as reflecting a new set of meanings which have taken over from the old, say, Capitalism replacing Christianity. But actually, the change is more drastic. It is more like cacophony replacing meaning as such. The shape of the city no longer manifests a single over-arching meaning, but on the one hand, individual great buildings each monumentalize some corporation or triumphant entrepreneur, while on the other, vast areas of the city form a crazy quilt of special purpose constructions—factories, malls, docks—following each some fragmentary instrumental rationality. Rare are the successful whole environments—New Delhi, Chandigar—built in the twentieth century.

On another level, the "atonal banshee of emerging egomania" unavoidably impinges through the ubiquity of advertising and the entertainment media, insistently calling us each to our own satisfaction and fulfillment, linking the powerful forces of sexual desire and the craving for wholeness, constitutive elements of our humanity, to products promoted to the status of icons, and in the process obscuring, emptying, and trivializing these forces themselves.

There is certainly a widespread sense of loss here, if not always of God, then at least of meaning. This manifests itself in the massive movement of people as tourists towards the still undamaged sites of earlier civilizations, with their temples, mosques, and cathedrals; as well as in the invocation of these historic sites in contemporary upscale suburbs—for instance, of Tuscany in Sandton, north of Johannesburg. Today's reality is easier to live while dreaming of being elsewhere, or in another stream of time.

But the implication of Wilson's passage, that modern conditions yield an experience of godlessness which secularist theories just ratify, is a bit too quick; and for more than one reason.

First, it quite overlooks other experiences of modernity: for instance, those of citizens of a nation whose political identity is defined in religious or confessional terms—the neo-Durkheimian predicament I described above; or else that of Methodists or Pentecostals, whose ability to meet the disciplines of contemporary life is bound up with Christian conversion, so that an order-sustaining morality is felt as inseparable from faith. The same unrelated jumble of rational economic actions by individual agents that may appear fragmentary and meaningless to one whose model is the mediaeval city may be lived by the believing entrepreneur or worker as the solid fruits of the disciplines of faith.

But second, even those who see godlessness here will not necessarily opt for the closed perspective on immanence. They may see this as a grievous lack, pointing to a transcendent integrative power which has been neglected.

And indeed, these two reactions may be combined: the celebration of capitalist entrepreneurship being taken as a positive sign of a faithful society, while the sexual excesses of the media bespeak a rebellion against God. It is this kind of double perception which underpins much of the "culture wars" in the contemporary U.S. Or again, we can think of the bitter opposition of the Christian right to gay marriage, which they see as an aberration in a society which hitherto has enshrined "Christian family values".

So the sense of the world as God-forsaken (or meaning-forsaken) doesn't necessarily transmute either logically or psychologically into the closed take on immanence, the belief that there is nothing beyond the "natural" order. The idea that it must be so comes partly from a confusion of disenchantment with the end of religion. This is widespread in the contemporary discussion. Indeed, the terms are sometimes used as synonyms. Even Weber seems to have fallen into this at times.

But I have been using the word here in a narrower sense: disenchantment is the dissolution of the "enchanted" world, the world of spirits and meaningful causal forces, of wood sprites and relics. Enchantment is essential to some forms of religion; but other forms—especially those of modern Reformed Christianity, both Catholic and Protestant—have been built on its partial or total denial. We cannot just equate the two.

The presence of something beyond (what we call today) the "natural" is more palpable and immediate, one might say, physical, in an enchanted age. The sacred in the strong sense, which marks out certain people, times, places and actions, in distinction to all others as profane, is by its very nature localizable, and its place is clearly marked out in ritual and sacred geography. This is what we sense, and often regret the passing of, when we contemplate the mediaeval cathedral. God-forsakenness is an experience of those whose ancestral culture has been transformed and repressed by a relentless process of disenchantment, whose deprivations can still be keenly felt. But it has been part of a move from one religious life to another, long before it came to be (mistakenly) seen by some as a facet of the decline of religion altogether.

Once we set aside the illusion which identifies religion and enchantment, what we have to retain from this whole movement is a certain direction of transformation in religious life itself. We have moved from an era in which religious life was more "embodied", where the presence of the sacred could be enacted in ritual, or seen, felt, touched, walked towards (in pilgrimage); into one which is more "in the mind", where the link with God passes more through our endorsing contested interpretations—for instance, of our political identity as religiously defined, or of God as the authority and moral source underpinning our ethical life.

The change mustn't be exaggerated. It is somewhat clearer on the level of official theology, the way in which the Churches understand their creeds. But there has always been rebellion on the level of popular religion. The Reformed churches always had to battle with (what they saw as) hold-overs from the old religion. The nineteenth-century, post-Restoration Catholic Church was "forced"—in the eyes of élites—to make allowance for a popular piety of pilgrimage, veneration of relics, apparitions of the Virgin, and the like. More generally, we see today the continuing power of pilgrimage, and in general what I have been calling the "festive". And more recently, in a strange dialectical reversal, we have Pentecostal movements, which integrate ecstatic prayer and miraculous healing, winning converts in traditional Catholic cultures where the established clerical élites look on these practices with suspicion and disdain. What would Calvin have said?

And all this doesn't take account of the continuing importance of "corporal works of mercy" in contemporary Christian practice.

But leaving these aspects and counter-movements aside, official Christianity has gone through what we can call an "excarnation", a transfer out of embodied, "enfleshed" forms of religious life, to those which are more "in the head". In this it follows in parallel with "Enlightenment", and modern unbelieving culture in general. The issue here is not how many positive invocations of the body we hear; these abound in many forms of atheist materialism, as also in more Liberal Christianity. The issue is whether our relation to the highest—God for believers, generally morality for unbelieving Aufklärer—is mediated in embodied form, as was plainly the case for parishioners "creeping to the Cross" on Good Friday in pre-Reformation England.[16] Or looking to what moves us towards the highest, the issue is to what degree our highest desires, those which allow us to discern the highest, are embodied, as the pity captured in the New Testament verb 'splangnizesthai' plainly is.

By contrast, we can look at the "enlightened" ethics of today. On one side, we have a Humean stream, which does indeed, have a place for feeling in ethics, the reaction of sympathy, but accords this no power to discern its good or bad uses. This a calculating reason must determine. And in certain extreme variants, even the most basic "gut" feelings, like our horror at infanticide, are ruled irrelevant. On the other side, we have the Kantian stream, which derives our moral obligations from a consideration of ourselves as pure rational agents.

Modern enlightened culture is very theory-oriented. We tend to live in our heads, trusting our disengaged understandings: of experience, of beauty (we can't really accept that it's telling us anything, unless about our own feelings); even the ethical: we think that the only valid form of ethical self-direction is through rational maxims or understanding. We can't accept that part of being good is opening ourselves to certain feelings; either the horror at infanticide, or agape as a gut feeling.

But the effect of Reform has been that much of modern Western Christianity has been following the same path.

But surely, one might argue, what I have been calling the immanent frame isn't simply neutral. To live in this frame is to be nudged in one direction rather than another. There is a sense in which this is quite true. The immanent frame has come about through the development of certain practices and theoretical insights. The bent of these has been to make us see ourselves as living in impersonal orders, naturally, socially, and ethically, as I described in Chapter 7. This of itself lent greater plausibility to Deism, as against orthodox Christianity; and later this has been drawn on to support atheism, and materialism. Or to take another example, the protocols of modern "scientific" and analytic thinking privilege the impersonal "view from nowhere", the standpoint which is "experience-far". So it tends to make us systematically devalue insights which might challenge the understanding of impersonal order, insights which might arise, for example, out of prayer, or in love relations. In our epoch, the most prestigious, well-established experience-far, impersonal order is that developed out of natural science. Taken on its own terms, as the whole story about us and our world, this can easily be seen as supporting materialism.

So in one sense it is true that living within this frame pushes us to the closed perspective. But this is the sense in which living within the frame is living according to the norms and practices that it incorporates. However, I have been arguing all along that the actual experience of living within Western modernity tends to awaken protest, resistances of various kinds. In this fuller, experiential sense, "living within" the frame doesn't simply tip you in one direction, but allows you to feel pulled two ways. A very common experience of living here is that of being cross-pressured between the open and closed perspectives.

In the following pages, moreover, I want to argue a further point. It is not just that the frame doesn't as such tip us in one direction or the other, that its effect on each person will be coloured by the orientation they have been led to develop. But even when they come to feel it as obviously supporting closure, this doesn't constitute a valid argument. The sense of "obvious" closure is not a perception of rational grounding, but an illusion of what I have been calling "spin".

In other words, while the norms and practices of the immanent frame may incline to closure, this neither decides the effect that living within the frame in fact will have on us, nor even less does it justify the closed take. If this seems "obvious" to us, either in the sense of a surface appearance (as in Wilson's "godlessness" above), or in the sense of imposing itself on reason, this is because we have already taken up a certain stance to it.[17]

5

I want now to examine the illusion of the rational "obviousness" of the closed perspective. My aim is to explore the constitution in modernity of what I will call "closed" or "horizontal" worlds. I mean by this shapes of our "world" (in Heidegger's sense, that is, the "world" in its meaning for us) which leave no place for the "vertical" or "transcendent", but which in one way or another close these off, render them inaccessible, or even unthinkable.

This existence of these has become "normal" for us. But we can bring out again how remarkable this is, if we take a certain distance from it, and return to the major contrast which enframes the argument of this book: we need just to jump back 500 years in our Western civilization (a.k.a. Latin Christendom), as I suggested at the beginning. At that time, non-belief in God was close to unthinkable for the vast majority;[18] whereas today this is not at all the case. One might be tempted to say that in certain milieux, the reverse has become true, that belief is unthinkable. But this exaggeration already shows up the lack of symmetry. It is truer to say that in our world, a whole gamut of positions, from the most militant atheism to the most orthodox traditional theisms, passing through every possible position on the way, are represented and defended somewhere in our society. Something like the unthinkability of some of these positions can be experienced in certain milieux, but what is ruled out will vary from context to context. An atheist in the Bible belt has trouble being understood, as often (in a rather different way) do believing Christians in certain reaches of the academy. But, of course, people in each of these contexts are aware that the others exist, and that the option they can't really credit is the default option elsewhere in the same society, whether they regard this with hostility or just perplexity. The existence of an alternative fragilizes each context, that is, makes its sense of the thinkable/unthinkable uncertain and wavering.

This fragilization[19] is then increased by the fact that great numbers of people are not firmly embedded in any such context, but are puzzled, cross-pressured, or have constituted by bricolage a sort of median position. The existence of these people raises sometimes even more acute doubts within the more assured milieux. The polar opposites can be written off as just mad or bad, as we see with the present American culture wars between "liberals" and "fundamentalists"; but the intermediate positions can sometimes not be as easily dismissed.

What I want to try is to articulate some of the worlds from within which the believing option seems strange and unjustifiable. But this articulation involves some degree of abstraction—indeed, three kinds of abstraction, with the corresponding dangers.

(a) What I shall really be describing is not worlds in their entirety, but "world structures", aspects or features of the way experience and thought are shaped and cohere, but not the whole of which they are constituents. (b) I will not be describing the world of any concrete human beings. A world is something which people inhabit. It gives the shape of what they experience, feel, opine, see, etc. The world of the cross-pressured is different from that of the assured. But what I'm doing is trying to articulate certain world-types ("ideal types" in a quasi-Weberian sense), which may not, will almost surely not coincide with the totality of any real person's world. (c) Thirdly, the articulation involves an intellectualization; one has to get at the connections in lived experience through ideas, and very often ideas which are not consciously available to the people concerned, unless they are forced to articulate them themselves through challenge and argument.

Nevertheless, this effort, I believe is very worth while, because it enables us to see the way in which we can be held within certain world structures without being aware that there are alternatives. A "picture" can "hold us captive", as Wittgenstein put it, in the image I invoked a few pages back.[20] And by the same token, we can gain insight into the way two people or groups can be arguing past each other, because their experience and thought are structured by two different pictures.

What I want to try to lay out is world structures which are closed to transcendence. They arise within what I have been calling the "immanent frame", but give it as I said above a certain twist, a certain spin, not primarily as a conscious theoretical move, but rather through certain deep pictures, which give further specificity to the pictures which underlie the frame itself.

A good sense of how these function can be found in the example I spoke of earlier, that which provides the framework for modern epistemology. I am taking "epistemology" here as more than a set of theories which have been widespread, but also at the level of a structure in my sense, that is, an underlying picture which is only partly consciously entertained, but which controls the way people think, argue, infer, make sense of things.

At its most blatant this structure operates with a picture of knowing agents as individuals, who build up their understanding of the world through combining and relating, in more and more comprehensive theories, the information which they take in, and which is couched in inner representations, be these conceived as mental pictures (in the earlier variants), or as something like sentences held true in the more contemporary versions.

Characteristic of this picture are a series of priority relations. Knowledge of the self and its states comes before knowledge of external reality and of others. The knowledge of reality as neutral fact comes before our attributing to it various "values" and relevances. And, of course, knowledge of the things of "this world", of the natural order precedes any theoretical invocation of forces and realities transcendent to it.

The epistemological picture, combining as it does very often with some understanding of modern science, operates frequently as a CWS. The priority relations tell us not only what is learned before what, but also what can be inferred on the basis of what. They are foundational relations. I know the world through my representations. I must grasp the world as fact before I can posit values. I must accede to the transcendent, if at all, by inference from the natural. This can operate as a CWS, because it is obvious that the inference to the transcendent is at the extreme and most fragile end of a chain of inferences; it is the most epistemically questionable. And indeed, granted the lack of consensus surrounding this move, as against earlier steps in the chain (e.g., to "other minds"), it is obviously highly problematic.

Now I introduce the epistemological picture in order to bring out some features of the way CWS operate in our time, the way they are on one hand contested, and on the other maintain themselves.

We are all aware of the contestation, because some of the most famous twentieth-century philosophers have taken part in it. And referring to Heidegger and Merleau-Ponty as paradigm cases of the refutation of epistemology, we can see that this view has been comprehensibly turned on its head. (1) Our grasp of the world does not consist simply of our holding inner representations of outer reality. We do hold such representations, which are perhaps best understood in contemporary terms as sentences held true. But these only make the sense that they do for us because they are thrown up in the course of an ongoing activity of coping with the world, as bodily, social and cultural beings. This coping can never be accounted for in terms of representations, but provides the background against which our representations have the sense that they do. (2) As just implied, this coping activity, and the understanding which inhabits it, is not primarily that of each of us as individuals; rather we are each inducted into the practices of coping as social "games" or activities; some of which do indeed, in the later stages of development, call upon us to assume a stance as individuals. But primordially, we are part of social action. (3) In this coping, the things which we deal with are not first and foremost objects, but what Heidegger calls "pragmata", things which are the focal points of our dealings, which therefore have relevance, meaning, significance for us, not as an add-on but from their first appearance in our world. Later, we learn to stand back, and consider things objectively, outside of the relevances of coping.

(4) In later Heidegger, these significances include some which have a higher status, structuring our whole way of life, the ensemble of our significances. In the formulation of "das Geviert", there are four axes to this context in which our world is set: earth and sky; human and divine.

Although all those who follow something like this deconstruction of epistemology do not go along with this fourth stage, it is clear that the general thrust of these arguments is to utterly overturn the priority relations of epistemology. Things which are considered as late inferences or additions, are seen to be part of our primordial predicament. There is no getting behind them, and it makes no sense to contest them. The "scandal of philosophy" is not the inability to attain to certainty of the external world, but rather that this should be considered a problem, says Heidegger in *Sein und Zeit*. We only have knowledge as agents coping with a world, which it makes no sense to doubt, since we are dealing with it. There is no priority of the neutral grasp of things over their value. There is no priority of the individual's sense of self over the society; our most primordial identity is as a new player being inducted into an old game. Even if we don't add the fourth stage, and consider something like the divine as part of the inescapable context of human action, the whole sense that it comes as a remote and most fragile inference or addition in a long chain is totally undercut by this overturning of epistemology. By denying this fourth stage, the new outlook might lend itself to the construction of a new CWS, but it doesn't offer itself as a CWS in the same direct and obvious way as the epistemological picture did.

We can learn something general about the way CWS operate, suffer attack, and defend themselves, from this example. From within itself, the epistemological picture seems unproblematic. It comes across as an obvious discovery we make when we reflect on our perception and acquisition of knowledge. All the great foundational figures: Descartes, Locke, Hume, claimed to be just saying what was obvious once one examined experience itself reflectively.

Seen from the deconstruction, this is a most massive self-blindness. Rather what happened is that experience was carved into shape by a powerful theory which posited the primacy of the individual, the neutral, the intra-mental as the locus of certainty. What was driving this theory? Certain "values", virtues, excellences: those of the independent, disengaged subject, reflexively controlling his own thought-processes, "self-responsibly" in Husserl's famous phrase. There is an ethic here, of independence, self-control, self-responsibility, of a disengagement which brings control; a stance which requires courage, the refusal of the easy comforts of conformity to authority, of the consolations of an enchanted world, of the surrender to the promptings of the senses. The entire picture, shot through with "values", which is meant to emerge out of the careful, objective, presuppositionless scrutiny, is now presented as having been there from the beginning, driving the whole process of "discovery".[21]

Once you shift to the deconstructing point of view, the CWS can no longer operate as such. It seemed to offer a neutral point of view from which we could problematize certain values—e.g., "transcendent" ones—more than others. But now it appears that it is itself driven by its own set of values. Its "neutrality" appears bogus.

Put another way, the CWS in a sense "naturalizes" a certain view on things. It tells us, as it were, that this is just the way things are, and once you look at experience, without preconceptions, this is what appears. "Natural" is opposed here to something like "socially constructed"; and from the deconstructing point of view, you have to tell a quite different story of the rise of this outlook. It isn't just that one day people looked without blinkers and discovered epistemology; rather this is the way things could be made to look from within a new historical formation of human identity, that of the disengaged, objectifying subject. The process involves a re-invention, a recreation of human identity, along with great changes in society and social practices. There is no simple stepping out of an earlier such identity into the pure light of bare nature.

It is a feature of our contemporary CWS that they are understood by those who inhabit them in this naturalizing way. It also follows from this that those who inhabit them see no alternative, except the return to earlier myth or illusion. That's what gives them their strength. People within the redoubt fight as it were to the last, and feeblest, argument, because they cannot envisage surrender except as regression. The naturalizing emerges in a kind of narration they proffer of their genesis, which I want to call a "subtraction story".

But to develop this idea I should move to another, richer CWS, or constellation of CWS. It is what people often gesture at with an expression like the "death of God". Of course, this expression is used in an uncountable range of ways; I can't be faithful to all of them, nor even will I be simply following the originator of the phrase (though I think my version is not too far from his),[22] if I say that one essential idea which this phrase captures is that conditions have arisen in the modern world in which it is no longer possible, honestly, rationally, without confusions, or fudging, or mental reservation, to believe in God. These conditions leave us nothing we can believe in beyond the human—human happiness, or potentialities, or heroism.

What conditions? Essentially, they are of two orders: first, and most important, the deliverances of science; and then secondarily also, the shape of contemporary moral experience.

To take up the first, perhaps the most powerful CWS operating today, the central idea seems to be that the whole thrust of modern science has been to establish materialism. For people who cling to this idea, the second order of conditions, the contemporary moral predicament, is unnecessary or merely secondary. Science alone can explain why belief is no longer possible in the above sense. This is a view held by people on all levels; from the most sophisticated: "We exist as material beings in a material world, all of whose phenomena are the consequences of physical relations among material entities",[23] to the most direct and simple: Madonna's "material girl, living in a material world".

Religion or spirituality involves substituting wrong and mythical explanations, explaining by "demons".[24] At bottom it's just a matter of facing the obvious truth.[25]

This doesn't mean that moral issues don't come into it. But they enter as accounts of why people run away from reality, why they want to go on believing illusion. They do so because it's comforting. The real world is utterly indifferent to us, and even to a certain degree dangerous, threatening. As children, we have to see ourselves as surrounded by love and concern, or we shrivel up. But in growing up, we have to learn to face the fact that this environment of concern can't extend beyond the human sphere, and mostly doesn't extend very far within it.

But this transition is hard. So we project a world which is providential, created by a benign God. Or at least, we see the world as meaningful in terms of the ultimate human good. The providential world is not only soothing, but it also takes the burden of evaluating things off our shoulders. The meanings of things are already given. As a well-known contemporary theorist put it:

> I think that the notion that we are all in the bosom of Abraham or are in God's embracing love is—look, it's a tough life and if you can delude yourself into thinking that there's all some warm fuzzy meaning to it all, it's enormously comforting. But I do think it's just a story we tell ourselves.[26]

So religion emanates from a childish lack of courage. We need to stand up like men, and face reality.

Now the traditional unbelieving attack on religion since the Enlightenment contains this accusation of childish pusillanimity. It also involves an attack on religion as calling for terrible self-mutilation, actuated by pride. Human desire has to be checked, mortified. And then this mortification is often imposed on others, so that religion is the source of a terrible infliction of suffering, and the visiting of severe punishment, on heretics and outsiders. This belongs to the "moral" facet of the 'death of God' critique, which I will revert to in a moment. But for the science-driven facet, the basic reason for resisting the truth is pusillanimity.

Unbelief has the opposite features. The unbeliever has the courage to take up an adult stance, and face reality. He knows that human beings are on their own. But this doesn't cause him just to cave in. On the contrary, he determines to affirm human worth, and the human good, and to work for it, without false illusion or consolation. And that means that in his moral beliefs he is also counter-mortification. Moreover, he has no reason to exclude anyone as heretic; so his philanthropy is universal. Unbelief goes together with modern (exclusive) humanism.

So goes one story. The crucial idea is that the scientific-epistemic part of it is completely self-supporting. That's something the rational mind will be led to believe independent of any moral convictions. The moral attributions to one side or the other come when you are trying to explain why some people accept and others resist these truths. The connection between materialist science and humanist affirmation comes because you have to be a mature, courageous being to face these facts. As to why mature courage embraces benevolence, which figures here in the portrait of this humanism, the answer can simply be that left to ourselves we do want to benefit our fellow humans; or that we have developed this way culturally, and we value it, and we can keep this going if we set ourselves to it.

From the believer's perspective, all this falls out rather differently. We start with an epistemic response: the argument from modern science to all-around materialism seems quite unconvincing. Whenever this is worked out in something closer to detail, it seems full of holes. The best examples today might be evolution, sociobiology, and the like. But we also see reasonings of this kind in the works of Richard Dawkins, for instance, or Daniel Dennett.[27]

So the believer returns the compliment. He casts about for an explanation why the materialist is so eager to believe very inconclusive arguments. Here the moral outlook just mentioned comes back in, but in a different role. Not that, failure to rise to which makes you unable to face the facts of materialism; but rather that, whose moral attraction, and seeming plausibility to the facts of the human moral condition, draw you to it, so that you readily grant the materialist argument from science its various leaps of faith. The whole package seems plausible, so we don't pick too closely at the details.

But how can this be? Surely, the whole package is meant to be plausible precisely *because* science has shown . . . etc. That's certainly the way the package of epistemic and moral views presents itself to those who accept it; that's the official story, as it were. But the supposition here is that the official story isn't the real one; that the real power that the package has to attract and convince lies in it as a definition of our ethical predicament, in particular, as beings capable of forming beliefs.

This means that this ideal of the courageous acknowledger of unpalatable truths, ready to eschew all easy comfort and consolation, and who by the same token becomes capable of grasping and controlling the world, sits well with us, draws us, that we feel tempted to make it our own. And/or it means that the counter-ideals of belief, devotion, piety, can all-too-easily seem actuated by a still immature desire for consolation, meaning, extra-human sustenance.

What seems to accredit the view of the package as epistemically-driven are all the famous conversion stories, starting with post-Darwinian Victorians but continuing to our day, where people who had a strong faith early in life found that they had reluctantly, even with anguish of soul, to relinquish it, because "Darwin has refuted the Bible". Surely, we want to say, these people in a sense preferred the Christian outlook morally, but had to bow, with whatever degree of inner pain, to the facts.

But that's exactly what I'm resisting saying. What happened here was not that a moral outlook bowed to brute facts. Rather we might say that one moral outlook gave way to another. Another model of what was higher triumphed. And much was going for this model: images of power, of untrammelled agency, of spiritual self-possession (the "buffered self"). On the other side, one's childhood faith had perhaps in many respects remained childish; it was all too easy to come to see it as essentially and constitutionally so.

But this recession of one moral ideal in face of the other is only one aspect of the story. The crucial judgment is an all-in one about the nature of the human ethical predicament: the new moral outlook, the "ethics of belief" in Clifford's famous phrase, that one should only give credence to what was clearly demonstrated by the evidence, was not only attractive in itself; it also carried with it a view of our ethical predicament, namely, that we are strongly tempted, the more so, the less mature we are, to deviate from this austere principle, and give assent to comforting untruths. The convert to the new ethics has learned to mistrust some of his own deepest instincts, and in particular those which draw him to religious belief. The really operative conversion here was based on the plausibility of this understanding of our ethical situation over the Christian one with its characteristic picture of what entices us to sin and apostasy. The crucial change is in the status accorded to the inclination to believe; this is the object of a radical shift in interpretation. It is no longer the impetus in us towards truth, but has become rather the most dangerous temptation to sin against the austere principles of belief-formation. This whole construal of our ethical predicament becomes more plausible. The attraction of the new moral ideal is only part of this, albeit an important one. What was also crucial was a changed reading of our own motivation, wherein the desire to believe appears now as childish temptation. Since all incipient faith is childish in an obvious sense, and (in the Christian case) only evolves beyond this by being child-like in the Gospel sense, this (mis)reading is not difficult to make.[28]

Of course, the change was painful, because one could be deeply attached to this childhood faith, not just as part of one's past, but also to what it promised. Indeed, this continuing attraction can be an integral part of the new outlook, now figuring as temptation. We can understand the regret, the nostalgia that can accompany the conversion to unbelief, the sense that we do it reluctantly. A. N. Wilson argues in his book *God's Funeral* that the nineteenth century is full of regret and mourning around this very issue, and he cites the Hardy poem of the same title.[29] But the regret is often cast in the mould of sorrow at the loss of a more childish, but beautiful world. (This is, of course, another important late-Victorian theme, which was articulated so powerfully by Barrie in *Peter Pan*.) Hardy expresses both the regret and the childish nature of the lost world in his sympathetic figuration of the old faith in *The Oxen*:

> Christmas Eve, and twelve of the clock.
>   "Now they are on their knees"
> An Elder said as we sat in a flock
>   By the embers in hearthside ease.
>
> We pictured the meek mild creatures where
>   They dwelt in their strawy pen,
> Nor did it occur to one of us there
>   To doubt they were kneeling then.
>
> So fair a fancy few would weave
>   In these years! Yet I feel,
> If someone said on Christmas Eve,
>   "Come; see the oxen kneel
>
> In the lonely barton by yonder comb
>   Our childhood used to know,"
> I should go with him in the gloom,
>   Hoping it might be so.[30]

Moreover, the pain itself could work *for* the conversion. It has been noted how many of the crop of great Victorian agnostics came from Evangelical families. They transposed the model of the strenuous, manly, philanthropic concern into the new secular key. But the very core of that model, manly self-conquest, rising above the pain of loss, now told in favour of the apostasy.[31]

So I am less than fully convinced by the major thrust of the "death of God" account of the rise of modern secularity; its account in other words of the modern conditions of belief. What makes belief problematical, often difficult and full of doubts, is not simply "science".

It should be obvious that there are parallels between my critique of the "official story" here, and the deconstruction of epistemology. In both cases, what is being claimed is that some move is being passed off as a simple discovery, which in fact is much more like a new construction; a change that involves also a new sense of our identity and our place in the world, with its implicit values, rather than simply registering observable reality. (To say that these are "constructions" is not to say that the issues here are unarbitrable by reason; that is a "post-modern" fallacy; but their arbitration is much more complicated, like that between Kuhnian paradigms, and also involves issues of hermeneutical adequacy.)[32]

Where the classical epistemologists claimed it as an obvious truth of "reflection", or inner observation, that one was first of all aware of the ideas in our mind; the proponents of the death of God want to see Godlessness as a property of the universe which science lays bare. Where the deconstructors of epistemology want to show how this supposedly obvious truth of reflection in fact only appears so within a certain value-laden construal of agency; so here I am arguing that it is only within some understanding of agency, in which disengaged scientific enquiry is woven into a story of courageous adulthood, to be attained through a renunciation of the more "childish" comforts of meaning and beatitude, that the death of God story appears obvious.

And just as, once the epistemological story is properly in place, and comes to dominate the philosophical discourse, the new construal comes to seem more and more obvious and unchallengeable; so here with the courageous adult agency of disengagement. What was once one possible construction among others sinks to the level of a picture, in Wittgenstein's sense; that is, it becomes part of the unquestioned background, something whose shape is not perceived, but which conditions, largely unnoticed, the way we think, infer, experience, process claims and arguments. From within the picture, it just seems obvious that the order of argument proceeds from science to atheism, through a series of well-grounded steps. For the critic, who sees all too well how ill-grounded some of these steps are, the crucial role of the construal of agency becomes much more salient.

This story of the picture holding us captive may be convincing applied to those who are within an established culture of atheism; but how can it be that people who are converted to this outlook also seem to fall into the picture, and accept the official story? Because it is crucial to this outlook of "death of God" atheism that it understand itself as science-driven; to accept that it has espoused one view of adult agency among possible others would be to admit that there is something here which needs defense which has as yet received none. It is essential to this whole position that the construal of agency here remain at the level of a picture; just as it is essential to the whole tradition of mediational epistemology that the primacy of ideas or of sentences held true, or whatever it sees as the mediating elements, not be seen as one construal among others, needing defense. As long as these crucial enframing constructions remain pictures, they cannot be challenged; indeed, alternatives to them are impossible to imagine. That's what it means to remain captive.

This is not to deny that science (and even more "science") has had an important place in the story; and that in a number of ways. For one thing, the universe which this science reveals is very different from the centred hierarchic cosmos which our civilization grew up within; it hardly suggests to us that humans have any kind of special place in its story, whose temporal and spatial dimensions are mind-numbing. This, and the conception of natural law by which we understand it, makes it refractory to the interventions of Providence as these were envisaged in the framework of the earlier cosmos, and the connected understanding of the Biblical story. Seen in this light, "Darwin" has indeed, "refuted the Bible".

For another thing, the development of modern science has gone hand in hand with the modern understanding of the human epistemic predicament, which I described above in Chapter 7. This has generated its own ethic, that of the austere, disengaged reason I described above. But all this still doesn't amount to an endorsement of the official story, that the present climate of unbelief in many milieux in contemporary society is a response to the strong case for materialism which science has drawn up during the last three centuries.

The connection is rather that which I have been exploring in the first part of this chapter. Modern science, along with the many other facets described—the buffered identity, with its disciplines, modern individualism, with its reliance on instrumental reason and action in secular time—make up the immanent frame. This can be lived in many ways. Some are open to transcendence, and some move to closure. The two we have just been looking at which push to closure, seen as value-soaked construals of agency, draw on notions of the good which have unavoidably played a big role in the immanent frame: such as disengaged reason, the courage to let go of comforting illusions, the reliance on one's own reason against authority, to name just some. It is possible to live these in tandem with others, which modify or limit them; or one can make them central, without rival. Going this second route can easily lead you to the construals of agency which sustain the closed world systems I have just been examining. Living from out of this sense of agency gives a certain spin to the immanent frame, which then seems to reflect back to us the validity of our closed image of it. Science, modern individualism, instrumental reason, secular time, all seem further proofs of the truth of immanence. For instance, natural science is not just one road to truth, but becomes the paradigm of all roads. Secular time, seen as homogeneous and empty, is not just the dominant domain of present-day action, but is time itself. Our stance entrenches us in a picture, which we eventually become unable to challenge.

6

But now, a crucial part of my argument for the "deconstruction" of the death of God view, is that the arguments from natural science to Godlessness are not all that convincing. Leaving aside the challenge that someone might raise who found these arguments more compelling, we might object to my presumption in refusing the interpretation that death of God protagonists put on their own position. So what if the arguments aren't compelling, might they not nevertheless be the arguments which move them?

In fact, why shouldn't bad arguments have an important effect in history, as much if not more than good arguments? In a sense, this objection is well taken; and in a sense, therefore, the official story is also true. Since lots of people believe that they are atheists and materialists because science has shown these to be irrefutable, there is a perfectly good sense in which we can say that this is their reason.

But an explanation in terms of a bad reason calls for supplementation. We need an account of why the bad reason nevertheless works. This is not necessarily so, of course, in individual cases. Individuals can just take some conclusion on authority from their milieu. Just as we laypeople take the latest report about the micro-constitution of the atom from the Sunday paper, so we may take it on authority from a Sagan or a Dawkins that Science has refuted God. But this leaves still unexplained how an authority of this kind gets constituted. What makes it the case that we laypeople, as also the scientific luminaries, get so easily sucked into invalid arguments? Why do we and they not more readily see the alternatives? My proffered account in terms of the attraction of an over-all ethically-charged vision of agency is meant to answer this deeper question.

I am not arguing that an account of someone's action in terms of erroneous belief always needs supplementation. I may leave the house without an umbrella because I believe the radio forecast to be reliable, and it predicted fair weather. But the difference between this kind of case and the issue we're dealing with here, is first, that the weather, beyond the inconvenience of getting wet today, doesn't matter to me in anything like the same way, and second, that I have no alternative access to this afternoon's weather than the forecast.

This latter is not simply true in the question of belief in God. Of course, as a layperson, I have to take on authority the findings of paleontology. But I am not similarly without resources on the issue whether what science has shown about the material world denies the existence of God. Because I can also have a religious life, a sense of God and how he impinges on my existence, against which I can check the supposed claims to refutation.

I want to draw the Desdemona analogy. What makes *Othello* a tragedy, and not just a tale of misfortune, is that we hold its protagonist culpable in his too-ready belief of the evidence fabricated by Iago. He had an alternative mode of access to her innocence in Desdemona herself, if he could only have opened his heart/mind to her love and devotion. The fatal flaw in the tragic hero Othello is his inability to do this, imprisoned as he is in a powerful code of honour—an imprisonment undoubtedly aggravated by his outsider's status and sudden promotion.

The reason why I can't accept the arguments that "science has refuted God", without any supplement, as an explanation of the rise of unbelief is that we are on this issue like Othello, rather than the person listening to the forecast as he hesitates before the umbrella stand. We can't just explain what we do on the basis of the information we received from external sources, without seeing what we made of the internal ones.

All this doesn't mean that a perfectly valid description of an individual's experience might not be, that he felt forced to give up a faith he cherished, because (as he thought) the brute facts of the universe contradicted it. Because once you go this way, once you accept unbelief, then you will probably also accept the ideology which accords primacy to the external sources, which depreciates the internal ones as incompetent here, indeed, as likely sources of childish illusion—following our own modern code of honour, that of the adult, rational subject of knowledge. It now looks ex post facto as though there was no rational alternative—and so it seemed as well to Othello. But we who have seen this happen need a further account why Desdemona's testimony wasn't heard.

But Desdemona's voice must be very faint within the modern horizon. This is the new view of the human epistemic predicament which I described at the end of Chapter 7. We start from our understanding of human individuals united in societies of mutual benefit, and capable of grasping and controlling Nature, through the use of disengaged reason. In Newton's day, this could still yield arguments demonstrating a benevolent creator. But two hundred years later, both features of this conclusion were in question: first, that the existence of Design requires a creator, and that what is created shows evidence of benignity. The updated version of the horizon of argument often takes a materialist cast, which makes natural science the royal road to truth in all domains. From this point of view, considerations of experienced meaning can only be advanced in an argument about God or human purpose if they have already been scientifically validated. By the very nature of things, arguments in this frame tend to privilege the "experience-far" considerations of natural science over the experience-near. Desdemona's voice suffers from the blight of systematic mistrust.

Thus, once one has taken the step into unbelief, there are overwhelming reasons why one will be induced to buy into the official, science-driven story. And because we very often make these choices under the influence of others, on whose authority we buy the official story, it is not surprising that lots of people have thought of their conversion as science-driven, even perhaps in the most dramatic form. Science seemed to show that we are nothing but a fleeting life-form on a dying star; or that the universe is nothing but decaying matter, under ever increasing entropy, that there is thus no place for spirit or God, miracles or salvation. Something like the vision which Dostoyevsky had in the Museum in Basel before the Dead Christ by Hans Holbein,[33] of the absolute finality of death, which convinced him that there must be something more, might easily have the opposite effect, of dragging you down and forcing an abandonment of your faith.

But the question remains: if the arguments in fact aren't conclusive, why do they *seem* so convincing, where at other times and places God's existence just seems obvious? This is the question I'm trying to answer, and the "death of God" doesn't help me here; rather it blocks the way with a pseudo-solution.

So my contention is that the power of materialism today comes not from the scientific "facts", but has rather to be explained in terms of the power of a certain package uniting materialism with a moral outlook, the package we could call "atheist humanism", or exclusive humanism. What gives the package its power? I have been trying to answer this above in terms of certain values which are implicit in the immanent frame, such as disengaged reason, which pushed to the limit, generate the science-driven "death of God" story.

But we should also look at the second level of the "death of God" account, the one which starts from our contemporary moral predicament. The conclusion here is the same as with the argument from science, that we can no longer rationally believe in God; but the starting point is now the ethical outlook of the modern age.

Now it is true that a great deal of our political and moral life is focussed on human ends: human welfare, human rights, human flourishing, equality between human beings. Indeed, our public life, in societies which are secular in a familiar modern sense, is exclusively concerned with human goods. And our age is certainly unique in human history in this respect. Hence, perhaps not surprisingly, some people see no place in this kind of world for belief in God. A faith of this kind would have to make one an outsider, an enemy of this world, in unrelenting combat with it. Thus one is either thoroughly in this world, living by its premises, and then one cannot really believe in God; or one believes, and one is in some sense living like a resident alien in modernity. Since we find ourselves more and more inducted into it, belief becomes harder and harder; the horizon of faith steadily recedes.[34]

Now this adversarial picture of the relation of faith to modernity is not an invention of unbelievers. It is matched and encouraged by a strand of Christian hostility to the humanist world. We have only to think of Pius IX, fulminating in his *Syllabus* of 1864 against all the errors of the modern world, including human rights, democracy, equality, and just about everything our contemporary Liberal state embodies. And there are other, more recent examples, among Christians as well as believers in other religions.

But this convergence between fundamentalists and hard-line atheists doesn't make their common interpretation of the relation of faith to modernity the only possible one. And it is clear that there are many people of faith who have helped to build and are now sustaining this modern humanist world, and are strongly committed to the modes of human well-being and flourishing that it has made central. Once again, the "death of God" account leaps to a conclusion which is far from being warranted. It is possible to see modern humanism as the enemy of religion, just as it is possible to take science as having proved atheism. But since the conclusion is in neither case warranted, the question arises why so many people do so. And that brings me back to the central issue I've been raising.

This moral version of the "death of God" account seems plausible to many people, because they make an assumption about the rise of modernity, which helps to screen from them how complex and difficult this quest is. The assumption is what I have called "the view from Dover Beach": the transition to modernity comes about through the loss of traditional beliefs and allegiances. This may be seen as coming about as a result of institutional changes: e.g., mobility and urbanization erode the beliefs and reference points of static rural society. Or the loss may be supposed to arise from the increasing operation of modern scientific reason. The change may be positively valued—or it may be judged a disaster by those for whom the traditional reference points were valuable, and scientific reason too narrow. But all these theories concur in describing the process: old views and loyalties are eroded. Old horizons are washed away, in Nietzsche's image. The sea of faith recedes, following Arnold. This stanza from his *Dover Beach* captures this perspective:

> The Sea of Faith
> Was once, too, at the full, and round earth's shore
> Lay like the folds of a bright girdle furled.
> But now I only hear
> Its melancholy, long, withdrawing roar,
> Retreating, to the breath
> Of the night-wind, down the vast edges drear
> And naked shingles of the world.[35]

The tone here is one of regret and nostalgia. But the underlying image of eroded faith could serve just as well for an upbeat story of the progress of triumphant scientific reason. From one point of view, humanity has shed a lot of false and harmful myths. From another, it has lost touch with crucial spiritual realities. But in either case, the change is seen as a loss of belief.

What emerges comes about through this loss. The upbeat story cherishes the dominance of an empirical-scientific approach to knowledge claims, of individualism, negative freedom, instrumental rationality. But these come to the fore because they are what we humans "normally" value, once we are no longer impeded or blinded by false or superstitious beliefs and the stultifying modes of life which accompany them. Once myth and error are dissipated, these are the only games in town. The empirical approach is the only valid way of acquiring knowledge, and this becomes evident as soon as we free ourselves from the thraldom of a false metaphysics. Increasing recourse to instrumental rationality allows us to get more and more of what we want, and we were only ever deterred from this by unfounded injunctions to limit ourselves. Individualism is the normal fruit of human self-regard absent the illusory claims of God, the Chain of Being, or the sacred order of society.

In other words, we moderns behave as we do because we have "come to see" that certain claims were false—or on the negative reading, because we have lost from view certain perennial truths. What this view reads out of the picture is the possibility that Western modernity might be powered by its own positive visions of the good, that is, by one constellation of such visions among available others, rather than by the only viable set left after the old myths and legends have been exploded. It screens out whatever there might be of a specific moral direction to Western modernity, beyond what is dictated by the general form of human life itself, once old error is shown up (or old truth forgotten). E.g., people behave as individuals, because that's what they "naturally" do when no longer held in by the old religions, metaphysics and customs, though this may be seen as a glorious liberation, or a purblind enmiring in egoism, depending on our perspective. What it cannot be seen as is a novel form of moral self-understanding, not definable simply by the negation of what preceded it.

The analogy should be evident between the moral death of God story, and its science-driven stable-mate, as well as epistemology. All make a crucial move which they present as a "discovery", something we "come to see" when certain conditions are met. In all cases, this move only looks like a discovery within the frame of a newly constructed understanding of ourselves, our predicament and our identity. The element of "discovery" seems unchallengeable, because the underlying construction is pushed out of sight and forgotten.

In terms of my discussion a few pages ago, all these accounts "naturalize" the features of the modern, liberal identity. They cannot see it as one, historically constructed understanding of human agency among others.

On this "subtraction" view of modernity, as what arises from the washing away of old horizons, modern humanism can only have arisen through the fading of earlier forms. It can only be conceived as coming to be through a "death of God". It just follows that you can't be fully into contemporary humanist concerns if you haven't sloughed off the old beliefs. You can't be fully with the modern age and still believe in God. Or alternatively, if you still believe, then you have reservations, you are at last partly, and perhaps covertly, some kind of adversary.

But of course, as I have argued at length elsewhere,[36] this is a quite inadequate account of modernity. What has got screened out is the possibility that Western modernity might be sustained by its own original spiritual vision, that is, not one generated simply and inescapably out of the transition. But this possibility is in fact the reality.

The logic of the subtraction story is something like this: once we slough off our concern with serving God, or attending to any other transcendent reality, what we're left with is human good, and that is what modern societies are concerned with. But this radically under-describes what I'm calling modern humanism. That I am left with only human concerns doesn't tell me to take universal human welfare as my goal; nor does it tell me that freedom is important, or fulfillment, or equality. Just being confined to human goods could just as well find expression in my concerning myself exclusively with my own material welfare, or that of my family or immediate milieu. The in fact very exigent demands of universal justice and benevolence which characterize modern humanism can't be explained just by the subtraction of earlier goals and allegiances.

The subtraction story, inadequate though it is, is deeply embedded in modern humanist consciousness. It is by no means propounded only by the more simplistic theorists. Even such a penetrating and sophisticated thinker as Paul Bénichou subscribed to a version of it in his *Morales du grand siècle:* "L'humanité s'estime dès qu'elle se voit capable de reculer sa misère; elle tend à oublier, en même temps que sa détresse, l'humiliante morale par laquelle, faisant de nécessité vertu, elle condamnait la vie." (Humanity respects itself from the time that it is capable of overcoming its poverty. It tends to forget, along with its material distress, the humiliating morality by which, making a virtue of necessity, it condemned life.)[37] Modern humanism arises, in other words, because humans become capable of sloughing off the older, other-worldly ethics of asceticism.

Moreover, this story is grounded in a certain view of human motivation in general, and of the well-springs of religious belief in particular. This latter is seen as the fruit of misery and the accompanying self-renunciation is "making a virtue of necessity". Belief is a product of deprivation, humiliation and a lack of hope. It is the obverse of the human desire for flourishing; where we are driven by our despair at the frustration of this desire.

Thus human flourishing is taken as our perennial goal, even though under eclipse in periods of misery and humiliation, and its content is taken as fairly unproblematic, once one begins to affirm it.

This excessive reliance on a subtraction story is related to the object of my earlier complaint, in the first chapter, viz., that this kind of account gives too much place to changes in belief, as against those in experience and sensibility. We can see how these two mistakes (if they are such) are connected. The subtraction story gives too little place to the cultural changes wrought by Western modernity, the way in which it has developed new understandings of the self, its place in society, in space and in time. It fails to see how innovative we have been; its tendency is to see modernity as the liberating of a continuing core of belief and desire from an overlay of metaphysical/religious illusion which distorted and inhibited it.

But the new ways in which we experience our world and the human condition: for instance, as autonomous subjects, as beings who can revel in choice, as citizens among others in a sovereign people, as potentially in control of history; all these and others are only comprehensible if we see them in the context of the great cultural changes, the new understandings of self, agency, time, society which Western modernity has generated. By ignoring or flattening out all these changes, a subtraction story makes it hard to conceive the changes in human experience. It is left only with an account in terms of altered beliefs.

This is one kind of account of the rise of modern secularity, and my attempt in this book has been to offer another, I think more convincing one. What we are dealing with are what are often called "master narratives", broad framework pictures of how history unfolds. These have come under some considerable attack in our time, and are thought to be (ideally) a thing of the past.[38] But my contention will be that, so far from being passé, these master narratives are essential to our thinking. We all wield them, including those who claim to repudiate them. We need to be lucid about what we are doing, and ready to debate the ones we're relying on. Attempting to repudiate them just obfuscates matters.

I have been tracing the outlines of one such narrative, an account of the coming of modern secularity, which in its general form is widely and deeply implanted in modern humanist culture. It tends to have four connected facets: (a) the "death of God" thesis that one can no longer honestly, lucidly, sincerely believe in God; (b) some "subtraction" story of the rise of modern humanism; (c) a view on the original reasons for religious belief, and on their place in perennial human motivations, which grounds the subtraction story. These views vary all the way from nineteenth-century theories about primitives' fears of the unknown, or desire to control the elements, to speculations like Freud's, linking religion to neurosis. On many of these accounts, religion simply becomes unnecessary when technology gets to a certain level: we don't need God any more, because we know how to get it ourselves.[39] These theories are generally wildly and implausibly reductive.

They issue in (d) a take on modern secularization as mainly a recession of religion in the face of science, technology and rationality. In the nineteenth century, thinkers like Comte confidently predicted the supersession of religion by science, as did Renan: "il viendra un jour où l'humanité ne croira plus, mais où elle saura; un jour où elle saura le monde métaphysique et moral, comme elle sait déjà le monde physique" (a day will come when humanity will no longer believe, but it will know: a day when it will know the metaphysical and moral world, just as it already knows the physical one).[40] As against this confident projection into the future, today everybody thinks that the illusion has some future; but on the vision I'm describing here it is in for some more shrinkage.

These four facets together give an idea of what modern secularization often looks like from within the camp of exclusive humanism. Against this, I have been offering a rather different picture.[41]

7

I have been looking at the two sides of the "death of God" perspective, and the way in which they "naturalize" various facets of the emerging identity of Western modernity. It turns out that there is a shift in the centre of gravity of the two accounts. The first, or science-driven side, which argues for materialism, seems to be based on epistemological claims. Materialism itself is an ontological thesis: everything which is, is based on "matter", whatever that means. But the argument here is ultimately epistemological, in that the ontological thesis appeals to the successes of science. It is because the paradigm examples of valid knowledge in the modern world (supposedly) take the realities they study as made exclusively of matter, that we are supposed to conclude that everything is matter.

But even if the premise about modern science is true, the conclusion doesn't follow; and I argued that those who buy the argument are induced to overlook its shortcomings because they are convinced (again without full justification) by the whole take on the human ethical predicament which is part of the materialist package. This presents materialism as the view of courageous adults, who are ready to resist the comforting illusions of earlier metaphysical and religious beliefs, in order to grasp the reality of an indifferent universe. Now this take is linked to a story, that of our rising to the point where we become capable of identifying, and then resisting these earlier illusions. This is the story which Kant made famous in his influential definition of Enlightenment, as the emergence of human beings from a state of tutelage for which they were themselves responsible, a *selbstbeschuldigte Unmündigkeit* (a self-responsible nonage). The slogan of this age was: sapere aude! Dare to know.[42] A growth of knowledge was essential to come to this stage, but this was inseparable from a new form of courage, which allows us to take responsibility for our own take on reality and on our place in it.

This means that a crucial part of this new conviction rests on a narrative, a view of how we got to where we are. And when we get to the second, moral side of the "death of God" perspective, we find that narrative has moved front and centre. Here it takes the form of a subtraction story; but we can see how these two narrations, that of courageous coming to adulthood, and that of subtraction of illusion, belong together. They are two sides of the same coin. What we got rid of were the illusions, and it took courage to do this; what is left are the genuine deliverances of science, the truth about things, including ourselves, which was waiting all along to be discovered.

"Coming of age", subtraction, these are two faces of this powerful contemporary story. But it is much richer than these, and it would be useful to explore a bit further other facets. I want to look here at two widespread and rhetorically convincing narrations, which have sunk to the level of unchallenged common sense in many milieux; that is, have become background "pictures" in something like Wittgenstein's sense.

The first concerns mainly our social and political condition. I argued earlier that we now understand ourselves as living in societies which are made up of equal individuals. Our belonging to society has become disconnected from the various networks, especially kinship relations, which we are involved in, and particularly from those networks which involve hierarchical relations, especially of the kind which were central to pre-modern "feudal" society. This is not to say that networks and hierarchy do not exist, but only that the modern imaginary sees them as disconnected from social belonging at the level of the nation, or the economy, or the public sphere. We belong to these larger wholes directly, that is, our access to them is not mediated by these networks. These wholes are held together by a "sociability of strangers".[43]

This tells the bare bones of the story, and very much from the outside. The actual account of the transition as it has been lived, is often a story of great moral enthusiasm at a discovery, at a liberation from a narrower world of closer, claustrophobic relations, involving excessive control and invidious distinctions; and at the same time it has been lived as a liberation into a new broader space, in which masses of people come together outside of the old distinctions, and meet as fellow citizens, as fellow human beings, in a new enterprise, like that of the nation, or the revolutionary party, the "party of mankind". We mustn't forget, of course, that from the other side, the party of those who resisted these changes, it has often been experienced as a catastrophic break-down of the most crucial and elementary social bond.

The paradigm example here is the French Revolution, in which people were liberated out of their "estates" into the new space of "la nation", bonded by the new trinity of "liberty, equality, fraternity". There is an immensely powerful moral inspiration here, which has meant that this radical move has been repeated again and again; first of all, obviously in other "nations" which undertook revolutions, or at least constituted themselves anew on the new basis; and at the same time, this was happening in the new parties which aspired to lead these revolutions, whether they succeeded or not. The partisans, from nationalist movements like "Young Italy" in the early nineteenth century, right on through the revolutionary anarchist and Bolshevik parties of the twentieth century, and into the terrorist movements of today, see themselves as stepping out of the older, narrower, often network, certainly hierarchical structures, into a broader space of equal comradeship, foreshadowing the new space of the reconstituted nation, or the new purified Islam.[44]

We can see this also in a series of "youth cultures", which have involved a rebellion against the hierarchical role ascription of the family, and a shift to an identity as a member of a larger fraternal movement. The last great one which shook our societies in the West, in the 60s and 70s, was certainly of this kind, challenging authority and attempting to dissolve the distinctions between teacher and student, student and worker, men and women; between work and play, means and ends; all in order to enter a new order in which all could be human together. The Utopian nature of the enterprise may dominate our memory of it, but the direction of shift it called for, its membership in a chain of such shifts out of distinction into a new space of freedom and equality, should not be forgotten.

And it was preceded by a number of such movements earlier, particularly among minorities who felt disadvantaged in a larger society. Yuri Slezkine, in his profound book on Jews in Russia in the twentieth century, has documented this with great clarity. Young Jews were responding to the hope of a new kind of space, one of openness and equality, a space which would be universal, and which would leave behind forever what they came to see as the narrow, cramped life of the ghetto.[45]

If we focus on this powerful moral attraction of a new, less cluttered, more universal and fraternal space, we find something which has wide resonances in human history. Something like this has happened again and again: Buddha's followers stepping out of the caste dharma into the new space of the Sangha; those of Christ following the lead of the parable of the Good Samaritan, until Paul can say: "in Christ is neither Jew nor Greek, slave nor free, man nor woman"; those of Muhammad, who see the new space of Islam, as beyond all tribes and nations; likewise, the appeal of Stoicism.

The power which this kind of move seems to have for us as a species could tell us something important about ourselves, if only we could define it more exactly. I don't pretend to do that here, but it does seem to me that the power can't be explained just by the negative move, the breaking out from the skein of distinctions and restrictions. It is true that breaking free from them can produce great excitement, as we see in carnivals, for instance, or in some outbreaks of violence. Bataille has written about this kind of power. But this seems to me different from the steady sense of reaching something higher, which attaches to the moves I have been describing above, as well as to modern social imaginaries.

The power has to be accounted for partly, even largely, by the positive attraction of the space we are released into: the space of the search for Enlightenment, of salvation, or of submission to God, or the cosmopolis of Gods and humans, to take the four examples above.

What is the power which inheres in the modern spaces of stranger sociability? It must have something to do with the enhanced sense of collective power and efficacy which arises here. Coming together as a people, a nation promises a new kind of efficacy to those who associate in this way. Instead of being subject, the people is sovereign. Of course, this promise is often thwarted in fact, by élites, by bureaucratic structures, by the people's own apathy. And yet the promise is still there, two hundred years on, as we can measure perhaps in the bitterness of the disappointment, when it fails to materialize. And, of course, it is partly materialized, as one can see in comparing democratic societies to those ruled by irresponsible cliques of power-holders.

Something to do with this, but not everything. There is also the fact that this new kind of efficacy also presents itself as based on justice, equality, liberty, end even solidarity. It is the novel mix of these two goods, agency and justice, as we could sum them up, which accounts for the moral power of the new spaces.

Once this new form establishes itself as superior, normative, then the modern conceptions of justice, in terms of equality and non-discrimination, begin to take hold. The subtraction story would have it that we always shared these intuitions, only they were over-ridden and sidelined by various illusory metaphysical and religious doctrines endorsing hierarchy and élite rule. But this is not what happened. In the former differentiated and hierarchical societies, like pre-modern European kingdoms with their different orders, or the Ottoman Empire with its hierarchically arranged millets, there was another conception of justice, which was of course not always followed. It took as given the differences, and defined a justice between the orders or millets which took account of these. European peasants rebelling against landlords didn't usually challenge the fact of hierarchy, only an excessively repressive and exploitative application of it: the landlords were accused of illegitimately increasing burdens, of introducing corvée where there was none historically. Everywhere the "moral economy" took account of supposedly established custom, which was itself hierarchical.

Before justice could be conceived in the modern way, which makes, for instance, Rawls' work seem so truistic for many contemporaries, this whole way of understanding society had to give way before the modern one. A new kind of space had to be created, which had the immense combined draw of its superior efficacy, as well as its own forms of justice, liberty, and solidarity. Once more the attempt to understand the rise of modernity just in terms of subtraction, without taking account of new and unprecedented creation, grievously distorts.

Pre-moderns could be as untroubled by the fact of systemic inequality between orders and peoples and religious groups, which were part of the order of things, as contemporary ultra-liberals can be untroubled by a capitalism which generates a destitute underclass, which is also seen as part of an order in which the idle and undisciplined get their just deserts.

It is the power of these new spaces which explains how the shifts continue, recruiting new populations, but also taking the same ones through more and more radical challenges to hierarchy and difference. Once one moves into the new space, then almost any traditional difference can potentially be portrayed as an unjust imposition, granted that conditions are ripe. And so there can be a late-developing move for gender equality, well after the founding moves of the new social imaginary, but more immediately following women's entry into the work-force, their acquiring education, and so on. A new vector operates in modern history, and the possibility exists of challenging the fruit of previous revolutions on their inadequate fulfillment of their own principles—as the young did in the sixties. The vector is defined by a series of moves of the form "Xer than thou".

The shift from the earlier moves I cited: Buddhist, Christian, Stoic, Muslim, which are the classic steps in the Axial Revolution, on one hand, and the rise of the modern social imaginary on the other, brings into existence a different kind of individualism. The first, Axial moves were the charter for what Dumont calls "l'individu-hors-du-monde". The Bhikkhu, the monk, the sanyassin, the Sufi saint, steps outside the regular order of what still remains a hierarchical society. The modern shift is the charter for "l'individu-dans-le-monde"; the social "world" is now seen as made up of individuals, which associate for mutual benefit.

Four strong benchmarks of the new order are: liberty: the move is meant to liberate; power: it is meant to empower; mutual benefit: this is the basic point of the society; and reason: whether freedom, power, mutual benefit has been achieved, or how to achieve them, is meant to be arbitrable by rational discussion. Their achievement is meant to be something demonstrable. These, as well as the basic premises of equality, and the foregrounding of rights, are the crucial constitutive concepts of the new understanding.

Now these are, of course, "Enlightenment" values. This is enough to set many people off on a narrative of political modernity which sees it as arising against, in combat with, and/or at the expense of "religion". But this needs to be examined more exactly.

It is indeed the case that this modern form arises in a struggle with the thicket of structures and rules which came before. The ancien régime operated on a number of easily identifiable counter-values: (1) those which made the structures and rules valuable in themselves, say, because based on the cosmic order, or the real differences between groups, races, genders; (2) the notion that there is something higher, more important than mutual benefit; and (3) some features of the human good were actually condemned: for instance, sensuality; hence a disposition to asceticism.

Now all these have been defended by Churches and other religious leaders, as I described above. The Catholic Church under Pio Nono is a sufficiently persuasive example of this, and there are many others. So the secularist reading is far from an invention. But it is also far from the whole story. The origins of the modern idea of moral order among Christian (or at least theist) thinkers, like Locke; the existence of Christian Democracy in our day; all these show that oppositions (1) and (3) from a religious perspective are far from a necessary feature of reality. (2) of course is something that any religious belief with a transcendent dimension would have to retain, but then it is far from obvious that this threatens what is good in the Enlightenment package above. On the contrary, it may even offer some insight into the limitations of these Enlightenment values taken as totally sufficient.

So the story of the rise of modern social spaces doesn't need to be given an anti-religious spin. But there are motivations to go this way; and like any spin, we can easily see how the wide acceptance of one such, and the relegation of religion which this involves, could harden into a "picture", which appears obvious and unchallengeable. The point of tracing this facet of the narrative of modern secularity is not that it shows this to be any better founded than the story of materialism and science or that of modernity as subtraction. Rather it is that taking up this facet shows how once a secularist spin has been taken, this anti-religious story has all the force and moral power which attach to the inauguration of these spaces of citizen sociability.

I mentioned above the modern idea of a people as agent of collective empowerment. But the power of this new space also has another aspect. The people as "nation" is often seen as the bearer of a certain language or culture. The world is lived and sung in a way which is special to our nation and its language. Such is the basic idea behind the Herderian notion of the nation. So the desire to join this new space can also have this other meaning: that one wants to get close to the source of this special way of living and singing. This can be the "people", in the sense of the common people, unspoiled by the élites (who may have capitulated, and are talking French or English among themselves, despising the common tongue). Or it may be that the process of bringing the genius of the language to expression in high culture is already begun; and very often this process is seen as issuing from the work of a foundation figure, a Dante, Shakespeare, Goethe, Pushkin, Mickiewicz, Petöfi. The new space is then defined by speaking (or perhaps writing in) this newly enhanced vernacular. Slezkine discusses this phenomenon in an interesting way.[46]

8

There is another facet of this narrative of secularity which it is worth mentioning here, because of its ubiquity and importance in the "closed" spin on immanence. The story line here is this: once human beings took their norms, their goods, their standards of ultimate value from an authority outside of themselves; from God, or the gods, or the nature of Being or the cosmos. But then they came to see that these higher authorities were their own fictions, and they realized that they had to establish their norms and values for themselves, on their own authority. This is a radicalization of the coming to adulthood story as it figures in the science-driven argument for materialism. It is not just that freed from illusion, humans come to establish the true facts about the world. It is also that they come to dictate the ultimate values by which they live.

Of course, these two formulations can come very close to the same thing for someone who holds that it is science, in some sense, which establishes what is morally right. Utilitarians often hold something like this: it is axiomatic that the right thing to do is to act so as to bring about the greatest happiness (to adopt this traditional formulation), and it is up to the various special sciences, as well as commonsense empirical investigation, to establish what will in fact bring this about. In this case, the dramatic claim to establish our own standards comes down to the thought that we no longer receive these norms from an authority outside of us, but rather from our own scientific investigations. We might say that we take them from reason, or from our own reason. But it is clear that we don't decide ourselves what is right; this is determined by the facts of the case.

In a parallel way, Kant would claim that while we legislate the moral law, this is established by reason; only now it is not just the facts of the case, but the nature of reason, which requires that we act on universalizable maxims. We can't decide what is right, but only will to follow it, acting out of our nature as rational agents, as against beings with desires.

But part of the dramatic force of this narrative line is lost here. What is striking about it is the claim to issue the norms we live by on our own authority. This thought can set off a tremor, a frisson in us, as we sense how much we are defying an age-old sense of higher, more-than-human authority; and at the same time, it can galvanize us with a sense of our own responsibility, and the courage we need to take it up. Beyond this, we can be struck by the sense that we stand, as it were, before a normative abyss, that this blind, deaf, silent universe offers *no* guidance whatever; we can find here an exhilarating challenge, which inspires us, which can even awaken a sense of the strange beauty of this alien universe, in the face of which we stake our claim as legislators of meaning.

This same story can be told at different levels of radicality. At its most humdrum, a contemporary Humean might reflect on Hume's debunking of rational vision as the basis for morality. This rather resides in ordinary human sentiment, in a certain innate propensity to approve and disapprove of actions in function of their conducing or not to the happiness and well-being of humans. Our innate feelings of sympathy ensure that we will not be actuated here merely by our own happiness, but rather by the general utility.

Now here we are plainly not able to decide what is good and right. This is determined, for one part, by our innate tendency to approve what brings happiness, and for another part, by our reason insofar as we use this to determine what does in fact conduce to human welfare. But seen from another side, it is clear that this position departs crucially from traditional ethics. It not only debunks the claim that our standards are determined by something higher, be it the will of God, or the nature of the cosmos, or the Idea of the Human, or whatever, but it also dissipates the aura of irrecusable authority which depends on this higher source. Our moral impulses are natural, just like all our other impulses; they are part of how human beings function de facto, like our sexual constitution, and our need for self-esteem and recognition, and all the rest.

But of course, moral demands claim to be higher, over-riding, to be those we really ought to listen to, even when other desires clamour to ignore them. That is part of what we mean by morality. And by and large a Humean moral philosopher will not want to reject this claim; she will aspire to live her life in response to it. But then she will be aware that it is not the universe, or God, but ultimately she herself who is assenting to accord moral demands this status. In this sense, some kind of decision is called for.

And this decision requires a certain kind of courage; because so deeply ingrained in our history and culture, perhaps even in our make-up, is the connection between higher source and over-riding claim, that the debunking of all outside sources can easily induce in us a failure of nerve. We have to have the courage to re-affirm on our own authority (some of) the moral rules which used to hold as commands of God or Nature.

Now we can generalize this notion of self-authorization beyond the narrowly Humean moral philosophy, and we come to the position ably articulated by Isaiah Berlin at the end of his "Two Concepts of Liberty":

> In the end, men choose between ultimate values; they choose as they do, because their life and thought are determined by fundamental moral categories and concepts that are, at any rate over large stretches of time and space, a part of their being and thought and sense of their own identity.

Here Berlin invokes "the ideal of freedom to choose ends without claiming eternal validity for them". He acknowledges that this was not recognized in the past, and may not be in the future, "but no sceptical conclusions seem to me to follow".

> Principles are not less sacred because their duration cannot be guaranteed. Indeed, the very desire for guarantees that our values are eternal and secure in some objective heaven is perhaps only a craving for the certainties of childhood or the absolute values of our primitive past. "To realise the relative validity of our convictions", said an admirable writer of our time, "and yet to stand for them unflinchingly, is what distinguishes a civilised man from a barbarian." To demand more than this is perhaps a deep and incurable metaphysical need; but to allow it to determine one's practice is a symptom of an equally deep, and more dangerous, moral and political immaturity.[47]

The narrative line I have been describing is beautifully invoked here: from childhood to adulthood, from barbarity to civilization, we climb to the point of being capable of self-authorization. But it is clear that, although there are important choices to be made (Berlin is well known for his thesis of the irreducible conflict between values), nevertheless much of what we accept as normative is deeply anchored in our past and identity.

Self-authorization can be given a more radical twist, if we think of the values which we endorse as not so continuous with our past and what we have become. Authors who sense themselves to be in a revolutionary situation can more easily see themselves as espousing a more radically new position; say, a new humanism, over against a theistic ethic, or one based on the Great Chain of Being; or a humanism of a particular temper, over against other, more influential forms.

We find a stance of this latter kind in Albert Camus, for instance, whose humanism was partly defined in opposition to the "progressive", Communist-leaning, revolutionary humanism espoused by Sartre. In Camus, the sense is strong that this self-authorization takes place over against a universe which is silent and indifferent, and which defeats all attempts to find some meaning in it. It is in this sense the site of "absurdity". But realizing this fully, and rising to the challenge, and espousing one's own ethic in the teeth of this absurdity, can yield the courage and inspiration to struggle against the force of meaningless adversity. Dr. Rieux in *La Peste* is an exemplary hero of this stance. To project some false meaning onto the plague, for instance, that humans are being punished for their sins, is not only to give in to illusion, but also to lay down one's arms in the struggle.

Camus' position, because of its articulacy and rhetorical force, is worth examining in a little more detail. His crucial move is to articulate the sense of the human condition, after the end of religious-metaphysical illusions, with the notion of the "absurd". The absurd "naît de cette confrontation entre l'appel humain et le silence déraisonnable du monde"[48] (the absurd is born of this confrontation between the human call and the unreasonable silence of the world).[49] We feel called to happiness, *jouissance*. This is not just a desire, but a sense that this is our normal condition; that this is what we are designed for. And beyond that, we feel an imperious demand in us to make sense of the world, to find some unified meaning in it. We have, in other words, an intuition about the meaning of things, written into our inescapable life experience.

But then the claims to fulfillment and meaning are brutally denied by an indifferent universe. It owes us nothing, and its operations randomly favour and then crush our aspirations. The nascent sense of meaning meets an enigma which defies all over-all meaning. The attempts at sense-making are continually and utterly frustrated. This is the contradiction which Camus names "absurd".

Of course, there is a seeming contradiction in this claim itself. Those who are chary of Camus' dramatization of the human condition have not been slow to point this out. If the point is that, contrary to Christianity and a host of metaphysical views, the universe is indifferent and void of meaning, it doesn't make sense to speak of absurdity either. Absurdity exists where there is reason to expect meaning, and nonsense appears instead. How can there be an expectation of meaning in a universe which is by hypothesis devoid of it?

Camus' point here is phenomenological. It is part of our life-experience to expect, strive, hope for happiness and meaning. Seen in the view from nowhere, the universe is just indifferent, and there is no point speaking of the absence of meaning. But as we live it, the expectation, the demand for meaning is ineradicable; the universe as lived is "absurd". "Ce monde en lui-même n'est pas raisonnable . . . Mais ce qui est absurde, c'est la confrontation de cet irrationnel et de ce désir éperdu de clarté dont l'appel résonne au plus profond de l'homme."[50] (This world in itself is not reasonable. . . . But what is absurd is the confrontation between this irrational reality and the wild longing for clarity whose call resonates in the depths of the human heart.)[51]

To make the demand for meaning is not an optional stance. It is central to our humanity:

> Je peux tout nier de cette partie de moi qui vit de nostalgies incertaines, sauf ce désir d'unité, cet appétit de résoudre, cette exigence de clarté et de cohésion. Je peux tout réfuter dans ce monde qui m'entoure, me heurte ou me transporte, sauf ce chaos, ce hasard roi et cette divine équivalence qui naît de l'anarchie.[52]

> (I can negate everything of that part of me that lives on vague nostalgias, except this desire for unity, this longing for resolution, this need for clarity and cohesion. I can refute everything in my surrounding world that clashes with me or enraptures me, except this chaos, this sovereign chance and this divine equivalence that springs from anarchy.)[53]

How to respond to this? The traditional response has been to negate absurdity, to affirm cosmic meaning. Or perhaps better put, throughout its whole early development, the human race lived within socially-constructed projections of meaning on the world which quite occluded the issue which we moderns have to face. One way to react today is to try to rehabilitate these projections, or devise new ones. Continuing belief in Christianity is an attempt to retain an old form, but orthodox revolutionary Marxism represents a new attempt to do the same thing. In the end of history, after the Revolution, everything will make sense (if we forget details like accidents and premature death).

Another strategy is to downplay the importance of the earthly happiness we desire and feel ourselves made for. The fact that this is frustrated is not all that important, because we have something much more important to strive for: salvation, the Revolution. Obviously, these two go together, they are two sides of the same coin. To affirm that the universe is meaningful, when it negates the first-off claim that we make of it in our desire for happiness, must mean to displace the sought-for meaning elsewhere. Something else matters more than our ordinary fulfillment.

Camus rejects both facets of this strategy. We must never denigrate happiness, "il faut aimer la nature, avoir une sagesse de la vie dans l'immédiat et pas dans le lointain" (we must love nature, have a wisdom of life in its immediacy, and not from a distance).[54] This is what Camus referred to as his "Hellenism". We can see something of the same idea as other modern critics have raised with the idea of "paganism", we try to go back behind the transformation perspective of Christianity, and once more restore ordinary human flourishing to its rightful place as our highest end.

Taking up this utterly lucid stance, we have a sense of our own dignity as clear-sighted beings, capable of facing the painful truth. Camus speaks of "honour":

> Noblesse oblige à l'honneur. Mais l'homme oblige à la noblesse. . . . Vigny a très bien vu que l'honneur était la seule morale possible pour l'homme sans Dieu. Les raisons de l'homme ne tiennent pas debout. C'est l'homme qui tient debout à leur place.[55]

> (Nobility obliges one to honour; but being a man obliges one to nobility. . . . Vigny saw very well that honour was the only possible morality for the man without God. For man's reasons cannot stand by themselves; it is man who stands by himself in their place.)[56]

But this is not all. To have rehabilitated ordinary happiness binds us to all; it brings us together with others in an effort to fight for this happiness wherever it is endangered. This is a fight which we will lose in the end, but which allows for many provisional victories. These are all we have; we shouldn't squander them.

In this response, we see the negation of a third feature which Camus sees in religio-metaphysical projections of meaning; not only covering up the absurd, not only denigrating happiness, but also denying the fulfillments of whatever meaning we believe in to those who refuse to accept our creed. To free oneself of these projections is to be able to accede to a real universality. "Il faut bien . . . faire ce que le christianisme n'a jamais fait: s'occuper des damnés."[57] (One must . . . do what Christianity has never done: take care of the damned.)[58]

Camus is expressing here his variant of what we called in the earlier discussion this sense of breaking out into a new space between human beings, which carries with it a new wider solidarity. This is the space he calls "la révolte". "Il me semble trouver dans le mouvement de la révolte le lieu commun où les hommes se rejoignent."[59] (I believe we find in the movement of revolt the common ground on which men can unite.) Revolt against what? Against absurdity itself; instead of just passively bearing the denial of our aspirations to happiness; and avoiding even more the false solutions which cover up the absurd and promise some illusory substitute to a favoured group, the effective rebellion means fighting the battles we can fight, for the limited, provisional happiness we can achieve, wherever this is to be found, and whoever will be the beneficiaries, without exclusion. "Sachant qu'il n'est pas de causes victorieuses, j'ai du goût pour les causes perdues: elles demandent une âme entière, égale à sa défaite comme à ses victoires passagères."[60] (Knowing that there are no victorious causes, I have a taste for lost causes. They demand a soul without fissure, the equal of defeat, as well as of its temporary victories.)[61]

This passionate sense that the provisional, limited happiness and well-being should never be sacrificed in the name of the great over-all solution, was what made Camus unable to follow Sartre in his support for Communism, and brought about the painful rupture between the two erstwhile friends and allies.[62]

So revolt, which Camus says at one point "n'est que l'assurance d'un destin écrasant, moins la résignation qui devrait l'accompagner" (is but the assurance of a crushing fate, minus the resignation that ought to accompany it), is the only stance worthy of the human being. To take it up "lui restitue sa grandeur. Pour un homme sans oeillères, il n'est pas de plus beau spectacle que celui de l'intelligence aux prises avec une réalité qui le dépasse. Le spectacle de l'orgueil humain est indépassable. . . . Appauvrir cette réalité dont l'inhumanité fait la grandeur de l'homme, c'est du même coup l'appauvrir lui-même."[63] ([This stance] restores to life its greatness. For a man without blinkers, there is no finer sight than that of an understanding at grips with a reality which transcends it. The sight of human pride is unsurpassable. . . . To impoverish that reality whose inhumanity constitutes human greatness is tantamount to impoverishing man himself.)[64]

There is an inspiring ideal of courage, akin to Stoicism, in this position, which we find renewed in a number of ways in our time. One struggles for the good, with no guarantees of success, indeed, even with a certainty of ultimate failure; not only in the sense that the indifferent universe will ultimately do away with all the works of humankind, but also because one will accept no transcendent hope beyond history, that works of good will can be taken up into eternity. It is the very height of human morality, because at the apex of ungrounded self-authorization, to be totally committed to the right, even in the face of certain defeat. Derrida espoused a position somewhat like this.

Camus, Derrida, and others ended up authorising an ethic which has deep roots in our civilization, a humanism which takes up some variant of the modern moral order, that our actions and structures should conduce to the benefit of all. But Nietzsche conceived of a kind of self-authorization which deliberately rejected universal benefit, egalitarianism, democracy, as so many obstacles on the road to self-overcoming. Here we have another pitch of radicality, which is ready to make a total break with the founding principles of our civilization. This is not a mere recasting of these, however far-reaching, as one sees with Marx, but a head-on rejection. From this sense of radical self-authorization an exhilarating sense of freedom, power and beauty can arise, as we can see in this closing passage from *The Will to Power:*

And do you know what "the world" is to me? Shall I show it to you in my mirror? This world: a monster of energy, without beginning, without end; a firm, iron magnitude of force that does not grow bigger or smaller, that does not expend itself but only transforms itself; as a whole, of unalterable size, a household without expenses or losses, but likewise without increase or income; enclosed by "nothingness" as by a boundary; not something blurry or wasted, not something endlessly extended, but set in a definite space as a definite force, and not a space that might be "empty" here or there, but rather as force throughout, as a play of forces and waves of forces, at the same time one and many, increasing here and at the same time decreasing there; a sea of forces flowing and rushing together, eternally changing, eternally flooding back, with tremendous years of recurrence, with an ebb and a flood of its forms; out of the simplest forms striving towards the most complex, out of the stillest, most rigid, coldest forms towards the hottest, most turbulent, most self-contradictory, and then again returning home to the simple out of this abundance, out of the play of contradictions back to the joy of concord, still affirming itself in this uniformity of its courses and its years, blessing itself as that which must return eternally, as a becoming which knows no satiety, no disgust no weariness: this my *Dionysian* world of the eternally self-creating, the eternally self-destroying, this mystery world of twofold voluptuous delight, my "beyond good and evil", without goal, unless the joy of the circle itself is a goal; without will, unless a ring feels good will towards itself—do you want a *name* for this world? A *solution* for all its riddles? A *light* for you, too, you best-concealed, most intrepid, most midnightly men?—*This world is the will to power—and nothing besides!* And you yourselves are also this will to power—and nothing besides![65]

The dawning sense in modern times that we are in a meaningless universe, that our most cherished meanings find no endorsement in the cosmos, or in the will of God, has often been described as a traumatic loss, a second and definitive expulsion from paradise. But in Nietzsche's portrayal, virtually a hymn of praise, we sense another reaction: exhilaration. It is partly the very spectacle of immensity and power, but there is also the almost giddy sense that in this massive turbulence, all meaning is up to us. This can appear as the ultimate emancipation, freeing us from all exogenous significance.

So we see that the narrative of self-authorization can be told in many registers, some very radical. But the story is often told without distinguishing between these different forms, as a kind of generic story, pointing to the obvious fact that, with the demise of God and the meaningful cosmos, we are the only authorising agency left. Thus Alain Renaut:

> L'*humanisme,* c'est au fond la conception et la valorisation de l'humanité comme capacité d'*autonomie*—je veux dire . . . que ce qui constitue la modernité, c'est ce fait que l'homme va se penser comme la source de ses représentations et de ces actes, comme leur fondement (sujet) ou encore comme leur auteur . . . L'homme de l'humanisme est celui qui n'entend plus recevoir ses normes ou ses lois ni de la nature des choses (Aristote), ni de Dieu, mais qui les fonde lui-même à partir de sa raison et de sa volonté. Ainsi le droit naturel moderne serait-il un droit subjectif, posé et défini par la raison humaine (rationalisme juridique) ou la volonté humaine (volontarisme juridique).[66]

> (Fundamentally, *humanism* is the conception and valorization of humanity in its capacity for *autonomy.* What I mean . . . is that what constitutes modernity is the fact that man thinks of himself as the source of his representations and acts, as their foundation (subject) or their author. . . . The man of humanism is the one who no longer receives his norms and laws either from the nature of things (Aristotle) nor from God, but who establishes them himself on the basis of his reason and will. Thus modern natural right is a subjective right, posited and defined by human reason (juridical rationalism) or by human will (juridical voluntarism).

Self-authorization is just taken here as an axiomatic feature of modernity, whether it be through reason or will. This is a tremendously widespread narrative nowadays; it crops up everywhere. Wherever it is accepted, it in turn seems to make the closed take on immanence equally axiomatic. The entire ethical stance of moderns supposes and follows on from the death of God (and of course, of the meaningful cosmos). This gives a twist to the story of modernity as adulthood, which imparts drama, a call to steadfast courage, even the exhilaration of total emancipation.

The sense that we have reached maturity in casting aside faith can be played out in the register of disengaged reason, and the need to accept the deliverances of neutral science, whatever they be. This was the thrust of the first set of CWSs which I described above. But there can also be the sense that adulthood above all means being able to face the loss of meaning in things, being ready to find or project meaning in face of a universe which itself is without sense. Here the virtues may not, or not simply, be those of disengaged reason, and scientific responsibility. Indeed, the sense may be that we have to avoid a too simple reliance on science in the search for meaning. The main virtue stressed here is the imaginative courage to face the void, and to be energized by it to the creation of meaning. Nietzsche and his followers are crucial protagonists of this spin on immanence. And Camus, as we saw above, offered another very influential version of it.[67]

But how coherent is this view of the creation of meaning and value in face of the void? Certainly, as an account of what happened in the early stages of modernity, it verges on fantasy. If you had tried to explain to Locke or Grotius that this is what they were doing, they would have stared at you in incomprehension.

But leaving this aside, how coherent is the claim itself? Can the values we take as binding really be invented? Or in the less radical version of Berlin, where we admit that they emerge from our past and our identity, what does it mean to endorse them in their temporality and relativity? Of course, I see that my standard for a good human life has no application before or after there are humans. I also can recognize that the ethic of authenticity I endorse made no sense to people in other cultures and times. But that doesn't prevent me from thinking that these standards are rooted in what we are, even in human nature, to use the traditional expression, and that they need to be sought after, discovered, better defined, rather than being endorsed.[68]

Moreover, what are we to make of the aura surrounding these standards, the fact that they command my admiration and allegiance? That is, after all, what the references to God and the cosmos were attempting to make sense of. It is not at all clear that Humeans, Kantians, let alone Nietzscheans, can offer a more convincing account of this than the traditional ones.

And finally, who has decreed that the transformations we can hope and strive for in human life are restricted to those which can be carried out in a meaningless universe without a transcendent source?

The narratives of self-authorization, when examined more closely, are far from self-evident; and yet their assuming axiomatic status in the thinking of many people, is one facet of a powerful and widespread CWS, imposing a closed spin on the immanent frame we all share.

9

I have been outlining four facets of a take on modernity which make it appear as a closed immanent order. I have called these "closed world structures", because they (wrongly) make this take seem obvious, unchallengeable, axiomatic. These facets are in a sense variants on a narrative of coming of age, moving from a childlike to an adult consciousness. In the first facet, which makes the claim that science has shown that God cannot exist, or at least that religion is irrelevant to life, the story of maturation is in the background, but it plays a crucial role in the acceptance of this way of thinking. The second is a narrative of subtraction, but this too is minimally argued, and serves more as the unnoticed background to the narratives people tell. The third and fourth offer fuller narratives, with a lot of rich detail, of the rise of modern political-moral spaces, on one hand, and of the authorization of values by the autonomous self. But they are linked together as stories of maturation, of which they present different sides.

I have articulated these facets in some detail, partly in order to show that they function as unchallenged axioms, rather than as unshakeable arguments, and that they rely on very shaky assumptions, are often grounded on illegitimate naturalizations of what are in fact profound cultural mutations, and in general survive largely because they end up escaping examination in the climate in which they are taken as the undeniable framework for any argument. But my goal has also been to give some sense of how lively and powerful these narrations can be, how exciting and engaging, in particular the last two, and how they associate the closed take with various virtues, mainly those of courageous, clear-sighted adulthood. It is easy to see how, if no other considerations impinge, they could generate anticipatory confidence in a take of closure within the immanent frame. But as supposed conclusive proofs they don't make the grade.

The narrative dimension is extremely important, because the force of these CWS comes less from the supposed detailed argument (that science refutes religion, or that Christianity is incompatible with human rights), and much more from the general form of the narratives, to the effect that there was once a time when religion could flourish, but that this time is past. The plausibility structures of faith have collapsed, once and for all, irreversibly. We see this sense among many nineteenth century figures, concerning faith in a personal God (as against some kind of impersonal force). Arnold thought that the older form of religion was irretrievably a thing of the past, as did Hardy, and in another way, William James.

And the same kind of supposition is widespread today, now in favour of atheism, or materialism, relegating all forms of religion to an earlier era. In a certain sense, the original arguments on which this narrative rests cease to matter, so powerful is the sense created in certain milieux, that these old views just *can't* be options for us.

I could in fact have gone much farther in exploring further facets of the outlook of closed immanence. I discussed in detail the epistemological doctrines associated with it, but a lot needs to be said as well about the widespread take on moral philosophy today, with its exclusive focus on questions of obligatory action, the question of what is the right thing to do. It in fact abandons wider issues of the nature of the good life, of higher ethical motivation, of what we should love. The wider focus is evident in the founding philosophies of Western ethics, in the ancient world. But modern discussions, which tend to concentrate on the range of doctrines descended from Utilitarian thinkers and Kant, have very much narrowed the field.[69] Of course, underlying this change are massive shifts in the understanding of human agency and the human good, but these deeper changes are pushed into the background and "naturalized", so that it just seems evident that what is centrally at stake in morals must be either utility, or utility plus the requirements of freedom, and/or those of rational argument. In any of these formulations, the basis of ethics is seen as something obvious, and there seems no call to examine the understanding of the incomparably higher underlying all this, much less raise the question whether it points to something transcendent.

And, of course, there are other modes of CWS, powered by other senses of agency and our predicament. But enough has been said to give the flavour of this stance to modernity.

Now in milieux in which this stance dominates, it can seem very hard to understand why anyone can believe in God, unless through a failure of reason, or a culpable self-indulgence. And yet even there, as in the islands of unchallenged faith, there is a lively sense that the alternative exists, and some nagging doubts may be induced by this.

In a sense, the alternative can't disappear, because it is part of the official story itself. Following some of the versions of the "secularization" story, religion should just eventually disappear altogether, as we saw in the quote from Renan a few paragraphs ago. The illusion is finally dispelled, and humanity puts it behind them. As we could argue that particular forms of belief or particular religious functions have quite disappeared. We could perhaps imagine a humanity for whom "religion" just meant one of the "higher" forms, which had completely forgotten about shamans and shamanism. (I'm not sure that even this can really be relegated in this way, but we can imagine it for the sake of argument.)

Or in the contemporary form proposed by Bruce above, the prospect that religion might disappear under the force of scientific refutation is abandoned, but the prediction is that in humanity's search for meaning in the future, religious answers will be relegated to the margins.

But religion as a whole disappear or be marginalized in this fashion? At first sight, there seems to be a difficulty with this, in that the very self-understanding of unbelief, that whereby it can present itself as mature, courageous, as a conquest over the temptations of childishness, dependency or lesser fortitude, requires that we remain aware of the vanquished enemy, of the obstacles which have to be climbed over, of the dangers which still await those whose brave self-responsibility falters. Faith has to remain a possibility, or else the self-valorizing understanding of atheism founders. Imagining that faith might just disappear is imagining a fundamentally different form of non-faith, one quite unconnected to identity. It would be one in which it would be as indifferent and unconnected to my sense of my ethical predicament that I have no faith, as it is today that I don't believe, for instance, in phlogiston, or natural places. This I suppose is something like what Bruce is predicting.

Perhaps some people see themselves as approaching this condition today; people who say: "I'm not religious", in the same tone of voice as they might say: I don't like turnips, or Elvis Presley. My guess is that if pressed to look at the issues, even they would begin to sense that they stood in one or other relation to faith as an identity-defining issue. And certainly the argument about faith and unbelief which circulates in our culture, the moves from one to the other which people make, are all understood on this ethically-charged level. Religion remains ineradicably on the horizon of areligion; and vice versa. This is another indication that the "official story" needs to be understood on a deeper level, as I have been suggesting above.

10

All this may perhaps give us a sense of what it can mean to stand in the Jamesian open space I spoke of above (section 3), where the winds blow, where one can feel the pull in both directions. To stand here is to be at the mid-point of the cross-pressures that define our culture.

The experience in this space may take many forms. But I want to single out two versions, which each reflect a direction one may be leaning. The first is familiar from the preceding discussion; those who want to opt for the ordered, impersonal universe, whether in its scientist-materialist form, or in a more spiritualized variant, feel the imminent loss of a world of beauty, meaning, warmth, as well as of the perspective of a self-transformation beyond the everyday. The attraction of these cherished goods is closely linked to the past, often to the childhood of the chooser—which is, of course, what helps ultimately to discredit them. Even after the die is cast, the force of these rejected aspirations recurs in the form of regret and nostalgia. Which is why the nineteenth century shows that continuing strand of regret, even bereavement, which Wilson spoke of,[70] one of whose most poignant expressions is Hardy's poem *God's Funeral*:

> 'So, toward our myth's oblivion,
> Darkling, and languid-lipped, we creep and grope
> Sadlier than those who wept in Babylon,
> Whose Zion was still an abiding hope.
>
> 'How sweet it was in years far hied
> To start the wheels of day with trustful prayer,

To lie down liegely at the eventide
And feel a blest assurance he was there!

    'And who or what shall fill his place?
Whither will wanderers turn distracted eyes
For some fixed star to stimulate their pace
Towards the goal of their enterprise?' . . .[71]

This sense of loss can perhaps never be stilled, only swept away or swallowed up (and for how long?) in the exhilaration of total emancipation.

The second version is what those experience whose strongest leanings move them towards at least some search for spiritual meaning, and often towards God. These are haunted by a sense that the universe might after all be as meaningless as the most reductive materialism describes. They feel that their vision has to struggle against this flat and empty world; they fear that their strong desire for God, or for eternity, might after all be the self-induced illusion that materialists claim it to be.

This has been a familiar predicament during the last two centuries. Czeslaw Milosz, following Erich Heller, speaks of the "Romantic crisis of European culture", unleashed by "the dichotomy between the world of scientific laws—cold, indifferent to human values—and man's inner world".[72] This may not be the best name for this stream of sensibility, but Milosz captures the sense of threat to the central meanings of life, as well as the refusal to confine these to a lost past, and the determination to recover a new way of expressing and validating these meanings. His prime examples—and there are many others—are Blake, Goethe, and Dostoyevsky, but of course the list has to include Milosz himself.

The understanding that this is a continuing struggle, that the vindication of faith is not complete emerges, for instance, in Dostoyevsky's famous saying that if he had to choose between Christ and the truth, he would choose Christ.[73] Confidence here must remain always anticipatory. Parallel to the continuing regret of ex-believers is this sense that the struggle for belief is never definitively won.

These two forms of experience stand among the many which belong to what Milosz, following Heller, calls the "Disinherited Mind".

16 Cross Pressures

1

It is clear what part this discussion of closed world structures plays in my broader argument about theories of secularization. I would like to claim that the force of these narratives of closed immanence helps explain why mainstream theory so often operates with the "basement" it does, to use the terminology of Chapter 12. At its foundation is the assumption that the world is proceeding towards an overcoming or relegation of religion. This master narrative enframes the particular theoretical claims which constitute the theory.

The vector which I want to offer in its place, at least for Western society (and that is what my arguments in this book focus on) is more complicated. We have undergone a change in our condition, involving both an alteration of the structures we live within, and our way of imagining these structures. This is something we all share, regardless of our differences in outlook. But this cannot be captured in terms of a decline and marginalization of religion. What we share is what I have been calling "the immanent frame"; the different structures we live in: scientific, social, technological, and so on, constitute such a frame in that they are part of a "natural", or "this-worldly" order which can be understood in its own terms, without reference to the "supernatural" or "transcendent". But this order of itself leaves the issue open whether, for purposes of ultimate explanation, or spiritual transformation, or final sense-making, we might have to invoke something transcendent. It is only when the order is "spun" in a certain way that it seems to dictate a "closed" interpretation.

The consequences of this change for religion have been complex and multi-directional. I have argued that the developments of Western modernity have destabilized and rendered virtually unsustainable earlier forms of religious life, but that new forms have sprung up. Moreover this process of destabilization and recomposition is not a once-for-all change, but is continuing. As a result the religious life of Western societies is much more fragmented than ever before, and also much more unstable, as people change their positions during a lifetime, or between generations, to a greater degree than ever before.

The salient feature of Western societies is not so much a decline of religious faith and practice, though there has been lots of that, more in some societies than in others, but rather a mutual fragilization of different religious positions, as well as of the outlooks both of belief and unbelief. The whole culture experiences cross pressures, between the draw of the narratives of closed immanence on one side, and the sense of their inadequacy on the other, strengthened by encounter with existing milieux of religious practice, or just by some intimations of the transcendent. The cross pressures are experienced more acutely by some people and in some milieux than others, but over the whole culture, we can see them reflected in a number of middle positions, which have drawn from both sides.

Here's where we can see the four facets of the story of closed immanence I examined above beginning to come apart. I treated them in the last section as facets of the same story, and that is indeed, how many people see them, and live and think within them. But the first one, which adopts a science-based materialism, often in company with the subtraction story which downplays cultural change and invention, also arouses a lot of resistance. Materialism is too closely bound up with reductionist views, in which thought, intentions, desires and aspirations are supposed to be reductively explained either in terms of mechanism, or in terms of more basic motivations.

Materialism, as I argued above, has many forms. Two forms are particularly common in human science: First, mechanistic explanation (M.1); this means really that we eschew meanings and teleology in our explanations; we only allow for efficient causation. This kind of theory also has a penchant for atomistic accounts, in which causal contact is punctual, in time and space. But there is also what I might call "motivational materialism" (M.2): we speak of motivated action, but only base our explanations on the lower motives, not moral aspirations, for instance, or in general, strong evaluations. Ordinary "vulgar" Marxism is the best-known example of this. M.2 "follows" from M.1, in the sense that eschewing meanings fits better with it, but strictly speaking M.1 shouldn't allow us to speak of motives at all. However, in the scientific imagination, our basic motives can seem like segmental drives, a primitive "push" with very little emotional understanding, hence minimum meanings, just desire triggered by an object. B. F. Skinner and other behaviourists seemed to take them this way.

What is going for this? On one level, "Science", that is, the success of post-Galilean explanations. But also there is the bias introduced by taking the external view, the view from nowhere, where we can take in the whole universe in panorama.[1] This is by its very nature a view which is experience-far. From way out there, we all seem like ants, destined to come and go without trace; like other species.

This preference for the universal, impersonal order now seems to us a preference for materialism, because that is how we have come to see the universal order. But this reading has developed and grown in the last centuries; it becomes strong only in the nineteenth century. Before we had an earlier variant, visible in the growth of Deism, or even of Spinozism.

But this standpoint is also ethically driven. First, it takes courage; we have to resist the blandishments of comforting meaning, as according to the standard narrative did Copernicus, Darwin, Freud. It is also supported by the ethical aura surrounding disengagement.

And there is also a moral stance. Religion and metaphysics supposedly turn us away from a concrete concern for human desire, suffering and happiness. There seems to be a strange inference here, caricatured by Solovyov: "Man descends from the apes, therefore we must love each other". But the inference can seem to go through if one brings in the modern morality of mutual benefit: people ought to relate in such a way as to mutually enhance their several projects of life, and as we saw above, religion can be painted as the enemy of this principle, overriding or upsetting the order of benefit by its otherworldly demands. Moreover, the principle itself can be seen as self-evident, once you take the disengaged stance to human affairs, which by definition is impartial. So we have to jettison God and Plato. Of course, Nietzsche shows where this ape argument can go when you reject the MMO. But for the Enlightenment mainstream, a commitment to this order seems to be integral to the stance of scientific disengagement itself.

But there are also various grounds of repulsion from this. These crystallize around ideas of what the greatness, or as I have been describing it here, the fullness of human life consists in. The uneasy sense that they express is that the reductive materialist account of human beings leave no place for fullness as they understand it. Here are some of the definitions of fullness that trigger this reaction.

(1) There is the sense that we aren't just determined, that we are active, building, creating, shaping agents. Leibniz and Kant were crucial defenders of this view. This is both an insight into how we actually work, and also an ethical repulsion against denying this.

(2) There is also a spiritual objection: we have higher ethical/spiritual motives, for instance, Kant's "Achtung für das Gesetz"; Jaurès, Arnold, and others also take similar positions against reduction.

(3) Then there are aesthetic objections: Art, Nature moves us; we have a deeper sense of meaning; we can't see our "aesthetic" responses as just another form of pleasurable reaction. They have a deeper significance.

Now all of these can lead people to return to, or re-affirm, an orthodox faith. If this is what denying God leads to, then it seems a bad move. But many of those who share this negative reaction to materialism also want to define themselves against orthodox religion, or at least Christianity. They seek a middle way. It can be some kind of "spiritual", or theistic position, which departs from orthodox Christianity, as we see with Kant, Arnold, and Jaurès; or it can be an attempt to find some other basis for ethics (issue 2), starting from intuitions we have about human dignity, which in some way is not susceptible of reduction.

Of course, I am taking it as axiomatic that everyone, and hence all philosophical positions, accept some definition of greatness and fullness in human life. So it is not the case that materialists deny ethics, for instance, as they are often accused of doing by their critics. The driving forces behind materialism are ethical and moral as we just saw. It is rather that their explanation of how we can square their account with these forms of fullness seems terribly implausible to many others: how one can believe in a materialist reduction of thinking and conceptual spontaneity (issue 1), for instance; or a materialist account of motivation and the validity of ethics (issue 2); or how some reductive account of the way coloured surfaces trigger a certain reaction in the brain can make sense of our response to Rembrandt (issue 3).

Here are three nodal points around which the swirling debates in our culture gather. Here are three forms of human achievement which most people want somehow to hold on to, to defend as possible. A major question for all positions which take their stand in immanence, whether materialistic or not, is: how can one account for the specific force of creative agency, or ethical demands, or for the power of artistic experience, without speaking in terms of some transcendent being or force which interpellates us? And this question is further modulated by whatever we believe human motivation consists in. The more we feel bound by our ontological beliefs to approximate our nature to that of other animals, the more difficult or contested our account is going to be. But in general these positions try to give an intra-psychic account of the force of our ethical and aesthetic experience.

Freud is a good example. On one hand, one of his favourite sayings was: "das Moralische versteht sich von selbst" (morality is self-evident),[2] giving expression to the seemingly obvious link between scientific disengagement and the modern moral order which I mentioned a few paragraphs ago. On the other, he opened a whole new hermeneutic field in which the appeal for us of works of art could be understood in terms of our intra-psychic economy.

Here are three fields of polarization, or cross pressure, which are operative on the contemporary scene. They take their start from some doctrine, or perhaps feature of contemporary society, that can plausibly be presented as a consequence, or at least an accompaniment, of the decline of religion, but which many people find repugnant or unacceptable. Reductive materialism was this starting point in the examples we have just discussed. This point is, of course, at first grist for the mill of the defenders of orthodoxy, and is taken up as such. But it frequently happens that those who object to it also include many who reject this orthodoxy. Hence the cross pressure.

This might make more persuasive my claim that the debate in our society has to be understood as suspended between the extreme positions, of orthodox religion and (in contemporary terms) materialist atheism. It is not that middle positions don't abound; not even that the number of people in such positions are not very considerable. It is rather that these positions define themselves (as we always do) by what they reject, and in our case, this almost invariably includes the extreme positions. Our culture would have to have evolved out of all recognition, were either of these to drop so far out of sight that this would no longer be true. In this sense, the cross pressure defines the whole culture.

We can also see how my claim that the culture is suspended between the extreme positions in no way involves that all, or even most, of its members are. Most people may be ensconced in a relatively untroubled way in one or other position, whether extreme or middle. That is not the point, which is rather that these positions themselves are defined in a field in which the extreme ones, transcendental religion on one hand, and reductive materialism on the other, are crucial reference points.

As well as inspiring the creation of new positions, new ways of rejecting religion which avoid the repugnant consequence, these cross pressures can lead to a condition where many people hesitate for a long time in their attitude to religion. The previous paragraphs offer examples of new creations. But a movement to and fro, and/or a long term hesitancy can also result.

Take for example the savage violation of human rights perpetrated by the Nazi régime. In response to this violent rejection of what people were willing to call the standards of "Christian civilization" (even very unorthodox figures like Winston Churchill), there was a movement of return to religion in many European countries after the War. In Germany, the protection of religion was seen as a bulwark of human rights. Fifty years of European secularity, and the rise of religiously-inspired terrorism, have persuaded quite a number that there is no such tight connection. And yet still many Germans whose outlook is quite secular continue to pay the confessional tax which they could easily relieve themselves of by declaring themselves *konfessionslos*. When asked why, they often reply that "they want the church to give moral guidance for their children," or that "they see the church as important for the moral fabric of society".[3]

We find a similar pattern among many Québécois parents after the "Quiet Revolution". They had utterly ceased to practise themselves, but they were reluctant to abandon religious education in the schools, lest their children lose their sense of values.

But where they don't lead simply to prolonged uncertainty or havering, cross pressures of this kind have been responsible for a host of new positions, which constitute what I have been calling the "Nova". We are torn between an anti-Christian thrust and a repulsion towards some (to us) extreme form of reduction; so we invent new positions. In a sense, even the original Deist impersonal order can be seen in this light, because it didn't want to let go of the goodness of creation as a Lucretian-inspired atheism would have.

And there are other lines of cross pressure in our world, with other starting points, that is notions or forms of life which have been generated along with the rejection of religion, and which many people recoil from, even those who no longer want to accept the old religion. One such starting point is a doctrinaire utilitarianism, where all value is homogenized in terms of utility consequences, and the difference between higher and lower motivations denied. From its first appearance, this provoked a reaction, notably expressed by Rousseau, followed by Kant, and alive today in the various versions of neo-Kantianism. Another, connected starting point is a thoroughgoing stance towards nature and the world as simply instrument and raw material for human purposes. The reactions against this are evident, above all in the ramifying ecological movements, and also in the anguished questioning about the limits of medical research and engineering of the human make-up. Many of those who raise these questions are believers, but many are not, but find themselves seeking common ground with those who are.

One of the key human motivations I mentioned above that almost everyone wants to find a place for was the moral one. But there is another reaction against the disciplined moral order of modernity, which sees this as what we need to escape. The disciplines of morality or good order threaten to crush our spontaneity, or our creativity, or our desiring natures. We find a rebellion of this kind in the Romantic period, and with Nietzsche it takes the radical form of a debunking rejection of modern morality itself, with its privileging of equality, happiness, the reduction of suffering. This morality was the enemy of the controlled unleashing of the Will to Power, where Apollonian order would be at the service of Dionysian force. Nietzsche propounded a new ethic, but it was one in which the moral as defined in Western modernity had no place. This is one source of what I described above as the "immanent counter-Enlightenment".

The consequences of this protest in the art, culture and thought of the West have been very important. The search for the Dionysian has been continuing and attractive, through such twentieth century thinkers as Bataille and Foucault, among others. But this has been the source of another dimension of cross pressure. It is not just that features of the Nietzschean critique can be appropriated by religious critics of modern liberal civilization (e.g., Mounier in *L'Affrontement Chrétien*).[4] It is also that most moderns cannot but feel a profound allegiance at least to the basic principles of the modern moral order. Hence the attempts by contemporary neo-Nietzscheans to couple their critique of discipline and order with a radical critique of modern society as based on power and inequality. We see this in one way with Foucault and Connolly,[5] in another with Derrida.

2

In these cross-pressured fields, what is the debate ultimately about? One crucial choice which the immanent frame offers us is whether or not to believe in some transcendent source or power; for many people in our Western culture, the choice is whether to believe in God. To many it may not seem like a choice, because it has been foreclosed by their milieu, or their affinities, or their deep moral orientations; but the culture of immanence itself leaves the choice open; it is not foreclosed by undeniable arguments. Many however, end up taking a stand one way or another. What are the crucial issues determining this stand?

In the last chapter, I described various narratives of secularity; I told these stories partly to show that there is no apodictic proof here, but also to show what is attractive to its proponents about various forms of unbelief. As I indicated in the previous section, I believe that there is no escaping some version of what I called in an earlier discussion "fullness"; for any liveable understanding of human life, there must be some way in which this life looks good, whole, proper, really being lived as it should. The utter absence of some such would leave us in abject, unbearable despair. So it's not that unbelief shuns Christian ideas of fullness for nothing at all; it has its own versions.

The swirling debate between belief and unbelief, as well as between different versions of each, can therefore be seen as a debate about what real fullness consists in. The debate has two facets. Take a debate between two kinds of unbelief; on one hand, a standard utilitarian position; beings have certain needs and desires: for instance, prosperity, a family where people grow up healthy and adjusted, good times with friends and family; and against this, we have one of those heroic positions, which in our culture often owe a great deal to Friedrich Nietzsche: for instance, that ordinary happiness is a "pitiable comfort" (ein erbärmliches Behagen), there is something much higher in life. Or it might be the heroic humanism of a Dr. Rieux, in Camus' *La Peste,* who acts for the good of his fellow creatures, in spite of the absurd, even in the last instance, the ultimate futility of all such action.

So on one level, it seems that the "heroic" critique to, say, a Humean is that the satisfactions she seeks for self and others are real, but there is something higher in life which she is missing out on. But the critique in the other direction seems to take up a different issue: it calls into question the supposed satisfaction itself. The sense of a "high" that the heroic figure finds in his action is seen as suspect. The charge might be (and often is) that the "high" here consists largely of a self-dramatization; we play a drama to ourselves in which are lonely heroes; it is all a great show. In fact, what it covers over is an inability to find satisfaction in the ordinary human pleasures and fulfillments. There is some maladjustment here; perhaps the person is unable to commit to a stable relationship; perhaps he needs the adrenaline of high-risk action; he is unable to love; this is how the critique might run. The alleged fulfillment would itself be branded as unreal, non-genuine.

There is a parallel among Christians. There are some that claim the superiority of the vocations of self-denial over the ordinary ones, in this way analogous to the heroic stance of a Nietzsche. Most people would probably agree that the real Christian position sees both as potentially genuine. But a critique could still be made of someone who embraced such a "heroic" vocation that his motivation was impure; his real motivation in entering it was the sense of superiority it conferred; and that would not be the real "fulfillment" here; it would be to this extent a non-genuine simulacrum.

So one kind of critique says: I see a genuine fullness here, that is, something which is deeper, solider than the run of ordinary life, but I want to point out that there are things which yield a still higher, deeper, more powerful fullness; you shouldn't be making your present fullness the whole goal of your life. Then there is another critique which says: I see the kind of fullness you're supposing, and I also see that you are getting some kick out of this, but the two are not the same. You think you're getting fulfillment, but you're fooling yourself, passing yourself off with a simulacrum. This, either because although there is a genuine variety of this fullness, you haven't got it (the case of the ascetic monk who is getting a high out of being so heroic and self-denying); or more radically, because this kind of fullness is a mirage: a possible Humean critique of Nietzsche, for instance: the whole thing is a self-played drama, which covers something much less admirable.

And this is, of course, also the form of the Nietzschean critique of Christianity: you think you are renouncing out of love, but in fact your motives are a witch's brew concocted of fear, envy, resentment and hatred for the powerful, beautiful and successful.

We might think that the first kind of critique is reserved to the "downward" direction, where "higher" aspirations rate "lower" ones—where both sides might agree to this way of ranking, although the Humeans would use these words in ironic scare quotes. While the debunking critique generally proceeds "upward". But this isn't necessarily so. Take the clever, successful, fast-living dealer in images (say, in advertising). He may have a great sense of satisfaction in having been clever enough to devise immensely successful advertising slogans, which have made various rather ordinary products fashionable. He has made money, attracted women, achieved a certain fame; he is capable of working hard, and then playing hard in fashionable resorts. This is real living. Like Nietzsche, he sees that not everybody can hack this, most people's lives are enmired in grayness, but his glitters.

A "downward" critique, say, from someone whose entrepreneurial effort includes building inexpensive but effective wells for villagers in the Sahel, might brand this as non-genuine; on analogous grounds to some of the "upwards" critiques above: the satisfaction depends on how you play it to yourself, or how you can get an admiring audience to see it; it is all tinsel, or smoke and mirrors. The fashionable products don't really increase human welfare. It's all a game we play with ourselves and a like-minded milieu, in this respect like the faux heroics of the lonely warrior. Meanwhile, you're sacrificing real things: really useful production, real relationships in a series of glitzy affairs, real enjoyment of nature in the life-style of the resort. And the proof of all this is that it can't last; it can't fill a whole life; when the powers fade, it leaves emptiness behind.

Something analogous was the thrust of the Augustinian Christian critique of the pagan life of warrior fame and glory. The fulfillments of pride are all judged as, ultimately, empty.

We can see that the debate here is about what has been called "the ends of life". It is an ethical debate, continuous with the one we find Plato and Aristotle intervening in at their time. And it concerns both what proposed possibilities are real: can people really renounce out of love, and not always just fear-resentment? Can the life of glitz be made to last forever?; and partly what real possibilities are genuine fulfillments, or the highest such fulfillments. These two aspects are inextricably interwoven.

The debate between metaphysico-religious positions is driven mainly by people's sense of their ethical predicament in this sense. It is this which largely determines the positions they adopt, those they turn away from, the conversions they undergo from one to another; the cross-pressure they feel between two which are both unacceptable, which pushes them to devise a new position, and which drives the Nova. Even when it seems to be driven by something else, and perhaps partly is, an important role is being played by this debate. This is what I argued above in the case of conversions to unbelief which seem to turn on (and in the mouths of the converts are said to be decided) by a thought of the kind: "science has proven . . ."—e.g., that everything is matter, that God cannot exist. I argued that even there, a crucial role is played by our sense of the human moral predicament, that is, both our attraction to the ethic of the austere, courageous knower of reality, and our sense that our residual draw to faith was less an indication of a real possibility than a residual weakness, a craving for comfort in face of the meaningless world.

The ethical dimension of the debate is clearly in evidence when we look at the important forms of religion today: for instance, the "neo-Durkheimian form" where religion is part of political identity; and/or the sense that religion is a crucial bulwark of a civilizational-moral way of life. What we are identifying with in both cases—what our nation stands for, our way of life—has a crucial ethical dimension. But there is a sense in which the ethical debate can't be entered into in its purest form in these cases. Our attachment to a certain ethical definition of fullness is bolstered by our belonging to a broader society to which we sense an emotional allegiance, and this brings other motivations into play, those of identity pride, for instance, which may be alien to the ethic which supposedly defines us.

Imagine someone who feels himself to be part of a "nation under God" (a certain American identity), or une République laïque (French Jacobin). It becomes all the harder for such people to change their ethico-religious views—to become agnostic in the first case, Catholic in the second—because they feel they are betraying their identity and their comrades-in-identity. Underlying this, is something less mentionable by either, that they feel they belong to a superior kind of human being in virtue of their belonging each to their own kind of republic, farther ahead than the rest of the human race, who do not really enjoy liberty, or reason and liberty, equality, fraternity.

Now the point is *not* that espousing the ethical position and belonging to a society go together. They almost always do, and certainly for a Christian becoming a believer means belonging to the Church. The problem is that the motivations which arise around my membership and militate against my changing my ethical views may not be those which the ethical position declares central. Take the American: to remain Christian out of chauvinistic pride in American superiority would hardly be to act for Christian reasons. And even the more laudable sense of solidarity would have to have its limits, in the case that the U.S. was wreaking serious harm in the world. We would have the makings of an "upwards" critique analogous to that mentioned above, where a possible fulfillment in an ascetic vocation is being missed because the motive for engaging in it is wrong.

And a similar point can be made concerning both the pride and solidarity of the Jacobin. Perhaps a certain way of dealing with religion (headscarves in schools) is not right, even though it seems impeccably "republican" and "laïque". Where should the real principles of equality and human rights tell you to come down?

It follows, of course, that the motivations for sticking with a doctrine because I want to stick with a Church can also be deviant to the doctrine. This is too obvious a phenomenon to need further argument. Christian history is full of Church chauvinism.

My main point here is not to berate such chauvinism (though a severe critique cannot do any harm in our present predicament), but to point out that the struggle with this issue as a clearly ethico-religious struggle, where one is forced to weigh what fulfillments are genuine and possible, and which are higher, can only with difficulty take place in such a context. Other, alien motivations systematically intervene. It is this systematic nature which makes the difference. Alien motivations are always intervening as we struggle with these issues, but not in a massive and organized way as they do where identities are at stake.

A similar point can be made by people who think that religion is essential for civilizational-moral order, even when they don't identify and take pride in it (say, the French nobility after the Restoration, who switched from incredulity to at least overt belief, chastened by the experience of the Revolution). Here again, something alien, that is, a fear of social disorder, tends to muddy the water of any inward ethico-religious debate.

Now since more and more people in our day have been shaken out of either religiously defined neo-Durkheimian identities, or else a marriage of religion with civilizational-moral order (both, for instance, have decisively weakened in Europe), more and more people are in a space where they can be induced to reconsider whatever their position has been, in relative freedom from alien considerations. These still impinge (how can I disappoint mother when I don't go to communion? How will I face the guys when I do?), but they are less likely to be merged and confused with genuinely valid reasons to go one way or another.

I want to stress again that the crucial debate in modern culture turns not just on rival notions of fullness, but on conceptions of our ethical predicament. As I argued in the last chapter, this latter conception is broader. It includes not only an understanding of fullness, but also:

(a) Some idea of what the motivations are which can carry us towards it; these may sometimes be implicit in the very notion of fullness—as in the Christian case where agape is both path and destination—but this is not always so.
(b) The motivations which bar our way to it: we saw that this was a locus of a key issue for those who felt that science had refuted their faith; their tendency to be moved by certain thoughts or images towards belief was branded as an obstacle to the adult goal of correct, responsible belief.

(c) There will also be some notion of how integrally fullness can be achieved; is it merely an ultimate, even utopian ideal which no human will reach in its entirety, but which can be approximated? Or is an integral transformation possible which will realize it totally? The goal of serenity in a troubled world, as conceived by exclusive humanism, is often one of the first type, whereas the end of detachment as understood in Buddhism is conceived as a complete transformation.

(d) Closely related to (c) is another cluster of issues: to what extent can the negative motivations under (b) be vanquished? Will they always remain, although they can be diminished? Or can they really be transformed, or gone beyond? Plainly Buddhism and also Christianity make the latter claim, but some versions of exclusive humanism do so too, while others clearly do not. Marxism, following an important strand in Rousseau, seemed to promise that humans would quite overcome their attachment to private interest distinct from the general good; but various modes of liberalism see this prospect as utterly illusory.

(e) Closely linked to (d) is another issue: if the negative motivations (b) cannot be utterly set aside, what are the costs of denying or over-riding them? Does this require serious sacrifice, even mutilation of human life?

All of these aspects may be taken up in the debate. (b) already figured in our account of conversions to scientific materialism, but we will see how issues (a), as well as (c), (d), and (e), can be sites of controversy, as we look at certain facets of this debate, as we see it around us in our culture.

3

Obviously, a whole book needs to be written about this, to add to those which have been, because a lot remains to be said in this domain. But I have space here only to indicate certain general features of the debate, the ones which emerge as salient out of the story—the "master narrative"—that I've been telling here.

Reverting to the dimensions of cross pressure, (1)–(3), mentioned above, holders of the intermediate positions shy away from materialist reductionism, because of some crucial feature of fullness—our being active, creative agents; our being moral subjects; our ability to respond to beauty—which they see as incompatible with the reductionist ontology. But the question can still be put: can you really give ontological space for these features short of admitting what you still want to deny, for instance, some reference to the transcendent, or to a larger cosmic force, or whatever? In other words is the intermediate position really viable?

This is an issue in category (a) above, in the sense that it asks whether we can make sense of the motivations which our understanding of fullness supposes.

Take the third area for example, that of our being moved by beauty, in art and nature. One kind of question is this: can the experience be made sense of in an ontology excluding the transcendent? At first blush, it appears obvious that it can, at least in part. Take a theory like Freud's, where the force for us of certain works of art is explained in terms of the feelings which arise in the depths of our psyche. Once we grant that something like the Oedipal drama is an essential phase of our psychic development, how could its evocation in *Oedipus Rex* fail to evoke tremors and a profound sense of recognition in the spectators?

Again, I mentioned earlier how nineteenth and twentieth century materialism recaptures some of the sense of wonder and depth in contemplating the whole of nature which we could find in the ancient world in the writings of Lucretius. The wonder is not only at the stupendous whole, but at the way in which we emerge, in one way fragile and insignificant, and yet capable of grasping this whole. Pascal's theme of the human being as a thinking reed can be played as well in an atheist and materialist register. One can even say that a kind of piety arises here, in which we recognize that for all our detachment in objectivating thought, we ultimately belong to this whole, and return to it. In the moving obituary for his colleague and mentor, William Hamilton, Richard Dawkins writes of his friend's wish at his death "to be laid out on the forest floor in the Amazon jungle and interred by burying beetles as food for their larvae":

> "Later, in their children, reared with care by horned parents out of fist-sized balls moulded from my flesh, I will escape. No worm for me, or sordid fly: rearranged and multiple, I will at last buzz from the soil like bees out of a nest—indeed, buzz louder than bees, almost like a swarm of motor bikes. I shall be borne, beetle by flying beetle, out into the Brazilian wilderness beneath the stars."[6]

One might say, that so articulated, this sense of wonder, and piety of belonging, is not just compatible with a naturalist, immanentist perspective, it supposes it; it is an intrinsic part of such a perspective.

If we think of this sense of wonder as at least in part aesthetic (the piety verges perhaps on the "religious"), then does not this example, like the previous Freudian one, put paid to doubts about finding space for our aesthetic experience (of both beauty and the sublime) within an immanentist ontology; in the case of

Dawkins and Hamilton, even a materialist one? Undoubtedly yes, but as I said above, only in part.

I say this, first because the power and genuineness of this experience of wonder doesn't exclude the possibility that something similar, perhaps even richer, might be recovered in the register of religious belief, as we see for example with Pascal. And second, there are other modes of aesthetic experience, whose power seems inseparable from their epiphanic nature, that is their revealing something beyond themselves, even beyond nature as we ordinarily know it. Bede Griffith's experience that I cited in the first chapter would be an example. And there are certain works of art—by Dante, Bach, the makers of Chartres Cathedral: the list is endless—whose power seems inseparable from their epiphanic, transcendent reference. Here the challenge is to the unbeliever, to find a non-theistic register in which to respond to them, without impoverishment.

Of course, it is not an easily decidable question, whether such registers can be found; certainly it is hard to arbitrate inter-subjectively, although each one of us has a reading of his/her own experience which inclines us to our own answer. And it is the harder because of the feature of post-Romantic art which I mentioned in an earlier chapter, whose subtler language allows us to manifest an order in things while leaving our ontological commitments relatively indeterminate. The way in which Wordsworth could be the paradigm poet for so many in the nineteenth century, across an ontological spectrum ranging from orthodox Christians to atheists, including Eliot and Hardy, illustrates this point.

But we can also see the cross pressure here in the place that poetry and their love of it held in the lives of many unbelievers. Not only Wordsworth, but especially Hardy and Housman (the latter much read by Hamilton, according to Dawkins).[7] It is interesting that a major articulator of contemporary unbelief, faced with the accusation that his age and milieu are lacking depth, points to its love of Hardy and Housman.[8]

I am not claiming in any way to decide the issue here about aesthetic experience, only to point out the considerations which weigh with each one of us, as we find ourselves leaning one way or another. And I would like to make some remarks about the second issue above, that of moral agency, in the same spirit. The question arises here of what ontology can underpin our moral commitments, which for most of us constitute a crucial "fulfillment", in the sense I'm using it here, that is, a mode of the higher, of fullness which we are called on to realize.[9] The birth of a middle position like Kant's comes from the negative judgment, that a purely materialist ontology, as well as a utilitarian account of ethics, cannot make sense of our moral experience.

This kind of issue continues as a live question for us; parallel to the case of aesthetic experience, we can ask what ontology do we need to make sense of our ethical or moral lives, properly understood. The Kantian solution itself can be challenged on these grounds, especially in relation to its reliance on the notion of principle or law, as well as its radical distinction between feeling (inclination) and moral motivation.

I'd like to mention another example here, this time of a challenge which has been levelled against a neo-Humean reconstruction of morality. I raise this because it touches on a theme which has emerged as central in my narrative, a crucial feature of the Modern Moral Order as it has come to be understood, its endorsing of universal human rights and welfare as one of our crucial goals. I want to understand this as our stepping into a wider, qualitatively different sense of inter-human solidarity, involving a break and partial replacement of earlier, narrower ties. In this respect, the move is analogous to certain precedent ones in history, inaugurated, for instance, by the Buddha, by Stoicism, by the New Testament preaching ("In Christ is neither Jew nor Greek, slave nor free, male nor female"), and by Muhammad. The break consists not only in that we greatly extend the range of solidarity, but also in that what it means to be bound together changes, often radically. It is one thing to be part of a differentiated, hierarchical society of orders, quite another to be citizen of a modern "nation". The relationship of "fraternité", as understood in the Revolution, only applied in this latter, horizontal space. It was intrinsically tied to the other terms in the trinity: "Liberté, Égalité, Fraternité".

The Humean understanding of this same historical development, in terms of our innate tendency to sympathy, sees this as moving from the narrower circles in which we lived at the beginning of history, and extending gradually as we collaborate in larger and larger circles, and hence enlarge our horizons, ending ultimately with (what we now call) "globalization", in a universal ethic.[10] There is no sense of the qualitative break in this account, of the sense of acceding to the higher that we experience when we break from or relativize a narrower and lower belonging for a higher solidarity.

I am thinking of the sense that Ernest Hemingway articulated in *For Whom the Bell Tolls,* experienced by his protagonist Robert Jordan:

a feeling of consecration to a duty toward all of the oppressed of the world that would be as difficult and embarrassing to speak about as religious experience and yet it was as authentic as the feeling you had when you heard Bach, or stood in Chartres Cathedral or the Cathedral at Leòn and saw the light coming through the great windows.[11]

I don't want to pursue this point to an utterly convincing conclusion. More pertinently, I don't think I can. I just want to identify the kind of issue at stake here:

whether our moral or ethical life, properly understood, can really be captured by the accounts which fit with our favoured ontology. In this case, we are starting from Hume's attempt to understand morality as a species of "natural" human sentiment among others, rather than as something that reason perceives as an intrinsically higher demand. The issue I raise here, without definitively answering, is whether such a "naturalist" account can make sense of the phenomenology of universalism, the sense of breaking out of an earlier space and acceding to a higher one, the sense of liberation, even exaltation which accompanies this move. The same question could be raised about a sociobiological account, which supposes a tendency in us, induced by evolution, to act in solidarity with our in-group, often through savage hostility to outsiders; and then explains the development of a universalist ethic by the gradual extension of what we define as the "in-group".

The issue of what causes, or lies behind, or (if this is possible) justifies these qualitative shifts in the space of solidarity, together with the sense of moral ascent, remains unresolved to general satisfaction (though I have my own—theistic—hunches). But I put it on the table here, first, in order to illustrate the kind of issue, parallel to the ones about concerning aesthetics, which arises also for ethics: the issue of how to align our best phenomenology with an adequate ontology, how to resolve a seeming lack of fit such as the one just described, either by enriching one's ontology, or by revising or challenging the phenomenology. And I raise it second, because this phenomenon of a qualitative step in space and nature of solidarity is one of the crucial features of modernity, which stands out in the story about secularity which I have been telling. I want to raise the whole issue of how to do justice to this step later on from another angle. But first, I turn to another important aspiration of modernity which this account has made central.

I refer to the aspiration to wholeness, particularly as it emerges in the reaction against the disciplined, buffered self in the Romantic period. The protest here is that the rational, disengaged agent is sacrificing something essential in realizing his ideals. What is sacrificed is often described as spontaneity or creativity, but it is even more frequently identified with our feelings, and our bodily existence. Taking Schiller as a paradigm example, the complaint is that our rational, formal power of abstract thinking, and of positing moral rules, has dominated and suppressed feeling, the demands of bodily existence, the concrete form, and the beautiful. The remedy is not just to reverse the priority, and sacrifice reason for feeling, or even to reach some kind of fair trade-off between them. It is rather, to move to a higher stage in which the drive to form and the drive to content ("Stofftrieb") are harmoniously united. This is in fact a realm of freedom, but also of beauty, which together constitute what Schiller calls "play".

There might seem a problem with taking a writer of the 1790s, critical of narrow rationalism, as articulating a generally accepted aspiration of our civilization. Surely the followers of Schiller and Goethe are only one party, in standing polemic with the aspirants to rational control and instrumental reason within modern culture. Yes, but this aspiration, not to sacrifice the bodily, the sensual, is something more general, and it surfaces among the partisans of maximal instrumental reason as well. What else should this reason aim at than the maximization of human desire? And doesn't this require that we set aside all hankering after illusory "higher" goals, like spiritual purity, or the dedication to virtue? So argued the proponents of the radical Enlightenment. These too were aiming at wholeness and harmony; only they proposed to reach it not by synthesizing a drive to higher form with desire; but rather by debunking all such higher drives, and finding a way to render all sensual, ordinary desires compatible with each other, both within and between human agents.

So the demand for wholeness, which forbids us to sacrifice the body, becomes central to much of the culture which we inherit from the eighteenth century, albeit this goal is conceived in radically different ways. Let's look at the crucial difference. For the radical Enlightenment, for Helvétius, Holbach, Bentham, not sacrificing the body meant giving ordinary sensual desire its outlet, its space where it could be fulfilled on its own terms. Of course, this would mean that some of the negative features which attach to this in our society, where we are pitted against others, and forced to grab what we want in opposition to others, would be overcome in the rational organization of society. But there would be no question of transforming sensual desire itself.

In the Schillerian model, by contrast, this desire is transformed. What it is when in conflict with the drive to form is one thing; what emerges when the two are fused or harmonized is another. Desire is fused with higher meaning when it unites with form, and this yields beauty.

Each side sees the other as deviating from the common goal. For the radicals, any talk of fusing or transforming desire is just another attempt to sideline the sensual in the name of some specious "higher". For the followers of Schiller, leaving desire in its untransformed state is precisely abandoning it to its degraded form. This can't be what it means to rescue the body.

This is one of the deepest unresolved issues of our modern Western culture, which surfaced again in the sexual revolution of the later twentieth century. In a sense its roots go back to the very foundations of this culture. In one way, one could argue that this understanding of wholeness which has to include a crucial place for the body is a legacy of our Christian civilization. Certainly, it would not have been conceivable in the spiritual outlook of late Hellenic and Roman civilization, which Christian faith then partly transformed, in the way I described above (Chapter 7), the transformation so well charted by Peter Brown.[12] But then on the other hand, the development of Reformed Christianity and on a longer scale, of post-Axial religion in general, has worked to sideline the body again.

Let's take the longer perspective first and look at what the Axial turn involved. Viewing this schematically (perhaps over simply) we might say: "Before" we have religious life in an enchanted world, but also a kind of acceptance of the two sides of things: the way the world (and hence also some gods/spirits) can be gracious, giving, sources of blessing; and in other ways (with other, or even sometimes the same gods/spirits) can be harsh, cruel, destructive. In the formulation of a contemporary scholar, the outlook was that:

> There will always be light and dark, hot and cold, night and day. Duality was the way the world was, and there is no disputing or changing that. From their point of view, these opposing forces had to exist for there to have been a world. The constant conflict and interplay of good and evil, light and dark, night and day, was a given and not something to try to resist. It was the nature of the universe.[13]

Over against this, the Axial religions offered routes of escaping/taming/overcoming this maelstrom of opposed forces. They offered a path towards a fuller, higher good.

In many cases, it was a good quite beyond ordinary human flourishing, and perhaps even incompatible with making this flourishing our highest end (e.g., Buddhist anatta). But it promised a transformation in which we would find our deepest and fullest end in this higher good, and even one in which the struggle of forces would be transcended (the lion lying down with the lamb), or tamed into a coherent, harmonious order (Confucian human-heartedness).

This introduced a tremendous strain and conflict into religious life, which wrack higher civilizations. The highest aspirations can be seen as just denying, crushing ordinary human desire, often branded as impulses that reduce us, or alienate us. There are two facets to their doing this. One is that they deny these desires, hem them in, demand that people control and restrict them very severely: for instance, they demand that their followers live up to a sexual ethic in which much must be renounced; or else that unruly warrior societies be pacified, aggression strongly controlled and reigned in, pride humbled. This is the facet of ethical demands.

The other side of these reforms we might call the "disenchanting" facet. These impulses are seen in purely negative terms. They are obstacles to the good. They are denied any depth resonance in the spiritual world.

For instance, in earlier periods sexual intercourse could be connected to the higher world through rituals and institutions like temple prostitution and sacred marriage. At the same time, in archaic, pre-Axial forms, ritual in war[14] or sacrifice consecrates violence; it relates violence to the sacred, and gives a kind of numinous depth to killing and the excitements and inebriation of killing; just as it does through the rituals mentioned above for sexual desire and union.

In other words, what we call today sex and violence could also be ways of connecting to the spirits/gods or the higher world. We could resonate with this world also in these dimensions of life. The corollary is that the higher world has both kinds of Gods, cruel and lascivious, as well as kind and chaste; Aphrodite and Mars, as well as Artemis and Athena. This is the moral "ambivalence" of the pre-Axial world I referred to above.

With the coming of "higher", post-Axial religions, this kind of numinous endorsement is more and more withdrawn. We move towards a point where, in some religions, violence has no more place at all in the sanctified life, or its analogues. This is true of Christianity, of Buddhism; and we find in Hinduism a steady spread of the demands of ahimsa, so that even jatis who were previously allowed and expected to kill animals, now try to rise through abandoning these practices.

This is the double wound suffered by these whole registers of human desire, inflicted by the high aspirations of post-Axial religion: ethical suppression, on one hand, and a disenchanting reduction to a mere impulse to vice, on the other, whose only significance is the negative one, that it stands in the way of virtue.

No wonder there is a continued rebellion against this wound. Suppressed modes of fulfillment return, even in enchanted form, in the "higher" religions. Carnival is one example. Another range can be seen in the whole gamut of forms of holy war. Various forms of sanctified and purifying violence recur, as we see in Christendom with the Crusades. This now seems to us profoundly at odds with the spirit of Christianity, a spirit which early mediaeval bishops were aware of on one level, when they tried to restrain noble bellicosity, and proclaim truces of God. But they were nevertheless induced to preach Crusades by falling back into scapegoat mode: the infidel was the servant of darkness, and therefore deserved the most utter hostility, in the name of the Prince of Peace.

In our day, modern unbelief often reacts to the wound by taking up the cause of "paganism".[15] It defends desire against the Christian demand for transformation. Various facets of the Enlightenment can be seen in this light.[16] There is a debunking materialist and utilitarian version, as with Helvétius. It revokes the ethical suppression of sensuality; but it ignores the disenchanting facet; rather it reinforces it. Desire is just desire. And the same thing recurs in Kant. Both Utilitarianism and Kantianism can be seen as a continuation of post-Axial reform with a vengeance. Sex may be seen as a natural fulfillment, as long as it doesn't get in the way of the morality of mutual respect. Violence is usually seen in a totally negative light. In our society, one often hears proposals to train it out of children by forbidding war toys, and shaming young men.

On the other hand, many Romantics took up paganism in a deeper sense, wanting to undo the disenchantment of desire, as well as the ethical suppression. So there is a nostalgia for older rituals, and societies in which these rituals were central, and they integrated us through our desire and fulfillment with nature and the cosmos. And so we have the powerful category of the "Dionysian", championed most famously by Nietzsche, but also evident in Bataille, Deleuze, Foucault and others. This is not just a call for release of desire, sexual as well as violent and destructive, but also the attempt to recover a profound resonance of these desires, the way they can offer us escape from our disciplinary prison into ecstasy. The sense is that we are too much in our heads, we are deeply excarnated, and we need to undo this. These modes of escape have a deep analogy—at least a felt resonance for us moderns—to earlier pre-Axial rituals. Think of the tumultuous, conflictual reception of "Le Sacre du Printemps" in Paris in 1913.[17]

At its worst—blindest, deafest, densest, say, materialist utilitarianism—Western modernity suppresses both poles of the religious. It inflicts the double wound on the pre-Axial; and it pours scorn on post-Axial religions. But we might see it as another kind of post-Axial reform, seeking to establish a form of life which is unqualifiedly good, another mode of harmonious order. It is perhaps the most insensitive of all post-Axial forms towards the resonances of the pre-Axial. Like many other such post-Axial forms, it is intolerant of its rivals, the religions, even as these often are of each other.

And even under the rule of well-ordered liberal societies, the repressed returns: scapegoating violence, fascination with sexual vice.

I have been trying to put the aspiration to wholeness, and to the rescue of the body, in the context of this longue durée of our religious history. But I want now to place it in relation to the shorter history which has been the main subject of this book, the various movements of Reform in Latin Christendom. In fact what I left out of the potted history of the last paragraphs was the way that various post-Axial religions have tried to avoid the movement to what I call "excarnation", the transfer of our religious life out of bodily forms of ritual, worship, practice, so that it comes more and more to reside "in the head". The resistance to excarnation takes various forms. Yogic practice is one example. But we also see a host of earlier rituals which have been continued with a new meaning or transformed. In the classic equilibrium of the "higher" civilizations, prior to the Reform of Latin Christendom, many of the pre-Axial forms of collective ritual were integrated into the new religion; and the new disciplines of the minority of religious "virtuosi" also had an important place for bodily expression; not just yogic practice, but also the rituals and forms of cenobitic life.

The aim is, not to return to the earlier sacralizations of sex and violence, but to find new forms of collective ritual; rites of passage; individual and small group disciplines of prayer, fasting, devotion; modes of marking time; new ways of living conjugal sexual life; and new works of healing and sharing, which could give bodily and at times public expression to the worship of God; or the search for Nirvana, or for Moksha.

In the (for me crucial) case of Pre-Reformation Latin Christendom, there were the specifically Christian celebration of the Mass, the rituals of the liturgical year, like Candlemas, and "creeping to the Cross" on Good Friday; the Christian rites of passage; a new sexual ethic; an ambivalent attitude to war; a definition of the "corporal works of mercy" institutionalized in the life of certain religious orders. And then, of course, there were a whole host of ceremonies and rituals which bespoke a pre-Christian origin, albeit somewhat transformed and integrated into Church practice, but these trailed off into a contested margin, where things went on which were highly suspect to the clergy, and of dubious evangelical warrant.

But this equilibrium, like all those of the "higher" civilizations issuing from the Axial revolution, was very unstable. It was not just the semi-pagan fringe of dubious practices to ward off spirits or ensure good health, or a marriage partner which gave offense. It was also that the high post-Axial demands sat uneasily with the life most people led. The high sexual ethic never quite fit with the actual ethic of peasant communities. They agreed in condemning adultery, but not about pre-marital sex, as I mentioned in an earlier chapter. Not to speak of the way in which the clergy and monks themselves failed to live up to their vows; or the way in which earthly power could turn the "magic" of the Church to its own ends, bolstering political power and élite privilege; or inversely, clerical power could try to accumulate property and subjugate the political.

It is easy to see how this pre-Reformation condition could seem negatively to justify the most radical Reform. But in fact the direction of this Reform was towards a far-reaching excarnation; that is one of the main contentions of this book. Older pre-Axial practices were swept away in a wide-ranging disenchantment. Among Protestants, the central ritual of the Mass was abolished as itself an example of illicit "magic". Carnival was suppressed. The uses of music, dancing, drama, were curtailed to various degrees of severity in the Church, and often put under heavy pressure in lay society. Some rites of passage were abolished or downgraded (marriage ceased to be a sacrament for some Protestant churches).

At the same time, a disengaged stance of rational analysis and control towards the self introduces another facet of excarnation. As Descartes argued, we need to distance ourselves from our embodied understanding of things, in order to achieve clear and distinct knowledge. Right action is then understood as what emerges from this clear understanding. So it is not defined as what comes from properly ordered desire, but rather as what disengaged reason demands of desire, to which desire has to be trained to be docile.[18]

If we think of the three levels of human linguistic-communicative activity in its broadest sense: one of bodily habitus and mimicry, one of symbolic expression in art, poetry, music, dance; and one of prose, descriptive language; we can say that ab-original religious life was mainly couched in the first two, but that the culture which emerges from modern Western Reform has largely abandoned these, and confines itself to the third. In this way, it parallels what modern disengaged reason has done to morality. In both cases, the key is to grasp correct prepositional truth—about God and his Christ in one case, about correct action in the other. In the first case, right worship follows, but the forms that it takes are secondary, and can be varied at will. In the second case, a successful imposition of reason brings about right action, but what this amounts to is to be known purely by reason—either the calculation of utility consequences, or the universalizability of the maxim. In no case, is a paradigm bodily emotion seen as *criterial* for right action—as in the case of New Testament agape.

I have offered a caricature of modern Western religion; or rather, an ideal type which defines a direction that much of it has been drawn into. Enough to provoke powerful reactions, Catholic to various forms of Protestantism, Methodists and Pietists to established Protestant Churches in the eighteenth century, Pentecostalists to all the above in our day. So the reality is much more checkered. But the tendency has been there, and continues to work; and lots of people have come to the end of this road, in various forms of Deism, Unitarianism, awe before some impersonal order.

What does this mean for our discussion above? Let me return to the point where we were opposing radical Enlighteners with Schiller's approach to the question: what does it mean to achieve wholeness by rescuing the body? We can understand better first why this is a demand that speaks to us. We can understand this not only in the light of the thrust to excarnation which we can trace back to the Axial period, but which becomes increasingly powerful in the Western drive to Reform. We can also understand why it speaks to us, because there is something in Christian civilization which resists excarnation.

But because there is something in the actual Reform of Latin Christendom which has pushed this excarnation farther than ever before in human history, we can see both why the aspiration to overcome it must be an invitation to struggle; and also why this overcoming is so differently understood. The pressure and suppression has been both against bodily desires, of sex and violence in particular; but it also has steadily tended to exclude bodily desire as an expression of the higher, of fullness. There has been both ethical suppression, and disenchanting reduction. One party accepts the reduction, and directs its fire purely against the suppression; the other, in this following Schiller wants to undo the reduction.

Who is right? How can one say definitively? But if we look at the sexual revolution of the 1960s, it's clear that it was the Schillerian position which brought people into the streets. Hugh Hefner and *Playboy* might be thought to represent the other pole: sensuality is good as such. But among the revolutionaries, even those who might have subscribed verbally to the Hefnerian formula plainly entertained utopian hopes of a new kind of world, in which unrestricted sexual activity would help to release a new kind of fraternity. One of these steps into a new and wider space of solidarity that I spoke of above was what was hoped for as part of the package with sexual freedom. I have already discussed the illusions involved here, but these events say something about the power of the Schillerian mode, of the hope to undo reduction and not just suppression. Of course, hope by itself doesn't show anything about what transformations are possible.

Or can it sometimes? We need to look now at the different answers to the disappointed hopes of wholeness, and the issue whether or how this should be abandoned.

It is easy to understand how the hope for wholeness and the rescue of the body has been used in the struggle between faith and unbelief. We have seen how Enlightenment has turned it against religion: this has allegedly been frustrating a perfectly available harmony of our ordinary desires, by its insistence of chasing supposed higher goods, which lead to senseless mortification. But central to Christian faith is the hope of an ultimate reconciliation of humans and God, and that in the (resurrected) body.

Each side thus turns around and makes the accusation of unrealizable utopia to the other. Unbelievers scoff at the Christian parousia as a pipe-dream. But as long as Enlighteners keep alive hopes of their own harmony, they will find Christians (and lots of others) warning them against unreal Utopianism. We have to consider two dimensions of Utopia, which correspond to the two facets of modern moral/ethical consciousness we have been examining here: not just the harmony between body and spirit, or bodily desire and our highest aspirations; but also the harmony between all human beings so harmonized, which brings in our attachment to the ethic of universal rights and well-being. These two have usually gone together; the hopes of the students of 1968 were in this regard not at all exceptional. The same kind of double harmony (within each and among all) has also been sought by Schiller, by radical revolutionaries, and in Marxism. In the heyday of Revolution, there were voices at least purportedly Christian, like de Maistre, who warned against the unreal hopes on which masses were betting their lives. And similarly in relation to twentieth-century Communism.

The picture changes, however, when these hopes are dashed. We are living in such an age, in the aftermath of the 60s and 70s, and even more in the wake of the collapse of Marxist Communism. It is hard to believe that either kind of harmony is now on the cards. How does this alter the debate?

For those who cannot accept the Christian hope of a reconciliation beyond history, and who cannot any more believe in the various formulae of double harmony in our earthly condition, the conclusion might seem clear: abandon all hopes of such harmony. But this leaves a lot indeterminate. What more modest hopes are left? And can one really bring oneself to abandon both these goals? Does not a great deal of our political activity take as its goal, if only as an idea of reason, a world order in which peoples live together in equality and justice? Does not a great deal of our efforts at healing take as a goal the wholeness of the person? How easily can we set these goals aside?

While Freud, for instance, in this following Schopenhauer, that great enemy of the Romantic idea of wholeness, asks us utterly to abandon the goal of psychic harmony, we don't need to go this far. There are plenty of less ambitious forms of social unity than Communism (liberalism offers many such); and purported ways of overcoming psychic conflict which don't go all the way with Schiller. It is these which are now on the agenda in our post-Utopian age (but for how long will this last?).

We can see from this example of the ideal of wholeness how issues of ranges (c) to (e) in our list above are crucial, that is, questions about whether this ideal can be integrally reached, about the motives which stand in its way, and about the possible costs of trying to attain it. We will be looking at these in a more acute form in the next chapter.

17 Dilemmas 1

i. Humanism and "Transcendence"

As we examined the aspiration to wholeness, whether directed against the hegemony of calculating reason, or the "higher" demands of Platonist or Christian asceticism, we saw that it was intrinsically linked to an aspiration to rescue the body, or to rehabilitate ordinary human desire. We also saw that it entered in different ways into the polemic between Christian faith and unbelief.

I want to look at this polemic in a little more detail, as it unfolds in our (for the moment, anyway) anti-Utopian phase. I will start by examining how the aspiration to rehabilitate the body and desire figures in an accusation against faith, and more particularly Christian faith, that it intrinsically and by its very nature frustrates this aspiration. I believe that this examination will show that things are not necessarily what they seem, and that the polemic between religion and secular humanism ends up pointing to a set of dilemmas which both of these outlooks have to face.

1

One obvious fruit of this desire to rehabilitate the ordinary, the bodily in modern culture has been the affirmation of the essential goodness, innocence of our original, spontaneous aspirations. Evil tends to be seen as exogenous, as brought on by society, history, patriarchy, capitalism, the "system" in one form or another. As David Martin puts it, the "mobile, shifting, hedonistic, technicist" mentality that one encounters in the dominant metropolitan culture today "has no sense of personal guilt and yet possesses an excoriating sense of collective sin."[1]

One of the most striking fruits of this sense of innate human innocence has been the transfer of so many issues which used to be considered moral into a therapeutic register. What was formerly sin is often now seen as sickness. This is the "triumph of the therapeutic",[2] which has paradoxical results. It seems to involve an enhancement of human dignity, but can actually end up abasing it.

I want to examine this a bit further. What we have here is a shift in framework: certain human struggles, questions, issues, difficulties, problems are moved from a moral/spiritual to a therapeutic register. What exactly is involved here?

It's not that sickness and health haven't been used as metaphors for moral and spiritual failure/fullness: think of the therapeutic image in Plato, or the image of the "sin-sick soul". But the difference perhaps lies here: in the spiritual register, the "normal", everyday, beginning situation of the soul is to be partly in the grip of evil. Something heroic or exceptional is required to get beyond this; most of us are in the middle range, where we're struggling. So there is a kind of human "normalcy" which is defined for this middle range.

The basis for this is that there is a certain form of dignity in sin, evil. It is a kind of search for the good, but deviated by catastrophic, culpable error. Ultimately, there is nothing to this; it is just wrong; its glory and prestige turn out to be empty, tawdry. But within the error, there is a certain appearance of greatness, glory, which has a certain consistency. Hence the idea of normalcy in this middle range.

As against this, just being sick has no dignity. It may be culpable (how people think of contracting AIDS), or it may be without blame. But it is pure failure, weakness, lack, diminishment.

Now depth-psychological notions of mental illness fit somewhere between these clearly distinguished categories. There is an element of illusion sometimes; things appear other than they are. But this error may be devoid of any dignity. It may just be our inability to grow up and see things from an adult perspective. Or just a compulsion; or a blind, uncontrollable reaction. The Lucifer story has no place in its aetiology.

So healing doesn't involve conversion, a growth in wisdom, a new, higher way of seeing the world; or at least, these are not the hinges of healing, though they may be among its results.

There are, of course, intermediate phenomena. There are kinds of therapy, of a humanist depth-psychological kind, where the various complexes come close to being seen as understandable reactions of limited beings; where the therapy partly involves changing your vision of things. These approach the spiritual. But what keeps them on the therapy side is that the original aetiology has no Lucifer element. There is no choice, where there is at least apparent worth and dignity on the wrong side— or at least attraction to apparent worth and dignity; there doesn't have to be choice in the sense of election between alternatives. The original fall is entirely in the nature of compulsions, or modes of imprisonment.

So the difference is this: evil has the dignity of an option for an apparent good; sickness has not. This dignity is conceded, even in the discourse of conversion that purports to show evil up as false good, and hence really empty, really only a kind of alienation. It is conceded not in the text, but in the context, in the manner of address, which recognizes the power of the opponent.

Now the pathos involved in the triumph of the therapeutic is this: One reason to throw over the spiritual perspective evil/holiness was to reject the idea that our normal, middle-range existence is imperfect. We're perfectly all right as we are, as "natural" beings. So the dignity of ordinary, "natural" existence is even further enhanced. This ought to have liberated us from what were recognized frequently as the fruits of sin: impotence, division, anguish, spleen, melancholy, emptiness, incapacity, paralyzing gloom, acedia, etc. But in fact these abound.

Only now, as afflictions of beings destined for middle-range normalcy, they must be seen as the result of sickness. They must be treated therapeutically. But the person being treated is now being approached as one who is just incapacitated. He has *less* dignity than the sinner. So what was supposed to enhance our dignity has reduced it. We are just to be dealt with, manipulated into health.

From another angle: casting off religion was meant to free us, give us our full dignity of agents; throwing off the tutelage of religion, hence of the church, hence of the clergy. But now we are forced to go to new experts, therapists, doctors, who exercise the kind of control that is appropriate over blind and compulsive mechanisms; who may even be administering drugs to us. Our sick selves are even more being talked down to, just treated as things, than were the faithful of yore in churches.

Obviously, this difference can be mitigated to the extent that (a) the cure is a "talking cure", and calls on the co-operation of the patient as co-agent in the cure; and that (b) the sickness, compulsion, constrained place is understood as (i) something all flesh is heir to, so we aren't talking down as from a higher plateau of the healthy, and as (ii) being humanly understandable as a predicament to have fallen into, something we can understand people being drawn into, for which we can feel the sympathy of equals—"I so understand how easy it would be to fall into that". Here we are edging towards something like the dignity of sin. For instance, Winnicott, with his appreciation of the middle range, in which "good enough" mothering takes place; and also other humanist therapists.

So the therapeutic turn, the move from a hermeneutic of sin, evil, or spiritual misdirection, to one of sickness, has at best ambiguous results for human dignity. And it also has important consequences for our self-understanding. I mentioned above what were formerly seen as the fruits of spiritual misdirection: anguish, spleen, melancholy, emptiness, and to on, continue in our therapeutic age. But now they are often read, not as signs of such misdirection, or of our lack of contact with spiritual reality, but simply as pathologies.

A spiritual perspective will suppose that somewhere, deep down, we will feel drawn to recognize and live in relation to what it defines as spiritual reality. We may feel drawn to it, may pine for it, feel dissatisfied and incomplete without it. People speak of "divine discontent", of a "désir d'éternité". This may be buried deep down, but it is a perpetual human potential. So even people who are very successful in the range of normal human flourishing (perhaps especially such people) can feel unease, perhaps remorse, some sense that their achievements are hollow. From the perspective of those who deny this supposed spiritual reality, this unease can only be pathological; it is totally non-functional; it can only hold us back. The denial of much traditionally understood spiritual reality has been a crucial factor in the therapeutic turn.

So the turn offers a radically different understanding of our experiences of unease, anguish, emptiness, division, and the like. In one case, they may be telling us something important; they may be revealing some lack or misdirection in our lives. In the other, they are akin to illness, and as such may be *symptomatic* of some mistaken direction (as my high blood pressure is a consequence of my too rich diet); they don't constitute a (perhaps largely confused and masked) *perception* of this misdirection.

So which perspective is chosen not only affects how others (doctors, helpers) will treat you, but also how you will treat yourself. In one case, the unease needs to be further understood, worked through, perhaps in prayer or meditation; in the other it needs to be got rid of, or at least rendered mild enough to be lived with.

Psychoanalysis may seem, and partly is, an intermediate phenomenon. Unlike behavioural therapies, or those relying mainly on drugs, it involves a hermeneutic, an attempt to understand the meaning of our unease. But its goal is the same; the hermeneutic delves into the unavoidable, deep psychic conflicts in our make-up. But these have no moral lesson for us; the guilt or remorse points to no real wrong. We strive to understand them in order to reduce their force, to become able to live with them. On the crucial issue, what we have morally or spiritually to learn from our suffering, it is firmly on the therapeutic side: the answer is "nothing".

The struggle between a "spiritual" and a therapeutic reading of our psychic suffering doesn't only oppose religion to unbelief. There are plenty of cases within the general range of unbelief in which a "higher" more "heroic" view of human life is in contest with one which stresses the fulfillments of ordinary desire. I raised some of these issues earlier in discussing the kinds of critiques which the "higher" addresses to the "lower" and vice versa. So we may judge that offering people the satisfactions of gainful employment, reasonable prosperity, consumer choice, exciting media, may be enough to assure a stable modern democracy, but still deplore the loss of a more exalted view of life, in which heroic action, or political self-rule, or great philanthropic dedication, was seen as a higher fulfillment. (Something like this view seems central to Francis Fukuyama's celebrated book on the "end of history".)[3]

Now presumably someone with these views would find nothing pathological in a highly successful professional, with a high income, feeling an uneasy sense that something crucial was missing in his life; and would see the attempt to get rid of this sense through treatment as a travesty of the human condition.

But in any case, one can see how this battle between the two perspectives can be crucial for how one lives one's life. If I am talked into believing that my deep unease, which is perhaps badly disorganizing my professional or married life, is just pathology, this can easily be accompanied by a sense of shame or inadequacy, that my psychological hang-ups are ruining my own life. This shame may be relieved by the thought that ultimately all this is organically caused. And this, plus the easy availability of cheap drugs, helps to drive so much psychotherapy towards the chemical.

We can see how fateful the issue is for a human life. To worry endlessly about the meaning of an unease whose whole basis is really organic is to have wasted time and effort and to have incurred unnecessary suffering. But to have tried to get rid of an unease that one really needed to understand is crippling; the more so in that within the culture of the therapeutic, the various languages, ethical and spiritual, in which this understanding can be couched become less and less familiar, less and less available to each new generation.

Put in other terms, it is a commonplace that human beings are powerfully drawn to fullness under some or other definitions. And most people will concur that these aspirations can themselves be the source of deep troubles; for instance, strong moral demands can impact on our lives in the form of crippling guilt, which may incapacitate us in our actions and responses, including the moral ones. But a crucial feature of a purely immanentist therapy is that the cure of these incapacities is held to involve—or even demand—our repudiation of, or at least distancing from, any aspirations to the transcendent, like religious faith. These produce incapacity not adventitiously, because we have become wrongly situated to them in our lives, but essentially. A cure which involves getting rid of them is quite conceivable, if not mandatory. Whereas from the spiritual perspective, that the demands of faith can produce crippling conflicts reflects not their gratuitous nature, but our real (fallen) predicament; the goal must be to find a more adequate response to the spiritual reality, not to flee it.

Of course, to simplify things, I have been speaking as if one could speak either of a "spiritual" or a "pathological" reading. In fact, an element of pathology often, one might even say, virtually always, enters into our unease. Evil, the turning away from the good, also generates pathology, in the sense of blind, compulsive seeking of lesser goods, even evils. So the spiritual or ethical perspective allows for, even requires the diagnosis of pathologies, as Dostoyevsky has shown. The issue is whether one can speak of pathology alone, or whether there is also a spiritual or ethical hermeneutic to be made.

Many of our actual incapacities are in a range where they can be treated either way. They have compulsive elements which can respond to therapy. But they also affect us as responsible choosers of wrong, evil. The therapeutic revolution has brought a number of insights, approaches. It is just as a total metaphysic that it risks generating perverse results: its attempts to treat our ailments can end up further stifling the spirit in us, and fastening other incapacities more firmly on us.

I have been discussing the relevance of the therapeutic turn for (1) the way we are treated (in both senses of this term), and (2) the way we understand ourselves.

But there is a third related difference between the two outlooks. If we see our impotences, incapacities, divisions, as the fruit of sin, evil, moral inadequacy, we will expect to find them in virtually all human beings; we will expect them to be overcome in rare cases only at the ultimate pinnacle of sanctity. But if we see them as the result of sickness, owing to avoidable traumas, faulty upbringing, lack of the right kind of support, and the like, we will expect a lot more people to attain to "normalcy", somewhere in the middle range as far as moral perfection is concerned, having got rid of their unease, or learned to live with it. The intersection of full capacity and humanity will be set at a lower altitude. But for spiritual outlooks of the transformation perspective, Christianity and Buddhism, say, the point where we achieve our full human capacity, beyond pathological and other confusions about our spiritual condition, is placed well beyond the level of recognized human flourishing. It is a distinctly minority phenomenon. We shall see the importance of this third distinction later on, in looking at the relation of spirituality to a stable political order.

The therapeutic approach disambiguates the complex, contradictory nature of evil, which does indeed involve a lesser capacity, but is always also the condition of a responsible agent. This disambiguation is supposed to be a clear step forward; but in fact it introduces us into a field of dilemmas, because the reality itself is complex, ambiguous.

2

Against this background, I want to look at the case against Christianity, that it denies or hampers human fulfillment. But first we should remind ourselves again of a paradoxical feature of this debate between religion and its rejection. If we take the critique of religion by unbelievers, it seems to come from two opposite directions.

On one hand, religion actuated by pride or fear sets impossibly high goals for humans, of asceticism, or mortification, or renunciation of ordinary human ends. It invites us to "transcend humanity", and this cannot but end up mutilating us; it leads us to despise and neglect the ordinary fulfillment and happiness which is within our reach. This is one of the major criticisms that emerges out of the first group of axes, the "Romantic" set that I described in Chapter 8.

On the other hand, the reproach is levelled that religion cannot face the real hard facts about nature and human life: that we are imperfect beings, the product of evolution, with a lot of aggression and conflict built into our natures; that there is also much which is horrible and terrible in human life which can't just be wished away. Religion tends to bowdlerize reality. This emerges from the second group of axes, the "tragic" set.

I said there is a paradox here, but not a contradiction. We can see how the two kinds of criticism could be rendered consistent, on a certain reading. The impossible transformations which are seen as mutilating us in one indictment, are those which are childishly utopian on the other.

But even if not contradictory, there is a strain between these two lines of attack. This is clear when we reflect that the second one mainly holds against the more "liberal", "Deist" forms of Christianity which were the ante-chamber to the turn to exclusive humanism. No one would dream of levelling a charge of bowdlerizing against Calvin for instance. Any view which sends the major part of humanity to unending unspeakable suffering in Hell can't be charged with covering up the dark side of things.

At the same time, the first attack is mainly in place against that more savage "old-time religion", and is less and less apposite, the more we move towards the "Deist" pole.

Not only that, but the bowdlerizing charge holds as well against unbelieving humanisms which have too rosy a view of the harmony of interests, or the power of human sympathy; while the mutilating attack holds in spades against certain forms of atheist humanism which have driven the destructive attempts at total reform which litter the history of the twentieth century.

A better way of formulating things would be to say, not that Christianity falls under both these criticisms, but rather that it is the scene of an internal struggle of interpretations, whereby some seek to avoid one, but thereby fall more directly under the other, and others do the reverse. The problem for Christian faith seems to be more like a dilemma, that it seems hard to avoid one of these criticisms without impaling oneself on the other—granted, that is, that one wants to avoid both.

But then one suspects that something similar may be true of unbelief. Unbelieving views may sell human beings short, in underestimating their ability to reform; but they may also put the bar too high, and justify some very destructive attempts at change. The issue is whether there is a place to stand between these errors, just as the analogous question may be put to Christian faith.

Or perhaps on examination, it will appear that there is more than one dilemma which both sides have to face, one concerned with transcendence and human fulfillment, and the other with the violent and aggressive dimensions of human nature.

But the general shape of the struggle seems to be this, that both sides are at grips with similar dilemmas, each within a very different understanding of the human predicament. In the one-sided heat of the debate, this generally disappears from view, and huger rocks are thrown by either side than are safe for dwellers in glass houses.

Let's look at each of these critiques in turn.

(A) Martha Nussbaum has given voice to the first critique, a warning against attempts to "transcend humanity", in a very interesting and frequently persuasive way.[4] Developing from, but not confining herself to the argument she developed in *The Fragility of Goodness*,[5] she sees the roots of our desire to transcend our ordinary condition in the unease and fear we experience in our finitude, our limitations, our neediness, our vulnerability.

One can distinguish two things wrong with this aspiration, as one surveys her arguments. On one hand, the desire to transcend, in at least some of its forms, must defeat itself. It starts as a human desire to offset the limits which often make our lives miserable and our world threatening. But if comprehensively granted, the wish would lift us altogether out of the human condition. Nussbaum makes this point effectively in discussing Odysseus' refusal of Calypso's offer to stay on her island, to enjoy an unending and secure love with a goddess, in order to return to a mortal human woman and a life beset by risk. On first hearing of the alternatives, we may think he is crazy; the fear and vulnerability in us leaps at the offer; but as we consider it further we see that human love, caring, mutual support is inseparable from the limited and threatened human condition. Calypso's unending, danger-free life lacks all the meaning that the once-for-allness of human existence, with its key turning points, its moments to seize or lose, in short its human temporality, confers. In choosing this remedy to risk, we would in a sense be "changing the subject", not improving our human lives, but going for something else altogether.[6]

She drives home this point with the example of athletic competition. This a straining against limits; each champion wants to push a bit father the world record in her field. But if we imagine being able to transcend our limits altogether, move great distances immediately and effortlessly, change shapes at will, what point would remain to athletic contests? Greek Gods would have no need for them. An athlete's aspiration to have the powers of Hermes deconstructs itself.[7]

Of course, this particular bit of ancient Greek fantasizing about divine immortality may not seem very relevant; how do you set about becoming a Greek god? But

Nussbaum's point is to get us to see in the extreme case what is already there in less total aspirations; such, for instance, as Plato's as described in the *Symposium,* for a love which would no longer be attached to particular human beings, but only to the Beautiful, to the Good itself. In this aspiration, are we not forgoing something that makes human life valuable? Are we not forsaking human excellence and striving after some alien life-form?

This is not without connection with Nussbaum's continuing polemic against a certain way of doing philosophy, entirely in disengaged mode and in general terms, keeping its distance from the particular, from the experience of the emotions, and hence from the narratives which best convey these. Her arguments here have been tremendously important, and rightly influential.

But there is another charge against the aspiration to transcend, not just that it is futile and self-defeating, but that it actually damages us, unfits us for the pursuit of human fulfillment. It does this by inducing in us hate and disgust at our ordinary human desires and neediness. It inculcates a repulsion at our limitations which poisons the joy we might otherwise feel in the satisfactions of human life as it is.

Here the enemy is not so much Greek polytheistic fantasy and Greek philosophy, but Christianity, especially in its Augustinian forms. Here Nussbaum takes up one of the central themes, one of the constitutive polemics of our secular age, as I am trying to describe it. Hatred at Christianity for having defamed, polluted, rendered impure ordinary human sensual desire is one of the most powerful motivations which impelled people to take the option for an exclusive humanism once this became thinkable. In her discussion of this in *Love's Knowledge,*[8] Nussbaum offers a genealogy of this position which has a pre-Christian starting point, in Epicurus and Lucretius, but the tone of her revulsion at Christian disgust at the body and ordinary fulfillment comes much closer to Voltaire and Nietzsche, whom she also invokes. And indeed, we could argue that Lucretius has become important for us in the last few centuries precisely because he has helped to articulate the polemics in Christian and post-Christian culture.

Nussbaum seems to approve of the task that Nietzsche set himself, whose negative side, in her words, was "the thorough, detailed dismantling of religious beliefs and teleological desires through the techniques of debunking genealogy, mordant satire, horrific projection."[9] The question arises, is this a desirable goal? Is it even a possible goal? In view of the importance of Christian universalism and agape in the constitution of the modern idea of moral order, ought we really to hope for the utter uprooting of all the beliefs and desires which Christianity has inculcated in our civilization? Perhaps Nietzsche saw the full scope of this question, and was ready to give an affirmative answer, because he wanted to jettison not only body-hatred, but pity, the relief of suffering, democracy, human rights. But how many are ready to follow him the whole way?

I think that in exploring this question, it is useful not to be dragged immediately into the polemics, because this tends to drive us into polarized positions and these, I suspect, turn out to be unsustainable, because we are all, rightly, more cross-pressured than they allow (yes, even Nietzsche, though he went to great lengths to find a place to stand outside this culture).

I want to take up the issues in two phases: first looking at the idea(s) of "transcending humanity", and the extent to which we can or want to repudiate them as such; and then later examining the place of Christianity in this whole debate.

Can we just renounce the aspiration to transcend, and return to "immanent" life? It sometimes sounds as though this is what Nussbaum is proposing. But in her William James lecture, she argues that the matter is "more complex" than this.[10] "There is a great deal of room, within the context of a human life . . . , for a certain sort of aspiration to transcend our ordinary humanity." But what we need is "transcendence . . . of an *internal* and human sort."[11]

Surely Nussbaum is right here, but it transfers the argument to a new plane, and raises the question whether her internal-external distinction will be able to make the discriminations we want.

She is right, but in order to do justice to the position she here distances herself from, we have to see why people have been tempted to hold it. We have to invoke one of the constitutive experiences of modernity. Indeed, the homecoming of Odysseus, from the realm of the monstrous, the threatening, of the limit situation, to the joys of ordinary life with its rhythmed flow of time, might even be taken as a paradigm image of this experience. Only with us, the monstrous and threatening has often been self-inflicted and self-imposed, or at least the imposition of other, deluded human beings.

This was the experience of many in the Reformed churches, when they rehabilitated the satisfactions of ordinary life, in marriage and productive vocation, from what they saw as the unjustified denigration implicit in the Catholic evaluation of the monastic vocation as following "counsels of perfection".[12] Actuated by pride, people had dedicated themselves to unreal ideals of an austerity to which they were not called by God, turning aside from the ordinary human path in which they were supposed to do his will. This revolt offered a kind of template in which later, more radical revisions could be shaped, including those which rejected Christianity altogether as sacrificing the joys of ordinary sensual, bodily existence in the name of illusory ideals of abstinence and renunciation. In recent centuries, and especially the last one, countless people have thrown off what has been presented to them as the demands of religion, and have seen themselves as rediscovering the value of the ordinary human satisfactions that these demands forbade. They had the sense of coming back to a forgotten good, a treasure buried in everyday life.

Not only religion has been the perceived object of this kind of rebellion. Millions of people were dragooned in the last century in the name of impossible ideals of social transformation. They longed to return to what they saw as the normal, the ordinary, the satisfactions of unmobilized human life. I remember an Estonian, circa 1990, telling me that for 45 years no one had lived a normal life in his country. There was no trouble understanding what he meant.

Whatever one thinks of the doctrinal issues involved, between Catholics and Protestants, Christians and unbelievers, one should recognize the positive force and value of these homecomings to the ordinary. There is an important human experience here, one which has been repeated again and again in modernity, and one which in itself, in spite of its doctrinal dressing, is very often profoundly positive, for it involves the rediscovery and affirmation of important human goods.

What is recovered in these moments of return is a sense of the value of unspectacular, flawed everyday love, between lovers, or friends, or parents and children, with its routines and labours, partings and reunions, estrangements and returns.[13] Now we can have a strong sense of rediscovery here even without having been carried away in an aspiration to transcendence, just because one can easily undervalue the riches of the ordinary in relation to more exciting or flashy achievements and fulfillments in life—a career full of conflict and adventure, or a passionate and dramatic love affair. (But perhaps these are exciting ultimately because of our yearning for transcendence.) And then our partner falls sick, or suffers a near-fatal accident, and we suddenly realize what this love means to us. Much of our literature recounts the recovery of the unspectacular ordinary, for instance, the novels of Jane Austen.

Rilke captured something of this in the second *Duino Elegy*, reflecting on the figures on Attic tombs:

> Gedenkt euch der Hände,
> wie sie drucklos beruhren, obwohl in den Torsen die Kraft steht.
> Diese Beherrschten wussten damit; so weit sind wirs,
> dieses ist unser, uns *so* zu beruhren; stärker
> stemmen die Götter uns an. Doch dies ist Sache der Götter.
>
> (Remember the hands,
> how weightlessly they rest, though there is power in the torsos.
> These self-mastered figures know: We can go this far,
> and this is ours, to touch one another this lightly; the gods
> can press down harder upon us. But that is the gods' affair.)[14]

This is one of the recurring insights of modernity; recurring, because it constantly needs to be rescued from forgetfulness; and constitutive of modernity, because of the importance in our culture of the affirmation of ordinary life.

Now it is perfectly understandable that someone who has won their way back to the ordinary out of some great project of self-surpassing should want to say something like: "a pox on all transcendence". This doesn't make such a slogan right, or even coherently tenable. But one has to respect and value the experience out of which it comes. Less nobly, other people, philosophers or ideologues, may trade on the power of this experience to win support through a sweeping rejection of transcendence. But this shouldn't make us forget the value of the experience itself.

Faced with this slogan, the reaction ought to be complex, including the following elements: (a) the slogan is wrong, (b) but it comes from a real and important experience which should not be denigrated, and thus (c) one must resist it, but can't simply stigmatize it as total error.

Why is it wrong? For the reasons that Nussbaum adduces when she adopts her more nuanced position. There are directions where we want to transcend; indeed, it would be almost impossible to imagine a human life in which all of these were rejected.

But we can't simply save the slogan by adding a qualifier to it: "a pox on all 'external' transcendence"; not unless we can give a clear sense to the distinction invoked here. What could we mean by "external" transcendence? Not of course, simply the rather absurd desire to become like Olympians (absurd for us, I mean, it made sense to the ancient Greeks). But taking off from what is wrong with that, as Nussbaum so well describes it, we might eschew all transformations which would wrench us out of the human mould, so that certain human goods and excellences would no longer be possible for us. As Greek gods could no longer pursue athletics and politics, and could not therefore have the characteristic ends and goods implicit in these activities.

We might use this criterion to reject Plato's idea of love in the *Symposium*, because it seems to render unimportant or merely ancillary all love for particular human beings. So friendship and sexual love would drop out of a way of life reformed in keeping with it. All moderns might agree here, but this doesn't mean that this criterion will always serve uncontroversially to divide permitted from unpermitted transcendences.

As Nussbaum points out in the Introduction to *Love's Knowledge,* there seems to be a tension between ethical demands and those of erotic love.[15] The way in which sexual love demands privacy and exclusivity, and can thus easily generate anger and jealousy, seems in tension with the aspiration to a more universal love and concern, one decentred from the self. Here it seems hard to say, well so much the worse for ordinary, embodied erotic love—hard that is, for us; Plato does seem to be saying this, and for something like the reasons just stated. But it also seems hard to say, let's declare the aspiration to a more universal, decentred concern as a forbidden, "external" form of transcendence. It indeed, seems "external" on the criterion just suggested—carrying through on it as an ultimate, exclusive demand would seem to sideline an important component of our lives, viz., erotic love, or any love where exclusion and hence jealousy and anger are in play. But it is now less clear that the distinction so defined can decide the matter for us. The revised slogan fails.

Or take another case. We have been engaged in this century with attempts to establish a lasting peace through some world order. But war has been the occasion, as well as of unspeakable horrors, of actions of great nobility. It calls forth a certain kind of dedication and courage which is hard to match elsewhere. Belonging to the generation which were children going on teenagers during the Second World War, it still seems to me undeniable that, even taking account of the full complexity and murkiness of human motivation, there were people who laid their lives on the line so that others could be free, and even greater horrors avoided. That is why our age, in which many have taken seriously the Kantian project of a Perpetual Peace, has also seen repeated attempts to define a "moral equivalent of war". This recognizes that, as things stand now, the end of war would remove an important occasion for human excellences: heroism, dedication, the defense of the weak.

Now some thinkers have responded to this by renouncing the type of transcendence here: war must continue, because it's essential for human excellence. Hegel is a striking case, but others have taken the same line in this century, like Ernst Jünger. They declare perpetual peace "external" in the meaning of the above discussion. But I cannot accept this line. Nor can I accept the comforting view of the other side that war breeds nothing but horrors and destruction, although plainly it does lots of this.

What emerges from all this is that the issue of transcending humanity is not all that easy to resolve. Not only is it hard to draw a clear line between acceptable and unacceptable ways of transcending, whether we make the distinction turn on externality versus internality or on anything else. But we may have to confess to being in a dilemma in certain cases, not knowing with unqualified certainty whether a given way is to be embraced or not.

What does emerge from this is that a slogan like "a pox on all transcendence", even with a qualifier before the last word, can't resolve all our problems. Renouncing all ways of transcending en bloc isn't on. Even such fierce enemies of Christian transcendence as Nietzsche, maybe especially such, are full of exhortations to "self-overcoming"; would want us to stifle pity in ourselves, in short would hardly leave us as we are, with our list of goods and excellences unimpaired.

We might take a line like that of Nel Noddings,[16] and renounce everything which competes with the values of nurturance, and love for those around us; but this too leaves out a great deal that we are now attached to, which attachments we would have to "transcend".

But if aspirations to transcendence cannot simply be eliminated, including those which are problematic, are hard to evaluate, or even put us in a dilemma, then maybe we cannot simply condemn outright those who propose these ways, even where we want to say that they are wrong.

Take the Christian hatred of the body and desire that Nussbaum discusses in her Beckett chapter.[17] I too want to condemn this, consider it a terrible deviation. But if we look at one of its points of origin in early Christian monasticism, as described by Peter Brown,[18] we can see that it comes from a sense that the life of sexuality and procreation was part of a concern for one's own family and its descendance, a concern with lineage, property and power which, while not bad in itself, was a barrier to a wholesale giving of oneself to the love of God. In other words, renunciation was part of an attempt to find a fuller response to the agape of God as seen in Christ, to take part in a fuller, more all-embracing love. This is close to the perspective in which we should see the dedication of Saint Francis of Assisi; and it reminds us of the battles that the Church has waged throughout the ages with the power of lineages, from Pope Hildebrand in the Investiture controversy to the friar who marries Romeo and Juliet without the knowledge of their feuding parents.

Today we can see how these reasons for renunciation could slide in a later period into a negative obsession with the body, a disgust-cum-fascination with desire, which is the phenomenon which Beckett picks up on and Nussbaum describes.

Perhaps we should renounce this aspiration to a fuller love on these grounds? I confess that this to me would be an even greater mutilation of the human than the cramped modern Catholicism which Beckett may be parodying. In any case, the argument for this has to be made, not just assumed.

But if we don't renounce it, then our response to this cramped, desire-obsessed mode of spirituality has to be as nuanced as that to its polar adversary above, and similarly threefold: (a) of course, we have to say that and where it's wrong, but (b) we have to acknowledge that it arises partly out of a genuine and valuable aspiration, one to a fuller love, and thus (c) we cannot simply condemn it root and branch, as though it could be undiscriminatingly destroyed and rooted out; we have in fact to overcome it while preserving what is valuable in its roots.

This is the ground of the unease I expressed above at just launching into a polemic on this issue. The polemic easily polarizes to the point where one side raises the slogan of "a pox on all transcendence", and the other replies with a reactive defense of all the cramped, obsessed deviations which are pilloried by their opponents. This is a situation which arises all too frequently in the culture wars in the United States, and elsewhere. Perhaps this is what Arnold meant to invoke in his celebrated image of ignorant armies clashing by night.

Among those who embrace the polemic against transcendence, the various aspirations to something higher have to be seen as twisted, sick, or actuated by gratuitous ill-will. These aspirations are either demonized, as in certain humanist attacks against Christianity as an anti-human force for evil, or else diminished by being seen as pathological.

In this latter case, we have an instance of the triumph of the therapeutic, with the two characteristic features I mentioned in the discussion above. First, deviation from the "normal", acceptable modes of human fulfillment is not recognized as being animated by another, albeit mistaken, image of the good; and second, the "normalcy" is within the reach of the person of average endowment; it is not something which only a small élite of the virtuous can attain.

Curiously if perhaps not entirely consistently, therapizing and demonizing can go together, as in certain humanist attacks on religion. Lives of renunciation are condemned as pathological, but at the same time, their inculcation in the laity is seen as part of the strategy of a clerical will to power. (Consistency can perhaps be regained by situating the pathology in the laity and the will to power in the clergy.)

Now this kind of anti-transcendent humanism often gives a reading of "immanence" which sets the bar rather high. It incorporates much of what we understand as civilized discipline, of spontaneous conformity with the modern moral order, as part of the generally available non-pathological "normal." This is perhaps not surprising, since as I argued above, the original opening for exclusive humanism came in a culture in which these disciplines of civilization had become indeed, second nature for many people. This is why they felt natural and within easy reach of the average person.

But however understandable, this stance makes this kind of humanism frequently dismissive of, and sometimes cruel to deviants, classing them as misfits or people actuated by ill-will. Contemporary examples can be found in some of the policies generated by "political correctness", which impose either mandatory re-education or harsh punishments, or both, on deviants from the various "codes", who are frequently accused of "racism" or "misogyny" for the least infractions.

All this underscores how problematic are the distinctions, not only between internal and external transcendence, but even transcendence/immanence itself. When the bar of normal behaviour is set high enough, "immanence" may no longer seem the right term. Of course, I want to retain the notion of transcendence, along the lines of my original distinction between exclusive and inclusive humanisms, for the purposes of my principal thesis. But here I want to point out how extremely unclear and unsatisfactory is the notion of "transcendence" implicit in this polemic against Christian faith as a negation of human bodily fulfillments; and also to show how some very demanding kinds of exclusive humanism easily generate a counter-reaction from within unbelief itself.

To declare the disciplines of civilized life, under the rule of law, and in conformity with the moral order of freedom and mutual benefit, as "normal" in the sense of non-pathological; or to see the aspiration to this mode of life as an "internal" transcendence; this is to class the various resistances to these disciplines: the impulses to violence, aggression, domination; and/or those to wild sexual licence, as mere pathology or under-development. These are simply to be extirpated, removed by therapy, re-education or the threat of force. They do not reflect any essential human fulfillments, even in a distorted form, from which people might indeed be induced to depart through moral transformation, but which cannot simply be repressed without depriving them of what for them are important ends, constituent of their lives as human beings. This is the stance behind the paternalistic psychic engineering which Anthony Burgess pilloried in *A Clockwork Orange*.

Or the issue could be put in relation to the triumph of the therapeutic. If the violence, aggression, sexual licence can be seen as mere pathology or under-development, something one can be cured or educated out of, then we lose nothing essential in being "normalized". But if we see them as actions the agents concerned could experience as essential fulfillments, then even if we think they would benefit from a moral transformation such that they would no longer see them this way, we cannot delude ourselves that we are simply doing them a favour in submitting them to therapy or re-education. We may, indeed, have to restrain them in various ways for the sake of others' safety or the general peace, but we would have to recognize that we were forcing them to incur a sacrifice for the general good.

The background to the distinction, between the therapeutic and ethical perspectives, has to be developed further in order to see what is at stake. The modern therapeutic perspective develops partly out of the Enlightenment (in inspiration, Lockean) idea that the human agent is malleable; on the basis of certain fundamental motivations (e.g., seeking pleasure, avoiding pain), the agent can be trained to identify his ends in a variety of different ways. To redefine these ends through re-education thus does not force him to abandon an intrinsic direction of his being; and if it ends up making him better able to adjust to everyone else, it can lead to greater harmony, greater general desire-fulfillment, and thus a gain all around.

The other source of the triumph of the therapeutic is the desire to do away with the category of sin, which attributes at some level an ill will to the sinner. The deviant is a victim of bad training or illness; he is not there as an agent endorsing his lamentable, destructive behaviour, someone we should therefore condemn; rather, he is caught in a cycle of compulsion, from which we can liberate him through therapy.

This second, deculpabilizing motive fits well with the malleability idea, but doesn't require it. The triumph of the therapeutic has often accompanied much more complex anthropologies which suppose great rigidities in human character formation, such as psychoanalysis.

But both of these sources are in conflict with the anthropology underlying the major ethical theories of our tradition, going back to the ancients, as well as with various religious outlooks. These differ among themselves, particularly in regard to the place they give to evil, but they agree in seeing the sinner or wrong-doer as pursuing something he senses as his good, either because he (mistakenly) thinks this is so (ancient variant), or because he perversely feels drawn to embrace evil (a variant which arises with Christianity). This wrong-doing, this "missing the mark" (*hamartia,* as it is called both in Aristotle and the Greek Bible), is usually seen as something very difficult to understand, perhaps ultimately inexplicable, even mysterious.

But it clearly escapes the purely environmental account of the malleability view. However much bad training and bad habits may have to do with our choice for the wrong (as Aristotle for instance argues), it ends up being something in which we invest our whole being, vision and desire. Good early training is thus not a sufficient condition of good character, which has to be nourished by admirable examples, and later even ethical reflection, according to Aristotle. But this very investment of our being through vision and desire is what makes our eventual transformation something which goes beyond the therapeutic. However much Plato invokes this image of the cure for ethical change, it is clear that he himself sees something like a "conversion"[19] in the turn to the good.

In modern terms, ethical transformation involves engaging both the will and the vision of the agent. It is beyond the reach of a therapy designed to cure an agent who doesn't endorse his deviancy, beyond the reach of an education which inculcates knowledge and capacities; it can be resistant to force and terror.

This can allow us to appreciate how a humanism of "civilized", moral conduct, which sees the resistances to it as mere pathology or under-development, when seen in the ethical perspective appears as a denigration, even dehumanization of the deviants it identifies and proposes to recondition.[20]

(B) Now this brings us into the domain of the other range of objections to religion, those which comes from the "tragic" direction. For it was inevitable that the "normalizing" humanism raise profound objections from all those who rebelled at its reductive take on the aggressive, combative, licentious dimensions of human life. These included those who wanted to condemn aggression, but saw the issue in the framework of the ethical anthropology. But the most virulent objections came from those who saw something to celebrate in aggression and sometimes also in sexual licence. Far from condemning the urge to fight, dominate, even inflict suffering,

Nietzsche saw them as expressions of the will to power. Their denigration by modern humanism, in the name of equality, happiness and an end to suffering, was what was degrading the human being, reducing human life to something no longer worth living, spreading "nihilism". In our day, this attack against civilizing humanism has been taken up by Michel Foucault, whose term 'normalization' I have borrowed in the above discussion. This was the (not really explicit) ethical meaning behind the much trumpeted "end of man";[21] as it is the point of the denunciation of "humanism" among many post-modernists.

This modern humanism provokes attacks along all the axes of the "tragic" range. For some (Tocqueville, Nietzsche, Sorel, Jünger), it voids life of its heroic dimension. For others (the above, but also in his own way Isaiah Berlin, as well as Bernard Williams), this humanism tends to hide from itself how great the conflict is between the different things we value. It artificially removes the tragedy, the wrenching choices between incompatibles, the dilemmas, which are inseparable from human life. It creates the impression that all good things come together effortlessly; but it only achieves this by denaturing and downgrading some of the goods which stand in the way of the preferred basket of liberal values.

Or again, the attack may come against the idea of happiness or fulfillment implicit in this humanism. By discrediting the refractory drives as pathological or under-developed, civilizing humanism implies that the proper human fulfillment will be, for the "normal", conflict-free. An untroubled happiness attends this normalcy, because nothing important need be sacrificed for it.

For the ethical perspective, this kind of untroubled harmony is indeed possible, but only at the pinnacle of human achievement; this is not something which could ever be statistically "normal", just as it could never be defined as normal in the sense of non-pathological. Most religious outlooks run parallel here to the ethical one. Full self-harmony will never be the lot of most humans, let alone "l'homme moyen sensuel".

For Nietzscheans, as for those who believe themselves to have grounds in biology and the theory of evolution for seeing aggression, or gender difference, or hierarchy, as deeply rooted in our natures, harmony will be unattainable, and it is even a kind of culpable weakness to believe in it or strive for it. The belief in untroubled happiness is not only a childish illusion, but also involves a truncation of human nature, turning our backs on much of what we are. They see something contemptible in this ideal, as I noted above in the previous section.

Now this set of critiques is hurled not only at normalizing humanism, but also at religion. In a way, this may seem wildly inappropriate. Hasn't Christian preaching always repeated that it is impossible to be fully happy as a sinful agent in a sinful world? Certainly this illusion can't be laid at the door of Christian faith, however much contemporary Christians may be sucked into this common view of the "pursuit of happiness" today.

But in another way, there clearly is a point to the charge. Because the idea either that aggression is ineradicable because in our genes (sociobiology), and/or that it is something which we ought to celebrate rather than trying to overcome (Nietzsche), is certainly incompatible with the Christian faith and hope, with any recognizable Christian eschaton. Christianity posits a possible transformation here which is rejected by Nietzscheanism and scientism alike. So it stands accused of an unreal optimism, of substituting hope for reality sense, of propagating a comforting myth about human beings which obscures the hard truth. In this, it is held to be the ancestor of normalizing humanism, as Nietzsche never tires of saying. And we have seen the historical sense in which this is true, in which this humanism emerged from a certain (reduced) reading of Christian faith.

Now here the argument shows a strange cross-over. When Nietzscheans reproach Christians for refusing to see how much humans cannot but affirm themselves through aggression, because they are so attached to a cleaned-up, "spiritualized" picture of the human potential, they are running closely parallel to the reproach above that Christianity can't accept our sensual nature. This is one of the key arguments of exclusive humanism in its rejection of Christian transcendence; and now a similar point is raised against this humanism itself by its deadliest enemies.

3

All this is rather confusing, and suggests that we need a new, more nuanced map of the ideological terrain. Modern culture is not just the scene of a struggle between belief and unbelief. We have seen that the arguments against religion come from two rather different angles; that even at first glance, they don't all hold against all variants of religion; that although the two directions of attack can be aligned somewhat from a Nietzschean perspective, as in the preceding paragraph, they ultimately carry us to very different conclusions. The camp of unbelief is deeply divided—about the nature of humanism, and more radically, about its value.

I want to offer another framework to understand these struggles, not as a struggle between two protagonists, but rather as a three-cornered, even perhaps four-cornered battle. The entry of what I called above "the immanent counter-Enlightenment", which challenges the humanist primacy of life, has greatly complicated the scene.

There are secular humanists, there are neo-Nietzscheans, and there are those who acknowledge some good beyond life. Any pair can gang up against the third on some important issue. Neo-Nietzscheans and secular humanists together condemn religion and reject any good beyond life. But neo-Nietzscheans and acknowledgers of transcendence are together in their absence of surprise at the continued disappointments of secular humanism, together also in the sense that its vision of life lacks a dimension. In a third line-up, secular humanists and believers come together in defending an idea of the human good, against the anti-humanism of Nietzsche's heirs.

A fourth party can be introduced to this field if we take account of the fact that the acknowledgers of transcendence are divided. Some think that the whole move to secular humanism was just a mistake, which needs to be undone. We need to return to an earlier view of things. Others, in which I place myself, think that the practical primacy of life has been a great gain for human kind, and that there is some truth in the self-narrative of the Enlightenment: this gain was in fact unlikely to come about without some breach with established religion. (We might even be tempted to say that modern unbelief is providential, but that might be too provocative a way of putting it.) But we nevertheless think that the metaphysical primacy of life espoused by exclusive humanism is wrong, and stifling, and that its continued dominance puts in danger the practical primacy.

I have rather complicated the scene in the last paragraph. Nevertheless, the simple lines sketched earlier still stand out, I believe. Both secular humanists and anti-humanists concur in one part of the Enlightenment narrative, that is, they see us as having been liberated from the illusion of a good beyond life, and thus enabled to affirm ourselves. This may take the form of an Enlightenment endorsement of benevolence and justice; or it may be the charter for the full affirmation of the will to power—or "the free play of the signifier", or the aesthetics of the self, or whatever the current version is. But it remains within the same climate which has relegated the beyond to the status of past illusion. For those fully within this climate, transcendence becomes all but invisible.

Of course, we might want to set aside this three-cornered picture, on the grounds that contemporary anti-humanism isn't a significant enough movement. If one just focusses one's attention on certain fashionable professors of comparative literature, this might seem plausible. But my sense is that the impact of this third stream in our culture and contemporary history has been very powerful, particularly if we take account of Fascism, as well as of the fascination with violence which has come to infect even Enlightenment-inspired movements, such as Bolshevism (and this is far from being the only such case). And can we exempt the gory history of even "progressive", democratic nationalism?

If we do adopt the three-cornered picture, however, some interesting questions arise. Explaining each is somewhat of a challenge for the others. In particular, anti-humanism is not easy to explain from the Enlightenment perspective. Why this throwback, on the part of people who are "liberated" from religion and tradition?

From the religious perspective, the problem is the opposite. There is a too quick and too slick explanation right to hand: The denial of transcendence is bound to lead to a crumbling and eventual break-down of all moral standards. First, secular humanism, and then eventually its pieties and values come under challenge. And in the end nihilism.

I am not saying that there is no insight at all in this account. But it leaves too much unexplained. Anti-humanism is not just a black hole, an absence of values, but also a new valorization of death, and sometimes violence. And some of the fascination it re-articulates for death and violence reminds us forcefully of many of the phenomena of traditional religion. It is clear that this fascination extends well beyond the borders of anti-humanism. As I just mentioned, we can see it also in the heirs of the Enlightenment; but also unmistakably recurring again and again in the religious tradition. Gulag and the Inquisition stand testimony to its perennial force.

But this sharp rebuttal to a too self-indulgent religious explanation poses once again a problem for exclusive humanism. If there is something perennial, recurring, here, whence comes it? We don't lack for immanent theories of a human propensity to evil, all the way from sociobiology to Freudian speculations on a death principle. But these have their own counter-Enlightenment thrust: they put a severe limit on any hopes for improvement. They tend to cast doubt on the central Enlightenment idea that we are in charge of our fate.

At the same time, from the perspective of transcendence, some considerations seem obvious:

Exclusive humanism closes the transcendent window, as though there were nothing beyond. More, as though it weren't an irrepressible need of the human heart to open that window, and first look, then go beyond. As though feeling this need were the result of a mistake, an erroneous world-view, bad conditioning, or worse, some pathology. Two radically different perspectives on the human condition. Who is right?

Well, who can make more sense of the life all of us are living? Seen from this angle, the very existence of modern anti-humanism seems to tell against exclusive humanism. If the transcendental view is right, then human beings have an ineradicable bent to respond to something beyond life. Denying this stifles. And in fact, even for those who accept the metaphysical primacy of life, this outlook can itself come to seem imprisoning. It is in this sense, rather than in the rather smug, self-satisfied view that unbelief must destroy itself, that the religious outlook finds anti-humanism unsurprising.

From within this outlook, we might be tempted to speculate further, and to suggest that the perennial human susceptibility to be fascinated by death and violence, is at base a manifestation of our nature as homo religiosus. From the point of view of someone who acknowledges transcendence, it is one of the places this aspiration beyond most easily goes when it fails to take us there. This doesn't mean that religion and violence are simply alternatives. On the contrary, it has meant that most historical religion has been deeply intricated with violence, from human sacrifice down to inter-communal massacres. Because most historical religion remains only very imperfectly oriented to the beyond. The religious affinities of the cult of violence in its different forms are indeed palpable.

What it might mean, however, is that the only way fully to escape the draw towards violence lies somewhere in the turn to transcendence, that is, through the full-hearted love of some good beyond life. Here we enter on a terrain, that of religion and violence, which has been explored in a very interesting way by René Girard. I want to return to this below.[22]

But whatever explanatory view we adopt, I hope I have said something to accredit the notion that no serious attempt to understand the Enlightenment today can do without a deeper study of the immanent counter-Enlightenment. The classical scenarios of the two-sided struggle keeps in the shade everything we can learn about these two major protagonists through their differences from and affinities to this third contestant that they have somehow conjured in their midst.

4

ii. Against Mutilation

What emerges from the above is that thinking out the attacks on religion of exclusive humanism shows up some deep differences in the camp of unbelief. This itself is not necessarily a problem: in principle, one of these views could be right and the other simply wrong. But my sense is that each side, the "humanist" and the "Nietzschean", raises deep difficulties for the other. It is not all that easy to abandon benevolence, equality, the goals of humanism. And yet the immanent revolt is often powerfully motivated. There are some unresolved dilemmas here.

They arise from that crucial complex of issues for any conception of the human ethical predicament that we identified in the last chapter: whether its notion of fullness is integrally realizable, whether the obstacles to it, the negative motivations can be fully overcome; and if not, whether over-riding them involves an unacceptable sacrifice (issues (c), (d) and (e)).

We may speak of dilemmas, of tensions, or even of attempts to square the circle. Whatever we call it, the basic form seems to be this: how to define our highest spiritual or moral aspirations for human beings, while showing a path to the transformation involved which doesn't crush, mutilate or deny what is essential to our humanity? Let us call this the "maximal demand".

Why is this demand important to us? I suggest we can find the reasons for this in our aspiration to wholeness, which I tried to articulate in the previous chapter. Running through modern culture is the sense of the wrong we do, in pursuing our highest ideals, when we sacrifice the body, or ordinary desire, or the fulfillments of everyday life. Why is this given such an important place? After all, Plato in the *Republic* seemed quite prepared to sideline the (in his culture too) central human desires to form families, own property, and hand this on to one's children; all in the name of a higher, fuller harmony in the state.

Of course, the ancients were far from agreeing on this. Aristotle strongly criticizes Plato's attempt to excise certain ordinary fulfillments from the good life, and in the *Politics*, Book 2, utterly rejects the Platonic proposal to abolish the family and private property. But the reasons in our case come to us from our origins in Christian culture. A religion of Incarnation cannot simply sideline the body. The "pity" ascribed to Jesus in the Gospel is a gut feeling; the eschatological perspective is for bodily resurrection. The Reformation accent on ordinary life goes much farther than Aristotle, not only making the sphere of production and the family part of the good life, but giving it a dignity which Aristotle had not accorded it. It is not surprising that a central tradition of Catholic philosophy from the Middle Ages grounded itself on Aristotle's philosophy.

The critique of Christianity has taken this centrality of the body, the ineliminability of our ordinary bodily fulfillments, and turned it against the faith itself, stigmatising it as a transform of Platonism. Nietzsche often invokes this filiation; and Nussbaum draws on it in her critique discussed above. What makes this critique so devastating is just that our culture in general so strongly endorses this centrality. And this is why the maximal demand has force for us: ideals cannot be pursued at the expense of purging, or denigrating, ordinary fulfillments.

The burden of the, admittedly sketchy, discussion in the preceding pages is that this demand is not all that easy to meet. We have to face the possibility that this may not be realizable, that squaring our highest aspirations with an integral respect for the full range of human fulfillments may be a mission impossible. That, in other words, we either have to scale down our moral aspirations in order to allow our ordinary human life to flourish; or we have to agree to sacrifice some of this ordinary flourishing to secure our higher goals. If we think of this as a dilemma, then perhaps we have to impale ourselves on one horn or the other.

I interpret the two, seemingly contradictory accusations against religious faith, that it respectively, leads to a mortification of ordinary human life, and that it bowdlerizes or sanitizes human nature, as really pointing to this dilemma. The combined accusation is: you have conceived our highest aspirations in such a way that to realize them you will have to mutilate humanity (the mortifying reproach); so naturally, you are induced surreptitiously to scale down your demands, and also to hide from yourselves the full power of human sensuality and aggression, so that ordinary and redeemed humanity can be brought within hailing range of each other—you thus merit the bowdlerizing reproach. In reality this sets out a dilemma: you only escape one horn by impaling yourself on the other.

Now the exclusive humanists who make these accusations against religion often seem to assume that they themselves escape them: that they have found a suitable definition of our highest aspirations which escapes the dilemma, which fully respects ordinary human flourishing. The burden of the above argument is that this is often an illusion. Their highest aspirations too run the risk of mortifying ordinary human life. They hide this from themselves, either because they under-rate how far we are from their goal—they underestimate human depravity, to use the traditional language—and so deserve the bowdlerizing reproach; or they are cavalier about the costs of reaching the goal, and hence deserve the mortifying reproach.

And of course, one can make both these mistakes at once, as we can see with the more mechanistic forms of Enlightenment moral engineering, those which see human nature as fundamentally malleable, the views of a Helvétius, for example. Because they see the issue of reform as merely a matter of forming the right habits, and making the right mental connections, ordinary human nature is not that far from the goal. They reject the doctrine of original sin as exaggerating human depravity. (So they bowdlerize.) But just for this reason, they are unable to see how terribly their social engineering will impact on human beings whose desires and aspirations are not so easily shaped from outside. (So their actual politics mutilate.)

We can, in other words, paradoxically impale ourselves on both horns, make both mistakes at once. And this is in fact the criticism frequently made of the more reductive streams which come from the Enlightenment. They set their sights low: they aim to produce a world in which each in serving himself will also benefit others; interests will harmonize. So humans will at last be satisfied, and the restless search for improvement will at last find a stable form. History will be at an end. This kind of outlook is implicit in much of the optimistic discourse today about free trade and globalization: when market democracies are established everywhere, there will be no more reason to fight. A reign of endless peaceful production and mutual enrichment will have dawned.

Now for many people, this is to pitch our aspirations too low. Fukuyama himself refers to this as an age of the "last men". And the spate of criticism on this score has been steady since the eighteenth century: Rousseau, Kant, Marx, Nietzsche; the list could be extended almost indefinitely. But at the same time, critics have often pointed out that these reductive theories fail altogether to recognize wide ranges of human motivation: the search for meaning, for self-affirmation, the demands of dignity and the wounds of humiliation, not to speak of the wilder ranges of sexual desire and the love of battle. They see them as either containable peccadilloes, or in their more threatening forms as pathology. Thus they fail altogether to measure the real costs of suppressing them or stamping them out. They take the (in Foucault's sense) normalized for fulfilled human beings.

Less reductive forms of exclusive humanism do not share these disabilities. Among other departures from the reductive mechanistic mode, they see a crucial fulfillment in rational freedom, and/or in moral autonomy, and/or aesthetic experience, as we saw in the previous chapter. But this doesn't mean that they have found a formulation of our highest aspirations which can meet the maximal demand. The literature is rich and complex, ever since the Romantic period, of those who have assessed the cost in emotional spontaneity and self-expression of the disciplines of rational freedom, or moral autonomy. Schiller is a case in point.

There are those who have followed Schiller and looked for a transformation—in Schiller's case, to the aesthetic dimension, to the realm of beauty—which could bring the two sides of our nature together, and meet the maximal demand. And, of course, revolutionaries like Marx have followed the same path. But these hopes are highly problematic, and those with a less reductive view of human motivation tend to despair of the maximal demand, to recognize that it sets us a mission impossible, and that it is more prudent, and less destructive to scale down our aspirations. We are tempted to have recourse to a "liberalism of fear", where the basic goal is to limit the infliction of suffering.

Or else we follow Nietzsche and repudiate a basic constraint on the maximal demand: that it reconcile higher aspirations and ordinary fulfillments for *everyone*. Once this universal requirement is set aside, the way is open to see that an élite of the truly exceptional is capable of bidding for excellence either without sacrifice, or in joyful acceptance of it. The fact that this achievement may weigh heavily on the masses is neither here nor there. Those Nietzsche has influenced, thinkers of the immanent counter-Enlightenment, have not been so quick to reject universalism, but they do want to open a space for the wilder, more unbounded forms of self-affirmation which the disciplines of modern humanism have repressed.

5

It thus remains very much an open question whether a form of exclusive humanism can be designed which can meet the maximal demand. But what about Christian faith? It is better equipped to meet it? It may appear that this is so, just because Christianity looks to a much fuller transformation of human life, such that it becomes possible to conceive of transfiguring even the most purblind, self-absorbed and violent. But this is a transformation which cannot be completed in history. In the nature of things, Christianity offers no global solution, no general organization of things here and now which will fully resolve the dilemma, and meet the maximal demand. It can only show ways in which we can, as individuals, and as churches, hold open the path to the fullness of the kingdom.

So Christians don't really "have the solution" to the dilemma, in the sense that we usually take this, and that for two reasons: first, the direction they point to cannot be demonstrated as right; it must be taken on faith; and second, related to this, we can't exhibit fully what it means, lay it out in a code or a fully-specified life form, but only point to the exemplary lives of certain trail-blazing people and communities.

But this understates the difficulties. That Christianity has often been seen as another form of Platonism, even worse in that it seems to give such an important place to punishment and sacrifice, is not just a function of the denseness or ill-will of the critics. The Gospel message doesn't fit into the categories which have come down to us through ages of human history, and is recurrently being twisted, even by its own adherents, to make sense in these terms.

This means that there are clearly wrong versions of Christian faith. But it doesn't mean that we can give a single right version to replace them. The hold of these categories which come to us through our history, including that of our pre-Axial religious life, is so great that we have trouble thinking through what the Christian revelation means. The wrong categories often come more "naturally" to us. So we operate with a certain amount of unclarity and confusion. This is the condition of doing theology.

That being said, we can identify certain misprisions, some of which can be more or less concisely laid out; others require that we disentangle the Christian message from the matrix of our earlier history.

One important locus of distortion surrounds the very notion of transformation. Plato would have responded to our reproach about sacrificing the body and ordinary life with contempt. The transformation he foresees, in which one becomes a real lover of wisdom, means that some things which mattered very much to us before cease to do so. That is in the nature of a far-reaching transformation. It's no use protesting that our present desires will be frustrated; these will disappear, because we will come to see that they aren't really important, not part of what is required to realize the Idea of a human being, which in turn means to come fully into attunement with the Idea of the Good.

And surely any far-reaching transformation will have this feature, that goals and fulfillments which matter now will fall away later. So if we want to defend the value of the life of "l'homme moyen sensuel", then we have to renounce any such major transformation. So runs the anti-Platonic logic of the radical Enlightenment. How then can Christians speak of transformation without becoming closet Platonists?

It is clear that any ethical view which allows for a transformation of our being will have this feature: things which the unregenerate desire will no longer move the transformed. Even the most reductive theory, which sees our desire as fixated on our own pleasure (such as Helvétius, once again), will allow for this: better training, or more understanding of the real conditions of achieving satisfaction, will remove any interest we had in, say, robbing our neighbours to fulfill our needs. More far-reaching transformations will involve one's losing whole categories of desire.

Arguably, in a Christian perspective, the saint will have lost interest in the ego-soothing homage of praise and admiration, which we normally crave, or in the display of macho power. The Platonizing error is to draw the distinction between what can be well lost, and what is essential to us, around the dividing line of our desire as such, and particularly bodily desire. (Of course, the real Plato of the *Republic* doesn't propose that we lose these desires, only that they become and remain perfectly docile to reason.) In the Christian perspective, by contrast, the agape which will ultimately sideline and make irrelevant the satisfactions of ego-boosting is itself bound up with a compassion which is itself incarnate as bodily desire. The transformation moves through a quite different axis, not that of body/soul, but rather that of "flesh/spirit", and these are quite unrelated. The fact that they are still frequently identified, by Christians as well as non-Christians, that "flesh" comes to be seen as synonymous with "body", is a testimony to how powerful the older categories remain in our life and thinking. Nor is this simply a hang-over from the past. One can argue that the disciplines of disengaged reason have given a new force to the body/mind split in modernity.

Another misprision occurs around the category of sacrifice. This is obviously a central category: Jesus gave up his life to save humans. The Christian is often called on to renounce something important. In tandem with the first misprision, Christian renunciation can easily slide towards a more Platonic or Stoic ideal. We renounce certain life fulfillments because they are "lower", because in the final analysis they are not what human life is really about, but ultimately obstacles to our real goal. What is sloughed off doesn't really matter. But this makes nonsense of the sacrifice of Christ. It is precisely because human life is so valuable, part of the plan of God for us, that giving it up has the significance of a supreme act of love. A contrast between the deaths of Socrates and Christ brings this point out with great clarity. In one case, the serenity of the philosopher about to drink the hemlock, assuring his friends that he was going to a better place; in the other, the agony in the garden, the prayer to Father that the cup might pass, only then swallowed up in the affirmation that "thy will be done".

This idea often seems hard to understand. It would be easy to understand why you should give up the fullness of flourishing, if there were something wrong with it. And that's how unbelief reads Christian renunciation, as a negative judgment on human fulfillment.

And in this, it follows much of Christian sensibility over the ages, which has also been uneasy about many aspects of human flourishing, has been uncertain and ambivalent about them. Take sexual fulfillment for instance. For centuries, the mediaeval church taught that sexual intercourse was essentially to be directed to procreation, and you shouldn't enjoy it too heartily even then. The Reformers tried to rehabilitate sexual relations among married couples, but in practice the emphasis on its being carried out to the glory of God put a damper on sexual pleasure.

I am not trying to be condescending about our ancestors, because I think that there is a real tension involved in trying to combine in one life sexual fulfillment and piety. This is only in fact one of the points at which a more general tension, between human flourishing in general and dedication to God, makes itself felt. That this tension should be particularly evident in the sexual domain is readily understandable. Intense and profound sexual fulfillment focusses us powerfully on the exchange within the couple; it strongly attaches us possessively to what is privately shared. We come close here to the point raised by Nussbaum that I quoted above. It was not for nothing that the early monks and hermits saw sexual renunciation as opening the way to the wider love of God.

Now that there is a tension between fulfillment and piety should not surprise us in a world distorted by sin, that is, separation from God. But we have to avoid turning this into a constitutive incompatibility. This, however, is what both exclusive humanism on one hand, and the sensibility of much conservative Christianity on the other, tend to do. The first take for granted that what is dedicated to God must detract from human fulfillment. The second are so focussed on the denial and restriction of desire that they easily fall into a mirror image of the secular stance: following God means denying yourself.

Both these positions seem coherent. The tension is between them, but seems absent within them. But if you hold that fulfillment and piety are not constitutively incompatible; and also that following God may often involve renunciation, you hold a position that can seem inconsistent, and is in considerable tension. The tension doesn't just come from the fact that the big battalions often are fighting it out on the understanding that one of these goals must yield to the other. It also comes from the real difficulty of combining the two goals, as I illustrated above with sexuality. It is after all, more than anything else, this real existential tension which has given rise to the ideological polarization, though of course this polarization certainly helps to worsen the tension.

This brings us to a third misprision, now not specifically about Christianity, but which affects our ethical thinking in general. We tend to see certain desires as good, such as love of our neighbour, generous sentiments towards others, etc.; and others as bad, such as pride, a propensity to violence, and the like. The goal must be to eradicate the bad ones and encourage the good. It is in this spirit that parents are often induced to keep their sons away from war toys, or to bowdlerize traditional children's tales, which are frequently violent.

This is indeed how things may look to the most reductive Enlightenment theories, where the goal is to stamp in good habits and stamp out bad. But in any theory which allows for a more far-reaching transformation, the reality is more complex. What have to be transformed are the desires themselves. Sexual desire has to grow into a more profound, more fully engaging love; self-affirmation into a devotion to those we love, sympathy has to become more awake to the real predicament of those around us, and so on. If this process has even started in any one of us—and this must be the case for at least one of these directions of growth—then our reality is complex. It can no longer be a question just of stamping out something, or stamping in something else. Thus simply putting an end to my sex life does away with the bad, obsessive self-absorbed aspects, but also ends the whole process of growth. This process can be guided, inflected, accelerated, but not simply interrupted. In Biblical terms, the wheat and the tares are so inextricably interwoven that the latter cannot be ripped out without also damaging the former.[23] This fundamental ambivalence of human reality, in all but the limit case of absolute evil (and is this really possible for us?), must always be kept in mind.

Having made these three points, we get to the really difficult matters. Those which accuse religion of denying and mutilating ordinary human sensuous life aren't simply victims of the Platonizing illusion, or a misunderstanding of the nature of sacrifice. Christian transformation is also from another point of view salvation. And salvation points to the possibility of damnation, and hence of divine punishment. The idea that such severe retribution awaits the unregenerate has also helped to accredit the picture of religion as negating and censuring ordinary human fulfillment. In order to cast further light here, we have to look back into the murky process whereby the Christian revelation emerged from and partly rejected earlier understandings of sacrifice and divine violence.

(A) In one sense the charge seems undeniable. As far back as we can look, we see that religion often involves sacrifice, in some fashion or other. We need to give up something; it can be to placate God, or to feed God, or to get His favour. But this demand can also be spiritualized or moralized: we are radically imperfect, below what God wants. So we need to sacrifice the bad parts; or sacrifice something in punishment for the bad parts.

The sense of unworthiness is playing an important role here. But humans have also always been under threat from destructive forces. There are fierce hurricanes, earthquakes, famines, floods. And then also in human affairs, there are wildly destructive people and actions: invasions, sackings, conquests, massacres. Or perhaps we feel the menace of ultimate entropy.

It may be that these are given a meaning by being subsumed into the terrible demands of baleful fate, which is ours in virtue of what we owe to the gods, or of our imperfections. This account fits the Nietzschean idea that we want to give a meaning to suffering in order to make it bearable. But we could also see it the other way around: the sense of lack, of our falling short is primitive; and we need to give a shape to it. Not: first suffering; then we look for a meaning; so suffering becomes punishment; but: first deserving punishment (or the sense of falling short); so we look for certain modes of suffering to give a shape to all this; or a sense of how we can make it up. So our punishment becomes identified with this suffering. In this way, natural destructive forces come to be seen as wild and full of a spirit of destruction.

Religion can thus mean that we identify with these demands/fates. So we see destruction as also divine, as with Kali-Shiva. And when you can bring yourself to identify with it, you are renouncing all the things which get destroyed, purifying yourself. Wild destruction is given a meaning and a purpose. In a sense it is domesticated, becomes less fearful in one way, even as it acquires part of the terror of the numinous.

This of course, involves submitting to an external, higher will, purpose, or demand; it requires decentring. But there is also a way of dealing with violence and destruction, and the terrible fears they arouse in us, which gives us a sense of power, of being in control. It is a central part of the warrior ethic. We face down the fear of destruction; we accept the possibility of violent death. We even see ourselves as in advance already claimed by death: we are "dead men on leave". Think of the symbolism in naming a regiment after the death's head: the "Totenkopf" battalion of the Prussian army.

Then we live in the element of violence, but like kings, unafraid, as agents of pure action, dealing death; we are the rulers of death. What was terrifying before is now exciting, exhilarating; we're on a high. It gives a sense to our lives. This is what it means to transcend.

One way of dealing with the terror stills the turbulence of violence, either depriving it of its numinous power, or identifying it with some higher such power, which is ultimately benign. The other keeps the numinous force of violence, but reverses the field of fear; what previously made us cower now exhilarates; we now live by it, transcend normal limits through it. This is what animates battle rage, berserker fury, which makes possible feats of arms undreamed of in our everyday mode.

There are also ways of combining these two responses, as in some cultures with human sacrifice. On one hand, we submit to the god to whom we offer our blood; but the sacrificers also become agents of violence; they do it instead of just submitting to it; they wade in blood and gore, but now with sacred intent. Because it combines the two strategies for dealing with this terror, there is nothing more satisfying than a sacred massacre. René Girard has explored this terrain, where religion and violence meet.[24]

So religion since way back has been involved with sacrifice and mutilation; through the sense of the obligation to offer something of our substance to God, heightened by our imperfections; and through our strategies for dealing with the deep inner tremors that violence and destruction awake in us, identifying them with the divine, or internalizing their numinous power, or both.

But there has also been a counter-movement, one which tried to break or at least purify this connection. Ancient Judaism starts a critique of this sacred levy on us. There are false gods; and their toll is a sheer robbery with violence, as with the sacrifices to Baal. This is not what God wants, as he signifies to Abraham on Mount Moriah.

This critique applies to the unspiritualized, unmoralized forms of sacrifice, where we just need to placate the Gods or spirits. But the Christian tradition retains various spiritualized forms, where the sacrifice is part of the road to perfection, or is our response to the kenosis (self-emptying) of God. We can become "eunuchs for the kingdom". Later, however, some of these roads will also be taxed with falseness, as when the Reformation denounces the "higher" renunciative vocations of Catholicism.

Now as we saw above, the anthropocentric turn in modern Christianity, followed by the unbelief which emerges from it, push this line of critique farther and farther. It portrays the older forms of Christian faith, and eventually religion as such, as a false spiritual perfectionism which sacrifices real, healthy, breathing, loving human beings enjoying their normal fulfillment on the altars of false Gods. All religion is ultimately Moloch drinking blood from the skulls of the slain.[25] The Old Testament critique of the Phoenician cults is now extended to faith in the transcendent as such.

At this point, anything beyond exclusive humanism can become a target for this criticism, as we saw with the critique of transcendence by Nussbaum and others.

The slide here, which takes us out of faith altogether, can perhaps be understood in this way: one central constituent of Christian revelation is that God not only wills our good, a good which includes human flourishing, but was willing to go to extraordinary lengths to ensure this, in the becoming human and suffering of his son. Now this constituent came to be read in such a way that it more and more excluded sacrifice and divinely ordained suffering, to the point where the central beliefs in God's sacrifice and suffering began to seem untenable.

If the good that God wills for us doesn't just include, but consists entirely in human flourishing, what sense does it make to sacrifice some part of this in order to serve God? This link between sacrifice and religion is broken. And the other stream of traditional Christian piety, which reads the violence and destruction in the world as part of the ultimate, fulfilled divine plan, and/or internalizes it as the power of rage, now becomes close to incomprehensible.

Internalization is out of the question, because the idea of human flourishing according to the modern moral order has no place for violence and rage, but only for pacific mutual benefit. Indeed, the disciplines of this civilizing order have involved repressing and marginalizing this violence, and above all, denying it any numinous power. It is rather degraded to the level of the pathological, as we saw above.

But nor does there seem to be any place for divine violence, as it were, destruction and suffering as part of the fulfilled divine plan. A God who purposes nothing but our human flourishing couldn't want to inflict this. It would make no sense. God, if anything, must be on our side in trying to repress and desacralize human violence. How could he himself give it positive meaning? And granted the interweaving of the two strategies above, the way in which a sense of destruction as from God licences our joyful participation as agents of God, engaged in sacred massacre, the repudiation of human violence seems to require the denial of divine destruction.

So in this anthropocentric climate, where we keep any idea of the spiritual, it must be totally constructive, positive. It can't accommodate Kali, and is less and less able to allow for a God who punishes. The wrath of God disappears, leaving only His love.

On the older view, wrath had to be part of the package. The sense of salvation was inseparable from that of our having fallen, being degraded. This in turn was inseparable from that of deserving punishment; deserved punishment has to be meted out. God owes this to his honour, as we saw earlier (Chapter 6). So some people fry in Hell; and the others are only saved because Christ offered "satisfaction" for them. This was the heart of the juridical-penal understanding of the atonement.

But in the anthropocentric climate, this no longer makes sense, and indeed, appears monstrous. True, an earlier phase, which I called above "Providential Deism", preserves the idea of rewards and punishments beyond the grave. And this made sense as a helpful measure to keep us on the path towards our own good, as we saw, for instance, with Locke. But as the feeling wanes that we need this kind of external prop, the last reason for divine violence, as punishment/pedagogy, disappears.

So there is a particularly strong attack against this whole dimension of the old theology, which gave a place to divine violence as punishment or trial. Hence the striking modern phenomenon, which has been described as "the decline of Hell".

And hence what was for a long time and remains for many the heart of Christian piety and devotion: love and gratitude at the suffering and sacrifice of Christ, seems incomprehensible, or even repellent and frightening to many. To celebrate such a terrible act of violence as a crucifixion, to make this the centre of your religion, you have to be sick; you have to be perversely attached to self-mutilation, because it assuages your self-hatred, or calms your fears of healthy self-affirmation. You are elevating self-punishment, which liberating humanism wants to banish as a pathology, to the rank of the numinous. This you hear frequently today.[26]

Of course, the Crucifixion can't be read out of the story at this late date; but it has to be an *accident de parcours;* not the main point. This fits well with the whole shift within the anthropocentric climate in the significance given to the life of Christ: what is important is not what he *does* (atone, conquer death, take captivity captive), but rather what he *says* or *teaches*. The slide to Unitarianism, and then beyond this to a humanism of which Christ can be one of the "prophets", belongs to this massive shift in the centre of gravity of the life of Jesus.

Of course, in doing this we are giving up the age-old attempts to cope with the fear and unease at the numinous resonance of violence and destruction by placing them within the divine plan. And this has a price. Suffering imposed by humans, particularly in the name of transcendent ideals, has a meaning: a negative one, as something we strive to get rid of. But extraneous suffering must be meaningless. We can't admit it has meaning without falling back into one of these views of suffering as right and necessary, as sent to try or punish or improve us.

And that is one of the reasons why the modern age is so concerned about the issue of meaning, as we shall explore further below. And it gives us part of the explanation why this age of the anthropocentric turn is one in which the issue of theodicy has taken such great importance.

There is an obvious connection, which can be put by saying that all the suffering which used to be given meaning and purpose as divine violence now poses a question for God; indeed, for just about any god, but most acutely for one who is supposed to have human flourishing as his major purpose. But we could also see the link in another way. The older view saw destruction and violence as an ineradicable part of our world and condition. The fact that the divine plan gave some meaning to it, and some ultimate path beyond it, was sufficient grounds for gratitude. Our new stance allows us to imagine a world shorn of violence and suffering, at least as a conceivable long-term goal. The destructive forces which confront us are nothing but obstacles on the path to this goal. It is a legitimate question to God, why they are there in the first place, if he too seeks this goal for us.

Again, we could put this in a third way, which links up with the discussion in an earlier section. The older stance grasps the world from within our condition of limitation and vulnerability. But to imagine how it could be comprehensively reformed requires that we stand outside it, see it as a system, laid out before us in a tableau or "world picture", in which we could then project various alterations. This is the standpoint from which the issues of theodicy cannot but arise, granted we recognize God at all.

Now I described unbelieving thought as being in something of a tension or dilemma above, pushing towards a humanist programme which tends to pathologize the obstacles to its realization, while it comes up repeatedly against the revulsion at the reductiveness of this stance, and generates what I called the immanent revolt.

But the anthropocentric turn puts Christian faith as well in something of a tension or dilemma, which has some connections or parallels with those of unbelief. On one hand, Christianity is inconceivable without sacrifice, without the possibility of some positive meaning to suffering. The Crucifixion cannot be sidelined as merely a regrettable by-product of a valuable career of teaching.

Yes, of course. But then isn't the answer easy? Just undo the anthropocentric turn; recover the insight that God has a purpose for us beyond just the best human flourishing we can manage in our present condition; recover the insight that we are fallen beings and can be raised.

This is certainly part of the answer. But this is not to say that our goal is just to return to the status quo ante Providential Deism. For one thing, the Christian faith, at least in Latin Christendom, was heavily invested in what I am calling the hyper-Augustinian juridical-penal framework.

Just to remind ourselves of what I am trying to outline here: there are at least two key mysteries that Christian faith turns on: one is why we are in the grip of evil, why we were/are somehow incapable of helping ourselves to overcome this condition, and become the kind of creatures which we know we were made to be; the other is how the sacrifice of Christ broke through this helplessness, and opened a way out. The first phenomenon has been understood in the West by the notion of original sin. The second has been called the atonement, and the dominant understanding in Latin Christendom for centuries fell within a peculiarly juridical-penal framework: in sinning, we deserved punishment and hence were lost to God. A big debt had to be paid. God had this debt paid for us by his own son, and thus opened the way for many of us to return.

One might think that an alert Christian faith would recognize that we will never be able to sound these mysteries, that any attempt to explicate them through some particular set of concepts, like 'original sin', 'paying the debt', or 'giving satisfaction',[27] will be approximate, and problematic at some points, and that we must at all costs avoid pushing the logic of any of these concepts recklessly to their ultimate conclusions, no matter how paradoxical or repulsive.

We have in a sense to operate with several different images in thinking of the mysteries of the Faith. Like any images or metaphors, they reveal something important, but the analogies cannot be pressed indefinitely without distortion. So the juridical-penal story does capture our fault. But there is another image, even the paradigm one, that of redemption, where the redeemer buys the captive out of imprisonment. Unlike the juridical-penal, there is no sense that the payment here is due anyone, certainly not the captor; any more than protection money is "owed" the mafia. The juridical metaphor, with its central figure of debt, can't be pushed to the limit without invalidating the (even more central) redemption metaphor. To do so is to forget that, while each image adds something, it is only through a whole range of these that we can even distantly hope to capture something of God's work in the world.

A similar point can be made about the wrath of God. When we sin, we provoke God's anger. This does carry something important about the way that sin cuts us off from God, and also about what a terrifying condition this is, and our responsibility in bringing this about. But one can't push the logic of the anger image through all its ramifications. When I'm mad at you for what you've done to me, I want to punish you, even cut you off, have nothing more to do with you. When we apply all this to God, we step across a line which makes nonsense of key Christian doctrines, carried by other images and stories, particularly here the tale of the prodigal son.[28]

But this restraint requires a kind of intellectual humility, and this seems to have been in short supply in Latin Christendom, which has been the scene of total, almost obsessive identification with certain favourite schemes, driven to any wild or repellent consequences, justifying murderous schisms. One thinks of Calvin's horrible doctrine of double predestination here, but the Catholic side has not been far behind in this hubristic rage to define.

Both sides drew from their common hyper-Augustinian roots the general or widely held consensus that the majority of the human race will be damned. The missionaries in post-Conquest Latin America felt that they had to inform their new converts that the ancestors of these latter were excluded forever from God's salvation. One could go on and on. It is sufficient to say that these consequences of the hyper-Augustinian framework were repellent to many consciences in earlier ages, and that they helped to propel many people outside the faith and into exclusive humanism as the anthropocentric turn gathered force.

Now I recognize that many believers today still want to affirm the full hyper-Augustinian package, e.g., conservative Catholics and some fundamentalist Protestants. But there is also a broader band of Christian belief and sensibility for which the decline of Hell is a positive doctrinal change. There can be no question for these people of a simple return to the status quo ante Deismo.

If I speak from out of this religious understanding, in which I place myself, then this modern turn has brought some positive benefits; in say, detaching our view of the first mystery (original sin) from an obsessive sense of human depravity; and in giving us a distance from the juridical-penal view of the atonement.

But a change has also occurred at a more fundamental level. Our hyper-Augustinian ancestors were part of a religious culture in which it was normal to find divine meaning to suffering and destruction. All previous human cultures had done so, and it seemed almost inconceivable to understand/experience the world in other terms. The break of modernity means that this kind of reading no longer can be taken for granted.

I mean this on two levels: not only that there are alternatives, which construe the dangers and misfortunes which befall us as purely contingent, something that only small minorities (e.g., Epicureans, and some other philosophers) did in the past. But also that the question arises whether readings in terms of divine violence are not a dangerous temptation.

I mentioned above the all-too-human tendency to colonize divine violence with our own. If such and such a conquest is God's punishment for our sins, then we are coming close to giving the conquerors a divine mission. This may be without danger when the instruments of God's wrath are outsiders, e.g., Mongol or Turkish invaders of Christendom. But those within who fight against the infidel, who suppress heresy, and punish offenders, can begin to see themselves too as having a divine mandate. The violence of God can be all too easily appropriated by the warrior cultures which internalize the numinous force of violence.

Expropriated divine violence is also a mechanism of exclusion. We are on God's side, and by definition they—the infidel, heretic, wrong-doer, adversary of our community—are not. We reach absurdities, like the last great convulsion of what was still Christian Europe, in the First World War, where each side confidently enrolled God among its supporters. We are not far from the spiritual temptation of believing that we are right and blessed, because we conquer.

Perhaps then the modern turn was right in taking the critique of divine violence, which begins with the Biblical denunciation of the sacrifices to Baal, right up to the point of challenging the very concept itself. Perhaps there is something deeply wrong with all hermeneutics of suffering as divine. Perhaps we are wrong to seek a meaning here.

But surely for a Christian the suffering of Christ has meaning, and by extension that of martyrs and saints? Yes, but on the traditional view this meaning fitted into an already existing framework of significance, whereby suffering was seen as punishment or pedagogy, the economy of which was altered by Christ's sacrifice.

We could start somewhere quite different, see suffering and destruction as often themselves devoid of meaning, and see the self-giving of Christ to suffering as a new initiative by God, whereby suffering repairs the breach between God and humans, and thus has not a retrospective or already established, but a transformative meaning.

We start with the fact of human resistance to God, closure towards God who could heal the consequences of this resistance, which we call sin. This is the first mystery. God's initiative is to enter, in full vulnerability, the heart of the resistance, to be among humans, offering participation in the divine life. The nature of the resistance is that this offer arouses even more violent opposition, not a divine violence, more a counter-divine one.

Now Christ's reaction to the resistance was to offer no counter-resistance, but to continue loving and offering. This love can go to the very heart of things, and open a road even for the resisters. This is the second mystery. Through this loving submission, violence is turned around, and instead of breeding counter-violence in an endless spiral, can be transformed. A path is opened of non-power, limitless self-giving, full action, and infinite openness.

On the basis of this initiative, the incomprehensible healing power of this suffering, it becomes possible for human suffering, even of the most meaningless type, to become associated with Christ's act, and to become a locus of renewed contact with God, an act which heals the world. The suffering is given a transformative effect, by being offered to God.

A catastrophe thus can become part of a providential story, by being responded to in a certain way; its meaning lies not in its antecedents, but in what is drawn out of it; just as the ultimate meaning of the Fall was the Incarnation that was God's response to it (hence its paradoxical description as a "felix culpa"). Neither the Lisbon earthquake nor the Boxing Day tsunami, neither the second World War nor Hiroshima, can be understood with reference to their antecedents as punishment; but they are given meaning through God's steadfast resolve not to abandon humanity in its worst distress.

The tension, awkwardness, even sometimes dilemma of this kind of modern Christian consciousness is that it tries to detach the central truths of the faith, about sin and atonement, from their familiar Latin-Christian backdrop, from the hyper-Augustinian juridical-penal reading, and the hermeneutics of divine violence, suffering as punishment or pedagogy. On one hand, many people find these hard to believe, or to square with their sense of God; on the other, so many of the official formulations of the faith still seem to be involved with them, and their hold on our imagination is still strong.

Our sin is our resistance to going along with God's initiative in making suffering reparative. We are deeply drawn towards God, but we also sense how following him will dislocate and transform beyond recognition the forms which have made life tolerable for us. We often react with fear, dismay, hostility. We are at war with ourselves, and responding differently to this inner conflict, we end up at war with each other. So it is undoubtedly true that the result of sin is much suffering. But this is by no means distributed according to desert. Many who are relatively innocent are swept up in this suffering, and some of the worst offenders get off lightly. The proper response to all this is not retrospective book-keeping, but making ourselves capable of responding to God's initiative.

But now if that's what sin is, then one can sympathize with a lot of the modern critique of a religion which focusses on the evil tendencies of human nature, and the need for renunciation and sacrifice. This is not because humans are in fact angelic, or there is no point to sacrifice. It's just that focussing on how bad human beings can be, even if it's to refute the often over-rosy views of secular humanists with their reliance on human malleability and therapy, can only strengthen misanthropy, which certainly won't bring you closer to God; and propounding sacrifice and renunciation for themselves takes you away from the main point, which is following God's initiative. That this can involve sacrifice, we well know from the charter act in this initiative, but renunciation is not its point. Indeed, the focus on renunciation can often give grist to the mill of the second misprision above, which misreads renunciation as the giving up of what is not valuable anyway.

But at the same time, this Christian consciousness cannot follow exclusive humanism in making human flourishing its only goal. There is a point in giving it all up, if one can contribute to repairing the breach with God.

Now this understanding is hard to hang on to, because of the second and third misprisions above. Renunciation slides towards finding its point in a purification from the bad things we don't really need anyway; and our life as lived on the road to a deeper transformation loses its ambivalence, and divides neatly into the good and bad parts, where the latter are, of course, to be "renounced". As I described above, the real existential tension in our lives between growth towards God and the hold of long-standing narrower habits and forms can easily polarize out into the good and bad bits, and listed in a schedule of do's and don'ts.

This modern Christian consciousness thus lives in a tension, that may feel at times like a dilemma, between what it draws from the development of modern humanism, and its attachment to the central mysteries of Christian faith. It endorses the decline of Hell, the rejection of the juridical-penal model of the atonement, and any hermeneutic of divine violence, as well as affirming the full value of human flourishing. But it cannot accept the self-enclosure in immanence, and is aware that God has given a new transformative meaning to suffering and death in the life and death of Christ. God's initiative has given a new sense to renunciation, which has to be recovered beyond the deforming encrustations of religious anti-humanism.

The wrath of God, which in the juridical-penal model was read as the condign response to an offence to God's "honour", is now seen as the inseparable accompaniment of a rejection of God's love, and the consequent isolation and division among sinners. Hell, the ultimate separation from God, must remain a possibility for human freedom, but all the presumptuous certainty that it is inhabited must be abandoned.

This is a difficult position, not just for the sociological reason that it cuts across the battle lines between belief and unbelief; but for the deeper existential reason that the tension between fulfillment and dedication to God is still very much unresolved in our lives.[29] It is supremely difficult to exhibit in one's life the compatibility one proclaims between the human and the divine. One reads this in the lives of exceptional individuals, but cannot easily refract it in one's own, so that others can read it there too. The polemicists on both sides of the battle line find it easier to live down to their one-sided views, or perhaps more accurately, to hide from themselves how much they contradict existentially what they proclaim ideologically.

The compatibility espoused by the modern Christian consciousness is not an achievement but an act of faith, in God's plan, and in the transformation he can and will wreak. This is its essential weakness for some, but for its protagonists what makes it ultimately credible.

iii. Roots of Violence

6

(B) So there is a certain parallel between the dilemmas of believers and unbelievers in this domain. Above we saw how exclusive humanism tends towards a rejection of the aspiration to transcendence; and yet it has trouble setting it aside altogether, as the problematic attempt to define an "internal transcendence" by Nussbaum testifies. Now we see how in its own way, modern belief feels an analogous tension between human flourishing and the demands of God.

Is there similarly a parallel in the other locus of tension, that between the demands of the pacific moral order and aggressive self-affirmation, the desire to break out of the narrow confines of discipline, even the love of violence and wild sexual licence? The tendency to class these obstacles to peaceful order as mere pathology, or primitive under-development, and to treat them as dispensable through therapy and conditioning, provokes a reaction, the revolt immanent to unbelief that I described above. The repudiation of this wild side of our being is seen by Nietzsche and others as a manoeuvre on all fours with the Christian "spiritual" rejection of sensuality. They are both self-mutilations in the name of a morality of slaves.

At first sight, it might appear that there would be no analogous problem on the Christian side. And this for the reason that Nietzsche and exclusive humanists keep proclaiming, that Christians have, in the doctrine of "original sin", the resources to declare many of the widespread tendencies of (statistically) "normal" human life as depraved. What goes for sensuality goes for violence. An appeal for our aggressive instincts on the grounds that we shouldn't mutilate our own being would be of no effect.

But a modern Christian consciousness is no longer so quick to solve its problems with the label "depravity". It is aware of the tensions between (fallen) nature and the demands of God, but it also sees how inextricably interwoven human self-affirmation is with its distorted forms, how—to recur to the Biblical image—the wheat and tares are together until the harvest, and how long is the process of reaching this harvest. This consciousness is thus able to sense a difficulty here, analogous to that felt by unbelievers. Because of this complex interweaving, the moves towards God and the resistance to him are often hard to disentangle.

The question is this: how to understand certain powerful desires, sometimes even to the point of frenzy: wild sexuality, berserker rage, love of battle, slaughter? When we experience these, we are like wild beasts, we think. These desires are not only deeply unsettling, but also destructive. They militate against: benevolence, the binding of wounds, peace, goodness; and also: long-lasting love, fidelity, bringing up children, caring. And of course, sanctity.

How to understand this opposition? And particularly, the wild side of it?

This wild side seems particularly strong, at least in cultures we know, among men, particularly young men. One can see their attraction to militias, fighting organizations, guerrillas, and the like. And we also note the propensity of this kind of semi-organized group violence to turn to rape, pillage, massacre. This seems to appeal as a powerful form of self-assertion, the cult of the macho.

At the antipodes of religion, we think. And this seems true for "higher" religions. But violence, and sometimes sexuality, gets itself a place among many "primitive" religions, and not only there; as I was saying in the last chapter in relation to pre-Axial religion.

What to make of this? One common approach in our culture is the disengaged, objectifying "scientific" one. The propensity to violence can be understood in biological, evolutionary terms. It is in some ways "wired into" us.

Can we understand violence in biological terms, or must we have recourse to the meta-biological? I am using "meta" here in one of the original senses of its use in "metaphysical", what is "after" or "beyond" the physical. What is "meta" the biological in this sense? We could put it this way: the biological is what we share with other animals, we need food, shelter, sex; and other things that we alone seek, but which serve needs analogous to those of other animals: like clothes for warmth. We enter the realm of the meta-biological when we come to needs like that for meaning. Here we can no longer spell out what is involved in biological terms, those with animal analogues, nor state in these terms what kinds of things will answer this need, like a sense of purpose, or of the importance or value of a certain kind of life, or the like.

We can have sociobiological accounts of both sex and violence. We can imagine that our ancestors had to develop propensities for fighting and if necessary killing outsiders to their clans, or otherwise they would not have survived; just as we have such accounts of man-woman pair-bonding, which allowed more offspring to survive. Perhaps we might think that this explains phenomena of today, like nationalist mobilizations to war, which justify ruthless attacks on the enemy; or the importance of love and marriage in all human societies. That our evolutionary history has contributed something to who we are today must in some sense be true. The issue about sociobiology is just how much it explains.

Even sociobiologists must be aware that we have created elaborate meta-biological matrices around both love and war; that we have notions about real, profound love; or about war for a just cause. The issue is: do these matrices of self-understanding explain anything important about our behaviour in these domains? In particular, these matrices are cultural; they vary between society and society. Is it important to understand the variations in order to grasp why we do what we do, or are the main features of our actions in these domains adequately accounted for in terms of our common evolutionary inheritance?

No one would want to deny that these varying cultural matrices are crucial to understanding the moral and religious outlooks of different societies. Perhaps we have to go to the meta-biological level in order to understand the ways in which each culture struggles to control the powerful, disruptive forces of sex and violence. But these forces themselves could perhaps be understood in purely biological terms. This way of dividing up the field goes easily along with notions of categorical violence as a "throwback"; culture evolves, and brings higher and higher standards of moral behaviour. We now live with and partly by, notions of human rights which are incomparably more demanding than in previous civilizations; but the old drives lurk there still, waiting for certain extreme conditions which will allow them to break out. We can even add a Freudian twist to this take on things: the advance of civilization brings with it ever more stringent standards which place an ever heavier interdict on violent behaviour. Previous outlets, like Carnivals, riots, public and ritualized executions, bull fights, fox hunting, and other things we now consider barbarous, have all fallen under interdict. This adds to the sense of release and the surge of excitement which accompanies outbreaks of categorical violence, when they are at last permitted.

Within this explanatory division of labour, we could think of explaining the violence itself on a purely biological level, as something that presumably remains the same in human life, even as culture "advances". We note that men, even more frequently young men, are usually the perpetrators, and that can point us to a hormonal explanation. Does it all comes down to testosterone? But this seems radically insufficient. It's not that body chemistry is not a crucial factor, but that it never operates alone in human life, but only through the meanings that things have for us. The hormonal explanation doesn't tell us why people are susceptible to certain meanings. It could at best explain just the brute fact of violence, whenever we're crossed, for instance; like: why men are violent in relationships, more than women. But even that is questionable, because of findings, like those of James Gilligan, that humiliation is an important causal factor in individual violence.[30]

And when we come to categorical violence, we see that meta-biological factors often play a decisive role. Yes, young men are often drawn to it; but we also see that they are all the more drawn when they are unemployed, just hanging around, and see no meaningful future for themselves, as in the refugee camps of Palestine. It is the matrices of meaning that their lives are embedded in which offer them the sense of vibrant purpose, which can galvanize them and give significance to their lives. Moreover, it is these matrices which designate who is compatriot, and who is the enemy.

And then there is what has sometimes been called, a bit euphemistically, the "excess" which often accompanies this violence. This can give to its perpetrators a "high", which both allows and tempts us beyond all permissible limits. As a perceptive observer puts in a recent book:

> The god-like empowerment over other human lives and the drug of war combine, like the ecstasy of erotic love, to let our senses command our bodies. Killing unleashes within us dark undercurrents that see us desecrate and whip ourselves into greater orgies of destruction. The dead, treated with respect in peacetime, are abused in wartime. They become pieces of performance art. Corpses were impaled in Bosnia on the side of barn doors, decapitated, or draped like discarded clothing over fences. They were dumped into rivers, burned alive in homes, herded into warehouses and shot and mutilated, or left

on the roadside. Children could pass them on the street, gape at them and walk on.[31]

We are tempted to explain this kind of outbreak of barbarity in the way this term suggests, as throwbacks to earlier, less civilized times. This is, I believe, a dangerous illusion. But even if it were true, this wouldn't mean that the archaic here is to be explained in terms of biology and not of culture.

We might be tempted to explain the high here, the wild abandon by the fact that these underlying drives are severely reigned in, and even repressed in modern civilization, which makes for the high energy of sudden release when we can let go. And this view may be strengthened when we note how the release of violence can also be a kind of aphrodisiac, unchaining sexual desire, and giving the perpetrators an erotic aura.[32]

But even when we go back to "barbaric" times, prior to the heavy interdictions of modern civilization, we find that these two drives were from the earliest times interwoven with meta-biological meaning. As I mentioned in an earlier section, sexuality was connected to the sacred, through rituals like sacred marriage, or temple prostitution. Categorical violence, in the form of war, goes deep in human history. Keegan argues that at first it too was largely ritualized.[33] This limited the damage. (The irony is that "progress" has meant greater destruction, because of "rational" action.) And then there is the rich and varied history of human sacrifice.

So not only our struggles to control unchained sexual desire and violence need to be understood in meta-biological terms; these "drives" themselves have to be grasped through the matrices of meaning which give them shape in our lives. This is something we could easily have inferred, in fact, from the historic interweaving of religion and violence briefly reviewed in section 5 above.

7

Obviously, Christianity requires some kind of meta-biological account of our impulsions to violence. Meanings are susceptible to different interpretations, and hence to a change in direction in a way that genetically hard-wired dispositions are not. But this is not to say that such accounts must support the Christian notion of transformation. We have to remember that this is (at least) a three-cornered debate. There are accounts of the meaning of violence which are inspired by Nietzsche, and belong to the immanent counter-Enlightenment in the sense that they want to rehabilitate the impulsions to violence, destruction, and orgiastic sexuality.

Our whole understanding of the debate in this area would be foreshortened, if we didn't take account of some of these. I want briefly to mention two, which while influenced by Nietzsche, want to maintain a universalist perspective, and avoid relegating the mass of the "all-too-human" to a lesser category.

The first is Georges Bataille. I draw my account of his views mainly from his *Théorie de la religion.*[34]

Animals live in boundary-less continuity with their world. Humans have the power to separate out objects and identify them as "things" *(choses)*, in Bataille's sense. In the first place, they identify instrumental objects. These endure, alongside and in interaction with each other, but without flowing into each other in boundless continuity.

The human world is made of such enduring things, and indeed, our instrumental action is aimed at making it endure. Our own death has no proper place in this order, except as something to be staved off as long as possible.

But we are living beings, and sense the continuity. In the continuity which we share with animals, death is part of life. As living beings we have a longing to live in the continuity, for what Bataille calls "intimacy" (l'intimité). It draws us. But to humans in a stable order of things, this continuity is a threat, the ultimate threat of disruption, and its worst form, death. For the same reason, it is the site of the sacred in human life, which both fascinates and attracts, but also evokes horror: "l'intimité est sainte, sacrée et nimbée d'angoisse" (intimacy is holy, sacred, and suffused with anxiety).[35]

In the same way, we are ambivalent about death: both the break in our enduring world which we fight to ward off, and also the break-out of the world of things into continuity-intimacy. So it brings sadness, but also a kind of joy; our tears frequently express our loss, but "dans d'autres cas les larmes répondent par contre au triomphe inespéré, à la chance dont nous exultons, mais toujours de façon insensée, bien au delà du souci d'un temps à venir"[36] (on the other hand, tears are in some cases a response to unexpected triumph, to the fortune at which we exult, but always in an extravagant way, well beyond any concern for the future).

But this not Keats' being "half in love with easeful death". We come close in death to a break-out from the objectified, thingly order when we deal death, in violence. The draw to death is also a pull to violence, to destructions, to an untamed sexuality, the direct reversal and denial of our careful, instrumental effort to make the thing-order endure. It is a kind of abandonment, an instantaneous "consumption" (Bataille says "consumation", "using up", rather than "consommation").

This abandonment takes us out of the domain where everything is instrumental for something else, into a realm of activity which has its end in itself, that of "les dépenses dites improductives" (so-called unproductive expenditures):

Le luxe, les deuils, les guerres, les cultes, les constructions de monuments somptuaires, les jeux, les spectacles, les arts, l'activité sexuelle perverse (c'est-à-dire détournée de la finalité génitale) représentent autant d'activités qui . . . ont leur fin en elles-mêmes.[37]

(Luxury, mourning, war, religious worship, the construction of sumptuary monuments, games, spectacles, arts, perverse sexual activity (i.e., diverted from its genital function)—all these represent activities which . . . have their end in themselves.)[38]

The original, archaic religious form of this break-out is the sacrifice. The victim may be killed, but the point is not the killing itself, but abandoning and giving.

Ce qui importe c'est de passer d'un ordre durable, où toute consumation des ressources est subordonnée à la nécessité de durer, à la violence d'une consumation inconditionnelle.[39]

(What is important is to pass from a lasting order, in which all consumption of resources is subordinated to the need for duration, to the violence of unconditional consumption.)[40]

The sacrificer is saying, in effect,

Intimement, j'appartiens, moi, au monde souverain des dieux et des mythes, au monde de la générosité violente et sans calcul, comme ma femme appartient à mes désirs.[41]

(*Intimately,* I belong to the sovereign world of gods and myths, to the world of violent uncalculated generosity, just as my wife belongs to my desires.)[42]

Dans ses mythes étranges, dans ses rites cruels, l'homme est dès l'abord à la recherche de l'intimité perdue.[43]

(In his strange myths, in his cruel rites, man is from the beginning in search of lost intimacy.)[44]

Left to itself, this impulse would devour everything, like fire (which is thus one of the symbols and means of sacrifice). So somehow, sacrifice or any religious feast must simultaneously release and limit this opening to intimacy, drunkenness, chaos, sexual orgies, destruction; the community must have also a sense of where this has to stop, in order not to disappear.[45]

In this we have the fundamental contradiction of early religious life, which can never be overcome, even though the later, higher forms, emerge out of an attempt to escape it. Intimacy means escaping from the order of things, but the feast is being orchestrated by a community, which itself wants to survive as a super-thing. Military societies can try to escape this by turning the violence outward, instrumentalizing it to the survival of one's own community. The reaction against utilitarian preservation takes more sublimated forms, like the glory that the warrior seeks, even at the risk of his life, or the luxury and ornament which he surrounds himself with; but all this cannot really compensate for the direct plunge into self-release.

Then higher forms of religion arise, which place intimacy beyond the world, in a supersensible realm, and see the divine, or the intelligible world as fully compatible with the order of enduring things; indeed, the divine, or the order of intelligible ideas endorses the preservation of people and institutions. The code which expresses this endorsement, we think of as morality. It is rational, because you can work out by reason what is required to conserve the enduring order. Now violence, and the hankering for violence, is seen as evil, the enemy of God and of order. The original sacred, which was profoundly ambivalent, source of both benefit and harm, is now split into a pure divine, usually seen as beyond the world, and a principle of evil, which somehow inheres in the physical world.

But this just places the divine, the principle of intimacy, beyond the world, and hence farther than ever from us. This cannot satisfy human beings. Moreover this divine is supposedly something we can get closer to by various operations: disciplines, good works, which means we are treating it as though it was another reality which we can produce by instrumental action.

The final stage is reached when this last contradiction is overcome, in the Protestant principle of sola fide: good works can do nothing to bring salvation. But this finally liberates the realm of instrumental action and production from any ulterior goal. Now we have a form of economy is which production exists for its own sake, or rather its surplus is steadily used to make production more effective and plentiful. We have reached the stage of modern capitalism. (The debt to Weber is evident here.)

We have entered fully "le règne des choses" (the reign of things), "la souveraineté de la servitude" (the sovereignty of servitude). "L'homme s'éloigne de lui-même" (Man grows estranged from himself).[46] (We are reminded of Weber's "iron cage".) The fundamental principle which underlies the whole movement is this:

ce que [la vie humaine] admet d'ordre et de réserve n'a-t-il de sens qu'à partir du moment où les forces ordonnées et réservées se libèrent et se perdent pour des fins qui ne peuvent être assujeties à rien dont il soit possible de rendre des comptes. C'est seulement par une telle insubordination, même misérable, que l'espèce humaine cesse d'être isolée dans la splendeur sans condition des choses matérielles.[47]

(what [human life] allows in the way of order and reserve has meaning only from the moment when the ordered and reserved forces liberate and lose themselves for ends which cannot be subordinated to anything which can be accounted for [sc., in terms of gains and losses]. However wretched, it is only by such insubordination that the human race ceases to be isolated amid the unconditional splendour of material things.)[48]

This liberation is also what really unites human beings. "Tout transparaît, tout est ouvert et tout est infini, entre ceux qui consument intensément."[49] (Everything shows through, everything is open and infinite between those who consume intensely.)[50]

In place of the discredited faiths of the past, we have to find new forms of creative destruction to meet the deep need which religion has been striving to fulfill. Intimacy must find some expression.

The solution here is less clear than the problem, which is brilliantly outlined. We can see the basic intuition: the sense of immediacy and communion that can be reached in disorder, violence, sexual orgy, is an anthropological constant, a deep and ineradicable need. The attempts to train humans out of it, leave it behind us in the disciplines of civilization, are not only bound to fail, but also represent a mutilation of human life.

Drawing on Marcel Mauss, and Alexandre Kojève, Bataille's thought has obviously been shaped by the reaction against the disciplined, instrumental, objectivizing stance of modernity. His picture of the liberation of "intimacy" is drawn in stark contrast to this. His theory opens avenues for thinking about the place of violence and sacrifice in pre-Axial religions, however difficult it may be to follow it as an interpretation of the post-Axial. But this may make it all the more useful for understanding what the post-Axial age has repressed and lost.

But there is also a quite different way in which we can rehabilitate the impulse to violence and destruction. In the framework of a post-Schopenhauerian vision of things, we can even drown the pain in beauty. That humans inflict pain and suffering on others is part of the very way of things, the way the dark and inhuman in the universe resonates in us. To see this is to intuit the tragedy at the basis of human life. There is a certain beauty in this way, and a joy in seeing and assenting to it. The superior being can say "yea" to this way, and this is his joy, in Nietzsche's view.

This idea, of a reconciliation with violence and suffering through a beauty born of its necessity, recurs again and again in modern culture. It comes forth more often in literature than in philosophy, but it is a powerful presence nonetheless. There are hints of it in Melville, Conrad, and Faulkner; and also Hemingway, where a male, self-affirming love of struggle, of being up against odds, of showing courage and determination, is given depth and resonance by being related to something profoundly anchored in us and in our world, and thus transfigured through necessity.

A contemporary writer, Cormac McCarthy, has seized the public imagination in a series of novels in which visions of this kind appear, sometimes put in the mouths of minor characters:

> He said that men believe death's elections to be a thing inscrutable yet every act invites the act which follows and to the extent that men put one foot before the other they are accomplices in their own deaths as in all such facts of destiny. He said that moreover it could not be otherwise that men's ends are dictated at their birth and that they will seek their deaths in the face of every obstacle. He said that both views were one view and that while men may meet death in strange and obscure places which they might well have avoided it was more correct to say that no matter how hidden or crooked the path to that destruction yet they would seek it out.[51]

An even more powerful statement of the stark beauty behind the cruel ways of the universe is present in the poetry of Robinson Jeffers.

Jeffers came to his poetic vocation in Carmel, on the California coast. This was, for him, the end of our civilization, not only its limit in space, but the end of its Westward advance through time. The end: the place a cycle ends, and a new one might begin. In this place one can sense the roots of human life and civilization in the vast universe from which we arise.

Jeffers' poetry is nourished by a feeling for this life which pulses through the universe, and from it, as part of it, through us. There is a link here to Wordsworth and the Romantics, the sense of a great current which runs through the cosmos. But the vision is utterly different. Jeffers is willing to call this current "God", a kind of pantheistic God, who *is* the universe, and feels and sees it through us and his other creatures. To grasp this whole, to communicate with this current of life, is to have a vision of immense beauty, but it is also one of sacrifice, suffering, and a kind of indifferent cruelty. There is something reminiscent here of Nietzsche, speaking about his idealized warriors, before the "slave rebellion in morals", as like great predators.[52]

> God is like a hawk gliding among the stars . . .
>> He has a bloody beak and harsh talons,
>>> he pounces and tears . . .
> One fierce life ("Double Axe")

He has no righteousness
No mercy, no love ("At the Birth of an Age")[53]

Humans are dwarfed by this universe. We could and should turn and see, even worship the magnificent beauty of this whole.

I believe that the beauty and nothing else is
    what things are formed for. Certainly the world
Was not constructed for happiness nor love nor wisdom. No, nor for pain,
    hatred and folly. All these
Have their seasons; and in the long year they balance each other, they
    cancel out. But the beauty stands. ("Invasion," 583–584)[54]

But humans are prone to an invincible narcissism; they turn inwards, are concerned with themselves and their affairs, think that these are really important to the cosmos, or to God. Jeffers scorns Christianity, as the most influential form of this self-important illusion.

This narcissism breeds a self-separation from the world, and a kind of enjoyment of cruelty, which Jeffers sees as perverted, very different from the indifferent infliction of pain that is part of the life of nature. Some of Jeffers' poems articulate an acceptance, a calm communion with this vision of the whole:

ROCK AND HAWK

Here is a symbol in which
Many high tragic thoughts
Watch their own eyes

This gray rock, standing tall
On the headland, where the sea wind
Lets no tree grow

Earthquake-proved, and signatured
By ages of storms; on its peak
A falcon has perched.

I think, here is your emblem
To hang in the future sky;
Not the cross, not the hive,

But this; bright power, dark peace;
Fierce consciousness joined with final
Disinterestedness;

Life with calm death; the falcon's
Realist eyes and act
Married to the massive

Mysticism of stone,
Which failure cannot cast down
Nor success make proud. (502)

But in some of his poetry, particularly his narrative verse, we break beyond our own self-absorption, and communicate with the full intensity of the life we spring from through the dramatic action of the central figure, almost always a woman, in a way which draws on, and sometimes even rewrites Greek tragedy, or which builds on ancient notions of a Mother Goddess, dealing both life and death. Intense stories of incest and death by fire, as in *Tamar;* or cleansing violence, as in *The Women at Point Sur.*

Come storm, kind storm.
Summer and the days of tired gold
Are bitter blue and more ruinous
The leprous grass, the sick forest,
The sea like a whore's eyes,
And the noise of the sun,
The yellow dog barking in the blue pasture,
Snapping sidewise
. . . . .
You are tired and corrupt,
You kept the beast under till the fountain's poisoned,
He drips with mange and stinks through the oubliette window.
The promise-breaker war killed whom it freed
And none living's the cleaner. Yet storm comes, the lions hunt
In the night stripped with lightning. It will come: feed on peace
While the crust holds: to each of you at length a little
Desolation: a pinch of lust or a drop of terror:
Then the lions hunt in the brain of the dying: storm is good, storm is good,
       good creature,
Kind violence, throbbing throat aches with pity. (149–150)

As with Kali, or Durga, this female sakti of violence, through madness, murder, suicide, cleanses and purifies the all-too-human. We reconnect with the underlying current of life and death through the vivid invocation of this power.

8

But whether the propensity to violence is biological or metaphysical, this still leaves an enigma that any Christian understanding must explain: how can human nature as we know it be in the image of God?

Here's a hypothesis from within a Christian perspective: humans are born out of the animal kingdom, to be guided by God; and the males (at least the males) with a powerful sex-drive, and lots of aggression. As far as this endowment is concerned, the usual evolutionary explanation could be the correct one. But being guided by God means some kind of transformation of these drives; not just their repression, or suppression, keeping the lid on them; but some real turning of them from within, conversion, so that all the energy now goes along with God; the love powers agape, the aggression turns into energy, straining to bring things back to God, the energy to combat evil.

What is evil? Not just the point zero, that is, not being yet transformed. But another reaction to this point zero, which is the point of being a human animal and feeling this call to transformation, starting to be educated by God. There is now something higher in one's life, a dimension of something incomparably higher, which one can't turn one's back on totally, a dimension of longing and striving which one can't ignore.

Evil is capturing this for something less than, other than God. This is a tremendously powerful temptation. It is constitutive of human life as we know it that it has felt and succumbed to this temptation. Modes of life are built around this succumbing. The untransformed is endowed with some higher, even numinous power. So the self-feeling of power becomes pride, philotimo; but also the wild frenzy of killing, or sex, can be endowed with the numinous.

This is the fallen condition. There are two dimensions. God is slowly educating mankind, slowly turning it, transforming it from within. (There is heavy borrowing here from the perspective of Irenaeus.) But at the same time, the pedagogy is being stolen, has been misappropriated, and misapplied; the education is occurring in this field of resistance.

The resistance takes certain historic forms. Certain facets of our untransformed lives are endowed with numinous power; these forms get established, and then get handed down. Partly in the obvious ways that cultural traditions continue. The kids see the soldiers marching with drums and trumpets, and are dying to grow up and be soldiers, do great deeds. But they also transmit in a more mysterious way, as though they entered into a kind of human milieu in which we all bathe, and influence us even where there is no normal "contact". (The devil is often invoked to explain this.)

Now God's pedagogy operates in this field of opposition. In this field, it can be a positive step, bringing us back closer to God, if the numinosity around some untransformed practice is bent back, brought into some kind of relation of service to God; even though one might suppose that the ultimate goal would be to leave this practice behind altogether. One can't leap altogether to the end. That's the truth of the slow pedagogy.

But on the other hand, there can and must also be leaps. Otherwise no significant forward steps will be made in the response to God. Sometimes, one has to break altogether with some historic forms. Abraham is our paradigm for this.

Thus we have human sacrifice in many religions. This has to be seen in a double framework: on one hand, it is a way of giving numinous power to our desire to control, kill, inflict violence. This numinously concentrates into blood-lust, the pleasure in violence, a kind of inebriation; the untransformed desire concentrates in itself, generates its own numinosity, as I described in the earlier discussion, instead of opening itself to God's transforming action.

On the other hand, given all this, channelling this into sacrifice is a way of turning this back to divinity. It makes some kind of move, concession, to the divine pedagogy.

Something similar can be said about sacred marriage, or temple prostitution.

The revelation to Abraham breaks with these. And with revelation comes a gift of power. We reject human sacrifice altogether; God is leading us higher. But we still don't manage to leap right to the end. Violence is still given a place; now a double place. It is there outside, in those pagan practices which have been declared abominable, like sacrificing children to Baal. But since these have to be combatted, it is now also inside, in our mobilizing as warriors to struggle against this paganism, defending the boundary against it. There is still holy violence, as I discussed earlier. The numinosity is no longer intrinsic to it; there is no longer a hallowing of battle lust in itself; but still the arms are blessed. And there is a danger here; that an unadmitted self-concentration can take place here, and bring us to atrocities which will be done in the name of God. Perhaps some of these are reported in the Old Testament?[55]

There was a further revelation with Christ, and a new gift of power. The victimhood of God, and the change it wrought, transforms the relation of violence and holiness. But in important ways, we slid back in Christendom, and maybe this wasn't entirely avoidable. So there is still blessed violence. This is justified by the idea that there is an outside, an external boundary to God's people. Violence is done to men who ultimately resist God, his sworn enemies.

But from the beginning, perhaps especially in the beginning, there is unease in Christianity about this violence. Later in Christendom, they coped with it in the usual way, by differentiation with complementarity. The Christian soldier is blessed; but the clergy cannot draw blood.

There is also violence to oneself in mortification. This is part of the struggle against our resistance to God.

We can see that the place for sanctioned, sanctified violence goes along more easily with non-universalism. This gives an ineradicable niche for violence in the universe. The underlying idea is something like this: humans can choose; they should choose for God, but they have to be able to choose against. Choosing all the way against means being the enemy of God, doing him violence, and thus also suffering his violence. Why this latter? Because God can't really declare the path of refusal wrong without rejecting it; and he can't really reject it without somehow punishing it. He owes it to his honour. He's stuck with a kind of logical-metaphysical necessity to punish the rejecters. This is a crucial premise of the juridical-penal view.

This brings us to another dimension of violence. Because we have taken the turn of numinizing it, the turn of self-concentration, we sense it there in the human milieu. It both beckons us as a means of self-affirmation, or giving numinous force to our lives; and also terrifies us. It terrifies because awful things can be inflicted on us, but also because with the other side of ourselves, our "higher" sides, we fear being sucked into it; we fear its temptation, like that of wild sexuality. (It is an advantage of both Bataille's and Jeffers' views that they try to make sense of this ambivalence, both the fascination and the anguish.)

These are the sources of the fear and inner trouble that we feel in relation to violence and destruction, which I invoked in my earlier discussion. We might be able to explain a certain propensity to aggression from out of our evolutionary background; but the inner resonance and terror, which so strongly motivates the ways we institutionalize violence in our lives, in religion, war and punishment, this we only feel because we are already in the field of God's pedagogy. It is only in this field that violence has a numinous dimension in the first place.

Now as we saw earlier, these fears/unease can be reduced once we can see this violence as somehow part of the plan of things which conduces to or is compatible with salvation: Shiva, Kali, destruction as the left hand of God. Or else, violence as the necessary outburst of divine love, crushing those who ultimately refuse. Dante's Hell was made not only by divine power and supreme Wisdom, but also by primal love.[56]

There is a truth in this latter view, but it is not incompatible with universalism; because the refusal does breed violence, condemns us to live in violence. And the relations of violence precipitate out at any one time victims and persecutors, sheep and goats, those guilty of inflicting harm and those who suffer it. *Must* there thus be damned, as well as saved? The question is, whether this distinction between harmers and harmed is God's last word, whether the transforming power can go farther, can chase the violence into its ultimate lair, and conquer it. We might see God as the supreme tennis player, who responds to our bad moves with new ways of countering them.[57]

By contrast, seeing the violence as part of the ultimate, fulfilled divine plan, as the destiny of evil-doers, allows us to participate in our own version, cheering on the punishment of these evil-doers; or else, even inflicting it as God's militia. Hence the endorsement of sacred massacres. Modern universalism, "the decline of Hell", has knocked out this prop, and this seems to be a gain.

Does this Christian hermeneutic of violence offer a way out of the dilemmas of exclusive humanism? In a way, perhaps yes; in another way, no.

Let's look again at the tensions between the various humanist positions. The modern idea of order wants to ban violence altogether, and in certain versions wild sex. In the objectifying view which comes from the Enlightenment, violence has no more numinous cover whatever, whether implicit in the cosmos or through serving God. Or else it can preserve something like a numinous aura, when deployed in the service of the Revolution, or la Patrie, and its telos is to bring about the final stage in which it will disappear. I will return to this secular version of sacred massacre below. But leaving this aside, on a common Enlightenment view violence and wild sex can be seen as just raw thuggery, sensuality, something utterly primitive, to be overcome, whose attraction belongs properly only to the most primitive stage of human development.

Now in reducing violence to pathology or primitivism, we take an external stance to our most powerful desires, dividing ourselves, and repudiating these powerful drives. The metaphysical/numinous dimension of sex and violence is lost.

Several motives push us in this direction. There is not only the hold of reductive materialist modes of explanation. This is important, and has more than one motive. Many are attracted to them not only on epistemological or metaphysical grounds, but also because, say, a purely biological approach might offer some way of modifying them, suppressing tendencies to violence by behavioural therapy (as in *Clockwork Orange*), or more profoundly through genetic engineering.

But we also frequently have a strong practical motivation. We are both repelled by violence and fear its ravages in our lives. In our desire to combat it, it is tempting to be as dismissive and degrading as we can, to see it as mere depravity (in a spiritual perspective), or pathology (in an exclusive humanist one). In the terms of my discussion in the previous chapter, it is tempting to accompany our ethical suppression of violence with a disengaging reduction of the propensity to it. To resist this reduction may make you seem to collude with the glorifiers of violence, and you will be accused of undercutting the immediate and urgent agenda of control, which is supposed to be furthered by a dismissive, reductive account of the drives.

And if, as it will undoubtedly turn out, this reductive account doesn't yield any techniques of control or diminution of violent tendencies, if violence as rooted in biology or evolution comes to seem an irreducible constant, then it will appear all the more urgent to control behaviour, and hence to avoid any recognition of its possible human meanings.

But this whole reductive approach, as I have argued in the previous pages, seems quite inadequate. It is not only theoretically dubious, in view of the obvious importance of meta-biological factors, but it may also be practically counter-productive. The attempt to control behaviour in a climate of contempt and disgust at the motives of the controlled may just provoke revolt and a stronger affirmation of violence.

And indeed, this inadequacy has provoked reactions and protests which resonate throughout modern culture, as we have already seen. In face of the merely clinical, disengaged, desiccating view, the Romantic axis of critique has sought a way of affirming again what is powerful and comes from deep down within us. Something which comes from the depths has its own kind of numinosity in the Romantic age, and in those who write and create in its aftermath. The primitive has power, on which we need to draw, or before which we stand in awe, even as we may have to limit it, resist it. In Schopenhauer's transposition of Romantic depths as the Will, these are the site of wild and formless striving, of violence and unrestrained sexuality. These are the depths invoked in Conrad's heart of darkness; in early Stravinsky; in the whole age of the Primitive. These illustrate the immense power of the post-Romantic, Schopenhauerian influence on art and thought at the turn of the twentieth century. In different ways, the search was to recover a sense of the numinous in the human depths, including sexuality and aggression, a power which could be tapped through aesthetic presentation.

And the multiplication of new positions continues. Freud tried to recuperate these aesthetic insights for "science", reading the power of art in terms of his intra-psychic dynamics. In Dostoyevsky, on the other hand, we find a new Christian response informed by Romanticism. Nietzsche's "Jasagen" of the wild dimensions which humanism reduced has been widely followed in the twentieth century, for instance, by Michel Foucault; as also in different ways by Bataille and Jeffers, as we have seen.

But herein lies the difficulty. These explorations of the depth meaning of violence tend either to yield an affirmation, even glorification of it; or else to show how ineradicable it is. Put in other terms, we could say that they generally tend to show the draw to violence to be too deeply anchored to be rooted out, whether they rejoice in this prospect (Nietzsche) or take it with a resigned pessimism (Freud).

Theoretically, a meta-biological account of the draw to violence in terms of its meaning could open the way to a possible redefinition or transformation of this meaning which might take us beyond it. Bataille, for instance, seems to want to explore this possibility. Once we are free from all theological illusions, as well as from the reification of "le règne des choses" (the reign of things), we can accede to a new form of immediacy which is not based on destruction.[58] Elsewhere he speaks of a mysticism "sans forme et sans mode".[59] But while his aim seems clear here, the solution remains elusive.

Now the Christian meta-biological account I've been describing here does open such a perspective of transformation. This is the sense in which I could answer yes to the question above: does Christianity take us out of the space of dilemmas that exclusive humanism seems unable to escape? But the answer could also be no. And not just because for many the nature of the transformation suggested here may be as opaque as Bataille's. It is also that in another way, this view makes a certain kind of dilemma central to our experience.

The kind of transformation I am talking about here is not just a matter of plasticity: that you train them differently and they turn out to like helping old ladies cross the street. That would be the level zero environmentalism of Locke and the Aufklärung which the various reactions above are against. The transformation is much more mysterious, and involves offering another spiritual direction.

But if you allow for this possibility, then you are often perplexed in face of what I have been calling the wild dimensions in human life, sex and aggression. You cannot simply deny their numinous or metaphysical dimension, because you see that from the beginning they have been caught up in the divine pedagogy. The various forms they have taken in human life express responses to this pedagogy. In different ways, these responses express resistance to God, an attempt to capture and inflect the path of agape he calls us on, and bend it into something we find easier to live with.

But that doesn't mean that these forms are simply all bad. They are bad qua inflections, but are good qua responses to God's call. We have to recognize the fundamental ambivalence of human reality, which the third misprision above totally loses sight of. Moreover, these forms are far from being all equally bad and good. Some need to be resisted more fiercely than others. On top of this, there is a movement of God's pedagogy through history, so that some forms which are utterly unconscionable now, were more excusable earlier, such as sacred war, or even human sacrifice.

This means that we have to respond on two levels to the resonances of violence in us. In the immediate context, we have to defend the innocent against attack. We had to fight the Nazis, end militia-driven civil wars, punish crimes against the person, silence calls to violence, and the like. This is all in the nature of damage control.

On another level, we have to think of how we can collaborate with God's pedagogy, help along the turning into the directions of God's plan. We certainly can't do this by denying their numinous meaning, by reducing them to pathology. This can only break the contact with those who are moved by them, and push them into sullen resistance. But we can't do this by celebrating them either, as something intrinsically human, regardless of the form they take. Nor does it help to reify them as genetically given, set in the biological concrete of our DNA.

If you see these drives in this transformative perspective, you can't adopt a simple unambivalent stance to them, as both normalizing, therapizing humanists, and Nietzscheans do, each in their own way. To the first, you will seem to line up with the second, and probably vice versa. So there is not only a tension due to your bivalent perspective on the drives to sex and violence; but also one which can arise between what seem to be the demands of the immediate agenda, and those of the more transformative one.

The force of numinous violence is among us, in football riots, street gangs, motorcycle gangs, and so on. Its liberating effects can be celebrated in modern theory, in the paths opened by Nietzsche, as with Bataille and Caillois. Not to speak of Jünger. In the face of this, we are tempted to offer reductive and objectifying accounts. But a Christian perspective forbids us taking this kind of satisfying distance from it all. Indeed, perhaps it allows us to see that taking this distance, just because it mobilizes us more effectively to crush these outbreaks, and make over the perpetrators through compulsion, also helps awaken and legitimate the hostility and aggression in us, so that we are the more ready to believe and participate in our own kind of "holy" violence, even in a secular, liberal framework.

If all this is true, then here too, in dealing with sexuality and violence, even as above in the issue of fulfillment and transcendence, Christian belief faces tensions, difficulties, even dilemmas. And these have a certain parallel to those which arise for unbelief.

But then something rather unexpected has arisen out of our discussion of the polemic between belief and unbelief. If we take the two main axes of the critique of religion by unbelief, we find that, far from pointing to an evident answer, they rather show that both protagonists face profound difficulties and dilemmas, and indeed, of basically parallel kinds.

It is not clear that exclusive humanism can find answers to these dilemmas, or can meet the maximal demand. When this becomes evident, there is sometimes triumphalist rejoicing in the Christian camp. But this is ill-founded. Yes, Christians have some intimations of how one might get beyond these dilemmas, but these are not only in the realm of faith, in the sense of the "anticipatory confidence" I described earlier (Chapter 15), but are not of the kind which could be decanted into a general code or programme.

But there is worse: in the context of the immanent frame, where so much turns on codes and structures, this inability to offer solutions is a painful predicament, which makes one feel inadequate and irrelevant to the great discussion. So that Christians are often induced to claim more than they should, and to begin to offer "answers"; and in doing so, they fall into the same kind of blindness that reductive humanism suffers from.

And so one frequently finds that the Christian life is identified with a certain "normal" morality, for instance, that of self-reliant work and "family values", and/or this morality is seen as largely realized in a "Christian" polity. Deviants are branded, not as pathological, but as "evil". This avoids, indeed, the flattening of the therapeutic turn, but is also profoundly distortive, falling into the third misprision and washing out the ambivalences in all of our lives, while rejecting much that it good along with the harmful (much wheat along with the tares, in Biblical language).

But it's not an accident that "Christians" fall into similar deviations to those of "secular humanists". As I have tried to show throughout this book, we both emerge from the same long process of Reform in Latin Christendom. We are brothers under the skin.

Both sides need a good dose of humility, that is, realism. If the encounter between faith and humanism is carried through in this spirit, we find that both sides are fragilized; and the issue is rather reshaped in a new form: not who has the final decisive argument in its armory—must Christianity crush human flourishing? must unbelief degrade human life? Rather, it appears as a matter of who can respond most profoundly and convincingly to what are ultimately commonly felt dilemmas.

I want to return to this below in a further discussion of the nature of modern violence. But in order to get to that, we have to probe further the issue of the meanings of violence, its meta-biological motivations. No one is even near a final theory in this domain, though a number of interesting suggestions have been mentioned. In order to cast further light on our motivations, I have to introduce some other features of the contemporary debate.

18 Dilemmas 2

iv. Beyond Misanthropy and Violence?

9

I have been trying to describe the conflicted field of debate between belief and unbelief in Western culture today. I characterized this first, as a field under cross pressure between extreme positions, represented by orthodox religion on one hand (that is, originally by Christianity and Judaism, but now more and more joined by Islam, Hinduism, Buddhism, and other faiths), and hard-line materialistic atheism on the other. Cross pressure doesn't mean that all or even most people in this culture feel torn, but rather that virtually all positions held are drawn to define themselves at last partly in relation to these extremes.

Second, I argued that a crucial, and under-mentioned, set of considerations in this debate concern our views about our ethical predicament.

Third, I have argued that this debate, rather than being one between clearly opposed, internally self-consistent positions, actually tends on closer examination into a struggle between two rival attempts to construe and come to terms with certain common dilemmas: between aspirations to transcendence (in the broader sense of Nussbaum's discussion: I have normally been using the term in a narrower sense in this book) and the cherishing of ordinary human desires; between the demand to understand and respect the meta-biological roots of human violence and the imperative moral demand to end it.

I also singled out two important reference points of the debate in Western modernity: our allegiance to the modern moral order and universal human rights and well-being on one hand, and our aspiration to wholeness, and the rehabilitation of the body and desire, on the other.

We see from all this how life in a secular age (in sense 3) is uneasy and cross-pressured, and doesn't lend itself easily to a comfortable resting place. This is what we see in the polemic, but it emerges also if we look at a range of concerns that are endemic to this age, those which touch on the issue of meaning in life.

Luc Ferry's recent exploration of this question is very interesting.[1] What we do always has a point; we undertake various projects, and in-between we keep going the routines which sustain our lives. Through all this, something may be growing: a life of love; children who are becoming adults and then leaving to live their own lives; we may be getting better at some valuable and useful activity. But we can also be struck by a question of what this all adds up to; what is the meaning of it all? Or since the individual projects and the recurring routine all have their purpose, the question comes as a higher order one: what is the meaning of all these particular purposes? "Le 'sens du sens'—la signification ultime de toutes ces significations particulières—nous fait défaut."[2] (The meaning of meaning—the ultimate significance of all these particular meanings—is lacking.)[3]

Now at this point, reactions tend to differ. Some people hold that one shouldn't ask this meta-question, that one should train oneself not to feel the need. It is true that refusing the question could be part of a spiritual training, one very much oriented to a beyond, on the grounds that any answer we give is bound to be distortive and partial, and will screen from us the real point of things. But as a way of defending exclusive humanism, this move has serious drawbacks. Lots of people don't want to ask the meta-question; but once it arises for someone they will not easily be put off by the injunction to forget it—unless it is part of some discipline which will in fact bring them to an answer, as in the training I've just mentioned.

That is because it arises out of a sense that there are goals which could engage us more fully and deeply than our ordinary ends. It is the same sense which I invoked in the first chapter, that somewhere there is a fullness or richness which transcends the ordinary, which is now recurring, but in an interrogative mode, as something sought for. This will not easily be uprooted from the human heart.

A much more effective response will be to try to give an answer which remains within the natural-human domain, either by showing that one of our present purposes actually has the fullness and depth we seek; or by proposing something which goes beyond the usual scope of our lives, but which remains immanent. It is something of this latter kind which Luc Ferry attempts in his book. He sees in the succouring of human life and well-being universally a goal which really transcends the ordinary ambit of life. And he cites moving testimony how service in organizations like Médecins Sans Frontières has effectively given a strong sense to life for many young people.[4] It is as he argues a kind of transcendence of our ordinary existence, but one which is "horizontal", not "vertical".[5] He evens wants to use the term 'sacred' (very much in the French tradition, as we have seen); but this doesn't take us outside the human domain; on the contrary, it is very much part of the human life-form to propose such ends which transcend the ordinary. "C'est par la position des valeurs hors du monde que l'homme s'avère véritablement homme."[6] (It is by positing extraworldly values that man proves himself truly human.)[7]

This answer draws in part on Kant, and in more general terms it recurs to the modern discovery/invention of intra-human sources of motivation for universal benevolence, which I described in the previous segment. Ferry's answer to the meaning of life resonates with us because these sources have become part of our inheritance. It is a powerful answer. Whether it is enough for us will depend partly on whether we sense that it captures the full force of the call we feel to succour human beings as human; whether there is something still left out which is articulated, for instance, in the language of the human as image of God.

I have discussed this question elsewhere.[8] But here I want to explore further the unease which Ferry has alluded to. It is a central feature of our "secular", that is, cross-pressured, pluralist world, in which the attractions of immanence are very strong. If we could get a clearer view of the lines of force which traverse this world, of the shape of spiritual experience within it, we would come closer to what I have been seeking here in this work, an understanding of what it is to live in an age of secularity 3.

Raising the issue of meaning as Ferry does is a good place to start. It is indeed a feature of our age, unlike any previous ones, that we can feel the loss of meaning as a real threat. But to remain here would be to leave things at too abstract a level. This fits with a certain, unbelieving view of our predicament, that what human beings need or crave is meaning, any meaning, anything which negates or escapes meaninglessness; whereas for different religious views, the need or aspiration is always seen in more specific terms: for God, for Nirvana, to overcome duality. Influential theories of religion have been built on this generalized, abstract definition of what humans seek in faith—a definition which is, of course, compatible with all the answers offered to this quest being illusions. As I stated above, Weber's understanding of religion seems to start from this premise, as does Gauchet's very interesting theory.[9]

We have another recent statement of this view from Richard Lewontin, in a discussion of the reasons why some Christians reject the theory of evolution:

> What is at issue here is whether the experience of one's family, social, and working life, with its share of angst, pain, fatigue, and failure, can provide meaning in the absence of a belief in an ordained higher purpose. The continued appeal of a story of the divine creation of human life is that it provides, for those for whom the ordinary experience of living does not, a seductive relief from what Eric Fromm called the Anxiety of Meaningless. The rest is commentary.[10]

I'm not saying this view is simply false; it does capture important phenomena. But it is partial, because too abstract. The human need for meaning also takes on more specific, concrete forms; and I believe these can be read in our present predicament, even by those without a faith commitment—although such a commitment probably prepares you better to notice them.

Indeed, there is something absurd about the idea that our lives could be focussed on meaning as such, rather than on some specific good or value. One might die for God, or the Revolution, or the classless society, but not for meaning. This term designates a universal, which is intended to capture what draws a host of different people to their respective religio-metaphysical-moral options.

Sometimes, a purported universal of this sort can be put forward as a "higher" replacement for a number of more particular goods. The (Christian, Islamic, or liberal) missionary says to the members of various tribes: what underlies your sense that the lives of some particular range of people are to be respected is really a dim sense of the universal, that human life as such must be preserved. The call is to convert to the wider perspective. But this kind of thing is inconceivable in the case of "meaning" as such.

This universal category doesn't belong to the agent's perspective, but rather appears to the (generally disenchanted) observer, who notes that different peoples centre their lives in different things, in many (perhaps all) cases without objective warrant. The conclusion which can be drawn is that the universal need is for some such centre, regardless of what it is, provided only it can be believed in.

Obviously, important general questions are at stake in this reading of contemporary spiritual experience. Just as my reading of the rise of modern secularity played off against a theory of epistemological primacy which underpinned the "death of God" scenario; so here the picture I want to offer of our present concerns and debates will conflict with certain popular general theories of religion. I mean by this, theories of what humans seek in religion.

This is not to say that I will be offering my own such general theory. On the contrary, it would perhaps be better at the outset to come clean, and say that I doubt very much whether any such general theory can even be established. I mean a theory which can gather all the powerful élans and aspirations which humans have manifested in the spiritual realm, and relate them to some single set of underlying needs or aims or tendencies (whether it be the desire for meaning or something else). The phenomena are much too varied and baffling for that; and even if they were more tractable, we would have to stand at the end of history to be able to draw such conclusions.

I think rather that we are faced with different spiritual traditions, in which new forms are initiated in history which capture the allegiance of people and give a certain shape to their spiritual hunger. These are then carried down and reshaped, so that successor versions in the same society/culture usually bear some strong resemblance to what preceded them. I have argued that this is true for exclusive humanism in relation to Christian faith, in the centrality of benevolence, for instance. I have even argued that exclusive humanism couldn't have arisen without this analogue to agape. But no one could argue from this that all viable spiritual views have to have an agape-analogue. The contrary is obviously the case.

None of us stands at the point of view of the universal. Our attachment to our own faith cannot come from a universal survey of all others from which we conclude that this is the right one. It can only come from our sense of its inner spiritual power, chastened by the challenges which we will have had to meet from other faiths.

But I think in addition to this general appeal to caution in the face of the immense variety of religious forms, there is a specific reason to be wary of this general theory of religion as motivated by the search for meaning. This is because, as I argued above, it belongs so clearly to the observer's perspective. Anyone genuinely "into" some good or value must see this particular good as having worth; this is what he is moved by. As a modern, he may also find a certain reflexive stance unavoidable, whereby he sees that this is his "meaning", that is, it is to him what some quite other good is to his neighbour, what gives his life order and sense. (How he puts this together with his first-order sense of the validity of the value in question is another, more complicated issue.)

It is easy to understand why, after religious views have been challenged, and even rendered for many people ineligible, the sense of what has been *lost* may centre around the issue of meaning. The "disenchanted" world does indeed, seem a world without meaning. But this doesn't mean that through all the ages of religious life in all its variety, this was the driving factor in the constitution and preservation of religious forms. There is a fallacious inference behind the untroubled adoption of this theory of religious motivation. Just because this looms as big issue for *us* in a secular age, it is all too easy to project it on all times and places. But there is in the end something incoherent in this move. It will certainly not help us at all to understand why, for instance, certain kinds of shamanism arose in paleolithic times, nor why Europe was torn apart over the issue of salvation by faith in the sixteenth century.

Having said this, I want to try to explore some of the spiritual hungers and tensions of secular modernity, as they become visible in the light of the story I've been telling of its genesis.

1. When we break down the hunger for meaning into more concrete needs, one is for an answer to the problem of suffering and evil. I don't mean a theodicy; by definition, unbelievers have no place for this. I mean how to live with it.

We can be overwhelmed when we are made aware of all the suffering there is in the world; and more than this, the loss, dispersal, evil, blindness; or the distorted and thwarted and self-mutilating humanity; or the dullness, emptiness, flatness.

This is, as it were, a condition which arises even in a disenchanted world: we are unprotected; now not from demons and spirits, but from suffering and evil as we sense it raging in the world. There are unguarded moments when we can feel the immense weight of suffering, when we are dragged down by it, or pulled down into despair. Being in contact with war, or famine, or massacre, or pestilence, will press this in on us.

But beyond suffering, there is evil; for instance, the infliction of suffering, the cruelty, fanaticism, joy or laughter at the suffering of the victims. And then what is almost worse, the sinking into brutality, the insensible brute violence of the criminal. It's almost like a nightmare. One wants to be protected, separated from this. But it can creep under your guard and assail you, even in a disenchanted world.

I'm not claiming that all humans feel this. This, or at least our particular forms of it, belong to us in our civilization, and the fact that we have been shaped by a long past marked by a spirituality of agape and ethics of benevolence has a lot to do with it. But it is widely felt need, or better, a way in which we are vulnerable, in which the world can "get to us".

The negative, self-defensive response to this is to shut a lot of it out; don't watch the evening news for a while, concentrate on something else. More corrosively, throughout history we have been good at cancelling the horror by telling ourselves that these people are not really like us; maybe they don't really mind the poverty and squalor as we would; or maybe they're bad, they're evil, and they deserve it; or they brought it on themselves through their sloth and fecklessness. Or else we paint a brighter picture of things, in which the suffering is occluded; for instance, we distance ourselves through an external, aestheticized vision of the natives in their meaningful, thick culture.

All this numbs the sense of something deeply wrong, of a world so out of joint that it is almost unbearable to contemplate it. These exclusionary or distancing reactions keep us from being overwhelmed; they keep us sane.

But there is also a positive response to this; when you feel able to act, to do something to heal the world; when you can feel part of the solution and not simply part of the problem. We can have this sense from acting on a small scale, feeling that we are holding up our end in our immediate surroundings, and therefore doing our bit to "tikkun olam", to use the pithy Hebrew expression, which we might render as "healing the world". We might be doing this by working, for instance, in a productive job, especially by being in a "helping" profession. When people seek a "meaningful" job, one that will help answer the question of the meaning of their lives, this sense of being part of the solution is often an important element. Ferry's analysis seems to dovetail with mine at this point.

One important issue in our lives is: how much do we cope with the sense of the world's misery by the various defensive, exclusionary moves, and how much by the practices of tikkun?

Now in a certain way a strategy of distancing is implicit in the modern disengaged stance. You see the problem, but you don't allow it to get to you. You can allow in a certain compassion, concern, but you don't let yourself be overwhelmed by it. These are the dispassionate facts about where human beings are now. As for evil, this gets even less to you. Your compassion for these hardened criminals is conditioned by the limits of an ameliorative programme. If they can be rehabilitated, then this must be done. Otherwise, they can be written off.

So distancing works both by holding oneself back from being engulfed by suffering, and also by exclusion based on the limits of practical action. You can't worry about what can't be changed.

The positive side, what this distancing preserves, is the sense of yourself as disengaged subject, moved by impersonal benevolence; the liberal self, benevolent towards all mankind, but within the limits of the reasonable and possible, is capable of facing the facts of unavoidable suffering and evil, and writing them off inwardly. You have to be able to face these things; hence your hostility to the unreal Christian hope. The satisfaction can come from being able to order the world to a certain extent, to bring about some good. This sense of efficacy entrenches the identity of the benevolent disengaged subject, and showing it as worthy, justifies the shutting out.

Another form that this distancing can take we see, for instance, in the Bolshevik stance. This has similar roots to the liberal, the benevolent disengaged sense. But there also is a tremendous sense of power, in exercising titanic control over history. All benevolence is now invested in this all-powerful ameliorative action; so that what is out of reach of this can be sacrificed, or ruthlessly set aside. This allows one to be brutal, to transgress principles of universal respect for innocent human life; and this in a way that liberalism cannot follow, where the sense of our limitation enforces negative checks: at least one should refrain from inflicting suffering or death. But while the illusion lasts that one has tremendous power to do good, the sense of efficacy in benevolence entrenches the disengaged-benevolent identity. One is sure of being part of the solution; and so is no longer part of the problem. This is especially strong in the heady moments of Revolution, or when one joins the CP.

What goes on here is a double process: On one side, there is the sense of being part of the solution, answering the human problem, fighting back evil and suffering, which answers suffering and evil with effective remedies, and so keeps one from being engulfed. But also, the cutting off of gut-sympathy with suffering and evil through disengagement and the stance of control means that we no longer feel implicated in this. These are not our people any more. These foolish, backward, self-inflicting savages, or these brutal killers, or the blind, egoistic bourgeois exploiters, and the cruel, brutal White Guards; we deny kinship with them. We do this through the disengagement of scrutiny, and through the stance of control.

Moving along a spectrum from the Bolshevik, we can come to a stance which has abandoned universal benevolence and the moral order of mutual benefit. This is a Nietzschean stance, which rejects equality and benevolence because it sees them as levelling, and catering to the lowest in us, to comfort and security. It seeks heroism. A form of this can connect to the titanic, as in Jünger's *Der Arbeiter* phase.[11] Or it can take a milder form of élite rule by Übermenschen, where everything subserves their heroism and dedication to excellence.

Here the first positive part of the answer is no longer benevolence, but the idea that the human type demands realization of its excellence, and only the few can do this; so they must go ahead. The rest can perhaps get some satisfaction in knowing that they subserve this, but if not, they have to be sacrificed. The enemy here is not suffering, but a sinking into sloth, mediocrity, meaninglessness. The second process, marking one's distance, comes from the élitism of this outlook. Only the excellent truly count.

The animus here against liberalism/socialism is the Nietzschean one, that they make their major end succouring the weak, ending suffering, bringing about equality. They stifle the need of the highest spirits for excellence, self-overcoming, risk, heroism. You are ready to put your life on the line: Hegel's "Daransetzen"; you are ever ready to "have at them": Jünger's "Draufgängertum".[12] These superior beings are eager to affront suffering in their drive to a higher life; and they are ready to face death. They reverse the field of fear. They hold to a warrior ethic. Precisely for this reason, they have to fight off the temptation of pity. They have to steel themselves against engulfment, and take the cold distance of disengagement.

So their answer to the power of evil, at least for part of it, the drive to violence, is to internalize it, and baptise it, as it were, consecrate it to the striving for excellence; marrying the Übermensch, the primitive, and the highest. This is a modern variant of that internalization/concentration of the numinous in violence that I spoke of in the previous section. Again Jünger of the '20s seems to be tempted onto this path. This is the dark side of his Nietzscheanism, which was vulgarized in Nazi racism.

Then there is the victim scenario. This can colonize the Left. All evil is projected onto the others; they alone are the victimizers; we are pure victim. The liberal self feels relatively innocent, because (a) it sees the whole picture clearly, and (b) it is part of the solution. But this is compatible with recognizing some degree of one's own fault in the disorder of the world. The victim scenario, on the other hand, a kind of deviant, secularized Christianity, achieves total innocence, at the cost of projecting total evil on the other. This can justify Bolshevik-type ruthlessness, as well as titanic action. We can see how this carries out both processes, which distance us from evil: we are part of the solution, and we are utterly other than those who inflict harm. We have no part with them.

So we can see various forms of modern unbelief as powered by our recoil from suffering and evil. Something replaces the spirit world of yore, even for the buffered self which has shut it out. That is, there is still something we need protection from. This is not to say that everyone is driven to invest heavily in one of the strategies mentioned above. We see this total investment with active Bolsheviks and dedicated victims, for instance. But lots of people may only take up these positions lightly and tentatively; many haver between more than one; and may mainly defend themselves against engulfment by narrowing their focus, plunging into their lives, seeking Pascalian distraction. Plunging into life isn't necessarily an escape. We moderns are less capable of narrowing our focus, because the media and the global meta-topical spaces we inhabit often force the plight of even far-away others into our attention.

Some of these strategies involve taking on what seems to be evil: sanctifying violence, war, sacrifice of others, denial of their equal humanity. In this, they seem the opposite of religion and Christianity. But, as I pointed out above, lots of historical Christianity has succeeded in incorporating these elements: the drive to order at all costs, militancy, driving out and destroying heretics, and the like. True, Christian faith was always held back by certain limits which Nazis could override, but the sanctifying of violence was there nonetheless. Historical Christianity has shown a variety of mixtures, marrying a practice of tikkun with various exclusionary moves against the damned, the pagan, the unbeliever, the heretic, the irremediably tepid.

Belief and unbelief confront each other today on the ground of this common need, in a context where we are less and less comfortable with our venerable repertories of exclusionary moves. Looking at the exclusionary practices of Christianity over history, some people are sure that a humanistic response will enable us to maximize healing over exclusion. But then the question may arise whether any humanistic view, just because it is woven around a picture of the potential greatness of human beings, doesn't tempt us to neglect the failures, the blackguards, the useless, the dying, those on the way out, in brief, those who negate the promise. Perhaps only God, and to some extent those who connect themselves to God, can love human beings when they are utterly abject. The work of Mother Teresa in Calcutta brings this question to mind.

The debate on this issue can be carried further. I have tried to do so elsewhere.[13] But what ought to be clear is just how hard it is to come to a decisive conclusion on these matters, which are nevertheless raised for us by some of our deepest intuitions about meaning in life. The issue of whether this must drive us beyond the human domain remains very much open.

But what emerges most strongly from this reflection on suffering and evil is the challenge it poses to both sides, to disintricate their practices of tikkun from their strategies of exclusion. On one side, it points to a purified Christian alternative, where one could aim to dwell in the suffering and evil without recoil, sure of the power of God to transform it. One is part of the solution by being there and praying, being there and affirming the good which is never absent. You see the good through the eyes of God.

One must also be there with these unbelieving solutions, affirming the good, and combatting the demonic. There is perhaps a new, as yet untravelled road from them to God, a way of "making straight the way of the Lord".

On the other side, there is a chastened, negative Liberalism, which has learned from the excesses of its own demonic potentiality. Practice decency, avoid suffering, fight oppression. Isaiah Berlin has been an important figure here, as has in another way Judith Shklar. There is a certain deep wisdom here.[14]

10

I will return in the next chapter to this question of the spiritual tensions of secular modernity, but for now I want to revert to the very incomplete discussion of the previous sections: what about violence and religion? This is something very much on our minds today in a time of theologically-inspired terrorism. Of course, we have also seen terrible violence powered by atheistic and/or anti-Christian ideologies, like Marxist-Leninism and Nazism. But this still doesn't dispose of the issue. The very conclusion that I argued for above, that the sources of categorical violence are metaphysical rather than biological, seem to put the spotlight on metaphysical or religious views which condone or encourage killing.

The concern that I have been articulating above, how we live with evil, and avoid being engulfed by it, allows us to take further the discussion of religion and violence in section 5 above, and cast light on its continued involvement with violence.

Killing, as we saw, could be given a place along with the other aspects of life in pre-Axial religions. There was a time to make war and a time for peace; or there were people whose task (one might say "dharma") it was to make war. There were gods of war; and sacred killing in sacrifice; as well as gods and goddesses of peaceful activity. But the move to Axial religions generally brought a primacy of peace over war, even though many features of the pre-Axial continued in the "higher" religions. War, or violence, came to be seen in many cases as the result of evil. Certainly this was the case with Christianity.

So how does sacred killing survive? How does it recur in the "higher" religions, seemingly in defiance of their founding principles? How does Christian civilization re-invent persecution, in the form for instance of anti-Semitism? How does it preach holy war, in the form of the Crusades?

I can't discuss this at anything like the length it deserves here.[15] But briefly put, the answer is that sacred killing recurs because it offers a form of purification. The stronger we feel that we are somehow involved in evil, for instance, the more we feel overwhelmed by the chaos and evil of the world, as I discussed in the last section, the more tempting it is to reach for a mode of projection, in which the evil is concentrated outside of us, in a contrast case. This makes of us the pure, and even more strikingly so if we are fighting manfully against these carriers of impurity and disorder. Moreover, since God is the source of purity, in so fighting, we identify with him; we are on his side.

This is the essence of what we might call the "scapegoat mechanism".[16] We can perhaps understand this as a convergence point between two formations: One is the response of ensuring ourselves that we are good/ordered by identifying a contrast case from which we separate ourselves. We draw the line between us. This can be expressed in terms of purity/pollution, the self-affirming contrast. The second is the strength and spiritual force which comes from identifying with numinous violence, the violence of the Gods; identifying actively, in some form of sacred massacre. We can have the self-affirming contrast without the sacred massacre; e.g., the Indian caste system. But when they come together, the result is peculiarly powerful.

This sacred killing powered by the contrast comes in two major forms, if this rather over-simplified grid can be imposed on a host of complex phenomena. There is the scapegoat mechanism as such (SM), where we turn on, kill or expel an outsider (contrast case) who is within, who has eroded the boundary. And then there is the Crusade, where we go to war with a contrast case outside. The latter, in addition to fusing together numinous violence and purity, also realizes another powerful synthesis: it bonds the warrior stance, as lord of death, with the higher cause of numinous violence. So it both gathers all this potentially disintegrating violence into a higher unity, and also gives the warrior self-affirmation a higher meaning and purpose. The Crusades are a paradigm case, a "solution" to the grinding conflict between Christian faith and the aristocratic-warrior way of life of the rulers of mediaeval society; to the perpetual battle of the Church to impose a "peace of God" on an unruly and bellicose nobility.

So numinous violence can recur even in religious cultures that were founded on the rejection of earlier forms of sacred killing, or human sacrifice. They recur, because even drawing on the new definitions of purity and goodness, people make use of these to establish and protect their own sense of purity, their separation from the bad.[17] Do these people oppose the Prince of Peace? Let's go and smash them! We have the self-given assurance of being that Prince's most faithful followers, even while we violate his teaching.

But this doesn't simply recreate the status quo ante of the Axial Age. Before and after there was identification with numinous violence. But what was involved changed radically. Numinous violence doesn't mean necessarily identifying with the good. In the pre-Axial period, the gods were both benign and malign; some mainly one, some mainly the other, most often both. "Benign" here is measured in relation to ordinary human flourishing: life, health, prosperity, many descendants. We have often to trick and propitiate these higher beings (hence the importance of the "trickster" figure). But the Axial Revolution tended to place the Divine on the side of the ultimate good; while at the same time redefining this as something which goes beyond what is understood as ordinary human flourishing: Nirvana, Eternal Life.

Some forms of the Axial transformation bring God closer to a conception of morality; some code which is justified and made sense of in terms of this higher Good, as with Plato. We also see this with the God invoked by the Prophets, who frequently enjoins us to forget sacrifice, and succour the widows and orphans.

So violence is now on a new footing. It is in the service of the Higher. And this means it can be all the more implacable, ruthless and thorough. Where much earlier warfare was ritualized, and hence limited, post-Axial sacred killing will become more and more rationalized and limitless.

This "progress" continues, because sacred killing not only survives, or reinvents itself after the Axial Revolution; it also does so after the modern secular Revolutions which were meant to sweep away "fanaticism", religious persecution, and Crusades; in short all the religiously-induced, senseless killing of the past. We can see this in the paradigm case of the French Revolution, in which once again the purity of republican "virtue" is to be defended by the elimination of its enemies. And once again, the killing is now seen to be more rational (directed against targets that really deserve it), clean, clinical and technological (the guillotine), and to bring about the real reign of good. This will be the reign of peace: Robespierre in his vote on the new constitution, sided with those who wanted to ban the death penalty. The disconnect between the final goals and the sacred killing which was meant to encompass it couldn't be more striking.

And when we move into the twentieth century, we can see a revolutionary violence, boosted by rational technology which dwarfs the horrors of all earlier ages.[18]

In an important sense, the modern disengaged rational and secular world goes even farther in this direction than the religious civilization it rejected. The last limits are swept aside. There are no reasons to stay your hand when the target encompasses only evil, filth, the negative. As Stalin put it: "Who's going to remember all this riff-raff in ten or twenty years' time?"[19]

Morality rationalizes. That is, the code is based on some conception of what the good or right is, related to human well-being. This brings with it some notion of responsibility. We punish wrong-doers. We move away from the ambivalences of early religion; where the sacred brought both boon and danger; where we can worship the victim of the sacrifice afterwards.

In the Christian context, identifying with divine violence became identifying with the (of course, righteous) wrath of God. And so we persecute heretics. Also witchcraft trials participate formally in this logic; however based on murderous fantasies.

The modern moral order, and the disenchanted, rationalized world, should put an end to all this. There is no place for the Wrath of God; and even among believers there has been a "Decline of Hell".

But moralizing may make things worse; and the question arises whether we don't invent new murderous fantasies in the enlightened, disenchanted world. How "dated" is this violence, precisely the "excess"?

Note how in the modern world, the original sacrifice of victims, who are both sacred and dangerous, sources of trouble and of healing, is broken apart. This yields (a) the scapegoat who is entirely wrong, evil; as in witchcraft, anti-Semitism; and (b) the purely righteous sacrifice: the brave young men fallen in battle, an idea ultimately derived from Christianity.[20]

What does all this tell us about the relation of violence and religion? Is religion the main instigator of categorical violence? Well, it would certainly appear that since the very beginning of human culture, religion and violence have been closely interwoven. And there certainly are cases today where the connection holds.

But on the other hand, when we examine more closely some of what we might call the religious uses of violence, in particular its appeal to scapegoat mechanisms, and the self-affirmation of our purity by identifying all evil with the enemy outside (or provisionally within, but who therefore needs to be expelled), we find that all this can easily survive the rejection of religion, and recurs in ideological-political forms which are resolutely lay, even atheist. Moreover, it recurs in them with a kind of false good conscience, an unawareness of repeating an old and execrable pattern, just because of the easy assumption that all that belonged to the old days of religion, and therefore can't be happening in our Enlightened age.

But more than this, if religion has from the beginning been bound up with violence, the nature of the involvement has changed. In archaic, pre-Axial forms, ritual in war or sacrifice consecrates violence; it relates violence to the sacred, and gives a kind of numinous depth to killing and the excitements and inebriation of killing; just as it does through other rituals for sexual desire and union.

With the coming of "higher", post-Axial religions, this kind of numinous endorsement is more and more withdrawn. We move towards a point where, in some religions, violence has no more place at all in the sanctified life, or its analogues, as I remarked above in section 3.

But nevertheless, as we have seen, various forms of sanctified and purifying violence recur. We get a phenomenon like the Crusades. This is profoundly at odds with the spirit of Christianity, which early mediaeval bishops were aware of on one level, when they tried to restrain noble bellicosity, and proclaim truces of God. But they were nevertheless induced to preach Crusades by falling back into scapegoat mode: the infidel was the servant of darkness, and therefore deserved the most utter hostility, in the name of the Prince of Peace.

There remained nonetheless a profound ambivalence. These holy campaigns were supposed to act under stricter rules than ordinary war; clergy were not themselves supposed to take up arms. But basically, we have the mould in which Robespierre will later fit. An enemy of the death penalty once the Republic is established, he is willing to wade through blood to set it up in all its purity. The illusion is that one can separate before and after, within and without. Purity will reign within and during the Kingdom/Republic, but savagery will rule our relations to what is without or before this realm of peace.

Post-Axial religions often suffer from a profound bad faith, even hypocrisy. But in this, they are not alone. They have been followed by some of the militant secular ideologies in this, as well as that hybrid phenomenon of our day, confessionally-defined nationalisms (BJP's Hindutva, George W. Bush's nation bringing liberty to the world, following God's will for humanity).

But these higher religions and ideologies want to use violence to affirm their own purity, while depriving it altogether of the numinous depth that archaic and earlier forms endowed it with. Violence is ugly and savage, but it must nevertheless be used by noble and dedicated warriors. We are constantly repressing one half of what we deep down know about the world of war and violence; and we are constantly being surprised when confronted by the savagery of our own valiant soldiers, be it in My Lai, or Abu Ghraib.

The modern world, religious and secular, suffers from a deep rift in its self-understanding, an ideological blindness of massive proportions; something which is brilliantly anatomized by Chris Hedges in his harrowing book.[21]

And so, once again, both faith and secular thinking face a similar challenge, which they have trouble conceiving, let alone dealing with effectively. I want to return to this below, after the discussion in the following section.

11

Like all earlier notions of the moral basis of social order—like the orders of hierarchical complementarity, or ancient law—the modern idea of moral order tends to be seen by its adherents as self-stabilizing. That is, conformity to it lends cohesion to society, which becomes self-sustaining.

In modern society, this stability is meant to be based on the basic principle of the modern idea, that is, that the properly ordered society brings together individuals in such a way that their reciprocal action redounds to their mutual benefit. This, as we saw, has been differently conceived. At the beginning views which we could call minimalist were put forward, say, by Locke, and later on by the mainstream of the eighteenth-century Enlightenment. I call them minimalist, in that they were not terribly demanding of altruism or a strong sense of solidarity; given the right structure, and conformity with certain rules of mutual respect of rights, mutual benefit would flow from each person's pursuing their own best interests. This has been known as the view that society can be stabilized via a "harmony of interests".

Later, in reaction to these, we see versions which accentuate the importance of citizen bonding, of a strong common identification with the general will, and which put a greater emphasis on solidarity. Rousseau and Marx are crucial thinkers in this stream of thinking.[22] Or else, there are versions which demand a much higher level of altruism, which is very often conceived as universal, transcending all boundaries. Kant, and also Marx in his own way, are key authors in this stream, while Hegel tried in his own way to marry Rousseau and Kant.

In all these versions, the well-ordered society is seen as self-stabilizing. This is not just true of the "harmony of interests" variant. A contemporary thinker profoundly influenced by Kant, John Rawls, could also hold that the "well-ordered" society tended to win the allegiance of its members, and thus sustain itself.[23] Kant, universalist as he was, tended to extend the effect to the international sphere: republican societies, run by bourgeois tax-payers, who—unlike irresponsible princes out for glory—knew and felt the costs of war, would be more and more reluctant to wage war on each other. Mankind could hope for a coming age of Perpetual Peace.[24]

But views of the minimalist range are hardly superseded. Indeed, they have if anything become more prominent and prevalent after the implosion of Communism. A common view today is that the spread of free markets, liberal societies and democratic forms of rule will ensure a golden age for humankind, promising universal peace and growing well-being for all. People need to be trained in the disciplines and methods of self-reliance, entrepreneurship, respect for rights, and democratic government; but these are things they already hanker after, and once acquired they never want to lose.

Our whole view of ourselves, based on our modern understanding of morality, and an ordered, disciplined society of mutual benefit, is that we have moved (in some favoured countries), and are moving (in other, less favoured ones) to a civilization which entrenches democracy and human rights. What is the basis of this confident prospect?

The answer is to hold that "normally", once these régimes are established, we are quite happy with them. Deviations have always been the result of error, superstition, or bad conditions. Once these are overcome, we are happy in this civilization, for reasons which were first adumbrated in the Enlightenment of the eighteenth century: because we are motivated by enlightened self-interest, and ultimately see the harmony of interests which modern democratic and market societies realize; and/or because of some deep-programmed sympathy in our nature.

Of course, various things can disturb this harmony: excessive egoism, pride, the competitive search for power and reputation; as well as various "vices": desire, drink, different addictions, etc. But the idea is often that these can be contained by stronger motives of a positive kind mentioned above. So we settle into stable democracy.

Thus we often hear it said that globalization and economic growth will turn societies in which violence seems to be endemic into peaceful democracies, because people will have more constructive outlets for their energies (this is the burden of many of Thomas Friedman's op-ed pieces in *The New York Times*). A similar sense of the satisfactions of liberal market democracies underlies Francis Fukuyama's declaration of an End of History (albeit with a certain disquiet at the loss of higher human goals).

But the sad record of continuing violence troubles this prospect. Why is it still with us? Why are we still perpetuating it ourselves? No one yet has totally convincing answers to these questions, which we face in common, whatever our metaphysical or religious beliefs.

One part of the answer is certainly this: the more minimalist rules which are supposed to guarantee harmony are inherently morally instable. The code of honest, free competition, mutual respect of rights and democratic rule, is meant to be strengthened once applied by the fact that people are in fact benefited by it, and become more firmly attached to it. This expectation is what the optimistic prospects of neo-liberal globalization are based on. Now there is obviously some truth to this in our present age, but there are clearly massive flaws.

It is not just that the operation of the freest markets produces terribly negative consequences for some people, at least in the short and medium run. (In the long run, all this is supposed to iron out, but we know what Keynes had to say about this supposed consolation.) It is also that even to ensure the benefit to the majority, in the best circumstances, requires a degree of probity, and allegiance to the common interest, which the rules of the free market don't guarantee. CEOs who cheat employees of their pensions, firms which pursue ecologically irresponsible policies to the brink of global disaster; the list could be extended.

It seems we need a stronger ethic, a firmer identification with the common good, more solidarity, if we are really to enter the promised land of a self-sustaining ethical code, or even meet the basic condition of the modern moral order, that our interaction really be of mutual benefit. So can't the response be simply to rewrite the code, put in a bit more Rousseau or Marx?

But we are all now painfully aware of the problems involved in this. Too great central control can undercut the prosperity that everyone desires, and can also threaten freedom. The solidarity can't be just managed from on high, but must be something people really identify with. But modern examples of strong common identity, the most prominent of which is nationalism, also pose their own problems, frequently being hostile to diversity, or mobilizing against outsiders. Indeed, they can easily become sites of one or other form of the scapegoat mechanism I discussed in the previous section, that is, the way we shore up our own sense of moral integrity by projecting evil onto some Other, and frequently come to entrench our own conviction of purity and self-righteousness by waging violent persecution or war against this Other.

This whole domain, of the social ethic which can bind a society together, is very problematic, and is the site of multiple dilemmas. Of course, the lack of a strong sense of social solidarity could be compensated by a higher level of general altruism, which would also, one hopes, act as a hedge against exclusionary practices, war and persecution, even where solidarity is strong.

As far as the latter hope is concerned, it will be shaken by the discussion of the previous section, which shows how the scapegoat mechanism can recreate itself even within forms of modern universalist humanism. The case is clear enough for Jacobinism and Bolshevism, but one hears echoes of a similar stance behind much of the rhetoric on the "War on Terror" even in contemporary liberal societies, including justifications of war and even torture to eliminate totally the carriers of evil. It would appear that any conception of purity can suffer the subversion of the scapegoating move, whereby our own righteousness is guaranteed by our violent combat against those projected as evil; even the "purity" defined in terms of human rights and democracy.

But how about the first hope: altruism as a supplement to bonds of solidarity which are too weak, not only within societies, but even more on a global scale, where they are clearly inadequate to sustain policies based on the general interest?

It is clear that altruism on a global scale plays a bigger role in our era than ever before, not only in the private sector, in the form of humanitarian aid, and the action of NGOs like Médecins Sans Frontières, but also on the governmental level. We have only to think of the recent G8 initiative to greatly increase the level of aid to Africa. But that raises the issue of the moral sources underlying these initiatives.

In Chapter 16, I raised the question whether we could make sense of our feeling of obligation to all human beings in terms of various accounts offered by modern naturalist philosophies. And I expressed some doubts about the Humean account in terms of a human sympathy which gradually spreads in wider and wider circles. Could the ontology here of moral sentiment match the phenomenology? I thought not. That account seemed defective, because it didn't have a way of explaining our sense of obligation, our sense that we were breaking with an older, narrower, less satisfactory mode of solidarity.

But here we are asking another question. Even though we have a defective account of what moves us, we may still be strongly motivated. People in fact agree on a politics of solidarity, or on humanitarian action, for a wide range of reasons; where one is an atheist humanist, another a Christian, another a Muslim, and so on. This is of the essence of a modern polity which operates on an "overlapping consensus". But within this, we can still ask which is more satisfactory as a basis, not now as an account of how it could come to exist, as in the earlier discussion, but rather as what I have called a "moral source". I mean by that considerations which (for us) inspire us to embrace this morality, and the evoking of which strengthens our commitment to it.[25]

Here the issue concerns what we need to carry through on what the morality demands of us. Does our reason for embracing it motivate us to carry out what it calls for, or might it perhaps be that it crucially weakens us in face of some of the obstacles and distractions which lie in our way?

It is very likely that the answers to these two questions are closely linked. The right answer to our first question, what can best explain our moral aspirations and action, will identify our real underlying motivation, rather than the ideologically induced pictures of it which we have come to accept. This is the motivation which underlies our highest aspirations, and also our best practice, where we really live up to the demands we make of ourselves. But then the chances are that recognizing this motivation, and becoming more clearly and acutely aware of it, will strengthen our attachment to this ethic, and our resolve to act on it. Coming to clarity on "why we are doing this" can help identify and neutralize other extraneous motives—such as self-righteousness, contempt and hatred of wrong-doers, and a sense of civilizational superiority—which may muddy action and lead us away from our goals. And it will characteristically also inspire us and strengthen our resolve. A motivation which has this kind of potential to empower I want to call a "moral source".

Now I mentioned earlier that the main accounts offered in the Enlightenment period of our willingness to enter this broader space of universal solidarity were based on the universal sympathy which I just touched on, on one hand, and the way in which, on the other, our rising above our particularity to a universal view brought us to a sort of universal benevolence. On this account, the very assuming of the stance of the impartial spectator cannot but induce us to desire universal well-being.

But if we move beyond an explanatory account and seek an identification of moral sources, we have to go a bit further. Why does grasping the general perspective make you act for the good of all? Plainly, as a matter of fact, not everybody does. What are those agents missing who lamentably fall short of this demand?

The answer that flows from the Humean account would be that our sympathy is too restricted. Our ability to feel solidarity ranges over too narrow a scope. Presumably we might help overcome this defect by learning more about distant others, or exposing ourselves to television coverage of some disaster which works directly in our emotions. But this is not quite the same as invoking a moral source. We link up here with the earlier discussion of Humean sympathy as an explanation for solidarity. The alleged extension of sympathy with civilizational development and wider contact is just a fact about us; what it doesn't account for is our sense that there is something higher, nobler, more fully human about universal sympathy. It is this sense of universal solidarity as higher which can operate as a moral source; helping us set aside extraneous motivations, and inspiring us to act.

So what account of what is higher here can function as such a source? One answer invokes our sense of dignity as agents capable of grasping the universal perspective—or as rational agents, to put the point in a frequently-invoked way. To live up to our capacity as beings capable of this universal insight, we ought to act also universally, however this is conceived. It may be in terms of our aiming at the general happiness (Utilitarianism), or it may be in terms of our acting on universalizable maxims (Kant). But in both cases, we can say that we owe it to our own dignity to act this way, and this is what the moral source consists in. That is, this is what one can appeal to, in oneself or another, to bring us into line with what we ought to do.

Descartes, in his appeal to "générosité" as the keystone of the other virtues, began this modern anchoring of morality in dignity. Of course, as the term in its original sense implies, this was a very old basis for ethical action, central to the warrior and noble honour ethics. You have to live up to your status, and not behave as though you were from one of the lower orders. Only with Descartes, the appeal is both internalized, and made universal. The higher order you belong to is not one of external rank, but of rational agency; and in that all humans (potentially) share. Enlightenment universalism follows in his footsteps.[26]

The weight which reposes on this sense of dignity is, of course, the less where there really is sympathy motivating you to act for another's good; and also where there is a lively sense of common interest, backed by a doctrine of the harmony of interests, or by some hope of achieving a universal double harmony, within and between people. But once belief in these earlier props fades, as it tends to do in this post-Utopian age, the main appeal becomes one to my dignity. I would be ashamed, as a rational being, to act for petty private advantage. Or transposed into a more disabused and disillusioned language, as a fully lucid human being, seeing the absurdity in things, I cannot but want to fight this by acting to relieve the suffering of human beings in general, as with Dr. Rieux in *La Peste*. As Camus put it in the quote I cited above: "Vigny a très bien vu que l'honneur est la seule morale possible pour l'homme sans Dieu"[27] (Vigny saw very well that honour is the only possible morality for man without God).[28]

And the farther one moves to a "post-modern", "anti-humanist" position, the more a passionate commitment to universal rights is without grounding in the nature of things, and without hope of reward or fulfillment, the more unmotivated in traditional terms this commitment is, as with Derrida for instance, then the more it is plainly powered by a sense of dignity, the sense of a demand laid on us by our very lucidity.

This seems admirable and heroic. And in a way it undoubtedly is. But a question arises of whether it is an adequate source, that is, whether it can really motivate us to carry through on our aspiration to universal human dignity and well-being.

This brings us to the issue I raised very briefly in the last chapter of *Sources*.[29] The more impressed one is with this colossal extension of a Gospel ethic to a universal solidarity, to a concern for human beings on the other side of the globe, whom we shall never meet or need as companions or compatriots; or, because that is not the ultimately difficult challenge, the more impressed we are at the sense of justice we can still feel for people we do have contact with, and tend to dislike or despise; or at a willingness to help people who often seem to be the cause of their own suffering; the more we contemplate all this, the more surprise we can feel at people generating the motivation to engage in these enterprises of solidarity, of international philanthropy, or the modern welfare state. Or to bring out the negative side, the less surprised one is when the motivation to keep them going flags, as we see in the present hardening of feeling against the impoverished and disfavoured in many Western democracies.

We could put the matter this way. Our age makes higher demands of solidarity and benevolence on people today than ever before. Never before have people been asked to stretch out so far, and so consistently, so systematically, so as a matter of course, to the stranger outside the gates. A similar point can be made, if we look at the other dimension of the affirmation of ordinary life, that concerned with universal justice. Here too, we are asked to maintain standards of equality which cover wider and wider classes of people, bridge more and more kinds of difference, impinge more and more in our lives. How do we manage to do it?

Or perhaps we don't manage all that well; and the interesting and important question might run: how could we manage to do it? But at least to get close to the answer to this, we should ask: how do we do as well as we do, which after all, at first sight seems in these domains of solidarity and justice much better than previous ages?

1. Well, one way is that performance to these standards has become part of what we understand as a decent, civilized human life. We live up to them to the extent we do, because we would be somewhat ashamed of ourselves if we didn't. They have become part of our self-image, our sense of our own worth. And alongside this, we feel a sense of satisfaction and superiority when we contemplate others—our ancestors, or contemporary illiberal societies—who didn't or don't recognize them. This is basically the principal moral source that I have just outlined above, the one enshrined in Enlightenment-based exclusive humanism.

But we sense immediately how fragile this is as a motivation. It makes our philanthropy vulnerable to the shifting fashion of media attention, and the various modes of feel-good hype. We throw ourselves into the cause of the month, raise funds for this famine, petition the government to intervene in that grisly civil war; and then forget all about it next month, when it drops off the CNN screen. A solidarity ultimately driven by the giver's own sense of moral superiority is a whimsical and fickle thing. We are far in fact from the universality and unconditionality which our moral outlook prescribes.

We might envisage getting beyond this by a more exigent sense of our own moral worth; one that would require more consistency, a certain independence from fashion, careful, informed attention to the real needs. This is part of what people working in NGOs in the field must feel, who correspondingly look down on us TV-image-driven givers, as we do on the lesser breeds who don't respond to this type of campaign at all.

2. But the most exigent, lofty sense of self-worth has limitations. I feel worthy in helping people, in giving without stint. But what is worthy about helping people? It's obvious, as humans they have a certain dignity. My feelings of self-worth connect intellectually and emotionally with my sense of the worth of human beings. Here is where modern secular humanism is tempted to congratulate itself. In replacing the low and demeaning picture of human beings as depraved, inveterate sinners, in articulating the potential of human beings for goodness and greatness, humanism has not only given us the courage to act for reform, but also explains why this

philanthropic action is so immensely worthwhile. The higher the human potential, the greater the enterprise of realizing it, and the more the carriers of this potential are worthy of our help in achieving it.

But philanthropy and solidarity driven by a lofty humanism, just as that which was driven often by high religious ideals, has a Janus face. On one side, in the abstract, one is inspired to act. But on the other, faced with the immense disappointments of actual human performance, with the myriad ways in which real, concrete human beings fall short of, ignore, parody and betray this magnificent potential, one cannot but experience a growing sense of anger and futility. Are these people really worthy objects of all these efforts? Perhaps in face of all this stupid recalcitrance, it would not be a betrayal of human worth, or one's self-worth, if one abandoned them. Or perhaps the best that can be done for them is to force them to shape up.

Before the reality of human shortcomings, philanthropy—the love of the human—can gradually come to be invested with contempt, hatred, aggression. The action is broken off, or worse, continues, but informed now with these new feelings, and becomes progressively more coercive and inhumane. The history of despotic socialism, i.e., twentieth-century communism, is replete with this tragic turn, brilliantly foreseen by Dostoyevsky over 100 years ago ("Starting from unlimited freedom, I have arrived at unlimited despotism"),[30] and then repeated again and again with a fatal regularity, through one-party régimes on a macro level, to a host of "helping" institutions on a micro level from orphanages to boarding schools for aboriginals.

The ultimate stop on the line was reached by Elena Ceausescu in her last recorded statement before her murder by the successor régime: that the Rumanian people had shown themselves unworthy of the immense untiring efforts of her husband on their behalf.

The tragic irony is that the higher the sense of potential, the more grievously real people fall short, and the more severe the turn-around will be which is inspired by the disappointment. A lofty humanism posits high standards of self-worth, and a magnificent goal to strive towards. It inspires enterprises of great moment. But by this very token it encourages force, despotism, tutelage, ultimately contempt, and a certain ruthlessness in shaping refractory human material. Oddly enough, the same horrors which Enlightenment critique picked up in societies and institutions dominated by religion.

And for the same causes. The difference of belief here is not crucial. Wherever action for high ideals is not tempered, controlled, ultimately engulfed in an unconditional love of the beneficiaries, this ugly dialectic risks repeating itself. And of course, just holding the appropriate religious *beliefs* is no guarantee that this will be so.

3. A third pattern of motivation, which we have seen repeatedly, this time in the register of justice rather than benevolence: We have seen it with Jacobins, Bolsheviks, and today with the politically correct left, as well as the so-called "Christian" right. We fight against injustices which cry out to heaven for vengeance. We are moved by a flaming indignation against these: racism, oppression, sexism, or leftist attacks on the family or Christian faith. This indignation comes to be fuelled by hatred for those who support and connive with these injustices; and this in turn is fed by our sense of superiority that we are not like these instruments and accomplices of evil. Soon we are blinded to the havoc we wreak around us. Our picture of the world has safely located all evil outside of us. The very energy and hatred with which we combat evil proves its exteriority to us. We must never relent, but on the contrary double our energy, vie with each other in indignation and denunciation. This is the dialectic of sacred killing which I discussed in sections 5 and 10.

Another tragic irony nests here. The stronger the sense of (often correctly identified) injustice, the more powerfully this pattern can become entrenched. We become centres of hatred, generators of new modes of injustice on a greater scale, but we started with the most exquisite sense of wrong, the greatest passion for justice and equality and peace.

A Buddhist acquaintance of mine from Thailand briefly visited the German Greens. He confessed to utter bewilderment. He thought he understood the goals of the party: peace between human beings, and a stance of respect and friendship by humans towards nature. But what astonished him was all the anger, the tone of denunciation, of hatred towards the established parties. These people didn't seem to see that the first step towards their goal would have to involve stilling the anger and aggression in themselves. He couldn't understand what they were up to.[31]

The blindness is typical of modern exclusive secular humanism. This modern humanism prides itself on having released energy for philanthropy and reform; by getting rid of "original sin", of a lowly and demeaning picture of human nature, it encourages us to reach high. Of course, there is some truth in this. But it is also terribly partial, terribly naïve, because it has never faced the questions I have been raising here: what can power this great effort at philanthropic reform? This humanism leaves us with our own high sense of self-worth to keep us from backsliding, a high notion of human worth to inspire us forward, and a flaming indignation against wrong and oppression to energize us. It cannot appreciate how problematic all of these are, how easily they can slide into something trivial, ugly or downright dangerous and destructive.

A Nietzschean genealogist can have a field day here. Nothing gave Nietzsche greater satisfaction than showing how morality or spirituality is really powered by its direct opposite; e.g., that the Christian aspiration to love is really motivated by the hatred of the weak for the strong. Whatever one thinks of this judgment on Christianity, it is clear that modern humanism is full of potential for such disconcerting reversals: from dedication to others to self-indulgent, feel-good responses, from a lofty sense of human dignity to control powered by contempt and hatred, from absolute freedom to absolute despotism, from a flaming desire to help the oppressed to an incandescent hatred for all those who stand in the way. And the higher the flight, the greater the potential fall.

Perhaps after all, it's safer to have small goals, not too great expectations, be somewhat cynical about human potentiality from the start. This is undoubtedly so, but then one also risks not having the motivation to undertake great acts of solidarity, and combat great injustices. In the end, the question becomes a maximin one: how to have the greatest degree of philanthropic action with the minimum hope in mankind. A figure like Dr. Rieux in Camus' *La Peste* stands as a possible solution to this problem. But that is fiction. What is possible in real life?

The reflections of the last paragraphs show how philanthropy, in actual practice, can breed misanthropy. But one also sees a powerful streak of misanthropy in modern culture quite independent of any real experience of trying to help, or to change the conditions of life. There is a kind of misanthropy in principle, as it were, which declares the worthlessness of human life; it sees itself as taking a heroic stance and finally declaring what both Christians and humanists try to hide from themselves and from us all. In a recent book,[32] Nancy Huston studies the extraordinary phenomenon in twentieth century literature, that some of the most popular authors espoused the bleakest and most unconditional misanthropy, and were read and applauded by a wide public, most of whose members were never tempted to live by this outlook.

She cites, for instance, Samuel Beckett, Thomas Bernhard, Emil Cioran, Imre Kertesz, Milan Kundera. A common source for many of them was Schopenhauer, the great pessimist, who did indeed, make his own the famous line from Calderón's *La vida es sueño*: "pues el delito mayor del hombre es haber nacido"—the great crime of humans is to have been born. But in fact Schopenhauer identifies as a crime not so much being born—that is rather seen as a great misfortune; rather it is giving birth which is to be condemned. This kind of misanthropy utterly rejects and despises human generation, reproduction, the whole business of forming families and having children; which stance often carries with it a certain misogyny. Women are a danger to men, because they entrap them into continuing the whole process of generation, which Schopenhauer saw as the continued striving of the Will to multiply its carriers.

What can seem puzzling here is that this extreme pessimism continues to attract such attention, applause, literary prizes, media attention. Nancy Huston offers some interesting explanations of this. Plainly she is right that there is something heroic in this stance, even though one might condemn it on other grounds, and that this wins admiration. "Portant l'auréole de la douleur puissance *x*, ses adeptes sont nos Christs en croix, nos saints torturés, nos martyrs stoïques, magnifiques et magnifiés", in the disenchanted world of modernity.[33] (Wearing the halo of pain to the *n*th power, its followers are our Christs on the cross, our tortured saints, our stoic martyrs, magnificent and glorified.) I would add another reason. Plainly many of us are ambivalent about the philanthropic solidarity we profess, and this for a host of reasons, including those discussed above. Ambivalence is increased by an unquiet conscience: we are not doing all that we ought to in the light of our ideals and aspirations. There is a certain pleasure in seeing these trashed so thoroughly, giving vent to the suppressed side of our ambivalence, expressing our resentment at the way we are all nudged into hypocrisy by the norms of political correctness—and all in a plausibly deniable way, since after all we are only "enjoying literature".[34]

But supposing we wanted to liberate ourselves from this sneaking sympathy with misanthropy? Huston offers considerations which ought to achieve this. She points us to the experience of having children, bringing them up. "J'ai vu la lente émergence du langage, de la personnalité, l'hallucinante construction d'un être, sa façon d'ingurgiter le monde, de le faire sien, d'entrer en relation avec lui: . . . *j'ai vu que c'était passionant*."[35] (I saw the slow emergence of language, or personality, the incredible construction of a being, its way of ingesting the world, of making it its own, of entering into relation with it: . . . *I saw that it was profoundly moving*.)

I find this true and moving indeed. I'm sure it describes a widespread experience. But this brings us back to our earlier question. This sense of awe, surprise, tenderness, which moves us so much when a new human being emerges, finds herself, what does it reflect? It's plain that people can refuse to see it, like the midwife, Arina Prokhorovna, in Dostoyevsky's *The Possessed;* when Shatov cries out in wonder at the new baby, "It's the mystery of the appearance of a new being, a great and inexplicable mystery. . . . There were two, and suddenly there is a third, a new spirit; . . . a new thought and a new love . . . so uncanny . . . there is nothing higher in the world," Arina Prochorovna replies laughing, "What a fuss you're making . . . It's simply the further development of the organism, and nothing more, there is no mystery, . . . otherwise every fly would be a mystery. And let me tell you something. Superfluous human beings should not be born."[36]

When you don't fend off this insight, what are you seeing? What way of articulating this insight really does it justice? What captures it at its most powerful? What can enable it to work most powerfully on us and direct our lives? Our two questions above, that of explaining our moral responses, and that of identifying our moral sources, are once again closely interlinked.

A Christian would say that what the parent sees in the growing child is some facet of the image of God. But it is not obvious to everyone that you need metaphysical or spiritual terms to make sense of this insight. However, it's equally not obvious that the opposite is the case, and that this is a reaction which can just be explained naturalistically. We ought to see this as a question needing further enquiry, clarification, exploration; and moreover as an important such question. Relating this to the above discussion on the sources of universal solidarity, the issue might be put this way: how can the moving insight that most of us can easily recognize in relation to our own children somehow inform and energize our stance to human beings as such?

Instead, the whole issue of our depth motivation to philanthropy is often taken as easily resolved; either by our beliefs—for some people in God, for others in Kantian morality or human rights; or else from another angle, by our "natural" feelings of sympathy or (as in this case) wonder.

But, as I said earlier, just having appropriate beliefs is no solution to the dilemmas of philanthropic practice I described above. And sympathy can so easily be blocked by ideology, even (though rarely) in the case of one's own children, but certainly when it comes to others'. In fact, the transformation of high ideals into brutal practice was demonstrated lavishly in Christendom well before modern humanism came on the scene. So what can one do?

How can we become agents on whom misanthropy has no hold, in whom it awakens no connivance? There is, of course, a Christian account of this, which I just invoked above. This cannot be a matter of guarantee, only of faith. It can be described in two ways. Either as a love/compassion which is unconditional, that is, not based on what you the recipient have made of yourself; or as one based on what you are most profoundly, a being in the image of God. They obviously amount to the same thing. In either case, the love is not conditional on the worth realized in you just as an individual, or even in what is realizable in you alone. That's because being made in the image of God, as a feature of each human being, is not something that can be characterized just by reference to this being alone. Our being in the image of God is also our standing among others in the stream of love which is that facet of God's life we try to grasp, very inadequately, in speaking of the Trinity.

There is also another issue here. We can look at Christian agape and, say, Camus' affirming human happiness in the face of the absurd, as two alternative ways of sustaining the same kind of philanthropic action, such as humanitarian action or a defence of human rights. Here are two stances that will typically be adopted by different people in an overlapping consensus. That was the main focus of the above discussion. But they also reflect very different ethical views, radically different conceptions of human life.

I spoke above of the heroism of the modern misanthropic stance. The heroism consists in continuing to live in face of the perceived meaninglessness and worth-lessness of life. But the related position of a Camus, where the response to the meaningless universe is continued philanthropic action, seems even more heroic. Indeed, it seems even more heroic than, say, Christian martyrdom, because the gift of self, in living for others, even more in dying for them, is bereft even of the hope of return which the martyr still has, in the restored life of the Resurrection. It is the absolute heroism.

This partly accounts for the great prestige of this position in our day; and if as I have held, the convincing force of modern atheism lies more in its ethical stance than in epistemological considerations, this is no small matter.

It may seem that this claim to superiority is unanswerable; even the Crucifixion is trumped by a yet more gratuitous giving.

But is this the ultimate measure of excellence? If we think of ethical virtue as the realization of lone individuals, this may seem to be the case. But suppose the highest good consists in communion, mutual giving and receiving, as in the paradigm of the eschatological banquet. The heroism of gratuitous giving has no place for reci-procity. If you return anything to me, then my gift was not totally gratuitous; and besides, in the extreme case, I disappear with my gift and no communion between us is possible. This unilateral heroism is self-enclosed. It touches the outermost limit of what we can attain to when moved by a sense of our own dignity. But is that what life is about? Christian faith proposes a quite different view.[37]

Let's return to Nancy Huston's insight above, as we see the child awakening, be-coming another free being. This is, in fact, one side of something bigger. The child is being led by a parent along a path of growth. But this is not just a service per-formed by one human being for another. It only succeeds where it is other and more than this, where a bond of love arises. This is a bond where each is a gift to the other, where each gives and receives, and where the line between giving and receiv-ing is blurred. We are quite outside the range of "altruistic" unilateralism.

Could it be that, in a very different way, something analogous lies behind the sense of solidarity between equals that pushes us to help people, even on the other side of the globe? The sense here would be that we are somehow given to each other, and that ideally, at the limit, this points us towards a relationship where giving and receiving merge.

Once again, our concern here is dual. On one hand, we want to discover what the moving force is here, to give an account which does justice to it. On the other, we sense that getting it right will help to strengthen it, and to liberate it from the motives I described above which so easily colonize philanthropy and turn it into its opposite.

Now one might conclude that this kind of response to the image of God in others is not really a possibility for us humans, and one might not be able to make sense of this notion of our being given to each other. I think this can be real for us, but only to the extent that we open ourselves to God, which means in fact, overstepping the limits set in theory by exclusive humanisms. If one does believe that, then one has something very important to say to modern times, something that addresses the fragility of what all of us, believer and unbeliever alike, most value in these times.

But if not, then it may appear that the awe-inspiring, Stoic courage of a Camus or a Derrida must be our highest aspiration. Without a "leap of faith", of anticipatory confidence, one way or another, this question remains moot. But *if* the act of faith in God should be well-founded, then one must see this Stoic courage in a new light. It is still admirable as human self-overcoming in Nietzsche's sense—as is its cousin, root-and-branch Schopenhauerian misanthropy—but it is achieved at the expense of turning oneself, and possibly many others, away from the path towards a much more powerful and effective healing action in history.[38]

12

In both the last sections, the argument came to a point where we had to look beyond the question of what the code ought to be, whether minimalist, or based more on solidarity, or altruism, and raised the issue of the deeper motivation needed to carry through on the code. This arose negatively in section 10, where the issue arises: how can we combat or overcome the temptation to shore up self-righteousness through scapegoating? It arose more positively in section 11, where we were looking for adequate moral sources for the high contemporary standards of altruism.

In both these cases, we went beyond the scope of much moral thinking which has emerged out of the modern conception of moral order. This has tended to focus precisely on codes, both moral codes, on one hand, and sets of institutions and rules, on the other. In the original minimalist version of moral order as self-sustaining through a harmony of interests, this eclipse of the issue of moral motivation was quite understandable; the basis of stability and social order was enlightened self-interest. "Interest" was the basic continuing motivation, which needed only to be steered in the right direction through good habits and/or enlightened views.

Of course, this eclipse of the issue of motivation, which would have been incomprehensible to the ancients, was challenged by the later more demanding versions of moral order, stressing solidarity and/or altruism. Both Rousseau and Kant made the question of motivation central: amour-propre versus the general will; a will moved by inclination versus one moved by reason. But contemporary thinking, even in its neo-Kantian forms, seems to have moved again away from this insight.

Thus a great deal of effort in modern liberal society is invested in defining and applying codes of conduct. First, at the highest theoretical level, much contemporary moral theory assumes that morality can be defined in terms of a code of obligatory and forbidden actions, a code moreover which can be generated from a single source or principle. Hence the major importance in our philosophy departments of the battle between Utilitarians and (post)-Kantians; they agree that there must be a single principle from which one can generate all and only obligatory actions, but they wage a vigorous polemic over the nature of this principle. On one hand, there are those who opt for some or other mode of calculation of utility (rule utilitarianism, act utilitarianism, utilities as preferences, etc.). On the other hand, we find those whose criterion lies in some form of universality: be it the original Kantian sort (acting by universalizable maxims), or more sophisticated modern versions, as for example: that norm is right which is agreed by all those affected (Habermas); or that act is right which you could justify to those affected (Scanlon). The constant here is the identification of morality with a unified code, generated from a single source.

But if you move out of the academy into the political realm, you are struck with a similar (and related) code-fixation. This is interwoven with the legal entrenchment of certain fundamental principles of our society, whose most prominent and visible form is the constitutionalization of various charters of rights and non-discrimination, which is a central feature of our world. This leads to a more and more elaborate definition of legally binding codes. But this approach extends in spirit beyond the political sphere. It is taken for granted that the way to achieve certain important collective goods, like tolerance and mutual respect, lies in a code of behaviour, like the "speech codes" which some campuses have put in place. The contours of disrespect are codified, so that they can be forbidden, and if necessary sanctioned. Thus will our society march forward.

What's wrong with this? Why can't our moral/ethical life ever be adequately captured in a code? Here are some of the reasons:

1. The Aristotle reason: situations, events are unforeseeably various; no set of formulae will ever capture all of them. Any pre-fixed code will have to be adjusted to new situations. That is why the good person with phronesis really operates on a deep sense of the goods concerned, plus a flexible ability to discern what the new situation requires.

2. The plurality of goods (also Aristotle): there is more than one good; this is not recognized by Kant and Bentham, and all those who try to derive morality from a single source-principle. These goods can conflict in certain circumstances: liberty

and equality; justice and mercy; commutative justice and comity; efficient success and compassionate understanding; getting things done bureaucratically (requiring categories, rules) and treating everyone as a unique person; and so on.

3. Now this feature (2) intensifies (1). It creates dilemmas; and dilemmatic situations differ in non-predictable ways. So we need phronesis even more. We need a sense of the two goods in conflict here, and of the weight of each demand in the tension in relation to its own kind. If one is really weighty, and the other relatively trivial, we know which way to lean.

So different examples of the "same" dilemma call for different resolutions. But there is more. It is in the nature of dilemmas that even in a concrete case, they may admit of more than one solution. That is, the "same" dilemma, defined by the goods in conflict, and in this concrete case, may admit of more than one solution, like quadratic equations with two unknowns. Why?

Because we are not only dealing with goods (justice and mercy, liberty and equality), but with the claims of certain people, certain agents. How they chose, or can be induced to treat their own claims can have a fateful effect on the outcome. Someone has suffered a historical wrong; commutative justice demands redress. But there are other considerations. What might be considered full redress, if we just look at the nature of the wrong, will have other effects, which may be damaging to parties who are either innocent, or whose guilt is not all that total. This is obviously what arises in cases of historical redress: reparations payments to historical victims; or in cases of transition from a despotic exploitative régime to a more open, democratic, egalitarian one. In this latter case, we have also to consider the effects of full reparations on the future co-existence of the descendants of exploiters and exploited in the new régime.

Now one "right" solution might be an all-things-considered award to the victims, in a context where the two parties remain locked in conflict, at arm's length. But if they can be brought together, can talk, become motivated to try to find some good future basis for their common existence, then one may emerge with quite a different "award", or solution. Cases of contemporary transitional justice come to mind, like the Truth and Reconciliation Commission in South Africa. Of course, big questions arise about this: did the victims really agree? Who exactly were the victims? Were they rushed, pushed, forced into conceding too much? And so on. But the basic idea behind this kind of procedure was to get the ex-victims to accept that they could have a maximum of one kind of closure (the truth about what happened) at the cost of renouncing a lot that they could quite legitimately claim of another kind: punishment of the perpetrators, an eye for an eye. The aim was to find an "award" which allowed also for a reconciliation, and therefore living together on a new footing.

The important point here is this: that one reason dilemmas admit of more than one solution is that they are frequently also conflicts between claimants, and these can be differently seen or interpreted by those involved. But further, by moving the interpretations in a certain direction, the same dilemma can be resolved in a less costly way to the two goods. That is, one resolution may be the only right one here, because the parties remain rigidly hostile and opposed to each other, insisting on their full "rights"; as a result, the "award" to the victim is on one sense higher, therefore hurting the perpetrator more; but the resulting hostility also deprives the victims and their successors of the goods of comity and collaboration. As against this, the operation of a TRC can lift us to a new point where the issue is not so totally zero-sum. It can bring about, in relation to the first situation of total hostility, a win-win move.

4. Generalizing this, we can see that some dilemmas have to be understood in a kind of two-dimensional space. The horizontal space gives you the dimension in which you have to find the point of resolution, the fair "award", between two parties. The vertical space opens the possibility that by rising higher, you'll accede to a new horizontal space where the resolution will be less painful/damaging for both parties.

Examples of this abound in modern politics. A "fair" resolution for Bosnia after the terrible mutual killing is perhaps this strange tri-partite state with separate cantons and a triune presidency, and a great deal of uncertainty and instability. But imagine that, over time, some trust can be re-established between the parties; then one can see the possibility of moving towards a more normal federal system.

That is why the great benefactors in politics are those whose charismatic interventions help a society to move up in this space; Mandela, Tutu come to mind, as the above example suggests.

Put another way, we can say that dilemmas of this kind are also trilemmas, or double dilemmas. First, we have to judge between claims A and B; but then we also have to decide whether we will go for the best "award" between A and B on the level we're now on, or try to induce people to rise to another level. Great leaders here have a mixture of shrewd judgment of where people can be induced to go, as well as great charismatic power to lead them there. Mandela again comes to mind.

The vertical dimension I've been talking about here is one of reconciliation and trust. And this, incidentally, is one of the central themes of a Christian understanding of these dilemmas. The above discussion indeed shows how Christian faith can never be decanted into a fixed code. Because it always places our actions in two dimensions, one of right action, and also an eschatological dimension. This is also a dimension of reconciliation and trust, but it points beyond any merely intra-historical perspective of possible reconciliation. It can, however, inspire vertical moves in history, like those of Mandela and Tutu. (Tutu's faith commitment is well known; I don't know what Nelson Mandela actually believes, but his whole move was obviously deeply inspired by Christianity, if only historically; forgiveness is a key category, however downplayed as a term here.)

The New Testament is full of indications of this. Take the owner of the vineyard who invited workers in at the beginning of the day, then successively at later hours until the end. His proposal to pay everyone one denarius is obviously outrageous as a suggestion for the basis of wages policy in a stable society; hence the protests of those who came at the beginning of the day. But the parable opens the eschatological dimension of the Kingdom of God: at the height of that vertical space, that's the only appropriate distribution. God operates in that vertical dimension, as well as being with us horizontally in the person of Christ.[39]

But that means that there aren't any formulae for acting as Christians in the world. Take the best code possible in today's circumstances, or what passes for such. The question always arises: could one, by transcending/amending/re-interpreting the code, move us all vertically? Christ is constantly doing that in the Gospel. That's why there is something extremely troubling about the tendency of some Christian churches today to identify themselves so totally with certain codes (especially sexual norms), and institutions (liberal society).

But to return to the main line of argument, invoking the vertical dimension brings us in another way back to the missing perspective in modern moral philosophy, that of moral motivation. For clearly moving higher in the dimension of reconciliation and trust involves a kind of motivational conversion, and ability to forgo the satisfactions of retribution, or the security which comes from keeping a distrustful distance from the neighbour. It involves people bonding in a new way, whether this vertical path we are moving along is understood in a Christian way or not.

So the "code fetishism", or nomolatry, of modern liberal society is potentially very damaging. It tends to forget the background which makes sense of any code: the variety of goods which the rules and norms are meant to realize, and it tends to make us insensitive, even blind, to the vertical dimension. It also encourages a "one size fits all" approach: a rule is a rule. One might even say that modern nomolatry dumbs us down, morally and spiritually.

13

Now this discussion surely has relevance to the issue we left in suspense at the end of section 10, that of scapegoating violence. Does all this tell us anything about how to lessen violence, or get rid of it? Have we a hope of doing this?

Let us consider first Kant's hypothesis which I mentioned above, although he wasn't the only person to hold it. This is the view that ordered, democratic societies will become less violent; won't go to war with each other, and presumably won't suffer civil wars. There is some truth to this, as we saw in section 11. Modern disciplined order has had some effect. But as we saw in the same section, the peace is fragile, for a host of reasons; partly because there are certain success conditions of economic order; partly because of tensions of exclusion and rivalry which remain sub-violent, but generate hostility. And then there is the problem that some societies have great trouble acceding to the category of ordered democratic polities.

So any programme to overcome violence must contain at least two objectives: (1) build such ordered democratic polities; (2) try to make their benefits spread as wide as possible, e.g., by preventing the formation of desperate, excluded groups; particularly young men.

But this programme seems radically incomplete, in face of the carry-over or better re-editing of older forms of scapegoating, and holy war to our day. Can we do something to fight these? Is there a third element to our programme?

One answer might be: let us note the metaphysical/religious roots of this categorial, purificatory violence. So how do we get rid of it? It is religious, or at least, metaphysical; and so we will only get rid of it by totally overcoming the religious dimension in our existence. The problem up to now is that many of the main builders of a supposedly secular Republic, the Lenins and the Robespierres, have not really liberated themselves from this incubus as they thought they had.

Thus it seems clear from the phenomena reviewed above that just proposing some non-religious theory, like modern humanism, doesn't really do the trick. The religious forms seem to reconstitute themselves. So we would have to fight for a real, thoroughgoing disenchantment, a total escape from religion. But how do we do this? Is this really possible?

This suggests another answer: all the above shows that the religious dimension is inescapable. Perhaps there is only the choice between good and bad religion. Now there is good religion. For instance, there is Girard's take on Old and New Testaments, as the source for a counter-story to the scapegoat narrative, which shows the victim to be innocent.[40] And we can say something analogous about the Buddha, for instance.

Thus we can point to the Gospel picture of a Christian counter-violence: a transformation of the energy which usually goes into scapegoat purification; transformation which reaches to overcome the fear of violence not by becoming lord of it, by directing it as an annihilating force against evil, but which aims rather to overcome fear by offering oneself to it; responding with love and forgiveness, thereby tapping a source of goodness, and healing.

But an analogous point to the one just made about humanism can be made about these religious positions. Just adopting some religion, even an in principle "good" one, doesn't do the trick. Christianity is responsible for "le souci de la victime" in the modern world. But we see how this can be colonized by the religion of purification of scapegoats. Do we want to protest that this is a secularized variant? Then how about the long, dreary and terrible history of Christian anti-Semitism? Seen in a Girardian light, this is a straight betrayal of the Gospel; an 180 degree reversal. So just believing in these "good" religions doesn't overcome the danger.

Both sides have the virus, and must fight against it.

Where does this leave us in our search for a third kind of measure in our programme? We noticed a pattern in the paradoxical reversals above. The goodness which inhabits our goal, or our vision of order, is somehow undone when it comes to struggling to realize it. Robespierre's republic without a death penalty somehow energizes a programme of escalating butchery; and similar things can be said for the Herderian order of nations co-existing in diversity, or the goal of rescuing all victims. The paradox is, that the very goodness of the goal defines us, its builders and defenders as good, and hence opens the way to our grounding our self-integrity on a contrast case who must be as evil as we are virtuous. The higher the morality, the more vicious the hatred and hence destruction we can, indeed must wreak. When the Crusade comes to its fullness in the moralism of the modern world, even the last vestiges of chivalric respect for an enemy, as in the days of Salah-ud-din and Richard Coeur de Lion, have disappeared. There is nothing left but the grim, relentless struggle against evil.

There is no general remedy against this self-righteous reconstitution of the categorizations of violence, the lines drawn between the good and evil ones which permit the most terrible atrocities. But there can be moves, always within a given context, whereby someone renounces the right conferred by suffering, the right of the innocent to punish the guilty, of the victim to purge the victimizer. The move is the very opposite of the instinctive defense of our righteousness. It is a move which can be called forgiveness, but at a deeper level, it is based on a recognition of common, flawed humanity.

In Dostoyevsky's *The Possessed*, the slogan of the scientistic revolutionaries who would remake the world is "no one is to blame". That is the slogan of the disengaged stance to reality, of the therapeutic outlook. What this slogan hides is another stance which projects the blame entirely on the enemy, giving ourselves the power to act that comes from total righteousness. Opposed to this is the insight that Dostoyevsky's potentially redemptive characters struggle to: "we are all to blame".[41]

It is this restoration of a common ground which defines the kind of move I am talking about. It opens a new footing of co-responsibility to the erstwhile enemy.

This brings us back to the example of Nelson Mandela I mentioned above. There was great political wisdom there. Because following the only too understandable path of revenge would have made it impossible to build a new, democratic society. It is this reflection which has pushed many leaders after periods of civil war in history to offer amnesties. But there was more than that here. Amnesties have the flaw that they usually involve suppressing the truth or at least consciousness of the terrible wrongs that have been done, which therefore fester in the body politic. Mandela's answer was the Truth and Reconciliation Commission, one which is meant to bring terrible deeds to light, but not necessarily in a context of retribution. Moreover, the deeds to be brought to light were not only those of the former ruling side. Here is the new ground of co-responsibility which this Commission offered.

No one knows if this will ultimately work. A move like this goes against the utterly understandable desire for revenge by those who have suffered, as well as all the reflexes of self-righteousness. But without this, and even more the extraordinary stance of Mandela from his first release from prison, what one might call his renunciation of the rights of victimhood, the new South Africa might never have even begun to emerge from the temptations to civil war which threatened and are not yet quite stilled.[42]

There are other examples in this whole field of transitions from despotic and often murderous régimes, inseparable from the spread of democracy. The Polish case also comes to mind, and the strong advice of people like Adam Michnik to forgo the satisfactions of retribution in the name of building a new society. The Dalai Lama's response to Chinese oppression in Tibet offers another striking case.

It is in moves of this kind that we need to seek the third element in our programme. They follow neither of the lines suggested above, in that, although they clearly derive a lot from the religious traditions involved, they are not necessarily the fruit of a personal religious faith. But however motivated, their power lies not in suppressing the madness of violent categorization, but in transfiguring it in the name of a new kind of common world.

19 Unquiet Frontiers of Modernity

14

I'd like to return now to Ferry's meta-question about "le sens du sens", the sources of deeper meaning in our lives. At the beginning of the previous chapter, I began to explore one such source, and the hunger it responds to. I mean our aspiration to separate ourselves from evil and chaos, and to anchor ourselves in the good. We saw what ambiguous fruit this aspiration could produce, not just in the answers we might deem religious, but in the various immanent humanisms and antihumanisms as well. I want now to mention a few other sources of meaning, or domains of life in which we seek such sources. This examination cannot decide the issue between belief and unbelief, any more than the discussion of the previous sections did. But it can bring into view certain sites of unease with the closed perspective on the immanent frame.

2. Let's look at another way to answer Ferry's question: we could try to show how deep and powerful are the meanings of ordinary life, the satisfactions of love, of work, the enjoyment of the natural world, the riches of music, literature, art. This sense of the value of ordinary living is one of the constitutive elements of modern culture, as I argued in the discussion about transcendence above. It was incorporated into the Enlightenment, and then it was further deepened in the Romantic period. Romantic art and sensibility added further depth to relations of sexual love, seen now as intense communication; to our relation to nature, which speaks to us as life to life; to our sense of time and the past.

But the depth and fullness of ordinary life has been articulated for us in an art which constantly seems to transgress the limits of the natural-human domain. The Romantic sense of nature, for instance, is hard to separate from images of a larger force, or a current of life sweeping through all things. These images, central for instance to Wordsworth's poetry, as in the passage quoted above, break the carefully erected boundaries of the buffered identity, which neatly divide mind from nature.

But these are after all just images, metaphors? Perhaps. But for what? The temptation is to say here that what they describe are our deep *feelings* about nature. The problem with this is that it comes close to treating feelings as just brute sensations, whereas the feelings involved here present themselves more as affectively-charged *perceptions* of the natural world which surrounds us. Does naturalism involve a reduction of all such perceptions just to raw feelings? If not, can we find an alternative language to render these perceptions which doesn't burst the categories of the buffered self? It's not clear that the answer to this last question is positive.

This connects up to a salient fact about our modern culture, that so many of the works which move us, and articulate something important about our lives, are connected to our religious tradition. I noted above how tourist itineraries are drawn to the cathedrals and temples of the past. This might be just because people are fascinated by the past, and the only past we have is religious. That would also explain our being moved today by Bach or by the *Missa Solemnis*. This is a possible account, but I find it unconvincing. From another standpoint, one might say that this is only one of a number of ways in which the old religion has not been fully replaced in a supposedly "secular" age.

Once again, my aim is not to fight the issue to a conclusion, but rather to show how difficult this is.

3. I mentioned above our sense of time and the past. Living in a world of secular time, that is, in which the older awareness of higher times has receded, has allowed new senses of time and memory to grow.

Perhaps the best way to try to grasp the change in time experience is in terms of the alterations in our understandings of order. Our forebears lived in a world of multiple times, hierarchically related. The social orders of hierarchical complementarity in which they lived only made sense within this multi-layered time. A doctrine like that of the King's Two Bodies becomes bizarre nonsense in the uniform, secular time of modernity.

In particular, the notion of complementarity or necessary alternation between elements of opposed, or at least unequal, value supposes that society is set in a cosmos in which such complementarities reign, governed by a time which is not a homogeneous container, indifferent to its content, but is multiform and kairotic. This is the kind of world in which Carnival, an interlude in which established order is reversed, and the "world turned upside down", could make sense. This order itself is in a complementary relation to something beyond order, and this alternation recognizes the beyond, and gives it its due. Victor Turner tried to articulate this relation in terms of "structure" and "anti-structure".[1]

But successive waves of modern reform, in the name of religion or "civility", have striven through organization and discipline to create a human order in which the good need make only tactical and contingent concessions to the bad or the less good. The disciplines of "civility" (for which we significantly now use the process word 'civilization') have crucially contributed to the erasure of complementarity. In so doing, they have taken us from a world in which higher times made everyday sense, to one in which the monopoly of secular time over public space is unchallenged.

We can trace this same process from another angle, if we look briefly at the development of our central modern forms of society: the public sphere, the economy, the democratic state.

Modern nation states are "imagined communities", in Benedict Anderson's celebrated phrase.[2] We might say that they have a particular kind of social imaginary, that is, socially shared ways in which social spaces are imagined. There are two important features of the modern imaginary, which I can best bring out by contrasting them in each case with what went before in European history.

First, there is the shift from hierarchical, mediated-access societies to horizontal, direct-access societies. And secondly, the modern social imaginary no longer sees the greater trans-local entities—nations, states, churches—as grounded in something other, something higher, than common action in secular time. This was not true of the pre-modern state. The hierarchical order of the kingdom was seen as based in the Great Chain of Being. The tribal unit was seen as constituted as such by its law, which went back "since time out of mind", or perhaps to some founding moment which had the status of a "time of origins" in Eliade's sense.

What is immensely suggestive about Anderson's account is that it links these two features. It shows how the rise of direct-access societies was linked to changing understandings of time, and consequently of the possible ways of imagining social wholes. Anderson stresses how the new sense of belonging to a nation was prepared by a new way of grasping society under the category of simultaneity:[3] society as the whole consisting of the simultaneous happening of all the myriad events which mark the lives of its members at that moment. These events are the fillers of this segment of a kind of homogeneous time. This very clear, unambiguous concept of simultaneity belongs to an understanding of time as exclusively secular, as I argued in an earlier segment.

A purely secular time-understanding allows us to imagine society "horizontally", unrelated to any "high points", where the ordinary sequence of events touches higher time, and therefore without recognizing any privileged persons or agencies— such as kings or priests—who stand and mediate at such alleged points. This radical horizontality is precisely what is implied in the direct access society, where each member is "immediate to the whole".

From this we can measure how inexorably the modern age has led us more and more to understand or imagine ourselves exclusively in secular time. This has partly come about through the multiple changes that we call collectively "disenchantment". It has been immeasurably strengthened by the legacy of the drive for order which has become part of what we understand by civilization. This has made us take a stance towards time as an instrument, or as a resource to be managed, and hence measured, cut up, regulated. The instrumental stance by its very nature homogenizes; it defines segments for some further purpose, but recognizes no intrinsic qualitative differences. This stance has built the rigid time frame in which we all live.

But on top of this, the pure secular time of simultaneity and succession is the medium of the different forms of the modern social imaginary. We are enveloped in both our public and private lives by a pervasive time-ordering which has no place for the higher times of earlier ages.

But this hasn't simply been a "homogeneous, empty time". It is doubtful if humans could ever live exclusively in this. Time for us continues to be marked by cycles, through which we orient ourselves. Even those who are most thoroughly immersed in the packed, measured schedules of a demanding career—perhaps especially they—can be totally at a loss if their routine is interrupted. The frame gives a sense to their lives, distinguishing different moments from each other, giving each its sense, creating mini-kairoi to mark the passage of time. It's as though we humans have a need for gathered time, in one form or another.

Now, one way in which this has been met in our age is narrative, a more intense telling of our stories, as individuals and as societies. On the first level, autobiography—a genre in a sense pioneered by Augustine, and then left fallow for 14 centuries before it is taken up by Rousseau—has become one of the most prominent fields of modern writing.

On the social level, our interest in history grows ever more intense. But not only this, on the political level, we need to make sense of our national stories.

The move to a horizontal, direct-access world, interwoven with an embedding in secular time, had to bring with it a different sense of our situation in time and space. In particular it brings different understandings of history and modes of narration.

I have discussed the narrativity of the nation, and the related categories of Revolution and Progress, in Chapter 4. These have become crucial constituents of our social imaginary in the secular age.

For narration is one way of gathering time. It shapes the flow of time, "de-homogenizes" it, and marks out kairotic moments, like the times of revolution, liberation, 1789, 1989.

And so we can also gather by commemorating. The commemorating itself becomes a kind of kairotic moment in little, since we come together out of our dispersal in order to celebrate founding events in common. We have a more intense sense of the unity of our story, because we're now sharing it.

But there are other moments when we find ourselves together, without a programme, as it were. Millions of people discover, for instance, that they are not alone in feeling what they do at the death of Princess Diana. They find themselves together in the actions of mourning, and these now fuse into a vast common tribute, creating a new kairotic moment, a turning point in the stories of many individuals, and in the common understandings of society. These moments can be very powerful, even dangerously so.

But they seem to answer a deeply felt need in modern society. I spoke in Chapter 13 about these new forms of "horizontal" social imaginary, which do not sustain common actions, but rather set up spaces of mutual display. Spaces of this kind are of greater and greater importance in modern urban society, just because so many people rub shoulders in mutual anonymity. A host of urban monads hover on the boundary between solitude and communication; and because they stand on this cusp they may sometimes flip over into common action, as with the cheering crowd at a football game, or a rock festival. There is a heightened excitement at these moments of fusion, which seem to respond to some important felt need of today's "lonely crowd".

Some moments of this kind are, indeed, the closest analogues to the Carnival of previous centuries. They can be powerful and moving, because they witness the birth of a new collective agent out of its formerly dispersed potential. They can be heady, exciting. But unlike Carnival, they are not enframed by any deeply entrenched if implicit common understanding of structure and counter-structure. They are often immensely riveting, but frequently also "wild", up for grabs, capable of being taken over by a host of different moral vectors, either utopian revolutionary, or xenophobic, or wildly destructive; or they can crystallize on some deeply felt, commonly cherished good, like ringing the key chains in Wenceslas Square; or as in the case of the Di funeral, celebrating in an out-of-ordinary life the ordinary, fragile pursuit of love and happiness.

Remembering the history of the twentieth century, replete with the Nürnberg rallies and other such horrors, one has as much cause for fear as hope in these "wild" kairotic moments. But the potentiality for them, and their immense appeal, is perhaps implicit in the experience of modern secular time. The "festive", as I described it earlier, is a crucial feature of modern life.

In the above discussion, we identified two ways in which time can be given shape in our world. The first is by cycles, routines, recurring forms in our lives: the daily round, the week, the year with its seasons, times of heightened activity, vacations.

The second is through narrations of change, growth, development, realization of potential. These have their once-for-all moments: of founding, revolution, liberation. Outside of these stand moments of "wild", unprogrammed, often unpredictable coming together, when mutual display turns into common action. These can be very powerful because they can have the feel of a "revolutionary" moment, when some latent common ground is first discovered, and thus perhaps a new way of being together inaugurated. They feel, at least for this moment, like nodal points, and this is part of their sometimes overwhelming appeal.

The cycle and the once-for-all are complexly related and mutually dependent. For one thing, the great nodal points are then repeatedly celebrated: the 4th of July, the 14th of July, the 3rd of May. This celebration is essential if the narrative is to remain alive, relevant, formative. In addition, some of the "wild" nodal points are or become or arise from celebrations.

But if the once-for-all has to be repeated to remain alive, it is also true that the cycles depend on the once-for-all for their meaning and force. One could argue that something like this has always been true. Humans have virtually always marked out cycles of time: day, month, year, and longer periods like the "Great Years" of the Stoics which end in a general conflagration. But the many repeatable segments are related to the one continuing order, or transcendent principle, and it is this which gives them their significance. The Stoic Great Year represents the unfolding and then return to origin of a single principle; the many instances for Plato are only what they are in relation to the one Idea.

In virtually all pre-modern outlooks, the meaning of the repeated cycles of time was found outside of time, or in higher time or eternity. What is peculiar to the modern world is the rise of an outlook where the single reality giving meaning to the repeatable cycles is a narrative of human self-realization, variously understood as the story of Progress, or Reason and Freedom, or Civilization or Decency or Human Rights; or as the coming to maturity of a nation or culture. The routines of disciplined work over the years, even over lifetimes, the feats of invention, creation, innovation, nation-building, are given a larger meaning through their place in the bigger story. Let's say I am a dedicated doctor, engineer, scientist, agronomer. My life is full of disciplined routines. But through these I am helping to build and sustain a civilization in which human well-being will be served as never before in history; and the perhaps small discoveries and innovations which I manage to make will hand on the same task to my successors at a slightly higher level of achievement. The meaning of these routines, what makes them really worth while, lies in this bigger picture, which extends across space but also across time.

An important feature of the modern world is that these narratives have come under attack. It is the claim of a certain trendy "post-modernism" that the age of

Grand Narratives is over, that we cannot believe in these any more.[4] But their demise is the more obviously exaggerated in that the post-modern writers themselves are making use of the same trope in declaring the reign of narrative ended: ONCE we were into grand stories, but NOW we have realized their emptiness and we proceed to the next stage. This is a familiar refrain.

So deeply has the narrative of human progress become embedded in our world that it would indeed be a frightening day in which all faith in it was lost. Its embedding is attested in much everyday vocabulary, in which some ideas are described as 'progressive', others as 'backward'; some views are those of today, others are positively 'mediaeval'; some thinkers are 'ahead of their time', others are still in a previous century, etc.

But although total collapse is not the issue, it is also true that the narratives of modernity have been questioned, contested, attacked, since their inception in the eighteenth century. From the very beginning, there were protests about the flatness, insipidity, lack of inspiration about the goal of progress, ordinary human happiness. For some, the very fact that all transcendent perspectives had been set aside was enough to condemn this goal as inadequate. But others who were also committed unbelievers taxed it with levelling down human life, with leaving no place for the exceptional, the heroic, the larger-than-life. Progress meant equality, the lowest common denominator, the end of greatness, sacrifice, self-overcoming. Nietzsche has been the most influential articulator of this line of attack in our culture.

Or else the disciplines of civilization were seen as confining and denying inspiration, deep feeling, the powerful emotions which gave life its meaning. They represent a prison which we have to break out of. Since the Romantic period repeated attacks have been made from this quarter.

Running through all these attacks is the spectre of meaninglessness; that as a result of the denial of transcendence, of heroism, of deep feeling, we are left with a view of human life which is empty, cannot inspire commitment, offers nothing really worth while, cannot answer the craving for goals we can dedicate ourselves to. Human happiness can only inspire us when we have to fight against the forces which are destroying it; but once realized, it will inspire nothing but ennui, a cosmic yawn.

This theme is indeed special to modernity, as I argued above. In earlier years, it would have seemed bizarre to fear an absence of meaning. When humans were posed between salvation and damnation, one might protest at the injustice and cruelty of an avenging God, but not that there were no important issues left.

So constitutive is this worry to modernity, that some thinkers have seen the essence of religion in the answers it offers to the question of meaning. I believe, as I argue above, that these theories are in an important way off the track. They imply that the main point of religion is solving the human need for meaning. In taking this stance, they absolutize the modern predicament, as though the view from here were the final truth on things (as well as offering a view which can't fully make sense from the first-person standpoint). In this way, they constitute in a sense offshoots from the narrative of progress. But the intuition they start from is uncontestable: that the issue about meaning is a central preoccupation of our age, and its threatened lack fragilizes all the narratives of modernity by which we live.

But even aside from this congenital fragility, the narratives of modernity encounter increasing doubt and attack in the nineteenth and twentieth centuries. In part, this is because the actual achievements of civilization—industrial wastelands, rampant capitalism, mass society, ecological devastation—begin to look more and more questionable. But there is also the splitting of the original Enlightenment goal into more and more different variants. These sometimes arise to respond to earlier critiques, such as versions of human well-being which include expressive fulfillment; or else they respond to the problematic realizations of civilization, as the communist vision hoped to overcome the depredations of capitalism.

On top of all this, some of the earlier notions of order, which still had a lot of residual power in the Age of Enlightenment, notions like the Great Chain of Being, and of the Divine-human history of salvation, lose much of their force. Much of the poetry and art of the Romantic period can only be understood against the background of this eclipse. The older notions of order had provided a set of reference points for poetic language, a range of subjects for painting which had an understood force. Now the artistic languages which relied on these reference points and force begin to weaken. Poetry is in search of "subtler languages", built without reference to a publicly accepted vision of things;[5] art is in search of newly defined subjects. I have described this development in Chapter 10.

But unsupported by a believable narrative, or by other, earlier conceptions of order, the disciplined routines of everyday life in civilization become highly problematic. On one hand, they can come to seem a prison, confining us to meaningless repetition, crushing and deadening whatever might be a source of meaning. This sense was already present in the critique of the Romantic period, but it comes to recur more insistently as we approach the contemporary age.

Or else, these routines themselves can fail to integrate our lives; this either because we are expelled from them, or not allowed to enter them, or remain outside them—through unemployment, forced idleness, or an inability/unwillingness to take on the disciplines. But then the very shape of everyday time, the local shape of time at the present moment, is in danger of being lost. Time disintegrates, loses all meaningful connection, becomes leaden or endless.

Or else again, the routines are still there, but they fail to unite our life across their repeatable instances. They cannot give unity to the whole span of a life, much less unite our lives with those of our ancestors and successors. But this has always been an important part of the meaning of repeatable cycles. They connect us in a continuity, and thus knit together their different instances in a larger single pattern across time.

Part of what it has normally meant for the patterns and cycles in my life to have meaning and validity for me is that they are those of my forebears. These patterns are one with theirs, in the sense of qualitatively the same. But not only this, they are continuous with theirs, segments of the same story. It was part of their life pattern that they handed this on to me; it is part of my life pattern that I honour them through re-enactment, that I remember them in reliving the pattern, and that I hand them on. These different enactments are not discontinuous. They connect; they gather into an unbroken story.

That the repeatable cycles of life connect over time, and make a continuity, is an essential condition of a life having meaning. Just this kind of connection was assured by earlier modes of gathering in the eternal; as it is also provided by strong modern narratives of human self-realization. But where the credibility and force of these narratives weaken, the unity comes under threat.

Now with hindsight, we can hold that this threat of disunity and meaninglessness was implicit in the original move to a purely secular time, to a life lived unconnected with higher times, and against the background of a cosmic time which at least as far as human affairs are concerned can be described as "homogeneous and empty". But it is clear that for a long time, the residual force of earlier views, and the power of strong narratives, held this threat at a distance. It is around the middle of the nineteenth century, and of course only among artistic and cultural élites, that one begins to see some awareness of a kind of crisis of time consciousness.

We can see it in the three modes I have just mentioned. The sense of imprisonment in the routine is articulated by the great Weberian image of the iron cage. This is a kind of imprisonment in the banal, the "alltäglich". (Indeed, the word we translate in English as the "routinization" of charisma is "Veralltäglichung".)[6]

The sense of the disintegration of everyday time, its hardening into a kind of leaden endlessness, was movingly articulated by Baudelaire. It is the essence of what he calls "spleen", "ennui".

Proust is the most brilliant articulator of the lost connection across time, but also the inventor of new experience-immanent ways of restoring it. Living in a world of secular time, that is, in which the older awareness of higher times has receded, has allowed, indeed, induced new senses of time and memory to grow. One of the most striking of these is created before our eyes in *A la Recherche*, which builds towards the creation of a "subtler language" in which it can be formulated. What Proust gives us is a sense of a higher time, built out of the sensibility of a modern living in the flow of secular time. The connections between widely spaced moments are not mediated by the order of being, or sacred history; they are made to appear in the mundane sensual experience of the madeleine, and the rocking paving stone.

What arises through the sense of loss in these three dimensions is the need to re-discover a lived time beneath or beyond the objectified time-resource of the disci-plined order of civilization. It is out of lived experience that we either find the way to break out of the Iron Cage, or to transfigure the world of ennui, or to reconnect the lost time.

While writers explore the loss and grope towards transfigurations, philosophy begins tentatively to thematize lived time, first with Bergson, and later with Heidegger.

15

4. The above are just some of the ways in which our modern time-experience re-sponds to the recession of higher times. To enumerate them all would require a much more wide-ranging study of contemporary culture, and in particular, our stances towards death. But together they perhaps give us cause to speak of a "désir d'éternité" in human beings, a desire to gather together the scattered moments of meaning into some kind of whole.[7] And maybe this emerges in another way as well, in face of death.

One of the things which makes it very difficult to sustain a sense of the higher meaning of ordinary life, in particular our love relations, is death. It's not just that they matter to us a lot, and hence there is a grievous hole in our lives when our part-ner dies. It's also because just because they are so significant, they seem to demand eternity. A deep love already exists against the vicissitudes of life, tying together past and present in spite of the disruptions and dispersals of quarrels, distractions, mis-understandings, resentments. By its very nature it participates in gathered time. And so death can seem a defeat, the ultimate dispersal which remains ungathered.

"Alle Lust will Ewigkeit." I interpret Nietzsche's famous line to mean, not: we're having such a good time, let's not stop; but rather: this love by its nature calls for eternity.

It is significant that the salient feature of death today, the major drama around it, is this separation of loved ones. Ariès has shown that it was not always so. In the late mediaeval and early modern ages, the great issue was the judgment soon to be faced by the person dying. And before that, the dead were in a sense still in a sort of com-munity with the living. So that Ariès distinguishes the periods under the titles: "la mort de nous", "la mort de moi", and "la mort de toi".[8]

Just because Hell has faded, but love relationships are central to the meaning of our lives, we live with the greatest anguish la mort de toi.

Now the implication of much atheist discussion of Christian or in general religious ideas of eternal life is that it is another facet of the childish attitude which takes its wishes for reality, that growing up means abandoning this. Death is final ("an eternal sleep", in the words of a French revolutionary dechristianizer). We have to start from here in order to direct our attention to this world, and making it fit for humans.

This dismissive attitude often assumes that our desire for eternity is simply one to live on, not to have our lives stop. It is this kind of desire which the famous Epicurean reasoning is supposed to still: as long as you're aware of the problem, you're alive; when you're dead, it will no longer be a problem for you. But there is something shallow about this understanding of what's wrong with death.

If we could separate happiness as a thing of the moment from any meaning, then we could enjoy some great moments now, and after pass on to some great moments later; rather as we enjoy good meals. Maybe in the old days, there was another kind of cuisine. We regret mildly its passing. But there is good food now, so let's tuck in.

But that's just the problem. The deepest, most powerful kind of happiness, even in the moment, is plunged into a sense of meaning. And the meaning seems denied by certain kinds of ending. That's why the greatest crisis around death comes from the death of someone we love.

Alle Lust will Ewigkeit; not just because you might want it to go on and on, as with any pleasant experience. Rather, all joy strives for eternity, because it loses some of its sense if it doesn't last.

And when you look back on your life together, those happy moments, those travels in the sun, were bathed in the awareness of other years, other travels, which seemed to come alive in the present one. This is the Great Return, the real "ewige Wiederkehr"; not just the recurrence of something similar, but the return of what was undying in that moment. This is what Proust seems to reach to, and not just the recall of what is lost forever.

But even just holding in memory is akin to keeping the time alive; even more if you can write about it, capture it in art. Art aspires to a certain kind of eternity, to be able to speak to future ages. But there are also other lesser modes or substitutes for eternity. One can make the eternal be the clan, the tribe, the society, the way of life. And your love, and the children who come from it, have their place in the chain; as long as you have preserved, or better enhanced, that tribe or way of life, you've handed it on. In that way, the meaning continues.

This just shows how joy strives for eternity, even if all that is available is a lesser form of it; and even if something is left out that matters to us highly individuated moderns, as the particular things that meant most to us are gradually lost in the general impact we've made. And of course, this eternity can't preserve those who are really forgotten, or those who haven't left their mark, or those who have been damned, excluded. There is no general resurrection in this "eternity" of grateful posterity. This is what exercised Benjamin, the unfilled need to rescue those who were trampled in history.

Now all this doesn't show that the faith perspective is correct. It just shows that the yearning for eternity is not the trivial and childish thing it is painted as. The Epicurean answer copes with (some facets of) "la mort de moi", but not at all "la mort de toi", or the death of meaning.

And so what? Doesn't the fact that this is a serious, an unstillable longing just show up even more the courage you need to be a clear-sighted atheist? Perhaps, but it also shows how the yearning for eternity reflects an ethical insight, the one expressed in the Nietzschean phrase, which could be put negatively, that death undermines meaning. Something important is lost when one forgets this. There is, after all, a kind of cross pressure here.

This connection of death with meaning is reflected in two often-discussed features of human life as we understand it today. The first is the way in which facing death, seeing one's life as about to come to an end, can concentrate the issue of what we have lived for. What has it all amounted to? In other words, death can bring out the question of meaning in its most acute form. This is what lies behind Heidegger's claim that an authentic existence involves a stance of "Sein-zum-Tode", being towards death.

The second is the way that those bereaved, or left behind, struggle to hold on to the meaning they have built with the deceased, while (unavoidably) letting go of the person. This is what funeral rites have always been meant to do, whatever other goals they have served. And since a crucial way of doing this is to connect this person, even in their death, with something eternal—or at the very least ongoing—the collapse of a sense of the eternal brings on a void, a kind of crisis. This we see today. The prospect that the person who has died is called to an eternal life, "in sure and certain hope of the Resurrection", is either denied, or held in a kind of uncertain suspense by those close to him. And yet other kinds of continuing reality may not be really meaningful to him and his mourners. The ongoing political society, for instance, will certainly do for the deceased statesman; the continuing life of our town for the departed mayor. But many people were not connected in that way to these levels of society; they lived in them relatively unknown, and they themselves didn't feel closely bound within them. It's not clear what ongoing reality we can latch on to.

There is a sense of void here, and of deep embarrassment. But at the same time, we have the greatest difficulty finding a way of marking this, a ceremony for death which will speak to our strongest feelings. Ferry speaks of the "banalité du deuil" to-day;[9] we very often feel awkward at a funeral; don't know what to say to the bereaved; are often tempted to avoid the issue if we can. And at the same time, even people who otherwise don't practice have recourse to religious funerals; perhaps because here at least is a language which fits the need for eternity, even if you're not sure you believe all that.

Sylvette Denèfle points out, in her study of unbelievers in France, that the hardest point of their "creed" for them to hold to is the thought that there is no life after death. A half of her sample are unsound on this, a quarter expressing the belief that something continues, and another quarter trimming. What is hardest of all for them is the death of loved ones.[10]

We don't know how to deal with death, and so we ignore it as much and for as long as possible. We concentrate on life. The dying don't want to impose their plight on the people they love, even though they may be eager, even aching to talk about what it means to them now that they face it. Doctors and others fail to pick up on this desire, because they project their own reluctance to deal with death onto the patient. Sometimes the dying will ask that their loved ones make no fuss over them, hold no ceremony, just cremate them and move on; as though they were doing the bereaved a favour in colluding in their aversion to death. The aim can be to glide through the whole affair, smoothly and as much as possible painlessly, for both dying and bereaved, an ideal portrayed (with some ambivalence) in the film *Les Invasions Barbares*. The cost is a denial of the issue of meaning itself, something which can never be totally suppressed in any case.

In this very embarrassed, confused avoidance, the deep link of death and meaning is nevertheless exhibited.

I return to the other connection of death and meaning, mentioned above, the notion that death, in particular the moment of death, is the privileged site from which the meaning of life can be grasped. Death can offer a vantage point, beyond the confusion and dispersal of living.

A need for meaning, a desire for eternity, can press us against the boundaries of the human domain. But death in another way can offer a way to escape the confinement of this domain, to breathe the air beyond.

We can see this, if we follow a line of thought and sensibility, which grows up within the world of unbelief in the nineteenth century. It represents, in a sense, an attack on certain key Enlightenment values, but from within. It is what I described above as the "immanent revolt".

It is the revolt from within unbelief, as it were, against the primacy of life. Not now in the name of something beyond, but really more just from a sense of being confined, diminished by the acknowledgement of this primacy.

And as I said earlier, one of the crucial themes of this revolt has been a rediscovery of the centrality of death in human life.

A paradigm figure of this transition is Mallarmé. Like his Parnassan predecessors, he identifies the search for the Ideal, for Beauty, with a turning away from life:

> Ainsi, pris du dégoût de l'homme à l'âme dure
> Vautré dans le bonheur, où ses seuls appétits
> Mangent. . . .
> Je fuis et je m'accroche à toutes les croisées
> D'où l'on tourne l'épaule à la vie, et béni,
> Dans leur verre, lavé d'éternelles rosées,
> Que dore le matin chaste de l'Infini.
>
> Je me mire et me vois ange! et je meurs, et j'aime
> —Que la vitre soit l'art, soit la mysticité—
> A renaître, portant mon rêve en diadème,
> Au ciel antérieur où fleurit la Beauté!
> ("Les Fenêtres", 21–32)
>
> (Thus, seized with disgust for the man of hard heart,
> Sprawled in the happiness in which only his appetites
> Feed, . . .
> I flee, clinging to all the window frames
> From which one can turn one's back on life;
> And blessed in their glass, bathed in eternal dews,
> Adorned by the chaste morning of the Infinite.
>
> I gaze at myself and I see an angel! And I die, yearning
> —Be the window pane art, be it mysticism—
> To be reborn, bearing my dream as a diadem,
> Under the former sky where Beauty once flourished.)[11]

In this early poem, you can still see the earlier religious sources of this dissatisfaction with bare life. The image of the window, invoked repeatedly in different forms, divides the universe into a lower and higher. The lower is likened to a hospital, life is a kind of putrefaction; but above and beyond is the river, the sky, and the images which invoke this are still saturated with the resonances of the religious tradition: Infini, ange, mysticité.

But later, after his crisis, Mallarmé emerges with something like a materialist view of the universe. Underneath everything we see is le Rien, le Néant. But the poet's vocation is none the less imperious. He will even speak of it in terms which borrow from the Romantic tradition of an original, perfect language. (Poetry is concerned with "l'explication orphique de la Terre".)

In terms of belief, Mallarmé has joined the Enlightenment, and even a rather extreme, materialist version of it. But in terms of the point of human existence, he couldn't be farther removed from it. The primacy of life is decisively rejected, treated with revulsion. What emerges is something like a counter-primacy of death.

It is clear that for Mallarmé the realization of the poetic vocation, achieving the purified language, essentially involves something like the death of the poet; certainly the overcoming of all particularity, but this process, it seems, is consummated only in actual death: "Tel qu'en Lui-même enfin l'éternité le change." (Such that, in Himself, eternity transforms him.)

Tout ce que, par contre coup, mon être a souffert, pendant cette longue agonie, est inénarrable, mais heureusement je suis parfaitement mort, et la région la plus impure où mon Esprit puisse s'aventurer est l'Éternité, mon Esprit, ce Solitaire habituel de sa propre Pureté, que n'obscurcit plus même le reflet du Temps.[12]

(All that my being has suffered as a reaction during that slow death is beyond recounting, but fortunately I am utterly dead, and the most impure region where my spirit can venture is Eternity—my Spirit, that recluse accustomed to dwelling in its own Purity, which is no longer darkened even by the reflection of Time.)[13]

Mallarmé becomes the first great modern poet of absence ("aboli bibelot d'inanité sonore" [voided bauble of resounding futility]), followed in that by others, including Eliot and Celan: the absence, clearly, of the object "Sur les crédences, au salon vide: nul ptyx" (atop the sideboards in the empty room: no ptyx), but this is something which can only be attained via the absence, in a sense the death, of the subject ("Car le Maître est allé puiser des pleurs au Styx / Avec ce seul objet dont le Néant s'honore" [For the Master has gone to draw tears from the Styx / With this sole object in which Nothingness takes pride]).[14] A strange parallel is set up with the earlier religious tradition, but within the framework of denied transcendence.

Death and the moment of death have an ineradicable place in the religious traditions: death as the giving up of everything, of one's very self, in Christianity; the hour of death as a crucial moment, therefore ("pray for us now and at the hour of our death"); a status it has as well in most Buddhist traditions. In Christian terms: the locus of death, as the place where one has given everything, is the place of maximum union with God; and therefore, paradoxically, the source of most abundant life.[15]

In this new post-Mallarmé perspective, the locus of death takes on a new paradigm status. The Christian paradox drops away: death is no longer the source of life. But there is a new paradox: there seems to be a renewed affirmation of transcendence, of something beyond flourishing, in the sense of a point to life beyond life. But at the same time, this is denied, because this point has absolutely no anchorage in the nature of reality. To search for this point in reality is to encounter only le Néant.

This paradoxical idea, which we could call immanent transcendence, is one of the principal themes of the immanent counter-Enlightenment. Death offers in some sense the privileged perspective, the paradigm gathering point for life. This idea recurs again and again in our culture—not necessarily derived from Mallarmé. Heidegger's Sein-zum-Tode, which I mentioned above, is a famous example, but the theme is taken up in rather different forms in Sartre, Camus, and Foucault, was echoed in "the death of man" fad, and so on. And in the variant which spoke of "the death of the subject", the paradoxical affinities with certain religious outlooks—perhaps most obviously Buddhism—were patent.

Alongside that, and interwoven with it, is the other kind of revolt against the primacy of life which I described above *(Subtler)*, of which the most influential proponent has undoubtedly been Nietzsche. It is significant that the most important antihumanist thinkers of our time—e.g., Foucault, Derrida, behind them, Bataille—all draw heavily on Nietzsche.

16

But I don't want to pursue this here. I have discussed it at greater length elsewhere.[16] My aim in the last pages has been to raise a number of ways in which our modern culture is restless at the barriers of the human sphere. I have mentioned: the search for meaning, the deepening of our sense of life through our contact with nature and art, death as a denial of the significance of love, but also death as an escape from the confines of life, to the paramount vantage point in which life shows its meaning.

Before I dealt with a number of dilemmas and demands which both faith and exclusive humanism have to deal with. These demands include: finding the moral sources which can enable us to live up to our very strong universal commitments to human rights and well-being; and finding how to avoid the turn to violence which returns uncannily and often unnoticed in the "higher" forms of life which have supposedly set it aside definitively. Rather than one side clearly possessing the answers that the other one lacks, we find rather that both face the same issues, and each with some difficulty.

The more one reflects, the more the easy certainties of either "spin", transcendental or immanentist, are undermined.

I could have mentioned many other such points of pressure on our fixed positions; but I hope that the basic point has been made more plausible: the present fractured expressivist culture, with its advancing post-Durkheimian understanding, seems very inhospitable to belief. Our world is ideologically fragmented, and the range of positions are growing as the nova effect is multiplied by expressive individualism. There are strong incentives to remain within the bounds of the human domain, or at least not to bother exploring beyond it. The level of understanding of some of the great languages of transcendence is declining; in this respect, massive unlearning is taking place. The individual pursuit of happiness as defined by consumer culture still absorbs much of our time and energy, or else the threat of being shut out of this pursuit through poverty, unemployment, incapacity galvanizes all our efforts.

All this is true, and yet the sense that there is something more presses in. Great numbers of people feel it: in moments of reflection about their life; in moments of relaxation in nature; in moments of bereavement and loss; and quite wildly and unpredictably. Our age is very far from settling in to a comfortable unbelief. Although many individuals do so, and more still seem to on the outside, the unrest continues to surface. Could it ever be otherwise?

The secular age is schizophrenic, or better, deeply cross-pressured. People seem at a safe distance from religion; and yet they are very moved to know that there are dedicated believers, like Mother Teresa. The unbelieving world, well used to disliking Pius XII, was bowled over by John XXIII. A Pope just had to sound like a Christian, and many immemorial resistances melted. Il fallait y penser. It's as though many people who don't want to follow want nevertheless to hear the message of Christ, want it to be proclaimed out there. The paradox was evident in the response to the late Pope. Many people were inspired by John Paul's public peripatetic preaching, about love, about world peace, about international economic justice. They are thrilled that these things are being said. But even many Catholics among his admirers didn't feel that they must follow all his moral injunctions. And in an expressive, post-Durkheimian world, this is not a contradiction. It makes perfect sense.

Such are the strange and complex conditions of belief in our age.

20 Conversions

In the last chapter, I was trying to describe the contemporary debate, largely through examining unbelieving positions, and their critiques of religion. But here I want to get another perspective on this debate, and look briefly at some of those who broke out of the immanent frame; people who went through some kind of "conversion".

In some cases, people went through a kind of self-authenticating, one might say "epiphanic" experience, like Bede Griffiths whom I quoted in the first chapter. Another example of this kind of experience comes from Vaclav Havel:

> Again, I call to mind that distant moment in [the prison at] Hermanice when on a hot, cloudless summer day, I sat on a pile of rusty iron and gazed into the crown of an enormous tree that stretched, with dignified repose, up and over all the fences, wires, bars and watchtowers that separated me from it. As I watched the imperceptible trembling of its leaves against an endless sky, I was overcome by a sensation that is difficult to describe: all at once, I seemed to rise above all the coordinates of my momentary existence in the world into a kind of state outside time in which all the beautiful things I have ever seen and experienced existed in a total "co-present"; I felt a sense of reconciliation, indeed of an almost gentle assent to the inevitable course of events as revealed to me now, and this combined with a carefree determination to face what had to be faced. A profound amazement at the sovereignty of Being became a dizzy sensation of tumbling endlessly into the abyss of its mystery; an unbounded joy at being alive, at having been given the chance to live through all I have lived through, and at the fact that everything has a deep and obvious meaning—this joy formed a strange alliance in me with a vague horror at the inapprehensibility and unattainability of everything I was so close to in that moment, standing at the very "edge of the infinite"; I was flooded with a sense

of ultimate happiness and harmony with the world and with myself, with that moment, with all the moments I could call up, and with everything invisible that lies behind it and has meaning. I would even say that I was somehow "struck by love", though I don't know precisely for whom or what.[1]

It goes without saying that for most people who undergo a conversion there may never have been one of those seemingly self-authenticating experiences, like Bede's or Havel's; but they may easily take on a new view about religion from others: saints, prophets, charismatic leaders, who have radiated some sense of more direct contact.

This sense that others have been closer is an essential part of the ordinary person's confidence in a shared religious language, or a way of articulating fullness. These may be named figures, identified paradigms, like Francis of Assisi, or Saint Teresa; or Jonathan Edwards, or John Wesley; or they may figure as the unnamed company of (to oneself) unknown saints or holy people. In either case (and often these two are combined), the language one adheres to is given force by the conviction that others have lived it in a more complete, direct and powerful manner. This is part of what it means to belong to a church.

But we need to enlarge our range of examples of what this more direct contact might involve. I started off with a kind of experience of fullness, those of Bede and Havel. Analogous to these perhaps, and more powerful, are the visions of mystics, like Teresa. But we can't confine ourselves to this kind of closeness to the place of fullness. Perhaps more important in the Christian tradition has been another kind of contact, illustrated by St. Francis: what is striking about Francis is that he was seized by a sense of the overpowering force of God's love, and a burning desire to become a channel of this love. His story also includes visions, for instance, of this love of God in Nature (brother sun and sister moon); but the salient inspiring feature of his life emerges in the story of his conversion, how he was moved to abandon everything in his life for the love of God. We might say that what moved Francis was not so much the kind of vision of God's power "out there", as in the "epiphanic" moments of Bede and Havel, but the heightened power of love itself which God opened to him. The transformation beyond our usual scope was a crucial part of what seized him; not as a greater personal power (this is a danger of deviation), but as a participation in God's love.

Here too, someone in the "middle condition" can have a dim sense of what this kind of love could be like, be drawn to it, and be confirmed in this conviction by, say reading a life of Francis.

We need to enlarge our palette of such points of contact with fullness, because we are too prone in our age to think of this contact in terms of "experience"; and to think of experience as something subjective, distinct from the object experienced; and as something to do with our feelings, distinct from changes in our being: dispositions, orientations, the bent of our lives, etc. That is, "experience" may have a causal effect on these latter, but it is defined separately from them. This notion of experience, as distinct both from the object and the continuing nature of the subject (experiencer), is quintessentially modern, and springs from the modern philosophy of mind and knowledge which comes down to us from Descartes and other writers of the seventeenth century. We see the influence of this in William James' work.

This notion of experience already distorts in the case of the events that Bede and Havel recount; because what they experienced (in one ordinary sense of this word) was defined for them in terms, on one hand of the deeper reality they were now open to, and on the other, this reality was understood as life-changing. The very nature of this experience is distorted, if we try to see it as an entity distinct from object or agent.

But there is less temptation to do this, if we look at the conversion of Francis. Granted, here too, there were "experiences", of joy, of liberation; but it's clear that the core of the event was its heart-transforming, life-changing nature. Something similar may be seen in the life of that second Teresa, Thérèse de Lisieux.

So we need to enlarge our palette of points of contact with fullness; there are those which involve a contemplative grasp of this fullness (Bede, Havel, epiphanies of Loyola, Jonathan Edwards); as well as visions of the negative absence of fullness: desolation, emptiness, and the like. And then there are those which consist in life-changing moments, being "surprised by love". This distinction can be, of course, merely notional; that is, the same event may partake of both.

These by no means exhaust the range. The two types of event discussed so far involve individuals. But there is another kind of experience-cum-transformation which can occur in a moment of collective ritual or celebration. This is what I called earlier the "festive"; and which was very much stressed by Durkheim: moments of "collective effervescence", which can bond the members of a society, or send them off in a new direction, or open them to fullness. This type of event goes back, of course, into the very dawn of human religion; but it is precisely the kind of thing which has been marginalized in religion in the modern West, which has as we saw above displaced the center of gravity of the religious life away from it.

Now, however it comes about, whether it happens suddenly or gradually, there are certain features of such conversions today which reflect our times. One arises from the nature of what they are conversions out of. Many great conversions, or to put it differently, many of the great founding moves of a new spiritual direction in history, involve a transformation of the frame in which people thought, felt and lived before. They bring into view something beyond that frame, which at the same time changes the meaning of all the elements of the frame. Things make sense in a wholly new way. We can think of the change that Jesus wrought in the pre-existing notion of the Messiah in his society, of the way the Buddha transformed the understanding of what it was to go beyond the chain of rebirth; within Christianity, we can cite the way in which Francis transformed the understanding of what it meant to respond to God's love, the new mystical tradition founded by Saint Teresa, and so on. There was something very disruptive of existing habits of thought, action, and piety. We have the analogue of a "paradigm change" in science, only one that affects the central issues of our lives.

Contemporary conversions often have this feature, even where the only life influenced may be the convert's own. But they involve the same kind of paradigm shifts. Think of moving from an immanent therapeutic perspective to a spiritual one, as I described the difference above, in which God, good and evil are now taken as serious realities. The internal economy of the immanent theory, say a Freudian one, in which the various forces which count are purely intra-psychic, and are rooted in the patient's desires and fears, is now disrupted. The genesis of guilt, alienation, internal division is now found at least in part in the aspiration to something transcendent. So Walker Percy's conversion to Catholicism was based in part on a shift in anthropology. Catholicism "considers the human agent part angel, part beast". This view of a deeply divided being, "a creature suspended between two infinities" replaced the orthodox scientific view of the human being as a mere "organism in an environment".[2]

Or again, take the shift in moral perspective which Dostoyevsky helped make, and which I drew on in much of the discussion of the previous chapters. Dostoyevsky raised about the political reformers of his day the question of their depth motivations, and their relation to good and evil. Their self-perception of their motivation was that they wanted to improve the lot of humankind, and that they were actuated by benevolence, or in the case of the more radical revolutionaries, by a scientific detachment which of itself brought impartiality and a commitment to the general good. Dostoyevsky stepped totally outside of their universe of discourse, of their ontology of possible motives, in finding the roots of their moral excitement, of their steely resolve, of their willingness to use violence at a quite different level, which they could never acknowledge. Where Shatov in *The Possessed* sees the wonder of a new creation in a baby that has just been born, the midwife sees only "a further development of the organism".

Francis of Assisi also upset the parameters of his time, but these concerned what people understood as what God wants. The system he upset was much more porous, had a place for him to say what he wanted. By contrast, these moderns are all breaking beyond systems which their opponents see as totalities in a new sense; they are systems of immanent order which can be explained and accounted for in their own terms. That is what the modern idea of the "natural", counterposed to the "supernatural" means. It is possible, even tempting to make a claim on behalf of this, that there is no need whatever to go beyond it to understand our world. And because in some very prestigious cases, like the systems tracked by natural science, the generally shared understanding, by believer and unbeliever alike, is that they can in fact be explained in their own terms, it is easy to decree that the totality of sense-making is captured by the currently dominant theoretical terms.

Attempting to make a paradigm change beyond this (as against a shift between paradigms within natural science) is in some sense bucking the limits of generally accepted language. The terms in which the paradigm shift can be made are suspect, and difficult to credit; they either belong to outlooks which can be discredited as "pre-modern" (e.g., God, evil, agape); or else one has to have recourse to a new "subtler language", whose terms on their own don't have generally accepted referents, but which can point us beyond ordinary, "immanent" realities. Indeed, what may have to be challenged here is the very distinction nature/supernature itself.

This is why so many influential converts in the last two centuries have been writers and artists. Literature is one of the prime loci of expression of these newly-discovered insights; newly-discovered because people come at them from out of the immanent order, either from the belief that this order is all there is, or at least from a powerful sense of the pressure that this order exerts on us all. Flannery O'Connor, not admittedly a convert, but one who felt this pressure keenly, spoke of "the conflict between an attraction for the Holy and the disbelief in it that we breathe in the air of our times". And she spoke of how in her kind of realism, to which she sometimes applied the term "grotesque", the writer uses "an extreme image to join an instance from everyday life with 'a point not visible to the naked eye, but believed in by him firmly, just as real to him, really, as the one that everybody sees'". That "point not visible" is the point outside the self-contained system of everyday explanation, the one in relation to which all our ordinary meanings change, the hinge of the paradigm shift. The artist takes us "past psychology and sociology 'towards the limits of mystery'".[3]

The convert's insights break beyond the limits of the regnant versions of immanent order, either in terms of accepted theories, or of moral and political practice (and you need to go beyond both at once in order to raise the issues about the roots of violence I raised in the preceding chapter). And this may require her to invent a new language or literary style. She breaks from the immanent order to a larger, more encompassing one, which includes it while disrupting it.

But this raises another crucial issue. The larger order (say, of God and his

Church) disrupts the existing order. But is there another ideal relation between this larger order, and the established political, cultural, intellectual orders of society? Is the ideal relation one in which there is no lack of fit, in which the two cohere perfectly? This ideal has often haunted converts in the last centuries. They look back and see the glorious past of Christendom, be it in the European Middle Ages, or in the early modern period, or in the time before the French Revolution, or before the Reformation; or even, as with the American "Christian Right", the age they want to restore is only a few decades in the past. Their grievance against the established order (or "le désordre établi", to quote a favourite phrase of Maurras and Action Française) is that it is out of joint, both with itself and with the higher order; and indeed, the two go together, because it could only get back in true with itself by recovering contact with this higher, more encompassing order.[4]

A great many converts have felt this, at least as a temptation, even where it wasn't their main reason for converting. It was strong in the followers of Action Française, but we can also see it for instance in Christopher Dawson, in Hilaire Belloc, to some degree in G. K. Chesterton, although without the nostalgic dimension, and in T. S. Eliot (who, not coincidentally, admired Maurras).

Several strands came together in this. For some, like Dawson and Eliot, it seemed clear that the deepest sources of European culture were in Christianity, and that this culture must lose force and depth to the extent that moderns departed from it.[5] Another strand identified the basic error of modernity in subjectivism, that is, in philosophies which stressed the powers of the free individual subject, constructing his scientific and cultural world. Eliot also took up this theme, but the best known articulation of this critique came from the pen of Jacques Maritain. In particular, his *Trois Réformateurs* lined up Luther, Descartes, and Rousseau as targets, three highly influential figures who progressively had contributed to the apotheosis of the modern subject.[6] The great and necessary remedy was a renewed Thomistic philosophy which would once more bring about a recognition of objective reality. This philosophy can liberate because it forces us "to lift our heads", to consider "the object as other" ("l'objet en tant qu'autre"); it makes me subordinate myself to "a being independent from myself".[7]

For Maritain, this philosophical standpoint was identified with "intelligence", and we can see here one of the reasons for his alliance with Maurras throughout the teens and early 20s of the century. For "l'intelligence" was one of the key slogans of the Maurrasian party, defined in similar terms as a rejection of modern subjectivism, but then further spelled out as demanding an unremitting hostility to liberalism, and to the "idol" of democracy, as well as an affirmation of the primacy of Catholicism, and the recovery of the power of the state through a restored monarchy.[8] This was the poisoned fruit from which Maritain had to struggle to liberate himself.

But the Maurrasian constellation was not the only way of working out this notion of "intelligence". The close link between rational thought and anti-subjectivism was also prominent in the work of other famous converts in the twentieth century, who didn't link this stand to ultra-Right politics, figures like Chesterton, or Ronald Knox in England for example.[9]

The third interwoven strand in this complex was often the most fateful for its political consequences; this was the idea that Christianity was essential for order itself. The modern world, through its subjectivism and its denial of its moral roots, was falling into ever deeper disorder. As Evelyn Waugh put it in an article of 1930:

> It seems to me that in the present state of European history the essential issue is no longer between Catholicism, on one side, and Protestantism, on the other, but between Christianity and Chaos. . . . Civilization—and by this I do not mean talking cinemas and tinned food, nor even surgery and hygienic houses, but the whole moral and artistic organization of Europe—has not in itself the power of survival. It came into being through Christianity, and without it has no significance or power to command allegiance. . . . It is no longer possible . . . to accept the benefits of civilization and at the same time deny the supernatural basis on which it rests.[10]

The Christian religion, or in some cases, Catholicism as the only bulwark against a menacing disintegration and disorder; this theme was woven together with that of the deep roots of European culture, and that of the dangers of self-indulgent subjectivism. Then these three were united to a critique of the flatness of modern civilization, which sees "the final triumph of the Hollow Men, who, knowing the price of everything and the value of nothing, had lost the ability to *feel* or *think* deeply about anything".

This was a very powerful amalgam. It tied the intuition that the immanent frame was confining, even stifling, and left something vital out, with a backward look to the deep roots of culture and order. There was something very seductive about this amalgam, but also something very troubling. The latter factor emerged with time, and led some prominent converts to break out of it. This seems to have been the case with Thomas Merton, for instance.[11] And it certainly is what happened to Maritain.

I will return to the latter below, but for the moment, I want to remark that, in relation to this amalgam, the Western convert (one might say, "reconvert") to Christianity is in a unique situation. It is hard to conceive of a new Christian in Africa or Asia thinking in these terms. The hold of the former Christendom on our imagination is immense, and in a sense, rightly so. So the sense can easily arise, that the task of breaking out of the dominant immanentist orders today is already defined by the model of Christendom. Of course, the issue remains open of how much we can actually go back, but this earlier civilization gives us both our paradigm language, which we are seeking, and perhaps also the model of a society and culture which is not in tension with, but fully expresses the Faith.

Of course, the backward look here may deceive. How closely did life in the actual society, whether in the Middle Ages, or le Grand Siècle, or nineteenth-century America, reflect "Christian values"? The fact that society paid obeisance to these, unlike what we see today, was no guarantee of actual conformity to them. But at a deeper level, we should ask what we might expect this conformity to consist in. In the mediaeval period itself, it was generally understood that the full demands of Christian life would never be met, outside of isolated pockets of sanctity, in history, but only in the Parousia, at the end of time. It was recognized that there were structural features of our existence here, for instance, the existence of states, and of private property, which were inseparable from our fallen condition; these were necessary to mitigate some of the disastrous effects of the Fall, but just for this reason, they couldn't be projected forward into the eschaton.

This meant that the two orders in which the Christian lived, the City of God and the earthly city, to use Augustine's expression, could never be totally in true with each other. There were strains. And this was reflected in differential rules of action, which may seem to us today to be hypocritical or inconsistent. So war was allowed in certain circumstances, but clergy should not take part in combat. The Church itself could not use force to fight heresy, but this was left to the "secular arm". And it is true that these arrangements easily pass over into mere expedients to protect the appearances of ecclesiastical innocence and non-involvement. But within the then-regnant outlook there was no totally comfortable way of smoothly combining the demands of the two orders.

A central part of my story in earlier chapters is the way in which the drive to Reform tended to bring these demands closer to each other. The thrust of Reform was to make a Church in which everyone should show the same degree of personal commitment and devotion which had hitherto been the stance of a dedicated élite. This would be a Church in which all genuine members (excluding the damned) should strive integrally to fulfill the Gospel. To carry through on this Reform required that one define a way of life open to everyone which would amount to such an integral fulfillment; and this couldn't help but bring about a definition of the demands of Christian faith closer into line with what is attainable in this world, with what can be realized in history. The distance between the ultimate City of God and the properly Christian-conforming earthly one has to be reduced.

If one carries this rapprochement of the two orders to its ultimate end point, one falls into a kind of Deism, in which the Incarnation loses its significance, Jesus becomes a great teacher expounding the demands of God, and what these demands consist in is a morality which allows us to live here in peace and harmony, a version in other words of the modern moral order. The whole point of true religion is to propound this morality; this sets the limits of the transformation we are called to. The "next world" now has a different function, not to complete a path of "theiosis" begun here, but to provide rewards and punishments which fulfill the demands of justice on our actions in history. The tension between the two orders quite disappears.

My claim in the earlier chapters was that, although few went on to this logical conclusion, and orthodox Christianity maintained the understanding of two non-coincident orders, nevertheless mainline Christianity in the West was deeply affected by this narrowing of the gap, especially but certainly not only in Protestant societies. And the gap in some ways narrowed even further in the nineteenth and twentieth centuries, as the sense of civilizational superiority, which grew with Western colonial power, became interwoven with a sense of Christendom as the bearer of this civilization. Missionaries brought Christianity to the non-Western world, often with the sense that they were also bringing the bases of future prosperity, progress, order, and (sometimes also) democracy and freedom. It became hard for many to answer the question, what is Christian faith about? The salvation of humankind, or the progress wrought by capitalism, technology, democracy? The two tended to blend into one. Even harder did it become to distinguish between salvation and the establishment of good moral order.

An American Methodist Bishop "told an audience in 1870 that he foresaw in the not-too-distant future an America that would be 'without an adulterer, or a swearer, or a Sabbath-breaker, or an ingrate, or an apostate, or a backslider, or a slanderer; hundreds of homes without a prodigal, a quarrel or heartburn, or a bitter tear'. . . . Thirty years later, the head of the American Board for Foreign Missions declared that 'Christianity is the religion of the dominant nations of the earth. Nor is it rash to prophesy that in due time it will be the only religion in the world'. . . . A Baptist leader 'wrote in 1909 that, of the three "great facts" of modern society'—Christianity, the state, democracy—Christianity was 'the most potent force in our modern civilization.'"[12] I quoted in Chapter 12 the Duke of Devonshire who, in a speech to raise money for the London Church Fund, asked his audience: "Can you imagine for one moment what England would have been like today without those churches and all that those churches mean? . . . Certainly it would not have been safe to walk the streets. All respect, decency, all those things which tend to make modern civilization what it is would not have been in existence."

In other words, the ideal of Christendom has tended to evolve since the age of

Dante. Then there was a strong sense of the gap and inescapable tension between the ultimate order of the Parousia, which is in gestation today, on one hand, and the established order of civilization as we live it, on the other. In many Christian milieux in modern times, that gap has narrowed, and the tensions lost sight of.

2

Is this a loss? One can argue that it is. First, in that in identifying the Christian life with a life lived in conformity with the norms of our civilization, we lose sight of the further, greater transformation which Christian faith holds out, the raising of human life to the divine (theiosis). Secondly, as Ivan Illich has so forcefully argued, something is lost when we take the way of living together that the Gospel points us to and make of it a code of rules enforced by organizations erected for this purpose. I want to follow Illich's argument a bit more fully, because as should become evident, his story is quite close to the one I have been trying to tell in these pages. Indeed, I have learned a lot from him.[13]

This understanding is rooted in a Christian faith. Illich, who had earlier been a priest, remained a Catholic Christian, orthodox in his theology, but profoundly original and iconoclastic in his understanding of the Church in history. He saw the actual development of the Christian churches and of Christian civilization (what we used to call "Christendom") as a "corruption" of Christianity.

Scholars agree that the Christian church which arose in the ancient world was a new kind of religious association, that it created around itself new "service" institutions, like hospitals and hospices for the needy. It was heavily engaged in the practical works of charity. This kind of activity remained important throughout the long centuries of Christendom, until in the modern era, these institutions have been taken over by secular bodies, often by governments. Seen within the history of Western civilization, the present-day welfare state can be understood as the long-term heir to the early Christian church.

Now most people, whether Christian or not, would see this as a positive credit to Christianity, as a "progressive" move in history for which the Church is responsible. Without necessarily denying that good has come from this, Illich sees also its dark side. In particular, he sees in the way this has worked out a profound betrayal of the Christian message.

Illich starts right off in Chapter 1 to explain this, using what is perhaps the most famous story from the New Testament, the parable of the Good Samaritan. This arises out of a discussion of the meaning of the precept from the Ten Commandments: Love your neighbour as yourself. A scribe asks Jesus: "but who is my neighbour?", and Jesus' answer is the story. A traveler is robbed and beaten and left by the side of the road. A priest and a Levite—that is, important figures in the Jewish community—pass by "on the other side". Finally a Samaritan—that is, a despised outsider—comes, and he takes up the man, binds his wounds, and takes him to recuperate at a nearby inn.

So what kind of answer is this to the original question? We moderns tend to think that it's obvious. Our neighbours, the people we ought to help when they're in this kind of plight, are not just the fellow members of our group, tribe, nation; but any human being, regardless of the limits of tribal belonging. We can generalize this, and say that all human beings, without discrimination, are the proper beneficiaries of our help, which ought to be given generously, following the example of the Samaritan. This story can be seen as one of original building blocks out of which our modern universalist moral consciousness has been built.

So we take in the lesson, but we put it in a certain register, that of moral rules, how we ought to behave. The higher moral rules are the universal ones, those which apply across the whole human species. We concentrate on the move out of the parochial. But in Illich's view, in this we are missing what is essential here. What the story is opening for us is not a set of universal rules, applying anywhere and everywhere, but another way of being. This involves on one hand a new motivation, and on the other, a new kind of community.

Illich's take on the parable can be put in this way: there are earlier forms of religious and social life which (a) are based on a strong sense of "we", more fundamental than the "I", hence a notion of insider/outsider, and (b) have a sense of the demonic, both the powers of darkness which surround us, and the spirits which protect us against them.

These pre-modern ways of life also (c) have a strong sense of the fitting, of proportion. This means (i) that the things in the world have their appropriate form that they must live out, or live up to (one way of articulating this is the Plato-Aristotle notion of Forms), and (ii) they are set in a cosmos, where different parts correspond to other parts, and on different levels: heaven and earth, up and down, male and female, etc. (chapter 9).

The Gospel opens up a new way, which breaks open these limits. The parable of the Samaritan illustrates this. So far, Illich agrees with the standard view. The Samaritan is moved by the wounded man; he moves to act, and in doing so inaugurates (potentially) a new relation of friendship/love/charity with this person. But this cuts across the boundaries of the permitted "we's" in his world. It is a free act of his "I". Illich's talk of freedom here might mislead a modern. It is not something he generates just out of himself; it is that he responds to this person. He feels called to respond, however, not by some principle of "ought", but by this wounded person himself. And in so responding, he frees himself from the bounds of the "we". He also acts outside of the carefully constructed sense of the sacred, of the demons of darkness, and various modes of prophylaxis against them which have been erected in "our" culture, society, religion (often evident in views of the outsider as "unclean").

This shakes up the cosmos and the proportionalities which are established in it in "our" society, but it does not deny proportionality. It creates a new kind of fittingness, belonging together, between Samaritan and wounded Jew. They are fitted together in a disymmetric proportionality (chapter 17, p. 197) which comes from God, which is that of agape, and which became possible because God became flesh. The enfleshment of God extends outward, through such new links as the Samaritan makes with the Jew, into a network, which we call the Church. But this is a network, not a categorical grouping; that is, it is a skein of relations which link particular, unique, enfleshed people to each other, rather than a grouping of people together on the grounds of their sharing some important property (as in modern nations, we are all Canadians, Americans, French people; or universally, we are all rights-bearers, etc.). It resembles earlier kin networks in this regard. (In a tribe, the important thing is not the category we share in, but that I am related to this person as my father, that as my uncle, that other as my cousin, etc. Which is why anthropologists discover to their surprise that in "primitive" societies in the Amazon, say, people had words for the different roles, moieties, clans, etc., but no name for the whole group.)[14] But it is unlike tribal kinship groups in that it is not confined to the established "we", that it creates links across boundaries, on the basis of a mutual fittingness which is not based on kinship but on the kind of love which God has for us, which we call agape.

The corruption of this new network comes when it falls back into something more "normal" in worldly terms. Sometimes a church community becomes a tribe (or takes over an existing tribal society), and treats outsiders as Jews treated Samaritans (Belfast). But the really terrible corruption is a kind of falling forward, in which the church develops into something unprecedented. The network of agape involves a kind of fidelity to the new relations; and because we can all too easily fall away from this (which falling away we call "sin"), we are led to shore up these relations; we institutionalize them, introduce rules, divide responsibilities. In this way, we keep the hungry fed, the homeless housed, the naked clothed; but we are now living caricatures of the network life. We have lost some of the communion, the "conspiratio", which is at the heart of the Eucharist (chapter 20). The spirit is strangled.

Something new emerges out of all this: modern bureaucracies, based on rationality, and rules. Rules prescribe treatments for categories of people, so a tremendously important feature of our lives is that we fit into categories; our rights, entitlements, burdens, etc., depend on these. These shape our lives, make us see ourselves in new ways, in which category-belonging bulks large, and the idiosyncratically-enfleshed individual becomes less relevant, not to speak of the ways in which this enfleshed person flourishes through his/her network of friendships. For Illich, there is something monstrous, alienating about this way of life. The monstrous comes from a corruption of the highest, the agape-network. Corrupted Christianity gives rise to the modern.

Illich's vision goes beyond this understanding of the bureaucratic hardening of the Church, which happened relatively early on, and affects most branches of the Church, even Oriental ones. He sees that the process was taken much farther in Latin Christendom. We see it in the criminalization or judicialization of sin and its remission (chapter 5). Rules, oughts, and punishments take over more and more. But he also sees it in a series of developments which everyone recognizes as central to Western modernity, but which are hard to conceptualize: things like the growth of an objectifying standpoint on everything, including human life, which steadily becomes more and more dominant.

We see this in what he calls the medicalization of the body. The medical knowledge of the body, which tracks the way our organs work, the various chemical processes which underlie these workings, and so on, involves our taking a standpoint outside ourselves. They devalue and set aside the lived body and its experience. This is not the source of real, scientific knowledge, and it must be set aside if we want really to understand what is going on within us. We get trained to see ourselves from the outside, as it were, as objects of science. But this doesn't just displace lived experience, it also alters it. The sense of imbalance, of not being "dans mon assiette", for instance, is no longer taken as a primary phenomenon, but just as a symptom of some underlying malfunction; and so is not attended to any more in the same way. Instead, I become more acutely aware of the things I am trained to see as important symptoms of life-threatening malfunction.

So medicalization alters our phenomenology of lived experience, suppressing certain facets of this experience, making other recessive, bringing out still others. But it also covers its tracks; we don't see that we're being led to see/feel ourselves in different ways, we just believe naïvely that this is experience itself; we imagine that people have always experienced themselves this way. And we are baffled by accounts of earlier ages.

Illich follows this development of the decentred, outside view through a series of often startling analyses: e.g., the development of the gaze, our eventual capture by a view of ourselves as we show up in media images, or in X-ray imaging, or in various ways of representing underlying processes visually, on graphs, etc. ("visiotypes"; pp. 158–160). We are in the process alienated from our anchoring in the world, in real fleshly reality; which we can only recover access to through the lived body, whose testimony is being distortively shaped or even denied by "virtual" reality.

Similarly in his tracing of our self-conception as users of tools, as separable instruments; and then into our sense of ourselves as parts of systems (chapter 13). We move ever farther away from the lived body. This is the process I spoke about earlier with the term "excarnation".

This takes us ever farther away from the network of agape. This can only be created in enfleshment. Agape moves outward from the guts; the New Testament word for "taking pity", *splangnizesthai,* places the response in the bowels. We cease being able to make sense of this the more we go along with these alienating self-images. Resurrection only makes sense when we take seriously enfleshment (p. 214), i.e., overcome excarnation.

But the alienating view is also partly a creation of Christianity. There is a desire for power here, of course, but also the aspiration to help, heal, make life better. (Bacon links the new science to "improving the condition of mankind".) It is another monstrous creation of (corrupted) Christianity. And the corruption of the best is the worst (Corruptio optimi pessima).

Illich's text here also offers a very deep insight, still in some ways inchoate, of our fears of darkness, and the powers of evil. In the earliest forms of religious life, we kept these at bay partly by propitiating them, and partly by turning for protection to benign spirits, eventually God. The new path of the Gospel invites us to step out of the old protections, erected by the old "we's", confident in our impunity before these forces. But this impunity is the obverse side of our fidelity to the network of agape; and as we turn our back on that, try to "organize", to regulate the network, we fall away, and the fears recur. But now in a new register; we face them more and more alone, without the "cover" of the old collective protections (chapter 6).

This drives us further in the direction of objectification/disenchantment. Science just negates, denies this whole dimension of dark forces. We are now reassured, our fears calmed. But our sense of them remains in two ways: first, the fascination with the idea of such forces, and benign counter-forces; so much of popular stories, films, art, recreates them (Star Trek, Lord of the Rings, Matrix, Pullman, Harry Potter). We give ourselves frissons, while still holding the reality at bay. Second, they re-emerge in modes of diabolical evil which we find ourselves involved in (Holocaust, genocides, Gulags, killing fields, etc.).

We can see that Illich's story is not just about Christianity, but also about modern civilization. The latter is in some way the historical creation of "corrupted" Christianity. This in many ways comes close to the story I have been trying to tell: how the modern secular world emerged out of the more and more rule-bound and norm-governed Reform of Latin Christendom.

This civilization has pushed to its farthest limits the move which Illich describes as the corrupting of Christianity: that is, in response to the failure and inadequacy of a motivation grounded in a sense of mutual belonging, it erects a system. This incorporates (a) a code or set of rules, (b) a set of disciplines which make us internalize these rules, and (c) a system of rationally constructed organizations (private and public bureaucracies, universities, schools) to make sure that we carry out what the rules demand. All these become second nature to us, including the decentring from our lived experience which we have to carry through in order to become disciplined, rational, disengaged subjects. From within this perspective, the standard account of the Good Samaritan story appears just obvious: it is a stage on the road to a universal morality of rules.

Modern ethics illustrates this fetishism of rules and norms. Not just law, but ethics is seen in terms of rules (Kant). The spirit of the law is important, where it is, because it too expresses some general principle. For Kant, the principle is that we should put regulation by reason, or humanity as rational agency, first. In contrast, as we have seen, the network of agape puts first the gut-driven response to this person. This can't be reduced to a general rule. Because we can't live up to this, we need rules. "Because of the hardness of your hearts". It's not that we could just abolish them. But modern liberal civilization fetishizes them. We think we have to find the RIGHT system of rules, norms, and then follow them through unfailingly. We can't see any more the way these rules fit badly our world of enfleshed human beings, we fail to notice the dilemmas they have to sweep under the carpet: for instance, justice versus mercy; or justice versus a renewed relation—the kind of dilemma which post-Apartheid South Africa faced, and which the Truth and Reconciliation Commission was meant to meet, as an attempt to get beyond the existing codes of retribution. We connect up here with the discussion in Chapter 18, section 12.[15]

In this perspective, something crucial in the Samaritan story gets lost. A world ordered by this system of rules, disciplines, organizations can only see contingency as an obstacle, even an enemy and a threat. The ideal is to master it, to extend the web of control so that contingency is reduced to a minimum. By contrast, contingency is an essential feature of the story as an answer to the question that prompted it. Who is my neighbour? The one you happen across, stumble across, who is wounded there in the road. Sheer accident also has a hand in shaping the proportionate, the appropriate response. It is telling us something, answering our deepest questions: *this* is your neighbour. But to hear this, we have to escape from the monomaniacal perspective in which contingency can only be an adversary requiring control. Illich develops this theme profoundly in chapters 3 and 4.

* * *

What is Illich telling us? That we should dismantle our code-driven, disciplined, objectified world? Illich was a thoroughgoing radical, and I don't want to blunt his message. I can't claim to speak for him, but this is what I draw from his work. We can't live without codes, legal ones which are essential to the rule of law, moral ones which we have to inculcate in each new generation. But even if we can't fully escape the nomocratic-judicialized-objectified world, it is terribly important to see that that is not all there is, that it is in many ways dehumanizing, alienating; that it often generates dilemmas that it cannot see, and in driving forward, acts with great ruthlessness and cruelty. The various modes of political correctness, from Left and Right, illustrate this every day.

As does also the continued pull to violence in our world. Codes, even the best codes, are not as innocent as they seem. They take root in us as an answer to some of our deepest metaphysical needs, that for meaning, for instance, or that for a sense of our own goodness. The code can rapidly become the crutch for our sense of moral superiority. This is, of course, another important theme of the New Testament, as we see with the parable of the Pharisee and the Publican.

Worse, this moral superiority feeds on the proof offered by the contrast case, the evil, warped, inhuman ones. We even give our own goodness its crowning proof when we wage war on evil. We will do battle against axes of evil and networks of terror; and then we discover to our surprise and horror that we are reproducing the evil we defined ourselves against.

Codes, even the best codes, can become idolatrous traps, which tempt us to complicity in violence. Illich can remind us not to become totally invested in the code, even the best code of a peace-loving, egalitarian, liberalism. We should find the centre of our spiritual lives beyond the code, deeper than the code, in networks of living concern, which are not to be sacrificed to the code, which must even from time to time subvert it. This message comes out of a certain theology, but it could be heard with profit by everybody.

I have been arguing, in part following Illich, that there has been a long-standing tendency in the West to slide towards an identification of Christian faith and civilizational order. This not only makes us lose sight of the full transformation that Christians are called to, but it also makes us lose a crucial critical distance from the order which we identify as Christendom, whether it be the one at present established, or some earlier one which we are fighting to restore.

Illich thinks that this take-over of Christianity by an order which negates its spirit is *the* mystery of evil (*mysterium inequitatis,* pp. 169–170). Even if one doesn't go this far, one can see the dangers inherent in it. The belief that God is on our side, that He blesses *our* order, is one of the most powerful sources of chauvinism. It can be a fertile inspiration to violence. For our enemies must be His enemies, and these surely must be fought with every means at our disposal. That is the danger that the Catholic Church eventually perceived, which led to the Papal condemnation of Action Française in 1926. And this in spite of the fact that the particular civilizational order which this movement was struggling for, a restored Catholic monarchy, was highly attractive to many churchmen. Maurras tried to reassure his Catholic followers with his slogan "Politique, d'abord", implying that the political alliance was merely provisional, and didn't imply an identity of goal; but in fact what was going on was a kind of integral fusion of faith and political programme, which nourished a kind of conflict which hovered constantly on the edge of violence, with Maurras calling for the assassination of Republican politicians.

The Papal condemnation was the occasion of Maritain's break with Maurras, and his move towards a very different position, one in which he came to see the reconstruction of Christian civilization in novel terms; not as a return to Christendom, that is, to a single civilization homogeneously and integrally Christian, but limited to one area. Rather he sought a unity of Christian culture on a global scale, but in a dispersed network of Christian lay institutions and centres of intellectual and spiritual life. "Au lieu d'un château fort dressé au milieu des terres, il faudrait penser à l'armée des étoiles jetées dans le ciel."[16] (Instead of a fortified castle erected in the middle of the land, we must think of an army of stars thrown into the sky.) The central feature of this new culture will be "l'avènement spirituel, non pas de l'ego centré sur lui-même, mais de la subjectivité créatrice" (the spiritual advent, not of the self-centred ego, but of creative subjectivity).[17] This new understanding of philosophy and the modern condition reached its fullest expression in Maritain's *Humanisme Intégral*.[18]

3

If we return to the conversions (or reconversions) to Christianity in the past two centuries, we can discern two tendencies in the light of this discussion. These are often accompanied by an acute sense that the present immanent orders of psychological or moral self-understanding are deeply flawed, and an awareness of a larger order which can alone make sense of our lives. Larger order and established order are out of true. But the ultimate significance of this may be seen in two ways. On one hand, this lack of fit can be seen as a fact just about the present order, something that could be overcome by establishing another order, a real Christendom, whose paradigm will usually be identified in our past. Or on the other hand, we could see this gap as endemic in the human historical condition itself. On this view, there must always be this gap and tension between the demands of Christian faith and the norms of civilization, even the very best of civilizations.

This issue has not always been clear in the lives and thought of converts. As we saw above, some have moved from one view to the other, as with Thomas Merton and Jacques Maritain. Others have leaned both ways, at different moments and in different phases of their thought. In general, the more alienated from the modern age, the more fiercely one condemns it, the more likely one is to adopt the first view, and to pine for a really Christian order. Whereas those that believe that there is something uniquely valuable and important about the civilization of democracy and human rights, if they have not lost totally their sense of distance, as with the nineteenth and early twentieth century figures I quoted above, will take the second path. They will become modern civilization's "loyal opposition".

This critical distance from what we might judge to be "the least bad civilization so far" may also lead them to place themselves differently in history. Those who identify totally with our times can easily accept a straight theory of progress. We have nothing to learn from past epochs; insofar as they were different from ours, we can set them aside as irrelevant. The polar opposition of these "progressives" are those who want to return to some past paradigm: *they* (the Middle Ages, or the seventeenth century, or the pre-60s America) got it right, and we have to repudiate whatever in modern times deviates from that standard. In Christian terms, it is easy to see an "age of faith" in one of these earlier times and to idealize it; just as the Protestant clergy I quoted above played the "progressive" card in Christian terms and saw the new civilization as the triumph of Christianity.

But those who take the critical distance from a civilization they will nevertheless defend can see things differently. Perhaps there is no "golden age" of Christianity. Perhaps the different phases and societies where Christian faith has existed are all "unmittelbar zu Gott", in the famous phrase that Ranke applied to the ages of history. They differ because each mode of Christian life has had to climb out of, achieve a certain distance from its own embedding in its time (in the "saeculum", one might want to say). But far from allowing these modes to be neatly ranked, this is the difference which enables them to give something to each other.

These different approaches, out of different embeddings, we can call "itineraries" to the Faith. I can perhaps give a livelier sense of what I mean here by new itineraries, and of the issues which can arise around them, if we look at a particular example. Charles Péguy is a paradigm example of a modern who has found his own path, a new path.

We can see this first of all in that he comes out of or through a very modern concern; one might say a modern protest at a crucially modern development.

The modern development is what we have been calling "excarnation", in particular the exaltation of disengaged reason as the royal road to knowledge, even in human affairs. The proper road to knowledge is by objectification, even in history; this he thinks is an entrenched prejudice of the thinkers of his time. By "objectification", I mean grasping the matter studied as something quite independent of us, where we don't need to understand it all through our involvement with it, or the meanings it has in our lives. The past is thus another country, and our "objective" understanding of it might be that of anyone, whether they descend from this past or not. We should grasp it in "a view from nowhere".

This view of what knowledge is tends to favour, without necessarily generating, a view of humanity which is "objectified" in another sense, that is, understood as on all fours with non-human objects, understood in mechanistic terms, and in a determinist framework.

This whole approach, Péguy strongly rejected. He was thus deeply influenced by Bergson, who offered perhaps the major philosophical challenge to this view at that moment in France. One of Bergson's main lines of attack struck at the consciousness of time that was central to the objectifying view. Instead of thinking of time as analogous to space, where moments lie alongside each other, we have to take account of the lived time of durée, in which we bridge different (objectively distinguishable) moments, and connect them in a single stream, as we experience in action, or in hearing a melody. The mechanistic outlook fails to understand the present; it sees it just as a momentary phase in a continuing process; whereas on the Bergsonian view, "le présent a une épaisseur qui est exactement celle de la liberté dans le monde", as Emmanuel Mounier puts it.[19] (The present has a depth that is exactly that of freedom in the world.)

This kind of bridge between past, present, and future that we experience in action (this doctrine anticipates in a way Heidegger's famous analysis of the three ekstaseis),[20] we also experience in another way in what Bergson calls "memory".

Péguy, building on Bergson, distinguishes history (the objectifying kind) and memory: "L'histoire consiste essentiellement à passer au long de l'événement. La mémoire consiste essentiellement, étant dedans l'événement, avant tout à n'en pas sortir, à y rester, et à le remonter en dedans."[21] (History consists essentially in running alongside the event. Being inside the event, memory consists essentially above all not in going outside of it, but in remaining there and reliving it from within.)

This kind of understanding, by "memory", was of crucial importance for Péguy, because he saw himself as emerging out of a millennial culture of France, moreover a culture of its people, rather than of élites, the way of life of peasants and artisans. To grasp this was to plunge oneself in it, to bring to mind the way one was inducted into it, through the multiple practices of making, sowing, reaping, praying. The issue of how this was to be grasped was crucial for Péguy because, as the first of his popular milieu to have the good fortune to be educated, he felt a need, really a vocation incumbent on him, to articulate this way of life.[22] To approach it "historically" would be to denature it. The formation of a people and its culture over the ages was a long process of handing down and thus shaping its key practices, and hence was best understood on the analogy of an action, and therefore in the kind of understanding of time which was appropriate to action, and this for him was memory in his Bergson-derived sense.

This, moreover, was not just an issue of how to study the past, but had important practical significance. What was at stake was not just how to know the past, but how to relate to it. A crucial distinction for Péguy lay between a life dominated by fixed habits, and one in which one could creatively renew oneself, even against the force of acquired and rigidified forms. The habit-dominated life was indeed, one in which one was determined by one's past, repeating the established forms which had been stamped into one. Creative renewal was only possible in action which by its very nature had to have a certain temporal depth. This kind of action had to draw on the forms which had been shaped in a deeper past, but not by a simple mechanical reproduction, as with "habit", rather by a creative re-application of the spirit of the tradition.

We can see how Péguy confused his contemporaries, and was almost impossible to place. This left socialist Dreyfusard, a believer in revolution and in the Republic, passionately insisted on the need to root one's action in the millennial, including Catholic, past of France. So is he a reactionary? But he also passionately denounced the clerical, anti-Dreyfusard party, precisely for their desire to re-impose old forms: monarchy, clerical dominance, in their outmoded form, without ever considering how the tradition had grown and changed.

For Péguy the millennial tradition of France included the Revolution. This sounds less paradoxical as soon as one takes into account that this was a tradition of the French *people,* not of élite institutions. In a political field in which the Left believed in (objectifying) science and progress, which relegated the past to oblivion; and the Right was fighting to go back to the institutions of the ancien régime, it is no wonder that Péguy's was a lonely voice, and his thought was constantly travestied by friend and foe alike.

A crucial concept for Péguy was *fidélité,* a faithfulness to the tradition which precisely excluded just going back. Going back was a betrayal, because it replaced a creative continuation of the past with a mechanical reproduction of it. This is what we do when we act habitually, and there is no point trying to replace today's habits with those of yesterday. Moreover, the very attempt to engineer such a change means treating society as an inert object to be shaped, precisely the stance which Péguy meant to avoid. In his final judgment both Left and Right suffered from the same incapacity, they both wanted to engineer reality, be it to the new blueprints of "reason", or the ancient tried model of "tradition". They couldn't appeal to the creative action of the people.

To be inspired by a real living tradition of this kind was to be moved by a "mystique". This word created from the very beginning much confusion. One might think that he might have used the term "ideal". But as Mounier put it, he shied away from this latter term, precisely because it risked "de faire oublier que le spirituel est seul éminemment réel" (to make us forget that the spiritual is the only eminent reality).[23] Otherwise put, all valid ideals are already anchored in a deep tradition, in ways of life which have already been lived. They can't enter history like a newly invented plan which sweeps reality aside, or shapes it from above. The validly new is a recreation of a tradition. That is why he could see the Republic, and later socialism, as the re-expression of the French popular tradition, in profound continuity with it.

But an initiative started under this inspiration can degenerate, can be taken over by a party that seeks power, or a new order of fixed norms and habits. Then the "mystique" degenerates into what Péguy called "une politique", which he uses in this profoundly derogatory sense. The cause of Dreyfus was one of liberty and justice, but then it became a political programme, the basis of new rules of constraint (e.g., ramming through the separation of Church and State), responding to considerations of raison d'État and party favoritism.

Péguy becomes in the end convinced that this decline is inevitable. Hence his famous phrase: "Tout commence en mystique et finit en politique": what starts as "mystique" will finish as "politique".[24] This became part of a more general belief that there was a basic tendency in human life for the creative to fall into the mechanical and habitual, for our spiritual arteries to harden as time goes on. Modernity itself, which favours the disengaged and objectifying, is an instance of this hardening. "Ce qui était pour nous, pour nos pères, un instinct, une race, des pensées, est devenu pour eux [politicians] des propositions, . . . ce qui était pour nous organique est devenu pour eux logique."[25] (What for us, for our fathers, was an instinct, ancestry, living thoughts, have become for them [politicians] propositions . . . what was for us organic has become for them logical.)

Péguy's return to faith was partly the response to this very distressing insight. But before discussing this return, we should look at a few other facets of his thought.

We have already seen that, in spite of his appeal to tradition, in spite of his use of such terms as "race", Péguy was not of the Right, was not an ally of Barrès for instance. He was profoundly republican and socialist. And it is also true that in spite of his appeal to the millennial tradition of French Catholicism, he was neither of the clerical party, nor easily subsumable within the regnant Tridentine Catholicism, with its emphasis on rules, on obedience to authority, not to speak of its suspicion of the flesh and the people.

Thus authentic action, which links us to and continues our past, is seen as freedom by Péguy. It is the highest freedom to be moved by one's mystique, as against being organized and mobilized, and constrained by political authority to follow the rules; even when these latter claim to realize the mystique, we have already fallen into a politique.

Secondly, there is a plurality of such mystiques which have inspired human beings. Péguy himself was moved by more than one. Mounier speaks of four in his case: "l'antique [his love of Greek thought and culture], la juive [his admiration for Jews and Judaism],[26] la socialiste, la chrétienne".[27] More than one such animating, already incarnate ideal can fit together in one life. And different individuals, and also peoples each have their own vocation to the universal, to follow their own path faithfully. As Mounier puts it, "pour chaque homme, pour chaque peuple, suivre sa mystique ce sera découvrir en lui son *genium,* sa vocation, puis leur garder une fidélité sans défauts, non parce qu'ils sont siens, mais parce qu'ils sont un appel vers une plus haute destinée"[28] (for each man, as for each people, to follow his *mystique* will be to discover in himself his *genium* and his vocation, and then to cleave to them with an unfailing fidelity, not because they are his own, but because they are a call toward a higher destiny).

This, of course, doesn't mean that all such ideals are compatible. But, and this brings us to a third point, Péguy's ideal of a "cité harmonieuse", which he conceived as a socialist, and never abandoned as an ultimate destination to aim at, incorporates the aim of a loyal co-operation between the defenders of such ideals, honest about their disagreements, but never having recourse to force or exclusion.[29] This is how Péguy himself lived with his diverse circle of friends.

Fourthly, as one can already surmise from this last point, Péguy has no place in his theology for Hell. He is a universalist about salvation. In Mounier's words: "Aucun vivant, dans la cité harmonieuse, n'était étranger, ni les sages, ni les saints, des cultures périmées, ni mêmes les animaux. . . . Il ne fallait pas qu'il y eût un absent au salut éternel."[30] (In the harmonious city, no living creature was an outsider, not the wise men nor the saints of outmoded cultures, not even the animals. . . . There should be no one absent from eternal salvation.)

We can readily understand, in the light of these differences, how much Péguy was out of sympathy with the whole authoritarian style of the Catholic church of his day. He was, of course, outraged when the works of Bergson were put on the Index, but his reply also showed how bizarre and absurd he considered the Index to be.[31]

We can also see how far he was from the code-fixation of the Church, with its complicated menu of minor and major faults: "Ce qu'on nomme la morale est un enduit qui rend l'homme impermeable à la grace" (What is termed morality is a coating that makes man impermeable to grace); "Rien n'est plus contraire à ce qu'on nomme (d'un nom un peu honteux) la religion comme ce qu'on nomme la morale. . . . Et rien est aussi sot (puisque rien n'est aussi Louis-Philippe et aussi Monsieur Thiers) que de mettre comme ça ensemble la morale et la religion" (Nothing is more contrary to what is termed [somewhat shamefacedly] religion than what is termed morality. . . . And nothing is as foolish [because nothing is so Louis-Philippe and so Monsieur Thiers] as putting morality and religion together like that). And in more lapidary fashion: "La morale a été inventée par les malingres. Et la vie chrétienne a été inventée par Jésus-Christ."[32] (Morality was invented by sickly people. Christian life was invented by Jesus Christ.)

And it is not surprising that he has a better understanding of the ambivalent mutual involvement of good and evil in history: "Ce qu'il y a de redoubtable dans la réalité de la vie, ce n'est pas la juxtaposition du bien et du mal: c'est leur interpénétration, c'est leur mutuelle incorporation, leur nourriture mutuelle, et parfois leur étrange, leur mystérieuse parenté."[33] (What is formidable in the reality of life is not the juxtaposition of good and evil; rather it is their interpenetration, their mutual incorporation, their mutual sustenance, and sometimes their strange and mysterious kinship.)

Considering all this, it is not surprising that Péguy, for all his profound Catholic roots, passed a period alienated from the Church; and this was partly prolonged, after his re-conversion, by his sense of solidarity with his wife, who did not convert. (Putting this solidarity above the obligation to practice was another not very Tridentine thing to do, but this step wasn't frivolously taken, and it cost Péguy a lot.)

And yet it wasn't really surprising that Péguy, "mauvais sujet" though he was, returned to Catholicism. In a sense he never left it. Péguy hankered after a time of creative action, linking different periods together, but he had an acute sense of how impossible this was to attain humanly, in face of the seemingly irresistible slide into the mechanical and the habitual, the punctual present which is determined by the past, but no longer in living relation to it. All this pointed towards a Christian idea of eternity. Not the Platonic, or Plotinian notion, of an eternity beyond time, but the prospect of a redeemed or gathered time, in which all moments are reconnected in the same movement. What was perhaps lacking before the (re)conversion was hope, and it is not surprising that afterwards he raises hope to the highest rank among the virtues.[34]

Also profoundly Catholic was his notion of how we acceded to that eternity, through a communion, with God, but through the church. Like the porches of many mediaeval cathedrals, the image is of a chain, in which the faithful are connected through their local saints, up to Mary, to Christ and God.

> Nul n'est aussi compétent que le pécheur en matière de chrétienneté. Nul si ce n'est le saint. Et en principe, c'est le même homme. . . . Le pécheur tend la main au saint, puisque le saint donne la main au pécheur, Et tous ensemble, l'un par l'autre, l'un tirant l'autre, ils font une chaîne qui monte jusqu'à Jésus, une chaîne de doigts indéliables. . . . Celui qui n'est pas chrétien, c'est celui qui ne donne pas la main.

> (No one is as knowledgeable as the sinner in matters of Christianity. No one if not the saint. And in principle, it's the same person. . . . The sinner extends his hand to the saint, since the saint reaches out to help him. And all together, the one through the other, the one pulling the other, they form a chain that rises up to Jesus, a chain of fingers that can't be disconnected. . . . The one who is not Christian is the one who does not offer his hand.)

And later,

> On n'est pas chrétien parce qu'on est à un certain niveau moral, intellectuel, spirituel même. On est chrétien parce qu'on est d'une race *remontante,* d'une certain race mystique, d'une certaine race spirituelle et charnelle, temporelle et éternelle, d'un certain *sang.*[35]

> (One is not Christian because one is at a certain moral, intellectual, or even spiritual level. One is Christian because one belongs to a race *which is re-ascending,* to a certain mystical race that is spiritual and carnal, temporal and eternal; in other words, because one is of a certain *blood.*)

The words 'race' and 'sang' appear there, which was the cause of great misunderstanding later, particularly when one thinks of what happened not long after in European history.[36] But the point here is to underline the carnal, the notion that the spiritual is always incarnate, and that in chains which cut across time. It reflects how for Péguy, his Christian faith is animated by his profound rejection of modern excarnation. This is, as it were, the path by which he rejoins the faith of the Incarnation.

And the crucial concept here is communion, the "joining of hands", in other words, the communion of saints, to which we are all connected.

4

It is not hard to recognize in Péguy some of the themes which became central to the reforms of Vatican II, the rehabilitation of freedom, of the church as people of God, the openness to other faiths, among others. And indeed, there was a line of influence here. Much of the crucial theological writing which laid the intellectual groundwork for the Council came from France. I am thinking of Congar, Daniélou, de Lubac. Their prime intellectual sources were the Fathers, but they emerged from a milieu of Catholic thought and sensibility which had been marked by Péguy.[37]

So the question arises of what we are to make of the kind of challenge which Péguy made to an established Catholic tradition, in this case, the one which was defined at the Council of Trent, modified by the shocks of the Revolution, the Restoration, and the nineteenth century. This is ultimately the same question as, what should we make of the reform of Vatican II?

Now there are two clear perspectives in which this can be seen. On one hand, we can postulate that what is at stake here is the ultimately and totally right understanding of Catholic Christianity. Then the issue is, who got it right, Vatican II or Trent, and/or in which respect? In this case, the kind of reflection I've been making here, in which I have been trying to get clear Péguy's path to the Faith, what he emerged through and out of, as it were, the outcrop of rock from which he made the leap, only has importance in explaining how he got it wrong, or how he got it right.

We would be dealing with his background in the way that is familiar from many debates in secular history. For instance, the way in which believers in Progress argue that earlier ages couldn't have been expected to see certain truths which are obvious to us, because they lacked certain knowledge, or a freedom from prejudices, and the like; or from the other side, the way supporters of traditional ways may argue that in the contemporary condition of moral decay, when the most basic decencies are under attack, we cannot expect that young people will be able to see the value of what has been lost. We describe backgrounds and perspectives, in other words, as epistemically privileged or deprived, as good or bad vantage points to discern some single truth.

The second framework in which we can understand this kind of study postulates that what is at stake is complementary insights. Neither is simply right or wrong about a single issue, but each bring a fresh perspective which augments and enriches our understanding. The issue is to see how these different insights fit together, and for this purpose filling out the background, the social/intellectual/spiritual context from which an insight comes can be very illuminating.

We can see that the issue here is closely linked to that we discussed in the previous section, whether we recognize a "golden age" of Christianity in the recent or more distant past (or for certain churches in the nineteenth century, even in the present), on one hand; or we see them as different, complementary but not clearly rankable approaches, on the other.

Which postulate should we make? I don't think we can simply choose. The reality is more complex, but plainly there is some of each. There are clearly issues on which Péguy's views just contradict earlier established beliefs, and Vatican II changes the reigning ideas surrounding Vatican I: like the importance of freedom, the value of democracy, the centrality of human rights, the judgments made on other faith traditions, and so on. But this doesn't exhaust the question of how to think of the relation between these two historical forms of Catholic faith.

Pius IX was just wrong to think that democracy and human rights were incompatible with Christianity, or even inferior social contexts for the flourishing of faith. But that doesn't mean that Catholics suspicious of democracy in the nineteenth century might not have seen some of its dangers and weaknesses more clearly than we do as children of the twentieth century, who had to defend democracy against various gruesome forms of tyranny.

We rightly condemn such general principles as "error has no rights" as confused and dangerous, and reject the modes of censorship which they justified, but that doesn't mean that a spiritual discipline of obedience cannot have great value in certain conditions.

Or, to take a non-doctrinal issue: the whole way in which certain modes of abstention, like fasting, abstaining from meat on Friday, and so on, were made part of a code, and applied as a matter of obligation, was stifling and needed to be challenged; but that doesn't mean that we haven't lost something important with the passing of these collective acts of abstention from the life of the Church, as Eamon Duffy has strongly argued.[38]

We have to grasp these historical differences bi-focally; in one way, we are dealing with right/wrong issues, in which each change is a gain or loss of truth; in another with different avenues of approach to the faith from out of very different ways of life. A total focus on the first can blind us to the second. And this would be a great loss. This is partly because understanding another approach can free us from the blindness that attends a total embedding in our own.

Christians today, for example, have to climb out of an age in which Hell and the wrath of God are often very faintly felt, if they are understood at all. But they live in a world where objectification and excarnation reign, where death undermines meaning, and so on. We have to struggle to recover a sense of what the Incarnation can mean. But Jonathan Edwards, for instance, three centuries ago, lived in a world where the wrath of God was a powerful presence, and where the difficulty was to come to an adequate sense of God's universal love. One can respond to this difference polemically, and judge that one or other was bang-on right, and the other quite wrong. We condemn Edwards as caught in an old mode, or ourselves as having watered down the faith.

But we can also see it in another light. Neither of us grasps the whole picture. None of us could ever grasp alone everything that is involved in our alienation from God and his action to bring us back. But there are a great many of us, scattered through history, who have had some powerful sense of some facet of this drama. Together we can live it more fully than any one of us could alone. Instead of reaching immediately for the weapons of polemic, we might better listen for a voice which we could never have assumed ourselves, whose tone might have been forever unknown to us if we hadn't strained to understand it. We will find that we have to extend this courtesy even to people who would never have extended it to us (like Jonathan Edwards)—in that respect, perhaps we have made some modest headway towards truth in the last couple of centuries, although we can certainly find precedents in the whole history of Christianity. Our faith is not the acme of Christianity, but nor is it a degenerate version; it should rather be open to a conversation that ranges over the whole of the last 20 centuries (and even in some ways before).

This, of course, leaves us with an immense set of messy, hermeneutical issues: how the different approaches relate to each other; how they relate together to questions of over-arching truth. We will never be without these issues; the belief that they can be finally set aside by some secure instance of authority, whether the Bible or the Pope, is a dangerous and damaging illusion.[39]

What this fragmentary and difficult conversation points towards is the Communion of Saints. I'm understanding this not just as a communion of perfected persons, who have left their imperfections behind them; but rather as a communion of whole lives, of whole itineraries towards God. The whole itinerary is what we constantly retell in the lives of the saints. These include even the moments of betrayal, as the Gospel story retells the moment when Peter disavowed Christ. This is not wiped out by Peter's subsequent life. But God's response was such that the bitter sorrow he felt when the cock crew was a step towards his apostolic life after Pentecost. God made even this a stepping stone towards sanctity, and in this meaning it belongs integrally to his life as a saint.

Itineraries consist not only of sins. My itinerary crucially includes my existence embedded in a historic order, with its good and bad, in and out of which I must move towards God's order. The eschaton must bring together all these itineraries, with their very different landscapes and perils.

And this gives us a second reason not to let the issue of final truth occlude the difference of itineraries. It is that the Church, as a communion of different peoples and ages, in mutual understanding and enrichment, is damaged, limited, and divided by an unfounded total belief in one's own truth, which really better deserves the name of heresy.

I have described two different meanings we can give to the sense the contemporary convert has that she must move outside the established order. One sets us to look for the perfectly adequate historic order; the other invites us to a conversation which can reach beyond any one such order. The goal in this case is not to return to an earlier formula, inspiring as many of these will undoubtedly be; there will always be an element of imitation of earlier models, but inevitably and rightly Christian life today will look for and discover new ways of moving beyond the present orders to God. One could say that we look for new and unprecedented itineraries. Understanding our time in Christian terms is partly to discern these new paths, opened by pioneers who have discovered a way through the particular labyrinthine landscape we live in, its thickets and trackless wastes, to God.

5

Péguy was my key example, but in fact pioneers abound of new itineraries in Western modernity; there are those whose paths have been marked in literature, from Dostoyevsky, to those whom we have been discussing in this chapter, as well as others too numerous to mention. But I should like to discuss briefly one other major figure, Gerard Manley Hopkins.

Hopkins offers, indeed, a striking example of a surprising new itinerary. Like Péguy, he starts from the modern, more exactly post-Romantic predicament. He felt keenly the threat of a narrowing and reduction of human life in a culture centred on disciplined instrumental reason. We lose contact with the natural world surrounding us, and at the same time, with a higher dimension in our own lives. He was at one in this regard with an important stream of the thought and sensibility of his age; with Ruskin in his sense that the contemporary age has lost a perception of beauty in the world around us; and that this is intimately connected with a system of economic exploitation. But also with Pater in the search to recover an aesthetic dimension in contemporary life.

Further, he shares the post-Romantic intuition that art, and in particular poetry, is a key element in this recovery. One way of conceiving the importance of poetry was through a theory of language, which originates with thinkers of the Romantic generation in Germany: the Schlegel brothers, and Novalis, for instance, building on the work of Hamann and Herder.

Their poetics arises out of a sense of the constitutive power of language. It starts in the Hamann-Herder understanding that words don't just acquire meaning through designating things we already experience. On the contrary, speech, linguistic expression, makes things exist for us in a new mode, one of awareness or reflection ("Besonnenheit", to use Herder's term).

This idea is then transformed by the writers of the 1790s into a new understanding of poetics. In much ordinary speech, words do indeed seem to function according to the old, designative view. Forgetting the global relation to the world that language itself constitutes, we can easily believe that words like, for instance, 'hand', 'stick', 'water', just stand for things we already know. But for a range of higher things, the "infinite", the "invisible", our predicament is obviously different.

This emerges perhaps most clearly in their doctrine of the "symbol". The crucial point about the "symbol" was that it was that whereby alone a domain was disclosed; we could say: that whereby alone certain meanings come to exist for us. The highest things, things to do with the infinite, with God, with our deepest feelings, can only be made objects of thought and consideration for us through expression in symbols. How can the infinite be brought to the surface, to appearance (Erscheinung)? asks A. W. Schlegel. "Nur symbolisch, in Bildern und Zeichen" (only symbolically, in pictures and signs), he answers. Poetry is what achieves this: "Dichten . . . ist nichts anderes als ein ewiges Symbolisieren: wir suchen entweder für etwas Geistiges eine äussere Hülle oder wir beziehen ein Äusseres auf ein unsichtbares Inneres."[40] (Poetry . . . is nothing other than a perpetual symbolizing: either we seek an external covering for something spiritual, or else we relate something external to an invisible interior.)

We can get a better sense of what was meant by these higher, "invisible" things, if we think, as a first approximation, of the things that couldn't figure in our experience at all if we weren't language beings. Take 'spirit' (Ruach, Pneuma). Well, wind would be there for us, even if we had remained pre-linguistic animals; we might seek shelter from it. And breathing would be there, as we gasp for breath running.

But spirit? Not that gift, that rushing, that onset of strength to reach for something higher, something fuller. This sense of the force of the incomparably higher only takes shape for us in the name. Spirit enters our world through language; its manifestation depends on speech. The term 'spirit' is a symbol in Schlegel's sense. And the uses of language whereby these words are first launched into circulation are called in the above quote "Dichten", the creation of poetry.

On this view, there is something performative about poetry; through creating symbols it establishes new meanings. Poetry is potentially world-making; that is, the understanding of poetics which comes down to us from the 1790s.

Understanding poetics in this way brings about a shift of register, which opens up a new gamut of possibilities. Think of 'Spirit' again: it enters our world through the

Bible and related texts and sayings, its reality fixed in narrative and doctrine. The new poetics involves a reflexive move, which points to the way the Bible itself is not a simple narration of events which were already there for, e.g., the people of Israel, before they were recorded. It points to the way that these events themselves have been made manifest, and given shape, in language. This reflexive turn, so typical of modernity, brings an awareness of the conditions of awareness, of making the "Invisible" manifest.

A gamut of possibilities opens here. Reflexive awareness can bring about subjectivism, and a collapse of transcendence, but doesn't need to. At one, subjectivist, extreme, the manifestations in language can be seen just as effects of language. The poet's straining to find the right word is not seen as an attempt to be faithful to a reality beyond language. At another point on the spectrum, this language is understood as an attempt to define something which transcends language, but is still quite intra-worldly. The poet articulates human nature, or the human condition. Then at the other extreme, the full, original understanding is retained: our language strives to render God, or something which transcends humanity.

All too often, it is just assumed that the reflexive turn of modern poetics entails or inevitably issues in the first, subjectivist stance. But there is no necessity to this. What is crucial to the new "subtler" languages of post-Romantic poetics, as I argued in an earlier chapter, was that they permit a kind of suspension or indeterminacy of ontological commitments. It can remain unsettled where on the above spectrum a poet situates himself. In other words, it is in the very nature of this modern poetics, where the semantics of its language is constructed, as it were, within the poetic work itself, to allow for an ontological indeterminacy. The language *can* be taken in more than one sense, ranging from the fullest ontological commitment to the transcendent to the most subjective, human-, even language-centred. We can see this in the reception of Wordsworth's poetry in the nineteenth century.[41]

This indeterminacy is permitted, but not required. A new poetic language can serve to find a way back to the God of Abraham. And that is what one sees in Hopkins (and later, for instance, in Eliot). In this kind of case, the poetry has a double source, as Seamus Heaney has suggested.[42] On one hand, the poetic images strive to articulate experience, almost one might say, to gain relief from the "acute discomfort" of powerful but confused feeling, as Eliot put it; on the other, they strive to make sense of, to make once more experientially real, the action of God which has already been captured in a theological language honed by tradition. The ultimate insight captured in the poem is a fusion of the two, which transforms both; that is, the experience is given a deeper meaning, and the work of God acquires a new kind of experiential reality.

Sometimes for Hopkins the two modes of access are distributed in different parts of the poem; in some of his sonnets, the octave articulates experience, while the sestet attempts to fuse this with doctrine. Where the fusion is less than fully successful, the poem doesn't fully hold together; it works marvellously where the images of the octave transmute into a vibrant medium of theological insight—as with "Windhover", for instance.

Returning to the discourse about language in this post-Romantic context, the complaint is often made that language as we ordinarily use it has been flattened, emptied. That is, the ordinary use of language in our age operates with it as though its only function were the instrumental one of designating already recognized elements. The constitutive, revelatory power of language is totally sidelined and ignored, or even denied. This understanding of language-use is correlative with a stance in which we treat things, and even each other, in purely instrumental terms.

This is often spoken of as a flattening, or impoverishment of *language,* and not simply as an inadequate understanding of language on the part of (some of) its users. This also follows from the understanding of language I'm describing here. Through language in its constitutive use (let's call it Poetry), we open up contact with something higher or deeper (be it God, or the depths of human nature, desire, the Will to Power, or whatever) through language. Poetry can be seen as an event with performative force, words which open up contact, make something manifest for the first time. But what is this event?

Outside of the most subjectivistic interpretations I reviewed above, it has an objective side: something language-transcendent is manifested, set free. But it also has an inescapably subjective aspect. This reality is made manifest to us, who speak this language, have this sensibility, have been prepared by previous speech or experience. So this new word resonates in/for us; that the word reveals what it does is ALSO a fact about us, even though it is more than this. It *could* in principle eventually resonate for everyone, but only because they will have been inducted into the language and the human meanings within which it can resonate. This is the sense of Shelley's phrase "subtler language", in which he describes the medium of modern poetry. Unlike the references of earlier poems, which were guaranteed by established public meanings (the Chain of Being, Divine history, and the like), modern poetry doesn't rely on already recognized structures. It opens new paths, "sets free" new realities, but only for those for whom it resonates.[43]

This is what makes for the fragility of this "poetic" language. What reveals by resonation can cease to. The language may go dead, flat, become routinized, a handy tool of reference, a commonplace, like a dead metaphor, just unthinkingly invoked. We see this, of course, with traditional religious language, as also its opposite. The opposite, the continuing, ever-renewed force of a language, can be sustained in a living religious tradition. "Come Holy Spirit, our hearts inspire", sing generations of worshippers, ever-renewing the fullness of meaning. But these same prayers can become dead, routine; people just go through the motions when saying/singing them; or else they take an aura of comfort, of the familiarity of our links with family, lineage, past, which has little to do with their original revelatory force.

In the light of this new understanding of language, this deadness, routine, which used to be seen as a lack in the worshipper, can now be situated in our language, not now seen as an ideal code, but as the medium that circulates among us, here and now in our society. The very demand for authenticity—quintessentially modern—seems to drive us towards new languages, which *can* resonate within us.

In relation to the poetic tradition itself, the danger looms that poetic language lose its force, like all those Shakespearean or Biblical metaphors buried in ordinary speech, that it become leveled down; in other words, that the difference between ordinary, routine, everyday descriptive and calculating-operative speech, on one hand, and poetic creation on the other, be lost; the second absorbed into the first. In relation to the literary canon, the idea is that great poetry, in order to resonate again, needs a new context; otherwise put, it needs a range of contemporary voices, which can serve as its interlocutors, with which it can resonate. Otherwise its force is in danger of being lost.

This fear of language going dead, of its losing its resonance, is recurrent in modern culture, and not just in relation to literature. We see it in Heidegger, for instance, in his contrast between empty conformist "Gerede" ("idle talk") and authentic speech. It is a quintessentially modern worry, because it depends on the modern sense of the potential of language as Poetry (Dichtung), and the resulting distinction between creative and ordinary speech. Only in relation to this high vocation of poetic language, can this fear of falling arise. The fear is of a loss of the performative power. It is coeval with modern poetics. It was expressed by the founding thinkers of the 1790s, and has recurred ever since, along with the hope that new poetic creation can reverse the fall. This was the sense of Mallarmé's homage to Edgar Allen Poe for having assumed the vocation of "donner un sens plus pur aux mots de la tribu".[44] The apprehension that language is in constant danger of being lowered, besmirched, becoming inauthentic, is ever-recurring. We see it in different ways in the early twentieth century with Karl Kraus and George Orwell. In the realm of art, a word has been coined for this collapse into banality and empty sentiment: kitsch.

But there are a couple of features of this fragility of language which have been especially thematized in the twentieth century, and which were of crucial importance to Hopkins. The original Romantic idea of the poet as creator and seer could suggest a monological view. The resonance which really matters is that in the poet's soul or being. But more and more a dialogical understanding of language (implicit in the founding theories of Hamann, Herder, and Humboldt) makes its way, and it becomes clear that the resonances which matter are those which link speaker and hearer, writer and readers, and eventually (perhaps) whole communities. Poets may fail to be heard, but the end of the writing is to reach others and to effect a coming together in the Being revealed, or set free.[45]

Parallel to the isolation of the "I" is the focus on the single poetic Word. Just as there is a partial insight behind monologism (a single poet creates), so there is some truth in this focus on a single word. The breakthrough to renewed performative power can come to fruition in a crucial moment, even a word. Some neologism, or new turn of phrase, seems to concentrate in itself the power of a new language; we can think of Hopkins' "inscape", for instance.

But the partiality of this view comes clear when we see how this concentrated breakthrough in a word is only made possible through a host of others, references, invocations, questionings, against which background the performative power can act in this word. Just as resonance occurs not in the single poet but between him/her and a Thou, so the power to make us resonate builds through a whole constellation, before erupting (as it may) in a single word or phrase. Just as the poem as a whole can make us resonate, but only thanks to the whole inter-textual setting; the kind indeed, that we constantly try to build anew so that our classics can continue to live for us.

The meaning in the chain of meanings: there is something much more here than the banal Saussurean observation that the meaning of each term depends on the skein of distinctions in which it is set. "Dans la langue, il n'y a que des différences et pas de termes positifs."[46] (In language there are only differences with no positive terms.) 'Red' would mean something different were there no notions of 'scarlet' or 'crimson'. Here we're talking about how a word can serve to open a new space, reveal a new reality, make contact with the hidden or lost. And this power only comes against a whole background of complementary meanings, which is itself altered by the introduction of the new word.

There is another way of formulating this issue of the restoration of language in the post-Romantic tradition, which also has to be read in the light of this holism of meaning. This is the Kabbalistic-inspired theme of the Name. In the original Adamic language, words captured the nature of the reality they designated. This is a theme invoked in the twentieth century, for instance, by Adorno and Benjamin.

It might sound as though what is degenerate and inadequate in modern language is just the Saussurean feature that words are "unmotivated", that is, there is no more reason to call this animal 'dog', than there is to refer to it as 'chien', or 'Hund'. But it would be absurd to think that poetry might re-invent single words which in this sense "represented" the reality they help us talk about. If however, we see that what is at stake here is the whole poetic image, then an important point emerges. Hopkins in "Windhover" captures the Kestrel in flight, not in a single word, but in the diction, rhythm, and words of his poem; and beyond this, he captures something of the action of God.

So there are three issues, or perhaps three ways to put the same issue, which are inherent in this understanding of language and poetry: (1) that our language has lost, and needs to have restored to it, its constitutive power; (2) that the loss of this power means that we can indeed, deal instrumentally with the realities which surround us, but that their deeper meaning, the background in which they exist, the higher reality which finds expression in them, remain ignored and invisible; put in different terms, (3) it means that our language has lost the power to Name things in their embedding in this deeper/higher reality.

And of course, (4) this incapacity of language is a crucial facet of an incapacity of being, that our lives are reduced, flattened. "All is seared with trade; bleared, seared with toil . . ."[47]

This is the context in which I want to see Hopkins. He felt strongly the ugliness, "the *sordidness* of things",[48] in the urban industrial world which had grown in England. Indeed, he felt this perhaps too keenly: his judgment on this world was too global and undiscriminating, and his turning for a remedy towards unspoiled nature sometimes resembled a panic flight. In any case, he did see a close attention to the forms of nature as an essential antidote to the hideous and deforming environment of industrial Britain, whose continued extension he (rightly) feared.

> What would the world be, once bereft
> Of wet and wildness? Let them be left,
> O let them be left, wildness and wet;
> Long live the weeds and the wilderness yet.[49]

The attention to natural forms can uncover a deeper reality to which we are more and more blinded in this civilization. At a first level, this reality is what is articulated in Hopkins' key terms 'instress' and 'inscape'. The basic insight is somewhat related to Aquinas, in that the existence of things which surround us is not understood simply as an inert fact, but rather as a kind of action. Each thing has an inner tension (an instress) by which it realizes and maintains its proper form (its inscape). This, of course, draws on the Platonic-Aristotelian idea that whatever exists has a proper form. But Hopkins was inspired by Duns Scotus, and went beyond this. A given thing partakes not only of the form of its kind, as tree, or bird; it also has its own particular inscape, its "haecceitas", its "thisness", to use Scotus' expression.

Hopkins speaks of the "oneness" of a thing. Writing of a tree, he tells of "the inscape markedly holding its most simple and beautiful oneness up from the ground". He will also speak of a "self" in this context: "self is the intrinsic oneness of a thing".[50]

Much of Hopkins' poetry can be said to Name the inscape of things. Its constitutive force makes this reality appear; it reveals and celebrates the force of particular existents, as in his celebrated poem "Windhover":

> I caught this morning morning's minion, king-
> > dom of daylight's dauphin, dapple-dàwn-drawn Falcon, in his riding
> > Of the rolling level ûndernéath him steady àir, and striding
> High there, how he rung upon the rein of a wimpling wing
> In his ecstasy! Then off, forth on a swing,
> > As a skate's heel sweeps smooth on a bow-bend: the hurl and gliding
> > Rebuffed the bog wind. My heart is in hiding
> Stirred for a bird—the achieve of, the mastery of the thing![51]

But Hopkins is pointing to something beyond this. Beyond his robust grasp on inscape is a more fragile hold on a depth perspective, of God's action and our ultimate redemption. The particular existence of each thing is what it has from God:

> Glory be to God for dappled things –
> > For skies of couple-colour as a brinded cow;
> . . . . .
> All things counter, original, spare, strange;
> > Whatever is fickle, freckled (who knows how?)
> > > With swift, slow, sweet, sour, adàzzle, dîm;
> He fathers-forth whose beauty is past change:
> > > > > > Pràise hîm.[52]

And a thing can have its particular being only in relation to God. Applied to ourselves as personal beings, this means that we can only be ourselves in communion with God, which means that we discern the particularity that God has chosen for us, and ratify it, choose it in our turn. The self gives a "sigh of content". The alternative is to close within ourselves;

> Self yeast of spirit a dull dough sours. I see
> The lost are like this, and their scourge to be
> As I am mine, their sweating selves; but worse.[53]

Being really ourselves requires an abandonment, a letting go, a sacrifice. So that the moment at which Christ enters most fully our lives is (if we allow it) the moment of our death. Thus the nun on the deck of the sinking *Deutschland* "was calling 'O Christ, Christ, come quickly'".[54] Death and Resurrection are inextricably linked. The most fearsome destruction can also be seen as a gentle spring.

> Surf, snow, river and earth
> Gnashed: but thou art above, thou Orion of light;
> Thy unchancelling poising palms were weighing the worth,
> Thou martyr-master: in thy sight
> Storm flakes were scroll-leaved flowers, lily showers—sweet heaven was
> astrew in them.[55]

We can never know God. The one who lies behind Creation can never be grasped directly. His "elected silence"[56] leaves us without certain knowledge.

> We guess; we clothe Thee, unseen King,
> With attributes we deem are meet;
> Each in his own imagining
> Sets up a shadow in thy seat;[57]

But we can have a sense of him in his creation; not just in the inscapes of particular things, but also in the cosmos, and the power we sense behind it. Hopkins, like Claudel, has a strong sense of the power of God in the grandeur of the universe:

> The world is charged with the grandeur of God
> It will flame out, like shining from shook foil;[58]

But this insight, this deeper perspective on things beyond their inscape, is fragile. It can fail us, and Hopkins was prone to fall into despondency, which seems to have been particularly deep during his last five years, which he spent in Ireland.

> I wake and feel the fell of dark, not day.
> What hours, O what black hours we have spent
> This night! What sight you, heart, saw; ways you went!
> And more must, in yet longer light's delay.
> . . . . .
> I am gall, I am heartburn. God's most deep decree

Bitter would have me taste: my taste was me;
Bones built in me, flesh filled, blood brimmed the curse.[59]

Through this dry time, Hopkins refused to give in to despair: "No I'll not, carrion comfort, Despair, not feed on thee". With utter determination, he continued to pray: "Mine, O thou lord of life, send my roots rain".[60]

Hopkins, like Péguy, starts from a modern predicament, and also ends up in previously uncharted terrain. This is not so in the sense that his thinking deviates in any way from Christian orthodoxy. On the contrary, he resists strongly the slide towards a religion of impersonal order, which the nineteenth century inherited from eighteenth-century Deism, and which many of its leading figures remade for their own time—immensely influential figures like Arnold and Emerson. In fact, the desire to reconnect with the orthodox tradition was a central concern for Hopkins, pulling him first towards the High Church party and Tractarianism, and then later motivating his conversion to Catholicism.

Rejecting any doctrinal compromise with the spirit of his age, Hopkins returns decisively to the central Christian focus on communion as the goal of God's action in Creation. God didn't just make us so that we could live according to the laws of his creation, but to participate in his love. What is striking is the way Hopkins brings to the fore once again the deep connection between this telos of communion and a recognition of the particular in all its specificity. Something like this connection was already palpable in the spirituality of St. Francis of Assisi; and of course, it was brought out explicitly by the great Franciscan thinker Duns Scotus, who inspired Hopkins. But the Jesuit poet renews it in the wholly different context of the nineteenth century, where the universe, vast in time and space, has already quite broken out of the dimensions, as well as the Platonic-Aristotelian conceptuality of the mediaeval cosmos. So that Hopkins' vision of God at work in the particular inscape, as well as in the overwhelming and often destructive action of a measureless universe, is quite unprecedented.[61] It could only happen in our time; but it certainly didn't have to happen. There is nothing inevitable in this response to the universe as we now understand it. Hopkins was graced with a rare insight. He paced out an itinerary which is in more than one sense ground-breaking.

So lonely a road both as poet and as Christian, so unratified in his time, that he could feel at moments unable to reach the end.

birds build—but not I build; no, but strain,
Time's eunuch, and not breed one word which wakes.[62]

But in another moment of discouragement, where he laments how much he feels a stranger, not just in Ireland, but in his own country which has not understood him, he sounds a slightly different note.

> Only what word
>
> Wisest my heart breeds dark heaven's baffling ban
> Bars or hell's spell thwarts. This to hoard unheard,
> Heard unheeded, leaves me a lonely began.[63]

We recognize today how immensely that unheard word was worth "hoarding". Hopkins was himself aware of this, and at moments, he was ready to wait.

6

I have spent a great deal of time on literary figures in this chapter, but the gamut of new itineraries is much wider than this. There are also those who have found new paths of prayer or action, like Charles de Foucauld, John Maine, Jean Vanier, Mother Teresa, and Thérèse de Lisieux,[64] to name just a few. And many of these are and will remain unknown to the general public. Indeed, I have just scratched the surface.

The issue is, what to make of it. As a matter of fact, all the people I have been talking about in this chapter were in one clear sense impeccably orthodox Catholics. So it is quite legitimate to see them as in continuity with their predecessors. From this it is just a step to saying that what really matters is the continuity, and not the new paths broken. What is significant about these people is the contribution they made to restoring a previously established, then grievously challenged Church order; their idiosyncratic deviations are neither here nor there.

Or else "progressives" might think that some of these supposed "deviations" have actually finally got the faith right, and we can relegate earlier "traditional" versions to partly erroneous foreshadowing of the real thing.

Either one of these stances adopts the first framework that I described in section 4 above, the one which postulates one single paradigm of Christian order, whether to be found in some past era ("traditionalists"), or in the present age ("progressives").

I hope I have contributed a little in this discussion to making clear how much is lost in this perspective, the rich variety of paths to God which it negates or casts into shadow. But this full variety can only come to light if we adopt the other framework, and see the unity of the church as stretching into eternity across all time, such that the paradigm itineraries that it gathers can't be identified with those of any one age.[65]

The issue is ultimately one of whether one gives a decisive privilege to one historically-embedded order of Christian life, be it past or present, or whether one refuses paradigmatic status to any.

Unfortunately, as we can readily understand in the light of the story I've been telling, the issue between these two ways of relating to historically embedded orders is not likely to be resolved calmly and in mutually respectful exchange. We saw above the importance of modes of faith today that are tied to political identities, and/or notions of civilizational-moral order. People who are drawn to these forms may sometimes be led to sympathize with the first response, looking for and latching on to a historic order which can be seen as fully blessed. This is by no means inevitable. Many people, for instance, for whom conversion has meant that they can put some order in their lives, end or escape chaos, for whom the sense that "not everything is permitted" was a liberating force, nevertheless are not tempted to latch on to a new model of Christendom. In some circumstances, for instance, Pentecostals in contemporary Brazil or Africa, this doesn't even make much sense.

But where the firm identification with a present or past order is consolidated, faith can all too easily become defined in terms of certain codes and loyalties (or these codes and loyalties are boosted by their consecration in religion), and those who fall outside these tend to appear more easily as renegades than fellow Christians from whom one may have something to learn.

And so we have the contemporary Kulturkampf, particularly in the U.S.A., in which some churches are induced to take on the "secular world" on some issues of sexual ethics, often narrowly defined; which leads to a condemnation of other Christians who are reluctant to be recruited into this Crusade, and hence to a kind of civil war in the Church. This becomes all the more difficult to appease, since Christian churches are now global, no longer simply Western bodies, and many of the issues play out very differently on other continents.

Here is one great source of division. There is another, which is related. I mentioned above the response to excarnation, the felt need to rehabilitate the body. This has led to one kind of reaction in Western culture, a celebration of the value of sensual desire. But this can only undo one facet of excarnation, the ethical suppression of the sexual/sensual, it cannot touch the disenchanting reduction. This can easily go along with, indeed, in a sense encourages the lifting of all limits on sensuality.

To undo the reduction would be to rediscover the way in which life in our natural surroundings, as well as bodily feeling, bodily action, and bodily expression, can be channels of contact with fullness. Earlier religious life was full of such bodily modes and rituals. But it is precisely these which have tended to be sidelined with the advance of Reform, through more cerebral forms of Christian faith and ritual, and then into the disciplined, disengaged secular world. But the aspiration here will not be denied, and it is not surprising that the fastest-growing form of Christianity, Pentecostalism, very often makes an important place for bodily rituals, particularly of healing. But this runs against what many Western Christians see as the great achievement of religious Reform over the whole modern period. Another important potential source of conflict lies here.[66]

These two areas of conflict are connected, in that the major struggle over codes lies in the area of sexual ethics; and sexuality is a crucial dimension of our bodily existence. Making theological sense of this once again will undoubtedly involve another look at certain issues of sexual ethics: contraception, in the Catholic case, and homosexuality, among others. But it demands much more than this. We have to recover a sense of the link between erotic desire and the love of God, which lies deep in the Biblical traditions, whether Jewish or Christian, and find new ways of giving expression to this. And since the contemporary sexual revolution, as I mentioned above (Chapter 13), has made issues of sexual identity central, this rediscovery or re-articulation has to explore once more the question of gender identities, male and female, and how they figure in the God-human relation. There are two ways of evading or short-circuiting this exploration: one is to consider the differences of gender identity as trivial, or quite malleable, or freely determinable by individuals; and the other is to fix on one, supposedly eternal and unchangeable, definition of the difference, which for instance von Balthasar seems to have done.

These two extreme positions mirror the polar over-simplifications which bedevil the Nature/Nurture debate, that either everything must be decided by environmental factors; or everything must be determined by heredity. It should be obvious by now that human culture doesn't work that way: it always involves some interpretation and redefinition, but against a background of human constants. Because these are always appearing under a new guise, from society to society and from age to age, they are easier to identify than they are to characterize. But sexual life involving in some form both differences and attraction is undoubtedly one of them. Here as in other nodal points of human culture, one needs a sense both of the continuing background and the changing forms.

And one needs both these today in order to explore again the profound interpenetration of eros and the spiritual life. This terribly fraught area in Western Christendom, where the sexual meets the spiritual, urgently awaits the discovery of new paths to God.[67]

7

Having wisely noted in several places in this book the impossibility of prediction, I cannot stop myself from speculating nevertheless. Or perhaps better, I want to lay out two alternative futures, which depend on two fundamental assumptions about the place of the spiritual in human life, respectively that underlying mainstream theory, and the one which has been the basis of my narrative.

I have been trying to say something about secularity 3, that is, the conditions of belief in our age. I have told a long story, because I believe that one can only get a handle on this if one comes at it historically. It is not that one or other view simply follows from the story, but rather that, in the way I tried to explain in Chapter 12, one's story only makes sense in the light of a certain understanding of the place of the spiritual in our lives. Reasoning runs in both directions. One's sense of human spiritual life will suggest certain ways of telling our story; but then on the other side, the plausibility or implausibility of the story will give support or cast doubt on one's view of the spiritual. My claim throughout has been that the view implicit in mainstream theory, its "basement" in the terms of Chapter 12, has been rendered less plausible in the light of the actual order of events and processes in Western society that we usually call "secularization".

So I have an excuse to speculate. Talking about two futures will help to illustrate and make clearer the depth assumptions of the two views.

One future, which flows out of mainline secularization theory, sees religion shrinking further and further. Of course, no one expects it to disappear totally, giving way to science, as the old generation of rationalist atheists did (see the quotes from Renan and Comte in Chapter 15). Most atheists accept today that there will always be a certain degree of "irrationality", or at least inattention to science, and the wildest ideas will always have defenders. But we will get to a point, as formulated by Steve Bruce, where the number of people who go for some form of religious faith will be what you might expect if we started from scratch, and everybody invented their own explanation for things.

The basic supposition here is that religious, transcendent views are erroneous, or at least have no plausible grounds. Once we have outgrown the legacy of the past, they could only re-enter our world through the wilder, more gratuitous inventions of minorities.

I foresee another future, based on another supposition. This is the opposite of the mainstream view. In our religious lives we are responding to a transcendent reality. We all have some sense of this, which emerges in our identifying and recognizing some mode of what I have called fullness, and seeking to attain it. Modes of fullness recognized by exclusive humanisms, and others that remain within the immanent frame, are therefore responding to transcendent reality, but misrecognizing it. They are shutting out crucial features of it. So the structural characteristic of the religious (re)conversions that I described above, that one feels oneself to be breaking out of a narrower frame into a broader field, which makes sense of things in a different way, corresponds to reality.[68] It can easily be that an earlier sense of fullness is now given a new and deeper meaning, as we saw with Bede Griffiths, who first read his school field epiphany in the light of a Wordsworthian Romanticism, and then came to see it in Christian terms.

The shutting out is, however, very understandable. Conversion, breaking out into the broader field, normally makes one aware of how much we are always shutting out. Those who believe in the God of Abraham should normally be reminded of how little they know him, how partial is their grasp of him. They have a long way to go. (Of course, the fanatics among them forget this and revert to living in another bubble, enjoying a false confidence in their own hard-edged truths.)

And all these shuttings out, those of atheists and those of believers, can be strongly motivated. "Human kind cannot bear much reality" (Eliot). We would all be shaken, destabilized, made distraught, by seeing God face to face, all of a sudden, now. We need to shut him out, to some degree, for the sake of a minimum equilibrium. The difference lies in where this equilibrium point falls for us. If I am right that our sense of fullness is a reflection of transcendent reality (which for me is the God of Abraham), and that all people have a sense of fullness, then there is no absolute point zero. But there is a crucial point where many come to rest in our civilization, defined by a refusal to envisage transcendence as the meaning of this fullness. Exclusive humanism must find the ground and contours of fullness in the immanent sphere, in some condition of human life, or feeling, or achievement. The door is barred against further discovery.

But the bar against discovery is not confined to atheists. Many believers (the fanatics, but also more than these) rest in the certainty that they have got God right (as against all those heretics and pagans in the outer darkness). They are clutching onto an idol, to use a term familiar in the traditions of the God of Abraham.

Too much reality is not only destabilizing; it can be dangerous. It will be so to the extent that we try to overcome our disorientation by the false certainty of closure, and then try to shore up this certainty by projecting the chaos and evil we feel in ourselves onto some enemy, in the manner I described in Chapter 18. We assure ourselves of our integral goodness by aggressive action against evil. I fight pollution, therefore I am pure.

So religious faith can be dangerous. Opening to transcendence is fraught with peril. But this is particularly so if we respond to these perils by premature closure, drawing an unambiguous boundary between the pure and the impure through the polarization of conflict, even war. That religious believers are capable of this, history amply attests. But atheists can as well, once they open themselves to strong ideals, such as a republic of equals, a world order of perpetual peace, or communism. We find the same self-assurance of purity through aggressive attack on "axes of evil", among believers and atheists alike. Idolatry breeds violence.

So, on these suppositions, what does the future look like? Of course, this cannot be foretold in any detail; and moreover, things will almost certainly work out differently in different societies. But its general structure would be this: whatever the equilibrium point which dominates in any milieu, it will always be fragile. Some will want to move further "inward", towards a more immanentist position, for all the reasons rehearsed earlier in this book; and some will find the present equilibrium confining, even stifling, and will want to move outward.

In societies where the general equilibrium point is firmly within immanence, where many people even have trouble understanding how a sanè person could believe in God, the dominant secularization narrative, which tends to blame our religious past for many of the woes of our world, will become less plausible over time. This will happen in part because it will be clear that other societies are not following suit, and thus that this master narrative isn't about universal humanity; and also because many of the ills for which "religion" was supposedly responsible aren't going away. Of course, the plausibility of the narrative can be sustained by stigmatizing the religious societies as hostile to modern values, as many Europeans tend to do today with the United States; and even more with "Islam". But unless we sink to a real "clash of civilizations", this way of lending plausibility to the secularization narrative will give out sooner or later.

At the same time, this heavy concentration of the atmosphere of immanence will intensify a sense of living in a "waste land" for subsequent generations, and many young people will begin again to explore beyond the boundaries. Where this will lead, no one can predict, although perhaps the intimations of Mikhaïl Epstein, which I described at the end of Chapter 14, may turn out to be prescient.

There is also another feature of the "future of the religious past"[69] which the story I have been telling suggests. This is that much of our past which our modern narratives tell us is firmly behind us cannot thus simply be abandoned. Both the mainline Christian and the secularist narratives are happy to relegate certain features of the human religious past. Both see the Axial revolutions as unambiguously positive events, so that "polytheism", or "paganism" (to speak in Judeo-Christian terms) belong to a world well-lost. To which Protestants (and also to some degree certain Catholics) would add the Reformation (or its Catholic variant), which allegedly completed the work of the Axial turn, and which rid us of the relics of paganism and idolatry. So far the two main narratives run together. Then the secularist story breaks ranks and adds a further step forward, in which religion as such is shed, like an old skin, and we move out into the sunlight of reason.

More pessimistic variants of these narrations allow for the fact that whatever faults and inadequacies were responsible for these earlier phases may still be operative in human life. Idolatry may be a continuing temptation of the human heart; or irrationality and hence religious belief may be something which most humans have trouble doing without. Hence the relegation may not be complete. But at our best, we can do without these relics.

My story in this book suggests something different from these narrations, even in their pessimistic versions. Much of our deep past cannot simply be laid aside, not just because of our "weakness", but because there is something genuinely important and valuable in it. Recognizing this fact, in our present culture, usually means being anti-Christian, embracing some of the values of "paganism", or "polytheism". Peter Gay, in his celebrated book on the Enlightenment,[70] spoke of it as a "modern paganism". This may not capture the whole phenomenon, but he was undoubtedly on to an important strand in it. It is the strand which led John Stuart Mill to exalt "pagan self-assertion" over "Christian self-denial", or to take a very different example, led Nietzsche to oppose "Dionysius" to "the Crucified One".[71] This polemical stance is usually fully reciprocated by Christians who see themselves attacked.

But this simple opposition doesn't do justice to the facts; at least this is what the story suggests that I've been trying to tell. It's not that I want to put the two opposed positions on the same footing; that I would, for instance, be just as happy had the breakthrough to Jewish monotheism never occurred. It is rather that this, and later breakthroughs—like the long process of Reform in Latin Christendom which I've been dealing with here—were carried through in such a way (and perhaps it couldn't have been otherwise) that they crushed or sidelined important facets of spiritual life, which had in fact flourished in earlier "paganisms", for all their faults.

The repression and marginalization of one such facet is the process that I've been referring to here as "excarnation", the steady disembodying of spiritual life, so that it is less and less carried in deeply meaningful bodily forms, and lies more and more "in the head". It's not that I'm trying to say that Christianity, for instance, is inferior to paganism in that, whatever else it has, it lacks the full sense of embodiment of the earlier forms it displaced. Rather I am saying that Christianity, as the faith of the Incarnate God, is denying something essential to itself as long as it remains wedded to forms which excarnate.

Excarnation is also connected to a fear and therefore repression of sexuality, and hence an avoidance, or too timid treatment of questions of sexual identity, as I argued in the previous section.

Another negative feature of both axial breakthroughs and Reform has been its tendency to homogenize. The urge to reform has often been one to bring all of life under the sway of a single principle or demand: the worship of the One God, or the recognition that salvation is only by faith, or that salvation is only within the church. And this Reform has frequently been carried through by ironing out or sidelining whatever in human life might seem not to consort easily with this single demand. The insight which people try to express today through invoking the superiority of "polytheism" is just this, that these earlier cultures allowed for the integrity of different facets of life and their demands in a way that modern religious or moral outlooks have lost. Different gods—Artemis, Aphrodite, Mars, Athena—force us to respect the integrity of different ways of life: celibacy, sexual union, war, the arts of peace, which life according to a single principle often ends up denying.

Once again, it is not a matter of returning to an earlier form—worshipping Mars for instance—but of becoming aware how easily a Procrustean drive can come to inhabit a movement for Reform. In all of these there lurks a proto-totalitarian temptation. Luther and Calvin were surely right to condemn the ideology of spiritual superiority which infected late-mediaeval monasticism, but they ended up discrediting celibate vocations as such, greatly reducing the range of Christian lives. And their Reformation has helped to produce, via another stage of "reform", today's secular world, where renunciation is not just viewed with suspicion—to a certain degree that is always healthy and necessary—but is off the radar altogether, just a form of madness or self-mutilation. We end up from all this with a narrower, more homogeneous world of conformity to a hedonic principle.

The point is, once more, not that we need to leaven Christianity with a dose of paganism, but that our Christian life itself has suffered a mutilation to the extent that it imposes this kind of homogenization. The Church was rather meant to be the place in which human beings, in all their difference and disparate itineraries, come together; and in this regard, we are obviously falling far short.

The lesson to be drawn from this is that these moments of ascent, where what I called a couple of chapters ago "God's pedagogy" takes us higher, are often (maybe always) in their "really existing" historical form highly ambiguous, incurring important losses as well as invaluable gains. The indispensable step forward can in its concrete form impose unacceptable sacrifices. This is a reason to be wary of these mainline narratives of simple, cost-free supersession, whether narrated by Christians, or by protagonists of the Enlightenment.[72]

In fact, it is precisely these claims fully to supersede the problematic past which blind us to the ways in which we are repeating some of its horrors in our own way, as we saw two chapters ago in the troubling history of the recreation of scapegoating violence both in Christendom, and in the modern secular world.

The account I'm offering here has no place for unproblematic breaks with a past which is simply left behind us. In this I believe that I am following an insight of Robert Bellah, which he is working out in detail in a forthcoming book on the religious development of humanity, and which he formulates in the slogan: "nothing is ever lost".[73]

This is another way in which the story of how we got here is inextricably bound up with our account of where we are, which has been a structuring principle of this work throughout.

Epilogue: The Many Stories

I would like to situate my story of Western "secularization" in relation to other historical accounts, which trace the changes in philosophical or theological outlook or theory that ended up producing our present predicament. These seem on one level very different, but I don't believe that there is a real conflict with mine.

There is one such current today, with which I have great deal of sympathy. I'm thinking of the scholarship which links the critique of mediaeval "realism" (as with Aquinas), and the rise of nominalism, possibilism, and a more voluntarist theology in Scotus, Occam, and others with the thrust towards a secular world.

The link has been made between nominalism and the rise of mechanistic science, as also the growing force of the new instrumental stance of human agency.[1] And certainly nominalism contributed to the development of a clear distinction between nature and supernature, immanent order and transcendent reality, which as we have seen has been an essential intellectual background of modern secularity. The instrumental stance, in turn, contributes to the new turn inward as a base for a triumphant grasp of the world, intellectually and practically.

All these help generate the powerful modern ontic dualism: Mind over against a mechanistic, meaning-shorn universe, without internal purposes such as the older cosmos had.[2]

All these together—science, mechanism, the instrumental stance—contribute to disenchantment. The mechanization of the Weltbild is a high-level cousin of Entzauberung in the sense in which I've been using the term here: the decline and withering of beliefs and practices that call on spirits and moral forces.

It is easy to see secularity arising in this context. There is a direct causal relation to Entzauberung, which is one part of the story. And there was obviously complicity with Reform, which helped along Entzauberung, and helped to destroy the mediaeval-Christian cosmos. Indeed, the anti-realism which helped to empty this cosmos of Ideas and Forms had clearly theological motives.

Rémi Brague's story, of "la sagesse du monde" and its decline, fits here.[3]

From the mechanization of the world picture, and the atrophy of a sense of God as connected to a meaningful cosmos, the sense falls away of a hierarchy of being, and we lose the context for a philosophy of analogy, and hence for a certain understanding of our (limited) access to a knowledge of God. Indeed, we might following John Milbank see this new "univocal" understanding of being, predicated alike of God and of creatures, as the crucial shift from which other changes flow.[4]

Once this move has been made, God becomes more easily conceivable as a very big and powerful Being, in fact, as the supreme Artificer, and his Providence more immediately understood in terms of its remarkable general Design. Our access to the will of God through his Design is crucial to the story of the Modern Moral Order, and to the new neo-Durkheimian understandings of God's presence among us.

We can easily see how the way was prepared for the remaining elements in our story, and particularly the rise of a culturally hegemonic notion of a closed immanent order.

Let's call this the Intellectual Deviation (ID) story. We can see that it fits in a way with mine, but that it develops things which I have barely mentioned, and also leaves out the things which I have spent the most time on. Now I believe that this story explicates some very important truths, and draws some crucial connections. But I don't think this can suffice as the main story behind secularity. There is another important piece, which deals with the thrust to complete the Axial revolution; I mean Reform, which strives to end the post-Axial equilibrium, that is, the balance and complementarity between pre- and post-Axial elements in all higher civilizations. It is this process, occurring in Latin Christendom, that I have been focusing on, through the various social and cultural changes which have been generated on the way. Let's refer to this as the Reform Master Narrative (RMN).

Briefly summed up, Reform demanded that everyone be a *real, 100 percent* Christian. Reform not only disenchants, but disciplines and re-orders life and society. Along with civility, this makes for a notion of moral order which gives a new sense to Christianity, and the demands of the faith. This collapses the distance of faith from Christendom. It induces an anthropocentric shift, and hence a break-out from the monopoly of Christian faith.

My case is not only that RMN is clearly important, and obviously provided the framework for eighteenth-century break-out; but also that ID by itself wasn't enough:

(a) ID deals with changes in theoretical understanding, mainly among learned and related élites. What we lack is a story of how secularity (1, 2, or 3) emerges as a mass phenomenon. Of course it could simply be (i) trickle-down all the way, or (ii) the upsetting effect of the great changes: migration, industrialization, urbanization, etc. But manifestly (i) a good part of the "trickle-down" occurs via the spreading social imaginary, and (ii) we have already shown how just institutional changes depend for their effect on how they are lived/understood; our story of the modern social imaginary helps to explain how these were understood.

(b) ID in fact was originally a move within Christian doctrine; it found Christian reasons for the changes we described; indeed, it was originally inspired by these reasons; but unlike RMN, it didn't provide motives for turning on Christianity in anger (though Blumenberg doesn't think so?).

(c) Science, and especially mechanistic materialism, doesn't provide such reasons until much later; after Darwin, when the whole picture of the universe as a benign, providential creation is called into question. Biblical chronology is upset; the argument from Design goes; negative results occur for theodicy. Then later, mechanistic materialism calls all religion into question; this barely surfaces in the eighteenth century, becomes much more powerful in the nineteenth. Earlier the idea of a universe profoundly out of joint, where there is suffering and destruction, from which God seeks to redeem us, wasn't such an obvious target for anti-theodicy arguments. Disorder can be seen as the wrath of God, without being seen as direct punishing intervention.

(d) Of course, the move to a Christianity of good mechanistic Design can be seen as a distortion, a loss of crucial depth. The Radical Orthodox are right that we need some Plato-type understanding of what we are made for. But the mere dumbing-down of faith doesn't necessarily lead to secularity; otherwise there would be little faith left. However, once a break-out occurs, all these dumbings-down contribute to a sense of the inescapable immanent frame. The growing intellectual hegemony of impersonal orders is a case in point.

I would see our two stories, ID and RMN, as complementary, exploring different sides of the same mountain, or the same winding river of history. ID clarifies some of the crucial intellectual and theological connections. But we need RMN to upset the unilinear story, to show the play of destabilization and recomposition. The understanding of social imaginaries is crucial to explain these.

One might object: this may be right about the diachronic story; but now we're at endpoint, to which both ID and RMN contribute, could we not just fix the contemporary situation in terms of the deviations identified in ID? But history cannot be separated from the situation it has brought about. We have to understand religious/spiritual life today in all its different thrusts, resistances, and reactions, e.g., to discipline, homogenization. Thus we need both ID and RMN to explain religion today.

Notes

Introduction

1. This, of course, was until recently the standard view of what I'm calling secularity 1. We may indeed challenge some of its details, such as the notion of religion as "private". See José Casanova, *Public Religions in the Modern World* (Chicago: University of Chicago Press, 1994).

In his more recent work, Casanova has clarified further the complexity of what I am calling here secularity 1. He distinguishes on one hand, secularization as the alleged privatization of religion (which he still wants to contest), from secularization "as differentiation of the secular spheres (state, economy, science), usually understood as 'emancipation', from religious institutions and norms." He identifies this as "the core component of the classic theories of secularization, which is related to the original etymological-historical meaning of the term. It refers to the transfer of persons, things, meanings, etc., from ecclesiastical or religious to civil or lay use, possession or control." See his forthcoming book distinguishing what is valid from what is false in mainline secularization theories.

2. "La religion est partout"; see the discussion in Danièle Hervieu-Léger, *Le Pèlerin et le Convert* (Paris: Flammarion, 1999), pp. 20–21.

3. An important strand of the contemporary theory of secularization, following Max Weber, concentrates on this "differentiation" and "autonomization" of the different spheres, driven by a process of "rationalization". See Peter Berger, *The Sacred Canopy* (New York: Doubleday, 1969); and Olivier Tschannen, *Les Théories de la sécularisation* (Genève: Droz, 1992), chapter IV. I shall offer a partial critique of this outlook later on.

4. The schoolboy was George Macaulay Trevelyan. The saying is invoked by Owen Chadwick, *The Secularization of the European Mind in the Nineteenth Century* (Cambridge: Cambridge University Press, 1975), p. 164.

5. Bede Griffiths, *The Golden String* (London: Fount, 1979), p. 9.

6. Peter Berger, *A Far Glory: The Quest for Faith in an Age of Credulity* (New York: Free Press; Toronto: Maxwell Macmillan Canada; New York: Maxwell Macmillan International, 1992), pp. 128–129.

7. Schiller, *Letters on the Aesthetic Education of Man,* ed. and trans. Elizabeth Wilkinson and L. A. Willoughby (Oxford: Clarendon Press, 1967), chapter 15.

8. 'Fullness' has come to be my shorthand term here for the condition we aspire to, but I am acutely aware how inadequate all words are here. Every possible designation has something wrong with it. The glaring one in the case of 'fullness' is that according to one very plausible spiritual path, visible clearly in Buddhism, for instance, the highest aspiration is to a kind of emptiness *(sunyata)*; or to put it more paradoxically, real fullness only comes through emptiness. But there is no perfect terminological solution here, and so with all these reservations I let the word stand.

9. See Hans Joas, *Braucht der Mensch Religion?* (Freiburg: Herder, 2004), especially pp. 12–31 and 50–62, for an interesting discussion of (potentially) religious experience and its articulations.

10. In this pencil sketch of a phenomenology of moral/spiritual experience, with three "places", high, low, and middle, there is obviously an immense amount left out. It is clear, for instance, that we also experience the force of moral/spiritual demands in a host of other places, for instance in the judgments we make on actions of others and ourselves, admiring some, being pained or indignant at others. The moral dimension saturates our ordinary lives, and is present in them in a host of ways.

11. *La Peste, Le Mythe de Sisyphe.*

12. Birgit Meyer, *Translating the Devil* (Trenton: Africa World Press, 1999), p. 181.

13. I've borrowed this term from Schiller's famous distinction between "naïve" and "sentimental" poetry, because of the obvious parallels between his contrast and the one I'm drawing here. See Schiller, "Über naïve und sentimentalische Dichtung", in *Sämtliche Werke*, Volume 5 (München: Carl Hanser Verlag, 1980), pp. 694–780.

14. See Hubert Dreyfus, *Being in the World* (Cambridge, Mass.: MIT Press, 1991); and John Searle, *The Construction of Social Reality* (New York: The Free Press, 1995).

15. Ludwig Wittgenstein, *On Certainty*, ed. G. E. M. Anscombe and G. H. von Wright, trans. Denis Paul and G. E. M. Anscombe (Oxford: Blackwell, 1969).

16. Marie-Anne Lescourret, *Claudel* (Paris: Flammarion, 2003), chapter 3.

17. Of course, this idea had its forerunners in ancient times, with the Epicureans, for instance; but, I would argue, not with Aristotle, whose God played a crucial role, as pole of attraction, in the cosmos. But it is first in the modern West, especially with post-Galilean science, that the immanent order becomes more than a theory; it is rather the background to all our thinking.

18. See the Dalai Lama, *Ancient Wisdom, Modern World: Ethics for the New Millennium* (London: Little, Brown, 1999).

19. In a sense, I seem here to be implicitly taking a stand on an issue which tends to divide theorists of "secularization", the question of how to define 'religion'. For some, the account is functional, in terms of what religion does for people or society, e.g., help "integration". For others, the definition ought to be substantive, and most of these want to make some reference to supernatural beings or forces criterial. The choice makes a big difference as to the kind of theory propounded. On a functional view, it is possible to argue that religion hasn't declined in a "secular" age, because one is willing to include all

sorts of contemporary phenomena, even including rock concerts and football matches, as religious. On the substantive view, some decline is undeniable. See the interesting discussion in Danièle Hervieu-Léger, *La Religion pour Mémoire* (Paris: Cerf, 1993), chapters 2 and 3.

I don't mean to argue in the abstract that one of these definitions is better than another; just that the interesting question for me concerns religion in a substantive sense. Only I have chosen my own way of circumscribing the phenomenon, finessing the reference to the "supernatural", because the distinction natural/supernatural is far from universal, and only arises really in the Western tradition (with the possible exception of Islam), via the place accorded to human flourishing.

20. See the *Daedalus* volumes edited by Shmuel Eisenstadt, "Early Modernities", Summer 1998, Volume 127, Number 3; and "Multiple Modernities", Winter 2000, Volume 129, Number 1; and also Dilip Parameshwar Gaonkar, ed., *Alternative Modernities* (Durham: Duke University Press, 2001).

21. I am also aware of the opposite danger, that one could neglect the interconnections between the process of secularization in different civilizations. Peter van der Veer has already criticized me on this score, for neglecting the way in which colonialist perceptions of non-European societies nourished their conceptions of religion. See van der Veer, *Imperial Encounters* (Princeton: Princeton University Press, 2001).

22. Harvard University Press, 1989.

1. The Bulwarks of Belief

1. See *Sources of the Self* (Harvard University Press, 1989), chapter 7.

2. "There was a force in all things, animate, and, to our view, inanimate: water, trees, substances, words; and there was a mutual influence among things. There were also human and supra- or extra-human beings, who exercised power of different kinds and at different levels: saints, witches, ghosts, spirits and less palpable entities." Stephen Wilson, *The Magical Universe* (London: Hambledon & London, 2000), p. xvii.

3. This term "porous" is also used by Stanley Tambiah in his interesting contrast between Western and Ayurvedic medicine in their treatment of mental illness. In the latter, the "empirical individual is . . . seen as porous and open to outside influences all the time"; in S. Tambiah, *Magic, Science, Religion, and the Scope of Rationality* (Cambridge: Cambridge University Press, 1990), p. 134. I believe Tambiah is making substantively the same distinction as I am trying to define here. The discussion in his book connects this distinction with what he sees as two different ways of relating to our world, "two orientations to our cosmos", to which he gives for short the titles "participation" and "causality". All human beings are capable of both, but different civilizations and forms of life give very different weights to them; see *Magic,* especially chapter 5.

4. See the discussion of possession in Birgit Meyer, *Translating the Devil* (Trenton: Africa World Press, 1999), pp. 205–206.

5. Eamon Duffy, *The Stripping of the Altars* (New Haven: Yale University Press, 1992), chapter 8.

6. Jonathan Sumption, *Pilgrimage: An Image of Mediaeval Religion* (London: Faber & Faber, 1975), p. 78.

7. William Bouwsma, *John Calvin* (New York: Oxford University Press, 1988), p. 34.

8. Quoted in Wilson, *The Magical Universe,* p. 38.

9. Jean Delumeau, *La Peur en Occident* (Paris: Fayard, 1978), p. 221.

10. Ibid., p. 393.

11. I believe that substantially the same point was argued by Lucien Febvre in his celebrated book on Rabelais; see Lucien Paul Victor Febvre, *Le problème de l'incroyance au XVIe siècle, la religion de Rabelais* (Paris: A. Michel, 1947).

12. Peter Brown, *The Body and Society* (New York: Columbia University Press, 1988), chapters 4, 7.

13. Keith Thomas, *Religion and the Decline of Magic* (London: Weidenfeld, 1971), pp. 34–35.

14. Preserved Smith, *Erasmus* (New York: Ungar, 1923 [1962]), p. 57. See also ibid., p. 294, for an Erasmian spoof, supposedly the "complaints" of the Virgin Mary at the importuning of her devotees.

15. Of course, as Wilson points out (*The Magical Universe,* pp. 31–33), Carnivals were also fertility rites, but I am concerned here with their order-reversing aspect.

16. This is not to say that the mock violence didn't also convey a lot of real animosity, particularly between social groups. And it also could occur that the dramatized aggression could spill over into the real thing, either spontaneously or sometimes by design. For a case of this latter, see E. Le Roy Ladurie, *Le Carnaval de Romans* (Paris: Gallimard, 1979).

17. Natalie Zemon Davis, *Society and Culture in Early Modern France* (Stanford: Stanford University Press, 1975).

18. Quoted in Peter Burke, *Popular Culture in Early Modern Europe* (New York: New York University Press, 1978), p. 202.

19. Mikhail Mikhaïlovich Bakhtin, *Rabelais and His World,* trans. Helene Iswolsky (Cambridge, Mass.: MIT Press, 1968).

20. Victor Turner, *The Ritual Process: Structure and Anti-Structure* (Ithaca: Cornell University Press, 1969), and *Dramas, Fields, and Metaphors* (Ithaca: Cornell University Press, 1978).

21. Turner, *Dramas,* p. 237.

22. Turner, *The Ritual Process,* pp. 101, 171; see also the Apo ceremony of the Ashanti, pp. 178–181.

23. Turner, *Dramas,* p. 234.

24. Arnold van Gennep, *Rites of Passage* (London: Routledge, 1960).

25. Turner, *The Ritual Process,* p. 93.

26. Mona Ozouf, *La Fête Révolutionnaire* (Paris: Gallimard, 1976), pp. 102–108. See also

Michel Vovelle, *La mentalité révolutionnaire: société et mentalités sous la révolution française* (Paris: Editions sociales, 1985).

27. Ozouf, *La Fête Révolutionnaire,* p. 88. Translation modified from Mona Ozouf, *Festivals and the French Revolution,* trans. Alan Sheridan (Cambridge, Mass.: Harvard University Press, 1985), p. 72. Rousseau gives the clearest statement of this principle in the *Lettre à M. d'Alembert,* where he contrasts modern theatre and the public festivals of a true republic. These latter take place in the open air. He makes it clear that the identity of spectator and performer is the key to these virtuous assemblies:

> Mais quels seront les objets de ces spectacles? qu'y montrera-t-on? Rien, si l'on veut. Avec la liberté, partout où régne l'affluence, le bien-être y régne aussi. Plantez au milieu d'une place un piquet couronné de fleurs, rassemblez-y le peuple, et vous aurez une fête. Faîtes mieux encore: donnez les spectateurs en spectacle; rendez-les acteurs eux-mêmes; faîtes que chacun se voie et s'aime dans les autres, afin que tous en soient mieux unis.

See *Du Contrat Social* (Paris: Garnier, 1962), pp. 224–225.

28. Quote from Cabanis in Ozouf, *La Fête Révolutionnaire,* pp. 336–337. Translation modified from Mona Ozouf, *Festivals and the French Revolution,* p. 279.

29. I have discussed this at greater length in "Iris Murdoch and Moral Philosophy", in Maria Antonaccio and William Schweiker, eds., *Iris Murdoch and the Search for Human Goodness* (Chicago: University of Chicago Press, 1996).

30. See Turner's discussion of liminality and art in our age, in *Dramas,* pp. 254–257; and *The Ritual Process,* pp. 128–129.

31. Victor Turner makes this point effectively, in *Dramas,* pp. 268–270; as does Bernice Martin in her penetrating study of the expressive revolution of the Sixties and after, *A Sociology of Cultural Change* (Oxford: Blackwell, 1981). She draws on Turner's key concepts of anti-structure and liminality to show the aporiai which inevitably arise when one tries to make these the self-sufficient basis of human life. These aporiai provide her the conceptual grid for her insightful reading of the twists, turns, and conflicts that have defined and bedeviled this revolution ever since.

32. Walter Benjamin, *Illuminations* (London: Fontana, 1973), p. 263. Benedict Anderson shows the crucial importance of this understanding of time to the modern social imaginary. See *Imagined Communities* (London: Verso, 1991), chapter 2. I return to this question in Chapter 4.

33. In *Imagined Communities* (London: Verso, 1983), pp. 28–31.

34. Jean Guitton, *Le Temps et Éternité chez Plotin et Saint Augustin* (Paris: Vrin, 1933), p. 235.

35. Martin Heidegger, *Sein und Zeit* (Tübingen: Niemeyer, 1927), Second Division, chapter 3, section 65.

36. Guitton, *Le Temps et Éternité,* chapter 5.

37. Ibid., pp. 236–237.

38. Mircea Eliade, *The Sacred and the Profane: The Nature of Religion,* trans. Willard R. Trask (New York: Harcourt Brace, 1959).

39. Victor Turner also makes this point, that the pilgrim goes into a higher time; see *Dramas,* p. 207.

40. "Some say, that ever 'gainst that season comes
    Wherein our Saviour's birth is celebrated,
    The bird of dawning singeth all night long:
    And then, they say, no spirit can walk abroad;
    The nights are wholesome; then no planets strike,
    No fairy takes, nor witch hath power to charm,
    So hallow'd and so gracious is the time."
    Hamlet, Act I, scene I; lines 158–164.

41. *Die Protestantische Ethik und der Geist des Kapitalismus* (Weinheim: Beltz Athenäum, 2000), p. 153; English translation: *The Protestant Ethic and the Spirit of Capitalism,* trans. Talcott Parsons (New York: Scribner, 1958), p. 181.

42. *Ethics,* X.7.

43. Pierre Chaunu, *Le Temps des Réformes* (Paris: Fayard, 1975), p. 172.

44. Thomas, *Religion and the Decline of Magic,* p. 47.

45. Richard Fletcher, *The Barbarian Conversion* (New York: Henry Holt, 1997).

46. Thomas, *Religion and the Decline of Magic,* pp. 163–166.

47. Cf. John Bossy, *Christianity in the West: 1400–1700* (Oxford: Oxford University Press, 1985), chapter 1.

48. Ronald C. Finucane, *Miracles and Pilgrims: Popular Beliefs in Mediaeval England* (Totowa, N.J.: Rowman & Littlefield, 1977), pp. 196 ff.

49. Duffy, *The Stripping of the Altars,* p. 234.

50. Ibid., pp. 236–237, 241, 246.

51. Preserved Smith, *Erasmus,* p. 70.

52. Duffy, *The Stripping of the Altars,* chapter 8.

53. Philippe Ariès, *L'Homme devant la Mort* (Paris: Seuil, 1977), Book I, part 2; Jean Delumeau, *Le Péché et la Peur* (Paris: Fayard, 1983), passim.

54. Delumeau, *Le Péché et la Peur,* pp. 78–79.

55. Chaunu, *Le Temps des Réformes,* p. 189. Chaunu cites J. Huizinga, *Le déclin du Moyen Age,* who in turn attributes the quote to Odo of Cluny (who in all likelihood did not see *Crash*).

56. Translation modified from Johan Huizinga, *The Autumn of the Middle Ages,* trans. Rodney J. Payton and Ulrich Mammitzsch (Chicago and London: University of Chicago Press, 1996), p. 160.

57. Jean Delumeau, *La Peur en Occident* (Paris: Fayard, 1978), pp. 75–87 (hereafter cited as *Peur*).

58. Jean Delumeau, *Le Péché et la Peur* (Paris: Fayard, 1983), p. 45 (hereafter cited as *Péché*).

59. Delumeau, *Péché,* chapter 2.

60. Delumeau, *Peur,* chapter 2.

61. Delumeau, *Péché,* pp. 245, 490.

62. John Bossy, *Christianity in the West* (Oxford: Oxford University Press, 1985), p. 126.

63. Ibid., p. 126.

64. Chaunu, *Le Temps des Réformes,* pp. 192 ff.

65. Ibid., pp. 196 ff.

66. Duffy, *The Stripping of the Altars,* pp. 328, 336–337.

67. Ibid., p. 361.

68. Ibid., pp. 16–18, 26, 124–125.

69. Thomas, *Religion and the Decline of Magic,* pp. 30–31.

70. Smith, *Erasmus,* p. 57.

71. Chaunu, *Le Temps des Réformes,* pp. 205–209.

72. Anne Hudson, *The Premature Reformation* (Oxford: The Clarendon Press; New York: Oxford University Press, 1988), pp. 165–166, 303.

73. Quoted in Chaunu, *Le Temps des Réformes,* pp. 428–429; from Strohl, 243.

74. Delumeau, *Péché,* chapter 11.

75. Ibid., pp. 471–472.

76. Ibid., pp. 613–614, quoting Bunyan and Calvin.

77. Ibid., p. 563, Christopher Love.

78. Quoted in Smith, *Erasmus,* pp. 391–392.

79. *L'Institution de la Religion Chrestienne,* I.i.

80. Ibid., III.xiii.2; quoted in William Bouwsma, *John Calvin* (Oxford: Oxford University Press, 1988), p. 141.

81. Ibid., III.xiii.

82. Ibid., II.i.4.

83. A relativization of Augustine's explanation, as one attempt among many to give language to a mystery we can never sound, wouldn't reverse the verdict of his debate with Pelagius. This latter denies the enigma of incapacity altogether. There is no mystery here to find language for. Augustine was at least right in identifying the question, whatever one thinks of his answer.

84. *L'Institution de la Religion Chrestienne,* IV.xv.305.

85. Ibid., III.xix.

86. Bouwsma, *John Calvin,* p. 144.

87. Thomas, *Religion and the Decline of Magic,* chapter 3.

88. There is, of course, warrant for this in the Bible. See, for instance, Paul's Epistle to the Romans, 1, 28–31; and his Galatians, 5, 19–23.

89. See Philip Gorski, *The Disciplinary Revolution* (Chicago: University of Chicago Press, 2003), pp. 19–22.

90. Bouwsma, *John Calvin,* p. 218.

91. Delumeau, *Péché,* chapter 19.

92. I am postulating a long-term vector in Latin Christendom towards Reform, beginning perhaps as far back as the Hildebrandine reforms of the eleventh century, then running through both Catholic and Protestant Reformations. What keeps this vector going is a question which is hard to answer, but I think its general direction is undeniable. John O'Malley, in *Trent and All That* (Cambridge, Mass.: Harvard University Press, 2000), pp. 17–18, argues that originally reform dealt with discipline and mores, and the idea was to bring about a return to the original rule or canons, either of the church, or of some religious order, which had supposedly slipped into laxity. I think this is the kernel of the idea, but in the great tradition which I am calling Reform (with a capital "R"), it is connected with two others. The first is a change in religious life itself, towards greater personal devotion, and/or discipline, as well as a more Christocentric focus for these; the second is the goal I have just described in the text: to make over *all* Christians, so that they meet these higher standards of dedication and commitment. It was these two aspects that made Reform not simply a return to past purity (although this was frequently invoked), but an engine of genuine novelty and unprecedented change. It was also these two aspirations which may help account for the continuing thrust of the movement over so many centuries and phases.

Diarmaid MacCulloch also sees a continuity between the Hildbrandine reforms of the twelfth century and the later Reformation. These early measures can be seen as founding moves in "the formation of a persecuting society"; "undeniably there was an attempt to use Europe's clergy to spearhead an intensive and unprecedented regulation of the whole of society". MacCulloch, *Reformation* (London: Allen Lane, 2003), pp. 27–28.

93. Bronislaw Geremek, *La potence et la pitié: l'Europe et les pauvres du Moyen Age à nos jours,* trans. Joanna Arnold-Moricet (Paris: Gallimard, 1987).

94. Delumeau, *Péché,* pp. 146–152.

95. Delumeau, *Peur,* passim.

2. The Rise of the Disciplinary Society

1. Quoted in M.-D. Chenu, *La Théologie au XIIe Siècle* (Paris: Vrin, 1957), pp. 25–26.

2. Aquinas, *The Summa Contra Gentiles,* trans. The English Dominican Fathers (London: Burns Oates & Washbourne Ltd., 1928).

3. Cf. Chenu, *Théologie,* p. 184.

4. We are now talking about the highest intellectual constructions, but we can see an analogy to the enchanted world as lived by the common people, where the primacy of reciprocal action also left no room for an understanding of things as instantiating exceptionless laws.

5. *Liber XII Questionum,* c.2, P.L., 172, 1179, quoted in Chenu, *Théologie,* p. 24.

6. From M.-D. Chenu, *Nature, Man, and Society in the Twelfth Century: Essays on New Theological Perspectives in the Latin West,* trans./ed. Jerome Taylor and Lester K. Little (Chicago and London: University of Chicago Press, 1968), p. 8.

7. Quoted in ibid., p. 170.

8. From ibid., p. 117.

9. See, for instance, W. Ullman, *Principles of Government and Politics in the Middle Ages* (New York: Barnes and Noble, 1966), pp. 300 ff.

10. See the discussion of the monastic model of the apostolic life in Chenu, *Nature, Man, and Society,* pp. 226–233.

11. See ibid., chapter X.

12. Louis Dupré, *Passage to Modernity* (New Haven: Yale University Press, 1993), pp. 36–41.

13. See the discussion in Chenu, *Nature, Man, and Society,* chapter XI.

14. See John Hale, *The Civilization of Europe in the Renaissance* (New York: Atheneum, 1993), pp. 219 ff.

15. Ficino, *Platonic Theology,* trans. Josephine I. Burroughs, in *Journal of the History of Ideas* 5 (1944), p. 65; quoted in Stephen Greenblatt, *Renaissance Self-Fashioning: From More to Shakespeare* (Chicago: University of Chicago Press, 1980), p. 18.

16. This includes, but goes beyond, the important "monopoly of the legitimate use of physical force" of which Weber speaks. See "Politics as a Vocation", in H. H Gerth and C. Wright Mills, eds., *From Max Weber* (New York: Oxford University Press, 1946), p. 78.

17. John Hale, *The Civilization of Europe in the Renaissance* (New York: Macmillan, 1993), pp. 362.

18. Ibid., pp. 367–368.

19. Ibid., p. 366. This term 'polite' is, of course, another borrowing from the Greek term which 'civil' translates.

20. Ibid., p. 367. See the statue of Charles V, triumphing over savagery.

21. Ibid., pp. 369–371.

22. See "Des Cannibales", in Michel de Montaigne, *Essais* (Paris: Garnier-Flammarion, 1969), Volume 1, chapter XXXI, pp. 251–263.

23. Justus Lipsius, *Six Bookes of Politickes,* trans. William Jones (London: 1594, p. 17); quoted in Hale, *Civilization of Europe,* p. 360.

24. Jean Calvin, *Job,* Sermon 136, p. 718, quoted in Michael Walzer, *The Revolution of the Saints* (Cambridge, Mass.: Harvard University Press, 1965), p. 31.

25. Which is not to say that they didn't meddle at all; just that their successfully imposing order was not a mark of sanctification. On the contrary, their view called for a continuing gap between the mores of world and cloister. The same is true of Byzantine monks, who notoriously meddled, often in a threatening and semi-violent way.

26. Quoted in Philip Benedict, *Christ's Churches Purely Reformed* (New Haven: Yale University Press, 2002), p. xvi.

27. Henry Crosse, *Virtue's Commonwealth;* quoted in Walzer, *Revolution of the Saints,* p. 208.

28. Quoted in Walzer, ibid., pp. 211–212.

29. Dod and Cleaver, *Household Government,* sig. X3; quoted in Walzer, *Revolution of the Saints,* p. 216.

30. Baxter, *Holy Commonwealth* (London, 1659), p. 274; quoted in Walzer, *Revolution of the Saints,* p. 224.

31. See John Bossy, *Christianity in the West: 1400–1700* (Oxford: Oxford University Press, 1985), pp. 40–41.

32. See Bronislaw Geremek, *La potence et la pitié: l'Europe et les pauvres du Moyen Age à nos jours,* trans. Joanna Arnold-Moricet (Paris: Gallimard, 1987), p. 32.

33. Ibid., pp. 180 ff.

34. Michel Foucault, *Folie et déraison: Histoire de la folie à l'âge classique* (Paris: Plon, 1961).

35. Geremek, *La potence et la pitié,* pp. 40–41.

36. Ibid., pp. 277–278. See also Philip Gorski, *The Disciplinary Revolution* (Chicago: University of Chicago Press, 2003), pp. 63–64.

37. Perkins, *Works* (London, 1616), I, 755; quoted in Walzer, *Revolution of the Saints,* p. 213.

38. Geremek, *La potence et la pitié,* pp. 186, 201.

39. Peter Burke, *Popular Culture in Early Modern Europe* (New York: New York University Press, 1978), p. 209.

40. Ibid., p. 212.

41. Ibid., p. 217.

42. Ibid., p. 270.

43. Ibid., p. 271.

44. Ibid., p. 221.

45. Of course, this didn't mean "police-state" in the modern sense. 'Polizei' (another term derived from 'polis') "had the connotation of administration in the broadest sense, that is, institutional means and procedures necessary to secure peaceful and orderly existence for the population of the land." Marc Raeff, *The Well-Ordered Police State* (New Haven: Yale University Press, 1983), p. 5.

46. Ibid., pp. 61, 86–87, 89.

47. Ibid., p. 87.

48. Ibid., p. 178.

49. See Philip Gorski, *The Disciplinary Revolution* (Chicago: University of Chicago Press, 2003), chapters 2 and 3. Even Frederick the Great was impressed when, after the hard-won victory at Leuthen, his troops broke spontaneously into the hymn "Nun Danket alle Gott". "Mein Gott", said the free-thinking monarch, "welche Kraft hat die Religion!" Hans-Joachim Schoeps, *Preussen* (Frankfurt: Ullstein, 1992), p. 74.

50. Michel Foucault, *Surveiller et Punir* (Paris: Gallimard, 1975), Part III, chapter 1.

51. Stephen Greenblatt, *Renaissance Self-Fashioning* (Chicago: University of Chicago Press, 1980).

52. *Discours de la Méthode*, Part II, in *Oeuvres de Descartes*, ed. Charles Adam et Paul Tannery (hereafter A&T) (Paris: Vrin, 1973), Volume VI, p. 62.

53. "Das mittelalterische System endet in einer solchen Phase der verselbständigten Objektivierung, der vom Humanen isolierten Verhärtung. Was hier 'Selbstbehauptung' genannt wird, ist der Gegenzug der Rückholung der verlorenen Antriebe, der neuen Konzentration auf das Interesse des Menschen an sich selbst." Hans Blumenberg, *Die Legitimität der Neuzeit* (Frankfurt: Suhrkamp, 1983), Volume 1, p. 209. Translation: *The Legitimacy of the Modern Age*, trans. Robert M. Wallace (Cambridge, Mass.: MIT Press, 1983), pp. 177–178.

54. Quotations here from Dupré, *Passage to Modernity*, pp. 48–49, 51, 124–125, from whose very enlightening discussion I have drawn here.

55. We have to allow for a similar multiplicity of sources when it comes to the mechanization of the world picture itself. We could argue that the homogenization of space and time which we see in the development of perspective in Italian painting in the fifteenth century, and which was discussed above on p. 96, was one of the facilitators of the new understanding of a universe entirely in secular time. But we can't assume that the reasons for this change in representation had anything to do with a drive to mechanization, or a rejection of the cosmos shaped by Form.

56. Gerhard Oestreich, *Neostoicism and the Early Modern State* (Cambridge: Cambridge University Press, 1982), pp. 29, 35.

57. Ibid., p. 19. Translation modified from Justus Lipsius, *A Discourse on Constancy in Two Books* (London: Printed for Humphrey Mosley, 1654).

58. *De vita beata*, VII, 15, 7; quoted in Oestreich, *Neostoicism*, p. 22.

59. Erasmus, *Enchiridion*, chapter 14, p. 104.

60. Quoted in Oestreich, *Neostoicism*, p. 19; as also the (modified) translation.

61. See ibid., p. 53.

62. Max Weber, *Die Protestantische Ethik und der Geist des Kapitalismus* (Weinheim: Beltz Athenäum, 2000), p. 119; see the translation by Talcott Parsons, *The Protestant Ethic and the Spirit of Capitalism* (New York: Scribner, 1958), p. 151.

63. See Oestreich, *Neostoicism*, pp. 72–73.

64. See ibid., p. 8.

65. See James Madison in the *Federalist Papers*, no. 10; Madison argued, of course, that this new situation was an advantage.

66. As was argued by Hegel, and by Benjamin Constant. See Charles Taylor, *Hegel* (Cambridge: Cambridge University Press, 1975), pp. 395–396; and Benjamin Constant, "De la liberté des anciens comparée à celle des modernes", in Constant, *De l'Esprit de Conquête et de l'Usurpation* (Paris: Flammarion, 1986), pp. 265–291.

67. See Walzer, *Revolution of the Saints*, pp. 225, 227.

68. Raeff, *Well-Ordered Police State*, p. 177.

69. This corresponds to an important stage in the disappearance of an age-old under-

standing, one which goes way beyond our civilization, and which Rémi Brague has described in his interesting book, *La Sagesse du Monde* (Paris: Seuil). In the form it comes to us from the Greeks we are part of a cosmos, where the term implies more than our contemporary word "universe". It implies that the whole is ordered, and that this order tends to maintain itself, that the forms are at work in reality, as I put it above. This is as true of humans and their life, as it is of any other part of the universe.

True, there are also imperfections in human life, and in the Aristotelian version, these apply to the whole sub-lunar world. Only the upper world, the "sky", instantiates the order perfectly; and so it makes sense to call on us to imitate this, and in so doing turn away from our deviant practices (ibid., pp. 128–136, 152–171. Plato famously makes a call of this kind in *Republic* VII (500).

But the idea still is that in imitating heaven, we are following the bent of our nature, working with a self-realizing form. With the new artificialist stance, this latter idea falls away. The human order must be constructed by will. But the notion of the extra-human cosmos as offering us a model can still continue, even beyond the scientific revolution, which put paid to the conception of the world as expressing or manifesting forms, as we shall see in the next section. Perhaps one might argue that it still continues, for instance, in certain ecological movements. However, in recent centuries it is more and more rivaled by pictures of nature, "red in tooth and claw", as an anti-model. And besides, the mechanist conception of the universe can no longer consist with the idea of a real "wisdom of the cosmos", other than as a weak metaphor (ibid., Part IV).

70. Hugo Grotius, *De jure belli ac pacis*. Translation: *The Rights of War and Peace*, trans. A. C. Campbell (New York and London: Walter Dunne, 1901), Book I, Introduction, paragraph 10, p. 21.

71. Hugo Grotius, *On the Law of War and Peace (De jure belli ac pacis)*, trans. Francis W. Kelsey (Oxford, 1925); Prolegomena, paragraph 11, p. 13.

72. John Locke, *Second Treatise of Civil Government*, chapter 5.

73. Benedict Anderson, *Imagined Communities* (London: Verso, 1991), p. 24, quoting Walter Benjamin, *Illuminations* (London: Fontana, 1973), p. 263.

74. Letter to Elizabeth, 18 May 1645, A&T, IV, 202; English translation in *Descartes: Philosophical Letters*, trans. Anthony Kenny (Oxford: Oxford University Press, 1970); hereafter cited as *Letters*.

75. Letter to Elizabeth, 1 September 1645, A&T, IV, pp. 286–287.

76. *Republic*, 500.

77. I fully accept the overtones of this last phrase, not because I want to saddle modernity with the worst perversions of the twentieth century, not at all, but to mark the fact that these perversions were a twist given to a crucial theme of our age.

78. Letter to Queen Christina of Sweden, 20 November 1647, A&T, V, 85; English translation in *Letters*, p. 228. See also his *Traité des Passions de l'âme* (hereafter cited as *TPA*), art. 152.

79. *TPA,* art. 153, A&T, XI, 445–446; English translation: *The Philosophical Works of Descartes,* trans. E. S. Haldane and G. R. T. Ross (hereafter H&R) (Cambridge: Dover, 1955), I, 401–402. Descartes is following du Vair in this internalization of the honour ethic. Du Vair was partway there. "Le vraye honneur est l'esclat d'une belle & vertueuse action, qui rejaillit de nostre conscience à la veuë de ceux avec qui nous vivons, & par une reflexion en nous-mesmes, nous apporte un tesmoignage de ce que les autres croyent de nous, qui se tourne en un grand contentement d'esprit"; and so "L'ambition est une bien douce passion, qui se coule aisément és esprits les plus genereux." *La Philosophie Morale,* pp. 267–268.

80. *TPA,* art. 161, A&T, XI, 454; H&R, I, 406. See also arts. 156 and 203.

81. I have discussed Descartes' turn at greater length in *Sources of the Self* (Cambridge, Mass.: Harvard University Press, 1989), chapter 8.

82. Letter to Elizabeth, 1 September 1645, A&T, IV, 286, *Letters,* p. 170.

83. Norbert Elias, *Über den Prozess der Zivilisation* (Frankfurt: Suhrkamp, 1978); English translation: *The Civilizing Process* (Oxford: Blackwell, 1994). Numbers in parentheses in the text are page references to the German edition; if preceded by an 'E', they refer to the English translation.

84. See this discussion in my *Sources of the Self,* chapter 8.

85. Ibid., chapter 17.

86. John McManners, "Enlightenment: Secular and Christian", in J. McManners, ed., *The Oxford History of Christianity* (Oxford: Oxford University Press, 1990), pp. 277, 298.

87. Quoted in Erwin Panofsky, *Renaissance and Renascences in Western Art* (Stockholm: Almquist & Wiksells, 1965), p. 120.

3. The Great Disembedding

1. See his "Religious Evolution", chapter 2 of *Beyond Belief* (New York: Harper & Row, 1970).

2. Godfrey Lienhardt, *Divinity and Experience* (Oxford: Oxford University Press, 1961), pp. 233–235.

3. Ibid., p. 292.

4. Robert Bellah, in his recent article "What is Axial about the Axial Age?" in *Archives européennes de Sociologie* 46 (2005), no. 1, pp. 69–89, makes a similar point about what he calls "tribal religion": "Ritual in tribal societies involves the participation of all or most members of the group" (69). He contrasts these with "archaic societies", which term designates the large-scale states that arose in the ancient world, and subjugated many of the smaller face-to-face societies. These were hierarchical, and their crucial rituals focussed on crucial figures, kings or priests. But the face-to-face rituals continued, down at the base, and in Bellah's mind, do so right up to our time. I have been greatly helped here by the much richer account of religious development in Robert Bellah's work: first in his "Religious Evolution", in his collection *Beyond Belief*; and more recently in the article quoted above. The contrast I

want to make in this chapter is much simpler than the series of stages which Bellah identifies; the "tribal" and the "archaic" are fused in my category of "early" or "pre-Axial" religion. My point is to bring into sharp relief the disembedding thrust of the Axial formulations.

5. See, e.g., Lienhardt, *Divinity and Experience,* chapter 3; Roger Caillois, *L'Homme et le Sacré* (Paris: Gallimard, 1963), chapter 3.

6. This is a much commented feature of aboriginal religion in Australia; see Lucien Lévy-Bruhl, *L'Expérience mystique et les Symboles chez les Primitifs* (Paris: Alcan, 1937), pp. 180 ff.; Caillois, *L'Homme et le Sacré,* pp. 143–145; W. E. H. Stanner, *On Aboriginal Religion* (see note 14 below). The same connection to the land has been noted with the Okanagan in British Columbia; see J. Mander and E. Goldsmith, *The Case against the Global Economy* (San Francisco: Sierra Club Books, 1996), chapter 39.

7. John Stuart Mill, *On Liberty,* in Mill, *Three Essays* (Oxford: Oxford University Press, 1975), p. 77.

8. See, for instance, S. N. Eisenstadt, ed., *The Origins and Diversity of Axial Age Civilizations* (Albany: State University of New York Press, 1986); see also Bellah, "What is Axial about the Axial Age?"

9. Karl Jaspers, *Vom Ursprung und Ziel der Geschichte* (Zürich: Artemis, 1949). In using these terms, "Axial" and "post-Axial", I am groping for an expression to distinguish two quite different forms of religious life, one of which goes back much longer than the other. But I am not necessarily accepting much of what Jaspers associated with this term. For instance, I have no final view on whether we can identify a particular "Axial Age" *(Achsenzeit)* when these important changes occurred in civilizations far removed from each other more or less simultaneously. The issue of what these important changes consist in has recently come back to the centre of scholarly attention, along with the renewed concern with defining different civilizational traditions, after a long infertile period in which Western thinkers remained spell-bound by the extraordinary idea that there was a single path, from "tradition" to "modernity", which all societies were bound to travel, but some much earlier than others. See, for instance, Johann Arnason, S. N. Eisenstadt, and Björn Wittrock, *Axial Civilizations and World History* (Leiden: Brill, 2005). I don't want to take a stand in their very interesting debates, for instance, that between Eisenstadt and Wittrock, about which changes were crucial to the transitions. For my purposes in this book, the contrast between pre- and post-Axial is defined by the features I enumerate in the text.

10. Francis Oakley, *Kingship* (Oxford: Blackwell, 2006), p. 7. Bellah makes a fundamentally similar point, I believe, in his recent paper "What is Axial?": "Both tribal and archaic religions are 'cosmological', in that supernature, nature and society were all fused in a single cosmos" (p. 70).

11. Oakley, *Kingship,* pp. 50–57. See also Rémi Brague, *La Sagesse du Monde* (Paris: Fayard, 1999), pp. 219–239.

12. See Cho-Yun Hsu, "Historical Conditions of the Emergence and Crystallization of the Confucian System", in S. N. Eisenstadt, ed., *Axial Age Civilizations,* pp. 306–324.

13. In this sense, I agree with Shmuel Eisenstadt's formulation of one of the key changes of the Axial period, "the emergence, conceptualization and institutionalization of a basic tension between the transcendental and mundane orders"; with, of course, the understanding that the "transcendental" order itself changes when the tension arises. S. N. Eisenstadt, ed., *Axial Age Civilizations*, p. 1.

14. W. E. Stanner, "On Aboriginal Religion", a series of six articles in *Oceania*, vols. 30–33, 1959–1963; the expression quoted figures in article II, vol. 30, no. 4, June 1960, p. 276. See also by the same author "The Dreaming", in W. Lessa and E. Z. Vogt, eds., *Reader in Comparative Religion* (Evanston: Row, Peterson, 1958), pp. 158–167.

15. Article VI, *Oceania*, vol. 33, no. 4, June 1963, p. 269.

16. See Marcel Gauchet, *Le désenchantement du monde* (Paris: Gallimard, 1985), chapter 2. Robert Bellah ("What is Axial?", p. 70) also stresses the importance of these "archaic societies".

17. Louis Dumont, "De l'individu-hors-du-monde à l'individu-dans-le-monde," in *Essais sur l'individualisme* (Paris: Seuil, 1983).

18. I want to take account of Stanley Tambiah's reservations about Dumont's formula "individual outside the world" in relation to the Buddhist renouncer; see S. J. Tambiah, "The Reflexive and Institutional Achievements of Early Buddhism", in S. N. Eisenstadt, ed., *Axial Age Civilizations*, p. 466. The bhikkhu is outside the "world", in the sense of the life of the society-relating-to-cosmos-and-gods. But this doesn't prevent, even perhaps renders inevitable, (a) a new kind of sociability in which renouncers come together (the Sangha), and (b) relations of complementarity between renouncers and those in the world, whereby the latter can have some part in what the renouncers are directly seeking ("merit"), or even (although this may appear a deviation) whereby the spiritual power of monks can be directed to the ordinary life-goals of the laity.

19. Chapter 2, section 3.

20. See Francis Fukuyama, *Trust* (New York: Free Press, 1995).

21. Ivan Illich, *The Corruption of Christianity*, publication of the Canadian Broadcasting Corporation in the series "Ideas", January 2000. See also *The Rivers North of the Future: The Testament of Ivan Illich*, as told to David Cayley (Toronto: Anansi, 2005). I will return to this issue of "corruption" in the last chapter.

22. See René Girard, *Je vois Satan tomber comme l'éclair* (Paris: Grasset, 1999).

4. Modern Social Imaginaries

1. This chapter draws on my *Modern Social Imaginaries* (Durham: Duke University Press, 2004), to which the reader is referred for more detail in the argument. I have obviously drawn heavily on the pioneering work of Benedict Anderson in his *Imagined Communities* (London: Verso, 1991), as well as on work by Jürgen Habermas and Michael Warner, and on that of Pierre Rosanvallon and others, which I shall acknowledge as the argument unfolds.

2. John Locke, in the *Second Treatise on Government,* chapter II, defines the state of Nature as a condition "wherein all the Power and Jurisdiction is reciprocal, no one having more than another: there being nothing more evident, than that Creatures of the same species and rank promiscuously born to all the same advantages of Nature, and the use of the same faculties, should be equal one amongst another without Subordination or Subjection, unless the Lord and Master of them all, should by any manifest Declaration of his Will set one above another, and confer on him by evident and clear appointment an undoubted Right to Dominion and Sovereignty." See *Locke's Two Treatises of Government,* ed. Peter Laslett (Cambridge: Cambridge University Press, 1967), II, chapter II, para. 4, p. 287.

3. See J. G. A. Pocock, *The Ancient Constitution and the Feudal Law,* 2nd ed. (Cambridge: Cambridge University Press, 1987).

4. The term "moral economy" is borrowed from E. P. Thompson, "The Moral Economy of the English Crowd in the Eighteenth Century", *Past and Present* 50 (1971), pp. 76–136.

5. *Macbeth,* 2.3.56; 2.4.17–18 (see my *Sources of the Self,* p. 298).

6. Quoted in Louis Dupré, *Passage to Modernity* (New Haven: Yale University Press, 1993), p. 19.

7. "The sun will not overstep his measures; if he does, the Erinyes, the handmaids of Justice, will find him out." Quoted in George Sabine, *A History of Political Theory,* 3rd ed. (New York: Holt, Rinehart & Winston, 1961), p. 26.

8. *Locke's Two Treatises,* I, chapter IX, para. 86, p. 223.

9. Ibid., II, chapter II, para. 6, p. 289; see also II, chapter XI, para. 135, p. 376; and *Some Thoughts concerning Education,* para. 116.

10. *Locke's Two Treatises,* II, chapter 5, para. 34, p. 309.

11. See *Peasants into Frenchmen* (London: Chatto & Windus, 1979), chapter 28.

12. See the discussions in Hubert Dreyfus, *Being in the World* (Cambridge, Mass.: MIT Press, 1991); and John Searle, *The Construction of Social Reality* (New York: The Free Press, 1995); drawing on the work of Heidegger, Wittgenstein, and Polanyi.

13. The way in which the social imaginary extends well beyond what has been (or even can be) theorized is illustrated in Francis Fukuyama's interesting discussion of the economics of social trust. Some economies find it difficult to build large-scale non-state enterprises, because a climate of trust which extends wider than the family is absent or weak. The social imaginary in these societies marks discriminations—between kin and non-kin—for purposes of economic association, which have gone largely unremarked in the theories of the economy that we all share, including the people in those societies. And governments can be induced to adopt policies, legal changes, incentives, etc., on the assumption that forming enterprises of any scale is there in the repertory, and just needs encouragement. But the sense of a sharp boundary of mutual reliability around the family may severely restrict the repertory, however much it might be theoretically demonstrated to people that they would be better off changing their way of doing business. The implicit "map" of social space has deep fissures,

which are profoundly anchored in culture and the imaginary, beyond the reach of correction by better theory. Francis Fukuyama, *Trust* (New York: Free Press, 1995).

14. Mikhail Bakhtin, *Speech Genres and Other Late Essays* (Austin: University of Texas Press, 1986).

15. This doesn't mean that Utopias don't deal in their own kind of possibility. They may describe far-off lands or remote future societies which can't be imitated today, which we may never be able to imitate. But the underlying idea is that these things are really possible in the sense that they lie in the bent of human nature. This is what the narrator of More's book thinks: the Utopians are living according to nature (Bronislaw Baczko, *Les Imaginaires Sociaux* [Paris: Payot, 1984], p. 75). This is also what Plato thought, who provided one of the models for More's book, and for a host of other "Utopian" writings.

16. Immanuel Kant, *Kritik der reinen Vernunft*, "Von dem Schematismus der reinen Verständnisbegriffe", Berlin Academy Edition (Berlin: Walter de Gruyter, 1968), Volume III, pp. 133–139.

17. Leslie Stephen, *History of English Thought in the 18th Century* (Bristol: Thoemmes, 1997), Volume 2, p. 72.

18. *Mémoires*, p. 63, cited in Nanerl Keohane, *Philosophy and the State in France* (Princeton: Princeton University Press, 1980), p. 248.

19. Keohane, *Philosophy and the State,* pp. 249–251.

20. Of course, a large and complex thesis lies behind this flip reference. The basic idea is that Baroque culture is a kind of synthesis of the modern understanding of agency as inward and poietic, constructing orders in the world, and the older understanding of the world as cosmos, shaped by Form. With hindsight, we tend to see the synthesis as instable, as doomed to be superseded, as it was in fact.

But whatever the truth of this, we can see in Baroque culture a kind of constitutive tension, between an order which is already there, and is hierarchical, and agents who continue and complete it through their constructive activity, and hence tend to understand themselves as acting out of themselves, and thus in this respect as situated outside of hierarchy and thus equal. Hence hybrid formulations such as those of Louis above.

I have learned much from the very interesting description of Baroque art in Louis Dupré's *Passage to Modernity* (New Haven: Yale University Press, 1993), pp. 237–248. Dupré speaks of the Baroque as the "last comprehensive synthesis" between human agency and the world in which it takes place, where the meanings generated by this agency can find some relation to those we discover in the world. But it is a synthesis filled with tension and conflict.

Baroque churches focus this tension not so much on the cosmos as static order, but on God whose power and goodness are expressed in the cosmos. But this descending power is taken up and carried forward by human agency, creating "the modern tension between a divine and a human order conceived as separate centres of power" (p. 226).

Baroque culture, Dupré argues, is united by "a comprehensive spiritual vision. . . .

At the centre of it stands the person, confident in the ability to give form and structure to a nascent world. But—and here lies its religious significance—that centre remains vertically linked to a transcendent source from which, via a descending scale of mediating bodies, the human creator draws his power. This dual centre—human and divine—distinguishes the Baroque world picture from the vertical one of the Middle Ages, in which reality descends from a single transcendent point, as well as from the unproblematically horizontal one of later modernity, prefigured in some features of the Renaissance. The tension between the two centres conveys to the Baroque a complex, restless, and dynamic quality" (237).

21. Keohane, *Philosophy and the State,* pp. 164–167.

22. I have discussed this at greater length in *Sources of the Self* (Cambridge, Mass.: Harvard University Press, 1989), chapter 13.

23. Albert Hirschman, *The Passions and the Interests* (Princeton: Princeton University Press, 1977). I am greatly indebted to the discussion in this extremely interesting book.

24. Alexander Pope, *Essay on Man,* III, 9–26, 109–114; IV, 396.

25. See the interesting discussion in Mary Poovey, *A History of the Modern Fact* (Chicago: University of Chicago Press, 1998), chapter 3.

26. See J. B. Schneewind, *The Invention of Autonomy* (Cambridge: Cambridge University Press, 1998), Part I; and Pierre Manent, *La Cité de l'Homme* (Paris: Fayard, 1994), Part I.

27. Philip Carter, *Men and the Emergence of Polite Society* (London: Longman, 2001), chapters 3 and 4; Anna Bryson, *From Courtesy to Civility* (Oxford: Oxford University Press, 1998), chapter 7.

28. Indeed, what we now consider the heights of Enlightenment social science, from Montesquieu to Ferguson, was not monochrome; these writers drew not only on the modern mode of objectifying science, but also on the traditional republican understanding. Adam Smith not only formulated the "Invisible Hand", he also pondered the negative consequences of the extreme division of labour for citizenship and martial spirit "of the great body of the people"; *The Wealth of Nations* (Oxford: Clarendon Press, 1976), Volume 2, p. 787. And Ferguson, the author of one of the most influential stadial theories of commercial society, studied the conditions in which such societies could succumb to "corruption"; Adam Ferguson, *Essay on the History of Civil Society* (New Brunswick, N.J.: Transaction Books, 1980), Parts V and VI.

29. Translated by Thomas Burger (Cambridge, Mass.: MIT Press, 1989); German original: *Strukturwandel der Öffentlichkeit* (Neuwied: Luchterhand, 1962).

30. Cambridge, Mass.: Harvard University Press, 1990.

31. *Letters,* chapter 1.

32. This indicates how far the late eighteenth century notion of public opinion is from what is the object of poll research today. The phenomenon that "public opinion research" aims to measure is, in terms of my above distinction, a convergent unity, and doesn't need to emerge from discussion. It is analogous to the opinion of mankind. The ideal underlying the eighteenth century version emerges in this passage from Burke, quoted by Habermas (*Struc-*

tural Transformation, pp. 117–118): "In a free country, every man thinks he has a concern in all public matters; that he has a right to form and deliver an opinion on them. They sift, examine and discuss them. They are curious, eager, attentive and jealous; and by making such matters the daily subjects of their thoughts and discoveries, vast numbers contract a very tolerable knowledge of them, and some a very considerable one. . . . Whereas in other countries none but men whose office calls them to it having much care or thought about public affairs, and not daring to try the force of their opinions with one another, ability of this sort is extremely rare in any station of life. In free countries, there is often found more real public wisdom and sagacity in shops and manufactories than in cabinets of princes in countries where none dares to have an opinion until he comes to them."

33. Habermas, *Structural Transformation*, p. 119.

34. *Letters*, p. 41.

35. See Fox's speech, quoted in Habermas, *Structural Transformation*, pp. 65–66: "It is certainly right and prudent to consult the public opinion. . . . If the public opinion did not happen to square with mine; if, after pointing out to them the danger, they did not see it in the same light with me, or if they conceived that another remedy was preferable to mine, I should consider it as my due to my king, due to my Country, due to my honour to retire, that they might pursue the plan which they thought better, by a fit instrument, that is by a man who thought with them. . . . but one thing is most clear, that I ought to give the public the means of forming an opinion."

36. Cited in Habermas, *Structural Transformation*, p. 117.

37. Ibid., p. 82.

38. See *Letters*, pp. 40–42. Warner also points to the relationship with the impersonal agency of modern capitalism (pp. 62–63), as well as the closeness of fit between the impersonal stance and the battle against imperial corruption which was so central a theme in the colonies (pp. 65–66), in the framing of this highly over-determined mode.

39. *Letters*, p. 46.

40. See E. Kantorowicz, *The King's Two Bodies* (Princeton: Princeton University Press, 1957).

41. For an extra-European example of this kind of thing, see Clifford Geertz's *Negar* (Princeton: Princeton University Press, 1980), where the pre-Conquest Balinese state is described.

42. I have this picture of pre-modern time-consciousness, involving different modes of higher time, in "Die Modernitaet und die saekulare Zeit," in *Am Ende des Milleniums: Zeit und Modernitaeten*, ed. Krzysztof Michalski (Stuttgart: Klett Kotta, 2000), pp. 28–85.

43. As a matter of fact, excluding the religious dimension is not even a necessary condition of my concept of secular here, let alone a sufficient one. A secular association is one grounded purely on common action, and this excludes any divine grounding *for this association,* but nothing prevents the people so associated from continuing a religious form of life;

indeed, this form may even require that, e.g., political associations be purely secular. There are for instance *religious* motives for espousing a separation of church and state.

44. Mircea Eliade, *The Sacred and the Profane* (New York: Harper, 1959), pp. 80 ff.

45. Anderson borrows a term from Benjamin to describe modern profane time: he sees it as a "homogeneous, empty time". 'Homogeneity' captures the aspect I am describing here, that all events now fall into the same kind of time; but the "emptiness" of time takes us into another issue: the way in which both space and time come to be seen as "containers" which things and events contingently fill, rather than as constituted by what fills them. This latter step is part of the metaphysical imagination of modern physics, as we can see with Newton. But it is the step to homogeneity which is crucial for secularization, as I am conceiving it.

The step to emptiness is part of the objectification of time which has been so important a part of the outlook of the modern subject of instrumental reason. Time has been in a sense "spatialized". Heidegger has mounted a strong attack on this whole conception in his understanding of temporality; see especially *Sein und Zeit* (Tübingen: Niemeyer, 1926), Division 2. But distinguishing secularity from the objectification of time allows us to situate Heidegger on the modern side of the divide. Heideggerian temporality is also a mode of secular time.

46. This was not as big a step as it might seem, because in the understanding of the colonists, the rights they enjoyed as Britons were already seen as concrete specifications of "natural" rights; see Bernard Bailyn, *The Ideological Origins of the American Revolution* (Cambridge, Mass.: Harvard University Press, 1992), pp. 77–78, 187–188.

47. "Nul ne craint aux États-Unis, comme c'est le cas en France, que le rapport de délégation puisse être assimilé à une pure forme de domination"; Pierre Rosanvallon, *La Démocratie inachevée* (Paris: Gallimard, 2000), p. 28. This profound agreement on forms of representation didn't obviate very vigorous debates on structures, as we can see in the raging controversies around the new federal Constitution. It even allowed some profound issues to be raised about the nature of representation; see Bailyn, *Ideological Origins of the American Revolution,* chapter V. Nor did this basic agreement prevent popular uprisings against laws voted by assemblies, as with Shay's Rebellion. The point was that these rebellions were not attempting to set up rival modes of legitimacy; they were rather the last resort against what were seen as crying injustices which a system, however legitimate, could still enact. In this, they were rather analogous to the uprisings in ancien régime France, which will be discussed below. See the interesting treatment in Patrice Gueniffey, *La Politique de la Terreur* (Paris: Fayard, 2000), pp. 53–57.

48. François Furet, *La Révolution Française* (Paris, 1988).

49. See Simon Schama, *Citizens* (New York: Knopf, 1989), chapter 4.

50. Orlando Figes, *A People's Tragedy* (London: Penguin, 1997), pp. 98–101, 518–519.

51. Locke had already developed an embryonic form of this mechanism. In his chapter on property, he assures us that "he who appropriates land to himself by his labour, does not lessen but increase the stock of mankind. For the provisions serving to the support of hu-

mane life, produced by one acre of inclosed and cultivated land, are (to speak much within compasse) ten times more, than those, which are yielded by an acre of Land, of an equal richnesse, lying wast in common. And therefore he, that incloses Land and has a greater plenty of the conveniencys of life from ten acres, than he could have had from an hundred left to Nature, may truly be said, to give ninety acres to Mankind." *Second Treatise of Civil Government*, V.37.

52. *Du Contrat Social*, Book I, chapter 6.

53. Ibid., Book I, chapter 8; English translation from *The Essential Rousseau*, trans. Lowell Bair (New York: Signet, 1974), p. 21.

54. Ibid.; English from *The Essential Rousseau*, p. 20.

55. "Profession de foi du vicaire savoyard", *Émile* (Paris: Éditions Garnier, 1964), pp. 354–355; English translation by Barbara Foxley, in Jean-Jacques Rousseau, *Émile* (London: Dent, 1911), p. 254.

56. Quoted by Georges Lefebvre, in *Quatre-Vingt-neuf* (Paris: Éditions Sociales, 1970), pp. 245–246.

57. Montesquieu, *L'Esprit des Lois*, Book IV, chapter 5.

58. François Furet, *Penser la Révolution française* (Paris: Gallimard, 1978), p. 276.

59. Jean Starobinski, *Jean-Jacques Rousseau: La Transparence et l'Obstacle* (Paris: Gallimard, 1971).

60. J.-J. Rousseau, *Lettre à d'Alembert sur les spectacles*, in *Du Contrat Social* (Paris: Classiques Garnier, 1962), p. 225; English translation by Allan Bloom, in Jean-Jacques Rousseau, *Politics and the Arts* (Ithaca: Cornell University Press, 1968), p. 126. We can see from this how the transparency that Rousseau seeks is the enemy of "representation" in all its forms, whether it be political, theatrical, or linguistic. For certain two-place relations, transparency and unity demand that the same term figure in both places. These include the relation 'x governs y', as well as 'x portrays something before y'.

61. Mona Ozouf, *La fête révolutionnaire* (Paris: Gallimard, 1976).

62. Patrice Gueniffey, *La Politique de la Terreur*, makes good use of this distinction in his discussion.

63. Furet, *Penser*, pp. 271 ff.

64. I have explained this in greater detail in *Modern Social Imaginaries*, chapter 8.

65. Pierre Rosanvallon, *Le Sacre du Citoyen* (Paris: Gallimard, 1992); and *Le Modèle politique français* (Paris: Seuil, 2004).

66. Benedict Anderson, *Imagined Communities* (London: Verso, 1991).

67. Ibid., p. 37.

68. Martin Heidegger, "Die Zeit des Weltbildes", in *Holzwege* (Frankfurt: Niemeyer, 1972).

69. I have borrowed this terminology from Craig Calhoun; see, for instance, his "Nationalism and Ethnicity" in *American Review of Sociology*, no. 9 (1993), p. 230. The discussion in this section owes a great deal to Calhoun's recent work.

70. This has been admirably traced by Eugen Weber, *Peasants into Frenchmen* (London: Chatto, 1979).

71. Ibid.

5. The Spectre of Idealism

1. See G. A. Cohen, *Karl Marx's Theory of History* (Oxford: Oxford University Press, 1979), on whose analysis I draw in the succeeding paragraphs.

2. Adam Smith, *The Wealth of Nations* (Oxford: The Clarendon Press, 1976).

3. Marcel Mauss, *Essai sur le don,* in Mauss, *Sociologie et Anthropologie* (Paris: Quadrige/ P.U.F., 1999), Part II.

4. This is the transition which Michael Mann, in his impressive *The Sources of Social Power,* Volume I (Cambridge: Cambridge University Press, 1986), pp. 458–463, speaking of the English case, calls the move from the "coordinated to the organic state". He links it, in the context of the constitutional régimes of this period (England, Holland), to the creation of what he calls the "class-nation" (p. 480).

5. This is the process that Anna Bryson describes in her brilliant *From Courtesy to Civility* (Oxford: Oxford University Press, 1998). I have learned a great deal from this book.

6. Quoted in ibid., p. 70.

7. Bryson also makes this point; see ibid., p. 72.

8. See J. G. A. Pocock, *The Machiavellian Moment* (Princeton: Princeton University Press, 1975).

9. See Philip Carter, *Men and the Emergence of Polite Society* (London: Longman, 2001), pp. 25, 36–39.

10. See, for example, Adam Ferguson, *An Essay on the History of Civil Society* (London: Transaction Books, 1980).

11. See Albert Hirschman, *The Passions and the Interests* (Princeton: Princeton University Press, 1977).

12. See J. G. A. Pocock, *Barbarism and Religion* (Cambridge: Cambridge University Press, 1999); Karen O'Brien, *Narratives of Enlightenment* (Cambridge: Cambridge University Press, 1997); and Pierre Manent, *La Cité de l'Homme* (Paris: Fayard, 1994), Part I.

6. Providential Deism

1. In this part of the book, I am trying to deal with the phenomenon which Marcel Gauchet calls "la sortie de la religion"; see his *Le désenchantement du monde* (Paris: Gallimard, 1985). Needless to say, I treat it somewhat differently, but I have gained a lot from his account.

2. Matthew Tindal, *Christianity as Old as the Creation* (London, 1730), p. 14.

3. Roger Mercier, *La Réhabilitation de la Nature humaine, 1700–1750* (Villemonble: La Balance, 1960), pp. 105, 274–277.

4. *The Reasonableness of Christianity* (London, 1695), pp. 287–289.

5. Francis Hutcheson, *A System of Moral Philosophy,* facsimile reproduction of the 1755 edition (Hildesheim: Georg Olms, 1969), p. 184.

6. John McManners, "Enlightenment: Secular and Christian", in J. McManners, ed., *The Oxford History of Christianity* (Oxford: Oxford University Press, 1990), pp. 282–283.

7. Quoted in E. C. Mossner, *Joseph Butler and the Age of Reason* (New York: Macmillan, 1936), p. 8.

8. Michael Buckley, S.J., *At the Origins of Modern Atheism* (New Haven: Yale University Press, 1987).

9. See, for instance, Gordon Rupp, *Religion in England 1688–1791* (Oxford: The Clarendon Press; New York: Oxford University Press, 1986), p. 276, and James Downey, *The Eighteenth Century Pulpit* (Oxford: The Clarendon Press, 1969), p. 226. Downey puts it, "As defined by Archbishop Tillotson and practised by Latitudinarians throughout the eighteenth century, religion ceased to be a *mysterium tremendum et fascinans*. The church seemed to become almost a society for the reformation of manners, a place where kindred spirits met to have their moral sensibilities tuned to a finer pitch" (p. 10).

10. Quoted in Gerald Robertson Cragg, *Puritanism to the Age of Reason: A Study of Changes in Religious Thought within the Church of England, 1660–1700* (Cambridge: Cambridge University Press, 1950), p. 78n2. See also his Sermon, "His Commandments are not Grievous": "The laws of God are reasonable, that is, suitable to our nature and advantageous to our interest"; quoted in Downey, *The Eighteenth Century Pulpit,* pp. 14–15, also p. 26.

11. Clarke, commenting on the New Testament, argues that in these civilized days we are required "only to retrench our vain and sinful expenses; not to sell *all* and give to the poor, but to be charitable out of the superfluity of our plenty; not to lay down our lives, or even the comfortable enjoyments of life, but to forsake the unreasonable and unfruitful pleasures of sin." Quoted in Leslie Stephen, *History of English Thought in the 18th Century* (Bristol: Thoemmes, 1997), Volume 2, p. 340.

12. Quoted in Cragg, *Puritanism to the Age of Reason,* p. 97.

13. Henri Bremond, *Histoire Littéraire du sentiment religieux en France, depuis la fin des guerres de religion jusqu'à nos jours* (Paris: A. Colin, 11 volumes, 1967–1968).

14. Louis Dupré, *Passage to Modernity* (New Haven: Yale University Press, 1993), pp. 223–230.

15. See Henri Bremond, *Histoire Littéraire,* Volume 4, *La Conquête mystique: l'école de Port-Royal.*

16. See Edward Gibbon, *The History of the Decline and Fall of the Roman Empire,* chapter XXXVI (London: Penguin Edition, 1994), II, p. 418.

17. Matthew Tindal, *Christianity as Old as the Creation,* p. 16.

18. Quoted from Perry Miller, *The New England Mind: The Seventeenth Century* (Cambridge, Mass: Harvard University Press, 1967), p. 41.

19. To be fair to Tindal and Deists, the distrust of disinterested love was much more widespread, and played an important part in more orthodox Augustinian theology. Bossuet

justifies his vigorous persecution of Fénelon's "amour pur" by arguing that God's law has to hold us at least partly out of self-interest.

20. *L'Institution de la religion Chrestienne,* Book III, chapter 19.

21. This way had been prepared by the preaching of Tillotson, whose polemic against Papist "idolatry", against transubstantiation and the authority of the Church, prepared the ground for the arguments of later writers who were frankly anti-Christian; Leslie Stephen, *History of English Thought in the 18th Century,* Volume 1, pp. 78–79; E. C. Mossner, *Bishop Butler and the Age of Reason* (New York: Macmillan, 1936), pp. 22–23.

22. Tindal, *Christianity as Old as the Creation,* chapter 4.

23. Whichcote was drawing here on the Greek fathers, with their notion of theiosis.

24. See "Die Zeit des Weltbildes", *Holzwege* (Frankfurt: Niemeyer, 1972).

25. Francis Hutcheson, *A System of Moral Philosophy,* p. 217.

26. "À commencer depuis les dernières années du Cardinal de Richelieu jusqu'à celles qui ont suivi la mort de Louis XIV, il s'est fait dans nos arts, dans nos esprits, dans nos moeurs, comme dans notre gouvernement, une révolution générale, qui doit servir de marque éternelle à la véritable gloire de notre patrie"; quoted in J. G. A. Pocock, *Barbarism and Religion* (Cambridge: Cambridge University Press, 1999), Volume II, p. 86.

27. As Pocock remarks, speaking of 'manners' and 'moeurs' together: "This keyword denoted a complex of shared practices and values, which secured the individual as social being and furnished to society surrounding him with an indefinitely complex and flexible texture; more powerfully even than laws, manners rendered civil society capable of absorbing and controlling human action and belief, even when grounded in the allegedly immediate experience of divine presence." *Barbarism and Religion,* Volume II, pp. 19–20.

28. Quoted in Pocock, *Barbarism and Religion,* Volume II, p. 203.

29. "There arose a systematic and resolute identification of the religious with the social, equally compatible with liberal and with absolutist views of the political authority with which society was governed; the distinction was of secondary importance compared with the paramount need to maintain that the spirit manifested itself, and even became incarnate, only through social channels, reasonable, humane and obedient to authority, and never in ways subversive of the human and sociable order." Pocock, *Barbarism and Religion,* Volume I, p. 26.

30. Abbé Raynal, *Histoire philosphique et politique des établissements et du commerce des Européens dans les Deux Indes* (1770); quote taken from the edition of Geneva, 1780, t.X, pp. 127 ff.; quoted in Marcel Gauchet, *La Religion dans la démocratie* (Paris: Gallimard, 1998), pp. 34–35.

31. Gibbon, *The History of the Decline and Fall of the Roman Empire,* Volume 1, p. 56.

32. Ibid., Volume 1, p. 524.

33. Ibid., Volume 3, p. 90.

34. H.-X. Arquillière, *L'Augustinisme politique* (Paris: Vrin, 1934).

35. This is at least the view of Francis Oakley; see his *Kingship* (Oxford: Blackwell, 2006), pp. 91, 98–99.

36. Arquillière quotes Isidore of Seville: "Ceterum, intra ecclesiam, potestates necessariae non essent, nisi ut, quod non prevalet sacerdos efficere per doctrine sermonem, potestas hoc imperet per discipline terrorem." *L'Augustinisme politique*, p. 142.

37. John O'Malley, *Trent and All That* (Cambridge, Mass.: Harvard University Press, 2000), describes this continually recurring culture of reform; see especially chapter 1.

38. Marcel Gauchet also gives a crucial importance to this long drive for Reform, which runs through the late Middle Ages and the early modern time, in the "disenchanting of the world", although I'm not sure if we don't conceive it slightly differently. See *Le désenchantement du monde* (Paris: Gallimard, 1985), pp. 221–231.

39. "This world: a monster of energy, without beginning, without end; . . . out of the simplest forms striving toward the most complex, out of the stillest, most rigid, coldest forms toward the hottest, most turbulent, most self-contradictory, and then again returning home to the simple out of this abundance, out of the play of contradictions back to the joy of concord, still affirming itself in this uniformity of its courses and its years, blessing itself as that which must return eternally, as a becoming which knows no satiety, no disgust, no weariness: this my *Dionysian* world of the eternally self-creating, the eternally self-destroying, this mystery world of the twofold voluptuous delight, my "beyond good and evil", without goal, unless the joy of the circle itself is a goal; without will, unless a ring feels good will towards itself—do you want a *name* for this world? . . . *This world is the will to power—and nothing besides!* And you yourselves are also this will to power—and nothing besides!" *The Will to Power*, trans. Walter Kaufmann and R. J. Hollingdale (New York: Random House, 1967), para. 1067.

40. Quoted in Ross Harrison, *Bentham* (London: Routledge, 1983), p. 276 (see my *Sources of the Self*, p. 331).

41. *Pompée*, II.i.370–373.

42. Modified from *Pompey*, trans. Katherine Philips (Dublin: Samuel Dancer, 1663).

43. *Mes Pensées*, 1131–1132, quoted in Mercier, *La Réhabilitation de la Nature humaine*, p. 252.

44. Quoted in ibid., pp. 382–383.

45. *De l'Esprit des Lois*, IV.2.

46. Translation slightly modified from *The Spirit of the Laws*, trans./ed. Anne M. Cohler, Basia Carolyn Miller, and Harold Samuel Stone (Cambridge: Cambridge University Press, 1989), pp. 31 f.

47. *Mes Pensées*, 1285, quoted in Mercier, *La Réhabilitation de la Nature humaine*, pp. 249–250.

48. Quoted in Ronald Clark, *Bertrand Russell* (London: Cape, 1975), p. 190 (see *Sources of the Self*, pp. 407–408).

49. "Zwei Dinge erfüllen das Gemüth mit immer neuer und zunehmender Bewunderung und Ehrfurcht, je öfter und anhaltender sich das Nachdenken damit beschäftigt: der bestirnte Himmel über mir und das moralische Gesetz in mir." *Kritik der praktischen Vernunft*, Berlin Academy Edition (Berlin: de Gruyter, 1968), V, 161.

50. For discussions of pitié, see *Discours sur l'origine et les fondements de l'inégalité parmi les hommes,* ed. Garnier-Flammarion (Paris, 1971), pp. 197–198, and *Émile,* ed. Classiques-Garnier (Paris, 1964), p. 261. See also the paean to "conscience" by the *vicaire savoyard* in ibid., pp. 354–355.

51. *De l'Homme,* II.vi, pp. 146–147 (see *Sources of the Self,* p. 328).

52. Rousseau, *Discours sur l'origine et les fondements de l'inégalité.*

53. I return to a discussion of this kind of move in human history, into a new, more universal space which inspires us to a new kind of moral action; see Chapter 15, section 7.

54. John Rawls, in his *Theory of Justice,* makes it an important condition of a correct theory that it stabilize itself over time, that is, that in a society in which justice in this form is established, the commitment to it will grow rather than decline. I will discuss this expectation of self-stabilization more fully later, in Chapter 17.

55. *Sources of the Self* (Cambridge, Mass.: Harvard University Press, 1989).

56. See ibid., chapter 11.

57. Ibid., chapters 15, 20.

58. Jean Delumeau, *Le Péché et la Peur* (Paris: Fayard, 1983), chapter 8.

59. The more radical Deists also joined in this repulsion at hyper-Augustinian Christianity, putting it on a level with Atheism. Jefferson wrote: "I can never join Calvin in addressing *his* god. He was indeed, an atheist, which I can never be; or rather, his religion was daemonism. If ever a man worshipped a false god, he did. The being described in his five points, is not the god whom you and I acknowledge and adore, the creator and benevolent governor of the world; but a daemon of malignant spirit. It would be more pardonable to believe in no god at all, than to blaspheme him by the atrocious attributes of Calvin." Paine took the same line in his *Age of Reason:* "As to the Christian system of faith, it appears to me as a species of Atheism—a sort of religious denial of God. It . . . is as near to Atheism as twilight is to darkness." Quoted in Michael Buckley, S.J., *At the Origins of Modern Atheism* (New Haven: Yale University Press, 1987).

60. David Hume, *Enquiry concerning the Principles of Morals,* Section IX, para. 219; in David Hume, *Enquiries,* ed. L. A. Selby-Bigge (Oxford: The Clarendon Press, 1902), pp. 269–270. Hume's point might be sharpened into the rhetorical question: "Would you invite St. Francis to dinner?" In fact, even Francis' protector, Cardinal Ugolino, had reason to ask himself this question. On one occasion, when Francis had been induced, rather reluctantly, to dine at the Cardinal's table, with various nobles, knights, and chaplains, he left discreetly beforehand, and begged in the streets. Returning to the dinner, he handed around some of the crusts and other alms he had received. The Cardinal was, needless to say, deeply offended. There was a point to this eccentric behaviour, of course; it all related to the impending Papal approval of the more radically ascetic features of the Franciscan Rule. But it might perhaps have been more delicately made. See Adrian House, *Francis of Assisi* (London: Chatto, 2000), p. 244.

61. "Innerweltliche Askese", in *Die Protestantische Ethik und der Geist des Kapitalismus*

(Weinheim: Beltz Athenäum, 2000), p. 119; see the translation by Talcott Parsons, *The Protestant Ethic and the Spirit of Capitalism* (New York: Scribner, 1958), p. 151.

62. Quoted in Mercier, *La Réhabilitation de la Nature humaine,* p. 59. Later, the Epicurean tradition was taken up in a kind of synthesis with Stoicism, which allowed it to become part of an activist creed, by Maupertuis, for instance; and in that form takes its place in the mainstream Enlightenment; see Mercier, ibid., pp. 345–346.

63. Leslie Stephen, *History of English Thought in the 18th Century,* Volume 1, pp. 447–448.

7. The Impersonal Order

1. Bernard Williams, *Truth and Truthfulness* (Princeton: Princeton University Press, 2002), chapter 7.

2. See, for instance, Étienne B. de Condillac, *Essai sur l'origine des Connoissances humaines* (Paris: Vrin, 2002); Lord Monboddo, *Of the Origin and Progress of Language* (Edinburgh, 1786); J. G. Herder, *Abhandlung über den Ursprung der Sprache* (Reclam, 1966), English translation: *Essay on the Origin of Language* (Chicago: University of Chicago Press, 1966).

3. Baruch Spinoza, *Tractatus Theologico-politicus,* trans. S. Shirley (Leiden: Brill, 1989).

4. H. R. Trevor-Roper, ed., *The Decline and Fall of the Fall of the Roman Empire,* by Edward Gibbon (New York: Twayne, 1963), p. x.

5. I owe a lot here to the brilliant discussion in J. G. A. Pocock's *Barbarism and Religion* (Cambridge: Cambridge University Press, 1999). An interesting account of the "Enlightened narrative" occurs in Volume 2, chapter 25.

6. E.g., ibid., pp. 84, 201.

7. Edward Gibbon, *The History of the Decline and Fall of the Roman Empire* (Penguin Books, 1994), Volume 3, pp. 515, 516.

8. Pocock, *Barbarism and Religion,* Volume I, p. 75.

9. Spinoza, *Tractatus Theologico-politicus;* see also Yirmiahu Yovel, *Spinoza and Other Heretics,* Volume 1, *The Marrano of Reason* (Princeton: Princeton University Press, 1989), pp. 131–132.

10. Peter Brown, *The Body and Society* (New York: Columbia University Press, 1988), p. 34.

11. Ezekiel 36:6, quoted in Brown, *The Body and Society,* p. 35. See also the New Testament references to "the hardness of your hearts"; also Kallistos Ware, *The Kingdom of the Heart,* the John Main Lectures 2002, published by the World Community for Christian Meditation (London, 2002).

12. See Brown, *The Body and Society,* passim, for a penetrating account of this change.

13. R. F. Capon, *An Offering of Uncles: The Priesthood of Adam and the Shape of the World* (New York: Sheed and Ward, 1967).

14. Martha Nussbaum, in her very interesting discussion of Augustine, *Upheavals of Thought* (Cambridge: Cambridge University Press, 2001), pp. 536–539, shows how he sees his life as changed by chance encounters. A person can "happen across" himself. See also Peter Brown, *Augustine of Hippo,* 1967 edition (Berkeley: University of California Press, 1967), p. 155.

15. Nussbaum, *Upheavals of Thought,* p. 528.

16. See John Zizioulas, *Being as Communion* (Crestwood, N.Y.: St. Vladimir's Seminary Press, 1985), chapter 1.

17. See Alexis de Tocqueville's famous chapter on this transition, in *La Démocratie en Amérique* (Paris: Garnier Flammarion, 1981), Volume II, Part 2, chapter 2, pp. 125–127.

18. David Martin, *Christian Language and Its Mutations* (Aldershot: Ashgate, 2002), p. 175.

19. See Ivan Illich, *The Corruption of Christianity,* publication of the Canadian Broadcasting Corporation in the series "Ideas", January 2000. See also *The Rivers North of the Future: The Testament of Ivan Illich,* as told to David Cayley (Toronto: Anansi, 2005). I will return to this issue of "corruption" in the last chapter.

20. Jerry Schneewind, *The Invention of Autonomy* (Cambridge: Cambridge University Press, 1998).

21. The tension I've been describing here between impersonal orders and faith in a personal God is part of what has accredited the idea that Christian faith was more at home in the Middle Ages. But this is a terrible illusion. *This* source of tension was not there; but as the reference to the importance of the Christian warrior should make clear, other tensions were. The most superficial acquaintance with mediaeval history, and the knock-down, drag-out struggles between Popes and Kings, should put paid to this idea.

22. See my *Sources of the Self* (Cambridge, Mass.: Harvard University Press, 1989), pp. 159–164.

23. See Francis Oakley, "Christian Theology and the Newtonian Science", *Church History* 30 (1961), pp. 433–457.

24. See my discussion in "Understanding the Other: A Gadamerian View on Conceptual Schemes", in Jeff Malpas et al., eds., *Gadamer's Century: Essays in Honour of Hans-Georg Gadamer* (Cambridge, Mass.: MIT Press, 2002), pp. 279–297.

25. Adam Smith, *The Wealth of Nations* (Oxford: Clarendon Press, 1976); Adam Ferguson, *Essay on the History of Civil Society* (New Brunswick, N.J.: Transaction Books, 1980), Parts V and VI.

26. Martin, *Christian Language and Its Mutations,* p. 173.

27. See J. G. A. Pocock, *Barbarism and Religion,* on the slide out of orthodoxy among refugee Huguenots in Holland, e.g., Jean Leclerc and Jacques Bernard.

28. George Tyrrell, *Christianity at the Cross-Roads* (1909), quoted in Alister McGrath, *The Twilight of Atheism* (New York and London: Doubleday, 2004), p. 140.

29. Nicholas Lash, *Holiness, Speech and Silence* (Burlington, Vt.: Ashgate, 2004).

30. La Mettrie, *L'Homme Machine,* quoted in McGrath, *Twilight of Atheism,* p. 33.

31. Stanley Hauerwas, *With the Grain of the Universe* (Grand Rapids: Brazos Press, 2001), chapter 1. See also Michael Buckley, *At the Origins of Modern Atheism* (New Haven: Yale University Press, 1987).

32. See the discussion in Hauerwas, *With the Grain,* chapter 1; also Alasdair MacIntyre, *Three Rival Versions of Moral Enquiry* (Notre Dame, Ind.: University of Notre Dame Press, 1990); John Milbank, *Theology and Social Theory,* 2nd ed. (Oxford: Blackwell, 2006); Catherine Pickstock, *After Writing* (Oxford: Blackwell, 1998); Fergus Kerr, *Aquinas* (Oxford: Blackwell, 2001); David Burrell, *Analogy and Philosophical Language* (New Haven: Yale University Press, 1973).

8. The Malaises of Modernity

1. E. P. Thompson, *The Making of the English Working Class* (Harmondsworth: Penguin Books, 1968), p. 13.

2. John Hale, *The Civilization of Europe in the Renaissance* (New York: Atheneum, 1994), p. 360.

3. So much so, that this now anthropocentrized sense of civilization develops its own genetic story, in which its religious antecedents are played down. The rise of this consciousness is seen as a fruit of the Renaissance, arising in a normal process of maturation out of the humanism of the late mediaeval period. The Reformation is either ignored, or else it appears as a stage in the process, through a very one-sided portrait, in which its individuating, liberating attack on mediaeval Catholic authority and the sacred is anachronistically presented just as a sort of proto-Enlightenment, the features of the later, anthropocentric "liberal" Protestantism being read back into the founding age.

A story like this can be told, in which freedom and reason broaden down from precedent to precedent, a kind of Whig history of the buffered self. There is some truth to it, because the pious drive to order did eventually mutate into the anthropocentric version. And as always in these matters, the chronology is not neat. There were important figures in the tradition who, even early on, seem to be developing an ethic of constructed order somewhat at a distance from the theological sources. I am thinking, for instance, of Justus Lipsius, and what we call "neo-Stoicism", where the sources in ancient philosophy are explicitly acknowledged (discussed in Chapter 2). Characteristically, Lipsius managed to slide back and forth between Catholic and Protestant milieux, so that his ultimate allegiance is still in some doubt, which probably means that this issue didn't mean all that much to him. In this, he prefigures Leibniz, but a whole century before.

But this Whig story leaves out something essential. First this, that the main motor of the drive for order and disenchantment was the religious one. If it had been left to exceptional figures like Lipsius, who could draw on a largely ancient-philosophical inspiration, the transformation would have taken a lot longer, and maybe not come at all. The movements which could draw masses of people, cultivated or not, into the slip-stream of disenchantment were the religious ones, Catholic and Protestant.

Secondly, as a result of this, the new humanism bears the mark of its origins, as I argued above; not only in being committed to goals of active, instrumental ordering of self and world, but also in the central place within it of universalism and benevolence.

Notwithstanding all this, and in spite of its crucial deficiencies, it is possible to put together a story of the slow, incremental, linear advance of disenchantment and anthropocentrism.

4. See the discussion in Peter Berger, *A Far Glory: The Quest for Faith in an Age of Credulity* (New York: The Free Press, 1992), pp. 37 ff. Of course, "fragilization" here means only that the issue of a possible change of belief is kept alive for us in a way which has few precedents in earlier ages; and as a consequence, there are more "conversions" in both directions in the lives of individuals, and between generations. But this says nothing about the firmness or depth of the faith (or atheist belief) once espoused. On the contrary, the faith which confronts alternatives can be deeper and stronger. See Chapter 15, note 19, where I take up an objection which Hans Joas makes to Berger in this regard.

5. Max Weber, "Science as a Vocation", in H. H. Gerth and C. Wright Mills, eds., *From Max Weber* (New York: Oxford University Press, 1946), p. 155.

6. Luc Ferry, *L'Homme-Dieu ou le sens de la vie* (Paris: Grasset, 1996), p. 19. I discuss this at greater length in Chapter 18.

7. Jean-Paul Sartre, *La Nausée* (Paris: Gallimard, 1938).

8. See César Graña, *Modernity and Its Discontents* (New York: Harper Torchbooks, 1964).

9. See Mona Ozouf, *La fête révolutionnaire* (Paris: Gallimard, 1976).

10. *Letters on the Aesthetic Education of Man,* ed. and trans. Elizabeth Wilkinson and L. A. Willoughby (Oxford: Clarendon Press, 1967), Letter VI.

11. Ibid., Letter XV.

12. *Philosophical Regimen,* in *Life, Unpublished Letters, and Philosophical Regimen of Anthony, Earl of Shaftesbury,* ed. Benjamin Rand (London: S. Sonnenschein, 1900), p. 54.

13. Nicholaus Ludwig von Zinzendorf, in *M. Aug. Gottlieb Spangenbergs Apologetische Schluss-Schrift . . .* (Leipzig and Görlitz, 1752); photographically reprinted as Nikolaus Ludwig von Zinzendorf, *Ergänzungsbände zu den Hauptschriften,* ed. Erich Beyreuther and Gerhard Meyer, vol. 3 (Hildesheim, 1964), p. 181.

14. F. Schiller, *Letters on the Aesthetic Education of Man,* ed. and trans. Elizabeth Wilkinson and L. A. Willoughby (Oxford: Clarendon Press, 1967).

15. M. H. Abrams in his remarkable discussion of this period points out how widespread and important these spiral narratives were; see *Natural Supernaturalism* (New York: Norton, 1971), especially chapters 3 and 4. He also points out how much they drew from earlier models, including Christian understandings of Heilsgeschichte.

16. Michael Buckley, *At the Origins of Modern Atheism* (New Haven: Yale University Press, 1987).

17. *Zur Genealogie der Moral*, III, 28: "Die Sinnlosigkeit des Leidens, *nicht* das Leiden, war der Fluch, der bisher über der Menschheit ausgebreitet lag" (München: Goldmann, Gelbe Taschenbücher), Volume 991, p. 135.

18. See the interesting discussion of Max Weber in the insightful study by Eyal Chowers, *The Modern Self in the Labyrinth* (Cambridge, Mass.: Harvard University Press, 2004), chapter 3. See also Marcel Gauchet, *Le désenchantement du monde* (Paris: Gallimard, 1985).

19. Alexis de Tocqueville, *La Démocratie en Amérique* (Paris: Garnier Flammarion, 1985), Volume II, Part IV, chapter 6, pp. 383–388.

20. See *Also Sprach Zarathustra,* Zarathustra Vorrede, section 5 (München: Goldmann, Gelbe Taschenbücher), Volume 403, p. 16.

9. The Dark Abyss of Time

1. The Platonic derived theory of things as manifestations of the ideas can consort easily with the popular beliefs about enchantment. Both can make sense of the notion that meaningful causal forces inhere in the objects around us. Plato-inspired views about the cosmos could serve as the high culture, theorized pendant to popular enchantment.

2. See Paolo Rossi, *The Dark Abyss of Time,* trans. Lydia Cochrane (Chicago: University of Chicago Press, 1984), pp. 108–109. Did Buffon borrow from Shakespeare? Consider this speech from *The Tempest,* where Prospero questions Miranda about what she remembers: "What sees thou else / In the dark backward and abyss of time?" (Act I, Scene II, ll. 49–50). I owe this reference to Lindsay Waters.

3. Denis Diderot, *Le Rêve de d'Alembert,* in *Oeuvres,* p. 299.

4. Modified from *D'Alembert's Dream,* trans. Jacques Barzun and Ralph H. Bowen, in *Rameau's Nephew and Other Works* (Indianapolis and London: Hackett, 2001), p. 117.

5. Ibid., chapter 22.

6. Michael Buckley, *At the Origins of Modern Atheism* (New Haven: Yale University Press, 1987).

7. Rossi, *The Dark Abyss,* p. 69.

8. Ibid., pp. 42–44.

9. See, for instance, the "rapture" novels of Tim LaHaye and Jerry Jenkins. The first in the series was *Left Behind: A Novel of the Earth's Last Days* (Wheaton, Ill.: Tyndale House, 1995).

10. Condillac cited in Rossi, *The Dark Abyss,* pp. 44–45.

11. See Rossi, *The Dark Abyss,* chapter 7, and Stephen Jay Gould, *Time's Arrow, Time's Cycle* (Cambridge, Mass.: Harvard University Press, 1987), chapter 2.

12. Rossi, *The Dark Abyss,* chapter 26.

13. Ibid., pp. 36–37.

14. Ibid., p. 185.

15. Clarence Glacken, *Traces on the Rhodian Shore* (Berkeley: University of California Press, 1967), p. 117. The quote here is reproduced by Glacken from Mircea Eliade, *Cosmos and History* (New York: Harper, 1959).

16. Glacken, *Traces on the Rhodian Shore,* pp. 312–313.

17. Ibid., pp. 481, 483.

18. Ibid., p. 310.

19. Roderick Nash, *Wilderness and the American Mind* (New Haven: Yale University Press, 1973), pp. 11–13.

20. Rossi, *The Dark Abyss,* p. 112.

21. Simon Schama, *Landscape and Memory* (New York: Knopf, 1995), pp. 424–433.

22. Ibid., p. 433.

23. Ibid., pp. 449, 453.

24. Edmund Burke, *A Philosophical Enquiry into the Origins of our Ideas of the Sublime and Beautiful* (London: R. and J. Dodsley, 1757), Book IV, chapter vii; Immanuel Kant, *Kritik der Urteilskraft,* Berlin Academy Edition (Berlin: Gruyter, 1968), Volume V, p. 262.

25. This is closely related to what I identified as axis II.3 in the sketch of the previous chapter.

26. Burke, *Philosophical Enquiry;* Kant, *Kritik,* pp. 261–262.

27. Schama, *Landscape and Memory,* chapter 9.

28. Charles Rosen, "Now, Voyager", in *The New York Review of Books,* November 6, 1986, p. 58.

29. Quoted from Nash, *Wilderness and the American Mind,* chapter 3.

30. Ibid., pp. 61–62.

31. Quoted from Max Oelschlaeger, *The Idea of Wilderness* (New Haven: Yale University Press, 1991), p. 148.

32. Ibid., pp. 152–153, 158.

33. Glacken, *Traces on the Rhodian Shore,* pp. 198–199.

34. This connects with axis III.1 in my sketch above.

35. Rossi, *The Dark Abyss,* chapter 17.

36. Johann Gottfried Herder, *Vom Erkennen und Empfinden der menschlichen Seele,* in *Herders Sämmtliche Werke,* ed. Bernard Suphan, 15 vols. (Berlin: Weidmann, 1877–1913), VIII, 200.

37. Quoted in M. H. Abrams, *The Mirror and the Lamp* (Oxford: Oxford University Press, 1953), p. 65.

38. *Tintern Abbey,* ll. 100–102.

39. Friedrich Hölderlin, *Hyperion* (Frankfurt-am-Main: Fischer, 1962), Book I, second letter, p. 9.

40. As A. N. Wilson puts it in a recent work, "If one had to isolate a single all-consuming

idea which has taken hold of the human race in the post-political era in which we now live, it is the interrelatedness of natural forms—the fact that we all live on this planet together—human beings, mammals, fish, insects, trees—all dependent on one another, all very unlikely to have a second chance of life either beyond the grave or through reincarnation, and therefore aware of the responsibilities incumbent upon custodians of the Earth"; in *The Victorians* (London: Hutchinson, 2002), p. 230.

41. Oelschlaeger, *The Idea of Wilderness*, p. 158.

42. Henry David Thoreau, *Walden* (Princeton: Princeton University Press, 1973), pp. 210, 219; quoted in Schama, *Landscape and Memory*, p. 571.

43. "Walking", pp. 228–229; quoted in Oelschlaeger, *The Idea of Wilderness*, pp. 165–166.

44. "Zwei Dinge erfüllen das Gemüth mit immer neuer und zunehmender Bewunderung und Ehrfurcht, je öfter und anhaltender sich das Nachdenken damit beschäftigt: *der bestirnte Himmel über mir und das moralische Gesetz in mir.*" *Kritik der praktischen Vernunft*, Berlin Academy Edition (Berlin: Walter Gruyter, 1968), p. 161.

45. Marcel Gauchet, *L'inconscient cérébral* (Paris: Seuil, 1992).

46. I have tried to explain this change in *Sources of the Self* (Cambridge, Mass.: Harvard University Press, 1989), chapter 11, pp. 189–190.

47. Ibid., pp. 19–22, 37–38.

48. Ibid., p. 72.

49. See the discussion in Nash, *Wilderness and the American Mind*, p. 23. Nash quotes Alexis de Tocqueville, *Journey to America*, ed. J. P. Mayer, trans. George Lawrence (New Haven: Yale University Press, 1960), p. 335; and *Democracy in America*, ed. Phillips Bradley (New York: Knopf, 1945), Volume 2, p. 74.

50. Chapter 4 of Randy Connolly's unpublished doctoral dissertation makes this point. But it is also accessible in Randy Connolly, "The Rise and Persistence of the Technological Community Ideal," *Online Communities: Commerce, Community Action, and the Virtual University*, ed. Chris Werry and Miranda Mowbray (Upper Saddle River, N.J.: Prentice Hall, 2001).

10. The Expanding Universe of Unbelief

1. Charles Baudelaire, "Correspondances", in *Les Fleurs du Mal;* see his *Oeuvres Complètes* (Paris: Gallimard, Pléiade edition, 1975), p. 11.

2. Earl Wasserman, *The Subtler Language* (Baltimore: Johns Hopkins University Press, 1968), pp. 10–11.

3. Thus Wordsworth tells of how he
> would stand
> If the night blackened with a coming storm,
> Beneath some rock, listening to notes that are

The ghostly language of the ancient earth
Or make their dim abode in distant winds.
        (*The Prelude*, ll. 307-311)

4. Charles Rosen and Henri Zerner, *Romanticism and Realism* (New York: Norton, 1984), p. 58.

5. Ibid., pp. 68 ff.

6. Ibid., p. 67.

7. F. Schiller, *Letters on the Aesthetic Education of Man,* ed. and trans. Elizabeth Wilkinson and L. A. Willoughby (Oxford: Clarendon Press, 1967).

8. Ibid., letter 16.

9. Hans Urs von Balthasar, *Herrlichkeit (The Glory of the Lord)* (Einsiedeln: Johannes Verlag, 1962).

10. I have found the discussion very helpful in David Martin, *The Breaking of the Image: A Sociology of Christian Theory and Practice* (Oxford: Basil Blackwell, 1980), pp. 135 ff.

11. Stefan Collini, *Public Moralists: Political Thought and Intellectual Life in Britain, 1850–1930* (Oxford: Clarendon Press, 1991), p. 74.

12. G. Lessing, *Werke,* ed. Pedersen and von Olshausen, Volume 23, p. 49. The ditch is uncrossable, because "zufällige Geschichtswahrheiten können der Beweis von notwendigen Vernunftwahrheiten nie werden"; ibid., p. 47.

13. Samuel Hynes, *The Edwardian Turn of Mind* (London: Pimlico, 1968), p. 139.

14. Collini, *Public Moralists,* p. 192.

15. Douglas Hofstadter, "Reductionism and Religion", in *Behavioral and Brain Sciences* 3 (1980), p. 434.

16. The awe, but also the sense of connection, emerges in these reflections of Charles Lindbergh: "I know myself as mortal, but this raises the question: 'What is I?' Am I an individual, or am I an evolving life stream composed of countless selves? . . . As one identity, I was born in AD 1902. But as AD twentieth-century man, I am billions of years old. The life I consider as myself has existed through past eons with unbroken continuity. Individuals are custodians of the life stream—temporal manifestations of far greater being, forming from and returning to their essence like so many dreams. . . . I recall standing on the edge of a deep valley in the Hawaiian island of Maui, thinking that a life stream is like a mountain river—springing from hidden sources, born out of the earth, touched by stars, merging, blending, evolving in the shape momentarily seen." He sums up: "I am form and I am formless. I am life and I am matter, mortal and immortal. I am one and I am many—myself and humanity in flux. . . . After my death, the molecules of my being will return to the earth and sky. They came from the stars. I am of the stars." Quoted in Gore Vidal, "The Eagle is Grounded", in *The Times Literary Supplement,* no. 4987, October 30, 1998, p. 6.

We can see how Lindbergh stands fully within the modern cosmic imaginary. His experience of nature, e.g., on Maui, immediately suggests to him the depth of the universe and our dark genesis from it.

17. Michel Foucault, *Les Mots et les Choses* (Paris: Gallimard, 1966).

18. Martin Marty, *The Modern Schism* (New York: Harper, 1969).

19. See *Sources of the Self* (Cambridge, Mass.: Harvard University Press, 1989), chapter 13.

20. Alexis de Tocqueville, *La Démocratie en Amérique* (Paris: Garnier Flammarion, 1981), Volume II, Part 2, chapter 2, p. 385.

21. Hegel makes this feature of the traditional honour ethics central to his dialectic of the master and the slave. In the original struggle for recognition between warriors, each shows that he is worthy of such recognition precisely by setting his life at hazard. The key to dignity is this "Daransetzen". *Phänomenologie des Geistes,* chapter IV.

22. James Miller, *The Passion of Michel Foucault* (New York: Simon & Schuster, 1993).

11. Nineteenth-Century Trajectories

1. J. S. Mill, *Autobiography* (New York: Columbia University Press, 1960), p. 60.

2. See Simon Heffer, *Moral Desperado: A Life of Thomas Carlyle* (London: Weidenfeld & Nicholson, 1995).

3. A. Abbott Ikeler, *Puritan Temper and Transcendental Faith: Carlyle's Literary Vision* (Columbus: Ohio State University Press, 1972), pp. 72–80.

4. Heffer, *Moral Desperado,* p. 293.

5. *Sartor Resartus* (Berkeley: University of California Press, 2000), p. 144.

6. A. N. Wilson, *God's Funeral* (New York: Norton, 1999), p. 62.

7. *Sartor,* p. 124.

8. Quoted in Ikeler, *Puritan Temper,* p. 55 (from the "Hero as Prophet").

9. Park Honan, *Matthew Arnold: A Life* (New York: McGraw-Hill, 1981), p. 88.

10. Ibid., pp. 126–127.

11. Ibid., p. 140.

12. *Culture and Anarchy* (New York: AMS Press, 1970), p. 48.

13. *The Poems of Matthew Arnold,* ed. Kenneth Allott (London: Longmans, 1965), pp. 518–534.

14. Ibid., pp. 285–294.

15. Lionel Trilling, *Matthew Arnold* (New York: Norton, 1939), chapter IV.

16. *Culture and Anarchy,* Preface, p xi.

17. Ibid., p. 11.

18. Ibid., p. xiv.

19. Ibid., p. xli.

20. Clinton Mahann, *Matthew Arnold: A Literary Life* (London: Macmillan, 1998), p. 112.

21. Mrs. Humphry Ward, *Robert Elsmere* (Lincoln: University of Nebraska Press, 1967). Page references in the text are to this edition.

22. Lionel Trilling, in his interesting discussion of *Robert Elsmere* in his *Matthew Arnold* (New York: Norton, 1939), p. 308, makes this point very tellingly.

23. See the "Editor's Introduction" to *Robert Elsmere*, p. xix.

24. Wilson, *God's Funeral*, p. 4. Wilson takes the title of his book from a poem by Thomas Hardy, which eloquently expresses the sense of mourning and loss at the decline of the faith.

25. See the very interesting discussion in J. W. Burrow, *The Crisis of Reason* (New Haven: Yale University Press, 2000), Prologue.

26. See Steve Bruce, *God Is Dead* (Oxford: Blackwell, 2002), p. 42. I discuss this view in the next chapter.

27. Quoted in Jane Millgate, *Macaulay* (London/Boston: Routledge and Kegan Paul, 1973), p. 137.

28. George Otto Trevelyan, *The Life and Letters of Lord Macaulay* [1876], enlarged and complete edition (London: Longmans, Green, 1908), p. 33.

29. Macaulay's values in this regard can be gleaned from the inscription he composed for the statue in Calcutta of his friend and ally, Lord William Bentinck:

> To William Cavendish Bentinck,
>> Who, during seven years, ruled India with eminent Prudence,
>>> Integrity and Benevolence:
>> Who, placed at the head of a great Empire, never laid aside the
>>> simplicity and moderation of a private citizen:
>> Who infused into Oriental despotism the spirit of British Freedom:
>> Who never forgot that the end of Government is the happiness
>>> of the Governed:
>> Who abolished cruel rites:
>> Who effaced humiliating distinctions:
>> Who gave liberty to the expression of public opinion:
>> Whose constant study it was, to elevate the intellectual and moral
>>> character of the Nations committed to his charge.

Quoted in Millgate, *Macaulay*, p. 64.

30. Stefan Collini, *Public Moralists: Political Thought and Intellectual Life in Britain, 1850–1930* (Oxford: Clarendon Press, 1991), pp. 91–95; quotes from p. 94. The sense of the superiority of English civilization was expressed also in terms of this kind of character-formation; e.g., Marshall, who claimed that "more self-reliant habits, more forethought, more deliberateness and free choice" are exhibited by the English than by any others (p. 92). England's "national character" was frequently invoked to explain its political and economic success (pp. 107 ff.).

31. Collini, *Public Moralists*, pp. 186–187, 193.

32. Ibid., pp. 71–72, 74–79.

33. Ibid., pp. 101–103.

34. Ibid., p. 74.

35. Noel Annan, *Our Age* (London: Fontana, 1990), p. 58.

36. Mary Trevelyan Moorman, *George Macaulay Trevelyan: A Memoir* (London: Hamish Hamilton, 1980), pp. 30–31.

37. Ibid., pp. 50–51.

38. David Cannadine, *G. M. Trevelyan, A Life in History* (London: HarperCollins, 1992), pp. 147–148.

39. Moorman, *George Macaulay Trevelyan,* p. 40.

40. Ibid., p. 216n5.

41. Ibid., p. 232.

42. Ibid., pp. 210–211.

43. See Denis Donoghue, *Walter Pater* (New York: Knopf, 1995), p. 52; see also chapter 27.

44. Quoted in Annan, *Our Age,* p. 107.

45. Ibid., pp. 118–119.

46. Samuel Hynes, *A War Imagined* (London: Pimlico, 1990), p. 280.

47. Ibid., p. 328.

48. Quoted in ibid., p. 342.

49. Ibid., pp. 342 ff.

50. Paul Fussell, *The Great War and Modern Memory* (New York: Oxford University Press, 1975), p. 161. Fussell also gives an illuminating lexicon of this "heightened" language, pp. 21–22.

51. Noel Annan, *Our Age* (London: Fontana, 1990).

52. Ibid., pp. 14, 17, 18, and chapters 2 and 3.

53. Ibid., p. 18.

54. Ibid., chapter 4.

55. Ibid., p. 18.

56. Ibid., p. 608.

57. Quoted in Émile Poulat, *Où va le Christianisme?* (Paris: Plon/Mame, 1996), pp. 140–141.

58. Robert Wohl, *The Generation of 1914* (Cambridge, Mass.: Harvard University Press, 1979), pp. 8–9.

59. Ibid., p. 217.

60. Quoted in Hynes, *A War Imagined,* p. 12.

61. Modris Eksteins, *Rites of Spring* (Toronto: Lester & Orpen Dennys, 1989), pp. 316–317.

12. The Age of Mobilization

1. Robert Tombs (*France: 1814–1914* [London: Longman, 1996], p. 135) places the high water mark at 1880; for their part, Gérald Cholvy and Yves-Marie Hilaire (*Histoire religieuse de la France contemporaine: 1800/1880* [Paris: Privat, 1985], p. 317) set it earlier,

around 1860. I have split the difference. Ralph Gibson (*A Social History of French Catholicism 1798–1914* [London: Routledge, 1987], p. 230) concurs on this timing.

2. Callum Brown, "A Revisionist Approach to Religious Change", in Steve Bruce, ed., *Religion and Modernization* (Oxford: Oxford University Press, 1992).

3. Roger Finke, "An Unsecular America", in Bruce, ed., *Religion and Modernization*.

4. Olivier Tschannen, *Les théories de la sécularisation* (Genève: Droz, 1992), chapter IV.

5. Perhaps what we need here is a sharper concept of differentiation, distinguishing on one hand a decline of what we might call "saturation", and a genuine side-lining of religion. A society is religiously saturated when the reference to God or the spirits arises inevitably in all facets of its life: we pray before we hunt, we commune with the spirits of the deer; and also when we meet to decide where to hunt, what to plant, etc. The earliest societies were certainly of this type. As Danièle Hervieu-Léger puts it, in these societies "la religion est partout"; see *Le Pèlerin et le Converti* (Paris: Flammarion, 1999), pp. 20–21. The core of the concept of differentiation is the antonym to saturation in this sense: "religion" precipitates out as one "sphere" among others. Now a society can undergo "differentiation", in this sense, as with our modern economy, medicine, etc., and still be very much shaped by its dominant religious form. Differentiation as non-saturation is very different from "differentiation" as a component of "secularization". The difference between a religiously saturated society, and one which is differentiated but still religiously shaped, roughly corresponds to what I distinguish below as "ancien régime" and "mobilization" forms of religious presence.

6. Max Weber, *Die Protestantische Ethik und der Geist des Kapitalismus* (Weinheim: Beltz Athenäum, 2000), English translation: *The Protestant Ethic and the Spirit of Capitalism*, trans. Talcott Parsons (New York: Scribner, 1958); Marcel Gauchet, *Le désenchantement du monde* (Paris: Gallimard, 1985); Peter Berger, *The Sacred Canopy: Elements of a Sociological Theory of Religion* (Garden City, N.J.: Doubleday, 1967).

7. José Casanova, *Public Religions in the Modern World* (Chicago: University of Chicago Press, 1994), pp. 5, 20, 211.

8. Roger Finke, "An Unsecular America", pp. 154 ff.

9. See the discussions in Hugh McLeod, *Secularization in Western Europe, 1848–1914* (New York: St. Martin's Press, 2000), Introduction; and *European Religion in the Age of Great Cities, 1830–1930* (London: Routledge, 1995), Introduction; also Callum Brown, *The Death of Christian Britain* (London: Routledge, 2001).

10. Steve Bruce, "Pluralism and Religious Vitality", in Steve Bruce, ed., *Religion and Modernization* (Oxford: Oxford University Press, 1992), pp. 170–194. Ralph Gibson, in his *A Social History of French Catholicism 1789–1914* (London: Routledge, 1989), pp. 170–180, discusses "la carte Boulard", the map drawn up in 1947 by Chanoine Boulard, showing the great regional differences in religious practice in France. François Furet called this map "one of the most crucial and most mysterious documents on France and her history". The mystery resides in the fact that this map closely mirrors maps that can be drawn up of related differences in the nineteenth century, and even in the eighteenth. These long-standing differ-

ences make it very difficult to map levels of practice onto social and economic variables; the effects of these vary too much from region to region. Part of the explanation for these differences lies "in the history of French Catholicism before the Revolution. . . . It is probably necessary to go back to the Catholic Reformation, or indeed, (in many cases) to the all-too-often undocumented social history of the Middle Ages" (p. 177). Yves-Marie Hilaire, *Une Chrétienté au XIXe Siècle?* (Lille: PUL, 1977), Volume 1, p. 552, makes an analogous point. Some of the explanation for differences in practice in the different regions of the North of France goes back to "les efforts de la Réforme catholique, poursuivis méthodiquement au XVIIIe siècle dans les diocèses de Boulogne et de St Omer à l'ouest et dans celui de Cambrai à l'est. . . . Un Partz de Pressy à Boulogne, un Fénelon à Cambrai, aidés par un clergé nombreux et actif, semblent avoir durablement marqué leur diocèse."

11. For instance, Michael Hornsby-Smith, "Recent Transformations in English Catholicism: Evidence of Secularization?" in Bruce, ed., *Religion and Modernization,* pp. 118–123; David Martin, "Towards Eliminating the Concept of Secularization", in J. Gould, ed., *Penguin Survey of the Social Sciences* (Harmondsworth: Penguin Books, 1965), pp. 169–182. Martin has since propounded his own version of a secularization thesis, but mindful of his earlier critique.

12. David Martin, *Religious and Secular,* p. 67.

13. Bruce, *Religion and Modernization,* pp. 1–2.

14. Steve Bruce, *Religion in Modern Britain* (Oxford: Oxford University Press, 1995), p. viii.

15. Ibid., pp. 132–133. This is a common view. Hugh McLeod quotes the Dutch saying: "Artificial fertilisers make atheists", in H. McLeod, "Secular Cities?" in Bruce, ed., *Religion and Modernization,* p. 61. And Rudolph Bultmann: "We cannot use electric lights and radios and, in the event of illness, avail ourselves of modern medical and clinical means and at the same time believe in the spirit and wonder world of the New Testament"; from *New Testament and Mythology and Other Basic Writings,* ed. and trans. Schubert M. Ogden (Philadelphia: Forest Press, 1984), p. 4.

16. There is something to be said for understanding the deep differences in unthought between believers and unbelievers in our civilization as analogous to a cultural difference. Just as the scholars of culture A may have trouble understanding culture B, without challenging their hitherto unquestioned background categories, so here; with the difference that in our case both believers and unbelievers tend to operate within categories that screen out (different) aspects of the complex reality we are both living in today. I will develop this point in Part V.

17. E.g., Bryan Wilson, "Reflections on a Many-Sided Controversy", in Bruce, ed., *Religion and Modernization,* p. 210.

18. See note 9 above.

19. I adopt Hugh McLeod's distinction between "orthodox" and "revisionists" in his discussion in the Introduction to H. McLeod, ed., *European Religion in the Age of Great Cities.*

20. Roy Wallis and Steve Bruce, "Secularization: The Orthodox Model", in Bruce, ed., *Religion and Modernization,* pp. 10–11. See also Bruce, *Religion in the Modern World* (Oxford: Oxford University Press, 1996), p. 7. David Martin offers a similar definition: "By 'religious' I mean the acceptance of a level of reality beyond the observable world known to science, to which are ascribed meanings and purposes completing and transcending those of the purely human realm." *A General Theory of Secularization* (New York: Harper, 1978), p. 12.

21. This is not to say that there might not be other kinds of reflection for which a broad definition might be useful, as we see with the work of Danièle Hervieu-Léger: *La Religion pour Mémoire* (Paris: Cerf, 1993), and *Le Pèlerin et le Converti* (Paris: Flammarion, 1999). Sometimes it helps in understanding our society to bring out the common elements between different outlooks, which straddle what we normally see as the secular/religious divide. But for my purposes here, I need the narrower concept.

22. Bruce, *Religion and Modernization,* p. 6. Sometimes the phenomenon is defined as "the diminishing of the social significance of religion". Wallis and Bruce quote Wilson approvingly to this effect on page 11. But there is not really a contradiction here. Both phenomena occur. But I prefer the focus on individual belief, not only because it is often not easy to compare the social significance of religion in different societies and different ages, but also because many of the examples which Bryan Wilson gives for declining social significance plainly causally depend on declining belief—either fewer people believing, or their believing less strongly and intensely. See his "Reflections on a Many-Sided Controversy", in Bruce, ed., *Religion and Modernization,* pp. 195–210.

23. Of course, this is an utterly Christian account of such a higher perspective; but there are analogous forms in many other religions: going beyond the self connects one to the Mahakaruna, or great compassion, a transformation way beyond ordinary flourishing (indeed, negating one of the main conditions of what is ordinarily seen as flourishing, viz., the continuing self); the call to submit to God in Islam which empowers humans in a way unavailable in any other fashion. And so on.

24. Bruce, *Religion in the Modern World,* p. 26.

25. Ibid., p. 39.

26. Wallis and Bruce, "Secularization: The Orthodox Model", p. 17. Cf. also Bruce, *Religion in the Modern World,* p. 62.

27. We are in the general domain that people have talked about in terms of alternative "Master Narratives". A Master Narrative is an account which embeds the events it makes sense of within some understanding of the general drift of history. This in turn is intimately linked with a certain view of the gamut of human motivations. Examples are the various Enlightenment stories of progress, the Marxist story, stories of modernity as decadence and loss of moral cohesion, and the like.

28. Bruce, *Religion in the Modern World,* p. 58.

29. See the passage from Paul Bénichou, quoted in chapter 1.

30. Quoted in Sylvette Denèfle, *Sociologie de la Sécularisation* (Paris-Montréal: l'Harmattan, 1997), pp. 93–94.

31. See Bruce, *Religion in the Modern World,* pp. 38, 49, 58.

32. Ibid., p. 4.

33. Ibid., p. 58.

34. Steve Bruce, *God Is Dead* (Oxford: Blackwell, 2002), p. 42.

35. As a matter of fact, you don't have to have faith to believe in the continuing saliency of independent religious motivation. You could think that evolution had played a cruel trick on the human race, and given us an unquenchable thirst for transformation to which no objective possibility corresponded. This seems to me the next most likely hypothesis after theism, and still more plausible than the Disappearance Thesis.

36. As Ralph Gibson puts it, discussing the case of nineteenth-century France, in his *A Social History of French Catholicism* (London: Routledge, 1989, p. 227): "It has been customary to see this period as one of dechristianization, in which the hold of the Catholic faith on the hearts and minds of French men and women, and its ability to determine their behaviour, steadily declined, as France underwent a process of 'modernization' of which not only secularization but also the decline of religious belief were necessary aspects. This vision is, however, a product of that innocent faith in modernity which caused so many Catholics to applaud Pius IX's condemnation of 'liberty, progress, and modern civilization'. In as far as France did undergo a process of modernization . . . , it was not necessarily incompatible with Catholicism. There were in fact a number of contradictory forces at work in France in the nineteenth century, resulting in an evolution of Catholic behaviour which was far from being linear. The old image of linear dechristianization needs most definitely to be consigned to the rubbish-heap of history."

37. I owe a lot to the interesting discussions in the works of McLeod, Brown, Blatschke, Raeidts, van Rooden, Wolffe, and others.

38. See Keith Thomas, *Religion and the Decline of Magic* (New York: Scribner, 1971).

39. John Wolffe, *God and Greater Britain* (London: Routledge, 1994), pp. 80–82. Similar descriptions of the composite nature of popular religion can be found in James Obelkevich, *Religion and Rural Society: South Lindsey 1825–1875* (Oxford: Oxford University Press, 1976), chapter VI; Sarah Williams, *Religious Belief and Popular Culture in Southwark* (Oxford: Oxford University Press, 1999), chapters 3 and 4; and for France in Philippe Boutry, *Prêtres et Paroisses au pays du curé d'Ars* (Paris: Cerf, 1986), Part III, chapter 2, and Yves Hilaire, *Une Chrétienté au XIXe Siècle?* (Lille: PUL, 1977), Volume 1, chapter XI.

40. Obelkevich, *Religion and Rural Society,* chapter VI. Jeffrey Cox, *The English Churches in a Secular Society* (New York: Oxford University Press, 1982), p. 95, also seems to share this view; he talks of "old non Christian accretions", and "semi-pagan superstition".

41. Robert Lane Fox, *Pagans and Christians* (New York: Knopf, 1986).

42. Boutry, *Prêtres et Paroisses,* pp. 346–354. Sarah Williams, *Religious Belief,* pp. 100,

107–108. Yves-Marie Hilaire makes a similar point about "le bon prêtre", and points particularly to the reputation of those who put their lives at risk to help others in the cholera epidemics; *Une Chrétienté,* chapter VII.

43. Wolffe, *God and Greater Britain,* p. 78; Sarah Williams, "Urban Popular Religion and Rites of Passage", in Hugh McLeod, ed., *European Religion in the Age of Great Cities;* also Williams, *Religious Belief,* chapter 4.

44. Hilaire, *Une Chrétienté,* Volume 2, pp. 631–633, speaks of the christianisme "festif" of the popular strata.

45. The creation of new cults continues today, sometimes in symbiosis, sometimes in opposition to the Church in Mexico, as Claudio Lomnitz' work on "La Santa Muerte" shows; see Claudio Lomnitz, *Death and the Idea of Mexico* (New York: Zone Books, 2005), pp. 483–497.

46. See Eamon Duffy, *The Stripping of the Altars* (New Haven: Yale University Press, 1992).

47. Boutry, *Prêtres et Paroisses,* Part I, chapter 2, shows how in the Department of Ain a majority rural clergy looked with great suspicion on the whole way of life of the small class of workers which was beginning to assemble in a limited number of centres. Receiving an individual salary, and seemingly unintegrated into a recognizable community, the workers appeared virtually condemned to a life of dissipation. They needed to be taken in hand. This approach obviously repelled workers.

48. See Eugen Weber, *Peasants into Frenchmen* (London: Chatto, 1979), chapter 19; and Boutry, *Prêtres et Paroisses,* passim.

49. Weber, *Peasants into Frenchmen,* pp. 281–282.

50. See, for instance, Hugh McLeod, *European Religion,* pp. 11–18.

51. Ernst Kantorowicz, *The King's Two Bodies* (Princeton: Princeton University Press, 1997).

52. I described these more fully above in Chapter 1.

53. See Robert Bellah, "Civil Religion in America", in *Beyond Belief: Essays on Religion in a Post-Traditional World* (New York: Harper & Row, 1970), chapter 9.

54. E.g., *Tongues of Fire* (Oxford: Blackwell, 1990), and *A General Theory of Secularization* (Oxford: Blackwell, 1978).

55. See Gordon Wood, *The Radicalism of the American Revolution* (New York: Vintage, 1993).

56. But even so, the very poor tended to be less touched by these movements in England than the more skilled workers. See Hugh McLeod, *Secularization in Western Europe, 1848–1914* (New York: St. Martin's Press, 2000), chapter 3; also his *Religion and the People of Western Europe 1789–1989* (Oxford: Oxford University Press, 1997), chapter 4; and David Hempton, *Religion and Political Culture in Britain and Ireland* (Cambridge: Cambridge University Press, 1996), p. 29 and chapter 6.

57. I have drawn here, i.a., on the valuable discussions in Hugh McLeod, *Religion and the*

People of Western Europe, pp. 36–43; John Wolffe, *God and Greater Britain,* pp. 20–30; and David Hempton, *Religion and Political Culture,* chapter 2.

58. See Joyce Appleby, *Inheriting the Revolution* (Cambridge, Mass.: Harvard University Press, 2000), p. 206.

59. Callum Brown, *The Death of Christian Britain* (London: Routledge, 2001).

60. See David Martin, *Tongues of Fire,* and *Pentecostalism: The World Their Parish* (Oxford: Blackwell, 2002).

61. Sociologists have noticed similar effects flowing from strong (re)conversions to Islam in contemporary France; see Danièle Hervieu-Léger, *Le Pèlerin et le Converti* (Paris: Flammarion, 1999), pp. 142–143.

62. Linda Colley, *Britons* (New Haven: Yale University Press, 1992). See also Wolffe, *God and Greater Britain;* and David Hempton, *Religion and Political Culture in Britain and Ireland* (Cambridge: Cambridge University Press, 1996), chapters 5 and 7.

63. The connection of Christianity with decency in England has been noted by David Martin, *Dilemmas of Contemporary Religion* (Oxford: Blackwell, 1978), p. 122.

64. This whole issue of violence in modernity deserves further extensive treatment, especially taking account of the pathbreaking work of René Girard.

65. A very good summary of the different paths has been given by David Martin, in *On Secularization: Towards a Revised General Theory* (Aldershot: Ashgate, 2005).

66. Boutry, *Prêtres et Paroisses,* p. 487.

67. Ibid., p. 506.

68. Ibid., pp. 344, 459–460. Sarah Williams picks up on something similar in turn of the century Southwark, a consensually enforced code of practice, locally referred to as "public opinion"; *Religious Belief,* pp. 37–38.

69. It also held together a schismatic parish of ex-Jansenists, who refused to reconvert individually. They all agreed that "il ne faut pas quitter la religion de nos pères"; "le respect humain" demanded this. Boutry, *Prêtres et Paroisses,* p. 522.

70. Ibid., p. 567. The shift from "mentalité" to "opinion" is just a facet of the making over of non-élite communities in the nineteenth century on the principles of élite culture. Obelkevich, *Religion and Rural Society,* pp. 91–102, notices something similar in South Lindsey. The self-policing (through charivari or "rough music"), egalitarian village community, where people sought not privacy but to be one with the crowd, gave way slowly to a society of self-disciplined individuals.

71. Boutry tells of the "attitudes de réserve, de méfiance, de refus même" of clergy in the face of many of the practices of folk religion; *Prêtres et Paroisses,* p. 481. McLeod (*Religion and the People of Western Europe,* pp. 64–65) quotes the bitter statement of another French curé in 1907: "Not a single man does his Easter Duties, but it's a curious fact that they all take part in processions."

72. Obelkevich, *Religion and Rural Society,* pp. 83–84.

73. Maurice Agulhon, *La République au village* (Paris: Le Seuil, 1979), p. 172.

74. From Maurice Agulhon, *The Republic in the Village: The People of the Var from the French Revolution to the Second Republic,* trans. Janet Lloyd (Cambridge: Cambridge University Press; and Paris: Editions de la Maison des Sciences de l'Homme, 1982), p. 101.

75. Ibid., p. 644, also pp. 578–595 and 625–651.

76. Ibid., p. 626.

77. See Carl Strikwerda, "A Resurgent Religion", in McLeod, ed., *European Religion,* chapter 2. For other interesting insights into Belgian Catholicism, see Vincent Viaene, *Belgium and the Holy See from Gregory XVI to Pius IX 1831–59: Catholic Revival, Society and Politics in 19th Century Europe* (Leuven/Brussels/Rome, 2001), pp. 157–215.

78. Boutry also speaks of the campaigns of curés against "les abus", principally la danse, le cabaret et le travail le dimanche; *Prêtres et Paroisses,* p. 579.

79. Ralph Gibson, *A Social History of French Catholicism* (London: Routledge, 1989), p. 144.

80. See the interesting discussion in Thomas Kselman, *Miracles and Prophecies in Nineteenth Century France* (New Brunswick, N.J.: Rutgers University Press, 1983), chapter 6.

81. The sense of civilizational superiority also underpinned Imperialism, and gave it the good conscience of "the white man's burden". This sense of rightfully assuming the burden of rule over "backward" peoples later shifted its basis; it was justified on racial grounds, or on grounds of the Enlightened culture of Europeans.

> Where England's flag flies wide unfurl'd
> All tyrant wrongs repelling,
> God made the world a better world
> For man's brief earthly dwelling.

This was put more prosaically by Disraeli's Colonial Secretary in 1878, who spoke of the British duty to supply "our native fellow-subjects . . . with a system where the humblest may enjoy freedom from oppression and wrong equally with the greatest; where the light of religion and morality can penetrate into the darkest dwelling places". And the role of Evangelicals in spreading benign British rule—in India, and Africa (Livingston, Gordon)—was known and highly appreciated by Evangelicals at home. See Wolffe, *God and Greater Britain,* pp. 194, 221–222; also McLeod, *Secularization in Western Europe,* pp. 237, 239–240; and Hempton, *Religion and Political Culture in Great Britain and Ireland,* chapter 8.

82. Boutry, *Prêtres et Paroisses,* p. 344; see also p. 380, where he speaks of the self-given "mission morale, sociale, et pour tout dire civilisatrice de l'Église dans le monde". Hilaire, *Une Chrétienté,* Volume 1, p. 305, evokes the same idea.

83. Jeffrey Cox, *The English Churches in a Secular Society* (New York: Oxford University Press, 1982), p. 271; Duke of Devonshire quote, pp. 109–110.

84. See Olaf Blaschke, "Europe between 1800 and 1970: A Second Confessional Age", paper for a conference on "Master Narratives", April 2002; as yet unpublished (as far as I know)

85. See Peter Raedts, "The Church as Nation State: A New Look at Ultramontanist Ca-

tholicism (1850–1900)", paper for a conference on "Master Narratives", April 2002; as yet unpublished (as far as I know).

86. See Olaf Blaschke, "Europe between 1800 and 1970"; also Hugh McLeod, *Secularization in Western Europe*, pp. 208–209, 224–225. There are also certain analogies with the rich social life organized around Sunday Schools in England; see David Hempton, *Religion and Political Culture in Britain and Ireland*, pp. 124–125.

13. The Age of Authenticity

1. See Robert Wuthnow, *Loose Connections* (Cambridge, Mass.: Harvard University Press, 1998), pp. 1–2; also Alan Wolfe, *One Nation, After All* (New York: Viking, 1998), chapter 6; Gertrude Himmelfarb, *One Nation, Two Cultures* (New York: Knopf, 1999), pp. 20 ff; Robert Putnam, *Bowling Alone* (New York: Simon & Schuster, 2000).

2. Putnam, *Bowling Alone,* holds that the decline in "social capital" is real; whereas this is contested by Wuthnow, *Loose Connections,* who sees the declining older forms being replaced by new kinds of "looser" connections. See also Wolfe, *One Nation,* pp. 252–253; and John A. Hall and Charles Lindholm, *Is America Breaking Apart?* (Princeton: Princeton University Press, 1999), pp. 121–122. Whereas the critics may be right about associations in general, Putnam seems to be onto something important in the sphere of political participation. The new lobbies and single-issue organizations operate rather differently from the older membership associations.

3. See Putnam, *Bowling Alone,* section III; Wuthnow, *Loose Connections,* chapter 4.

4. Cf. Richard Hoggart, *The Uses of Literacy* (London: Chatto & Windus, 1957).

5. Cf. Yves Lambert, *Dieu Change en Bretagne* (Paris: Cerf, 1985).

6. See *The Malaise of Modernity* (Toronto: Anansi, 1991).

7. Quoted from Samuel Hynes: *The Edwardian Turn of Mind* (Princeton: Princeton University Press 1968), p. 325.

8. Michel Winock, *Le Siècle des Intellectuels* (Paris: Seuil, 1997), chapter 17.

9. See David Brooks, *Bobos in Paradise* (New York: Simon & Schuster, 2000), pp. 117–124; Alan Ehrenhalt, *The Lost City: The Forgotten Virtues of Community in America* (New York: Basic Books, 1994), pp. 60–64; the Tillich quote is on page 61.

10. F. Schiller, *Letters on the Aesthetic Education of Man,* ed. and trans. Elizabeth Wilkinson and L. A. Willoughby (Oxford: Clarendon Press, 1967); see especially letter VI.

11. François Ricard has given an excellent description of the sense of entering a new age with unprecedented possibilities; see his penetrating essay on the early baby boomers, *La Génération Lyrique* (Montréal: Boréal, 1992).

12. Brooks, *Bobos in Paradise,* chapters 3, 5, 6; the quote is from page 134.

13. For a good treatment of these polarizing mechanisms, see James Davison Hunter, *Culture Wars* (New York: Basic Books, 1991), and *Before the Shooting Begins* (New York: The Free Press, 1994). Alan Wolfe, *One Nation,* attempts to minimize the divisions.

14. Hunter, *Before the Shooting Begins,* p. 118.

15. Ibid., Part III.

16. Ehrenhalt, *The Lost City.*

17. Ibid, p. 2

18. See *Modern Social Imaginaries* (Durham: Duke University Press, 2004).

19. Émile Durkheim, *Les Formes élémentaires de la Vie religieuse,* 5th ed. (Paris: PUF, 1968).

20. See Danièle Hervieu-Léger, *La Religion pour Mémoire* (Paris: Cerf, 1993), chapter 3, esp. pp. 82 ff.

21. Achille Mbembe in his fascinating analysis of contemporary Johannesburg, "Aesthetics of Superfluity" (*Public Culture,* vol. 16, no. 3 [2004], Duke University Press, pp. 373–405), describes whole mall environments in the new upscale north end of the urban area, Melrose Arch and Montecasino [*sic*]. These form the dreamed of elsewhere to which shoppers are linked. In artful imitations, even including a careful treatment of the stone to make it look weathered through centuries, they place us in Tuscany. This is both a centre of first-world design, but also in its mediaeval roots it bespeaks the integrated community that modern consumer capitalism is dissolving. Shoppers there can square the circle emotionally, and enjoy both the excitement of expanding choice and the nostalgically desired community with a long past of deep meanings (pp. 393 ff.).

22. Pun intended. The oblique reference here is to Naomi Klein's path-breaking book, *No Logo: Taking Aim at the Brand Bullies* (Toronto: Vintage Canada, 2000).

23. Jean-Louis Schlegel makes the point that the values which constantly emerge from studies of young people today are: "droits de l'homme, tolérance, respect des convictions d'autrui, libertés, amitié, amour, solidarité, fraternité, justice, respect de la nature, intervention humanitaire"; *Esprit,* no. 233, June 1997, p. 29. Sylvette Denèfle concurs for her sample of French unbelievers: *Sociologie de la Sécularisation* (Paris: L'Harmattan, 1997), chapter 6. Tolerance is for them the key virtue (pp. 166 ff.).

24. Michael Sandel, *Democracy's Discontent* (Cambridge, Mass.: Harvard University Press, 1996), pp. 209–210.

25. Michel Winock, *Le siècle des intellectuels* (Paris: Seuil, 1997), p. 582.

26. One might argue that this identity shift helps explain the falling rate of participation in voting, not only in the U.S. but almost everywhere in the Atlantic world. This decline is stronger among the younger cohorts (see Putnam, *Bowling Alone,* chapter 14). The disengagement is probably not simply direct, that is, unattached individuals losing interest in politics, but also indirect: people have dropped out of the movements and organizations that used to link them to politics. For instance, the decline of class consciousness, and hence class movements, like Trade Unions, in certain countries (e.g., the U.K., France) breaks the link that connected many people to the political system. Their link to the whole was via a class identity and a certain understanding of class struggle. A world in which there are fewer and

fewer people linked through identity to the "Labour Movement", or the PCF, is probably also one in which the level of abstention rises.

27. I think my analysis here comes close to that of Marcel Gauchet, where he talks of the present time in France as "une troisième époque de la laïcité"; *La Religion dans la Démocratie* (Paris: Gallimard, 1998), p. 74. See also his *La Condition Historique* (Paris: Stock, 2003), chapter 12. This latter book places the development in the context of a profound and illuminating theory of human history.

28. François Furet, *Le Passé d'une Illusion* (Paris: Gallimard, 1996), points out how remarkable the allegiance was, and the sense of belonging that sustained it.

29. The excellent book by José Casanova, *Public Religions in the Modern World* (Chicago: University of Chicago Press, 1994), shows how diverse our religious predicament is. If we ever came to live in a predicament totally defined by the post-Durkheimian understanding, there would probably be no further space for religion in the public sphere. Spiritual life would be entirely privatized, in keeping with the norms of a certain procedural liberalism which is very widespread today. But Casanova traces in fact a "deprivatization" of religion, that is, an attempt by churches and religious bodies to intervene again in the political life of their societies. Instances are the Christian Right and the Catholic bishops' letters in the U.S.A., which I have just mentioned. It is unlikely (and also undesirable) that this kind of thing will ever cease. But the situation in which these interventions take place is defined by the end of a uniform Durkheimian dispensation, and the growing acceptance among many people of a post-Durkheimian understanding.

30. Luc Ferry in his very interesting *L'Homme-Dieu ou le sens de la vie* (Paris: Grasset, 1996), chapter 1, picks up on this phenomenon under the title "le refus de l'Autorité". I agree with much of what he says, but I think he over-intellectualizes this reaction by relating it directly to Descartes, instead of seeing its expressivist roots.

31. Sir George Trevelyan, in a lecture at the Festival for Mind, Body, and Spirit, quoted in Paul Heelas, *The New Age Movement* (Oxford: Blackwell, 1996), p. 21. The injunction, one might say, represents only a New Age outlook. But in this respect, the various New Age movements accentuate much more widely held attitudes, as Heelas argues in chapter 6. In 1978, for instance, a Gallup poll found that 80 percent of Americans agreed that "an individual should arrive at his or her own religious beliefs independent of any churches or synagogues" (Heelas, p. 164); also cited in Robert Bellah et al., *Habits of the Heart* (Berkeley: University of California Press, 1985), p. 228.

32. Yves Lambert, *Dieu Change en Bretagne* (Paris: Cerf, 1985), p. 373. Danièle Hervieu-Léger makes a similar point to mine here. She speaks of the recession in the contemporary world of the fear of want: "Que se passe-t-il pour la religion dans une société où l'on a l'assurance de manger à sa faim, quoi qu'il arrive?", in *Chrétiens, tournez la page* (Paris: Bayard, 2002), p. 97.

33. Religious sociologists had already noticed that the high level of practice in certain re-

gions of France was tied to living within the parish. Migration to the cities generally had a devastating effect. As Gabriel Le Bras put it, "Je suis convaincu que sur cent ruraux qui s'établissent à Paris, il y en a à peu près 90 qui, au sortir de la gare Montparnasse, cessent d'être des pratiquants." Quoted in Danièle Hervieu-Léger, *Vers un nouveau Christianisme?* (Paris: Seuil, 1986), p. 37.

34. Ibid.

35. Lambert, *Dieu Change en Bretagne,* pp. 385ff.

36. David Hempton, *Religion and Political Culture in Britain and Ireland* (Cambridge: Cambridge University Press, 1996), pp. 18 and 132–133.

37. J. S. Mill, *On Liberty;* see Hugh McLeod, *Religion and the People of Western Europe,* p. 114; Jeffrey Cox, *The English Churches in a Secular Society,* p. 275.

38. David Martin, *Pentecostalism* (Oxford: Blackwell, 2002), pp. 14–15. Gertrude Himmelfarb, *One Nation, Two Cultures,* makes a similar point. "In disparaging the Puritan ethic, the counterculture undermined those virtues that might better have served the poor. The underclass is thus not only the victim of its own 'culture of poverty', it is also the victim of the upper-class culture around it. The kind of casual delinquency that a white suburban teenager can absorb with relative impunity may be literally fatal to a black inner city teenager" (p. 26). Of course, what is absurd is the exclusive attribution of causal responsibility for poverty to "permissive" culture, when flagrantly unjust policies of neglect and regressive income distribution have contributed so heavily to the plight of the American poor.

39. Of course, the sexual revolution could itself be taken as the axis of a master narrative or subtraction story, and was frequently interpreted in this way in the 1960s (see, for instance, Reich, *The Greening of America*). Parallel to stories like: science shows that religion is wrong, and once people remove the obstacles to seeing this, they can't go back; or: people in the end want autonomy, and once they see through the false reasons underlying authority, they can't go back; so there is a possible story: people desire unchecked sexual fulfillment, and once they see that they have been denied this by unfounded restrictions, there is no going back. This is certainly how things felt to a lot of young people in, say, Berkeley, or the Latin Quarter, in 1968. But this outlook hasn't worn very well. In fact, most people quickly perceived that things are much more complicated.

40. Martin, *Pentecostalism,* pp. 98–106.

41. See Callum Brown, *The Death of Christian Britain* (London: Routledge, 2001), especially chapters 4 and 5.

42. I have discussed this at greater length elsewhere, in my *Modern Social Imaginaries* (Durham: Duke University Press, 2004).

43. Philippe Boutry, *Prêtres et Paroisses au pays du curé d'Ars* (Paris: Cerf, 1986), p. 578.

44. Ibid., Part III, chapters 1 and 4. There are also interesting discussions of this gender split in practice in Hugh McLeod, *Secularization and the People of Western Europe* (Oxford: Oxford University Press, 1997), p. 128; in Leonore Davidoff and Catherine Hall, *Family Fortunes* (London: Routledge, 1987), chapter 2; and in Thomas Kselman, "The Varieties of

Religious Experience in Urban France", in Hugh McLeod, ed., *European Religion in the Age of Great Cities, 1830–1930* (London: Routledge, 1995), chapter 6.

45. Quoted in Brown, *Death of Christian Britain,* p. 180.

46. See Yves-Marie Hilaire, *Une Chrétienté au XIXe Siècle?* (Lille: PUL, 1977), Volume 1, pp. 74–80.

47. Grace Davie, *Religion in Modern Europe* (Oxford: Oxford University Press, 2000), pp. 63–64.

48. John Bossy, *Christianity in the West, 1400–1700* (Oxford: Oxford University Press, 1985), p. 35; Ralph Gibson, *A Social History of French Catholicism 1789–1914* (London: Routledge, 1989), p. 24.

49. Bossy, *Christianity in the West,* p. 37.

50. Jean Delumeau, *Le Péché et la Peur* (Paris: Fayard, 1983); also Gibson, *A Social History,* pp. 241 ff.

51. Quoted in Gibson, *A Social History,* p. 246.

52. E. Germain, *Parler du salut?* (Paris: Beauchesne, 1967), p. 295; quoted, along with a very interesting discussion, in Gibson, *A Social History,* p. 244.

53. Gibson, *A Social History,* p. 188; Delumeau, *Le Péché et la Peur,* chapter 17, pp. 517–519, 525.

54. John D'Emilio and Esther B. Freedman, *Intimate Matters* (New York: Harper & Row, 1988), p. 4; and Steven Seidman, *Romantic Longings* (New York and London: Routledge, 1991), pp. 23–24.

55. Seidman, *Romantic Longings,* pp. 26–27.

56. Susan Sontag, *Illness as Metaphor* (New York: Picador, 2001).

57. *Ethics,* Book 6.

58. Beth Bailey, *Sex in the Heartland* (Cambridge, Mass.: Harvard University Press, 1999), chapter 8.

59. Seidman, *Romantic Longings,* chapter 5.

60. D'Emilio and Freedman, *Intimate Matters,* pp. 312 ff.; Seidman, *Romantic Longings,* chapter 5.

61. David Martin, *Pentecostalism,* p. 21.

14. Religion Today

1. Alan Ehrenhalt, *The Lost City* (New York: Basic Books, 1955), pp. 220–228. See also Robert Wuthnow, *After Heaven* (Berkeley: University of California Press, 1998), chapter 2.

2. Quoted in Wade Clark Roof, *Spiritual Marketplace* (Princeton: Princeton University Press, 1999), p. 222.

3. Ibid., p. 86.

4. Ibid., pp. 21–24.

5. Paul Heelas, Linda Woodhead, et al., *The Spiritual Revolution* (Oxford: Blackwell,

2004), p. 26. This study is set in a community in England. It is clear that the themes here are very similar to those invoked in the U.S., or indeed, anywhere today in the Atlantic world.

6. Roof, *Spiritual Marketplace,* pp. 92, 106.

7. Ibid., chapters 1 and 2.

8. Ibid., p. 137.

9. Ibid., pp. 9 and 40: "In a very real sense, self-fulfillment became a trap: with so much emphasis upon the self—with its inflated images of being special, unique, and only potentially realized—maintaining the self became a 'burden', a psychological crisis brought on by one's own self-delusions."

10. Heelas, Woodhead, et al., *The Spiritual Revolution.*

11. Ibid., p. 31.

12. Ibid., p. 81.

13. Ibid., p. 26.

14. Ibid., p. 88.

15. Ibid., p. 16.

16. Henri Bremond, *L'Histoire littéraire du sentiment religieux en France, depuis la fin des guerres de religion jusqu'à nos jours* (Paris: A. Colin, 11 volumes, 1967–1968); see Volume 1: *L'humanisme dévot.*

17. St. François speaks of a "recueillement amoureux de l'âme en Dieu"; see *Traité de l'Amour de Dieu* (Paris: Monastre de la Visitation, n.d.), Book VI, chapters vi–xi, pp. 250–267.

18. Jean Lacouture, *Jésuites: 1, Les Conquérants* (Paris: Seuil, 1991), pp. 21–22.

19. Wuthnow, *After Heaven,* chapter 1.

20. Michael Hornsby-Smith, "Recent Transformations in English Catholicism", in S. Bruce, ed., *Religion and Modernization,* chapter 6.

21. See Steve Bruce, *Religion in the Modern World* (Oxford: Oxford University Press, 1996), pp. 33, 137 ff.; Sylvette Denèfle, *Sociologie de la Sécularisation* (Paris: L'Harmattan, 1997).

22. For instance, the *Gallup Political & Economic Index* (394, June 1993) reports that in Britain 40 percent believe in "some sort of spirit or lifeforce", as opposed to 30 percent who have faith in a "personal God"; cited in Heelas, Woodhead, et al., *The Spiritual Revolution,* p. 166. Analogous figures have been found in Sweden and France; see Danièle Hervieu-Léger, *Le Pélerin et le Converti* (Paris: Flammarion, 1999), pp. 44–46.

23. The move of many Western societies into what I have been calling a "post-Durkheimian" dispensation has obviously facilitated their move towards "multi-culturalism", at the same time as this has become a more urgent issue because of the increasing diversity of their populations. But multi-culturalism has also produced strains, which are often exacerbated by the continuing hold of one or another "Durkheimian" understanding on important segments of the population. Christian conservatives are made edgy by rampant expressivism in the U.S.A.; and many French people find it hard to see their country as con-

taining an important Muslim component, so long have they related to it as an essentially Catholic country, or one defined by the constitutive tension between Catholicism and "laïcité".

24. Hervieu-Léger, *Le Pèlerin et le Converti*, pp. 41, 56; Grace Davie, *Religion in Britain since 1945: Believing without Belonging* (Oxford: Blackwell, 1994). A discussion of the special Scandinavian pattern can be found in Hervieu-Léger, *Le Pèlerin et le Converti*, p. 57; and Grace Davie, *Religion in Modern Europe* (Oxford: Oxford University Press, 2000), p. 3.

25. William James, *The Varieties of Religious Experience* (Penguin Books, 1982).

26. Hervieu-Léger, *Le Pèlerin et le Converti*, pp. 100–108.

27. See the very interesting discussion in Robert Wuthnow, *After Heaven*, chapter 7, "The Practice of Spirituality".

28. Another way of putting the whole development since 1500 would be in terms of these different kinds and levels of religious life. At the beginning of this period, there was a single church. This (a) unified (in paleo-Durkheimian fashion) the whole society; (b) its local associations (parishes) were the site of face-to-face religious sociability, and (c) it was the matrix within which some might pursue a more private devotional life. Now these three forms of religious practice can exist totally dissociated from each other. People can be "into" one, without engaging the other. But we must stress: this *can* be the case. Not everyone will live this dissociation. I owe this formulation to José Casanova (private communication).

29. See Grace Davie, *Religion in Britain since 1945;* and John Wolffe. The term "diffusive Christianity" was coined by Jeffrey Cox, *The English Churches in a Secular Society, Lambeth 1870–1930* (New York: Oxford University Press, 1982), chapter 4.

30. John Wolffe, *God and Greater Britain* (London: Routledge, 1994), pp. 92–93. David Hempton, *Religion and Political Culture in Britain and Ireland* (Cambridge: Cambridge University Press, 1996), pp. 136–137, gives another account of this diffused understanding of Christianity, while stressing that all the terms we invent to describe it, including "believing without belonging", and "diffusive Christianity" itself, are insufficiently flexible to capture the complex reality. Hempton also points out the importance of religious music, particularly hymn-singing, in this culture.

31. Wolffe, *God and Greater Britain.* Boutry makes a parallel remark about the period 1840–1860 in the Ain Department (but this was not exceptional in this respect in France): "Jamais peut-être, dans la longue histoire de l'Église catholique, la réalité vécue du ministère n'aura aussi exactement coïncidé avec son idéal; jamais l'existence des curés de villages ne sera approchée d'aussi près du modèle du 'bon prêtre', élaboré quelque trois siècles plus tôt par les Pères du Concile de Trente." Boutry, *Prêtres et Paroisses*, p. 243.

32. Grace Davie, *Religion in Britain since 1945*, pp. 69–70. For the figures, see her tables, pp. 46–50.

33. Ibid., pp. 88–91.

34. Peter Berger, "Religion and the West", in *The National Interest* (Summer 2005), 80, pp. 113–114.

35. E.g., Grace Davie, *Europe: The Exceptional Case* (London: Darton, Longman & Todd, 2002), p. 46.

36. Steve Bruce, *Religion in the Modern World* (Oxford: Oxford University Press, 1996), chapter 6.

37. See José Casanova, "Immigration and Religious Pluralism: An EU/US comparison", note 20, in Thomas Banchoff, ed., *The New Religious Pluralism and Democracy* (Oxford: Oxford University Press, 2006). I have learned a great deal from Casanova's discussion here and elsewhere.

38. Ibid.

39. Again, there is a similarity to a thesis of Martin's; see David Martin, *Pentecostalism* (Oxford: Blackwell, 2002), pp. 56, 68.

40. This is the thesis of José Casanova, in his "Ortodoxías seculares y heterodoxías religiosas en la modernidad", pp. 18–20. This thesis will be expounded in his forthcoming book on what is valid and what is false in the traditional secularization thesis.

41. This is close to the thesis outlined by Martin, if I understand him correctly, in *Pentecostalism*, p. 53.

42. In fact, we cannot but be astonished at the chauvinism of intellectuals and academics on both sides at the outbreak of the First World War. A large number of German professors published a manifesto explaining that their nation's struggle was in the name of Kultur. To which a number of French Catholic scholars responded in November identifying the real cause of the terrible conflict: "La philosophie allemande, avec son subjectivisme de fond, avec son idéalisme transcendental, avec son dédain des données du sens commun, avec ses cloisons étanches entre le monde du phénomène et celui de la pensée, entre le monde de la raison et celui de la morale ou de la religion, n'a-t-elle pas préparé le terrain aux prétentions les plus extravagantes d'hommes qui, pleins de confiance en leur propre esprit et se tenant eux-mêmes pour des êtres supérieurs, se sont cru le droit de s'élever au-dessus des règles communes, ou de les plier à leur fantaisie?" Maritain, in his winter course of 1914–15 at the Institut Catholique, proclaimed that a French victory "signifierait, non pas immédiatement sans doute, mais dans ses consequences éloignées, la victoire de la civilisation et de la foi catholique sur le naturalisme de la *Kultur* germano-protestante"; Philippe Chenaux, *Entre Maurras et Maritain* (Paris: Cerf, 1999), pp. 18–19, 201.

43. Perhaps a "control case" can be found in the societies of the old British Commonwealth: Canada, Australia, New Zealand. Like the U.S., and (almost) from the beginning, they have been in the Age of Mobilization. But their faith-related neo-Durkheimian definitions haven't fared as well. Either they lived in a "British" identity, which has since decayed in the "mother country" as well as the ex-colony; or (as in the case of Québec), they have undergone a turn-over which much more resembles the European model. But above all, they are not hegemonic powers, and in one case are constantly reminded of this fact by their proximity to the nation which is. So it is not surprising to find the figures for religious belief/

practice somewhat between European and U.S. ones. It is also not surprising that the issue of gay marriage, while it has been upsetting for Conservatives in Canada as well, has not awakened the same degree of heat and indignation in Canada as in our neighbour to the South.

44. This "hot" identity may also help to explain the differences between Europe and America that emerged on the occasion of the recent war in Iraq. Some commentators have tried to capture this in the memorable phrase: "Americans are from Mars, Europeans from Venus". See Robert Kagan, *Of Paradise and Power* (New York: Taylor and Francis, 2003).

45. William James, *The Varieties of Religious Experience* (New York: Random House, 1999).

46. Up till now, we have been comparing the U.S. with European societies, but perhaps another aspect will emerge if we compare it with the European Union; because this, in its gradual self-definition, has taken steps of its own in the direction of secularity 1, most notably the refusal to integrate God in the new, highly contested constitution. See Peter Berger, "Religion in the West", in *The National Interest,* Summer 2005, pp. 112–119. Berger sees the E.U. as an agency of secularization: "Integration into Europe means signing on the Eurosecularity" (p. 113); but more precisely put, we could say that integration into Europe encourages further the decline in power of whatever neo-Durkheimian identities existed.

Comparing the two political structures, we can say that for many Americans the neo-Durkheimian link between God and nation is strong; whereas for Europeans, not only is the link discredited in individual countries, but on the continental level, the plurality of confessions in which the older patriotisms were embedded poses an additional obstacle. In this way, "God" can be seen to threaten European integration, while still fostering American patriotism.

Thinking of the issue on the European level also shows how another of the factors mentioned above operates with greater force. European societies have tended to follow along behind their élite cultures more than American, we said above. But this effect is magnified at the "European" level, where the running has been entirely made by these élites—with consequences which have emerged recently in referenda in various states on the Continent.

47. *Esprit,* June 1997, pp. 45–47.

48. In using this rather vague expression, I am not trying in any way to define some kind of anthropological constant, a timeless definition of the human religious sense. I believe this is quite beyond our powers, at least today. The forms and modes of religion are much too varied across history. "Eternity" is a meaningful term in the religious traditions which have defined Latin Christendom; hence my use of it here. The claim is that religion in this register still has a powerful draw on people today.

49. It seems to me that the three-stage picture that I'm developing here is well captured in Hugh McLeod's paper "The Register, the Ticket and the Website", an as yet unpublished paper. But I wouldn't want to presume his agreement with the way I work it out here.

50. John Rawls, *Political Liberalism* (New York: Columbia University Press, 1993).

51. José Casanova, *Public Religions in the Modern World* (Chicago: University of Chicago Press, 1994).

52. Grace Davie, *Religion in Britain since 1945,* pp. 149 ff. Also Grace Davie, *Religion in Modern Europe,* pp. 53–54.

53. Grace Davie, *Religion in Britain since 1945,* pp. 123–124.

54. Paul Valadier, in *Esprit,* June 1997, pp. 39–40.

55. Mikhaïl Epstein, "Minimal Religion", and "Post-Atheism: From Apophatic Theology to 'Minimal Religion'", in Mikhaïl Epstein, Alexander Genis, and Slobodanka Vladiv-Glover, *Russian Postmodernism: New Perspectives in Post-Soviet Culture* (New York/Oxford: Berghahn Books, 1999). See also Jonathan Sutton, "'Minimal Religion' and Mikhaïl Epstein's Interpretation of Religion in Late-Soviet and Post-Soviet Russia", in *Studies in East European Thought,* February 2006. I am grateful to Jonathan Sutton for making me aware of Epstein's work.

56. Ibid., pp. 167–168.

57. Ibid., p. 386.

58. Ibid., p. 362.

15. The Immanent Frame

1. See Hubert Dreyfus and Charles Taylor, *Retrieving Realism* (forthcoming).

2. I have discussed this at greater length in *Sources of the Self* (Cambridge, Mass.: Harvard University Press, 1989).

3. Norbert Elias, *Über den Prozess der Zivilisation* (Frankfurt: Suhrkamp, 1978); English translation: *The Civilizing Process* (Oxford: Blackwell, 1994).

4. See especially *Surveiller et Punir* (Paris: Gallimard, 1975).

5. Max Weber, *Die Protestantische Ethik und der Geist des Kapitalismus* (Weinheim: Beltz Athenäum, 2000), p. 119; see translation by Talcott Parsons, *The Protestant Ethic and the Spirit of Capitalism* (New York: Scribner, 1958).

6. Max Scheler, *Gesammelte Werke,* Volume 6 (Bern/Munich: Francke Verlag, 1960), p. 205.

7. I mean, let me repeat, an order which can be understood in its own terms, without reference to interventions from outside; the issue of whether we have to suppose some higher creative power behind it remains disputed, of course.

8. Yves-Marie Hilaire, *Une Chrétienté au XIXe Siècle?* (Lille: PUL, 1977), Volume 2, pp. 631–633.

9. See René Rémond, *L'Anticléricalisme en France* (Paris: Fayard, 1976).

10. Albert Camus, *Noces* (Alger: Charlot, 1938).

11. Claude Chauvin, *Renan* (Paris: Desclée de Brouwer, 2000).

12. Cf. *The Varieties of Religion Today* (Cambridge, Mass.: Harvard University Press, 2002), p. 59.

13. "Ein Bild hielt uns gefangen", Ludwig Wittgenstein, *Philosophische Untersuchungen*, para. 115.

14. "Wer dies Schicksal der Zeit nicht männlich ertragen kann, dem muss man sagen: Er kehre lieber schweigend . . . in die weit und erbarmend geöffneten Arme der alten Kirche zurück." "Wissenschaft als Beruf", in Max Weber, *Gesammelte Aufsätze zur Wissenschaftslehre* (Tübingen: Mohr, 1982), p. 612; "Science as a Vocation", trans. H. Gerth and C. W. Mills, *From Max Weber* (London: Routledge, 1991), p. 155.

15. A. N. Wilson, *God's Funeral* (London: Norton, 1999), p. 12.

16. Eamon Duffy, *The Stripping of the Altars* (New Haven: Yale University Press, 1992).

17. "Obvious" needs to be further defined; we might distinguish a primary and a secondary sense. The primarily obvious is what you don't need any special training or education to know. We could say that it is equivalent to Macaulay's what "every schoolboy knows"; except that these things can turn out to be false, so we have to use "obvious" in a different sense, such that things can *seem* obvious, without really being so. The seemingly obvious is "what every schoolchild knows" (for any given culture).

As against this, we have the way in which some things can appear more and more obvious as a result of long experience and/or personal development, as older people can sometimes see the illusions of young people's loves or ideals. Of course, here too this "seeing through" can also turn out to be false, so we should allow for the seems/is distinction here too.

But the point is, that the secondary is a different kind of obviousness, because it only shows up in our world as a result of experience/development. Its domain is what people have often designated as "wisdom". Belief in God may be secondarily obvious, never primarily so (as might have seemed the claim behind the "proofs" for God's existence). As a result of experience, prayer, and practice, what was initially a mere leap of faith comes to be more and more clear and undeniable. In this (secondary) sense, for the saint, the existence of God may come to seem "obvious"—but never to the point where there is no further need of anticipatory confidence. Only people in the grips of "spin" think that the existence or non-existence of God is obvious in a primary sense. See my "Faith and Reason".

18. See Lucien Febvre, *Le Problème de l'Incroyance au XVIe siècle, la religion de Rabelais* (Paris: A. Michel, 1947).

19. A further word is necessary to clarify my concept of "fragilization". Hans Joas in his "Glaube und Moral im Zeitalter der Kontingenz" (in Hans Joas, *Braucht der Mensch Religion?* [Freiburg: Herder, 2004]) argues against a similar fragilization thesis put forward by Peter Berger in *Sehnsucht nach Sinn* (Frankfurt/Main, 1994). But I don't think there is any disagreement between Joas and myself on this. This is because the notion of "fragilization" (my word) is somewhat different between myself and Berger. I mean by this that greater proximity of alternatives has led to a society in which more people change their positions, that is, "convert" in their lifetimes, and/or adopt a different position than their parents. Life-time and intergenerational switches become more common. But this has

nothing to do with a supposed greater fragility of the faith they end up with (or decide to remain with), as Berger seems to imply. On the contrary, the faith arising in this contemporary predicament can be stronger, just because it has faced the alternative without distortion. It is common in all ages, and in ours as well, to find a "crutch" for one's faith in some depreciating story about the alternatives. So Protestants and Catholics walked around for centuries with highly negative stereotypes about the other, which didn't really resist examination. One reaction to fragilization in my sense can be an increasing reliance on such crutches. So one hears "arguments" today from believers about the possible immoral and violent consequences of atheism (look at Stalin, Pol Pot, etc.); and then counter-arguments from "secularists" warning against the same consequences flowing inevitably from religion (look at Torquemada, the Crusades, etc., etc.). All such "arguments" represent triumphs of selective attention over reality. Recently even so intelligent a person as Slavoj Žižek claimed that "'godless' atheist liberals" in the West are more tolerant of Muslims than Christians (see "Atheism is a legacy worth fighting for", *International Herald Tribune*, March 14, 2006, p. 6). In fact, when it comes to Islam-bashing, the record of both these groups is pretty shameful these days.

In fact, a faith which can throw away such crutches is much stronger, more rooted in its own sources. It is one of the advantages of our modern predicament that it can and does push people to jettison such demeaning defences. In this I fully agree with Joas.

20. "Ein Bild hielt uns gefangen", *Philosophical Investigations*, para. 115.

21. See Dreyfus and Taylor, *Retrieving Realism*, for a fuller discussion of modern epistemology and its deconstruction.

22. The "death of God" reference is from *The Gay Science*, para. 125. Later on, Nietzsche says: "Man sieht, *was* eigentlich über den christlichen Gott gesiegt hat: die christliche Moralität selbst, der immer strenger genommene Begriff der Wahrhaftigkeit, die Beichtväterfeinheit des christlichen Gewissens, übersetzt und sublimiert zum wissenschaftlichen Gewissen, zur intellektuellen Sauberkeit um jeden Preis. Die Natur ansehn, als ob sie ein Beweis für die Güte und Obhut eines Gottes sei; die Geschichte interpretieren zu Ehren einer göttlichen Vernunft, als beständiges Zeugnis einer sittlichen Weltordnung und sittlicher Schlussabsichten; die eignen Erlebnisse auslegen, wie wir fromme Menschen lange genug ausgelegt haben, wie als ob alles Fügung, alles Wink, alles dem Heil der Seele zuliebe ausgedacht und geschickt sei: Das ist numehr *vorbei,* das hat das Gewissen *gegen* sich, das gilt allen feineren Gewissen als unanständig, unehrlich, als Lügnerei, Feminismus, Schwachheit, Feigheit" (para. 357). It will be clear later on where my interpretation agrees with Nietzsche's.

23. Richard Lewontin, *New York Review of Books*, January 9, 1997, p. 28.

24. Lewontin's article again, quoting from Carl Sagan.

25. This materialism, for all the lack of sophistication of the arguments for it, is actually rather complex. One can distinguish different species of materialism which inhabit the for-

ests of modern scientific speculation. Besides just plain materialism (which approaches the status of a truism), there are mechanistic materialism, economic materialism, "billiard-ball" materialism, and so on. I have discussed this at greater length in my comment on Vincent Descombes' work; see my contribution to the Symposium: Vincent Descombes, *The Mind's Provisions* (Princeton: Princeton University Press, 2001), "Descombes' Critique of Cognitivism", in *Inquiry* 47 (2004), pp. 203–218.

26. Stephen Jay Gould, quoted in Frederick Crews, "Saving us from Darwin, part II", in *New York Review of Books,* October 18, 2001. This doesn't reflect Gould's more nuanced position, as set out in, for instance, *Rocks of Ages: Science and Religion in the Fullness of Life* (New York: Ballantine Books, 1999).

27. Dawkins' reasons for believing that science can sideline religion hardly inspire confidence. They draw heavily on an oversimple distinction between "faith" and "science". "A case can be made that faith is one of the world's great evils, comparable to the smallpox virus but harder to eradicate. Faith, being belief that isn't based on evidence, is the principal vice of any religion." As for science, it "is free of the main vice of religion, which is faith." But to hold that there are *no* assumptions in a scientist's work which aren't already based on evidence is surely a reflection of a *blind* faith, one that can't even feel the occasional tremor of doubt. Few religious believers are this untroubled. Dawkins' quotes are taken from Alister McGrath, *The Twilight of Atheism* (London and New York: Doubleday, 2004), p. 95.

28. Sometimes proponents of the materialist view are quite lucid about their prior ontological commitments. So Richard Lewontin: "Our willingness to accept scientific claims that are against common sense is the key to understanding the real struggle between science and the supernatural. We take the side of science *in spite of* the patent absurdity of its constructs, *in spite of* its failure to fulfill many of its extravagant promises of health and life, *in spite of* the tolerance of the scientific community for unsubstantiated just-so stories, because we have a prior commitment, a commitment to materialism."

"It is not that the methods and institutions of science somehow compel us to accept a material explanation of the phenomenal world but, on the contrary, that we are forced by our a priori allegiance to material causes to create an apparatus of investigation and a set of concepts that produce material explanations, no matter how counterintuitive, no matter how mystifying to the uninitiated. Moreover that materialism is absolute, for we cannot allow a divine foot in the door." Richard Lewontin, in *New York Review of Books,* January 9, 1997; quoted in *First Things,* June/July 2002.

29. A. N. Wilson, *God's Funeral,* speaking of the loss of faith in this period: "This is the story of bereavement as much as of adventure" (p. 4).

30. *The Complete Poems of Thomas Hardy,* ed. James Gibson (London: Macmillan, 1976), poem no. 403, p. 468.

31. See Stefan Collini, *Public Moralists: Political Thought and Intellectual Life in Britain, 1850–1930* (Oxford: Clarendon Press, 1991).

32. Of course, this change in view about our moral predicament connects to, that is, both supports and is supported by the powerful narrative of our "coming of age" in a world of immanent order. I return to the important place of this master narrative below.

33. I am grateful to Martin Warner for correcting me on this. The painting turns up in *The Idiot* (Part 3, chapter 6), and the Prince says of it (Part 2, chapter 4): "Some people may lose their faith by looking at that picture".

34. Friedrich Nietzsche, in *The Gay Science,* para. 125, the famous passage about the madman who announces the death of God, also makes use of this horizon image.

35. *Dover Beach,* ll. 21–28.

36. *Sources of the Self* (Cambridge, Mass.: Harvard University Press, 1989).

37. *Morales du grand siècle* (Paris: Gallimard, 1948), p. 226. Translation modified from Paul Bénichou, *Man and Ethics: Studies in French Classicism,* trans. Elizabeth Hughes (Garden City, N.Y.: Doubleday, 1971), p. 251.

38. J.-F. Lyotard, *La Condition post-moderne: rapport sur le savoir* (Paris: Éditions de Minuit, 1979).

39. There is a more sophisticated version of this in Steve Bruce, *Religion in Modern Britain* (Oxford: Oxford University Press, 1995), pp. 131–133.

40. Quoted in Sylvette Denèfle, *Sociologie de la Sécularisation* (Paris/Montréal: L'Harmattan, 1997), pp. 93–94.

41. If I can manage to tell this story properly, then we will see that there is some, phenomenal, truth to the "death of God" account. A humanism has come about which can be seen, and hence lived, as exclusive. And from within this, it can indeed seem plausible that science points us towards a materialist account of spirit. The "death of God" is not just an erroneous account of modern secularity on a theoretical level; it is also a way we may be tempted to interpret, and hence experience, the modern condition. It is not the explanans I am looking for, but it is a crucial part of the explanandum. In this role, I am very far from wanting to deny it.

42. Immanuel Kant, "Was ist Aufklärung?" in *Kants Werke,* Akademie Textausgabe (Berlin: Walter de Gruyter, 1968), Volume VIII, p. 33; "Enlightenment is man's emergence from his self-imposed nonage. Nonage is the inability to use one's own understanding without another's guidance." In "What Is Enlightenment?", trans. Peter Gay, in Gay, *The Enlightenment: A Comprehensive Anthology* (New York: Simon & Schuster, 1973), p. 384.

43. See Michael Warner, *Publics and Counterpublics* (New York/Cambridge, Mass.: Zone Books [distributed by MIT Press], 2002).

44. Syed Qutb, *Milestones,* trans. S. Badrul Hasan (Karachi: International Islamic Publishers, 1981).

45. Yuri Slezkine, *The Jewish Century* (Princeton: Princeton University Press, 2004), chapter 3, especially pp. 140–170.

46. Ibid., pp. 65 ff., 96–100.

47. Isaiah Berlin, *Four Essays on Liberty* (Oxford: Oxford University Press, 1969), pp. 171–172.

48. Albert Camus, *Le Mythe de Sisyphe* (Paris: Gallimard, Folio essais, 1942), p. 46.

49. Modified from *The Myth of Sisyphus,* trans. Justin O'Brien (Penguin Books, 1975), pp. 31 f.

50. Ibid., p. 39.

51. Modified from *The Myth of Sisyphus,* trans. O'Brien, p. 26.

52. Ibid., p. 75.

53. Modified from *The Myth of Sisyphus,* trans. O'Brien, p. 51.

54. Olivier Todd, *Albert Camus* (Paris: Gallimard, 1996), p. 536. Translation modified from Olivier Todd, *Albert Camus: A Life,* trans. Benjamin Ivry (New York: Alfred A. Knopf, 1997), p. 296.

55. Ibid., pp. 457–458.

56. From Todd, *Albert Camus: A Life,* p. 252.

57. Ibid., p. 396.

58. From Todd, *Albert Camus: A Life,* p. 214.

59. Ibid., p. 397.

60. Camus, *Le Mythe de Sisyphe,* p. 119. A little later in the same work, Camus says: "Comment ne pas comprendre que dans cet univers vulnérable, tout ce qui est humain et n'est que cela prend un sens plus brûlant? Visages tendus, fraternité menacée, amitié si forte et si pudique des hommes entre eux, ce sont les vraies richesses puisqu'elles sont périssables" (p. 122).

61. Modified from *The Myth of Sisyphus,* trans. O'Brien, p. 80.

62. See Ronald Aronson, *Camus & Sartre* (Chicago: University of Chicago Press, 2004).

63. Camus, *Le Mythe de Sisyphe,* pp. 79–80.

64. Modified from *The Myth of Sisyphus,* trans. O'Brien, p. 54.

65. Friedrich Nietzsche, *The Will to Power,* trans. Walter Kaufmann and R. J. Hollingdale (New York: Random House, 1967), para. 1067 (1885), pp. 549–550.

66. *L'ère de l'individu: contribution à une histoire de la subjectivité* (Paris: Gallimard, 1989), p. 53; italics in original. Quoted in Vincent Descombes, *Le complément du sujet* (Paris: Gallimard, 2004), p. 401.

67. But people of this orientation are often not in a CWS at all; that is, they recognize that they are offering one interpretation of the human condition among many. This is particularly so when they see the limitations of scientism.

68. Vincent Descombes, in *Le complément du sujet,* makes a very telling criticism of Renaut's notion of autonomy as self-authorization, in the chapters following the quote I cited above.

69. I have discussed and criticized this in *Sources of the Self,* Part I.

70. See note 28 above.

71. *The Complete Poems of Thomas Hardy,* ed. James Gibson (London: Macmillan, 1976), poem 267, pp. 327–328.

72. Czeslaw Milosz, *The Land of Ulro* (New York: Farrar, Straus, Giroux, 1984), p. 94. Milosz draws on Erich Heller's essay "Goethe and the Idea of Scientific Truth", from his collection, *The Disinherited Mind.*

73. Milosz, *The Land of Ulro,* p. 52.

16. Cross Pressures

1. Martin Heidegger, "Die Zeit des Weltbildes", in *Holzwege* (Frankfurt am Main: Klostermann, 1950).

2. Ernest Jones, *Sigmund Freud, Life and Work,* Volume 2, *Years of Maturity 1901–1919* (London: The Hogarth Press, 1955), p. 463.

3. Peter Berger, "Religion and the West", in *The National Interest* (Summer 2005), 80, Research Library, p. 116.

4. Emmanuel Mounier, *L'Affrontement Chrétien* (Paris: Seuil, 1945).

5. William Connolly, *The Terms of Political Discourse* (Princeton: Princeton University Press, 1983).

6. Richard Dawkins, "Forever Voyaging", *Times Literary Supplement,* August 4, 2000, p. 12.

7. Ibid.

8. Noel Annan, *Our Age* (London: Fontana, 1991), p. 608. I referred to this exchange above; see Chapter 11.

9. I am obviously using the term 'fulfillment' in a broader sense than the ordinary word, which is usually reserved for whatever fulfills our personal needs and aspirations. Here I want to extend it to whatever realizes (what we see as) the highest and fullest form of life, even if this demands the sacrifice of personal "fulfillment". I chose this term, partly because I need some such generic category for my argument, and secondly because of the role I had already given to "fullness". But nevertheless I write with trepidation, because I know how hard it is to escape misinterpretation, short of reprinting this note on every page.

10. David Hume, *Enquiry concerning the Principles of Morals,* Section IX, paras. 222–224, in David Hume, *Enquiries,* ed. L. A. Selby-Bigge (Oxford: Clarendon Press, 1902), pp. 272–276; see also p. 274, note 1, for Hume's understanding of the transition from savagery to civilization.

11. Quoted in Piers Brendon, *The Dark Valley* (New York: Knopf, 2000), p. 405.

12. Peter Brown, *The Body and Society* (New York: Columbia University Press, 1988).

13. *Books & Culture,* January–February 2002 (Carol Stream, Ill.), p. 13.

14. John Keegan, *A History of Warfare* (London: Hutchinson, 1993).

15. John Stuart Mill, *On Liberty,* in Mill, *Three Essays* (Oxford: Oxford University Press, 1975), p. 77.

16. Cf. Peter Gay's interesting book *The Enlightenment: An Interpretation,* whose first volume is subtitled: *The Rise of Modern Paganism* (New York: Knopf, 1966).

17. Modris Eksteins, *Rites of Spring* (Toronto: Dennys, 1989), Act I, 1.

18. See the discussion of Descartes' *Traité des Passions* in my *Sources of the Self* (Cambridge, Mass.: Harvard University Press, 1989), chapter 8.

17. Dilemmas 1

1. David Martin, *The Dilemmas of Contemporary Religion* (New York: St. Martin's Press, 1978), p. 94.

2. Philip Rieff, *The Triumph of the Therapeutic: Uses of Faith after Freud* (New York: Harper & Row, 1966).

3. Francis Fukuyama, *The End of History and the Last Man* (New York: Free Press, 1992).

4. Reference here is to her William James Lecture, "Transcending Humanity", published as chapter 15 of Martha Nussbaum, *Love's Knowledge* (New York: Oxford University Press, 1990; cited hereafter as *LK*). But I shall also draw on the discussion in chapter 12 of this work, as well as on her Gifford Lectures, as reported by Fergus Kerr, *Immortal Longings* (Notre Dame: University of Notre Dame Press, 1997), whose treatment of these issues I have found very helpful.

5. Cambridge University Press, 1986.

6. *LK,* pp. 365–367.

7. Ibid., p. 372.

8. Chapter 12, "Narrative Emotions".

9. *LK,* p. 307.

10. Ibid., p. 378.

11. Ibid., p. p. 379; italics in original.

12. I have discussed this in *Sources of the Self* (Cambridge, Mass.: Harvard University Press, 1989), chapter 13.

13. Nussbaum invokes this in her Gifford Lectures, in the love of Leopold and Molly Bloom in *Ulysses;* see Fergus Kerr, *Immortal Longings,* pp. 4–5.

14. R. M. Rilke, *Duino Elegies, II: The Selected Poetry of Rainer Maria Rilke,* trans. Stephen Mitchell (New York: Vintage, 1984), p. 161.

15. *LK,* pp. 50–53.

16. Nel Noddings, *Caring: A Feminine Approach to Ethics and Moral Education* (Berkeley: University of California Press, 1984).

17. *LK,* chapter 12.

18. *The Body and Society* (New York: Columbia University Press, 1988).

19. "periagoge"; see *Republic,* Book VII, 518E–519A.

20. This issue was famously raised by Anthony Burgess in *A Clockwork Orange* (New York: W. W. Norton, 1963).

21. See *Les Mots et les Choses* (Paris: Gallimard, 1967).

22. See René Girard, *La Violence et le Sacré* (Paris: Grasset, 1972); and *Le Bouc émissaire* (Paris: Grasset, 1982).

23. See the Gospel according to Matthew, chapter 13, verses 24–30.

24. See Girard, *La Violence et le Sacré* and *Le Bouc émissaire.*

25. Marx uses this expression of class society and its exploitation, but he would have been happy to extend it to the renunciative thrust of those religions which reflected and supported class society.

26. See also the discussion of Luce Irigaray's attempts to invoke a religion which wouldn't need sacrifice in Fergus Kerr, *Immortal Longings,* p. 102.

27. See the critique of the inadequacies of a theology of satisfaction in Karl Rahner, *On the Theology of Death* (Freiburg: Herder; Montreal: Palm Publishers, 1961), pp. 58–63.

28. See the discussion about the wrath of God in Herbert McCabe, *God, Christ and Us* (London: Continuum, 2003): "We need images, especially conflicting images" (pp. 15–16). McCabe points out (p. 61) that Aquinas also argued this need for many images (*Summa Theologiae,* Ia, 1, 9).

29. This is especially the case with sexual fulfillment. The confusion can perhaps be lessened by serious thought about the relation between erotic desire and the love of God, and about the place of gender identities in our relation to God. I will raise this matter briefly below, in "Conversions," section 6.

30. James Gilligan, *Violence* (New York: Vintage, 1996).

31. Chris Hedges, *War Is a Force That Gives Us Meaning* (New York: Public Affairs, 2002), p. 89. Jonathan Glover points to the same sense of excitement at power which some people experience in combat. War, he quotes a Vietnam veteran, "is, for men, at some terrible level the closest thing to what childbirth is for women: the initiation into the power of life and death. It's like lifting off a corner of the universe and looking at what's underneath"; in *Humanity* (New Haven: Yale University Press, 2000), p. 56.

32. Hedges also notes this, in *War Is a Force,* pp. 98–105.

33. John Keegan, *A History of Warfare* (London: Hutchinson, 1993).

34. Georges Bataille, *Théorie de la religion* (Paris: Gallimard, 1973).

35. Ibid., p. 71.

36. Ibid., p. 65.

37. Georges Bataille, *La Part Maudite* (Paris: Minuit, 1967), p. 33.

38. Modified from "The Notion of Expenditure", in *Visions of Excess: Selected Writings, 1927–1939,* ed. and trans. Allan Stoekl (Minneapolis: University of Minnesota Press, 1985), p. 118.

39. Bataille, *Théorie de la religion,* p. 66.

40. From Bataille, *Theory of Religion,* trans. Robert Hurley (New York: Zone Books, 1989), p. 49.

41. Ibid., p. 59

42. Ibid., p. 44.

43. Bataille, *La Part Maudite*, pp. 113–115.

44. Modified from *The Accursed Share: An Essay on General Economy*, trans. Robert Hurley (New York: Zone Books, 1991), p. 57.

45. Bataille, *Théorie de la religion*, pp. 71–75.

46. Ibid., p. 123.

47. Bataille, *La Part Maudite*, p. 53.

48. Modified from "The Notion of Expenditure," in *Visions of Excess*, ed./trans. Allan Stoekl, p. 128.

49. Ibid., pp. 115–116.

50. From *The Accursed Share*, trans. Robert Hurley, pp. 58 f.

51. A. O. Scott, "The Sun Also Sets", review of *Cities of the Plain, Vol. 3, The Border Trilogy*, by Cormac McCarthy, in *The New York Review of Books*, September 24, 1998.

52. "Sie sind nach Aussen hin, dort wo das Fremde, *die* Fremde beginnt, nicht viel besser als losgelassene Raubthiere. Sie geniessen da die Freiheit von allem socialen Zwang, sie halten sich in der Wildniss schadlos für die Spannung, welche eine lange Einschliessung und Einfriedigung in den Frieden der Gemeinschaft giebt, sie treten in die Unschuld des Raubthier-Gewissens *zurück*, also frohlockende Ungeheuer, welche vielleicht von einer scheusslicher Abfolge von Mord, Niederbrennung, Schändung, Folterung mit einem Übermuthe und seelischen Gleichgewichte davongehen, wie als ob nur ein Studentenstreich vollbracht sei, überzeugt davon, dass die Dichter für lange Etwas zu singen und zu rühmen haben." *Zur Genealogie der Moral*, Erste Abhandlung, 11; in *Nietzsches Werke* (Berlin: Walter de Gruyter, 1968), Sechste Abteilung, Zweiter Band, pp. 288–289.

53. Quoted in James Karman, *Robinson Jeffers* (San Francisco: Chronicle Books, 1987), p. 51.

54. Page references are to *The Collected Poetry of Robinson Jeffers*, ed. Tim Hunt (Stanford: Stanford University Press, 2001).

55. See 1 Samuel 15, where Saul is deposed because he failed to kill all the Amalekites.

56. "Fecemi la divina Potestate, / La somma Sapienza e 'l Primo Amore"; *Inferno*, Canto III, ll. 5–6.

57. The image is from R. F. Capon, *An Offering of Uncles: The Priesthood of Adam and the Shape of the World* (New York: Sheed and Ward, 1967).

58. Bataille, *Théorie de la religion*, p. 132.

59. "Cela revient en fait, comme dans l'expérience des mystiques, à une contemplation intellectuelle 'sans forme et sans mode'". *La Part Maudite*, pp. 271–273.

18. Dilemmas 2

1. Luc Ferry, *L'Homme-Dieu ou Le sens de la vie* (Paris: Grasset, 1996).

2. Ibid., p. 19.

3. From Luc Ferry, *Man Made God: The Meaning of Life*, trans. David Pellauer (Chicago and London: University of Chicago Press, 2002), p. 7.

4. Ferry, *L'Homme-Dieu,* pp. 204–205.

5. Ibid., p. 124.

6. Ibid., pp. 240–241.

7. Modified from Ferry, *Man Made God,* trans. Pellauer, p. 139.

8. See "A Catholic Modernity?", in James Heft, ed., *A Catholic Modernity?* (New York: Oxford University Press, 2001).

9. Marcel Gauchet, *Le désenchantement du monde* (Paris: Gallimard, 1985).

10. Richard Lewontin, in the *New York Review of Books,* October 20, 2005, p. 53.

11. Ernst Jünger, *Der Arbeiter: Herrschaft und Gestalt* (Hamburg: Hanseatische Verlagsanstalt, 1932).

12. G. W. F. Hegel, *Die Phänomenologie des Geistes* (Hamburg: Felix Meiner Verlag, 1952), p. 144; Ernst Jünger, *In Stahlgewittern. Aus dem Tagebuch eines Stosstruppführers* [original publication 1920] (Berlin: E. S. Mittler & Sohn, 1924).

13. See "A Catholic Modernity?", in James Heft, ed. *A Catholic Modernity?*

14. Jeffrey Alexander's new book (*The Civil Sphere* [New York: Oxford University Press, 2006], especially chapter 4) examines the discourse of the civil sphere, the common normative understanding which holds liberal democratic societies together. This discourse expresses and entrenches codes, which endorse certain motives, relations and institutions, and condemn others as contrary to the ethos of the society. Alexander sees these codes as reflecting notions of purity and pollution, that is, the negatively coded features are really seen as corrupting and profoundly undermining our society. Alexander's point is that, while it is hard to imagine a modern democracy surviving without such a code, it also inevitably offers a dangerous source of social exclusion, of inhuman modes of "purification". I believe there is a link here to my discussion of the scapegoat phenomenon.

15. I have tried to lay out a fuller account in "Notes on the Sources of Violence: Perennial and Modern", in James L. Heft, ed., *Beyond Violence: Religious Sources of Social Transformation in Judaism, Christianity, Islam* (New York: Fordham University Press, 2004), pp. 15–42.

16. I have obviously borrowed here from the very interesting works of René Girard; see *La Violence et le Sacré* (Paris: Grasset, 1972); *Le Bouc Émissaire* (Paris: Grasset, 1982), *Je vois Satan tomber comme l'éclair* (Paris: Grasset, 1999).

17. Something of this connection is articulated by Frantz Fanon, but horrifyingly, not as a critique, but as a justification of purifying violence. This is how Sartre articulates this glorification of anti-colonial war:

> It is man re-creating himself. . . . no gentleness can efface the marks of violence: only violence itself can destroy them. The native cures himself of colonial neurosis by thrusting out the settler through force of arms. When his rage boils over, he rediscovers his lost innocence and he comes to know himself in that he himself creates himself. . . . Once begun, it is a war that gives no quarter. You may fear or be feared; that is to say, abandon yourself to the dissociations of a sham existence or conquer your birthright of

unity. When the peasant takes a gun in his hands, the old myths grow dim and the prohibitions are one by one forgotten. The rebel's weapon is the proof of his humanity. For in the first days of the revolt you must kill; to shoot down a European is to kill two birds with one stone, to destroy an oppressor and the man he oppresses at the same time: there remain a dead man and a free man.

Quoted in Ronald Aronson, *Camus & Sartre* (Chicago: University of Chicago Press, 2004), p. 222.

18. Perhaps this could be seen as a reflection of a development that Balthasar formulates theologically: that after Calvary "evil loses whatever it had of 'pagan innocence': . . . ill is done and even celebrated for its own sake, and fascinates like the snake-engirdled head of Medusa"; Aidan Nichols, *No Bloodless Myth: A Guide through Balthasar's Dramatics* (Edinburgh: T&T Clark, 2000), pp. 208–209.

19. Quoted in Jonathan Glover, *Humanity: A Moral History of the Twentieth Century* (New Haven: Yale University Press, 2000), p. 256.

20. It is in this context that I would like to understand the thesis about monotheism and violence of Regina Schwartz's interesting and suggestive work, *The Curse of Cain* (Chicago: University of Chicago Press, 1997). I am suggesting that the phenomenon is perhaps more widespread and general than she proposes.

21. *War Is a Force Which Gives Us Meaning* (New York: Public Affairs, 2002).

22. See the interesting book by Hauke Brunkhorst on the crucial importance of solidarity to modern thought: *Solidarität: Von der Bürgerfreundschaft zur globalen Rechtsgenossenschaft* (Frankfurt: Suhrkamp, 2002).

23. John Rawls, *A Theory of Justice* (Cambridge, Mass.: Harvard University Press, 1971).

24. See Immanuel Kant, *Zum ewigen Frieden,* in *Kants Werke,* Akademie Textausgabe (Berlin: Walter de Gruyter, 1968), Volume VIII, pp. 341–386; English translation: "Perpetual Peace", in H. Reiss, ed., *Kant's Political Writings* (Cambridge: Cambridge University Press, 1970). Arguably, this depended more on harmony of interests considerations, which Kant still accepted, even though they were no longer central to his ethical theory.

25. I have discussed this at greater length in *Sources of the Self* (Cambridge, Mass.: Harvard University Press, 1989), Part I.

26. I have discussed this further in ibid., chapter 8.

27. See Chapter 15, note 49.

28. From Olivier Todd, *Albert Camus: A Life,* trans. Benjamin Ivry (New York: Alfred A. Knopf, 1997), p. 252.

29. *Sources of the Self,* chapter 25. I have drawn here on my discussion in "A Catholic Modernity?", in *A Catholic Modernity,* ed. James Heft.

30. Fyodor Dostoyevsky, *The Devils,* trans. David Magarshack (Harmondsworth: Penguin Books, 1971), p. 404.

31. A conversation with Sulak Sivaraksa.

32. Nancy Huston, *Professeurs de désespoir* (Paris: Actes Sud, 2004).

33. Ibid., p. 347.

34. But plainly an adequate account of this phenomenon would have to delve much deeper, into our times and into the human heart; as we can see from Huston's more sympathetic treatment of Samuel Beckett. See also, for instance, Czeslaw Milosz on Gombrowicz, in *The Land of Ulro* (New York: Farrar, Straus, Giroux, 1985), section 12.

35. Ibid., p. 45; italics in original.

36. The passage can be found in a slightly different translation in *The Demons,* trans. Richard Pevear and Larissa Volokhonsky (New York: Vintage, 1995), Part Three, chapter 5, section vi, pp. 592–583.

37. See the discussion of Derrida and Lévinas in John Milbank, *Being Reconciled* (London: Routledge, 2003), chapter 8. See also Robert Spaemann, *Glück und Wohlwollen* (Stuttgart: Klett Cotta, 1989).

38. One might think that "optimistic" perspectives, those which hope for far-reaching transformations of human life, are more epistemically chancy than "pessimistic" views. One would need much less anticipatory confidence to espouse the latter. But if this means that one is less exposed to tragic error as a "pessimist", then it isn't correct. One kind of disaster attends trying a transformation which is in fact impossible. But there is another kind of loss, in which a positive change which is attainable is aborted from the beginning through the refusal to believe in it. Thus it might seem smarter, or safer, never to trust anyone else, but certain kinds of mutually empowering relations with others will never grow in a climate of thick mutual mistrust. Examples stretch all the way from love to the forms of political power which Hannah Arendt wrote about.

39. See Matthew 20, verses 1–16. In a profound discussion of another parable, that of the Good Samaritan, Paul Thibaud makes the remark that the Samaritan's response should not simply be seen as a one-off act. It inaugurates a new relation. "Cette relation s'étend dans le temps, elle peut connaître des étapes comme le montre l'évocation de la convalescence à l'auberge, elle inaugure un temps meilleur, unissant les protagonistes dans la perspective d'un avenir commun. L'horizon qui s'offre n'est pas un horizon apocalyptique, comme dans nombre d'autres paraboles évangéliques, c'est un horizon historique, d'amélioration du monde." See Thibaud, "L'Autre et le Prochain", in *Esprit,* June 2003, pp. 13–24. I might add, and Thibaud might well agree here, that this historical horizon makes sense for Christians in relation to the deeper, apocalyptic one.

40. See note 16 above, especially René Girard, *Je vois Satan tomber comme l'éclair.*

41. This is the insight that Shatov comes to, faced with the generosity of Arina Prokhorovna, for all her reductive views on human life; see *The Demons,* Part Three, chapter 5, section iii, p. 584.

42. For an interesting discussion of the advantages and dangers of a Truth Commission of this kind, see Rajeev Bhargava, "Restoring Decency to Barbaric Societies", in Robert Rotberg and Dennis Thompson, eds., *Truth and Justice* (Princeton: Princeton University Press, 2000), pp. 45–67.

19. Unquiet Frontiers of Modernity

1. Victor Turner, *The Ritual Process: Structure and Anti-Structure* (Ithaca, N.Y.: Cornell University Press, 1969), and *Dramas, Fields, and Metaphors* (Ithaca, N.Y.: Cornell University Press, 1978).

2. Benedict Anderson, *Imagined Communities: Reflections on the Origin and Spread of Nationalism* (London: Verso, 1983; second edition, 1991).

3. Ibid., p. 37.

4. See especially J.-F. Lyotard, *La Condition post-moderne: rapport sur le savoir* (Paris: Éditions de Minuit, 1979).

5. The term is Shelley's, but adopted by Earl Wasserman in a very interesting way. See his book *The Subtler Language* (Baltimore: Johns Hopkins University Press, 1968). For a further discussion of this concept of 'subtler language', see Chapter 10 above, and also my *Sources of the Self* (Cambridge, Mass.: Harvard University Press, 1989), Part V.

6. See the extremely interesting exploration of this theme, on Weber and other writers, in Eyal Chowers, *The Modern Self in the Labyrinth* (Cambridge, Mass.: Harvard University Press, 2004).

7. An expression used by Chantal Millon-Delsol in *Esprit,* no. 233, June 1997, p. 45.

8. Philippe Ariès, *L'Homme devant la mort* (Paris: Seuil, 1977).

9. Luc Ferry, *L'Homme-Dieu ou Le sens de la vie* (Paris: Grasset, 1996), p. 12.

10. Sylvette Denèfle, *Sociologie de la Sécularisation* (Paris: L'Harmattan, 1997), chapter 7.

11. Translation modified from *Stéphane Mallarmé: Selected Poems,* trans. Henry Weinfield (Berkeley: University of California Press, 1994), p. 12.

12. Letter of May 14, 1867, to Henri Cazalis, reproduced in *Correspondance Mallarmé 1862–1871* (Paris: Gallimard, 1959), p. 240.

13. Modified from *Selected Letters of Stéphane Mallarmé,* ed. and trans. Rosemary Lloyd (Chicago and London: University of Chicago Press, 1988), p. 74.

14. Translations modified from *Stéphane Mallarmé: Selected Poems,* trans. Henry Weinfield (Berkeley: University of California Press, 1994), p. 69.

15. See the discussion on Hopkins below, in Chapter 20.

16. See "The Immanent Counter-Enlightenment", in Ronald Beiner and Wayne Norman, eds., *Canadian Political Philosophy* (Don Mills, Ont./New York: Oxford University Press, 2001), pp. 386–400.

20. Conversions

1. Vaclav Havel, *Letters to Olga* (New York: Knopf, [1984], 1988), pp. 331–332. Quoted by Bellah, *Religious Evolution,* pp. 8–9.

2. Paul Elie, *The Life You Save May Be Your Own* (New York: Farrar, Straus, Giroux, 2003), p. 160. I am quoting here mostly Elie, though the phrase "organism in an environment" is Percy's.

3. Once again, I am following the penetrating discussion in Elie, *The Life You Save,* pp. 155, 312. Double quotes are Elie's text; single quotes enclose expressions of O'Connor.

4. This turn towards the past, which Norman Cantor referred to as the "retro-medieval" outlook, drew great numbers of writers, and not only Catholic converts; e.g., Henry Adams. See Elie, *The Life You Save,* pp. 6–7 and 97.

5. "I am talking about the common tradition of Christianity which has made Europe what it is, and about the common cultural elements which this common Christianity has brought with it. . . . It is in Christianity that our arts have developed; it is in Christianity that the laws of Europe have—until recently—been rooted. It is against a background of Christianity that all our thought has significance." T. S. Eliot, *Notes Towards the Definition of Culture* (London, Faber & Faber, 1962), p. 122; quoted in Joseph Pearce, *Literary Converts* (London: HarperCollins, 1999), p. 264.

6. Jacques Maritain, *Trois Réformateurs* (Paris: Plon, 1925).

7. Jean-Luc Barré, *Jacques et Raïssa Maritain* (Paris: Stock, 1997), p. 256.

8. Philippe Chenaux, *Entre Maurras et Maritain* (Paris: Cerf, 1999), p. 91.

9. See Joseph Pearce, *Literary Converts,* chapter 15.

10. Ibid., pp. 166–167. See also Ian Ker, *The Catholic Revival in English Literature, 1845–1961* (South Bend: University of Notre Dame Press, 2003), p. 191.

11. See Paul Elie, *The Life You Save.*

12. Richard Neuhaus, "The Public Square", in *First Things,* March 2005, p. 60. The Methodist Bishop sounds like a prime example of the (now outmoded) "pre-millennial" outlook, but we can see lots of examples of this elision of Christian faith and democratic civilization among today's "post-millennials" as well.

13. *The Rivers North of the Future: The Testament of Ivan Illich,* as told to David Cayley (Toronto: Anansi, 2005). Page and chapter references in the text are to this work.

14. See Greg Urban, *Metaphysical Community: The Interplay of the Senses and the Intellect* (Austin: University of Texas Press, 1996), chapter 2, pp. 28–65.

15. I have also developed this further in "The Perils of Moralism" (forthcoming).

16. Jean-Luc Barré, *Jacques et Raïssa Maritain,* p. 396.

17. Ibid., p. 398.

18. Paris: Éditions Montaigne, 1936.

19. Emmanuel Mounier, *La Pensée de Charles Péguy* (Paris: Plon, 1931), p. 144.

20. Martin Heidegger, *Sein und Zeit* (Tübingen: Niemeyer, 1927), Second Division, chapter 3, section 65.

21. *Clio, dialogue de l'histoire et de l'âme païenne,* VIII, 285–286, quoted in Mounier, *La Pensée de Charles Péguy,* p. 82.

22. As Albert Béguin put it, as the first of his line who had learned to read, "il se retourne vers les ancêtres taciturnes, et mesure son privilège de venir premier manifester par la parole ce qui s'était conserver intact dans la succession de ceux qui ne s'exprimaient que par les gestes et les grands actes solonnels de la vie"; Albert Béguin, *La Prière de Péguy,* 4th ed. (Paris:

Seuil, 1948), p. 19. Béguin is describing a passage in Péguy's *Note Conjointe sur Monsieur Descartes*. Mounier quotes from the same work: "L'homme se replonge dans le silence de sa race et de remontée en remontée il y trouve le dernier prolongement que nous puissions saisir du silence éternel de la création première"; *Note Conjointe*, IV, 92–96; Mounier, *La Pensée de Charles Péguy*, p. 91.

23. Mounier, *La Pensée de Charles Péguy*, p. 106.

24. *Notre jeunesse*, IV, 59; quoted in Mounier, *La Pensée de Charles Péguy*, p. 115.

25. Ibid., IV, 51; quoted in Mounier, *La Pensée de Charles Péguy*, p. 109.

26. See an excellent discussion of what this meant to Péguy in Alain Finkielkraut, *Le Mécontemporain* (Paris: Gallimard, 1991), pp. 40 ff.

27. Mounier, *La Pensée de Charles Péguy*, p. 107.

28. Ibid. We can see here an idea which has parallels to Herder's notion that each person and each people "hat sein eigenes Maass", the core of the modern ideal of authenticity. This is another facet of Péguy which is quintessentially modern.

29. As Mounier puts it, "La cité harmonieuse, qui oublie toutes les luttes passées, ne connaît pas d'exclusions, et reçoit tous les hommes de toutes les cultures, de toutes les vies intérieures, de toutes les religions, de toutes les philosophies." *La Pensée de Charles Péguy*, p. 46.

30. Ibid., pp. 182–183.

31. *Note Conjointe*, quoted and discussed in Alexander Dru, *Péguy* (London: Harvill, 1956), pp. 98–103.

32. *Note Conjointe*, IX, 104–106; *l'argent, suite*, XIV-9, 135; quote in Mounier, *La Pensée de Charles Péguy*, pp. 132–133.

33. *Les récentes œuvres de Zola*, II, 130, quoted in Mounier, *La Pensée de Charles Péguy*, pp. 204–5.

34. See *Le Porche de la deuxième Vertu*, in Charles Péguy, *Oeuvres poétiques complètes* (Paris: Gallimard, Éditions Pléiade, 1975), pp. 527–670. See the discussion in Mounier, *La Pensée de Charles Péguy*, pp. 192 ff.

35. *Un nouveau théologien*, quoted in Albert Béguin, *La Prière de Péguy*, p. 42. Also Mounier, *La Pensée de Charles Péguy*, p. 189 (attributed to *nouveau théologien*, XIII, 257–258).

36. This is, of course, not the only problem with Péguy's invocation of "race" in the sense of nation. He was clearly not in any sense a racist, but one may quarrel with his nationalism, and particularly with his acceptance of the War, in which he lost his life. His critique of modern rootlessness plainly also has its dangers.

37. Von Balthasar, who wrote in the wake of these theologians, also gives an important place to Péguy; see his *Herrlichkeit*, Volume 2 (Einsiedeln: Joannes Verlag, 1962), pp. 769–880.

38. Eamon Duffy, *Faith of our Fathers* (London: Continuum, 2004).

39. The pre-history of Vatican II shows how this ability to connect with the Christian

faith of another age can help us to relate our own. An inflexible conception of the Church, of its authority, of the philosophical sources it could call on, found expression in an intransigent condemnation of "modernism". All this was narrowing the permitted intellectual life of the Catholic Church and digging an ever deeper trench between it and the world. The way beyond this impasse was found in a return to the Patristic sources, particularly the Greek fathers, in the works among others of Henri de Lubac and Yves Congar. These sources not only were the basis for renewed definitions of the church and the supernatural, but also made it possible to recover the connections between theology and mystical life, and between both of these and the lived experience of our age. Speaking of these sources, a recent author says: "Théologie en actes, qui sourd de l'experience des premières communautés chrétiennes, et théologie mystique, où les symboles joue un rôle capital, elle comble l'appétit du vécu et du mystère des contemporains que décourage le brouet rationalisant, sinon rationaliste, de l'enseignement délivré sous l'étiquette thomiste, enseignement qui soumet la prolifération de la vie à un carcan thomiste. Théologie de l'histoire du salut et théologie sensible aux tribulations de l'histoire de l'Église, elle confère à l'histoire un sens qu'ils [sc. les nouveaux théologiens] cherchent à tâtons, et dont l'anhistorisme de la scolastique tardive est bien incapable." Étienne Fouilloux, *Une Église en quête de liberté* (Paris: Desclée de Brouwer, 1998), p. 185.

40. *Die Kunstlehre*, 81–82; I have chosen 'symbol' as the key word, even though it was not the only one used, and the usage within and across writers was varied and not always consistent. Sometimes the word 'allegory' was used for the same thing; which was highly confusing, since 'symbol' as a vehicle for this key idea was defined in contrast to 'allegory' (under another description). Confusion is potentially further compounded by the fact that this term is also used in a host of different ways by others (its use in the expression 'symbolic logic' seems utterly antipodal to the sense it bears for the Romantics). But we need a word for our discussion, and let it be 'symbol'.

41. See Stephen Gill, *Wordsworth and the Victorians* (Oxford: Clarendon Press, 1998).

42. See Seamus Heaney, "The Fire i' the Flint", in *Preoccupations* (London: Faber & Faber, 1980), pp. 79–97.

43. I have developed this point further in *Sources of the Self* (Cambridge, Mass.: Harvard University Press, 1989), chapter 21.

44. "Le Tombeau d'Edgar Poe", line 6.

45. This idea of the importance of the addressee, even beyond our contemporaries the super-addressee, was also developed by Mikhail Bakhtin.

46. Ferdinand de Saussure, *Cours de Linguistique générale* (Paris: Payot, 1978), pp. 155–156.

47. "God's Grandeur"; see *Gerard Manley Hopkins: Selected Poetry*, ed. Catherine Philips (Oxford: Oxford University Press, 1995), p. 114.

48. This phrase quoted by Norman White, in his *Hopkins: A Literary Biography* (Oxford: Oxford University Press, 1992), p. 125.

49. "Inversnaid", *Selected Poetry*, ed. Philips, p. 138.

50. Von Balthasar, *The Glory of the Lord*, p. 357. Hopkins' Scotism seems to prefigure in an eerie way the "minimal religion" which Mikhaïl Epstein discerns in post-atheist Russia. This, reacting against the concern for the "distant one" of atheist communism, is primarily concerned with our relations with our neighbours, particular people. For Epstein, there is a theological vision underlying this. "Minimalist theology . . . eschews pantheistic assumptions. God is not in everything, but in each thing, in the *eachness* of every thing." "The true subject of theology is the world of singularities, the uniqueness of all things created in the image of the single Creator." "Each thing is unique only by virtue of the fact that God is unique." See Mikhaïl Epstein, "Minimal Religion", in Mikhaïl Epstein, Alexander Genis, and Slobodanka Vladiv-Glover, *Russian Postmodernism: New Perspectives in Post-Soviet Culture* (New York/Oxford: Berghahn Books, 1999), pp. 167–169.

51. *Selected Poetry*, ed. Philips, p. 117.

52. "Pied Beauty", *Selected Poetry*, ed. Philips, p. 117.

53. "I wake and feel", *Selected Poetry*, ed. Philips, p. 151. See the discussion in von Balthasar, *The Glory of the Lord*, pp. 379–380, 383–384.

54. "The Wreck of the Deutschland", stanza 24, line 191; *Selected Poetry*, ed. Philips, p. 104.

55. Ibid., stanza 21, lines 164–169; *Selected Poetry*, ed. Philips, p. 103. See von Balthasar, *The Glory of the Lord*, p. 387.

56. "The Habit of Perfection", *Selected Poetry*, ed. Philips, p. 79.

57. "Nondum", *Selected Poetry*, ed. Philips, p. 80.

58. "God's Grandeur", *Selected Poetry*, ed. Philips, p. 114; see also "The Starlight Night", ibid.; and especially "That Nature is a Heraclitean Fire", ibid., p. 163.

59. "I wake and feel", *Selected Poetry*, ed. Philips, p. 151. The three lines after the last quoted here were quoted above, beginning "Selfyeast of spirit", note 13.

60. "Carrion Comfort", *Selected Poetry*, ed. Philips, p. 153; and "Justus quidem tu es, Domine", ibid., p. 165. Walter Ong argues cogently that Hopkins' periods of despondency cannot be understood as a loss of faith. "Everything Hopkins says and everything in his ascetical background suggests that Hopkins' point-blank thrust into the suffering self, far from being a threat to Christian faith that somehow made God 'disappear', in fact provided an opportunity to know more deeply what the faith entailed and to embrace the faith's full consequences with a degree of explicit awareness unattainable before." Walter J. Ong, *Hopkins, the Self and God* (Toronto: University of Toronto Press, 1986), p. 152.

61. See again "That Nature is a Heraclitean Fire", in order to get a sense of how much Hopkins' universe was beyond the dominant cosmos ideas of the Middle Ages and early modernity; *Selected Poetry*, ed. Philips, p. 163. See also the discussion in Ong, *Hopkins*, pp. 156–159.

62. "Justus quidem tu es, Domine . . .", *Selected Poetry*, ed. Philips.

63. "To seem the stranger", *Selected Poetry*, ed. Philips, p. 151.

64. Thérèse's path starts also from our modern condition. This is not like the earlier one, in which there are indeed "sinners", who live with only a faint sense of God and Christ, without relating to Him; but where nevertheless "everyone", that is, the whole society, believes. Rather we live in a world in which the negation of God is a real option, adopted by millions. See Fernand Ouellette, *Je serai l'Amour* (Montreal: Fidès, 1996):

"Thérèse est pénétrée depuis longtemps de 'tristesse métaphysique'. C'est bien sur ce terrain-là que se joue son drame intime. La tristesse est liée à la conscience qu'elle a, depuis son enfance, de la souffrance du Christ et du rejet de son amour par les hommes. . . . Marcel Moret conclut que 'c'est cette tristesse proprement métaphysique des temps modernes que Thérèse, par un dessein mystérieux de la Providence, a eu entre autres pour vocation d'assumer sous les apparences de la joie et de la consolation'" (323). Her experience of this lack of faith, as void, doesn't lead her to try to close herself off from it; her aim is rather to live in it, wanting still to believe, and to be with God. This is her "petite voie" (336). "[On] ne peut travailler efficacement au salut des âmes qu'en endurant les souffrances même des pécheurs, et en partageant avec eux le 'pain de l'épreuve'" (337).

As Michel de Certeau puts it, "l'itinéraire de Thérèse de Lisieux commence avec un vouloir absolu ('je choisis tout') et s'achève dans la 'nuit' qui marque la fin de sa vie avec un foi réduite à 'ce que JE VEUX CROIRE'"; *La Fable Mystique* (Paris: Gallimard, 1982), p. 236n55.

65. See Rowan Williams' critique of the search for a Christian golden age: "The whole idea that there is a *privileged* era for being a Christian is a strange one"; in *Why Study the Past?* (London: Darton, Longman, Todd, 2005), p. 105.

66. There is an interesting discussion of this whole matter in Alister McGrath, *The Twilight of Atheism* (New York: Doubleday, 2004), chapter 8.

67. See the interesting discussion in Rupert Short, *God's Advocates* (London: Darton, Longman and Todd, 2005), interviews with Janet Martin Soskice, pp. 24–42, and Sarah Coakley, pp. 67–85.

68. This accounts for the sense of being hemmed in, contained, in the contemporary secular world, that one finds among many writers with a faith commitment. Josef Pieper speaks of the "dome (die Kuppel) of the workaday world", which can imprison us. Sophists, pseudo-philosophers, screw down the dome more tightly. We need to burst beyond it. See *The Philosophical Act*, in *Leisure the Basis of Culture*, trans. Alexander Dru (Indianapolis: The Liberty Fund, 1999), pp. 69–71; *Was Heisst Philosophieren?* (Einsiedeln: Johannes Verlag, 2003), pp. 19–21.

69. See my article of this title in Hent de Vries, ed., *Religion—The Concept* (Fordham University Press, forthcoming).

70. Peter Gay, *The Enlightenment: An Interpretation* (New York: Knopf, 1966).

71. John Stuart Mill, *On Liberty*, in Mill, *Three Essays* (Oxford: Oxford University Press, 1975), p. 77. Friedrich Nietzsche: "—Hat man mich vestanden?—Dionysos gegen den

Gekreuzigten." See "Ecce Homo", in *Nietzsches Werke* (Berlin: Walter de Gruyter, 1969), Sechste Abteilung, Dritter Band, p. 372.

72. It goes without saying that this applies also to Christianity's claims to "supersede" Judaism. To the extent that this kind of claim is made on behalf of Christian faith, to that extent the faith is occulted, even mutilated. But also, more generally, I hope it will be evident how my (admittedly ill-defined) notion of "God's pedagogy" differs from a view like Lessing's (see *Die Erziehung des Menschengeschlechts*). It's not just that the "course" doesn't end in a Deistic-inspired moralism, but more fundamentally, since the pedagogy turns on deepening our sense of the mysteries of sin and atonement, it never properly "ends" at all: there is no era of satisfied graduates, who can look down condescendingly on the imperfect grasp of their less-advanced predecessors. See a discussion of the Deist-type version in Nicholas Boyle, *Sacred and Secular Scriptures* (Notre Dame: University of Notre Dame Press, 2005), chapters 1 and 2.

73. Robert Bellah, "What Is Axial about the Axial Age?", in *Archives Européennes de Sociologie,* 46, no. 1, pp. 69–89; the quote is on p. 72. The whole argument is developed at length in Robert Bellah, *Religion in Human Evolution: From the Paleolithic to the Axial Age* (forthcoming).

Epilogue: The Many Stories

1. See Francis Oakley, "Christian Theology and the Newtonian Science", *Church History* 30 (1961), pp. 433–457.

2. These connections have been explored at a very high level in the work of John Milbank and Catherine Pickstock, often spoken of as proponents of "Radical Orthodoxy". See, for instance, John Milbank, *Theology and Social Theory,* 2nd edition (Oxford: Blackwell, 2005); Catherine Pickstock, *After Writing* (Oxford: Blackwell, 1998); John Milbank and Catherine Pickstock, *Truth in Aquinas* (London: Routledge, 2001); John Milbank, Catherine Pickstock, and Graham Ward, eds., *Radical Orthodoxy* (London: Routledge, 1999).

3. Rémi Brague, *La Sagesse du Monde* (Paris: Fayard, 1999).

4. See John Milbank, in Rupert Shortt, *God's Advocates* (London: Darton, Longman & Todd), p. 108.

Index